The 1994 Information Please® Business Almanac & Desk Reference

The 1994 Information Please® Business Almanac & Desk Reference

Seth Godin, Editor

HOUGHTON MIFFLIN COMPANY
Boston • New York

ISBN: 0-395-64384-8

ISSN: 1070-4639

Printed in the United States of America

DOW 10 9 8 7 6 5 4 3 2

Contents

How to Use This Book

There are five easy ways to access the *Almanac*:

Chapter by Chapter

The front and back inside covers give a map of the organization of the *Almanac*, together with page numbers for each chapter. At the start of each chapter you'll find a listing of every article contained in the chapter.

The Table of Contents

The *Almanac* is organized in much the same way a company is. Information about doing business abroad is in the International section, while data on brand names and ad agencies is listed under Marketing. The Table of Contents lists each chapter, together with the name of each article in that chapter.

The Company and Publication Index

Top Reference Sources

The Heading Index

Every company referred to in the *Almanac* is indexed at the end of the book.
Every article and every Top Reference Source in the *Almanac* is indexed as well.

Feedback

The editors of the *Almanac* would like to hear from you. Tell us your likes and dislikes, and let us know what information you'd like to see included in future volumes. While we can't answer every letter, we promise that each suggestion will be carefully reviewed and included wherever possible.

To reach the editorial staff:

Internet:	Sethwood@AOL.com
CompuServe:	76004,2554
Fax:	(914) 664-4615
Mail:	Box 660, Yonkers, NY 10710

Editorial and Production Staff

Editor in Chief:	Seth Godin
Consulting Editor:	Michael Cader
Senior Editors:	Ellen Kenny Lisa DiMona Margery Mandell
Associate Editor:	Megan O'Connor
Production Editor:	Julie Maner
Finance Editor:	Margaret Talcott
Editorial Assistance:	Joyce Bermel
Proofreading:	Bill Hartford Julie Monahan Pat Goff
Technical Layout:	Martin Erb
Data Entry:	Vic Lapuszinski Byron Stone
Research:	Kate Grossman José Arroyo
Design:	Charles Kreloff
Glossary:	Marcia Layton
Template Design:	Lisa Jahred
Troubleshooting:	Steve Ketchum
Security:	Lucy Wood
Houghton Mifflin:	Steve Lewers Bob Moses Marnie Patterson Kristin Robbins Bob Enos Greg Mrozek Pat McTiernan Doug Eisenhart Bill Trippe Steve Vana-Paxhia Bruce Frost
Output:	Graphics Express
Maps:	MicroMaps

Acknowledgments

More than 500 people contributed valuable insights, information and advice to the creation of this Almanac. This is a partial list of those who were so gracious in their help.

REFERENCE SOURCES:

Access EPA, U.S. Government Printing Office
Accountant's Desk Handbook, Prentice Hall
Accountant's Handbook of Formulas and Tables, Prentice Hall
Accounting Desk Book, Prentice Hall
Accounting Today
Advertising Age
Air Traveler's Handbook, St. Martin's Press
Aircraft, Airports and Airways, U.S. Government Printing Office
Almanac of Business and Industrial Financial Ratios, Prentice Hall
AMA Guide for Meeting and Event Planners, Gale Research
AMA Handbook of Key Management Forms, American Management Association
AMA Management Handbook, American Management Association
American Academy of Actuaries Yearbook, American Acedemy of Actuaries
The American Almanac 1992-1993, The Reference Press
American Almanac of Jobs and Salaries, Avon Books
American Business Climate and Economic Profiles, Gale Research
American Demographics
American Export Register, Thomas International Publishing
An American Guide to Doing Business in Australia, PacRim Publishing
American Lobbyists Directory, Gale Research
Americans with Disabilities Act Handbook, John Wiley & Sons
Annual Asset Survey, Salomon Brothers
Annual of Advertising, Editorial and Television Art and Design, Art Directors Club
Architectural Record, McGraw-Hill
Auto Rental News, Bobit Publishing
Aviation Daily
Barron's National Business and Financial Weekly, Dow Jones-Irwin
Best's Insurance Reports, A.M. Best Company
Best's Review, A.M. Best Company
The Better World Investment Guide, Prentice Hall
Beyond Race and Gender, American Management Association
Billboard's International Talent and Touring Directory, Billboard Publications
Book Publishing, Practicing Law Institute
Broadcasting & Cable Market Place, R.R. Bowker
Bulletin to Management, Bureau of National Affairs
Business Aviation Magazine
Business Forms on File, Facts on File
Business Information Alert, Alert Publications
Business One Irwin Business & Investment Almanac, Business One Irwin
Business Protocol, John Wiley & Sons
Business Rankings and Salaries Index, Gale Research
Business Statistics, U.S. Government Printing Office
Business to Business Directory, NYNEX Information Resources
Business Week
Buyers Laboratory Test Reports: Reports on Office Products, Buyers Laboratory
C.Q. Almanac, Congressional Quarterly
Career Information Center, Glencoe Publishing
Cavalcade of Acts & Attractions, Amusement Business
Celebrity Directory, Axiom Information Resources
Census of Manufactures, U.S. Government Printing Office
College Blue Book: Occupational Education, Macmillan
Commerce Business Daily, U.S. Government Printing Office
Commercial Atlas & Marketing Guide, Rand McNally
Commodity Futures Trading Commission Monthly Reports, U.S. Government Printing Office
Communication Systems and Computer Networks, Halsted Press
The Complete Investor: Instruments, Markets and Methods, Richard D. Irwin

Comprehensive Day Care Programs, Professional Society
Computers and Computing Information Resources Directory, Gale Research
Consultants and Consulting Organizations Directory, Gale Research
Consumer Reports Travel Buying Guide 1992, Consumer Reports
Consumer Reports Travel Letter, Consumers Union of the United States
Consumer Sourcebook, Gale Research
Consumers Index to Product Evaluations & Information Sources, Pierian Press
Copyright Basics, U.S. Government Printing Office
Copyrights, Patents, and Trademarks, TAB Books
Corporate Guide to Parental Leaves, Catalyst
Crain's New York Business
Datapro Directory of Microcomputer Software, Datapro Research Corporation
Datapro Office Products Evaluation Service, Datapro Research Corporation
Design and Drafting News, American Design and Drafting Association
Design for a Livable Planet, HarperCollins
Direct Marketing Association Statistical Factbook , Direct Marketing Association
Direct Marketing Magazine
Directory of Accredited Home Study Schools, National Home Study Council
Directory of Conventions, Bill Communications
Directory of Lawyers and Law Firms by Specialty, West Publishing
Directory of Leading U.S. Export Management Companies, Bergano Book Company
Directory of Mailing List Companies, Todd Publications
Directory of Mail Order Catalogues, Grey House Publishing
Directory of U.S. Importers/Exporters, Journal of Commerce
Discount Store News, Lebhar-Friedman
Dow Jones Guide to Real Estate Investing, Dow Jones-Irwin
Dow Jones-Irwin Guide to Bond & Money Market Investments, Dow Jones-Irwin
Dow Jones-Irwin Guide to Fine Gems and Jewelry, Dow Jones-Irwin
Dow Jones-Irwin Guide to Put & Call Options, Dow Jones-Irwin
Dun's Employment Opportunities Directory, Dun's Marketing Services
Economic Indicators , U.S. Government Printing Office
The Economist
Employee Benefits and the Computer, Advanced Personnel Systems
Employment and Earnings, U. S. Department of Labor
Employment Coordinator, Research Institute of America
Employment, Hours, and Earnings: United States 1909-1984, U.S. Government Printing Office
ENR, McGraw-Hill
Entrepreneur and Small Business Problem Solver, John Wiley & Sons
Environmental Almanac, Houghton Mifflin
The Europa World Year Book, Gale Research
Executive Compensation Alert, Research Institute of America
Executive Excellence, Institute for Principle-Centered Leadership
Executive Recruiter News, Consultants News
Export Profits: A Guide for Small Business, Upstart Publishing
Export Programs: A Business Directory of U.S. Government Resources, Trade Promotion Coordinating Committee, U.S. Department of Commerce
Exportise, Small Business Foundation of America
FAA Statistical Handbook of Aviation, U.S. Government Printing Office
Federal Register, U.S. Government Printing Office
The Five Minute Interview, John Wiley & Sons
50 Simple Things You Can Do to Save the Earth, Earthworks Press
Forbes FYI, Forbes
Foreign Trade Barriers, Office of the United States Trade Representative
43 Proven Ways to Raise Capital for Your Small Business, Enterprise Publishing
The Foundation Directory, The Foundation Center
Foundation Giving, 1992 , The Foundation Center
Foundation Grants Index, The Foundation Center
Franchise Bible: A Comprehensive Guide, The Oasis Press/PSI Research
Franchise Opportunities Guide 1993 Edition, International Franchise Association
Frequent Flyer
Fundamentals of Business Law, Prentice Hall
Futures Magazine
Futures Market Dictionary, Prentice Hall
Garbage Magazine

Gift and Decorative Accessory Buyers Directory, Geyer McAllister Publications
Green Book–International Directory of Marketing Research Companies and Services, American Marketing Association
Guerrilla Financing, Houghton Mifflin
Guerrilla Marketing, Houghton Mifflin
Handbook For Raising Capital, Dow Jones-Irwin
Handbook of Business Information, Libraries Unlimited
Harvard Business Review
Herschell Gordon Lewis on the Art of Writing Copy, Prentice Hall
Hiring the Best, Bob Adams
Historical Statistics of the U.S., Colonial Times to 1970, U.S. Government Printing Office
How To Buy Foreign Stocks and Bonds: A Guide for the Individual Investor, HarperCollins
How To Develop an Effective Company Security Program, Dartnell
How To Do Business With Russians, Quorum Books
How To Fire an Employee, Facts on File
How to Form Your Own Corporation Without a Lawyer for Under $75.00, Enterprise • Dearborn
How To Read the Financial Pages, Warner Books
HR Magazine
Hudson's Subscription Newsletter Directory, Hudson's
The Hulbert Financial Digest, Hulbert Financial Digest
ID Magazine
Inc Yourself, Warner Books
Incentives Magazine
Incorporating Your Business, Contemporary Books
Industry, the Environment, and Corporate Social Responsibility, Council of Planning Librarians
Industry Week
Information for the Private Sector and State and Local Governments, EEOC
Information Please Almanac, Houghton Mifflin
The Insider's Guide to Franchising, AMACOM
Institutional Investor
International Directory of Corporate Affiliations, Reed Publishing
International Marketing Handbook, Gale Research
Investing in Employee Health, Jossey-Bass
Investment Dealers' Digest, IDD Information Services
Investor's Daily
The Investor's Dictionary, John Wiley & Sons
Journal of Accountancy
The Kennedy Directory, Consultants News
Kiplinger's Personal Finance Magazine
Law and Legal Information Directory, Gale Research
Law Dictionary for Non-Lawyers, West Publishing
Lawyers Almanac, Prentice Hall
The Legal Guide for Starting and Running a Small Business, Nolo Press
Legal Research: How to Find and Understand the Law, Nolo Press
Legal Thesaurus, Macmillan
Lesko's Info-Power, Information USA
The Lobbying Handbook, Professional Lobbying Consulting Center
Louis Rukeyser's Business Almanac, Simon & Schuster
MacUser
MacWeek
Mail Order Business Directory, B. Klein Publications
Mail Order Product Guide, B. Klein Publications
Managing Foundations Assets, The Foundation Center
Meetings and Conventions, Reed Travel Group
Mid-Session Review, Office of Management and Budget
The Money Charity Honor Roll, Money Magazine
Money Magazine
Employment & Trends , U.S. Office of Personnel Management
Moody's Bank and Finance Manual, Moody's Investors Service
Moody's Bond Record, Moody's Investors Service
Moody's Handbook of OTC Stocks, Moody's Investors Services
Nation's Business, Chamber of Commerce of the United States
National Directory of Corporate Giving, The Foundation Center
National Directory of Women-Owned Business Firms, Business Research Services

The National Law Journal, New York Law Publishing Company
National Report for Training and Development, American Society for Training and Development
National Roster of Realtors Directory, Stamats Communications
New Business Incorporations, Dun & Bradstreet
New York Public Library Book of Chronologies, Prentice Hall
New York Public Library Desk Reference, Webster's New World
New York State Bar Association Lawyer Referral and Information Service, New York State Bar Association
Newsletter on Annual Reports, Sid Cato
The Newsletter on Newsletters, Newsletter Clearinghouse
The 90 Minute Hour, Houghton Mifflin
1991 Licensing Business Databook, EPM Communications
1993 Adweek Client/Brand Directory, AdWeek
1993 Guide to Worldwide Postal-Code & Address Formats, Marian Nelson
NonProfit Times, John McIlquham
Nutshell
Occupational Outlook Handbook, U.S. Government Printing Office
OEL Insider, Office of Export Licensing, Bureau of Export Administration
Office Administration Handbook, Dartnell
On Location National Film and Videotape Production Directory, On Location Publishing
100 Highest Yields, Robert Heady
Opportunity in Mexico: Small Business Guide, Small Business Administration
Packaging Buyer's Guide, Cahners Publishing
Pacs and Lobbies Newsletter
The Partnership Book: How to Write a Partnership Agreement, Nolo Press
Patent It Yourself, Nolo Press
PC Week
Pensions and Other Retirement Benefits Plans, Bureau of National Affairs
Pensions & Investment Age
Personal Selling Power Magazine
Personnel and Human Resource Management, West Publishing
Personnel Management Abstracts, Personnel Management Abstracts Publishers
Playthings Magazine
Pocket Station Listing Guide, National Association of Television Program Executives
Poor's Register of Corporations, Directors and Executives, Standard and Poor's
Practical Guide to Credit and Collection, AMACOM
Pratt's Guide to Venture Capital Sources, Venture Economics
Protect Your Company From A to Z, Business Research Publications
Publishers Weekly
Racism and Sexism in Corporate Life, Free Press
Radio and Records Magazine
Rand McNally Bankers Directory: International, Rand McNally
Rating America's Corporate Conscience, Addison-Wesley
Rating Guide to Franchises, Facts on File
RCRA Orientation Manual , U.S. Government Printing Office
Recycling in the States 1990 Review, National Solid Waste Management Association
Report of the National Critical Technologies Panel, Executive Office of the President
Resource Recycling
Robert Half on Hiring, Plume
S & P 500 1991 Directory/Equities, Standard & Poor's
Security Dealer Magazine
Security Magazine, Cahners Publishing
Selected Data on Research and Development in Industry: 1990, National Science Foundation
Site Selection Magazine
Small Business Forms, LawPrep Press
Small Business Handbook, Prentice Hall
Small Business Sourcebook, 2nd ed, Gale Research
Software Reviews On File, Facts on File
The Source Book of Franchise Opportunities, Richard D. Irwin
Specialty Advertising Business, Specialty Adverstising Association International
Spot Television Rates and Data, Standard Rate and Data Service
Standard Legal Forms and Agreements for Small Businesses, Self Counsel Press
Starting and Operating A Clipping Service, Pilot Books
State and Metropolitan Area Databook, 1991, U.S. Government Printing Office
Statistical Abstract of the United States, U.S. Government Printing Office

Stocks, Bonds, Bills and Inflation: 1991 Yearbook, Ilbbotson Associates
Success Magazine
Successful Payroll Management, Prentice Hall
Superbrands, AdWeek
Survey of Current Business, U.S. Dept. of Commerce, Bureau of Economic Analysis
The Telecommuting Resource Guide, Pacific Bell
Ten-Second Business Forms, Bob Adams
Thomas Register of American Manufacturers, Thomas Publishing Company
Thomas Register's Inbound Traffic Guide, Thomas Publishing Company
Thorndyke Encyclopedia of Banking and Financial Tables, Warren, Gorham & Lamont
Trademark Management: A Guide For Executives, Clark Boardman Company
Tradeshow Services Directory
Trading Company Sourcebook, National Federation of Export Associations
Training Magazine, Lakewood Publications
Travel Industry World Yearbook, Child and Waters
The Ultimate College Shopper's Guide, Addison-Wesley
U.S. Customs Guide for Private Flyers, U. S. Customs Service
U.S. EEOC Combined Annual Report 1986-1988, U.S. Government Printing Office
U.S. Leading Export Management Companies, Bergano Book Company
U.S. News and World Report
Understanding Wall Street, TAB Books, Liberty House Division
UNESCO Statistical Yearbook, UNIPUB
The Universal Almanac, Andrews & McMeel
USA Today
Variety's Directory of Major U.S. Show Business Awards, R.R. Bowker
Variety's Who's Who in Show Business, R.R. Bowker
Venture Capital: Where To Find It 1992-1993 NASBIC Membership Directory, National Association of Small Business Investment Companies
Venture Economics , SDC Publishing
Vest Pocket CEO, Prentice Hall
Vest Pocket MBA, Prentice Hall
Vital Business Secrets for New and Growing Companies, Dow Jones-Irwin
The Wall Street Journal
Wall Street Words, Houghton Mifflin
Washington Representatives, Columbia Books
What Every Executive Better Know About the Law, Simon & Schuster
Who Owns What is in Your Head?, Elseview-Dutton
Who's Who in Venture Capital, John Wiley & Sons
Who's Who of Customs Brokers and Forwarding Agents, National Customs Brokers and Forwarding Agents Association
Workers' Relocation: A Bibliography, Vance Bibliographies
Working Woman
Worksite AIDS Education and Attitudes Toward People with the Disease, Georgia Institute of Technology
Worksite Wellness, Prentice Hall
Your Rights in the Workplace, Nolo Press
The Zen of Hype, Citadel Press

Thanks to the Following Individuals:

Burt Aronson; Rick Telberg, Accounting Today, Jim English, AdWeek; Jim McBride, Affiliated Warehouse Companies; Sakota Hudson, American Bankers Association; Christine Levit, American Express Travel Management Services; Dennis Smith, Liz Wainger, American Institute of Architects; Cathy Hunt, American Recycling Market Directory; Mitch Metzner, American Red Cross; Tom Mariam, American Stock Exchange; Ed Hendricks, Association of Management Consulting Firms; Bill Huffman, Battelle; Sherry Brown, Black Enterprise Magazine; Ken Brown, Bookazine; Margaret Bryant; Bill Alterman, Bureau of Labor Statistics; Dana Alexander, Bureau of Labor Statistics; Craig Howell, Bureau of Labor Statistics, Office of Producer Price Indexes; Diane Pardee, Business Committee for the Arts; Gary J. Steller, Business Franchise Guide; Ronnie Drakman, Business Insurance Magazine; Kate Rice, Business Traveler International; Mark Rose, Cass Communications; Renee Matthews, CDA Investment Technologies; Mark Morrow, CEEM Information Services; Mark Kerrigan, Celebrity Service International; Anita Liskey, Chicago Board of Trade; Richard Sandor, Chicago Board of Trade; Bonnie Greenberg & Pat Campbell, Chicago Board Options Exchange; Annette Wallace, Chicago Mercantile Exchange; Walter Sanders, Citicorp Diners Club; Nick Memoli, Commodity Futures Trading Commission; Karla Kelley, Commodity Price Charts; Herschell Gordon Lewis, Communicomp; Alex Nikiforchuk, CompuServe; Kathleen Dempsey, Corporate Real Estate Executive; Melissa Abernathy, Corporate Travel; David Jackson & Constance Thomas, D.C. Department of Finance and Revenue; Page Thompson, DDB Needham; Ken Bertsch, Deadlines; Dr. Roger Stephens, Department of Labor, Ergonomics Division; Bill Mosley, Department of Transportation; Roger Tucker, Design Access; Linda Arnold, Dow Jones-Irwin; Rita Grenville, E.I. Du Pont De Nemours and Company; Cable Newhouse, Entertainment Weekly; Elizabeth Wallace, Entrepreneur Group; Nicholas I. Morgan, Environmental Protection Agency; George Bolduc, Federal Aviation Administration; John Lipari, Federal Drug-Free Workplace Helpline; Beverly Berger, Federal Laboratory Consortium; Robin Roberts, Financial World Magazine; David Berry, FIND/SVP; Stewart Stern, Findex Directory; Betty Franklin, Forbes; Margo Keltner, Fortune; Katy Weigel & Lisa Calveria, Frank Russell; Toby Taylor, Futures Industry Association; William Godin, Hard Manufacturing; Richard Sailer, Goodyear; John Cogell, Grant Thornton; Liz DeIuliis, Grant Thornton Survey of Manufacturers; Carl Frankel, Green MarketAlert; Nancy Riviere, Greeting Card Association; Don White, Health Insurance Association of America; Leon Henry; Susan Spinale, Inc. Magazine; Karen Berube, Industrial Designers Society of America; Brett Bush, Infomercial Marketing Report; Bob Bergenzer, Information Resources; Randy Petersen, Inside Flyer; Michael J. Wax, Institute of Clean Air Companies; Mark Baven, Institute of Management & Administration; Steve Heusuk, Institute of Real Estate Management; David Krohn, Institute of Scrap Recycling Industries; Joseph Belth, Insurance Forum; Jean Salvatore, Insurance Information Institute; Dianna Losey, Interior Design Magazine; Becky Hyde, International Association of Exposition Managers; Robin Conn, International Asssociation of Convention and Visitors Bureaus; Tom West, International Business Brokers Association; Holly Chanatry and Carla Kruytbosch, International Business Magazine; Nicole L'Heureux, International Chamber of Commerce; Peter Tropper, International Finance Corporation; John Reynolds, International Franchise Association; Martha McDonald, International Quality and Productivity Center; Sheila Baker, International Trade Administration; Betty Hart, Investment Company Institute; Jim Olsen, J.D. Power and Associates; Andy Churchill, Jobs for the Future; Linda Horzwarth, Johnson & Johnson; Maryann Hogensen, Licensing Executive Society; Julie Friedlander, Lipper Analytical Services; Kyra Coury, LNA/Arbitron Multimedia Services; Laverne Henig & Clive Gershen, London Stock Exchange; Kathy Mahan, Manufacturers' Agents National Association; Mary Flowers, Manufacturers' Alliance for Productivity and Innovation; Jenny Marino, Manufacturing Technology Centers Program; Steven Levitt, Marketing Evaluations; Jane King, MCI Communications; Susan Ross & Jody Beutler, Mergerstat Review; Dauna Williams & Mia Colasuonno, Merrill Lynch; Phil Galdi, Merrill Lynch Portfolio Strategies; Anita Liskey, MidAm Commodity Exchange; Chris Gronkiewicz & Judy Fagan, Midwest Stock Exchange; Robert Tucker & Marie Salazar, Moody's Investor Services; Gordon Richards, National Association of Manufacturers; Carol Nashe, National Association of Radio Talk Show Hosts; Jeff Stafford, National Association of Realtors' Library; Fred Nichols, National Coalition for Advanced Technology; Beth Daley, National Committee for Responsive Philanthropy; Sharon Hadary, National Foundation for Women Business Owners; Joanne Overmann, National Institute of Standards and Technology; Dolores Redman, National Labor Relations Board; Jeff Montack, National Leadership Coalition on AIDS; Diane Shockey, National Materials Exchange Network; Daniel O'Connor, National Real Estate Index Market Monitor; Kathleen Meade, National Recycling Coalition; Joan Silinsh, National Register Publishing Company; John Jenkowski, National Science Foundation; Lawrence Rausch, National Science Foundation; Christine Boltz, National Solid

Waste Management Association; K. Brian McNamara, NESA; Justine Trowbridge & Steven Wheeler, New York Stock Exchange; Gene Nichols, Nichols/Feren; Judy Freed, Nightingale-Conant; Mark Duff, NIKKEI; Carol Weisner, Office of Solid Waste, U.S. Environmental Protection Agency; Larry Cole, Ogilvy & Mather; Talie Bar-Nadav, Organization Resources Counselors; Jennifer Stevens, Outdoor Advertising Association; Betty Manning, Pacific Stock Exchange; Sabine Schramm, Pensions & Investments; Jamie Farmer, Philadelphia Stock Exchange; Anne L. McKay, Pitney Bowes; Kelly Maynard, Professional Convention Management Association; Tracey George, R.R. Bowker; Fran Schwartz, Ravelle Brickman P.R.; Tracy Gross, RCRA Hotline; Abigail Roeder-Johnson, Roeder-Johnson; Pete Packer & Julie Pearman, Runzheimer International; Ed Flanagan, Sales and Marketing Executives of Greater New York; Michael Giliberto, Salomon Brothers; Carol Greenhut, Schonfeld and Associates; John Heine, Securities and Exchange Commission; Karen SanAntonio, Securities Industry Association; Patty Schmidt, Security Distributing & Marketing; Nancy Reder, Select Committee on Children, Youth and Family; Susan Shapiro, Simmons Market Research Bureau; Bobbie Middendorf, Small Business Legal Handbook; Nancy Thatcher, Solid Waste Assistance Program; John Branscome & Glenn Goldberg, Standard & Poor's; Michelle Peters, Strategies for Tenant Representation; John Schneider, Suburban Publishing of Connecticut; Steven Gold, Tax Foundation; Phil Barnett, The Cincinnati Stock Exchange; Chris Atwood, The Corporate University; Graef S. Crystal, The Crystal Report; John Holusha, The New York Times; Connie Lee Whelan, The Schechter Group; Donna Westermeyer, The Second Hulbert Financial Digest Almanac and Newsletter; Patrick Duck, U.S. Department of Commerce, Census Bureau, Business and Investment Branch; Sally Carson, U.S. Department of Commerce, International Trade Administration, Office of Trade & Economic Analysis; Pam Nacy, U.S. Dept. of Commerce, Economics and Statistics Administration, Office of Business Analysis; Mary Davis, U.S. International Trade Commission; Matt Roberts, Union Pen Company; Fred Eikelberg, Value Line; Laurie Googel, Van Nostrand Reinhold; Eileen Mooney, Voice Processing Magazine; Ed Welch; Ed Hansen, William M. Mercer Co.; David Dollata, Wilshire Associates; Helen Norton, Women's Legal Defense Fund; Karen Mazotta, Working Mother; Larry Delaney, World Trade Magazine; Susan Severance, Your Company Magazine; Allan Ripp, Zagat's Directory; Barbara Zimmerman.

Thanks to the Following Companies and Organizations:

A.C. Nielsen Company, Abelow Response, AFL-CIO, Air Charter Guide, Air & Waste Management Association, Airship International, Alcohol and Drug Problems Association of North America, Allstate Legal Supply, American Association of Advertising Agencies, American Bar Association, American Car Rental Association, American Civil Liberties Union, American Express Airfare Management Unit, American Institute of Certified Public Accountants, American Management Association, American Marketing Association, American Paper Institute, American Society for Quality Control, American Society of Journalists and Authors (ASJA), Army Career & Alumni Program, Art Network, Association for Science, Technology and Innovation, Association of Executive Search Consultants, Association of National Advertisers, Association of Small Business Development Centers, AT&T, Bacon's Information, BEI Entertainment Marketing, Blenheim Franchise Shows, Bloomberg, Boston Stock Exchange, Buck Consultants, Bureau of Labor Statistics, Business Owners and Managers Association, Business Travel News, Business Trend Analysts, Career Track, Charter Pacific Bank, Chronicle of Philanthropy, Chrysler Corporation, Citibank, Coffee Sugar Cocoa Exchange, Color Marketing Group, Cooperative Education Association, Corporate Resources Group, Council of State Governments, Council on Economic Priorities, Credit Research Foundation, Earth Share, Effie Awards - American Marketing Association, New York Chapter, Emergency Planning and Community Right to Know Act Information Hotline, Environmental Action Coalition, Environmental Federation of New York, Environmental Protection Agency, Export-Import Bank of the United States, Families & Work Institute, FASB Financial Accounting Standards Board, Federal Aviation Administration, Federal Elections Commission, Federal Information Center, Federal Reserve, Federal Reserve Board, Federal Trade Commission, Federal Trade Commission, Financial World, Find SVP, Fredonia Group, Freedom of Information Clearinghouse, Frost and Sullivan, Grant Thornton Survey of American Manufacturers, Harvard Business Services, Hay/Huggins Company, Human Factors Society, IDD Information Services, Inflight Food Service Association, Ingels, Institute of International Education, Institute of Outdoor Advertising, Internal Revenue Service, International Advertising Association, International Air Passengers Assocation, International Swap Dealers Association, Loose Leaf Binder Company, Luce Press Clippings, Magazine Publishers of America,

Meeting Planners International, Morgan Stanley Capital Internationals, Mt. Vernon Public Library, NASDAQ, National AIDS Clearing House, National Airline Passengers Association, National Association of Broadcasters, National Association of Business Travel Agents, National Association of Realtors, National Governors' Association, National Insurance Association, National Organization for Women, National Real Estate Investor, National Speakers Association, New York Cotton Exchange, New York Department of Health, New York Mercantile Exchange, New York State Attorney General's Office, New York State Division of Alcoholism and Alcohol Abuse, Northwestern National Life, O'Dwyer's Directory of Public Relations Firms, Office of Federal Contract Compliance Programs, Organization for Economic Cooperation and Development (OECD), Overseas Private Investment Corporation, Package Design Council International, Prestige Product Placement, Printbooks, Professional Dynametric Programs, Public Relations Society of America, Publishers Information Bureau, QCI Training & Educational Materials & Services, Rogers and Cowan, Royal Wholesale Banner, Safety Short Productions, Sheshunoff Information Services, Small Business Administration, Small Business Foundation of America, Specialty Advertising Association of Greater New York, Starch INRA Hooper, Stratospheric Ozone Information Hotline, The Advanced Technology Program, U.S. Department of Commerce, The Conference Board, The Foundation Center, The Kleid Company, The Licensing Letter - EPM Communications, The Malcolm Baldrige National Quality Awards, The One Club, The Spy Store, The World Bank, Toastmasters International, Tokyo Stock Exchange, Trademark Research Corporation, Trademark Searches/Thomson & Thomson, Tradewell, U.S. Department of Commerce, Bureau of Economic Analysis, U.S. Department of Commerce, Trade Information Center, U.S. Department of Health and Human Services, U.S. Department of Justice, Internal Security Division, U.S. Department of State, U.S. Post Office, U.S. Trademark Association, UPP EnterTainment, Urban Land Institute, VR Business Brokers, Walter Karl Companies, Walters International Speakers Bureau, Washington Speakers Bureau, White Plains Public Library, World Map Company.

A particular thank you to Jim English of AdWeek Magazine for his consistent support.
Thanks to the Almanac board of advisors: Abby Roeder-Johnson, Barry Bronfin, Beth Emme, Carl Sangree, Chip Conley, Chris Everly, Dan Lovy, Frank Sisco, Jay Levinson, William and Lenore Godin, Neil and Emily Epstein, Eric and Marjorie Bryen, Linda Litner, Lisa Orden Zarin, Kim Takal, Steven Greenstein, Lynne Gordon, Steve Dennis, Nancy Pellowe–Dennis.

Steve Lewers, Bob Enos and Bob Moses were responsible for much of the vision that helped us refine the almanac and bring it to its present form.

Finally, thanks to Helene, Lisa, Jerry, Joe, Mark, Scott and all of the other spouses who were so willing to be patient, insightful and supportive.

Maps

Atlanta

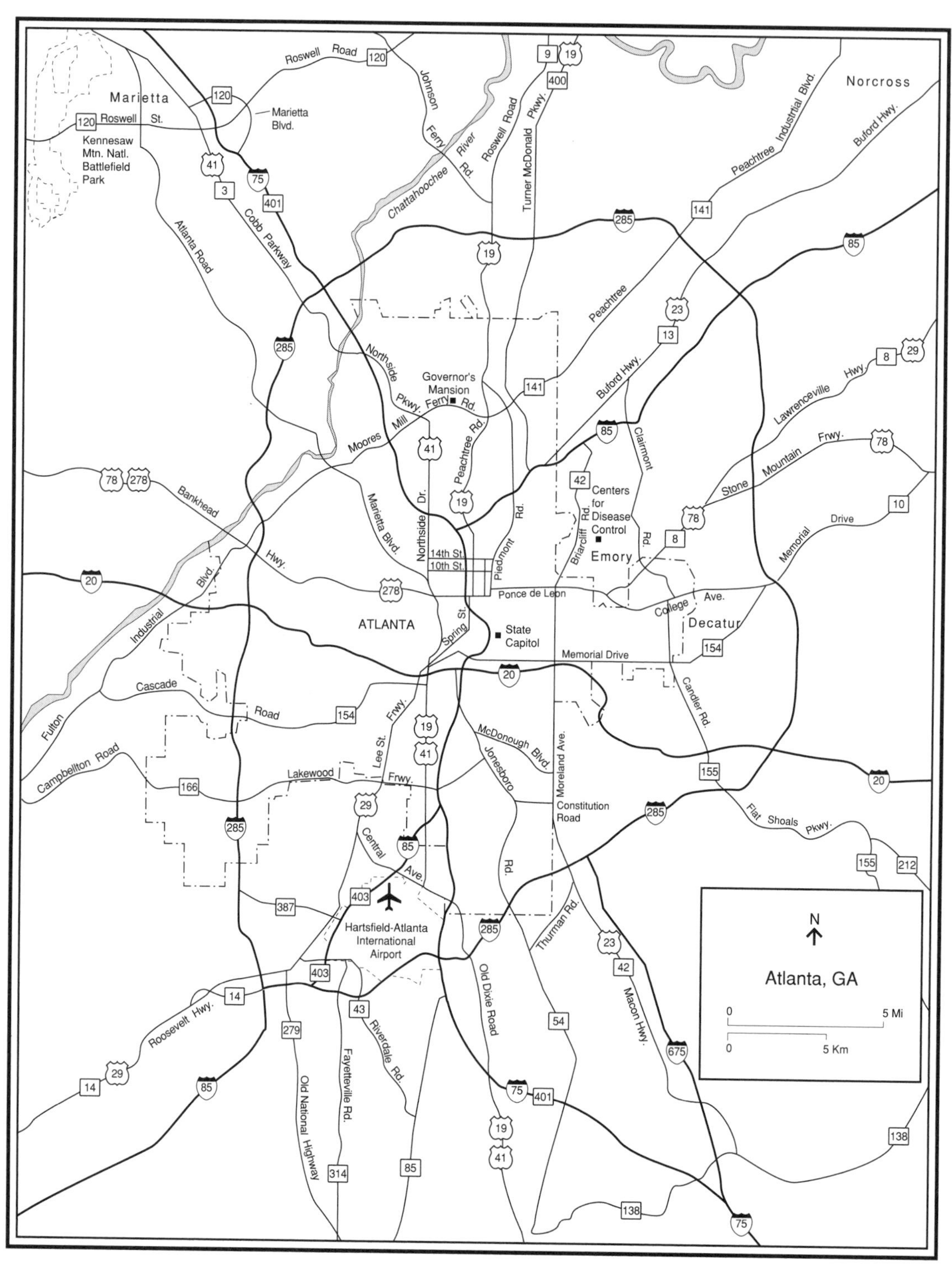

Marietta
Roswell Road
Roswell St.
Marietta Blvd.
Kennesaw Mtn. Natl. Battlefield Park
Johnson Ferry Rd.
Chattahoochee River
Roswell Road
Turner McDonald Pkwy.
Norcross
Peachtree Industrial Blvd.
Buford Hwy.
Atlanta Road
Cobb Parkway
Peachtree
Buford Hwy.
Northside Pkwy.
Governor's Mansion
Ferry Rd.
Moores Mill
Peachtree Rd.
Lawrenceville Hwy.
Clairmont
Stone Mountain Frwy.
Bankhead Hwy.
Marietta Blvd.
Northside Dr.
Piedmont Rd.
Centers for Disease Control
Briarcliff Rd.
Memorial Drive
Emory
14th St.
10th St.
Ponce de Leon
College Ave.
Industrial Blvd.
ATLANTA
Spring St.
State Capitol
Decatur
Memorial Drive
Cascade Road
Fulton
Lee St. Frwy.
McDonough Blvd.
Jonesboro Rd.
Candler Rd.
Moreland Ave.
Campbellton Road
Lakewood Frwy.
Constitution Road
Flat Shoals Pkwy.
Central Ave.
Hartsfield-Atlanta International Airport
Thurman Rd.
Roosevelt Hwy.
Old Dixie Road
Riverdale Rd.
Macon Hwy.
Fayetteville Rd.
Old National Highway
N
Atlanta, GA
0
5 Mi
0
5 Km

Boston

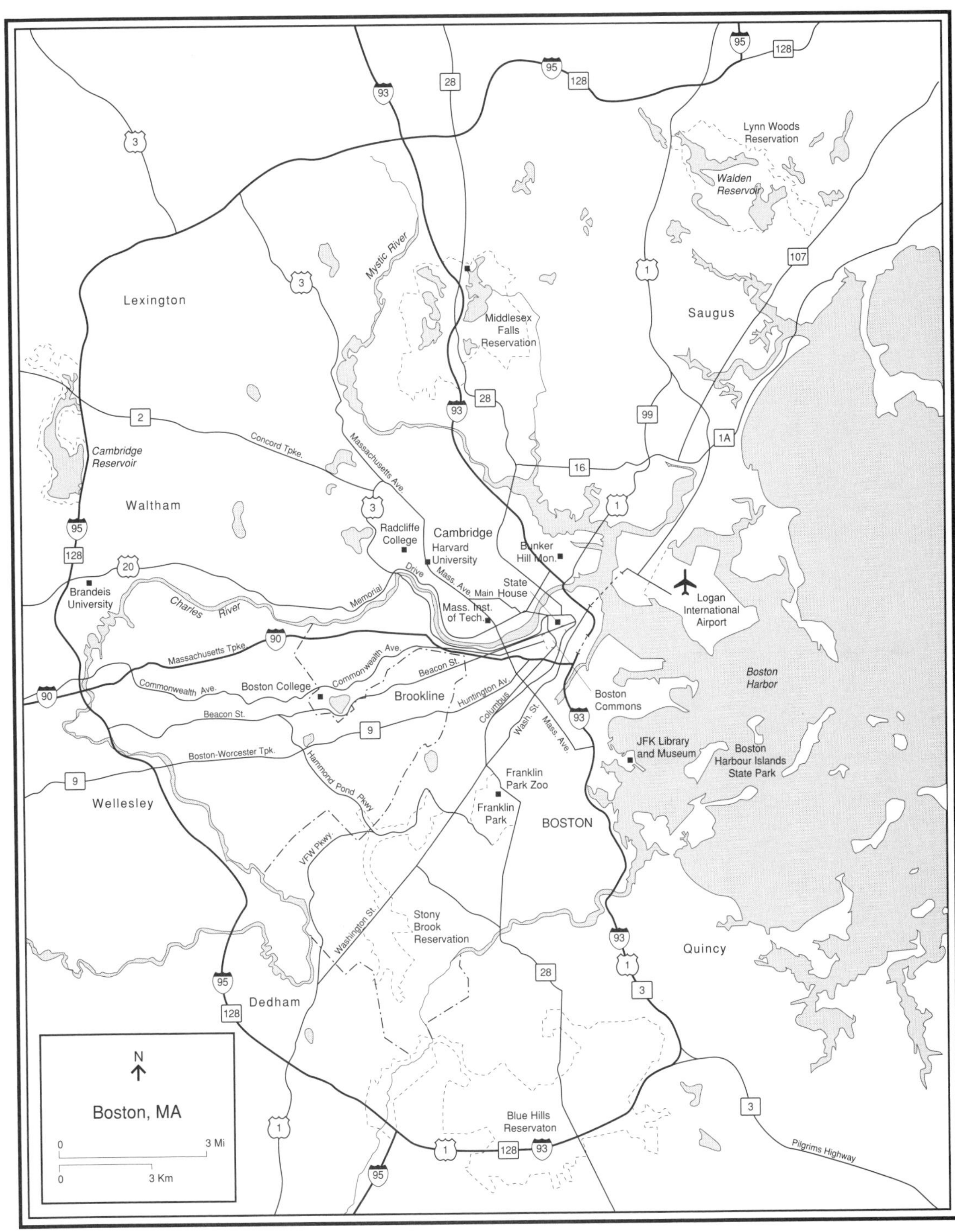
Lexington
Lynn Woods Reservation
Walden Reservoir
Mystic River
Middlesex Falls Reservation
Saugus
Cambridge Reservoir
Concord Tpke.
Massachusetts Ave.
Waltham
Radcliffe College
Cambridge
Harvard University
Bunker Hill Mon.
Brandeis University
Charles River
Memorial Drive
Mass. Ave.
Main
State House
Mass. Inst. of Tech.
Logan International Airport
Massachusetts Tpke.
Commonwealth Ave.
Beacon St.
Boston College
Brookline
Huntington Av.
Boston Commons
Boston Harbor
Columbus
Wash. St.
Mass. Ave.
Boston-Worcester Tpk.
Hammond Pond Pkwy.
JFK Library and Museum
Boston Harbour Islands State Park
Wellesley
Franklin Park Zoo
Franklin Park
BOSTON
VFW Pkwy.
Stony Brook Reservation
Washington St.
Quincy
Dedham
N
Boston, MA
0
3 Mi
0
3 Km
Blue Hills Reservaton
Pilgrims Highway

Chicago

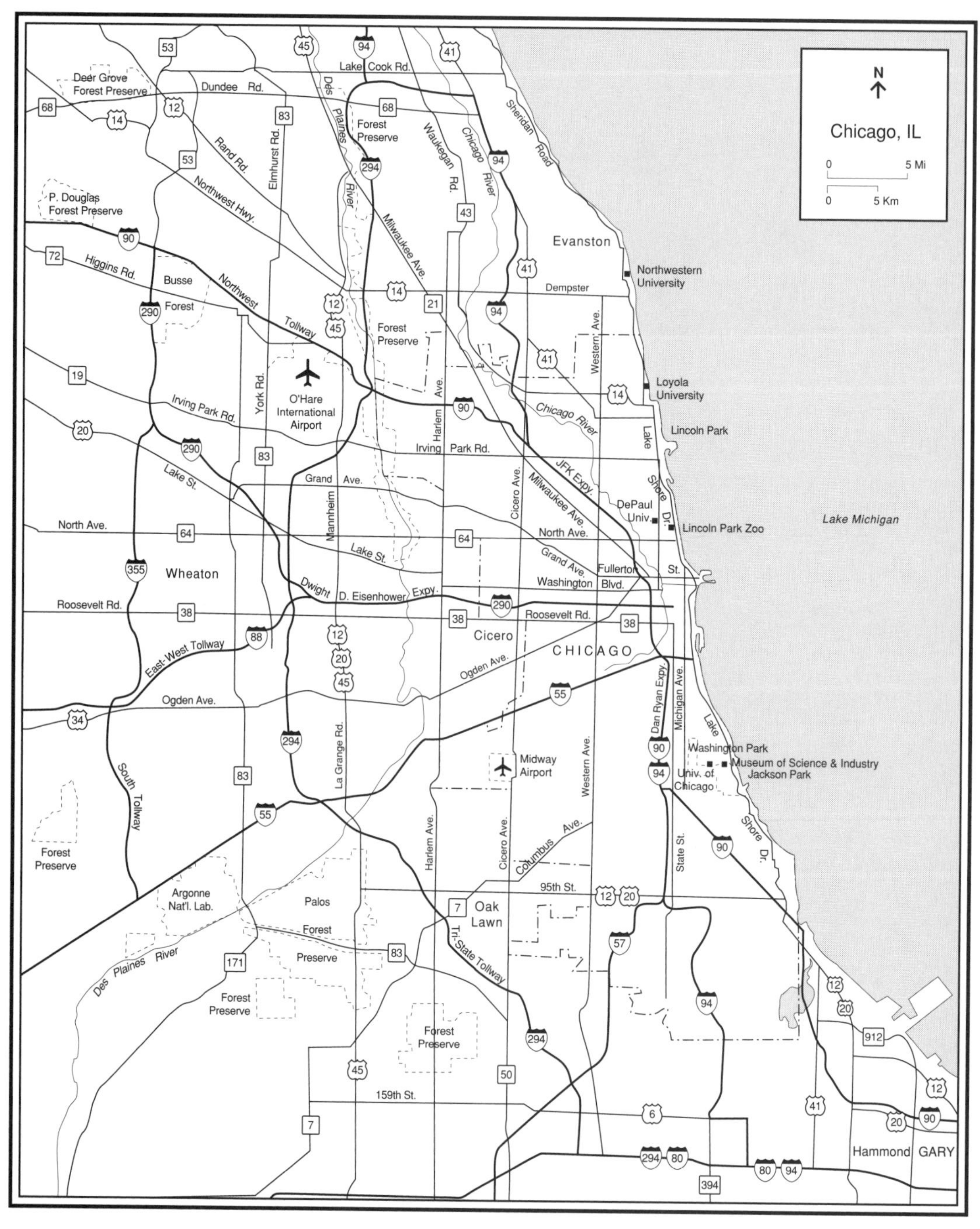
N
Chicago, IL
0 5 Mi
0 5 Km
Deer Grove Forest Preserve
Dundee Rd.
Lake Cook Rd.
Sheridan Road
Des Plaines River
Forest Preserve
Waukegan Rd.
Chicago River
Rand Rd.
Elmhurst Rd.
Northwest Hwy.
P. Douglas Forest Preserve
Milwaukee Ave.
Evanston
Northwestern University
Dempster
Higgins Rd.
Busse Forest
Northwest Tollway
Western Ave.
Loyola University
Irving Park Rd.
York Rd.
O'Hare International Airport
Harlem Ave.
Chicago River
Lincoln Park
Lake Shore Dr.
Irving Park Rd.
Lake St.
Grand Ave.
JFK Expy.
Cicero Ave.
Milwaukee Ave.
DePaul Univ.
Lincoln Park Zoo
Lake Michigan
North Ave.
Mannheim
North Ave.
Wheaton
Lake St.
Grand Ave.
Fullerton St.
Washington Blvd.
Dwight D. Eisenhower Expy.
Roosevelt Rd.
Roosevelt Rd.
Cicero
CHICAGO
East-West Tollway
Ogden Ave.
Ogden Ave.
Dan Ryan Expy.
Michigan Ave.
Lake
Washington Park
Museum of Science & Industry
Jackson Park
Univ. of Chicago
Midway Airport
La Grange Rd.
Western Ave.
South Tollway
Forest Preserve
Harlem Ave.
Cicero Ave.
Columbus Ave.
State St.
Shore Dr.
Argonne Nat'l. Lab.
Palos Forest Preserve
95th St.
Oak Lawn
Tri-State Tollway
Des Plaines River
Forest Preserve
Forest Preserve
159th St.
Hammond
GARY

Cleveland

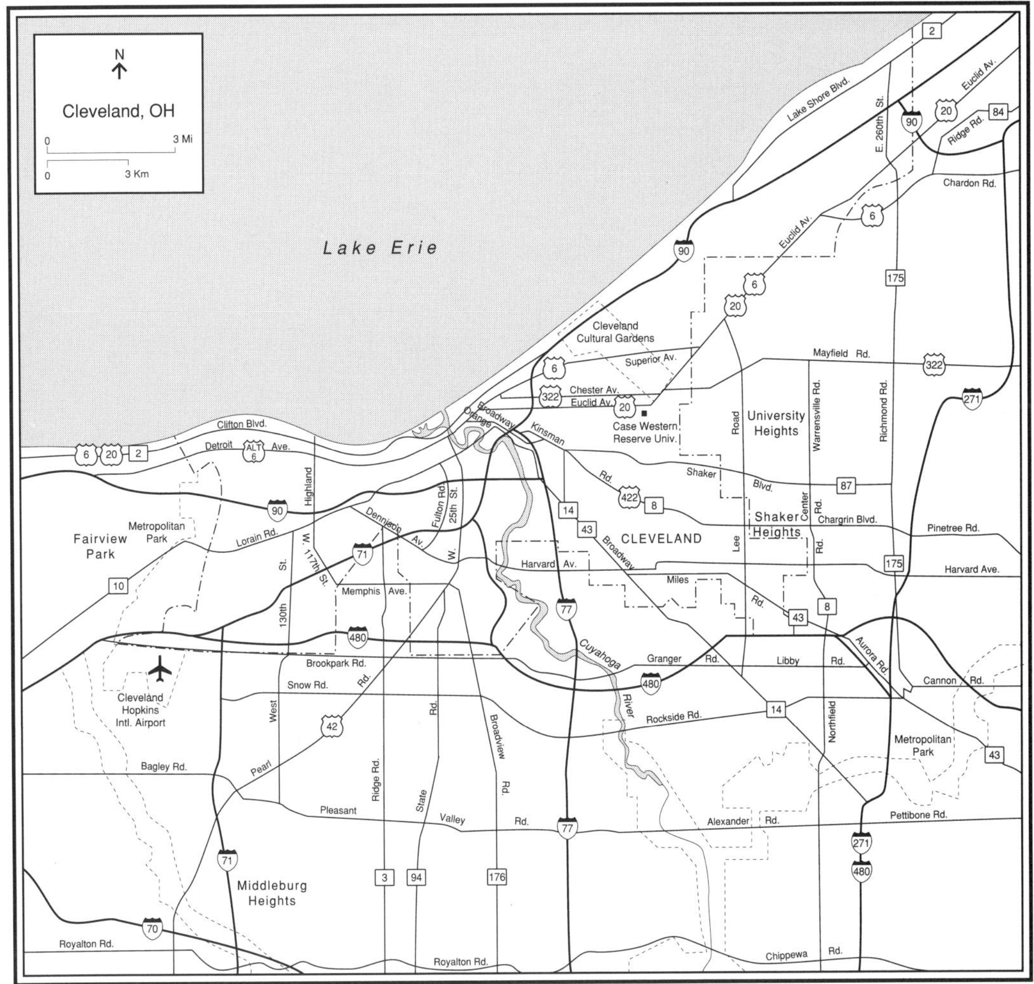
N
Cleveland, OH
0
3 Mi
0
3 Km
Lake Erie
Lake Shore Blvd.
E. 260th St.
Euclid Av.
Ridge Rd.
Chardon Rd.
Cleveland Cultural Gardens
Superior Av.
Chester Av.
Euclid Av.
Case Western Reserve Univ.
Mayfield Rd.
University Heights
Warrensville Rd.
Richmond Rd.
Clifton Blvd.
Detroit Ave.
Highland
Kinsman
Broadway
Orange
Shaker Blvd.
Fairview Park
Metropolitan Park
Lorain Rd.
Denison Av.
Fulton Rd.
W. 25th St.
CLEVELAND
Shaker Heights
Chargrin Blvd.
Pinetree Rd.
Harvard Av.
Harvard Ave.
W. 117th St.
130th St.
Memphis Ave.
Miles
Lee Rd.
Center Rd.
Brookpark Rd.
Snow Rd.
Granger Rd.
Libby Rd.
Aurora Rd.
Cannon Rd.
Cuyahoga River
Cleveland Hopkins Intl. Airport
West
Rockside Rd.
Northfield
Metropolitan Park
Bagley Rd.
Pearl Rd.
Ridge Rd.
State Rd.
Broadview Rd.
Pleasant Valley Rd.
Alexander Rd.
Pettibone Rd.
Middleburg Heights
Royalton Rd.
Royalton Rd.
Chippewa Rd.

Columbus

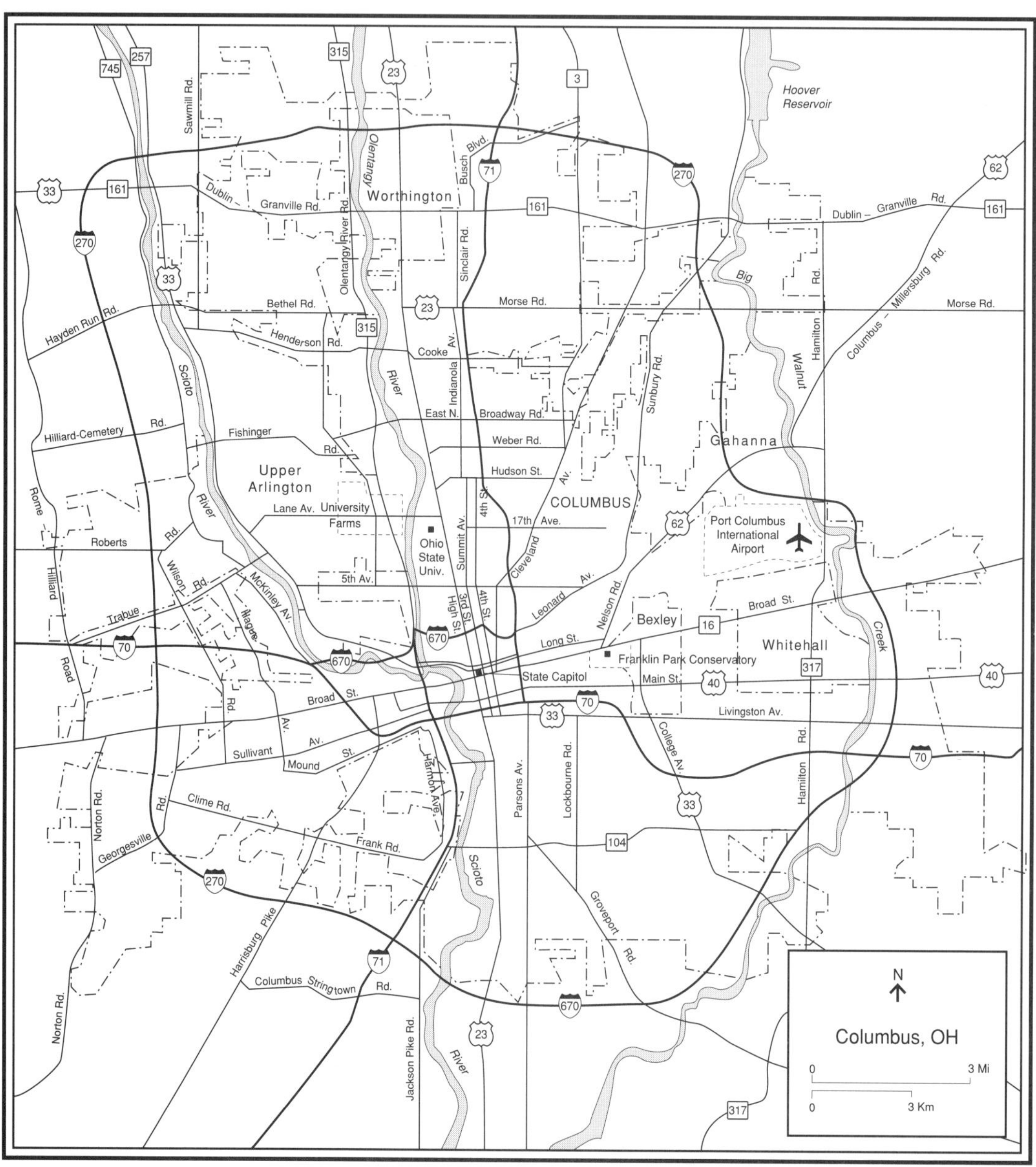
Hoover Reservoir
Worthington
Upper Arlington
COLUMBUS
Gahanna
Bexley
Whitehall
Ohio State Univ.
University Farms
Port Columbus International Airport
Franklin Park Conservatory
State Capitol
Scioto River
Olentangy River
Big Walnut Creek
Dublin - Granville Rd.
Morse Rd.
Bethel Rd.
Henderson Rd.
Hayden Run Rd.
Hilliard-Cemetery Rd.
Fishinger Rd.
Lane Av.
Roberts Rd.
Trabue Rd.
Broad St.
Sullivant Av.
Mound St.
Clime Rd.
Frank Rd.
Georgesville Rd.
Harrisburg Pike
Columbus Stringtown Rd.
Jackson Pike Rd.
Parsons Av.
Lockbourne Rd.
Groveport Rd.
College Av.
Livingston Av.
Main St.
Long St.
Leonard Av.
Nelson Rd.
Cleveland Av.
Sunbury Rd.
Hamilton Rd.
Columbus - Millersburg Rd.
Sawmill Rd.
Olentangy River Rd.
Sinclair Rd.
Busch Blvd.
Indianola Av.
Summit Av.
High St.
3rd St.
4th St.
Cooke Rd.
East N. Broadway Rd.
Weber Rd.
Hudson St.
17th Ave.
5th Av.
McKinley Av.
Wilson Rd.
Hague Av.
Harmon Ave.
Rome Hilliard Road
Norton Rd.
Columbus, OH
N
0 3 Mi
0 3 Km

Dallas–Fort Worth

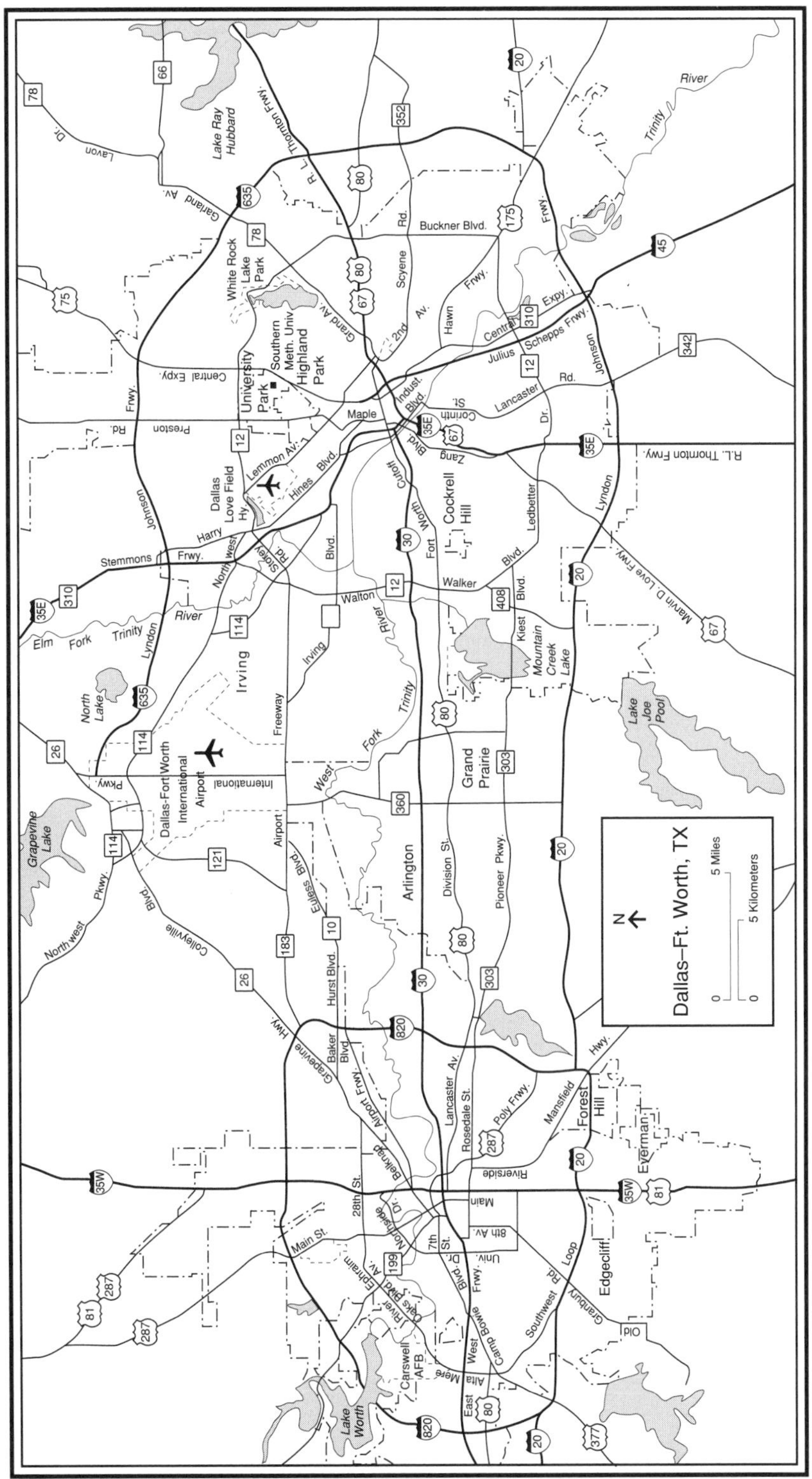

Denver

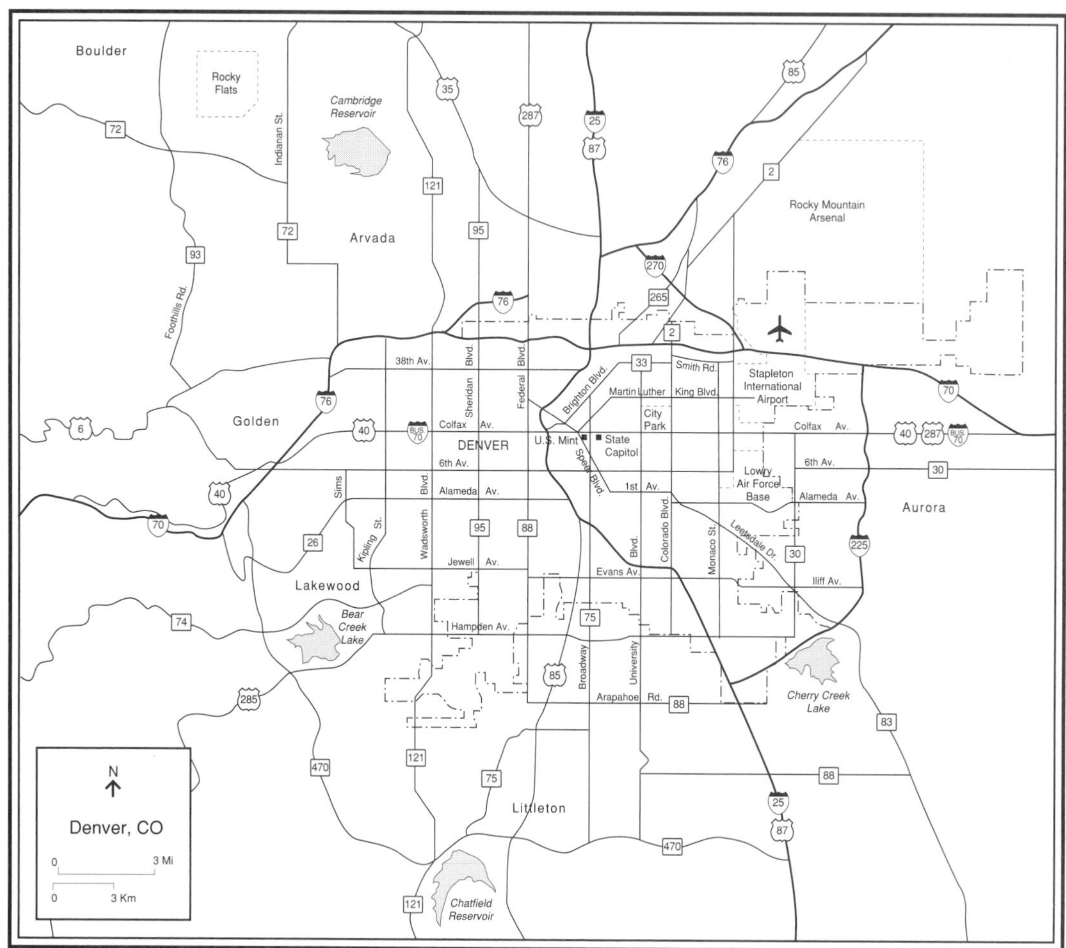
Boulder
Rocky Flats
Cambridge Reservoir
Arvada
Rocky Mountain Arsenal
Golden
DENVER
U.S. Mint
State Capitol
City Park
Stapleton International Airport
Lowry Air Force Base
Aurora
Lakewood
Bear Creek Lake
Cherry Creek Lake
Littleton
Chatfield Reservoir
Indianan St.
Foothills Rd.
38th Av.
Sheridan Blvd.
Federal Blvd.
Brighton Blvd.
Smith Rd.
Martin Luther King Blvd.
Colfax Av.
6th Av.
Alameda Av.
Sims
Kipling St.
Wadsworth Blvd.
Jewell Av.
Speer Blvd.
1st Av.
Colorado Blvd.
Monaco St.
Leetsdale Dr.
Evans Av.
Iliff Av.
Hampden Av.
Broadway
University Blvd.
Arapahoe Rd.
N
Denver, CO
0 3 Mi
0 3 Km

Detroit

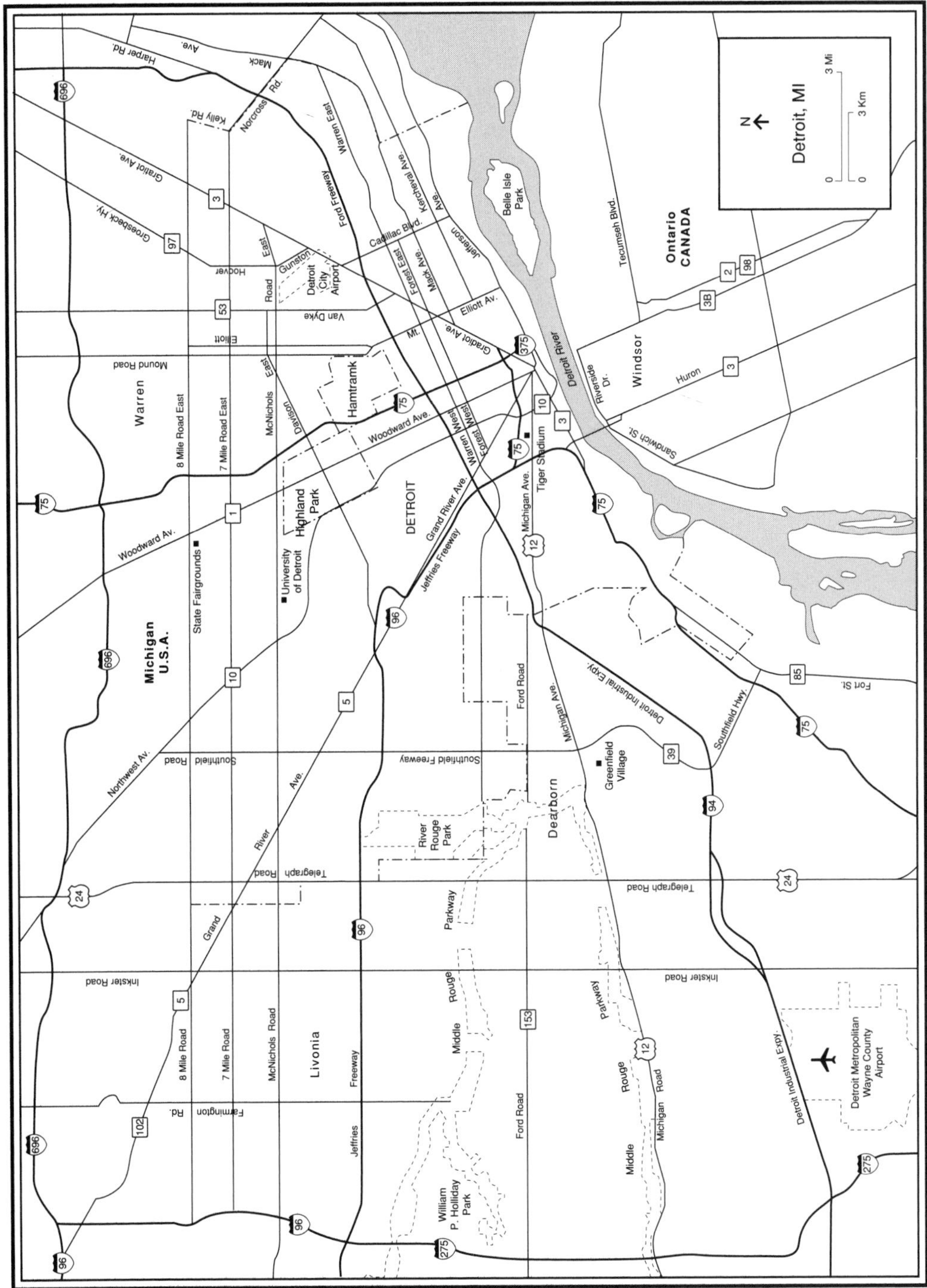
Detroit, MI
N
0 3 Mi
0 3 Km
Ontario
CANADA
Windsor
Michigan
U.S.A.
DETROIT
Warren
Hamtramck
Highland Park
Dearborn
Livonia
Detroit River
Belle Isle Park
Tiger Stadium
University of Detroit
State Fairgrounds
Greenfield Village
Detroit City Airport
River Rouge Park
William P. Holliday Park
Detroit Metropolitan Wayne County Airport
Harper Rd.
Mack Ave.
Kelly Rd.
Norcross Rd.
Gratiot Ave.
Groesbeck Hy.
Hoover
Van Dyke
Elliott
Mound Road
8 Mile Road East
7 Mile Road East
McNichols East
Davison
Gunston
East Road
Warren East
Ford Freeway
Kercheval Ave.
Cadillac Blvd.
Forest East
Mack Ave.
Jefferson Ave.
Elliott Av.
Mt. Elliott Ave.
Gratiot Ave.
Woodward Ave.
Woodward Av.
Warren West
Forest West
Grand River Ave.
Jeffries Freeway
Michigan Ave.
Ford Road
Detroit Industrial Expy.
Southfield Hwy.
Fort St.
Southfield Freeway
Southfield Road
Northwest Av.
Grand River Ave.
Telegraph Road
Parkway
Inkster Road
Middle Rouge Parkway
8 Mile Road
7 Mile Road
McNichols Road
Jeffries Freeway
Farmington Rd.
Michigan Road
Tecumseh Blvd.
Riverside Dr.
Huron
Sandwich St.
696
75
96
275
94
24
12
375
3
97
53
1
10
5
102
153
39
85
2
98
3B

Honolulu

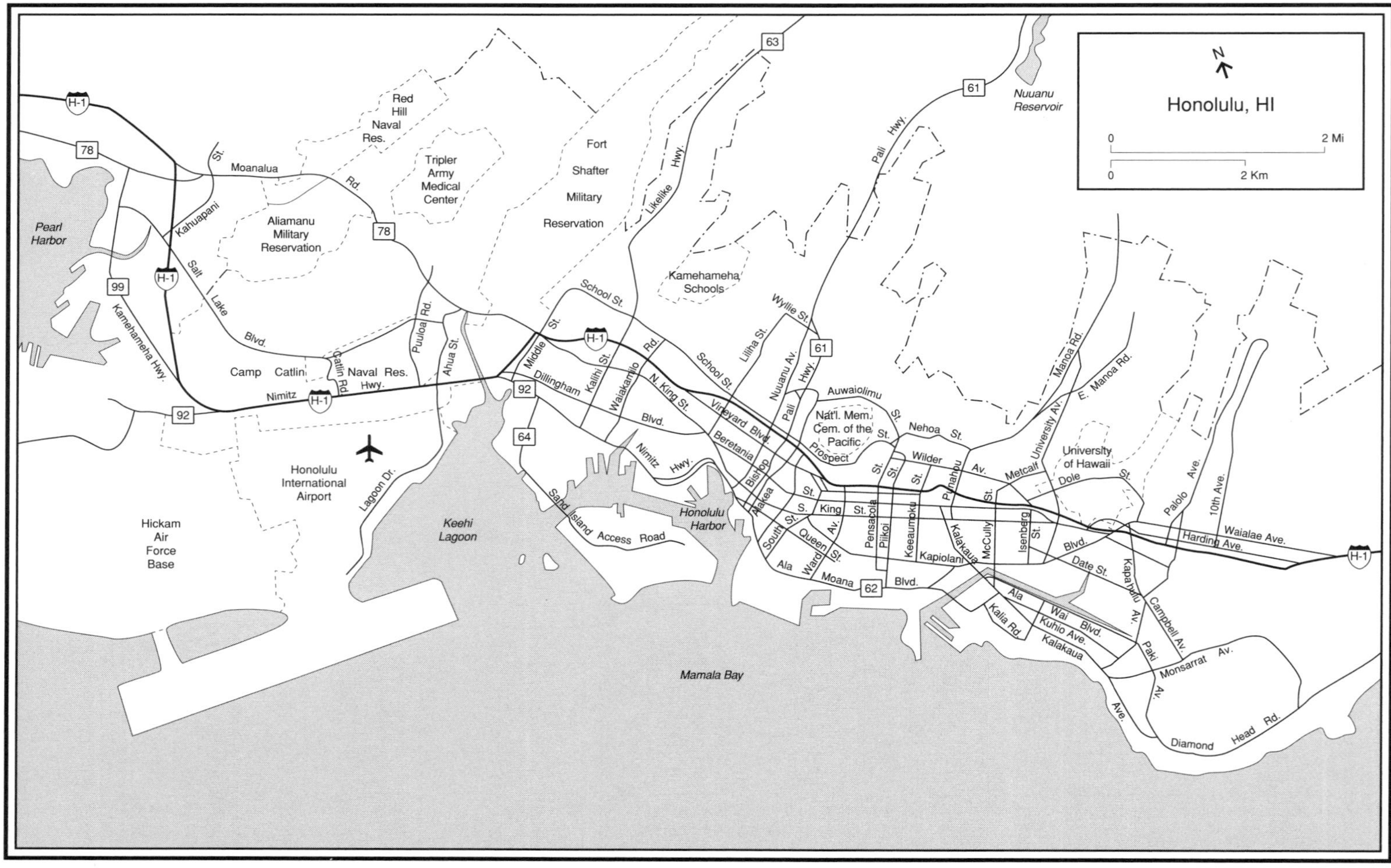
N
Honolulu, HI
0
2 Mi
0
2 Km
Nuuanu Reservoir
Pali Hwy.
Likelike Hwy.
Fort Shafter Military Reservation
Red Hill Naval Res.
Tripler Army Medical Center
Aliamanu Military Reservation
Moanalua Rd.
St.
Kahuapani
Salt Lake Blvd.
Pearl Harbor
Kamehameha Hwy.
Camp Catlin
Catlin Rd.
Naval Res. Hwy.
Nimitz
Puuloa Rd.
Ahua St.
Honolulu International Airport
Lagoon Dr.
Hickam Air Force Base
Keehi Lagoon
Sand Island Access Road
Honolulu Harbor
Mamala Bay
Kamehameha Schools
School St.
Middle St.
Dillingham Blvd.
Kalihi St.
Waiakamilo Rd.
N. King St.
Nimitz Hwy.
Vineyard Blvd.
Beretania
Bishop
Alakea
Liliha St.
Nuuanu Av.
Wyllie St.
Pali Hwy.
Auwaiolimu St.
Nat'l. Mem. Cem. of the Pacific
Prospect St.
Nehoa St.
Wilder Av.
S. King St.
South St.
Queen St.
Ward Av.
Ala Moana Blvd.
Pensacola St.
Piikoi St.
Keeaumoku St.
Punahou St.
Kapiolani Blvd.
Kalakaua
McCully St.
Isenberg St.
Metcalf St.
University Av.
Manoa Rd.
E. Manoa Rd.
University of Hawaii
Dole St.
Palolo Ave.
10th Ave.
Waialae Ave.
Harding Ave.
Date St.
Kapahulu Av.
Campbell Av.
Ala Wai Blvd.
Kalia Rd.
Kuhio Ave.
Kalakaua Ave.
Paki Av.
Monsarrat Av.
Diamond Head Rd.
H-1
61
62
63
64
78
92
99

Houston

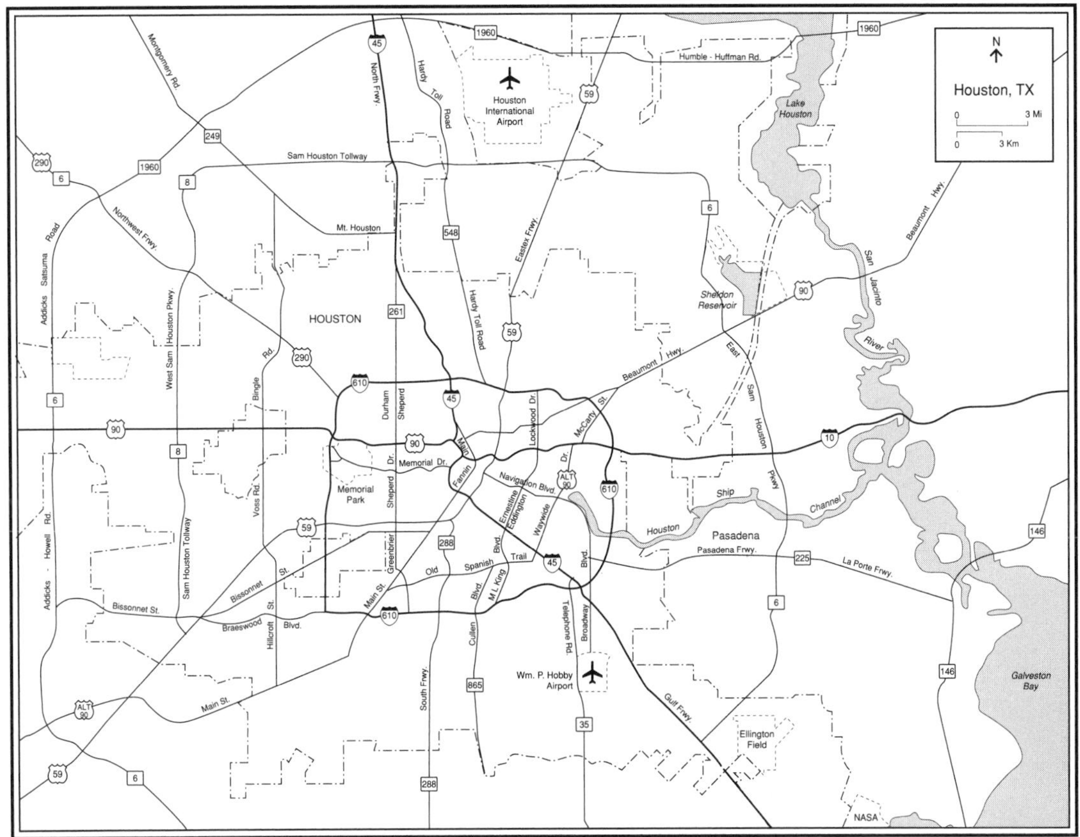
Houston, TX
N
0 3 Mi
0 3 Km
HOUSTON
Houston International Airport
Wm. P. Hobby Airport
Ellington Field
NASA
Lake Houston
Sheldon Reservoir
San Jacinto River
Houston Ship Channel
Galveston Bay
Pasadena
Memorial Park
Sam Houston Tollway
Mt. Houston
Humble - Huffman Rd.
Montgomery Rd.
Northwest Frwy.
North Frwy.
Hardy Toll Road
Eastex Frwy.
Beaumont Hwy.
East Sam Houston Pkwy.
Addicks - Satsuma Road
Addicks - Howell Rd.
West Sam Houston Pkwy.
Sam Houston Tollway
Bingle Rd.
Voss Rd.
Durham
Shepherd Dr.
Memorial Dr.
Main
Fannin
Lockwood Dr.
McCarty St.
Navigation Blvd.
Ernestine
Eddington
Waywide Dr.
Old Spanish Trail
Greenbrier
Bissonnet St.
Braeswood Blvd.
Hillcroft St.
Main St.
M L King Blvd.
Cullen Blvd.
Telephone Rd.
Broadway Blvd.
South Frwy.
Gulf Frwy.
Pasadena Frwy.
La Porte Frwy.
1960
45
59
249
290
6
8
548
261
610
90
10
ALT 90
288
225
146
865
35

Indianapolis

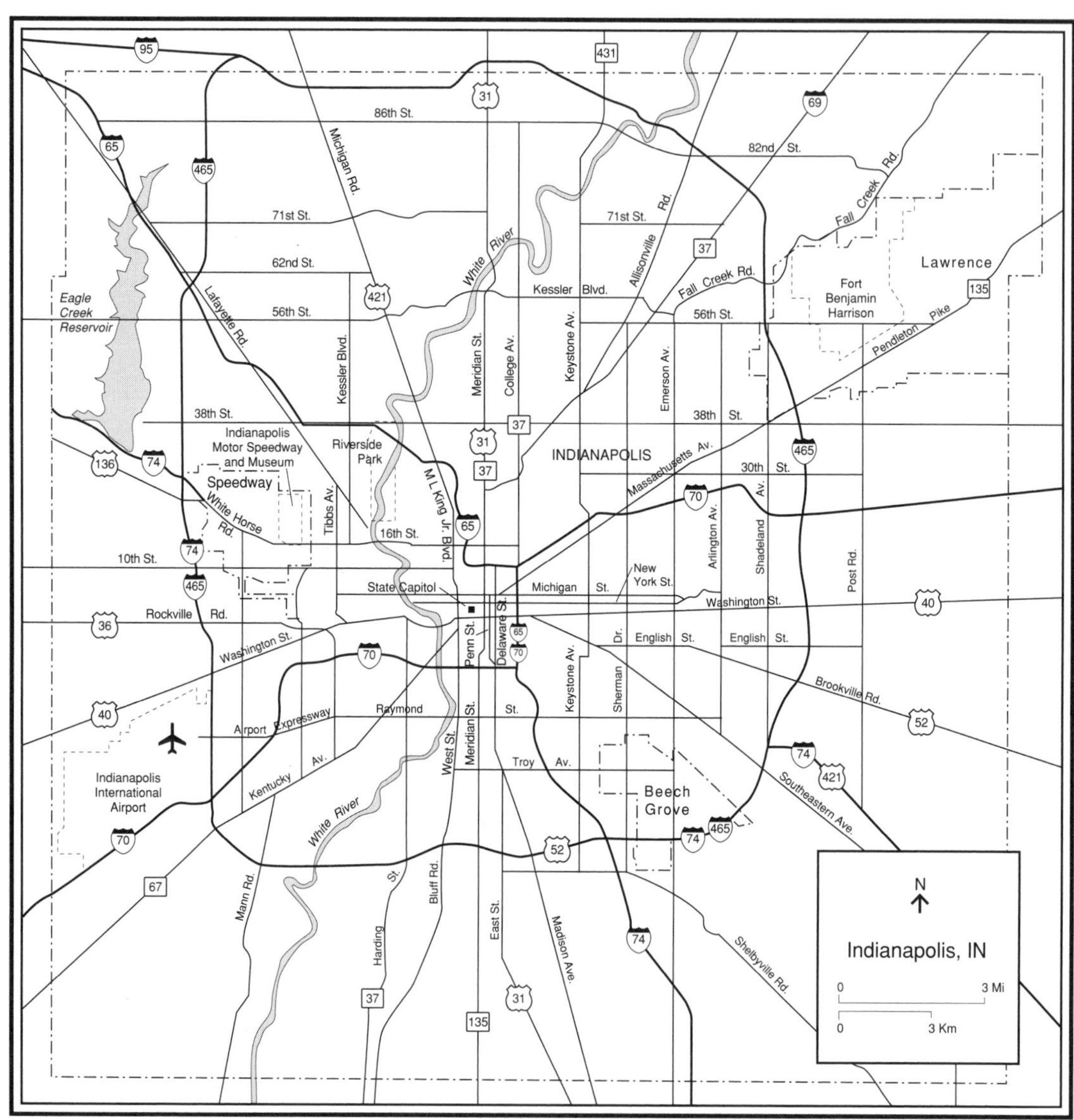

SAVE $25

DON'T MISS ANOTHER DEADLINE

Choice Courier Systems is now offering NEXT FLIGHT service. NEXT FLIGHT service enables you to fly your packages and documents immediately to any city in the United States.

Open your account today by calling (800) 223–1986, ext. 4000. When we issue you an account number, one phone call to the NEXT FLIGHT Control Center is all it will take to place your order.

First time shippers only. Send this coupon, with payment, with your invoice.

SAVE $10

Zig Ziglar

AMERICA'S FOREMOST SPEAKER

Zig Ziglar is the author of the only New York Times bestseller on selling. He has spoken all over the world, and changed the lives of millions of people. His books, videotapes and audiotapes on selling, goalsetting, positive mental attitude and success have sold millions of copies.

Mention this coupon when you order any Zig Ziglar product selling for more than $60 and take a $10 discount on your total order. See reverse side for details.

Save money on your next mailing!

Since 1975, *Cross Country Compute*r has specialized in computer outsourcing and data processing services for all types of business and consumer support and competitve prices.

Save money on your next mailing project. We will review your project with you absolutely free!

Mention this ad to recieve *Free Zip Processing*

SAVE 15%

Dartnell Business Services

SALES TRAINING AND NEWSLETTERS

Use this coupon to save 5% on Dartnell Marketing Publications' newsletter services, or save 15% on your first purchase from the Dartnell Corporate Training, Self–Development and Business Information Catalog.

New Subscribers Only. Send this coupon, with payment, to the address on the other side.

SAVE $19

THE MAGAZINE FOR INFORMATION EXECUTIVES

CIO, the technology management magazine for information executives, bridges the gap between technical IT news publications and general business magazines. Every issue contains case studies on successful implementations of technology applications and articles that detail information management trends as they pertain to important business issues such as quality, customer service and innovation. *CIO* is must reading for all executives.

New Subscribers Only. Send this coupon, with payment, to the address on the other side.

SAVE $33

Personal Selling Power

The how-to magazine for creating a more effective sales team. Receive practical ideas that improve selling skills, boost motivation, reduce sales cost and increase sales. Eight action packed issues a year.

Business Almanac Special
Get a three-year subscription at only $66 instead of the regular rate of $99. Plus, receive a FREE copy of the hardcover best seller *Superacheivers* (a $21 value) as a special bonus.

New Subscribers Only. Send this coupon, with payment, to the address on the other side.

FIRST SHIPMENT FREE!*

Just open a DHL preferred shipper account and get your first Express Document shipment absolutely FREE.

Call DHL at 1 800 228-3552 ext. 705

WE'LL TAKE IT FROM HERE™

New Customers Only.

SAVE $12

Success!

SUCCESS! is written for those seeking to achieve and succeed in life. Indepth tips on reaching your business and personal goals are featured in every issue. Profiles of successful entrepreneurs and hands-on tips you can use every day make SUCCESS! an important part of your life.

New Subscribers Only. Send this coupon, with payment, to the address on the other side.

Get Motivated Now.

For more information on all of Zig Ziglar's exciting programs, call (800) 527-0306. Don't wait another minute.

Please mention code: OTHR–BACOUP

One phone call is all it takes to place your order, NEXT FLIGH
service will do the rest:

- Pick Up Your Package
- Delivery
- Tracking
- Proof of Delivery

Name ______

Address ______

Company ______

City ______ State ____ Zip ____

Phone ______

For newsletters call Dartnell Boston at (800) 468-3038

For your free Corporate Training Catalog call or write Dartnell Chicago:

Dartnell Corporation
4660 N. Ravenswood Avenue
Chicago, IL 60640
(800) 621-5463

Get One Free Zip correction, Zip+4 appending, car-rt and delivery point barcoding with any list creation and maintenance. Offer valid for new accounts only, one file per company.

For more information call:
Lisa Phillips
Cross Country Computer Corp.
75 Corporate Drive.
Happauge, NY 1178-2021
(516) 231-4200

To save $33 off your three year subscription to *Personal Selling Power* and receive the hardcover book *Superacheivers* (a $21 dollar value) send this coupon with your check for $66 to :

PERSONAL SELLING POWER
1127 International Parkway
PO Box 5467
Fredricksburg VA 22403-0467

Or, call toll free:
(800) 752-7355
In VA call :
(703) 752-7000

There is no risk. If *Personal Selling Power* does not deliver 100% of what you expect, simply write to the above address and receive a prompt and courteous refund of the unused part of your subscription. (You may even keep the free bonus book!)

Yes, enter my one year subscription t
CIO magazine and bill me later for only $59, a savings of 24% off the basic rate of $78.

Name ______

Frm ______

Address ______

City ______ State ____ Zip ____

Send this coupon, with payment, to:
CIO Magazine, Attn: Circulation Department,
P.O. Box 9208, Framingham, MA 01701

This is a domestic rate only (Canada & U.S.) the foreign rate is $175 U.

Save $12

Success! has a newsstand price of $25 a year. Subscribe with this coupon and pay just $12.97 for ten issues. Call (800) 234-7324 to subscribe.

WE'LL TAKE IT FROM HERE℠

Call DHL at (800) 228-3552 ext. 705

*Offer good for new DHL customers only.
Valid only on a domestic or international Express Document shipment (up to 30 pages or 8 oz.) originating in the United States.

ave $100+ CompuServe

The Working–From–Home Forum. The Entrepreneur's Forum. The Investors Forum. These are just a few of the many online products ideal for the small business entrepreneur. Now, you can discover the exciting world of CompuServe at the low start up price of just $25 for your membership kit.

For only $25 your membership includes software, a $25 usage credit, a free subscription to CompuServe magazine and one free month of popular basic services. Offer expires September 30, 1994

ew Subscribers Only. Mention this coupon when you call the number on the other side.

Save $10 UPDATE: The Executive's Purchasing Advisor

Published by Buyer's Laboratory, Inc., the nation's leading independent office products testing lab, *Update: The Executive's Purchasing Advisor* educates readers on how to make wise purchases of all types of office products. Use this coupon to get $10 off the $95 subscription price of this 16-page monthly newsletter.

New Subscribers Only. Send this coupon, with payment, to the address on the other side.

ave $75 Starch Tested Copy

Drawing from the world's largest print ad database, this unique newsletter presents the most up–to–date analysis (with actual examples) of print advertising. Find out what really works in print advertising, what doesn't, and why, and learn the answers to the most asked advertising questions of the day. Save $75 off the regular price of $250 a year.

ew Subscribers Only. Send this coupon, with payment, to the address on the other side.

SAVE $25 Hudson's Subscription Newsletter Directory

The specialized newsletter press–read by America's most influential readers. 4,247 prime newletters, by subject, category, name, company, phone, fax, editor, publisher, subscription price, frequency, founding dates and press release information. Also, 240 multiple publishers. Save $25 off the regular price of $128.

New Subscribers Only. Send this coupon, with payment, to the address on the other side.

AVE $50 American Business Publishing

Timely Information on Critical Issues

- *The Executive Report on Managed Care*—
  News on HMOs, PPOs, IPAs, UR Programs and more.
- *Employee Assistance Program Management Letter*—
  Briefings on issues surrounding EAPs.
- *Employers' Health Benefits Management Letter*—
  Advice on balancing employee satisfaction, healthcare quality & cost containment.
- *Travel Expense Management*—
  Effective, proven advice on saving corporate travel dollars.

ew Subscribers Only. Send this coupon, with payment, to the address on the other side.

SAVE $47 Business and the Environment

BATE puts your organization on the cutting...and profitable...edge of the corporate environmental movement. Its news coverage cuts across national boundaries and industry sectors to bring you the best of what's working and provide critical benchmarking information. Monthly since 1990. $497 in North America.

(120*CO8H1)

New Subscribers Only. Send this coupon, with payment, to the address on the other side.

AVE $40 From the STATE CAPITALS

From the STATE CAPITALS newsletters cover state government activities across the nation. 18 separate titles–taxes, economic development, employee policies and much more. You select the subjects–we provide the weekly reports on activities concerning those subjects.
Subscriptions $215 to $295. See other side.

New Subscribers Only. Send this coupon, with payment, to the address on the other side.

MIC/ Tech–Microcomputers

An electronic information service providing detailed performance and pricing on personal computers, laptops, notebooks, servers, and workstations. Updated monthly, runs on IBM PCs and compatibles and Apple MACs. Send this coupon with a check for $795 to the address on the other side.

New Subscribers Only. Send this coupon, with payment, to the address on the other side.

FREE UPDATE

On January 15, 1994, the editors of *The Information Please Business Almanac and Desk Reference* will publish a 32-page update to this book. You can get a **free** copy by mailing or faxing this coupon to:

BOX 660
Yonkers, NY 10710
•
fax (914) 664-4615

Please Send A Free Update To:

Name ____________________

Company ____________________

Address ____________________

City ____________ State ______ Zip ______

Phone ____________ Fax ____________

Limit one per address. Please allow four weeks for delivery.

This Almanac will soon be available on Floppy Disk.

HERE'S HOW TO WIN A FREE COPY:

Imagine how useful the information in the *Almanac* would be running on your computer. You can instantly access hundreds of thousands of pieces of data, incorporate information into reports and letters, even find phone numbers for critical business contacts and government agencies.

As we go to press, Houghton Mifflin Company is finalizing plans for a computerized version of the *Almanac*. For details, and for a chance to win a free copy of the Almanac on disk, just fill in the coupon at right and send this card to the address on the other side. You don't even have to pay for the stamp.

Please Send FREE Information To:

Name ______________________

Company ______________________

Address ______________________

City ____________ State ______ Zip ______

Phone ____________ Fax ____________

Limit one entry per address. In the sole discretion of Houghton Mifflin, winner may receive an equivalent prize in cash or books. No purchase necessary. To enter without purchasing, send a facsimile of this form to the address on the other side.

FREE UPDATE

On January 15, 1994, the editors of *The Information Please Business Almanac and Desk Reference* will publish a 32-page update to this book. You can get a **free** copy by mailing or faxing us the coupon below. Sorry, only one update per address.

Mail or fax this form to:

BOX 660
Yonkers, NY 10710
•
fax (914) 664-4615

Please Send A Free Update To:

Name ______________________

Company ______________________

Address ______________________

City ____________ State ______ Zip ______

Phone ____________ Fax ____________

Limit one per address. Please allow four weeks for delivery.

Free Update. Floppy Disk.

Don't Delay.

NO POSTAGE
NECESSARY
IF MAILED
IN THE
UNITED STATES

BUSINESS REPLY MAIL

FIRST CLASS MAIL PERMIT NO. 2166 BOSTON, MA

POSTAGE WILL BE PAID BY ADDRESSEE

ATT: SOFTWARE DEPARTMENT - 11TH FLOOR
HOUGHTON MIFFLIN COMPANY
222 BERKELEY ST
BOSTON MA 02116-9330

Kansas City

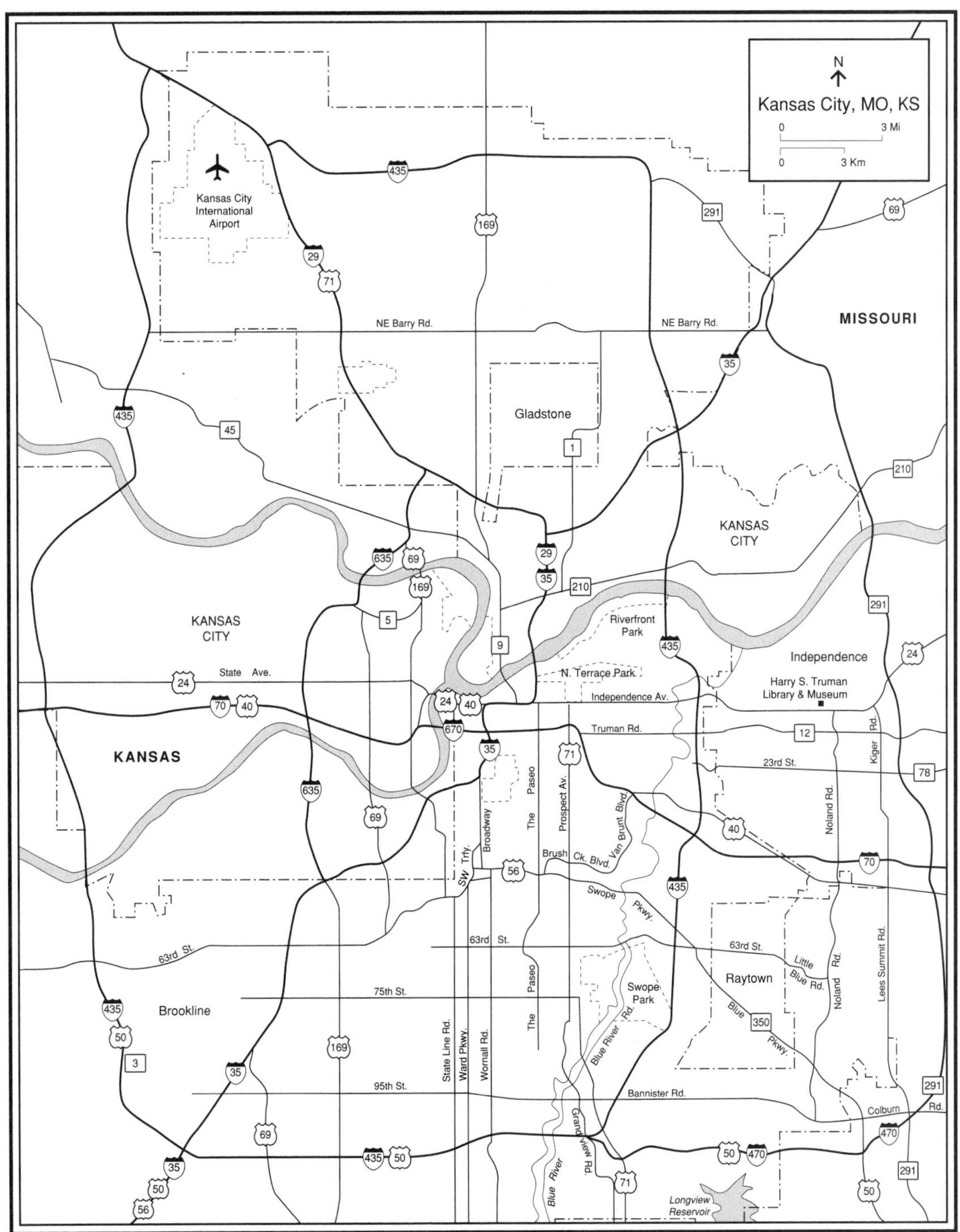
N
Kansas City, MO, KS
0 3 Mi
0 3 Km
Kansas City International Airport
MISSOURI
NE Barry Rd.
NE Barry Rd.
Gladstone
KANSAS CITY
KANSAS CITY
Riverfront Park
Independence
Harry S. Truman Library & Museum
N. Terrace Park
Independence Av.
State Ave.
Truman Rd.
23rd St.
KANSAS
Kiger Rd.
Noland Rd.
Broadway
The Paseo
Prospect Av.
Van Brunt Blvd.
Brush Ck. Blvd.
SW Trfy.
Swope Pkwy.
63rd St.
63rd St.
63rd St.
Raytown
Little Blue Rd.
Noland Rd.
Lees Summit Rd.
75th St.
Brookline
Swope Park
Blue River Rd.
Blue Pkwy.
State Line Rd.
Ward Pkwy.
Wornall Rd.
The Paseo
95th St.
Bannister Rd.
Colburn Rd.
Grandview Rd.
Blue River
Longview Reservoir

Los Angeles

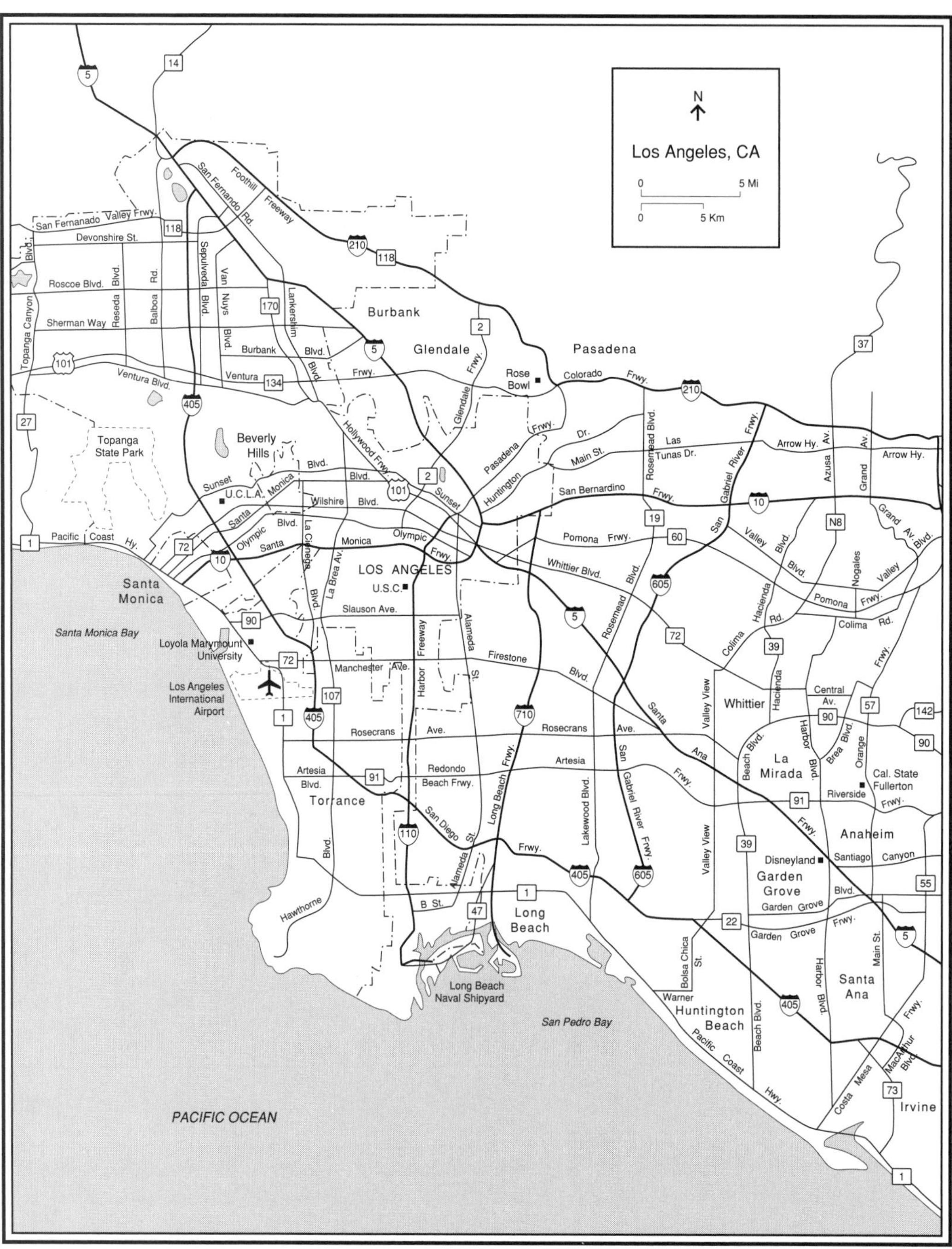
N
Los Angeles, CA
0
5 Mi
0
5 Km
San Fernando Valley Frwy.
Devonshire St.
Roscoe Blvd.
Sherman Way
Reseda Blvd.
Balboa Rd.
Sepulveda Blvd.
Van Nuys Blvd.
Topanga Canyon Blvd.
San Fernando Rd.
Foothill Freeway
Lankershim Blvd.
Burbank Blvd.
Ventura Blvd.
Ventura Frwy.
Burbank
Glendale
Pasadena
Rose Bowl
Colorado Frwy.
Glendale Frwy.
Hollywood Frwy.
Pasadena Frwy.
Topanga State Park
Beverly Hills
Sunset Blvd.
U.C.L.A.
Santa Monica Blvd.
Wilshire Blvd.
Olympic Blvd.
Santa Monica Frwy.
Pacific Coast Hy.
Santa Monica
Santa Monica Bay
La Cienega Blvd.
La Brea Av.
LOS ANGELES
U.S.C.
Slauson Ave.
Harbor Freeway
Alameda St.
Firestone Blvd.
Manchester Ave.
Loyola Marymount University
Los Angeles International Airport
Rosecrans Ave.
Artesia Blvd.
Redondo Beach Frwy.
Torrance
San Diego Frwy.
Long Beach Frwy.
Hawthorne Blvd.
B St.
Long Beach
Long Beach Naval Shipyard
San Pedro Bay
PACIFIC OCEAN
Huntington Dr.
Main St.
Las Tunas Dr.
Rosemead Blvd.
San Bernardino Frwy.
Pomona Frwy.
Whittier Blvd.
Santa Ana Frwy.
San Gabriel River Frwy.
Lakewood Blvd.
Arrow Hy.
Azusa Av.
Grand Av.
Valley Blvd.
Hacienda Rd.
Colima Rd.
Nogales
Pomona Frwy.
Valley View
Whittier
Central Av.
Beach Blvd.
La Mirada
Harbor Blvd.
Brea Blvd.
Orange
Cal. State Fullerton
Riverside Frwy.
Anaheim
Disneyland
Santiago Canyon
Garden Grove
Garden Grove Frwy.
Bolsa Chica St.
Warner
Huntington Beach
Pacific Coast Hwy.
Santa Ana
Main St.
Costa Mesa Frwy.
MacArthur Blvd.
Irvine
5
14
118
210
170
101
134
405
27
2
1
72
10
90
107
91
110
47
710
19
60
605
39
22
37
N8
57
142
55
73

Miami

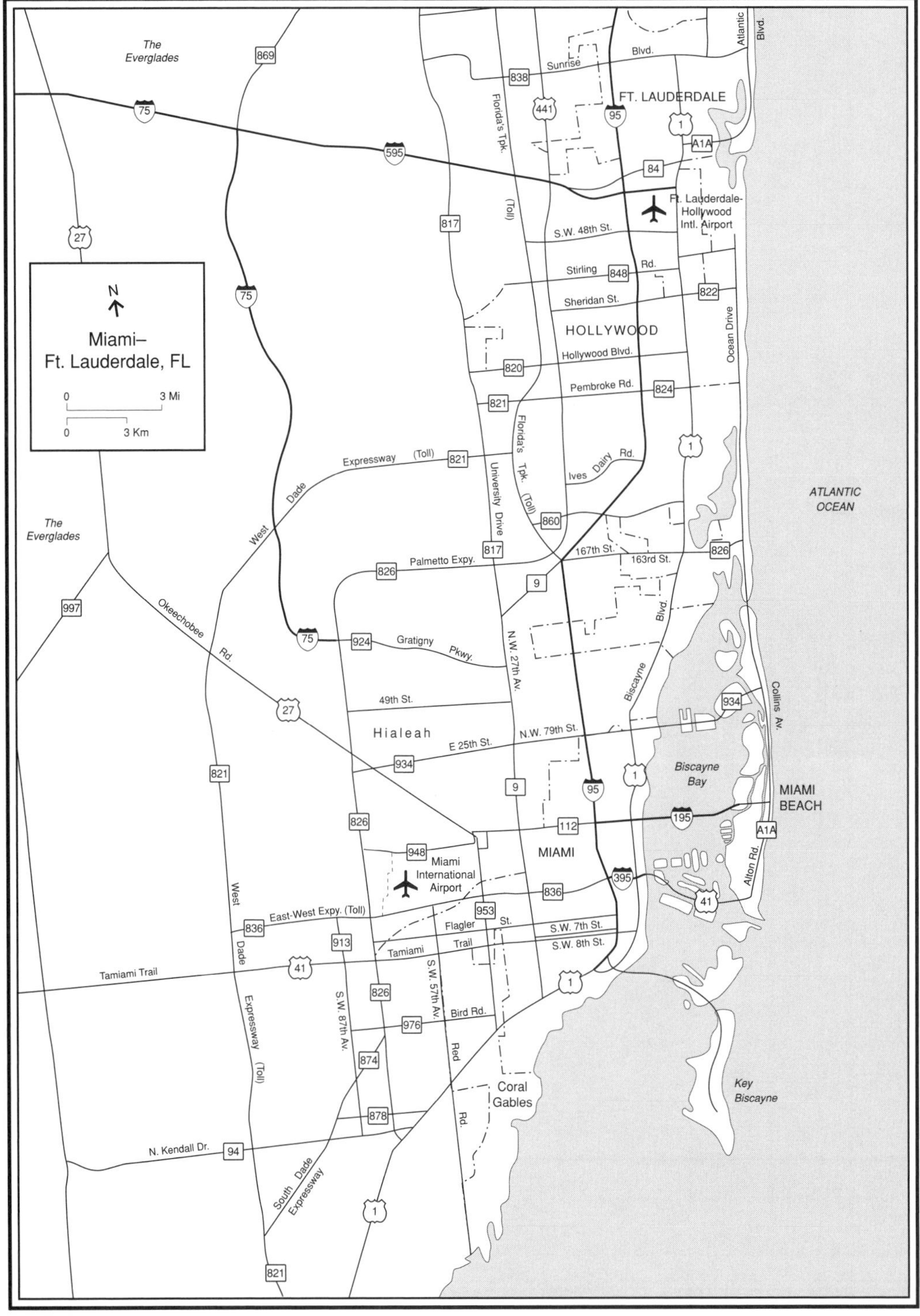
The Everglades
869
Sunrise Blvd.
838
441
95
FT. LAUDERDALE
1
A1A
75
595
84
Florida's Tpk. (Toll)
Ft. Lauderdale-Hollywood Intl. Airport
817
S.W. 48th St.
27
Stirling Rd.
848
N
Miami–Ft. Lauderdale, FL
0 3 Mi
0 3 Km
75
822
Sheridan St.
HOLLYWOOD
Ocean Drive
Hollywood Blvd.
820
Pembroke Rd.
824
821
Florida's Tpk. (Toll)
Expressway (Toll)
821
Ives Dairy Rd.
West Dade
University Drive
ATLANTIC OCEAN
The Everglades
860
817
167th St.
826
Palmetto Expy.
163rd St.
826
9
997
Okeechobee Rd.
Blvd.
75
924
Gratigny Pkwy.
N.W. 27th Av.
Biscayne
Collins Av.
27
49th St.
934
Hialeah
N.W. 79th St.
E 25th St.
934
821
9
95
1
Biscayne Bay
MIAMI BEACH
195
826
112
A1A
948
MIAMI
Alton Rd.
Miami International Airport
395
836
West Dade Expressway (Toll)
836
East-West Expy. (Toll)
953
41
913
Flagler St.
S.W. 7th St.
Tamiami Trail
S.W. 8th St.
Tamiami Trail
41
S.W. 57th Av.
826
1
S.W. 87th Av.
Bird Rd.
976
Red Rd.
874
Coral Gables
Key Biscayne
878
N. Kendall Dr.
94
South Dade Expressway
1
821

Minneapolis

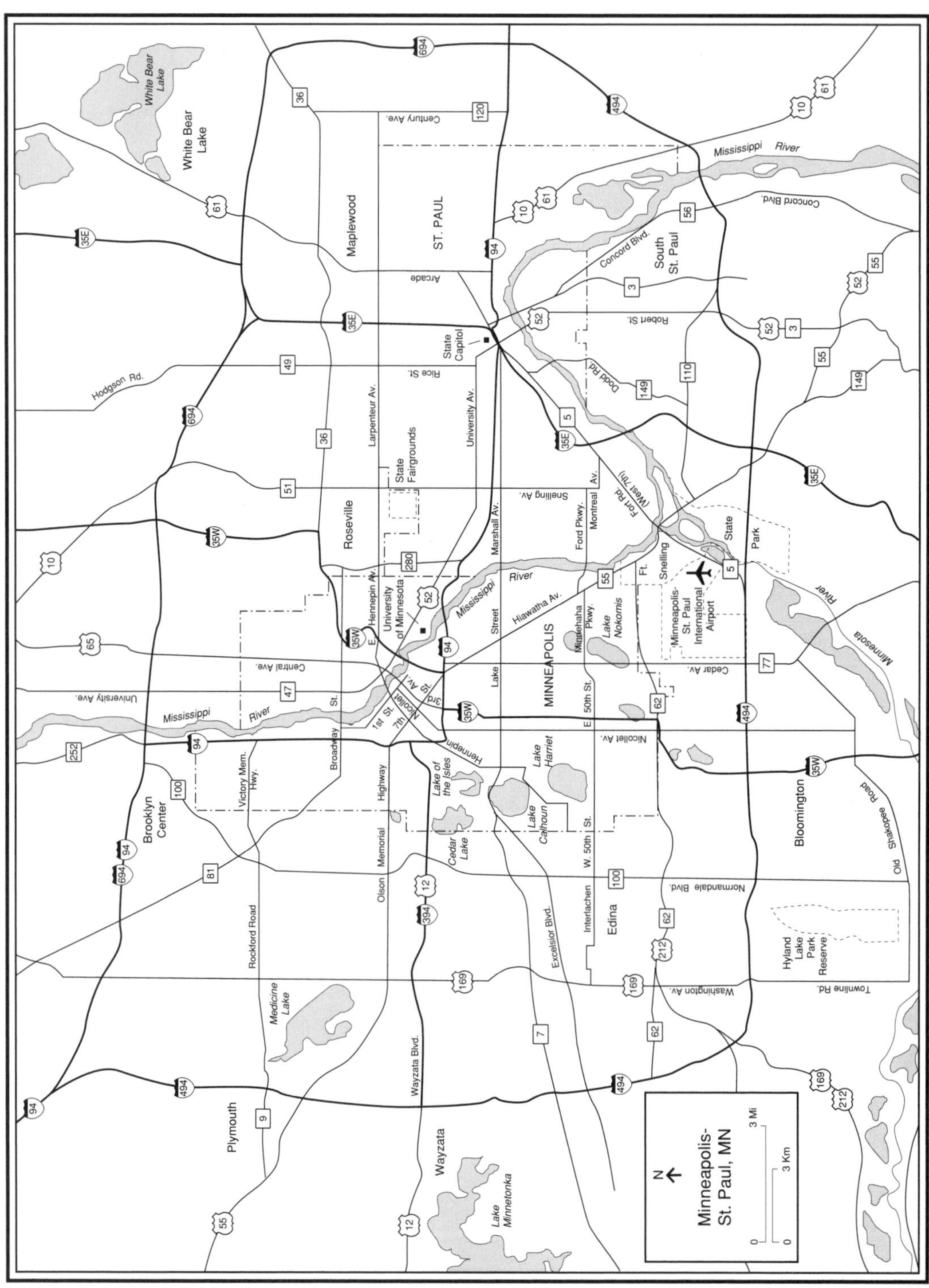

New Orleans

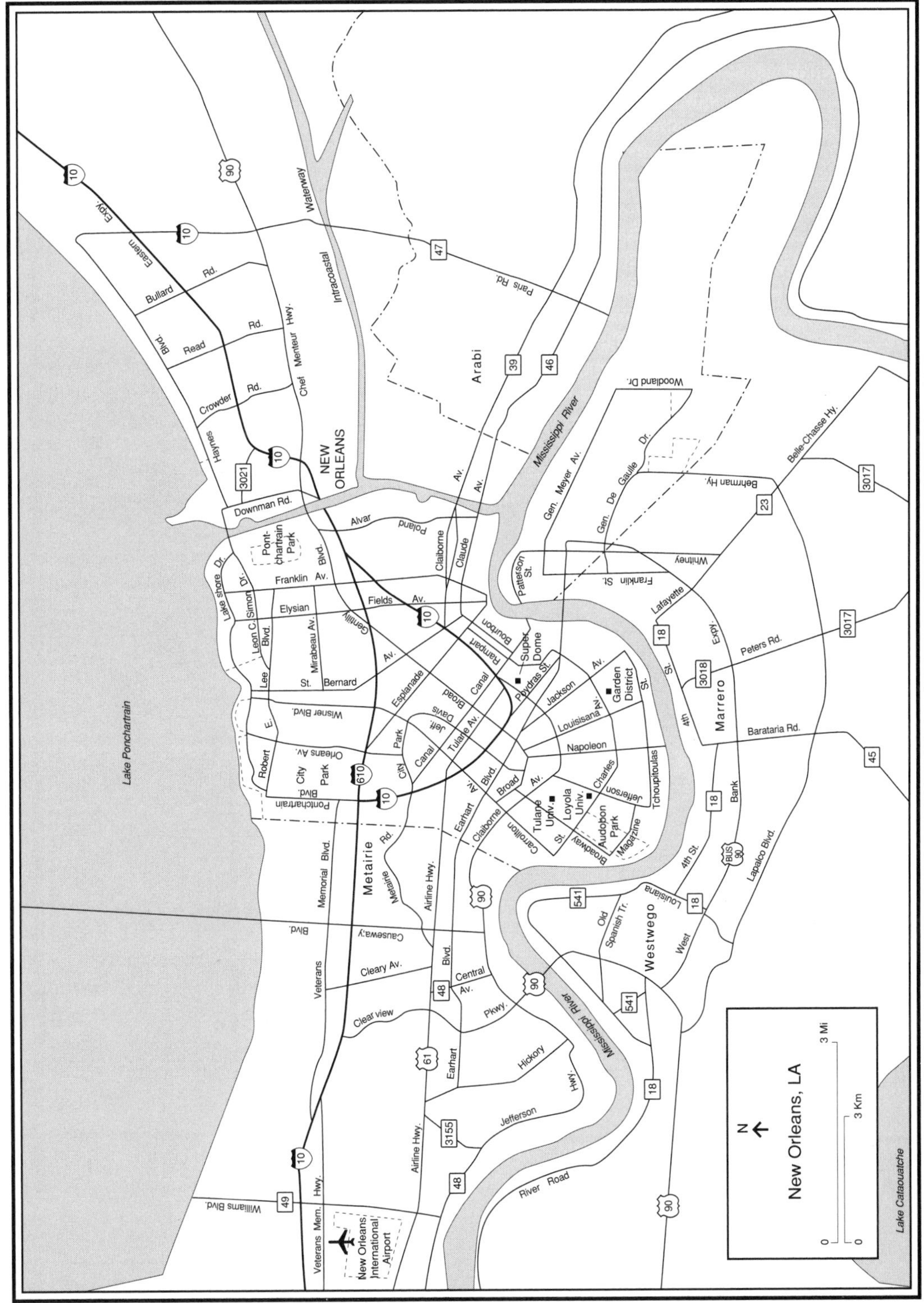
New Orleans, LA
Lake Ponchartrain
Lake Cataouatche
Mississippi River
Intracoastal Waterway
NEW ORLEANS
Arabi
Metairie
Marrero
Westwego
New Orleans International Airport
Superdome
Garden District
Tulane Univ.
Loyola Univ.
Audobon Park
City Park
Pontchartrain Park
0 3 Mi
0 3 Km

New York

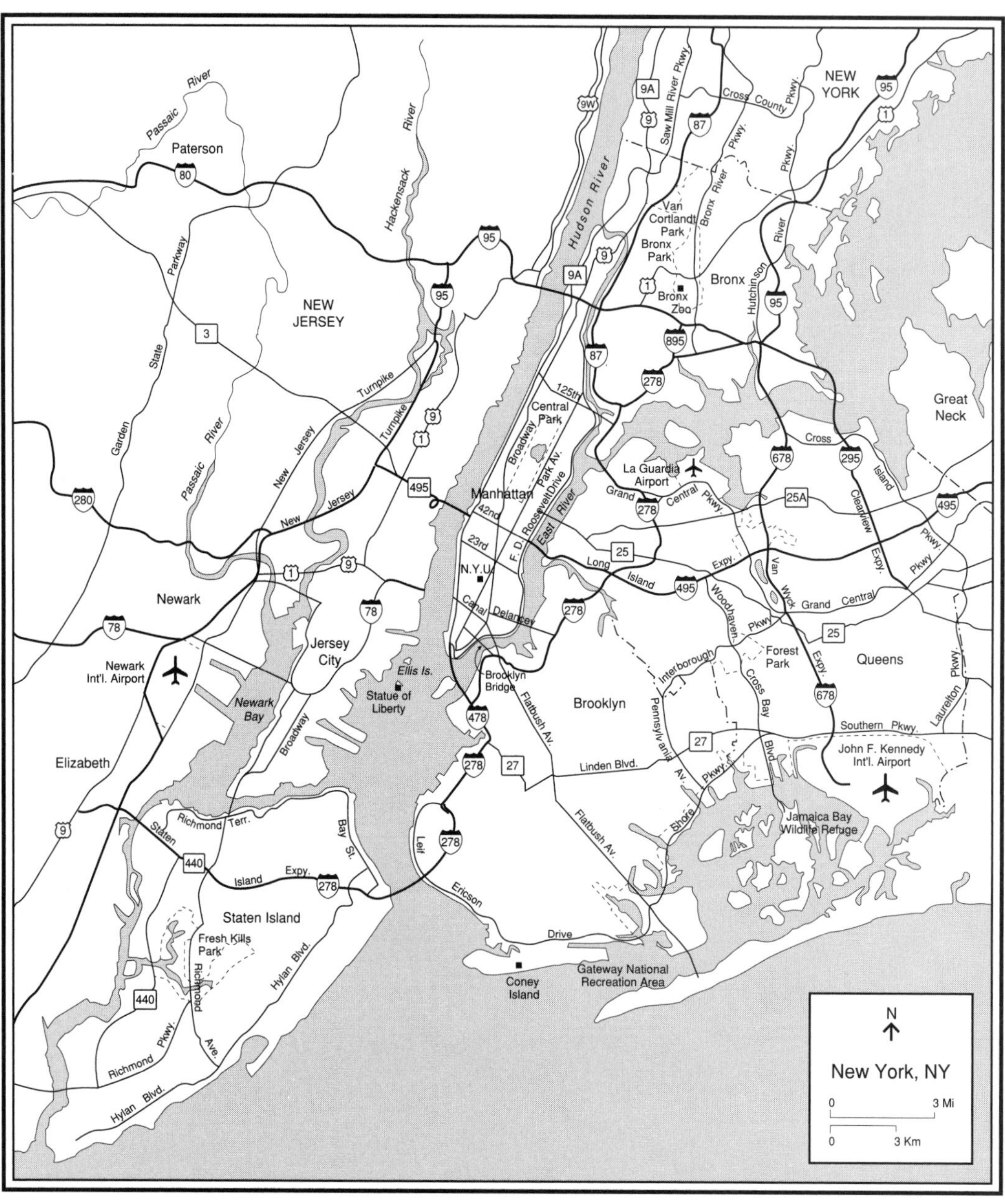
Passaic River
Paterson
Hackensack River
Hudson River
NEW JERSEY
Garden State Parkway
Passaic River
New Jersey Turnpike
Newark
Newark Int'l. Airport
Elizabeth
Newark Bay
Jersey City
Ellis Is.
Statue of Liberty
Manhattan
Central Park
N.Y.U.
Broadway
Park Av.
F.D. Roosevelt Drive
East River
125th
42nd
23rd
Canal
Delancey
Brooklyn Bridge
Flatbush Av.
Brooklyn
Linden Blvd.
Pennsylvania Av.
Shore Pkwy.
Leif Ericson Drive
Coney Island
Gateway National Recreation Area
Staten Island
Richmond Terr.
Staten Island Expy.
Bay St.
Fresh Kills Park
Richmond Ave.
Richmond Pkwy.
Hylan Blvd.
Saw Mill River Pkwy
Cross County Pkwy.
NEW YORK
Van Cortlandt Park
Bronx Park
Bronx River
Bronx Zoo
Bronx
Hutchinson River Pkwy.
La Guardia Airport
Grand Central Pkwy.
Long Island Expy.
Woodhaven Pkwy.
Interborough
Forest Park
Cross Bay Blvd.
Van Wyck Expy.
Queens
Cross Island Pkwy.
Clearview Expy.
Great Neck
Southern Pkwy.
Laurelton Pkwy.
John F. Kennedy Int'l. Airport
Jamaica Bay Wildlife Refuge
N
New York, NY
0 3 Mi
0 3 Km

Philadelphia

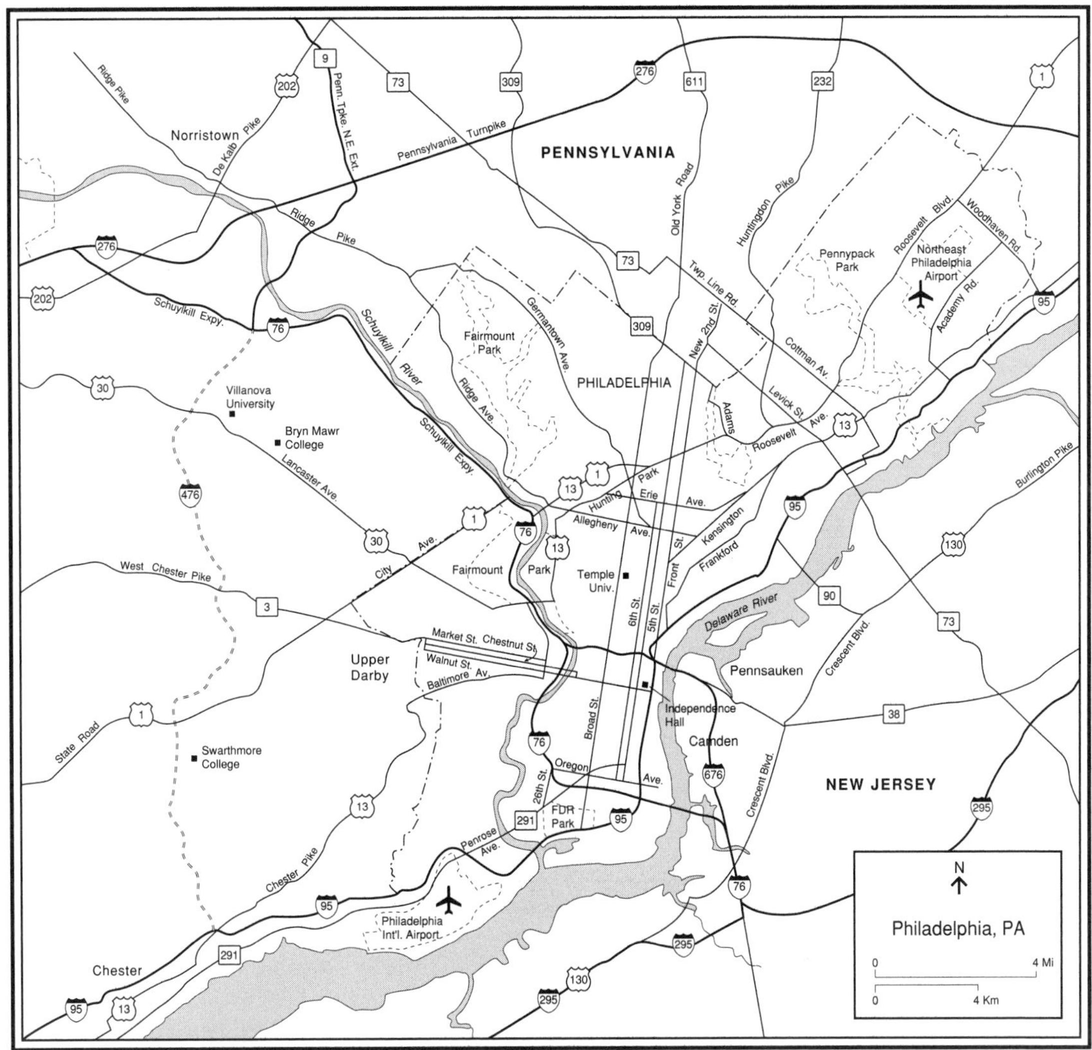

Phoenix

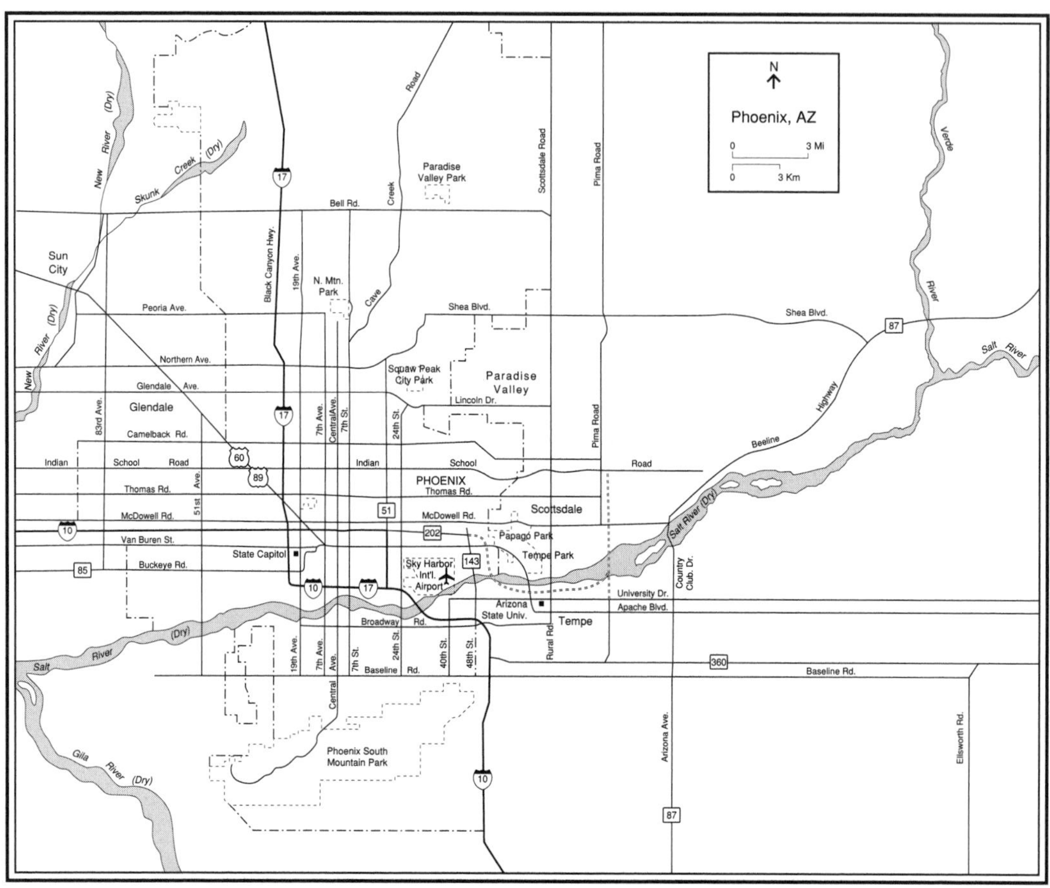
Phoenix, AZ
N
0 3 Mi
0 3 Km
Sun City
Glendale
PHOENIX
Scottsdale
Paradise Valley
Tempe
New River (Dry)
Skunk Creek (Dry)
Salt River (Dry)
Gila River (Dry)
Verde River
Salt River
Bell Rd.
Peoria Ave.
Northern Ave.
Glendale Ave.
Camelback Rd.
Indian School Road
Thomas Rd.
McDowell Rd.
Van Buren St.
Buckeye Rd.
Shea Blvd.
Lincoln Dr.
Broadway Rd.
Baseline Rd.
University Dr.
Apache Blvd.
Black Canyon Hwy.
Cave Creek Road
Scottsdale Road
Pima Road
Beeline Highway
83rd Ave.
51st Ave.
19th Ave.
7th Ave.
Central Ave.
7th St.
24th St.
40th St.
48th St.
Rural Rd.
Country Club Dr.
Arizona Ave.
Ellsworth Rd.
Paradise Valley Park
N. Mtn. Park
Squaw Peak City Park
Papago Park
Tempe Park
State Capitol
Sky Harbor Int'l. Airport
Arizona State Univ.
Phoenix South Mountain Park
17
10
60
89
51
202
143
85
87
360

Pittsburgh

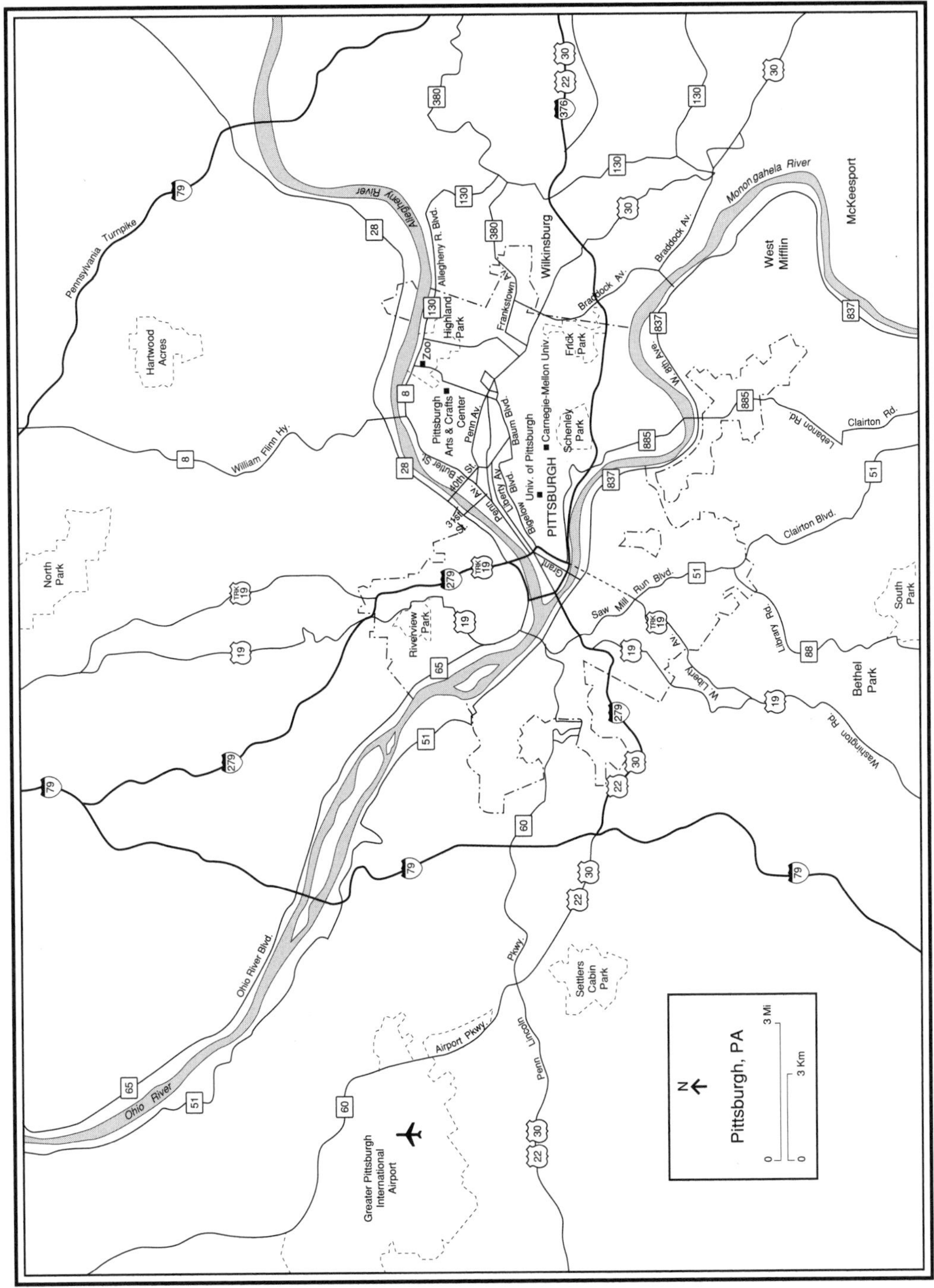
Pennsylvania Turnpike
Hartwood Acres
William Flinn Hy.
North Park
Allegheny River
Allegheny R. Blvd.
Highland Park
Zoo
Pittsburgh Arts & Crafts Center
Penn Av.
Butler St.
40th St.
31st St.
Frankstown Av.
Wilkinsburg
Baum Blvd.
Liberty Av.
Bigelow Blvd.
Univ. of Pittsburgh
Carnegie-Mellon Univ.
PITTSBURGH
Schenley Park
Frick Park
Braddock Av.
Monongahela River
West Mifflin
McKeesport
W. 8th Ave.
Lebanon Rd.
Clairton Rd.
Clairton Blvd.
Grant
Saw Mill Run Blvd.
W. Liberty Av.
Library Rd.
South Park
Bethel Park
Washington Rd.
Riverview Park
Ohio River Blvd.
Ohio River
Airport Pkwy.
Pkwy.
Penn Lincoln
Settlers Cabin Park
Greater Pittsburgh International Airport
Pittsburgh, PA
N
0
3 Mi
0
3 Km

St. Louis

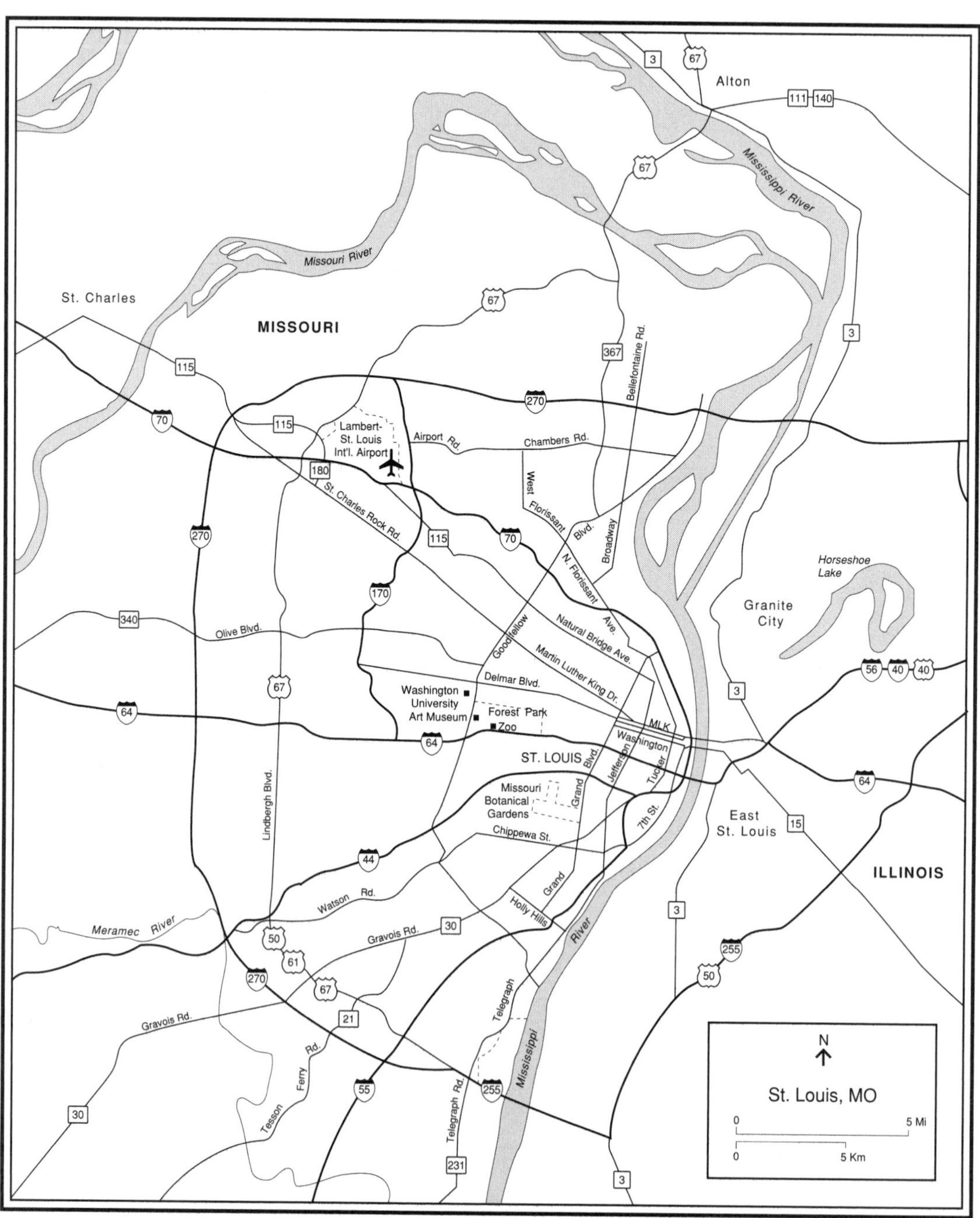

Alton
Mississippi River
Missouri River
St. Charles
MISSOURI
Bellefontaine Rd.
Lambert-St. Louis Int'l. Airport
Airport Rd.
Chambers Rd.
West Florissant Blvd.
Broadway
St. Charles Rock Rd.
N. Florissant Ave.
Horseshoe Lake
Granite City
Olive Blvd.
Goodfellow
Natural Bridge Ave.
Martin Luther King Dr.
Delmar Blvd.
Washington University Art Museum
Forest Park
Zoo
MLK
Washington
ST. LOUIS
Grand Blvd.
Jefferson
Tucker
Missouri Botanical Gardens
7th St.
East St. Louis
Lindbergh Blvd.
Chippewa St.
ILLINOIS
Watson Rd.
Grand
Holly Hills
Meramec River
Gravois Rd.
River
Telegraph
Gravois Rd.
Ferry Rd.
Tesson
Telegraph Rd.
Mississippi
St. Louis, MO
N
0
5 Mi
0
5 Km

San Diego

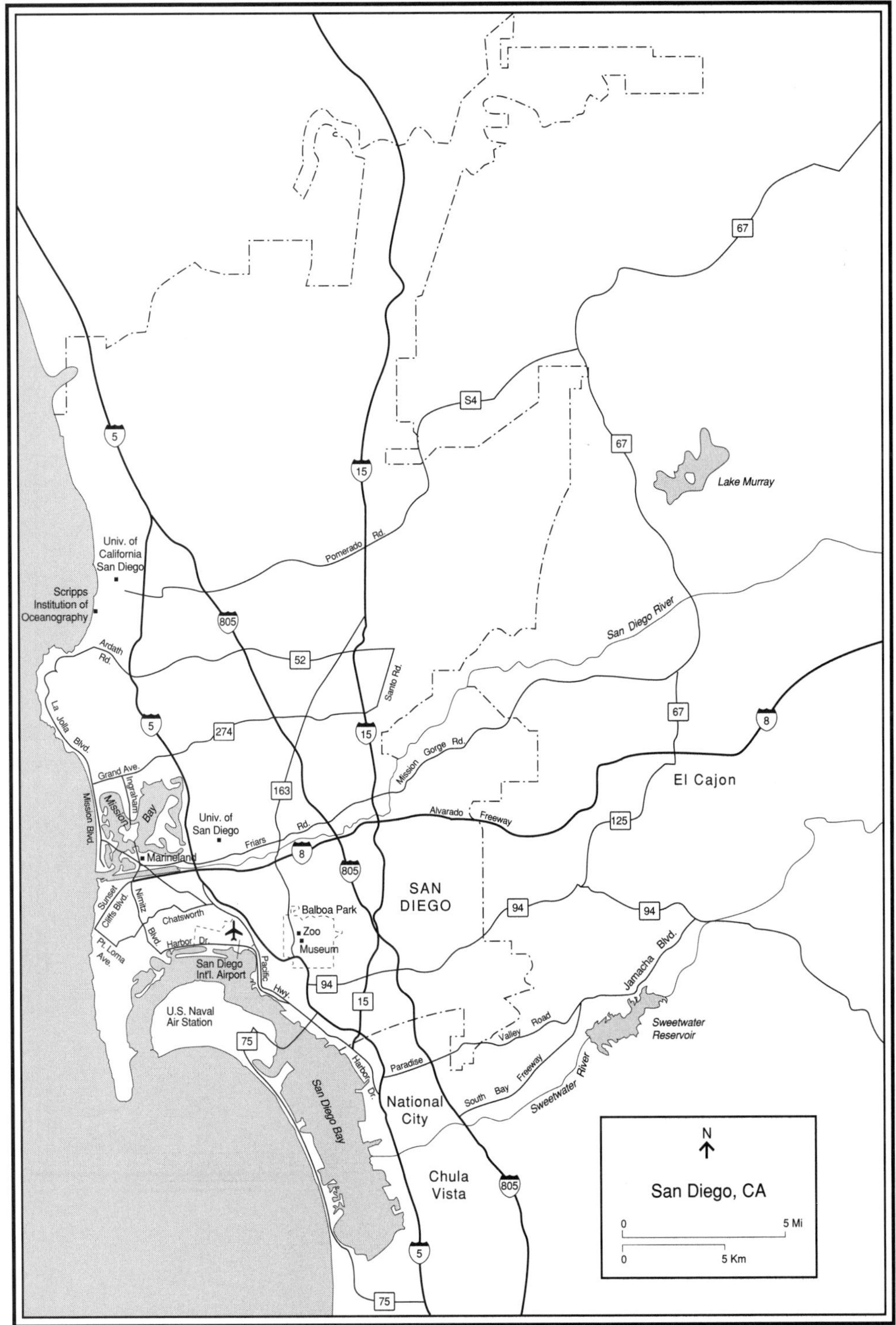

Univ. of California San Diego
Scripps Institution of Oceanography
Lake Murray
Pomerado Rd.
San Diego River
Ardath Rd.
Santo Rd.
La Jolla Blvd.
Mission Gorge Rd.
Grand Ave.
Ingraham
Mission Bay
Mission Blvd.
Univ. of San Diego
Friars Rd.
Alvarado Freeway
El Cajon
Marineland
Sunset Cliffs Blvd.
Nimitz Blvd.
Chatsworth
Harbor Dr.
Balboa Park
Zoo
Museum
SAN DIEGO
Pt. Loma Ave.
San Diego Int'l. Airport
Pacific Hwy.
Jamacha Blvd.
U.S. Naval Air Station
Valley Road
Sweetwater Reservoir
Harbor Dr.
Paradise
South Bay Freeway
Sweetwater River
San Diego Bay
National City
Chula Vista
N
San Diego, CA
0 5 Mi
0 5 Km

San Francisco

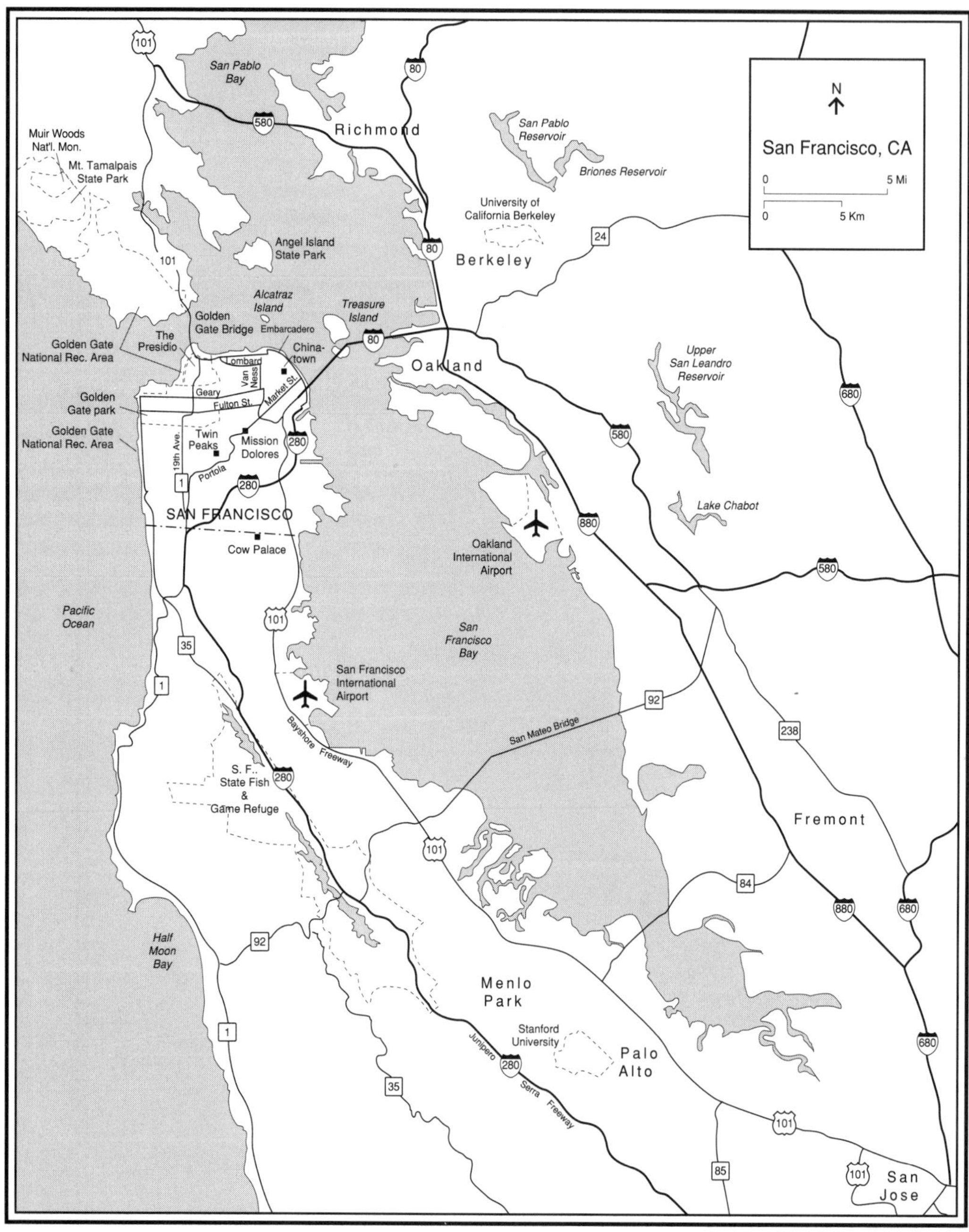

Seattle

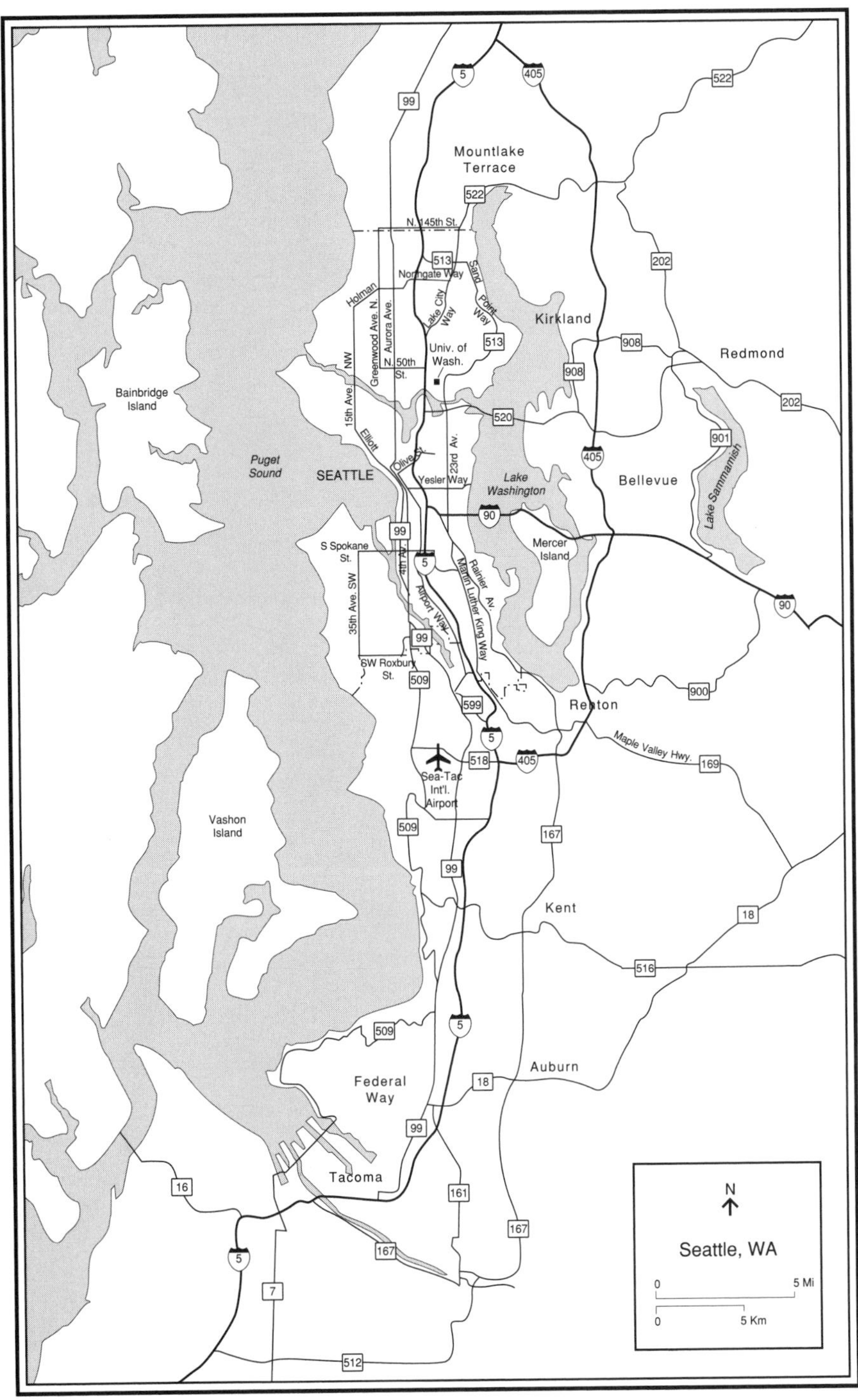

Mountlake Terrace
N. 145th St.
Northgate Way
Holman
Greenwood Ave. N.
Aurora Ave.
Lake City Way
Sand Point Way
Kirkland
Redmond
Univ. of Wash.
N. 50th St.
15th Ave. NW
Bainbridge Island
Puget Sound
SEATTLE
Elliott
Olive St.
23rd Av.
Yesler Way
Lake Washington
Bellevue
Lake Sammamish
Mercer Island
S Spokane St.
35th Ave. SW
4th Av.
Airport Way
Rainier Av.
Martin Luther King Way
SW Roxbury St.
Renton
Maple Valley Hwy.
Sea-Tac Int'l. Airport
Vashon Island
Kent
Auburn
Federal Way
Tacoma
Seattle, WA
N
0
5 Mi
0
5 Km
5
405
522
99
513
202
908
520
901
90
900
599
509
518
169
167
18
516
161
16
7
512

Washington, DC

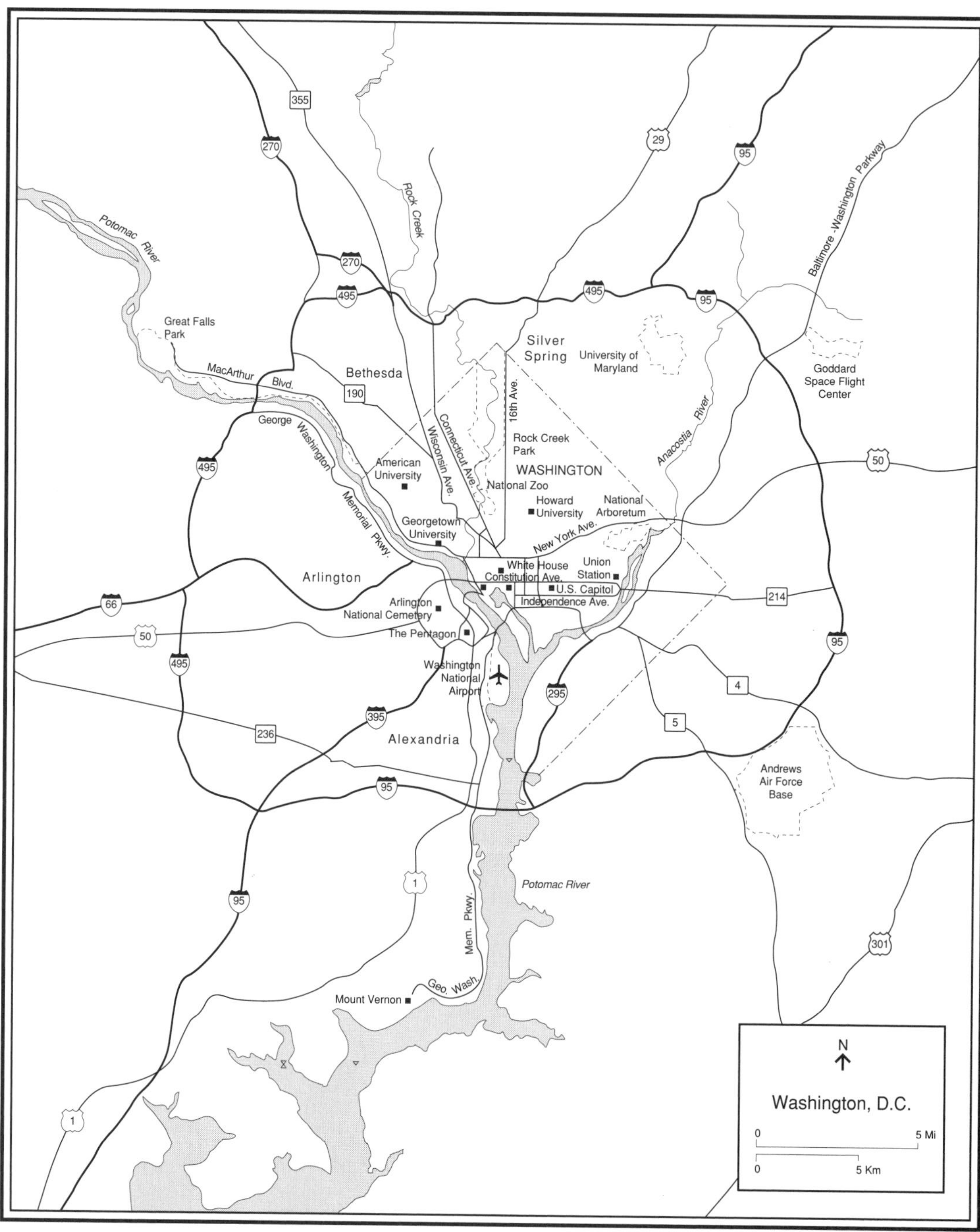

Africa

RUSSIA
UKRAINE
KAZAKHSTAN
Aral Sea
FRANCE
North Atlantic
Black Sea
SPAIN
TURKEY
Caspian Sea
Tangier
Oran
Algiers
Constantine
Tunis
Rabat
Casablanca
MOROCCO
Marrakech
Ghardaia
TUNISIA
Mediterranean Sea
Tripoli
Banghazi
IRAQ
IRAN
Alexandria
Cairo
Canary Islands (SPAIN)
Tindouf
ALGERIA
La'youn
LIBYA
EGYPT
WESTERN SAHARA
Al Jawf
Aswan
SAUDI ARABIA
Tamanrasset
MAURITANIA
MALI
NIGER
Port Sudan
Red Sea
Nouakchott
Faya-Largeau
Agadez
Nema
Tombouctou
CHAD
SENEGAL
Dakar
Banjul
GAMBIA
GUINEA BISSAU
Bissau
Niamey
Zinder
Lake Chad
Khartoum
Asmera
El Fashir
Bamako
BURKINA
Ouagadougou
N'Djamena
Kano
Maiduguri
SUDAN
DJIBOUTI
Djibouti
Berbera
SOMALIA
GUINEA
Conakry
Freetown
SIERRA LEONE
BENIN
NIGERIA
Addis Ababa
TOGO
IVORY COAST
GHANA
Wau
ETHIOPIA
Monrovia
LIBERIA
Abidjan
Accra
Lome
Porto Novo
Lagos
CENTRAL AFRICAN REPUBLIC
CAMEROON
Douala
Yaounde
Bangui
Juba
Lake Turkana
Malabo
EQUATORIAL GUINEA
UGANDA
Lake Albert
KENYA
Mogadishu
Bata
Sao Tome
Libreville
Kisangani
Kampala
Lake Victoria
Nairobi
SAO TOME & PRINCIPE
GABON
CONGO
ZAIRE
RWANDA
Kigali
BURUNDI
Bujumbura
Indian Ocean
Brazzaville
Kinshasa
Mombasa
Pointe-Noire
Cabinda (ANGOLA)
Kananga
Kalemie
TANZANIA
Dar es Salaam
South Atlantic
Lake Tanganyika
Luanda
Mbeya
Kasama
Lubumbashi
MALAWI
Lake Nyasa
Lobito
Luena
Kitwe
ANGOLA
ZAMBIA
Lilongwe
Nacala
Lusaka
Namibe
Lake Kariba
Mahajanga
Harare
MOZAMBIQUE
Antananarivo
ZIMBABWE
Beira
Mauritius
Port Lewis
NAMIBIA
Bulawayo
MADAGASCAR
Saint Denis
Reunion (FRANCE)
BOTSWANA
Windhoek
Toliara
SOUTH AFRICA (Walvis Bay)
Gaborone
Pretoria
Maputo
Johannesburg
Mbabane
Luderitz
SWAZILAND
Maseru
LESOTHO
Durban
SOUTH AFRICA
Cape Town
Port Elizabeth
1000 Km
1000 Mi.

Asia

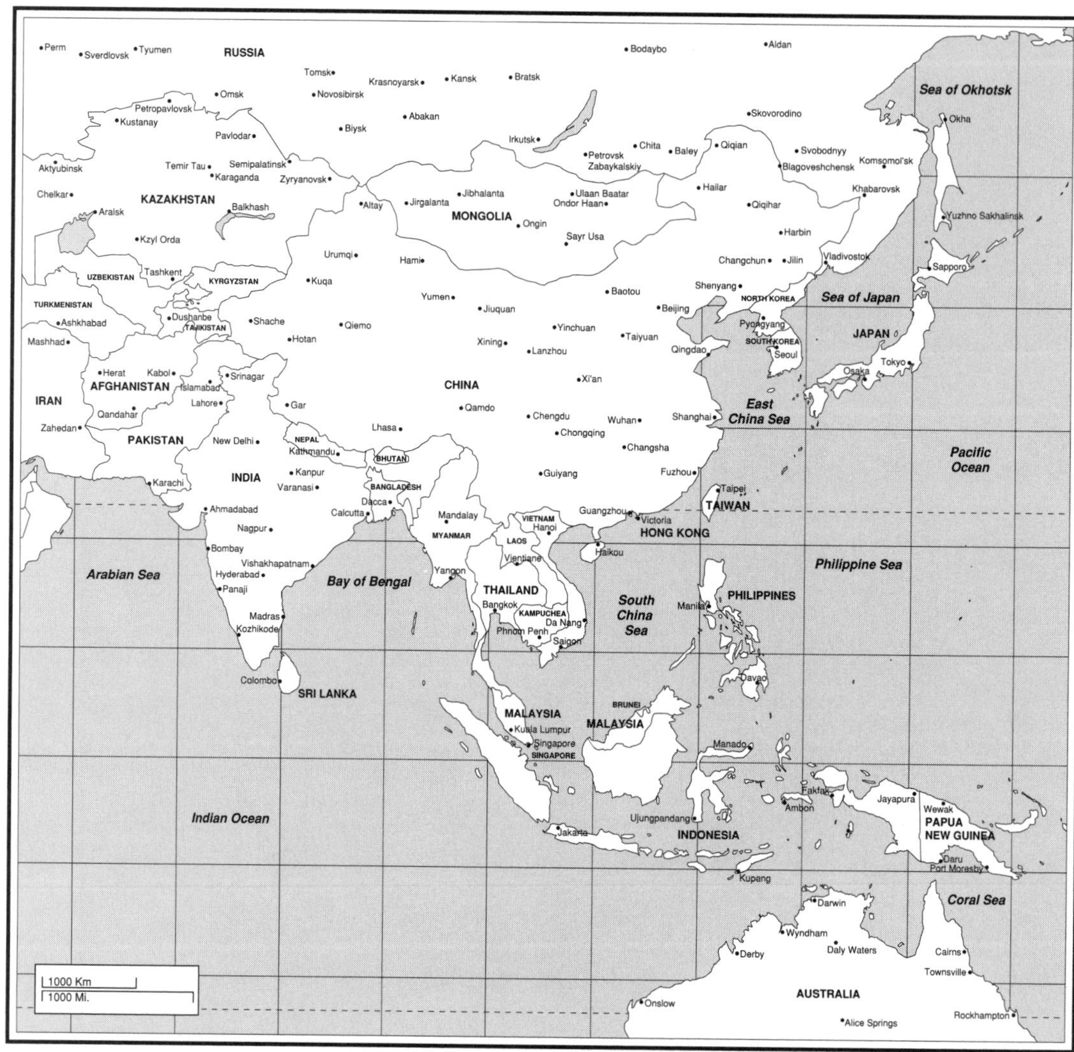
Perm
Sverdlovsk
Tyumen
RUSSIA
Bodaybo
Aldan
Tomsk
Krasnoyarsk
Kansk
Bratsk
Omsk
Novosibirsk
Petropavlovsk
Kustanay
Abakan
Biysk
Pavlodar
Irkutsk
Skovorodino
Sea of Okhotsk
Okha
Chita
Petrovsk Zabaykalskiy
Baley
Qiqian
Svobodnyy
Blagoveshchensk
Komsomol'sk
Aktyubinsk
Temir Tau
Semipalatinsk
Karaganda
Zyryanovsk
Chelkar
KAZAKHSTAN
Balkhash
Aralsk
Altay
Jirgalanta
Jibhalanta
MONGOLIA
Ongin
Ulaan Baatar
Ondor Haan
Hailar
Qiqihar
Khabarovsk
Yuzhno Sakhalinsk
Kzyl Orda
Sayr Usa
Harbin
Urumqi
Hami
Changchun
Jilin
Vladivostok
Sapporo
UZBEKISTAN
Tashkent
KYRGYZSTAN
Kuqa
Yumen
Baotou
Shenyang
NORTH KOREA
Sea of Japan
TURKMENISTAN
Ashkhabad
Dushanbe
TAJIKISTAN
Shache
Qiemo
Jiuquan
Beijing
Pyongyang
Mashhad
Hotan
Yinchuan
Taiyuan
JAPAN
Xining
Lanzhou
Qingdao
SOUTH KOREA
Seoul
Herat
Kabol
Srinagar
Tokyo
AFGHANISTAN
Islamabad
CHINA
Xi'an
Osaka
IRAN
Lahore
Gar
Qamdo
East China Sea
Qandahar
Chengdu
Wuhan
Shanghai
Zahedan
PAKISTAN
New Delhi
Lhasa
Chongqing
NEPAL
Kathmandu
BHUTAN
Changsha
Pacific Ocean
INDIA
Kanpur
Guiyang
Fuzhou
Karachi
Varanasi
BANGLADESH
Taipei
TAIWAN
Dacca
Ahmadabad
Calcutta
Mandalay
VIETNAM
Hanoi
Guangzhou
Victoria
HONG KONG
Nagpur
MYANMAR
LAOS
Haikou
Bombay
Vishakhapatnam
Vientiane
Philippine Sea
Arabian Sea
Hyderabad
Yangon
Bay of Bengal
Panaji
THAILAND
South China Sea
PHILIPPINES
Bangkok
Manila
Madras
KAMPUCHEA
Kozhikode
Da Nang
Phnom Penh
Saigon
Colombo
SRI LANKA
Davao
BRUNEI
MALAYSIA
Kuala Lumpur
MALAYSIA
Singapore
SINGAPORE
Manado
Fakfak
Jayapura
Wewak
Ambon
PAPUA NEW GUINEA
Indian Ocean
Ujungpandang
Jakarta
INDONESIA
Daru
Port Moresby
Kupang
Darwin
Coral Sea
Wyndham
Derby
Daly Waters
Cairns
Townsville
1000 Km
1000 Mi.
AUSTRALIA
Onslow
Alice Springs
Rockhampton

Australia

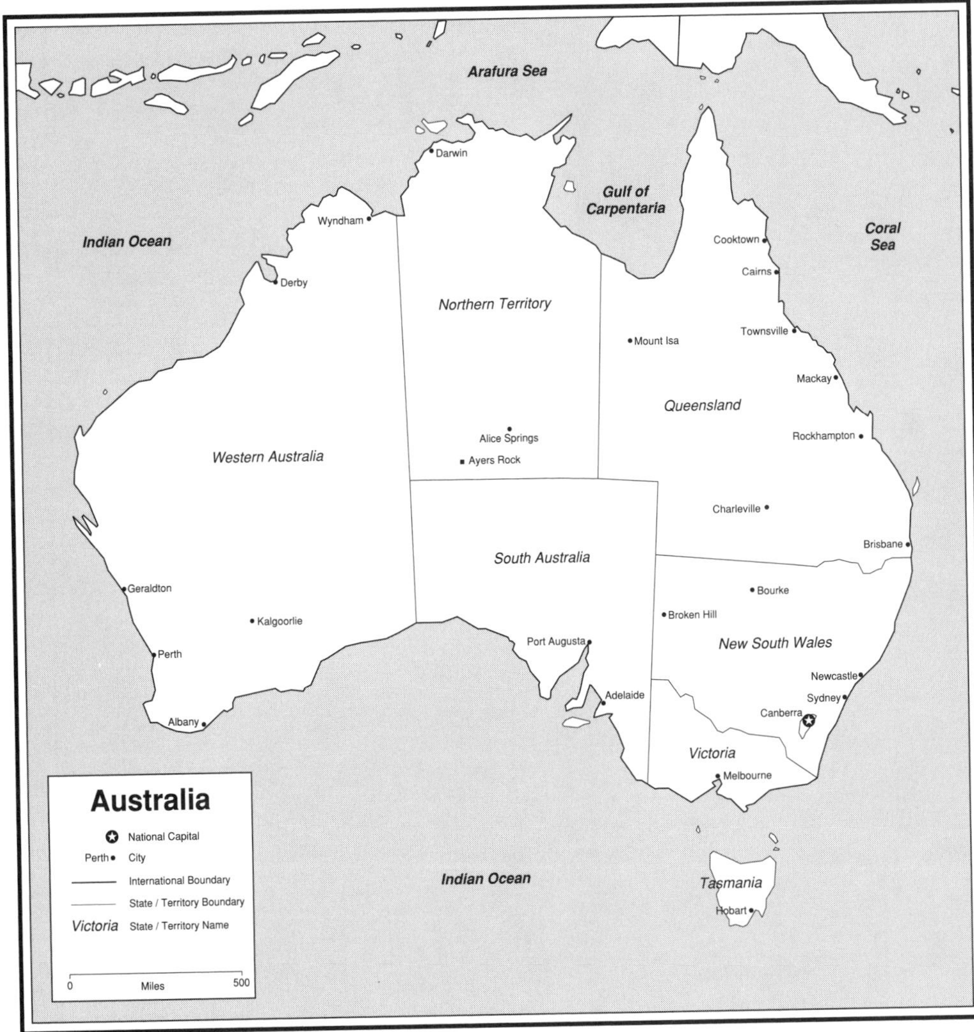
Arafura Sea
Darwin
Gulf of Carpentaria
Coral Sea
Indian Ocean
Wyndham
Derby
Northern Territory
Cooktown
Cairns
Townsville
Mount Isa
Mackay
Queensland
Rockhampton
Alice Springs
Ayers Rock
Western Australia
Charleville
Brisbane
South Australia
Bourke
Broken Hill
Geraldton
Kalgoorlie
Port Augusta
New South Wales
Perth
Newcastle
Adelaide
Sydney
Canberra
Albany
Victoria
Melbourne
Australia
National Capital
Perth City
International Boundary
State / Territory Boundary
Victoria State / Territory Name
0 Miles 500
Indian Ocean
Tasmania
Hobart

Canada

RUSSIA
Arctic Ocean
Beaufort Sea
GREENLAND (DENMARK)
ICELAND
UNITED STATES
Baffin Bay
Dawson
Victoria Island
Yukon Territory
Great Bear Lake
Baffin Island
Pacific Ocean
Whitehorse
Northwest Territories
Great Slave Lake
Yellowknife
Labrador Sea
Lake Athabasca
British Columbia
Hudson Bay
Alberta
Churchill
Newfoundland
Edmonton
Saskatchewan
Manitoba
Victoria
Vancouver
Calgary
Saskatoon
St. John's
Quebec
Regina
Lake Winnipeg
Ontario
Winnipeg
P.E.I.
Sydney
New Brunswick
Canada
National Capital
Calgary City
International Boundary
Provincial Boundary
Quebec Province Name
Thunder Bay
Lake Superior
Quebec
Fredericton
Halifax
Montreal
Nova Scotia
Lake Huron
Ottawa
Lake Michigan
Toronto
Lake Ontario
Atlantic Ocean
UNITED STATES
Lake Erie
0 Miles 500

Europe

Hammerfest
Murmansk
Reykjavik
ICELAND
Kiruna
Norwegian Sea
Oulu
SWEDEN
FINLAND
Trondheim
Sundsvall
Gulf of Bothnia
NORWAY
Tampere
North Atlantic Ocean
Helsinki
St. Petersburg
Bergen
Gavle
Oslo
RUSSIA
Tallinn
Stockholm
ESTONIA
Moscow
Aberdeen
North Sea
Riga
Goteborg
LATVIA
Edinburgh
DENMARK
Baltic Sea
Belfast
IRELAND
Newcastle
Copenhagen
LITHUANIA
Dublin
Vilnius
Minsk
Tver
Liverpool
Gdansk
U. K.
Rostock
BYELARUS
NETH.
Hamburg
Cardiff
Poznan
Warsaw
Amsterdam
Hannover
Berlin
London
POLAND
GERMANY
BELGIUM
Kyiv
English Channel
Leipzig
Bruxelles
Bonn
UKRAINE
Le Havre
Frankfurt
Prague
Krakow
Lviv
LUX.
Paris
CZECHOSLOVAKIA
Strasbourg
Nantes
Vienna
Bratislava
MOLDOVA
Munich
Chisinau
Odesa
FRANCE
Budapest
AUSTRIA
Bern
SWITZERLAND
HUNGARY
Cluj-Napoca
Geneva
Bordeaux
Pecs
ROMANIA
Ljubljana
SLOVENIA
Zagreb
CROATIA
Bay of Biscay
Lyon
Milan
Venice
Constanta
Black Sea
BOSNIA
Sarajevo
Belgrade
Bucharest
Bilbao
SERBIA
Varna
Marseille
Florence
Porto
ANDORRA
BULGARIA
ITALY
MONTENEGRO
Sofiya
PORTUGAL
Madrid
Barcelona
Skopje
Titograd
MACEDONIA
Istanbul
Lisbon
Rome
Adriatic
Tirana
SPAIN
Thessaloniki
Naples
Tyrrhenian Sea
ALBANIA
TURKEY
Valencia
Aegean
GREECE
Cagliari
Sevilla
Ionian Sea
Malaga
Mediterranean Sea
Patrai
Athens
Palermo
CYPRUS
250 Km
250 Mi.
CRETE

Mexico

UNITED STATES
Gulf of Mexico
Bahia de Campeche
North Pacific Ocean
Gulf of California
Golfo de Tehuantepec
Isla de Cozumel
Isla Cedros
Islas Marias
BELIZE
GUATEMALA
HONDURAS
EL SALVADOR
Tijuana
Mexicali
Ensenada
Baja California Norte
San Quintin
Puerto Penasco
Nogales
Sonora
Hermosillo
Guaymas
Cuidad Obregon
Santa Rosalia
Loreto
Baja California Sur
La Paz
San Lucas
Los Mochis
Culiacan
Sinaloa
Mazatlan
Ciudad Juarez
Chihuahua
Ojinaga
Chihuahua
Delicias
Hidalgo del Parral
Durango
Durango
Piedras Negras
Coahuila
Monclova
Torreon
Saltillo
Nuevo Laredo
Nuevo Leon
Monterrey
Matamoros
Tamaulipas
Cuidad Victoria
Ciudad Mante
Tampico
Zacatecas
Zacatecas
San Luis Potosi
San Luis Potosi
Aguascalientes
Nayarit
Tepic
Guadalajara
Jalisco
Colima
Colima
Manzanillo
Guanajuato
Leon
Queretaro
Pachuca
Poza Rica
Mexico City
Toluca
Cuernavaca
Tlaxcala
Xalapa
Puebla
Veracruz
Orizaba
Morelia
Michoacan
Lazaro Cardenas
Guerrero
Chilpancingo
Acapulco
Puebla
Veracruz
Oaxaca
Oaxaca
Puerto Escondido
Salina Cruz
Coatzacoalcos
Villahermosa
Chiapas
Tuxtla Gutierrez
Comitan
Tapachula
Progreso
Merida
Yucatan
Campeche
Campeche
Quintana Roo
Chetumal
Mexico
National Capital
Leon • City
Internaional Boundary
State (estado) Boundary
Jalisco State (estado) Name
0 Miles 300
Key to states in central Mexico
1 Aguascalientes
2 Guanajuato
3 Queretaro
4 Hidalgo
5 Mexico
6 Distrito Federal
7 Morelos
8 Tlaxcala

Russia

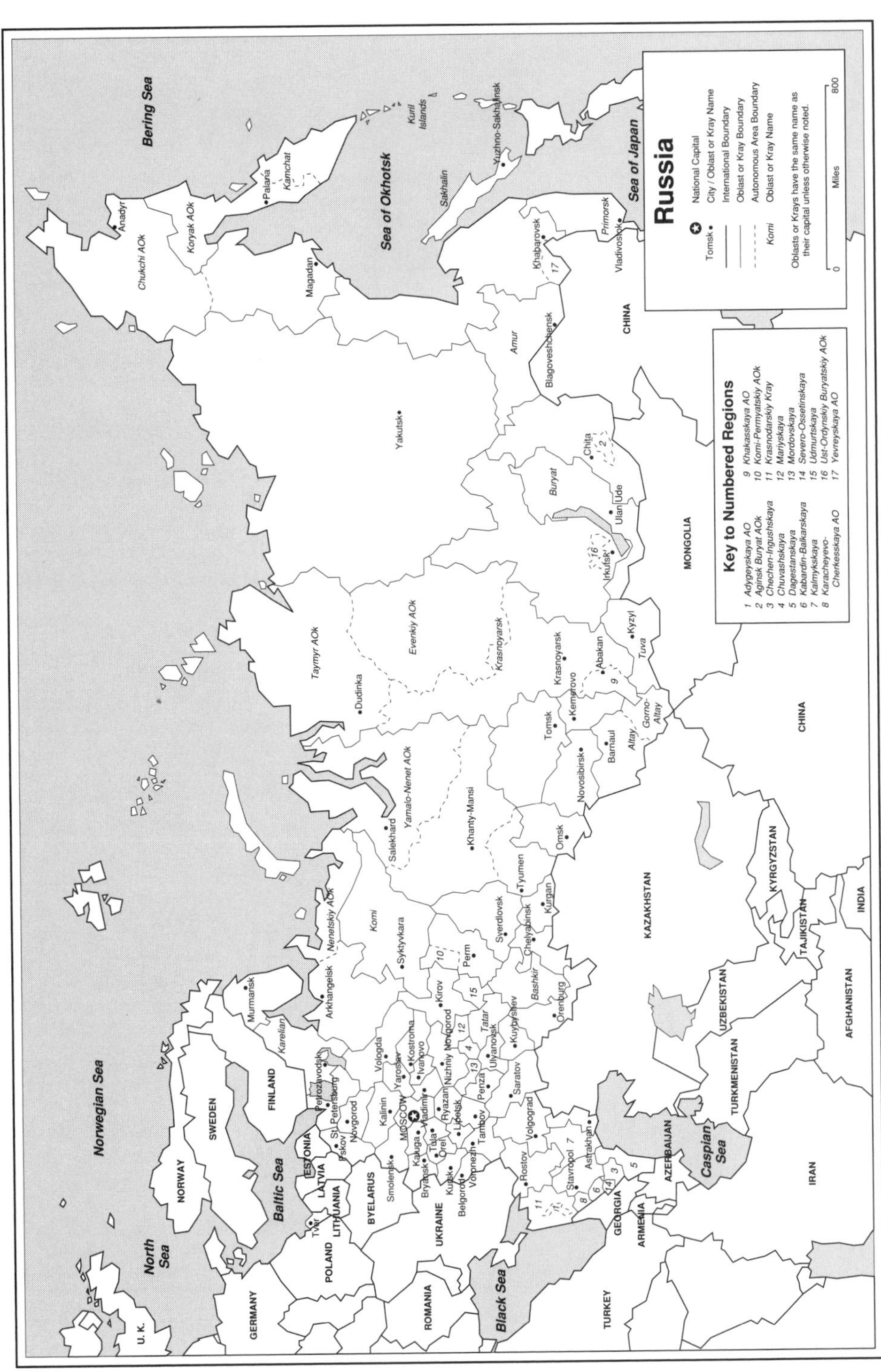
Russia
National Capital
Tomsk • City / Oblast or Kray Name
International Boundary
Oblast or Kray Boundary
Autonomous Area Boundary
Komi Oblast or Kray Name
Oblasts or Krays have the same name as their capital unless otherwise noted.
0 Miles 800
Key to Numbered Regions
1 Adygeyskaya AO
2 Aginsk Buryat AOk
3 Chechen-Ingushskaya
4 Chuvashskaya
5 Dagestanskaya
6 Kabardin-Balkarskaya
7 Kalmykskaya
8 Karacheyevo-Cherkesskaya AO
9 Khakasskaya AO
10 Komi-Permyatskiy AOk
11 Krasnodarskiy Kray
12 Mariyskaya
13 Mordovskaya
14 Severo-Osetinskaya
15 Udmurtskaya
16 Ust-Ordynskiy Buryatskiy AOk
17 Yevreyskaya AO
Bering Sea
Sea of Okhotsk
Kuril Islands
Sakhalin
Sea of Japan
Norwegian Sea
North Sea
Baltic Sea
Black Sea
Caspian Sea
Anadyr
Chukchi AOk
Koryak AOk
Palana
Kamchat
Magadan
Yuzhno-Sakhalinsk
Khabarovsk
Primorsk
Vladivostok
Blagoveshchensk
Amur
Yakutsk
Chita
Buryat
Ulan Ude
Irkutsk
Taymyr AOk
Evenkiy AOk
Krasnoyarsk
Dudinka
Abakan
Kyzyl
Tuva
Kemerovo
Gorno-Altay
Altay
Barnaul
Tomsk
Novosibirsk
Omsk
Yamalo-Nenet AOk
Salekhard
Khanty-Mansi
Tyumen
Kurgan
Chelyabinsk
Sverdlovsk
Nenetskiy AOk
Komi
Syktyvkara
Perm
Bashkir
Orenburg
Kirov
Tatar
Kuybyshev
Ulyanovsk
Saratov
Penza
Volgograd
Astrakhan
Stavropol
Rostov
Murmansk
Arkhangelsk
Karelian
Petrozavodsk
Vologda
Yaroslav
Kostroma
Ivanovo
Nizhniy Novgorod
Vladimir
Ryazan
Lipetsk
Tambov
Voronezh
Kalinin
MOSCOW
Kaluga
Tula
Orel
Bryansk
Kursk
Belgorod
Smolensk
Novgorod
St. Petersburg
Pskov
Tver
NORWAY
SWEDEN
FINLAND
ESTONIA
LATVIA
LITHUANIA
BYELARUS
UKRAINE
POLAND
GERMANY
ROMANIA
TURKEY
GEORGIA
ARMENIA
AZERBAIJAN
U. K.
KAZAKHSTAN
UZBEKISTAN
TURKMENISTAN
KYRGYZSTAN
TAJIKISTAN
AFGHANISTAN
INDIA
IRAN
MONGOLIA
CHINA

South America

United States

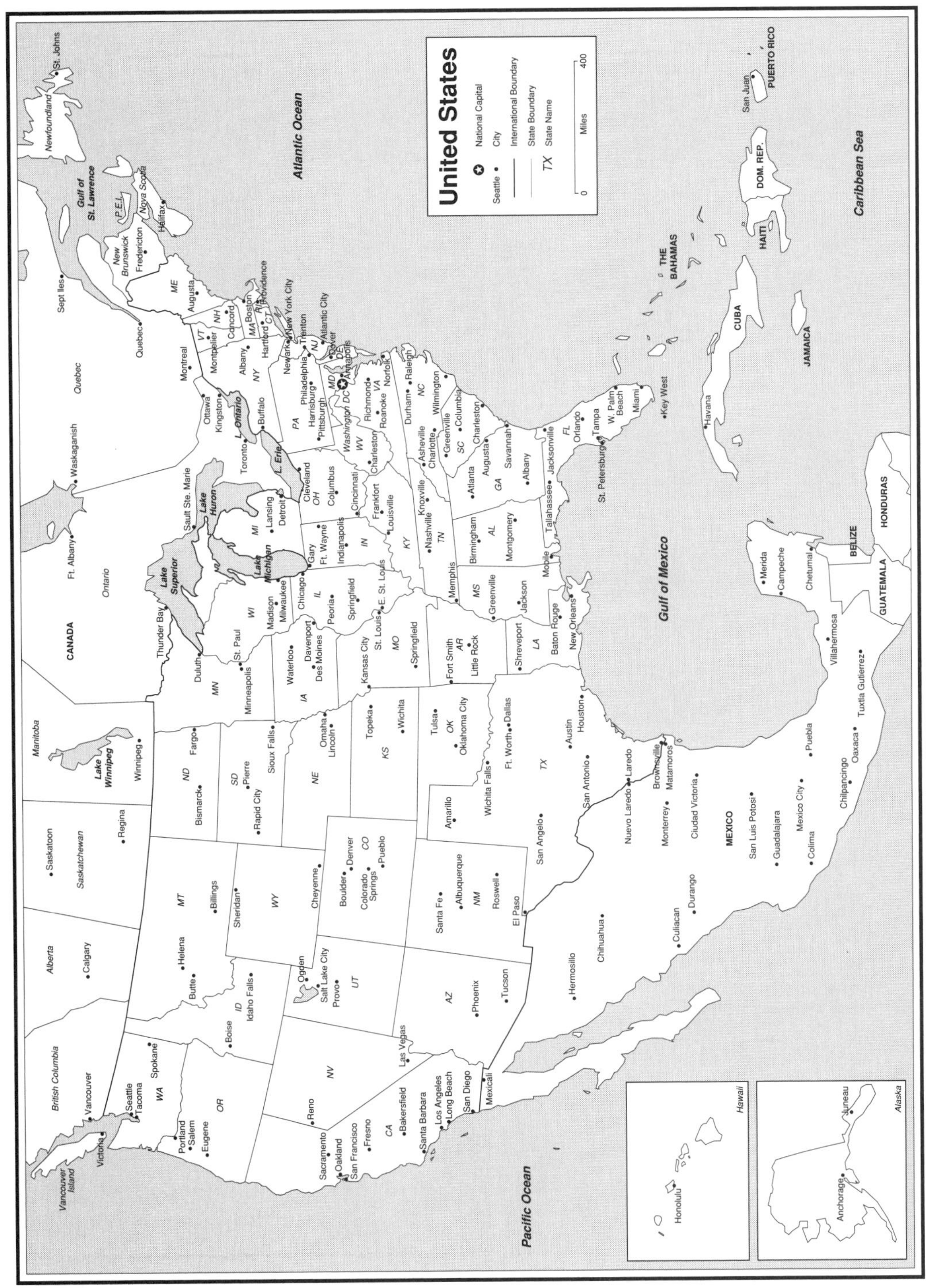

Mileage Table

	Atlanta	Baltimore	Boston	Chicago	Cincinnati	Cleveland	Columbus, OH	Dallas	Denver	Detroit	Houston	Indianapolis	Los Angeles	Miami	Milwaukee	Minneapolis	New York	Norfolk	Philadelphia	Phoenix	Pittsburgh	Portland, OR	Sacramento	St. Louis	San Antonio	San Diego	San Francisco	Seattle	Tampa	Washington, DC
Atlanta		576	945	606	374	555	569	728	1204	596	693	434	1939	595	669	906	761	515	665	1581	526	2165	2085	483	872	1885	2131	2175	406	546
Baltimore	576		368	619	428	313	411	1213	1497	407	1243	514	2321	946	639	933	185	160	89	1992	209	2349	2386	735	1404	2287	2447	2325	843	30
Boston	945	368		864	750	561	767	1557	1761	630	1605	814	2601	1258	857	1120	184	467	281	2293	494	2528	2627	1043	1759	2578	2693	2485	1184	398
Chicago	606	619	864		264	314	354	800	898	233	945	177	1739	1197	67	333	730	714	675	1436	411	1733	1776	258	1041	1718	1839	1713	1012	609
Cincinnati	374	428	750	264		221	110	810	1076	229	885	98	1893	949	317	595	583	484	505	1564	255	1968	1970	307	1022	1858	2029	1956	773	409
Cleveland	555	313	561	314	221		147	1019	1209	94	1105	260	2045	1081	327	620	417	434	361	1732	106	2038	2090	485	1239	2019	2153	2012	928	309
Columbus, OH	569	411	767	354	110	147		1046	1277	209	1228	178	2252	1198	455	762	567	577	473	1917	185	2439	2200	433	1327	2255	2457	2460	999	407
Dallas	728	1213	1557	800	810	1019	1046		644	984	247	760	1230	1118	852	852	1385	1209	1298	866	1064	1611	1427	550	247	1167	1459	1655	926	1188
Denver	1204	1497	1761	898	1076	1209	1277	644		1132	884	984	846	1712	905	691	1626	1558	1563	589	1297	982	895	777	793	837	952	1015	1510	1482
Detroit	596	407	630	233	229	94	209	984	1132		1091	230	1971	1147	237	527	500	528	452	1666	201	1946	2006	439	1213	1949	2071	1919	983	405
Houston	693	1243	1605	945	885	1105	1228	247	884	1091		862	1385	953	1004	1057	1425	1206	1332	1017	1129	1839	1619	688	191	1308	1643	1889	779	1216
Indianapolis	434	514	814	177	98	260	178	760	984	230	862		1808	1022	237	501	658	580	584	1485	323	1870	1877	229	984	1777	1937	1858	838	498
Los Angeles	1939	2321	2601	1739	1893	2045	2252	1230	846	1971	1385	1808		2334	1749	1531	2460	2362	2392	368	2127	833	373	1586	1206	109	337	953	2150	2302
Miami	595	946	1258	1197	949	1081	1198	1118	1712	1147	953	1022	2334		1259	1501	1097	803	1013	1966	1013	2693	2545	1068	1140	2260	2577	2717	205	920
Milwaukee	669	639	857	67	317	327	455	852	905	237	1004	237	1749	1259		296	736	745	688	1456	430	1711	1772	317	1095	1733	1838	1687	1075	632
Minneapolis	906	933	1120	333	595	620	762	852	691	527	1057	501	1531	1501	296		1017	1042	976	1274	724	1420	1512	447	1097	1528	1584	1393	1305	928
New York	761	185	184	730	583	417	567	1385	1626	500	1425	658	2460	1097	736	1017		296	97	2141	333	2436	2505	885	1582	2432	2569	2402	1011	214
Norfolk	515	160	467	714	484	434	577	1209	1558	528	1206	580	2362	803	745	1042	296		212	2023	329	2445	2453	782	1378	2322	2509	2428	716	141
Philadelphia	665	89	281	675	505	361	473	1298	1563	452	1332	584	2392	1013	688	976	97	212		2068	266	2397	2448	810	1492	2361	2510	2368	919	118
Phoenix	1581	1992	2293	1436	1564	1732	1917	866	589	1666	1017	1485	368	1966	1456	1274	2141	2023	2068		1808	1009	646	1258	841	302	649	1105	1782	1972
Pittsburgh	526	209	494	411	255	106	185	1064	1297	201	1129	323	2127	1013	430	724	333	329	266	1808		2140	2183	551	1273	2099	2245	2116	873	204
Portland, OR	2165	2349	2528	1733	1968	2038	2439	1611	982	1946	1839	1870	833	2693	1711	1420	2436	2445	2397	1009	2140		477	1702	1711	933	550	130	2490	2341
Sacramento	2085	2386	2627	1776	1970	2090	2200	1427	895	2006	1619	1877	373	2545	1772	1512	2505	2453	2448	646	2183	477		1673	1459	481	85	605	2351	2372
St. Louis	483	735	1043	258	307	485	433	550	777	439	688	229	1586	1068	317	447	885	782	810	1258	551	1702	1673		785	1551	1728	1703	868	716
San Antonio	872	1404	1759	1041	1022	1239	1327	247	793	1213	191	984	1206	1140	1095	1097	1582	1378	1492	841	1273	1711	1459	785		1126	1478	1771	969	1377
San Diego	1885	2287	2578	1718	1858	2019	2255	1167	837	1949	1308	1777	109	2260	1733	1528	2432	2322	2361	302	2099	933	481	1551	1126		446	1050	2079	2268
San Francisco	2131	2447	2693	1839	2029	2153	2457	1459	952	2071	1619	1937	337	2577	1838	1584	2569	2509	2510	649	2245	550	85	1728	1478	446		678	2384	2433
Seattle	2175	2325	2485	1713	1956	2012	2460	1655	1015	1919	1889	1858	953	2717	1687	1393	2402	2428	2368	1105	2116	130	605	1703	1771	1050	678		2513	2320
Tampa	406	843	1184	1012	773	928	999	926	1510	983	779	838	2150	205	1075	1305	1011	716	919	1782	873	2490	2351	868	969	2079	2384	2513		813
Washington, DC	546	30	398	609	409	309	407	1188	1482	405	1216	498	2302	920	632	928	214	141	118	1972	204	2341	2372	716	1377	2268	2433	2320	813	

Business Law & Government

Legal Issues in Hiring and Firing

THE 1986-1988 COMBINED ANNUAL REPORT of the Equal Employment Opportunity Commission states that three of the four most frequently cited charges received by the EEOC were related to hiring and firing practices. In 1988 alone 49.5% of these complaints were directed against an employer's discharge practices, followed by 17.8% regarding terms of employment, and 8.8% pertaining to hiring practices. Hiring and firing procedures should be carefully reviewed to assess the potential liability hidden within established practices.

Hiring

Hiring, in many cases, begins with a job application. Many of the questions found on traditional applications for employment have become sources of discrimination suits. A non-discriminatory job application should not contain questions about the following:

- Race, age, sex, religion, and national origin. An employer can ask if an applicant is 18 years of age or older and has a legal right to work in this country either through citizenship or status as a resident alien.
- Marital status, maiden name, number, names, and ages of children or other dependents.
- Employment of the spouse and child-care arrangements unless such queries are made of both male and female applicants.
- A woman's pregnancy or related condition.
- Arrest records which did not result in convictions. It is permissible to inquire about convictions or pending felony charges.
- The existence, nature or severity of a disability. An employer may ask about an applicant's ability to perform specific job functions.
- An applicant's height and weight, except in specific professions such as law enforcement, when valid guidelines have been established for various national organizations.
- Organizational affiliations except those pertaining to professional memberships related to the specific job.
- Military history unless the job requires such a background.
- Status as a high school graduate. It is permissible to request the applicant to supply the details of his or her educational history.
- Lowest salary acceptable for a specific position.

An interview can often be more litigiously threatening than the employment application, because uninformed interviewers often ask seemingly harmless questions which may, in fact, be discriminatory. An interviewer may casually ask a 32-year-old female applicant if she anticipates having a family. If she responds affirmatively and subsequently is not hired, she could file suit for discriminatory hiring practices. Experts say the general rule of thumb is: if a question does not have anything to do with the job, or is not vital to determining the applicant's ability to perform the responsibilities associated with the job, do not ask it.

Firing

Improperly handled employee terminations generate a significant number of lawsuits against corporations. Complete and accurate records of such actions protect the interests of both the employer and the former employee.

Firing generates stress for the employee being discharged, the individual who does the terminating and the employees who remain with the company. There are several concepts to consider before, during and after the discharge is completed which can significantly affect the attitudes and reactions of all involved as well as the vulnerability of the employer.

Before Firing an Employee

- Be sure the action is approved by top management and conforms to written company policy. Corporate legal advice may be sought regarding severance conditions for higher level employees.
- Except in a for-cause dismissal, an employee is entitled to a documented, concise explanation of the reasons for his or her dismissal. Plan the interview carefully to anticipate responses and diffuse reactions.
- Federal law requires a 60-day advance notification of employees affected by layoffs and plant or office closings. Prematurely early notification may significantly affect production and possibly invite undesirable reactions.
- Consider the possibility of an irrational response by a dismissed employee. Take the necessary precautions to change security codes, access codes to computers and entry to the corporate premises.

Legal Issues in Hiring and Firing (cont'd)

Handling a Termination

- Be honest and completely clear about the reasons for discharge. Avoid personal statements which might degrade or humiliate the individual, or vague statements which might suggest that the situation is reversible.
- It is sometimes helpful to have another individual, such as a professional from human resources, present as a witness and a support for the employee, particularly if emotional reactions are anticipated.
- Present a precise explanation of severance pay procedures, benefits continuation forms, pension or profit-sharing payouts and other available assistance, such as outplacement counseling. In larger corporations, the human resources department handles the filling out of the necessary forms and documents.
- Allow the individual to remove personal belongings at a low-visibility time, after hours or on a weekend. Prepare a checklist of company property that should be accounted for, including keys, credit cards, ID cards, computer disks.
- Respond to all questions and discuss the cover story to be presented when future employers inquire about the individual. Be prepared with a version that is supportive of the employee but does not threaten the company's credibility.

After Firing an Employee

- Document the termination in writing immediately, detailing conversation, reactions and emotional tone of both parties. This is essential for response to any future challenge to the termination.
- Inform the staff or co-workers of the termination by word of mouth or by memo. In the case of for-cause termination, the incident should be mentioned only briefly, in a non-defamatory manner. If performance is the reason, experts suggest that simply stating that the employee and the organization have agreed to part company should suffice.
- In the case of staff reduction or layoffs, the remaining staff should be assured that downsizing was warranted and that no additional layoffs are anticipated at this time. (If additional reductions are expected, employees should be informed that such an action may be required, and that they will be informed on or before a specific date.)
- Invite employees who have additional questions and concerns to meet with specified representatives of the company privately.
- Inform clients or customers who deal with the discharged individual that the company will continue to serve their needs. When necessary, name a specific individual who will replace the terminated employee.

Non-Compete Agreements

LOSING A VALUED EMPLOYEE is disconcerting. Discovering that the individual has defected to a competitor and has taken proprietary information with him or her is shocking and infuriating. Considerable damage can result when an employee takes invaluable company information such as proposed new product lines or strategic planning, and ultimately gives the competition an unfair advantage. Small and large businesses alike are faced with the problem of reducing the risk of losing more than an employee.

One commonly adopted solution is requiring a new hiree to sign a non-compete agreement. Such a document is an agreement between the employer and employee stating that, should the employee choose to leave the company, he or she will not go to work for a competitor for a specified period of time, frequently two years.

A non-compete document is particularly useful for employees who have access to critical information, either through job responsibility or through social interactions with owners or high-level executives. While the signed agreement does not provide fool-proof protection against such disruption, it deters this type of action by forcing the employee to reconsider the temptations. A signed document is an excellent reminder of one's responsibility.

A standard non-compete agreement might read this way:

"Employee agrees as a condition of employment that, in the event of termination for any reason, he/she will not engage in a similar or competitive business for a period of two years, nor will he/she contact or solicit any customer with whom Employer conducted business during his/her employment. This restrictive covenant shall be for a term of two years from termination, and shall encompass an area within a 50-mile radius of Employer's place of business."

Additional clauses might specify the protections desired by an individual business.

Non-Compete Agreements (cont'd)

"Employee agrees that Employer's customer lists, processes, manufacturing techniques, sales materials, and pricing information constitute the sole and exclusive property of Employer, and that same are 'trade secrets' under the law. Employee promises that under no circumstances shall he/she disclose same, during or after the term hereof, and upon violation of this provision Employee agrees that Employer shall be entitled to an injunction, compensatory and punitive damages, and reimbursement for its counsel fee."

Source: What Every Executive Better Know About the Law

It is important to note that non-compete agreements may be illegal in Montana, Nevada, North Dakota, and Oklahoma. Such agreements may be invalid or limited in Colorado, Florida, Hawaii, Louisiana, Oregon, South Dakota, and Wisconsin. While there is no federal law regarding non-compete agreements, employers should consult state regulations before using such a contract.

Recommended Resource

What Every Executive Better Know About the Law
by Michael Trachtman
Simon and Schuster

Employment Contracts

AN EMPLOYMENT CONTRACT spells out the conditions of employment including wages, hours and type of work.

Depending upon the level of employment, the responsibility of the new employee and the nature of the business, the conditions of employment should be detailed regarding the following elements:

- Term of employment.
- Duties of the employee including general and specific responsibilities and performance of duties.
- Compensation including monthly salary, automobile expenses, relocation and moving expenses, and a one-time bonus inducement if used. Details such as bonus or incentive plans, stock options, salary deferment plans, disability benefits, and health and retirement plans may or may not be spelled out.
- Confidentiality required of the employee regarding employer's operating expenses, pricing formulas, procedures, trade secrets, and proprietary information. This confidentiality extends to employee lists, customer lists or prospective customers who become clients of the organization during the individual's term.
- A non-compete clause as described above.
- Provisions for termination including a violation of responsibility, an inability to perform duties, reorganization or low company profits. Higher-level employees frequently have a clause included in the contract to state a certain amount of money, often from six to twelve months of salary, which will be paid to the employee in the event of termination by disagreement or dispute.

While an employer can overload the employment contract without good reason, it is important to remember that any item not covered in the original employment contract falls under common law rights. Consequently, an employee owns the rights to all ideas, inventions or discoveries unless he or she was specifically hired to develop those ideas or inventions. If the idea or invention is the incidental result of his employment, then the rights belong to the employee unless otherwise specified in the employment contract.

The Top Reference Sources

The Entrepreneur & Small Business Problem Solver
John Wiley & Sons, $24.95
(212) 850–6000

Written by marketing professor William A. Cohen, this is a comprehensive guide for entrepreneurs and managers of small businesses. Sections include financial problem solving, legal aspects of going into business, sources of capital, buying insurance, leasing equipment, financial management.

Also included are sections on market research, introducing new products, advertising and publicity, business plans, recruiting, protecting your ideas, and computers.

Contracts

JUST AS A BUSINESSPERSON scans the corporate environment for potential legal pitfalls within the organization, so too, he or she must similarly judge the potential liability of decisions involving outside individuals or businesses. While a written contract is not necessary for every action and decision taken by a businessperson, it can prove invaluable when:

- Disputes arise over delivery dates or option terms;
- Clear, precise written proof is required to resolve litigation;
- Complex details are anticipated and dealt with on paper instead of in the courtroom.

There are several instances when it is in an executive's own best interests to have a simple written agreement on file. First, a boilerplate model of a basic agreement should be kept on file and used when a company hires a consultant or independent contractor. Second, a letter of agreement should be used when an executive wants to create a "written handshake" which states the essentials of the agreement without becoming mired in details. Such an agreement states the simple facts in writing, and is confirmed and accepted when signed and returned to the sender.

This simple document should:

- Identify both parties and the role of each in the agreement;
- Describe the nature of the agreement;
- State payment terms, time expectations and other contingencies of the agreement;
- In the case of independent contractors, the document should include a clause prohibiting the disclosure to a competitor of any work created for this employer.

An early warning system of liability sensitivity requires prudence rather than panic. It isn't necessary to call an attorney before making every decision. Such hesitation affects the spontaneity of business agreements. Yet it is wise to have boilerplate documents reviewed by counsel prior to being used for the first time. When in doubt regarding a simple agreement, it is worth the peace of mind to consult an attorney. Counsel should be sought when complex situations are involved, such as incorporation, partnership, lease agreements, real estate agreements, debt collection, litigation, and labor/management relations.

The Small Business Administration (SBA) provides useful information through Business Development Specialists who can provide useful information and direction in response to telephone queries. To find a nearby District Office call (800) 827-5722.

Recommended Resource

Small Business Legal Handbook
by Robert Friedman
Enterprise Dearborn Publishing Co.
(800) 533-2665

Intellectual Property

IF AN INTRUDER STEALS A WORD PROCESSOR or piece of equipment from a factory, the owner becomes acutely aware of the loss. Yet the daily misuse of a company's intellectual property, including its logo or trademark, constitutes theft as well and can be far more damaging. An organization's intellectual property is protected by trademarks (on the company name or logo), patents (on its inventions or product designs) and copyrights (on the literary, musical or photographic products) generated by or for the company.

Trademarks

A trademark is potentially the most valuable asset of an organization. It is a word, symbol, design, or combination of these elements which identifies one's products and services and distinguishes them from others in the marketplace. The identity created by a distinct trademark is priceless in the customer loyalty and product awareness it generates. Trademarks extend the company's public image not only through the product or service, but also through printed material, packaging and advertising which bear that mark.

An owner can protect a trademark by common law or by federal registration. Common law protection begins with the first use of a mark and is indicated by ™ while Federal registration requires a more complicated procedure.

Why Register a Trademark?

An unregistered trademark (™) is protected by common law only within states where it is used. When a trademark is used in interstate commerce, experts suggest that it is in the owner's best interests to register the trademark (®) with the Federal Patent and Trademark Office (PTO). Such registration guarantees ownership of the mark and entitlement to its

Intellectual Property (cont'd)

use throughout the nation. It can be devastating to a corporation to establish a product name and trademark recognition only to find that its use is challenged by a previously unknown owner. Imagine the effect on Apple Computer if they suddenly discovered, six months after the first computer rolled off the assembly line, that their trademark rainbow apple with one bite missing was legally in use by an obscure organic fruit grower in California. Registration protects against litigation and liability as well as costly damages. When a trademark is to be used in a complicated manner, it is wise to consult a lawyer regarding the value of federally registering the mark.

Once a trademark is registered, ownership continues for a renewable period of ten years. Midway through the first decade, however, the owner must file an affidavit of intent to continue use of the trademark. In the absence of such documentation, the registration is cancelled.

Life Cycle of a Trademark

Whenever a new business is begun or a new product line is established in an existing company, a unique name, trademark or logo is created. A corporate trademark, name or symbol evolves out of the following process:

- Possible names are suggested in brainstorming sessions, by use of software designed to generate names or by name-creation consultants.
- Suggestions are screened via trademark directories or on-line research systems to determine the existence of conflicting U.S. federal, state or international trademark registrations or applications. (See below.)
- Candidates that survive the initial screening are subjected to professional trademark searches and reports on the availability of use of the desired trademark.
- An application and filing fee is presented to the Patent and Trademark Office (PTO) of the U.S. Department of Commerce and is reviewed by its federal staff.
- If no opposition or conflict is found in the application review process, the trademark is presented in the PTO's Official Gazette for opposition or challenge.
- Having survived this last hurdle, the owner of the proposed trademark is permitted to register the trademark. All subsequent use of the trademark should include the symbol ® as notification that the trademark is protected under federal trademark law. It is important to note, however, that a mark may be challenged for up to five years under federal law.

How to File an Application for Registration

The trademark owner can apply for registration independently or may be represented by an attorney. The risks associated with the financial advantages of self-representation include the possibility of having the application rejected and forfeiting the application fee if the PTO attorney discovers a conflicting mark. However, with some reasonable preparation, an enterprising individual can complete the application form and proceed through at least the initial stages of the procedure.

If a reasonably thorough search is conducted and no conflicting marks are uncovered, the application may be completed and submitted with the fee to the PTO for review.

Application for registration requires:

- A completed application form.
- A drawing of the mark to be used.
- Specimens showing intended use of the mark.
- Filing fee.

The PTO has documented all the pertinent information about trademark registration applications and filing requirements in a useful booklet called "Basic Facts About Trademarks."

All correspondence with the PTO, as well as requests for this booklet, can be addressed to:

The Commissioner of Patents and Trademarks
Washington, DC 20231

Contact Options

Information hotlines:

General Trademark or Patent Information
(703) 308-4367

Automated (Recorded) General Trademark or Patent Information
(703) 557-INFO

Automated Line for Status Information on Trademark Applications
(703) 305-8747 and (703) 305-8752

Copyright Information (Library of Congress)
(202) 479-0700

Almanac Fact

The Copyright Clearance Center is a non-profit organization created to ease the process of securing copyright permission and collecting fees. Thousands of publishers and users of business magazines, newsletters, books, technical and trade journals, and other publications register with the CCC and allow it to grant permission and collect fees for the right to reproduce copyrighted materials.

Copyright Clearance Center, 27 Congress St., Salem, MA 01970 (508) 744-3350; Fax: (508) 741-2318.

Intellectual Property (cont'd)

PTO FORM 1478:

Trademark/Service Mark Application, Principal Register, with Declaration

Mark ....
(Identify the mark)

Class No. ....
(If known)

TO THE ASSISTANT SECRETARY AND COMMISSIONER OF PATENTS AND TRADEMARKS:

....
(Applicant name)

....
(Applicant business address)

Applicant Entity: (Check one and supply requested information)

☐ Individual: ....
(Citizenship – Country)

☐ Partnership: ....
(Partnership Domicile – State and Country)

....
(Names and Citizenship (Country) of General Partners)

....

☐ Corporation: ....
(State (Country, if appropriate) of Incorporation)

☐ Other: ....
(Specify Nature of Entity and Domicile)

....

GOODS AND/OR SERVICES

Applicant requests registration of the above-identified trademark/service mark shown in the accompanying drawing in the United States Patent and Trademark Office on the Principal Register established by the Act of July 5, 1946 (15 U.S.C. 1051 et. seq., as amended.) for the following goods/services: ....

....

....

BASIS FOR APPLICATION:

Check one or more, but NOT both the first AND second boxes, and supply requested information.

☐ Applicant is using the mark in commerce on or in connection with the above identified goods/services. (15 U.S.C. 1051(a), as amended.) Three specimens showing the mark as used in commerce are submitted with this application.

- Date of first use of the mark anywhere: ....
- Date of first use of the mark in commerce which the U.S. Congress may regulate: ....
- Specify the type of commerce: ....
(e.g., interstate, between the U.S. and a specified foreign country)
- Specify manner or mode of use of mark on or in connection with the goods/services: ....
(e.g., trademark is applied to labels, service mark is used in advertisements)

☐ Applicant has a bona fide intention to use the mark in commerce on or in connection with the above identified goods/services. (15 U.S.C. 1051(b), as amended.)

Specify intended manner or mode of use of mark on or in connection with the goods/services: ....
(e.g., trademark will be applied to labels, service mark will be used in advertisements)

☐ Applicant has a bona fide intention to use the mark in commerce on or in connection with the above identified goods/services, and asserts a claim of priority based upon a foreign application in accordance with 15 U.S.C. 1126(d), as amended.

....

☐ Applicant has a bona fide intention to use the mark in commerce on or in connection with the above identified goods/services and, accompanying this application, submits a certification or certified copy of a foreign registration in accordance with 15 U.S.C. 1126(e), as amended.

....
(Country of registration)

....
(Registration number)

DECLARATION

The undersigned being hereby warned that willful false statements and the like so made are punishable by fine or imprisonment, or both, under 18 U.S.C. 1001, and that such willful false statements may jeopardize the validity of the application or any resulting registration, declares that he/she is properly authorized to execute this application on behalf of the applicant; he/she believes the applicant to be the owner of the trademark/service mark sought to be registered, or, if the application is being filed under 15 U.S.C. 1051(b), he/she believes applicant to be entitled to use such mark in commerce; to the best of his/her knowledge and belief no other person, firm, corporation, or association has the right to use the above identified mark in commerce, either in the identical form thereof or in such near resemblance thereto as to be likely, when used on or in connection with the goods/services of such other person, to cause confusion, or to cause mistake, or to deceive; and all statements made of his/her own knowledge are true and all statements made on information and belief are believed to be true.

.... (Date)	.... (Signature)
.... (Telephone Number)	.... (Print or Type Name and Position)

INSTRUCTIONS AND INFORMATION FOR APPLICANT

To receive a filing date, the application must be completed and **signed by the applicant** and submitted along with:

1. The prescribed fee for each class of goods/services listed in the application;
2. A drawing of the mark in conformance with 37 CFR 2.52;
3. If the application is based on use of the mark in commerce, three (3) specimens (evidence) of the mark as used in commerce for each class of goods/services listed in the application. All three specimens may be the same and may be in the nature of: (a) labels showing the mark which are placed on the goods; (b) a photograph of the mark as it appears on the goods, (c) brochures or advertisements showing the mark as used in connection with the services.

Verification of the application–The application must be signed in order for the application to receive a filing date. Only the following person may sign the verification (Declaration) for the application, depending on the applicant's legal entity: (a) the individual applicant; (b) an officer of the corporate applicant; (c) one general partner of a partnership applicant; (d) all joint applicants.

Additional information concerning the requirements for filing an application are available in a booklet entitled **Basic Facts about Trademarks**, which may be obtained by writing:

U.S. DEPARTMENT OF COMMERCE
Patent and Trademark Office
Washington, D.C. 20231

Or by calling: (703) 557-INFO

Trademark Searches

THE KEY TO THE SUCCESSFUL adoption of a trademark lies in the trademark search. This process ensures that a desired trademark does not infringe on another existing mark. An informal search can be performed independently and is particularly useful when screening suggestions for trademarks. Searches are generally conducted through computer subscriber databases such as Compu-Mark, Dialog or IntelliGate, using a personal computer, modem and printer.

At a cost of between $5 and $10 per search, an individual may uncover duplicate, conflicting trademarks. A search may also be conducted in a state patent and trademark depository library using Cassis, the free government on-line system. Finally, a search may be made in the library used by the PTO. This facility is located on the second floor of the South Tower Building, 2900 Crystal Dr., Arlington, VA 22202. Note: while these libraries have CD-ROMs containing a database of both registered and pending trademarks, in written descriptions, they do not contain the graphics of the actual design marks.

While the informal, independent search described above is a sound preliminary step, it is critical to ensure that the search process has been comprehensive. A successful challenge to the use of a trademark can result in staggering damages, legal costs and loss of profits by the party found guilty of infringement. This financial devastation could be compounded by the expense of removing the offending trademark from all advertising materials, labels and packaging, printed corporate stationary, checks, price lists, catalogues, and any other place in which the mark is displayed.

The wise alternative to an informal search is the use of professional trademark-search services, such as those listed below. These organizations offer a wide range of services designed to determine the availability of a trademark or trade name for use. Such services also monitor the marketplace for infringement of trademark use, supervise the maintenance of an existing trademark and advise a client regarding the possible acquisition of a specific mark. The value of such a service lies in the thoroughness with which trademark candidates are investigated from among common law sources, pending applications and actual registrations. Investigations can extend to the state, national or international marketplace, and can be performed in the preliminary screening stage as well as during the critical pre-filing period. Using such a service in the preliminary design stages of trademark development can save dollars in a costly design budget.

Once a trademark is secured, these agencies can provide additional services such as monitoring the activity of competitors, including the application for new marks from within a specific industry.

Contact Options

Thomson & Thomson
500 Victory Rd.
North Quincy, MA 02171-1545
(800) 692-8833 or (617) 479-1600
Fax: (617) 786-8273
Trademark Search Service

Trademark Research Corporation
300 Park Ave. S.
New York, NY 10010
(800) 872-6275 or (212) 228-4084
Fax: (212) 228-5090
Trademark Search Service

Additional organizations may be listed in the Business to Business pages of your telephone directory.

Filing for a Copyright

THE COPYRIGHT LAW is important to business individuals from two perspectives: as an owner and as a potential user of registered material. A copyright is used to protect the rights of the author of published or unpublished literature, music and lyrics, drama, choreography, graphics and other art forms, motion pictures, and sound recording.

A revision in the copyright law no longer requires copyright owners to mark their works in a special way to qualify for protection. However, many copyright owners continue to indicate their ownership in the work by using a © to indicate copyright protection.

The copyright registration process originates with an application form obtained from the U.S. Copyright Office. Form TX is the most commonly used application for most business uses and covers non-dramatic literary works such as fiction, nonfiction, textbooks, reference works, directories, catalogues, advertising copy, and computer programs.

Other Common Forms and Their Uses:

- Form PA: Material to be performed, including music (with accompanying lyrics), choreography, motion pictures, audio-visuals.
- Form VA: Visual arts. "Pictorial, graphic, or sculptural works," graphic arts, photographs, prints and art reproductions, maps, globes, charts, technical drawings, diagrams, and models.
- Form SR: Sound recordings.

Filing for a Copyright (cont'd)

Once the application is completed, it should be sent with the $20.00 application fee, payable to the Register of Copyrights, Copyright Office, Library of Congress, Washington, DC 20559. After the copyright has been issued, the owner has three months to supply two copies of the registered work, one for registration and one for the Library of Congress, to the Copyright Office.

Confusion arises concerning what can and cannot be copyrighted. Phrases, slogans, ideas, and mottoes cannot be copyrighted. Neither can blank forms, methods, systems, concepts, and names of products. Occasionally a business owner will attempt to copyright a product or service name, only to be informed that such registration is covered under trademark law rather than copyright law.

Fair Use

The general rule of thumb is that up to 250 words of text from a book or long article may be used without securing permission for such use. Be very careful of poetry, songs, famous individuals and endorsements, however. Recent case law has made some works (like directories) more open to fair use, and others (like a star's singing style) less open.

Contact Option

Copyright Office
Public Information Office
(202) 707-3000
Copyright Information and Brochures

To obtain specific copyright forms, call the Forms Hotline (202) 707-9100.

Software Publishers Assocation Piracy Hotline
(800) 388-7478

FORM TX
UNITED STATES COPYRIGHT OFFICE

REGISTRATION NUMBER

TX TXU

EFFECTIVE DATE OF REGISTRATION

Month Day Year

DO NOT WRITE ABOVE THIS LINE. IF YOU NEED MORE SPACE, USE A SEPARATE CONTINUATION SHEET.

1

TITLE OF THIS WORK ▼

PREVIOUS OR ALTERNATIVE TITLES ▼

PUBLICATION AS A CONTRIBUTION If this work was published as a contribution to a periodical, serial, or collection, give information about the collective work in which the contribution appeared. Title of Collective Work ▼

If published in a periodical or serial give: Volume ▼ Number ▼ Issue Date ▼ On Pages ▼

2

a NAME OF AUTHOR ▼ DATES OF BIRTH AND DEATH Year Born ▼ Year Died ▼

Was this contribution to the work a "work made for hire"? ☐ Yes ☐ No

AUTHOR'S NATIONALITY OR DOMICILE Name of Country OR { Citizen of ▶ Domiciled in ▶

WAS THIS AUTHOR'S CONTRIBUTION TO THE WORK Anonymous? ☐ Yes ☐ No Pseudonymous? ☐ Yes ☐ No If the answer to either of these questions is "Yes," see detailed instructions.

NATURE OF AUTHORSHIP Briefly describe nature of the material created by this author in which copyright is claimed. ▼

NOTE

Under the law, the "author" of a "work made for hire" is generally the employer, not the employee (see instructions). For any part of this work that was "made for hire" check "Yes" in the space provided, give the employer (or other person for whom the work was prepared) as "Author" of that part, and leave the space for dates of birth and death blank.

b NAME OF AUTHOR ▼ DATES OF BIRTH AND DEATH Year Born ▼ Year Died ▼

Was this contribution to the work a "work made for hire"? ☐ Yes ☐ No

AUTHOR'S NATIONALITY OR DOMICILE Name of country OR { Citizen of ▶ Domiciled in ▶

WAS THIS AUTHOR'S CONTRIBUTION TO THE WORK Anonymous? ☐ Yes ☐ No Pseudonymous? ☐ Yes ☐ No If the answer to either of these questions is "Yes," see detailed instructions.

NATURE OF AUTHORSHIP Briefly describe nature of the material created by this author in which copyright is claimed. ▼

c NAME OF AUTHOR ▼ DATES OF BIRTH AND DEATH Year Born ▼ Year Died ▼

Was this contribution to the work a "work made for hire"? ☐ Yes ☐ No

AUTHOR'S NATIONALITY OR DOMICILE Name of Country OR { Citizen of ▶ Domiciled in ▶

WAS THIS AUTHOR'S CONTRIBUTION TO THE WORK Anonymous? ☐ Yes ☐ No Pseudonymous? ☐ Yes ☐ No If the answer to either of these questions is "Yes," see detailed instructions.

NATURE OF AUTHORSHIP Briefly describe nature of the material created by this author in which copyright is claimed. ▼

3

YEAR IN WHICH CREATION OF THIS WORK WAS COMPLETED This information must be given in all cases. ◀ Year

DATE AND NATION OF FIRST PUBLICATION OF THIS PARTICULAR WORK Complete this information ONLY if this work has been published. Month ▶ Day ▶ Year ▶ ◀ Nation

4

See instructions before completing this space.

COPYRIGHT CLAIMANT(S) Name and address must be given even if the claimant is the same as the author given in space 2.▼

TRANSFER If the claimant(s) named here in space 4 are different from the author(s) named in space 2, give a brief statement of how the claimant(s) obtained ownership of the copyright.▼

DO NOT WRITE HERE OFFICE USE ONLY

APPLICATION RECEIVED

ONE DEPOSIT RECEIVED

TWO DEPOSITS RECEIVED

REMITTANCE NUMBER AND DATE

MORE ON BACK ▶ • Complete all applicable spaces (numbers 5-11) on the reverse side of this page. • See detailed instructions. • Sign the form at line 10.

DO NOT WRITE HERE

Page 1 of ______ pages

Filing for a Copyright (cont'd)

EXAMINED BY

FORM VA

CHECKED BY

☐ CORRESPONDENCE Yes

☐ DEPOSIT ACCOUNT FUNDS USED

FOR COPYRIGHT OFFICE USE ONLY

DO NOT WRITE ABOVE THIS LINE. IF YOU NEED MORE SPACE, USE A SEPARATE CONTINUATION SHEET.

5

PREVIOUS REGISTRATION Has registration for this work, or for an earlier version of this work, already been made in the Copyright Office?
☐ **Yes** ☐ **No** If your answer is "Yes," why is another registration being sought? (Check appropriate box) ▼
☐ This is the first published edition of a work previously registered in unpublished form.
☐ This is the first application submitted by this author as copyright claimant.
☐ This is a changed version of the work, as shown by space 6 on this application.
If your answer is "Yes," give: **Previous Registration Number** ▼ **Year of Registration** ▼

6

DERIVATIVE WORK OR COMPILATION Complete both space 6a & 6b for a derivative work; complete only 6b for a compilation.
a. **Preexisting Material** Identify any preexisting work or works that this work is based on or incorporates. ▼

See instructions before completing this space.

b. **Material Added to This Work** Give a brief, general statement of the material that has been added to this work and in which copyright is claimed. ▼

7

DEPOSIT ACCOUNT If the registration fee is to be charged to a Deposit Account established in the Copyright Office, give name and number of Account.
Name ▼ **Account Number** ▼

CORRESPONDENCE Give name and address to which correspondence about this application should be sent. Name/Address/Apt/City/State/Zip ▼

Area Code & Telephone Number ▶

Be sure to give your daytime phone ◀ number.

8

CERTIFICATION* I, the undersigned, hereby certify that I am the
Check only one ▼
☐ author
☐ other copyright claimant
☐ owner of exclusive right(s)
☐ authorized agent of ______
Name of author or other copyright claimant, or owner of exclusive right(s) ▲

of the work identified in this application and that the statements made by me in this application are correct to the best of my knowledge.

Typed or printed name and date ▼ If this is a published work, this date must be the same as or later than the date of publication given in space 3.

date ▶

Handwritten signature (X) ▼

9

MAIL CERTIFICATE TO

Name ▼

Number/Street/Apartment Number ▼

City/State/ZIP ▼

Certificate will be mailed in window envelope

Have you:
- Completed all necessary spaces?
- Signed your application in space 8?
- Enclosed check or money order for $10 payable to *Register of Copyrights?*
- Enclosed your deposit material with the application and fee?

MAIL TO: Register of Copyrights, Library of Congress, Washington, D.C. 20559.

* 17 U.S.C. § 506(e): Any person who knowingly makes a false representation of a material fact in the application for copyright registration provided for by section 409, or in any written statement filed in connection with the application, shall be fined not more than $2,500.

☆U.S. GOVERNMENT PRINTING OFFICE: 1987—181-531/40,025

April 1987—60,000

Trademark Protection

"ASPIRIN," "THERMOS," "CELLOPHANE," "shredded wheat," "nylon," and "zipper" are examples of the greatest danger facing a trademark holder. Each was once a registered but, unfortunately, poorly protected trademark. Public misuse caused the trademark name to degenerate to a generic term describing the class or nature of an article. Subsequently, the holder was denied the renewal of trademark rights, and the product name became simply a generic term for competitors' products.

A company or individual holding trademark rights should take the following precautions:

- Make sure the mark being used isn't already in use. Protect interests through a trademark search by a professional search organization.
- Use the trademark symbol ™ to indicate that it is the company's selected mark.
- Once registration is complete, use the ® symbol to indicate that the trademark is officially registered.
- Consider the services of a trademark search firm to monitor the valid and unscrupulous use of the mark.
- Notify in writing anyone who is misusing a trademark.
- In all advertising, use the trademark as an adjective modifier, rather than as a noun or a verb. Xerox®, for example, is careful to remind the public that Xerox® is a type of photocopier, rather than a process of duplicating a document.

Properly protected, a trademark can last indefinitely.

Patents

A PATENT IS A GOVERNMENT-GRANTED RIGHT which allows the holder to exclude all others from making, using, or selling the registered inventions. Patents are issued to the original inventor, joint inventors, legal representatives or guardians for a non-renewable period of 17 years. The patent grant allows the owner to pursue litigation against anyone who makes, uses or sells the patented invention without the written permission of the patent holder. However, patents also lend prestige to a product and are sometimes secured to impress financial investors or consumers of the product.

Three Types of Patents

- Utility patents cover new inventions that serve a particular useful function, such as Velcro fasteners, paper clips, and automatic transmissions.
- Design patents protect the unique design or shape of an object which is used for an ornamental or aesthetic purpose, such as a computer icon or the shape of a desk lamp. Design patents are granted for only 14 years.
- Plant patents are issued to an individual who has invented or discovered and produced asexually (from a seed) a new variety of plant, such as a flower. This patent type has been extended to include living cells or cell combinations as produced in biochemical research facilities.

The formula for determining the appropriate patent type, design or utility, is simple. Can the invention function without this feature? If the answer is yes, then a design patent is the appropriate protection.

Seven Important Points about Patents

- Patents are issued for objects or inventions, not ideas. Mental concepts and abstract ideas are not patentable. Protection for written materials and ideas are covered under copyright law while company logos and corporate marks are protected under trademark laws.
- A patent is not necessary to market an invention commercially. An inventor may make, use or sell an invention without the benefit of a patent, provided it is not covered by an existing patent currently held by another individual.
- It is a criminal offense to use the words "patent pending" in advertising if the patent application is not active.
- If a patent is desired, patent application must be made within one year from the time the invention is first commercialized or the right to patent is lost.
- Patented products are not superior products. A patent only guarantees that the product is significantly different from others similar to it. Superiority is determined by the user rather than by the inventor.
- Until the invention is commercialized and in widespread use, the patent has little value. However, consider where Polaroid would be today if Dr. Edwin Land had not patented the company's products.
- Patent protection is only as good as the vigilance one maintains against infringers. The value of a patent lies in its offensive power which becomes apparent when a patent holder warns a violator to discontinue the unauthorized use of the invention or risk litigation. (Unfortunately, all too often the party with the most money prevails.) In court proceedings, patent holders are certainly looked upon more favorably than violators. However, the burden of vigilance falls upon the patent holder.

Obtaining a Patent

It is safest to file a patent application before an invention is commercialized. Applications are filed with the Patent and Trademark Office (PTO) and include drawings of the invention, specifications, description, explanation of use, and a sworn declaration of origin.

Determining the patentability of the invention and meeting the requirements for application are complex processes that experts feel warrant the assistance of a patent attorney, a lawyer who has a degree in physical science or engineering. A list of attorneys and patent agents (qualified experts in patent applications and procedures who can practice before the Patent and Trademark Office but do not possess a law degree) is available in the following government publication:

Patent Attorneys and Agents Registered to Practice Before the U.S. Patent and Trademark Office
#003-004-00573-4, $21.00
U.S. Government Printing Office
Washington, DC 20402
(202) 783-3238

The explicit directions for filing application materials and the required fees are available from:

Commissioner of Patents and Trademarks
Washington, DC 20231

Recommended Resource

Patent It Yourself
by David Pressman
Nolo Press
(800) 992-6656

Work for Hire

IF EXECUTIVE RALPH HIRES ENGINEER SUSAN to create a super gizmo, who owns the rights to the super gizmo? If Susan tinkers in the company laboratory and develops a super widget, who owns the rights to her invention? Suppose, however, that Susan develops the super widget at home using all her own materials. Does Ralph have any rights and ownership to the super widget?

Law journals are full of cases in which employees and employers waged legal battles about the rights to inventions developed by the employee. According to experts, common law provides that the employer may assume title for those inventions developed within the scope of the individual's employment, particularly if "inventing" was included in the job description. In the absence of a contract, ownership of an invention which is outside the scope of the inventor's employment belongs to the inventor, but the employer is given "shop right," or the license to use the invention without paying royalties. If the invention was developed without the employer's resources and is outside the realm of the employer's business, the employer has no rights whatsoever to the employee's invention.

To avoid such disputes and the resulting litigation, the "work for hire" clause was introduced into employment contracts. Such agreements supersede the common law and clear up the misunderstandings regarding the exact nature of the employee's work responsibilities.

A "work for hire" clause entitles the employer to take ownership of all ideas, inventions and discoveries made by the employee as a condition of employment. It is not uncommon to include a clause in the contract which states that employees agree to sell for the sum of $1.00 any inventions, ideas and/or improvements developed during the term of employment which relate to products, methods, designs, and equipment used by the company or any of its subsidiaries. The following is an example of a "work for hire" clause.

________________, hereby certifies that (the "Work") was specially commissioned by and is to be considered a "work made for hire" under the Copyright Act of 1976, as amended, for __________ ("Company"), and that company is entitled to the copyright thereto.

Without limiting the foregoing, for good and valuable consideration, receipt of which is hereby acknowledged, the undersigned hereby assigns and transfers to the Company, its successors and assigns, absolutely and forever, all right, title and interest, throughout the world in and to the Work and each element thereof, including but not limited to the copyright therein, for the full term of such copyright, and any and all renewals or extensions thereof, in each country of the world, together with any and all present or future claims and causes of action against third parties arising from or related to the Work and the copyrights therein, and the right to use and retain the proceeds relating to such claims and causes of action.

Rights in the Workplace

TREATING EMPLOYEES WITH RESPECT and fairness is critical for two reasons. First, it establishes a company's reputation for fairness and impartiality. This reputation is carefully scrutinized by individuals both within and outside of the organization and is a vital factor in keeping and attracting desirable employees. The second, equally important reason is that identifying and safeguarding employee rights reduces the possibility of the company becoming embroiled in charges of discrimination, lengthy litigation and costly settlements.

Employee rights fall into three categories: the right to job security, the right to fair treatment by the employer and the right to fair treatment in the workplace.

Right to Job Security

This right protects the employee from "termination at will" or the previously popular employer practice of discharging an individual for virtually any reason. Legislation, including Title VII of the Civil Rights Act of 1964 and more recent anti-discrimination laws, is being cited in courts around the country in disputes about employee rights.

Court rulings have determined that an employee cannot be fired for:

- Whistle blowing regarding employer policies or violations of laws;
- Complaints or testimony regarding violations of employee rights;
- Lawful union activities;
- Filing claims for workers' compensation;
- Filing charges of unfair labor practices;
- Reporting OSHA violations;
- Garnishment for indebtedness.

Justifiable terminations should be spelled out in an employee handbook or personnel manual. Some of these reasons include:

Rights in the Workplace (cont'd)

- Incompetence or failure to respond to training;
- Gross insubordination;
- Repeated unexcused absences or lateness;
- Sexual harassment;
- Verbal abuse;
- Physical violence;
- Falsification of records;
- Theft;
- Drunkenness on the job.

Right to Fair Treatment by Employer

Fair treatment of employees includes honoring their rights to privacy and providing feedback regarding their performance in order to enable them to successfully meet job requirements. Examples of employee privacy include:

- The right to refuse a polygraph or drug test as a condition for employment;
- The right to access employment records. Although federal agencies and only six states have laws regarding this right, over 50% of major national companies now have written guidelines for allowing employees access to their personnel files;
- The right to prohibit release of information regarding the employee to other organizations without the employee's consent.

Fair treatment of the employee is guaranteed by:

- The right to specific information regarding company expectations and prohibitions as stated in an Employee Manual;
- The right to due process procedures including consistent rules and protocol for grievances;
- The right to a progressive system of discipline including: an oral warning, a written warning, suspension, transfer or demotion, and, as a last resort, discharge.

Right to Fair Treatment Within the Workplace

Executives often forget that their employees are entitled to an environment in which they are treated with fairness and respect by their fellow workers. Among these workplace rights are:

- The right to equal and impartial treatment by other employees regardless of race, sex, age, national origin, disability, religion;
- The right to be free from sexual harassment;
- The right to information about a plant or office closing. The Plant Closing Act of 1988 requires employers to provide affected employees with 60 days notification of a plant closing;
- The right to knowledge about workplace hazards ranging from warnings about chemicals used in the company to necessary safety precautions and simple guidelines for avoiding accidents.

Federal legislation protects employee rights, and it is the responsibility of the employer to be informed regarding the interpretation of these laws. Violations of workplace rights make the employer liable to charges of discriminatory practices.

Recommended Resource

Beyond Race and Gender
by R. Roosevelt Thomas, Jr.
AMACOM (American Management Association)
(212) 586-8100

Sexual Harassment

ALTHOUGH NOT A NEW WORKPLACE PROBLEM, the most frequently discussed current employment issue is sexual harassment. Studies over the last ten years indicate that 40% to 70% of women interviewed have been exposed to inappropriate sexual behavior on the job. The 1991 Justice Clarence Thomas confirmation hearings raised American consciousness about the issue while the publicity regarding the litigation between Dr. Francis Cooney, an esteemed brain surgeon, and her employer, Stanford University Medical School, demonstrated the presence of harassment at all levels in the workplace. Consequently, every employer must develop an awareness of situations which constitute sexual harassment, and an understanding of accountability and liability.

Sexual harassment is defined in one of two ways: (1) *quid pro quo* situations, and (2) those circumstances which create a "hostile environment." In the first category, an individual's employment, advancement or benefits are dependent upon the employee's submission to unwelcome sexual advances or behavior, including demands for sexual favors, unwanted touching, leering, and sexually suggestive gestures.

The second category, a hostile environment, is created when the victim is subjected to offensive behavior which consistently affects his/her work performance. Such behavior includes sexually explicit graffiti, offensive sexual epithets, abusive language, or vulgarities.The differences between incidents of bad taste and those of sexual harassment are based upon the frequency of behavior, the severity of the incident, the reaction of the victim, and the harasser's recognition of the victim's response.

Sexual Harassment (cont'd)

According to the Civil Rights Act of 1991, the potential for employer liability may be unlimited. Employers are liable for the sexual harassment actions of their supervisors, and their liability may extend to the behavior of other employees. Legal experts point out that employers are held responsible if the employer knows or should have been aware of the harassment and took no steps to correct the situation.

In order to avoid liability, an employer should take the following preventive steps:

- Adopt and implement a company policy against sexual harassment;
- Inform all employees about that policy;
- Train all supervisory staff to recognize a hostile environment and to respond sensitively to a complaint of harassment;
- Establish procedures for handling sexual harassment complaints;
- Take investigative and corrective action on any complaints, including discharge of the offender, when warranted.

How to Handle a Sexual Harassment Complaint

1. The charge should be reported immediately to the company official designated by corporate policy.

2. The designated official should conduct a thorough, documented, but confidential investigation, informing only those individuals considered essential to the investigatory process. Subsequent interviews should be conducted with witnesses or others with knowledge of the incident(s).

3. All information regarding the investigation should be documented and kept in a separate file.

4. Once the investigation is complete, the victim should be informed that appropriate disciplinary action has been taken. The victim does not need to be informed of the exact nature of the discipline.

5. The victim should be reassured that he or she will not be subject to retaliation and that he or she has legitimately pursued employee rights.

Discrimination

TITLE VII OF THE CIVIL RIGHTS ACT OF 1964 prohibits discrimination based on race, color, religion, sex, or national origin. Under this law, companies employing 15 or more individuals are prevented from discriminating in the areas of:

- Hiring and firing
- Compensation and promotion
- Transfer or layoff
- Job advertisements and recruitment
- Testing
- Training and apprenticeship programs
- Use of company facilities
- Fringe benefits, retirement plans and disability leave.

Amendments to the Civil Rights Act of 1964

Illegal discrimination is further prohibited by the following amendments to Title VII, which are monitored by the Equal Employment Opportunity Commission (EEOC):

- The Equal Pay Act (EPA) requires that an employer pay all employees equally for equal work, regardless of gender. The law covers situations where men and women perform jobs which require equal skill, effort and responsibility. The exception to this law is a pay system which is based on a factor other than gender, such as seniority, or the quantity or quality of items produced or processed. Thus, Jessica cannot be hired as a reservations agent at a base rate which is lower or higher than that of Randy who was hired 2 months earlier. However, Jessica can be hired at a base rate which is lower than Tom, who has been a reservations agent for five years and has received annual salary increases in return for five years of service to the company.
- The Age Discrimination in Employment Act (ADEA) of 1967 protects persons 40 years of age or older from discriminatory practices in hiring, firing, promotions, pay, and reduction in pension benefits.
- The Older Workers Benefit Protection Act of 1990 was established to discourage employers from targeting older workers for staff cutting programs. It prohibits employers from requiring employees who accept a severance pay package, or an early retirement plan, to sign away their rights to pursue legal action against age-based discrimination.
- The Pregnancy Discrimination Act prohibits employers from refusing to hire a pregnant woman,

Discrimination (cont'd)

terminating her employment based on her pregnancy or forcing her to take a maternity leave. The law also requires that a pregnant woman be allowed the same medical leave rights available to other employees for medical conditions. An employer may not refuse to provide health care insurance benefits for pregnancy, if such insurance is provided for other medical conditions.

Note: While Title VII forbids an employer from refusing to grant men the same child care leave rights as women, experts report that only 8% of U.S. companies offer the same option to male employees. Individual states, however, have specific laws regarding parental rights for childbirth, adoption and parental-responsibility leaves. The prudent employer will investigate such specific state laws either through the local library or in recommended resources.

Americans with Disabilities Act (ADA) enacted on July 26, 1992, prohibits discrimination against qualified individuals who are defined as persons "with a physical or mental impairment that substantially limits one or more major life activities." While job applicants may not be questioned about the existence, nature or severity of a disability, they may be asked about their ability to perform specific job functions.

Medical examinations may be a condition of employment, but only if all entering employees in the same category are requested to submit to the same exams. Likewise, medical examinations of current employees must be job-related and consistent with the employer's business needs. The ADA does not cover employees or applicants who are currently using illegal drugs. Tests for illegal use of drugs are not subject to the ADA's restrictions on medical examinations.

Often Overlooked Applications of Title VII

There are several other applications of Title VII that may be unknown to employers:

- An employer is required to reasonably accommodate the religious practices of an employee or prospective employee through flexible scheduling, voluntary substitutions or swaps, job reassignments and lateral transfers, unless to do so would create undue hardships on the employer.
- An employee whose religious practices prohibit payment of union dues to a labor organization cannot be required to pay the dues, but may pay an equal sum to a charitable organization.
- Pregnant employees must be permitted to work as long as they are able to perform their jobs. They may not be prohibited from returning to work for a predetermined length of time after childbirth.
- Leave for child care must be granted on the same basis as leave granted to employees for other non-medical reasons, such as non-job-related travel or education.
- English-only rules in the workplace may constitute illegal discrimination unless an employer can demonstrate that such a practice is necessary for conducting business. In such a situation, employees have to be told when they must speak English and the consequences for violating the rule.
- An "eligible small business" can receive a 50% tax credit for expenditures exceeding $250, but not in excess of $10,250, if those expenses are incurred in order to modify existing environments to comply with the requirements of the Americans with Disabilities Act.

Informing Employees of EEOC Regulations

An employer is expected to post notices describing the federal laws prohibiting job discrimination based on race, color, sex, national origin, religion, age, and disability, and describing the provisions of the Equal Pay Act. The EEOC provides a poster summarizing the laws and procedures for filing a complaint.

Contact Option

Equal Employment Opportunity Commission
Office of Communications and Legislative Affairs
1801 L St., NW
Washington, DC 20507
(800) 669-3362 or (202) 663-4264
Provides posters and fact sheets on discrimination law

Recommended Resource

Your Rights in the Workplace
by Dan Lacey
Nolo Press
(800) 992-6656

Almanac Fact

A 1992 Gallup survey shows that companies with twenty or fewer employees rarely provide employee leave or unpaid parental leave, forty-two percent of companies with 21 to 500 employees let workers take time off from the job.

Source: Gallup Organization

AIDS

THE 1990s BROUGHT THE BUSINESS WORLD a startling realization of the presence of AIDS in the workplace. The Centers for Disease Control (CDC) reports that more than 1 million people are infected with the HIV virus in the United States. While 200,000 people have died from AIDS in this country, many more are living with both diagnosed and undiagnosed HIV virus, which can precede the onset of AIDS. The impact on business is staggering in terms of both direct costs (increased costs in medical benefits, short-term and long-term disability coverage and increased Medicaid costs), as well as indirect costs (lost productivity, lost talent and increased recruitment and training expenses).

Individuals living with HIV/AIDS are protected under the Americans With Disabilities Act of 1990 and consequently it is illegal for businesses with 15 or more employees to discriminate against applicants or workers because they are infected with HIV or suffering from AIDS. Companies covered by ADA are expected to make reasonable accommodations in order to permit affected employees to continue working. These accommodations include extended leave policies, reassignment to available positions within the company and flexible work schedules.

Understanding the responsibilities required by law and responding to the very human needs of those employees living with HIV and those who work alongside these individuals, is a daunting task. There are three organizations dedicated to assisting large and small businesses in formulating policy, providing education and planning and responding to the immediate concerns of companies who suddenly find themselves face to face with this situation.

The American Red Cross

The American Red Cross will provide facilitators/instructors or train staff members of an individual company to provide a company training program on HIV/AIDS. This consists of a minimum one-hour presentation on the facts of HIV/AIDS infection and transmission. In addition, the Red Cross offers expanded presentations on the rights and responsibilities of businesses, the facts of disclosure, and a particularly useful training program for managers and supervisors. The Red Cross provides assistance to companies in policy planning.

The National Headquarters of the American Red Cross advises that interested individuals should first contact the local chapter of the American Red Cross to obtain advice and plan a program suited to the needs of the specific organization. If there is no local branch of the ARC, the AIDS Education staff at the National Headquarters of the American Red Cross will provide assistance.

American Red Cross National Headquarters
431 18th St., NW
Washington, DC 20006
AIDS Education Division
(202) 434-4074

The CDC's National AIDS Clearing House

The CDC's National AIDS Clearing House is a new referral service established under the National AIDS Information and Education Program. This service has divisions for information, education and experimental drug programs as well as a new division called Business Response to AIDS Resource Service. This division will provide information and local non-health care referrals to individuals in the business community anywhere in the nation. Their referrals regarding business policy and programs, training programs, legal questions, and insurance issues, are made on the local, state and national level. In addition they will refer inquiries to the appropriate state HIV coordinator.

The CDC National AIDS Clearing House
(800) 458-5231

The National Leadership Coalition on AIDS

The National Leadership Coalition on AIDS offers technical assistance and guidance to businesses in establishing policies and programs tailored to the individual needs of companies ranging from IBM to small businesses. They will send free literature to companies and individuals seeking to be proactive rather than reactive in the face of increasing HIV throughout the workplace. This particular organization is most useful in determining the specific needs of the company seeking to assist its employees. Its information agents offer clear, supportive direction to any and all inquiries regarding people living with HIV/AIDS. They are equipped to meet the immediate and long-term needs of any organization and are most interested in doing so. The Coalition will also provide a free copy for the first request of any printed materials which they publish on the topic of HIV/AIDS.

The National Leadership Coalition on AIDS
1730 M St., NW, Suite 905
Washington, DC 20036
(202) 429-0930

Acting as Your Own Lawyer

A MAN WHO ACTS AS HIS OWN ATTORNEY has a fool for a client. Obviously, the originator of this quote never had to pay a sizeable legal fee in return for a simple, routine legal procedure.

Armed with general interest, the time to conduct preliminary research and a desire to save corporate funds, an ambitious business owner can conduct many of his or her own legal matters. The prudent business owner, however, should be aware of the times when one does and does not require the services of an attorney. The key lies in realizing that the most basic business situation can become complicated and require the guidance of an attorney. The following are some examples of such legal situations:

- Choosing among sole proprietorship, partnership or corporation;
- Structuring a partnership agreement;
- Establishing a corporation;
- Dealing with stock and security laws;
- Registering trademarks, copyrights and patents;
- Filing for licenses or permits on federal, state and local levels;
- Fulfilling the basic tax requirements for small businesses;
- Purchasing real estate or a business;
- Leasing real estate or equipment;
- Negotiating a lease;
- Insuring a business;
- Hiring employees and independent contractors;
- Handling labor disagreements;
- Dealing with customer litigation;
- Extending credit and collecting debts;
- Planning for an estate;
- Dealing with criminal proceedings;
- Handling bankruptcy and reorganization proceedings.

In order to determine the extent to which an individual can handle any one of the above situations, he or she should:

- Understand the basic issues;
- Have a clear understanding of the forms and procedures involved in completing the legal transaction;
- Determine which if any aspects of the process can be handled by the individual without legal help;
- Evaluate the complexities and honestly assess the need for legal assistance;
- Decide if it is worthwhile in terms of time and savings to proceed independently.

Recommended Resources

The Legal Guide for Starting and Running a Small Business
by Fred S. Steingold
Nolo Press
(800) 992-6656 or (510) 549-1976

Small Business Legal Handbook
by Robert Friedman
Enterprise Dearborn
(800) 554-4379

The Partnership Book: How to Write a Partnership Agreement
by Denise Clifford and Ralph Warner
Nolo Press
(800) 992-6656 or (510) 549-1976

Legal Research: How to Find and Understand the Law
by Stephen Elias and Susan Levinkind
Nolo Press
(800) 992-6656 or (510) 549-1976

Another outstanding resource is the United States Small Business Administration (SBA). This federal organization is devoted to offering assistance to existing businesses or to aspiring entrepreneurs. The SBA provides information on financial assistance, management, obtaining government contracts, counseling services and offers many low-cost publications. By calling a local office of the SBA or its toll-free national number (800) 827-5722, the caller can request a list of available publications. These handy publications can be ordered at a low price and provide useful background information.

Almanac Fact

In 1990, 113 product liability cases had verdicts paying $1 million or more.

Source: Jury Verdict Research

Incorporation

New Business Incorporations (Thousands)

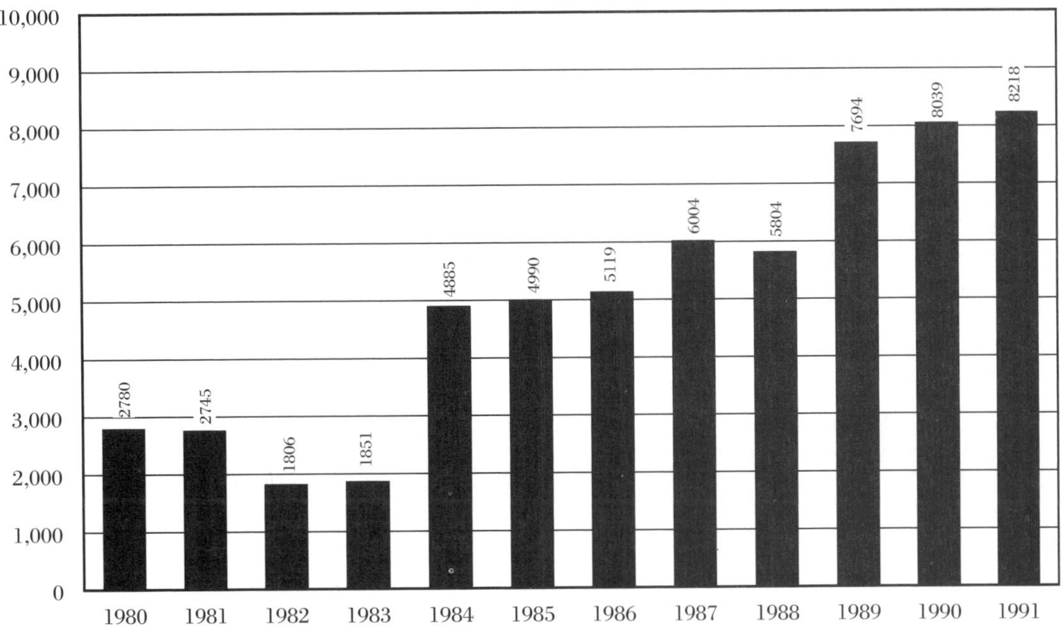

Source: Statistical Abstract

SINCE ITS INCEPTION IN THE UNITED STATES over 300 years ago, the corporation has continued to grow and flourish as a legal entity. Experts note that in North America, over 50,000 new corporations are formed each month, testifying to sustained commercial growth.

A business owner must choose from among the three types of legal structures (sole proprietorship, partnership and corporation) when establishing a new firm. The table above demonstrates the growth of business corporations, as a popular choice in the U.S. during the last decade.

Forming a corporation can appear to be a formidable task requiring legions of legal assistance, but there are many resources available to those seeking such a legal structure for their businesses. The primary step is to recognize the basic procedure of incorporating. The basic steps include:

- Select and reserve a corporate name;
- Prepare and file Articles of Incorporation;
- Select the Board of Directors;
- Establish corporate bylaws;
- Record the minutes of the first meeting of the Board of Directors;
- Establish a corporate bank account;
- Issue stock certificates to shareholders;
- Create a corporate record book;
- Conform to individual state requirements on incorporation;
- Review bulk sales laws which pertain to the corporation.

The business owner who possesses neither the time nor the inclination to perform these procedures independently, can either enlist the services of a lawyer or can utilize the services of organizations which deal directly with the individual owner in the incorporation process. Such specialists in incorporation can answer a business owner's questions over the telephone and can act as an agent for the company. For nominal fees advertised at $75.00 to $300.00, based on required services, these groups will help the organization choose from among the general, the closed and the non-stock corporation, and will guide the owner through the procedures to incorporation.

Contact Options

Corporate Agents Inc.
1013 Centre Rd., P.O. Box 1281
Wilmington, DE 19899
(800) 877-4224 or (302) 998-0598
Fax: (302) 998-7078
Incorporation Consultant

Incorporation (cont'd)

Harvard Business Services, Inc.
25 Greystone Manor
Lewes, DE 19958
(800) 345-2677
Incorporation Consultant

The more adventurous individual can secure the guidance of several good publications and perform the process on his or her own. These and other self-help books contain step-by-step descriptions of the procedures and, in some cases, provide specimens of the required forms.

Recommended Resources

How to Form Your Own Corporation Without a Lawyer for Under $75.00
by Ted Nicholas
Enterprise Dearborn
(800) 554-4379

The Legal Guide for Starting and Running a Small Business
by Fred S. Steingold
Nolo Press
(800) 992-6656 or (510) 549-1976

Prepared Legal Forms

THE PRESENCE OF THE PHOTOCOPIER as well as the personal computer and its powerful software have threatened the survival of all but the heartiest of suppliers of legal forms and documents. The enterprising business owner can produce the most commonly used documents through a combination of a reasonably powerful PC, a hard disk and laser printer. The catalogues from suppliers usually contain a listing of software available to produce blank electronic forms.

The business owner who infrequently uses legal forms can select either local stationers dealing with legal documents or one of the well-known suppliers of legal forms. Upon request they will send a catalogue and order form.

Contact Options

Blumberg's Law Products (Excelsior Legal, Inc.)
62 White St.
New York, NY 10013
(800) 221-2972 or (212) 431-5000
Legal Supply Source

Standard Legal Forms and Agreements for Small Businesses
Self-Counsel Press, Inc.
1704 N. State St.
Bellingham, WA 98225
(800) 663-3077 or (206) 676-4530
Standard Legal Form Templates

Important Documents for All Firms

CORPORATE RECORDS ARE A VITAL COMPONENT in an organization's self-defense program. Such documents can ensure that the protective umbrella of the corporation will serve the officers, the employees, the board of directors and the stockholders.

All businesses should have the following documents in a corporate kit. This is merely a collection of documents held together in a loose-leaf notebook or in a more formal corporate document holder available from a supplier of law products.

The following should be included in the corporate kit:

- Articles of Incorporation;
- Amendments to the Articles of Incorporation;
- Minutes of the Stockholders and Board of Directors Meetings;
- Bylaws of the Corporation;
- List of the Corporation's Shareholders;
- Corporate Secretary's Affidavit of Verification of Corporate Shares of Stock;
- All Directors Resolutions;
- All Stockholders Resolutions;
- Record of Dividends;
- Outstanding Loans;
- Contracts;
- Ledgers including Accounts Receivable, Accounts Payable and General Inventory;
- Insurance Policies;
- Resolutions regarding salaries and bonuses of top executives;
- Employment Contracts and Agreements;
- Stock Option Plans;
- Medical-Dental Expense Plans;
- Verification of citizenship or right to work according to the Immigration and Reform Control Act (IRCA) of 1986.

Employee Handbook

WHILE MOST EMPLOYERS ARE AWARE of the importance of adhering to the law when hiring, firing and paying employees, few recognize the legal value of the employee handbook. This document outlines the company's expectations of all employees and, when signed by the employee, acknowledges agreement to conform to those policies and practices.

A prudent employer will carefully prepare the employee handbook to present specific company policy on the following important topics:

- Administrative policies such as hours, security and safety procedures.
- Wage and salary information regarding salary increases, shift differential, non-scheduled work reimbursement, pay periods and checks, overtime, deduction types, annual evaluation policy.
- Benefits including parking, paid holidays, vacation policy, sick leave and personal leave policy, workman's compensation, and details of the health care and insurance plans.
- Personnel policies including hiring, performance appraisal, disciplinary procedures, resignation, severance pay, and grievance procedures.
- Causes for immediate dismissal including:
  Falsification of records, particularly application for employment;
  Incompetence in performance despite additional training;
  Repeated or gross insubordination;
  A pattern of unexcused absence or lateness;
  Abusive or threatening language to supervisors or other employees;
  Sexual harassment;
  Unauthorized possession of firearms on the company premises;
  Physical violence or attempted injury to another employee or visitor;
  Drunkenness on the job;
  Theft of company property or property of another employee;
  Receiving three notices of reprimand during any one-year period.

The Top Reference Sources

The Copyright Handbook
Nolo Press, $24.95
(510) 549-1976

This is a very thorough guide to copyright procedures that includes a good summation of copyright laws and requirements. Chapters are included on registration, completing all the necessary forms, what copyright protects, what copyright does not protect, works made for hire, jointly authored works, compilations, automated databases, fair use privilege, uses that are less likely to be deemed fair, fair use and the photocopy machine, obtaining permission to use copyrighted material, and much more.

Finding a Lawyer

WHILE LARGE CORPORATIONS have equally large legal firms on retainer to answer legal questions and monitor all legal transactions, the small business owner frequently cannot afford this luxury. He or she must analyze the specific needs of the company and carefully enlist the services of a legal professional. Selecting a good lawyer whose skills, experience and rapport match the needs of the business should begin with a recognition of the legal matters which may require an attorney's assistance.

Services Provided by a Business Lawyer

- Review partnership agreements or incorporation documents;
- Review proposed leases;
- Interpret zoning ordinances regarding land use;
- Evaluate employment agreements or advise regarding difficult terminations;
- Assist in patent, copyright, trademark, and business name proceedings;
- Represent the company interests in lawsuits or arbitrations;
- Review documents regarding business or real estate sale or purchase;
- Draft or evaluate estate planning documents such as wills and trusts;
- Advise on public offerings of corporate stock.

How to Select the Right Lawyer

Selecting a lawyer to represent business interests is no casual task, but a business owner should not be intimidated by the process. By following some basic steps, an individual can accumulate a list of prospective attorneys.

- Talk to people in the business community and ask whose legal services they've used and, more important, why they've made those selections.
- Ask a trusted banker, accountant, insurance agent, or real estate broker for a recommendation.
- Inquire among friends, relatives and business associates for candidate suggestions.
- Solicit the advice of the director of the local chamber of commerce.
- Visit a law librarian to ascertain the names of authors of business law books who may practice in the area. Such recommendations while potentially more difficult to obtain may nonetheless be particularly useful for unusual, specialized businesses.
- If a continuing legal education program (CLE) is available in the area, ask the director to suggest the names of well-qualified individuals.
- In many states, the bar association will provide a Lawyer Referral and Information Service. Where available, the service offers the caller a referral to a local lawyer who provides the type of legal services needed by the caller. Participating lawyers will usually agree to provide an initial consultation for a nominal fee. The rest is up to the individual and the attorney. It is important to note that the state bar associations can provide names of attorneys, but they cannot provide evaluations on these individuals.

Checking Out the Suggestions

After compiling a list of candidates, it is wise to seek additional information from the Martindale-Hubbell Law Directory, available at most law libraries and some local public libraries. This directory offers a compilation of biographical information, education, professional organizations, and the specialties of all listed lawyers. Each individual is also given a confidential rating solicited from lawyers and judges. While some ratings are not published at the behest of a lawyer or because one is not available, the information and rating system can serve to narrow the list considerably.

Interview Prospective Candidates

The final step in the selection process is to request interviews from several good prospects, making clear the purpose of the interview and thus avoiding consultation fees. It is important to look for experience, rapport, accessibility, and value by assessing the interview in terms of the following criteria:

- Does the candidate understand your field and the needs of your business?
- How accessible is this attorney to client phone calls, questions, document review?
- Is this attorney willing to assist in your business legal education, or is he or she proprietary and secretive about legal matters?
- Is this candidate willing to allow you to defray some legal costs by performing negotiations and preparing preliminary drafts of documents, and willing to advise, review and fine tune transactions when necessary?
- Is the candidate a practical problem solver or likely to become mired in legalistic technicalities?

Finding a Lawyer (cont'd)

- Is the prospective attorney willing to leave the control of the business to you, as owner, and serve as advisor in legal matters?
- Which services are billed by flat fees, contingency fees, annual fees, and hourly charges? Is the billing method clear and concise?
- Are all your questions answered?
- Is the individual clear and understandable in his or her answers?
- Do you feel comfortable and compatible with this individual?

Recommended Resource

The Legal Guide for Starting and Running A Small Business
by Fred S. Steingold
Nolo Press
(800) 992-6656

State Bar Association Directory

State	Bar Association Telephone
Alabama	(205) 269-1515
Alaska	(907) 272-7469
Arizona	(602) 252-4804
Arkansas	(501) 375-4605
California	(415) 561-8200
Colorado	(303) 860-1115
Connecticut	(203) 721-0025
Delaware	(302) 658-5278
District of Columbia	(202) 223-6600
Florida	(904) 222-3729
Georgia	(404) 527-8700
Hawaii	(808) 537-1868
Idaho	(208) 342-8958
Illinois	(217) 525-1760
Indiana	(317) 639-5465
Iowa	(515) 243-3179
Kansas	(913) 234-5696
Kentucky	(502) 564-3795
Louisiana	(504) 566-0930
Maine	(207) 622-7523
Maryland	(301) 685-7878
Massachusetts	(617) 542-3602
Michigan	(517) 372-9030
Minnesota	(612) 333-1183
Mississippi	(601) 948-4471
Missouri	(314) 635-4128
Montana	(406) 442-7763

State	Bar Association Telephone
Nebraska	(402) 475-7091
Nevada	(702) 382-2200
New Hampshire	(603) 224-6942
New Jersey	(908) 249-5000
New Mexico	(505) 842-6132
New York	(518) 463-3200
North Carolina	(919) 828-0561
North Dakota	(701) 255-1404
Ohio	(614) 487-2050
Oklahoma	(405) 524-2365
Oregon	(503) 620-0222
Pennsylvania	(717) 238-6715
Puerto Rico	(809) 721-3358
Rhode Island	(401) 421-5740
South Carolina	(803) 799-6653
South Dakota	(605) 224-7554
Tennessee	(615) 383-7421
Texas	(512) 463-1400
Utah	(801) 531-0660
Vermont	(802) 223-2020
Virginia	(804) 786-2061
Virgin Islands	(809) 778-7497
Washington	(206) 448-0441
West Virginia	(304) 342-1474
Wisconsin	(608) 257-3838
Wyoming	(307) 632-9061

Source: 1991-92 ABA Directory

The Top Reference Sources

The Legal Guide for Starting and Running a Small Business
Nolo Press, $19.95
(800) 992-6656

This book contains legal information the small business owner needs to know about partnerships, corporations, buying businesses, franchises, licenses, permits, leases, contracts, hiring and firing, customer relations, independent contractors, insurance and taxes.

Useful sample forms and letters are also included throughout.

Law Firm Fees

THE PRUDENT BUSINESS PERSON will investigate the cost of legal services just as he or she would carefully scrutinize estimates for any other service. It is important to question and understand the conventional fee structure used by attorneys, in order to intelligently estimate a bill for legal services.

There are five basic types of fees:

- Flat fees are charged for a standard service such as incorporation of a small business, divorce, and bankruptcy.
- Contingency fees are usually based on positive results in some legal action such as bill collection. A percentage of the amount recovered becomes the attorney's fee.
- Annual or monthly retainers are negotiated when an attorney agrees to perform all the legal work required by a corporation. This is used when the work is predictable and does not require extensive time away from the office.
- Hourly charges are frequently used for cases such as lawsuits and estate planning.
- Other fees that may be included in the charges are process service fees, investigations, court costs, travel expenses, long distance calls, expert testimony, medical reports, appraisals and out-of-pocket expenses.

Different services are billed in different ways. A higher hourly rate by an experienced lawyer can result in a lower charge than the bill from a less expensive but inexperienced lawyer. Charges are relative to the experience and legal knowledge of the members of a legal firm who may work on the case. They range from the highest fees for senior members of the firm, and decrease for the work of the associate attorney and the legal assistant. The lowest rates are assigned to the work of the paralegal staff who prepare routine documents under the supervision of a lawyer.

Fees can also be altered by the routine or special circumstances of the case, as well as the unexpected results of preliminary procedures and the experience and legal knowledge required to complete the proceedings.

During the first consultation (the fee for which may be waived by the attorney), the prospective client should collect enough information to agree upon a billing method. Some ideas for discussion during this meeting might be:

- If a retainer agreement is used, it should specify that, wherever possible, routine work should be done at the appropriate staff level. Final documents should be reviewed by the next qualified level of attorney.
- If an associate is handling the case, the client should not be billed for office conferences during which the inexperienced attorney is instructed or has his or her work reviewed by a senior counsel.
- The client should request a clear explanation of travel and waiting time rates and should not be billed at the same rate as litigation proceedings.
- If hourly charges are selected, it is a wise precaution to place a cap on the fee and to plan for a meeting to discuss a future course of action and additional fees.
- How is research charged? If the research for this assignment is used to educate the junior attorney, the expense should not be borne by the client.
- How are overhead charges such as copies, messenger services, overnight mail services charged to the client? While multiple copies of necessary documents can be billed to a client account, single house copies of a document should not be billed. Messenger and overnight mail service charges should not accrue due to procrastination on the part of the attorney, but rather as a result of valid, emergency changes.
- How are overtime charges accrued? If the overtime services of the law office staff are a direct result of proceedings in connection with the client's interests, the overtime may be billed to the client. However, if because of the volume of work, the lawyer requires a secretary to clear up a backlog, the client should not be billed for the secretary's overtime. The invoice should state the reason for the overtime and the nature of the work done during the overtime period.
- How are document revisions charged? Since documents are frequently stored on word processors, small changes can be easily and quickly inserted without considerable expense to either the firm or the client. If extensive revisions are the result of valid discussions between the two contracting parties, fees for such changes are valid.
- Experts suggest that to ensure that erroneous charges are not included in the invoice, the client should initially request copies of each letter or document for which the firm is billing. This allows the client a framework for a discussion of a bill which is unclear or seems unreasonably high. If the client has a copy of the lawyer's actual work product, the lawyer will be more disposed to charge a more reasonable fee.

Law Firm Billing

15 Largest Law Firms (by Partners, Associates)

Firm	Headquarters	Partners	Associates
Baker & McKenzie	Chicago	497	989
Jones, Day, Reavis & Pogue	Cleveland	407	665
Skadden, Arps, Slate, Meagher & Flom	New York	228	743
Gibson, Dunn & Crutcher	Los Angeles	231	418
Sidley & Austin	Chicago	284	380
Morgan, Lewis & Bockius	Philadelphia	253	387
Fulbright & Jaworski	Houston	282	342
Morrison & Foerster	San Francisco	234	399
Pillsbury Madison & Sutro	San Francisco	223	389
Weil, Gotshal & Manges	New York	146	473
Shearman & Sterling	New York	132	426
Mayer, Brown and Platt	Chicago	241	322
O'Melveny & Myers	Los Angeles	179	343
Latham & Watkins	Los Angeles	220	337
Vinson & Elkins L.L.P.	Houston	227	289

Source: National Law Journal

Cities with at least three law firms in the top 250 where the firms show the greatest growth in size:

Milwaukee
Richmond
Baltimore
Washington, DC
Cincinnati
Boston
Pittsburgh
Minneapolis/St. Paul

Cities with at least three law firms in the top 250 where the firms shows the greatest decrease in size:

Dallas
Houston
St. Louis
Los Angeles
Cleveland
Atlanta
Seattle
Detroit

Source: National Law Journal , September 28, 1992

Specialty Law Firms

FINDING A LAW FIRM that deals with the specific needs of a company can appear to be a formidable process. A simple way to accomplish this process is to call the county or state bar association. Ask if they have a lawyer referral system. If it is available, ask for a list of attorneys or firms which handle the particular specialty you need.

Frequently these services will provide a printed listing of attorneys by specialty. The referrals include attorneys who have agreed to offer an initial consultation for a nominal fee to the prospective client.

Almanac Fact

The U.S. law firm with the largest gross revenues is Skadden, Arps, with $490,000,000 in 1991.

Source: The American Lawyer, July 1992

U.S. Law Firms with Foreign Offices

	Argentina	Australia	Belgium	Brazil	Canada	China	Egypt	England	France	Germany	Hong Kong	Hungary	Indonesia	Italy	Japan	Lithuania	Mexico	Netherlands	Poland	Portugal	Russia	Saudi Arabia	Singapore	Spain	Sweden	Switzerland	Taiwan	Turkey
Baker & McKenzie	•	•	•	•	•	•	•	•	•	•	•	•		•	•		•	•	•		•	•	•	•		•	•	
Bryan Cave								•		•												•						
Cleary, Gottlieb,			•					•	•	•	•				•													
Coudert Brothers		•	•	•		•		•	•		•				•						•		•					
Cravath, Swaine & Moore								•																				
Davis Polk & Wardwell								•	•	•					•													
Debevoise & Plimpton								•	•			•																
Dechert Price & Rhoads			•					•																				
Dewey Ballantine								•				•																
Dorsey & Whitney			•					•																				
Fulbright & Jaworski								•			•																	
Gibson, Dunn & Crutcher			•					•	•		•				•							•						
Graham & James								•		•	•			•								•						
Hogan & Hartson			•					•	•										•									
Hunton & Williams			•																•									
Jones, Day			•					•		•	•				•							•				•	•	
Kaye, Scholer			•								•																	
Kelley Drye & Warren			•												•													
Latham & Watkins								•																				
LeBoeuf, Lamb			•					•													•							
Mayer, Brown & Platt			•					•							•													
McDermott, Will & Emory																•												
Milbank, Tweed								•			•				•						•		•					
Morgan, Lewis & Bockius			•					•		•					•													
Morrison & Foerster			•					•			•				•													
O'Melveny & Myers			•					•							•													
Shearman & Sterling					•			•	•	•		•			•												•	
Sidley & Austin								•							•								•					
Simpson Thacher								•							•													
Skadden, Arps		•	•		•			•	•	•	•	•			•						•							
Squire, Sanders								•				•																
Sullivan & Cromwell		•						•	•		•				•													
Vinson & Elkins L.L.P.								•											•		•							
Weil, Gotshal & Manges			•									•							•									
White & Case			•					•	•	•		•	•		•		•		•		•	•	•		•			•
Wilson, Elser, Moskowitz								•							•													

Federal Information Centers

KNOWING EXACTLY WHOM TO CALL is the first step in obtaining information. When an individual is searching for information from the Federal Government, the task of finding the appropriate office can be overwhelming. The General Services Administration has set up a public service clearinghouse for just such needs. The Federal Information Center is a telephone service that is staffed with individuals who can direct a caller to the appropriate federal agency.

The attractive feature of this service is the availability of regional offices serving the larger metropolitan areas of over 35 states. If one is not available in a certain location, the individual can call the main FIC center at (301) 722-9098.

U.S. Federal Information Centers

State	Telephone	Metropolitan Area Served
AK	(800) 729-8003	Anchorage
AL	(800) 366-2998	Birmingham, Mobile
AR	(800) 366-2998	Little Rock
AZ	(800) 359-3997	Phoenix
CA	(800) 726-4995	Los Angeles, San Diego, San Francisco, Santa Ana
CA	(916) 973-1695	Sacramento
CO	(800) 359-3997	Colorado Springs, Denver, Pueblo
CT	(800) 347-1997	Hartford, New Haven
DC	(202) 566-1937	Washington metropolitan area
FL	(800) 347-1997	Fort Lauderdale, Jacksonville, Miami, Orlando, St. Petersburg, Tampa, W. Palm Beach
GA	(800) 347-1997	Atlanta
HI	(800) 733-5996	Honolulu
IA	(800) 735-8004	All points in Iowa
IL	(800) 366-2998	Chicago
IN	(800) 366-2998	Gary
IN	(800) 347-1997	Indianapolis
KS	(800) 735-8004	All points in Kansas
KY	(800) 347-1997	Louisville
LA	(800) 366-2998	New Orleans
MA	(800) 347-1997	Boston
MD	(800) 347-1997	Baltimore
MI	(800) 347-1997	Detroit, Grand Rapids
MN	(800) 366-2998	Minneapolis
MO	(800) 366-2998	St. Louis
MO	(800) 735-8004	Other points in Missouri
NC	(800) 347-1997	Charlotte
NE	(800) 366-2998	Omaha
NE	(800) 735-8004	Other points in Nebraska
NJ	(800) 347-1997	Newark, Trenton
NM	(800) 359-3997	Albuquerque
NY	(800) 347-1997	Albany, Buffalo, New York, Rochester, Syracuse
OH	(800) 347-1997	Akron, Cincinnati, Cleveland, Columbus, Dayton, Toledo
OK	(800) 366-2998	Oklahoma City, Tulsa
OR	(800) 726-4995	Portland
PA	(800) 347-1997	Philadelphia, Pittsburgh
RI	(800) 347-1997	Providence
TN	(800) 347-1997	Chattanooga
TN	(800) 366-2998	Memphis, Nashville
TX	(800) 366-2998	Austin, Dallas, Fort Worth, Houston, San Antonio
UT	(800) 359-3997	Salt Lake City
VA	(800) 347-1997	Norfolk, Richmond, Roanoke
WA	(800) 726-4995	Seattle, Tacoma
WI	(800) 366-2998	Milwaukee

Regulatory Agencies

Consumer Product Safety Commission
Washington, DC 20207
(301) 504-0580

Environmental Protection Agency
401 M St., SW
Washington, DC 20460
(202) 260-4454

Equal Employment Opportunity Commission
Office of Communications and Legislative Affairs
1801 L St., NW
Washington, DC 20507
(800) 669-EEOC (669-3362) or (202) 663-4264

Federal Communications Commission
1919 M St., NW
Washington, DC 20554
(202) 632-7000

Federal Deposit Insurance Corporation
550 17th St., NW
Washington, DC 20429
(202) 898-6996

Federal Energy Regulatory Commission
825 N. Capitol St., NW
Washington, DC 20426
(202) 208-1371

Federal Reserve System
20th and C Sts., NW
Washington, DC 20551
(202) 452-3215

Federal Trade Commission
6th St. and Pennsylvania Ave., NW
Washington, DC 20580
(202) 326-2222

Food and Drug Administration
5600 Fishers Lane
Rockville, MD 20857
(301) 443-3170

Immigration and Naturalization Service
U.S. Dept. of Justice
425 Eye St., NW, Room 7116
Washington, DC 20536
(800) 777-7700 or (202) 633-3228

Interstate Commerce Commission
12th St. and Constitution Ave., NW
Washington, DC 20423
(202) 927-5350

National Labor Relations Board
1717 Pennsylvania Ave., NW
Washington, DC 20570
(202) 632-4950

Occupational Safety and Health Administration
200 Constitution Ave., NW
Washington, DC 20210
(202) 523-8151

Securities and Exchange Commission
450 5th St., NW
Washington, DC 20549
(202) 272-2650

National Credit Union Administration
1776 G St., NW
Washington, DC 20456
(202) 682-9650

National Transportation Safety Board
490 L'Enfant Plaza, SW
Washington, DC 20594
(202) 382-6600

Pension Benefit Guaranty Corporation
2020 K. St., NW
Washington, DC 20006
(202) 778-8840

Resolution Trust Corporation
801 17th St., NW
Washington, DC 20006
(202) 416-4387

Small Business Administration
409 3rd St., SW
Washington, DC 20416
(202) 205-6740

United States International Trade Commission
500 E St., SW
Washington, DC 20436
(202) 205-1000

U.S. Postal Service (Current Rates, Fees and Services)
475 L'Enfant Plaza SW
Washington, DC 20260
(202) 268-2284

Regulatory Agencies (cont'd)

Federal Offices:

Bureau of Export Administration (Commerce Dept.)
14th and Constitution Ave., NW
Washington, DC 20230
(202) 377-2721

Economic Development Administration
(Commerce Dept.)
14th and Constitution Ave., NW
Washington, DC 20230
(202) 377-5113

Patent and Trademark Office (Commerce Dept.)
Washington, DC 20231
(703) 557-4636

Office for Civil Rights (Health and Human Services Dept.)
330 Independence Ave., SW
Washington, DC 20201
(202) 619-0585

Social Security Administration (Health and Human Services Dept.)
6401 Security Blvd.
Baltimore, MD 21235
(410) 965-7700

Public Health Service (Health and Human Services Dept.)
200 Independence Ave., SW
Washington, DC 20201
(202) 245-6867

Government National Mortgage Association
(Housing and Urban Development Dept.)
451 7th St., SW
Washington, DC 20410
(202) 708-0980

Employment Standards Administration
(Labor Dept.)
200 Constitution Ave., NW
Washington, DC 20210
(202) 523-8743

Employment and Training Administration
(Labor Dept.)
200 Constitution Ave., NW
Washington, DC 20210
(202) 523-6871

Pension and Welfare Benefits Administration
(Labor Dept.)
200 Constitution Ave., NW
Washington, DC 20210
(202)523-8921

Veterans' Employment and Training Services
(Labor Dept.)
200 Constitution Ave., NW
Washington, DC 20210
(202) 523-9116

Internal Revenue Service (Treasury Dept.)
1111 Constitution Ave., NW
Washington, DC 20224
(800) 829-1040

United States Customs Service (Treasury Dept.)
1301 Constitution Ave., NW
Washington, DC 20229
(202) 566-8195

Hotlines:

Small Business Export/Import Advisory Service
(800) 424-5201 or (202) 566-8860

Small Business Administration Answer Desk

This connects the caller to an interactive voice unit which directs touch-tone phone users to a directory of services and information publications.
(800) 827-5722 or (202) 653-7561

Trade Regulation Enforcement
Federal Trade Commission
Enforcement Division
6th & Pennsylvania Ave., NW
Washington, DC 20580

The Top Reference Sources

Congressional Quarterly's Washington Information Directory
Congressional Quarterly, $89.95
(202) 887-8500

This directory lists the departments and agencies of the federal government, congressional committees, and private, nonprofit organizations in the nation's capital.

Each chapter covers a broad subject area, such as health, energy or science. Entries include the name, address, and telephone number of the organization; the name and title of the best person to contact for information; and a brief description of the work performed by the organization.

State Information Offices

EACH STATE HAS AN INFORMATION OFFICE staffed by operators who can direct the caller to the appropriate office based on his or her stated purpose. The Information Office numbers for each of the state offices are as follows:

State Information Office Phone Numbers

State	Telephone
Alabama	(205) 261-2500
Alaska	(907) 465-2111
Arizona	(602) 255-4900
Arkansas	(501) 371-3000
California	(916) 322-9900
Colorado	(303) 866-5000
Connecticut	(203) 240-0222
Delaware	(302) 736-4000
District of Columbia	(202) 727-1000
Florida	(904) 488-1234
Georgia	(404) 656-2000
Hawaii	(808) 548-6222
Idaho	(208) 334-2411
Illinois	(217) 782-2000
Indiana	(317) 232-1000
Iowa	(515) 281-5011
Kansas	(913) 296-0111
Kentucky	(502) 564-3130
Louisiana	(504) 342-6600
Maine	(207) 289-1110
Maryland	(301) 974-2000
Massachusetts	(617) 727-2121
Michigan	(517) 373-1837
Minnesota	(612) 296-6013
Mississippi	(601) 359-1000

State	Telephone
Missouri	(314) 751-2000
Montana	(406) 444-2511
Nebraska	(402) 471-2311
Nevada	(702) 885-5000
New Hampshire	(603) 271-1100
New Jersey	(609) 292-2121
New Mexico	(505) 827-4011
New York	(518) 474-2121
North Carolina	(919) 733-1110
North Dakota	(701) 224-2000
Ohio	(614) 466-2000
Oklahoma	(405) 521-1601
Oregon	(503) 378-3131
Pennsylvania	(717) 787-2121
Rhode Island	(401) 277-2000
South Carolina	(803) 734-1000
South Dakota	(605) 773-3011
Tennessee	(615) 741-3011
Texas	(512) 463-4630
Utah	(801) 533-4000
Vermont	(802) 828-1100
Virginia	(804) 786-0000
Washington	(206) 753-5000
West Virginia	(304) 348-3456
Wisconsin	(608) 266-2211
Wyoming	(307) 771-7011

OSHA

THE OCCUPATIONAL SAFETY AND HEALTH Administration (OSHA) is the arm of the U.S. Department of Labor which deals with maintaining health and safety in the workplace. Established under the OSHA act of 1970, this agency was set up to:

- Reduce workplace hazards.
- Establish minimum standards for health and safety for industries.
- Regularly inspect workplace sites to ensure compliance with standards. Note: Any business with ten or fewer employees is not subject to these inspections. However, OSHA produces a checklist for self-inspections of premises which can assist the small business owner in maintaining a hazard-free workplace.
- Maintain a systematic method of reporting incidents of on-the-job or work-related illnesses or injuries, including those which entitle an individual to compensation.

In order to provide businesses with information about OSHA requirements, free consultation assistance is available to employers. Representatives of OSHA will assist in identifying specific and potential hazards which may exist in the workplace. They will also assist in implementing health and safety programs, particularly concerning issues such as maintaining a smoke-free environment. To obtain a list of free OSHA publications as well as information regarding on-site consultation, interested individuals should contact:

OSHA (cont'd)

OSHA Publications
Occupational Safety and Health Administration
Department of Labor
200 Constitution Ave., NW, Room N4101
Washington, DC 20210
(202) 523-9667

To obtain information regarding the OSHA programs, and to be referred to the appropriate department of OSHA, the interested individual should call the Information Office at OSHA at (202)523-8151.

The upside of the OSHA safety regulations is a program called Voluntary Protection Program (VPP) which rewards companies for maintaining safer workplace environments. Those companies which have effective health and safety programs, and a lower than average injury and illness rate, may be eligible for the program. The benefits for participants in the program are reduced worker compensation costs, a reduction in workday injuries with potential for reduced insurance rates, and possible automatic exemption from OSHA's programmed inspections.

Georgia Power Company is reported to have enjoyed a $4 million annual reduction in worker's compensation premiums during the 9-year period it has been in the VPP program. Although this example is a very large corporation, the beneficial effect of an effective health and safety program can trickle down to the bottom line in any company through increased productivity and reduced compensation costs.

To find out about the program write or call:

Occupational Safety and Health Administration
Department of Labor
200 Constitution Ave., NW, Room N3700
Washington, DC 20210
(202) 523-7266

Statistics collected by the Insurance Information Institute suggest that awareness of safety in the workplace is beginning to produce favorable results in the reduced number of accidental deaths.

Accidental Deaths in the U.S.

	1991	1990	% Change
All Accidents	88,000	93,000	-5
Motor Vehicles	43,500	46,800	-7
Home	20,500	21,000	-2
Work	9,900	10,600	-7
Public	18,000	18,500	-3

Source: National Safety Council

The Top Reference Sources

Access EPA
U.S. Government Printing Office, $21
(202) 783-3238
Stock # 055-000-00406-4

First published in 1991, this annual directory of U.S. Environmental Protection Agency (EPA) and other public sector environmental information resources contains information for everyone interested in the environment.

Chapters include major EPA dockets, clearinghouses and hotlines, major EPA environmental databases, library and information services, state environmental libraries, alternate state environmental contacts, and EPA scientific models.

Government Income and Spending

Federal Budget Outlays: 1945 to 1992 ($ billions)

Year	Total Outlays	Human Resource	National Defense	Outlays as % of GNP	Receipts	Surplus or Deficit (-)
1945	92,712	1,859	82,965	43.6	45,159	-48,720
1950	42,562	14,221	13,724	16.0	39,443	-4,702
1955	68,444	14,908	42,729	17.7	65,451	-4,091
1960	92,191	26,184	48,130	18.2	92,492	510
1965	118,228	36,576	50,620	17.6	116,817	-1,605
1966	134,532	43,257	58,111	18.2	130,835	-3,068
1967	157,464	51,272	71,417	19.8	148,822	-12,620
1968	178,134	59,375	81,926	21.0	152,973	-27,742
1969	183,640	66,410	82,497	19.8	186,882	-507
1970	195,649	75,349	81,692	19.8	192,807	-8,694
1971	210,172	91,901	78,872	19.9	187,139	-26,052
1972	230,681	107,211	79,174	20.0	207,309	-26,423
1973	245,707	119,522	76,681	19.2	230,799	-15,403
1974	269,359	135,783	79,347	19.0	263,224	-7,971
1975	332,332	173,245	86,509	21.8	279,090	-55,260
1976	371,779	203,594	89,619	21.9	298,060	-70,499
1976*	95,973	52,065	22,269	21.4	81,232	-13,336
1977	409,203	221,895	97,241	21.2	355,559	-49,745
1978	458,729	242,329	104,495	21.1	399,561	-54,902
1979	503,464	267,574	116,342	20.6	463,302	-38,178
1980	590,920	313,374	133,995	22.1	517,112	-72,689
1981	678,249	362,022	157,513	22.7	599,272	-73,916
1982	745,755	388,681	185,309	23.8	617,766	-120,003
1983	808,380	426,003	209,903	24.3	600,562	-207,977
1984	851,846	432,042	227,413	23.0	666,457	-185,586
1985	946,391	471,822	252,748	23.8	734,057	-221,623
1986	990,336	481,594	273,375	23.5	769,091	-237,898
1987	1,003,911	502,196	281,999	22.5	854,143	-169,257
1988	1,064,140	533,404	290,361	22.1	908,954	-193,897
1989	1,144,169	568,668	303,559	22.1	990,691	-206,132
1990	1,251,778	619,327	299,331	22.9	1,031,308	-220,470
1991	1,323,011	689,691	273,292	23.5	1,054,264	-268,746
1992 est.	1,475,439	776,900	307,304	25.2	1,075,706	-399,733

**Represents Transitional Quarter, July-Sept.*

Source: 1992 Statistical Abstract

Government Income and Spending (cont'd)

Gross Federal Debt: 1945 to 1992 ($ billions)

Year	Total Debt	Federal Gov't. Account	The Public	Federal Reserve System	Debt as % of GNP
1945	260,123	24,941	235,182	21,792	122.5
1950	256,853	37,830	219,023	18,331	96.3
1955	274,366	47,751	226,616	23,607	71.0
1960	290,525	53,686	236,840	26,523	57.3
1965	322,318	61,540	260,778	39,100	47.9
1966	328,498	64,784	263,714	42,169	44.5
1967	340,445	73,819	266,626	46,719	42.8
1968	368,685	79,140	289,545	52,230	43.4
1969	365,769	87,661	278,108	54,095	39.4
1970	380,921	97,723	283,198	57,714	38.5
1971	408,176	105,140	303,037	65,518	38.7
1972	435,936	113,559	322,377	71,426	37.8
1973	466,291	125,381	340,910	75,181	36.4
1974	483,893	140,194	343,699	80,648	34.2
1975	541,925	147,225	394,700	84,993	35.6
1976	628,970	151,566	477,404	94,714	37.0
1976*	643,561	148,052	495,509	96,702	35.9
1977	706,398	157,295	549,103	105,004	36.5
1978	776,602	169,477	607,125	115,480	35.8
1979	828,923	189,162	639,761	115,594	33.9
1980	908,503	199,212	709,291	120,846	34.0
1981	994,298	209,507	784,791	124,466	33.3
1982	1,136,798	217,560	919,238	134,497	36.2
1983	1,371,164	240,114	1,131,049	155,527	41.3
1984	1,564,110	264,159	1,299,951	155,122	42.4
1985	1,816,974	317,612	1,499,362	169,806	46.0
1986	2,120,082	383,919	1,736,163	190,855	50.7
1987	2,345,578	457,444	1,888,134	212,040	53.0
1988	2,600,607	550,507	2,050,252	229,218	54.4
1989	2,867,538	677,214	2,190,324	220,088	55.9
1990	3,206,347	795,906	2,410,441	234,410	58.7
1991	3,598,993	911,751	2,687,242	258,591	64.0
1992 est.	4,077,510	1,000,227	3,077,283	NA	69.5

NA–Not Available

**Represents Transitional Quarter, July-Sept*

Source: 1992 Statistical Abstract

The Top Reference Sources

The Information Please Almanac
Houghton Mifflin, $7.95
(800) 225-3362

This best-selling almanac includes a multitude of facts and statistics, from complete World Series statistics to Census results, from global warming to personal finance.

Use this reference for fast access to background information and facts on election results, major world events, first aid techniques, the American economy, media, postal rates, famous personalities, health and nutrition, and countries (from Afghanistan to Zimbabwe).

Government Income and Spending (cont'd)

Annual Percentage Change in Receipts, Outlays, and Debt: 1945 to 1992

Year	Receipts	Outlays	Gross Federal Debt	Outlays, Off-Budget
1945	3.2	1.5	27.5	0.1
1950	0.1	9.6	1.7	0.5
1955	-6.0	-3.4	1.3	4.0
1960	16.7	0.1	1.1	10.9
1965	3.7	-0.3	2.0	16.5
1966	12.0	13.8	1.9	19.7
1967	13.7	17.0	3.6	20.4
1968	2.8	13.1	8.3	22.3
1969	22.2	3.1	-0.8	25.2
1970	3.2	6.5	4.1	27.6
1971	2.9	7.4	7.2	32.8
1972	10.8	9.8	6.8	36.9
1973	11.3	6.5	7.0	45.6
1974	14.0	9.6	3.8	52.1
1975	6.0	23.4	12.0	60.4
1976	6.8	11.9	16.1	69.6
1976	X	X	X	19.4
1977	19.3	10.1	12.3	80.7
1978	12.4	12.1	9.9	89.7
1979	16.0	9.8	6.7	100.0
1980	11.6	17.4	9.6	114.3
1981	15.9	14.8	9.4	135.2
1982	3.1	10.0	14.3	151.4
1983	-2.8	8.4	20.6	147.1
1984	11.0	5.4	14.1	165.8
1985	10.1	11.1	16.2	176.8
1986	4.8	4.6	16.7	183.5
1987	11.1	1.4	10.6	193.8
1988	6.4	6.0	10.9	202.7
1989	9.0	7.5.	10.3	210.9
1990	4.1	9.4.	11.8	225.1
1991	2.2	5.7.	12.2	241.7
1992 est.	2.0	11.5	13.3	251.5

X– Not Applicable

Source: 1992 Statistical Abstract

The Top Reference Sources

43 Proven Ways to Raise Capital for Your Small Business
Enterprise Publishing
(800) 533-2665

Author Ted Nicholas demonstrates how to raise capital when you have little or no assets to pledge. You will also learn the best place to begin when establishing a good credit rating, how to make the right first impression with an investor or creditor, eight types of bank loans and how to get each one, along with ten common mistakes to avoid when you are seeking financing. The easy-to-use format makes this complicated topic far simpler.

Government Income and Spending (cont'd)

Federal Receipts by Source ($ millions): 1980 to 1992

Source	1980	1985	1989	1990	1991	1992 est.	1980 % Distrib.	1992 est. % Distrib.
TOTAL RECEIPTS	517,112	734,057	990,691	1,031,308	1,054,264	1,075,706	100.0	100.0
Indiv. income taxes	244,069	334,531	445,690	466,884	467,827	478,749	47.2	44.5
Corp. income taxes	64,600	61,331	103,291	93,507	98,086	89,031	12.5	8.3
Social insurance	157,803	265,163	359,416	380,047	396,016	410,863	30.5	38.2
Employment taxes	138,748	234,646	332,859	353,891	370,526	383,663	26.8	35.7
Old-age and survivors insurance	96,581	169,822	240,595	255,031	265,503	271,784	18.7	25.3
Disability insurance	16,628	16,348	23,071	26,625	28,382	29,138	3.2	2.7
Hospital insurance	23,217	44,871	65,396	68,556	72,842	79,007	4.5	7.3
R.R. retirement/ pension fund	2,323	2,213	2,391	2,292	2,371	2,329	0.4	0.2
R.R. social security equivalent acct.	NA	1,391	1,407	1,387	1,428	1,405	NA	0.1
Unemployment insur.	15,336	25,758	22,011	21,635	20,922	22,547	3.0	2.1
Other retirement contributions	3,719	4,759	4,546	4,522	4,568	4,653	0.7	0.4
Excise taxes	24,329	35,992	34,386	35,345	42,402	46,098	4.7	4.3
Federal funds	15,563	19,097	13,147	15,591	18,275	21,170	3.0	2.0
Alcohol	5,601	5,562	5,661	5,695	7,364	8,219	1.1	0.8
Tobacco	2,443	4,779	4,378	4,081	4,706	4,897	0.5	0.5
Windfall profits	6,934	6,348	-	-	-	-	1.3	-
Ozone depletion	NA	-	-	360	562	662	-	0.1
Other taxes	585	261	317	2,460	2,549	4,343	0.1	0.4
Trust funds	8,766	16,894	21,239	19,754	24,127	24,928	1.7	2.3
Highways	6,620	13,015	15,628	13,867	16,979	17,387	1.3	1.6
Airport and airway	1,874	2,851	3,664	3,700	4,910	5,193	0.4	0.5
Black lung disability	272	581	563	665	652	627	0.1	0.1
Hazardous substance response	-	273	883	818	810	825	-	0.1
Aquatic resources	-	126	187	218	260	278	-	-
Leaking underground storage	-	-	168	122	123	145	-	-
Vaccine injury compensations	-	-	99	159	81	120	-	-
Oil spill liability	-	-	-	143	254	283	-	-
Estate and gift taxes	6,389	6,422	8,745	11,500	11,138	12,063	1.2	1.1
Customs duties	7,174	12,079	16,334	16,707	15,949	17,260	1.4	1.6
Fed. reserve deposits	11,767	17,059	19,604	24,319	19,158	18,507	2.3	1.7

NA–Not Available

Source: 1992 Statistical Abstract

The Top Reference Sources

The Statistical Abstract of the United States
U.S. Government Printing Office, $29
(202) 783-3238

Since 1878, the Statistical Abstract has been the authorititave summary of statistics on the social, political, and economic organization of the United States.

Compiled by the U.S. Bureau of the Census, it includes a representative selection of statistics widely used by public officials, business analysts, educators, librarians, research workers, and students. Source notes for each table and a guide to statistical publications are also included.

Governors, Mayors, Congress

U.S. Governors

State	Governor	Phone
Alabama	-	(205) 242-7100
Alaska	Walter J. Hickel	(907) 465-3500
Arizona	Fife Symington	(602) 542-4331
Arkansas	Jim Guy Tucker	(501) 682-2345
California	Pete Wilson	(916) 445-2841
Colorado	Roy R. Romer	(303) 866-2471
Connecticut	Lowell P. Weicker, Jr.	(203) 566-4840
Delaware	Tom Carper	(302) 739-4101
Florida	Lawton Chiles	(904) 488-2272
Georgia	Zell Miller	(404) 656-1776
Hawaii	John Waihee	(808) 586-0034
Idaho	Cecil D. Andrus	(208) 334-2100
Illinois	Jim Edgar	(217) 782-6830
Indiana	Evan Bayh	(317) 232-4567
Iowa	Terry E. Branstad	(515) 281-5211
Kansas	Joan Finney	(913) 296-3232
Kentucky	Brereton Jones	(502) 564-2611
Louisiana	Edwin W. Edwards	(504) 342-7015
Maine	John R. McKernan, Jr.	(207) 289-3531
Maryland	William Donald Schaefer	(301) 974-3901
Massachusetts	William F. Weld	(617) 727-3600
Michigan	John Engler	(517) 373-3400
Minnesota	Arne Carlson	(612) 296-3391
Mississippi	Kirk Fordice	(601) 359-3100
Missouri	Mel Carnahan	(314) 751-2151
Montana	Marc Racicot	(406) 444-3111
Nebraska	E. Benjamin Nelson	(402) 471-2244
Nevada	Bob Miller	(702) 687-5670
New Hampshire	Steve Merrill	(603) 271-2121
New Jersey	James J. Florio	(609) 292-6000
New Mexico	Bruce King	(505) 827-3000
New York	Mario M. Cuomo	(518) 474-8390
North Carolina	Jim Hunt, Jr.	(919) 733-4240
North Dakota	Ed Schafer	(701) 224-2200
Ohio	George V. Voinovich	(614) 466-3555
Oklahoma	David Walters	(405) 521-2342
Oregon	Barbara Roberts	(503) 378-3111
Pennsylvania	Robert P. Casey	(717) 787-2500
Puerto Rico	Rafael Hernandez-Colon	(809) 721-7000
Rhode Island	Bruce G. Sundlun	(401) 277-2080
South Carolina	Caroll A. Campbell, Jr.	(803) 734-9818
South Dakota	George S. Mickelson	(605) 773-3212
Tennessee	Ned McWherter	(615) 741-2001
Texas	Ann W. Richards	(512) 463-2000
Utah	Mike Leavitt	(801) 538-1000
Vermont	Howard Dean	(802) 828-3333
Virginia	L. Douglas Wilder	(804) 786-2211
Washington	Mike Lowry	(206) 753-5000
West Virginia	Gaston Caperton	(304) 348-2000
Wisconsin	Tommy G. Thompson	(608) 266-2211
Wyoming	Michael J. Sullivan	(307) 777-7434

Governors, Mayors, Congress (cont'd)

Mayors of Major U.S. Cities

Major Cities	Mayor	Phone
Atlanta	Maynard Jackson	(404) 330-6100
Baltimore	Kurt Schmoke	(410) 396-3835
Boston	Raymond L. Flynn	(617) 725-4000
Buffalo	James D. Griffin	(716) 851-4841
Chicago	Richard M. Daley	(312) 744-3300
Cincinnati	Dwight Tillery	(513) 352-3000
Cleveland	Michael R. White	(216) 664-2220
Columbus	Greg Lashevtka	(614) 645-7671
Dallas	Steve Bartlett	(214) 670-4054
Denver	Wellington E. Webb	(303) 640-2721
Detroit	Coleman A. Young	(313) 224-3400
Hartford	Carrie S. Perry	(203) 722-6610
Honolulu	Frank F. Fasi	(808) 523-4141
Houston	Bob Lanier	(713) 247-2200
Indianapolis	Stephan Goldsmith	(317) 327-3600
Jacksonville	Edward Austin	(904) 630-1776
Los Angeles	Tom Bradley	(213) 485-2121
Memphis	W.W. Herenton	(901) 576-6000
Miami	Xavier Suarez	(305) 250-3500
Milwaukee	John O. Norquist	(414) 278-2200
Minneapolis	Donald Fraser	(612) 673-2100
Nashville	Philip N. Bredesen	(615) 862-6000
New Orleans	Sidney Barthelemy	(504) 586-4000
New York	David Dinkins	(212) 788-3000
Norfolk	Mason C. Andrews	(804) 441-2679
Orlando	Glenda Hood	(407) 226-2221
Philadelphia	Edward Rendell	(215) 686-2181
Phoenix	Paul Johnson	(602) 262-7111
Pittsburgh	Sophie Masloff	(412) 255-2626
Portland, OR	Vera Katz	(503) 823-4120
Sacramento	Joseph Serna, Jr..	(916) 264-5407
St. Louis	Vincent C. Schoemehl, Jr.	(314) 622-3201
Salt Lake City	Dee Dee Corradini	(801) 535-7704
San Antonio	Nelson Wolff	(512) 299-7060
San Diego	Maureen O'Connor	(619) 236-6330
San Francisco	Frank Jordan	(415) 554-6141
Seattle	Norman Rice	(206) 684-4000
Tampa	Sandra W. Freedman	(813) 223-8251
Washington, DC	Sharon Pratt Kelly	(202) 727-6319

Source: U.S. Conference of Mayors

Almanac Fact

A survey of 200 printers in 15 U.S. cities shows that demand for business cards has risen 19.1% between 1989 and 1992.

Source: Rolodex

Governors, Mayors, Congress (cont'd)

Directory of U.S. Senators

Senator	State	Party	Phone
Murkowski, Frank H.	AK	R	(202) 224-6665
Stevens, Ted	AK	R	(202) 224-3004
Heflin, Howell	AL	D	(202) 224-4124
Shelby, Richard C.	AL	D	(202) 224-5744
Deconcini, Dennis	AZ	D	(202) 224-4521
McCain, John	AZ	R	(202) 224-2235
Bumpers, Dale	AR	D	(202) 224-4843
Pryor, David	AR	D	(202) 224-2353
Boxer, Barbara	CA	D	(202) 224-3553
Feinstein, Dianne	CA	D	(202) 224-3841
Brown, Hank	CO	R	(202) 224-5941
Campbell, Ben N.	CO	D	(202) 224-5852
Dodd, Christopher J.	CT	D	(202) 224-2823
Lieberman, Joseph L.	CT	D	(202) 224-4041
Biden, Joseph R., Jr.	DE	D	(202) 224-5042
Roth, William V., Jr.	DE	R	(202) 224-2441
Graham, Bob	FL	D	(202) 224-3041
Mack, Connie	FL	R	(202) 224-5274
Coverdell, Paul	GA	R	(202) 224-3643
Nunn, Sam	GA	D	(202) 224-3521
Akaka, Daniel K.	HI	D	(202) 224-6361
Inouye, Daniel K.	HI	D	(202) 224-3934
Craig, Larry E.	ID	R	(202) 224-2752
Kempthorne, Dirk	ID	D	(202) 224-6142
Moseley Braun, Carol	IL	D	(202) 224-2854
Simon, Paul	IL	D	(202) 224-2152
Coats, Dan	IN	R	(202) 224-5623
Lugar, Richard G.	IN	R	(202) 224-4814
Grassley, Charles E.	IA	R	(202) 224-3744
Harkin, Tom	IA	D	(202) 224-3254
Dole, Robert	KS	R	(202) 224-6521
Kassenbaum, Nancy	KS	R	(202) 224-4774
Ford, Wendell H	KY	D	(202) 224-4343
McConnell, Mitch	KY	R	(202) 224-2541
Breaux, John B	LA	D	(202) 224-4623
Johnston, J. Bennett	LA	R	(202) 224-5824
Cohen, William S.	ME	R	(202) 224-2523
Mitchell, George J.	ME	D	(202) 224-5344
Mikulski, Barbara A.	MD	D	(202) 224-4654
Sarbanes, Paul S.	MD	D	(202) 224-4524
Kennedy, Edward M.	MA	D	(202) 224-4543
Kerry, John F.	MA	D	(202) 224-2742
Levin, Carl	MI	D	(202) 224-6221
Riegle, Donald W., Jr.	MI	D	(202) 224-4822
Durenberger, Dave	MN	R	(202) 224-3244
Wellstone, Paul	MN	D	(202) 224-5641
Bond, Christopher S.	MO	R	(202) 224-5721
Danforth, John C.	MO	R	(202) 224-6154
Cochran, Thad	MS	R	(202) 224-5054
Lott, Trent	MS	R	(202) 224-6253

Senator	State	Party	Phone
Baucus, Max	MT	D	(202) 224-2651
Burns, Conrad	MT	R	(202) 224-2644
Exon, J. James	NE	D	(202) 224-4224
Kerrey, J. Robert	NE	D	(202) 224-6551
Gregg, Judd	NH	R	(202) 224-3324
Smith, Bob	NH	R	(202) 224-2841
Bradley, Bill	NJ	D	(202) 224-3224
Lautenberg, Frank R.	NJ	D	(202) 224-4744
Bingaman, Jeff	NM	D	(202) 224-5521
Domenici, Pete V.	NM	R	(202) 224-6621
Bryan, Richard H.	NV	D	(202) 224-6244
Reid, Harry	NV	D	(202) 224-3542
D'Amato, Alfonse M.	NY	R	(202) 224-6542
Moynihan, Daniel P.	NY	D	(202) 224-4451
Faircloth, Lauch	NC	R	(202) 224-3154
Helms, Jesse	NC	R	(202) 224-6342
Conrad, Kent	ND	D	(202) 224-2043
Dorgan, Byron L.	ND	D	(202) 224-2551
Glenn, John	OH	D	(202) 224-3353
Metzenbaum, Howard	OH	D	(202) 224-2315
Boren, David L.	OK	D	(202) 224-4721
Nickles, Don	OK	R	(202) 224-5754
Hatfield, Mark O.	OR	R	(202) 224-3753
Packwood, Bob	OR	R	(202) 224-5244
Specter, Arlen	PA	R	(202) 224-4254
Wofford, Harris	PA	D	(202) 224-6324
Chafee, John H.	RI	R	(202) 224-2921
Pell, Claiborne	RI	D	(202) 224-4642
Hollings, Ernest F.	SC	D	(202) 224-6121
Thurmond, Strom	SC	R	(202) 224-5972
Daschle, Thomas A.	SD	D	(202) 224-2321
Pressler, Larry	SD	R	(202) 224-5842
Mathews, Harlan	TN	D	(202) 224-4944
Sasser, Jim	TN	D	(202) 224-3344
Krueger, Bob D.	TX	D	(202) 224-5922
Gramm, Phil	TX	R	(202) 224-2934
Bennett, Robert F.	UT	R	(202) 224-5444
Hatch, Orin G.	UT	R	(202) 224-5251
Jeffords, James M.	VT	R	(202) 224-5141
Leahy, Patrick J.	VT	D	(202) 224-4242
Robb, Charles S.	VA	D	(202) 224-4024
Warner, John W.	VA	R	(202) 224-2023
Gorton, Slade	WA	R	(202) 224-3441
Murray, Patty	WA	D	(202) 224-2621
Feingold, Russell D.	WI	D	(202) 224-5323
Kohl, Herb	WI	D	(202) 224-5653
Byrd, Robert C.	WV	D	(202) 224-3954
Rockefeller John D., IV	WV	D	(202) 224-6472
Simpson, Alan K.	WY	R	(202) 224-3424
Wallop, Malcolm	WY	R	(202) 224-6441

Governors, Mayors, Congress (cont'd)

House of Representatives

Congressman	State	Party	Phone
Young, Don	AK	R	(202) 225-5765
Bachus, Spencer T., III	AL	R	(202) 225-4921
Bevill, Tom	AL	D	(202) 225-4876
Browder, Glen	AL	D	(202) 225-3261
Callahan, Sonny	AL	R	(202) 225-4931
Cramer, Robert E. , Jr.	AL	D	(202) 225-4801
Everett, Terry	AL	R	(202) 225-2901
Hilliard, Earl F.	AL	D	(202) 225-2665
Coppersmith, Sam	AZ	D	(202) 225-2635
English, Karan	AZ	D	(202) 225-2190
Kolbe, Jim	AZ	R	(202) 225-2542
Kyl, Jon	AZ	R	(202) 225-3361
Pastor, Ed	AZ	D	(202) 225-4065
Stump, Bob	AZ	R	(202) 225-4576
Dickey, Jay	AR	R	(202) 225-3772
Hutchinson, Y. Tim	AR	R	(202) 225-4301
Lambert, Blanche M.	AR	D	(202) 225-4076
Thornton, Ray	AR	D	(202) 225-2506
Faleomavaega, Eni F.H.	AS	C	(202) 225-8577
Baker, William P.	CA	R	(202) 225-1880
Becerra, Xavier	CA	D	(202) 225-6235
Beilenson, Anthony C.	CA	D	(202) 225-5911
Berman, Howard L.	CA	D	(202) 225-4695
Brown, George E., Jr.	CA	D	(202) 225-6161
Calvert, Ken	CA	R	(202) 225-1986
Condit, Gary A.	CA	D	(202) 225-6131
Cox, Christopher	CA	R	(202) 225-5611
Cunningham, Randy	CA	R	(202) 225-5452
Dellums, Ronald V.	CA	D	(202) 225-2661
Dixon, Julian C.	CA	D	(202) 225-7084
Dooley, Calvin M.	CA	D	(202) 225-3341
Doolittle, John T.	CA	R	(202) 225-2511
Dornan, Robert K.	CA	R	(202) 225-2965
Dreier, David	CA	R	(202) 225-2305
Edwards, Don	CA	D	(202) 225-3072
Eshoo, Anna G.	CA	D	(202) 225-8104
Fazio, Vic	CA	D	(202) 225-5716
Filner, Bob	CA	D	(202) 225-8045
Gallegly, Elton	CA	R	(202) 225-5811
Hamburg, Dan	CA	D	(202) 225-3311
Harman, Jane	CA	D	(202) 225-8220
Herger, Wally	CA	R	(202) 225-3076
Horn, Stephen	CA	R	(202) 225-6676
Huffington, Michael	CA	R	(202) 225-3601
Hunter, Duncan	CA	R	(202) 225-5672
Kim, Jay	CA	R	(202) 225-3201
Lantos, Tom	CA	D	(202) 225-3531
Lehman, Richard H.	CA	D	(202) 225-4540
Lewis, Jerry	CA	R	(202) 225-5861
Martinez, Matthew G.	CA	D	(202) 225-5464
Matsui, Robert T.	CA	D	(202) 225-7163
McCandless, Alfred A.	CA	R	(202) 225-5330
McKeon, Howard	CA	R	(202) 225-1956
Miller, George	CA	D	(202) 225-2095
Mineta, Norman Y.	CA	D	(202) 225-2361

Congressman	State	Party	Phone
Moorhead, Carlos J.	CA	R	(202) 225-4176
Packard, Ron	CA	R	(202) 225-3906
Panetta, Leon E.	CA	D	(202) 225-2861
Pelosi, Nancy	CA	D	(202) 225-4965
Pombo, Richard W.	CA	R	(202) 225-1947
Rohrabacher, Dana	CA	R	(202) 225-2415
Roybal-Allard, Lucille	CA	D	(202) 225-1766
Royce, Edward R.	CA	R	(202) 225-4111
Schenk, Lynn	CA	D	(202) 225-2040
Stark, Fortney Pete	CA	D	(202) 225-5065
Thomas, William M.	CA	R	(202) 225-2915
Torres, Esteban Edward	CA	D	(202) 225-5256
Tucker, Walter R., III	CA	D	(202) 225-7924
Waters, Maxine	CA	D	(202) 225-2201
Waxman, Henry A.	CA	D	(202) 225-3976
Woolsey, Lynn C.	CA	D	(202) 225-5161
Allard, Wayne	CO	R	(202) 225-4676
Hefley, Joel	CO	R	(202) 225-4422
McInnis, Scott	CO	R	(202) 225-4761
Schaefer, Dan	CO	R	(202) 225-7882
Schroeder, Patricia	CO	D	(202) 225-4431
Skaggs, David E.	CO	D	(202) 225-2161
DeLauro, Rosa L.	CT	D	(202) 225-3661
Franks, Gary A.	CT	R	(202) 225-3822
Gejdenson, Sam	CT	D	(202) 225-2076
Johnson, Nancy L.	CT	R	(202) 225-4476
Kennelly, Barbara B.	CT	D	(202) 225-2265
Shays, Christopher	CT	R	(202) 225-5541
Castle, Michael N.	DE	R	(202) 225-4165
Norton, Eleanor Holmes	DC	C	(202) 225-8050
Bacchus, Jim	FL	D	(202) 225-3671
Bilirakis, Michael	FL	R	(202) 225-5755
Brown, Corrine	FL	D	(202) 225-0123
Canady, Charles T.	FL	R	(202) 225-1252
Deutsch, Peter	FL	D	(202) 225-7931
Diaz-Balart, Lincoln	FL	R	(202) 225-4211
Fowler, Tillie K.	FL	R	(202) 225-2501
Gibbons, Sam	FL	D	(202) 225-3376
Goss, Porter J.	FL	R	(202) 225-2536
Hastings, Alcee L.	FL	D	(202) 225-1313
Hutto, Earl	FL	D	(202) 225-4136
Johnston, Harry	FL	D	(202) 225-3001
Lewis, Tom	FL	R	(202) 225-5792
McCollum, Bill	FL	R	(202) 225-2176
Meek, Carrie P.	FL	D	(202) 225-4506
Mica, John L.	FL	R	(202) 225-4035
Miller, Dan	FL	R	(202) 225-5015
Peterson, Douglas	FL	D	(202) 225-5235
Ros-Lehtinen, Ileana	FL	R	(202) 225-3931
Shaw, E. Clay, Jr.	FL	R	(202) 225-3026
Stearns, Cliff	FL	R	(202) 225-5744
Thurman, Karen L.	FL	D	(202) 225-1002
Young, C.W. Bill	FL	R	(202) 225-5961
Bishop, Sanford D., Jr.	GA	D	(202) 225-3631
Collins, Michael A.	GA	R	(202) 225-5901

Governors, Mayors, Congress (cont'd)

House of Representatives

Congressman	State	Party	Phone
Darden, George (Buddy)	GA	D	(202) 225-2931
Deal, Nathan	GA	D	(202) 225-5211
Gingrich, Newt	GA	R	(202) 225-4501
Johnson, Don	GA	D	(202) 225-4101
Kingston, Jack	GA	R	(202) 225-5831
Lewis, John	GA	D	(202) 225-3801
Linder, John	GA	R	(202) 225-4272
McKinney, Cynthia A.	GA	D	(202) 225-1605
Rowland, J. Roy	GA	D	(202) 225-6531
Underwood, Robert A.	GU	C	(202) 225-1188
Abercrombie, Neil	HI	D	(202) 225-2726
Mink, Patsy T.	HI	D	(202) 225-4906
Crapo, Michael D.	ID	R	(202) 225-5531
LaRocco, Larry	ID	D	(202) 225-6611
Collins, Cardiss	IL	D	(202) 225-5006
Costello, Jerry F.	IL	D	(202) 225-5661
Crane, Philip M.	IL	R	(202) 225-3711
Durbin, Richard J.	IL	D	(202) 225-5271
Evans, Lane	IL	D	(202) 225-5905
Ewing, Thomas W.	IL	R	(202) 225-2371
Fawell, Harris W.	IL	R	(202) 225-3515
Gutierrez, Luis V.	IL	D	(202) 225-8203
Hastert, J. Dennis	IL	R	(202) 225-2976
Hyde, Henry J.	IL	R	(202) 225-4561
Lipinski, William O.	IL	D	(202) 225-5701
Manzullo, Donald A	IL	R	(202) 225-5676
Michel, Robert H.	IL	R	(202) 225-6201
Porter, John Edward	IL	R	(202) 225-4835
Poshard, Glenn	IL	D	(202) 225-5201
Reynolds, Mel	IL	D	(202) 225-0773
Rostenkowski, Dan	IL	D	(202) 225-4061
Rush, Bobby L.	IL	D	(202) 225-4372
Sangmeister, George E.	IL	D	(202) 225-3635
Yates, Sidney R.	IL	D	(202) 225-2111
Burton, Dan	IN	R	(202) 225-2276
Buyer, Stephen E.	IN	R	(202) 225-5037
Hamilton, Lee H.	IN	D	(202) 225-5315
Jacobs, Andrew, Jr.	IN	D	(202) 225-4011
Long, Jill L.	IN	D	(202) 225-4436
McCloskey, Frank	IN	D	(202) 225-4636
Myers, John T.	IN	R	(202) 225-5805
Roemer, Tim	IN	D	(202) 225-3915
Sharp, Philip R.	IN	D	(202) 225-3021
Visclosky, Peter J.	IN	D	(202) 225-2461
Grandy, Fred	IA	R	(202) 225-5476
Leach, Jim	IA	R	(202) 225-6576
Lightfoot, Jim	IA	R	(202) 225-3806
Nussle, Jim	IA	R	(202) 225-3301
Smith, Neal	IA	D	(202) 225-4426
Glickman, Dan	KS	D	(202) 225-6216
Meyers, Jan	KS	R	(202) 225-2865
Roberts, Pat	KS	R	(202) 225-2715
Slattery, Jim	KS	D	(202) 225-6601
Baesler, Scotty	KY	D	(202) 225-4706
Barlow, Thomas J., III	KY	D	(202) 225-3115

Congressman	State	Party	Phone
Bunning, Jim	KY	R	(202) 225-3465
Mazzoli, Romano L.	KY	D	(202) 225-5401
Natcher, William H.	KY	D	(202) 225-3501
Rogers, Harold	KY	R	(202) 225-4601
Baker, Richard H.	LA	R	(202) 225-3901
Fields, Cleo	LA	D	(202) 225-8490
Hayes, James A.	LA	D	(202) 225-2031
Jefferson, William J.	LA	D	(202) 225-6636
Livingston, Bob	LA	R	(202) 225-3015
McCrery, Jim	LA	R	(202) 225-2777
Tauzin, W. J. (Billy)	LA	D	(202) 225-4031
Andrews, Thomas H.	ME	D	(202) 225-6116
Snowe, Olympia J.	ME	R	(202) 225-6306
Bartlett, Roscoe G.	MD	R	(202) 225-2721
Bentley, Helen Delich	MD	R	(202) 225-3061
Cardin, Benjamin L.	MD	D	(202) 225-4016
Gilchrest, Wayne T.	MD	R	(202) 225-5311
Hoyer, Steny H.	MD	D	(202) 225-4131
Mfume, Kweisi	MD	D	(202) 225-4741
Morella, Constance A.	MD	R	(202) 225-5341
Wynn, Albert Russell	MD	D	(202) 225-8699
Blute, Peter	MA	R	(202) 225-6101
Frank, Barney	MA	D	(202) 225-5931
Kennedy, Joseph P., II	MA	D	(202) 225-5111
Markey, Edward J.	MA	D	(202) 225-2836
Meehan, Martin, T.	MA	D	(202) 225-3411
Moakley, John Joseph	MA	D	(202) 225-8273
Neal, Richard E.	MA	D	(202) 225-5601
Olver, John W.	MA	D	(202) 225-5335
Studds, Gerry E.	MA	D	(202) 225-3111
Torkildsen, Peter G.	MA	R	(202) 225-8020
Barcia, James A.	MI	D	(202) 225-8171
Bonior, David E.	MI	D	(202) 225-2106
Camp, Dave	MI	R	(202) 225-3561
Carr, Bob	MI	D	(202) 225-4872
Collins, Barbara-Rose	MI	D	(202) 225-2261
Conyers, John, Jr.	MI	D	(202) 225-5126
Dingell, John D.	MI	D	(202) 225-4071
Ford, William D.	MI	D	(202) 225-6261
Henry, Paul B.	MI	R	(202) 225-3831
Hoekstra, Peter	MI	R	(202) 225-4401
Kildee, Dale E.	MI	D	(202) 225-3611
Knollenberg, Joe	MI	R	(202) 225-4735
Levin, Sander M.	MI	D	(202) 225-4961
Smith, Nick	MI	R	(202) 225-6276
Stupak, Bart	MI	D	(202) 225-4735
Upton, Fred	MI	R	(202) 225-3761
Grams, Rod	MN	R	(202) 225-2271
Minge, David	MN	D	(202) 225-2331
Oberstar, James L.	MN	D	(202) 225-6211
Penny, Timothy J.	MN	D	(202) 225-2472
Peterson, Collin C.	MN	D	(202) 225-2165
Ramstad, Jim	MN	R	(202) 225-2871
Sabo, Martin Olav	MN	D	(202) 225-4755
Vento, Bruce F.	MN	D	(202) 225-6631

Governors, Mayors, Congress (cont'd)

House of Representatives

Congressman	State	Party	Phone
Clay, William (Bill)	MO	D	(202) 225-2406
Danner, Pat	MO	D	(202) 225-7041
Emerson, Bill	MO	R	(202) 225-4404
Gephardt, Richard A.	MO	D	(202) 225-2671
Hancock, Mel	MO	R	(202) 225-6536
Skeleton, Ike	MO	D	(202) 225-2876
Talent, James M.	MO	R	(202) 225-2561
Volkmer, Harold L.	MO	D	(202) 225-2956
Wheat, Alan	MO	D	(202) 225-4535
Espy, Mike	MS	D	(202) 225-5876
Montgomery, G.V.	MS	D	(202) 225-5031
Parker, Mike	MS	D	(202) 225-5865
Taylor, Gene	MS	D	(202) 225-5772
Whitten, Jamie L.	MS	D	(202) 225-4306
Williams, Pat	MT	D	(202) 225-3211
Barrett, Bill	NE	R	(202) 225-6435
Bereuter, Doug	NE	R	(202) 225-4806
Hoagland, Peter	NE	D	(202) 225-4155
Swett, Dick	NH	D	(202) 225-5206
Zeliff, William H., Jr.	NH	R	(202) 225-5456
Andrews, Robert E.	NJ	D	(202) 225-6501
Franks, Bob	NJ	R	(202) 225-5361
Gallo, Dean A.	NJ	R	(202) 225-5034
Hughes, William J.	NJ	D	(202) 225-6572
Klein, Herb	NJ	D	(202) 225-5751
Menendez, Robert	NJ	D	(202) 225-7919
Pallone, Frank, Jr.	NJ	D	(202) 225-4671
Payne, Donald M.	NJ	D	(202) 225-3436
Roukema, Marge	NJ	R	(202) 225-4465
Saxton, Jim	NJ	R	(202) 225-4765
Smith, Christopher H.	NJ	R	(202) 225-3765
Torricelli, Robert G.	NJ	D	(202) 225-5061
Zimmer, Dick	NJ	R	(202) 225-5801
Richardson, Bill	NM	D	(202) 225-6190
Schiff, Steven	NM	R	(202) 225-6316
Skeen, Joe	NM	R	(202) 225-2365
Bilbray, James H.	NV	D	(202) 225-5965
Vucanovich, Barbara F.	NV	R	(202) 225-6155
Ackerman, Gary L.	NY	D	(202) 225-2601
Boehlert, Sherwood L.	NY	R	(202) 225-3665
Engel, Eliot L.	NY	D	(202) 225-2464
Fish, Hamilton, Jr.	NY	R	(202) 225-5441
Flake, Floyd H.	NY	D	(202) 225-3461
Gilman, Benjamin A.	NY	R	(202) 225-3776
Hinchey, Maurice D.	NY	D	(202) 225-6335
Hochbrueckner, George J.	NY	D	(202) 225-3826
Houghton, Amo	NY	D	(202) 225-3161
King, Peter T.	NY	R	(202) 225-7896
LaFalce, John J.	NY	D	(202) 225-3231
Lazio, Rick	NY	R	(202) 225-3335
Levy, David A.	NY	R	(202) 225-5516
Lowey, Nita M.	NY	D	(202) 225-6506
Maloney, Carolyn B.	NY	D	(202) 225-7944
Manton, Thomas J.	NY	D	(202) 225-3965
McHugh, John M.	NY	R	(202) 225-4611
McNulty, Michael R.	NY	D	(202) 225-5076
Molinari, Susan	NY	R	(202) 225-3371
Nadler, Jerrold	NY	D	(202) 225-5635
Owens, Major R.	NY	D	(202) 225-6231
Paxon, Bill	NY	R	(202) 225-5265
Quinn, Jack	NY	R	(202) 225-3306
Rangel, Charles B.	NY	D	(202) 225-4365
Schumer, Charles E.	NY	D	(202) 225-6616
Serrano, Jose E.	NY	D	(202) 225-4361
Slaughter, Louise McIntosh	NY	D	(202) 225-3615
Solomon, Gerald B.H.	NY	R	(202) 225-5614
Towns, Edolphus	NY	D	(202) 225-5936
Velazquez, Nydia M.	NY	D	(202) 225-2361
Walsh, James T.	NY	R	(202) 225-3701
Ballenger, Cass	NC	R	(202) 225-2576
Clayton, Eva M.	NC	D	(202) 225-3101
Coble, Howard	NC	R	(202) 225-3065
Hefner, W. G. (Bill)	NC	D	(202) 225-3715
Lancaster, H. Martin	NC	D	(202) 225-3415
McMillan, J. Alex	NC	R	(202) 225-1976
Neal, Stephen L.	NC	D	(202) 225-2071
Price, David E.	NC	D	(202) 225-1784
Rose, Charlie	NC	D	(202) 225-2731
Taylor, Charles H.	NC	R	(202) 225-6401
Valentine, Tim	NC	D	(202) 225-4531
Watt, Melvin, L.	NC	D	(202) 225-1510
Pomeroy, Earl	ND	D	(202) 225-2611
Applegate, Douglas	OH	D	(202) 225-6265
Boehner, John A.	OH	R	(202) 225-6205
Brown, Sherrod	OH	D	(202) 225-3401
Fingerhut, Eric	OH	D	(202) 225-5731
Gillmor, Paul E.	OH	R	(202) 225-6405
Gradison, Willis D., Jr.	OH	R	(202) 225-3164
Hall, Tony P.	OH	D	(202) 225-6465
Hobson, David L.	OH	R	(202) 225-4324
Hoke, Martin R.	OH	R	(202) 225-5871
Kaptur, Marcy	OH	D	(202) 225-4146
Kasich, John R.	OH	R	(202) 225-5355
Mann, David	OH	D	(202) 225-2216
Oxley, Michael G.	OH	R	(202) 225-2676
Pryce, Deborah	OH	R	(202) 225-2015
Regula, Ralph	OH	R	(202) 225-3876
Sawyer, Thomas C.	OH	D	(202) 225-5231
Stokes, Louis	OH	D	(202) 225-7032
Strickland, Ted	OH	D	(202) 225-5705
Traficant, James A., JR.	OH	D	(202) 225-5261
Brewster, Bill K.	OK	D	(202) 225-4565
English, Glenn	OK	D	(202) 225-5565
Inhofe, James M.	OK	R	(202) 225-2211
Istook, Ernest J., Jr.	OK	R	(202) 225-2132
McCurdy, Dave	OK	D	(202) 225-6165
Synar, Mike	OK	D	(202) 225-2701
DeFazio, Peter A.	OR	D	(202) 225-6416
Furse, Elizabeth	OR	D	(202) 225-0855
Kopetski, Michael J.	OR	D	(202) 225-5711

Governors, Mayors, Congress (cont'd)

House of Representatives

Congressman	State	Party	Phone
Smith, Robert F. (Bob)	OR	R	(202) 225-6730
Wyden, Ron	OR	D	(202) 225-4811
Blackwell, Lucien E.	PA	D	(202) 225-4001
Borski, Robert A.	PA	D	(202) 225-8251
Clinger, William F., Jr.	PA	R	(202) 225-5121
Coyne, William J.	PA	D	(202) 225-2301
Foglietta, Thomas M.	PA	D	(202) 225-4731
Gekas, George W.	PA	D	(202) 225-4315
Goodling, William F.	PA	R	(202) 225-5836
Greenwood, James C.	PA	R	(202) 225-4276
Holden, Tim	PA	D	(202) 225-5546
Kanjorski, Paul E.	PA	D	(202) 225-6511
Klink, Ron	PA	D	(202) 225-2565
Margolies-Mezvinsky, M.	PA	D	(202) 225-6111
McDade, Joseph M.	PA	R	(202) 225-3731
McHale, Paul	PA	D	(202) 225-6411
Murphy, Austin J.	PA	D	(202) 225-4665
Murtha, John P.	PA	D	(202) 225-2065
Ridge, Thomas J.	PA	R	(202) 225-5406
Santorum, Rick	PA	R	(202) 225-2135
Shuster, Bud	PA	R	(202) 225-2431
Walker, Robert S.	PA	R	(202) 225-2411
Weldon, Curt	PA	R	(202) 225-2011
Romero-Barcelo, Carlos	PR	C	(202) 225-2615
Machtley, Ronald K.	RI	R	(202) 225-4911
Reed, Jack	RI	D	(202) 225-2735
Clyburn, James E.	SC	R	(202) 225-3315
Derrick, Butler	SC	D	(202) 225-5301
Inglis, Bob	SC	R	(202) 225-6030
Ravenel, Arthur, Jr.	SC	R	(202) 225-3176
Spence, Floyd	SC	R	(202) 225-2452
Spratt, John M., Jr.	SC	D	(202) 225-5501
Johnson, Tim	SD	D	(202) 225-2801
Clement, Bob	TN	D	(202) 225-4311
Cooper, Jim	TN	D	(202) 225-6831
Duncan, John J., Jr.	TN	R	(202) 225-5435
Ford, Harold E.	TN	D	(202) 225-3265
Gordon, Bart	TN	D	(202) 225-4231
Lloyd, Marilyn	TN	D	(202) 225-3271
Quillen, James H. (Jimmy)	TN	R	(202) 225-6356
Sundquist, Don	TN	R	(202) 225-2811
Tanner, John S.	TN	D	(202) 225-4714
Andrews, Michael A.	TX	D	(202) 225-7508
Archer, Bill	TX	R	(202) 225-2571
Armey, Richard K.	TX	R	(202) 225-7772
Barton, Joe	TX	R	(202) 225-2002
Bonilla, Henry	TX	R	(202) 225-4511
Brooks, Jack	TX	D	(202) 225-6565
Bryant, John	TX	D	(202) 225-2231
Chapman, Jim	TX	D	(202) 225-3035
Coleman, Ronald D.	TX	D	(202) 225-4831
Combest, Larry	TX	R	(202) 225-4005
de la Garza, E	TX	D	(202) 225-2531
DeLay, Tom	TX	R	(202) 225-5951
Edwards, Chet	TX	D	(202) 225-6105

Congressman	State	Party	Phone
Fields, Jack	TX	R	(202) 225-4901
Frost, Martin	TX	D	(202) 225-3605
Geren, Pete	TX	D	(202) 225-5071
Gonzalez, Henry B.	TX	D	(202) 225-3236
Green, Gene	TX	D	(202) 225-1688
Hall, Ralph M.	TX	D	(202) 225-6673
Johnson, E.B.	TX	D	(202) 225-8885
Johnson, Sam	TX	R	(202) 225-4201
Laughlin, Greg	TX	D	(202) 225-2831
Ortiz, Solomon P.	TX	D	(202) 225-7742
Pickle, J. J.	TX	D	(202) 225-4865
Sarpalius, Bill	TX	D	(202) 225-3706
Smith, Lamar S.	TX	R	(202) 225-4236
Stenholm, Charles W.	TX	D	(202) 225-6605
Tejeda, Frank	TX	D	(202) 225-1640
Washington, Craig A.	TX	D	(202) 225-3816
Wilson, Charles	TX	D	(202) 225-2401
Hansen, James V.	UT	R	(202) 225-0453
Orton, Bill	UT	D	(202) 225-7751
Shepherd, Karen	UT	D	(202) 225-3011
Sanders, Bernard	VT	I	(202) 225-4115
de Lugo, Ron	VI	C	(202) 225-1790
Bateman, Herbert H.	VA	R	(202) 225-4261
Bliley, Thomas J., Jr.	VA	R	(202) 225-2815
Boucher, Rick	VA	D	(202) 225-3861
Byrne, Leslie L	VA	D	(202) 225-1492
Goodlatte, Bob	VA	R	(202) 225-5431
Moran, James P.	VA	D	(202) 225-4376
Payne, L. F.	VA	D	(202) 225-4711
Pickett, Owen B.	VA	D	(202) 225-4215
Scott, Robert C.	VA	D	(202) 225-8351
Sisisky, Norman	VA	D	(202) 225-6365
Wolf, Frank R.	VA	R	(202) 225-5136
Cantwell, Maria	WA	D	(202) 225-6311
Dicks, Norman D.	WA	D	(202) 225-5916
Dunn, Jennifer B.	WA	R	(202) 225-7761
Foley, Thomas S.	WA	D	(202) 225-2006
Inslee, Jay	WA	D	(202) 225-5816
Kreidler, Mike	WA	D	(202) 225-8901
McDermott, Jim	WA	D	(202) 225-3106
Swift, Al	WA	D	(202) 225-2605
Unsoeld, Jolene	WA	D	(202) 225-3536
Barrett, Thomas M.	WI	D	(202) 225-3571
Gunderson, Steve	WI	R	(202) 225-5506
Kleczka, Gerald D.	WI	D	(202) 225-4572
Klug, Scott L.	WI	R	(202) 225-2906
Obey, David R.	WI	D	(202) 225-3365
Petri, Thomas E.	WI	R	(202) 225-2476
Roth, Toby	WI	R	(202) 225-5665
Sensenbrenner, F. James, Jr.	WI	R	(202) 225-5101
Mollohan, Alan B.	WV	D	(202) 225-4172
Rahall, Nick Joe, II	WV	D	(202) 225-3452
Wise, Robert E., Jr.	WV	D	(202) 225-2711
Thomas, Craig	WY	R	(202) 225-2311

Congressional Chairs

House Committees

Committee	Representative
Agriculture	E. de la Garza, TX
Appropriations	William H. Natcher, KY
Armed Services	Ronald V. Dellums, CA
Banking, Finance, and Urban Affairs	Henry B. Gonzalez, TX
Budget	Martin Olav Sabo, MN
District of Columbia	Fortney Pete Stark, CA
Education and Labor	William D. Ford, MI
Energy and Commerce	John D. Dingell, MI
Foreign Affairs	Lee H. Hamilton, IN
Government Operations	John Conyers, Jr., MI
House Administration	Charlie Rose, NC
Judiciary	Jack Brooks, TX
Merchant Marine and Fisheries	Gerry E. Studds, MA
Natural Resources	George Miller, CA
Post Office and Civil Svc.	William L. Clay, MO
Public Works and Trans.	Norman Y. Mineta, CA
Rules and Admin.	Joe Moakley, MA
Science, Space, and Technology	George E. Brown, Jr., CA
Select Intelligence	Dan Glickman, KS
Small Business	John J. LaFalce, NY
Standards of Official Conduct	Jim McDermott, WA
Veterans' Affairs	G.V. Montgomery, MS
Ways and Means	Dan Rostenkowski, IL

Senate Committees

Committee	Senator
Agriculture, Nutrition, and Forestry	Patrick J. Leahy, VT
Appropriations	Robert C. Byrd, WV
Armed Services	Sam Nunn, GA
Banking, Housing, and Urban Affairs	Donald W. Riegle, Jr., MI
Budget	Jim Sasser, TN
Commerce, Science and Transportation	Ernest F. Hollings, SC
Energy and Natural Resources	J. Bennett Johnston, LA
Environment and Public Works	Max Baucus, MT
Finance	Daniel P. Moynihan, NY
Foreign Relations	Claiborne Pell, RI
Government Affairs	John Glenn, OH
Judiciary	Joseph R. Biden, Jr., DE
Labor and Human Resources	Edward M. Kennedy, MA
Rules and Admin.	Wendell H. Ford, KY
Select Ethics	Richard H. Bryan, NE
Select Indian Affairs	Daniel K. Inouye, HI
Select Intelligence	Dennis DeConcini, AZ
Small Business	Dale Bumpers, AK
Special Aging	David Pryor, AK
Veterans' Affairs	John D. Rockefeller IV , WV

Joint Committees of Congress

Committee	Senator	Representative
Economic	Paul S. Sarbanes, MD	David R. Obey, WI
Library	Claiborne Pell, RI	Charlie Rose, NC
Organization of Congress	David L. Boren, OK	Lee H. Hamilton, IN
Printing	Wendell H. Ford, KY	Charlie Rose, NC
Taxation	Daniel Moynihan, NY	Dan Rostenkowski, IL

The Top Reference Sources

Your Rights in the Workplace
Nolo Press, $15.95
(510) 549-1976

Written by Dan Lacey, a workplace consultant, this book is an employee's guide to firing, and lay-offs, wages and overtime, maternity and parental leave, unemployment and disability insurance, workers' compensation, job safety, sex, race, and age discrimination. It also explains the latest changes in laws passed to protect workers.

While written from an employee's point of view, this book is also an excellent resource for ensuring that an employer doesn't violate the law.

Small Business Administration

ACCORDING TO U.S. GOVERNMENT STATISTICS, the number of small businesses in the United States has increased by 54% since 1980. These businesses also account for 50% of the private work force, contribute 44% of all sales in the country, and are responsible for 38% of the gross national product.

The Small Business Administration (SBA) is an independent government agency created by Congress to help small businesses grow and prosper. The SBA has over 100 offices that offer small firms financial assistance through guaranteed loans, management assistance, help in obtaining government contracts, counseling services, and many low-cost publications.

The SBA offers assistance to small businesses and pays particular attention to those owned by ethnic minorities, women, veterans, and others with special needs and circumstances. There are fact sheets available covering each of these and many more categories.

Contact Option

Small Business Answer Desk
(800) 827-5722 or (202) 653-7561
SBA Services

This hotline provides the caller with an automated menu of topics on relevant small business issues. Informative brochures will be sent upon request.

The SBA publishes over 100 business booklets that sell for modest fees (usually under $2.00). They address issues which concern prospective and existing small business owners. A free directory of Small Business Administration Publications may be obtained from the SBA Answer Desk or from any regional SBA office.

Getting an SBA Loan

SBA LOANS ARE AVAILABLE to small companies that have sought and been refused financing from other lending institutions prior to applying to the SBA for assistance. Most of the SBA loans are made through the guaranteed loan program, in which the private lender agrees to loan funds to the small business and the SBA agrees to guarantee 90% of a loan under $155,000 and up to 85% of a loan greater than that figure, up to a maximum of $750,000.

Although the interest rates on SBA guaranteed loans are negotiated between the borrower and lender, they are subject to SBA maximums and generally cannot exceed 2.75% over the New York prime rate.

The SBA also provides specialized loan guarantee programs which include:

- Export revolving lines of credit
- International trade loans
- Seasonal lines of credit
- Small general contractor financing
- Lender incentives for small loans of less than $50,000
- Pollution control loans
- Community development loans.

Direct loans of up to $150,000 by the SBA are very limited and are available only to applicants unable to secure an SBA-guaranteed loan. Before applying, a small business owner must seek financing from his or her bank of account and, in cities of over 200,000, from at least one other lender. Direct loan funds are available to businesses located in high-unemployment areas, or owned by low-income or handicapped individuals, Vietnam veterans or disabled veterans. Interest on direct loans is based on the cost of money to the federal government and is calculated quarterly.

Eligibility Requirements

To be eligible for SBA loan assistance, a company must be operated for profit and fall within size standards. It cannot be a business involved in the creation or distribution of ideas or opinions such as newspapers, magazines, and academic schools. It cannot be engaged in speculation or investment in rental real estate.

The SBA has other eligibility requirements which qualify a business as a small business:

- Manufacturing: the maximum number of employees may range from 500 to 1,500 depending on the type of product manufactured.
- Wholesaling: the maximum number of employees may not exceed 100.
- Services: the average annual receipts may not exceed $3.5 to $14.5 million depending on the industry.
- Retailing: the average annual receipts may not exceed $3.5 to $13.5 million, depending on the industry.
- Construction: general construction average annual receipts may not exceed $9.5 to $17 million depending on the industry.

Getting an SBA Loan (cont'd)

- Special trade construction: average annual receipts may not exceed $7 million.
- Agriculture: average annual receipts range from $1 to $3.5 million, depending on the industry.

Applying for an SBA Loan

To apply for a loan, a small business owner must do the following:

- Prepare a current business balance sheet listing all assets, liabilities, and net worth. Start-up businesses should prepare an estimated balance sheet including the amount invested by the owner and others.
- Prepare a profit and loss statement for the current period and the most recent three fiscal years. Start-up businesses should prepare a detailed projection of earnings and expenses for at least the first year of operation.
- Prepare a personal financial statement of the proprietor and each partner or stockholder owning 20% or more of the business.
- List collateral to be offered as security for the loan.
- List any existing liens.
- State the amount of the requested loan and the purposes for which it is intended.
- Present the above items to a selected lender. If the loan request is refused, the business owner should contact the local SBA office regarding the guaranteed-loan program.
- If the guaranteed loan is not possible, other loans may be available from the SBA.

Alternatives to an SBA Loan

ALTHOUGH THE SBA is perhaps the best known "friend" to the small business owner, there are several other governmental and private sector organizations which can offer financial assistance and guidance to individuals requiring it.

SBIC (Small Business Investment Companies) are privately organized and managed firms which make equity capital and long-term credit available to small, independent businesses. SBICs are licensed by the SBA but set their own policies and investment decisions. SSBICs (Special Small Business Investment Companies) invest specifically in socially and economically disadvantaged entrepreneurs. The SBIC can borrow up to four times its private capital through a federally guaranteed funding system, at an interest rate slightly above the cost of money to the U.S., making it an attractive and powerful source of capital for new and growing businesses.

The National Association of Small Business Investment Companies (NASBIC) is the national trade association for the 215 SBICs and 127 SSBICs. It publishes a directory of members, broken down by state, size of financing, industry preference, and geographical preference. The NASBIC directory is entitled: "Venture Capital: Where to Find It" and costs $10.00, made payable to NASBIC. Phone or credit card orders are not accepted.

To obtain the directory write to:
NASBIC Directory
POB 2039
Merrifield, VA 22116

For other questions or information, call or write:
National Association of Small Business
Investment Companies
1199 N. Fairfax St., Suite 200
Alexandria, VA 22314
(703) 683-1601

BDCs (Business Development Corporations) are groups affiliated with 30 various state governments and they differ from SBAs. BDCs agree to accept riskier loans, for longer terms. They frequently sell parts of these loans to others on the secondary loan market to offset the risk. Interest rates usually average 2 to 4% above the prime lending rate and some BDCs charge a flat fee.

To locate the BDC within a state, or to obtain assistance in locating other funding sources, an individual should write or call a specific state Small Business Development Center. The national organization will direct the caller to one of 750 state or regional centers. These centers provide assistance in the form of training, counseling, and research assistance in start-up, operation, and expansion of business in all 50 states. While the centers do not provide funding, they do refer individuals to the organizations that can offer the greatest assistance.

Association of Small Business Development Centers
1313 Farnum, Suite 132
Omaha, NE 68182-0472
(402) 595-2387

Other sources of information on obtaining funding include:

- State Economic Development Agencies provide useful information on business opportunities and assistance programs.
- City or County Development Agencies offer assistance in identifying sources of funding.
- Small Business Advocates in individual state governments provide guidance and direction to increase efficiency.

Small Business Support Agencies

EACH STATE HAS MANY DIFFERENT SERVICES available to provide assistance for prospective or existing small business owners. These agencies provide services ranging from financial counseling and funding to assistance in training, licensing, regulation, consulting, state contracts, and every other need of the small business.

Valuable types of support services include:

- A general information number that will offer a referral to the appropriate agency or individual who can provide assistance and information about start-up procedures as well as ongoing problem-solving assistance.
- A number for a Small Business Advocate whose function in the state is to help business owners operate efficiently within the state, particularly where bureaucratic red tape exists.

For each state listing below, the first number will provide the caller with general information regarding state programs, available information packets, and referrals to other agencies to meet the caller's business needs. The second listing within each state is the office of the Small Business Advocate which provides information and expertise in dealing with local, state, and federal agencies.

State-by-State Support Agencies

State	Economic Development Office	Small Business Advocate
AL	(205) 263-0048	(205) 263-0048
AK	(907) 465-2018	(907) 465-2018
AZ	(602) 255-5374	(602) 255-5371
AR	(501) 682-7500	(501) 371-5273
CA	(916) 445-6545	(916) 322-6108
CO	(303) 892-3840	(303) 892-3840
CT	(203) 566-4051	(203) 566-4051
DE	(302) 736-4271	(302) 736-4271
DC	(202) 727-6600	(202) 636-5150
FL	(904) 488-9357	(904) 487-4698
GA	(404) 656-6200	(404) 656-6315
HI	(808) 548-7645	(803) 548-4347
ID	(208) 334-2470	(208) 334-2470
IL	(312) 917-7179	(312) 917-2829
IN	(317) 634-1690	(317) 232-5295
IA	(515) 281-3251	(515) 281-8324
KS	(913) 296-3483	(913) 296-3481
KY	(502) 564-4252	(502) 564-4252
LA	(504) 342-5359	(504) 564-4252
ME	(800) 872-3838 ME only	(207) 289-2658
MD	(301) 333-6975	(301) 974-3514
MA	(617) 727-3221	(413) 545-6301
MI	(517) 373-6241	(517) 335-4720
MN	(612) 296-3871	(612) 296-3871
MO	(800) 523-1434	(314) 751-4982
MS	(601) 359-3449	(601) 359-3552
MT	(406) 444-3923	(406) 444-4380
NE	(402) 471-3782	(402) 471-3742

State	Economic Development Office	Small Business Advocate
NV	(702) 885-4325	(702) 885-4602
NH	(603) 623-550	(603) 743-3995
NJ	(609) 984-4442	(609) 292-0700
NM	(505) 827-0300	(505) 827-0300
NY	(800) 782-8369	(212) 309-0466
NC	(919) 733-4151	(919) 733-7980
ND	(701) 777-3132	(701) 224-2810
OH	(614) 644-8748	(614) 466-2718
OK	(405) 843-9770	(405) 841-5120
OR	(503) 373-1225	(503) 373-1200
PA	(717) 783-5700	(717) 783-5700
RI	(401) 277-2601	(401) 831-1330
SC	(803) 737-0400	(803) 734-1400
SD	(605) 394-5725	(605) 773-5032
TN	(615) 741-1888	(615) 741-2626
TX	(512) 472-5059	(512) 472-5059
UT	(801) 581-7905	(801) 581-7905
VT	(802) 828-3221	(802) 828-3211
VA	(804) 786-3791	(804) 786-3791
WA	(206) 753-5630	(206) 753-5632
WI	(608) 266-1018	(608) 263-7766
WV	(304) 348-2960	(304) 348-2960
WY	(307) 325-4827	(307) 777-7287

Almanac Fact

According to Dun & Bradstreet, of the total number of failed businesses involved in 1990 court proceedings with creditors, 41% were small businesses with liabilities of less than $5,000.

Minority Contracting Provisions

THE SBA OFFERS SPECIAL ASSISTANCE to help minority-owned small businesses grow and thrive. The agency acts as the prime contractor for a share of all awards made by federal agencies and subcontracts to firms owned by socially and economically disadvantaged Americans. This SBA program admits small and minority-owned businesses into a program which allows them to negotiate on special contracts. Sources of information include the regional and district offices of the SBA, as well as individual State Information Offices.

Winning Government Contracts

IN ONE RECENT YEAR, THE FEDERAL government and its purchasing agents and departments contracted for $184.2 billion worth of goods and services from the private sector. This represents 16% of the total federal outlay. Of that total, $31.6 billion or 17.2% was purchased directly from small businesses. The SBA reports that another $27.2 billion reached small businesses through subcontracts to large, prime contractors to the federal government.

Through the Procurement Automated Source System (PASS), the SBA electronically brings the resumes of qualified small businesses to the desks of thousands of government procurement officials, and large government prime contractors throughout the U.S.

The Matchmaker Trade Missions (co-sponsored with the U.S. Department of Commerce) links U.S. firms with potential foreign buyers in the global marketplace.

Once again, the SBA Answer Desk Hotline can provide prerecorded messages regarding business opportunities in the federal government sector. The local office of the SBA can also provide such information.

Small Business Answer Desk
(800) 827-5722 or (202) 653-7561

The Small Business Innovation Research Program administers a program among government agencies that provides grants to small businesses for innovation research and development. The Pre-Solicitation Announcement, published by the SBIR in March, June, September, and December lists the needs of 11 federal agencies for R&D activities.

Additional information is available through the:

Office of Innovation, Research & Technology, SBA
409 Third St., SW
Washington, DC 20416

Each business day, the GPO releases the *Commerce Business Daily* a publication that provides a daily list of U.S. government procurement invitations, contract awards, subcontracting leads, sales of surplus property, and foreign business opportunities. Each edition contains approximately 500–1,000 such notices and each notice appears in the CBD only once. While back issues are available in the public library, a subscription may be obtained for six-month or one-year time periods.

Information about the rates and service may be obtained from:

The Superintendent of Documents
Government Printing Office
Washington, DC 20402
(202) 783-3238
Fax: (202) 512-2233

Each state's Department of Economic Development also provides complete information about state contract opportunities available to small businesses. The Department of Economic Development in each state can advise about the availability of such a publication.

Almanac Fact

Small businesses employ 50 percent of the private workforce, contribute 44 percent of all sales, and are responsible for 38 percent of the GNP.

Source: Small Business Administration

Assistance from the Government

The Service Corps of Retired Executives (SCORE)

SCORE is a volunteer program of the SBA. The organization matches the skills and experience of the volunteers with a business that needs expert advice. Approximately 14,000 men and women business executives participate in the program and share their management and technical expertise with present and prospective owners and managers of small businesses.

Volunteers are members of 390 locally organized, self-administered chapters offering services in more than 700 locations throughout the U.S. There is no charge for the counseling, but there may be a nominal fee for the training programs. Volunteers offer counseling in distribution channels, expansion potential, product changes. They offer workshops to present and prospective small business entrepreneurs, within the local community. An individual currently operating a small business or contemplating a business start-up is eligible for help from SCORE. The service is not tied to any SBA loan. Any local office of the SBA can advise a caller of the availability of a SCORE program.

Small Business Development Centers (SBDCs)

This branch of the SBA sponsors 57 SBDCs in 50 states as well as the District of Columbia, Puerto Rico, and the Virgin Islands. Through a network of subcenters located at educational institutions, chambers of commerce, economic development corporations, and downtown storefronts, the state SBDCs provide up-to-date counseling and training, and deal with financial, marketing, production, organization, engineering, technical problems, and feasibility studies.

More specialized programs include services to inventors with patentable products, international trade centers for how-to export and import advice, business law information and guidance, procurement matching, venture capital formation, and small business incubators.

The location of a local SBDC can be found in the telephone directory under U.S. Government, Small Business Administration or by calling the SBA Answer desk (800) 827-5722 or (202) 653-7561.

Small Business Institute (SBI)

The SBA sponsors over 500 SBIs in all states and territories to offer small business owners an opportunity to receive intensive management counseling from qualified college-level business students working under expert faculty guidance. The studies focus on market studies, accounting systems, personnel policies, production design, product line diversification, exporting, expansion feasibility, and strategy. A local office of the SBA can advise the caller of the availability of an SBI in the area.

Lobbying

THERE ARE APPROXIMATELY 14,000 INDIVIDUALS in the nation's capital whose profession might be listed as "advocacy." They include persons who work to influence government policies and actions by advocating for their own or their client's interests. They work in government affairs or in public relations departments for trade associations, professional societies, labor unions, corporations, and a wide variety of special interest and public interest groups. Some are registered as lobbyists on Capitol Hill. Others, who represent foreign industry or governments, are registered with the Justice Department as foreign agents. Still others are part of the Executive Branch of the Federal Government and act as liaisons between that office and Congress.

The Justice Department requires agents representing foreign countries, foreign companies, and organizations to file forms in their Foreign Agents Registration Unit: (202) 514-1216. These files are open for public inspection at the Justice Department.

Lobbyists also register with the Clerk of the House of Representatives and Secretary of the Senate, indicating the party or individuals in whose interest he or she works, the length of employment, amount of reimbursement received by the lobbyist, and what expenses are covered by this reimbursement. Furthermore, the lobbyist must file quarterly financial reports stating the name and address of each individual who has made a contribution of $500 or more, and the total contributions made during the calendar year.

Political Action Committees

POLITICAL ACTION COMMITTEES are groups devoted to special interests. These groups raise and distribute funds for political candidates who support their specific concerns, as well as for lobbyists who represent their interests to legislators. PACs can be sponsored by a trade association, a union, special interest group, or a company.

Contact Options

Business Associated PACS:

AFL-CIO Committee on Political Education
(202) 637-5101

Americans for Free International Trade
(202) 659-8545

Business and Industry
(202) 833-1880

Political Interest Groups:

American Conservative Union
(202) 546-6555
Organization focused on defense, foreign policy, economics, and legal issues.

U.S. Chamber of Commerce
(202) 463-5604
Federation promoting the enaction of pro-business legislation.

Congressional Economic Leadership Institute
(202) 546-5007
Nonpartisan conduit for discussion between Congress and private sector.

Family Research Council
(202) 393-2100
Advocates the interests of the family in public policy formulation.

Foundation for Public Affairs
(202) 872-1750
Research and educational foundation to disseminate information on corporate public affairs programs.

Several organizations monitor the voting records of members of Congress on particular issues and publish the results periodically. Some of the organizations which might be of interest to the business community include:

American Federation of Labor
Congress of Industrial Organizations
(202) 637-5000

Common Cause
(202) 833-1200

Competitive Enterprise Institute
(202) 547-1010

National Federation of Independent Business
(202) 554-9000

National Taxpayers Union
(202) 543-1300

National Women's Political Caucus
(202) 898-1100

U.S. Chamber of Commerce
(202) 463-5604

The Top Reference Sources

What Every Executive Better Know About the Law
Simon & Schuster, $17.95
(212) 698-7000

Author Michael Trachtman has written a valuable book that explains in clear language what executives should know about law and legal interpretations.

Sample chapter titles include, "But We Had an Oral Agreement," "Let's Make a Deal," "The Nuts and Bolts of a Contract," "How to Look Good When the Deal Goes Bad," and "See You in Court." This book shows how to use the law to your advantage in most business situations.

Major Trade Associations

MOST MAJOR TRADE ASSOCIATIONS maintain an office in Washington, DC, to deal with legislative issues. Each office will refer the caller to the appropriate department.

Selected Associations and Telephone Numbers

Trade Association	Telephone Number
American Bankers Association	(202) 663-5000
American Council of Life Insurance	(202) 624-2000
American Electronics Association	(408) 987-4200
American Farm Bureau Federation	(312) 399-5700
American Financial Services Association	(202) 296-5544
American Health Care Association	(202) 842-4444
American Hotel and Motel Association	(202) 289-3100
American Institute of Certified Public Accountants	(212) 575-6200
American Insurance Association	(212) 828-7100
American Petroleum Institute	(202) 682-8000
American Retail Federation	(202) 783-7971
American Society of Association Executives	(202) 626-2723
American Society of Travel Agents	(703) 739-2782
American Trucking Association	(703) 838-1700
Associated Builders and Contractors, Inc.	(202) 637-8800
Associated General Contractors of America	(202) 393-2040
Association of American Publishers	(212) 689-8920
Automotive Parts and Accessories Association	(301) 459-9110
Automotive Service Industry Association	(312) 836-1300
Computer and Business Equipment Manufacturers Association	(202) 737-8888
Computer Software and Services Information Industry	(703) 522-5055
Electronic Industries Association	(202) 457-4900
Food Marketing Institute	(202) 452-8444
Grocery Manufacturers Association	(202) 337-9400
Health Industry Distributors Association	(202) 659-0050
Health Industry Manufacturers Association	(202) 452-8420
Independent Insurance Agents of America, Inc.	(212) 285-2500
Independent Petroleum Association of America	(202) 857-4722
Information Industry Association	(202) 639-8262
International Association for Financial Planning	(404) 395-1605
International Communications Industries Association	(703) 273-7200
National Association of Broadcasters	(202) 429-5300
National Association of Chain Drug Stores	(703) 549-3001
National Association of Convenience Stores	(703) 684-3600
National Association of Home Builders	(202) 822-0200
National Association of Realtors	(312) 329-8200
National Association of Wholesalers-Distributors	(202) 872-0885
National Automobile Dealers Association	(703) 821-7407
National Business Incubators Association	(717) 249-4508
National Forest Products Association	(202) 463-2700
National Home Furnishing Association	(919) 883-1650
National Industrial Transportation League	(703) 524-5011
National Restaurant Association	(202) 331-5900
National Retail Federation	(212) 244-8780
Printing Industries of America, Inc.	(703) 519-8100
Travel Industry Association of America	(202) 293-1433

Hiring a Lobbyist

THE MOST EFFECTIVE WAY TO HIRE A LOBBYIST is to contact a Washington, DC, law firm that represents national associations, labor unions, U.S. companies, registered foreign agents, lobbyists, or special interest groups. The following are the largest Washington legal firms (as noted by *Legal Times*) that represent special interest clients (as indicated by their listing in *Washington Representatives*, a compilation of such groups).

Recommended Resource

Washington Representatives (1992)
Arthur C. Close, J. Valerie Steele, and Curtis W. McCormick, Eds.
Columbia Books
(202) 898-0662

Largest Washington Legal Firms

Legal Firm	Telephone Number
Covington & Burling	(202) 262-6000
Arnold & Porter	(202) 872-6700
Hogan & Hartson	(202) 637-5600
Shaw, Pittman, Potts & Trowbridge	(202) 663-8000
Arent, Fox, Kintner, Plotkin & Kahn	(202) 857-6000
Akin, Gump, Hauer & Feld	(202) 887-4000
Wilmer, Cutler & Pickering	(202) 663-6000
Steptoe & Johnson	(202) 429-3000
Jones, Day, Reavis & Pogue	(202) 879-3939
Crowell & Moring	(202) 624-2500
Skadden, Arps, Slate, Meagher & Flom	(202) 371-7000
Howrey & Simon	(202) 783-0800
Morgan, Lewis & Bockius	(202) 467-7000
Dickstein, Shapiro & Morin	(202) 785-9700
Dow, Lohnes, & Albertson	(202) 857-2500
Patton, Boggs & Blow	(202) 457-6000
Sutherland, Asbill & Brennan	(202) 383-0100
Williams & Connolly	(202) 331-5000
Sidley & Austin	(202) 736-8000
McKenna & Cuneo	(202) 789-7500
Verner, Lipfert, Bernhard, McPherson & Hand	(202) 371-6000
Fried, Frank, Harris, Shriver & Jacobson	(202) 639-7000
Reed Smith Shaw & McClay	(202) 456-6100
Gibson, Dunn & Crutcher	(202) 955-8500
Baker & Hostetler	(202) 861-1500
Miller & Chevalier	(202) 626-5800
Winston & Strawn	(202) 371-5700
Kirkpatrick & Lockhart	(202) 778-9000
Swidler & Berlin	(202) 944-4300

Source: Legal Times

Almanac Fact

The law firm with the largest branch office in Washington, DC, is Dallas-based Akin, Gump, Hauer & Feld.

Starting Your Own PAC

Recommended Resources

PACs and Lobbies (a newsletter)
Published by Amward Publications
#2000 National Press Building
Washington, DC 20045
(202) 488-7227

The Lobbying Handbook
by John Zorak
Professional Lobbying Consulting Center
1111 14th St., NW, Suite 1001
Washington, DC 20005
(202) 898-0084

Government Publications

MORE THAN 15,000 BOOKS, PAMPHLETS, posters, periodicals, subscription services, and other government publications are available for purchase from the Superintendent of Documents, Government Printing Office (GPO). They range from "accidents" to "zoning" and deal with almost every facet of human life. Topics are selected to meet the informational needs of congressional staff members who require sound background in order to propose and prepare legislation. The topics are also a response to the needs and interests of the general public.

The all-time best seller list prepared by the GPO includes the following titles and the number of copies sold:

1. *Infant Care* (17,601,122)
2. *Metric Conversion Card* (3,934,539)
3. *Federal Benefits for Veterans and Dependents* (2,318, 681)
4. *United States Government Handbook* (1,682,978)
5. *Occupational Outlook Handbook* (1,602,849)
6. *Adult Physical Fitness* (1,438,902)
7. *Economic Report of the President* (1,282,278)
8. *Constitution of the United States* (1,049,263)

Other continuing titles which have a recurring demand include:

1. *Statistical Abstract of the United States*, 1992
2. *United States Industrial Outlook*, 1992
3. *Where to Write for Vital Records*
4. *Eating to Lower Your Blood Cholesterol*
5. *Backyard Mechanic, Vols. 1, 2, 3.*

Frequently, a legal or general information question arises that can be resolved by a call to a Federal agency. It is usually worthwhile to request that the agency send any available printed information on a specific topic. Most agencies will gladly oblige such a request. If a charge is attached to a document, the caller will be referred to the Government Printing Office (GPO) and will be given the name of the publication to order.

In addition, regional depository libraries are designated to store, and make available for public access, all federal documents which are given a depository status. There are 1,400 such libraries throughout the country. The reference desk of the local public library should be able to provide the caller with the location of the nearest depository library, where he or she will be assisted in locating the desired publication.

Free Government Resources

THE GOVERNMENT PRINTING OFFICE (GPO) is responsible for producing printed documents (or securing the printing services from outside vendors) for all the books, pamphlets, and documents generated by the agencies of the Federal Government. Over 15,000 titles are available to the public, and cover more than 200 subjects. Since it is impractical to have a single catalogue for all titles, the GPO has made available a "subject bibliography" for each of the over 200 topics. A list of all publications available from the GPO by subject and title is available by writing or calling to request a specific Subject Bibliography Index.

The following is a sampler of the subjects and order numbers to use when requesting a subject bibliography from the GPO:

Accidents and Accident Prevention (229)
Accounting and Auditing (42)
Adolescence
Children and Youth (35)
Aeronautics
Aircraft, Airports and Airways (13)
Aviation Information and Training Materials (18)
Federal Aviation Regulations (12)
Africa (284)

Free Government Resources (cont'd)

Free Government Resources (cont'd)

Free Government Resources (cont'd)

Free Government Resources (cont'd)

Livestock and Poultry (10)
Lumber
Trees, Forest Products and Forest Management (86)
Magnetic Tapes
Electronic Information Products (314)
Management
Business and Business Management (4)
Labor-Management Relations (64)
Personnel Management (Formerly Personnel Management, Guidance and Counseling) (202)
Wildlife Management (116)
Manufactures
Census of Manufactures (146)
Maps
Maps and Atlases (U.S. and Foreign) (102)
Surveying and Mapping (183)
Marine Corps Publications (237)
Marine Fishes
Fish and Marine Life (209)
Marketing Research (125)
Mathematics (24)
Medals
Coins and Medals (198)
Mediation
Labor-Management Relations (64)
Medicine and Medical Science (154)
Mental Health (167)
Metric System
Weights and Measures (109)
Middle East (286)
Military History (98)
Military Supplies
Procurement, Supply Cataloging and Classification (129)
Minerals
Census of Mineral Industries (310)
Mineral Yearbooks (99)
Minerals and Mining (151)
Minorities (6)
Monuments
National Park Service Handbooks (Formerly Historical Handbook Series) (16)
Presidents of the United States (140)
Motion Pictures, Films and Audiovisual Information (73)
Motor Vehicles (49)
Music (221)
NASA Educational Publications (222)
NASA Scientific and Technical Publications (257)
National and World Economy (97)
National Defense and Security (153)
National Institute of Standards and Technology (290)
National Parks and Reserves
National Park Service Handbooks (Formerly Historical Handbook Series) (16)
Public Buildings, Landmarks and Historical Sites of the United States (140)
National Security
National Defense and Security (153)
Naturalization
Immigration, Naturalization and Citizenship (69)
Naval Education Publications (173)
Naval History (U.S.) (236)
Navigation (29)
Nuclear Power
Atomic Energy and Nuclear Power (200)
Nurses and Nursing Care (19)
Nutrition
Food, Diet and Nutrition (291)
Occupations
Employment and Occupations (44)
Occupational Outlook Handbook (270)
Vocational and Career Education (110)
Oceanography (32)
Office of Personnel Management Publications (300)
Ornamental Horticulture
The Home (41)
Outdoor Recreation
Recreational and Outdoor Activities (17)
Outer Space
Astronomy and Astrophysics (115)
Space, Rockets and Satellites (297)
Paleontology
Earth Sciences (160)
Passports
Customs, Immunization and Passport Publications (27)
Travel and Tourism (302)
Patents and Trademarks (21)
Personnel Management (Formerly Personnel Management, Guidance and Counseling) (202)
Pest Control
Insects (34)
Pesticides, Insecticides, Fungicides, and Rodenticides (227)
Photography (72)
Physical Fitness (239)
Pictures
Posters, Charts, Picture Sets, and Decals (57)
Poetry and Literature (142)
Political Science
Census of Governments (156)
Pollution
Air Pollution (46)
Environmental Education and Protection (88)
Waste Management (95)
Water Pollution and Water Resources (50)
Population
Census of Population and Housing (181)
Census of Population and Housing, Block Statistics (311)
Census of Population and Housing, Census Tracts (312)
Postal Service (169)
Posters, Charts, Picture Sets, and Decals (57)
Poultry
Livestock and Poultry (10)
Power Resources
Atomic Energy and Nuclear Power (200)
Presidents of the United States (106)
Prices, Wages and Cost of Living (226)
Printing and Graphic Arts (77)
Procurement, Supply Cataloging and Classification (129)
Public and Private Utilities (298)
Public Buildings, Landmarks and Historical Sites of

Free Government Resources (cont'd)

Free Government Publications (cont'd)

United States Code (197)
United States Reports (25)
Universities and Colleges
Higher Education (217)
Publications Relating to the College Debate Topic (176)
Urban Renewal
Housing, Urban and Rural Development (280)
Veterans Affairs and Benefits (80)
Victims of Crimes
Crime and Criminal Justice (36)
Vital and Health Statistics (121)
Vocational and Career Education (110)
Vocational Guidance
Personnel Management (Formerly Personnel Management, Guidance and Counseling) (202)
Voting and Elections (245)
Wages
Prices, Wages and the Cost of Living (226)
War
American Revolution (144)
Civil War (92)
Military History (98)
Naval History (United States) (236)
Waste Management (95)
Water Pollution and Water Resources (50)
Weather (234)
Weights and Measures (109)
Wildlife Management (116)
Women (111)
Workers' Compensation (108)
Writing
Communications and Office Skills (Formerly Stenography, Typing and Writing) (87)
Yearbooks
Conservation (238)
Department of Agriculture Yearbooks (31)
Minerals Yearbooks (99)
Youth
Children and Youth (35)
Drug Abuse (163)

Although there is a fee charged for the actual books, the catalogues are free and useful in choosing titles to answer questions and add to a professional's office library.

Particularly useful is a larger catalogue called *"Books for Business Professionals."* This catalogue contains the titles of useful government publications dealing with general business, export, import, patents and trademarks, law, accounting and taxes, labor relations, law and statistics, and selling to the government.

To order specific titles, a caller may use the automated ordering system, which will connect him or her to an individual who can advise about the price and availability of any title produced by the GPO. Orders can be placed using credit cards or by sending checks or money orders to the GPO:
U.S. Government Printing Office
Washington, DC 20402
(202) 783-3238

Orders can also be placed with the main bookstore of the GPO or in any one of the other locations. These branches of the GPO Bookstores are open to the public for browsing, like any other bookstore, usually during normal business hours. The locations are listed on the next page.

The Top Reference Sources

How to Form Your Own Corporation Without a Lawyer for Under $75.00
Enterprise Dearborn, $19.95
(312) 836-4400

The kind of practical information provided in this book previously had to be bought from an attorney.

Author Ted Nicholas explains how to avoid the hassle of lawyers and how to save hundreds or even thousands of dollars by following simple instructions. The book includes a complete set of forms, a certificate of incorporation, minutes, bylaws, and more.

GPO Branch Bookstores

State	Address	City, State, Zip	Telephone
AL	2021 3rd Ave. N.	Birmingham, AL 35203	(205) 731-1056
CA	505 S. Flower St.	Los Angeles, CA 90071	(213) 239-9844
CA	450 Golden Gate Ave.	San Francisco, CA 94102	(415) 252-5334
CO	1961 Stout St.	Denver, CO 80294	(303) 844-3964
CO	720 N. Main St.	Pueblo, CO 81003	(719) 544-3142
DC	710 N. Capitol St., NW	Washington, DC 20401	(202) 512-0132
DC	1510 H St., NW	Washington, DC 20005	(202) 653-5075
FL	400 W. Bay St.	Jacksonville, FL 32202	(904) 353-0569
GA	275 Peachtree St., NE	Atlanta, GA 30343	(404) 331-6947
IL	219 S. Dearborn St.	Chicago, IL 60604	(312) 353-5133
MA	T.P. O'Neill Federal Bldg.	Boston, MA 02222	(617) 720-4180
MI	477 Michigan Ave.	Detroit, MI 48226	(313) 226-7816
MO	5600 E. Bannister Rd.	Kansas City, MO 64137	(816) 765-2256
NY	26 Federal Plaza	New York, NY 10278	(212) 264-3825
OH	1240 E. 9th St.	Cleveland, OH 44199	(216) 522-4922
OH	200 N. High St.	Columbus, OH 43215	(614) 469-6956
OR	1305 SW First Ave.	Portland, OR 97201	(503) 221-6217
PA	100 N. 17th St.	Philadelphia, PA 19103	(215) 597-0677
PA	1000 Liberty Ave.	Pittsburgh, PA 15222	(412) 644-2721
TX	1100 Commerce St.	Dallas, TX 75242	(214) 767-0076
TX	801 Travis St.	Houston, TX 77002	(713) 228-1187
WA	915 2nd Ave.	Seattle, WA 98174	(206) 442-4270
WI	517 E. Wisconsin Ave.	Milwaukee, WI 53202	(414) 291-1304

Freedom of Information Act

THE FREEDOM OF INFORMATION ACT (FOIA) became law in 1966 and guaranteed the public the right of access to information held by the federal government. According to the act, any individual may request and receive a document, file, or other record held by any agency of the federal government. The burden of proof has shifted from the individual to the government, and the law requires that the government justify the need for secrecy regarding a document. However, there are nine specific exemptions to the access rule, including national defense, foreign policy, trade secrets, and criminal investigations.

The Privacy Act of 1974 enhances the FOIA by permitting individuals access to records about themselves, which are held by federal agencies. Such information must be complete, accurate, and relevant; the law requires that each agency publish a description of its record system and forbids the agency from disclosing personal information except to the individual who is the subject of such information. Both laws permit the individual to request access to federal records regarding him or herself and allows the individual to appeal a denial of that request.

The FOIA sets a deadline of ten working days for replying to the information request and a twenty-day deadline on responding to the appeal. The initial request letter and the appeals letter, if necessary, should be clearly and simply written. The Freedom of Information Clearinghouse will provide a brochure detailing how to write a request as well as an appeals letter.

Recommended Resource

A User's Guide to the Freedom of Information Act
Freedom of Information Clearinghouse
P.O. Box 19367
Washington, DC 20036
(202) 833-3000

Communications

Area Codes

State	City	Code
Alabama	All Locations	205
Alaska	All Locations	907
Arizona	All Locations	602
Arkansas	All Locations	501
California	Bakersfield	805
	Fresno	209
	Los Angeles	213/818/310
	Oakland	510
	Orange County	714
	Pasadena	818
	Sacramento	916
	San Diego	619
	San Francisco	415
	San Jose	408
Colorado	Colorado Springs	719
	Denver	303
Connecticut	All Locations	203
Delaware	All Locations	302
DC	Washington	202
Florida	Fort Myers	813
	Jacksonville	904
	Miami	305
	Palm Beach	407
Georgia	Atlanta	404
	Columbus	406
	Savannah	912
Hawaii	All Locations	808
Idaho	All Locations	208
Illinois	Centralia	618
	Chicago	312
	Decatur	217
	Des Plaines	708
	Peoria	309
	Rockford	815
	Springfield	217
Indiana	Evansville	812
	Indianapolis	317
	South Bend	219
Iowa	Cedar Rapids	319
	Council Bluffs	712
	Des Moines	515
Kansas	Topeka	913
	Wichita	316
Kentucky	Bowling Green	502
	Louisville	502
	Newport	606
Louisiana	Baton Rouge	504
	New Orleans	504
	Shreveport	318
Maine	All Locations	207
Maryland	Baltimore	410
	Rockville	301
Massachusetts	Boston	617
	Springfield	413
	Worcester	508
Michigan	Detroit	313
	Grand Rapids	616
	Kalamazoo	616
	Lansing	517
	Marquette	906
Minnesota	Duluth	218
	Minneapolis	612
	Rochester	507
Mississippi	All Locations	601
Missouri	Kansas City	816
	St. Louis	314
	Springfield	417
Montana	All Locations	406
Nebraska	Lincoln	402
	North Platte	308
	Omaha	402
Nevada	All Locations	702
New Hampshire	All Locations	603
New Jersey	Atlantic City	609
	Elizabeth	908
	Newark	201
	Trenton	609
New Mexico	All Locations	505
New York	Albany	518
	Buffalo	716
	Great Neck	516
	Ithaca	607
	New York City	212/718
	Rochester	716
	Syracuse	315
	White Plains	914
North Carolina	Charlotte	704
	Raleigh	919
North Dakota	All Locations	701
Ohio	Akron	216
	Cincinnati	513
	Cleveland	216
	Columbus	614
	Dayton	513
	Toledo	419
Oklahoma	Oklahoma City	405
	Tulsa	918
Oregon	All Locations	503
Pennsylvania	Erie	814
	Harrisburg	717
	Philadelphia	215
	Pittsburgh	412
Rhode Island	All Locations	401
South Carolina	All Locations	803
South Dakota	All Locations	605
Tennessee	Chattanooga	615
	Memphis	901
	Nashville	615
Texas	Amarillo	806
	Dallas	214
	El Paso	915
	Fort Worth	817
	Galveston	409
	Houston	713
	San Antonio	512
Utah	All Locations	801
Vermont	All Locations	802
Virginia	Alexandria	703
	Richmond	804
Washington	Seattle	206
	Spokane	509
	Tacoma	206
West Virginia	All Locations	304
Wisconsin	Green Bay	414
	Madison	608
	Wausau	715
Wyoming	All Locations	307

International Dialing

TRAVELERS CAN SAVE MONEY by using an AT&T calling card when making calls from foreign countries to the United States. To reach an AT&T operator, an access code must be dialed. Note: Some pay phones do not offer this service. For any numbers not listed, call (816) 654-6000 collect from any country

USA Direct AT&T Service

Country	Code
Anguilla	1-800 872 2881
Argentina	001-800-200-1111
Aruba	800 1011
Australia	0014-881-011
Austria	022-903-011
Bahamas	1-800-872-2881
Bahrain	800-001
Belgium	078-11-0010
Bermuda	1-800-872-2881
Brazil	000-8010
British Virgin Islands	1-800-872-2881
Cayman	1872
Chile	00, 0312
China, PRC	10811
Colombia	980-11-0010
Costa Rica	114
Czechoslovakia	00-420-00101
Denmark	8001-0010
Dominica	1-800-872-2881
Dominican Rep.	1-800-872-2881
Egypt	510-0200
El Salvador	190
Finland	9800-100-10
France	19-0011
Germany	0130-0010
Gambia	001-199-220-0010
Ghana	0191
Greece	00-800-1311
Grenada	872
Guam	108-872
Guatemala	190
Haiti	001-800-872-2881
Honduras	123
Hong Kong	800-1111
Hungary	00-800-01111
India	000-117
Indonesia	00-801-10
Ireland	1-800-550-000
Israel	177-100-2727
Italy	172-1011
Jamaica	0800-872-2881
Japan	0039-111
Kenya	0800-10
Korea	009-11
Liberia	797-797
Macao	0800-111
Malaysia	800-0011
Mexico	95-800-462-4240
Netherlands	06-022-9111
Netherlands Antilles	001-800-872-2881
New Zealand	000-911
Norway	050-12011
Panama	109
Peru	##0
Philippines	105-11
Poland	0-010-480-0111
Portugal	05017-1-288
St. Kitts	1-800-872-2881
Singapore	800-0011
Spain	900-9900-11
Suriname	156
Sweden	020795-611
Switzerland	046-05-0011
Taiwan	0080-102880
Thailand	001-999-11111
United Kingdom	0800-89-0011
Uruguay	000410
Zimbabwe	110899
United States	(800) 321-0288
Countries not listed	(816) 654-6000 collect

Source: David McCormick, AT&T

NOTE: MCI and Sprint have recently announced similar services. For information on these codes, contact your carrier directly.

Canadian Area Codes

Province	City	Code
Alberta		403
British Columbia		604
Manitoba		204
New Brunswick		506
Newfoundland		709
Nova Scotia		902
Ontario	Ottawa	613
	Toronto	416
Quebec	Montreal	514
	Quebec	418
Saskatchewan		306

International Dialing Codes

Country	Access Code
Algeria	213
Argentina	54
Australia	61
Austria	43
Belgium	32
Belize	501
Bolivia	591
Brazil	55
Chile	56
China	86
Colombia	57
Costa Rica	506
Denmark	45
Ecuador	593
Egypt	20
Ethiopia	251
Finland	358
France	33
Germany	37
Greece	30
Guam	671
Guatamala	502
Haiti	509
Hong Kong	852
Hungary	36
Iceland	354
India	91
Indonesia	62
Iran	
Iraq	964
Ireland	353
Israel	972
Italy	39
Japan	81
Kenya	254
Korea	82
Kuwait	965
Lebanon	961
Liberia	231
Libya	218
Luxembourg	352
Malaysia	60
Malta	356
Monaco	33
Morocco	212
Netherlands	31
Netherlands Antilles	599
New Zealand	64
Nicaragua	505
Nigeria	234
Norway	47
Oman	968
Pakistan	92
Panama	507
Paraguay	595
Peru	51
Philippines	63
Poland	48
Portugal	351
Qatar	974
Romania	40
Saudi Arabia	966
Senegal	221
Singapore	65
South Africa	27
Spain	34
Sri Lanka	94
Sweden	46
Switzerland	41
Taiwan	886
Thailand	66
Trinidad	809
Tunisia	216
Turkey	90
Russia	7
United Kingdom	44
Uruguay	598
Vatican	39
Venezuela	58

NOTE: Dial 011 before dialing a country code.

Almanac Fact

Until 1993, the total number of international phone lines in Russia was 30.

Source: The New York Times

Zip Codes

Manhattan Zip Codes

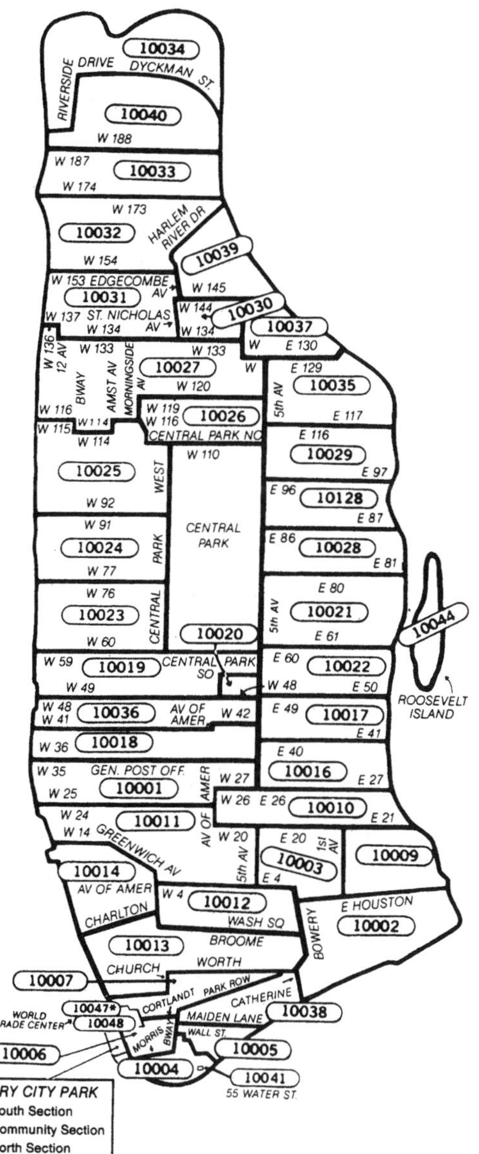

For fastest service, use the exact Zip Code for the destination address. The Zip Codes in this table will bring mail to the main post office in each city, which is faster than no Zip Code at all.

This table can also be used to send a batch of letters to a central Zip Code by Express Mail. The local postmaster will then deliver the individual letters locally, saving time and money.

To find a Zip Code for any location, call (800) 374-8777. After hours, call the Honolulu Post Office at (808) 423-3930.

Main Post Office Zip Codes

City	Zip Code
Atlanta	30301
Baltimore	21233
Boston	02101
Chicago	60601
Cincinnati	45202
Cleveland	44101
Columbus	43216
Dallas	75201
Denver	80201
Detroit	48231
Houston	77052
Indianapolis	46206
Los Angeles	90086
Miami	33101
Milwaukee	53201
Minneapolis	55401
New York	10001
Norfolk	23503
Philadelphia	19104
Phoenix	85201
Pittsburgh	15233
Portland	97208
Sacramento	95814
St. Louis	63166
San Antonio	78265
San Diego	92183
San Francisco	94142
Seattle	98101
Tampa	33602
Washington, DC (federal)	20500
Washington, DC (other)	20090

Postal Service

FOR MOST USERS, the United States Postal Service offers five classes of mail. From most expensive to least expensive, they are:

- *Express Mail:* overnight, seven days a week
- *Priority Mail:* two day service to most locations
- *First Class:* quick and relatively inexpensive
- *Third Class:* bulk mail—permit required
- *Fourth Class:* parcel post and books

In addition to these services, the Postal Service offers insurance, registration, certification, and (though rarely used) Special Delivery.

First Class Mail (single-piece letter rates)

Weight in oz.	Postage ($)
Postcard	0.19
1	0.29
2	0.52
3	0.75
4	0.98
5	1.21
6	1.44
7	1.67
8	1.90
9	2.13
10	2.36
11*	2.59

**For pieces weighing more than 11 oz., use priority mail service*

Priority Mail

Weight in lbs.	Postage ($)
1	2.90
2	2.90
3	4.10
4	4.65
5	5.45

Size requirements

Minimum size-pieces must meet the following requirements to be mailable in any class:

- All pieces must be at least .007 inch thick
- Pieces (except keys and identification devices) that are 1/4 inch or less thick must be:
  - rectangular in shape
  - at least 3 1/2 inches high
  - at least 5 inches long.

Pieces greater than 1/4 inch thick can be mailed even if they measure less than 3 1/2 by 5 inches

Non-Standard Mail

Mail that doesn't meet the above requirements is subject to a ten cent surcharge in addition to the applicable postage. For Presort First Class and carrier route First Class, the surcharge is $0.05 in addition to applicable surcharge.

Mail is characterized as non-standard, First-Class mail or single-piece Third Class mail if it weighs one ounce and:

- Any of the following dimensions are exceeded:

  Length: 11 1/2 inches

  Height: 6 1/8 inches

  Thickness: 1/4 inch, or
- The length divided by the height (aspect ratio) is less than 1.3 or more than 2.5

Second Class Mail

Second Class Mail is only available to newspapers and periodicals that have qualified for second-class mail privileges. This is a non-trivial task.

Third Class Mail

Third Class Mail is restricted to specific types of matter–circulars, books, catalogues and other printed materials–weighing less than 16 ounces. A permit is required, and the rules governing this class of service are numerous. Contact your postmaster for details.

Single-Piece Third Class Rates

Weight not exceeding (oz.)	Postage ($)
1	0.29
2	0.52
3	0.75
4	0.98
6	1.21
8	1.33
10	1.44
12	1.56
14	1.67
15	1.79

Fourth Class Mail

To the general public, Fourth Class is the cheapest postal rate available for anything weighing over one pound.

For authorized bulk users, there are subrates available for printed matter. This is a single rate charged to the company regardless of the zone.

The Fourth Class rates are based on the distance sent. There are some discounts available.

Postal Service (cont'd)

Special Services

- *Certified Mail* allows the sender to receive evidence of delivery for an extra fee. A mailing receipt and delivery record is sent from the destination post office. Available at a rate of $1.00 in addition to the applicable postage.
- *COD* (Collect on Delivery) The maximum value for COD service is $600.00. Consult postmaster for fees and conditions of mailing.

Insurance

Liability	Fee in addition to postage
.01 to 50.00	0.75
50.01 to 100.00	1.60
100.01 to 200.00	2.40
200.01 to 300.00	3.50
300.01 to 400.00	4.60
400.01 to 500.00	5.40
500.01 to 600.00	6.20

- *Registered Mail* allows the sender maximum protection and security. The letter is signed for at every step of the mailing process to insure that it has been delivered properly. The sender also receives a return receipt upon completion of delivery. There is an additional fee for registered mail.

Registered Mail Additional Fees

Value	Insured	Uninsured
1 to 100.00	4.50	4.40
100.01 to 500.00	4.85	4.70
500.01 to 1,000.00	5.25	5.05

- *Special Delivery* provides expedited delivery to specified zones. In virtually all cases, it is cheaper and faster to use Express Mail instead.
- *Special Handling* gives preferential handling to Third- and Fourth-Class packages. Packages less than 10 pounds are $1.80 extra. Those over 10 pounds are $2.50 more.

Additional Services

- *Certificate of Mailing* (for bulk mailing and firm mailing books, see postmaster.) Fifty cents per certificate.
- *Return Receipt* (available for COD, Express Mail, certified, insured for over $50.00, and registered mail). There are three levels of service:
- Requested at time of mailing, showing to whom (signature) and date delivered $1.00
- Showing to whom (signature), date, and address where delivered $1.35
- *Restricted Delivery* Not available for Express Mail $2.50
- *Return Receipt for Merchandise* (provides proof of delivery for merchandise shipments only. Cheaper but less secure than certified or registered mail.)
- Showing to whom (signature) and date delivered $1.10
- Showing to whom (signature), date, and address delivered $1.50

Express Mail

Express mail is available seven days a week and 365 days a year for mailable items up to 70 pounds in weight and 108 inches in combined length and width. Features include noon delivery between major business markets; merchandise and document reconstruction insurance; Express mail shipping containers; shipping receipts; special collection boxes; and such options as return receipt service; COD service; waiver of signature; and pickup service. Call (800) 222-1811 for pickup service at a rate of $4.50, no matter how many pieces.

Rates:
Up to 8 ounces $9.95
Up to 2 pounds $13.95
Over 2 pounds, consult your local postmaster.

Contact Option

U.S. Postal Service
(800) 222-1811
All rates included here are as of May, 1993. Call the postal service at the above number to confirm prices.

The Top Reference Sources

The Address Book
Perigee, $9.95
(212) 951-8400

This sixth edition of Michael Levine's best-selling book provides mailing addresses to over 3,500 celebrities, corporate executives, and other important people. From Hank Aaron, to ZZ Top, Levine's book is a must for homes and offices.

It also includes a celebrity birthday list.

Postal Service (cont'd)

International Air Mail—Small Packets and Printed Matter

Weight Not Over	Canada	Mexico	Western Hemisphere (except Canada & Mexico)	Europe	Asia/Africa	Pacific Rim
1 oz	0.38	0.40	0.70	0.85	0.93	0.95
2 oz	0.60	0.63	1.07	1.35	1.57	1.61
3 oz	0.82	0.85	1.44	1.85	2.21	2.27
4 oz	1.04	1.07	1.81	2.35	2.85	2.93
6 oz	1.48	1.51	2.18	3.01	3.76	3.85
8 oz	1.92	1.95	2.55	3.67	4.67	4.77
10 oz	2.36	2.39	2.92	4.33	5.58	5.69
12 oz	2.80	2.83	3.29	4.99	6.49	6.61
1 lb	3.12	3.55	4.03	6.31	8.31	8.45
1.8 lb	3.72	4.40	5.51	8.95	11.95	12.13
2 lb	4.32	5.25	6.99	11.59	15.59	15.81
2.8 lb	5.12	6.10	8.39	14.09	19.14	19.41
3 lb	5.92	6.95	9.79	16.59	22.69	23.01
3.8 lb	6.72	7.80	11.19	19.09	26.24	26.61
4 lb	7.52	8.65	12.59	21.59	29.79	30.21
Each additional 1/2 lb over 4 lbs	.80	.85	1.40	2.50	3.55	3.60

Postal Business Centers

The U.S. Postal Service maintains 63 Business Centers around the country. The sole function of these offices is to provide businesses with help and support in sending bulk mail.

Location	Phone Number
Anchorage, AK	(907) 564-2824
Birmingham, AL	(205) 521-0549
Little Rock, AR	(501) 227-6639
Phoenix, AZ	(602) 225-5454
Tucson, AZ	(602) 325-9815
Long Beach, CA	(310) 983-3068
Los Angeles, CA	(213) 586-1843
Oakland, CA	(510) 874-8600
Sacramento, CA	(916) 923-4357
San Diego, CA	(619) 574-5268
San Francisco, CA	(415) 550-6565
San Jose, CA	(408) 723-6260
Santa Ana, CA	(714) 662-6490
Van Nuys, CA	(818) 787-8948
Denver, CO	(303) 297-6118
Hartford, CT	(203) 525-1490
Jacksonville, FL	(904) 366-4892
Miami, FL	(305) 470-0803
Orlando, FL	(407) 826-5695
Tampa, FL	(813) 871-6245
Duluth, GA	(404) 717-3440
Honolulu, HI	(808) 423-3925
Des Moines, IA	(515) 283-7642
Aurora, IL	(708) 978-4455
Carol Stream, IL	(708) 260-5510
Chicago, IL	(312) 286-8226
Indianapolis, IN	(317) 464-6272
Wichita, KS	(316) 946-4650
Louisville, KY	(502) 454-1784
New Orleans, LA	(504) 589-1366

Location	Phone Number
Boston, MA	(617) 338-9725
Springfield, MA	(413) 731-0306
Detroit, MI	(313) 961-6574
Grand Rapids, MI	(616) 776-6144
Minneapolis, MN	(612) 349-4700
Kansas City, MO	(816) 374-9513
Saint Louis, MO	(314) 534-2678
Jackson, MS	(601) 360-2700
Greensboro, NC	(919) 655-9740
Omaha, NE	(402) 573-2101
Manchester, NH	(603) 644-3888
Edison, NJ	(908) 777-0565
Albany, NY	(518) 869-6526
Buffalo, NY	(716) 851-2800
Elmsford, NY	(914) 345-1237
Flushing, NY	(718) 321-5700
Hauppauge, NY	(516) 582-7516
New York, NY	(212) 425-2158
Oklahoma City, OK	(405) 720-2675
Portland, OR	(503) 294-2306
Pittsburgh, PA	(412) 359-7601
Providence, RI	(401) 276-5038
Columbia, SC	(803) 731-5900
Memphis, TN	(901) 576-2020
Nashville, TN	(615) 872-8383
Coppell, TX	(214) 393-6701
Houston, TX	(713) 226-3348
San Antonio, TX	(512) 590-5578
Salt Lake City, UT	(801) 974-2299
Merrifield, VA	(703) 207-6800
Richmond, VA	(804) 775-6224
Seattle, WA	(206) 625-7016
Milwaukee, WI	(414) 287-2522

Federal Express

FEDERAL EXPRESS INVENTED the mass-market overnight delivery business in 1973. They now serve 185 countries and deliver to virtually every location in America. There are three basic classes of service:

- *Priority Overnight Service*: Delivered the next business day by 10:30 A.M.
- *Standard Overnight Service*: Delivered by 3 P.M. the next business day.
- *Economy Two-Day Service*: Second-business-afternoon delivery by 4:30 P.M.

The maximum weight for all three classes of service is 150 pounds per package. The maximum size of 165 inches must be figured out by a formula: ((longest side) + (next longest x 2)) + (shortest side x 2). Other services offered include:

- *Overnight Freight Service:* Either by noon or 4:30 P.M. the next business day. For packages weighing more than 150 pounds up to 750 pounds or more with advanced approval. A confirmed flight reservation is required in advance.
- *Two-Day Freight Service:* Second business day delivery by 4:30 P.M. Each piece may weigh more than 150 pounds and up to 1,500 pounds, or more, with advanced approval. For delivery commitment to Hawaii call in advance.

Federal Express Standard Rates

Weight	Priority Overnight	Standard Overnight	Economy Two-Day
Letter up to 8 oz	15.50	11.50	NA
1 lb	22.50	15.50	13.00
2 lb	24.25	16.50	14.00
3 lb	27.00	17.50	15.00
4 lb	29.75	18.50	16.00
5 lb	32.50	19.50	17.00
6 lb	35.25	21.25	18.00
7 lb	38.00	23.00	19.00
8 lb	40.75	24.75	20.00
9 lb	43.50	26.50	21.00
10 lb	46.25	28.25	22.00

Note: All prices $2.50 less if dropped off at a service center. Rates as of April, 1993.

Special Services in addition to the regular service charge:

- *Saturday Delivery:* Priority overnight shipments dropped off on Friday (call for the latest drop-off time) can be delivered on Saturday. Saturday delivery is available for two-day service and must be dropped off by Thursday. (There is an extra charge of $10.00 per package.)
- *Saturday Pickup:* Priority and Standard packages can be picked up on Saturdays. There is a $10.00 charge per package. There is no additional charge if the package is dropped off at a Service Center.
- *C.O.D.:* Available to destinations in the U.S. including Hawaii and Alaska. A check or money order is collected on delivery. (charge is $5 per destination)
- *Dangerous Goods Service:* $10.00 per package.
- *Address Correction:* $5.00
- *Billing Special Handling Fee:* $5.00
- *SeaTiger Service:* For cargo shipped from Asia to destinations in North America, Latin America, or Europe. Shipments travel by ship to the US and then by air to their final destinations. For more information call (800) 421-7581.
- *Air Charter Services*: (800) 238-0181
- *Telecommunications for the Deaf:* (800) 238-7777
- *Transportation of Animals:* (800) 238-5355
- *International Service:* Federal Express serves more than 185 countries. It offers a variety of services. For more information call (800) 247-4747

Saving Money on Federal Express

- Drop off packages instead of requesting pickup. If your business ships ten packages a day, you're currently paying as much as $25 per day for pickups.
- Negotiate a discount. Call (800) 238-5355 and ask for the number of your sales rep. Request a face-to-face meeting, and feel free to talk about your other delivery options. There is flexibility built in to the rates.
- Use Standard Overnight instead of Priority.
- Routinely request verbal proof of delivery on all packages, and ask for a refund for all packages delivered late.

Recommended Resource

Federal Express
General information (800) 238-5355
Billing and pricing inquiries (800) 622-1147

United Parcel Service

UNITED PARCEL SERVICE (UPS) is one of the most cost-effective ways to move packages across the country. They offer four levels of service:

- Ground
- Three Day Select
- Second Day Air
- Next Day Air

In all instances, the maximum weight of the package is 70 pounds. The maximum size of 130 inches is figured out by a formula: ((longest side) + (next longest side x 2)) + (shortest side x 2).

Ground

Pricing on UPS ground service, the most inexpensive means of shipping most packages, is based on zones. The price of a given shipment changes depending on the origin and destination zip codes. The zone map used by UPS is different in every part of the country.

The charts on the next two pages give the price of sending one-pound and five-pound packages to and from major cities. These numbers are only a guideline–contact UPS for precise figures.

Three Day Select

This new service provides guaranteed three day service throughout the country. Rates are based on the origin and destination zip code. Call (800) 742-5877 for pricing.

Second Day Air (Blue)

All packages sent by this service within the 48 contiguous states are charged a flat rate.

Next Day Air (Red)

All packages sent by this service within the 48 contiguous states are charged a flat rate.

UPS Air Pricing

Weight (lbs.)	Second Day Air	Next Day Air
Letter	5.50	10.50
1	5.75	14.75
3	7.25	17.25
5	8.50	20.00
10	14.50	28.75

All rates as of April, 1993.

The costs above do not reflect pick up charges. With 24 hours notice, UPS will pick up any number of packages for a single fee of $5.00. For Air packages, UPS will pick up on the same day for a charge of $3.25 per package.

Contact Option

United Parcel Service
(800) 742-5877

The Top Reference Sources

Bacon's Newspaper/Magazine Directory
Bacon's Information, $250
(312) 922-2400

The 1993 edition of this annual directory of magazines and newspapers offers descriptive editorial profiles of leading consumer magazines and prominent trade publications.

The reference also contains a listing of Hispanic newspapers, ad rates, and an index of multiple publishers for daily newspaper chains.

United Parcel Service, (cont'd)

UPS Rates, 1 Pound Package, Ground Service

		Atlanta, 30301	Baltimore, 21233	Boston, 02101	Chicago, 60601	Cincinnati, 45202	Cleveland, 44101	Columbus, 43216	Dallas, 75201	Denver, 80201	Detroit, 48231	Houston, 77052	Indianapolis, 46206	LA, 90806	Miami, 33101	Milwaukee, 53201
Atlanta	30301	2.28	2.66	2.74	2.66	2.66	2.66	2.66	2.74	2.83	2.66	2.74	2.66	2.97	2.66	2.74
Baltimore	21233	2.66	2.28	2.66	2.66	2.66	2.43	2.66	2.83	2.91	2.66	2.83	2.66	2.97	2.74	2.74
Boston	02101	2.74	2.66	2.28	2.74	2.74	2.66	2.74	2.91	2.91	2.74	2.91	2.74	2.97	2.83	2.74
Chicago	60601	2.66	2.66	2.74	2.28	2.43	2.43	2.43	2.74	2.74	2.43	2.74	2.28	2.91	2.83	2.28
Cincinnati	45202	2.66	2.66	2.74	2.43	2.28	2.43	2.28	2.74	2.83	2.43	2.74	2.28	2.97	2.74	2.43
Cleveland	44101	2.66	2.43	2.66	2.43	2.43	2.28	2.28	2.74	2.83	2.28	2.83	2.43	2.97	2.83	2.66
Columbus	43216	2.66	2.66	2.74	2.43	2.28	2.28	2.28	2.74	2.83	2.43	2.74	2.28	2.97	2.74	2.66
Dallas	75201	2.74	2.83	2.91	2.74	2.74	2.74	2.74	2.28	2.74	2.74	2.43	2.74	2.83	2.83	2.74
Denver	80201	2.83	2.91	2.91	2.74	2.83	2.83	2.83	2.74	2.28	2.83	2.74	2.74	2.74	2.91	2.74
Detroit	48231	2.66	2.66	2.74	2.43	2.43	2.28	2.43	2.74	2.83	2.28	2.83	2.43	2.97	2.83	2.43
Houston	77052	2.74	2.83	2.91	2.74	2.74	2.83	2.74	2.43	2.74	2.83	2.28	2.74	2.83	2.74	2.74
Indianapolis	46206	2.66	2.66	2.74	2.28	2.28	2.43	2.28	2.74	2.74	2.43	2.74	2.28	2.91	2.83	2.28
Los Angeles	90086	2.97	2.97	2.97	2.91	2.97	2.97	2.97	2.83	2.74	2.97	2.83	2.91	2.28	2.97	2.91
Miami	33101	2.66	2.74	2.83	2.83	2.74	2.83	2.74	2.83	2.91	2.83	2.74	2.83	2.97	2.28	2.83
Milwaukee	53201	2.74	2.74	2.74	2.28	2.43	2.66	2.66	2.74	2.74	2.43	2.74	2.28	2.91	2.83	2.28
Minneapolis	55401	2.74	2.74	2.83	2.66	2.66	2.74	2.66	2.74	2.74	2.66	2.83	2.66	2.91	2.91	2.43
New York	10001	2.28	2.28	2.43	2.74	2.66	2.66	2.66	2.83	2.91	2.66	2.83	2.74	2.97	2.83	2.74
Norfolk	23503	2.66	2.43	2.66	2.74	2.66	2.66	2.66	2.83	2.91	2.66	2.83	2.66	2.97	2.74	2.74
Phil.	19104	2.74	2.28	2.43	2.74	2.66	2.66	2.66	2.83	2.91	2.66	2.83	2.66	2.97	2.74	2.74
Phoenix	85201	2.91	2.97	2.97	2.91	2.91	2.91	2.91	2.74	2.66	2.91	2.83	2.91	2.66	2.97	2.91
Pitt.	15233	2.66	2.43	2.66	2.66	2.43	2.28	2.28	2.83	2.83	2.43	2.83	2.66	2.97	2.74	2.66
Portland	97208	2.97	2.97	2.97	2.91	2.97	2.97	2.97	2.91	2.74	2.97	2.97	2.97	2.74	2.97	2.91
Sacramento	95814	2.97	2.97	2.97	2.91	2.97	2.97	2.97	2.91	2.74	2.97	2.91	2.97	2.66	2.97	2.91
St. Louis	63166	2.66	2.74	2.83	2.43	2.43	2.66	2.66	2.66	2.74	2.66	2.66	2.74	2.91	2.83	2.66
San Antonio	78265	2.74	2.83	2.91	2.83	2.83	2.83	2.83	2.43	2.74	2.83	2.43	2.74	2.83	2.83	2.83
San Diego	92183	2.97	2.97	2.97	2.91	2.97	2.97	2.97	2.83	2.74	2.97	2.83	2.91	2.28	2.97	2.91
San Fran.	94142	2.97	2.97	2.97	2.97	2.97	2.97	2.97	2.91	2.74	2.97	2.91	2.97	2.66	2.97	2.97
Seattle	98101	2.97	2.97	2.97	2.91	2.97	2.97	2.97	2.91	2.83	2.97	2.97	2.97	2.74	2.97	2.91
Tampa	33602	2.66	2.74	2.83	2.74	2.74	2.74	2.74	2.74	2.91	2.74	2.74	2.74	2.97	2.43	2.83
DC	20090	2.66	2.28	2.66	2.66	2.66	2.43	2.66	2.83	2.91	2.66	2.83	2.66	2.97	2.74	2.74

		Minneapolis, 55401	New York, 10001	Norfolk, 23503	Philadelphia, 19104	Phoenix, 85201	Pittsburgh, 15233	Portland, 97208	Sacramento, 95814	St. Louis, 63166	San Antonio, 78265	San Diego, 92183	San Francisco, 94142	Seattle, 98101	Tampa, 33602	DC, 20090
Minneapolis	55401	2.28	2.74	2.83	2.74	2.83	2.74	2.91	2.91	2.66	2.83	2.91	2.91	2.83	2.83	2.74
New York	10001	2.74	2.28	2.43	2.78	2.97	2.66	2.97	2.97	2.74	2.91	2.97	2.97	2.97	2.74	2.43
Norfolk	23503	2.83	2.43	2.28	2.43	2.97	2.66	2.97	2.97	2.74	2.83	2.97	2.97	2.97	2.74	2.28
Phil.	19104	2.74	2.78	2.43	2.28	2.97	2.43	2.97	2.97	2.74	2.91	2.97	2.97	2.97	2.74	2.28
Phoenix	85201	2.83	2.97	2.97	2.97	2.28	2.97	2.83	2.74	2.83	2.74	2.66	2.74	2.83	2.91	2.97
Pitt.	15233	2.74	2.66	2.66	2.43	2.97	2.28	2.97	2.97	2.66	2.83	2.97	2.97	2.97	2.74	2.43
Portland	97208	2.91	2.97	2.97	2.97	2.83	2.97	2.28	2.28	2.91	2.91	2.74	2.28	2.28	2.97	2.97
Sacramento	95814	2.91	2.97	2.97	2.97	2.74	2.97	2.28	2.28	2.91	2.91	2.66	2.28	2.74	2.97	2.97
St. Louis	63166	2.66	2.74	2.74	2.74	2.83	2.66	2.91	2.91	2.28	2.74	2.91	2.91	2.91	2.74	2.74
San Antonio	78265	2.83	2.91	2.83	2.91	2.74	2.83	2.91	2.91	2.74	2.28	2.83	2.91	2.91	2.74	2.83
San Diego	92183	2.91	2.97	2.97	2.97	2.66	2.97	2.74	2.66	2.91	2.83	2.28	2.66	2.83	2.97	2.97
San Fran.	94142	2.91	2.97	2.97	2.97	2.74	2.97	2.28	2.28	2.91	2.91	2.66	2.28	2.74	2.97	2.97
Seattle	98101	2.83	2.97	2.97	2.97	2.83	2.97	2.28	2.74	2.91	2.91	2.83	2.74	2.28	2.97	2.97
Tampa	33602	2.83	2.74	2.74	2.74	2.91	2.74	2.97	2.97	2.74	2.74	2.97	2.97	2.97	2.28	2.74
DC	20090	2.74	2.43	2.28	2.28	2.97	2.43	2.97	2.97	2.74	2.83	2.97	2.97	2.97	2.74	2.28

United Parcel Service, (cont'd)

UPS Rates, 5 Pound Package, Ground Service

		Atlanta, 30301	Baltimore, 21233	Boston, 02101	Chicago, 60601	Cincinnati, 45202	Cleveland, 44101	Columbus, 43216	Dallas, 75201	Denver, 80201	Detroit, 48231	Houston, 77052	Indianapolis, 46206	LA, 90806	Miami, 33101	Milwaukee, 53201
Atlanta	30301	2.61	3.31	3.51	3.31	3.31	3.31	3.31	3.51	3.83	3.31	3.51	3.31	4.44	3.31	3.51
Baltimore	21233	3.31	2.61	3.31	3.31	3.31	2.90	3.31	3.83	4.03	3.31	3.83	3.31	4.44	3.51	3.51
Boston	02101	3.51	3.31	2.61	3.51	3.51	3.31	3.51	4.03	4.03	3.51	4.03	3.51	4.44	3.83	3.51
Chicago	60601	3.31	3.31	3.51	2.61	2.90	2.90	2.90	3.51	3.51	2.90	3.51	2.61	4.03	3.83	2.61
Cincinnati	45202	3.31	3.31	3.51	2.90	2.61	2.90	2.61	3.51	3.83	2.90	3.51	2.61	4.44	3.83	2.90
Cleveland	44101	3.31	2.90	3.31	2.90	2.90	2.61	2.61	3.51	3.83	2.61	3.83	2.90	4.44	3.51	3.31
Columbus	43216	3.31	3.31	3.51	2.90	2.61	2.61	2.61	3.51	3.83	2.90	3.51	2.61	4.44	3.51	3.31
Dallas	75201	3.51	3.83	4.03	3.51	3.51	3.51	3.51	2.61	3.51	3.51	2.90	3.51	3.83	3.83	3.51
Denver	80201	3.83	4.03	4.03	3.51	3.83	3.83	3.83	3.51	2.61	3.83	3.51	3.51	3.51	4.03	3.51
Detroit	48231	3.31	3.31	3.51	2.90	2.90	2.61	2.90	3.51	3.83	2.61	3.83	2.90	4.44	3.83	2.90
Houston	77052	3.51	3.83	4.03	3.51	3.51	3.83	3.51	2.90	3.51	3.83	2.61	3.51	3.83	3.51	3.51
Indianapolis	46206	3.31	3.31	3.51	2.61	2.61	2.90	2.61	3.51	3.51	2.90	3.51	2.61	4.03	3.83	2.61
Los Angeles	90086	4.44	4.44	4.44	4.03	4.44	4.44	4.44	3.83	3.51	4.44	3.83	4.03	2.61	4.44	4.03
Miami	33101	3.31	3.51	3.83	3.83	3.83	3.51	3.51	3.83	4.03	3.83	3.51	3.83	4.44	2.61	3.83
Milwaukee	53201	3.51	3.51	3.51	2.61	2.90	3.31	3.31	3.51	3.51	2.90	3.51	2.61	4.03	3.83	2.61
Minneapolis	55401	3.51	3.51	3.83	3.31	3.31	3.51	3.31	3.51	3.51	3.31	3.83	3.31	4.03	4.03	2.90
New York	10001	2.61	2.61	2.90	3.51	3.31	3.31	3.31	3.83	4.03	3.31	3.83	3.51	4.44	3.83	3.51
Norfolk	23503	3.31	2.90	3.31	3.51	3.31	3.31	3.31	3.83	4.03	3.31	3.83	3.31	4.44	3.51	3.51
Phil.	19104	3.51	2.61	2.90	3.51	3.31	3.31	3.31	3.83	4.03	3.31	3.83	3.31	4.44	3.51	3.51
Phoenix	85201	4.03	4.44	4.44	4.03	4.03	4.03	4.03	3.51	3.31	4.03	3.83	4.03	3.31	4.44	4.03
Pittsburgh	15233	3.31	2.90	3.31	3.31	2.90	2.61	2.61	3.83	3.83	2.90	3.83	3.31	4.44	3.51	3.31
Portland	97208	4.44	4.44	4.44	4.03	4.44	4.44	4.44	4.03	3.51	4.44	4.44	4.44	3.51	4.44	4.03
Sacramento	95814	4.44	4.44	4.44	4.03	4.44	4.44	4.44	4.03	3.51	4.44	4.03	4.44	3.31	4.44	4.03
St. Louis	63166	3.31	3.51	3.83	2.90	2.90	3.31	3.31	3.31	3.51	3.31	3.31	3.51	4.03	3.83	3.31
San Antonio	78265	3.51	3.83	4.03	3.83	3.83	3.83	3.83	2.90	3.51	3.83	2.90	3.51	3.83	3.83	3.83
San Diego	92183	4.44	4.44	4.44	4.03	4.44	4.44	4.44	3.83	3.51	4.44	3.83	4.03	2.61	4.44	4.03
San Fran.	94142	4.44	4.44	4.44	4.44	4.44	4.44	4.44	4.03	3.51	4.44	4.03	4.44	3.31	4.44	4.44
Seattle	98101	4.44	4.44	4.44	4.03	4.44	4.44	4.44	4.03	3.83	4.44	4.44	4.44	3.51	4.44	4.03
Tampa	33602	3.31	3.51	3.83	3.51	3.51	3.51	3.51	3.51	4.03	3.51	3.51	3.51	4.44	2.90	3.83
DC	20090	3.31	2.61	3.31	3.31	3.31	2.90	3.31	3.83	4.03	3.31	3.83	3.31	4.44	3.51	3.51

		Minneapolis, 55401	New York, 10001	Norfolk, 23503	Philadelphia, 19104	Phoenix, 85201	Pittsburgh, 15233	Portland, 97208	Sacramento, 95814	St. Louis, 63166	San Antonio, 78265	San Diego, 92183	San Francisco, 94142	Seattle, 98101	Tampa, 33602	DC, 20900
Minneapolis	55401	2.61	3.51	3.83	3.51	3.83	3.51	4.03	4.03	3.31	3.83	4.03	4.03	3.83	3.83	3.51
New York	10001	3.51	2.61	2.90	2.61	4.44	3.31	4.44	4.44	3.51	4.03	4.44	4.44	4.44	3.51	2.9
Norfolk	23503	3.83	2.90	2.61	2.90	4.44	3.31	4.44	4.44	3.51	3.83	4.44	4.44	4.44	3.51	2.61
Phil.	19104	3.51	2.61	2.90	2.61	4.44	2.90	4.44	4.44	3.51	4.03	4.44	4.44	4.44	3.51	2.61
Phoenix	85201	3.83	4.44	4.44	4.44	2.61	4.44	3.83	3.51	3.83	3.51	3.31	3.51	3.83	4.03	4.44
Pitt.	15233	3.51	3.31	3.31	2.90	4.44	2.61	4.44	4.44	3.31	3.83	4.44	4.44	4.44	3.51	2.90
Portland	97208	4.03	4.44	4.44	4.44	3.83	4.44	2.61	2.61	4.03	4.03	3.51	2.61	2.61	4.44	4.44
Sacramento	95814	4.03	4.44	4.44	4.44	3.51	4.44	2.61	2.61	4.03	4.03	3.31	2.61	3.51	4.44	4.44
St. Louis	63166	3.31	3.51	3.51	3.51	3.83	3.31	4.03	4.03	2.61	3.51	4.03	4.03	4.03	3.51	3.51
San Antonio	78265	3.83	4.03	3.83	4.03	3.51	3.83	4.03	4.03	3.51	2.61	3.83	4.03	4.03	3.51	3.83
San Diego	92183	4.03	4.44	4.44	4.44	3.31	4.44	3.51	3.31	4.03	3.83	2.61	3.31	3.83	4.44	4.44
San Fran.	94142	4.03	4.44	4.44	4.44	3.51	4.44	2.61	2.61	4.03	4.03	3.31	2.61	3.51	4.44	4.44
Seattle	98101	3.83	4.44	4.44	4.44	3.83	4.44	2.61	3.51	4.03	4.03	3.83	3.51	2.61	4.44	4.44
Tampa	33602	3.83	3.51	3.51	3.51	4.03	3.51	4.44	4.44	3.51	3.51	4.44	4.44	4.44	2.61	3.51
DC	20090	3.51	2.90	2.61	2.61	4.44	2.90	4.44	4.44	3.51	3.83	4.44	4.44	4.44	3.51	2.61

Postal Abbreviations

Alabama	AL
Alaska	AK
American Samoa	AS
Arizona	AZ
Arkansas	AR
California	CA
Colorado	CO
Connecticut	CT
Delaware	DE
District of Columbia	DC
Florida	FL
Georgia	GA
Hawaii	HI
Idaho	ID
Illinois	IL
Indiana	IN
Iowa	IA
Kansas	KS
Kentucky	KY
Louisiana	LA
Maine	ME
Marshall Islands	TT
Maryland	MD
Massachusetts	MA
Michigan	MI
Minnesota	MN
Mississippi	MS
Missouri	MO
Montana	MT
Nebraska	NE
Nevada	NV
New Hampshire	NH
New Jersey	NJ
New Mexico	NM
New York	NY
North Carolina	NC
North Dakota	ND
Ohio	OH
Oklahoma	OK
Oregon	OR
Pennsylvania	PA
Puerto Rico	PR
Rhode Island	RI
South Carolina	SC
South Dakota	SD
Tennessee	TN
Texas	TX
Utah	UT
Vermont	VT
Virginia	VA
Virgin Islands	VI
Washington	WA
West Virginia	WV
Wisconsin	WI
Wyoming	WY

The Top Reference Sources

AT&T Toll-Free 800 Directory, Business Edition
AT&T, $4.99
(800) 522-6364

This essential reference is filled with over 120,000 toll-free 800 listings that will let you comparison shop from coast-to-coast, for free.

Listings are alphabetical by company name in the white pages, and by classified headings in the yellow pages.

Manhattan Address Locator

MANHATTAN'S GRID ADDRESS SYSTEM makes it easy to find the location of a building once you know its address.

To locate avenue addresses, take the address, cancel the last figure, divide by 2, add or subtract the key number below. The location is the nearest numbered cross street (approximately).

To find addresses on numbered cross streets, remember–numbers closest to Fifth Ave. are closest to zero.

Avenue	Key
Ave. A	Add 3
Ave. B	Add 3
Ave. C	Add 3
Ave. D	Add 3
1st Ave.	Add 3
2nd Ave.	Add 3
3rd Ave.	Add 10
4th Ave.	Add 8
5th Ave.	
Up to 200	Add 13
Up to 400	Add 16
Up to 600	Add 18
Up to 775	Add 20
From 775 to 1286	Cancel last fig. and subtract 18
Up to 1500	Add 45
Above 2000	Add 24
Ave. of the Americas	Subt. 12
7th Ave.	Add 12
Above 110th St.	Add 20
8th Ave.	Add 10

Avenue	Key
9th Ave.	Add 13
10th Ave.	Add 14
Amsterdam Ave.	Add 60
Audubon Ave.	Add 165
Broadway (23 to 192)	Subt. 30
Columbus Ave.	Add 60
Convent Ave.	Add 127
Central Park West	Divide by 10 and add 60
Edgecombe Ave.	Add 134
Ft. Washington Ave.	Add 158
Lenox Ave.	Add 110
Lexington Ave.	Add 22
Madison Ave.	Add 26
Manhattan Ave.	Add 100
Park Ave.	Add 35
Pleasant Ave.	Add 101
Riverside Drive (to 165)	Divide by 10 and add 72
St. Nicholas Ave.	Add 110
Wadsworth Ave.	Add 173
West End Ave.	Add 60
York Ave.	Add 4

The Top Reference Sources

The Elements of Style
Macmillan
(212) 702-2000

This classic reference by William Strunk, Jr., and E.B. White is a required text in most high school and college English classes.

In six brief chapters, the book explains the basic rules of grammar and punctuation, plus principles of composition, matters of form, and words and expressions commonly misused. A valuable book for anyone who writes.

Mailroom Phone Directory

AIR FREIGHT & PACKAGE SERVICE	
A.A. Freight Forwarding	(800) 922-2017
Air Afrique Cargo Sales	(800) 288-4950
Air Canada Cargo	(800) 443-6235
Air Cargo Expeditors	(800) 952-1700
Air Delivery Service International	(800) 368-0066
Airborne Express	(800) 222-3049
Airgroup Express	(800) 843-4784
America West Airlines	(800) 228-7862
American Airlines Freight	(800) 638-7320
Amtrak	(800) 523-6590
Austrian Airline Cargo Service	(800) 637-2957
Cannonball Air Couriers	(800) 323-6850
Caribbean Air Cargo	(800) 654-7640
Consolidated Air Service	(800) 362-1906
Continental Airlines Quickpak	(800) 421-2456
Delta Airlines	(800) 638-7333
DHL Worldwide Express	(800) 225-5345
Emery Worldwide ACF	(800) 443-6379
Federal Express	(800) 238 5355
Global Mail	(800) 426-7478
Griffin Express	(800) 648-2310
Hawaii Air Cargo	(800) 227-3540
J & B Fast Freight	(800) 841-8029
Japan Airlines Air Cargo	(800) 424-9235
KLM Royal Dutch Airlines Cargo	(800) 556-9000
Kuwait Airway Cargo Sales	(800) 221-6727
Moonlite Courier	(800) 872-4113
Nippon Cargo Airlines	(800) 622-2746
Philippine Airlines	(800) 227-6144
Primac Courier	(800) 232-6245
Priority Air Express	(800) 922-7637
Priority Courier Group	(800) 433-4675
Qantas Airways Limited	(800) 227-0290
Service by Air	(800) 662-0160
Sky Cab	(800) 631-5488
United Airlines	(800) 631-1500
United Parcel Service	(800) 742-5877
U.S. Express	(800) 468-1012
U.S. Postal Service	(800) 333-8777

DELIVERY SERVICES	
Jack Rabbit Delivery Service	(800) 782-8149
Coman Courier Service	(800) 824-6420
Condor Distribution Service	(800) 628-2055
Courier Network USA	(800) 443-9016
DeSantis Despatch	(800) 962-7260
Sky & Highway Transportation	(800) 328-1972
FACSIMILE COMMUNICATIONS	
Mita Copystar America	(800) 222-6482
Omnifax Facsimile	(800) 221-8330
Panafax Fax Machines	(800) 843-0080
Pitney Bowes Facsimile Systems	(800) 672-6937
Sharp	(800) 237-4277
Toshiba Facsimile Systems	(800) 468-6744
FACSIMILE TRANSMISSION SERVICE	
Corporate Limited	(800) 322-1017
Facsimile Services	(800) 621-8201
Faxnet Telecommunications	(800) 831-1140
Swift Global Communications	(800) 722-9119
FREIGHT FORWARDING	
Air Express International	(800) 432-1888
American Overseas Movers	(800) 292-3311
ATMC	(800) 822-2215
Challenger Freight Systems	(800) 225-2836
Consolidated Air Service	(800) 362-1906
Freight X Network International	(800) 327-9046
PAGING SYSTEMS	
American Paging	(800) 235-6245
Nationwide Paging	(800) 346-3968
Paging Services of America	(800) 472-0037
TELEPHONE CONFERENCE SYSTEMS	
AT&T Alliance Teleconference	(800) 544-6363
AT&T Classic Teleconference	(800) 232-1234
American Conferencing	(800) 852-8852
Conference Call Service	(800) 272-5663
Conference Call USA	(800) 654-0455
Darome Teleconferencing	(800) 922-1124

Source: AT&T Toll-Free 800 Directory

Almanac Fact

In the average office, 19 paper copies are made of each original document.

Source: Lawrence Livermore Labs

World Time Chart

Place	If it is 11:00 A.M. EST	Time +/- Hrs.
Afghanistan	8:30 P.M.	9.5
Albania ‡	5:00 P.M.	6
Algeria	5:00 P.M.	6
American Samoa	5:00 A.M.	-6
Andorra ‡	5:00 P.M.	6
Angola	5:00 P.M.	6
Anguilla	12:00 P.M.	1
Antigua	12:00 P.M.	1
Argentina ◊	1:00 P.M.	2
Aruba	12:00 P.M.	1
Australia ◊		
Northern Territories	1:30 A.M*	14.5
Western Australia	12:00 A.M*	13
Other	2:00 A.M*	15
Austria ‡	5:00 P.M.	6
Baffin Island	11:00 A.M	0
Bahamas †	11:00 A.M	0
Bahrain	7:00 P.M.	8
Baja California	8:00 A.M	-3
Bangladesh	10:00 P.M.	11
Barbados	12:00 P.M.	1
Barbuda	12:00 P.M.	1
Belgium ‡	5:00 P.M.	6
Belize	10:00 A.M	-1
Benin	5:00 P.M.	6
Bermuda †	12:00 P.M.	1
Bhutan	10:00 P.M.	11
Bikini Island	4:00 A.M*	17
Bolivia	12:00 P.M.	1
Bophuthatswana	6:00 P.M.	7
Borneo	12:00 A.M*	13
Botswana	6:00 P.M.	7
Brazil ◊		
Fernando de Noronha	2:00 P.M.	3
East	1:00 P.M.	2
West	12:00 P.M.	1
Territory of Acre	11:00 A.M	0
British Guyana	12:00 P.M.	1
British Virgin Islands	12:00 P.M.	1
Bulgaria ‡	6:00 P.M.	7
Burkina Faso	4:00 P.M.	5
Burma	10:30 P.M.	11.5
Burundi	6:00 P.M.	7
Cameroon	5:00 P.M.	6
Canada †		
Atlantic Time	12:00 P.M.	1
Eastern Time	11:00 A.M	0
Central Time	10:00 A.M	-1
Mountain Time	9:00 A.M	-2
Pacific Time	8:00 A.M	-3
Canary Islands ‡	4:00 P.M.	5
Cape Verde Islands	3:00 P.M.	4
Cayman Island	11:00 A.M	0
Central African Republic	5:00 P.M.	6
Chad	5:00 P.M.	6
Chile ◊	12:00 P.M.	1
China ◊	12:00 A.M*	13
Colombia	11:00 A.M	0
Congo	5:00 P.M.	6
Cook Islands ◊	6:00 A.M	-5
Costa Rica	10:00 A.M	-1
Crete	6:00 P.M.	7
Cuba ◊	11:00 A.M	0
Cyprus ‡	6:00 P.M.	7
Czech Republic	5:00 P.M.	6
Denmark ‡	5:00 P.M.	6
Djibouti	7:00 P.M.	8
Dominica	12:00 P.M.	1
Dominican Republic	12:00 P.M.	1
Ecuador	11:00 A.M	0
Egypt ◊	6:00 P.M.	7
El Salvador	10:00 A.M	-1
Equatorial Guinea	5:00 P.M.	6
Ethiopia	7:00 P.M.	8
Falkland Islands ◊	12:00 P.M.	1
Fiji	4:00 A.M*	17
Finland ‡	6:00 P.M.	7
France ‡	5:00 P.M.	6
French Antilles	12:00 P.M.	1
French Guyana	1:00 P.M.	2
French Polynesia		
Gambier Island	7:00 A.M*	-4
Marquesa Island	6:30 A.M	-4.5
Society Island	6:00 A.M	-5
Galapagos Islands	10:00 A.M	-1
Germany ‡	5:00 P.M.	6
Ghana	4:00 P.M.	5
Gibraltar ‡	5:00 P.M.	6
Great Britain ‡	4:00 P.M.	5
Greece ‡	6:00 P.M.	7

*Based on Eastern Standard Time. *Indicates time on the following day.*
NOTE: Countries around the world shift to daylight savings time on different schedules.
† Add one hour to time shown from April 1 to October 27. ‡ Add one hour to time shown from March 25 to September 22.
◊ See list "Non-Standard Daylight Savings" on page 114 for details for this country.

World Time Chart (cont'd)

Place	If it is 11:00 A.M. EST	Time +/- Hrs.
Greenland	1:00 P.M.	2
Mesters Vig	4:00 P.M.	5
Scoresby Sound	3:00 P.M.	4
Thule	12:00 P.M.	1
Grenada	12:00 P.M.	1
Guadeloupe	12:00 P.M.	1
Guam	2:00 A.M*	15
Guatemala	10:00 A.M	-1
Guinea-Bissau	4:00 P.M.	5
Guyana	1:00 P.M.	2
Haiti †	11:00 A.M	0
Hawaii †	6:00 A.M	-5
Hebrides Island, U.K.	4:00 P.M.	5
Honduras	10:00 A.M	-1
Hong Kong	12:00 A.M*	13
Hungary ‡	5:00 P.M.	6
Iceland	4:00 P.M.	5
India	9:30 P.M.	10.5
Indonesia		
Jakarta	11:00 P.M.	12
Central	12:00 A.M*	13
East	1:00 A.M*	14
Iran	7:30 P.M.	8.5
Iraq ◊	7:00 P.M.	8
Ireland ‡	4:00 P.M.	5
Isle of Man, U.K.	4:00 P.M.	5
Isle of Wight, U.K.	4:00 P.M.	5
Israel ◊	6:00 P.M.	7
Italy ‡	5:00 P.M.	6
Ivory Coast	4:00 P.M.	5
Jamaica †	11:00 A.M	0
Japan	1:00 A.M*	14
Jordan ◊	6:00 P.M.	7
Kamaran Island	7:00 P.M.	8
Kenya	7:00 P.M.	8
Korea	1:00 A.M*	14
Kuwait	7:00 P.M.	8
Laos	11:00 P.M.	12
Lebanon ◊	6:00 P.M.	7
Liberia	4:00 P.M.	5
Libya ◊	5:00 P.M.	6
Liechtenstein ‡	5:00 P.M.	6
Luxembourg ‡	5:00 P.M.	6
Madagascar	7:00 P.M.	8
Malawi	6:00 P.M.	7

Place	If it is 11:00 A.M. EST	Time +/- Hrs.
Malaysia	12:00 A.M*	13
Mali	4:00 P.M.	5
Malta ‡	5:00 P.M.	6
Marshall Islands	4:00 A.M*	17
Martinique	12:00 P.M.	1
Mauritius	8:00 P.M.	9
Mexico †		
Mexico City, Yucatan	10:00 A.M	-1
Baja S., N. Pacific Coasts	9:00 A.M	-2
Baja N. above 28th parallel	8:00 A.M	-3
Micronesia		
Kosrae, Ponape Islands	3:00 A.M	16
Truk, Yap Islands	1:00 A.M*	14
Monaco ‡	5:00 P.M.	6
Mongolia ‡	12:00 A.M*	13
Morocco	5:00 P.M.	6
Mozambique	6:00 P.M.	7
Mustique, St. Vincent	12:00 P.M.	1
Namibia	6:00 P.M.	7
Nepal	9:30 P.M.	10.5
Netherlands ‡	5:00 P.M.	6
Netherlands, Antilles	12:00 P.M.	1
New Britain (Papua N.G.)	2:00 A.M*	15
New Caledonia	3:00 A.M*	16
Newfoundland, Canada	1:30 P.M.	2.5
New Zealand ◊	4:00 A.M*	17
Nicaragua	10:00 A.M	-1
Nigeria	5:00 P.M.	6
Norfolk Island	3:30 A.M*	16.5
N. Sound Island, British V.I.	12:00 P.M.	1
Northern Ireland, U.K.	4:00 P.M.	5
Norway ‡	5:00 P.M.	6
Pakistan	9:00 P.M.	10
Panama	11:00 A.M	0
Papua New Guinea	2:00 A.M*	15
Paraguay ◊	12:00 P.M.	1
Peru ◊	11:00 A.M	0
Philippines	12:00 A.M*	13
Pitcairn Island	8:00 A.M	-3
Poland ‡	5:00 P.M.	6
Portugal ‡	4:00 P.M.	5
Azores	3:00 P.M.	4
Maderia	4:00 P.M.	5
Pr. Edward Is., Indian Ocean	7:00 P.M.	8
Pr. Edward Is., Canada	12:00 P.M.	1

*Based on Eastern Standard Time. *Indicates time on the following day.*
NOTE: Countries around the world shift to daylight savings time on different schedules.
† Add one hour to time shown from April 1 to October 27. ‡ Add one hour to time shown from March 25 to September 22.
◊ See list "Non-Standard Daylight Savings" on page 114 for details for this country.

World Time Chart (cont'd)

Place	If it is 11:00 A.M. EST	Time +/- Hrs.
Puerto Rico	12:00 P.M.	1
Qatar	7:00 P.M.	8
Romania ‡	6:00 P.M.	7
Russia		
Moscow, European Part	7:00 P.M.	8
Baku, Gorki, Arkhangelsk	8:00 P.M.	9
Sverdlovsk	9:00 P.M.	10
Tashkent	10:00 P.M.	11
Novosibirsk	11:00 P.M.	12
Taymyr Pen.	12:00 A.M*	13
Vladivostok	2:00 A.M*	15
Magadan, Sakhalin	3:00 A.M*	16
Kamchatka Pen.	4:00 A.M*	17
Saint Barthelemy	12:00 P.M.	1
Saint Croix, U.S. V.I.	12:00 P.M.	1
Saint Helena Island	4:00 P.M.	5
Saint John, U.S. V.I.	12:00 P.M.	1
Saint Kitts	12:00 P.M.	1
Saint Lucia	12:00 P.M.	1
Saint Thomas, U.S. V.I.	12:00 P.M.	1
Saint Vincent, Grenadines	12:00 P.M.	1
Saudi Arabia	7:00 P.M.	8
Scotland, U.K.	4:00 P.M.	5
Senegal	4:00 P.M.	5
Seychelles	8:00 P.M.	9
Shetland Islands, U.K.	4:00 P.M.	5
Sicily, Italy	5:00 P.M.	6
Sierra Leone	4:00 P.M.	5
Singapore	12:00 A.M*	13
Somali	7:00 P.M.	8
South Africa	6:00 P.M.	7
Spain ‡	5:00 P.M.	6
Sri Lanka	9:30 P.M.	10.5
Sudan	6:00 P.M.	7
Swaziland	6:00 P.M.	7
Sweden ‡	5:00 P.M.	6
Switzerland ‡	5:00 P.M.	6
Syria ◊	6:00 P.M.	7
Tahiti	6:00 A.M	-5
Taiwan	12:00 A.M*	13
Tanzania	7:00 P.M.	8
Thailand	11:00 P.M.	12
Tibet	10:00 P.M.	11
Tierra del Fuego	1:00 P.M.	2
Trinidad & Tobago	12:00 P.M.	1
Tunisia	5:00 P.M.	6
Turkey ‡	6:00 P.M.	7
Turks & Caicos Islands †	4:00 A.M*	17
Uganda	7:00 P.M.	8
United Arab Emirates	8:00 P.M.	9

Place	If it is 11:00 A.M. EST	Time +/- Hrs.
United Kingdom	4:00 P.M.	5
Uruguay	1:00 P.M.	2
USA †		
Eastern Time	11:00 A.M	0
Central Time	10:00 A.M	-1
Mountain Time	9:00 A.M	-2
Pacific Time	8:00 A.M	-3
Alaska Time	7:00 A.M	-4
Hawaii Time	6:00 A.M	-5
Vancouver Island	8:00 A.M	-3
Venezuela	12:00 P.M.	1
Vietnam	11:00 P.M.	12
Virgin Gorda, British.V.I.	12:00 P.M.	1
Virgin Islands	12:00 P.M.	1
Wales	4:00 P.M.	5
West Indies	12:00 P.M.	1
Zaire	5:00 P.M.	6
Zambia	6:00 P.M.	7
Zanzibar	7:00 P.M.	8
Zimbabwe	6:00 P.M.	7

Based on Eastern Standard Time.

**Indicates time on the following day.*

Non-Standard Daylight Savings

Country	Daylight Savings Time
Argentina	December 1–March 3
Australia	October 8–March 17
Brazil	December 1–March 3
Chile	October 8–March 10
China	April 15–September 15
Cook Islands	October 8–March 17
Cuba	March 18–October 6
Egypt	May 4–September 29
Falkland Islands	September 10–April 14
Iraq	May 4–September 29
Israel	April 29–September 1
Jordan	May 4–September 29
Lebanon	May 1–October 14
Libya	May 1–October 14
New Zealand	October 8–March 17
Paraguay	December 1–March 3
Peru	January 1–March 31
Syria	May 4–September 19

NOTE: Countries around the world shift to daylight savings time on different schedules. † Add one hour to time shown from April 1 to October 27. ‡ Add one hour to time shown from March 25 to September 22.

International Mailing

European Country Codes

The following codes for mailings into specified European countries have been adopted by the Postal Direct Marketing Service, an association of thirteen European Postal Administrations.

Code for country where mail is being sent:

Belgium	B
Denmark	DK
Finland	SF
France	F
Germany	D
Great Britain	GB
Ireland	IRL
Netherlands	NL
Norway	N
Portugal	P
Spain	(no code)
Sweden	S
Switzerland	CH

International Organizations Providing Postal Information

European Direct Marketing Association
Isabelle Van Durme
Membership Services Manager
34 Rue de Gouvernement Provisoire
1000 Brussels
Belgium
32 (2) 217 63 09
Fax: 32 (2) 217 69 85

Postal Direct Marketing Service
Ms. Hermina Mirteza
Information Centre
Lersnerstrasse 23
W-6000 Frankfurt/Main 1
Germany
49 (69) 1530 1108
Fax: 49 (69) 1530 1144

Universal Postal Union (U.P.U.)
Case Postale
3000 Berne 15
Switzerland
41 (31) 43 22 11
Fax: 41 (31) 43 22 10

International Postal Authorities Providing Postal-Code Directories and Information

Algeria
Secretariat d'Etat aux Postes et Telecommunications
Direction des Services Postaux
4 Boulevard Salah Bouakouir
Sept Merveilles
16000 Algiers
Algeria
(in French and Arabic)
213 (2) 71 12 20
213 (2) 61 49 97

Argentina
De Ingo. Ruben J. Vanzini
Jefe Div. Desarrollo de Sistemas
Postales - Direc. Gral. de Correos
Sarmiento 151
1000 Buenos Aires
Argentina
(in Spanish)
Main office numbers
54 (1) 312-1247
Fax: 54 (1) 311-3111, 311-4385

Australia
Mr. Deane Welsh
Mail Network Group
Australia Post Headquarters, GPO Box 1777Q
Melbourne Vic 3001
Australia
(in English)
61 (3) 204 7387
Fax: 61 (3) 663-3735

Austria
Bundesministerium für Offentliche
Wirtschaft und Verkehr
Generaldirektion fur die Postund
Telegraphenverwaltung
Postgasse 8
1011 Vienna
Austria
(Information about addressing in German. The directory is evidently out of print.)
43 (1) 515 51/1200
Fax: 43 (1) 512 3542

Bahrain
Mohammed Salman Khalaf
Chief Administration & Accounts
Ministry of Transportation
Postal Directorate, P.O. Box No. 1212

International Mailing (cont'd)

Manama
Bahrain
(Limited information in English about the code. No directory available.)
or
Najma Al Janahi
Director of CPR Directorate
Central Statistics Organisation
Central Population Register, P.O. Box 5995
Manama
Bahrain
973 535151
Fax: 973 728989

Belgium
Regie des Postes
Direction Generale 7
Service Commercial
Centre Monnaie
1000 Brussels
Brussels
(in French and Flemish)
32 (2) 219 3860
Fax: 32 (2) 218 4962

Bermuda
Mrs. Velda D. Smith
Assistant Postmaster General
Operations and Internal Affairs
General Post Office, Hamilton
Bermuda
(in English)
1 (809) 295-5151

Brazil
Vera Carvalho
Head of International Affairs
Entreprise Bresillenne des Postes et Telegraphes
SBN-Conjunto 03
Bloco A-11 Andar
70002-900 Brasilia-DF Brazil
Brazil
(in Portuguese. Authorities will input the new code, at no charge, if you supply computer tapes.)
55 (61) 225-0995
Fax: 55 (61) 224-1175

Canada
National Philatelic Center
Canada Post Corporation, Station 1
Antigonish NS B2G 2R8
Canada
(Address for ordering directory in English and French. Cost: $10.00.)

Postal Code Management
Canada Post Corporation
Ottawa On K1A OB1
Canada
(Use this address for information on computer tapes, mailing standards.)
1 (613) 734-7799
Fax: 1 (613) 993-7536

Costa Rica
Marjorie Romero
Direccion de Comercializacion
Ministerio de Governacion
Direccion Nacional de Cominicaciones
Apdo. Postal 8000
San Jose 1000
Costa Rica
(in Spanish)
506 239766
Fax: 506 539902

Czech Republic
Ing. Stepan Vojtus, CSc.
Chief of Department
Sprava Post a Telekomunikaci
Olsanska 5
125 03 Prague 3
Czech Republic
(General information, in Czech, about former Czechoslovakia)
142 (2) 6919 160
Fax: 42 (2) 714 1111
or
Sprava Post a Telekomunikaci
o.z. Vakus, zavod 01
Holeknova 10
125 07 Prague 5
Czech Republic
(Inquiries about names on tape.)

Denmark
Generaldirecktoratet for Postog Telegrafvaesenet
Postvaesenet
Bernstorffsgade 36
1566 Copenhagen V
Denmark
(in Danish)
45 (33) 932410
Fax: 45 (33) 937795

Egypt
Mr. Ahmed M. El Far
General Director of Organization and Management
Ministry of Communication
The National Postal Organization
General Headquarters
11511 Cairo
Egypt
(in Arabic; details in English)
20 (2) 3914156
Fax: 20 (2) 3934807, 3934809

El Salvador
Direccion General de Correos
Centro de Gobierno
San Salvador
El Salvador
503 71-1922

International Mailing (cont'd)

Finland
Tuomo Visakko
Systems Analyst
Post of Finland, P.O. Box 200
00521 Helsinki
Finland
(in Finish)
358 (0) 153-7632
Fax: 358 (0) 153-7728
(Printed material not available; this individual will respond to requests for information.)

France
Annie Vidal
Pour de Chef de Centre du Cesfic
Responsable du Pole Fonctionnel
15 Boulevard du General de Gaulle
92126 Montrouge Cedex
France
(in French)
33 (46) 57.08.14

Germany
Deutsche Bundespost
Postdienst
Generaldirektion
Postfach 30 00
W-5300 Bonn 1
Germany
(in German)
49 (228) 14-0
49 (228) 14-8872
49 (228) 14-8876

Greece
Hellenic Post (ELTA)
Direction of Production and Sales
Division of Production
101 88 Athens
Greece
(in Greek)
30 (1) 3243 311
Fax: 30 (1) 3223 595
30 (1) 3213 185

Guatemala
Doro Ofelia Milian Garcia
Jefe Seccion de Reclamos
Direccion General de Correos y Telegrafos
01501 Guatemala City
Guatemala
(In Spanish)
502 (2) 84693

Hungary
Mr. Sandor Molnar
Head of Division
Direction Generale des Postes
Krisztina Krt. 6-8, 1540 Budapest
Hungary
(in Hungarian)
36 (1) 155 05 50
Fax: 36 (1) 155 75 84
or
Mr. Jeno Kis Pal
(above address)
36 (1) 156 52 93

Iceland
Torfi Porsteinsson
General Directorate of Posts & Telecommunications
Postal Division
150 Reykjavik
Iceland
(in Icelandic)
354 (1) 63 60 00
Fax: 354 (1) 63 60 39

India
R. Kishore
Member of Postal Service Board
Department of Posts
Dak Tar Bhavan, Parliament St.
New Delhi 110001
India
(in English; but hard to obtain)
91 (11) 3711254, 3032638
Fax: 91 (11) 3714893

Indonesia
Drs. Soepardjiman, Bc.A.P.
Postal Planning Centre
Jl. Llre Martadinata 21
Bandung 40115
Indonesia
(details in English)
62 (22) 436479
Fax: 62 (22) 441292

Ireland
Orla McKibbin
Public Relations Executive
An Post, General Post Office
O'Connell St.
Dublin 1
Ireland
(in English; chart of Dublin codes)
353 (1) 728888
Fax: 353 (1) 723553

Israel
Jacqueline Vuysje
Director of Customer Relations
Israel Postal Authority
30 Rue Yafa, 91999 Jerusalem
Israel
(major cities in Hebrew; settlements in English)
972 (2) 290624/5/6/7/8
Fax: 972 (2) 254692

International Mailing (cont'd)

Italy
The Central Director for the Postal Services
Viale America No. 201
00144 Rome
Italy
(in Italian)
39 (6) 54601
Fax: 39 (6) 5405890

Japan
International Relations Office
Postal Bureau
Ministry of Posts and Telecommunications
32, Kasumigaseki 1-chome
Chiyoda-ku, Tokyo
100-90 Japan
(in English; directory of major cities)
81 (3) 3540-4392, 4378
Fax: 81 (3) 3593-9124

Great Britain
Department of Postal Administration
P.O. Box 106
Postal Headquarters, St. Helier
Mont Millais
Jersey, Channel Islands
Great Britain
(in English)
44 (534) 26262
Fax: 44 (534) 73690

Republic of Korea
Director
International Postal Division
Ministry of Communications
Bureau of Posts
Seoul 110-777
Republic of Korea
(in English)
82 (2) 750-2232
Fax: 82 (2) 750-2236

Liechtenstein
(see Switzerland)

Luxembourg
Mr Germain Kayser
Organization Service
Post Division
2998 Luxembourg
352 4991-645
352 48 12 14

Malaysia
Director General of Posts
Postcode and Mail Circulation
Planning Section, 8th Floor General Post Office
Dayabumi Complex
Jalan Cheng Lock
50670 Kuala Lumpur
Malaysia
(separate translation of details into English)
60 (3) 2741122
Fax: 60 (3) 2741275

Malta
Department of Posts
Valletta
Malta
(in English)
356 224421
Fax: 356 226191

Mexico
Ing. Jorge E. Aldana Margain
El Jefe Del Departmento
Gerencia de Desarrollo Postal y Asuntos Internacionales
Depto. de Asuntos Internacionales
Ofs. 1121 Netzahualcoyotl 109
Col. Centro
06082 Mexico
Mexico
(in Spanish)
52 (5) 578-5377
Fax: 52 (5) 709-8985, 9981

Morocco
Laheen Ouassou
Le Chef du Service de l'Acheminement
Minister of Postes and Telecommunications
Rabat
Morocco
(in French and Arabic)
212 (7) 762091, 762093
Fax: 212 (7) 705362

Nepal
Divakar Devkota
International Relations
Postal Service Department
Dillibazar
Kathmandu 44603
Nepal
(in English. cost: $20)
977 411353

The Netherlands
S. van der Wolf
PTT Post, Postbus 30250
2500 GG S-Gravenhage
The Netherlands
(details in English)
31 (70) 334 28 05
Fax: 31 (70) 334 28 03

New Zealand
Mr. Graeme Hogan
Product Manager Business Mail
Marketing (Letters) Group
51 Hurstmere Rd., P.O. Box 33-646
Takapuna Auckland
New Zealand
(in English)
64 (9) 486-7027
Fax: 64 (9) 486-7036

International Mailing (cont'd)

Norway
Norway Post
P.O. Box 1181 Sentrum
0107 Oslo
Norway
(in Norwegian)
47 (2) 40 90 50
Fax: 47 (2) 42 66 87

Republic of Panama
Gaspar Muir
Director de Servicios, Postales y Telgraficos
Apartado 3421 Panama 4
Republic of Panama
(in Spanish)
507 28-2343, 8586
Fax: 507 25-2827

Philippines
Jesus O. Dasmarinas
Chief
Public Relations and Marketing Staff
Department of Transportation and Communication
Postal Services Department
Liwasang Bonifacio
1000 Manila
Philippines
(in English)
63 (2) 47-14-11 to 14

Poland
Iwona Malkiewicz
Marketing Manager
Postal Authority - Poland
00-903 Warsaw 3
Poland
(in Polish)
48 (22) 20-26-81; 20-04-63
Fax: 48 (22) 20-47-13

Portugal
Mr. Luis Gaspar
International Relations Service
Correios de Portugal
R. Conde Redondo, 79-6
1192 Lisbon Codex
Portugal
(in Portuguese)
351 (1) 3154030, Ext. 1202
Fax: 351 (1) 534880

Saudi Arabia
Mr. Samir Hamed Banajah
The Kingdom of Saudi Arabia
Directorate General of Posts
Ministry of P.T.T.
Riyadh 11142
Saudi Arabia
(in English and Arabic)

Republic of Singapore
Mr. Zubir Hussain for Director of Postal Services
Singapore Telecom
International Relations
750 Chai Chee Rd. £05-00 Chai Chee Complex
Singapore 1646
Republic of Singapore
(in English)
65 4443680

Republic of South Africa
Mr. S.A.D. Schmidt
c/o General Manager
Postal Services
South African Post Office Ltd.
Private Bag X377
Pretoria 0001 Republic of South Africa
(in English and Afrikaans)
27 (12) 311-34
Fax: 27 (12) 325-61

Spain
Direccion Postal
Direccion de Asuntos Internationales
Organismo Autonomo Correos
Palacio de Comunicaciones
Plaza de Cibeles
28070 Madrid
Spain
(in Spanish)
34 (1) 5220931, 5322355
Fax: 34 (1) 5210227

Sweden
Bo Jevrell
Posten Brev Adressing
105 00 Stockholm
Sweden
(in Swedish/on CD)
46 (8) 781 10 00
Fax: 46 (8) 21 63 35

Switzerland
Miss R. Strebel
General Direktion PTT
PB 12 3030 Berne
Switzerland
(in French and German)
41 (31) 62 23 44
Fax: 41 (31) 62 53 59

Taiwan
Jacob C.K. Chu, Director
Customer Services Center
Directorate General of Posts
Taipei 10603
Taiwan
(in Chinese)
886 (2) 3921310, 3921319
Fax: 886 (2) 3513310

International Mailing (cont'd)

Thailand
Director of Postal Services
Communications Authority Thailand
99 Chaeng Wattana Rd., Don Muang
Bangkok 10002
Thailand
(in English)
66 (2) 5731454
Fax: 66 (2) 5731454

Tunisia
Nejib Boulares
Le Sous Directeur des Etudes et de la Plannication Postale
Ministere des Communication
Direction des Services Postaux
1030 Tunis
Tunisia
(in French and Arabic)
216 (1) 660 088
Fax: 216 (1) 354 628

Uruguay
Dra. Serranan Bassini
Directora de Division
Asesoria Internacional
Direction Nationale des Correos
Montevideo, Uruguay
(in Spanish)
598 (2) 96 10 05
Fax: 598 (2) 95 21 59

United Kingdom
Information about the postcode is free. There is a charge for the directories.
Information about Postcodes and Services:
Keith May
Customer Services Manager
Royal Mail, National Postcode Centre
3 & 4 St. Georges Business Centre
St. Georges Sq.
Portsmouth PO1 3AX
44 (705) 870307
Fax: 44 (705) 838518

Marketing (Large Businesses):
Stuart Pretty
Large Business Marketing Manager
Royal Mail, National Postcode Centre
3 & 4 St. Georges Business Centre
St. Georges Sq.
Portsmouth PO1 3AX
44 (705) 870307
Fax: 44 (705) 838518

Promotion of Postcodes/Information:
Steve Griffiths
Small Business Communications Mgr.
Royal Mail House 148-166 Old St.
London EC1V 9HQ
44 (71) 250-2057

Development of New Postcode Products:
Anne Wine
Product Development Manager
Royal Mail House
148-66 Old St.
London EC1V 9HQ
44 (71) 250-2307

United States
For information about services available from foreign postal authorities and information on international mailing:
Barry E. Burns
International Product Manager
International Business Department
United States Postal Service, Room 5437
475 l'Enfant Plaza SW
Washington, DC 20260
(212) 268-2276
Fax: (212) 268-5493

Printed Materials:
International Mail Manual
(subscription service: $16/year)
Postal Bulletin
(subscription service: $56/year domestic; $70/year international)
Superintendent of Documents
U.S. Government Printing Office
941 North Capitol St., NE
Washington, DC 20402
(202) 783-3238
Fax: (202) 512-2233

Military Overseas Zip Code Directory
National Address Information Center
Attn: Military APO/FPO Zip Codes
6060 Primacy Pkwy., Suite 101
Memphis, TN 38188
(800) 238-3150 (U.S. only)
Fax: (901) 767-8853 (free of charge)

1992 National Five-Digit ZIP Code & Post Office Directory (2 volumes)
Superintendent of Documents
U.S. Government Printing Office
732 N. Capitol St., NW
Washington, DC 20402
(202) 783-3238
Fax: (202) 572-2250
($15 soft cover; $20 hard cover)
(GPO stock # 039-000-00280-9)

Recommended Resource

1993 Guide to Worldwide Postal-Code & Address Formats
Marian Nelson, Editor
35 W. 90th St.
New York, NY 10024
(212) 362-9855

Corporate Administration

Charity and the Corporation

U.S. CORPORATIONS CONTRIBUTED just under $6 billion to nonprofit charitable organizations in 1990. In recent years, companies have continued to make increasingly larger contributions to foundations or organized projects. Studies indicate that during the 20 years from 1970 to 1990, contributions rose from $797 million to $5.9 billion.

Experts point out that the reasons for this largesse range from altruism to practical self-interest and include the following:

- To seek to improve the quality of life in a specific geographic region;
- To ensure a steady supply of future employees from within the community;
- To maintain a favorable corporate perception in the eyes of both employees and customers;
- To qualify for tax advantages by contributing to organizations that are registered with the IRS;
- To enhance a corporate image and influence the opinions of legislators.

Those who assess these trends predict that corporate contributions which have maintained a level of 1.7-1.9 percent of pre-tax income over the last 10 years will continue at this rate.

Recommended Resource

The Foundation Directory
The Foundation Center
79 Fifth Ave.
New York, NY 10003
(212) 620-4230

Supporters of the Arts & Charities

WHAT TYPES OF CHARITIES have been the recipients of corporate contributions? Research indicates that education has been the main focus of corporate charity. Thirty-eight percent of corporate giving has been directed to public education through programs directed at elementary through post-secondary education programs with a major focus given to the precollege level. Many of these contributions are in the form of human resources such as business/education partnerships. These projects provide personal involvement through programs designed to expand the horizons of the nation's youth in preparation for their participation in the work force.

Health and human services have received 26 percent of the corporate dollar while culture and arts have accounted for 11 percent. Civic and community activities have received 14 percent of the contributions with a major focus being on the environment.

Contact Options

Council on Foundations
1828 L St., NW, Suite 300
Washington, DC 20036
(202) 466-6512
Information on starting a philanthropic program.

The Foundation Center
79 Fifth Ave.
New York, NY 10003
(212) 620-4230
Information on foundations and corporate-giving programs.

Corporate Philanthropy: Where are the Dollars Going?

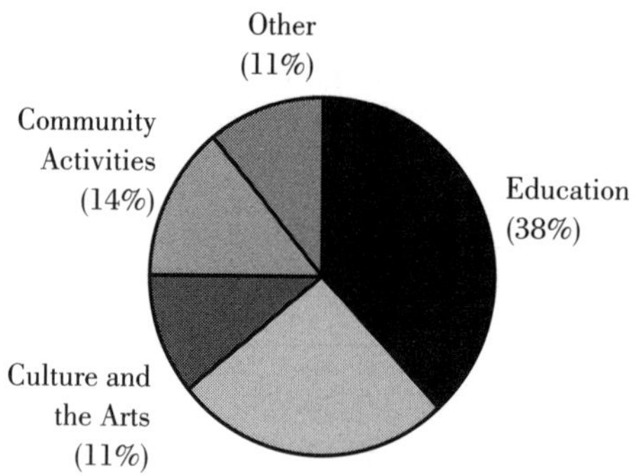

Source: The Conference Board

Charitable Contributions

CORPORATE CITIZENS ARE those businesses that recognize the interconnectedness between industry and the surrounding world. This awareness prompts these companies to make notable philanthropic contributions to charitable organizations that support the major categories of public education, health and human services, culture and arts, and civic and community activities.

There is sometimes a veil of secrecy regarding a corporation's charitable contributions. The National Committee for Responsible Philanthropy reports that of 200 of the largest profit-making corporations in the country, approximately 25 percent make no contribution information available to grant seekers or to the general public, even after requested to do so. This reluctance to disclose philanthropic information may be an attempt to discourage those seeking corporate hand-outs or may be an attempt to obscure the company's parsimony.

The Council on Economic Priorities profiled 100 companies and assessed their records of charitable contributions based on percent of pre-tax income budgeted for charity. According to the Council, an annual outlay of one percent of pre-tax dollars is considered an average charitable program. Fifty-nine of the 100 companies surveyed met or exceeded this criteria. The ratings that follow were determined by the amount of giving, based on worldwide taxable earnings, as well as corporate-giving programs which donated millions of dollars worth of drugs, equipment, medical supplies, or food products.

Company (% of pre-tax dollars to charity)

Ben & Jerry's Homemade (7.5)
Hewlett-Packard (5.2*)
Cummins Engine Company (5.0)
Dayton-Hudson (5.0)
H.B. Fuller (5.0)
Herman Miller (5.0)
Polaroid (4.0)
The Stride Rite (4.0)
Quaker Oats (3.0)
Sara Lee (2.9*)
General Mills (2.7*)
J.P. Morgan (2.6)
Digital Equipment (2.5)
Merck (2.5*)
Rouse (2.5)
Procter & Gamble (2.2*)
Atlantic Richfield (ARCO) (2.1)
Chambers Development (2.1)
Ashland Oil (2.0**)
Curtice-Burns (2.0**)
Chase Manhattan (2.0**)
Norwest (2.0**)
New York Times (2.0**)
Tasty Baking (2.0**)
Tektronix (2.0**)
Texas Instruments (2.0**)
Yellow Freight Systems (2.0**)
Colgate-Palmolive (2.0)
Huffy (2.0)
Tennant (2.0)
American Telephone and Telegraph (1.0-2.0)
General Mills (1.9)
International Business Machines (1.9)
Hershey Foods (1.8)
Minnesota Mining & Mfg. (3M) (1.8*)
Allied-Signal (1.7)
Deluxe (1.7)
General Electric (1.6*)
McDonnell Douglas (1.6)
Upjohn (1.6*)
American Express (1.5)
Lifeline Systems (1.5)
JC Penney (1.5)
PepsiCo (1.5)
Sara Lee (1.5)
Caterpillar (1.4)
H.J. Heinz (1.4*)
Kmart Corp. (1.4*)
Time Warner (1.4)
Eastman Kodak (1.3)
General Dynamics (1.3)
Apple Computer (1.2)
Kellogg Co. (1.2)
Pfizer (1.2)
Scott Paper (1.2)
Bristol-Myers Squibb (1.1)
Clorox (1.1)
The Coca-Cola (1.1)
General Electric (1.1)
General Motors (1.1)
Quaker Oats (1.1)
Rockwell International (1.1)
Sears, Roebuck (1.1)
Westinghouse Electric (1.1)
Campbell Soup (1.0)
Chevron Industries (1.0)
E.I. du Pont de Nemours (1.0)
Houghton Mifflin (1.0)
Liz Claiborne (1.0)
Merck (1.0)
Pitney Bowes (1.0)

**Companies including dollar value of in-kind gifts in charitable giving.*

***Greater Than 2.0%*

Source: The Better World Investment Guide

Almanac Fact

Fortune magazine produces an annual issue devoted to the most admired corporations in America. Corporate citizenship is one of the criteria upon which the candidates are judged. The top three corporations in 1992, based on their attention to community and environmental responsibility, were Merck, Johnson & Johnson, and Rubbermaid.

Source: "America's Most Admired Corporations," Fortune, February 10, 1992

The United Way and Alternatives

LAST YEAR, THE UNITED WAY raised more than $3 billion. With 2,100 autonomous local agencies and a host of more than 44,000 public service groups supported, the United Way continues to be a significant element in corporate philanthropy.

Less than 16% of the money raised by the United Way goes to cover overhead. Because of the large number of volunteers—many of them on loan from corporations—the United Way is able to keep costs low.

In an increasingly aware labor force, employees have expressed concern that the corporate-giving program selected for their company did not represent their charitable interests. As a result, alternative funds have been established. These are umbrella organizations that represent multiple charities with the same focus. Such programs offer an alternative to the donor who prefers to contribute to a specific type of cause not encompassed in another fund.

Contact Options

The United Way of America
(703) 836-7100

For the local agency in your area, check the white pages of your phone book.

Earth Share
(800) 875-3862

Represents 40 environmental organizations including American Farmland Trust, the National Audubon Society, the Rainforest Alliance, the Sierra Club Foundation, and the Wilderness Society.

Independent Charities of America
(800) 477-0733

Represents 244 organizations including Disabled American Veterans Charitable Service Trust, Toys for Tots and Ronald McDonald House.

International Service Agencies
(800) 638-8079

Represents 34 groups including CARE, the U.S. Committee of UNICEF, Save the Children, Project Hope, Catholic Relief Services, and Oxfam.

National/United Services Agencies
(800) 458-9505

Represents 65 organizations including the Make-a-Wish Foundation, the Children's Defense Fund, Farm Aid, Covenant House, the NAACP Legal Defense and Education Fund, and Phyllis Schlafly's Eagle Forum.

National Voluntary Health Agencies
(202) 467-5913

Represents Alzheimer's Association, the American Cancer Society, the Muscular Dystrophy Association and the National Kidney and Myasthenia Gravis foundations.

United Negro College Fund
(212) 326-1100

Represents 41 primarily African-American colleges and universities.

National Coalition of United Arts Funds
(212) 223-2787

Represents 60 funds which support symphonies, the ballet, zoos, museums, the theater, and historical societies.

Selecting an Alternative Fund

The National Committee for Responsive Philanthropy (NCRP) was organized in 1976 to make more information about philanthropic funds available to the public. As a watchdog group, the NCRP pressed for disclosure of foundation funds available and sought to create alternatives to the corporate charity fund-raising efforts of the United Way. As a result of the organization's efforts, alternative funds were established to organize charities not covered under the United Way. Employees are frequently offered a choice of target funds for their contributions, both through payroll deductions and from direct fund-raisers.

Apple Computer was one of the first Fortune 500 companies to offer employees the opportunity to contribute through their company to alternatives to the United Way. Other companies have followed suit as increasing awareness of employee preferences has occurred.

In order to find alternative funds in a particular area, interested individuals should contact the NCRP which assists in establishing such funds and provides a booklet describing each of the alternative funds.

Contact Options

National Committee for Responsive Philanthropy
2001 S St., NW, Suite 620
Washington, DC 20009
(202) 387-9177

The Top Charities

The Top 25 Charities Ranked by Income

Rank	Organization	Income ($ millions)	Administrative Costs (%)
1	Catholic Charities	1,538.6	9.7
2	Lutheran Social Ministry Organization	1,486.7	NA
3	American Red Cross	1,465.6	4.7
4	Young Men's Christian Association	1,438.5	NA
5	Salvation Army	1,215.5	17.1
6	UNICEF	821.0	8.4
7	Goodwill Industries of America	664.1	8.0
8	Association for Retarded Citizens	464.0	12.5
9	Boy Scouts of America	430.0	13.2
10	United Jewish Appeal	426.6	0.7
11	Shriners Hospitals for Crippled Children	413.9	2.1
12	Planned Parenthood	383.7	13.5
13	Jewish Community Centers Association	380.0	12.2
14	American Cancer Society	365.5	7.1
15	United Cerebral Palsy Association	359.9	12.7
16	CARE	293.5	2.4
17	National Easter Seal Society	288.5	9.9
18	American Heart Association	264.4	7.7
19	Boys and Girls Clubs of America	239.6	NA
20	Volunteers of America	239.2	12.5
21	Nature Conservancy	223.2	6.6
22	Catholic Relief Services	220.0	5.1
23	World Vision	215.5	7.6
24	City of Hope	157.0	10.2
25	March of Dimes	124.4	9.3

NA = not available

Source: The Non-Profit Times

Total income for these charities may come from public support, government support, investment, or member dues. The *Chronicle of Philanthropy* lists the top ten charities in 1991 based on contributions alone:

Rank	Organization	Contributions ($ millions)
1	United Jewish Appeal	668.1
2	Salvation Army	649.0
3	Second Harvest of Chicago	404.5
4	American Red Cross	386.1
5	Catholic Charities USA	368.3
6	American Cancer Society	346.3
7	American Heart Association	235.7
8	UJA Fed. of Philanthropies of NYC	235.5
9	YMCA of the USA	214.5
10	Boy Scouts of America	209.6

Almanac Fact

Roughly one-quarter of the nation's 200 largest profit-making corporations make no information on charitable contributions available to grant seekers or the public.

Source: National Committee for Responsive Philanthropy

Foundations and Grants

THERE ARE FOUR MAJOR types of foundations in operation throughout the country today.

Independent or Private Foundations

These foundations are frequently funded through the gift of an individual or a family. The foundations provide grants to individuals or institutions that meet the specific criteria for proposed application of philanthropic funds. The ten largest independent foundations and the total grant amounts are:

Foundation	Total Grants ($)
The Ford Foundation	227,828,194
The Pew Charitable Trusts	155,113,636
W.K. Kellogg Foundation	121,974,324
J.D. and C.T. MacArthur Foundation	115,675,981
The Robert Wood Johnson Foundation	112,022,743
Lilly Endowment, Inc.	107,930,515
The Andrew W. Mellon Foundation	74,467,370
The Rockefeller Foundation	74,414,356
The Annenberg Foundation	59,559,779
Kresge Foundation	48,792,000

Source: The Foundation Directory, 1992

Company-Sponsored Foundations

Company-sponsored foundations are funded by endowments and annual contributions of a profit-making corporation. These foundations are generally independent of the corporation. However, the grants awarded by the groups frequently reflect the interests of the corporation and are often made in the community in which the corporation is located.

The largest company–sponsored foundations, based on amount of gifts received, include:

Foundation	Gifts Received ($)
Procter & Gamble Fund	50,000,000
Alabama Power Foundation	25,000,000
General Cinema Corporation Charitable Foundation	24,854,375
US WEST Foundation	20,329,415
Georgia Power Foundation	20,000,000
Amoco Foundation	18,154,979
PepsiCo Foundation	18,000,000
GTE Foundation	17,693,782
Dayton Hudson Foundation	16,974,000
Southwestern Bell Foundation	16,095,200

Source: Foundation Giving, The Foundation Center, 1992

Community Foundations

Community foundations usually appeal to the general public for contributions that are used annually in support of ongoing local services. Their funds come from many sources rather than a single donor, and they are usually classified as public charities under tax law.

The top ten community foundations or public charities, based on total grants and total assets, are as follows:

Community Foundation	Total Grants ($)	Total Assets ($)
New York Community Trust	56,514,099	842,116,981
Chicago Community Trust	31,383,963	295,928,031
Cleveland Foundation	30,487,607	573,012,252
Communities Foundation of Texas	24,571,960	205,225,229
Marin Community Foundation	21,545,000	482,431,000
San Francisco Foundation	21,380,363	226,099,459
Boston Foundation	15,128,113	246,660,847
Columbus Foundation	11,439,352	150,581,845
St. Paul Foundation	11,144,298	152,250,345
Hartford Foundation for Public Giving	9,302,421	151,387,286

Operating Foundations

Operating foundations are organizations which use their resources for research or for a specific service. Funding usually comes from an endowment from a single source; however, the foundation is eligible for tax deductible contributions from the public. These groups provide few grants since the contributions are earmarked for specific purposes.

The largest operating foundations based on assets include:

Foundations	Assets ($)
J. Paul Getty Trust	3,691 billion
Norton Simon Foundation	288 million
Robert Welch Foundation	238 million
Amherst H. Wilder Foundation	206 million
Annie E. Casey Foundation	189 million
Norton Simon Art Foundation	165 million
Wunsch Americana Foundation	142 million
Charles F. Kettering Foundation	104 million
Russell Sage Foundation	97 million
Menil Foundation	93 million

Source: The Foundation Directory, 1992

Environmental Awareness

THE AVERAGE WORKER IN AN AMERICAN office is responsible for discarding 180 pounds of high-grade recyclable paper every year.

While federal laws are designed to protect the environment against unscrupulous industrial pollution, the corporate citizen can take steps to promote environmental awareness both within and outside of the company through the education of its employees.

Six Simple Projects for Office Conservation:

The following are some simple suggestions from conservation specialists regarding ways in which the corporate citizen can protect the environment:

- Ask employees to bring a coffee cup to work instead of using styrofoam or other disposable cups.
- Set up glass and aluminum recycling programs with containers in lunchrooms or next to beverage machines.
- Set up a paper recycling program with containers at each employee's desk or in central locations. The recyclable papers can be collected and placed in outdoor containers by the custodial staff.
- Investigate a two-sided copy machine to reduce the amount of paper used in copying reports.
- Investigate conducting an energy audit to determine what minor changes can result in significant savings in energy and dollars.
- Investigate water saving measures such as installing faucet aerators, and toilet water displacement devices.

Recommended Resources

50 Simple Things You Can Do to Save the Earth
by The Earthworks Group
Earthworks Press

Design for a Livable Planet
by Jon Naar
HarperCollins Publishing

Directing Corporate Dollars

National organizations will make presentations to companies to promote environmental programs that seek corporate funding. They will readily explain organized programs that can be set up to direct corporate dollars to preserving and enhancing the environment on a national and global level.

Contact Options

Earth Share
(800) 875-3862
Umbrella organization for 40 environmental groups.

Other independent regional organizations will provide information sessions to corporate employees regarding opportunities to extend their support throughout and beyond the workplace environment.

Environmental Action Coalition
625 Broadway
New York, NY 10012
(212) 677-1601

Individuals interested in directing their contributions and efforts to local environmental needs may contact one of several federations that operate in a variety of states. These environmental federations raise funds for regional conservation organizations and will frequently make presentations to corporate gatherings regarding such programs.

Contact Options

Environmental Federations by state:

Environmental Fund for Arizona
(602) 254-9330
Earth Share of California
(415) 882-9330
Nature Conservancy of Florida
(407) 628-5887
Environmental Fund for Georgia
(404) 934-0334
Environmental Fund for Illinois
(312) 939-1530
Environmental Fund for Indiana
(317) 685-8800
Environmental Fund for Michigan
(617) 332-1741
Minnesota Environmental Fund
(612) 379-3850
Missouri Coalition for the Environment
(314) 727-0600
Environmental Federation of New England
(617) 542-3363
Environmental Federation of New York
(518) 436-0421
Environmental Federation of North Carolina
(919) 687-4840
Environmental Federation of Oregon
(503) 223-9015
Environmental Fund for Pennsylvania
(215) 763-3602
Environmental Fund for Texas
(512) 472-5518
Environmental Fund for Virginia
(804) 977-4090
Earth Share of Washington
(206) 622-9840

Hiring the Disabled/Disadvantaged

THE AMERICANS WITH DISABILITIES ACT (ADA), July 26, 1992, prohibits discrimination against qualified individuals, defined as persons "with a physical or mental impairment that substantially limits one or more major life activities."

According to the U.S. Department of Education, Rehabilitation Services Administration, federal and state governments spent $1.9 billion in rehabilitation services designed to restore, preserve and develop the ability of disabled persons to function in productive activity. The responsible corporate citizen seeks ways to utilize the skills of all individuals. Advocates for such efforts point out that corporations can extend opportunities beyond the workplace into the community to allow disadvantaged or handicapped individuals the chance to perform jobs that will benefit the organization. A company may, for example, direct a corporate mailing project to a local organization that specializes in work/rehabilitation programs. Such groups are found in the Yellow Pages of the telephone book under "letter shop services."

Community Outreach

THE COUNCIL ON ECONOMIC PRIORITIES profiled 100 companies using a criterion of community outreach for a basis of judgment of corporate citizenship. Corporations receiving high marks included those that developed programs which promoted education, housing and/or volunteerism. Such companies invest in depressed neighborhoods, while others establish corporation foundations to fund programs that will support the community.

The companies with high scores in the area of community outreach include:

American Express
AT&T
Amoco
Apple Computer
Atlantic Richfield (ARCO)
Ben & Jerry's Homemade
Campbell Soup Company
Chevron Industries
Clorox
Delta Air Lines
Deluxe
Digital Equipment
Eastman Kodak
Ford Motor
H.B. Fuller
Gannett
General Mills
General Motors
Hawaiian Electric Industries
Herman Miller
Hershey Foods
Hewlett-Packard
IBM
Johnson & Johnson
Kellogg Co.
McDonalds
Merck
3M
JC Penney
PepsiCo
Pitney Bowes
Polaroid
Procter & Gamble
Quaker Oats
Rouse
Rubbermaid
Ryder System
Schering-Plough
Scott Paper
Sears, Roebuck
Time Warner
Walt Disney
Westinghouse Electric
Xerox

Source: The Better World Investment Guide

Recommended Resource

The Better World Investment Guide
Council on Economic Priorities
30 Irving Pl.
New York, NY 10003
(212) 420-1133

The Top Reference Sources

National Directory of Corporate Giving
The Foundation Center
(212) 620-4230

This directory profiles 1,791 companies making contributions to nonprofit organizations. It is intended for use by grantseekers in locating potential support, grantmakers in learning more about other grantseekers, scholars researching the field, journalists reporting on contributions activities of the corporate world, and everyone generally interested in philanthropy.

It lists company, address, contacts, financial data, types of philanthropic support, geographic limitations, and application information.

Corporate Responsibility

CORPORATE RESPONSIBILITY CAN BE expressed in a full range of business responses to the needs of society. It can be in the form of direct giving of funds to a targeted nonprofit organization. In addition, a corporation may elect to become directly involved in a project such as the Adopt-a-School Program in which corporations provide services rather than direct dollars to the target school or school district. The participating company supplies mentors, tutors, facilities, equipment, and technology in order to have a positive impact on the educational progress, and consequently exercises considerable control over its own benevolence.

Still other corporations establish company foundations that direct contributions to worthwhile programs or projects. This option offers companies more control over their contribution dollars and permits direction of these funds to specific areas or needs. The largest company-based foundations are listed in "Foundations and Grants." Advice on establishing a corporate foundation may be obtained from organizations that monitor and counsel foundations.

Contact Option

The Foundation Center
79 Fifth Ave., 8th Floor
New York, NY 10013
(212) 620-4230

Socially Conscious Investments

A HEIGHTENED SENSE OF CIVIC responsibility is being expressed in the types of investments selected by individual and corporate investors. Frequently investors will seek not only a return on their expenditure, but also a vehicle to express their concerns regarding corporate and public policies.

There are several investment funds that deal with socially and environmentally responsible companies.

Affirmative Investments Group
129 South St.
Boston, MA 02111
(800) 525-4847

Calvert Social Investment Fund
1700 Pennsylvania Ave., NW
Washington, DC 20006
(800) 368-2750
(301)951-4820

Dreyfus Third Century Fund
200 Park Ave.
New York, NY 10166
(212) 922-6000

Parnassus Fund
1427 Shrader St.
San Francisco, CA 94117
(800) 999-3505 or (415) 362-3505

Social Investment Forum
430 First Ave. N.
Minneapolis, MN 55401
(612) 333-8338

Socially Responsible Banking Fund
Vermont National Bank
P.O. Box 804-C
Brattleboro, VT 05301
(800) 544-7108

Working Assets Money Fund
230 California St.
San Francisco, CA 94111
(800) 533-3863

Recommended Resources

The Better World Investment Guide
Council on Economic Priorities
30 Irving Pl.
New York, NY 10003
(212) 420-1133

Design for a Livable Planet
By Jon Naar
Harper Collins Publishing
(800) 242-7737

Almanac Fact

At least $7.6 billion is now invested in socially-conscious money markets or mutual funds.

Source: The Better World Investment Guide

Public Interest Rankings

THE COUNCIL ON ECONOMIC PRIORITIES (CEP) is an independent public interest organization dedicated to researching and reporting on, among other issues, corporate social responsibility. Each year the CEP reviews hundreds of U.S. corporations and selects winners who meet standard criteria for excellence, improvement and innovation in the areas of charitable contributions, environmental concern, responsiveness to employees, equal opportunity and community outreach.

Contact Option

Council on Economic Priorities
30 Irving Pl.
New York, NY 10003
(212) 420-1133

CEP Corporate Conscience Awards

1990 Category	1990 Winner
Charitable Contributions	H.B. Fuller
Charitable Contributions	Stride Rite
Community Outreach	Foldcraft
Responsiveness to Employees	Time Warner
Equal Opportunity	Kellogg
Environment, Large Co.	Herman Miller
Environment, Small Co.	Smith & Hawken
Environment, honorable mention	H.J. Heinz

1991 Category	1991 Winner
Charitable Contributions	US West
Charitable Contributions	Tom's of Maine
Community Outreach	Supermarkets General Holdings
Community Outreach	Prudential Insurance
Responsiveness to Employees	Donnelley
Equal Opportunity	General Mills
Environment, Large Co.	Church & Dwight
Environment, Small Co.	Conservatree Paper

1992 Category	1992 Winner
Charitable Contrib., Large Co.	U.S. West
Charitable Contrib., Small Co.	Tom's of Maine
Community Outreach	Supermarkets General Holdings
	Prudential Insurance
Responsiveness to Employees	Donnelly
Equal Opportunity	General Mills
Environment, Large Co.	Church & Dwight
Environment, Small Co.	Conservatree Paper

1993 Category	1993 Winner
Community Involvement	Clorox Company
Equal Opportunity	Pitney Bowes
Responsiveness to Employees	Merck & Co.
	Quad/Graphics
Environment, Large Co.	Digital Equipment
Environment, Small Co.	Aveda Corp.
Special Recognition for Defense Conversion	Galileo Electro-Optics
	Kaman Aircraft
	Kavlico
	Science Applications International

CEP Corporate Conscience Dishonorable Mentions

Year	Company
1990	Exxon
	Perdue Farms
	USX Corporation
1991	American Cyanamid
	ConAgra
	Bristol-Myers
	Gerber Products
	Nestle/Carnation Foods

Year	Company
1992	Du Pont
	MAXXAM
	RJR Nabisco
1993	None Presented

Source: Council on Economic Priorities

Population Data

Resident Population by Age and State, 1991 (thousands)

Region, State	Total	Under 5	5 to 17 Years	18 to 24 Years	25 to 34 Years	35 to 44 Years	45 to 54 Years	55 to 64 Years	65 to 74 Years	75 to 84 Years	85 Years and over
U.S.	252,177	19,222	45,923	26,385	42,876	39,273	25,739	21,005	18,280	10,314	3,160
NORTH-EAST	50,976	3,672	8,470	5,252	8,636	7,962	5,381	4,560	4,027	2,297	719
ME	1,235	86	224	123	200	201	127	107	93	55	19
NH	1,105	85	195	112	197	188	114	86	73	41	14
VT	567	42	103	63	92	96	59	45	37	22	8
MA	5,996	431	943	669	1,083	940	606	500	459	272	93
RI	1,004	70	160	116	170	153	98	86	86	50	16
CT	3,291	237	527	327	571	526	362	289	256	147	48
NY	18,058	1,340	3,026	1,884	3,108	2,801	1,931	1,612	1,337	771	248
NJ	7,760	565	1,277	747	1,337	1,234	854	705	610	334	97
PA	11,961	816	2,014	1,211	1,878	1,823	1,231	1,131	1,077	605	176
MIDWEST	60,225	4,487	11,327	6,202	9,895	9,248	6,103	5,106	4,415	2,584	858
OH	10,939	796	2,023	1,129	1,768	1,690	1,130	969	837	454	141
IN	5,610	406	1,059	609	906	859	582	480	407	228	73
IL	11,543	887	2,111	1,193	1,977	1,777	1,184	967	821	478	150
MI	9,368	717	1,767	994	1,546	1,466	963	784	662	357	110
WI	4,955	362	949	505	813	763	490	413	360	225	76
MN	4,432	338	851	433	768	702	440	344	297	188	70
IA	2,795	193	532	283	419	413	276	247	228	147	56
MO	5,158	378	962	511	836	765	528	451	397	245	83
ND	635	46	127	67	100	94	57	52	47	33	11
SD	703	54	146	69	107	101	63	59	55	35	14
NE	1,593	120	315	156	251	240	151	134	118	77	30
KS	2,495	190	482	252	403	378	238	205	186	117	43
SOUTH	86,916	6,526	15,978	9,250	14,661	13,356	8,904	7,300	6,356	3,557	1,029
DE	680	51	117	75	120	104	70	60	51	25	7
MD	4,860	377	824	487	898	810	537	398	320	162	48
DC	598	43	78	76	120	95	61	49	44	26	8
VA	6,286	461	1,078	704	1,139	1,033	684	505	409	211	62
WV	1,801	106	331	187	256	282	193	174	156	89	26
NC	6,737	485	1,158	776	1,140	1,050	713	589	492	261	73
SC	3,560	270	668	411	594	549	366	295	251	124	32
GA	6,623	523	1,252	736	1,181	1,065	692	506	393	215	60
FL	13,277	915	2,083	1,202	2,120	1,916	1,333	1,276	1,395	817	221
KY	3,713	256	703	401	602	571	389	321	270	154	47
TN	4,953	346	884	530	812	776	538	437	362	207	61
AL	4,089	295	776	447	644	610	425	363	303	176	50
MS	2,592	202	549	299	393	364	249	213	180	110	33
AR	2,372	170	456	241	354	340	246	212	196	121	36
LA	4,252	339	894	465	697	634	411	338	277	153	45
OK	3,175	230	615	326	500	473	326	275	238	144	47
TX	17,349	1,457	3,512	1,888	3,091	2,684	1,671	1,289	1,021	563	172
WEST	54,060	4,538	10,149	5,681	9,684	8,707	5,351	4,039	3,482	1,875	554
MT	808	59	165	72	119	133	84	68	61	36	11
ID	1,039	82	236	103	152	160	102	79	71	42	12
WY	460	34	102	44	72	78	46	35	28	15	5
CO	3,377	258	625	338	607	602	351	255	200	106	34
NM	1,548	130	328	154	254	240	151	122	100	54	15
AZ	3,750	310	700	390	637	557	358	301	298	159	40
UT	1,770	174	468	208	278	238	142	107	91	50	14
NV	1,284	101	220	121	238	209	144	112	93	38	8
WA	5,018	383	932	489	859	856	526	383	341	190	58
OR	2,922	209	539	273	452	501	311	235	228	133	40
CA	30,380	2,651	5,512	3,312	5,704	4,835	2,965	2,214	1,874	1,009	305
AK	570	57	123	56	112	110	57	31	16	6	1
HI	1,135	89	199	120	201	187	114	94	81	38	11

Source: 1992 Statistical Abstract

Labor Force

Civilian Labor Force (millions) by Race, Hispanic Origin, Sex, and Age

Race, Sex, Age	1970	1980	1985	1990	1991	2000 (est.)	2005 (est.)
TOTAL	82.8	106.9	115.5	124.8	125.3	142.9	150.7
White	73.6	93.6	99.9	107.2	107.5	120.3	125.8
Male	46.0	54.5	56.5	59.3	59.3	64.5	66.8
Female	27.5	39.1	43.5	47.9	48.2	55.8	58.9
Black	9.2	10.9	12.4	13.5	13.5	16.5	17.8
Male	5.2	5.6	6.2	6.7	6.8	8.1	8.7
Female	4.0	5.3	6.1	6.8	6.8	8.4	9.1
Hispanic	NA	6.1	7.7	9.6	9.8	14.2	16.8
Male	NA	3.8	4.7	5.8	5.9	8.4	9.9
Female	NA	2.3	3.0	3.8	3.9	5.8	6.9
Male	51.2	61.5	64.4	68.2	68.4	75.9	79.3
16 to 19 years	4.0	5.0	4.1	3.9	3.6	4.4	4.6
20 to 24 years	5.7	8.6	8.3	7.3	7.3	7.2	8.0
25 to 34 years	11.3	17.0	18.8	19.8	19.6	17.3	17.0
35 to 44 years	10.5	11.8	14.5	17.3	17.9	20.4	19.2
45 to 54 years	10.4	9.9	9.9	11.2	11.5	16.5	18.6
55 to 64 years	7.1	7.2	7.1	6.8	6.7	7.8	9.7
65 years and over	2.2	1.9	1.8	2.0	2.0	2.2	2.3
Female	31.5	45.5	51.1	56.6	56.9	67.0	71.4
16 to 19 years	3.2	4.4	3.8	3.5	3.3	4.1	4.2
20 to 24 years	4.9	7.3	7.4	6.6	6.4	6.6	7.3
25 to 34 years	5.7	12.3	14.7	16.0	15.8	14.8	14.7
35 to 44 years	6.0	8.6	11.6	14.6	15.1	18.4	17.8
45 to 54 years	6.5	7.0	7.5	9.3	9.7	15.0	17.2
55 to 64 years	4.2	4.7	4.9	5.1	5.1	6.5	8.4
65 years and over	1.1	1.2	1.2	1.5	1.5	1.6	1.8

NA = not available

Source: 1992 Statistical Abstract

The Top Reference Sources

Commerce Business Daily
U.S. Government Printing Office, $325 a year
(202) 783-3238

This extremely useful publication contains a daily list of U.S. Government procurement invitations, contract awards, subcontracting leads, surplus property, and foreign business opportunities. It is essential reading for anyone who wants to obtain business from the government.

Labor Force (cont'd)

Labor Force Participation Rates (%) by Race, Sex, and Age

Race, Sex, Age	1970	1980	1985	1990	1991	2000	2005 (est.)
TOTAL	60.4	63.8	64.8	66.4	66.0	68.7	69.0
White	60.2	64.1	65.0	66.8	66.6	69.3	69.7
Male	80.0	78.2	77.0	76.9	76.4	76.7	76.2
Female	42.6	51.2	54.1	57.5	57.4	62.3	63.5
Black	61.8	61.0	62.9	63.3	62.6	65.7	65.6
Male	76.5	70.3	70.8	70.1	69.5	71.0	70.2
Female	49.5	53.1	56.5	57.8	57.0	61.2	61.7
Hispanic	NA	64.0	64.6	67.0	66.1	69.3	69.9
Male	NA	81.4	80.3	81.2	80.1	81.8	81.6
Female	NA	47.4	49.3	53.0	52.3	56.6	58.0
Male	79.7	77.4	76.3	76.1	75.5	76.0	75.4
16 to 19 years	56.1	60.5	56.8	55.7	53.2	57.4	57.7
20 to 24 years	83.3	85.9	85.0	84.3	83.4	85.5	86.1
25 to 34 years	96.4	95.2	94.7	94.2	93.7	93.9	93.6
35 to 44 years	96.9	95.5	95.0	94.4	94.2	93.7	93.4
45 to 54 years	94.3	91.2	91.0	90.7	90.5	90.5	90.3
55 to 64 years	83.0	72.1	67.9	67.7	66.9	68.2	67.9
65 years and over	26.8	19.0	15.8	16.4	15.8	15.8	16.0
Female	43.3	51.5	54.5	57.5	57.3	62.0	63.0
16 to 19 years	44.0	52.9	52.1	51.8	50.2	54.1	54.3
20 to 24 years	57.7	68.9	71.8	71.6	70.4	74.3	75.3
25 to 34 years	45.0	65.5	70.9	73.6	73.3	78.2	79.7
35 to 44 years	51.1	65.5	71.8	76.5	76.6	83.3	85.3
45 to 54 years	54.4	59.9	64.4	71.2	72.0	79.0	81.5
55 to 64 years	43.0	41.3	42.0	45.3	45.3	51.9	54.3
65 years and over	9.7	8.1	7.3	8.7	8.6	8.6	8.8

NA = not available

Source: 1992 Statistical Abstract

Labor Force Participation Rates (%) for Wives, Husband Present, by Age of Youngest Child

Presence, Age of Child	Total 1975	Total 1985	Total 1990	Total 1991	White 1975	White 1985	White 1990	White 1991	Black 1975	Black 1985	Black 1990	Black 1991
Wives, total	44.4	54.2	58.2	58.5	43.6	53.3	57.6	57.9	54.1	63.8	64.7	66.1
0 under 18	43.8	48.2	51.1	51.2	43.6	47.5	50.8	50.9	47.6	55.2	52.9	54.8
All under 18	44.9	60.8	66.3	66.8	43.6	59.9	65.6	66.2	58.4	71.7	75.6	76.5
Under 6	36.7	53.4	58.9	59.9	34.7	52.1	57.8	59.0	54.9	69.6	73.1	73.4
Under 3	32.7	50.5	55.5	56.8	30.7	49.4	54.9	55.9	50.1	66.2	67.5	70.3
1 yr., under	30.8	49.4	53.9	55.8	29.2	48.6	53.3	54.9	50.0	63.7	64.4	66.9
2 yrs.	37.1	54.0	60.9	60.5	35.1	52.7	60.3	58.9	56.4	69.9	75.4	77.8
3 to 5 yrs.	42.2	58.4	64.1	64.7	40.1	56.6	62.5	64.0	61.2	73.8	80.4	77.3
3 yrs.	41.2	55.1	63.1	62.2	39.0	52.7	62.3	61.2	62.7	72.3	74.5	81.0
4 yrs.	41.2	59.7	65.1	65.5	38.7	58.4	63.2	64.9	64.9	70.6	80.6	74.1
5 yrs.	44.4	62.1	64.5	67.1	43.8	59.9	62.0	66.5	56.3	79.1	86.2	79.1
6 to 13 yrs.	51.8	68.2	73.0	72.8	50.7	67.7	72.6	72.4	65.7	73.3	77.6	80.1
14 to 17 yrs.	53.5	67.0	75.1	75.7	53.4	66.6	74.9	76.0	52.3	74.4	78.8	77.6

Source: 1992 Statistical Abstract

Labor Force (cont'd)

Civilian Labor Force by Educational Attainment, Sex and Race

Civilian Labor Force	Total (thousands)	% Distribution Less than High School	% Distribution High School Graduates	Distribution 1-3 College Years	% Distribution 4+ College Years
TOTAL					
1970	61,765	36.1	38.1	11.8	14.1
1975	67,774	27.5	39.7	14.4	18.3
1980	78,010	20.6	39.8	17.6	22.0
1985	88,424	15.9	40.2	19.0	24.9
1988	94,870	14.7	39.9	19.7	25.7
1989	97,318	14.0	39.6	20.0	26.4
1990	99,981	13.3	39.4	20.8	26.5
1991	101,171	12.8	39.2	21.3	26.7
MALE					
1970	39,903	37.5	34.5	12.2	15.7
1975	41,628	28.9	36.1	14.8	20.2
1980	45,417	22.2	35.7	17.7	24.3
1985	49,647	17.7	36.9	18.3	27.1
1988	52,616	16.5	37.3	18.5	27.8
1989	53,668	15.7	36.9	19.2	28.2
1990	55,049	14.9	37.3	19.8	28.0
1991	55,554	14.5	37.1	20.3	28.2
FEMALE					
1970	22,462	33.5	44.3	10.9	11.2
1975	26,146	26.5	45.5	13.9	14.1
1980	32,593	18.4	45.4	17.4	18.7
1985	38,779	13.7	44.4	19.9	22.0
1988	42,254	12.4	43.3	21.2	23.1
1989	43,650	11.9	42.9	20.9	24.3
1990	44,932	11.2	42.1	22.1	24.6
1991	45,617	10.7	41.8	22.5	25.0
WHITE					
1970	55,044	33.7	39.3	12.2	14.8
1975	60,026	25.7	40.6	14.7	19.0
1980	68,509	19.1	40.2	17.7	22.9
1985	76,739	14.7	40.7	19.1	25.6
1988	81,886	13.8	40.1	19.7	26.4
1989	83,694	13.0	39.7	20.0	27.2
1990	85,882	12.5	39.4	20.8	27.3
1991	86,776	12.1	39.1	21.3	27.5
BLACK					
1970	6,721	55.5	28.2	8.0	8.3
1975	7,586	41.9	33.1	12.4	12.6
1980	7,731	34.7	38.1	16.3	11.0
1985	9,157	26.2	39.5	19.2	15.0
1988	9,985	22.6	43.0	19.2	15.2
1989	10,358	21.7	42.3	20.5	15.6
1990	10,711	19.4	43.0	21.8	15.8
1991	10,863	18.4	43.0	22.5	16.0

Source: 1992 Statistical Abstract

Labor Force (cont'd)

Self-Employed Workers (thousands) by Selected Characteristics

ITEM	1970	1975	1980	1985	1987	1988	1989	1990	1991
TOTAL SELF-EMPLOYED	7,031	7,427	8,642	9,269	9,624	9,917	10,008	10,160	10,341
INDUSTRY									
Agriculture	1,810	1,722	1,642	1,458	1,423	1,398	1,403	1,400	1,442
Nonagriculture	5,221	5,705	7,000	7,811	8,201	8,519	8,605	8,760	8,899
Mining	14	16	28	20	27	28	26	24	23
Construction	687	839	1,173	1,301	1,384	1,427	1,423	1,463	1,447
Manufacturing	264	273	358	347	354	394	406	429	420
Transportation & public utilities	196	223	282	315	335	345	323	302	318
Trade	1,667	1,709	1,899	1,792	1,841	1,823	1,882	1,859	1,879
Finance, insurance & real estate	254	335	458	558	597	624	621	635	619
Services	2,140	2,310	2,804	3,477	3,663	3,878	3,924	4,048	4,193
OCCUPATION									
Managerial & professional	NA	NA	NA	2,585	2,714	2,929	3,059	3,067	3,117
Technical, sales & admin. support	NA	NA	NA	2,059	2,139	2,155	2,195	2,252	2,245
Service occupations	NA	NA	NA	980	1,058	1,159	1,146	1,213	1,273
Precision prod., craft & repair	NA	NA	NA	1,611	1,680	1,674	1,648	1,680	1,697
Operators, fabricators & laborers	NA	NA	NA	568	595	604	585	568	584
Farming, forestry & fishing	NA	NA	NA	1,465	1,438	1,395	1,376	1,380	1,427

NA=not available

Source: 1992 Statistical Abstract

Employed Workers (thousands) by Work Schedules, Sex, and Age

Characteristic	1980	1985	1990	1991
TOTAL	99,303	107,150	117,914	116,877
FULL-TIME	82,562	88,534	97,994	96,575
Male	51,717	53,862	57,982	56,936
16 to 19 years old	2,017	1,437	1,343	1,085
20 to 24 years old	6,533	6,078	5,452	5,115
25 to 54 years old	35,644	39,207	44,229	43,947
55 years and over	7,521	7,139	6,959	6,789
Female	30,845	34,672	40,011	39,638
16 to 19 years old	1,456	1,069	975	785
20 to 24 years old	5,098	4,903	4,386	4,079
25 to 54 years old	20,395	24,838	30,485	30,696
55 years and over	3,897	3,862	4,166	4,079
PART-TIME	16,740	18,615	19,920	20,302
Male	5,471	6,028	6,452	6,657
16 to 19 years old	2,068	1,891	1,894	1,795
20 to 24 years old	999	1,261	1,174	1,306
25 to 54 years old	1,092	1,568	1,842	2,033
55 years and over	1,314	1,308	1,543	1,523
Female	11,270	12,587	13,468	13,645
16 to 19 years old	2,169	2,036	2,049	1,964
20 to 24 years old	1,456	1,738	1,611	1,733
25 to 54 years old	5,827	6,837	7,584	7,687
55 years and over	1,815	1,976	2,224	2,261

Source: 1992 Statistical Abstract

Labor Force (cont'd)

Unemployed Workers (thousands) by Work Schedules, Sex, and Age

Characteristic	1980	1985	1990	1991
TOTAL	7,637	8,312	6,874	8,426
LOOKING FOR FULL-TIME WORK	6,269	6,793	5,541	6,932
Male	3,703	3,925	3,264	4,211
16 to 19 years old	537	446	328	363
20 to 24 years old	994	857	582	736
25 to 54 years old	1,923	2,329	2,098	2,795
55 years and over	250	292	255	317
Female	2,564	2,868	2,277	2,721
16 to 19 years old	430	331	233	258
20 to 24 years old	636	636	439	481
25 to 54 years old	1,363	1,727	1,491	1,830
55 years and over	135	173	115	152
PART-TIME	1,369	1,519	1,332	1,494
Male	563	596	535	607
16 to 19 years old	377	360	301	346
20 to 24 years old	81	87	84	113
25 to 54 years old	54	79	89	88
55 years and over	52	70	61	60
Female	806	923	797	888
16 to 19 years old	326	330	286	323
20 to 24 years old	124	158	116	147
25 to 54 years old	299	359	323	347
55 years and over	57	75	72	71

Source: 1992 Statistical Abstract

Selected Labor Force Characteristics

Item	Number
OCCUPATION	
Executive, administrative & managerial	14,227,916
Professional specialty	16,305,666
Technicians & related support	4,257,235
Sales	13,634,686
Administrative support, including clerical	18,826,477
Private household	521,154
Protective service	1,992,852
Service, except professional & household	12,781,911
Farming, forestry & fishing	2,839,010
Precision production, craft & repair	13,097,963
Machine operators, assemblers & inspect.	7,904,197
Transportation & material moving	4,729,001
Handlers, equipment cleaners, laborers	4,563,134
INDUSTRY	
Agriculture, forestry and fisheries	3,115,372
Mining	723,423
Construction	7,214,763
Manufacturing, non-durable goods	8,053,234
Manufacturing, durable goods	12,408,844

Item	Number
Transportation	5,108,003
Communications, other public utilities	3,097,059
Wholesale trade	5,071,026
Retail trade	19,485,666
Finance, insurance and real estate	7,984,870
Business and repair services	5,577,462
Personal services	3,668,696
Entertainment and recreation services	1,636,460
Health services	9,682,684
Educational services	9,633,503
Other professional and related services	7,682,060
Public administration	5,538,077
CLASS OF WORKER	
Private wage and salary workers	89,541,393
Government workers	17,567,100
Local government workers	8,244,755
State government workers	5,381,445
Federal government workers	3,940,900
Self-employed workers	8,067,483
Unpaid family workers	505,226

Source:1990 Data, 1992 Statistical Abstract

Demographics

Civilian Employment Estimates (thousands)

Occupation	1990 Employment	2005 Low Growth Employment	2005 Moderate Growth Employment	2005 High Growth Employment
TOTAL	122,573	136,806	147,191	154,543
LARGEST JOB GROWTH				
Salespersons, retail	3,619	4,180	4,506	4,728
Registered nurses	1,727	2,318	2,494	2,648
Truck drivers, light and heavy	2,362	2,767	2,979	3,125
General managers and top executives	3,086	3,409	3,684	3,871
Janitors and cleaners	3,007	3,332	3,562	3,728
Nursing aides, orderlies, and attendants	1,274	1,700	1,826	1,934
Waiters and waitresses	1,747	2,110	2,196	2,262
Teachers: secondary school	1,280	1,575	1,717	1,849
Receptionists and information clerks	900	1,228	1,322	1,394
Systems analysts and computer scientists	463	769	829	864
Food preparation workers	1,156	1,442	1,521	1,585
Gardeners and groundskeepers, except farm	874	1,158	1,222	1,275
Accountants and auditors	985	1,235	1,325	1,385
Teachers, elementary	1,362	1,538	1,675	1,803
Teacher aides and educational assistants	808	999	1,086	1,165
Home health aides	287	512	550	582
Cooks, restaurant	615	840	872	898
Secretaries, except legal and medical	3,064	3,065	3,312	3,488
Lawyers	587	745	793	830
Marketing, advertising, and P.R.managers	427	582	630	659
Physicians	580	730	776	818
Financial managers	701	828	894	939
Teachers: preschool and kindergarten	425	555	598	636
Automotive mechanics	757	861	923	969
Electricians	548	652	706	748
FASTEST GROWING				
Home health aides	287	512	550	582
Systems analysts and computer scientists	463	769	829	864
Personal and home care aides	103	170	183	194
Medical assistants	165	268	287	306
Human services workers	145	231	249	264
Radiologic technologists and technicians	149	234	252	268
Medical secretaries	232	363	390	415
Psychologists	125	193	204	214
Travel agents	132	199	214	224
Correction officers	230	342	372	400
Flight attendants	101	146	159	168
Computer programmers	565	811	882	923
Management analysts	151	218	230	240
Child care workers	725	1,027	1,078	1,123
FASTEST DECLINING				
Electronic equipment assemblers, precision	171	78	90	92
Child care workers, private household	314	176	190	200
Cleaners and servants, private household	411	287	310	326
Switchboard operators	246	175	189	198
Typists and word processors	972	805	869	916

Source: 1992 Statistical Abstract

Demographics (cont'd)

Civilian Labor Force Status by Selected Metropolitan Area

Metropolitan Areas Ranked by Labor Force Size, 1990	Total Employed	Total Unemployed	Unemployment Rate
U.S. TOTAL	117,914.0	6,874.0	5.5
Los Angeles-Long Beach, CA	4,173.0	255.0	5.8
New York, NY	3,759.9	250.6	6.2
Chicago, IL	3,099.1	195.5	5.9
Philadelphia, PA-NJ	2,332.8	113.7	4.6
Washington, DC-MD-VA	2,134.4	75.4	3.4
Detroit, MI	1,990.0	160.7	7.5
Houston, TX	1,634.2	89.2	5.2
Boston, MA	1,481.6	79.2	5.1
Atlanta, GA	1,444.7	77.2	5.1
Dallas, TX	1,359.3	73.6	5.1
Minneapolis-St. Paul, MN-WI	1,350.2	60.0	4.3
Nassau-Suffolk, NY	1,349.2	53.6	3.8
Anaheim-Santa Ana, CA	1,336.4	46.4	3.4
St. Louis, MO-IL	1,197.0	75.2	5.9
Baltimore, MD	1,152.9	61.6	5.1
San Diego, CA	1,121.6	52.8	4.5
Seattle, WA	1,086.6	39.2	3.5
Oakland, CA	1,046.4	45.9	4.2
Phoenix, AZ	1,028.1	46.4	4.3
Riverside-San Bernadino, CA	1,001.0	70.6	6.6
Tampa-St. Petersburg-Clearwater, FL	965.8	52.1	5.1
Pittsburgh, PA	944.0	47.8	4.8
Cleveland, OH	909.1	45.7	4.8
Newark, NJ	901.4	51.1	5.4
Miami-Hialeah, FL	888.5	63.8	6.7
Denver, CO	853.2	41.1	4.6
San Francisco, CA	844.3	28.9	3.3
Kansas City, MO-Kansas City, KS	810.2	42.3	5.0
San Jose, CA	780.7	32.9	4.0
Cincinnati, OH-KY-IN	754.1	32.8	4.2
Milwaukee, WI	730.2	28.9	3.8
Columbus, OH	706.9	32.6	4.4
Sacramento, CA	703.6	35.5	4.8
Fort Worth-Arlington, TX	695.5	38.4	5.2
Bergen-Passaic, NJ	674.6	32.1	4.5
Portland, OR	655.2	28.7	4.2
Indianapolis, IN	642.7	28.0	4.2
Fort Lauderdale-Hollywood-Pompano Beach, FL	624.0	36.2	5.5
Charlotte-Gastonia-Rock Hill, NC-SC	624.1	22.6	3.5
Orlando, FL	606.5	34.0	5.3
Norfolk-Virginia Beach-Newport News, VA	594.4	29.5	4.7
San Antonio, TX	563.9	41.8	6.9
Middlesex-Somerset-Hunterdon, NJ	568.3	22.0	3.7
New Orleans, LA	544.4	33.1	5.7
Nashville, TN	511.6	21.1	4.0
Greensboro-Winston-Salem-High Point, NC	501.6	19.4	3.7
Louisville, KY-IN	494.1	26.6	5.1
Salt Lake City-Ogden, UT	490.1	21.0	4.1
Rochester, NY	491.1	18.9	3.7

Source: 1990 data, 1992 Statistical Abstract

Demographics (cont'd)

Average Hourly and Weekly Earnings in Current Dollars by Private Industry Group

Private Industry Group	1970	1980	1985	1989	1990	1991
AVERAGE HOURLY EARNINGS	3.23	6.66	8.57	9.66	10.02	10.34
Manufacturing	3.35	7.27	9.54	10.48	10.83	11.18
Mining	3.85	9.17	11.98	13.26	13.69	14.21
Construction	5.24	9.94	12.32	13.54	13.78	14.01
Transportation, public utilities	3.85	8.87	11.40	12.60	12.96	13.23
Wholesale trade	3.43	6.95	9.15	10.39	10.79	11.16
Retail trade	2.44	4.88	5.94	6.53	6.76	7.00
Finance, insurance, real estate	3.07	5.79	7.94	9.53	9.97	10.42
Services	2.81	5.85	7.90	9.38	9.83	10.24
AVERAGE WEEKLY EARNINGS	120.00	235.00	299.00	334.00	346.00	355.00
Manufacturing	133.00	289.00	386.00	430.00	442.00	455.00
Mining	164.00	397.00	520.00	570.00	604.00	631.00
Construction	195.00	368.00	464.00	513.00	526.00	534.00
Transportation, public utilities	156.00	351.00	450.00	490.00	504.00	511.00
Wholesale trade	137.00	267.00	351.00	395.00	411.00	425.00
Retail trade	82.00	147.00	175.00	189.00	195.00	200.00
Finance, insurance, real estate	113.00	210.00	289.00	341.00	357.00	373.00
Services	97.00	191.00	257.00	306.00	320.00	333.00

Source: 1992 Statistical Abstract

The Top Reference Sources

Martindale-Hubbell Law Directory
Reed, $605
(800) 521-8110

More than 800,000 lawyers are profiled in this 24-volume set.

In addition to providing valuable information on the background of any lawyer you may encounter, Martindale-Hubbell provides extensive cross-referencing to make it easier to find specialists in almost any area of the law.

Also included are digests of the statutory laws of all 50 states.

Unemployment

Unemployed Persons by Sex and Reason

Sex & Reason Unemployed	1980	1983	1984	1985	1986	1987	1988	1989	1990
Male	4,267	6,260	4,744	4,521	4,530	4,101	3,655	3,525	3,799
Job losers	2,649	4,331	2,976	2,749	2,725	2,432	2,078	1,975	2,208
Job leavers	438	386	375	409	520	494	503	495	511
Re-entrants	776	953	867	876	805	761	697	726	782
New entrants	405	589	526	487	480	413	376	328	298
Female	3,370	4,457	3,794	3,791	3,707	3,324	3,046	3,003	3,075
Job losers	1,297	1,926	1,445	1,390	1,308	1,134	1,014	1,008	1,114
Job leavers	453	444	449	468	494	471	480	529	503
Re-entrants	1,152	1,459	1,317	1,380	1,355	1,213	1,112	1,117	1,101
New entrants	468	627	584	552	549	506	440	349	357

Unemployed Persons: By Duration of Unemployment

Sex & Reason Unemployed	Total Unemployed	Less Than 5 Weeks Unemployed (%)	5 to 14 Weeks Unemployed (%)	15 Weeks or More Unemployed (%)
Male	4,817	36.5	32.4	31.1
Job losers	3,105	32.0	33.0	35.0
Job leavers	492	42.3	32.7	25.0
Re-entrants	865	44.2	31.0	24.7
New entrants	356	49.4	30.1	20.5
Female	3,609	44.9	32.2	22.9
Job losers	1,503	34.5	33.9	31.6
Job leavers	487	50.5	31.4	18.1
Re-entrants	1,222	52.0	30.6	17.4
New entrants	398	55.8	31.7	12.6

Unemployment Rates: By Industry

Industry	1975	1980	1985	1988	1989	1990	1991
ALL UNEMPLOYED	8.5	7.1	7.2	5.5	5.3	5.5	6.7
Industry							
Agriculture	10.4	11.0	13.2	10.6	9.6	9.7	11.6
Mining	4.1	6.4	9.5	7.9	5.8	4.8	7.7
Construction	18.0	14.1	13.1	10.6	10.0	11.1	15.4
Manufacturing	10.9	8.5	7.7	5.3	5.1	5.8	7.2
Transportation and public utilities	5.6	4.9	5.1	3.9	3.9	3.8	5.3
Wholesale and retail trade	8.7	7.4	7.6	6.2	6.0	6.4	7.6
Finance, insurance and real estate	4.9	3.4	3.5	3.0	3.1	3.0	4.0
Services	7.1	5.9	6.2	4.9	4.8	5.0	5.7
Government	4.1	4.1	3.9	2.8	2.7	2.6	3.2

Source: 1992 Statistical Abstract

Unemployment (cont'd)

Unemployment Rates: By Sex

Industry	Male 1980	Male 1991	Female 1980	Female 1991
ALL UNEMPLOYED	6.9	7.0	7.4	6.3
Industry				
Agriculture	9.7	11.6	15.1	11.8
Mining	6.7	8.6	4.5	3.4
Construction	14.6	15.9	8.9	10.1
Manufacturing	7.4	6.5	10.8	8.6
Transportation and public utilities	5.1	5.5	4.4	4.6
Wholesale and retail trade	6.6	7.2	8.3	8.0
Finance, insurance and real estate	3.2	3.8	3.5	4.0
Services	6.3	6.4	5.8	5.3
Government	3.9	3.3	4.3	3.1

Source: 1992 Statistical Abstract

Consumer Trends

Average Annual Consumer Expenditures, by household ($)

Item	1984	1985	1988	1989	1990	Avg. Annual % Change 1984-90	Avg. Annual % Change 1989-90
Total expenditures	21,975	23,490	25,892	27,810	28,369	4	2
Food, total	3,290	3,477	3,748	4,152	4,296	5	3
Food at home, total	1,970	2,037	2,136	2,390	2,485	4	4
Cereal and bakery products	262	283	312	359	368	6	3
Meats, poultry, fish, and eggs	586	579	551	611	668	2	9
Dairy products	253	266	274	304	295	3	-3
Fruits and vegetables	313	322	373	408	408	5	>.5
Other food at home	556	585	625	708	746	5	3
Food away from home	1,320	1,441	1,612	1,762	1,811	5	3
Alcoholic beverages	275	306	269	284	293	1	3
Tobacco products and smoking supplies	228	219	242	261	274	3	5
Housing, total	6,674	7,087	8,079	8,609	8,886	5	3
Shelter	3,489	3,833	4,493	4,835	5,032	6	4
Fuels, utilities and public services	1,638	1,648	1,747	1,835	1,890	2	3
Household operations and furnishings	1,241	1,282	1,477	1,546	1,557	4	1
Housekeeping supplies	307	325	361	394	406	5	3
Apparel and services	1,319	1,420	1,489	1,582	1,617	3	2
Transportation, total	4,304	4,587	5,093	5,187	5,122	3	-1
Vehicles	1,813	2,043	2,361	2,291	2,129	3	-7
Gasoline and motor oil	1,058	1,035	932	985	1,047	>.5	6
Other transportation	1,433	1,509	1,800	1,911	1,946	5	2
Health care	1,049	1,108	1,298	1,407	1,480	6	5
Life insurance	300	278	314	346	345	2	>.5
Pensions and Social Security	1,598	1,738	1,935	2,125	2,248	6	6
Other expenditures	2,936	3,269	3,426	3,857	3,806	4	-1

Source: 1992 Statistical Abstract

Consumer Trends (cont'd)

Average Annual Consumer Expenditures for Selected Metropolitan Statistical Areas

Metropolitan Statistical Area	Total Expendi-tures	Food	Total Housing	Shelter	Apparel & Services	Total Transport-ation	Health Care
Anchorage, AK	43,434	5,554	13,396	8,529	2,016	8,610	1,671
Atlanta, GA	32,760	4,158	10,775	6,401	2,108	5,543	1,798
Baltimore, MD	30,768	4,529	9,895	6,074	1,978	5,100	1,453
Boston-Lawrence-Salem, MA-NH	30,518	4,036	11,461	7,624	1,659	4,896	1,165
Buffalo-Niagara Falls, NY	24,530	4,530	7,759	4,511	1,315	4,513	1,162
Chicago-Gary-Lake County, IL-IN-WI	32,890	5,151	10,728	6,487	2,184	5,301	1,256
Cincinnati-Hamilton, OH-KY-IN	27,862	4,687	8,035	4,448	1,740	5,439	1,450
Cleveland-Akron-Lorain, OH	26,357	4,166	7,468	3,853	2,043	4,502	1,340
Dallas-Fort Worth, TX	34,534	4,530	10,296	5,453	1,982	6,948	1,552
Detroit-Ann Arbor, MI	28,658	3,760	9,521	5,644	1,262	5,883	1,157
Honolulu, HI	33,320	5,455	10,359	6,770	1,477	5,200	1,691
Houston-Galveston-Brazoria, TX	30,217	4,195	9,063	5,077	1,589	6,278	1,469
Kansas City, MO-Kansas City, KS	27,345	4,389	8,457	4,620	1,343	4,789	1,927
Los Angeles-Long Beach, CA	36,061	5,236	12,656	7,995	2,404	6,004	1,633
Miami-Fort Lauderdale, FL	33,205	4,926	10,470	6,204	1,587	6,839	1,742
Milwaukee, WI	26,021	3,966	8,724	5,548	1,544	4,396	1,088
Minneapolis-St. Paul, MN-WI	32,827	4,621	10,340	6,543	1,816	5,295	1,374
NY-Northern NJ-Long Island, NY-NJ-CT	32,680	5,120	11,169	6,968	2,290	4,866	1,490
Phil.-Wilmington-Trenton, PA-NJ-DE-MD	31,429	4,619	10,173	5,562	2,037	5,223	1,646
Pittsburgh-Beaver Valley, PA	26,168	4,292	8,324	3,936	1,646	4,138	1,208
Portland-Vancouver, OR-WA	27,467	3,866	8,773	5,467	1,440	4,758	1,291
St. Louis-East St. Louis-Alton, MO-IL-IA	27,491	3,813	8,793	4,386	1,340	4,888	1,428
San Diego, CA	32,024	4,351	11,642	7,179	1,849	5,019	1,285
San Francisco-Oakland-San Jose, CA	38,927	5,292	13,727	9,449	2,556	6,470	1,348
Seattle-Tacoma, WA	33,426	4,750	10,759	6721	1,667	5,761	1,578
Washington, DC-MD-VA	37,505	4,825	12,905	8,172	2,469	5,922	1,918

Source: 1990 data, 1992 Statistical Abstract

Per Capita Personal Income

Average Annual Pay by State ($)

State	1989 Avg. Annual Pay	1990 Avg. Annual Pay	1991 Avg. Annual Pay	% Change 1989-90	% Change 1990-91
U.S.	22,563	23,602	24,575	4.6	4.1
AL	19,593	20,468	21,287	4.5	4.0
AK	29,704	29,946	30,830	0.8	2.9
AZ	20,809	21,443	22,207	3.0	3.6
AR	17,418	18,204	19,008	4.5	4.4
CA	24,917	26,180	27,499	5.1	5.0
CO	21,940	22,908	23,981	4.4	4.7
CT	27,500	28,995	30,689	5.4	5.8
DE	23,268	24,423	25,647	5.0	5.0
DC	32,106	33,717	35,570	5.0	5.5
FL	20,072	21,032	21,991	4.8	4.6
GA	21,072	22,114	23,164	4.9	4.7
HI	21,624	23,167	24,104	7.1	4.0
ID	18,146	18,991	19,688	4.7	3.7
IL	24,212	25,312	23,310	4.5	3.9
IN	20,931	21,699	22,522	3.7	3.8
IA	18,420	19,224	19,810	4.4	3.0
KS	19,475	20,238	21,002	3.9	3.8
KY	19,001	19,947	20,730	5.0	3.9
LA	19,750	20,646	21,501	4.5	4.1
ME	19,202	20,154	20,870	5.0	3.6
MD	23,469	24,730	25,960	5.4	5.0
MA	25,233	26,689	28,041	5.8	5.0
MI	24,767	25,376	26,125	2.5	3.0
MN	22,155	23,126	23,961	4.4	3.6
MO	20,900	21,716	22,567	3.9	3.9
MS	17,047	17,718	18,411	3.9	3.9
MT	17,224	17,895	18,648	3.9	4.2
NE	17,690	18,577	19,372	5.0	4.3
NV	21,333	22,358	23,083	4.8	3.2
NH	21,553	22,609	23,600	4.9	4.4
NJ	26,780	28,449	29,992	6.2	5.4
NM	18,667	19,347	20,275	3.6	4.8
NY	27,303	28,873	30,011	5.8	3.9
NC	19,321	20,220	21,087	4.7	4.3
ND	16,932	17,626	18,132	4.1	2.9
OH	21,986	22,843	23,603	3.9	3.3
OK	19,533	20,288	20,968	3.9	3.3
OR	20,303	21,332	22,348	5.1	4.8
PA	22,313	23,457	24,393	5.1	4.0
RI	21,128	22,388	23,082	6.0	3.1
SC	18,797	19,669	20,439	4.6	3.9
SD	15,810	16,430	17,131	3.9	4.3
TN	19,712	20,611	21,541	4.6	4.5
TX	21,740	22,700	23,760	4.4	4.7
UT	19,362	20,074	20,874	3.7	4.0
VT	19,497	20,532	21,355	5.3	4.0
VA	21,882	22,750	23,804	4.0	4.6
WA	21,617	22,646	23,942	4.8	5.7
WV	19,788	20,715	21,356	4.7	3.1
WI	20,204	21,101	21,838	4.4	3.5
WY	19,230	20,049	20,591	4.3	2.7

Source: 1990 Statistical Abstract

Taxes

Real Family Income After Taxes, 1980 to 1992 ($)

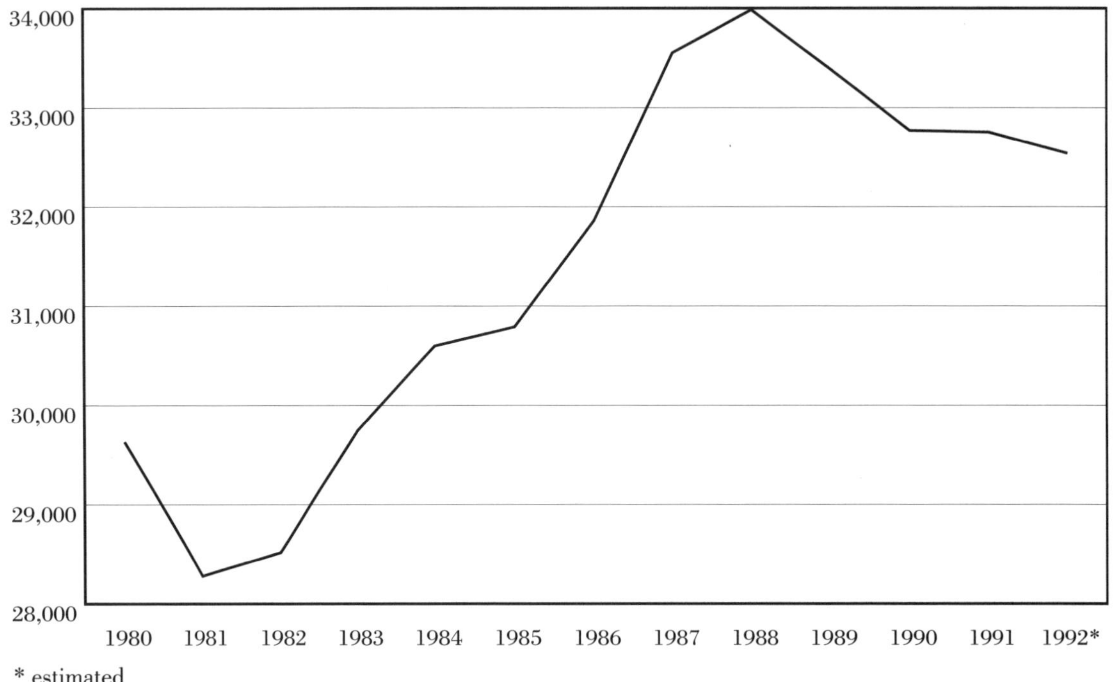

* estimated

Typical American Family Budget, 1992

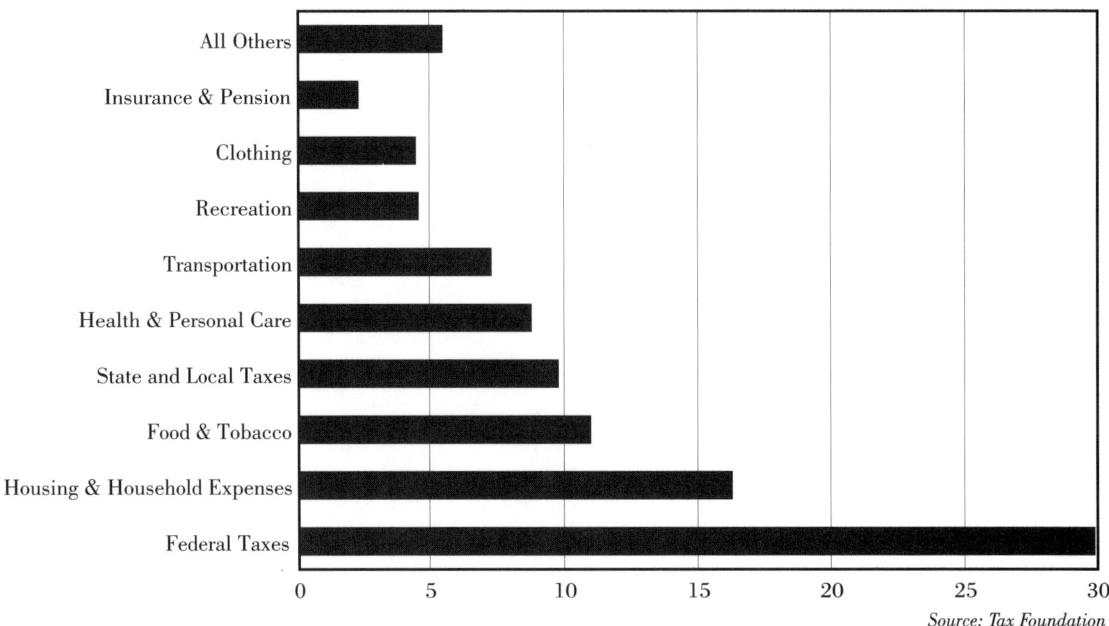

Source: Tax Foundation

State Taxes

Major State Taxes and Rates as of October 1, 1992

State	Corporate (%)	Individual (%)	General Sales and Use Tax (%)	Gasoline Tax (cents per gallon)	Cigarette Tax (cents per pack of 20)
Alabama	0.05	2 to 5	4	16	16.5
Alaska	1 to 9.4	none	none	8	29
Arizona	9.3	3.8 to 7	5	18	18
Arkansas	1 to 6.5	1 to 7	4.5	18.5	22
California	9.3	1 to 11	6	16	35
Colorado	5 to 5.1	5	3	22	20
Connecticut	11.5	4.5	6	26	45
Delaware	8.7	3.2 to 7.7	none	19	24
DC	10	6 to 9.5	6	20	50
Florida	5.5	none	6	11.6	33.9
Georgia	6	1 to 6	4	7.5	12
Hawaii	4.4 to 6.4	2 to 10	4	24.8 to 32.5	46
Idaho	8	2 to 8.2	5	22	18
Illinois	4.8	3	6.25	19	30
Indiana	3.4	3.4	5	15	15.5
Iowa	6 to 12	.4 to 9.98	5	20	36
Kansas	4	4.4 to 7.75	4.9	18	24
Kentucky	4 to 8.25	2 to 6	6	15	3
Louisiana	4 to 8	2 to 6	4	20	20
Maine	3.5 to 8.93	2 to 8.6	6	19	37
Maryland	7	2 to 6	5	23.5	36
Massachusetts	9.5	5.95	5	21	26
Michigan	2.35	4.6	4	15	25
Minnesota	9.8	6 to 8.5	6.5	20	48
Mississippi	3 to 5	3 to 5	7	18	18
Missouri	5	1.5 to 6	4.225	13	13
Montana	6.75	2 to 11	none	20	19.26
Nebraska	5.58 to 7.81	2.37 to 6.92	5	24	27
Nevada	none	none	6.5	23	35
New Hampshire	8	5	none	18	25
New Jersey	9	2 to 7	7	10.5	40
New Mexico	4.8 to 7.6	1.8 to 8.5	5	16	15
New York	9	4 to 7.875	4	8	39
North Carolina	7.75	6 to 7.75	4	21.9	5
North Dakota	3 to 10.5	2.67 to 12	5	17	29
Ohio	5.1 to 8.9	.743 to 6.9	5	21	18
Oklahoma	6	.5 to 7	4.5	17	23
Oregon	6.6	5 to 9	none	22	28
Pennsylvania	12.25	2.8	6	12	31
Rhode Island	9	4.125 to 9.92	7	26	37
South Carolina	5	2.5 to 7	5	16	7
South Dakota	none	none	4	18	23
Tennessee	6	6	6	22.4	13
Texas	none	none	6.25	20	41
Utah	5	2.55 to 7.2	5	19.5	26.5
Vermont	5.5 to 8.25	4.2 to 10.5	5	15	20
Virginia	6	2 to 5.75	3.5	17.5	2.5
Washington	none	none	6.5	23	34
West Virginia	9	3 to 6.5	6	15.5	17
Wisconsin	7.9	4.9 to 6.93	5	22.2	38
Wyoming	none	none	3	9	12

Source: Tax Foundation

State Taxes (cont'd)

Per Capita Federal Tax Burden by State, 1992

State	Per Capita Burden ($)	Total Tax State Rank	Per Capita State Rank
U.S. TOTAL	4,114	-	-
Alabama	3,116	24	44
Alaska	5,111	46	5
Arizona	3,216	25	41
Arkansas	2,980	32	47
California	4,457	1	11
Colorado	3,997	22	21
Connecticut	6,243	16	1
Delaware	5,129	43	4
DC	5,365	44	3
Florida	3,947	5	22
Georgia	3,555	12	33
Hawaii	4,455	37	12
Idaho	3,146	45	42
Illinois	4,776	4	9
Indiana	3,643	17	31
Iowa	3,678	30	30
Kansas	4,019	31	20
Kentucky	3,126	26	43
Louisiana	3,087	23	46
Maine	3,466	42	35
Maryland	4,842	13	8
Massachusetts	5,024	10	7
Michigan	4,188	9	16
Minnesota	4,182	20	18
Mississippi	2,499	33	51
Missouri	3,746	18	29
Montana	3,231	47	40
Nebraska	3,788	34	27
Nevada	4,183	35	17
New Hampshire	4,463	36	10
New Jersey	5,920	7	2
New Mexico	2,925	40	48
New York	5,041	2	6
North Carolina	3,468	14	34
North Dakota	3,263	50	38
Ohio	3,922	8	23
Oklahoma	3,275	29	37
Oregon	3,838	28	25
Pennsylvania	4,238	6	15
Rhode Island	4,293	41	13
South Carolina	3,115	27	45
South Dakota	3,231	48	39
Tennessee	3,437	21	36
Texas	3,630	3	32
Utah	2,787	39	50
Vermont	3,755	49	28
Virginia	4,171	11	19
Washington	4,268	15	14
West Virginia	2,883	38	49
Wisconsin	3,834	19	26
Wyoming	3,912	51	24

Source: Tax Foundation

Gross National Product

THE GROSS NATIONAL PRODUCT (GNP) is the total dollar value of all final goods and services produced for consumption in society during a particular time period. Its rise or fall thus measures economic activity based on the labor and production output within a country. The figures used to assemble data include the manufacture of tangible goods such as cars, furniture and bread, and the provision of services used in daily living such as education, health care and auto repair. Intermediate services used in the production of the final product are not separated since they are reflected in the final price of the goods or service. The GNP does include allowances for depreciation and indirect business taxes such as sales and property.

The Gross Domestic Product (GDP) measures output generated through production by labor and property which is physically located within the confines of a country. It excludes such factors as income earned by U.S. citizens working abroad, but does include factors such as the rental value of owner-occupied housing. In December, 1991 the Bureau of Economic Analysis began using the GDP rather than the GNP as the primary measure of United States production. This figure facilitates comparisons between the United States and other countries, since it is the standard used in international guidelines for economic accounting.

Money Supply, Yield Curve

PAPER MONEY AND COINS WERE originally used as the only mediums of exchange, but the sophistication of financial needs have expanded the types of financial instruments used today. In order to monitor the money supply, the Federal Reserve System, the nation's central bank and controller of the monetary policy of the country, uses 4 measures:

- M1 is the base measurement of the money supply and includes currency, coins, demand deposits, travelers checks from non-bank issuers, and other checkable deposits.
- M2 is equal to M1 plus overnight repurchase agreements issued by commercial banks, overnight Eurodollars, money market mutual funds, money market deposit accounts, savings accounts, time deposits less than $100,000.
- M3 is M2 plus institutionally held money-market funds, term re-purchase agreements, term Eurodollars, and large time-deposits.
- L, the fourth measure, is equal to M3 plus Treasury bills, commercial paper, bankers acceptances, and very liquid assets such as savings bonds.

The Top Reference Sources

The Vest-Pocket MBA
Prentice Hall, $11.95
(212) 698-7000

This handy reference contains all the formulas, guidelines, ratios and rules-of-thumb needed to evaluate and solve dozens of business problems.

The book contains scores of tables, graphs and charts.

Topics include balance sheet analysis, statistics, break even, working capital, budgeting techniques, margin analysis and more.

Economic Indicators

ECONOMIC INDICATORS ARE FIGURES used by forecasters to predict changes in market economics. There are eleven leading economic indicators used to track developments in areas which together predict changes in the overall level of the economy. These indicators are:

- The length of the average work week of production workers in manufacturing settings;
- The average weekly state unemployment insurance claims;
- New orders for consumer goods and materials based on 1982 dollars;
- Vendor performance or percentage of companies receiving slower deliveries from suppliers;
- Contracts and orders for equipment;
- Index of new private housing units;
- Changes in unfulfilled orders by manufacturers of durable goods;
- Changes in sensitive materials prices;
- Index of S&P 500 common stock prices;
- Money supply;
- Index of consumer expectations.

Producer Price Index

The Producer Price Index (PPI) measures prices at the wholesale level only. The PPI is viewed as a leading indicator of inflation.

Consumer Price Index

The Consumer Price Index (CPI) is also a leading economic indicator. Although changes are reported from month to month, the more meaningful analysis is found in charting the percent change from the same month in the prior year.

Other economic indicators include the index of industrial materials prices, the Dow Jones Commodity Spot Price Index, Futures Price Index, the Employment Cost Index, and the Hourly Compensation Index or the Unit Labor Cost Index as a measure of the change in cost to the labor factor of production. Long term interest rates are also used to measure changes in the cost of the capital factor of production.

The Conference Board

Noted for its carefully managed research program, the Conference Board generates the monthly "Consumer Confidence Survey" designated by the Department of Commerce as a leading economic indicator and predictor of recessions and recovery.

Other services offered consist of timely publications, data collection services for marketing executives, demographic information services, periodic consumer surveys, and over 100 annual conferences and seminars.

Recommended Resources

The Conference Board
845 Third Ave.
New York, NY 10022
(212) 759-0900

Economic Indicators
Council of Economic Advisors
Superintendent of Documents
Government Printing Office
Washington, DC 20402

Monthly publication of national and international economic statistics

The Top Reference Sources

The Conference Board
(212) 759-0900 or
(800) 872-6273

The Conference Board is a nonpartisan, nonadvocacy organization which published 20 special reports and more than 50 surveys a year. The Conference Board is supported by a membership of more than 2,000 organizations.

The Board offers monthly and quarterly surveys on consumer confidence and other macroeconomic topics, as well as special reports that discuss these topics in depth.

The Board also sponsors conferences and seminars of particular interest to chief executives and economists.

Price Indexes

TO TRACK THE EFFECTS OF PRICE INCREASES, the years 1982 to 1984 are set as a basis (equal to 100). A price index of 33, therefore, indicates that the price was one-third that of the average in 1982-1984

Consumer Price Indexes by Major Groups

Year	All Items	Energy	Food	Shelter	Apparel, upkeep	Trans.	Medical Care	Fuel Oil	Elect.	Piped gas	Phone	Commo-dities
1960	29.6	22.4	30.0	25.2	45.7	29.8	22.3	13.5	29.9	17.6	58.3	33.6
1961	29.9	22.5	30.4	25.4	46.1	30.1	22.9	14.0	29.9	17.9	58.5	33.8
1962	30.2	22.6	30.6	25.8	46.3	30.8	23.5	14.0	29.9	17.9	58.5	34.1
1963	30.6	22.6	31.1	26.1	46.9	30.9	24.1	14.3	29.9	17.9	58.6	34.4
1964	31.0	22.5	31.5	26.5	47.3	31.4	24.6	14.0	29.8	17.9	58.6	34.8
1965	31.5	22.9	32.2	27.0	47.8	31.9	25.2	14.3	29.7	18.0	57.7	35.2
1966	32.4	23.3	33.8	27.8	49.0	32.3	26.3	14.7	29.7	18.1	56.5	36.1
1967	33.4	23.8	34.1	28.8	51.0	33.3	28.2	15.1	29.9	18.1	57.3	36.8
1968	34.8	24.2	35.3	30.1	53.7	34.3	29.9	15.6	30.2	18.2	57.3	38.1
1969	36.7	24.8	37.1	32.6	56.8	35.7	31.9	15.9	30.8	18.6	58.0	39.9
1970	38.8	25.5	39.2	35.5	59.2	37.5	34.0	16.5	31.8	19.6	58.7	41.7
1971	40.5	26.5	40.4	37.0	61.1	39.5	36.1	17.6	33.9	21.0	61.6	43.2
1972	41.8	27.2	42.1	38.7	62.3	39.9	37.3	17.6	35.6	22.1	65.0	44.5
1973	44.4	29.4	48.2	40.5	64.6	41.2	38.9	20.4	37.4	23.1	66.7	47.8
1974	49.3	38.1	55.1	44.4	69.4	45.8	42.4	32.2	44.1	26.0	69.5	53.5
1975	53.8	42.1	59.8	48.8	72.5	50.1	47.5	34.9	50	31.1	71.7	58.2
1976	56.9	45.1	61.6	51.5	75.2	55.1	52.0	37.4	53.1	36.3	74.3	60.7
1977	60.6	49.4	65.5	54.9	78.6	59.0	57.0	42.4	56.6	43.2	75.2	64.2
1978	65.2	52.5	72.0	60.5	81.4	61.7	61.8	44.9	60.9	47.5	76.0	68.8
1979	72.6	65.7	79.9	68.9	84.9	70.5	67.5	63.1	65.6	55.1	75.8	76.6
1980	82.4	86.0	86.8	81.0	90.9	83.1	74.9	87.7	75.8	65.7	77.7	86.0
1981	90.9	97.7	93.6	90.5	95.3	93.2	82.9	107.3	87.2	74.9	84.6	93.2
1982	96.5	99.2	97.4	96.9	97.8	97.0	92.5	105.0	95.8	89.8	93.2	97.0
1983	99.6	99.9	99.4	99.1	100.2	99.3	100.6	96.5	98.9	104.7	99.2	99.8
1984	103.9	100.9	103.2	104.0	102.1	103.7	106.8	98.5	105.3	105.5	107.5	103.2
1985	107.6	101.6	105.6	109.8	105.0	106.4	113.5	94.6	108.9	104.8	111.7	105.4
1986	109.6	88.2	109.0	115.8	105.9	102.3	122.0	74.1	110.4	99.7	117.2	104.4
1987	113.6	88.6	113.5	121.3	110.6	105.4	130.1	75.8	110	95.1	116.5	107.7
1988	118.3	89.3	118.2	127.1	115.4	108.7	138.6	75.8	111.5	94.5	116.0	111.5
1989	124.0	94.3	125.1	132.8	118.6	114.1	149.3	80.3	114.7	97.1	117.2	116.7
1990	130.7	102.1	132.4	140.0	124.1	120.5	162.8	98.6	117.4	97.3	117.7	122.8
1991	136.2	102.5	136.3	146.3	128.7	123.8	177.0	92.4	121.8	98.5	119.7	126.6

The average for the years 1982-84 is set to equal 100.

Source: 1992 Statistical Abstract

Almanac Fact

The average cost of a dozen eggs in 1951 was $3.91. In 1991, the average cost was $.94. Tuition, room and board at Harvard were $7,424 in 1951. In 1991, tuition, room and board cost $22,080.

Source: Census Bureau

Price Indexes (cont'd)

Consumer Price Index for All Urban Consumers

Group	March 1991	March 1992
All items	135.0	139.9
Food	135.8	138.1
Alcoholic beverages	142.2	146.7
Apparel and upkeep	128.8	133.4
Men's and boys' apparel	123.0	127.4
Women's and girls' apparel	129.5	133.6
Footwear	120.8	124.9
Housing, total	132.6	136.6
Rent	142.0	146.4
Gas and electricity	110.8	111.5
Fuel oil, bottled gas	99.3	90.5
House operation	115.7	117.7
House furnishings	107.5	109.4
Transportation	122.3	124.4
Medical care	173.7	187.3
Personal care	133.6	137.9
Tobacco products	197.6	213.5
Entertainment	136.7	141.2
Personal and educational expenses	179.3	193.5

The average for the years 1982-84 is set to equal 100.

Producer Price Indexes by Major Commodity Groups

Commodity	1975	1980	1985	1989	1990	1991
All commodities	58.4	89.8	103.2	112.2	116.3	116.5
Farm products	77.0	102.9	95.1	110.7	112.2	105.7
Processed foods and feeds	72.6	95.9	103.5	117.8	121.9	121.9
Textile products and apparel	67.4	89.7	102.9	112.3	114.9	116.3
Hides, skins and leather products	56.5	94.7	108.9	136.3	141.7	138.9
Fuels and related products	35.4	82.8	91.4	72.9	82.2	81.2
Chemicals and allied products	62.0	89.0	103.7	123.1	123.6	125.6
Rubber and plastic products	62.2	90.1	101.9	112.6	113.6	115.2
Lumber and wood products	62.1	101.5	106.6	126.7	129.7	132.0
Pulp, paper and allied products	59.0	86.3	113.3	137.8	141.3	143.0
Metals and metal products	61.5	95.0	104.4	124.1	123.0	120.3
Machinery and equipment	57.9	86.0	107.2	117.4	120.7	123.0
Furniture and household durables	67.5	90.7	107.1	116.9	119.1	121.2
Non-metallic mineral products	54.4	88.4	108.6	112.6	114.7	117.2
Transportation equipment	56.7	82.9	107.9	117.7	121.5	126.4
Miscellaneous	53.4	93.6	109.4	NA	NA	NA

The average for the year 1982 is set to equal 100.

Source: 1993 Information Please Almanac

Almanac Fact

The average worker in Mexico City must work 37 minutes to earn enough money for a loaf of bread. He must work 235 minutes to earn enough for a Big Mac and large fries.

Source: Prices and Earnings Around the Globe

Time Spent at Work and Leisure

Non-Manufacturing Industries–Gross Average Weekly Earnings ($) and Hours Worked

Industry	1975 Earnings	1975 Hrs.	1985 Earnings	1985 Hrs.	1990 Earnings	1990 Hrs.	1991 Earnings	1991 Hrs.
Coal, lignite mining	284.53	39.2	630.77	41.4	740.52	44.0	771.52	44.7
Metal mining	250.72	42.3	547.24	40.9	602.07	42.7	640.07	42.9
Non-metallic minerals	213.09	43.4	451.68	44.5	524.12	45.3	529.85	44.6
Telephone communications	221.18	38.4	512.52	41.1	578.74	40.9	594.38	40.6
Radio and TV broadcasting	214.50	39.0	381.39	37.1	438.61	34.7	463.68	34.5
Electric, gas, sanitary svcs.	246.79	41.2	534.59	41.7	636.76	41.7	656.45	41.6
Local and suburban trans.	196.89	40.1	309.85	38.3	376.65	38.2	382.02	37.6
Wholesale trade	188.75	38.6	358.36	38.7	411.48	38.1	425.20	38.1
Retail trade	108.22	32.4	177.31	29.7	195.26	28.8	200.20	28.6
Hotels, tourist courts, motels	89.64	31.9	176.9	30.5	214.68	30.8	219.91	30.5
Laundries, dry clean., plants	106.05	35.0	198.7	34.2	232.22	34.0	239.33	33.9
Gen. building contracting	254.88	36.0	414.78	37.1	487.08	37.7	499.33	37.6

Manufacturing Industries–Gross Average Weekly Earnings ($) and Hours Worked

Industry	1975 Earnings	1975 Hrs.	1985 Earnings	1985 Hrs.	1990 Earnings	1990 Hrs.	1991 Earnings	1991 Hrs.
All manufacturing	189.51	39.4	385.56	40.5	422.27	40.8	455.03	40.7
Durable goods	205.09	39.9	415.71	41.2	468.76	41.3	483.34	41.1
Primary metal industries	246.80	40.0	484.72	41.5	550.83	42.7	562.53	42.2
Iron and steel foundries	220.99	40.4	429.62	40.8	484.99	42.1	492.96	41.6
Nonferrous foundries	190.03	39.1	388.74	41.8	413.48	40.3	429.14	40.6
Fabricated metal products	201.60	40.0	398.96	41.3	447.28	41.3	461.44	41.2
Hardware, cutlery, hand tools	187.07	39.3	396.42	40.7	440.08	40.9	454.40	40.9
Other hardware	133.46	40.2	385.40	41.3	448.63	40.6	460.18	40.6
Structural metal products	202.61	40.2	369.00	41.0	416.56	41.0	427.76	40.7
Electric & electronic equip.	180.91	39.5	384.48	40.6	420.65	40.8	436.71	40.7
Machinery, except electrical	219.22	40.9	427.04	41.5	494.34	42.0	507.49	41.7
Transportation equipment	242.61	40.3	542.72	42.7	592.20	42.0	619.70	41.9
Motor vehicles & equipment	262.68	40.6	584.64	43.5	619.46	42.4	648.04	42.3
Lumber and wood products	167.35	39.1	326.36	39.8	365.82	40.2	371.20	40.0
Furniture and fixtures	142.13	37.9	283.29	39.4	333.52	39.1	341.15	38.9
Nondurable goods	168.78	38.8	342.86	39.5	405.60	40.0	418.64	40.1
Textile mill products	133.28	39.2	266.39	39.7	320.40	40.0	336.98	40.6
Apparel & textile products	111.97	35.1	208.00	36.3	239.88	36.4	249.75	37.0
Leather & leather products	120.80	37.4	217.09	37.3	258.43	37.4	267.78	37.4
Food and kindred products	184.17	40.3	341.60	40.0	392.90	40.8	401.13	40.6
Tobacco manufactures	171.38	38.0	448.26	37.2	645.23	39.2	660.40	39.1
Paper and allied products	207.58	41.6	466.34	43.1	532.59	43.3	549.91	43.3
Printing and publishing	198.32	37.0	365.31	37.7	426.38	37.9	434.70	37.8
Chemicals & products	219.63	40.9	484.78	41.9	576.80	42.6	603.60	42.9
Petroleum & products	267.07	41.6	603.72	43.0	723.86	44.6	750.58	44.1

Source: 1993 Information Please Almanac

The 1993 Fortune 500

Rank	Company	Sales ($ millions)	Profits ($ millions)	Assets ($ millions)	Market Value ($ millions)
1	General Motors	132,774.9	-23,498.3	191,012.8	27,556.0
2	Exxon	103,547.0	4,770.0	85,030.0	78,556.5
3	Ford Motor	100,785.6	-7,385.0	180,545.2	24,090.4
4	International Business Machines	65,096.0	-4,965.0	86,705.0	31,571.8
5	General Electric	62,202.0	4,725.0	192,876.0	73,353.0
6	Mobil	57,389.0	862.0	40,561.0	27,019.8
7	Philip Morris	50,157.0	4,939.0	50,014.0	57,710.1
8	E.I. du Pont De Nemours	37,643.0	-3,927.0	38,870.0	31,556.6
9	Chevron	37,464.0	1,569.0	33,970.0	25,160.3
10	Texaco	37,130.0	712.0	25,992.0	16,301.1
11	Chrysler	36,897.0	723.0	40,653.0	11,557.5
12	Boeing	30,184.0	552.0	18,147.0	11,753.5
13	Procter & Gamble	29,890.0	1,872.0	24,025.0	36,501.3
14	Amoco	25,543.0	-74.0	28,453.0	26,986.5
15	PepsiCo	22,083.7	374.3	20,951.2	33,101.4
16	United Technologies	22,032.0	-287.0	15,928.0	5,709.1
17	Shell Oil	21,702.0	-190.0	26,970.0	N.A.
18	Conagra	21,219.0	372.4	9,758.7	6,675.4
19	Eastman Kodak	20,577.0	1,146.0	23,138.0	17,435.6
20	Dow Chemical	19,177.0	-489.0	25,360.0	15,128.7
21	Xerox	18,261.0	-1,020.0	34,051.0	7,866.7
22	Atlantic Richfield	18,061.0	801.0	24,256.0	18,593.9
23	McDonnell Douglas	17,513.0	781.0	13,781.0	2,150.6
24	Hewlett-Packard	16,427.0	549.0	13,700.0	19,358.4
25	USX	16,186.0	-1,826.0	17,252.0	N.A.
26	RJR Nabisco Holdings	15,734.0	299.0	32,041.0	9,502.7
27	Digital Equipment	14,027.0	-2,795.5	11,284.3	6,149.6
28	Minnesota Mining & Mfg.	13,883.0	1,233.0	11,955.0	23,436.6
29	Johnson & Johnson	13,846.0	1,030.0	11,884.0	26,461.8
30	Tenneco	13,606.0	-1,323.0	16,584.0	6,633.9
31	International Paper	13,600.0	86.0	16,459.0	7,822.1
32	Motorola	13,341.0	453.0	10,629.0	16,249.4
33	Sara Lee	13,321.0	761.0	9,989.0	14,590.8
34	Coca-Cola	13,238.0	1,664.0	11,052.0	56,037.6
35	Westinghouse Electric	12,100.0	-1,291.0	10,398.0	4,590.4
36	Allied-Signal	12,089.0	-712.0	10,756.0	9,399.8
37	Phillips Petroleum	11,933.0	180.0	11,468.0	7,514.2
38	Goodyear Tire & Rubber	11,923.6	-658.6	8,563.7	5,210.6
39	Georgia-Pacific	11,847.0	-124.0	10,890.0	5,815.3
40	Bristol-Myers Squibb	11,805.0	1,962.0	10,804.0	29,394.5
41	Anheuser-Busch	11,400.8	917.5	10,537.9	14,894.4
42	IBP	11,129.7	63.6	1,499.4	896.5
43	Rockwell International	10,995.1	-1,036.0	9,731.0	6,219.8
44	Caterpillar	10,194.0	-2,435.0	13,935.0	5,931.0
45	Lockheed	10,138.0	-283.0	6,754.0	3,547.2
46	Coastal	10,062.9	-126.8	10,579.8	2,646.9
47	Merck	9,800.8	1,984.2	11,086.0	42,926.3
48	Ashland Oil	9,595.8	-335.7	5,668.4	1,678.9
49	Aluminum Co. of America	9,588.4	-1,139.2	11,023.1	5,990.4
50	Archer Daniels Midland	9,344.1	503.8	7,524.5	8,532.5

The Fortune 500 (cont'd)

Rank	Company	Sales ($ millions)	Profits ($ millions)	Assets ($ millions)	Market Value ($ millions)
51	Weyerhaeuser	9,259.9	372.0	18,158.4	8,997.3
52	Unilever U.S.	9,216.8	N.A.	N.A.	N.A.
53	Citgo Petroleum	9,166.7	33.2	3,488.2	N.A.
54	Raytheon	9,118.9	635.1	6,015.1	7,393.5
55	Unocal	8,948.0	220.0	9,452.0	6,438.6
56	Occidental Petroleum	8,940.0	-591.0	17,877.0	6,036.6
57	American Brands	8,840.3	883.8	14,963.0	6,837.0
58	General Dynamics	8,731.0	815.0	4,222.0	3,578.4
59	Sun	8,626.0	-559.0	6,061.0	2,947.4
60	Monsanto	8,485.0	-88.0	9,085.0	6,399.7
61	Baxter International	8,471.0	441.0	9,549.0	8,125.9
62	Unisys	8,421.9	361.2	7,508.6	2,165.8
63	Textron	8,347.5	-355.4	18,366.8	3,787.1
64	TRW	8,311.0	-156.0	5,458.0	3,742.5
65	Hanson Industries NA	8,288.3	551.0	18,352.4	N.A.
66	Abbott Laboratories	7,894.2	1,239.1	6,941.2	21,300.5
67	American Home Products	7,873.7	1,460.8	7,141.4	19,362.6
68	General Mills	7,795.5	495.6	4,305.0	11,723.9
69	Ralston Purina	7,768.0	313.2	5,150.5	5,247.2
70	Emerson Electric	7,706.0	662.9	6,627.0	12,885.0
71	Texas Instruments	7,470.0	247.0	5,185.0	4,825.9
72	Pfizer	7,414.8	810.9	9,590.1	19,142.7
73	Whirlpool	7,309.4	205.0	6,118.0	3,658.9
74	Borden	7,142.6	-439.6	5,321.4	3,656.7
75	Kimberly-Clark	7,091.1	135.0	6,029.1	8,922.1
76	Apple Computer	7,086.5	530.4	4,223.7	6,509.0
77	Hoechst Celanese	7,044.0	-7.0	7,044.0	N.A.
78	Colgate-Palmolive	7,035.4	477.0	5,434.1	10,255.4
79	Deere	6,960.7	37.4	11,445.6	4,120.9
80	H.J. Heinz	6,628.5	638.3	5,931.9	11,310.2
81	CPC International	6,599.0	223.8	5,171.2	7,344.0
82	Miles	6,499.0	69.8	4,973.1	N.A.
83	W.R. Grace	6,329.6	-294.5	5,598.6	3,415.9
84	Eli Lilly	6,282.3	708.7	8,672.8	15,073.3
85	Campbell Soup	6,278.5	490.5	4,353.8	10,940.3
86	Honeywell	6,254.0	246.8	4,870.1	4,374.4
87	Kellogg	6,190.6	431.2	4,015.0	15,725.6
88	Union Carbide	6,167.0	-175.0	4,941.0	2,242.1
89	Cooper Industries	6,158.5	-228.7	7,575.6	5,882.7
90	North American Philips	6,138.0	49.8	3,045.1	N.A.
91	Amerada Hess	5,970.4	7.5	8,721.8	4,825.9
92	Martin Marietta	5,970.1	345.4	3,599.6	3,365.1
93	Intel	5,922.5	1,066.5	8,088.6	24,191.8
94	PPG Industries	5,857.7	319.4	5,661.7	7,161.8
95	Litton Industries	5,714.4	174.4	4,838.7	2,079.9
96	Reynolds Metals	5,620.3	-748.8	6,897.0	3,062.7
97	Warner-Lambert	5,597.6	644.0	4,077.0	9,000.1
98	Quaker Oats	5,586.0	247.6	3,039.9	4,978.9
99	Levi Strauss Associates	5,570.3	360.8	2,880.7	N.A.
100	Northrop	5,550.0	121.0	3,162.0	1,611.5

The Fortune 500 (cont'd)

Rank	Company	Sales ($ millions)	Profits ($ millions)	Assets ($ millions)	Market Value ($ millions)
101	Stone Container	5,533.0	-170.5	6,682.0	1,118.3
102	LTV	5,425.3	598.7	6,223.1	68.5
103	American Cyanamid	5,347.6	395.1	5,412.2	4,515.0
104	Gillette	5,190.1	513.4	4,189.9	13,127.6
105	Johnson Controls	5,164.7	123.0	3,179.5	1,893.3
106	Coca-Cola Enterprises	5,127.0	-186.0	8,085.0	1,810.8
107	BASF	5,042.4	-116.1	4,077.6	N.A.
108	Dana	5,036.1	-382.0	4,342.9	2,072.1
109	Champion International	4,950.3	-440.4	9,381.4	2,821.2
110	Scott Paper	4,886.2	167.2	6,299.6	2,900.6
111	Lyondell Petrochemical	4,805.0	16.0	1,215.0	2,080.0
112	Black & Decker	4,790.4	-333.6	5,391.9	1,512.3
113	James River Corp. of Virginia	4,747.6	-427.3	6,336.3	1,560.2
114	Mead	4,703.2	71.6	4,031.4	2,554.9
115	Chiquita Brands International	4,534.1	-284.0	2,880.6	716.4
116	Dresser Industries	4,282.8	-365.5	3,187.8	2,575.7
117	R.R. Donnelley & Sons	4,193.1	234.7	3,410.2	4,650.9
118	Tyson Foods	4,169.7	160.5	2,617.7	3,825.2
119	Compaq Computer	4,132.2	213.2	3,142.4	3,552.4
120	J.E. Seagram	4,130.0	437.0	9,315.0	N.A.
121	Eaton	4,109.0	-128.0	3,096.0	2,907.7
122	Rhône-Poulenc Rorer	4,095.9	438.3	3,858.3	6,344.5
123	Schering-Plough	4,094.2	720.4	4,156.6	11,745.6
124	Bethlehem Steel	4,012.8	-449.3	5,070.7	1,583.9
125	FMC	4,003.3	-75.7	2,826.6	1,678.6
126	Navistar International	3,892.0	-212.0	3,627.0	702.7
127	VF	3,864.6	237.0	2,712.4	3,227.8
128	Avon Products	3,847.6	175.0	1,735.7	4,506.9
129	American Standard	3,800.6	-57.3	3,135.9	N.A.
130	Ingersoll-Rand	3,783.8	-234.4	3,387.6	3,530.4
131	Crown Cork & Seal	3,780.7	155.4	3,825.1	3,221.3
132	Cummins Engine	3,749.2	-189.5	2,230.5	1,530.3
133	Corning	3,744.0	-12.6	4,286.3	6,637.6
134	Boise Cascade	3,732.2	-227.5	4,559.7	915.3
135	Owens-Illinois	3,718.4	-134.2	5,151.1	1,383.1
136	Amax	3,703.0	-284.3	6,049.8	1,660.7
137	Times Mirror	3,702.0	-66.6	4,327.3	4,210.8
138	Upjohn	3,668.9	324.3	4,604.9	4,822.8
139	Sun Microsystems	3,627.9	173.3	2,671.6	3,632.8
140	Masco	3,553.7	183.1	3,986.6	5,072.6
141	Grumman	3,503.9	-123.2	2,089.0	1,073.7
142	Inland Steel Industries	3,494.3	-815.6	3,146.5	758.0
143	Gannett	3,469.0	199.7	3,609.0	7,296.7
144	Pitney Bowes	3,460.0	100.2	6,498.8	6,621.0
145	Farmland Industries	3,438.0	N.A.	1,526.4	N.A.
146	Fina	3,408.8	-10.2	2,924.5	1,026.5
147	Kerr-McGee	3,392.0	-101.0	3,521.0	2,233.6
148	AMP	3,337.1	290.3	3,005.1	6,164.6
149	Agway	3,274.9	N.A.	1,829.3	N.A.
150	Air Products & Chemicals	3,242.7	271.0	4,491.6	5,030.3

The Fortune 500 (cont'd)

Rank	Company	Sales ($ millions)	Profits ($ millions)	Assets ($ millions)	Market Value ($ millions)
151	Hershey Foods	3,222.3	242.6	2,672.9	4,903.9
152	Varity	3,186.2	-178.0	3,179.8	961.0
153	Rohm & Haas	3,083.0	-5.0	3,445.0	3,801.2
154	Tyco Laboratories	3,066.5	95.3	2,451.5	2,105.5
155	Union Camp	3,064.4	76.2	4,739.1	3,080.0
156	Harris	3,041.9	75.2	2,483.8	1,415.3
157	Maytag	3,041.2	-315.4	2,501.5	1,471.8
158	Berkshire Hathaway	3,029.3	407.3	16,944.8	14,764.1
159	Jefferson Smurfit	3,000.2	-83.7	2,436.4	N.A.
160	Universal	2,989.0	70.7	1,261.4	978.5
161	Ethyl	2,975.0	255.0	9,204.3	3,254.9
162	Premark International	2,954.4	-79.3	1,958.8	1,476.3
163	Teledyne	2,890.8	33.2	1,535.9	1,122.1
164	Seagate Technology	2,888.7	63.2	1,816.6	1,091.5
165	Loral	2,881.8	121.8	2,658.6	2,145.4
166	Hercules	2,878.3	167.9	3,227.9	3,095.5
167	Owens-Corning Fiberglas	2,878.0	73.0	2,126.0	1,951.1
168	Illinois Tool Works	2,820.8	192.1	2,204.2	4,133.3
169	Geo. A. Hormel	2,813.7	95.2	913.0	1,843.2
170	EG&G	2,788.8	87.8	749.7	1,335.1
171	Paccar	2,761.4	65.2	2,809.3	2,054.7
172	Sherwin-Williams	2,759.5	62.9	1,729.9	2,859.1
173	Pennzoil	2,749.4	128.2	4,457.2	2,321.6
174	Temple-Inland	2,713.2	146.9	10,765.5	2,707.3
175	Reader's Digest Association	2,666.9	234.4	1,932.3	5,677.0
176	Mapco	2,644.2	100.7	1,911.7	1,546.5
177	Avery Dennison	2,622.9	80.1	1,684.0	1,538.8
178	Diamond Shamrock	2,602.6	8.7	1,297.5	592.0
179	Ultramar	2,595.5	56.3	1,792.4	796.5
180	Phelps Dodge	2,594.0	221.7	3,441.2	3,606.8
181	Land O'Lakes	2,561.8	N.A.	840.5	N.A.
182	Amdahl	2,553.7	-7.0	2,701.0	905.2
183	Armstrong World Industries	2,549.8	-234.2	2,009.8	1,239.3
184	Baker Hughes	2,544.6	5.0	3,212.9	3,243.4
185	Hasbro	2,541.1	179.2	2,082.8	2,735.1
186	B.F. Goodrich	2,530.6	-295.9	2,451.7	1,165.7
187	Ball	2,446.4	69.1	1,563.9	929.1
188	Engelhard	2,399.7	10.6	1,279.5	2,701.3
189	Total Petroleum	2,397.0	3.6	1,071.7	238.6
190	Whitman	2,397.0	59.8	2,062.8	1,579.8
191	Olin	2,386.0	9.0	2,030.0	846.2
192	Parker Hannifin	2,382.0	11.2	1,920.9	1,537.9
193	National Steel	2,373.3	-48.4	2,188.5	N.A.
194	McDermott	2,372.7	26.5	2,464.8	N.A.
195	Willamette Industries	2,372.4	81.6	2,527.4	2,273.5
196	Becton Dickinson	2,365.3	200.8	3,177.7	2,721.9
197	Westvaco	2,343.9	135.9	3,703.9	2,295.1
198	Knight-Ridder	2,334.6	40.9	2,458.1	3,173.5
199	Quantum Chemical	2,324.2	-287.5	3,153.9	383.3
200	Dean Foods	2,291.0	62.0	857.2	1,130.9

The Fortune 500 (cont'd)

Rank	Company	Sales ($ millions)	Profits ($ millions)	Assets ($ millions)	Market Value ($ millions)
201	Dover	2,291.0	129.7	1,426.1	2,676.2
202	International Multifoods	2,281.4	22.0	767.7	493.3
203	Conner Peripherals	2,273.5	121.1	1,904.7	869.7
204	Clark Oil & Refining	2,267.9	-5.1	787.8	N.A.
205	Maxxam	2,254.2	-7.3	3,125.0	273.9
206	Manville	2,241.5	14.8	3,630.0	1,180.0
207	Brunswick	2,227.7	-26.3	1,908.0	1,476.3
208	Collins & Aikman Group	2,226.7	-170.5	2,145.7	N.A.
209	Stanley Works	2,217.7	98.1	1,607.6	1,931.2
210	Louisiana-Pacific	2,192.0	176.9	2,206.0	3,959.2
211	Polaroid	2,168.2	99.0	2,008.1	1,318.4
212	Tosco	2,161.1	-74.5	962.9	706.2
213	Tribune	2,108.6	119.8	2,751.6	3,462.2
214	E-Systems	2,098.7	-69.5	1,253.6	1,266.3
215	Armco	2,084.0	-429.9	1,959.5	737.5
216	Burlington Ind. Equity	2,065.9	-182.5	1,676.0	1,015.1
217	Tandem Computers	2,058.3	-41.2	2,045.4	1,456.6
218	McGraw-Hill	2,050.5	28.6	2,508.1	2,898.9
219	Springs Industries	1,976.1	44.5	1,250.3	781.9
220	Dow Corning	1,955.7	-72.0	2,190.7	N.A.
221	York International	1,939.4	50.9	1,164.4	1,270.3
222	Gencorp	1,937.0	22.0	1,131.0	416.4
223	Asarco	1,932.4	-83.1	2,945.9	1,025.6
224	Morton International	1,929.4	144.5	2,110.9	3,233.6
225	Wang Laboratories	1,909.5	-356.6	1,065.9	138.9
226	Central Soya	1,907.7	28.0	892.1	N.A.
227	Arvin Industries	1,893.2	6.4	1,152.4	725.1
228	Pet	1,881.3	103.4	1,490.1	1,768.8
229	Mattel	1,880.2	143.9	1,260.3	2,126.7
230	Mid-America Dairymen	1,875.0	N.A.	389.7	N.A.
231	Sequa	1,868.3	N.A.	1,927.6	276.4
232	Fruit of the Loom	1,855.1	178.6	2,281.9	3,494.4
233	Sonoco Products	1,844.4	43.4	1,246.5	2,135.0
234	Dow Jones	1,824.7	107.6	2,372.0	3,068.4
235	Rubbermaid	1,810.3	164.1	1,326.6	5,246.8
236	Adolph Coors	1,805.7	-2.0	1,373.4	613.1
237	Echlin	1,793.1	64.3	1,241.2	1,441.2
238	Farmers Union Central Exchange	1,778.5	N.A.	1,055.9	N.A.
239	USG	1,777.0	-191.0	1,659.0	27.9
240	New York Times	1,773.5	-44.7	1,995.0	2,292.4
241	Shaw Industries	1,751.4	58.0	1,090.1	2,623.6
242	Witco	1,738.2	39.2	1,811.8	1,141.9
243	National Semiconductor	1,726.3	-120.1	1,148.9	1,214.3
244	Imcera Group	1,724.5	127.5	2,050.8	2,178.2
245	Bausch & Lomb	1,722.3	171.4	1,873.7	3,255.1
246	Clorox	1,717.0	98.7	1,614.8	2,619.8
247	Sundstrand	1,697.5	-121.7	1,803.8	1,378.0
248	Trinova	1,695.5	14.4	1,017.4	734.2
249	Murphy Oil	1,681.7	105.6	1,936.5	1,713.4
250	Masco Industries	1,678.3	38.4	1,877.3	766.3

The Fortune 500 (cont'd)

Rank	Company	Sales ($ millions)	Profits ($ millions)	Assets ($ millions)	Market Value ($ millions)
251	Burlington Resources	1,658.7	257.8	4,469.7	5,606.3
252	Freeport-McMoran	1,656.6	187.8	3,546.7	2,729.5
253	Cyprus Minerals	1,644.7	-333.6	1,683.2	1,613.9
254	Timken	1,642.3	4.5	1,738.4	904.8
255	National Service Industries	1,633.8	74.1	1,042.4	1,300.9
256	Harsco	1,633.1	84.3	991.2	1,088.1
257	General Signal	1,622.5	-83.2	1,226.0	1,268.8
258	Nucor	1,620.5	79.2	1,490.4	3,792.4
259	Duracell International	1,616.7	127.8	2,156.6	3,980.8
260	Fleetwood Enterprises	1,601.2	40.2	915.0	947.6
261	Newell	1,583.4	119.1	1,569.6	2,957.3
262	Crown Central Petroleum	1,576.3	-5.5	675.3	159.8
263	American Greetings	1,573.1	97.5	1,437.8	1,869.5
264	Cabot	1,562.2	62.2	1,554.5	706.4
265	Lubrizol	1,559.3	124.6	1,127.1	2,062.1
266	Reliance Electric	1,553.0	26.0	1,132.0	882.3
267	Deluxe	1,552.3	202.8	1,197.0	3,582.3
268	Great Lakes Chemical	1,538.2	232.7	1,732.0	5,570.0
269	Advanced Micro Devices	1,531.1	245.0	1,448.1	2,145.9
270	Storage Technology	1,521.5	15.5	1,709.9	990.7
271	LaFarge	1,511.2	-100.6	1,767.4	1,001.9
272	West Point-Pepperell	1,500.0	N.A.	N.A.	1,447.2
273	Bowater	1,495.6	-82.0	2,881.6	816.3
274	Nacco Industries	1,481.5	-85.9	1,664.3	445.7
275	McCormick	1,476.1	95.2	1,130.9	2,073.6
276	Interco	1,471.7	-48.9	1,250.1	693.8
277	Washington Post	1,463.8	127.8	1,568.1	2,813.9
278	Federal Paper Board	1,460.8	91.6	2,573.5	1,085.5
279	Hillenbrand Industries	1,438.2	116.3	1,935.2	3,248.9
280	Del Monte Foods	1,438.0	-58.0	1,215.0	N.A.
281	Lear Holdings	1,422.7	-22.2	799.9	N.A.
282	Harnischfeger Industries	1,401.0	56.7	1,507.7	496.4
283	Nalco Chemical	1,394.5	145.0	1,350.6	2,547.0
284	Coltec Industries	1,368.7	-42.2	828.8	1,231.2
285	Walter Industries	1,366.6	22.3	3,171.3	N.A.
286	M.A. Hanna	1,337.9	19.0	1,178.1	690.3
287	Potlatch	1,330.4	78.9	1,998.8	1,442.9
288	Thiokol	1,322.0	63.0	962.2	346.0
289	Oryx Energy	1,313.0	14.0	3,749.0	2,108.0
290	Gold Kist	1,312.0	N.A.	676.7	N.A.
291	Crane	1,307.0	24.3	630.2	816.4
292	Wm. Wrigley Jr.	1,301.3	141.3	711.4	3,967.4
293	Great American Mgmt. & Invest.	1,298.4	42.1	486.6	287.4
294	Tektronix	1,297.2	19.7	877.3	722.5
295	Raychem	1,296.3	-24.8	1,392.6	1715.3
296	Dresser-Rand	1,294.4	N.A.	733.7	N.A.
297	Gerber Products	1,293.1	127.6	893.7	2,334.7
298	Varian Associates	1,290.7	38.7	893.0	839.9
299	Tecumseh Products	1,286.7	-42.7	1,078.6	701.5
300	Rohr	1,283.3	1.5	1,364.0	169.9

The Fortune 500 (cont'd)

Rank	Company	Sales ($ millions)	Profits ($ millions)	Assets ($ millions)	Market Value ($ millions)
301	DWG	1,278.6	-7.5	881.7	411.3
302	Alliant Techsystems	1,274.4	38.8	521.8	236.3
303	Federal-Mogul	1,271.9	-83.7	1,099.5	375.0
304	Zenith Electronics	1,271.4	-105.9	578.6	227.0
305	Brown-Forman	1,263.8	146.4	1,193.5	2,190.6
306	E.W. Scripps	1,263.4	83.9	1,710.2	1,995.5
307	Amoskeag	1,247.9	5.3	934.9	87.3
308	Pentair	1,239.0	42.8	869.0	498.3
309	Valero Energy	1,234.6	83.9	1,759.1	952.1
310	Magnetek	1,229.8	22.2	917.0	589.4
311	United States Surgical	1,197.2	138.9	1,168.1	3,293.3
312	Trinity Industries	1,193.5	22.1	974.8	979.7
313	Medtronic	1,187.2	161.5	1,163.5	4,513.0
314	Standard Commercial	1,185.0	22.3	723.8	188.4
315	Intergraph	1,182.1	8.4	983.8	584.3
316	Bemis	1,181.3	57.0	742.7	1,300.8
317	Cooper Tire & Rubber	1,176.0	43.2	796.9	2,995.9
318	Figgie International	1,172.8	28.3	1,113.1	389.0
319	Leggett & Platt	1,170.5	62.5	678.0	1,416.9
320	Anchor Glass Container	1,163.3	3.3	1,321.7	N.A.
321	Fort Howard	1,151.4	-80.0	3,574.6	N.A.
322	Interstate Bakeries	1,145.9	15.6	573.6	345.9
323	Mark IV Industries	1,145.6	26.4	1,090.3	736.6
324	Savannah Foods & Industries	1,139.9	28.0	635.8	377.2
325	AG Processing	1,129.8	N.A.	416.4	N.A.
326	Amgen	1,128.4	357.6	1,374.3	4,532.8
327	Quantum	1,127.7	46.8	546.8	640.0
328	Data General	1,127.0	-62.5	940.5	458.6
329	Intl. Flavors & Fragrances	1,126.4	170.6	1,267.6	4,240.8
330	Ferro	1,107.4	58.8	696.5	893.7
331	Gateway 2000	1,107.1	70.0	269.3	N.A.
332	Harley-Davidson	1,106.0	53.8	522.2	1,291.4
333	J.M. Huber	1,102.3	43.0	871.4	N.A.
334	Unifi	1,091.4	62.6	804.9	2,007.4
335	Alberto-Culver	1,091.3	38.6	610.4	736.6
336	Ocean Spray	1,090.8	N.A.	577.2	N.A.
337	Dibrell Brothers	1,084.9	30.3	630.5	465.0
338	Weirton Steel	1,081.8	-31.8	1,005.4	180.2
339	Vulcan Materials	1,079.8	94.0	1,083.9	1,986.8
340	General Instrument	1,076.0	-53.0	1,727.5	2,030.1
341	Outboard Marine	1,070.0	1.9	997.1	402.2
342	Seaboard	1,060.7	31.1	483.5	360.0
343	IMC Fertilizer Group	1,058.5	-74.6	1,778.0	832.3
344	Thomas & Betts	1,057.2	50.9	1,117.1	1,251.9
345	Hartmarx	1,053.9	-220.2	512.0	222.0
346	Smithfield Foods	1,050.6	21.6	277.7	260.0
347	A.O. Smith	1,046.3	-17.3	769.0	409.1
348	SCI Systems	1,045.4	3.8	613.0	464.3
349	GAF	1,043.3	-167.9	2,092.4	N.A.
350	Briggs & Stratton	1,043.3	51.5	613.9	920.2

The Fortune 500 (cont'd)

Rank	Company	Sales ($ millions)	Profits ($ millions)	Assets ($ millions)	Market Value ($ millions)
351	Maxtor	1,038.9	7.1	445.2	215.1
352	Allegheny Ludlum	1,036.0	-78.4	871.2	1,183.3
353	Helene Curtis Industries	1,023.0	19.2	525.8	422.1
354	Pittway	1,019.4	47.4	574.0	578.5
355	UST	1,012.7	312.6	674.0	5,876.2
356	Terex	1,012.3	N.A.	N.A.	111.9
357	Ecolab	1,004.8	64.3	832.4	1,165.1
358	C.R. Bard	990.2	75.0	712.5	1,354.0
359	First Brands	988.5	23.4	836.0	689.9
360	Snap-On Tools	985.9	66.0	1,177.4	1,415.6
361	Thermo Electron	975.3	59.2	1,818.3	1,399.3
362	Worthington Industries	974.2	55.5	622.3	1,500.0
363	ITT Rayonier	973.7	-103.5	1,476.4	N.A.
364	Sunbeam/Oster	967.2	48.3	1,092.1	1,469.7
365	Dexter	957.6	38.2	782.0	622.9
366	Danaher	955.5	31.6	769.8	763.2
367	AST Research	951.1	68.5	580.6	454.6
368	Tesoro Petroleum	950.3	-65.9	446.7	56.3
369	Holnam	946.2	-28.6	1,353.1	438.7
370	Western Digital	940.0	-72.9	532.5	303.5
371	H.B. Fuller	933.7	35.6	561.2	537.8
372	Wheeling-Pittsburgh	933.3	-33.6	1,116.7	164.6
373	IMO Industries	929.2	-82.6	994.6	117.7
374	Brooke Group	928.6	N.A.	N.A.	36.1
375	Perkin-Elmer	919.7	58.8	801.3	1,243.0
376	Kellwood	917.1	22.8	538.0	400.1
377	NL Industries	915.8	-76.4	1,472.1	241.7
378	Beckman Instruments	913.6	43.8	738.4	682.8
379	Essex Group	910.6	1.3	706.0	N.A.
380	Consolidated Papers	905.3	12.4	1,487.0	1,719.7
381	CF Industries	903.5	N.A.	790.6	N.A.
382	Russell	899.1	81.9	964.9	1,316.1
383	Allergan	897.7	103.6	885.8	1,503.0
384	Nortek	895.0	-24.2	515.4	68.9
385	Dell Computer	889.9	50.9	559.6	1,093.6
386	Flowers Industries	888.7	31.7	462.1	691.3
387	Chesapeake	888.4	4.7	958.9	498.0
388	Universal Foods	883.4	41.7	702.1	879.5
389	Lukens	881.7	33.1	760.0	671.3
390	Jostens	876.4	61.4	565.4	1,269.3
391	Mitchell Energy	874.4	44.3	2,252.3	913.6
392	Silicon Graphics	866.6	-118.4	758.1	1,903.9
393	Lincoln Electric	862.3	-45.3	603.8	N.A.
394	UCC Investors Holding	856.6	-27.8	1,212.1	N.A.
395	JPS Textile Group	852.3	-10.9	563.7	N.A.
396	Magma Copper	833.3	55.3	1,156.5	736.1
397	Valhi	829.8	N.A.	N.A.	688.5
398	Wellman	828.2	52.3	997.0	710.9
399	Amsted Industries	827.1	15.3	522.1	N.A.
400	Gitano Group	826.5	-237.7	249.6	72.0

The Fortune 500 (cont'd)

Rank	Company	Sales ($ millions)	Profits ($ millions)	Assets ($ millions)	Market Value ($ millions)
401	Quaker State	821.3	-93.8	792.8	308.9
402	Clark Equipment	819.6	66.0	958.7	392.6
403	Pilgrim's Pride	817.4	-29.7	434.6	244.9
404	Herman Miller	809.7	-14.1	471.6	545.1
405	Hudson Foods	809.2	2.2	393.1	193.1
406	SPX	801.2	16.4	566.0	236.3
407	Hubbell	800.2	77.6	806.7	1,654.5
408	Cray Research	797.6	-14.9	1,021.3	742.3
409	Doskocil	796.1	-26.8	286.0	88.1
410	Safety-Kleen	795.9	45.6	1,006.4	1,261.5
411	Tri Valley Growers	795.1	N.A.	744.0	N.A.
412	Cincinnati Milacron	792.1	21.5	578.9	579.6
413	Louisiana Land & Exploration	787.4	-6.8	1,209.1	1,143.9
414	Kaman	784.7	17.4	443.4	217.2
415	Molex	782.1	67.5	849.7	1,953.2
416	Georgia Gulf	779.5	46.3	419.4	795.8
417	K-III Communications	778.2	-145.3	1,193.2	N.A.
418	Leslie Fay	777.4	N.A.	N.A.	102.3
419	Millipore	777.0	33.2	786.6	769.6
420	Ametek	776.2	44.4	594.7	640.9
421	Kendall International	774.9	226.9	733.3	472.6
422	Cone Mills	770.1	43.4	401.9	449.6
423	Tyco Toys	768.6	18.0	749.2	386.7
424	Applied Materials	757.1	39.5	853.8	1,736.7
425	Stanhome	744.1	46.7	415.6	652.5
426	Thorn Apple Valley	740.4	21.1	132.6	128.8
427	A. Schulman	738.9	43.8	428.0	867.2
428	Crystal Brands	736.3	-75.3	478.9	29.6
429	Maxus Energy	730.3	74.2	1,805.9	1,168.7
430	Abex	728.4	-203.0	738.1	79.0
431	International Controls	725.6	-7.6	476.4	N.A.
432	Insilco	725.4	31.3	547.7	N.A.
433	Meredith	724.6	-6.3	593.3	431.4
434	Gaylord Container	722.8	-132.5	901.7	173.2
435	UIS	714.4	39.1	464.2	N.A.
436	Hon Industries	712.3	38.7	322.7	918.5
437	Interlake	711.1	-27.7	511.3	79.8
438	Betz Laboratories	710.2	82.0	510.6	1,703.0
439	Delta Woodside Industries	705.5	40.0	524.8	356.8
440	Standard Register	705.2	26.0	482.5	581.4
441	Huffy	703.6	4.2	335.3	188.7
442	Union Texas Petroleum Holdings	700.7	13.6	1,580.6	1,957.9
443	Fisher-Price	695.5	41.3	455.2	799.6
444	Longview Fibre	691.4	32.1	930.3	982.0
445	Pall	690.5	92.7	912.9	2,097.6
446	Imperial Holly	690.2	-2.8	364.1	127.5
447	Tambrands	687.5	121.4	373.0	2,369.4
448	Stewart & Stevenson Services	686.4	35.7	477.9	1,093.5
449	Valspar	683.5	34.4	321.6	690.2
450	Carter-Wallace	681.1	45.7	582.2	1,219.0

The Fortune 500 (cont'd)

Rank	Company	Sales ($ millions)	Profits ($ millions)	Assets ($ millions)	Market Value ($ millions)
451	Homestake Mining	681.0	-175.8	1,145.2	1,709.6
452	Nerco	672.0	-551.2	1,170.9	456.2
453	Valassis Communications	671.0	74.4	292.7	746.9
454	NCH	670.8	39.4	470.8	546.8
455	Vishay Intertechnology	664.2	30.4	651.1	682.2
456	Dr Pepper/Seven-up	663.2	-140.1	668.1	1,157.5
457	Commerce Clearing House	659.4	-64.1	595.8	678.3
458	Prairie Farms Dairy	659.3	N.A.	197.5	N.A.
459	Standard Products	657.7	23.3	398.8	446.8
460	Coca-Cola Bottling Co. Consol.	655.8	-114.1	898.7	181.3
461	Banta	655.3	35.7	410.2	602.4
462	Sigma-Aldrich	654.4	95.5	N.A.	2,650.6
463	Sealy	654.2	10.0	780.3	N.A.
464	Baroid	648.1	17.7	560.1	512.3
465	Reynolds & Reynolds	647.5	39.2	521.8	748.8
466	Riceland Foods	647.5	N.A.	237.0	N.A.
467	Natl. Coop. Refinery Assn.	646.4	N.A.	463.6	N.A.
468	Oshkosh Truck	641.2	8.8	260.0	79.3
469	Blount	637.3	0.7	466.2	170.5
470	Toro	635.2	-23.8	421.3	234.3
471	Specialty Coatings International	635.0	22.2	393.8	N.A.
472	Anacomp	632.0	26.9	681.6	149.6
473	Newmont Mining	631.7	79.0	1,215.0	2,700.4
474	Warnaco Group	626.9	-20.2	629.6	590.5
475	Kimball International	624.4	38.6	422.0	656.4
476	Sun-Diamond Growers	623.2	N.A.	343.0	N.A.
477	Ply Gem	623.2	6.3	314.0	128.6
478	Giddings & Lewis	622.9	35.5	627.5	789.5
479	La-Z-Boy Chair	621.2	25.1	376.7	527.8
480	Joy Technologies	621.1	-14.2	574.7	263.9
481	AM International	620.4	-124.8	441.4	14.7
482	LSI Logic	617.5	-110.2	736.2	573.3
483	Loctite	617.1	72.3	557.4	1,586.6
484	Guilford Mills	614.9	24.9	414.3	353.1
485	Eagle-Picher Industries	612.2	28.9	419.4	24.8
486	Texas Industries	611.1	1.9	776.7	302.8
487	St. Joe Paper	610.7	15.6	1,388.3	1,261.9
488	Mary Kay Cosmetics	609.6	14.5	500.8	N.A.
489	Silgan	605.0	N.A.	N.A.	N.A.
490	Harman Intl. Industries	604.5	3.5	415.9	195.1
491	Bandag	602.4	82.8	469.2	1,552.2
492	Kennametal	594.5	12.9	472.2	339.1
493	Interface	594.1	12.3	534.1	215.8
494	Vigoro	594.1	41.9	411.4	470.0
495	Exide	593.6	6.7	463.7	N.A.
496	Arcadian	593.4	4.5	604.0	N.A.
497	Avondale Industries	592.0	-11.2	346.2	41.6
498	Carlisle	591.1	24.7	383.5	393.7
499	E.R. Carpenter	590.0	14.0	380.0	N.A.
500	Block Drug	585.3	57.3	649.6	947.1
	Totals	2,364,525.7	10.5	2,551,429.3	1,821,392.0

Source: Fortune Magazine, 1993

Inc. 500 Fastest Growing Companies

Rank	Company	1991 Sales ($ thousands)	1991 Profit Range	No. of Employees 1991	% Sales Growth 1987-91
1	Kingston Technology, Fountain Valley, CA	140,666	A	110	117,122
2	Gateway 2000, N. Sioux City, SD	626,798	C	1,193	41,355
3	M.D. Enterprises of Connecticut, New Haven, CT	83,212	D	163	35,767
4	Veragon, Houston, TX	34,125	F	110	33,687
5	Insight Distribution Network, Tempe, AZ	61,548	D	250	25,545
6	Sterling Healthcare Group, Coral Gables, FL	28,128	C	40	21,705
7	Indeck Energy Services, Buffalo Grove, IL	77,793	F	126	18,828
8	Communique Telecommunications, Ontario, CA	18,844	E	60	14,395
9	Technology Works, Austin, TX	28,264	D	100	12,747
10	Transitional Technology, Anaheim, CA	11,511	D	46	9,823
11	Parsons Technology, Hiawatha, IA	28,033	D	235	9,771
12	MacTemps, Cambridge, MA	13,447	D	72	9,437
13	Telephone Express, Colorado Springs, CO	18,451	C	80	8,771
14	Worthington Voice Services, Worthington, OH	9,134	A	9	8,599
15	Alliance Employee Leasing, Dallas, TX	174,618	E	37	8,029
16	Administaff, Kingwood, TX	298,360	D	11,380	7,316
17	Active Voice, Seattle, WA	11,531	B	90	7,152
18	Dunsirn Industries, Neenah, WI	9,754	C	62	7,125
19	Salepoint Systems, San Diego, CA	7,810	A	30	7,000
20	Mega-Sys, Greenwood, IN	7,703	D	13	6,967
21	Jelyn & Co., Fort Washington, PA	8,769	B	15	6,915
22	Powerfood, Berkeley, CA	10,970	D	56	6,714
23	MapInfo, Troy, NY	7,042	C	80	6,671
24	Metrica, San Antonio, TX	8,152	D	145	6,269
25	Shiva, Cambridge, MA	28,044	F	130	5,957
26	Parexel International, Waltham, MA	25,652	D	550	5,922
27	Corporate Express, Boulder, CO	36,413	F	167	5,909
28	McArthur/Glen Group, McLean, VA	24,000	F	124	5,754
29	MVM, Falls Church, VA	24,181	D	798	5,685
30	B&V Technology, Idaho Falls, ID	18,275	A	231	5,647
31	Mastech Systems, Pittsburgh, PA	13,513	B	247	5,438
32	Maximum Strategy, San Jose, CA	7,820	A	25	5,331
33	AAMP of America, Clearwater, FL	6,694	B	29	5,089
34	Florida Infusion, Palm Harbor, FL	21,931	B	16	5,060
35	Global Mail, Sterling, VA	8,803	C	45	5,018
36	Federal Investment, E. Providence, RI	12,629	B	20	4,972
37	Contract Manufacturer, Madill, OK	5,619	D	68	4,962
38	Glitterwrap, Westwood, NJ	10,404	D	75	4,926
39	StarPak, Denver, CO	12,930	D	125	4,779
40	Trigen Energy, White Plains, NY	44,930	D	195	4,595
41	Focus Healthcare Management, Brentwood, TN	11,521	D	200	4,564
42	Mustang Engineering, Houston, TX	15,286	C	230	4,546
43	Corporate Child Care Management, Nashville, TN	6,344	F	400	4,306
44	Staff Relief, Houston, TX	13,521	D	600	4,276
45	American Megatrends, Norcross, GA	70,210	A	114	4,165
46	Panoramic, Fort Wayne, IN	5,855	A	20	4,143
47	Melaleuca, Idaho Falls, ID	100,765	A	728	4,143
48	Adtran, Huntsville, AL	42,621	A	225	4,038
49	User Technology Associates, Arlington, VA	12,424	B	250	3,934
50	Micro-Frame Technologies, Ontario, CA	5,454	B	46	3,881

Profit Range: A-16% or more; B-11% to 15%; C-6% to 10%; D-1%-5%; E-break-even; F-loss

Inc. 500 Fastest Growing Companies (cont'd)

Rank	Company	1991 Sales ($ thousands)	1991 Profit Range	No. of Employees, 1991	% Sales Growth 1987-91
51	Tycom Limited Partnership, Santa Ana, CA	11,450	F	210	3,848
52	Conmec, Bethlehem, PA	19,401	D	110	3,819
53	Registry, Wellesley, MA	16,927	D	54	3,809
54	Presidio, Suitland, MD	4,087	E	15	3,792
55	Abacus, San Francisco, CA	30,276	D	103	3,615
56	Softub, Pacoima, CA	6,359	D	70	3,555
57	Select Ticketing Systems, Syracuse, NY	8,024	D	69	3,547
58	Kofax Image Products, Irvine, CA	10,342	F	96	3,503
59	CMG Health, Owings Mills, MD	10,442	F	95	3,381
60	Leasing Solutions, San Jose, CA	23,295	D	48	3,286
61	Ward Petroleum, Enid, OK	146,886	D	79	3,258
62	Auto Kontrols, Houston, TX	7,941	D	40	3,128
63	Compurex System, Easton, MA	15,123	D	16	3,064
64	Premiere Merchandising, Inglewood, CA	3,489	E	12	3,043
65	National Safety Associates, Memphis, TN	284,891	A	650	2,946
66	Fortitech, Schenectady, NY	5,223	C	18	2,902
67	Calais Home, Houston, TX	9,491	D	20	2,894
68	Abacus Technology, Chevy Chase, MD	12,407	C	104	2,890
69	Wind River Systems, Alameda, CA	17,085	C	125	2,871
70	EduCare Community Living, Austin, TX	13,685	C	328	2,862
71	Coldwater Creek, Sand Point, ID	10,869	A	54	2,814
72	Cadapult Graphic Systems, Paramus, NJ	4,125	D	8	2,785
73	Pacific Trading Overseas, Miami, FL	5,423	B	3	2,769
74	Cardboard Gold, Santa Ana, CA	11,154	C	16	2,760
75	Atlantic Coast Textiles, Atlanta, GA	3,322	D	8	2,739
76	Intl. Computers & Telecommunications, Rockville, MD	11,269	E	205	2,682
77	Grand Aire Express, Monroe, MI	3,808	A	41	2,640
78	Montgomery Development, Syracuse, NY	6,349	D	25	2,625
79	BitWise Designs, Schenectady, NY	2,928	D	10	2,611
80	Vermont Teddy Bear, Shelburne, VT	5,245	E	130	2,562
81	Item Products, Houston, TX	3,845	A	31	2,552
82	Tampa Bay Vending, Tampa, FL	2,747	A	35	2,541
83	Collegiate Sports Design, New Strawn, KS	4,294	F	6	2,534
84	Deneba Systems, Miami, FL	8,421	A	60	2,532
85	Complete Health Services, Birmingham, AL	159,651	D	410	2,483
86	Fiber Optic Technologies, Engelwood, CO	5,949	D	73	2,453
87	PAI, Oak Ridge, TN	7,454	C	65	2,453
88	Summit Marketing Group, Rochester, NY	4,516	D	159	2,451
89	Payroll 1 MidAtlantic, McLean, VA	2,549	B	52	2,424
90	Nationwide Remittance Centers, McLean, VA	9,899	F	175	2,412
91	MediServe Information Systems, Tempe, AZ	2,704	B	20	2,404
92	Cap Toys, Bedford Heights, OH	18,264	C	30	2,392
93	Tramex Travel, Austin, TX	14,764	D	37	2,365
94	Ma Laboratories, San Jose, CA	52,470	D	70	2,355
95	All Green, Marietta, GA	9,476	D	240	2,330
96	Goodman Music, Los Angeles, CA	10,968	D	40	2,305
97	Sonic Solutions, San Rafael, CA	5,787	A	30	2,301
98	Payroll 1, Royal Oak, MI	3,737	C	100	2,296
99	Center for Applied Psychology, King of Prussia, PA	4,373	D	18	2,290
100	SMTEK, Newbury Park, CA	9,204	D	85	2,284

Profit Range: A-16% or more; B-11% to 15%; C-6% to 10%; D-1%-5%; E-break-even; F-loss

Inc. 500 Fastest Growing Companies (cont'd)

Rank	Company	1991 Sales ($ thousands)	1991 Profit Range	No. of Employees 1991	% Sales Growth 1987-91
101	Business Computer Training Institute, Mill Creek, WA	8,801	D	162	2,266
102	Ethix, Beaverton, OR	19,412	A	341	2,236
103	Red Rose Collection, Burlingame, CA	6,345	C	54	2,233
104	JTS Enterprises, Houston, TX	18,864	D	3	2,209
105	Eastern Computers, Virginia Beach, VA	49,834	C	400	2,195
106	Allstar Builders, Miami, FL	4,860	B	18	2,182
107	MediCenter, Lawton, OK	12,516	B	92	2,172
108	Advanced Systems Technology, Atlanta, GA	11,669	D	155	2,166
109	Marathon Systems, San Francisco, CA	4,744	D	47	2,138
110	DSS, Carmel, CA	4,380	D	180	2,135
111	Data Storage Marketing, Boulder, CO	68,944	E	145	2,109
112	Vercon Construction, Greenville, SC	32,006	D	55	2,107
113	Proserve, Denver, CO	8,255	D	325	2,107
114	Earth Care Paper, Madison, WI	5,102	F	45	2,099
115	Symmetrix, Lexington, MA	18,884	C	115	2,098
116	Atlantic Network System, Cary, NC	2,814	D	8	2,081
117	Ribbon Outlet, Somerville, NJ	14,354	E	450	2,068
118	Corporate Staffing Resources, Elkhart, IL	12,938	D	60	2,011
119	Genpack USA, Bridgewater, MI	3,440	C	20	1,985
120	Copifax, Berlin, NJ	4,292	D	42	1,944
121	Intuit, Menlo Park, CA	44,539	C	242	1,926
122	Certified Abatement Systems, Houston, TX	4,010	A	25	1,915
123	D. J. King Trucking & Excavating, E. Windsor, CT	2,614	E	28	1,911
124	Microtest, Phoenix, AZ	17,209	B	108	1,894
125	SalesTalk, Mountain View, CA	7,359	D	40	1,889
126	Gensym, Cambridge, MA	10,499	C	90	1,885
127	Technical Management Services, Arlington, VA	6,109	C	90	1,877
128	Automated Systems Design, Roswell, GA	2,883	D	32	1,861
129	Gym Masters, Albany, CA	6,237	D	60	1,855
130	Digital Network Associates, New York, NY	5,633	B	20	1,842
131	MediSense, Cambridge, MA	89,782	F	786	1,840
132	Digidesign, Menlo Park, CA	13,881	B	84	1,833
133	Walklett Burns, Malvern, PA	2,140	D	30	1,794
134	Automation Partners International, San Francisco, CA	21,795	F	120	1,774
135	JRL Systems, Austin, TX	2,935	B	18	1,758
136	Advanced Computer Systems, Fairfax, VA	11,410	D	250	1,752
137	D&K Enterprises, Carrollton, TX	1,924	A	18	1,750
138	Bruce Co., Washington, DC	2,134	D	66	1,740
139	Thomas-Conrad, Austin, TX	30,614	D	225	1,724
140	Joe Koch Construction, Youngstown, OH	5,532	B	21	1,714
141	Spray Systems Environmental, Tempe, AZ	8,626	C	125	1,697
142	Coastal Environmental Services, Linthicum, MD	2,760	D	33	1,692
143	Design Automation Systems, Houston, TX	5,360	B	14	1,687
144	Johnson & Co. Wilderness Products, Bangor, ME	1,822	D	13	1,686
145	Pelton & Associates, Redondo Beach, CA	8,902	D	22	1,673
146	Advanced Cellular Systems, Graynaro, PR	8,066	D	39	1,673
147	ROW Sciences, Rockville, MD	19,798	D	300	1,641
148	Cutchall Management, Omaha, NE	3,324	C	60	1,631
149	Atkinson-Baker & Associates, Burbank, CA	3,860	D	30	1,631
150	Digital Instruments, Santa Barbara, CA	16,591	A	52	1,628

Profit Range: A-16% or more; B-11% to 15%; C-6% to 10%; D-1%-5%; E-break-even; F-loss

Inc. 500 Fastest Growing Companies (cont'd)

Rank	Company	1991 Sales ($ thousands)	1991 Profit Range	No. of Employees 1991	% Sales Growth 1987-91
151	Northwest Pine Products, Bend, OR	12,819	C	34	1,628
152	Waste Reduction Systems, Houston, TX	6,643	D	85	1,625
153	Command Medical Products, Ormond Beach, FL	3,118	F	130	1,613
154	H. J. Ford Associates, Arlington, VA	8,275	C	76	1,603
155	Computer One, Albuquerque, NM	7,507	D	16	1,587
156	Recom Technologies, San Jose, CA	9,172	D	209	1,583
157	Fanamation, Compton, CA	5,620	F	48	1,578
158	Taylor Medical, Beaumont, TX	81,061	F	500	1,574
159	Dickens Data Systems, Norcross, GA	35,800	C	85	1,565
160	Travelpro Luggage, Deerfield Beach, FL	4,090	A	15	1,556
161	David Mitchell & Associates, St. Paul, MN	6,671	C	100	1,555
162	Glenn-Runnion, Charlotte, NC	1,652	B	25	1,552
163	McGinnis Farms, Alpharetta, GA	7,109	D	44	1,538
164	Am-Pro Protective Agency, Columbia, SC	34,122	E	1,193	1,533
165	Loflin Environmental Services, Houston, TX	1,767	B	14	1,521
166	SWFTE International, Hockessin, DE	2,025	A	11	1,520
167	Palm Tree Packaging, Apopka, FL	2,150	D	17	1,517
168	Keypoint Technology, Walnut, CA	60,253	C	54	1,511
169	World-Wide Refinishing Systems, Waco, TX	2,974	A	20	1,499
170	Ithaca Software, Alameda, CA	2,801	B	29	1,491
171	MAR Oil & Gas, Santa Fe, NM	2,449	D	4	1,490
172	J. L. Honigberg & Associates, Chicago, IL	6,547	D	14	1,478
173	Regency Coffee, New Prague, MN	2,810	F	55	1,461
174	Custom Applications, Billerica, MA	5,209	B	38	1,441
175	American Fashion Jewels, S. San Francisco, CA	23,900	E	145	1,429
176	Creative Products, Fairburn, GA	4,711	D	109	1,420
177	Allied Holdings, Torrance, CA	30,485	F	200	1,419
178	Groundwater Protection, Orlando, FL	6,927	D	85	1,416
179	Three Springs, Huntsville, AL	5,029	A	89	1,415
180	PBR Consulting Group, Philadelphia, PA	5,019	D	52	1,412
181	Biosym Technologies, San Diego, CA	22,869	D	160	1,406
182	Gardner/Fox Associates, Bryn Mawr, PA	5,100	D	45	1,404
183	Maier Group, New York, NY	6,012	C	18	1,396
184	Action Temporary Services, Evansville, IN	1,896	D	7	1,393
185	S&W Foundation Contractors, Richardson, TX	2,014	D	45	1,392
186	Tova Industries, Louisville, KY	2,936	C	30	1,383
187	Hub City Florida Terminals, Orange Park, FL	21,738	D	14	1,375
188	U.S. Computer Maintenance, Farmington, NY	4,689	B	40	1,371
189	American Fastsigns, Dallas, TX	3,457	D	28	1,365
190	MRI Manufacturing & Research, Tucson, AZ	2,707	C	84	1,363
191	Combined Resource Technology, Baton Rouge, LA	1,489	A	13	1,360
192	Iconics, Foxborough, MA	7,250	A	50	1,347
193	Software Technical Services, Atlanta, GA	2,846	A	15	1,337
194	EMC Engineers, Denver, CO	3,687	D	43	1,335
195	R&R Recreation Products, Englewood Cliffs, NJ	3,377	C	4	1,325
196	Noble Oil Services, Sanford, NC	2,647	D	36	1,323
197	Micro Information Services, Mequon, WI	3,376	D	25	1,318
198	Shepard-Patterson, Conshohocken, PA	1,432	D	32	1,318
199	Gupta Technologies, Menlo Park, CA	21,295	D	141	1,318
200	Computer Service Supply, Londonderry, NH	2,418	C	14	1,306

Profit Range: A-16% or more; B-11% to 15%; C-6% to 10%; D-1%-5%; E-break-even; F-loss

Inc. 500 Fastest Growing Companies (cont'd)

Rank	Company	1991 Sales ($ thousands)	1991 Profit Range	No. of Employees 1991	% Sales Growth 1987-91
201	Fostec, Auburn, NY	2,009	D	28	1,305
202	DAZSER & DAZSER/MD, Tampa, FL	5,171	F	16	1,301
203	Comprehensive Technologies Intl., Chantilly, VA	33,298	D	547	1,298
204	Stamina Products, Springfield, MO	13,942	D	14	1,290
205	Union Pointe Construction, Salt Lake City, UT	7,934	D	18	1,289
206	Dominant Systems, Ann Arbor, MI	1,625	D	10	1,289
207	Country Originals, Jackson, MS	2,517	D	22	1,275
208	Audio Partners, Auburn, CA	1,579	D	9	1,273
209	American Packaging & Assembly, Albertson, NY	1,764	A	200	1,267
210	Peripheral Land, Fremont, CA	25,140	D	106	1,264
211	Taggart, Cody, WY	15,669	F	230	1,263
212	Metrographics Printing Fairfield, NJ	2,015	C	10	1,261
213	Securities Service Network, Knoxville, TN	4,636	D	73	1,260
214	St. Supery Vineyards & Winery, Rutherford, CA	3,453	F	60	1,249
215	U.S. Hospitality, Nashville, TN	1,385	A	18	1,245
216	Research Information Systems, Carlsbad, CA	3,868	A	45	1,243
217	Camelot Systems, Haverhill, MA	4,654	D	35	1,237
218	Piedmont Group, Oakland, CA	2,029	F	25	1,235
219	Fulton Computer Products, Rockville Centre, NY	13,276	C	20	1,229
220	Pet Ventures, Arlington, VA	5,829	F	70	1,228
221	IQ Software, Norcross, GA	7,795	A	70	1,226
222	HazWaste Industries, Richmond, VA	11,453	D	159	1,219
223	Small Systems Management, Wilmington, DE	2,294	D	7	1,218
224	Carlson Co., Newport Beach, CA	2,209	A	57	1,215
225	International Computer Graphics, Fremont, CA	23,576	D	28	1,209
226	Personnel Management, Shelbyville, IN	9,488	D	45	1,207
227	System Connection, Provo, UT	6,468	C	50	1,204
228	Telamon, Indianapolis, IN	9,490	D	40	1,204
229	Data Sciences, Roseville, MN	2,005	D	33	1,202
230	Fisher Industrial Services, Glencoe, AL	6,528	C	78	1,200
231	Neumann Developments, Janesville, WI	17,446	C	40	1,200
232	Van G. Miller, Waterloo, IA	3,060	A	13	1,197
233	Jackson Hewitt Tax Service, Virginia Beach, VA	4,447	A	72	1,197
234	Sonetics, Portland, OR	3,390	C	28	1,194
235	Diversified Pacific Construction, Irvine, CA	11,616	D	16	1,189
236	Impact Printhead Services, Austin, TX	6,683	B	104	1,180
237	Associated Family Photographers, Phoenix, AZ	24,658	D	700	1,173
238	J.B. Dollar Stretcher Magazine, Richfield, OH	1,565	C	7	1,162
239	Inside Communications, Boulder, CO	2,863	F	19	1,156
240	LBS Capital Management, Safety Harbor, FL	2,031	A	10	1,154
241	IVT Limited, Huntington Station, NY	2,665	C	4	1,151
242	Compusense, Bedford, NH	1,597	A	18	1,148
243	Ergodyne, St. Paul, MN	12,385	B	27	1,147
244	Electronic Ballast Technology, Torrance, CA	42,218	C	450	1,146
245	United Staffing, Troy, NY	33,761	F	42	1,141
246	Restek, Bellefonte, PA	6,455	A	61	1,137
247	Systems & Programming Solutions, Milwaukee, WI	1,519	B	25	1,135
248	Spray-Tech, Longwood, FL	17,070	D	110	1,131
249	Directed Electronics, Vista, CA	35,222	D	95	1,127
250	Coverall North America, San Diego, CA	18,302	D	125	1,127

Profit Range: A-16% or more; B-11% to 15%; C-6% to 10%; D-1%-5%; E-break-even; F-loss

Inc. 500 Fastest Growing Companies (cont'd)

Rank	Company	1991 Sales ($ thousands)	1991 Profit Range	No. of Employees 1991	% Sales Growth 1987-91
251	Computerized Diagnostic Imaging , Riverside, CA	10,413	B	60	1,127
252	DataLOK, Los Angeles, CA	3,174	B	41	1,125
253	Charter Oak Consulting Group, Hartford, CT	3,652	F	10	1,121
254	Delta Environmental Consultants, St. Paul, MN	44,528	D	509	1,116
255	Southern Audio Services, Baton Rouge, LA	8,951	C	61	1,116
256	Computer Equity, Chantilly, VA	11,922	D	49	1,115
257	Applied Computer Technology, Fort Collins, CO	5,384	D	25	1,113
258	Envoy Global, Portland, OR	3,969	D	30	1,110
259	Key Construction, Wichita, KS	12,489	C	50	1,097
260	Advantage Construction Arlington, TX	1,974	C	21	1,096
261	European Toy Collection, Portage, IN	2,342	D	9	1,095
262	National Catastrophe Adjusters, Indianapolis, IN	1,574	D	32	1,092
263	National Contract Staffing, Las Vegas, NV	24,952	D	20	1,088
264	Sentinel Systems, Hampton, VA	4,601	D	15	1,086
265	Hospitality Network, Henderson, NE	14,885	F	65	1,081
266	Barclays Law Publishers, S. San Francisco, CA	8,243	A	65	1,079
267	First Benefit, Anderson, IN	5,253	D	98	1,073
268	JMR Electronics, Northridge, CA	11,627	C	141	1,070
269	InfoSource, Winter Park, FL	1,506	E	42	1,067
270	Maritime Services, Hood River, OR	3,904	E	30	1,065
271	American Cargo Systems, Overland Park, KS	5,784	D	14	1,064
272	GS Industries, Pasadena, TX	2,001	D	10	1,063
273	Scientech, Idaho Falls, ID	21,489	D	198	1,062
274	A.M. Express, Escanaba, MI	1,754	D	24	1,062
275	Sahara, Bountiful, UT	15,143	C	27	1,056
276	Broadcast Plus Productions, Universal City, CA	1,564	C	2	1,050
277	Vector Engineering, Grass Valley, CA	2,135	D	32	1,048
278	World Travel Partners, Atlanta, GA	176,781	D	425	1,043
279	Lai, Venuti & Lai, Santa Clara, CA	1,745	C	12	1,041
280	Van Mar, East Brunswick, NJ	26,718	D	125	1,035
281	Vanguard Automation, Tucson, AZ	6,748	D	96	1,034
282	AST/The Data Group, Chalfont, PA	8,571	A	65	1,032
283	S. Cohen & Associates, McLean, VA	9,058	D	45	1,027
284	Achen-Gardner, Chandler, AZ	8,529	D	55	1,025
285	DataServ, Farmington Hills, MI	4,173	B	25	1,022
286	GET Travel, Walnut Creek, CA	4,025	D	20	1,021
287	Groundwater & Environmental Svcs., Wall, NJ	15,563	A	145	1,019
288	Huckell/Weinman Associates, Kirkland, WA	1,245	C	9	1,012
289	DCT Systems, St. Paul, MN	103,696	D	189	1,006
290	Auto-Soft, Bountiful, UT	5,537	B	45	1,001
291	Computer Communication, Waterbury, CT	9,796	B	16	999
292	Hernandez Engineering, Houston, TX	16,977	D	345	998
293	Design Fabricators, Boulder, CO	3,260	B	53	998
294	Label Technology, Merced, CA	3,137	D	30	997
295	Eastern Group, Alexandria, VA	52,794	D	90	990
296	Papa John's International, Louisville, KY	19,254	C	220	980
297	Communications, Marketing Atlanta, GA	2,085	C	43	980
298	Sonny Hill Motors, Platte City, MO	139,808	D	350	978
299	Binary Arts, Alexandria, VA	2,001	B	5	970
300	Electronic Label Technology, Tulsa, OK	15,340	D	63	964

Profit Range: A-16% or more; B-11% to 15%; C-6% to 10%; D-1%-5%; E-break-even; F-loss

Inc. 500 Fastest Growing Companies (cont'd)

Rank	Company	1991 Sales ($ thousands)	1991 Profit Range	No. of Employees 1991	% Sales Growth 1987-91
301	Artistic Impressions, Lombard, IL	7,519	C	38	962
302	ESW, Dyer, IN	1,411	C	30	961
303	MC Strategies, Atlanta, GA	4,046	C	110	959
304	Engineering Management , Rockville, MD	1,203	C	15	955
305	Govind & Associates, Corpus Christi, TX	7,545	D	170	955
306	USA Direct, Manchester, PA	18,164	C	331	954
307	Sterling Environmental Services, Amherst, NY	4,121	C	8	951
308	Evergreen Environmental Group, Crestwood, KY	4,230	A	29	950
309	Chico's, Fort Myers, FL	23,177	C	240	945
310	Fitec International, Memphis, TN	34,397	D	480	944
311	TL Care, San Francisco, CA	3,404	D	6	941
312	ABA Personnel Services, San Francisco, CA	4,408	D	12	937
313	United International Engineering, Albuquerque, NM	13,710	B	175	937
314	Aztech Controls, Mesa, AZ	6,252	C	20	935
315	Koch International, Westbury, NY	14,014	D	60	931
316	American Playworld, Ogden, UT	13,903	B	157	931
317	Z-Barten Productions, Culver City, CA	1,449	B	25	928
318	Siciliano, Springfield, IL	7,588	D	50	927
319	Main Street Muffins, Akron, OH	1,106	C	17	924
320	McCool's Carpet Outlet, Kokomo, IN	2,007	B	7	924
321	Barclays Oxygen Homecare, Englewood, CO	3,643	A	32	920
322	ESE, Marshfield, WI	2,540	D	25	916
323	Athletic Fitters, Eden Prairie, MN	8,115	B	41	916
324	Roux Associates, Huntington, NY	11,895	D	108	909
325	McNerney Heintz, Barrington, IL	9,357	C	171	904
326	Precision Response, Miami, FL	16,182	B	250	904
327	Canvasbacks, Milwaukee, WI	6,744	B	50	904
328	Fenders & More, Nashville, TN	9,742	D	55	903
329	Creative Producers Group, St. Louis, MO	1,403	B	10	902
330	Deckers, Carpinteria, CA	11,617	B	200	899
331	Medical Equipment Repair Services, Sarasota, FL	1,058	D	14	898
332	MWW/Strategic Communications, River Edge, NJ	3,138	C	24	893
333	Leopardo Construction, Glendale Heights, IL	55,248	D	105	890
334	Wasser Industries, Seattle, WA	3,722	D	7	887
335	Spec-line Laminated Products, Doraville, GA	1,457	B	31	884
336	Geerlings & Wade, Canton, MA	3,077	C	13	880
337	Nature's Recipe Pet Foods, Corona, CA	21,182	A	40	880
338	Safesite Records Management, Billerica, MA	6,366	F	152	875
339	Tri-Services, Chesapeake, VA	1,401	D	50	873
340	MMI of Mississippi, Crystal Springs, MS	2,698	A	14	871
341	Travel Store, Los Angeles, CA	23,670	D	40	868
342	Oreman Sales, Kenner, LA	61,987	C	72	868
343	Flexible Personnel, Fort Wayne, IN	7,964	F	29	868
344	Commonwealth, Cincinnati, OH	4,184	D	30	866
345	Staff Leasing, Bradenton, FL	154,447	D	11,310	864
346	North American Processing, Niles, IL	137,164	D	13	863
347	Touchstone Research Lab, Triadelphia, WV	2,291	D	23	859
348	Remote Control International, Carlsbad, CA	4,263	D	50	858
349	Southwest Royalties, Midland, TX	17,589	D	70	856
350	ERM-Rocky Mountain, Englewood, CO	4,750	B	56	856

Profit Range: A-16% or more; B-11% to 15%; C-6% to 10%; D-1%-5%; E-break-even; F-loss

Inc. 500 Fastest Growing Companies (cont'd)

Rank	Company	1991 Sales ($ thousands)	1991 Profit Range	No. of Employees 1991	% Sales Growth 1987-91
351	Applied Utility Systems, Santa Ana, CA	6,813	D	27	852
352	EDECO, Tulsa, OK	7,140	C	170	843
353	SoMat, Urbana, IL	1,750	D	10	841
354	Litle & Co., Salem, NH	45,954	D	101	841
355	Saturn Electronics Rochester Hills, MI	14,975	C	325	841
356	R&M Business Systems, Elk Grove Village, IL	3,534	C	38	840
357	System Resources, Burlington, MA	12,682	C	139	836
358	Metters Industries, McLean, VA	29,406	D	350	836
359	MDM Engineering, San Clemente, CA	10,135	C	125	836
360	Enecotech Group, Denver, CO	14,990	C	200	830
361	Griffis/Blessing, Colorado Springs, CO	1,116	A	25	830
362	Shields Health Care, Brockton, MA	28,372	A	120	829
363	Allsup, Belleville, IL	6,036	A	89	827
364	Teubner & Associates, Stillwater, OK	2,247	C	16	825
365	American International Construction, Houston, TX	20,245	D	200	821
366	Stretcho Fabrics, Hawthorne, NJ	10,015	D	7	820
367	Routing Technology Software, Vienna, VA	6,736	A	65	820
368	MBS Communications, Cheshire, CT	1,220	B	33	817
369	Team Spirit, Omaha, NE	13,470	B	90	817
370	Gravity Graphics, Brooklyn, NY	2,556	D	42	816
371	Hofgard Benefit Plan Administrators, Boulder, CO	1,370	F	28	813
372	S&S Management & Consulting, Somerset, MA	2,166	B	7	810
373	Saloom Furniture, Gardner, MA	5,740	C	65	807
374	Option Technologies, Mendota Heights, MN	995	C	7	805
375	Micro Dynamics, Silver Spring, MD	6,585	D	55	803
376	Datastorm Technologies, Columbia, MO	17,821	A	93	803
377	Genesis Automation, Shelton, CT	2,088	F	13	800
378	Refco Investments, Melrose Park, IL	1,178	A	4	799
379	Environmental Operations, St. Louis, MO	1,824	D	29	799
380	ABL Electronics, Hunt Valley, MD	3,204	D	39	792
381	Barry T. Chouinard, Northfield, VT	3,672	C	20	791
382	American Insurance Atlanta, GA	15,709	D	100	791
383	Commercial Benefits, Woodland Hills, CA	2,563	A	20	790
384	Compu-Call, N. Attleboro, MA	5,202	D	9	789
385	Terra Vac, San Juan, PR	14,244	C	32	789
386	Integratrak, Seattle, WA	2,186	B	27	789
387	Allen Systems Group, Naples, FL	8,198	C	120	788
388	Wek Enterprises, Buena Park, CA	7,358	D	35	783
389	EnviroSearch International, Salt Lake City, UT	2,111	D	39	783
390	Landex Construction, San Diego, CA	7,024	D	21	782
391	Traco Manufacturing, Orem, UT	2,827	B	14	778
392	Modern Technologies, Dayton, OH	32,936	C	477	777
393	Todisco Jewelry, New York, NY	4,003	D	100	772
394	Integrity Industries, Kingsville, TX	6,253	C	16	772
395	Penn Property & Casualty, Lemoyne, PA	3,690	D	10	770
396	Concord Holding, New York, NY	13,959	A	56	770
397	Knowledge Systems, Cary, NC	2,040	F	29	768
398	Heritage Asset Management Group, Dallas, TX	1,752	D	72	767
399	Asia Source, Fremont, CA	67,021	D	50	765
400	Logos Systems, Houston, TX	908	F	10	765

Profit Range: A-16% or more; B-11% to 15%; C-6% to 10%; D-1%-5%; E-break-even; F-loss

Inc. 500 Fastest Growing Companies (cont'd)

Rank	Company	1991 Sales ($ thousands)	1991 Profit Range	No. of Employees 1991	% Sales Growth 1987-91
401	Sun Coast Resources, Houston, TX	86,154	D	14	764
402	Zeiders Enterprises, Woodbridge, VA	3,515	D	90	764
403	Carretas, Albuquerque, NM	1,868	D	30	761
404	Marketing Profiles, Maitland, FL	8,379	C	53	760
405	Summit Builders, Phoenix, AZ	27,216	D	49	760
406	Microserv, Kirkland, WA	5,485	D	98	754
407	Optimation Technology, Rush, NY	1,441	C	25	753
408	Turbine Consultants, Milwaukee, WI	5,294	A	11	750
409	Oakville Forest Products, Oakville, WA	6,883	D	17	750
410	Strifler Group, Dallas, TX	2,200	A	30	749
411	Gulf Coast Hair Care, Panama City, FL	2,597	D	140	749
412	Kenley, Mason, OH	2,583	A	6	747
413	Plastronics Plus, E. Troy, WI	4,982	D	80	744
414	Nutech Laundry & Textiles, Hyattsville, MD	3,901	C	130	744
415	Western Fiberglass, Windsor, CA	2,074	F	30	740
416	Boston Preparatory, New York, NY	1,172	A	4	737
417	Field Brothers Construction, Marion, OH	12,115	C	155	736
418	HMA Behavioral Health, Worcester, MA	2,268	D	22	731
419	SVL Analytical, Kellogg, ID	3,068	D	75	727
420	OCS Group, Pittsford, NY	5,661	B	119	726
421	MIC Industries, Reston, VA	20,696	A	98	724
422	TME, Houston, TX	12,237	F	171	722
423	Design Basics, Omaha, NE	2,111	A	28	721
424	Arbor Systems, Carrollton, TX	2,611	C	16	721
425	Proteus, Albuquerque, NM	4,883	D	79	715
426	Lifetime Products, Clearfield, UT	27,133	C	218	715
427	Gale Group, Winter Park, FL	58,086	F	400	715
428	Bulk International, Troy, MI	16,251	D	138	714
429	Stone Computer & Copier Supply, Tulsa, OK	2,936	D	18	711
430	ATV, Cleveland, OH	21,404	D	52	710
431	Pioneer Software, Raleigh, NC	2,329	B	27	709
432	Florida Marketing International, Ormond Beach, FL	7,649	A	23	707
433	Bendco/Bending & Coiling, Pasadena, TX	4,360	D	53	704
434	Globaltec, Titusville, NJ	2,495	D	16	702
435	Bike Pro USA, Phoenix, AZ	1,024	D	26	700
436	Horizon Data, Reston, VA	10,382	C	50	700
437	Partnership Group, Lansdale, PA	7,413	D	100	699
438	Complete Property Services, Oldsmar, FL	2,435	B	25	698
439	Mattern Construction, Preston, CT	2,865	C	9	698
440	Quintiles Transnational, Morrisville, NC	30,461	C	320	697
441	Sunrise Terrace, Fairfax, VA	12,157	C	378	697
442	Sherikon, Chantilly, VA	14,128	D	193	696
443	Music Tech of Minneapolis, Minneapolis, MN	1,406	D	50	694
444	Northwest Micro, Beaverton, OR	7,395	D	19	694
445	U.S. Xpress, Tunnel Hill, GA	141,928	D	2,104	691
446	Magnet, Washington, MO	12,679	C	192	688
447	Loan Pricing, New York, NY	3,717	D	41	688
448	Energy Dynamics, New Berlin, WI	10,088	D	26	687
449	U.S. Structures, Richmond, VA	11,000	F	25	686
450	Univest Financial Group, Marietta, GA	16,500	A	78	686

Profit Range: A-16% or more; B-11% to 15%; C-6% to 10%; D-1%-5%; E-break-even; F-loss

Inc. 500 Fastest Growing Companies (cont'd)

Rank	Company	1991 Sales ($ thousands)	1991 Profit Range	No. of Employees, 1991	% Sales Growth 1987-91
451	Source Technologies, Charlotte, NC	5,436	D	16	683
452	Pleasant Co., Middleton, WI	64,263	B	228	683
453	Skender Construction, Palos Hills, IL	4,272	F	28	682
454	GreenLine, Bowling Green, OH	2,228	D	32	682
455	Zia Cosmetics, San Francisco, CA	1,247	D	16	679
456	Cadmus Group, Waltham, MA	6,453	D	90	676
457	Buschman, Cleveland, OH	1,310	A	11	675
458	Megasource, Bloomfield Hills, MI	7,162	A	63	673
459	Hazco Services, Dayton, OH	11,090	C	65	671
460	Schweitzer Engineering Laboratories, Pullman, WA	15,634	A	84	670
461	Humanix Temporary Services, Spokane, WA	2,663	D	9	670
462	PPOM, Southfield, MI	12,394	D	115	669
463	Executive Software, Glendale, CA	15,210	B	95	667
464	Schnaubelt Shorts, Coraopolis, PA	1,387	C	47	666
465	FourGen Software, Edmonds, WA	5,051	C	84	665
466	Forcum/Mackey Construction, Ivanhoe, CA	7,963	D	18	663
467	Home Care Affiliates, Louisville, KY	31,157	D	436	662
468	Harmony Schools, Princeton, NJ	2,663	D	104	661
469	Roelynn Business Products, Hazlet, NJ	1,041	D	6	660
470	Posi-Clean, Wheeling, WV	2,019	B	28	659
471	Mendez Excavation, Breckenridge, CO	2,906	B	35	659
472	Loop Restaurant, Jacksonville, FL	4,788	B	75	658
473	Creative Staffing, Miami, FL	7,144	D	24	658
474	Cucci International, Torrance, CA	2,930	C	34	657
475	Metalize Texas, Bastrop, TX	885	E	25	656
476	Diplomatic Language Services, Arlington, VA	2,750	D	122	655
477	SNL Securities, Charlottesville, VA	2,337	C	27	654
478	NationaLease Purchasing, Oakbrook Terrace, IL	23,664	D	12	654
479	CMS Communications, Bridgeton, MO	18,283	C	152	649
480	Authorized Cellular/Security One, Roseville, MI	1,828	B	20	646
481	Thomure Medsearch, St. Louis, MO	1,599	B	50	644
482	DCS Software & Consulting, Dallas, TX	4,439	D	90	644
483	Supplemental Health Care Services, Tonawanda, NY	6,515	F	1,100	641
484	AccSys Technology, Pleasanton, CA	3,256	D	22	640
485	Visual Concepts Media, Bloomfield, CT	826	D	6	638
486	De-Mar, Clovis, CA	3,109	B	35	632
487	J and M Laboratories, Dawsonville, GA	2,861	A	50	628
488	Monterey Homes, Scottsdale, AZ	20,528	D	30	627
489	American Teleconferencing Svcs., Overland Park, KS	3,462	D	43	627
490	Asosa Personnel, Tucson, AZ	4,087	D	22	627
491	National Business Group, Atlanta, GA	8,652	D	13	626
492	CareFlorida, Miami, FL	75,677	D	189	624
493	Dan Flickinger Inc., Seattle, WA	1,802	F	9	624
494	Reunion Time, Tinton Falls, NJ	2,511	C	11	622
495	Tracer Research, Tucson, AZ	8,943	C	93	620
496	Phoenix Controls, Newton, MA	7,662	D	74	618
497	Apogee Research, Bethesda, MD	3,065	D	35	614
498	Mastersoft, Scottsdale, AZ	2,043	A	16	614
499	Copyco, Deerfield Beach, FL	6,706	D	89	614
500	Falcon Microsystems, Landover, MD	138,938	D	249	606

Profit Range: A-16% or more; B-11% to 15%; C-6% to 10%; D-1%-5%; E-break-even; F-loss

Source: Inc. Magazine, 1992

Black and Women CEOs

The Black Enterprise 100

Rank	Company	Location	Staff	1991 Sales ($ millions)
1	TLC Beatrice International Holdings	New York, NY	5,000	1,542.00
2	Johnson Publishing	Chicago, IL	2,710	261.36
3	Philadephia Coca-Cola Bottling	Philadelphia, PA	1,000	256.00
4	H.J. Russell & Co.	Atlanta, GA	798	143.59
5	Barden Communications	Detroit, MI	332	91.20
6	Garden State Cable TV	Cherry Hill, NJ	300	88.00
7	Soft Sheen Products	Chicago, IL	537	87.90
8	RMS Technologies	Marlton, NJ	1,116	79.86
9	Stop Shop and Save	Baltimore, MD	600	66.00
10	The Bing Group	Detroit, MI	195	64.90
11	Technology Applications	Alexandria, VA	600	64.00
12	Trans Jones Inc., Jones Transfer Co.	Monroe, MI	983	61.20
13	Mays Chemical Co.	Indianapolis, IN	72	56.70
14	Pulsar Data Systems	Lanham, MD	48	53.00
15	Black Entertainment Television Holdings	Washington, DC	249	50.81
16	The Maxima Corp.	Lanham, MD	809	49.82
17	Network Solutions	Herndon, VA	450	48.80
18	Community Foods	Baltimore, MD	428	47.50
19	Pepsi-Cola of Washington DC, L.P.	Washington, DC	145	44.11
*	Johnson Products	Chicago, IL	224	44.00
*	Luster Products	Chicago, IL	315	44.00
*	Surface Protection Industries	Los Angeles, CA	200	44.00
23	Essence Communications	New York, NY	76	43.25
24	Granite Broadcasting	New York, NY	357	39.99
25	Westside Distributors	South Gate, CA	115	39.00
26	Grimes Oil	Boston, MA	18	36.00
27	Calhoun Enterprises	Montgomery, AL	582	35.80
28	Gold Line Refining	Houston, TX	51	35.72
29	Beauchamp Distributing	Compton, CA	117	34.50
30	The Gourmet Cos.	Atlanta, GA	1,551	34.30
*	Am-Pro Protective Agency	Columbia, SC	1,240	34.30
32	Rush Communications	New York, NY	60	34.00
33	Pro-Line Corp.	Dallas, TX	193	33.83
34	Integrated Systems Analysts	Arlington, VA	550	33.50
35	Wesley Industries	Flint, MI	300	32.50
36	The Thacker Organization	Decatur, GA	144	30.80
37	Automated Sciences Group	Silver Spring, MD	300	30.00
*	Input Output Computer Services	Waltham, MA	200	30.00
39	Brooks Sausage Co.	Chicago, IL	145	29.75
40	Orchem, Inc.	Cincinnati, OH	78	28.50
41	Crest Computer Supply	Skokie, IL	55	28.00
42	Yancy Materials	Woodbridge, CT	8	27.00
43	Metters Industries	McLean, VA	417	26.83
44	Trumark	Lansing, MI	200	26.50
45	Inner City Broadcasting	New York, NY	200	26.00
*	Premium Distributors Inc. of Washington, DC	Washington, DC	75	26.00
47	Restoration Supermarket	Brooklyn, NY	150	25.30
48	Queen City Broadcasting	New York, NY	130	25.20
49	Parks Sausage	Baltimore, MD	202	25.00
50	American Development	N. Charleston, SC	106	25.00

*=*tie*

Black and Women CEO's (cont'd)

Rank	Company	Location	Staff	1991 Sales ($ millions)
*	Superb Manufacturing	Detroit, MI	140	25.00
52	Systems Management American	Norfolk, VA	193	24.00
53	African Development Public Investment Corp.	Hollywood, CA	10	23.00
54	Regal Plastics	Roseville, MI	250	22.86
55	Dick Griffey Productions	Hollywood, CA	70	22.00
*	R.O.W. Sciences	Rockville, MD	300	22.00
57	Powers & Sons Construction	Gary, IN	65	21.66
58	Orpack-Stone	Herrin, IL	106	21.00
59	Advanced Consumer Marketing	Burlingame, CA	60	20.70
60	Summa-Harrison Metal Products	Mt. Clemens, MI	200	20.39
61	Burns Enterprises	Louisville, KY	450	20.00
*	V-Tech	Pamona, CA	200	20.00
*	Stephens Engineering	Lanham, MD	130	20.00
*	Navcom Systems	Manassas, VA	100	20.00
65	Simmons Enterprises	Cincinnati, OH	75	19.62
66	H.F. Henderson Industries	West Caldwell, NJ	175	19.20
67	Bronner Brothers	Atlanta, GA	200	19.00
*	Best Foam Fabricators	Chicago, IL	120	19.00
69	Dual & Associates	Arlington, VA	246	18.73
70	Telephone Advertising Corp. of America	Atlanta, GA	21	18.61
71	Viking Enterprises	Chicago, IL	165	18.50
72	C.H. James & Co.	Charleston, WV	25	18.00
73	Earl G. Graves Ltd.	New York, NY	63	17.45
74	Sylvest Management Systems	Lanham, MD	20	16.80
75	Accurate Information Systems	So. Plainfield, NJ	110	16.50
76	Terry Manufacturing	Roanoke, AL	280	16.00
77	A.L. Eastmond & Sons	Bronx, NY	135	15.40
78	A Minority Entity	Norco, LA	1,300	15.23
79	Drew Pearson Cos.	Addison, TX	27	15.00
80	Systems Engineering & Management Associates	Falls Church, VA	240	15.00
*	Solo Joint Inc. (D/B/A Cross Colours)	Los Angeles, CA	55	15.00
82	Consolidated Beverage	New York, NY	18	14.60
83	American Urban Radio Networks	New York, NY	80	14.00
84	Walter International Transportation	Jamaica, NY	25	13.60
85	Delta Enterprises	Greenville, MS	236	13.50
86	Carter Industrial Services	Anderson, IN	250	13.13
87	Watiker and Son	Zanesville, OH	130	13.00
88	Ozanne Construction	Cleveland, OH	45	12.90
89	Specialized Packaging International	Hamden, CT	6	12.77
90	James T. Heard Management	Cerritos, CA	295	12.70
91	Advance Inc.	Arlington, VA	200	12.50
92	Michael Alan Lewis Co.	Union, IL	78	12.38
93	Eltrex Industries	Rochester, NY	155	12.25
94	Tresp Associates	Alexandria, VA	186	12.00
95	Williams-Russell and Johnson	Atlanta, GA	180	11.30
96	Black River Manufacturing	Port Huron, MI	72	11.20
97	Mandex	Springfield, VA	180	11.04
98	William Cargile Contractor	Cincinnati, OH	57	11.00
99	RPM Supply Co.	Philadelphia, PA	20	10.83
100	Burrell Communications Group	Chicago, IL	115	10.51

**=tie*

Source: Black Enterprise

Black and Women CEO's (cont'd)

ACCORDING TO STATISTICS GENERATED by the National Foundation for Women Business Owners, women own at least 5.4 million businesses. *Working Woman* in conjunction with NFWBO ranked the top 25 women-owned businesses in the first annual salute to women business owners. To be considered, candidates had to own at least 20 percent of the stock in private companies and 10 percent in public ones and the women had to be top executives running the day-to-day operations.

Recommended Resource

National Foundation for Women Business Owners
1377 K St. NW, Suite 637
Washington, DC 20005
(301) 495-4975

The Top 25 Women-Owned Businesses

Rank	Owner	Business Name	1991 Sales ($ mil.)	Employees	% of Ownership
1	Antonia Axson Johnson	Axel Johnson Group, Stockholm	829	2,000	100
2	Gretchen Williams, Liz Minyard	Minyard Food Stores, Coppell, TX	700	6,100	33 each
3	Linda J. Wachner	Warnaco Group Inc., NY	548	11,800	14.4
4	Jenny Craig	Jenny Craig, Inc., Del Mar, CA	412	7,000	61
5	Donna W. Steigerwaldt	Jockey International, Kenosha, WI	450	5,000	>50
6	Susie Tompkins	Esprit De Corp, San Francisco, CA	450	1,400	>20
7	Norma Paige	Astronautics, Milwaukee, WI	415	4,700	Joint
8	Helen K. Copley	Copley Press, La Jolla, CA	405	3,500	100
9	Barbara Levy Kipper	Chas. Levy Co., Chicago, IL	350	1,700	100
10	Annabelle L. Fetterman	Lundy Packing Co., Clinton, NC	350	900	>20
11	Bettye Martin Musham	Gear Holdings, Inc., NY	280	30	>20
12	Linda Johnson Rice	Johnson Publishing, Chicago, IL	252	2,753	100
13	Dian Graves Owen	Owen Healthcare, Inc., Houston, TX	250	2,000	38.7
14	Carole Little	Carole Little, Inc, Los Angeles, CA	205	600	50
15	Lana Jane Lewis-Brent	Sunshine Jr. Stores, Inc., Panama City, FL	203	1,800	56
16	Ellen R. Gordon	Tootsie Roll Industries, Chicago, IL	200	1,400	49
17	Donna Karan	Donna Karan Co., NY	200	750	50
18	Dorothy Owen	Owen Steel Co., Columbia, SC	192	1,500	>20
19	Christel Dehaan	Resort Condominiums Int'l, Indianapolis, IN	180	2,300	100
20	Adrienne Vittadini	Adrienne Vittadini, Inc., NY	160	200	>50
21	Lillian Vernon	Lillian Vernon Corp., Mt. Vernon, NY	160	1,000	30
22	Helen Jo Whitsell	Copeland Lumber Yards Inc., Portland, OR	152	800	>50
23	Judy Sims	Software Spectrum, Garland, TX	146	260	19
24	Paula Kent Meehan	Redken Laboratories, Canoga Park, CA	140	830	51
25	Lois Rust	Rose Acre Farms, Seymour, IN	127	500	49

Source: Working Woman Magazine (May, 1992) and National Foundation for Women Business Owners. Reprinted with permission.

The Top Reference Sources

Working Woman
(212) 551-9500

This monthly magazine is focused on women and their careers.

Features provide guidelines on women's legal rights, management skills, career tactics and developments, plus how to maintain fitness and a positive self-image.

Regular surveys and statistical features, including an annual salary survey, make this an excellent resource.

The Forbes 400 Wealthiest Ranking

Name	Worth ($ mil)	Primary Sources
du Pont family	8,600	Du Pont (I)
Gates, William	6,300	Microsoft
Rockefeller family	5,500	Oil (I)
Kluge, John Werner	5,500	Metromedia
Walton, S. Robson	5,100	Wal-Mart (I)
Walton, John T.	5,100	Wal-Mart (I)
Walton, Jim C.	5,100	Wal-Mart (I)
Walton, Helen	5,100	Wal-Mart (I)
Walton, Alice L.	5,100	Wal-Mart (I)
Mellon family	5,000	(I)
Buffet, Warren	4,400	Stock market
Newhouse, Samuel Jr.	3,500	Publishing
Newhouse, Donald	3,500	Publishing
Redstone, Sumner	3,250	Movie theaters
Perelman, Ronald Owen	2,900	Leveraged buyouts
Arison, Ted	2,850	Cruise ships
Allen, Paul Gardner	2,800	Microsoft
Murdoch, Keith Rupert	2,600	Publishing
Van Andel, Jay	2,500	Amway
Phipps family	2,500	Steel (I)
DeVos, Richard Marvin	2,500	Amway
Perot, Henry Ross	2,400	Electronic data
Hillman, Henry Lea	2,400	Industrialist
Bronfman, Edgar Miles	2,350	Seagram Co.
Vogel, Jacqueline Mars	2,250	Candy
Mars, John Franklyn	2,250	Candy
Mars, Forrest Edward Sr.	2,250	Candy
Mars, Forrest Edward Jr.	2,250	Candy
Chambers, Anne Cox	2,100	Cox Enterprises (I)
Anthony, Barbara Cox	2,100	Cox Enterprises (I)
Turner, Robert (Ted)	1,900	Turner Broadcasting
Knight, Philip Hampson	1,900	Nike
Wexner, Leslie Herbert	1,800	The Limited
Packard, David	1,800	Hewlett-Packard
Pritzker, Jay Arthur	1,700	Financier
Pritzker, Robert Alan	1,700	Financier
Hillenbrand family	1,700	Caskets
Bass, Sid Richardson	1,700	Investments
Bass, Lee Marshall	1,700	Investments
Scripps (E.W.) family	1,600	Newspapers (I)
Gund family	1,600	Coffee, Banking (I)
Bancroft family	1,600	Dow Jones (I)
Annenberg, Walter H.	1,600	Publishing
Johnson, Samuel Curtis	1,500	Johnson Wax
Johnson, Edward family	1,500	Investments
Hunt, Ray Lee family	1,500	Oil (I)
Blaustein family	1,500	Oil (I)
Bechtel, Stephen Jr. (F)	1,500	Engineering
Tisch, Preston Robert	1,400	Loews Corp.

(I) = inheritance; (F) = family

Name	Worth ($ mil)	Primary Sources
Tisch, Laurence Alan	1,400	Loews Corporation
Smith family	1,400	Illinois Tool Works
Davis, Marvin Harold	1,400	Oil
Bass, Robert Muse	1,400	Investments
Getty, Gordon Peter	1,350	Oil (I)
Ziff, William Bernard Jr.	1,300	Publishing
LeFrak, Samuel Jayson	1,300	Real estate
Crown, Lester (F)	1,300	(I)
Chandler family	1,300	Times Mirror
Busch family	1,300	Anheuser-Busch
Bren, Donald Leroy	1,300	Real estate
Walton, James Lawrence	1,250	Wal-Mart
Koch, David Hamilton	1,250	(I)
Koch, Charles de Ganahl	1,250	(I)
Collier family	1,200	Real estate (I)
Donnelley family	1,170	R.R. Donnelley
Rockefeller, David Sr. (F)	1,100	(I)
Malone, Mary	1,100	Campbell Soup (I)
Kroc, Joan Beverly	1,100	McDonald's (I)
Kerkorian, Kirk	1,100	Investments
Heyman, Samuel J.	1,100	GAF Corp.
Hewlett, William Redington	1,100	Hewlett-Packard
Dorrance, John T. III	1,100	Campbell Soup (I)
Dorrance, Bennett	1,100	Campbell Soup (I)
Brown family	1,100	Whiskey (I)
Bass, Edward Perry	1,100	Investments
Ballmer, Steven Anthony	1,100	Microsoft
Schwan, Marvin Maynard	1,000	Ice cream
Rockefeller, Laurance (F)	1,000	(I)
Petrie, Milton	1,000	Petrie Stores
Murdoch, David Howard	1,000	Investments
Mellon, Paul	1,000	(I)
Lilly family	1,000	Pharmaceuticals
Lauder, Ronald Steven	1,000	Cosmetics
Lauder, Leonard Alan	1,000	Cosmetics
Lauder, Estée	1,000	Cosmetics
Hill, Margaret Hunt (F)	1,000	Oil (I)
Helmsley, Harry Brakmann	1,000	Real estate
Haas, Peter E. Sr. (F)	1,000	Levi Strauss
Fribourg, Michel (F)	1,000	Grain trader
de Young family	1,000	Newspapers
Dayton family	1,000	Dayton-Hudson
Johnson, Barbara Piasecka	990	(I)
Weyerhaeuser family	980	Timber (I)
Nordstrom family	970	Retailing
Wrigley, William	965	Wrigley's
Upjohn family	960	Upjohn (I)
Rockefeller, Winthrop Paul	950	(I)
Reynolds, Donald	950	Publishing

The Forbes 400 Wealthiest Ranking (cont'd)

Name	Worth ($ mil)	Primary Source
Pitcairn family	950	PPG Industries (I)
Hall, Donald Joyce	950	Hallmark Cards
Davidson, William	950	Guardian Industries
Albertson, Joseph	930	Albertson's
Simmons, Harold	900	Investments
Reed family	900	Lumber, paper
Feeney, Charles F.	900	Duty Free Shoppers
Cooke, Jack Kent	900	Real Estate
Anschutz, Philip	900	Oil
Houghton family	890	Corning Glass
Scripps (J.E.) family	880	Newspapers (I)
Temple family	860	Timber (I)
Geffen, David	850	Music
Gaylord, Edward	850	Broadcasting
Cargill, Margaret (F)	850	Cargill (I)
Cargill, James R. (F)	850	Cargill (I)
Jenkins family	845	Publix Super Markets
Bastian, Bruce W.	840	WordPerfect
Ashton, Alan C.	840	WordPerfect
Hearst, William (F)	825	(I)
Hearst, Randolph (F)	825	(I)
Horvitz family	815	Media (I)
Turner family	800	Real estate, apparel
Stuart family	800	Carnation (I)
Stern, Leonard	800	Pet supplies
Sorenson, James	800	Medical devices
Rich, Marc	800	Commodities
Noorda, Raymond J.	800	Novell
Meijer family	800	Retailing
Kleberg family	800	Real estate (I)
Hixon family	800	Electrical connectors
Green, Pincus	800	Commodities trader
Dedman, Robert Sr.	800	Country clubs
Carlson, Curtis	800	Entrepreneur
Bacardi family	800	Liquor
Tyson, Donald John	790	Tyson Foods
Soros, George	785	Money manager
Lykes family	770	Real estate, banking
Richardson family	765	Richardson-Vicks (I)
Pohlad, Carl Ray	765	MEI Corp.
Perenchio, Andrew	765	Television
Whitney, Betsey	750	(I)
Scaife, Richard	750	(I)
Lennon, Fred A.	750	Valves
Ford, William Clay	750	Ford Motor (I)
Duke, Doris	750	(I)
Mennen family	730	The Mennen Co.
Milliken, Roger (F)	725	Textiles
Louis, John Jeffrey	725	Johnson Wax (I)
Kauffman, Ewing	725	Marion Labs

Name	Worth ($ mil)	Primary Source
Hamilton, Dorrance	725	Campbell Soup (I)
Pigott family	710	Paccar (I)
Whittier family	700	Oil (I)
Moran, James Martin	700	Toyota
Lauren, Ralph	700	Apparel
Harbert, John III	700	Construction
Field, Frederick W.	700	Department stores (I)
Campbell family	700	Real estate (I)
Cafaro, William (F)	700	Shopping malls
Lindemann, George L.	685	Cable, cellular
Moore, Gordon Earle	680	Intel Corp
Davis, Shelby Cullom	680	Investment banking
Marcus, Bernard	675	Home Depot
Mead family	660	Consolidated Papers
Marriott family	660	Hotels, food service
Weber, Charlotte Colket	650	Campbell Soup (I)
Van Beuren, Hope Hill	650	Campbell Soup (I)
Icahn, Carl Celian	650	Financier
Clapp family	650	Weyerhaeuser (I)
Block family	650	Block Drug (I)
Andersen family	650	Windows
Magness, Bob John	640	Telecommunications
Frost, Phillip	630	Pharmaceuticals
Pulitzer family	620	Publishing (I)
Copley, Helen Kinney	620	Publishing
Jordan family	610	Publishing, retail (I)
Hoyt family	610	Carter-Wallace
Cook, Jane Bancroft (F)	610	Dow Jones (I)
Yates family	600	Oil
Wege family	600	Steelcase
Washington, Dennis	600	Entrepreneur
Tyson, Barbara	600	Tyson Foods
Smith (Charles E.) (F)	600	Real estate
Sarofim, Fayez Shalaby	600	Money management
Sammons family	600	Broadcasting (I)
Peltz, Nelson	600	Leveraged buyouts
May, Cordelia Scaife	600	(I)
Ingram, Erskine	600	Barges
Idema family	600	Steelcase
Hunting family	600	Steelcase
Hollingsworth, John D.	600	Textile machinery
Hess, Leon	600	Amerada Hess
Goldman family	600	Real estate (I)
Fisher, Doris F.	600	The Gap
Fisher, Donald George	600	The Gap
Fireman, Paul B.	600	Reebok
Durst family	600	Real estate
Bean (Gorman) family	600	L.L. Bean (I)
Batten, Frank Sr.	600	Publishing
Abraham, S. Daniel	600	Slim-Fast Foods

The Forbes 400 Wealthiest Ranking (cont'd)

Name	Worth ($ mil)	Primary Source
Smith, Richard Alan	575	General Cinema
Gore family	575	Gore-Tex
Ellison, Lawrence Joseph	575	Oracle Corp.
Graham family	565	Washington Post
Pictet, Marion (F)	560	Cargill (I)
MacMillan, Whitney (F)	560	Cargill (I)
MacMillan, W. Duncan (F)	560	Cargill (I)
MacMillan, John (F)	560	(I)
MacMillan, Cargill Jr. (F)	560	Cargill (I)
Keinath, Pauline (F)	560	Cargill (I)
Huizenga, Harry	560	Blockbuster Video
Gates, Charles (F)	560	Gates Corp.
Wirtz family	550	Real estate (I)
Simplot, John (F)	550	Potatoes
Monaghan, Thomas	550	Pizza
McGraw family	550	McGraw-Hill
Marshall, James II	550	Oil
Johnson, Charles	550	Franklin Resources
Huntsman, Jon Meade	550	Plastics
Edson, John Orin	550	Manufacturing
Cook, William Alfred	550	Catheters
Bennett, William	550	Circus Circus Ent.
Belk family	550	Retailing
Abramson, Leonard	550	U.S. Healthcare
Singleton, Henry Earl	545	Teledyne
Davis, James Elsworth	540	Winn-Dixie
Barbey family	540	VF Corp (I)
Moody, Robert Lee (F)	530	Amer. Nat'l. Insur.
Mitchell, George	530	Oil and gas
Greenberg, Maurice	530	American Int'l.
Disney, Roy Edward	530	Walt Disney (I)
Park, Roy Hampton	525	Park Comm.
Carver, Lucille	525	Bandag (I)
Tauber, Laszlo Nandor	500	Real estate
Rudin family	500	Real estate (I)
Rowling, Reese (F)	500	Oil and gas
Roberts, George R.	500	Leveraged buyouts
Rich, Robert Sr.	500	Food products
O'Connor family	500	(I)
Norris family	500	Lennox Int'l.
Murphy family	500	Oil
Moore, Jerry J.	500	Shopping centers
Lupton, John Thomas	500	Coca-Cola bottler
Levine, Stuart Robert	500	Cabletron Systems
Landegger family	500	Pulp mills (I)
Kravis, Henry R.	500	Leveraged buyouts
Kohlberg, Jerome Jr.	500	Leveraged buyouts
Koch, William	500	Oil services (I)
Koch, Frederick	500	Oil services (I)
Jacobs, Jeremy	500	Sports concessions

Name	Worth ($ mil)	Primary Source
Ilitch, Michael	500	Little Caesar Pizza
Hunt, Caroline (F)	500	Oil (I)
Hughes family	500	Real estate (I)
Hostetter, Amos Barr Jr.	500	Cont. Cablevision
Heinz, Teresa F.	500	H.J. Heinz
Haas, Josephine B. (F)	500	Levi Strauss
Haas, John Charles	500	Rohm & Haas
Haas, Fritz Otto	500	Rohm & Haas
Galvin, Robert William	500	Motorola
Flagler family	500	Oil (I)
Davenport, Elizabeth	500	Coca-Cola bottler
Cullen family	500	Oil (I)
Coulter, Wallace Henry	500	Blood counters
Blank, Arthur	500	Home Depot
Anderson, John Edward	500	Beverages
Ueltschi, Albert Lee	495	FlightSafety
Naify, Robert Allen	495	Tele-Communications
Coulter, Joseph	495	Blood counters
Taylor family	480	Publishing (I)
McClatchy family	480	Newspapers (I)
Kimmel, Sidney	480	Jones Apparel
Cowles (Gardner) family	480	Newspapers (I)
Sulzberger family	475	New York Times
Reid, Elizabeth Ann	475	Hallmark (I)
Marshall, Barbara Hall	475	Hallmark (I)
Goldman, Rhonda H. (F)	475	Levi Strauss
Brittingham family	475	Dal-Tile
Berry, John William Sr. (F)	475	Yellow Pages
Gonda family	470	Aircraft leasing
Frist, Thomas F. Jr. (F)	470	Hospital Corp.
Belfer, Arthur Bejer (F)	470	Oil
Russell family	465	Athletic wear
Lerner, Alfred	465	Banking
Ellis, Alpheus Lee	460	Banking
Close family	460	Textiles
Stephens, Jackson (F)	455	Investment banking
Skaggs, Leonard Jr.	455	American Stores
Watson family	450	Real estate
Swig family	450	Real estate
Solheim, Karsten	450	Golf clubs
Rosenwald family	450	Sears/Roebuck (I)
Lindner, Carl Jr. (F)	450	Insurance
Goodson, Mark	450	Game shows
Dillon family	450	Dillon, Read (I)
Broad, Eli	450	Housing
Terra, Daniel James	445	Lawter International
Stryker family	445	Medical supplies
Pew family	440	Sun Oil (I)
Silliman, Mariana du Pont	430	Du Pont Co. (I)
Rust, Eleanor du Pont	430	Du Pont Co. (I)

The Forbes 400 Wealthiest Ranking (cont'd)

Name	Worth ($ mil)	Primary Source
Pennington, William	430	Circus Circus
May, Irene du Pont	430	Du Pont (I)
Flint, Lucile du Pont (F)	430	Du Pont (I)
du Pont, Irénée Jr. (F)	430	Du Pont (I)
Dolan, Charles Francis	430	Cable television
de Menil family	430	Schlumberger (I)
Darden, Constance du Pont	430	Du Pont (I)
Bredin, Octavia du Pont	430	Du Pont (I)
Zell, Samuel	425	Real estate
Ford, Josephine Clay	425	Ford Motor (I)
Dart, William A.	425	Dart Container
Clark family	425	Singer Manuf.
Moores, John Jay	415	BMC Software
Hearst, George Jr. (F)	415	(I)
Hearst, David Jr. (F)	415	(I)
Cooke, Phoebe Hearst (F)	415	(I)
Benson, Craig Robert	415	Cabletron
Baoudjakdji, Millicent (F)	415	(I)
Wolfe family	410	Newspapers (I)
Ryan, Patrick George	410	Insurance
Milliken, Minot (F)	410	Textiles
Milliken, Gerrish (F)	410	Textiles
Kelly, William Russell	410	Kelly Services
Franchetti, Anne (F)	410	Milliken & Co.
Ward, Louis Larrick	400	Russell Stover
Unanue family	400	Goya Foods
Taylor, Jack Crawford	400	Auto rental
Taubman, Adolph Alfred	400	Real estate
Spanos, Alexander Gus	400	Real estate
Sommer, Viola	400	Real estate (I)
Segerstrom family	400	Real estate
Rose family	400	Real estate
Rollins family	400	(I)
McGovern, Patrick Joseph	400	Publishing
Marion, Anne Windfohr	400	(I)
Mandel, Morton L.	400	Premier Industrial
Mandel, Joseph C.	400	Premier Industrial
Mandel, Jack N.	400	Premier Industrial
Lurie, Robert Alfred	400	(I)
Lewis, Reginald F.	400	LBOs
Krehbiel, John Sr. (F)	400	Molex
Kelley family	400	Hotels
Johnson, Rupert Jr.	400	Franklin Resources
Jamail, Joseph Dahr Jr.	400	Pennzoil settlement
Huffington, Roy Michael	400	Oil
Hobby, Oveta Culp (F)	400	Media
Herb, Marvin	400	Coca-Cola bottler
Glazer, Guilford	400	Real estate
Freeman, Mansfield	400	American Int'l.
Fisher, Zachary (F)	400	Real estate
Fisher, Lawrence (F)	400	Real estate

Name	Worth ($ mil)	Primary Source
Farish family	400	Oil (I)
Dyson, Charles Henry	400	Conglomerator
Coors family	400	Beer
Comer, Gary	400	Land's End
Butt, Charles C.	400	Grocery stores
Bingham family	400	Publishing
Wexner, Bella Cabakof	395	The Limited
Spangler, Clemmie Jr. (F)	390	Investments
Reinhart, Dewayne B.	390	Food wholesaler
Rainwater, Richard	390	Investments
McCaw, Craig O.	390	McCaw Cellular
Perry, Claire Eugenia Getty	380	Oil (I)
McLane, Robert Drayton Jr.	380	Food wholesaling
Manoogian, Richard	380	Masco
Levine, Leon	380	Family Dollar
King family	380	King World Prod.
Getty, Caroline Marie	380	Inheritance (oil)
Earhart, Anne Getty	380	Inheritance (oil)
Watson (Thomas) family	375	IBM
Shorenstein, Walter	375	Real estate
Scharbauer, Clarence Jr.	375	Oil, land (I)
Hunt, Johnnie Bryan	375	J.B. Hunt
Engelhard, Jane B.	375	(I)
Cohn, Seymour	375	Real estate
Brennan, Bernard F,	375	Montgomery Ward
Wasserman, Lewis Robert	370	MCA
Keck, Howard Brighton	370	Superior Oil
Getty, Eugene Paul	370	Oil (I)
Fisher, Max Martin	370	Oil
Buffet, Susan	370	Berkshire Hathaway
Robinson, Jesse (F)	365	Banking
Mathile, Clayton Lee	360	Iams Co.
Hoiles, Harry Howard	360	Newspapers
Hardie, Mary Jane Hoiles	360	Newspapers
Farmer, Richard T.	360	Cintas Corp.
Culverhouse, Hugh Franklin	360	Real estate
Wagner, Cyril Jr.	350	Oil
Taper, Sydney Mark (F)	350	First Charter
Solomon, Russell	350	Tower Records
Sakioka, Katsumasa (F)	350	Real estate
Peery, Richard Taylor	350	Real estate
Mills, Alice du Pont (F)	350	Du Pont (I)
Milken, Michael (F)	350	Financier
McGlothlin, James (F)	350	Coal
Lebensfeld, Harry	350	UIS, Inc.
Kennedy family	350	(I)
Irvine family	350	Lawsuits (I)
du Pont, Alexis Jr. (F)	350	Du Pont (I)
Catsimatidis, John	350	Supermarkets
Brown, Jack	350	Oil

The Forbes 400 Wealthiest Ranking (cont'd)

Name	Worth ($ mil)	Primary Source
Bloomberg, Michael Rubens	350	Financial news
Arrillaga, John	350	Real estate
Allen, Herbert Anthony	350	Stock market
Allen, Herbert	350	Stock market
Allen, Charles Jr.	350	Stock market
Weis, Robert Freeman	345	Weis Markets
Naify, Marshall	345	Tele-Comm.
Norris, Diana Strawbridge	340	Campbell's (I)
Litwin, Leonard	340	Real estate
Haas, Peter E. Jr (F)	340	Levi Strauss
Connell, Grover	340	Equip. leasing
Solow, Sheldon Henry	330	Real estate
Gottwald, Floyd Dewey Jr.	330	Ethyl Corp.
Behring, Kenneth Eugene	330	Developer
Petersen, Robert Einar	325	Publishing
Markkula, Armas Clifford Jr.	320	Apple Comp.
Lund, Sharon Disney	320	Walt Disney (I)
Simmons, Richard Paul	315	Allegheny Ludlum
Goizueta, Roberto Crispulo	315	Coca-Cola
Autry, Orvon Gene	315	Broadcasting
Haas, Walter A. Jr.	310	Levi Strauss
Haas, Robert D. (F)	310	Levi Strauss
Gottwald, Bruce Cobb	310	Ethyl Corp.
Evans, James Emmett	310	Citrus grower
Dell, Michael	310	Dell Computer
Binger, Virginia McKnight	310	3M (I)
Weis, Sigfried	300	Weis Markets
Stempel, Ernest E.	300	AIG
Steinberg, Saul Philip	300	Financier
Spelling, Aaron	300	Television
Simon, Melvin	300	Shopping Ctrs.
Searle, William Louis	300	G.D. Searle
Searle, Daniel Crow	300	G.D. Searle
Saul, B. Francis II	300	(I)
Rinker, Marshall Edison Sr.	300	Concrete
Perdue, Franklyn Parsons	300	Perdue Farms
Pennington, Claude B.	300	Oil
Pearson, Edith du Pont (F)	300	Du Pont (I)
Pamplin, Robert Boisseau Sr.	300	Textiles
Pamplin, Robert Boisseau Jr.	300	Textiles
Moncrief, William Alvin Jr.	300	Oil
Milbury, Cassandra Mellon	300	(I)
Mellon, Timothy	300	(I)
Mellon, Seward Prosser	300	(I)
Mellon, Richard Prosser	300	(I)
McCaw, Keith W.	300	McCaw Cellular
McCaw, John Elroy Jr.	300	McCaw Cellular
McCaw, Bruce R.	300	McCaw Cellular
May, Peter	300	Leveraged buys
Maritz, William Edward (F)	300	Maritz Inc.
Lesher, Dean	300	Newspapers
Lawrence, M. Larry	300	Real estate

Name	Worth ($ mil)	Primary Source
Kovner, Bruce	300	Trading
Johnson, James	300	Johnson & Johnson (I)
Jacobs, Richard E.	300	Shopping centers
Hubbard, Stanley	300	Broadcasting
Hillman, Tatnall Lea	300	(I)
Hillman, Howard	300	(I)
Hammons, John	300	Hotels
Guccione, Robert	300	Publishing
Gallo, Julio	300	Wine
Gallo, Ernest	300	Wine
Forman, Michael	300	Real estate
Field, Marshall V	300	Dept. Stores (I)
Duke, Jennifer	300	Johnson & Johnson (I)
du Pont, Willis (F)	300	Du Pont (I)
Dixon, Suzanne	300	G.D. Searle & Co.
Dixon, Fitz Jr.	300	(I)
Davis, Artemus	300	Winn-Dixie
Currier, Michael S.	300	(I)
Currier, Lavinia M.	300	(I)
Currier, Andrea	300	(I)
Cosby, William Jr.	300	Television
Conover, Catherine	300	(I)
Congel, Robert J.	300	Shopping malls
Cantor, Bernard	300	Cantor Fitzgerald
Borg, Malcolm	300	Publishing
Andreas, Dwayne (F)	300	Archer-Daniels-Midland
Alexander, Norman	300	Sequa Corp.
Ackerman, Peter	300	Junk bonds
Blech, David	295	Biotech Investments
Evans, Thomas	290	Investments
Allbritton, Joe Lewis	290	Media
Leininger, James	285	Specialty hospital beds
Hyde, Joseph III	285	Auto parts
Howard, Robert	285	Publishing
Thorne, Oakleigh	280	Comm. Clearing House
Littlefield, Edmund	280	General Electric
Berry, Jack (F)	280	Citrus
Simon, William	275	Leveraged buyouts
Parker, Jack (F)	275	Real estate
O'Neill, Richard	275	Real Estate (I)
Milken, Lowell (F)	275	Financier
Fuqua, John Brooks	275	Investments
Avery, Alice (F)	275	Real Estate (I)
Keck, William II	270	Superior Oil Co.
Grainger, David	270	W.W. Grainger
Bass, Anne	270	Divorce
Kaiser, George B.	265	Gas
Clayton, James Lee	265	Mobile homes
Berkley, William	265	Food processing

Source: Forbes Magazine, 1992

**Note: Due to multiple entries, rankings have been omitted and more than 400 names appear.*

(F) = and Family; (I) = Inheritance

Business Plan Outline

THE BUSINESS PLAN IS A CRITICAL element in planning, growing and financing a business. Here is a sample outline created by Jan Wm. Zupnick, President of The Entrepreneurship Institute.

I. Overview
- A. Summary of Fundamental Elements Upon Which the Venture is Built
- B. Background and Critical Success Factors
  1. Introduction
     - a. Purpose
     - b. History of company
     - c. General description of products or services
     - d. Benefits
     - e. Objectives
     - f. Critical success factors
  2. Business Environment
     - a. Industry description
     - b. Regulatory climate
     - c. Market description
     - d. Competition
     - e. Barriers to achieving objectives
  3. Alternatives (existing businesses)
     - a. Business as usual
     - b. Growth through expansion
     - c. Growth through merger, acquisition, etc.
     - d. Contraction
     - e. Sell out
  4. Risks and Opportunities
     - a. Strengths
     - b. Weaknesses
- C. Description of Products and Services
  1. Description of Each Product or Service
  2. Uniqueness and Special Aspects
     - a. Features, advantages, benefits
     - b. Strengths and weaknesses
     - c. Patents, licenses, royalties
  3. Anticipated Changes (existing businesses)
     - a. Planned products and services
     - b. Discontinued products and services
     - c. Life cycles
     - d. Environment
  4. Product Strategy
     - a. Buy for resale
     - b. Make
       - – R & D
       - – Engineering
     - c. Unique or similar
     - d. Narrow or broad market
     - e. Quality

II. Marketing
- A. Critical Success Factors
- B. Strategy
- C. Market Analysis
  1. Economic Environment
  2. Industry Environment
  3. Customer Base
  4. Market Size, Geography
  5. Market Share
  6. Market Segment and Target Market
  7. Market Needs Analysis
  8. Market Opportunity Trend Analysis
  9. Technological Trends
  10. Growth Trends
  11. Government Regulations
- D. Competition
- E. Sales Tactics
- F. Pricing
- G. Promotion
- H. Packaging
  1. Physical Package for Products
  2. Product and Service Philosophy (Maintenance)
  3. Product or System Philosophy

III. Management and Operational Plan
- A. Management Team
  1. Organization Chart
  2. Key Management Personnel Descriptions
  3. Management Compensation & Ownership
  4. Board of Directors
  5. Supporting Professional Services
- B. Human Resources
  1. Number
  2. Recruitment
  3. Selection
  4. Skills
  5. Training
- C. Facilities and Equipment
  1. Plant, Offices, Warehouse
  2. Capacity, Percent Utilized
  3. Location
  4. Strategy & Plans
  5. Equipment
     - a. Production tools and machinery
     - b. Inspection equipment
     - c. Vendor quality assurance inspection

Business Plan Outline (cont'd)

IV. Financial Plan
- A. Financial Situation
  1. Financial History Highlights
  2. Present Financial Condition
  3. Credit Arrangements and Sources
  4. Revenue Projections
  5. Ratios and Comparative Analyses
     - a. Internal ratio analysis
     - b. External ratio analysis
     - c. Budget analysis
  6. Contingent Liabilities
  7. Insurance
  8. Tax Consideration
  9. Review and Control
- B. Financing Requirements
  1. Equity Policy Statement
  2. Capital Requirements
     - a. Amount
     - b. Purpose
  3. Funding Sources
     - a. Internal
     - b. External
     - c. List of potential sources
  4. Financing Proposal

V. Appendices
- A. Schedule of Major Events
- B. Personnel Resources, Key-Person Resumes
- C. Facilities and Equipment Data
- D. Financial History
- E. Revenue Forecast
- F. Product or Service Cost Analysis
- G. Expense Budgets
- H. Income Statement Projection
- I. Cash Flow Projection
- J. Balance Sheet Projection
- K. Financial Ratios
- L. Collateral
- M. Organization Chart
- N. Major Customers
- O. Principal Suppliers
- P. Insurance Coverages
- Q. Formats
- R. Other Supporting Documents and Data

Source: ©, The Entrepreneurship Institute

The Top Reference Sources

The Directory of Corporate Philanthropy
Gale Research, $365.00
(313) 961-6083

Compiled by the research staff of the Public Management Institute, this reference is a good source of factual information on the funding programs of the 580 American corporations with the most active philanthropic programs.

Entries include the address and phone number of each corporation, plus contact person, eligibility, number of grants made, application process, sample grants, and more.

Business Failures

Number of Business Failures by Industry

Industry	1985	1986	1987	1989	1990
TOTAL	57,253	61,616	61,111	50,361	60,432
Agriculture, forestry, fishing	2,699	2,649	3,766	1,540	1,727
Mining	796	921	627	351	381
Construction	7,005	7,109	6,735	7,120	8,072
Manufacturing	4,869	4,772	4,273	3,933	4,709
Food and kindred products	261	239	191	216	226
Textile mill products	110	72	73	75	101
Apparel, other textile products	338	287	265	204	318
Lumber and wood products	415	392	374	368	417
Furniture and fixtures	236	244	200	253	257
Paper and allied products	55	46	60	46	66
Printing and publishing	659	606	633	679	728
Chemicals and allied products	172	129	116	102	134
Petroleum refining	26	35	21	21	21
Primary metal products	122	133	107	71	114
Transportation equipment	197	226	175	190	240
Instruments and related products	110	140	112	108	119
Miscellaneous	271	267	241	206	269
Transportation, public utilities	2,536	2,565	2,236	2,115	2,610
Wholesale trade	4,836	4,869	4,336	3,687	4,376
Retail trade	13,494	13,620	12,240	11,120	12,826
Finance, insurance, real estate	2,676	2,797	2,550	2,932	3,881
Services	16,649	20,967	23,802	13,679	17,673

Source: Business Failure Record, Dun and Bradstreet

The Top Reference Sources

Corporate Meeting Planners
Reed Publishing
(908) 464-6800

This directory of corporate meeting planners lists approximately 18,090 meeting planners, together with their titles, for over 11,686 top companies in the U.S. Also included are the complete address, telephone number, and type of business for each firm.

Listings also include the number of meetings held during the calendar year, the months and seasons these meetings are held, the number of days, number of attendees, and the location.

50 Largest Companies Worldwide

The World's Largest Industrial Companies

Rank	Company	Country	Sales ($ millions)	Profits ($ millions)	Employees
1	General Motors	U.S.	123,780.1	-4,452.8	756,300
2	Royal Dutch/Shell Group	Britain/Netherlands	103,834.8	4,249.3	133,000
3	Exxon	U.S.	103,242.0	5,600.0	101,000
4	Ford Motor	U.S.	88,962.8	-2,258.0	332,700
5	Toyota Motor	Japan	78,061.3	3,143.2	102,423
6	IBM	U.S.	65,394.0	-2,827.0	344,553
7	IRI	Italy	64,095.5	-254.1	407,169
8	General Electric	U.S.	60,236.0	2,636.0	284,000
9	British Petroleum	Britain	58,355.0	802.8	111,900
10	Daimler-Benz	Germany	57,321.3	1,129.4	379,252
11	Mobil	U.S.	56,910.0	1,920.0	67,500
12	Hitachi	Japan	56,053.3	1,629.2	309,757
13	Matsushita Electric Industrial	Japan	48,595.0	1,832.5	210,848
14	Philip Morris	U.S.	48,109.0	3,006.0	166,000
15	Fiat	Italy	46,812.0	898.7	287,957
16	Volkswagen	Germany	46,042.2	665.5	265,566
17	Siemens	Germany	44,859.2	1,135.2	402,000
18	Samsung Group	South Korea	43,701.9	347.3	187,377
19	Nissan Motor	Japan	42,905.7	340.9	138,326
20	Unilever	Britain/Netherlands	41,262.3	1,842.6	298,000
21	ENI	Italy	41,047.3	872.0	NA
22	E.I. du Pont de Nemours	U.S.	38,031.0	1,403.0	133,000
23	Texaco	U.S.	37,551.0	1,294.0	40,181
24	Chevron	U.S.	36,795.0	1,293.0	55,123
25	Elf Aquitaine	France	36,315.8	1,737.1	86,900
26	Nestlé	Switzerland	35,583.7	1,722.3	201,139
27	Toshiba	Japan	33,232.5	855.4	162,000
28	Honda Motor	Japan	30,567.3	539.8	85,500
29	Philips Electronics	Netherlands	30,217.6	642.8	240,000
30	Renault	France	29,432.4	545.8	147,195
31	Chrysler	U.S.	29,370.0	-795.0	126,500
32	Boeing	U.S.	29,314.0	1,567.0	159,100
33	Abb Asea Brown Boveri	Switzerland	28,883.0	587.0	214,399
34	Hoechst	Germany	28,468.2	661.8	179,322
35	Peugeot	France	28,403.3	979.9	156,800
36	Alcatel Alsthom	France	28,390.7	1,095.9	213,100
37	BASF	Germany	28,130.4	627.0	129,434
38	Procter & Gamble	U.S.	27,406.0	1,773.0	94,000
39	NEC	Japan	26,675.4	384.9	117,994
40	Sony	Japan	26,581.4	825.1	112,900
41	Amoco	U.S.	25,604.0	1,484.0	54,120
42	Bayer	Germany	25,581.3	1,100.5	164,200
43	Daewoo	South Korea	25,362.6	NA	81,607
44	Total	France	25,361.7	1,030.3	56,156
45	PDVSA	Venezuela	24,000.0	NA	52,000
46	Mitsubishi Electric	Japan	23,976.3	564.5	97,002
47	Nippon Steel	Japan	23,141.6	641.8	54,062
48	Thyssen	Germany	22,465.0	294.1	148,557
49	Imperial Chemical Industries	Britain	22,339.4	958.4	128,600
50	United Technologies	U.S.	21,262.0	-1,021.0	185,100

Source: Fortune Magazine

50 Largest Companies Worldwide (cont'd)

Largest Companies in the World by Industry

Industry	Company	Country	Sales ($ millions)
Aerospace	Boeing	U.S.	29,314
Apparel	Levi Strauss Associates	U.S.	4,903
Beverages	PepsiCo	U.S.	19,771
Building materials	Saint-Gobain	France	13,311
Chemicals	E.I. dú Pont de Nemours	U.S.	38,031
Computers, office equipment	IBM	U.S.	65,394
Electronics, electrical equipment	General Electric	U.S.	60,236
Food	Philip Morris	U.S.	48,109
Forest products	International Paper	U.S.	12,703
Furniture	Johnson Controls	U.S.	4,566
Industrial and farm equipment	ABB Asea Brown Boveri	Switzerland	28,883
Jewelry, watches	Seiko	Japan	3,070
Metal products	Pechiney	France	13,198
Metals	IRI	Italy	64,096
Mining, crude-oil production	Ruhrkohle	Germany	14,902
Motor vehicles and parts	General Motors	U.S.	123,780
Petroleum refining	Royal Dutch/Shell Group	Britain/Netherlands	103,835
Pharmaceuticals	Johnson & Johnson	U.S.	12,447
Publishing, printing	Bertelsmann	Germany	9,104
Rubber and plastic products	Bridgestone	Japan	13,226
Scientific and photo equipment	Eastman Kodak	U.S.	19,649
Soaps, cosmetics	Procter & Gamble	U.S.	27,406
Textiles	Toray Industries	Japan	6,666
Tobacco	RJR Nabisco Holdings	U.S.	14,989
Toys, sporting goods	Yamaha	Japan	3,654
Transportation equipment	Hyundai Heavy Industries	S. Korea	6,823

Fortune Magazine, July 27, 1992, "The Global 500"

Worldwide Taxes

Percent of GNP Collected as National Taxes

Country	Percentage
France	43.8
Germany	38.1
Italy	37.8
Britain	36.5
Canada	35.3
Japan	30.6
U.S.	30.1

Range of Personal Tax Brackets in the Seven Industrialized Nations (%)

Country	Lowest	Highest
Britain	25	40
Canada	17	29
France	5	57
Germany	22	56
Italy	10	50
Japan	10	50
U.S.	15	28

Source: "OECD in Figures" 1992 Edition, supplement to The OECD Observer, No. 176, June/July, 1992

Balance of Trade with the World

National Trade Balances, 1990

Country	Goods and Services Imports ($ billions)	Goods and Services Exports ($ billions)
Australia	52.0	48.9
Austria	62.8	64.6
Belgium	136.8	143.0
Canada	143.0	144.8
Denmark	38.6	45.7
Finland	33.0	31.2
France	269.8	269.4
Germany	393.5	476.0
Greece	21.7	14.4
Iceland	2.1	2.2
Ireland	22.9	26.4
Italy	228.8	229.1
Japan	307.5	327.6
Luxembourg	8.6	8.6
Netherlands	144.0	158.1
New Zealand	12.9	12.2
Norway	38.9	46.6
Portugal	27.1	21.7
Spain	100.6	83.9
Sweden	68.1	69.1
Switzerland	81.7	82.9
Turkey	25.0	21.4
United Kingdom	262.7	239.6
United States	608.3	528.4

Source: "OECD in Figures" 1992 Edition, supplement to The OECD Observer, No. 176, June/July, 1992

U.S. Merchandise Trade with Japan ($ billions)

Commodities	Exports	Imports	Balance
Total merchandise trade			
1990	48.6	89.7	-41.1
1991	48.1	91.6	-43.5
Food and beverages			
1990	8.5	0.3	8.2
1991	8.6	0.3	8.3
Capital goods			
1990	14.4	34.4	-20.0
1991	15.1	36.1	-21.0
Automobile vehicles and parts			
1990	1.8	32.2	-30.4
1991	1.5	32.8	-31.3
Consumer goods			
1990	6.9	13.0	-6.1
1991	6.1	12.5	-6.4
Industrial supplies			
1990	15.2	8.4	6.8
1991	14.9	8.5	6.4
Other products			
1990	1.8	1.4	0.4
1991	1.9	1.4	0.5

Source: U.S. Department of Commerce, International Trade Administration

Balance of Trade (cont'd)

U.S. Merchandise Trade ($ billions)

Commodities	Exports	Imports	Balance
TOTAL TRADE			
1990 annual	393.6	495.3	-101.7
1991 annual	421.9	488.1	-66.2
1991			
I	407.1	474.9	-67.8
II	423.5	475.9	-52.4
III	419.8	497.5	-77.7
IV	440.7	506.4	-65.7
MANUFACTURES TRADE			
1990 annual	315.4	388.8	-73.5
1991 annual	345.4	393.1	-47.7
1991			
I	328.9	368.6	-39.7
II	358.3	379.9	-21.6
III	335.8	400.3	-64.5
IV	358.5	423.4	-64.9
AGRICULTURAL TRADE			
1990 annual	39.6	22.3	17.3
1991 annual	39.3	22.2	17.1
1991			
I	41.7	22.7	19.0
II	35.8	23.2	12.6
III	34.5	20.3	14.2
IV	45.3	22.4	22.9

Source: U.S. Department of Commerce, International Trade Administration

The Top Reference Sources

The Vest-Pocket CEO
Prentice Hall, $12.95
(212) 699-7000

This is a terrific little guidebook for handling nearly every business problem. Included are 101 innovative solutions to the most challenging problems facing today's decision makers, taken from some of the most successful corporations in the country. Highlights are Honeywell's 7 tactics for managing a product development team; Ernst & Whinney's customer service checklist; Boston Consulting Group's Growth Share Matrix; Price Waterhouse's application of Kawasaki Heavy Industries' "just-in-time" production system, among others.

Balance of Trade (cont'd)

Composition of U.S. Merchandise Trade ($ billions, annual rates)

	Exports	Imports	Balance
CAPITAL GOODS			
1990 annual	152.7	116.4	36.3
1991 annual	166.8	121.4	45.4
1991			
I	155.5	119.2	36.3
II	170.2	121.1	49.1
III	165.9	122.4	43.5
IV	175.7	122.9	52.8
CONSUMER GOODS			
1990 annual	43.3	105.7	-62.4
1991 annual	46.2	107.9	-61.7
1991			
I	46.4	100.4	-54.0
II	45.1	100.2	-55.1
III	44.7	110.4	-65.7
IV	48.4	120.6	-72.2
AUTOMOTIVE VEHICLES AND PARTS			
1990 annual	37.4	87.3	-49.9
1991 annual	40.2	85.3	-45.1
1991			
I	34.5	82.2	-47.7
II	41.3	79.0	-37.7
III	41.8	91.2	-49.4
IV	43.2	88.7	-45.5
FOOD AND BEVERAGES			
1990 annual	35.1	26.7	8.4
1991 annual	36.3	26.5	9.8
1991			
I	35.0	25.6	9.4
II	34.8	28.0	6.8
III	36.1	26.4	9.7
IV	39.4	26.3	13.1
PETROLEUM AND PRODUCTS			
1990 annual	7.7	62.2	-54.5
1991 annual	7.6	51.5	-43.9
I	10.2	52.9	-42.7
II	6.6	51.7	-45.1
III	6.2	52.0	-45.8
IV	7.4	48.9	-41.5
OTHER INDUSTRIAL SUPPLIES			
1990 annual	96.8	81.0	15.8
1991 annual	101.6	80.1	21.5
1991			
I	102.3	79.4	22.9
II	102.5	79.1	23.4
III	101.0	79.1	21.9
IV	100.9	82.6	18.3

Source: U.S. Department of Commerce, International Trade Administration

Balance of Trade (cont'd)

U.S. Merchandise Trade by Area ($ billions, annual rates)

	Exports	Imports	Balance
WESTERN EUROPE			
1990 annual	113.1	109.0	4.1
1991 annual	118.7	102.6	16.1
1991			
I	123.3	100.7	22.6
II	123.0	102.4	20.6
III	107.2	99.4	7.8
IV	121.4	108.0	13.4
JAPAN			
1990 annual	48.6	89.7	-41.1
1991 annual	48.1	91.6	-43.4
1991			
I	49.3	90.1	-40.8
II	48.5	84.5	-36.0
III	46.1	93.0	-46.9
IV	48.7	98.7	-50.1
CANADA			
1990 annual	83.7	91.4	-7.7
1991 annual	85.1	91.1	-6.0
1991			
I	80.7	86.4	-5.7
II	90.9	95.2	-4.3
III	82.3	88.5	-6.2
IV	88.0	94.4	-6.4
OPEC			
1990 annual	13.7	38.1	-24.4
1991 annual	19.1	33.0	-13.9
1991			
I	16.5	33.8	-17.3
II	18.8	32.4	-13.6
III	19.3	33.4	-14.1
IV	21.7	32.3	-10.6
OTHER DEVELOPING COUNTRIES			
1990 annual	113.6	142.4	-28.8
1991 annual	127.7	142.1	-14.4
1991			
I	118.5	129.6	-11.3
II	128.0	136.8	-8.8
III	128.7	149.4	-20.7
IV	135.6	152.5	-16.9
EAST EUROPE/FORMER U.S.S.R./COMMUNIST ASIA			
1990 annual	9.0	17.4	-8.4
1991 annual	11.1	20.8	-9.7
1991			
I	11.0	16.3	-5.3
II	10.1	17.6	-7.5
III	10.1	24.3	-14.2
IV	13.1	25.0	-11.9

Source: U.S. Department of Commerce, International Trade Administration

World Unemployment

World Unemployment Rates (%, 1990 and 1980)

Country	1990 Both Sexes	1980 Both Sexes	1990 Women	1980 Women	1990 Men	1980 Men	1990, 12 or More Months Unemployed	1980, 12 or More Months Unemployed
Australia	6.9	5.9	7.1	7.4	6.8	4.9	21.6	19.9
Austria	3.2	1.9	3.5	2.8	3.0	1.3	13.1	NA
Belgium	8.7	7.9	12.8	13.5	5.9	4.6	76.3	61.5
Canada	8.1	7.4	8.1	8.4	8.0	6.8	5.7	3.2
Denmark	8.3	6.0	8.9	8.3	7.7	4.2	25.9	3.2
Finland	3.4	4.6	2.8	4.6	4.0	4.6	6.9	27.0
France	9.0	6.3	12.0	9.4	6.7	4.2	43.9	32.6
Germany	6.2	3.2	7.4	4.3	5.4	2.5	49.0	28.7
Greece	7.5	2.8	12.3	4.1	4.6	2.2	52.4	20.6
Iceland	1.6	0.3	NA	NA	NA	NA	NA	NA
Ireland	13.7	7.3	10.0	7.0	15.5	7.4	67.3	38.2
Italy	10.8	7.5	17.0	13.0	7.2	4.7	70.4	51.2
Japan	2.1	2.0	2.2	2.0	2.0	2.0	19.1	16.4
Luxembourg	1.1	0.7	1.7	1.2	0.9	0.5	NA	NA
Netherlands	7.5	6.0	10.7	7.1	5.5	5.6	49.9	35.9
New Zealand	7.8	2.2	7.2	2.7	8.2	2.0	18.7	7.0
Norway	5.2	1.6	4.8	2.3	5.6	1.2	19.2	3.3
Portugal	4.6	7.7	6.6	13.3	3.1	4.0	48.3	NA
Spain	15.9	11.1	23.9	12.7	11.7	10.4	54.0	32.8
Sweden	1.5	2.0	1.5	2.3	1.5	1.7	4.8	5.5
Switzerland	0.5	0.2	0.6	0.3	0.5	0.1	NA	NA
Turkey	6.9	11.2	7.0		6.9		NA	NA
U.K.	5.5	5.6	3.3	4.2	7.1	6.6	40.8	29.5
United States	5.4	7.0	5.4	7.4	5.4	6.7	5.6	4.3

Source: "OECD in Figures" 1992 Edition, supplement to The OECD Observer, No. 176, June/July, 1992

The Top Reference Sources

Co-op Source Directory
National Register Publishing
(800) 323-6772

The Co-op Source Directory provides a comprehensive quick reference guide to manufacturers' cooperative advertising programs. It is divided into 52 product classifications under which co-op summaries appear alphabetically by manufacturer.

The summaries are detailed and include eligible media, regional variations, reimbursement methods, accrual, timing, international availability, media requirements, advertising aids, etc.

Corporate Office Space

Office Vacancy Rates

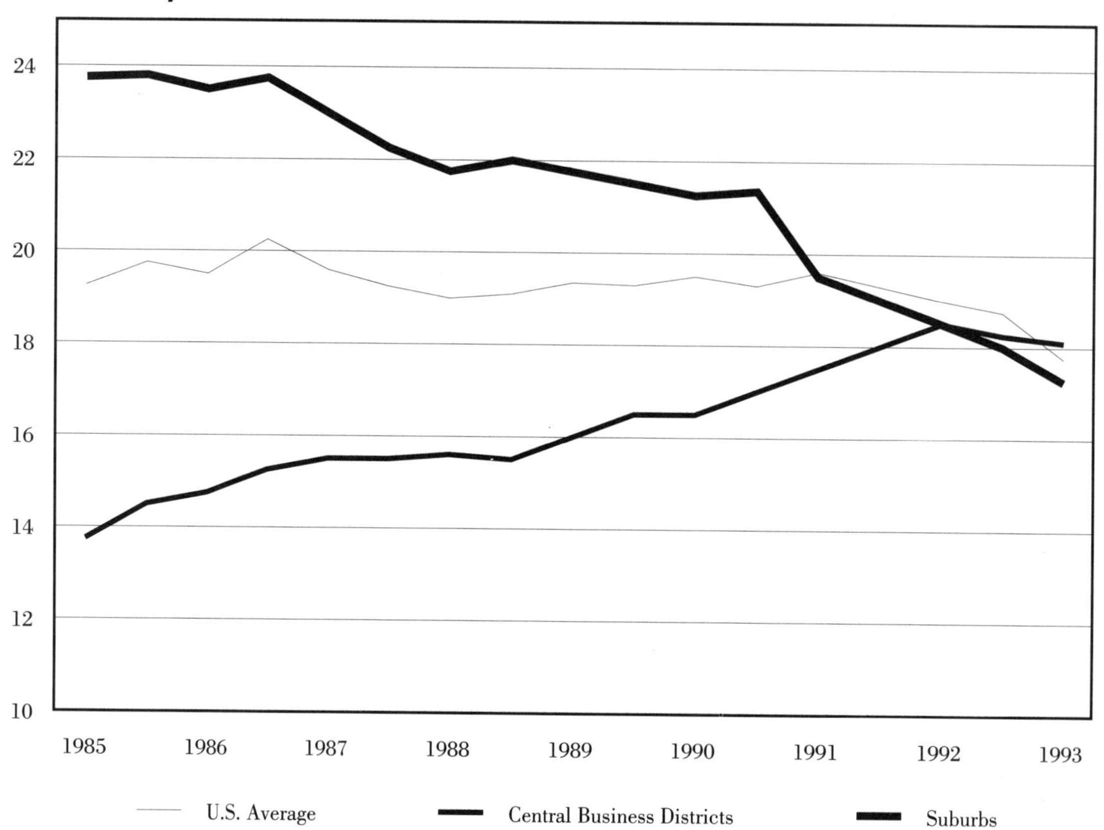

Metropolitan Office Markets Ranked by Vacancy Rates

Top Ten Markets

Rank	City	Vacancy June 1992
1	Honolulu	7.2
2	Las Vegas	12.5
3	San Francisco	12.7
4	Raleigh-Durham	13.2
5	San Jose	13.5
6	Seattle	13.8
7	Columbus	14.0
8	Portland	14.1
9	Sacramento	15.6
10	Pittsburgh	15.6

Bottom Ten Markets

Rank	City	Vacancy June 1992
1	West Palm Beach	29.5
2	Dallas	27.6
3	New Orleans	25.8
4	San Diego	25.3
5	Fort Lauderdale	25.1
6	Tampa	24.3
7	Houston	24.1
8	Tulsa	24
9	Miami	23.9
10	Ventura	23.7

Source: Salomon Brothers

Real Office Rents, Vacancy Rates

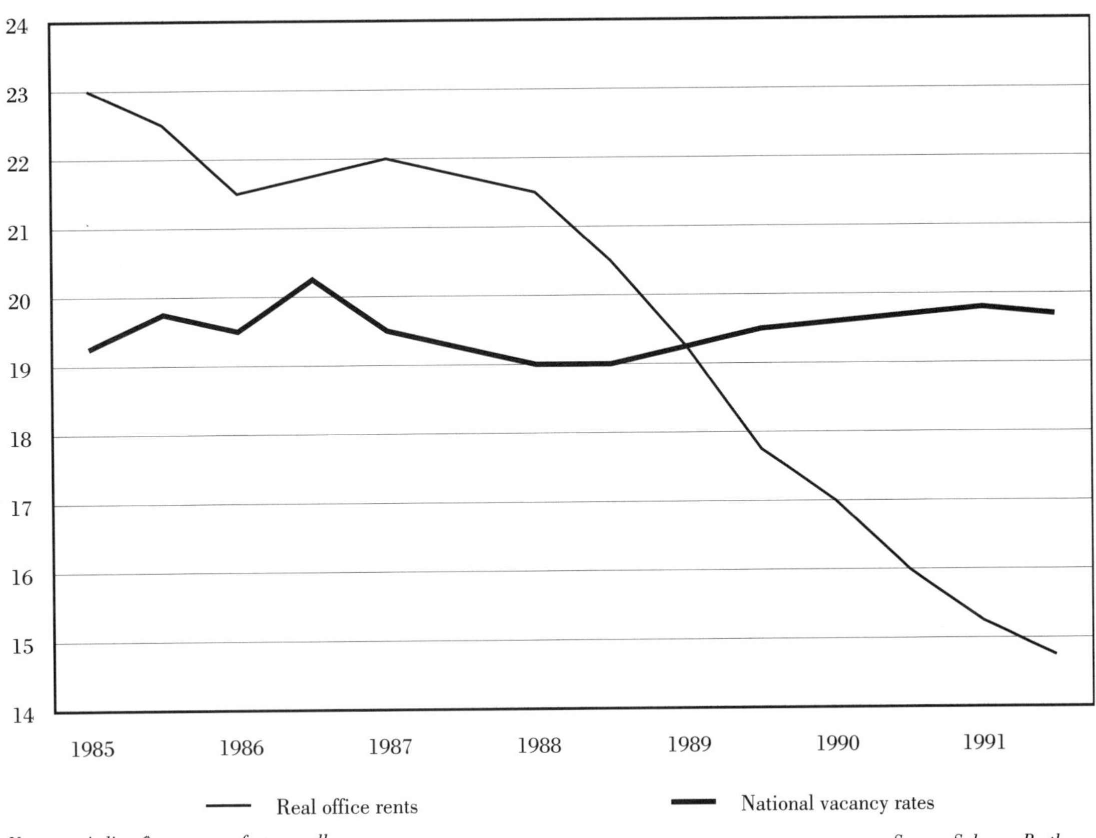

Note: y axis lists $ per square foot as well as vacancy rate in %.

Source: Salomon Brothers

The Top Reference Sources

Statistical Forecasts of the United States
Gale Research, $89.50
(313) 961-6083

This reference covers population, employment, labor, crime, education, health care, and other key areas. Statistics are compiled from a diverse range of sources, and data is presented in hundreds of charts, graphs, tables, and other statistical illustrations portraying both long- and-short term forecasts of future developments in the United States.

Vacancy Rates and Rental Costs

City	Total Office Inventory Surveyed	Office Occupancy Rate (%)	Rental Range ($ per Sq. Ft.)
Akron	1,479,646	82.3	9.00-21.50
Anchorage, downtown	2,865,838	91.4	7.80-30.00
Anchorage, suburban	4,360,539	91.4	7.80-30.00
Atlanta, downtown	42,703,402	79.7	NA
Atlanta, suburban	63,143,261	85.0	NA
Boston, downtown	36,289,539	82.5	NA
Boston, CBD	31,931,065	84.4	NA
Boston, city of	46,503,169	82.5	NA
Boston, south suburban	6,184,502	85.1	NA
Buffalo	7,327,409	78.5	7.00-12.00
Charlotte, downtown	9,726,518	82.3	18.42
Charlotte, suburban	11,205,496	78.5	13.92
Chattanooga	4,131,210	82.8	3.75-15.80
Chicago, downtown	102,180,403	76.2	2.50-41.00
Chicago, O'Hare corridor	3,527,720	77.6	9.00-26.86
Cincinnati, downtown	14,222,562	83.0	15.45
Cincinnati, suburban	8,133,590	80.9	13.98
Cleveland, downtown	22,500,000	78.7	14.00-20.50
Cleveland, suburban	13,000,000	83.8	NA
Corpus Christi	2,610,617	60.6	7.00-15.00
Dallas, downtown	31,364,900	68.8	15.00-16.50
Dallas, suburban	96,875,650	74.1	13.00-16.50
Denver, downtown	23,983,805	77.9	4.00-20.00
Denver, suburban	46,947,129	80.0	3.75-22.00
Detroit, downtown	13,252,973	80.2	10.17-19.34
Detroit, suburban	46,637,193	80.7	13.07-19.30
Fort Worth, downtown	7,328,147	82.4	8.00-18.00
Fort Worth, suburban	14,693,943	80.9	6.00-16.00
Hartford, downtown	11,595,539	73.3	9.93-29.45
Hartford, suburban	13,093,302	78.6	7.00-22.50
Indianapolis, downtown	10,833,700	80.0	8.50-23.00
Indianapolis, suburban	12,965,400	76.6	NA
Inland Empire: (Riverside/San Bernardino City)	7,083,696	82.5	9.00-24.00
Kansas City, downtown	12,438,415	78.6	8.50-22.00
Kansas City, suburban	22,017,555	86.6	10.00-21.00
Louisville, downtown	7,460,000	81.4	6.00-20.00
Louisville, suburban	5,590,000	86.0	6.50-17.00
Manhattan, downtown	91,200,000	77.9	28.82
Manhattan, midtown	189,200,000	82.8	33.54
Manhattan, midtown south	35,500,000	81.7	15.87
Milwaukee, downtown	12,511,204	80.6	NA
Milwaulkee, suburban	12,031,655	79.2	NA
Minneapolis, downtown	21,272,000	78.5	12.00-21.00
Minneapolis, suburban	20,500,000	79.5	12.50-21.00
New Orleans, downtown	16,051,421	72.4	6.00-20.00
New Orleans, suburban	5,313,807	88.6	10.00-19.00
Oakland/ East Bay	83,400,000	85.4	NA
Orange County	50,015,125	80.4	1.37-1.73
Phoenix, downtown	16,100,000	74.5	11.48-16.73
Phoenix, suburban	29,900,000	77.9	12.35-14.82

Vacancy Rates and Rental Costs (cont'd)

City	Total Office Inventory Surveyed	Office Occupancy Rate (%)	Rental Range ($ per Sq. Ft.)
Pittsburgh, downtown	23,603,000	82.2	6.30-28.50
Pittsburgh, suburban	11,704,000	85.7	7.00-21.50
Portland, downtown	15,226,609	85.8	11.06-19.75
Portland, suburban	9,331,857	86.0	NA
Sacramento, downtown	9,433,000	85.4	17.50-32.00
Sacramento, suburban	25,391,000	85.9	15.00-25.00
Saint Louis, downtown	11,393,697	79.5	10.23-20.41
Saint Louis, suburban	16,360,878	86.7	13.14-20.85
Saint Paul, downtown	6,800,000	79.0	9.00-21.00
Saint Paul, suburban	2,100,000	82.0	7.45-20.50
St. Petersburg/Pinellas City, downtown	1,608,858	62.2	10.00-29.00
St. Petersburg/ Pinellas County, suburban	5,994,413	73.1	8.00-22.00
San Jose, downtown	4,817,290	83.1	9.00-23.40
San Jose, suburban	23,234,822	85.2	9.00-43.20
Seattle, downtown	24,168,522	85.4	9.25-32.50
Seattle, suburban	6,571,638	84.7	9.00-18.25
Tampa Bay/Hillsborough Cty., downtown	6,212,692	72.5	10.00-29.00
Tampa Bay/Hillsborough Cty., suburban	13,207,924	83.7	8.00-22.00
Tulsa, downtown	6,443,646	86.7	8.50-15.00
Tulsa, suburban	7,505,235	82.8	8.00-14.00
Washington, DC, downtown	78,997,661	86.0	11.50-53.25
Suburban Virginia	71,434,418	82.0	5.50-39.00
Suburban Maryland	37,268,736	81.8	7.50-41.50

Source: 1992 North American Office Market Review, BOMA

Contact Options

BOMA Building Owners and Managers Assn.
1201 New York Ave., NW
Washington, DC 20005
(202) 408-2662

Society for Industrial and Office Realtors
777 14th St., NW, Suite 400
Washington, DC 20005
(202) 737-1150

Recommended Resource

ULI Market Profiles: 1992
Urban Land Institute
Washington, DC 20005
Urban Land Institute Economic report on 35 major locations plus 13 international markets for real estate development in residential, retail, hotel, office, and industrial sectors.

The Top Reference Sources

Comparative Statistics of Industrial and Office Real Estate Markets
Society of Industrial and Office Realtors
(202) 737-1150

This publication includes a detailed review and forecast of both industrial and office real estate markets, as well as an analysis of economic trends and their effect on industrial and office markets.

The book is compiled by a select group of SIOR members in major metropolitan areas in the U.S., Canada, and abroad. The book includes many charts and graphs.

Construction Starts

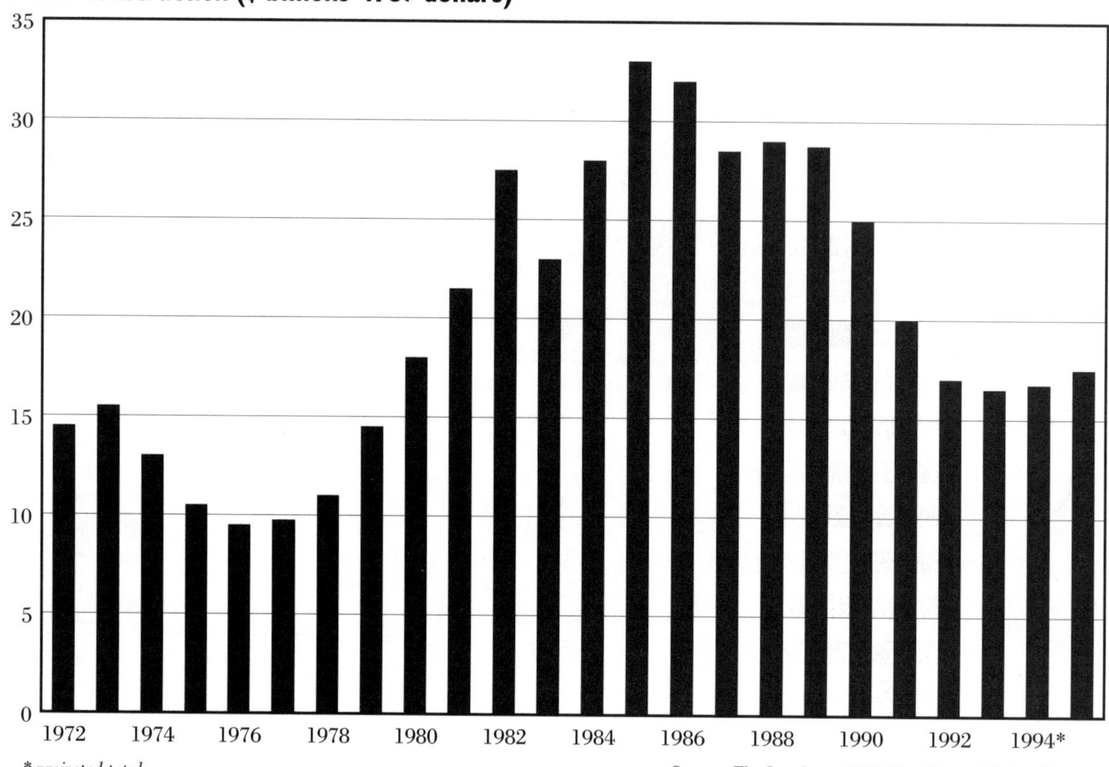

* *projected totals*

Source: The Landauer 1993 Real Estate Market Forecast

The Top Reference Sources

Construction Review
U.S. Government Printing Office, $24.00 a year
(202) 783-3238

This quarterly publication of the International Trade Administration canvasses the major construction series published by the Census Bureau and Bureau of Labor Statistics. It includes about fifty pages of statistics, from building permits to housing starts, construction materials to price indexes, plus one or two brief articles per issue.

Features include articles on world trade in building materials and non-residential building improvements in the United States.

Landauer Momentum Index

LANDAUER ASSOCIATES HAS RANKED 24 major metropolitan areas by their real estate momentum. This is computed as the prospective change in supply and demand balance for office space. The median value is set to 100–thus Phoenix has average momentum, while Orlando is expected to see a growth rate that outstrips supply.

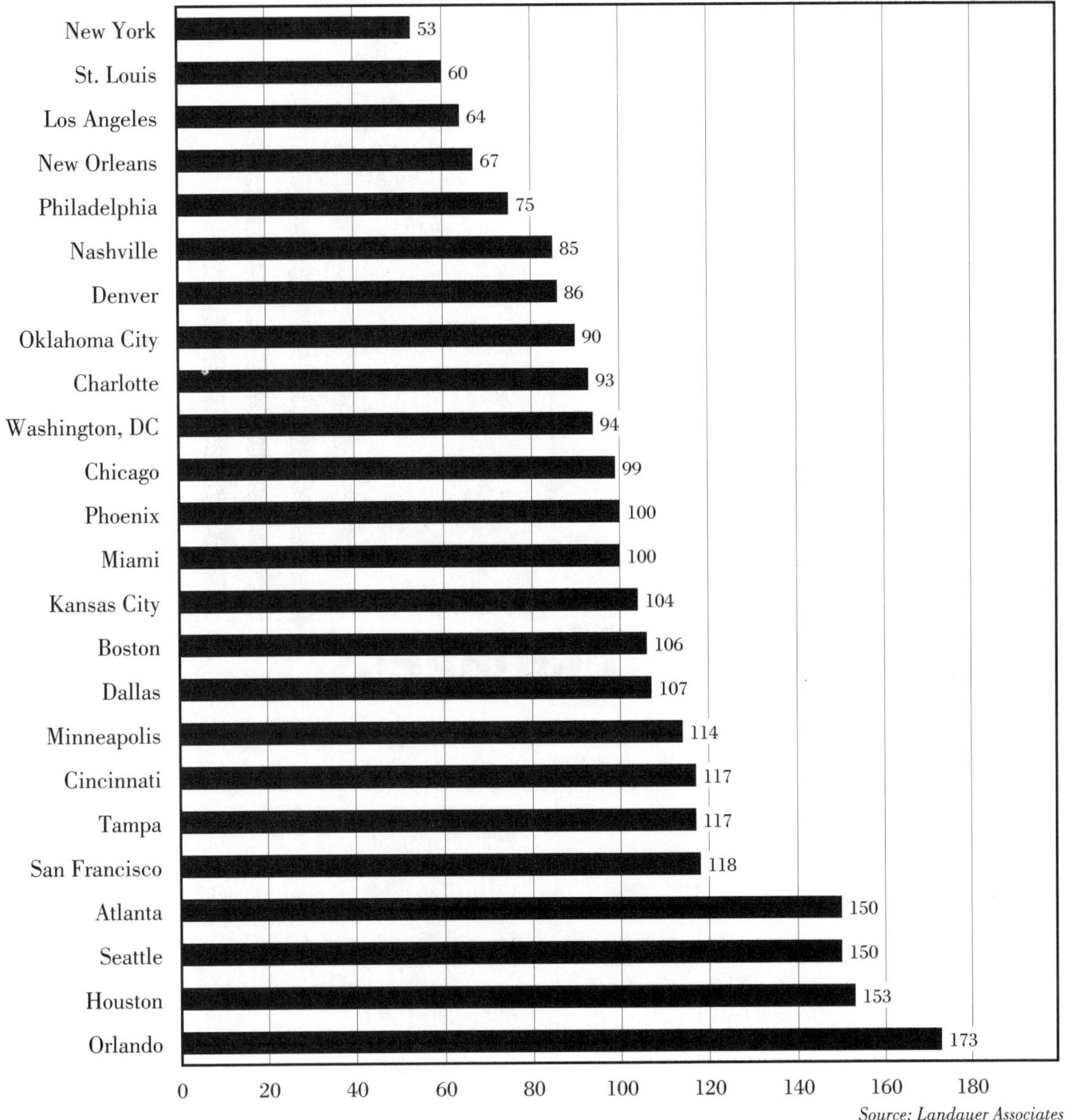

Source: Landauer Associates

Major Real Estate Developers

NATIONAL REAL ESTATE INVESTOR conducts an annual survey of real estate developers and ranks the respondents based on the total square feet under development in North America. The top ten listings from this survey are:

Homart Development Co.
55 W. Monroe, Suite 3100
Chicago, IL 60603
(312) 551-5000

Hines Interests Ltd. Partnership
2800 Post Oak Blvd.
Houston, TX 77056
(713) 621-8000

Melvin Simon & Associates, Inc.
P.O. Box 7033
Indianapolis, IN 46207
(317) 636-1600

The Edward J. DeBartolo Corp.
7620 Market St.
Youngstown, OH 44513
(216) 758-7292

Lincoln Property Co.
500 N. Akard, Suite 3300
Dallas, TX 75201
(214) 740-3300

Breslin Realty Development Corp.
500 Old Country Rd.
Garden City, NY 11530
(516) 741-7400

The Hutensky Group
City Place, 34th Floor,
Hartford, CT 06103
(203) 275-6600

The Cafaro Co.
2445 Belmont Ave.
Youngstown, OH 44504
(216) 747-2661

Zeckendorf Realty L.P.
55 E. 59th St.
New York, NY 10022
(212) 826-2900

Industrial Developments Int'l, Inc.
3443 Peachtree Rd., Suite 1050
Atlanta, GA 30326
(404) 233-6080

Major Property Managers

NATIONAL REAL ESTATE INVESTOR conducts an annual survey of property managers ranking the respondents based on the amount of space in their management portfolios. The following are the top ten listings from that survey:

Tramell Crow Co.
2001 Ross Ave., Suite 3500
Dallas, TX 75201
(214) 979-5100

Network Management Group International
7502 Greenville Ave., Suite 330, LB 44
Dallas, TX 75231
(214) 739-9090

Lincoln Property Co.
500 N. Akard, Suite 300
Dallas, TX 75201
(214) 740-3300

JMB Properties Co.,
900 N. Michigan Ave.
Chicago, IL 60601
(312) 915-2500

Cushman & Wakefield, Inc.
1180 Ave. of the Americas
New York, NY 10036
(212) 704-2260

The Edward J. DeBartolo Corp.
7620 Market St.
Youngstown, OH 44513
(216) 758-7292

Insignia Management Group
P.O. Box 1089
Greenville, SC 29602
(803) 239-1000

La Salle Partners
11 S. LaSalle St.
Chicago, IL 60603
(312) 782-5800

PM Realty Group
1177 W. Loop South, Suite 1200
Houston, TX 77027
(713) 966-3600

Grubb & Ellis
2800 Two Oliver Plaza
Pittsburgh, PA 15222
(412) 281-0100

Major Real Estate Lenders

The Top 50 Commercial Banks in Deposits

Rank	Bank Name	City Location	Telephone	Deposits as of June, 1992 ($)
1	Citibank, NA	New York	(800) 568-7904	126,826,000,000
2	Bank of America NT &SA	San Francisco	(415) 622-6320	111,406,000,000
3	Chemical Bank	New York	(212) 310-6161	76,260,000,000
4	Chase Manhattan Bank, NA	New York	(212) 552-2222	56,602,000,000
5	Wells Fargo Bank, NA	San Francisco	(415) 477-1000	43,021,541,000
6	Morgan Guaranty Trust Co.	New York	(212) 483-2323	38,323,864,000
7	Bank of New York	New York	(212) 495-1041	28,899,961,000
8	NationsBank of Texas, NA	Dallas	(214) 508-2130	25,895,987,000
9	First Union National Bank of Florida	Jacksonville	(904) 361-2265	22,404,451,000
10	First National Bank	Chicago	(312) 732-4000	22,052,000,000
11	Mellon Bank, NA	Pittsburgh	(412) 234-5000	21,663,829,000
12	Bankers Trust Co.	New York	(212) 250-2500	21,133,000,000
13	First National Bank	Boston	(617) 434-8155	19,199,901,000
14	Republic National Bank	New York	(212) 525-5000	17,344,441,000
15	NBD Bank, NA	Detroit	(313) 225-1000	16,657,428,000
16	First Interstate Bank of California	Los Angeles	(213) 614-4111	16,636,303,000
17	Continental Bank, NA	Chicago	(312) 828-2345	15,496,000,000
18	First Union National Bank of North Carolina	Charlotte	(704) 374-6161	13,693,771,000
19	Marine Midland Bank, NA	Buffalo	(716) 841-6762	13,620,160,000
20	Union Bank	San Francisco	(213) 236-7109	12,864,643,000
21	Seattle-First National Bank	Seattle	(206) 358-3000	12,755,439,000
22	National Westminster Bank USA	New York	(516) 531-7120	11,683,545,000
23	Bank One, Texas, NA	Dallas	(713) 751-6100	11,508,590,000
24	First Fidelity Bank, NA	Newark	(201) 565-3223	11,438,686,000
25	Pittsburgh National Bank	Pittsburgh	(412) 762-2331	11,281,559,000
26	CoreStates Bank, NA	Philadelphia	(215) 973-3512	11,041,259,000
27	Wachovia Bank of North Carolina, NA	Winston-Salem	(919) 770-5000	10,863,556,000
28	State Street Bank & Trust Co.	Boston	(617) 654-4000	10,628,514,000
29	Key Bank of New York	Albany	(518) 486-8159	10,536,341,000
30	NationsBank of Virginia, NA	Richmond	(804) 788-3034	10,154,060,000
31	NCNB National Bank of Florida	Tampa	(813) 224-5151	9,996,065,000
32	Comerica Bank	Detroit	(313) 222-3300	9,751,949,000
33	NationsBank of Georgia, NA	Atlanta	(404) 607-4109	9,125,825,000
34	Valley National Bank of Arizona	Phoenix	(602) 261-2461	9,050,646,000
35	Midlantic National Bank	Edison, NJ	(908) 321-2254	8,970,032,000
36	Maryland National Bank	Baltimore	(410) 605-6150	8,898,573,000
37	Meridian Bank	Reading, PA	(215) 320-2000	8,828,433,000
38	NationsBank of North Carolina, NA	Charlotte	(704) 386-8669	8,816,231,000
39	Connecticut National Bank	Hartford	(203) 728-2000	8,542,109,000
40	Bank of America, Arizona	Phoenix	(602) 262-8815	8,277,096,000
41	Society National Bank	Cleveland	(216) 689-3000	8,117,237,000
42	Manufacturers Bank, NA	Detroit	(313) 222-2402	8,067,479,000
43	Banco Popular de Puerto Rico	San Juan	(809) 765-9800	7,976,198,000
44	BayBank Middlesex	Burlington, MA	(617) 564-4266	7,904,394,000
45	Crestar Bank	Richmond, VA	(804) 782-5000	7,730,047,000
46	Bank of Hawaii	Honolulu	(808) 537-8272	7,584,773,000
47	Norwest Bank Minnesota, NA	Minneapolis	(612) 667-8123	7,570,902,000
48	First Bank, NA	Minneapolis	(612) 370-4141	7,544,060,000
49	Michigan National Bank	Farmington Hills	(313) 473-3200	7,483,739,000
50	Huntington National	Columbus, OH	(614) 463-4424	7,258,266,000

Source: American Banker

BOMA Standards

THE BUILDING OWNERS AND MANAGERS Association International (BOMA) is an organization whose purpose is to establish standards through which building owners, managers, tenants, appraisers, architects, lending institutions, and others can communicate and compute on a clear and understandable basis. To achieve that objective, BOMA publishes standards for measuring floor area, calculating and analyzing expenses and income for office buildings, as well as other related tasks. In addition, BOMA provides annual surveys of office space utilization, rental prices/square foot, vacancy rates, and the general rental market in major downtown and suburban locations throughout the nation as well as in Canada.

Contact Option

Building Owners and Managers Association International (BOMA)
1201 New York Ave., NW, Suite 300
Washington, DC 20005
(202) 408-2662

Financing Investment Real Estate

Sales Price of Real Estate (Percent Distribution)

Price Range ($)	All	Retail	Office	Industrial	Multifamily
0-250,000	29	25	27	25	25
250,001-500,000	21	28	13	19	24
500,001-1,000,000	18	19	21	17	22
1,000,001-2,000,000	14	17	23	8	9
2,000,001-5,000,000	13	8	10	25	18
5,000,001-10,000,000	4	3	6	6	2
10,000,001-20,000,000	-	-	-	-	-
>20,000,001	1	-	-	-	-
TOTAL	100	100	100	100	100

Capital Ranges of Real Estate (Percent Distribution)

Cap Rate Range	All	Retail	Office	Industrial	Multifamily
<7.00	5	-	-	7	7
7.01-8.00	2	-	7	-	3
8.01-9.00	8	-	-	6	18
9.01-10.00	16	17	20	20	13
10.01-11.00	28	41	20	27	31
11.01-12.00	20	9	46	20	11
12.01-13.00	7	8	-	-	7
13.01-15.00	14	25	7	13	10
TOTAL	100	100	100	100	100
Mean (Fall 1992)	10.95	11.5	11.15	11.14	10.42
Mean (Fall 1991)	10.3	10.48	11.57	9.64	10.02

Financing Investment Real Estate (cont'd)

Debt Coverage Ratios for Real Estate (Percent Distributions)

Debt Coverage Ratio Range	All	Retail	Office	Industrial	Multifamily
1.00-1.09	2	-	-	-	6
1.10-1.19	8	17	-	-	12
1.20-1.29	29	33	14	14	47
1.30-1.39	12	17	15	29	6
1.40-1.49	10	-	-	14	11
>1.50	39	33	71	43	18
TOTAL	100	100	100	100	100
Mean (Fall 1992)	1.47	1.41	1.65	1.59	1.32
Mean (Fall 1991)	1.24	1.25	1.25	1.26	1.21

Loan-to-Values for Real Estate (LTV's–Percent Distribution)

LTV Range	All	Retail	Office	Industrial	Multifamily
20-50	10	12	6	25	3
51-70	25	25	25	17	28
71-80	43	50	50	41	45
81-90	18	13	13	17	17
91-100	4	-	6	-	7
TOTAL	100	100	100	100	100
Mean (Fall 1992)	72.57	71.20	72.78	67.96	74.36
Mean (Fall 1991)	72.81	74.68	74.60	70.82	75.10

Loan Type for Real Estate (Percent of Respondents)

Loan Type	All	Retail	Office	Industrial	Multifamily
Fixed Rate	34	28	30	34	45
Adjustable Rate	16	8	18	21	24
Wraparound	2	17	2	3	29
Balloon	21	6	24	29	29
Equity Participation	-	17	-	3	-
TOTAL	100	100	100	100	100

Loan Sources for Real Estate (Percent Distributions)

Loan Source	All	Retail	Office	Industrial	Multifamily
Pension Fund	2	5	-	8	-
Insurance Company	7	-	7	12	8
S & L's	9	5	7	-	22
Commercial Banks	35	63	40	28	34
Syndication	-	-	-	-	-
Private Investors	6	-	7	12	-
Seller	35	22	21	40	36
Assumption	6	5	18	-	-
IRB	-	-	-	-	-
TOTAL	100	100	100	100	100

Source: National Association of Realtors, 1992

Leasing Negotiation Tips

ACCORDING TO Corporate Real Estate Executive, *some suggestions for successful real estate negotiation include:*

Techniques used during negotiations depend on whether you are in the "early," "middle," or "ending" phase of the process.

In the early phase of negotiations, it is important to develop basic trust, spell out realistic objectives, learn relevant facts, and establish procedural guidelines. Careful preparation will set the stage for this process. The one who is best prepared and who has anticipated objections, generally has the advantage right to the end.

There are certain tactics that help. For example, meeting at your place, if possible, or at a neutral location may eliminate distractions or interruptions, may allow you to plan seating or even lighting to your advantage. Because important decisions are best made at mid-day, scheduling the meeting over lunch would enable you to start with some small talk that may reveal more about the other person's needs and personality. Above all, schedule enough time.

The early phase is the time to ask a lot of questions, probe for information, concentrate on what the other party is saying, and how it is being said. Establish reasonable expectations. This is also the time to show how much both sides have in common, as well as learn about related problems. During this phase, listen carefully and attempt to get the other side to talk and make commitments. Save most of your talking for the middle phase when you will concentrate on problem solving.

During the middle phase of negotiations, explore alternatives to show you understand the other party's position. At this point, you can start to narrow down the issues and establish a positive tone and a sense of coming to an agreement. Keep asking the other party to explain the reasoning behind every demand and be ready to explain your own. Observe his eyes and body language carefully when he is making an important point. Try trading small compromises in return for larger ones.

Never concede anything to quickly; be sure each concession is fully appreciated and always made for something in return. Save your energy for what is important—which is usually the price.

Throughout negotiations, it is important to avoid common pitfalls. Don't ask for too little. If you don't ask, you don't get. Don't make excessive demands that destroy your credibility. Know exactly what you will settle for, or you will transfer control of negotiations to the other side. Be prepared to break a stalemate with new information or by changing the subject or by asking questions. Have a deadline to work against. If you are negotiating with more than one principal, leave something for the other principals to negotiate just prior to closing.

When it is time to wrap up the agreement, the parties should review together what is agreed upon and confirm that all the problems are resolved. This is not the time for you to bring up new issues. If you have everything you want, stop negotiating. As you get into the document stage, be prepared to illustrate to the party's lawyer how and why they have a good deal.

In working out the documents, ask the other party's lawyer to note any questions or give you any comments before changing the language. Once the other party is committed to its own language, it is more difficult to reverse direction.

Lastly, be available in person when the documents are prepared to answer any last minute questions or to resolve any remaining matters.

When the deal is done, analyze your approach. Remember that hard work, practice, and experience are essential for consistent success. And do not underestimate your ability to earn a reputation as an excellent negotiator.

Source: NACORE International, reprinted by permission.

Recommended Resources

Corporate Real Estate Executive
NACORE International
440 Columbia Dr., Suite 400
West Palm Beach, FL 33409
(407) 683-8111

Negotiating Commercial Real Estate Leases
by Martin Zankel
Dearborn Financial Publishing
Nontechnical guide to elements in leases and other related topics.

Tenant's Handbook to Office Leasing
by Stanley Wolfson
McGraw-Hill Professional Publishing Group.
Negotiating tips for leasing contracts enhanced by tables, charts, graphs, and forms.

Total Personal Income

Percent Change, First Quarter 1991-1992

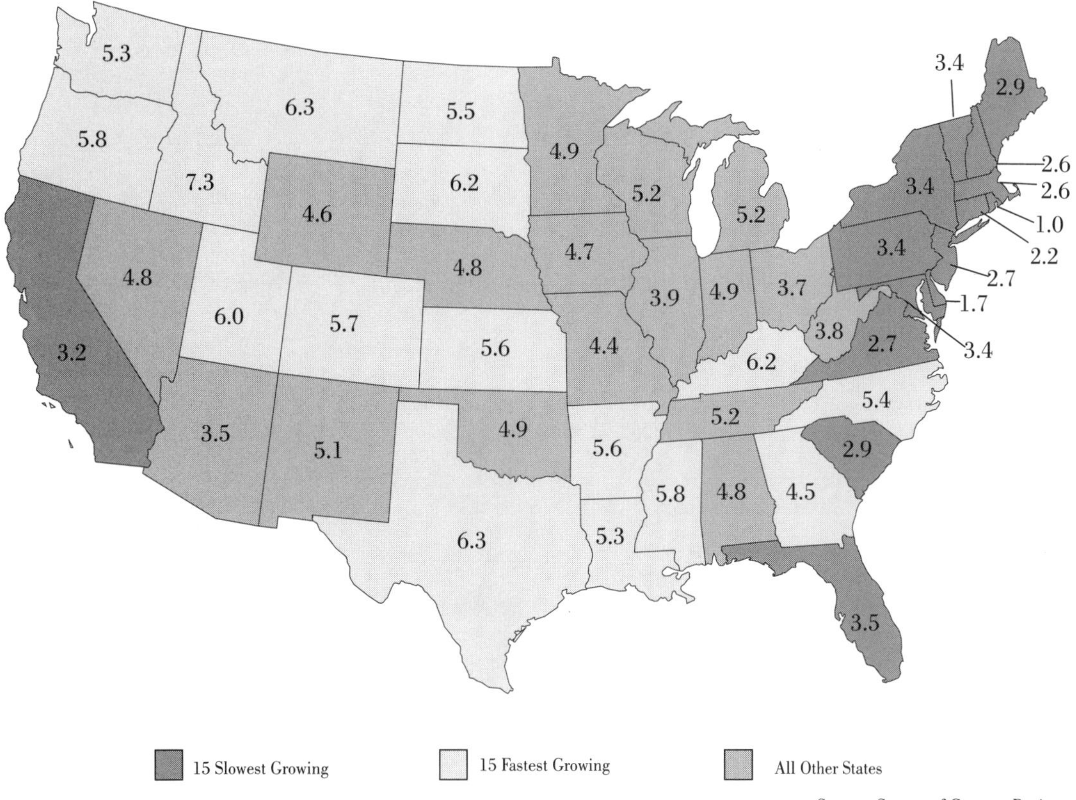

Source: Survey of Current Business

The Top Reference Sources

State and Metropolitan Area Data Book
U.S. Government Printing Office
(301) 763-4100

This publication is a supplement to *Statistical Abstract*, compiled by the Economics and Statistics Administration, Bureau of the Census. The data presented comes from over fifty federal and private agencies and represents some of the most up-to-date statistics available.

The statistics included cover a range of topics: commercial office space, manufacturers, personal income, housing, civilian labor force, farms, and retail trade.

Management Consulting Firms

Largest Management Consulting Firms in the U.S.

Firm	1991 Revenue ($ millions)	No. of Professionals	Telephone
Andersen Consulting	1,090	10,071	(312) 580-0069
Mercer Consulting Group	581	4,680	(212) 345-4500
Ernst & Young	551	3,384	(216) 861-5000
Deloitte & Touche	470	2,800	(212) 489-1600
Towers Perrin	441	2,300	(212) 309-3400
Booz-Allen & Hamilton	405	2,325	(212) 697-1900
Coopers & Lybrand	400	3,010	(212) 536-3306
McKinsey & Co.	400	1,000	(212) 446-7000
KPMG Peat Marwick	356	1,913	(212) 909-5000
Wyatt Co.	318	1,702	(617) 237-3900
Price Waterhouse	298	2,552	(212) 489-8900
Hewitt Associates	296	1,900	(312) 295-5000
American Management Systems	261	3,030	(703) 841-6000
CSC Consulting	226	1,875	(617) 661-0900
Alexander Consulting Group	175	800	(201) 460-6700
Arthur D. Little	151	1,000	(617) 864-5770
Gemini Consulting	146	442	(201) 285-9000
A. Foster Higgins	126	960	(212) 574-9000
Buck Consultants	122	810	(212) 330-1000
Milliman & Robertson	115	350	(206) 624-7940
Alexander Proudfoot	104	360	(407) 697-9600
A.T. Kearney	95	350	(312) 648-0111
RCG International	95	1,050	(212) 642-6000
Bain & Co.	88	300	(617) 572-2000
Hay Group	80	225	(215) 875-2300
Boston Consulting Group	75	260	(617) 973-1200
Kenneth Leventhal	64	317	(714) 644-7909
TSC	63	450	(312) 819-2250
The Segal Co.	58	476	(212) 251-5000
SRI International	53	310	(415) 326-6200
W.F. Corroon	52	500	(206)386-7988
Noble Lowndes	48	485	(201) 533-4500
Miller Mason & Dickenson	44	280	(415) 496-7400
George S. May International	39	300	(312) 825-8806
Grant Thornton	38	315	(212) 599-0100
BEI Holdings	38	420	(404) 315-6060
Kurt Salmon Associates	37	250	(404) 892-0321
Sandy Corp.	35	135	(313) 649-0800
Godwins International	33	301	(914) 747-2002
Kwasha Lipton	33	330	(201) 592-1300

Source: Consultant News

Almanac Fact

Receipts of management, consulting, and public relations firms reached an estimated $66.5 billion in 1992, an increase of almost 5 percent over 1991.

Source: U.S. Industrial Outlook

Business Brokers

THE TREND TOWARD INDEPENDENTLY OWNED and operated small- and medium-sized businesses is increasing dramatically. In fact, small companies created over 13 million jobs in the last decade.

Business brokers bring the buyers and sellers of these businesses together. When the companies that are for sale exceed $1 million in value, the negotiations are usually handled by mergers and acquisitions specialists. Smaller business deals–sales below $1 million–are handled by business brokers.

For sellers, business brokers:

- Advise on how to prepare a business for sale.
- Advise on pricing the business.
- Market the business to potential buyers.
- Keep the sale confidential to protect business standing.
- Pre-qualify prospects to find the right match.
- Negotiate the transaction.
- Manage the close.

For buyers, business brokers:

- Provide access to an inventory of businesses for sale.
- Answer questions about buying a business.
- Match buyer's interests, goals, and desires with the right business.
- Prepare buyers to act quickly when the right opportunity is uncovered
- Identify financing options.
- Manage the close.
- Support the transition.

Contact Options

International Business Brokers Association
P.O. Box 704
Concord, MA 01742
(508) 369-2490
The IBBA is a trade association that has a directory of its members arranged alphabetically and by location.

International Association of Merger and Acquisition Consultants
200 S. Frontage
Suite 103
Burr Ridge, IL 60521
(708) 323-0233

Business Brokers:

New England Business Advisors, Inc.
196 Danbury Rd., P.O. Box 786
Wilton, CT 06897
(203) 834-0070

Corporate Investment International
101 Wymore Rd., Suite 225
Altamonte Springs, FL 32714
(407) 682-9600

Georgia Business Associates, Inc.
2401 Lake Park Dr., Suite 350
Atlanta, GA 30080
(404) 319-6500

Hoganson Venture Group, Inc.
15 Salt Creek Ln., Suite 217
Hinsdale, IL 60521
(708) 887-4788

Finn & Associates, Inc.
545 North Woodlawn
Wichita, KS 67208
(316) 683-3466

UBI of Louisiana
4205 Canal St.
New Orleans, LA 70119
(504) 486-5375

Vernon A. Martin, Inc.
1 Corporate Pl., Ferncroft Village
Danvers, MA 01923
(508) 774-0160

Inexco Business Brokerage & Development
6200 28th St., SE
Grand Rapids, MI 49546
(616) 949-4374

Calhoun Companies
4930 W. 77th St., Suite 100
Minneapolis, MN 55453
(612) 831-3300

Opportunities in Business
3433 Broadway St., NE, Suite 555
Minneapolis, MN 55413
(612) 331-8392

Siegel Business Services, Inc.
One Bala Plaza, Suite 621
Bala-Cynwyd, PA 19004
(215) 668-9780

Business Brokers (cont'd)

Landmark Business Brokers
600 W. Park Row
Arlington, TX 76010
(817) 265-9188

Certified Business Brokers
10301 Northwest Freeway, Suite 200
Houston, TX 77092
(713) 680-1200

Country Business, Inc.
Box 1071
Manchester Center, VT 05255
(802) 362-4710

J.S. Keate & Co.
655 Eden Park Dr., Suite 160
Cincinnati, OH 45202
(513) 241-3700

Bluestem Resources Group, Inc.
1611 S. Utica Ave., Suite One
Tulsa, OK 74104
(918) 627-6500

The Hughes Group & Associates, Inc.
621 N. Robinson
Oklahoma City, OK 73102
(405) 232-5191

Probus/MBI Business Brokers & Consultants
307 Orchard City Dr., Suite 100
Campbell, CA 95008
(408) 370-9500

Geneva Business Services, Inc.
5 Park Plaza
Irvine, CA 92714
(714) 756-2200

Business Team, Inc.
3031 Tisch Way, Suite 400
San Jose, CA 95128
(408) 246-1102

DAP Business Services, Inc.
11314 South St.
Cerritos, CA 90701
(213) 402-2686

Colorado Business Consultants
899 Logan St., Suite 309
Denver, CO 80203
(303) 832-2020

Corporate Finance Associates
600 17th St.
Suite 710 N.
Denver, CO 80202
(303) 623-5600

VR Business Brokers
6 Boulderbrook Rd.
Wellesley, MA 02181
(617) 235-8025
VR has 82 franchises around the country, each independently owned and operated. It is the only national company of business brokers in the United States.

Architects/Designers

20 Largest Design Firms in the General Building Market by Domestic Billings, 1991

Hellmuth, Obata & Kassabaum, St. Louis, MO
CRSS, Houston, TX
Fluor Daniel, Irvine, CA
The Ellerbe Becket, Minneapolis, MN
Skidmore, Owings & Merrill, Chicago, IL
Burns and Roe Enterprises, Oradell, NJ
Law Cos. Group/Sir Alexander Gibb
Bechtel Group, San Francisco, CA
Professional Services Industries, Lombard, IL
United Engrs & Constrs, Philadelphia, PA
HKS, Dallas, TX
NBBJ, Seattle, WA
RTKL Associates, Baltimore, MD
The Austin Co., Cleveland, OH
Gensler & Assoc., San Francisco, CA
The Smith Group, Detroit, MI
Heery International, Atlanta, GA
Leo A. Daly, Omaha, NE
HDR, Omaha, NE
Holmes & Narver, Orange, CA

Source: Engineering News Record, April 6, 1992

Award Winners

Almost every year since 1907, the American Institute of Architects has awarded a gold medal to one architect for outstanding design work.

Year	Architect
1981	Josep Liuis Sert
1982	Romaldo Giurgola
1983	Nathaniel A. Owings
1985	William Wayne Caudill (posthumously)
1986	Arthur Erickson
1989	Joseph Esherick
1990	E. Fay Jones
1991	Charles W. Moore
1992	Benjamin Thompson
1993	Kevin Roche

Contact Option

The American Institute of Architects
1735 New York Avenue NW
Washington, DC 20006
(202) 626-7421

Choosing an Architect

THERE ARE MANY METHODS OF SELECTING an architect, ranging from formal design competitions to negotiated procurement to competitive bidding. You need to determine which approach fits your requirements and designate an individual or group to manage your selection process. To begin the selection process:

- Make a list of potential architects by asking colleagues for referrals.
- Contact your local chapter of the American Institute of Architects.
- Discover who designed projects similar to yours that appeal to you.

You may want to ask for qualifications and references at this stage. If the scope of the project is still indefinite, narrow the field based on what you learn.

You may want the architect to prepare a preliminary or full proposal explaining how he or she would approach your project. In that case, you may wish to send a written project description to the most promising firms; sending the same information to each architecture firm will make it easier to compare responses.

Decide how much cost information to request and when you want to request it; you may want to know only how the architect will charge for services, or you may need more–like preliminary estimates or even a detailed proposal. The choice is yours to make based on your needs and the nature of your project.

With your in-house team, or whichever staff you delegate to manage the project, review the information you have collected. Useful factors to consider include:

- The size of the firm and the amount of time it has been in practice
- Experience and past projects
- Their ability to work within budget/time schedules
- Cost of services
- Special expertise including experience in your project type, management ability, and knowledge of building codes/zoning regulations.

Beyond review of the proposal, you may also wish to:

- Visit at least one finished project of each architect under consideration.
- Call client references.

An interview can give you important information on how well you will be able to work with a potential architect. If the written material you have received doesn't tell you all you need to know to select a firm, here is one way to pursue the process further:

- Create a short list of perhaps three to five firms to interview.
- Decide who from your firm will be responsible for the interviewing and final selection.
- Allow at least an hour for the interview.
- Decide on location of interview. At your office the architect can gain a better understanding of you and your project; at the architect's office you can see how the architect and staff work.
- Make sure that the people you interview are the people who will actually be working on your project.

In making your final determination, look at:

- Design quality
- Technical competence
- Experience
- Cost
- Organization.

You will need to evaluate for yourself the weight to give each of the factors.

You will also be looking for an architect who:

- Is responsive to your needs
- Listens carefully
- Seems to understand your company
- Makes you feel comfortable.

You will be working with the architect for a long time and may work with him or her on future projects. It is important that you trust the architect's judgment and ability.

Recommended Resource

The American Institute of Architects
1735 New York Ave., NW
Washington, DC 20006
(202) 626-7461

In addition to its role as the national organization of architects, the AIA maintains local and regional offices that will work with a company to help it find an architect. To reach a local office, contact the national headquarters above.

Interior Design

EVERY JANUARY AND JULY, *Interior Design Magazine* ranks the top 100 design firms.

Contact Options

American Society of Interior Designers
608 Massachusetts Ave., NE
Washington, DC 20002
(202) 546-3480

ASID has local offices around the country and will make referrals for interior designers in any location.

Office Planners and Users Group
Box 11182
Philadelphia, PA 19136
(215) 335-9400

The Office Planners and Users Group (OPUG) is a loosely structured organization of office planners, facility managers, and administrative personnel whose responsibility encompasses planning and managing office facilities.

Interior Design's Top 25 Design Firms

Name of Firm	City	Telephone	Interior Design Fees ($ millions)	No. of Employees
Gensler & Associates/Architects	San Francisco, CA	(415) 433-3700	40.77	275
Interior Space International	Chicago, IL	(312) 454-9100	24.75	44
R.J. Pavlik	Ft. Lauderdale, FL	(305) 523-3300	18.37	42
RTKL Associates	Baltimore, MD	(410) 528-8600	18.15	63
Leo A. Daly	Omaha, NE	(402) 391-8111	17.26	27
Howard Needles Tammen & Bergendoff (HNTB)	Kansas City, MO	(816) 472-1201	17.25	19
Sverdrup Corporation	St. Louis, MO	(314) 436-7600	16.51	103
Hellmuth, Obata & Kassabaum	St. Louis, MO	(314) 421-2000	15.83	52
Swanke Hayden Connell Architects	New York, NY	(212) 977-9696	13.32	36
Smith, Hinchman & Grylls Associates	Detroit, MI	(313) 983-3600	13.03	18
KPF Interior Architects, PC	New York, NY	(212) 397-1100	11.00	47
ODA/Environetics International	New York, NY	(212) 221-7440	10.63	58
Perkins & Will	Chicago, IL	(312) 977-1100	10.16	39
Space Design International	Cincinnati, OH	(513) 241-3000	10.15	66
NBBJ Interiors	Seattle, WA	(206) 223-5555	10.12	21
Emery Roth & Sons Interior Design	New York, NY	(212) 753-1733	9.80	20
Ellerbe Becket	Minneapolis, MN	(612) 376-2000	9.40	26
HLW-Haines Lundberg Waehler	New York, NY	(212) 353-4600	9.10	42
STUDIOS Architecture	Washington, DC	(202) 736-5900	9.08	55
Retail Planning Associates (RPA)	Columbus, OH	(614) 461-1820	9.06	24
Walker Group/CNI	New York, NY	(212) 206-0444	8.57	58
SCR Design Organization	New York, NY	(212) 421-3500	8.30	38
Griswold, Heckel & Kelly Associates	Chicago, IL	(312) 263-6605	7.91	54
Interior Architects (IA)	San Francisco, CA	(415) 434-3305	7.89	48
The Phillips Janson Group Architects, P.C.	New York, NY	(212) 768-0800	7.88	57

The Top Reference Sources

Directory of Industrial Designers
Industrial Design Society of America, $75
(703) 759-0700

This annual directory lists 2,200 industrial designers by their specialty. It includes consumer products, appliances, heavy equipment, computers, toys, furniture, and medical instrument designers, as well as listings by geographical location and by employer.

Corporate Art

ESTABLISHING A CORPORATE ART COLLECTION is no longer the privilege of Fortune 500 companies alone. In recent years, more and more small- and mid-sized firms have begun to collect art, not only to create ambiance in their surrounding office space but because of its potential investment value.

As a result, an entire industry has developed to serve the needs of corporate art collections. The following directories provide information on what other companies are collecting as well as complete listings of the agents, dealers, and consultants who help companies choose their collections.

Recommended Resources

ARTnews International Directory of Corporate Art Collections
Published by ARTnews & International Art Alliance
P.O. Box 1608
Largo, FL 34649
(813) 581-7328

This annual directory provides an alphabetical listing by company of major national and international corporate art collections. Each listing includes a brief description of the corporation as well as information pertinent to the collection, including size, year begun, location, source of artwork, loan policy, and selection process.

Art Marketing Sourcebook
ArtNetwork
13284 Rices Crossing Rd.
P.O. Box 369
Renaissance, CA 95962
(800) 383-0677

This annual book is a full-color catalogue of the work of American artists, complete with personal profiles, names and addresses of the artists and their agents. It is used as a resource for galleries, publishers, private and corporate collectors, and consultants.

Directory of Fine Art Representatives and Corporations Collecting Art
Edited by Constance Franklin
Directors Guild Publishers
13284 Rices Crossing Rd.
P.O. Box 369
Renaissance, CA 95962
(800) 383-0677

This directory includes a geographical listing of art representatives, including area of specialization, target markets, years in business, and review standards, as well as a separate geographical listing and description of corporate collections.

Annual Reports

Sid Cato's Tips for Producing the Best Annual Report

- Make the cover demand readership, as does the cover of a weekly magazine. It should contain an action-inviting element such as a strong quote or theme statement.
- Use an action-oriented contents listing to create a positive feel for the company.
- Make sure there is a good company description as well as a financial highlights listing. This should contain a percentage-change column and the current average of at least 12 non-operational items.
- Include a forthright shareholder letter of approximately three pages. Companies do have bad years, and they should be confronted directly. The shareholder letter should begin with a photograph of the company's top executive.
- Include financial data and graphs captioned so their meaning is clear.
- List biographical data on officers and directors to inform stockholders about the people running the company.
- Provide forward-looking material so the reader knows where the company is headed.
- Create a feeling of honesty by describing the involvement of the company's chief executive officer.

Recommended Resource

Sid Cato's Newsletter on Annual Reports
P.O.Box 738
Waukesha, WI 53187
(414) 549-3200
Fax: (414) 549-4666

Annual Reports (cont'd)

Every year, *Institutional Investor* magazine picks what it considers to be the best annual reports in several categories including: most consistent effort, most improved report, best graphics, and best financial presentation. Here are some of the magazine's selections for 1992.

Best Annual Reports

AMR Corp.
Burlington Northern
Coca-Cola Co.
Consolidated Papers
General Electric Co.
Hannaford Brothers Co.
Knight-Ridder
Lubrizol Corp.
PepsiCo

Best Financial Presentation

Atlantic Richfield Co.
Capital Cities/ABC
CSX
Dresser Industries
General Mills
Minnesota Mining & Manufacturing Co.
National Medical Enterprises
Pall Corp./Philip Morris Co.
Phillips Petroleum Co.
Quaker Oats Co.
Vulcan Materials Co.

Best Graphics

Bristol-Myers Squibb Co.
General Electric Co.
International Paper Co.
Philip Morris Co.
United Healthcare Corp.

Most Consistent Effort

Albertson's
Atlantic Richfield Co.
Capital Cities/ABC
Deere & Co.
Dresser Industries
Fluor Corp.
Gillette Corp.
Golden West Financial Corp.
Loral Corp.
Masco Corp.
Merck & Co.
Monsanto Co.
Morton International
National Medical Enterprises
Philip Morris Co.
Quaker Oats Co.

Most Improved

Bank of Boston Corp.
Caterpillar
CBS
W.W. Grainger
Hercules
IBM Corp.
Mobil Corp.
Occidental Petroleum Corp.
Phillips Petroleum Corp.
Weyerhaeuser Co.

Source: Institutional Investor, September, 1992

Annual Report Designers & Writers

Contact Options

Graphic design firms specializing in annual reports:

The Conceptual Communications Group
10 E. 22nd St.
New York, NY 10010
(212) 302-7388

Addison Corporate Annual Reports
112 E. 31st St.
New York, NY 10016
(212) 889-2451

WYD Inc.
61 Wilton Rd.
Westport, CT 06880
(203) 227-2627

Little & Co.
1010 S. 7 St., Suite 550
Minneapolis, MN 55415
(612) 375-0077

Gunn Associates
275 Newbury St.
Boston, MA 02116
(617) 267-0618

Boller Coates Spadaro
445 W. Erie St.
Chicago, IL 60601
(312) 787-2783

Recommended Resource

Graphic Arts Monthly Printing Industry Sourcebook
Cahner's Publishing
(212) 645-0067

Finance

The Stock Market

AT THE EXPLOSIVE PEAK OF THE EIGHTIES, bull market, U.S. stock-trading volumes reached a record high of two-and-a-quarter trillion (1987). While for a time the stock outlook for the nineties appeared bleak, the early decade has taken investors by surprise. The markets have done more than rebound from that temporary and terrifying 508-point correction of October 19, 1987, the biggest drop ever. With indexes soaring, the 1991 and 1992 markets have set new records, demonstrating the astonishing strength and sustained power of America's financial system and corporations.

Market Value of Stocks on U.S. Exchanges

Year	Value of Stocks ($ thousands)
1985	1,119,419,614
1986	1,705,123,953
1987	2,284,165,520
1988	1,587,011,727
1989	1,844,768,135
1990	1,611,667,363

Source: U.S. Securities and Exchange Commission Annual Report, 1991

Volume of Stock Sales on U.S. Exchanges

Year	Stocks (shares in thousands)
1985	37,046,010
1986	48,337,694
1987	63,770,625
1988	52,533,283
1989	54,238,571
1990	53,337,731

Volume of Stock Sales by Exchange: 1990

Exchange	Stocks (shares in thousands)
AMEX	3,124,619
BSE	918,050
CSE	287,263
MIDW	2,511,409
NYSE	43,828,680
PSE	1,681,557
PHLX	978,576
SSE	7,576
CBOE	0

Source: NYSE Fact Book, 1991

Stock Sales on all U.S. Exchanges (total dollar volume in $ billions)

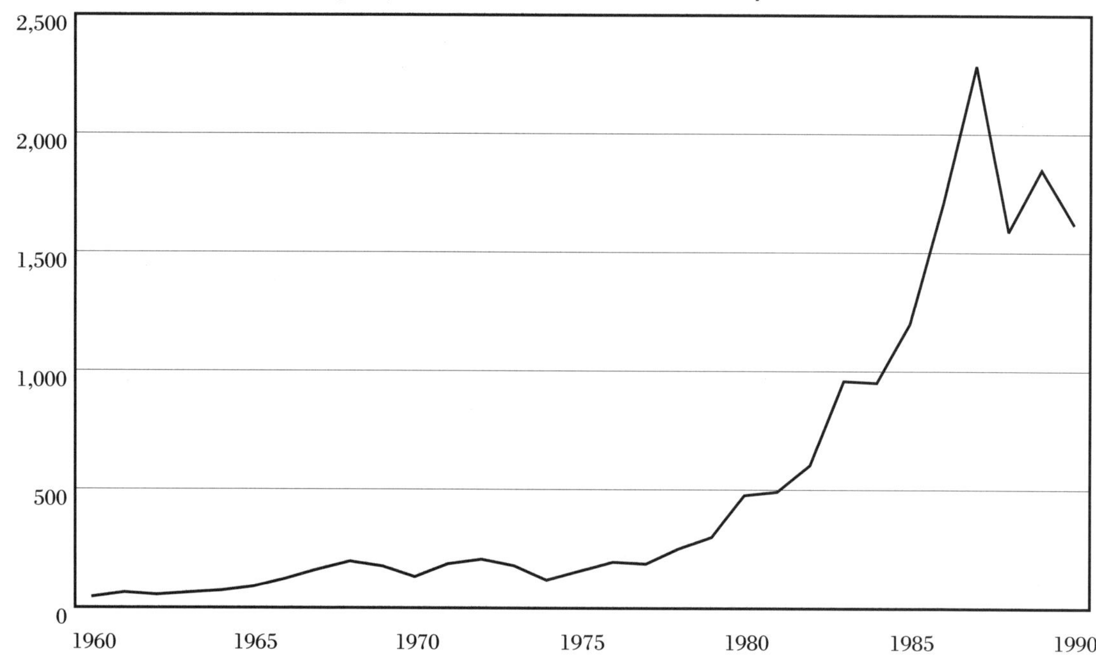

Source: U.S. Securities and Exchange Commission Annual Report, 1991

The Stock Market (cont'd)

Share Volume (%) by Exchange, 1945 to 1990

Year	NYSE	AMEX	MSE	PSE	PHLX	BSE	CSE	Others
1945	65.87	21.31	1.77	2.98	1.06	0.66	0.05	6.30
1950	73.32	13.54	2.16	3.11	0.97	0.65	0.09	3.16
1955	68.85	19.19	2.09	3.08	0.85	0.48	0.05	5.41
1960	68.47	22.27	2.20	3.11	0.88	0.38	0.04	2.65
1965	69.90	22.53	2.63	2.33	0.81	0.26	0.05	1.49
1970	71.28	19.03	3.16	3.68	1.63	0.51	0.02	0.69
1975	80.99	8.97	3.97	3.26	1.54	0.85	0.13	0.29
1980	79.94	10.78	3.84	2.80	1.54	0.57	0.32	0.21
1985	81.52	5.78	6.12	3.66	1.47	1.27	0.15	0.03
1986	81.12	6.28	5.73	3.68	1.53	1.33	0.30	0.02
1987	83.09	5.57	5.19	3.23	1.30	1.28	0.30	0.04
1988	83.74	4.95	5.26	3.03	1.29	1.32	0.39	0.02
1989	81.33	6.02	5.44	3.34	1.80	1.64	0.41	0.02
1990	81.86	6.23	4.68	3.16	1.82	1.71	0.53	0.01

Source: U.S. Securities and Exchange Commission Annual Report, 1991

New York Stock Exchange (NYSE)

OVER 80% OF AMERICAN SECURITIES are traded on the NYSE, the United States' oldest and largest exchange. In 1991, over 10,000 institutions managing $3.5 trillion in securities had access to and used the NYSE market.

New York Stock Exchange, Inc. (NYSE)
11 Wall St.
New York, NY 10005
(212) 656-3000
Founded: 1792
Members/Seats: 1,417 members; 1,366 seats
Companies/Issues listed: 1,885 companies; 2,426 issues

NYSE Record Reported Trades

Record	Date	No. Trades
Week Ending	10/23/87	840,246
Month	12/91	2,600,156
Year	1991	27,106,243

NYSE Record Volume

Record	Date	Volume (shares)
First Hour	6/17/88	158,630,000
Day	10/20/87	608,148,710
Year	1987	47,801,308,660

NYSE Record Value of Trading

Record	Date	Value of Trading ($ millions)
Day	10/19/87	20,993.0
Year	1987	1,873,597.2

Source: New York Stock Exchange Fact Book, 1991

Almanac Fact

The highest price paid for a membership seat on the NYSE is $1,150,000. This plateau was reached on September 21, 1987.

Source: New York Stock Exchange Fact Book, 1991

NYSE (cont'd)

NYSE Average Share Prices

End of Year	Average price ($)
1924	62.45
1950	39.86
1960	47.53
1970	39.61
1975	30.48
1976	35.03
1977	30.53
1978	29.84
1979	31.99
1980	36.87
1981	29.87
1982	33.03
1983	35.11
1984	32.31
1985	37.20
1986	36.89
1987	30.87
1988	32.26
1989	36.51
1990	31.08
1991	37.27

Source: New York Stock Exchange Fact Book, 1991

NYSE Seat Sales

Year	High ($)	Low ($)
1955	90,000	80,000
1960	162,000	135,000
1965	250,000	190,000
1970	320,000	130000
1971	300,000	145,000
1972	250,000	150,000
1973	190,000	72,000
1974	105,000	65,000
1975	138,000	55,000
1976	104,000	40,000
1977	95,000	35,000
1978	105,000	46,000
1979	210,000	82,000
1980	275,000	175,000
1981	285,000	220,000
1982	340,000	190,000
1983	425,000	310,000
1984	400,000	290,000
1985	480,000	310,000
1986	600,000	455,000
1987	1,150,000	605,000
1988	820,000	580,000
1989	675,000	420,000
1990	430,000	250,000
1991	440,000	345,000

Source: New York Stock Exchange Fact Book, 1991

NYSE Reported Share Volume, 1960 to 1991

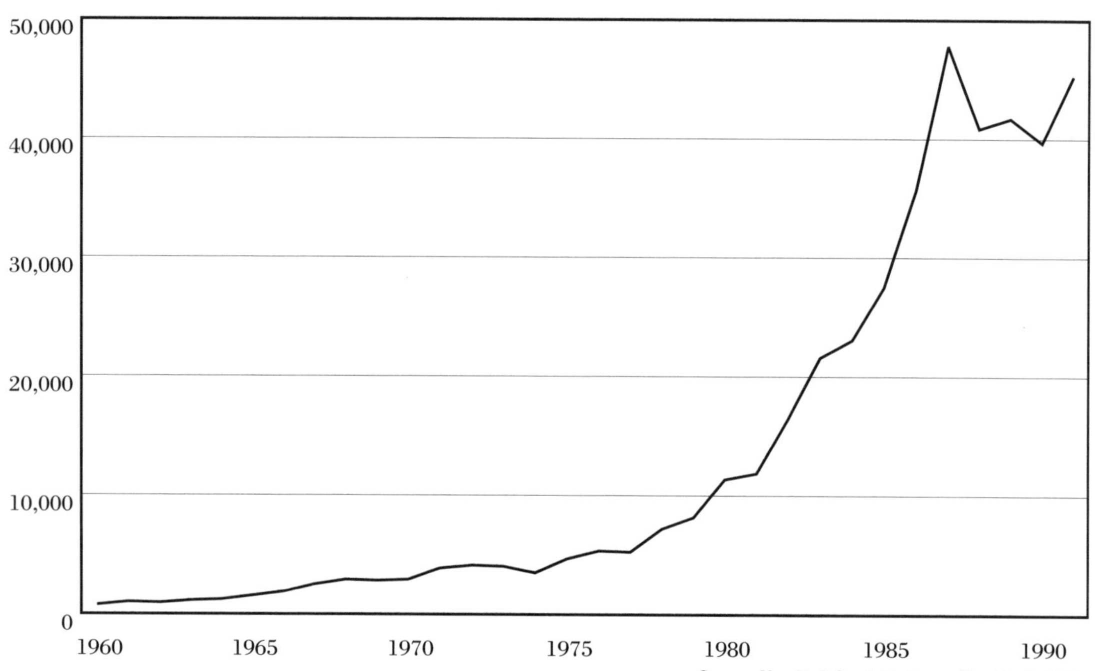

Source: New York Stock Exchange Fact Book, 1991

NYSE Stocks Rated

Ten Most Active NYSE Stocks, 1992

Stock	Share Volume
Glaxo	569,390,000
RJR Nabisco	543,230,000
General Motors	537,620,000
IBM	512,980,000
Philip Morris	472,410,000
Telefonos de Mexico	464,880,000
Citicorp	453,480,000
AT&T	428,890,000
Chrysler	427,790,000
Merck	406,010,000

Source: The New York Times

Ten Most Active NYSE Stocks, 1991

Stock	Share Volume
RJR Nabisco Holdings	531,882,100
Philip Morris	428,465,300
PepsiCo. Inc.	384,978,800
AT&T	383,113,400
American Express	369,776,600
IBM	357,535,100
Citicorp	316,200,200
General Electric	296,173,800
General Motors	296,173,800
Glaxo	270,103,800

Source: The Wall Street Journal

Ten Best Performers on the NYSE, 1992

Common Stock	Closing Price ($)	% Change from 1991
BancFlorida Financial	12.00	357.1
Equimark	8.13	261.1
Tandycrafts	28.88	260.9
Northeast Federal	6.63	231.3
Western Digital	8.63	228.6
Salant	9.50	204.0
Coachman Industries	17.25	200.0
Carriage Insustries	13.38	189.2
EMC	23.75	185.0
Diana	5.63	181.3

Source: New York Stock Exchange Fact Book, 1991

Ten Worst Performers on the NYSE, 1992

Common Stock	Closing Price ($)	% Change from 1991
El Paso Refinery	1.50	-83.1
GitanoGroup	3.63	-80.3
Robertson-Ceco	0.69	-78.0
Employee Benefits	12.00	-77.3
JWP	3.88	-75.0
Rymer Foods	1.38	-69.4
Crystal Brands	4.38	-68.8
Fabri-Centers	14.38	-66.7
PS Group	9.50	-68.6
Value Merchant	9.50	-68.6

Source: The Wall Street Journal

Transactions (%) in NYSE-Listed Stock on Participating Markets

Year	NYSE	AMEX	PSE	MSE	PHLX	BSE	CSE	NASD	INST	TOTAL
1981	82.42	0.00	6.41	4.54	3.85	0.91	0.87	0.96	0.02	100.00
1982	78.61	0.00	8.27	5.89	3.92	1.00	0.84	1.44	0.04	100.00
1983	77.68	0.00	8.58	6.81	3.88	1.25	0.49	1.28	0.04	100.00
1984	75.40	0.00	8.93	7.95	4.10	1.78	0.34	1.41	0.09	100.00
1985	74.24	0.00	9.51	8.16	3.82	2.17	0.32	1.70	0.10	100.00
1986	72.68	0.00	10.57	8.52	3.65	2.25	0.29	2.00	0.03	100.00
1987	73.60	0.00	9.31	8.94	3.50	2.32	0.26	2.05	0.02	100.00
1988	72.99	0.00	8.44	9.74	3.22	2.33	0.35	2.91	0.03	100.00
1989	69.23	0.00	8.35	10.43	3.39	3.16	0.44	4.98	0.03	100.00
1990	66.17	0.00	8.14	9.71	3.02	3.77	0.63	8.53	0.03	100.00
1991	67.33	0.00	8.12	8.03	2.84	3.37	0.74	9.53	0.03	100.00

Source: New York Stock Exchange Fact Book, 1991

NYSE Stocks Rated (cont'd)

50 Leading Stocks by Market Value

Company	Symbol	Listed Shares (millions)	Market Value 2/93 ($ millions)
Exxon	XON	1,813	110,582
General Electric	GE	927	78,754
Wal-Mart Stores	WMT	1,150	73,155
Philip Morris	MO	935	72,020
Coca-Cola	KO	1,692	70,848
American Telephone & Telegraph	T	1,326	67,604
Merck	MRK	1,367	59,459
Procter & Gamble	PG	730	39,247
Johnson & Johnson	JNJ	767	38,560
Bristol-Myers Squibb	BMY	532	35,863
PepsiCo	PEP	883	35,689
GTE	GTE	945	32,836
du Pont de Nemours	DD	674	31,781
International Business Machines	IBM	572	28,804
Mobil	MOB	440	27,755
American International Group	AIG	225	26,090
Abbott Laboratories	ABT	849	25,793
BellSouth	BLS	489	24,862
Chevron	CHV	356	24,759
Amoco	AN	496	24,189
Pfizer	PFE	332	24,100
American Home Products	AHP	355	23,897
Minnesota Mining & Manufacturing	MMM	236	23,748
Walt Disney	DIS	552	23,742
General Motors	GM	706	22,781
Bell Atlantic	BEL	436	22,359
Home Depot	HD	331	22,288
Southwestern Bell	SBC	301	22,266
Federal National Mortgage	FNM	282	21,551
Ameritech	AIT	294	20,934
Kellogg	K	310	20,695
McDonald's	MCD	415	20,239
Anheuser-Busch	BUD	340	19,822
Waste Management	WMX	496	19,724
Pacific Telesis	PAC	433	19,153
Ford Motor	F	441	18,654
Dow Chemical	DOW	327	18,728
Atlantic Richfield	ARC	161	18,445
NYNEX	NYN	213	17,835
Lilly (Eli)	LLY	293	17,788
Hewlett-Packard	HWP	252	17,587
Sears, Roebuck	S	387	17,566
Schlumberger	SLB	306	17,436
Royal Dutch Petroleum	RD	215	17,414
Schering-Plough	SGP	288	17,028
Texaco	TX	274	16,388
US West	USW	420	16,112
BankAmerica	BAC	346	16,070
Gillette	GS	277	15,774
Eastman Kodak	EK	374	15,113

Source: New York Stock Exchange

American Stock Exchange (Amex)

The American Stock Exchange, Inc. (Amex)
86 Trinity Pl.
New York, NY 10006
(212) 306-1000

Members/Seats: 661 regular members; 203 options principal members

Companies/Issues listed: 860 companies; 1,055 issues

The Amex list includes many younger, smaller firms and mid-size growth companies, oil, and high technology issues.

Typical Amex Company ($ millions)

	Average	Median
Total Assets	358.9	67.8
Shareholders' Equity	85.0	24.4
Sales	260.6	57.3
Market Value	184.4	31.3
Employees	1,774.0	440.0
Long-Term Debt	86.3	10.5
Shares Outstanding	14.4	5.4
Pre-Tax Income	5.2	1.5

Amex Volume Since 1960

Year	Volume ($)
1960	4,235,685,712
1965	8,874,874,754
1970	14,266,040,599
1975	5,678,028,284
1980	35,788,327,624
1981	24,520,205,419
1982	21,056,649,904
1983	31,237,023,941
1984	21,376,098,408
1985	27,838,566,791

Amex Volume Since 1960

Year	Volume ($)
1986	45,356,898,691
1987	50,469,993,686
1988	30,921,806,605
1989	44,401,174,619
1990	37,714,827,819
1991	40,919,297,189

Amex Record Volume

Record	Date	Volume
First Hour	10/20/87	143,432,760
Week	10/19/87	158,680,590
Year	1987	3,505,954,875

Prices Paid for Amex Seats Since 1960

Year	High ($)	Low ($)
1960	60,000	51,000
1965	80,000	55,000
1970	185,000	70,000
1975	72,000	34,000
1980	252,000	95,000
1981	275,000	200,000
1982	285,000	180,000
1983	325,000	261,000
1984	255,000	160,000
1985	160,000	115,000
1986	285,000	145,000
1987	420,000	265,000
1988	280,000	180,000
1989	215,000	155,000
1990	170,000	83,500
1991	120,000	80,000

Source: American Stock Exchange Fact Book, 1991

The Top Reference Sources

The Business One Irwin Business and Investment Almanac
Business One Irwin
(800)634-3966

Edited by Sumner N. Levine, this annual publication is a standard reference for the business and investment community. It includes major and group stock market averages, reviews of the major futures markets, charts for futures-traded commodities, the performance of mutual funds, and performance of leading economies.

The book also contains data on future employment opportunities, U.S. demographics, international stock price indexes, and consumer price indexes.

Amex Stocks Ranked

Ten Most Active Amex Stocks, 1992

Stock	Share Volume
Chambers Devel. "A"	105,820,000
Amdahl	102,890,000
U.S. Bioscience	81,660,000
Echo Bay Mines Ltd.	72,330,000
Sulcus Computer	71,970,000
Exploration Co. of La.	68,770,000
Hillhaven	66,600,000
Ivax	66,280,000
Fruit of the Loom	62,490,000
Interdigital Communications	51,040,000

Source: The New York Times

Ten Most Active Amex Stocks, 1991

Stock	Share Volume
Fruit of the Loom	67,600,000
Echo Bay Mines Ltd.	60,600,000
Amdahl Corporation	60,300,000
Wang Laboratories	51,700,000
The Hillhaven Corporation	51,300,000
Metro Mobile CTS, Inc.	42,600,000
Energy Service Co., Inc.	42,300,000
Hasbro, Inc.	38,000,000
Forest Laboratories, Inc.	35,600,000
B.A.T. Industries, p.l.c.	34,900,000

Source: Amex Fact Book, 1991

Best Performers on the Amex, 1992

Common Stock	Closing Price ($)	% Change from '91
Decorator Industries	14.88	561.1
Cavalier Homes	14.25	448.1
Andrea Electronics	22.38	411.4
Shelter Components	14.88	379.8

Source: The Wall Street Journal

Worst Performers on the Amex, 1992

Common Stock	Closing Price ($)	% Change from '91
Wang Laboratories "B"	0.38	-87.0
Nortankers	0.50	-81.8
First National Corp. (CA)	1.06	-81.1
Chambers Develop. "A"	6.88	-79.7

Source: The Wall Street Journal

Stocks Outstanding on the Amex, 1980 to 1991 in billions

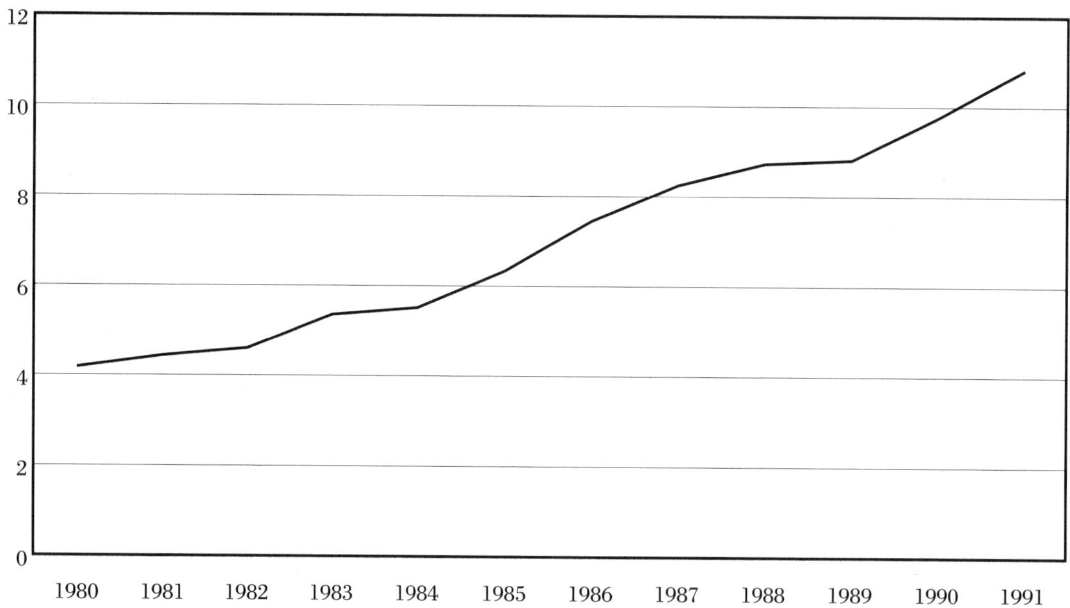

Source: Amex Fact Book, 1991

Amex Stocks Ranked (cont'd)

Amex Seat Sales, 1970 to 1991

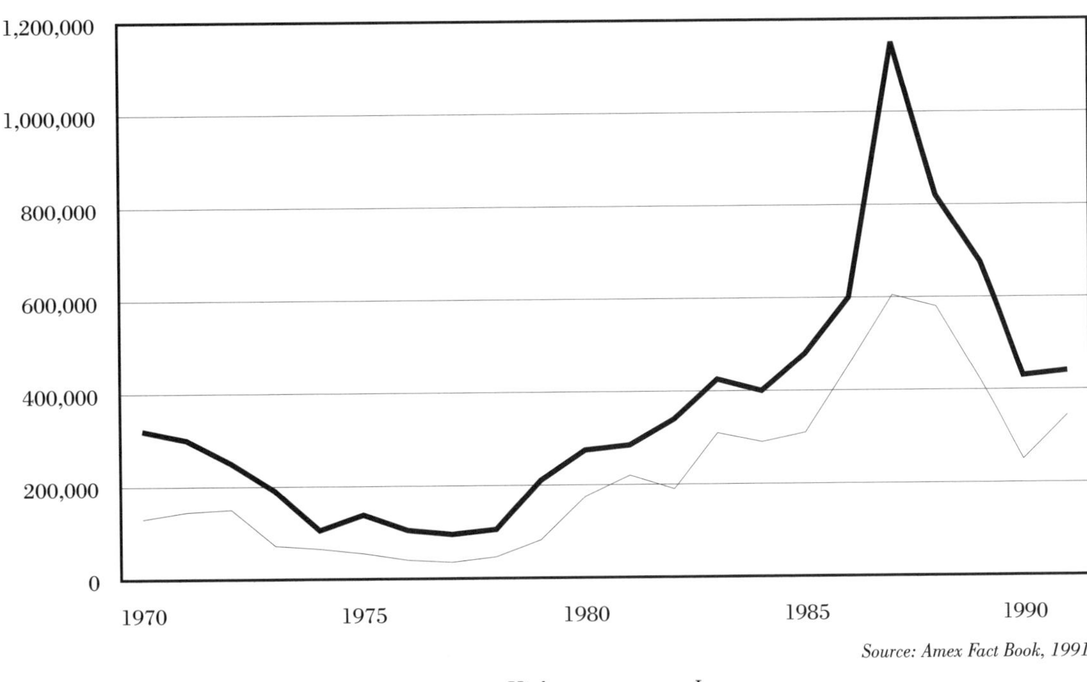

Source: Amex Fact Book, 1991

The Top Reference Sources

The Corporate Finance Sourcebook
National Register Publishing Company, $425
(708) 256-6067

This annual directory catalogs 19 sources of capital funding and management, including venture capital firms, private lenders, banks, trusts, commercial financing and factoring firms, pension managers, and accounting firms. Listings include the names and numbers of investment officers, industry preference, minimum to maximum investment limits, and lending criteria.

Over 3,600 firms and 20,000 key executives are included in this highly recommended publication.

The OTC Market: NASDAQ

SHARES OF SMALL AND RELATIVELY NEW companies are traded over-the-counter, in the OTC market. This market has no location: transactions are executed over telephones, private wires, and computers by a vast network of brokers and dealers. Sales and trading information on most (but not all) OTC transactions is received and stored by The National Association of Securities Dealers (NASD). The NASD transmits price and volume data on its computerized quote system: The National Association of Securities Dealers Automated Quotations System (NASDAQ).

The National Assoc. of Securities Dealers (NASD)
1735 K St., NW
Washington, DC 20006
(202) 728-8000
Members: 6,000

NASD is a not-for-profit association of brokers and dealers founded in 1939. A self-regulating organization, the NASD establishes standards of conduct for members trading through NASDAQ and other over-the-counter securities markets. Members of NASD may sell securities to each other at wholesale prices while selling retail to non-members.

NASDAQ is the third-largest market in the world, after the New York and Tokyo exchanges, and handles over 45% of all shares traded in the major U.S. markets. There are 5,5401 member firms, 29,137 branch offices, and 406,106 registered representatives on the NASDAQ. More than 4,100 companies have their stocks traded in the NASDAQ; statistics on over 5,300 domestic and foreign securities are transmitted through NASDAQ.

In 1991, the NASDAQ was the fastest-growing equity market in the United States. Listed companies include Apple Computer, Intel, Microsoft, LVMH Moët Hennessey, Louis Vuitton, Adolph Coors, and MCI Communications.

NASDAQ Volume Since 1981 ($ billions)

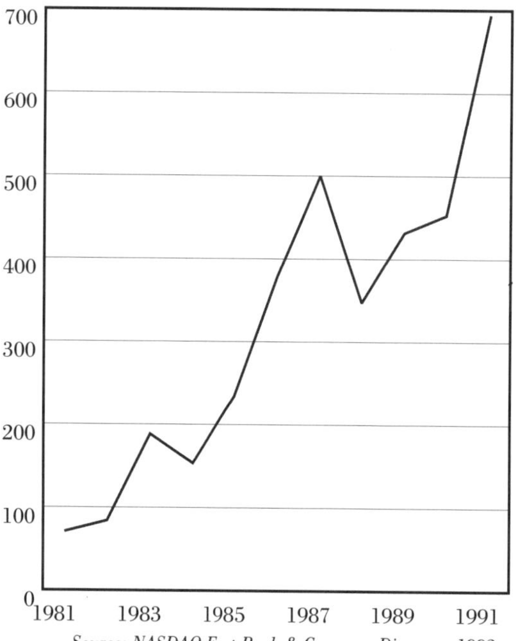

Source: NASDAQ Fact Book & Company Directory, 1992

NASDAQ Single Day Trading Records

Date	Share Volume
October 21, 1987	288,059,700
October 20, 1987	284,117,100
March 6, 1991	283,079,300
April 17, 1991	267,555,100
January 23, 1987	261,850,700

Profile of Typical NASDAQ Company

Total Assets ($ mil.)	546.7
Shareholders' Equity ($ mil.)	100.9
Total Revenues ($ mil.)	232.1
P/E ratio	43.0

Profile of Typical NASDAQ Issue

Share Price ($)	12.73
Number of Market Makers	10.5
Total Shares Outstanding ($ mil.)	9.9
Public Float (shares, $ mil.))	6.8
Market Value of Shares Outstanding ($ mil.)	125.6

Source: NASDAQ Fact Book, 1992

The OTC Market: NASDAQ (cont'd)

Ten Most Active NASDAQ Stocks, 1992

Stock	Share Volume
Intel	553,720,000
Tele-Commun. "A"	443,850,000
Novell	434,320,000
Microsoft	402,460,000
Seagate Technology	390,220,000
Sun Microsystems	384,360,000
Apple Computer	367,890,000
Oracle Systems	343,860,000
Telefonos de Mexico	339,400,000
Amgen	329,460,000

Source: The New York Times

Ten Most Active NASDAQ Stocks, 1991

Stock	Share Volume
Intel Corporation	554,312,000
Apple Computer	516,471,000
Sun Microsystems	398,252,000
MCI Communications Corp	365,636,000
Oracle Systems Corp.	341,722,000
Seagate Technology Inc.	312,761,000
Tele-Communications, Inc.	297,626,000
Microsoft Corporation	284,984,000
Amgen Inc.	248,200,000
U.S. Healthcare, Inc.	247,513,000

Source: NASDAQ Fact Book & Company Directory, 1992

Ten Best Performing NASDAQ Stocks, 1992

Common Stock	Closing Price ($)	% Change from 1991
DSC Communications	22.00	467.7
CFS Financial	19.50	457.1
Andover Bancorp	11.50	441.2
Newbridge Networks	41.25	441.0
Multi Bank Financial	24.50	429.7
Informix	36.25	427.3
KCS Energy	42.50	390.4
Key Tronic	10.38	388.2
Nam Ti Electronics	16.75	387.2
Autotate "A"	21.50	377.8

Source: The Wall Street Journal

Ten Worst Performing NASDAQ Stocks, 1992

Common Stock	Closing Price ($)	% Change from 1991
First Seismic	0.06	-98.2
Security Investment Group	0.06	-97.2
Millfred Trading	0.38	-94.1
R-Tek	0.50	-93.5
Cencor	0.50	-93.1
Sheffield Industries	1.38	-89.6
Everex Systems	.38	-88.9
Bioplasty	0.75	-87.0
Aegis Group PLC ADR	0.75	-87.0
Sequoia Systems	2.13	-86.0

Source: The Wall Street Journal

The Top Reference Sources

The NASDAQ Fact Book & Company Directory
National Association of Securities Dealers, $20
(202) 728-6900

Published annually, this book provides extensive data on the performance of NASDAQ securities and statistics on the NASDAQ market as a whole, as well as information to assist in contacting each company directly.

It is used as a resource by shareholders, corporations, investment analysts, brokerage firms, financial media, government, and educational institutions.

U.S Stock Exchanges

Pacific Stock Exchange (PSE)

618 S. Spring St.
Los Angeles, CA 90014

- Members listed: 551
- Hours: The PSE is the last full auction U.S. market to close, at 1:50PM Pacific Time, 50 minutes past the New York close.
- Volume: 2.0 billion shares (1989). In 1991, the PSE's average daily volume rose at the highest rate among all use exchanges: 23%
- Options: 13.9 million contracts (1989)

Midwest Stock Exchange (MSE)

440 LaSalle St.
Chicago, IL 60603
(312) 663-2222

- Founded: 1882 as the Chicago Stock Exchange. In 1949 the St. Louis, Cleveland, and Minneapolis-St. Paul exchanges merged with the Chicago exchange to form the Midwest Stock Exchange. The New Orleans Stock Exchange joined in 1959.
- Members/seats: 446 (including specialists, floor brokers and off-floor members)
- Companies/issues listed: 2,619

In 1991, block trades represented almost 43% of the total share volume. The average price per share was $28.18.

Midwest Stock Exchange All-Time Records

- Largest Trade to Date:
  Unocal Corporation, 7,000,000 shares
  March 27, 1985 (value: $336,000,000)
- Largest Trading Day:
  25,715,100 shares: November 30, 1987
- Largest Monthly Volume:
  352,154,000 shares: October 1987
- Largest Yearly Volume:
  3,320,219,000 shares: 1987

Boston Stock Exchange (BSE)

One Boston Pl.
Boston, MA 02109
(617) 723-9500

- Founded: 1834, the third oldest stock exchange in the United States
- Members/seats: 203 seats held by 144 member firms
- Companies/issues listed: 127 exclusive listings; over 2,100 issues total
- Volume: 4,000,00 shares traded daily

Trading Volumes on the Boston Stock Exchange

Year	Volume (in millions)
1987	777.0
1988	670.3
1989	781.2
1990	840.2
1991	899.1

Source: The Boston Stock Exchange Annual Report, 1991

Contact Options

The Cincinnati Stock Exchange, Inc. (CSE)
205 Dixie Terminal Building
Cincinnati, OH 45202
(513) 621-1410

Philadelphia Stock Exchange (PHLX)
1900 Market St.
Philadelphia, PA 19103
(215) 496-5000

Almanac Fact

If you stashed $100 in your mattress each month, it would take you 834 years to collect a million dollars.

Source: Fortune Guide to Investing in the 1990's

U.S. Exchange Markets

Foreign Stocks Listed on U.S. Exchanges

Exchange	No. Common Stocks	Value ($ millions)	No. Preferred Stocks	Value ($ millions)
New York	97	126,275	13	1,380
American	74	23,737	3	767
Boston	2	56	0	0
Pacific	2	33	0	0
TOTAL	175	150,101	16	2,147

The Various Markets of the U.S. Exchanges

	NYSE	AMEX	MSE	PSE	PHLX	BSE	CBOE	CBOT	CME
Equities	•	•	•	•	•	•			
Listed Options		•		•	•		•		
OTC Options	•	•		•	•		•		
Index Options	•	•		•	•		•	•	•
Index Futures	•								
Currency Options		•			•				•
AGRI Options									•
AGRI/Currency Futures								•	•
Options on AGRI/CURR Futures								•	

Recommended Resources

New York Stock Exchange Fact Book
New York Stock Exchange, Inc.
11 Wall St.
New York, NY 10005
(212) 656-3000

American Stock Exchange Fact Book
American Stock Exchange, Inc.
86 Trinity Pl.
New York, NY 10006
(212) 306-1000

NASDAQ Fact Book & Company Directory
The National Association of Securities Dealers, Inc.
1735 K St., NW, 8th Floor
Washington, DC 20006
(202) 728-8000

The Top Reference Sources

The Directory of Corporate Affiliations
National Register Publishing Company, $725
(708) 256-6067

Published annually, this directory gives a view-at-a-glance of the corporate structure of more than 5,000 major U.S companies and their 50,000 subsidiaries, divisions, and affiliates.

Parent company listings contain address, numbers, ticker symbols, stock markets, financial data, number of employees, sales, balance sheet data, SIC codes, a description of the company's line of business, key personnel, and members of the board. Also included are summaries of mergers and acquisitions and name changes.

Dividends and Splits

A COMPANY'S DIVIDEND PAYMENT to stockholders represents the stockholder's share of the company's net profits. The dividend amount is decided by the company's directors; it is fixed per share and typically paid quarterly in cash (mailed checks).

Cash Dividends on NYSE Listed Common Stocks

Year	Number of Issues Listed at Year End	Number Paying Cash Dividends During Year	Estimated Aggregate Cash Payments ($ millions)
1929	842	554	2,711
1935	776	387	1,336
1940	829	577	2,099
1945	881	746	2,275
1950	1,039	930	5,404
1951	1,054	961	5,467
1952	1,067	975	5,595
1953	1,069	964	5,874
1954	1,076	968	6,439
1955	1,076	982	7,488
1956	1,077	975	8,341
1957	1,098	991	8,807
1958	1,086	961	8,711
1959	1,092	953	9,337
1960	1,126	981	9,872
1961	1,145	981	10,430
1962	1,168	994	11,203
1963	1,194	1,032	12,096
1964	1,227	1,066	13,555
1965	1,254	1,111	15,302
1966	1,267	1,127	16,151
1967	1,255	1,116	16,866
1968	1,253	1,104	18,124
1969	1,290	1,121	19,404
1970	1,330	1,120	19,781
1971	1,399	1,132	20,256
1972	1,478	1,195	21,490
1973	1,536	1,276	23,627
1974	1,543	1,308	25,662
1975	1,531	1,273	26,901
1976	1,550	1,304	30,608
1977	1,549	1,360	36,270
1978	1,552	1,373	41,151
1979	1,536	1,359	46,937
1980	1,540	1,361	53,072
1981	1,534	1,337	60,628
1982	1,499	1,287	62,224
1983	1,518	1,259	67,102
1984	1,511	1,243	68,215
1985	1,503	1,206	74,237
1986	1,536	1,180	76,161
1987	1,606	1,219	84,377
1988	1,643	1,270	102,190
1990	1,683	1,303	101,778
1991	1,741	NA	103,150
1992	1,860	NA	123,385

Source: NYSE Fact Book, 1991

Dividends and Splits (cont'd)

Annual Number of Stock Splits on the NYSE

Year	Total
1982	146
1983	300
1984	178
1985	166
1986	272

Year	Total
1987	244
1988	104
1989	142
1990	105
1991	107

Block Trading

BLOCKS ARE LARGE HOLDINGS OF STOCK, usually 10,000 shares or more. Blocks are most likely owned by institutions; block trades usually occur between institutions.

Block Trading on the NYSE

Year	Total Transactions	% of Reported Volume
1965	2,171	3.1
1970	17,217	15.4
1975	34,420	16.6
1976	47,632	18.7
1977	54,27	22.4
1978	75,036	22.9
1979	97,509	26.5
1980	133,597	29.2
1981	145,564	31.8
1982	254,707	41.0
1983	363,415	45.6
1984	433,427	49.8
1985	539,039	51.7
1986	665,587	49.9
1987	920,679	51.2
1988	768,419	54.5
1989	872,811	51.1
1990	843,365	49.6
1991	981,077	49.6

Source: NYSE Fact Book, 1991

Block Trading on the Amex

Year	Number of Blocks	% of Total Dollar Volume
1970	2,260	6.9
1975	1,803	7.6
1980	9,895	11.5
1981	10,463	16.2
1982	12,330	17.9
1983	20,629	21.4
1984	18,820	29.2
1985	29,094	34.0
1986	44,421	35.4
1987	53,814	36.0
1988	39,865	36.7
1989	51,907	33.4
1990	60,830	37.7
1991	52,678	34.8

Source: Amex Fact Book, 1991

Initial Public Offerings

WHEN A COMPANY FIRST OFFERS ITS STOCK for sale to potential investors it conducts what is known as an initial public offering (IPO).

Total IPO Issuance on NYSE

Year	No. of Issues	Proceeds ($ millions)
1976	2	73.4
1977	2	63.2
1978	0	0.0
1979	0	0.0
1980	2	101.6
1981	1	60.0
1982	2	154.0
1983	14	1,141.7
1984	13	901.7
1985	25	3,994.4
1986	67	9,692.8
1987	72	17,983.0
1988	71	19,301.3
1989	64	10,816.1
1990	57	7,380.5
1991	87	17,406.1
1992	168	28,131.4
TOTAL	647	117,201.2

Total IPO Issuance on NASDAQ

Year	# of Issues	Proceeds ($ millions)
1976	3	79.7
1977	2	47.7
1978	0	0.0
1979	1	1.6
1980	0	0.0
1981	1	25.0
1982	2	12.1
1983	2	80.3
1984	4	167.1
1985	4	31.7
1986	9	199.2
1987	9	285.8
1988	24	284.0
1989	106	1,896.2
1990	139	2,304.7
1991	303	7,546.6
1992	416	10,935.1
TOTAL	1,025	23,896.9

Total IPO Issuance on Amex

Year	# of Issues	Proceeds ($ millions)
1976	2	9.9
1977	0	0.0
1978	0	0.0
1979	2	20.4
1980	1	9.6
1981	5	61.9
1982	0	0.0
1983	7	129.8
1984	9	113.6
1985	17	520.4
1986	53	2,316.9
1987	52	2,008.8
1988	36	2,226.3
1989	10	346.2
1990	9	344.3
1991	11	191.3
1992	10	350.2
TOTAL	224	8,649.5

Total IPO Issuances

Year	# of Issues	Proceeds ($ millions)
1975	6	189.4
1976	40	337.2
1977	32	221.6
1978	38	225.4
1979	62	398.4
1980	149	1,387.1
1981	348	3,114.7
1982	122	1,339.1
1983	686	12,466.4
1984	357	3,868.9
1985	355	8,497.6
1986	726	22,211.3
1987	553	26,838.2
1988	288	23,606.1
1989	248	13,691.4
1990	213	10,117.4
1991	402	25,144.2
1992	595	39,419.2
TOTAL	5,220	193,073.6

Source: Securities Data Company

Initial Public Offerings (cont'd)

20 Largest Domestic IPO's, 1985 to 1992 (excluding closed-end funds)

Date	Issuer	Offering Amount ($ millions)	# of Shares Offered (millions)	Offering Price ($)	Book Manager
10/30/87	British Petroleum	2,864.1	42.2	67.9	Goldman, Sachs
3/26/87	Consolidated Rail	1,456.0	52.0	28.0	Goldman, Sachs
5/20/86	Henley Group	1,190.0	56.0	21.3	Lazard Freres & Co.
7/27/92	Wellcome Group	1,067.5	70.0	15.3	Morgan Stanley
11/21/86	Coca-Cola Enterprises	1,001.4	60.6	16.5	Allen & Co
1/18/89	Lyondell Petrochemical	960.0	32.0	30.0	Goldman, Sachs
10/23/85	Fireman's Fund	824.0	32.0	25.8	Shearson Lehman Brothers
4/9/92	First Data	770.0	35.0	22.0	Lehman Brothers
9/12/85	Rockefeller Center Properties	750.0	37.5	20.0	Goldman, Sachs
1/22/91	MBNA	689.3	30.6	22.5	Goldman, Sachs
10/29/86	Commercial Credit	662.2	32.3	20.5	First Boston
2/26/92	HCA Hospital Corp. of Amer.	584.8	27.2	21.5	Goldman, Sachs
11/6/86	UNUM	561.5	22.0	25.5	Goldman, Sachs
12/11/91	Owens-Illinois	528.0	48.0	11.0	Morgan Stanley
12/12/91	HealthTrust Inc-The Hospital	511.0	36.5	14.0	Merrill Lynch & Co.
7/18/91	Exel	487.2	19.1	25.5	Goldman, Sachs
5/7/87	Shearson Lehman Bros. Hldg	476.0	14.0	34.0	Shearson Lehman Brothers
3/19/92	Burlington Industries Equity	469.4	33.53	14.0	Morgan Stanley
3/25/92	Coltec Industries	462.0	30.8	15.0	Morgan Stanley
9/28/87	ARCO Chemical	432.0	13.5	32.0	Goldman, Sachs

Source: Securities Data Company

The Top Reference Sources

S&P 500 Directory
Standard & Poor's, $39.95
(212) 208-1649

This annual fact book provides a good overview of the S&P 500 index, including background information and methodology. It includes a "year in review" section, plus a directory of S&P index products, and an A-Z listing of the S&P 500 companies.

S&P 500 company reports and statistical tables are also provided.

The World's Stock Exchanges

Stock Exchanges

Stock Exchange	Tokyo	New York	Toronto	U.K.	Frankfurt	Paris	Zurich
No. Stock-Listed Companies (D)	1,627	1,678	1,127	1,946	389	443	182
No. Stock-Listed Companies (F)	125	96	66	613	354	226	240
No. Listed Issues, Stocks(D)	1,634	2,174	1,539	2,029	484	482	335
No. Listed Issues, Stocks (F)	125	110	54	794	390	248	247
No. Listed Issues, Bonds (D)	1,311	2,709	14	2,722	5,728	2,573	1,502
No. Listed Issues, Bonds (F)	154	203	-	1,621	1,008	205	946
Total Mkt. Value, Stocks ($ mil.)	2,821,660	2,692,123	241,925	858,165	341,030	304,388	163,416
Total Mkt. Value, Bonds ($ mil.)	978,895	1,610,175	-	576,291	645,382	481,073	158,487
Trading Value, Stocks ($ mil.)	1,303,145	1,325,332	54,858	544,060	348,914	120,199	373,257
Trading Value, Bonds ($ mil.)	365,274	10,894	-	943,213	389,112	553,725	
No. of Member Firms	124	516	71	410	214	44	27

Stock Exchange	Amsterdam	Milan	Australia	Hong Kong	Singapore	Taiwan	Korea
No. Stock-Listed Companies (D)	260	220	1,085	284	150	199	699
No. Stock-Listed Companies (F)	238	-	37	15	22	-	-
No. Listed Issues, Stocks (D)	303	334	1,492	294	154	213	1,115
No. Listed Issues, Stocks (F)	307	-	46	15	23	-	-
No. Listed Issues, Bonds (D)	998	1,322	1,706	8	50	46	6,891
No. Listed Issues, Bonds (F)	168	19	-	4	105	-	-
Total Mkt. Value, Stocks ($ mil.)	148,553	148,766	108,628	83,279	34,268	98,854	110,301
Total Mkt. Value, Bonds ($ mil.)	166,308	588,757	46,433	656	98,698	6,551	71,353
Trading Value, Stocks ($ mil.)	40,845	42,317	40,173	34,728	20,279	706,695	75,525
Trading Value, Bonds ($ mil.)	51,978	31,916	11,489	33	1,303	227	4,819
No. of Member Firms	152	113	90	686	26	373	25

D=Domestic, F=Foreign

Source: Tokyo Stock Exchange Fact Book, 1992

Dollar Volume of Equity Trading in Major World Markets (U.S. $ billions)

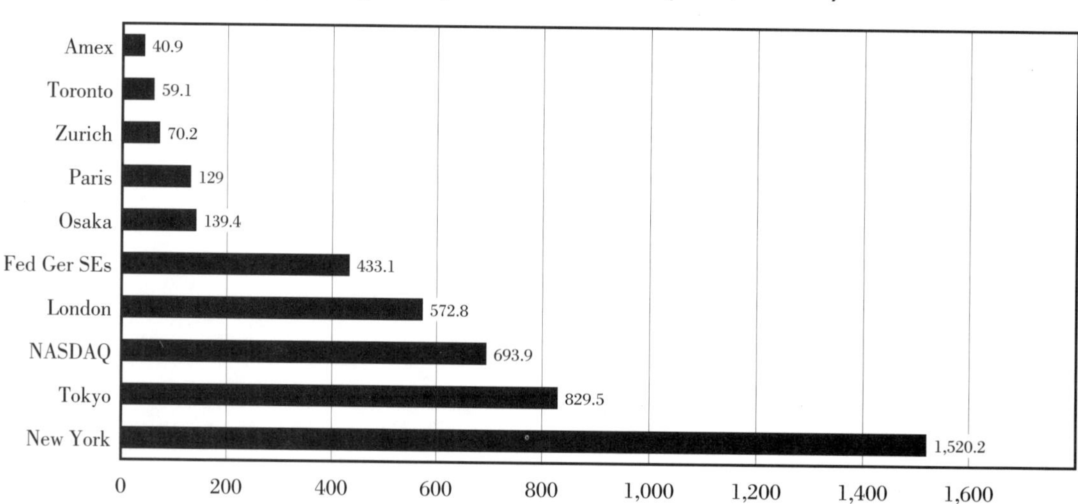

Source: 1992 NASDAQ Fact Book

The World's Stock Exchanges (cont'd)

1992 Best Performers on the World Stock Market

Country	P/E Ratio	In Home Currency	In Dollars
Hong Kong	14.6	22.2	22.9
Thailand	13.5	19.9	18.7
Switzerland	15.2	19.4	15.1
Britain	18.9	9.0	9.3
U.S. (S&P 500)	24.0	3.7	3.7

1992 Worst Performers on the World Stock Market

Country	P/E Ratio	In Home Currency	In Dollars
Netherlands	12.8	2.9	-0.9
France	14.9	-0.4	-4.2
Germany	14.4	-6.5	-10.0
Canada	17.2	-7.0	-15.7
Australia	20.1	-9.1	-17.2
Japan	38.2	-22.7	-22.0

Source: Barclays de Zoete Wedd Securities, Morgan Stanley Capital International

Major Foreign Exchanges

London Stock Exchange

The International Stock Exchange of the
United Kingdom and The Republic of Ireland
Old Broad Street
London, England EC2N 1HP

Irish Companies Listed on the London Exchange

Year	No. of Companies
1971	117
1972	205
1973	102
1974	14
1975	19
1976	18
1977	24
1978	35
1979	49
1980	35
1981	63
1982	59
1983	79
1984	87
1985	80
1986	136
1987	155
1988	129
1989	110
1990	120
1991	101
1992	60

Overseas Companies Listed on the London Exchange

Year	No. of Companies
1970	16
1971	28
1972	40
1973	51
1974	17
1975	10
1976	19
1977	15
1978	8
1979	15
1980	28
1981	28
1982	21
1983	36
1984	84
1985	18
1986	33
1987	34
1988	34
1989	49
1990	38
1991	20
1992	8

Source: London Stock Exchange

Major Foreign Exchanges (cont'd)

Largest New Companies Admitted to the London Stock Exchange

Date of Listing	Company	Proceeds (mil. pounds)
12/8/86	British Gas	5,434
12/3/84	British Telecommunications	3,916
12/5/88	British Steel	2,500
6/18/91	Scottish Power	1,956
10/10/86	TSB Group	1,496
5/20/87	Rolls-Royce	1,363
3/12/91	National Power	1,338
7/28/87	BAA	1,225
7/12/89	Abbey National	975
12/12/89	Thames Water	922
6/18/91	Scottish Hydro-Electric	920
2/11/87	British Airways	900
12/12/89	North West Water Group	854
12/12/89	Severn Trust	849
3/12/91	PowerGen	820
12/10/87	Eurotunnel/Eurotunnel S.A.	770
12/12/89	Anglian Water	707
12/11/90	Eastern Electricity	648
12/11/90	Southern Electric	648
7/17/92	MFI Furniture Group	629

Stock Offerings by London Stock Exchange

Date	Company	Price	Proceeds (mil. pds)
10/30/87	British Petroleum Co.	330p	1513
8/9/88	Guinness	430p	391
12/22/87	Midland Bank	475p	383
9/1/87	THORN EMI	695p	371
9/1/87	Trafalgar House	388p	316
7/14/87	Williams Holdings	785p	285
10/1/87	Pilkington	290p	266
7/1/87	Valor	330p	265
9/4/87	Smiths Industries	310p	223
8/27/92	Royal Bank of Scotland	$25	202
6/5/89	Barclays Bank	$25	200

Record Vendor Placings by UK Companies

Date	Acquiring Company	Acquired Company	Value of Offer (millions of pounds)
8/3/87	British Petroleum	Standard Oil Company	1,026
12/23/91	LASMO	Ultramar	1,008
2/25/88	British Petroleum	Britoil	874
11/25/91	BTR	Hawker Siddeley Group	818
3/27/92	Redland	Steetley	670
11/8/88	Mecca Leisure Group	Pleasurama	660
12/24/90	Wiggins Teape Appleton	Arjomari-Prioux SA	568
6/11/92	Dowty Group	TI Group	532
7/3/89	Carlton Communications	U.E.I.	511
3/5/91	Williams Holdings	Yale & Valor	450

Source: London Stock Exchange

The Top Reference Sources

Financial World
Financial World Partners, $36.00 a year
(212) 594-5030

This monthly magazine concentrates on business, economic, and financial topics. It includes a focus on the national economy and effects of Washington policy upon it, statistical analysis of stock, bond, and mutual fund activity, and the international industrial and financial arena. Highlights include the list of America's 200 Best Growth Companies.

Major Foreign Exchanges (cont'd)

Tokyo Stock Exchange

2-1 Nihombashi-Kabuto-Cho
Chuo-Ku, Tokyo 103
Tel: Tokyo 3666-0141

The Tokyo Stock Exchange is divided into two sections. Approximately 1,220 companies are listed in the First Section, the marketplace for stocks of larger companies. In the Second Section, the marketplace for smaller and newly-listed companies, approximately 420 companies are listed.

Ten Most Active Tokyo Stock Exchange Issues, 1991

Company	Reported Share Volume
Nippon Steel	1,770,000,000
Mitsubishi Heavy Industries	1,364,000,000
Hitachi Zosen	1,331,000,000
NKK	1,112,000,000
Hitachi	972,000,000
Sumitomo Metal Industries	970,000,000
Chiyoda	931,000,000
Mitsubishi Materials	866,000,000
Mitsui Ship Building	813,000,000
Honshu Paper	788,000,000

Source: Tokyo Stock Exchange Fact Book, 1992

Tokyo Stock Price Index (TOPIX) measures the performance of all stocks listed on the First Section of the Tokyo Stock Exchange. The TOPIX is separated as well into 28 sub-indexes by industry groups and size.

The Nikkei Stock Average is the Dow Jones Average of the Tokyo Stock Market, tracking the price movements of 225 large, well-known issues in the First Section of the Tokyo Stock Exchange. The stocks included represent a broad range of industries including foods, textiles, pulp and paper, chemicals, drugs, petroleum, rubber, glass and ceramics, iron and steel, non-ferrous metals, machinery, electrial equipment, shipbuilding, motor vehicles, transportation equipment, precision instruments, marine products, mining, construction, trade, retail stores, banks, securities, insurance, real estate, railroad and bus, trucking, sea transportation, air transportation, warehousing, communications, electric power, gas, and services.

The Top Reference Sources

Tokyo Stock Exchange Fact Book
Tokyo Stock Exchange
(212) 363-2350

This is a useful reference for anyone interested in following the Tokyo Stock Exchange.

It is made available in English by the New York Research Office of the Exchange.

Statistical data are provided, along with explanatory comments. The book also includes stock price trends, companies listed, commission rates, investors, etc.

Major Foreign Exchanges (cont'd)

Just as the Dow Jones Industrial Average is used as a barometer for stock market performance in the U.S., the FT-SE tracks the London Stock Exchange and the Topix and the Nikkei track the Tokyo Stock Exchange.

FT-SE Financial Times Index, 1984 to 1992

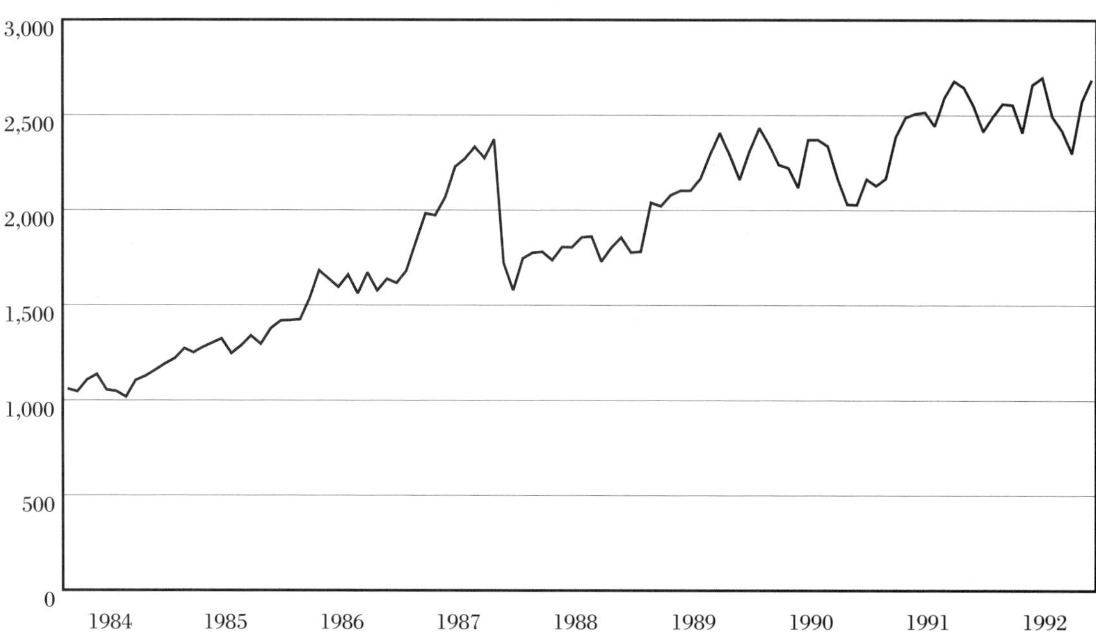

Source: The London Stock Exchange

Topix Performance, 1950 to 1991

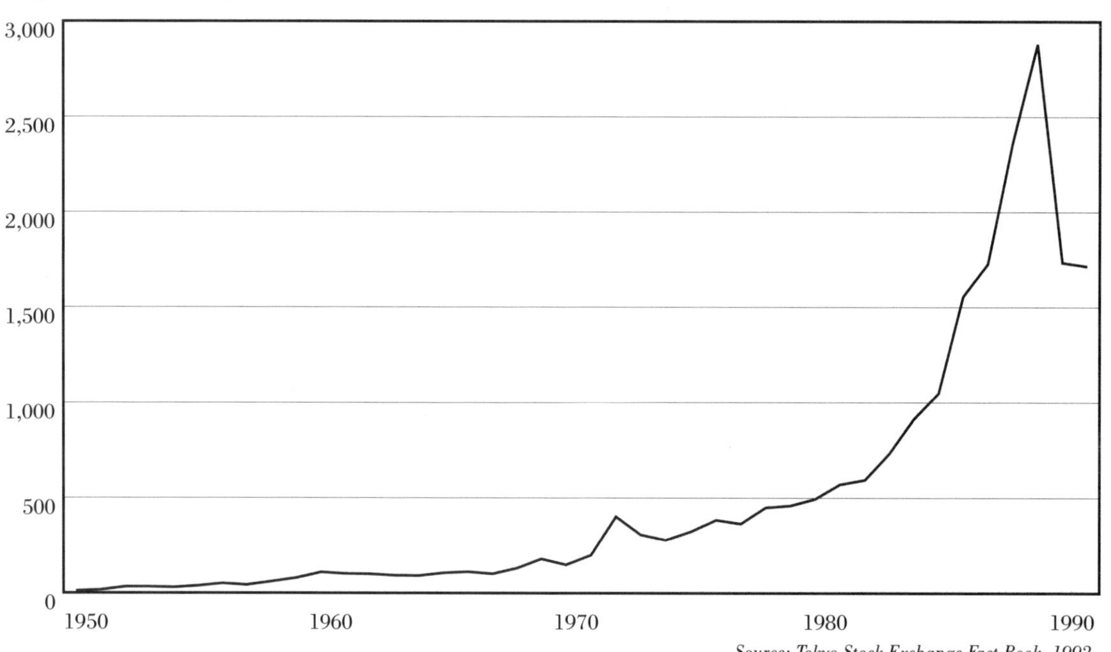

Source: Tokyo Stock Exchange Fact Book, 1992

Major Foreign Exchanges (cont'd)

The Nikkei Stock Average: Record One-Day Gains and Losses

Date	Average	Percent Gain or Loss
October 2, 1990	2298.41	+13.24
December 15, 1949	109.62	+11.29
October 21, 1987	2,3947.41	+9.30
April 16, 1953	355.03	+6.41
March 6, 1953	361.88	+6.31
October 20, 1987	2,190.08	-14.90
March 5, 1953	340.41	-10.00
April 30, 1970	2,114.32	-8.69
August 16, 1971	2,530.48	-7.68
December 14, 1949	98.50	- 6.97

Source: The Nikkei Stock Average Data Book, 1991

Nikkei Stock Average Performance

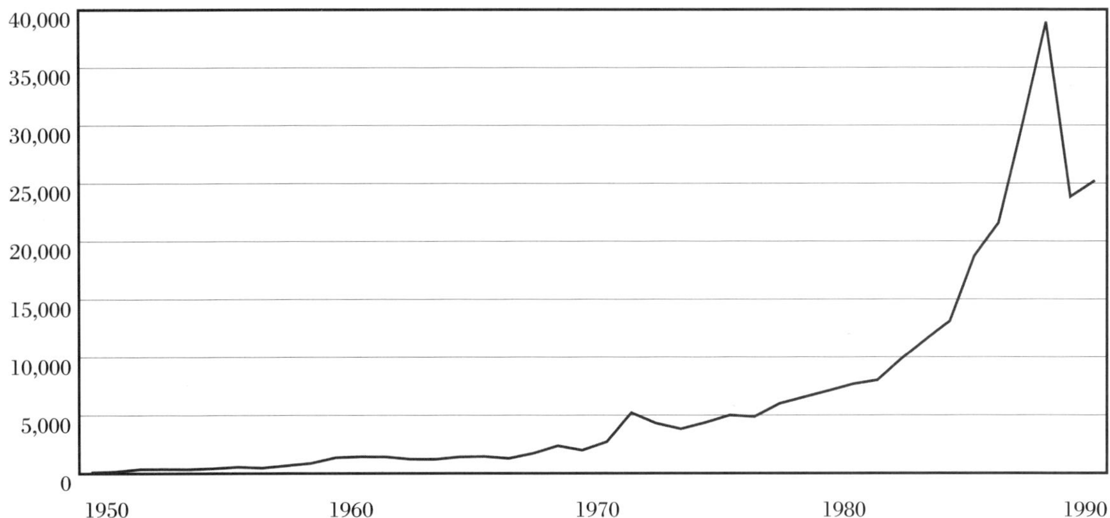

Source: The Nikkei Stock Average Data Book, 1991

The Top Reference Sources

The Nikkei Stock Average Data Book
Nihon Keizai Shimbun America
(212) 261-6240

This is a very useful reference for anyone interested in following the Nikkei Stock Average. It provides a thorough overview of the Stock Average, with performance charts, comparisons with other indexes, stock price rankings, lists of the most advanced and declined stocks, annual quotations, long term trends, average daily closing prices, largest losses and gains, etc.

Major Foreign Exchanges (cont'd)

Foreign Exchange Listings

Australia
Sydney Stock Exchange
Exchange Street
20 Bond St.
Australia Square
P.O. Box H224
Sydney, 2000
Index: Sydney All Ordinaries

Belgium
Brussels Stock Exchange
Palais de la Bourse
1000 Brussels
Index: Bel-20 Index

Canada
Toronto Stock Exchange
2 First Canadian Pl.
Toronto, Ontario M5X 1J2
Index: 300 Composite

France
Bourse De Paris
Paris Stock Exchange
4, Place de la Bourse
F-75080 Paris Cedex 02
Index: CAC 40

Germany
Frankfurter Wertpapierbore
Frankfurt Exchange
Börsenplatz 6, P.O. 100811
D-6000 Frankfurt am Main 1
Index: DAX 30

Hong Kong
Stock Exchange of Hong Kong
One and Two Exchange Square
Central Hong Kong
Index: Hang Seng

The Netherlands
Amsterdamse Effectenbeurs
Amsterdam Stock Exchange
Beursplein 5
1012 JW Amersterdam
Index: ANP-CBS General

Switzerland
Zurich Stock Exchange
Bleicherweg 5
P.O. Box CH-8021
Zurich
Index: Swiss Market

Foreign Investment (%) in Tokyo Stock Exchange

Source: Tokyo Stock Exchange Fact Book, 1992

The Dow Jones Averages

The Dow Jones Industrial Average

The Dow Jones Industrial Average ("the Dow") tracks price movements in 30 of the largest, blue-chip issues traded on the NYSE.

Allied-Signal
Aluminum Co. of America
American Express
AT&T
Bethlehem Steel
Boeing
Caterpillar
Chevron
Coca-Cola
Disney (Walt)
Du Pont
Eastman Kodak
Exxon
General Electric
General Motors
Goodyear
IBM
International Paper
McDonald's
Merck
Minnesota Mining and Manufacturing
Morgan (J.P.)
Philip Morris
Procter & Gamble
Sears
Texaco
Union Carbide
United Technologies
Westinghouse
Woolworth

The Dow Jones Transportation Average

The Dow Jones Transportation Average was originally of railroads alone. The current index, however, also reflects developments in the airline and trucking business in this mix of twenty transport companies:

AMR Corp.
Airborne Freight
Alaska Air
American President
Burlington Northern
Carolina Freight
Consolidated Freightways
Consolidated Rail
CSX Corporation
Delta Air Lines
Federal Express
Norfolk Southern
Roadway Services
Ryder Systems
Santa Fe Pacific
Southwest Airlines
UAL Corporation
Union Pacific
USAir
XTRA Corporation

The Dow Jones Utility Average

The Dow Jones Utility Average tracks 15 large electricity and natural gas utilities.

American Electric Power
Arkla
Centerior
Commonwealth Edison
Consolidated Edison
Consolidated Natural Gas
Detroit Edison
Houston Industries
Niagara Mohawk Power
Pacific Gas & Electric
Panhandle Eastern
Peoples Energy
Philadelphia Electric
Public Service Enterprises
SCE

Best Performing Dow Jones Industrials, 1992

Company	1992 close ($)	% change from 1991
Union Carbide	16.63	91.88*
Walt Disney	43.00	50.22
Allied-Signal	60.50	37.89
AT&T	51.00	30.35
McDonald's	48.75	28.29
Goodyear	68.38	27.80
Caterpillar	53.63	22.22
American Express	24.88	21.34
Sears	45.50	20.13
Woolworth	31.63	19.34

**Union Carbide's June 1992 spin-off of Praxair altered the stock price*

Source: *The Wall Street Journal*

The Dow Jones Averages (cont'd)

Worst Performing Dow Jones Industrials, 1992

Company	1992 close ($)	% change from 1991
IBM	50.38	-43.40
Westinghouse	13.38	-25.69
Merck	43.38	-21.85
Kodak	40.50	-16.06
Boeing	40.13	-15.97

Source: The Wall Street Journal

Dow Jones Industrial Average Performance Since 1900

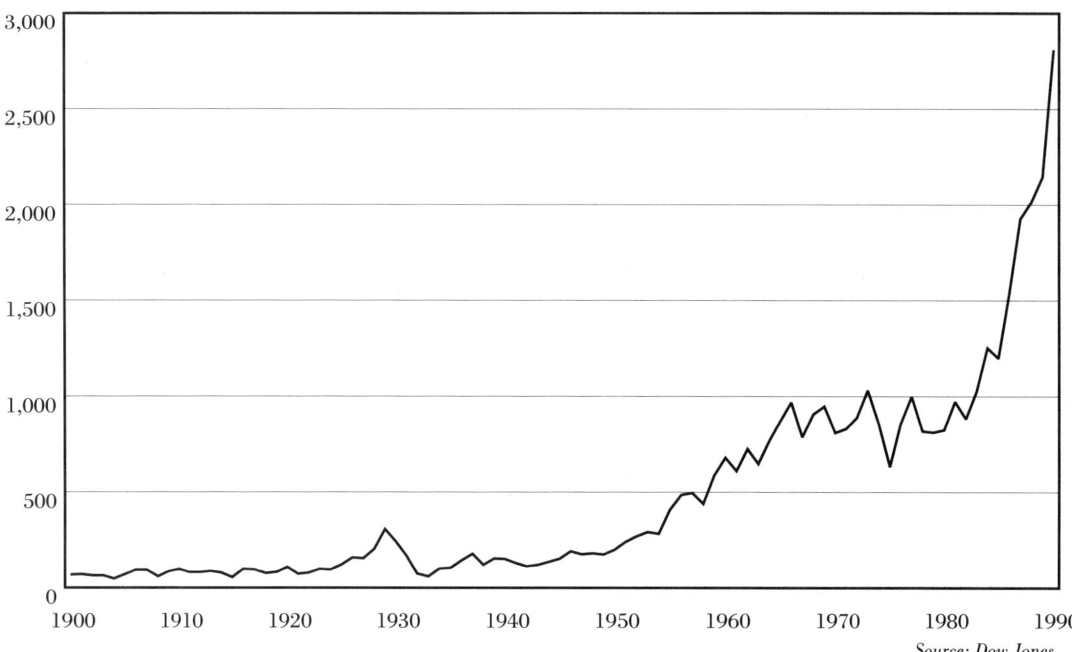

Source: Dow Jones

S&P 500 Index Performance, Yearly Close

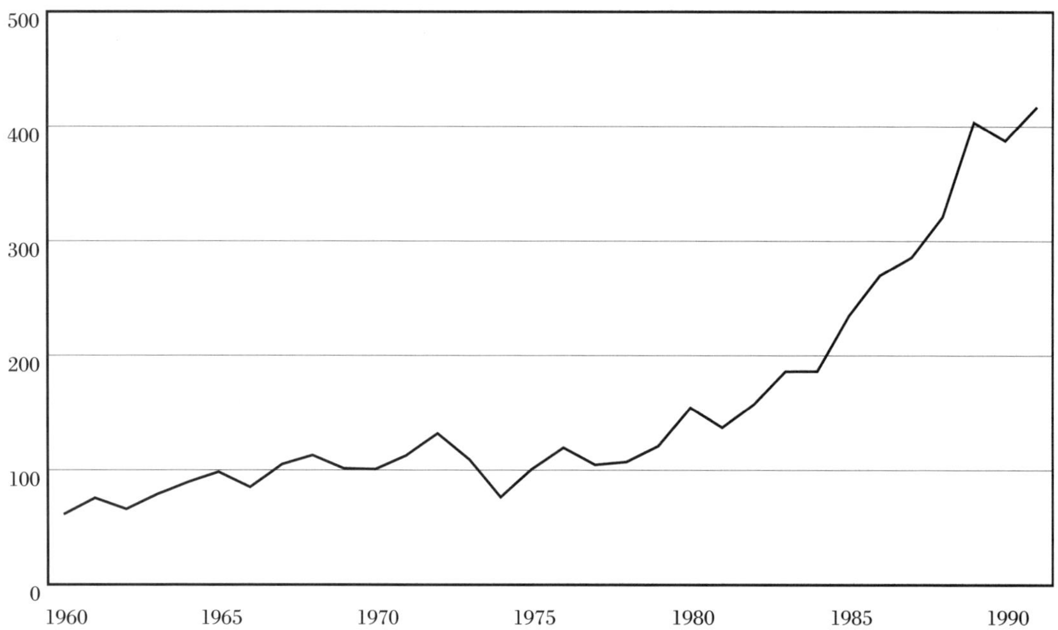

Source: S&P 500 Directory, 1992

Standard & Poor's 500

STANDARD & POOR'S 500 INDEX (S&P 500) represents approximately 80% of the value of all issues traded on the NYSE, reflecting the performance of 500 stocks including industrials, public utilities, transportation, and financial companies. Movement within each of these industry categories is tracked in sub-indexes.

The S&P 500 index is currently one of the 12 leading economic indicators cited by the U.S. Commerce Department.

S&P 500 Composite Stock Price Index

Ticker Symbol	Company Name
AMP	AMP Inc.
AMR	AMR Corp.
T	AT&T
ABT	Abbott Laboratories
AMT	ACME-Cleveland Corp
AMD	Advanced Micro Devices, Inc
AET	Aetna Life and Casualty, Co.
AHM	Ahmanson (H.F.) & Co.
APD	Air Products and Chemicals, Inc.
ACV	Alberto-Culver Company
ABS	Albertson's Inc.
AL	Alcan Aluminum Limited
ASN	Alco Standard Corporation
AAL	Alexander & Alexander Services
ALD	Allied-Signal
AA	Aluminum Co. of America
AZA	Alza Corp.
AMX	Amax Inc.
AMH	Amdahl Corporation
AHC	Amerada Hess
AMB	American Brands
ACY	American Cyanamid
AEP	American Electric Power
AXP	American Express
AGC	American General Corporation
AGREA	American Greetings
AHP	American Home Products
AIT	American Information Technologies
AIG	American International Group
ASC	American Stores
AIT	Ameritech Corp.
AN	Amoco Corporation
ANDW	Andrew Corp.
BUD	Anheuser-Busch Companies
AAPL	Apple Computer
ADM	Archer-Daniels-Midland
ALG	Arkla, Inc.
AS	Armco, Inc.
ACK	Armstrong World Industries
AR	Asarco, Inc.

Ticker Symbol	Company Name
ASH	Ashland Oil
ARC	Atlantic Richfield
ACAD	Autodesk
AUD	Automatic Data Processing
AVY	Avery Dennison Corporation
AVP	Avon Products
BHI	Baker Hughes Incorporated
BLL	Ball Corporation
BLY	Bally Manufacturing
BGE	Baltimore Gas & Electric
ONE	Banc One
BKB	Bank of Boston
BAC	BankAmerica
BT	Bankers Trust New York
BCR	Bard (C.R.)
BBI	Barnett Banks
BSET	Bassett Furniture Industries
BOL	Bausch & Lomb
BAX	Baxter International
BDX	Becton, Dickinson & Co.
BEL	Bell Atlantic
BLS	BellSouth
BMS	Bemis Company
BNL	Beneficial Corporation
BS	Bethlehem Steel
BEV	Beverly Enterprises
BMET	Biomet
BDK	Black & Decker
HRB	Block (H&R)
BV	Blockbuster Entertainment
BOAT	Boatmen's Bancshares
BA	Boeing
BCC	Boise Cascade
BN	Borden
BGG	Briggs & Stratton
BMY	Bristol-Myers Squibb
BFD	Brown-Forman
BG	Brown Group
BNS	Brown & Sharpe Mfg.
BFI	Browning-Ferris Industries
BRNO	Bruno's
BC	Brunswick
BNI	Burlington Northern
CVN	C&S/Sovran
CBS	CBS
CNA	CNA Financial
CPC	CPC International
CSX	CSX Corporation
CPB	Campbell Soup
CCB	Capital Cities/ABC
CPH	Capital Holding

Standard & Poor's 500 (cont'd)

Ticker Symbol	Company Name
CPL	Carolina Power & Light
CAT	Caterpillar
CTX	Centex
CSR	Central & South West
CHA	Champion International
CHRS	Charming Shoppes
CMB	Chase Manhattan Corporation
CHL	Chemical Banking
CHV	Chevron
C	Chrysler
CB	Chubb
CI	Cigna
CMZ	Cincinnati Milacron
CC	Circuit City Stores
CCI	Citicorp
CKL	Clark Equipment
CLX	Clorox
CGP	Coastal Corporation
KO	Coca-Cola
CL	Colgate-Palmolive
CG	Columbia Gas System
CMCSA	Comcast
CWE	Commonwealth Edison
CMY	Community Psychiatric Centers
CPQ	Compaq Computer
CA	Computer Associates International
CSC	Computer Sciences
CAG	Conagra
ED	Consolidated Edison Co. of New York
CNF	Consolidated Freightways
CNG	Consolidated Natural Gas
CRR	Consolidated Rail
CIC	Continental Corp.
CDA	Control Data
CBE	Cooper Industries
CTB	Cooper Tire & Rubber
ACCOB	Coors (Adolph)
CSFN	Corestates Financial
GLW	Corning Incorporated
CR	Crane
CYR	Cray Research
CCK	Crown Cork & Seal
CUM	Cummins Engine
CYM	Cyprus Minerals
DIGI	DSC Communications
DCN	Dana
DGN	Data General
DH	Dayton-Hudson
DE	Deere & Company
DAL	Delta Air Lines
DLX	Deluxe Corporation
DTE	Detroit Edison
DL	Dial Corporation
DEC	Digital Equipment
DDS	Dillard Department Stores
D	Dominion Resources
DNY	Donnelley (R.R.) & Sons
DOV	Dover Corporation
DOW	Dow Chemical
DJ	Dow Jones
DI	Dresser Industries
DUK	Duke Power
DNB	Dun & Bradstreet
DD	Du Pont De Nemours
EGG	EG & G
ESY	E-Systems
EFU	Eastern Enterprises
EK	Eastman Kodak
ETN	Eaton Corporation
ECH	Echlin
ECO	Echo Bay Mines
ECL	Ecolab
EMR	Emerson Electric
EC	Engelhard
ENE	Enron
ENS	Enserch
ETR	Entergy
EY	Ethyl Corp.
XON	Exxon
FMC	FMC
FPL	FPL Group
FJQ	Fedders
FDX	Federal Express
FNM	Federal National Mortgage
FBO	Federal Paper Board
FNB	First Chicago
FFB	First Fidelity Bancorp
I	First Interstate Bancorp
FRM	First Mississippi
FTU	First Union
FNG	Fleet/Norstar Financial Group
FLE	Fleetwood Enterprises
FLM	Fleming Companies
FLR	Fluor
F	Ford Motor
FWC	Foster Wheeler
GTE	GTE
GCI	Gannett Co.
GPS	The Gap
GCN	General Cinema Corporaton

Standard & Poor's 500 (cont'd)

Ticker Symbol	Company Name
GD	General Dynamics
GE	General Electric
GIS	General Mills
GM	General Motors
GRN	General Re
GSX	General Signal
GCO	Genesco
GPC	Genuine Parts
GP	Georgia-Pacific
GEB	Gerber Products
GFSA	Giant Food
GS	Gillette
GDW	Golden West Financial
GR	Goodrich (B.F.)
GT	Goodyear Tire & Rubber
GRA	Grace (W.R.) & Co.
GWW	Grainger (W.W.)
GAP	Great Atlantic & Pacific Tea Company
GLK	Great Lakes Chemical
GWF	Great Western Financial
GQ	Grumman Corp.
HAL	Halliburton Co.
HDL	Handleman Co.
JH	Harland (John H.)
HPH	Harnischfeger Industries, Inc.
HRS	Harris Corp.
HMX	Hartmarx Corp.
HAS	Hasbro, Inc.
HNZ	Heinz (H.J.) Company
HP	Helmerich & Payne, Inc
HPC	Hercules Incorporated
HSY	Hershey Foods Corp.
HWP	Hewlett-Packard Co.
HLT	Hilton Hotels Corp.
HD	Home Depot, Inc. (The)
HM	Homestake Mining Co.
HON	Honeywell Inc.
HI	Household International, Inc.
HOU	Houston Industries Incorporated
HUM	Humana Inc.
ITT	ITT Corporation
ITW	Illinois Tool Works Inc.
IMA	Imcera Group Inc.
N	Inco Limited
IR	Ingersoll-Rand Co.
IAD	Inland Steel Industries, Inc.
INTC	Intel Corp.
INGR	Intergraph Corporation
IK	Interlake Corporation (The)
IBM	International Business Machines Corp.

Ticker Symbol	Company Name
IFF	International Flavors & Fragrances
IP	International Paper Co.
JWP	JWP Inc.
JR	James River Corp. of Virginia
JP	Jefferson-Pilot Corp.
JCI	Johnson Controls, Inc.
JNJ	Johnson & Johnson
JOS	Jostens, Inc
KM	k Mart Corp.
KBH	Kaufman & Broad Home Corp.
K	Kellogg Co.
KMG	Kerr-McGee Corp.
KMB	Kimberly-Clark Corporation
KWP	King World Productions Inc.
KRI	Knight-Ridder, Inc.
KR	Kroger Co. (The)
LLY	Lilly (Eli) and Co.
LTD	Limited, Inc. (The)
LNC	Lincoln National Corp.
LIT	Litton Industries, Inc.
LIZC	Liz Claiborne, Inc
LK	Lockheed Corp.
LDG	Longs Drug Stores Corp.
LOR	Loral Corp.
LOTS	Lotus Development Corp.
LLX	Louisiana Land & Exploration Co.
LPX	Louisiana-Pacific Corp.
LOW	Lowe's Companies, Inc.
LUB	Luby's Cafeterias, Inc.
MAI	M/A-Com Inc
MCIC	MCI Communications Corp.
MNR	Manor Care, Inc.
MHC	Manufacturers Hanover Corp.
MHS	Marriott Corporation
MMC	Marsh & McLennan, Incorporated
ML	Martin Marietta Corp.
MAS	Masco Corp.
MAT	Mattel Inc.
MXS	Maxus Energy Corp,.
MA	May Department Stores Company (The)
MYG	Maytag Corporation
MDR	McDermott International, Inc.
MCD	McDonald's Corp.
MD	McDonnell Douglas Corp.
MHP	McGraw-Hill, Inc.
MCK	McKesson Corp.
MEA	Mead Corporation (The)
MDT	Medtronic, Inc.
MEL	Mellon Bank Corporation
MES	Melville Corp.

Standard & Poor's 500 (cont'd)

Ticker Symbol	Company Name
MST	Mercantile Stores Co., Inc
MRK	Merck & Co., Inc.
MDP	Meredith Corp.
MER	Merrill Lynch & Co., Inc.
MIL	Millipore Corp.
MMM	Minnesota Mining & Mfg. Co.
MOB	Mobil Corporation
MMO	Monarch Machine Tool Co.
MTC	Monsanto Company
MCL	Moore Corporation Limited
JPM	Morgan (J.P.) & Co. Inc.
MRN	Morrison Knudsen Corp.
MII	Morton International Inc.
MOT	Motorola, Inc.
NBD	NBD Bancorp, Inc.
NCB	NCNB Corp.
NL	NL Industries
NC	NACCO Industries
NLC	Nalco Chemical
NEC	National Education
NII	National Intergroup
NME	National Medical Enterprises
NSM	National Semiconductor
NSI	National Service Industries
NAV	Navistar International
NYTA	New York Times Company (The)
NWL	Newell
NEM	Newmont Mining
NMK	Niagara Mohawk Power
GAS	Nicor
NIKE	Nike
NOBE	Nordstrom
NSC	Norfolk Southern
NSP	Northern States Power
NT	Northern Telecom
NOC	Northrop
NOB	Norwest
NOVL	Novell
NUE	Nucor
NYN	NYNEX
OXY	Occidental Petroleum
OG	Ogden
OEC	Ohio Edison
OKE	Oneok
ORCL	Oracle Systems
ORX	Oryx Energy
GOSHA	Oshkosh B'Gosh
OM	Outboard Marine
OCF	Owens-Corning Fiberglass
PHM	PHM

Ticker Symbol	Company Name
PNC	PNC Financial
PPG	PPG Industries
PIN	PSI Resources
PCAR	Paccar
PET	Pacific Enterprises
PCG	Pacific Gas & Electric
PAC	Pacific Telesis Group
PPW	Pacificorp
PLL	Pall
PEL	Panhandle Eastern
PCI	Paramount Communications
PH	Parker Hannifin
JCP	Penney (J.C.) Company
PZL	Pennzoil
PGL	Peoples Energy
PBY	Pep Boys (Manny, Moe & Jack)
PEP	PepsiCo
PKN	Perkin-Elmer
PT	PET
PFE	Pfizer
PD	Phelps Dodge
PE	Philadelphia Electric
MO	Philip Morris
P	Phillips Petroleum
PBI	Pitney Bowes
PCO	Pittston
PDG	Placer Dome
PRD	Polaroid
PCH	Potlatch
PMI	Premark International
PCLB	Price
PA	Primerica
PG	Procter & Gamble
PRI	Promus
PEG	Public Service Enterprises
OAT	Quaker Oats
CUE	Quantum Chemical
RAL	Ralston Purina
RYC	Raychem
RTN	Raytheon
RBK	Reebok International
RLM	Reynolds Metals
RAD	Rite Aid
ROAD	Roadway Service
ROK	Rockwell International
ROH	Rohm & Haas
RDC	Rowan
RD	Royal Dutch Petroleum
RBD	Rubbermaid
RML	Russell

Standard & Poor's 500 (Cont'd)

Ticker Symbol	Company Name
RYAN	Ryan's Family Steak Houses
R	Ryder System
SCE	SCE
SPW	SPX
SAFC	SAFECO
SK	Safety-Kleen
STJM	St. Jude Medical
STPL	St. Paul Companies
SB	Salomon
SFR	Santa Fe Energy Resources
SFX	Santa Fe Pacific
SLE	Sara Lee
SGP	Schering-Plough
SLB	Schlumberger
SFA	Scientific-Atlanta
SPP	Scott Paper
VO	Seagram Company (The)
S	Sears
SPC	Security Pacific
SRV	Service Corporation International
SMED	Shared Medical Systems
SNC	Shawmut National
SHW	Sherwin-Williams
SHN	Shoney's
SKY	Skyline
SNA	Snap-On Tools
SNT	Sonat
SO	Southern
SBC	Southwestern Bell
SMI	Springs Industries
SWK	Stanley Works
STO	Stone Container
SRR	Stride Rite
SUN	Sun
STI	Suntrust Banks
SVU	Super Valu Stores
SYN	Syntex
SYY	SYSCO
TJX	TJX Companies (The)
TRW	TRW
TDM	Tandem Computers
TAN	Tandy
TEK	Tektronix
TCOMA	Tele-Communications
TDY	Teledyne
TIN	Temple-Inland
TGT	Tenneco
TX	Texaco
TXN	Texas Instruments
TXU	Texas Utilities
TXT	Textron
TNB	Thomas & Betts
TWX	Time Warner
TMC	Times Mirror

Ticker Symbol	Company Name
TKR	Timken
TMK	Torchmark
TOY	Toys R Us
TA	Transamerica
E	Transco Energy
TIC	Travelers Corp
TRB	Tribune
TNV	Trinova
TYC	Tyco Laboratories
UAL	UAL Corp.
FG	USF & G
USG	USG
UST	UST
MRO	USX-Marathon Group
X	USX-US Steel Group
UN	Unilever
UCC	Union Camp
UK	Union Carbide
UEP	Union Electric
UNP	Union Pacific
UIS	Unisys
USW	US West
UTX	United Technologies
UT	United Telecom of Kansas
UCL	Unocal
UPJ	Upjohn
U	USAir
USH	USLife
VFC	U.F. Corp.
VAT	Varity
WMT	Wal-Mart Stores
WAG	Walgreen
DIS	Walt Disney
WANB	Wang Laboratories
WLA	Warner-Lambert
WMX	Waste Management
WFC	Wells Fargo & Co.
WEN	Wendy's International
WX	Westinghouse Electric
WMOR	Westmoreland Coal
W	Westvaco
WETT	Wetterau
WY	Weyerhaeuser
WHR	Whirlpool
WH	Whitman
WMB	Williams Companies (The)
WIN	Winn-Dixie Stores
Z	Woolworth
WTHG	Worthington Industries
WWY	Wm. Wrigley Jr.
XRX	Xerox
YELL	Yellow Freight Systems Inc of Delaware
ZE	Zenith Electronics
ZRN	Zurn Industries

Standard & Poor's 500 (cont'd)

S&P 500 by Major Industry Group

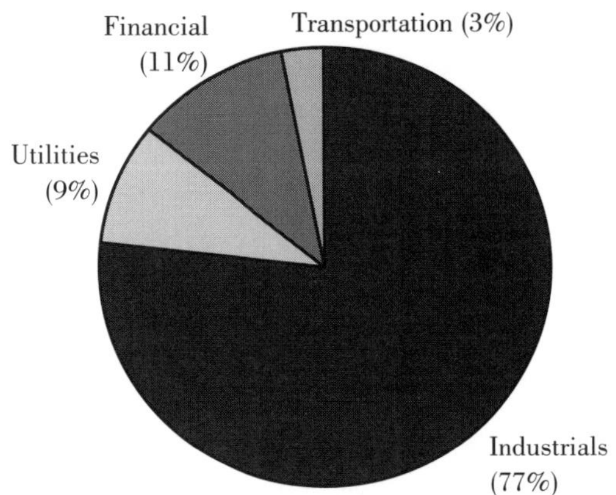

Source: S&P 500 Directory, 1991

Profile of Average S&P 500 Company

Revenues	$6,710 million
Net Income	$298 million
Earnings per Share	$2.12
Dividend Payout Ratio	56%
Stock Price (12/31/90)	$34 3/8
Dividend Yield (12/31/90)	4%
P/E (12/31/90)	16.3
Market Value (12/31/91)	$4,400 million

Source: S&P 500 Directory, 1991

Most Widely Held S&P Companies, 1991

Rank	Company	Number of Shareholders
1	AT&T (T)	2,486,000
2	BellSouth (BLS)	1,387,800
3	Bell Atlantic Corp. (BET)	1,151,000
4	NYNEX Corp. (NYN)	1,093,200
5	Ameritech (AIT)	1,082,600
6	Southwestern Bell (SBC)	1,051,200
7	US West Inc. (USW)	1,007,400
8	Pacific Telesis (PAC)	951,900
9	General Motors (GM)	915,600
10	International Business Machines (IBM)	789,000
11	Exxon Corp. (XON)	636,200
12	General Electric (GE)	515,000
13	Royal Dutch Petroleum (RD)	500,000
14	GTE Corp. (GTE)	442,000
15	Sears (S)	344,100
16	Ford Motor (F)	294,700
17	Pacific Gas & Electric (PCG)	287,000
18	Philadelphia Electric (PE)	282,600
19	Southern Co. (SO)	263,000
20	Mobil Corp. (MOB)	218,300

Source: S&P 500 Directory, 1992

Almanac Fact

After the breakup of AT&T, all seven of the Baby Bells remain the top companies in total number of shareholders.

Standard & Poor's

Standard & Poor's 500 (cont'd)

S&P 500 Index Performance, Yearly Close, P/E Ratio

Year	Close	Close P/E Ratio
1960	61.49	18.14
1961	75.72	22.47
1962	66.00	17.05
1963	79.25	18.69
1964	89.62	18.55
1965	98.47	17.87
1966	85.24	14.47
1967	105.11	18.57
1968	113.02	18.38
1969	101.49	16.45
1970	100.90	18.58
1971	112.72	18.72
1972	131.87	19.31
1973	109.14	12.32
1974	76.47	7.89

Year	Close	Close P/E Ratio
1975	100.88	11.80
1976	119.46	11.19
1977	104.71	9.01
1978	107.21	8.17
1979	121.02	7.47
1980	154.45	9.58
1981	137.12	8.29
1982	157.62	11.92
1983	186.24	12.64
1984	186.36	10.36
1985	234.56	15.39
1986	269.93	18.73
1987	285.86	14.09
1988	321.26	12.35
1989	403.49	15.31
1990	387.42	15.90
1991	417.09	26.12

Source: S&P 500 Directory, 1992

The Top Reference Sources

S&P MidCap 400 Directory
Standard & Poor's, $39.95
(212) 208-1649

Published for the first time in 1992, this annual directory is designed to provide money managers, analysts, institutional and individual investors, corporative executives, journalists, and observers of financial markets and the overall economy with a comprehensive and authoritative analysis of the growing, middle capitalization sector of the U.S. equities market.

The book includes a complete listing of the MidCap 400 companies, company reports, and statistical tables.

Composite Indexes

The Amex Market Value Index

The Amex Market Value Index is composed of all common stocks listed on the American Stock Exchange.

Amex Market Value Index Performance, Yearly Highs

Year	Index
1976	54.92
1977	63.95
1978	88.44
1979	123.54
1980	185.38
1981	190.18
1982	170.93
1983	249.03
1984	227.73
1985	246.13
1986	285.19
1987	365.01
1988	309.59
1989	382.45
1990	395.05

Source: Amex Fact Book, 1991

The Value Line Composite Index

The Value Line Composite Index tracks the performance of 1,700 stocks listed on the New York Stock Exchange, the American Stock Exchange, the Regional and Canadian Exchanges and the over-the-counter market.

The New York Stock Exchange Composite Index

The New York Stock Exchange Composite Index measures price movement of all NYSE-listed common stocks as well as performance in four subgroups: Industrial, Transportation, Utility and Finance.

NASDAQ Composite Index

The Nasdaq Composite Index indicates price movements of all domestic OTC common stocks listed on the NASDAQ system. The composite is broken down into six specialized industry indexes.

NASDAQ Composite Index Classifications

Index	Number of Issues	Market Value ($ billions)
Industrial	2,771	348.0
Other Finance	646	79.5
Bank	198	7.5
Insurance	121	18.2
Utility	157	44.1
Transportation	62	11.0
Total Composite	3,955	508.3
Total Unassigned	729	11.2
Total All NASDAQ	4,684	519.5

Source: NASDAQ Fact Book & Company Directory, 1992

NASDAQ Composite Index Market Value, 1981 to 1991

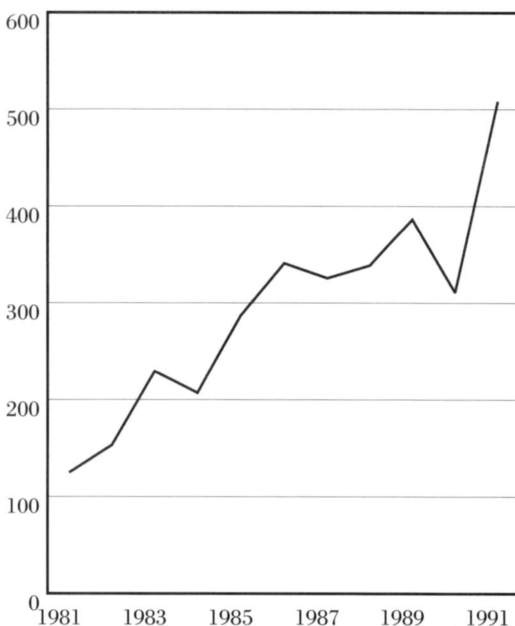

Source: NASDAQ Fact Book & Company Directory, 1992

The Amex Market Value Index

Index Performance

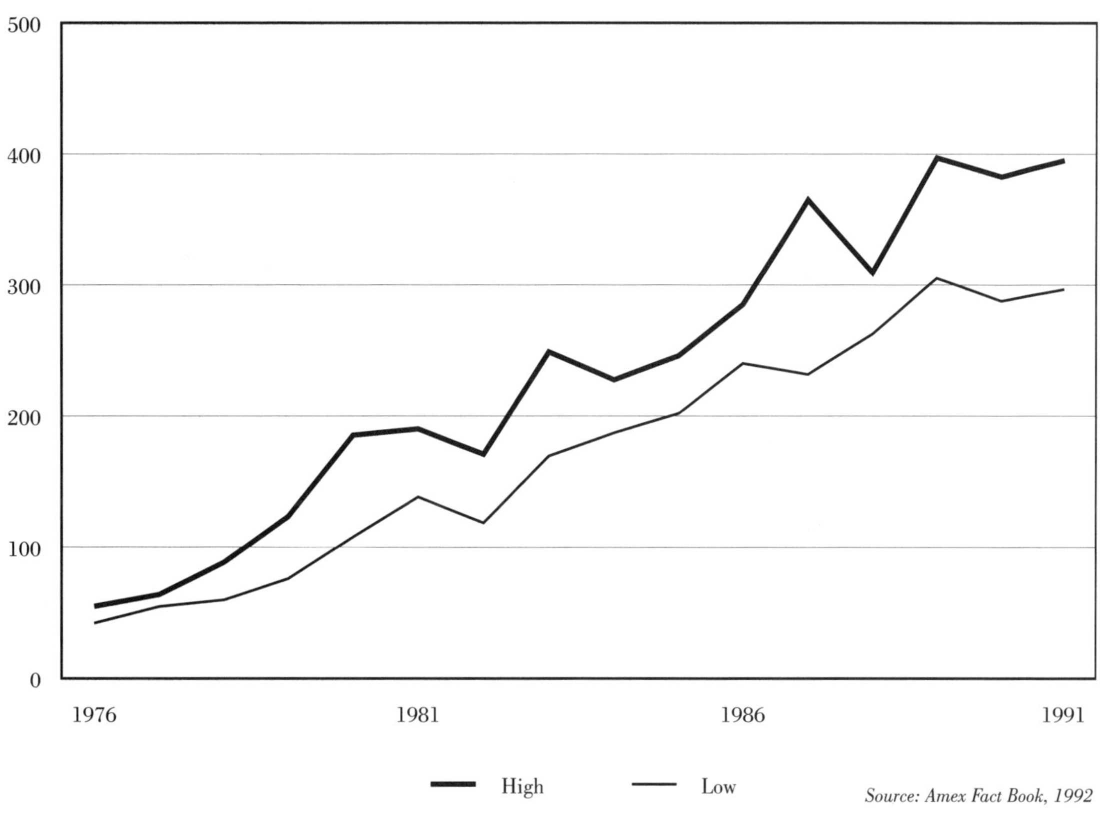

Source: Amex Fact Book, 1992

The Top Reference Sources

Pensions & Investments
Crain Communications ($150 a year)
(312) 649-5240

This newspaper of corporate and institutional investing includes informative articles on a range of investment topics.

Regular features include tracking the changes in the S&P 500, Russell 3000 Stock Index, Morgan Stanley Capital Internationals, and other stock indexes.

P&I also sponsors a number of surveys throughout the year, on topics as varied as the largest real estate investors to the popularity of Ross Perot.

The Wilshire 5000 Equity Index

THE WILSHIRE 5000 EQUITY INDEX measures price movements of all stocks listed on the New York Stock Exchange (85%) and American Stock Exchange (3%) and of most active over-the-counter stocks (12%), or all common equity securities for which pricing is available.

The Wilshire 5000 Equity Index

Source: Wilshire Associates

The Russell 2000 Index

THE RUSSELL 2000 INDEX TRACKS the stock prices of 2,000 small-capitalization companies (average market capitalization $155 million).

The Russell 2000 Index Performance

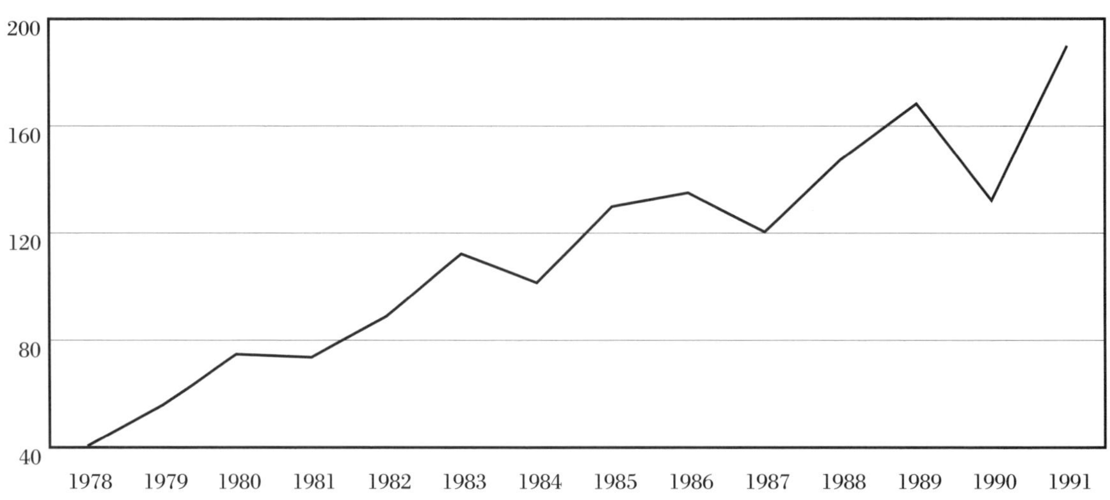

Source: Frank Russell Company, Tacoma, WA

Stock Indexes Performance

1992 Stock Indexes Performance

Index	High	Low	Close	% Change
DJIA	3413.21	3136.58	3301.11	4.17
DJ Equity Index	417.43	371.37	413.29	5.48
S&P 500 Index	441.28	394.50	435.71	4.46
NYSE Composite	242.08	217.92	240.21	4.69
NASDAQ Composite	676.95	547.84	676.95	15.45
Amex	419.00	364.90	399.23	1.06
Value Line	266.85	238.81	266.68	6.95

Source: The Wall Street Journal

Performance of Stock Indexes, Year-End

Year	Dow Jones Industrial Average	S&P 500	NYSE Composite	Amex Market Value	NASDAQ Composite	Value Line
1981	875.00	122.55	71.11	160.32	195.84	137.81
1982	1,046.54	140.64	81.03	170.30	232.41	158.94
1983	1,258.64	164.93	95.18	223.01	278.60	194.35
1984	1,211.57	167.24	96.38	204.26	247.35	177.98
1985	1,546.67	211.28	121.58	246.13	324.93	214.86
1986	1,895.95	242.17	138.58	263.27	348.83	225.62
1987	1,938.83	247.08	138.23	260.35	330.47	201.62
1988	2,168.57	277.72	156.26	306.01	381.38	232.68
1989	2,753.20	353.40	195.04	378.00	454.82	258.78
1990	2,633.66	330.22	180.49	308.11	373.84	195.99
1991	3,168.83	417.09	229.44	395.05	586.34	249.34

Source: Securities Industry Assoc. Fact Book, 1992

Performance of Stock Indexes, Annual Percent Change

Year	Dow Jones Industrial Average	S&P 500	NYSE Composite	Amex Market Value	NASDAQ Composite	Value Line
1981	-9.2	-9.7	-8.7	-8.1	-3.2	-4.4
1982	19.6	14.8	14.0	6.2	18.7	15.3
1983	20.3	17.3	17.5	31.0	19.9	22.3
1984	-3.7	1.4	1.3	8.4	-11.2	-8.4
1985	27.7	26.3	26.1	20.5	31.4	20.7
1986	22.6	14.6	14.0	7.0	7.4	5.0
1987	2.3	2.0	-0.3	-1.1	-5.3	-10.6
1988	11.8	12.4	13.0	17.5	15.4	15.4
1989	27.0	27.3	24.8	23.5	19.3	11.2
1990	-4.3	-6.6	-7.5	-18.5	-17.8	-24.3
1991	20.3	26.3	27.1	28.2	56.8	27.2

Source: Securities Industry Assoc. Fact Book, 1992

PE Ratio by Industry Group

Industry Performance: PE Ratio, Yields

Industry	PE Ratio 1992*	Yield
Publishing & Broadcasting	64	1.67
Beverages	39	1.80
Fuel	35	3.03
Computer Software & Services	29	0.37
Manufacturing	29	1.84
Paper & Forest Products	27	2.70
Transportation	27	1.43
Leisure Time Industries	26	1.08
Chemicals	24	2.75
Service Industries	23	1.38
Automotive	22	1.84
Discount & Fashion Retailing	22	1.10
Medical Products	22	1.39
Drug Retail and Distribution	21	1.44
Housing & Real Estate	21	1.54
Home Furnishings & Appliances	20	1.80
Telecommunications	20	3.90
Aerospace	19	3.06
Drugs & Research	19	2.60
Electrical & Electronics	19	1.70
Food	19	1.85
Health Care Services	18	0.67
Containers & Packaging	17	1.60
Conglomerates	16	2.78
Non-Bank Financial	16	2.46
Computers & Peripherals	15	0.65
Tobacco	15	2.33
Banks	13	2.82
Utilities & Power	5	5.30

**based on Nov. 30 stock price* *Source: Business Week*

Best, Worst Performing Industry Groups

Industry	% Change From 1991
Electronic Semiconductors	64.5
Automobiles	43.7
Entertainment	42.9
Miscellaneous Transportation	40.3
Other Major Banks	40.3
Manufactured Housing	38.2
Hotel/Motel	37.4
Retail–Speciality	33.2
Oil and Gas Drilling	31.7
Money Center Banks	31.7
Long-Distance Telecom	30.8
Life Insurance	30.1
Containers/Paper	-5.3
Alcoholic Beverages	-6.4
Oil Exploration and Production	-8.3
Retail–Speciality Apparel	-8.6
Gold Mining	-9.7
Airlines	-11.5
Coal	-11.6
Housewares	-12.0
Diversified Health Care	-15.5
Medical Products and Supplies	-15.8
Health Care Drugs	-20.8
Hospital Management	-25.4
Computer Systems	-30.1

Source: Standard & Poor's

The Top Reference Sources

Hulbert Financial Digest
Hulbert, $135
(703) 683-5905

There are literally hundreds of newsletters written for investors. In most cases, the primary source of income for the editor is not the stock market, but the revenue from the newsletter.

In order to separate the pros from the pretenders, the Hulbert Financial Digest keeps track of each newsletter's performance. Hulbert's compilations give the regular investor the data needed to choose the best advice available.

Financial Ratios by Industry

Five-Year Average Financial Ratios for Selected Industries

Financial Ratios	Food, Tobacco	Textile Mill Products	Paper, Allied Products	Printing, Publishing	Chemicals, Allied Products
Current Ratio	1.3	2.1	1.6	1.6	1.4
Quick Ratio	0.7	1.2	1.0	1.3	0.9
Long-term Debt to Equity (%)	91.7	98.3	77.5	71.9	50.9
Total Liabilities to Total Assets (%)	64.7	64.5	58.3	58.7	56.5
Total Liabilities to Equity (%)	184.6	184.5	141.6	142.3	130.1
Fixed Assets to Equity (%)	87.9	95.9	142.2	61.8	79.9
Current to Total Liabilities (%)	36.1	36.5	28.3	34.2	42.5
Cash Flow to Total Assets (%)	9.7	8.5	10.3	8.9	11.8
Short-term Debt to Total Assets (%)	7.1	8.0	3.9	4.3	6.7
Long-term Debt to Total Assets (%)	32.1	34.3	31.7	29.6	22.1
Equity to Total Assets (%)	35.3	35.4	41.7	41.3	43.5
Average Collection Period (days)	26.8	49.6	35.8	53.4	51.4
Inventory Turnover (times)	10.0	6.6	10.3	14.6	7.8
Fixed Assets Turnover (times)	4.3	4.3	1.8	4.0	2.7
Total Assets Turnover (times)	1.3	1.4	1.1	1.0	0.9
Profit Margin before Taxes (%)	7.1	3.6	7.4	7.6	11.5
Return on Assets before Taxes (%)	9.6	5.3	8.2	8.0	10.8
Return on Assets after Taxes (%)	6.4	3.4	5.3	4.9	7.6
Return on Equity before Taxes (%)	27.1	14.5	18.7	19.5	24.8
Return on Equity after Taxes (%)	18.1	9.1	12.3	11.9	17.6

Financial Ratios	Industrial Chemicals, Synthetics	Drugs	Petroleum, Coal Products	Rubber, Plastic Products	Stone, Clay, Glass Products
Current Ratio	1.4	1.2	1.0	1.4	1.5
Quick Ratio	0.9	0.8	0.7	0.8	1.0
Long-term Debt to Equity (%)	56.8	27.1	50.2	74.1	103.1
Total Liabilities to Total Assets (%)	57.5	51.9	57.4	65.5	66.5
Total Liabilities to Equity (%)	135.5	108.3	134.7	189.9	201.0
Fixed Assets to Equity (%)	95.8	58.6	128.6	105.7	130.5
Current to Total Liabilities (%)	38.7	55.6	32.4	50.4	33.2
Cash Flow to Total Assets (%)	11.5	15.8	10.5	8.9	6.3
Short-term Debt to Total Assets (%)	5.8	9.4	4.8	11.7	7.7
Long-term Debt to Total Assets (%)	24.1	13.0	21.4	25.6	34.2
Equity to Total Assets (%)	42.5	48.1	42.6	34.5	33.5
Average Collection Period (days)	56.6	48.2	33.9	49.7	51.1
Inventory Turnover (times)	7.9	7.6	15.0	8.0	8.8
Fixed Assets Turnover (times)	2.2	3.1	1.6	4.0	2.3
Total Assets Turnover (times)	0.9	0.9	0.8	1.4	1.0
Profit Margin before Taxes (%)	10.4	19.8	7.1	4.1	2.6
Return on Assets before Taxes (%)	9.4	17.1	6.0	6.0	3.1
Return on Assets after Taxes (%)	6.5	12.8	4.8	4.0	2.0
Return on Equity before Taxes (%)	21.9	35.4	14.0	16.7	8.3
Return on Equity after Taxes (%)	15.1	26.5	11.3	11.2	5.3

Financial Ratios by Industry (cont'd)

Financial Ratios	Primary Metal Industries	Iron, Steel	Nonferrous Metals	Fabricated Metal Products	Machinery, Except Electrical
Current Ratio	1.7	1.7	1.8	1.9	1.8
Quick Ratio	1.0	0.9	1.0	1.1	1.1
Long-term Debt to Equity (%)	81.0	151.7	57.0	58.9	37.3
Total Liabilities to Total Assets (%)	67.7	81.7	55.9	58.2	49.4
Total Liabilities to Equity (%)	210.4	458.5	127.0	139.4	98.0
Fixed Assets to Equity (%)	131.9	246.2	93.8	66.6	47.8
Current to Total Liabilities (%)	35.3	33.0	38.2	46.8	51.0
Cash Flow to Total Assets (%)	7.9	5.6	9.8	9.3	7.7
Short-term Debt to Total Assets (%)	4.8	4.6	5.1	6.8	5.8
Long-term Debt to Total Assets (%)	26.1	27.1	25.1	24.6	18.8
Equity to Total Assets (%)	32.2	18.3	44.1	41.8	50.5
Average Collection Period (days)	46.7	45.3	47.8	52.5	63.7
Inventory Turnover (times)	7.0	6.3	7.7	6.7	5.8
Fixed Assets Turnover (times)	2.8	2.8	2.8	5.1	4.1
Total Assets Turnover (times)	1.2	1.2	1.2	1.4	1.0
Profit Margin before Taxes (%)	4.0	1.8	6.1	5.1	4.7
Return on Assets before Taxes (%)	5.0	2.4	7.3	7.3	4.7
Return on Assets after Taxes (%)	3.5	1.2	5.4	5.0	3.4
Return on Equity before Taxes (%)	15.5	11.7	16.3	17.4	9.1
Return on Equity after Taxes (%)	10.7	5.1	12.1	12.0	6.6

Financial Ratios	Electrical, Electronic Equipment	Transportation Equipment	Motor Vehicles, Equipment	Aircraft, Guided Missiles, Parts	Instruments, Related Products
Current Ratio	1.5	1.3	1.4	1.2	1.7
Quick Ratio	0.9	0.7	1.0	0.4	1.0
Long-term Debt to Equity (%)	35.7	43.7	39.9	44.8	47.4
Total Liabilities to Total Assets (%)	55.4	64.1	58.9	69.7	53.2
Total Liabilities to Equity (%)	124.7	179.0	145.7	230.5	113.8
Fixed Assets to Equity (%)	50.5	70.5	70.6	66.3	53.6
Current to Total Liabilities (%)	59.3	57.9	45.9	72.1	45.5
Cash Flow to Total Assets (%)	8.3	6.9	7.1	6.6	10.2
Short-term Debt to Total Assets (%)	8.7	3.2	2.9	3.2	5.9
Long-term Debt to Total Assets (%)	15.9	15.6	16.2	13.6	22.1
Equity to Total Assets (%)	44.6	35.9	41.1	30.3	46.9
Average Collection Period (days)	57.8	54.8	52.8	51.4	60.8
Inventory Turnover (times)	5.5	5.2	12.9	2.5	5.9
Fixed Assets Turnover (times)	4.8	4.4	4.1	5.1	3.6
Total Assets Turnover (times)	1.1	1.1	1.2	1.0	0.9
Profit Margin before Taxes (%)	5.6	2.9	1.5	4.6	9.0
Return on Assets before Taxes (%)	6.2	3.5	2.5	4.7	8.1
Return on Assets after Taxes (%)	4.2	2.7	2.3	3.2	6.1
Return on Equity before Taxes (%)	13.9	9.2	5.1	15.6	17.1
Return on Equity after Taxes (%)	9.4	7.1	4.8	10.8	13.0

The financial ratios presented here are based on consistent, seasonally adjusted time series. Source data for the series are published in the Census Bureau's Quarterly Financial Report. *Corporations are classified in accordance with the* Standard Industrial Classification Manual, *1987. All corporations included in the report receive a greater portion of gross receipts from manufacturing than from other activities; final industry classification is determined by the major source of receipts within the manufacturing sector.*

Financial Ratios by Industry (cont'd)

In the calculations on the preceding pages, the federal government uses the following formulas. These formulas are valuable in evaluating the financial reports of any business.

Formulas for Financial Ratios

Current Ratio
Current assets/current liabilities. Measures short-term solvency.

Quick Ratio
Current assets less inventories/current liabilities. Measures short-term solvency.

Long-term Debt to Equity
Long-term debt/stockholders' equity. Measures the relationship of long-term debt to equity financing.

Liabilities to Assets
Total liabilities/total assets. Measures the proportion of assets provided by creditors, or the extent of leverage.

Liabilities to Equity
Total liabilities/stockholders' equity.
Measures the relationship of debt to equity financing.

Fixed Assets to Equity
Net property, plant and equipment/stockholders' equity. Indicates the relative investment in operational assets.

Current to Total Liabilities
Current liabilities/total liabilities. Indicates reliance on short-term as opposed to long-term debt.

Cash Flow to Total Assets
Net income after tax plus depreciation/total assets. Measures cash flow relative to assets.

Short-term Debt to Total Assets
Short-term debt/total assets. Indicates the reliance on short-term debt to support the asset structure.

Long-term Debt to Total Assets
Long-term debt/total assets. Indicates the reliance on long-term debt to support the asset structure.

Equity to Total Assets
Stockholders' equity/total assets. Measures the stockholders' share of total assets.

Average Collection Period
Accounts receivable/sales per day. Indicates the relative level and quality of accounts receivable.

Inventory Turnover
Net sales/inventory. Measures the relative efficiency of the use of inventory investment.

Fixed Assets Turnover
Net sales/net property, plant and equipment. Measures the relative efficiency of the use of property, plant and equipment.

Total Assets Turnover
Net sales/total assets. Measures the relative efficiency of the use of all assets.

Profit Margin
Net income/net sales. Measures the percent of profit per sales dollar.

Return on Assets
Net income/total assets. Measures the return on total investment.

Return on Equity
Net income/stockholders' equity. Measures the return on stockholders' share of total investment.

Source: U.S. Department of Commerce, Office of Business Analysis

The Top Reference Sources

The American Almanac
The Reference Press, $14.95
(800) 486-8666

This reference book is based on the *Statistical Abstract of the United States*, which is compiled annually by the Bureau of the Census and published by the U.S. Government Printing Office.

The American Almanac contains standard summary statistics on the social, political, and economic organization of the United States, from college enrollment to crop production to population growth rates. This handsome paperback volume is perhaps more reader-friendly than the *Statistical Abstract* and is also available in trade bookstores.

The Individual Investor

MORE SO THAN IN ANY BULL MARKET in history, individuals were active participants in the 1980's stock surge: between 1980 and mid-1990, the number of individual households investing in the stock market jumped more than 50 percent.

NYSE Individual Shareholders (thousands)

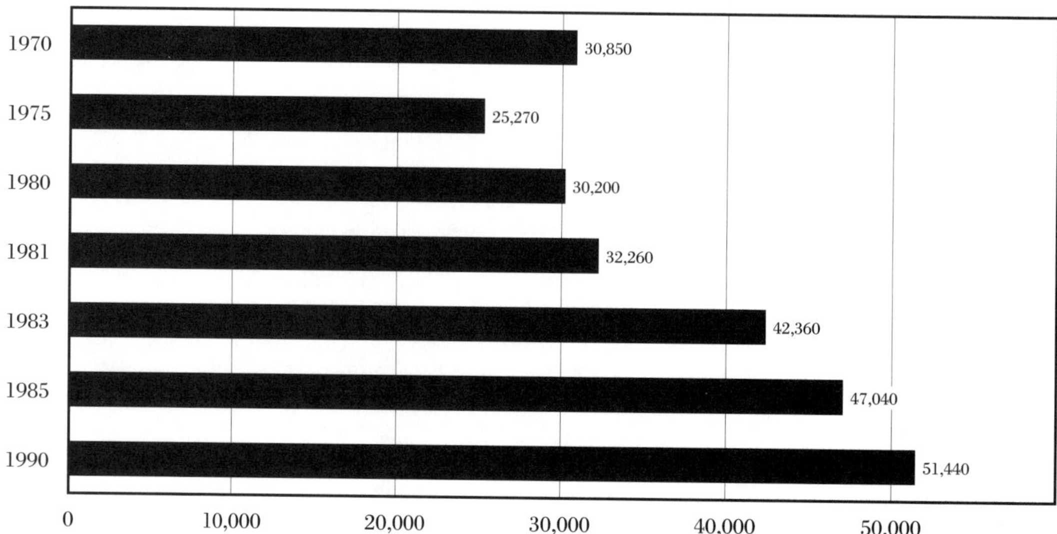

NYSE Individual Shareholders by Profession (thousands)

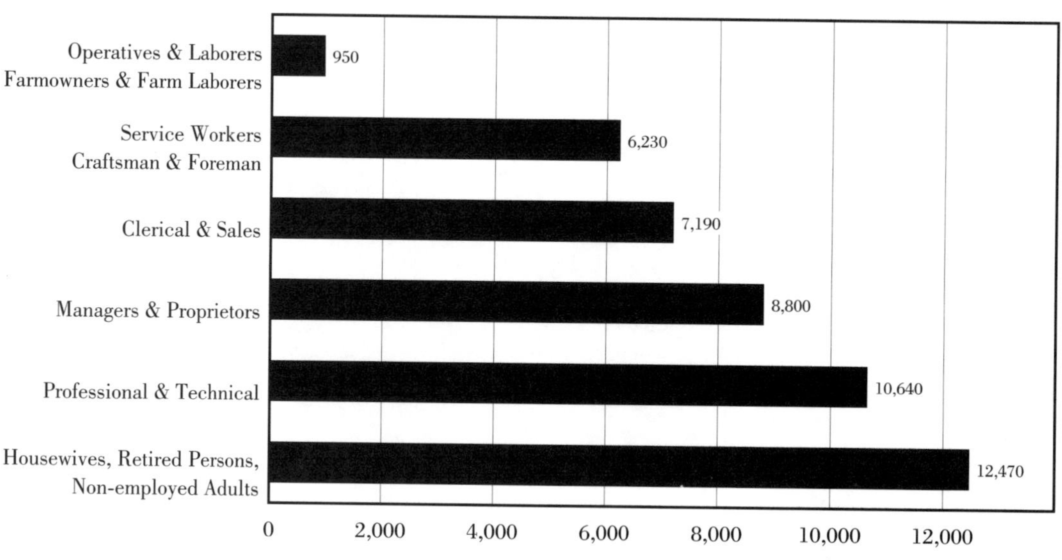

Source: NYSE Fact Book, 1991

Individual Investor (cont'd)

NYSE Shareholders by Age

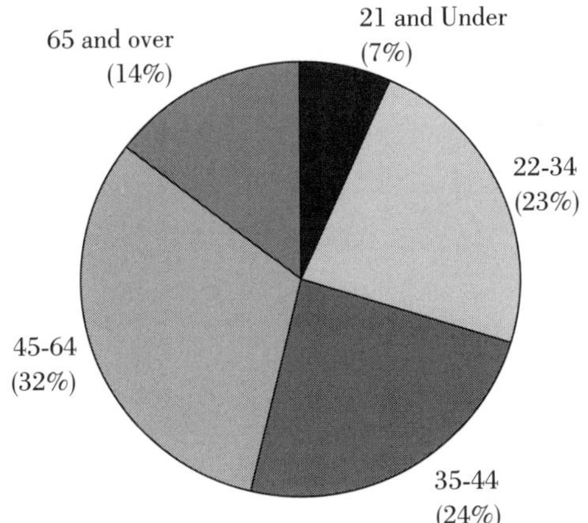

NYSE Shareholders by Education

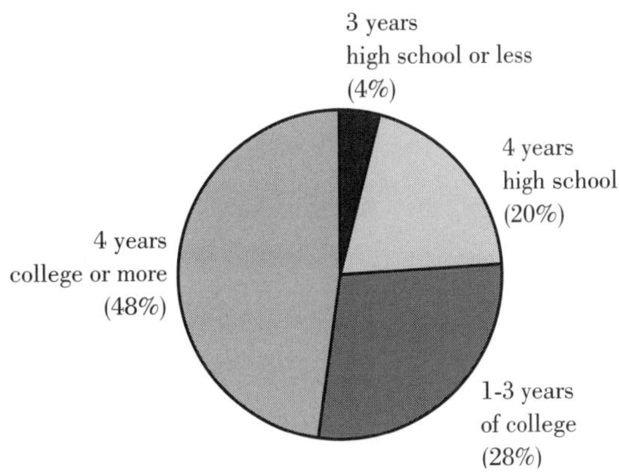

NYSE Shareholders by Portfolio Size ($)

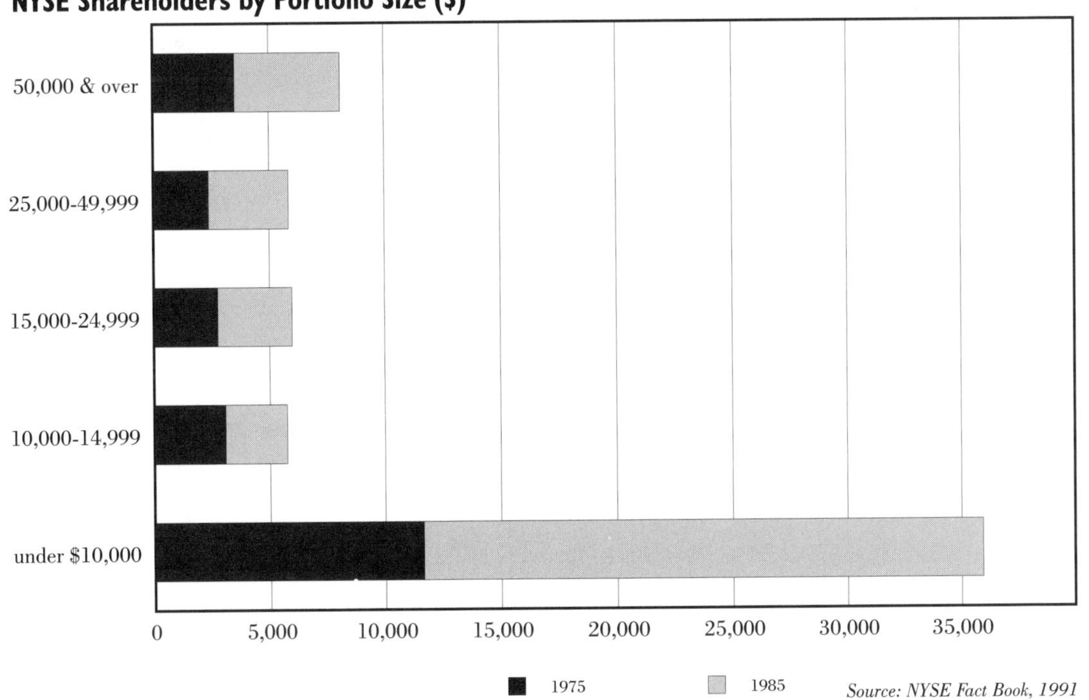

Source: NYSE Fact Book, 1991

Individual Investor (cont'd)

NYSE Shareholders by Metropolitan Region (thousands)

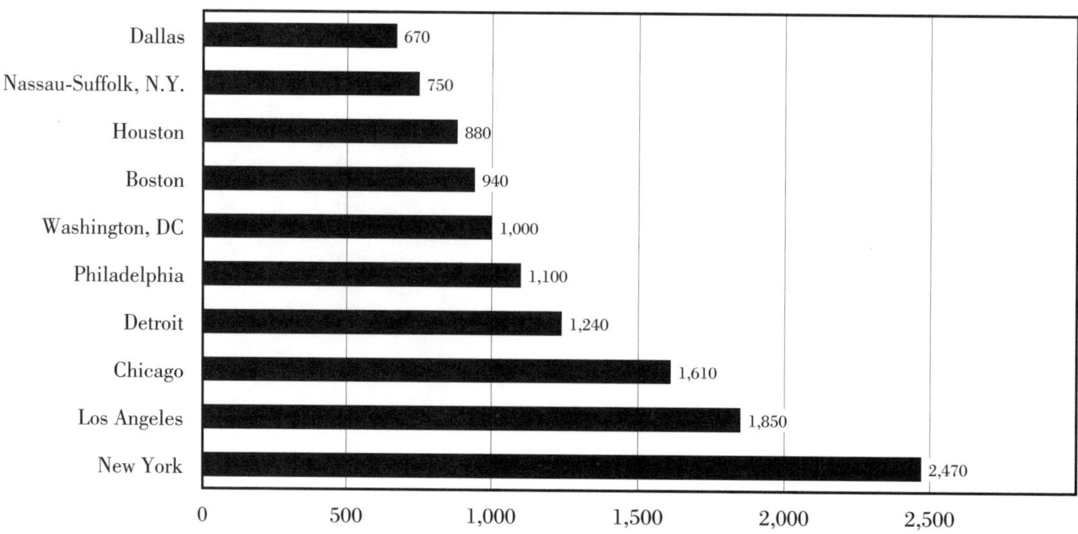

Source: NYSE Fact Book, 1991

The Institutional Investor

Mutual Fund and Equity Assets of Private Pension Funds, 1977 to 1992

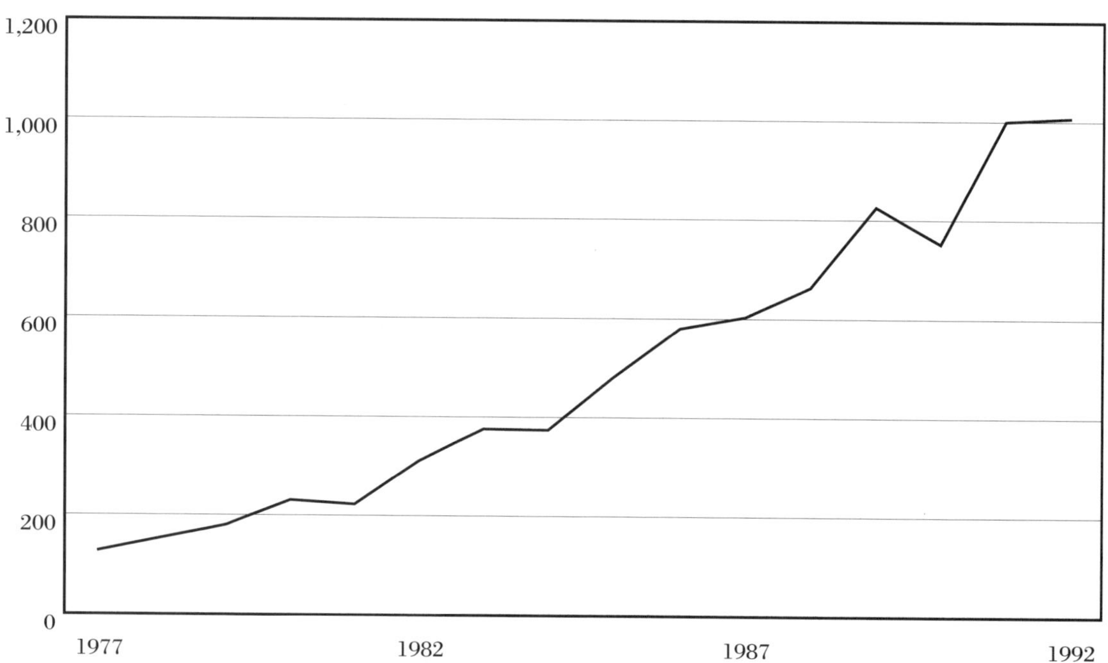

Source: Board of Governors, Federal Reserve System Flow of Funds

The Top Stock Analysts

Stock Research Departments Ranked

Rank	Stock Analyst
1	Donaldson, Lufkin & Jenrette
2	Goldman Sachs
3	Merrill Lynch
4	Lehman Brothers
5	Smith Barney
6	First Boston
6	Morgan Stanley
8	PaineWebber
9	Prudential Securities
10	Kidder Peabody
11*	Salomon Brothers
11	Wertheim Schroder
13	Sanford C. Bernstein
14	Cowen
15	Bear Stearns
16	Dean Witter Reynolds
16*	Oppenheimer
18	C.J. Lawrence
19	Montgomery Securities
20	Alex. Brown & Sons
20	County NatWest Securities
20*	International Strategy & Investment

*=*tie*

The Best Analysts: Stock Pickers

Rank	Name	Industry	Firm
1	Rebecca Barfield	Tobacco	First Boston
2	Thomas Brown	Banks/regional	DLJ
3	Stephen Girsky	Auto and rubber	PaineWebber
4	Robert Hageman	Nonferrous metals	Kidder Peabody
5	Russell Leavitt	Electrical/consumer	Salomon Brothers
6	Charles LoCastro	Chemicals/fertilizers	DLJ
7	George Shapiro	Aerospace	Salomon Brothers
8	Scott Smith	Info. tech./software	DLJ
9	George Thompson	Beverages	Prudential
10	Gary Yablon	Railroads	Wertheim

The Best Analysts: Written Reports

Rank	Name	Industry	Firm
1	Kenneth Abramowitz	Health care, medical supplies, tech.	Sanford C. Bernstein
2	Marc I. Cohen	Tobacco	Goldman Sachs
3	Stephen Girsky	Tire and rubber	PaineWebber
4	Jonathan Gra	Gov't sponsored enterprises, S&Ls	Sanford C. Bernstein
5	Emanuel Goldman	Tobacco	PaineWebber
6	Thomas Hanley	Banks/regional	First Boston
7	Daniel Lemaitre	Med. supplies and tech.	Cowen
8	Ernest Liu	Utilities	Goldman Sachs
9	Joel Price	Coal	DLJ
10	Barry Willman	Info.tech./mid.sys.	Sanford C. Bernstein

Source: Institutional Investor, 1992 All-America Research Team

Top Stock Analysts (cont'd)

The Best Analysts: Overall Service

Rank	Name	Industry	Firm
1	Barry Abramson	Utilities	Prudential
2	Marc D. Cohen	Coal	Kidder Peabody
3	Stephen Girsky	Tire and rubber	PaineWebber
4	Craig Kloner	Trucking	Goldman Sachs
5	Judah Kraushaar	Banks/money center	Merrill Lynch
6	John Phizackerley	Gold mining	Lehman Brothers
7	Daniel Rheingold	Telecom. services	Morgan Stanley
8	Daniel Roling	Coal	Merrill Lynch
9	Stanley Rubin	Electrical equipment	Merrill Lynch
10	Linda Runyon	Cellular	Kidder Peabody

Winners on the All-Star Research Team

Industry	Name	Firm
Advertising Agencies	Susan Decker	DLJ
Aerospace	George Shapiro	Salomon Brothers
Airlines	Paul Karos	First Boston
Autos & Auto Parts	Stephen Girsky	PaineWebber
Banks/Money Center	Thomas Hanley	First Boston
Banks/Regional	Thomas Brown	DLJ
Beverages	Emanuel Goldman	PaineWebber
Biotechnology	Teena Lerner	Lehman Brothers
Broadcasting	Dennis Leibowitz	DLJ
Building	Gregory Nejmeh	Lehman Brothers
Cellular	Dennis Leibowitz	DLJ
Chemicals	William Young	DLJ
Chemicals/Fertilizers	Charles LoCastro	DLJ
Chemicals/Specialty	Katharine Plourde	DLJ
Coal	Joel Price	DLJ
Cosmetics	Joseph Kozloff	Smith Barney
Defense Electronics	Elliott Rogers	Cowen & Co.
Electrical Consumer	Robert Cornell	Lehman Brothers
Electrical Equipment	David Altman	Goldman Sachs
Electronics	James Barlage	Smith Barney
Electronics/Connectors	Jerry Labowitz	Merrill Lynch
Engineering and Construction	Jeanne Gallagher Terrile	Merrill Lynch
Financial Services	Lawrence Eckenfelder	Prudential Securities
Food	Nomi Ghez	Goldman Sachs
Gaming and Lodging	John Rohs	Wertheim Schroder
Gold Mining	John Tumazos	DLJ
Gov't Sponsored Enterprises	Eric Hemel	Morgan Stanley
Health Care Services	Kenneth Abramowitz	Sanford C. Bernstein
Household Services	Jack Salzman	Goldman Sachs
Info. Tech./Mainframes	Steven Milunovich	Morgan Stanley
Info.Tech./Mid-Range Sys.	Laura Conigliaro	Prudential Securities
Info.Tech./PCs and Peripherals	Daniel Benton	Goldman Sachs
Info.Tech./Software and Comp. Svcs	Richard Sherlund	Goldman Sachs
Insurance/Life	Joan Zief	Merrill Lynch
Insurance/Non-Life	David Seifer	DLJ
Leisure Time	Harold Vogel	Merrill Lunch
Machinery	John McGinty	First Boston

Source: Institutional Investor, 1992 All-America Research Team

Top Stock Analysts (cont'd)

Industry	Name	Firm
Medical Supplies & Technology	Daniel Lemaitre	Cowen & Co.
Natural Gas	Curt Launer	DLJ
Nonferrous Metals	John Tumazos	DLJ
Oil/Domestic	Frank Knuettel	Prudential Securities
Oil/Exploration	Thomas Driscoll	Salomon Brothers
Oil/International	Bryan Jacoboski	PaineWebber
Oil Svcs. & Equipment	James Carroll	PaineWebber
Packaging	Cornelius Thornton	Goldman Sachs
Paper & Forest Products	George Adler	Smith Barney
Pharmaceuticals	Christina Heuer	Smith Barney
Photography & Elecronic Imaging	B. Alexander Henderson	Prudential Securities
Pollution Control	William Genco	Merrill Lynch
Publishing	Kevin Gruneich	First Boston
Railroads	Joel Price	DLJ
Restuarants	John Rohs	Wertheim Schroder
Retailing	Joseph Ellis	Goldman Sachs
Retailing/Food & Drug Chains	Debra Levin	Morgan Stanley
Retailing/Specialty	Joseph Ellis	Goldman Sachs
Savings & Loans	Jerry Gitt	Merrill Lynch
Steel	Michelle Applebaum	Salomon Brothers
Telecommunication Equipment	Jospeh Bellace	Merrill Lynch
Telecommunication Svcs.	Robert Morris III	Goldman Sachs
Textiles and Apparel	Deborah Bronston	Prudential Securities
Tire and Rubber	Stephen Girsky	PaineWebber
Tobacco	Rebecca Barfield	First Boston
Trucking	Craig Kloner	Goldman Sachs
Utilities	Ernest Liu	Goldman Sachs
Accounting	Patricia McConnell	Bear Stearns
Economics	Edward Hyman, Jr.	ISI Group
Market Timing	Robert Farrell	Merrill Lynch
Multi-Industry	David Moore	DLJ
Portfolio Strategy	Greg Smith	Prudential Securities
Small Growth Companies	L. Keith Mullins	Smith Barney
Quantative Research	Elaine Garzarelli	Lehman Brothers

Source: Institutional Investor, 1992 All-America Research Team

Recommended Resource

Institutional Investor
88 Madison Ave.
New York, NY 10022
(212) 303-3300

Almanac Fact

The Chicago Board Options Exchange is the world's largest options marketplace, accounting for approximately 92 percent of the U.S. options market share in 1992.

Source: CBOE

Corporate Activity

Announced U.S. Mergers and Acquisitions

Announcement Date	No. of Deals	Value ($ millions)
1982	1,931	56,035.1
1983	3,387	96,222.7
1984	3,619	169,652.5
1985	2,257	187,006.5
1986	3,114	212,976.1
1987	3,303	208,645.7
1988	3,894	335,680.8
1989	5,448	292,361.0
1990	5,640	178,939.8
1991	5,211	137,880.9
1992	5,476	128,351.4
INDUSTRY TOTALS	43,280	2,003,752.4

The Ten Largest Completed U.S. Merger & Acquisitions Deals, 1984 to 1991

Year Effective	Acquirer	Acquired	Attitude	Value ($ millions)
1989	Kohlberg Kravis Roberts & Co.	RJR Nabisco	Hostile	30,598.8
1990	Time Inc.	Warner Communications	Friendly	14,110.0
1988	Philip Morris Inc.	Kraft Inc.	Poison Pill	13,444.0
1984	Standard Oil of California	Gulf Oil Corp.	Friendly	13,400.0
1989	Bristol Myers Co.	Squibb Corp.	Friendly	12,094.0
1984	Texaco Inc.	Getty Oil Co.	Friendly	10,120.0
1989	Beecham Group PLC	SmithKline Beckman Group	Friendly	7,922.0
1991	AT&T	NCR Corp.	Hostile	7,893.4
1987	BP America Inc.	The Standard Oil Co.	Friendly	7,857.7
1991	Matsushita Electric Industrial	MCA Inc.	Friendly	7,406.0

The Ten Largest U.S. Merger & Acquisitions Deals Completed in 1992

Date Effective	Acquirer	Acquired	Attitude	Value ($ millions)
4/22/92	BankAmerica Corp	Security Pacific Corp.	Friendly	4,212.7
3/3/92	Altus Finance/Credit Lyonnais	Executive Life Insurance Co-Junk Bond Portfolio	Friendly	3,250.0
4/30/92	Bell Atlantic Corp.	Metro Mobile CTS Inc.	Friendly	2,464.0
6/5/92	Northeast Utilities	Public Service Co. of New Hampshire	Friendly	2,300.0
7/6/92	Shareholders	Praxair (a unit of Union Carbide)	Friendly	1,994.0
6/26/92	Time Warner Inc.	American Television & Communications Corp.	Friendly	1,699.5
9/30/92	American Re	American Re-Insurance Co. /Aetna Life & Casualty	Friendly	1,430.0
10/1/92	Emerson Electric Co.	Fisher Controls International	Friendly	1,275.0
3/16/92	Society Corp.	AmeriTrust Corp.	Friendly	1,186.0
10/30/92	Pennzoil Co.	Chevron PBC Inc.	Friendly	1,170.0

Source: Securities Data Company

Corporate Activity (cont'd)

Announced U.S. LBOs

Year	No. of Deals	Value ($ millions)
1982	22	2,343.8
1983	63	9,191.9
1984	122	13,810.4
1985	166	28,055.1
1986	245	39,161.3
1987	235	42,894.1
1988	309	93,551.7
1989	329	35,164.5
1990	204	12,031.7
1991	225	6,239.8
1992	239	10,182.7
INDUSTRY TOTALS	2,159	292,627.0

Announced U.S. Divestitures

Year	No. of Deals	Value ($ millions)
1982	441	11,622.2
1983	1,038	33,511.8
1984	1,140	49,463.6
1985	931	57,527.2
1986	1,205	79,766.6
1987	1,136	83,497.8
1988	1,446	120,811.1
1989	2,082	101,546.9
1990	2,251	78,845.0
1991	2,183	57,295.1
1992	2,090	57,411.5
INDUSTRY TOTALS	15,943	731,298.7

Source: Securities Data Company

S&P 500 Company Activity

Activity	1988	1989	1990	1991
Mergers and Acquisitions among companies in the index	9	10	8	5
Acquisition by company outside the index	14	15	2	2
Restructurings	1	4	2	1
Bankruptcies	3	0	2	3
Total Number of company changes	27	30	14	12

Source: S&P 500 Directory, 1992

The Top Reference Sources

Standard & Poor's Register of Corporations, Directors and Executives
Standard & Poor's
(212) 208-8702

Published since 1928, this annual, three-volume reference provides information on the nation's major corporations and their key staff.

Volume 1 profiles more than 55,000 corporations in alphabetical order. Volume 2 gives brief biographies of directors and executives. Volume 3 contains indexes by geography and industry, among others. Supplements are published in April, July, and October.

Securities and Exchange Commission

DURING 1991, THE SEC APPEARED in 50 reorganization cases filed under Chapter 11 of the Bankruptcy Code involving companies with aggregated stated assets of almost $27 billion and about 330,000 public investors. Counting these new cases, the agency was a party in 186 Chapter 11 cases during the year. In these cases, the stated assets totalled approximately $85 billion and involved about 1.1 billion public investors. Thirty-seven cases were concluded through confirmation of a plan of reorganization, dismissal, or liquidation, leaving 149 cases in which the Commission was a party at year-end.

Recommended Resource

United States Securities and Exchange Commission Annual Report
Superintendent of Documents
P.O. Box 371954
Pittsburgh, PA 15250
(202) 783-3238

Full Disclosure Reviews: Corporate Filings

Major Filing Review	1987	1988	1989	1990	1991
SECURITIES ACT REGISTRATIONS					
New Issuers	1,949	1,444	1,177	895	630
Repeat Issuers	775	640	604	635	776
Post-Effective Amendments	707	1,045	929	708	583
ANNUAL REPORTS					
Full Reviews	1,389	2,166	1,949	1,129	1,557
Full Financial Reviews	60	567	388	292	712
Tender Offers (14D-1)	201	254	188	95	37
Going Private Schedules	230	276	176	108	68
Contested Proxy Solicitations	65	93	84	75	65
MERGER/GOING PRIVATE					
Proxy Statements	248	314	291	240	188
Other	2,563	790	428	351	374

SEC Total Enforcement Actions Initiated

Type of Action	1987	1988	1989	1990	1991
TOTAL	303	252	310	304	320
Civil Injunctive Actions	144	125	140	186	171
Administrative Proceedings	146	109	155	111	138
Civil and Criminal Contempt Proceedings	13	17	15	7	10
Reports of Investigation	0	1	0	0	1

Source: U.S. Securities and Exchange Commission, Annual Report, 1991

The Top Reference Sources

Moody's Industrial Manual
Moody's Investors Service
(212) 553-1623

Moody's annual bound volume of their twice-weekly publication covers U.S., Canadian, and foreign companies listed on U.S. exchanges.

The listings include corporate history, subsidiaries, principal facilities, products, and financial data.

An excellent resource for broad background data on a wide array of companies.

Securities and Exchange Commission (cont'd)

Enforcement Cases Initiated by the SEC: By Program Area and Percentage

Program Area in Which a Civil Action or Administrative Proceeding Was Initiated	Total	% of Total Cases
SECURITIES OFFERING CASES		29
Non-Regulated Entity	40	
Regulated Entity	53	
TOTAL	93	
BROKER-DEALER CASES		22
Back Office	10	
Fraud Against Consumer	43	
Municipal Securities	2	
Other	14	
TOTAL	69	
ISSUER FINANCIAL STATEMENT AND REPORTING CASES		14
Issuer Financial Disclosure	40	
Issuer Reporting Other	4	
Issuer Related Party Transactions	7	
TOTAL	45	
Insider Trading Cases	34	11
Market Manipulation Cases	29	9
OTHER REGULATED ENTITY CASES		
Investment Advisors	14	
Investment Companies	6	
Total Other Regulated Entity Cases	20	7
Contempt Proceedings	10	3
Corporate Control Cases	6	2
Fraud Against Regulated Entities	4	1
Miscellaneous Disclosure/Reporting	3	1
DELINQUENT FILINGS		
Issuer Reporting	6	
Forms 3 & 4	1	
Total Delinquent Filing Cases	7	2
GRAND TOTAL	320	101

Note: the percentages add up to more than 100 due to the rounding of figures

SEC Litigation and Legal Activities: Increase in Matters Handled, 1990 to 1991

Action Taken	1990	1991	% Increase
Litigation Matters Opened	185	263	42
Litigation Matters Closed	126	247	96
Adjudication			
Cases Received	22	30	36
Cases Completed	18	39	117
Legislation			
Testimony	18	29	56
Comments to Congress and Others	26	29	12
Corporate Reorganization			
Disclosure Statements Reviewed	93	152	63
Disclosure Statements Commented On	57	92	61
Conduct Regulation Matters	87	249	186

Source: U.S. Securities and Exchange Commission, Annual Report, 1991

Bonds

BONDS ARE LONG-TERM debt obligations issued typically in $1,000 or $5,000 denominations by companies, governments (including the U.S. Treasury), municipalities, or federal agencies. The interest paid on these loans–the coupon or coupon rate–depends upon the amount of risk assumed by the buyer, the loan's backing, and the overall economic climate at the time of issuance. The range of rates offered at any given time is determined in relation to benchmark interest rates set by the U.S. Federal Reserve. But from the date of issuance, a bond's rate of interest remains fixed until maturity. While the prime interest rate may greatly fluctuate over the term of the bond, the rate of interest on the bond remains the same, providing a sure, steady source of income.

The term, repayment schedule, and security of bonds vary widely depending upon the financial needs of the issuer and the bond's intended use, as well as by the type of issuance.

Interest and Bond Yields, 1981 to 1992

Period	U.S. Treasury 3-Month Bills	U.S. Treasury 3-yr. Maturity	U.S. Treasury 10-yr. Maturity	High-Grade Muni Bonds	Corp. AAA Bonds	Prime Comm'l Paper	Discount Rate	Prime Rate	New-Home Mortge. Yields
1981	14.029	14.44	13.91	11.23	14.17	14.76	13.42	18.87	14.70
1982	10.686	12.92	13.00	11.57	13.79	11.89	11.02	14.86	15.14
1983	8.63	10.45	11.10	9.47	12.04	8.89	8.50	10.79	12.57
1984	9.58	11.89	12.44	10.15	12.71	10.16	8.80	12.04	12.38
1985	7.48	9.64	10.62	9.18	11.37	8.01	7.69	9.93	11.55
1986	5.98	7.06	7.68	7.38	9.02	6.39	6.33	8.33	10.17
1987	5.82	7.68	8.39	7.73	9.38	6.85	5.66	8.21	9.31
1988	6.69	8.26	8.85	7.76	9.71	7.68	6.20	9.32	9.19
1989	8.12	8.55	8.49	7.24	9.26	8.80	6.93	10.87	10.13
1990	7.51	8.26	8.55	7.25	9.32	7.95	6.98	10.01	10.05
1991	5.42	6.82	7.86	6.89	8.77	5.85	5.45	8.46	9.32
Nov	4.60	5.90	7.42	6.64	8.48	4.93	5.00	8.00	8.64
Dec	4.12	5.39	7.09	6.63	8.31	4.49	4.50	7.50	8.53
1992									
Jan	3.84	5.40	7.03	6.41	8.20	4.06	3.50	6.50	8.49
Feb	3.84	5.72	7.34	6.67	8.29	4.13	3.50	6.50	8.65
Mar	4.05	6.18	7.54	6.69	8.35	4.38	3.50	6.50	8.51
Apr	3.81	5.93	7.48	6.64	8.33	4.13	3.50	6.50	8.58
May	3.66	5.81	7.39	6.57	8.28	3.97	3.50	6.50	8.59
June	3.70	5.60	7.26	6.50	8.22	3.99	3.50	6.50	8.43
July	3.28	4.91	6.84	6.12	8.07	3.53	3.50	6.50	8.00
Aug	3.14	4.72	6.59	6.08	7.95	3.44	3.00	6.00	8.00
Sept	2.97	4.42	6.42	6.24	7.92	3.26	3.00	6.00	7.93
Oct	2.84	4.64	6.59	6.38	7.99	3.33	3.00	6.00	7.90
Nov	3.14	5.14	6.87	6.35	8.10	3.67	3.00	6.00	NA
1992 Week End:									
Nov 28	3.27	5.24	6.86	6.27	8.06	3.79	3.00	6.00	NA
Dec 5	3.31	5.35	6.91	6.28	8.06	3.86	3.00	6.00	NA
Dec.12	3.29	5.19	6.77	6.25	8.00	3.73	3.00	6.00	NA
Dec 19	3.26	5.25	6.79	6.29	7.99	3.71	3.00	6.00	NA

Source: Economic Indicators, The Council of Economic Advisers

Corporate and Taxable Bonds

CORPORATIONS ISSUE VARIOUS TYPES of debt securities to fund their operations and investments. Their short-term needs are filled by the issuance of commercial paper which can be bought only in $100,000 denominations with a maturity of 90 to 180 days. For the longer term of 20 to 30 years, companies issue bonds in denominations of $1,000 which can be classified by length of time until maturity, and by the type of security put up to secure the bond.

Debenture Bonds
A loan not secured by any particular asset but by the company's unpledged assets. The most common type of taxable bond, backed only by the company's word and financial capacity to meet regular principal and interest payments. High-yield and convertible bonds are examples of debentures.

High-Yield (Junk) Bonds
An unsecured loan rated higher in risk because of the uncertain financial strength of the issuing company; graded less than BBB.

Convertible Bond
A loan that can be converted at the owner's discretion from company debt into a designated amount of equity, e.g. from bonds into stock shareholdings.

Collateral Trust Bond
A loan backed by securities, other companies' stocks and bonds, held by the issuing company.

Mortgage Bond
A loan secured by a piece of real estate or fixed property, such as a factory, warehouse, or laboratory.

Equipment Trust Certificate
A loan secured by movable equipment, such as a fleet of trucks or a locomotive.

Income Bond
A loan that is repaid only when the company operates at a profit.

Senior and Junior or Subordinated Bonds
Loans that are classified by the issuer according to their seniority. Repayment to senior debt holders takes priority if the company enters into financial trouble.

Sinking Fund Bond
A loan that is retired through partial payments over time until final maturity. Repayment usually commences five to ten years after the date of issue.

Zero-Coupon Bonds
A corporate, municipal, or treasury bond that is sold at a deeply discounted price, at a fraction of its par value, but pays no interest until final maturity, typically decades from the date of issue.

Secondary markets for corporate bonds are made by investors trading primarily on the New York Stock Exchange and on the American Stock Exchange.

In January, 1993, the corporate bond market set a record for new issuance: $37.1 million total issues for the month, including sales by corporations and government agencies.

U.S. Domestic Corporate Investment Grade Debt, Sales Volume

Year	Proceeds ($ millions)	No. of Issues
1975	32,076.2	470
1976	27,547.0	382
1977	20,806.5	303
1978	16,119.7	208
1979	21,696.4	213
1980	34,038.2	363
1981	30,174.8	321
1982	32,578.1	417
1983	26,974.1	314
1984	33,531.1	307
1985	56,691.6	489
1986	109,165.0	829
1987	82,383.1	645
1988	77,040.6	515
1989	82,043.0	543
1990	77,240.1	539
1991	145,328.6	1,296
1992	182,531.1	1,322
INDUSTRY TOTALS	1,087,965.3	9,476

Source: Securities Data Company

Corporate and Taxable Bonds (cont'd)

U.S. Domestic Non-Investment Grade Debt, Sales Volume

Year	Proceeds ($ millions)	No. of Issues
1975	142.7	18
1976	700.4	30
1977	1,030.8	61
1978	1,588.2	83
1979	1,390.8	56
1980	1,374.2	45
1981	1,247.2	34
1982	2,466.7	53
1983	7,406.4	95
1984	14,002.7	131
1985	14,190.8	175
1986	31,905.6	226
1987	28,140.1	190
1988	27,718.8	160
1989	25,091.6	129
1990	1,394.9	10
1991	9,971.0	48
1992	37,942.0	235
INDUSTRY TOTALS	207,704.9	1,779

Source: Securities Data Company

Mortgage-Backed Bonds

Mortgage-Backed Securities, Sales Volume

Year	Proceeds ($ millions)	No. of Issues
1975	50.0	1
1976	74.6	1
1977	1,338.9	13
1978	1,251.7	19
1979	1,476.8	24
1980	500.2	8
1981	512.6	12
1982	1,264.8	37
1983	8,566.9	66
1984	12,069.2	117
1985	19,581.3	212
1986	57,827.0	372
1987	82,542.8	470
1988	98,866.8	621
1989	110,596.1	464
1990	133,996.5	474
1991	250,161.6	729
1992	377,801.2	999
INDUSTRY TOTALS	1,158,479.0	4,639

Source: Securities Data Company

Convertible Bonds

U.S. Domestic Convertible Bonds, Sales Volume

Year	Proceeds ($ millions)	No. of Issues
1975	1,490.5	21
1976	932.3	25
1977	495.7	17
1978	393.4	19
1979	724.1	31
1980	4,359.6	98
1981	4,652.9	92
1982	3,201.0	67
1983	6,120.3	113
1984	4,093.7	66
1985	7,484.6	139
1986	10,115.9	207
1987	9,863.6	148
1988	3,136.1	36
1989	5,519.9	63
1990	4,756.5	34
1991	7,478.6	49
1992	7,036.2	65
INDUSTRY TOTALS	81,855.1	1,290

Source: Securities Data Company

U.S. Government Securities

GUARANTEED BY THE U.S. GOVERNMENT and exempt from state and local income taxes, these securities are some of the safest you can purchase. But because of the near-absence of default risk they offer lower interest rates than do corporate issues. Government issues are actively traded on the over-the-counter market after their initial sale to large investors through an auction conducted by the Treasury.

Treasury Bills
Issued at a discount and repaid at face value at final maturity, T-bills pay no interest. They have the shortest maturation of all government securities: 91, 182 or 364 days. $10,000 minimum face value investment.

Treasury Notes
Maturing in the range of two to ten years, T-notes yield a steady stream of interest. $1,000 minumum purchase; most notes are sold in $5,000 denominations.

Treasury Bonds
Long-term government debt bearing interest, T-bonds generally mature in ten years or longer. Like T-notes they come in denominations of $1,000, $5,000, $10,000, $100,000, and $1,000,000 and are popular with traders and institutional investors. They are highly sensitive to interest-rate movements.

Zero-Coupon Government Bonds
Long-term government debt bearing interest, with all interest paid in a lump sum at the end of the term. Similar to other zero coupon bonds but tax free.

Flower Bonds
This limited series of bonds (the last issue was in 1971) can be redeemed at the time of the holder's death for the payment of estate taxes.

U.S. Savings Bonds
Unlike Treasury bills, notes, and bonds, U.S. Savings Bonds cannnot be traded in a secondary market. They are sold mostly to individual investors who buy them directly from the Treasury. The most popular variety of U.S. Savings Bond sells at a 50% discount from its face value and is entirely free of commissions.

U.S. Government Securities (cont'd)

Through the sale of securities, the U.S. Government has created more than $200 billion in debt yearly since 1985. Daily volume in U.S. Treasury Securities is up to $100 billion.

Federal Agency Issues

While the federal government does not back all these issues, they do authorize a variety of their agencies to issue debentures and notes to finance their operations, including:

- U.S. Post Office
- The Tennessee Valley Authority
- The Export-Import Bank
- The Federal Home Loan Mortgage Corporation (FHLMC or Freddie Mac)
- The Federal Intermediate Credit Bank (FICB)
- The Federal National Mortgage Association (FNMA or Fannie Mae)
- The Government National Mortgage Association (GNMA or GinnieMae).

As a group, these securities offer a higher rate of interest than direct U.S. Treasury obligations, even though the majority are backed by the full faith and credit of the U.S. Government. Certain issues are also exempt from state and local taxes.

Federal Agency Issues, Sales Volume

Year	Proceeds ($ millions)	No. of Issues
1975	3,795.1	35
1976	3,940.0	44
1977	4,419.2	38
1978	3,814.5	22
1979	2,672.9	19
1980	1,335.4	10
1981	3,689.5	25
1982	5,074.1	30
1983	3,057.3	20
1984	5,644.2	22
1985	5,306.4	27
1986	8,756.0	49
1987	7,392.2	48
1988	15,633.2	71
1989	27,059.3	106
1990	28,587.1	173
1991	45,245.2	273
1992	89,189.8	546
INDUSTRY TOTALS	264,611.6	1,558

Source: Securities Data Company

Municipal Bonds

ISSUED BY STATES, CITIES, TOWNS, COUNTIES, and their agencies, municipal bonds (often called munis or tax exempts) are free of federal tax and often from state and local tax in their state of issuance. A new municipal issue subject to federal tax was created out of The Tax Reform Act of 1986. Like corporate issues, municipal bonds are categorized by the form of collateral used to back them and to raise their revenue.

General Obligation Bonds (GO Bonds)
GO Bonds represent the largest group of municipal issues. Paid back by general revenues–secured by the government's tax revenue and its ability to impose new taxes–these bonds are only slightly less secure than similar government issues. By law, the government is required to levy taxes in order to pay their bondholders.

Revenue Bonds
Used in the development of toll roads, bridges, or tunnels, or any revenue-producing projects, these bonds are paid off by the revenues generated from the specific development. They typically offer a higher rate of interest than GO Bonds, as payment is more narrowly backed.

Municipal Bonds (cont'd)

Industrial Development Bonds
These specific bonds are issued by state and local governnments to fund the construction of new industrial parks, plants, or any development which might attract businesses and increase leasing revenue for the state. The financial strength of the private businesses involved in the project generally determines the quality of the bond. Most are now taxable under The Tax Reform Act of 1986.

Redevelopment Agency Bonds
Used for the construction of commercial projects, these bonds are secured by part of the property taxes levied on the development.

Airport Bonds
One type of airport bond is used toward, and secured by, general operations and usage. Another, much riskier bond, is tied specifically to facilities leased by individual airlines and is secured by the leasing contract itself.

Bond ratings are listed in Moody's Bond Record and Standard and Poor's Bond Guide. Weekly newsletters, Moody's Bond Survey, and CreditWeek (a publication of Standard and Poor's) offer more detailed information of select issues.

As newspapers and financial journals do not carry complete information on municipal bonds, current price, and trading data, investors must turn to specific bond publications to track these issues.

The bible of bond issuance, pricing, and trading is the annual publication *Moody's Municipal & Government Manual*. Organized by state, city, town, and political subdivision, the compendium lists all bond issues (including as well information on Federal Agency issues) and offers information critical to bond buyers, from state tax revenues and census figures to statistics on attendance at local schools. Updates to *Moody's Municipal* are published in a semi-weekly newsletter which lists new and changed issues as well as call notices.

Recommended Resources

The Blue List
Standard & Poor's
65 Broadway
New York, NY 10004
(212) 770-4000

The Daily Bond Buyer
The Weekly Bond Buyer
1 State Street Plaza
New York, NY 10004
(212) 943-8200

Bond Week
488 Madison Avenue
New York, NY 10022
(212) 303-3300

Short-Term Municipal Bond Issues, Sales Volume

Year	Proceeds ($ millions)	No. of Issues
1980	8,762.6	286
1981	13,790.8	464
1982	16,149.8	511
1983	18,870.4	541
1984	21,092.8	711
1985	21,141.4	790
1986	21,115.8	1,315
1987	19,752.1	1,199
1988	22,302.0	1,604
1989	28,834.1	2,351
1990	34,110.8	2,811
1991	43,159.9	3,611
1992	41,636.0	3,112
INDUSTRY TOTALS	310,718.5	19,306

Long-Term Municipal Bond Issues, Sales Volume

Year	Proceeds ($ millions)	No. of Issues
1980	41,247.3	1,411
1981	40,418.4	1,481
1982	70,485.9	2,384
1983	76,558.7	2,462
1984	95,070.2	2,857

Municipal Bonds (cont'd)

Year	Proceeds ($ millions)	No. of Issues
1985	201,439.9	5,606
1986	148,100.4	7,419
1987	101,460.3	6,816
1988	115,332.9	7,912
1989	121,928.8	8,842
1990	126,137.5	8,438
1991	171,031.9	10,566
1992	233,656.8	12,485
INDUSTRY TOTALS	1,542,869.1	78,679

Source: Securities Data Company

Bond Performance

Merrill Lynch Hi-Yield Master Index

Year	Return (%)
1985	24.61
1986	16.35
1987	4.69
1988	13.47
1989	4.23
1990	-4.38
1991	34.58
1992	18.16

Merrill Lynch Mortgage Master Index

Year	Return (%)
1983	9.51
1984	18.32
1985	25.45
1986	13.14
1987	3.53
1988	9.15
1989	14.60
1990	10.84
1991	15.78
1992	7.33

Merrill Lynch Agency Master Index

Year	Return (%)
1983	8.27
1984	14.52
1985	17.79
1986	13.87
1987	3.42
1988	4.47
1989	12.93
1990	9.90
1991	15.21
1992	7.27

Note: Includes Governments, U.S. Agencies (all Maturities)

Merrill Lynch Corporate Master Index

Year	Return (%)
1983	9.32
1984	16.21
1985	25.38
1986	16.30
1987	1.84
1988	9.76
1989	14.12
1990	7.37
1991	18.24
1992	9.12

Merrill Lynch Domestic Master Index

Year	Return (%)
1983	8.03
1984	15.20
1985	22.40
1986	15.22
1987	2.40
1988	8.04
1989	14.18
1990	9.10
1991	15.85
1992	7.58

Note: Includes Corporate-Government-Mortgage-Bond Index

Bond Performance (cont'd)

Merrill Lynch 1-10 Year Treasury Index

Year	Return (%)
1983	7.57
1984	14.18
1985	18.36
1986	13.20
1987	3.63
1988	6.33
1989	12.60
1990	9.50
1991	13.99
1992	6.94

Government, U.S. Treasury, Intermediate-Term, 1-9.99 years

Merrill Lynch 10+ Treasury Index

Year	Return (%)
1983	1.55
1984	14.95
1985	31.53
1986	23.99
1987	-2.66
1988	9.20
1989	18.90
1990	6.46
1991	18.43
1992	7.94

Governments, U.S. Treasury, Intermediate-Term, 10 years and over

Merrill Lynch 30 Year Treasury Strip

Year	Return (%)
1986	47.71
1987	-31.87
1988	-5.76
1989	28.41
1990	-4.02
1991	15.36
1992	5.67

Merrill Lynch Convertible Securities Index

Year	Return (%)
1988	12.81
1989	12.46
1990	-6.99
1991	31.96
1992	22.41

Convertible Securities (Bonds and Preferreds) All Qualities

Merrill Lynch Eurodollar Index

Year	Return (%)
1983	11.1
1984	12.68
1985	18.12
1986	13.89
1987	2.63
1988	8.90
1989	12.67
1990	9.37
1991	15.84
1992	8.04

Eurodollar Straight Bonds

Merrill Lynch 1-10 Year Treasury Index (% return)

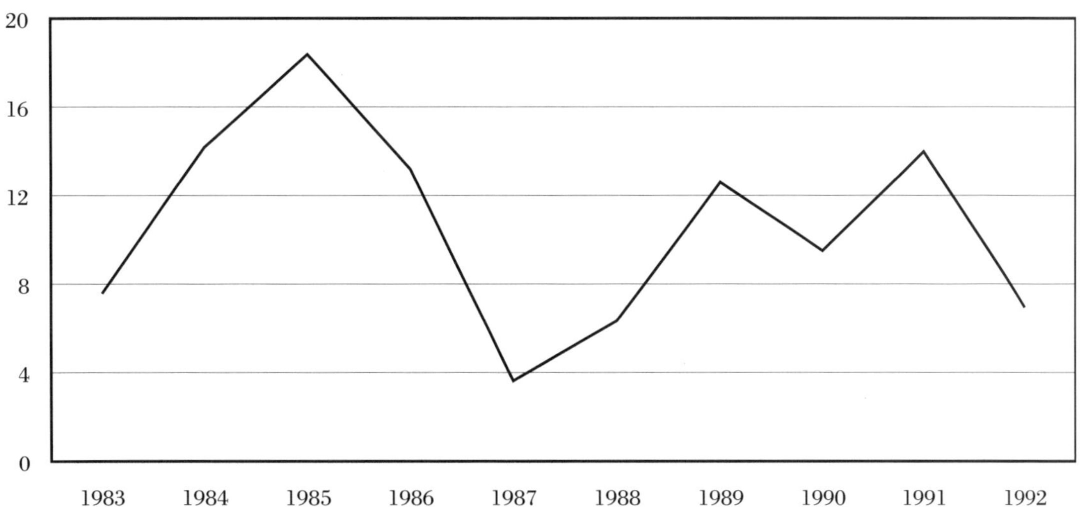

Source: Merrill Lynch

Bond Performance (cont'd)

New Security Issues of Corporations: By Type of Offering

Type of Bond Offering	1985	1987	1988	1989	1990
Total	203.7	326.1	353.1	320.0	298.8
Public, domestic	119.7	209.7	202.0	179.7	188.8
Private placement, domestic	46.2	92.1	127.7	117.4	87.0
Sold abroad	37.8	24.3	23.1	22.9	23.1

New Security Issues of Corporations: By Industry Group

Industry Group	1985	1987	1988	1989	1990
Manufacturing	63.6	60.9	70.3	76.2	52.6
Commercial and miscellaneous	17.2	49.8	62.8	49.5	40.0
Transportation	6.0	12.0	10.3	10.0	12.7
Public utility	13.6	23.0	20.8	18.7	17.6
Communication	10.9	7.3	5.6	8.5	6.6
Real estate and financial	92.3	173.1	183.3	157.2	169.2

Source: U.S. Bureau of the Census, Statistical Abstract of the United States, 1992

Ownership of Public Debt Securities by Private Investor

Investor	1980	1985	1986	1987	1988	1989	1990	1991
Total privately held	616	1,417	1,602	1,731	1,859	2,016	2,288	2,563
Commercial banks	112	189	198	194	185	165	172	222
Non-bank investors	504	1,228	1,405	1,537	1,674	1,851	2,117	2,341
Individuals	117	155	163	172	190	216	234	264
Insurance companies	24	81	102	108	119	125	142	168
Money market funds	4	25	29	15	12	15	46	80
Corporations	19	59	69	85	86	93	109	151
State and local governments	88	304	347	418	472	488	490	490
Foreign and international	130	225	263	300	362	393	422	458
Other investors	123	380	433	439	433	521	674	731

Source: Treasury Bulletin (quarterly), U.S. Department of the Treasury

Household Assets in the Credit Market Instruments

	1980	1985	1987	1988	1989	1990	1991
U.S. Government securities	241	448	492	622	739	822	838
Treasury issues	194	357	355	410	432	492	505
Savings bonds	73	80	101	110	118	126	138
Other Treasury	122	277	254	300	314	366	367
Agency issues	47	91	136	212	308	330	334
Tax-exempt obligations	102	305	398	465	527	549	554
Corporate and foreign bonds	31	19	91	52	65	195	178
Mortgages	107	127	165	182	213	226	248
Open-market paper	43	129	151	196	195	212	177

Source: Board of Governors of the Federal Reserve System

Bonds Listed on the New York Stock Exchange

	1980	1985	1986	1987	1988	1989	1990	1991
No. of issuers	1,045.0	1,010.0	951.0	885.0	846.0	794.0	743.0	706.0
No. of issues	3,057.0	3,856.0	3,611.0	3,346.0	3,106.0	2,961.0	2,912.0	2,727.0
Face value ($ bil.)	602.0	1,327.0	1,380.0	1,651.0	1,610.0	1,435.0	1,689.0	2,219.0
Market value ($ bil.)	508.0	1,339.0	1,458.0	1,621.0	1,561.0	1,412.0	1,610.0	2,227.0
Average price (%)	84.4	100.9	105.7	98.2	97.0	98.4	95.3	100.3

Source: U.S. Bureau of the Census, Statistical Abstract of the United States, 1992

Bond Performance (cont'd)

Foreign Purchases and Sales of U.S. Securities

Year and Country	Total	Treasury Bonds and Notes	U.S. Government Corporations Bonds	Corporate Bonds	Corporate Stocks
1980	15.8	4.9	2.6	2.9	5.4
1985	78.3	29.2	4.3	39.8	4.9
1987	69.4	25.6	5.0	22.5	16.3
1988	74.8	48.8	6.7	21.2	-2.0
1989	96.6	54.2	15.1	17.4	9.9
1990, TOTAL	19.4	17.9	6.3	10.4	-15.1
Japan	-16.9	-14.8	0.4	0.3	-2.9
United Kingdom	5.4	-2.0	2.0	8.4	-3.0
Canada	-1.8	-4.6	0.7	1.2	0.9
Germany	5.1	5.9	-	-0.4	-0.4
Netherlands Antilles	11.6	10.8	1.5	0.5	-1.1
Sweden	1.5	1.2	-	-	0.3
1991, TOTAL	61.1	22.5	9.8	17.7	11.1
United Kingdom	14.6	5.7	1.3	8.0	-0.3
Japan	2.9	-4.1	4.7	1.1	1.2
Canada	2.4	-2.7	0.3	1.0	3.8
Bermuda	-1.9	-2.2	-	0.5	-0.2
Netherlands Antilles	7.0	6.2	-	0.3	0.6
France	-0.2	-1.0	0.4	0.4	-

Source: Statistical Abstract

Tax Exempt Versus Taxable Yields

	Yields (%)								
Tax Bracket (%)	5.5	6.0	6.5	7.0	7.5	8.0	8.5	9.0	9.5
28	7.64	8.33	9.03	9.72	10.42	11.11	11.81	12.50	13.19
30	7.86	8.57	9.29	10.00	10.71	11.43	12.14	12.86	13.57
31	7.97	8.70	9.42	10.14	10.87	11.59	12.32	13.04	13.77
32	8.09	8.82	9.56	10.29	11.03	11.76	12.50	13.24	13.97
34	8.33	9.09	9.85	10.61	11.36	12.12	12.88	13.64	14.39
36	8.59	9.38	10.16	10.94	11.72	12.50	13.28	14.06	14.84
37	8.73	9.52	10.32	11.11	11.90	12.70	13.49	14.29	15.08
39	9.02	9.84	10.66	11.48	12.30	13.11	13.93	14.75	15.57

Example: A 6% tax exempt bond is equivalent to a 9.09% taxable bond for anyone in the 34% tax bracket.

Source: Statistical Abstract

U.S. Exchanges Listing Bonds

Exchange	No. of Listed Bonds	Market Value ($ millions)
American	259	29,423
Boston	2	33
Cincinnati	5	109
Midwest	0	0
New York	2,709	1,586,747
Pacific	81	3,246
Philadelphia	58	NA
Spokane	0	0
TOTAL	3,114	1,619,558

Source: U.S. Securities and Exchange Commission, Annual Report, 1991

Bonds on the NYSE

THE NYSE'S BOND MARKET IS THE LARGEST of all the U.S. exchanges, offering investors a selection of nearly 2,800 bonds issued by the U.S. government, U.S. corporations, foreign governments, foreign corporations, and international banks. In 1991, bond trading on the Exchange reached a record $12.7 billion. About 90% of the NYSE bond volume is in straight or non-convertible debt.

Groups Listing Bonds on the New York Stock Exchange

Major Group	Number of Issuers	Number of Issues	Par Value ($)	Market Value
U.S. companies	657	1,773	281,745	231,665
Foreign companies	18	28	5,085	5,330
U.S. government	1	786	1,916,998	1,974,508
International banks	6	96	12,047	11,794
Foreign governments	23	44	3,620	3,713
TOTAL	705	2,727	2,219,495	2,227,010

Source: NYSE Fact Book, 1991

25 Most Active Bonds on the New York Stock Exchange, 1991

Issue	Par Value of Reported Volume ($ thousands)
RJR Nabisco Capital	1,369,777
RJR Nabisco Holdings	792,096
RJR Nabisco Capital	417,779
Chrysler Corp.	322,767
RJR Nabisco Capital	303,187
Stone Container	265,743
General Motors Acceptance	230,690
Chrysler Auburn Hills	197,253
Chrysler Corp.	189,678
Unisys Corp.	163,304
General Motors Acceptance	160,800
USG Corp.	160,323
Chrysler Corp.	148,854
Chrysler Corp.	143,723
RJR Nabisco Holdings	140,423
RJR Nabisco Capital	135,075
Walt Disney	134,281
IBM Corp.	109,071
Occidental Petroleum	99,274
Owens-Illinois	98,072
Unisys Corp.	85,898
Stone Container	83,928
American Telephone & Telegraph	75,661
Pan American World Airways	70,794
Golden Nugget Finance	68,535

Source: NYSE Fact Book, 1991

Volume of Bond Trading on the NYSE

Year	Volume ($ millions)
1980	5,190
1983	7,572
1984	6,982
1985	9,046
1986	10,464
1987	9,727
1988	7,702
1989	8,836
1990	12,698

Source: Statistical Abstract

NYSE Bond Trading Activity Records

Most Active	Volume ($ millions)
DAYS	TOTAL VOLUME
February 6, 1991	158.4
February 7, 1991	128.1
February 5, 1991	124.3
July 17, 1990	113.9
January 29, 1990	111.8
January 30, 1991	108.3
July 16, 1990	105.2
February 8, 1991	102.0
February 11, 1991	99.1
February 13, 1990	98.7
MONTHS	AVG. DAILY VOLUME
February, 1991	88.9
March, 1991	62.4
July, 1990	55.0
YEARS	AVG. DAILY VOLUME
1991	50.2
1990	32.1
1986	41.4

Source: NYSE Fact Book, 1991

Bonds on the NYSE (cont'd)

Volume of Bond Trading on the NYSE ($ millions)

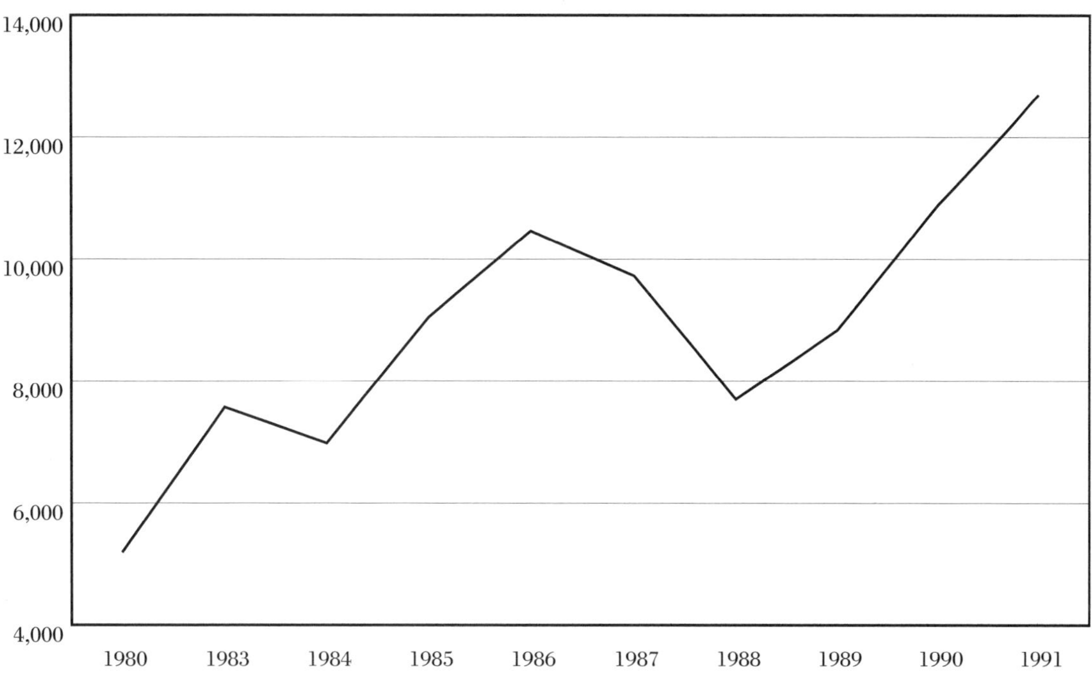

Source: U.S. Bureau of the Census, Statistical Abstract of the United States, 1992

The Top Reference Sources

The Corporate Directory of U.S. Public Companies
Gale/Walker's Western Research, $360
(800) 877-4253 (Gale)

This mammoth 2-volume set lists the essential facts on every U.S. public company (more than 9,500 in all) with sales greater then $5 million.

Entries include contact data, legal counsel, stock price range, SIC codes, major subsidiaries, and more.

Bonds on the NYSE (cont'd)

Largest Corporate Bond Listings on the New York Stock Exchange, 1991

Issue	Principal Amount ($ millions)	Listing Date
Eastman Kodak	3,200,000	10/9
RJR Nabisco Capital	1,500,000	4/19
U.S. West	1,450,000	6/21
AMR	1,300,000	3/12
Freeport-McMoRan	1,150,000	6/26
W.R. Grace & Co.	1,035,000	5/13
Owens-Illinois	1,000,000	12/13
Freeport-McMoRan	862,500	8/8
Marriott	776,260	6/12
FMC	752,140	8/2
Halliburton Company	728,170	3/13
American Telephone & Telegraph	676,000	12/13
Whirlpool Corp.	675,000	5/8
United Telecommunications	573,000	2/20
GPA Delaware	500,000	12/11
Tenneco Inc.	500,000	8/21
Rite Aid	460,000	7/19
Long Island Lighting	415,000	6/4
Long Island Lighting	415,000	6/4
Long Island Lighting	375,000	8/28
Freeport-McMoRan	373,000	2/5
Alaska Air Group	345,000	4/11
AMAX	300,000	6/13
Toyota Motor Credit	300,000	8/14
Unisys	300,000	1/8

Source: NYSE Fact Book, 1991

Bonds on the Amex

THE AMEX OPENED TRADING of U.S. Government securities, Treasury Notes and Bonds in 1975. As of December 31, 1991, 236 Corporate and 744 Government issues were listed, including U.S. Government Securities in odd-lot denominations, Treasury Notes (2 to 10 years maturity), Treasury Bonds (20 years or more maturity), Federal Agency Securities (Federal Home Loan Banks, Federal National Mortgage Association, Federal Farm Credits, and Federal Land Banks), one-year U.S. Treasury Bills, and three- and six-month Treasury Bills.

Corporate Bond Trading on the Amex

Year	Principal Amount ($ thousands)
1975	259,395
1980	355,723
1981	301,226
1982	325,145
1983	395,089
1984	371,857
1985	644,882
1986	810,151
1987	686,922
1988	603,882
1989	708,836
1990	767,118
1991	952,477

Government Bond Trading on the Amex

Year	Principal Amount ($ thousands)
1975	44,805
1980	761,228
1981	964,955
1982	1,392,736
1983	1,808,921
1984	2,086,817
1985	2,117,007
1986	2,421,255
1987	3,016,038
1988	3,691,901
1989	3,518,454
1990	2,719,710
1991	2,770,900

Source: Amex Fact Book, 1991

Bonds on the Amex (cont'd)

Corporate Bond Listings on the Amex

Year	No. of Issues	Principal Amount Outstanding ($)	Total Market Value ($)	Average Price ($)
1960	63	1,064,502,930	954,792,454	86.69
1965	98	1,422,110,590	1,319,703,311	92.80
1970	169	3,178,354,510	2,044,735,556	64.34
1975	197	4,421,821,224	2,998,605,993	67.82
1980	225	6,195,258,443	4,853,002,615	78.34
1981	237	6,863,444,443	4,894,243,593	71.31
1982	244	7,419,099,691	6,213,798,988	83.75
1983	262	8,764,565,391	7,443,389,349	84.93
1984	290	12,670,599,101	9,646,216,836	76.13
1985	347	22,853,452,911	17,655,245,818	77.25
1986	341	24,118,069,806	19,845,653,627	82.28
1987	324	25,461,827,026	19,069,341,030	74.89
1988	309	25,557,448,968	20,993,531,457	82.14
1989	279	27,279,065,889	21,443,266,531	78.61
1990	260	27,195,333,970	29,458,671,424	108.32
1991	236	25,415,012,661	18,859,931,447	74.21

Source: Amex Fact Book, 1991

Bond Ratings

WHILE BOND PRICES AND INTEREST RATES are broadly determined by bond categories (zero-coupon, convertible, income, for example); an issue's exact pricing and coupon are determined by a credit rating. Standard & Poor's and Moody's are the best known and most influential credit rating agencies. Their role as raters is to assess the risk of certain bonds through the study of all information provided to the public, and to assign grades to the issue and issuing company which accurately reflect the company's ability to meet the promised principal and interest payments.

While S&P warns investors that a credit rating is not a recommendation to purchase, sell, or hold a particular security, their initial ratings, and revised downgrades and upgrades, greatly affect the success of the issuance in the eyes of both issuers and holders. Bonds with higher ratings offer lower yields and easier money for the issuer. A lower rating usually results in a lower price on the bond–a less expensive purchase for the investor but a riskier investment. In 1991, those who gambled on lower-rated bonds (junk bonds) reaped the highest total returns: an average 34.5%. One year later, in a less outstanding year for bonds, junk debt took second place in the race for high returns, 18.2% compared to a 22.4% return on convertible debt.

Although somewhat different in their letter-usage, Standard & Poor's and Moody's both rate bonds in descending alphabetical order from A to C.

Standard & Poor's rates some 2,000 domestic and foreign companies; 8,000 munipical, state, and supranational entities; and 1,300 commerical-paper-issuing entities. Moody's rates 19,000 long-term debt issues; 28,000 municipals; and 2,000 commercial paper issuers.

Bond Rating Codes

	S&P	Moody's
Highest Quality	AAA	Aaa
High Quality	AA	Aa
Upper Medium Grade	A	A
Medium Grade	BBB	Baa
Somewhat Speculative	BB	Ba
Low Grade, Speculative	B	B
Low Grade, Default Possible	CCC	Caa
Low Grade, Partial Recovery Possible	CC	Ca
Default, Recovery Unlikely	C	C

Commodity and Future Contracts

Major Commodity Futures Traded on the U.S. Exchanges

Grains and Oilseeds
Barley
Corn
Flaxseed
Oats
Rapeseed
Rye
Sorghum
Soybean Meal
Soybean Oil
Soybeans
Wheat

Wood
Lumber, Plywood

Metals and Petroleum
Aluminum
Copper
Crude Oil
Gold
Heating Oil
Palladium
Petroleum
Platinum
Propane
Silver
Unleaded Gas

Livestock and Meat
Broilers
Feeder Cattle
Pork Bellies
Hogs
Live Cattle

Food and Fiber
Cocoa
Coffee
Cotton
Eggs
Orange Juice
Potatoes
Rice
Sugar

Major Financial Futures Traded on the U.S. Exchanges

Interest Rates
Certificates of Deposit
Commercial Paper
GNMA Certificates
T-bills
T-bonds
T-notes

Foreign Currencies
British Pound
Canadian Dollar
Deutsche Mark
Dutch Guilder
French Franc
Japanese Yen
Mexican Peso
Swiss Franc

Indexes
Consumer Price Index (CPI-W)
CRB Futures Index
Municipal Bond Index
NYSE Index
NYSE Beta Index
Standard & Poor's 500 Index
Standard & Poor's 100 Index
Standard & Poor's OTC Index
U.S. Dollar Index

Market Volume of Futures Trading (millions)

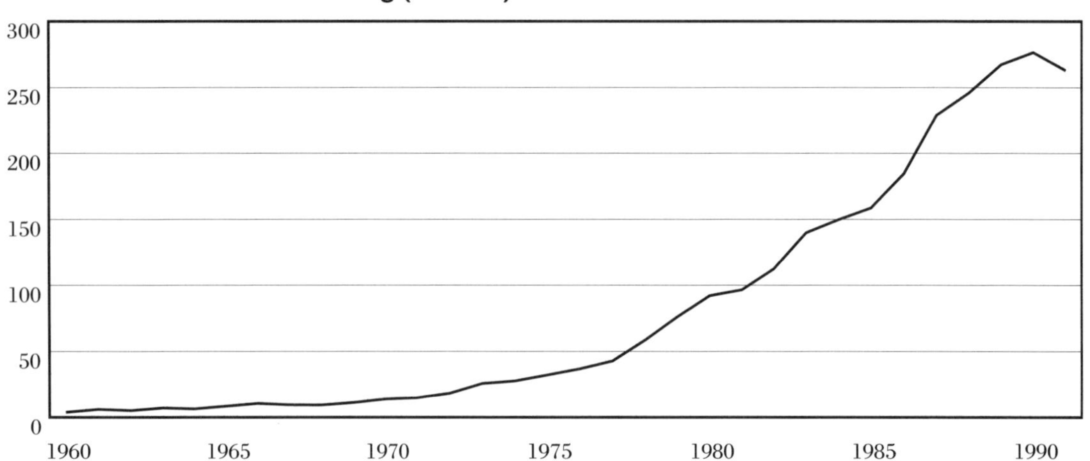

Source: Futures Industry Association

Commodity and Future Contracts (cont'd)

U.S. Futures Contracts Traded by Commodity Group

Rank	Commodity Group	Contracts	Percent
1987			
1	Interest Rate	97,506,007	42.60
2	Ag Commodities	43,366,454	18.95
3	Equity Indices	25,142,036	10.98
4	Energy Products	20,952,358	9.15
5	Foreign Currency/Index	20,940,817	9.15
6	Precious Metals	17,817,380	7.78
7	Non-Precious Metals	2,577,709	1.13
8	Other	573,923	0.25
	TOTAL	228,876,684	100.00
1988			
1	Interest Rate	102,618,415	41.74
2	Ag Commodities	60,473,648	24.60
6	Equity Indices	14,348,076	5.84
3	Energy Products	27,109,767	11.03
4	Foreign Currency/Index	22,162,799	9.01
5	Precious Metals	16,465,152	6.70
7	Non-Precious Metals	2,115,993	0.86
8	Other	577,440	0.23
	TOTAL	245,871,290	100.00
1989			
1	Interest Rate	123,657,483	46.25
2	Ag Commodities	54,051,698	20.21
6	Equity Indices	13,290,808	4.97
3	Energy Products	30,775,659	11.51
4	Foreign Currency/Index	26,965,702	10.08
5	Precious Metals	16,147,189	6.04
7	Non-Precious Metals	2,097,288	0.78
8	Other	398,451	0.15
	TOTAL	267,384,278	100.00
1990			
1	Interest Rate	123,419,532	44.63
2	Ag Commodities	57,088,348	20.64
6	Equity Indices	14,767,090	5.34
3	Energy Products	35,441,295	12.82
4	Foreign Currency/Index	28,880,894	10.44
5	Precious Metals	14,812,847	5.36
7	Non-Precious Metals	1,853,281	0.67
8	Other	272,217	0.10
	TOTAL	276,535,504	100.00
1991			
1	Interest Rate	119,764,959	45.56
2	Ag Commodities	52,229,512	19.87
5	Equity Indices	14,861,067	5.65
3	Energy Products	33,670,228	12.81
4	Foreign Currency/Index	28,715,961	10.92
6	Precious Metals	11,791,525	4.49
7	Non-Precious Metals	1,640,065	0.62
8	Other	221,706	0.08
	TOTAL	262,895,023	100.00

Source: Futures Industry Association

Commodity and Future Contracts (cont'd)

U.S. Futures: Contracts with Volume over 100,000

Rank	Contracts With Volume Over 100,000	1991 Contracts	Percent	1990 Contracts	Percent	1990 Rank
1	T-Bonds, CBOT	67,887,497	25.82	75,499,257	27.30	1
2	Eurodollar, CME	37,244,223	14.17	34,695,625	12.55	2
3	Crude Oil, NYMEX	21,005,867	7.99	23,686,897	8.57	3
4	S&P 500 Index, CME	12,340,380	4.69	12,139,209	4.39	4
5	Deutschemark, CME	10,928,693	4.16	9,169,230	3.32	8
6	Corn, CBOT	10,852,909	4.13	11,423,027	4.13	5
7	Soybeans, CBOT	9,013,739	3.43	10,301,905	3.73	6
8	Gold (100 oz.), COMEX	6,799,917	2.59	9,730,041	3.52	7
9	No. 2 Heating Oil, NY, NYMEX	6,680,171	2.54	6,376,871	2.31	11
10	T-Notes (10-Year), CBOT	6,341,432	2.41	6,054,222	2.19	12
11	Japanese Yen, CME	6,017,012	2.29	7,437,235	2.69	9
12	Swiss Franc, CME	5,835,480	2.22	6,524,893	2.36	10
13	Unleaded Regular Gas, NYMEX	5,509,926	2.10	5,205,995	1.88	14
14	Soybean Meal, CBOT	4,498,287	1.71	4,904,471	1.77	15
15	Sugar #11, CSC	4,268,546	1.62	5,424,801	1.96	13
16	Silver (5,000 oz.), COMEX	4,154,704	1.58	3,913,609	1.42	17
17	Soybean Oil, CBOT	4,018,544	1.53	4,658,302	1.68	16
18	Live Cattle, CME	3,792,824	1.44	3,797,376	1.37	18
19	British Pound, CME	3,745,617	1.42	3,410,333	1.23	19
20	T-Notes (5-Year), CBOT	3,386,161	1.29	2,532,828	0.92	21
21	Wheat, CBOT	3,146,844	1.20	2,876,270	1.04	20
22	T-Bills (90-Day), CME	2,012,079	0.77	1,869,610	0.68	23
23	Coffee C, CSC	1,772,648	0.67	1,774,050	0.64	25
24	High Grade Copper, COMEX	1,640,065	0.62	1,853,185	0.67	24
25	Cotton #2, NYCE	1,614,244	0.61	1,534,611	0.55	29
26	Live Hogs, CME	1,582,234	0.60	2,241,272	0.81	22
27	NYSE Composite Index, NYFE	1,486,166	0.57	1,574,641	0.57	27
28	Wheat, KCBT	1,412,510	0.54	1,136,234	0.41	33
29	T-Bonds, MIDAM	1,397,225	0.53	1,461,046	0.53	30
30	Soybeans, MIDAM	1,387,923	0.53	1,565,641	0.57	28
31	Cocoa (10 M Tons), CSC	1,233,519	0.47	1,635,917	0.59	26
32	Canadian Dollar, CME	1,139,397	0.43	1,408,799	0.51	31
33	Pork Bellies, CME	1,005,196	0.38	1,303,129	0.47	32
34	U.S. Dollar Index, NYCE	715,547	0.27	565,194	0.20	37
35	MMI Maxi, CBOT	702,927	0.27	951,325	0.34	34
36	Wheat, MGE	624,826	0.24	477,043	0.17	38
37	Platinum, NYMEX	604,646	0.23	820,934	0.30	35
38	Municipal Bond Index, CBOT	549,135	0.21	696,861	0.25	36
39	Feeder Cattle, CME	538,495	0.20	391,308	0.14	41
40	One Month LIBOR, CME	450,354	0.17			
41	Corn, MIDAM	433,480	0.16	455,289	0.16	39
42	Natural Gas, NYMEX	418,410	0.16	132,820	0.05	48
43	Oats, CBOT	354,953	0.14	433,567	0.16	40
44	Orange Juice (Frozen Conc.), NYCE	287,538	0.11	342,574	0.12	42
45	T-Notes (2-Year), CBOT	285,567	0.11	110,789	0.04	49
46	Nikkei 225, CME	246,948	0.09			
47	Lumber, CME	160,521	0.06	201,984	0.07	44
48	Wheat, MIDAM	153,949	0.06	147,033	0.05	46
49	Sugar #14, CSC	131,791	0.05	139,143	0.05	47
50	30-Day Interest Rate, CBOT	115,958	0.04			
51	Silver (1,000 oz.), CBOT	114,268	0.04	178,801	0.06	45
	Contracts w/Volume Over 100,000			327,512	0.12	
	Contracts w/Volume Under 100,000	853,731	0.32	1,042,795	0.38	
	TOTAL	262,895,023	100.00	276,535,504	100.00	

Source: Futures Industry Association

Options

BEFORE THE OPENING OF THE CHICAGO Board of Exchange (CBOE) in 1973, now the world's largest options exchange, options were traded on an unregulated basis through a limited number of firms specializing in them. Now options are listed and traded on five major U.S. exchanges and on most of the commodity exchanges.

Market Value of Options Sales on U.S. Exchanges: Non-Equity Options

Calendar Year	Non-Equity Options
1985	29,028,581
1986	47,887,805
1987	65,748,621
1988	35,455,956
1989	36,351,306
1990	51,793,712

Market Value of Options Sales on U.S. Exchanges: Equity Options

Calendar Year	Equity Options Traded
1985	29,952,739
1986	40,054,282
1987	53,123,325
1988	27,163,915
1989	40,423,407
1990	27,218,738

Source: U.S. Securities and Exchange Commission

Markets Listing Equity Options

Market	% Share
Chicago Board Options Exchange	42.19
American Stock Exchange	33.47
Philadelphia Stock Exchange	10.36
Pacific Stock Exchange	12.10
New York Stock Exchange	1.88
TOTAL	100.00

Markets Listing Index Options

Market	% Share
Chicago Board Options Exchange	91.88
American Stock Exchange	7.58
Philadelphia Stock Exchange	0.35
Pacific Stock Exchange	0.09
New York Stock Exchange	0.11
TOTAL	100.00

Markets Listing All Options

Market	% Share
Chicago Board Options Exchange	60.20
American Stock Exchange	21.07
Philadelphia Stock Exchange	11.14
Pacific Stock Exchange	6.54
New York Stock Exchange	1.05
TOTAL	100.00

Source: Chicago Board Options Exchange

U.S. Options Contracts Traded by Commodity Group

Rank	Commodities Group	Contracts	Percent
1991			
1	Interest Rate	31,015,006	49.86
2	Foreign Currency/Index	11,486,318	18.47
3	Ag Commodities	8,860,003	14.24
5	Precious Metals	2,462,854	3.96
6	Equity Indexes	1,863,125	3.00
4	Energy Products	6,405,652	10.30
7	Non-Precious Metals	97,163	0.16
8	Other	11,784	0.02
	TOTAL	62,201,905	100.00
1990			
1	Interest Rate	35,336,832	55.13
3	Foreign Currency/Index	8,588,796	13.40
2	Ag Commodities	9,580,512	14.95
5	Precious Metals	2,686,774	4.19
6	Equity Indexes	1,672,425	2.61
4	Energy Products	6,097,107	9.51
7	Non-Precious Metals	107,387	0.17
8	Other	33,261	0.05
	TOTAL	64,103,094	100.00

Options (cont'd)

Rank	Commodities Group	Contracts	Percent
1989			
1	Interest Rate	28,073,883	
2	Foreign Currency/Index	9,119,520	50.63
3	Ag Commodities	8,113,952	14.63
5	Precious Metals	2,366,450	4.27
6	Equity Indexes	1,201,111	2.17
4	Energy Products	6,316,183	11.39
7	Non-Precious Metals	234,035	0.42
8	Other	20,996	0.04
	TOTAL	55,446,130	100.00
1988			
1	Interest Rate	23,312,073	47.44
3	Foreign Currency/Index	7,623,383	15.51
2	Ag Commodities	8,832,658	17.98
5	Precious Metals	2,579,182	5.25
6	Equity Indexes	758,131	1.54
4	Energy Products	5,606,093	11.41
7	Non-Precious Metals	402,792	0.82
8	Other	23,178	0.05
	TOTAL	49,137,490	100.00
1987			
1	Interest Rate	25,842,477	55.95
2	Foreign Currency/Index	7,062,113	15.29
3	Ag Commodities	4,309,280	9.33
5	Precious Metals	3,008,214	6.51
6	Equity Indexes	2,083,926	4.51
4	Energy Products	3,260,642	7.06
7	Non-Precious Metals	612,850	1.33
8	Other	6,483	0.01
	TOTAL	46,185,985	100.00

Source: Futures Industry Association

U.S. Options: Contracts with Volume over 100,000

1991 Rank	Contracts with Volume over 100,000	1991 Contracts	Percent	1990 Contracts	Percent	1990 Rank
1	T-Bonds, CBOT	21,925,578	35.25	27,315,411	42.61	1
2	Eurodollar, CME	7,874,551	12.66	6,859,625	10.70	2
3	Deutschemark, CME	5,643,031	9.07	3,430,374	5.35	4
4	Crude Oil, NYMEX	4,968,742	7.99	5,254,612	8.20	3
5	Japanese Yen, CME	2,397,141	3.85	3,116,130	4.86	5
6	Soybeans, CBOT	2,165,167	3.48	2,089,382	3.26	8
7	Corn, CBOT	2,048,422	3.29	2,116,302	3.30	7
8	S&P 500 Index, CME	1,813,118	2.91	1,638,131	2.56	10
9	Sugar, CSC	1,512,976	2.43	2,393,016	3.73	6
10	U.S. Dollar Index, NYCE	1,418,298	2.28			
11	Gold (1,000 oz.), COMEX	1,398,451	2.25	1,931,804	3.01	9
12	Silver (5,000 oz.), COMEX	1,019,093	1.64	747,499	1.17	13
13	Swiss Franc, CME	998,002	1.60	1,130,447	1.76	11
14	T-Notes (10-Year), CBOT	890,293	1.43	936,754	1.46	12
15	Heating Oil, NYMEX	863,143	1.39	406,810	0.63	18
16	Live Cattle, CME	776,624	1.25	713,276	1.11	14
17	Wheat, CBOT	692,327	1.11	482,941	0.75	16
18	British Pound, CME	650,472	1.05	501,187	0.78	15
19	Unleaded Regular Gas, NYMEX	573,767	0.92	435,685	0.68	17
20	Coffee, CSC	411,550	0.66	282,566	0.44	22

Options (cont'd)

1991 Rank	Contracts with Volume over 100,000	1991 Contracts	Percent	1990 Contracts	Percent	1990 Rank
21	Cotton #2, NYCE	392,132	0.63	284,991	0.44	20
22	Canadian Dollar, CME	336,758	0.54	283,609	0.44	21
23	Feeder Cattle, CME	168,966	0.27	168,310	0.26	25
24	Cocoa (10 M Tons), CSC	163,610	0.26	344,944	0.54	19
25	T-Notes (5-Year), CBOT	129,389	0.21			
26	Soybean Meal, CBOT	116,433	0.19	181,429	0.28	23
27	Live Hogs, CME	112,338	0.18	171,306	0.27	24
	Contracts w/Volume Over 100,000			245,476	0.38	
	Contracts w/Volume Under 100,000	741,533	1.19	641,077	1.00	
	TOTAL	62,201,905	100.00	64,103,094	100.00	

Source: Futures Industry Association

U.S. Futures and Options Exchanges

The Various Markets of the U.S. Exchanges

	NYSE	AMEX	MSE	PSE	PHLX	BSE	CBOE	CBOT	CME
Equities	•	•	•	•	•	•			
Listed Options		•		•	•		•		
OTC Options	•	•		•	•		•		
Index Options	•	•		•	•		•	•	•
Index Futures	•								
Currency Options		•			•				•
AGRI Options									•
AGRI/Currency Futures								•	•
Options on AGRI/CURR Futures								•	

U.S. Futures Exchange Volume and Market Share, 1991 and 1990

1991 Rank	Exchange	1991 Contracts	Percent	1990 Contracts	Percent	1990 Rank
1	Chicago Board of Trade	111,311,333	42.34	120,769,784	43.67	1
2	Chicago Mercantile Exchange	87,135,012	33.14	84,837,757	30.68	2
3	New York Mercantile Exchange	34,353,073	13.07	36,357,871	13.15	3
4	Commodity Exchange	12,594,686	4.79	15,496,931	5.60	4
5	Coffee Sugar & Cocoa Exchange	7,406,618	2.82	8,973,911	3.25	5
6	MidAmerica Commodity Exchange	3,681,880	1.40	3,975,528	1.44	6
7	New York Cotton Exchange	2,700,171	1.03	2,746,209	0.99	7
8	New York Futures Exchange	1,547,372	0.59	1,656,968	0.60	8
9	Kansas City Board of Trade	1,498,220	0.57	1,187,083	0.43	9
10	Minneapolis Grain Exchange	627,348	0.24	478,077	0.17	10
11	Chicago Rice & Cotton Exchange	39,310	0.01	55,385	0.02	11
	TOTAL	262,895,023	100.00	276,535,504	100.00	

Source: Futures Industry Association

U.S. Futures and Options Exchanges (cont'd)

U.S. Options Exchange Volume and Market Share

1991 Rank	Exchange	1991 Contracts	Percent	1990 Contracts	Percent	1990 Rank
1	Chicago Board of Trade	28,125,965	45.22	33,461,799	52.20	1
2	Chicago Mercantile Exchange	20,993,604	33.75	18,156,855	28.32	2
3	New York Mercantile Exchange	6,433,641	10.34	6,100,856	9.52	3
4	Commodity Exchange	2,528,969	4.07	2,786,690	4.35	5
5	Coffee Sugar & Cocoa Exchange	2,088,136	3.36	3,020,526	4.71	4
6	New York Cotton Exchange	1,866,508	3.00	447,688	0.70	6
7	Kansas City Board of Trade	91,060	0.15	65,794	0.10	7
8	New York Futures Exchange	38,237	0.06	29,045	0.05	9
9	MidAmerica Commodity Exchange	29,663	0.05	29,310	0.05	8
10	Minneapolis Grain Exchange	6,122	0.01	4,531	0.01	10
	TOTAL	62,201,905	100.00	64,103,094	100.00	

Source: Futures Industry Association

Futures and Option Contracts by Exchange

American Stock Exchange

Options
- Computer Technology Index
- Institutional Index
- International Market Index
- Major Market Index (XMI)
- LT-20 Index
- Oil Index
- Chicago Board of Trade

Futures
- Corn
- Oats
- Soybeans
- Soybean Meal
- Soybean Oil
- Wheat
- Gold
- Silver
- U.S. Treasury Bonds
- U.S. Treasury Notes
- Two-Year U.S. Treasury Notes
- Five-Year U.S. Treasury Notes
- 30-Day Interest Rate
- Major Market Index-Maxi
- Municipal Bond Index

Options on Futures
- Corn
- Oats
- Soybeans
- Soybean Meal
- Soybean Oil
- Wheat
- Gold
- Silver
- U.S. Treasury Bonds
- U.S. Treasury Notes
- Five-Year U.S. Treasury Notes
- Municipal Bond Index
- Japanese Government Bonds

Chicago Board Options Exchange

Options
- Equities
- Long-Term Equities (on selected blue chips)
- Interest Rate (Long-Term, Short-Term)
- S&P 100 Stock Index
- S&P 500 Stock Index
- U.S. 30-Year Treasury Bonds
- U.S. Five-Year Treasury Notes

Chicago Mercantile Exchange

Futures and Options on Futures
- Cattle, Feeder
- Cattle, Live
- Hogs, Live
- Lumber
- Pork Bellies

Index and Option Market Division
- Futures and Options on Futures
- Nikkei 225 Stock Average
- Standard & Poor's 500 Stock Index

International Monetary Market Division
- Futures
- Australian Dollar
- British Pound
- Canadian Dollar
- Deutsche Mark
- Dollar/Deutsche Mark DIFF
- Dollar/Sterling DIFF
- Dollar/Yen DIFF
- Eurodollar Time Deposit
- Japanese Yen
- London Interbank Offered Rate
- Swiss Franc
- Treasury Bills

Options on Futures
- Australian Dollar
- British Pound
- Canadian Dollar
- Deutsche Mark
- Eurodollar Time Deposit (3 month)
- Japanese Yen
- Swiss Franc
- Treasury Bills (90 day)

Coffee, Sugar & Cocoa Exchange

Futures
- Cocoa
- Coffee C
- Sugar No. 11
- Sugar No. 14
- Sugar (White)

U.S. Futures and Options Exchanges (cont'd)

International Market Index

Options on Futures
- Cocoa
- Coffee C
- Sugar No. 11

Commodity Exchange Inc.

Futures
- Aluminum
- Copper
- Gold
- Silver

Options on Futures
- Copper
- Gold
- Silver

Kansas City Board of Trade

Futures
- Grain Sorghum
- Mini Value Line
- Stock Index
- Value Line
- Wheat (Hard red winter)

Options of Futures
- Wheat (Hard red winter)

MidAmerica Commodity Exchange

Futures
- Cattle, Live
- Hogs, Live
- Corn
- Oats
- CRCE Rough Rice
- Soybeans
- Soybean Meal
- Wheat (Soft winter)
- New York Gold
- New York Silver
- Platinum
- British Pound
- Canadian Dollar
- Deutsche Mark
- Japanese Yen
- Swiss Franc
- U.S. Treasury Bills (90-day)
- U.S. Treasury Bonds
- U.S. Treasury Notes

Options on Futures
- Soybeans
- Wheat (Soft winter)
- New York Gold
- Minneapolis Grain Exchange

Futures
- High Fructose Corn Syrup
- Oats
- Wheat (Hard red spring)
- Wheat (White)

Options of Futures
- Wheat (Hard red spring)
- New York Cotton Exchange

Futures and Options on Futures
- Cotton

New York Futures Exchange

Futures
- NYSE Composite Stock Index
- CRB Futures Price Index
- U.S. Treasury Bonds

Options on Futures
- NYSE Composite Stock Index
- CRB Futures Price Index
- New York Mercantile Exchange

Futures
- Crude Oil (Light sweet)
- Natural Gas
- No. 2 Heating Oil (New York)
- Palladium
- Platinum
- Propane
- Residual Fuel Oil
- Unleaded Gasoline

Options on Futures
- Crude Oil (Light sweet)
- No. 2 Heating Oil (New York)
- Unleaded Gasoline
- New York Stock Exchange

Options
- NYSE Composite Index

Pacific Stock Exchange

Options
- Financial News Composite Index
- Philadelphia Board of Trade

Futures
- Australian Dollar
- British Pound
- Canadian Dollar
- Deutsche Mark
- European Currency Unit
- French Franc
- Japanese Yen

National Over-the-Counter Index
- Swiss Franc

Philadelphia Stock Exchange

Options
- Australian Dollar
- British Pound
- Canadian Dollar
- Deutsche Mark
- European Currency Unit
- French Franc
- Gold/Silver Stock Index
- Japanese Yen

National Over-the-Counter Index
- Swiss Franc

Utility Index (European-style)

Value Line Index (European-style)

U.S. Futures and Options Exchanges (cont'd)

The American Stock Exchange (Amex)

86 Trinity Pl.
New York, NY 10006
(212) 306-1000

- Members/seats–661 regular members; 203 options principal members
- Companies/issues listed–860 companies listed, 1,055 issues
- 1991 Average Daily Volume–153,451 contracts
- Lists–258 individual stock options (including 68 options on OTC securities); long-term options with expirations up to three years on 21 actively-traded common stocks; four broad-based index options, including the Major Market Index (XMI); two industry-based options.

The Amex stock options programs began in January 1975 with the listing of six call options. In 1983 the program was expanded to include options on broad-market and industry-based stock indices. In 1985, the Amex launched trading of options on over-the-counter (OTC) securities.

10 Most Active Amex Options, 1991

Product	Average Daily Volume
Major Market Index (XMI)	15,355
Philip Morris Companies, Inc.(MO)	11,445
The Walt Disney Company (DIS)	5,972
Amgen Inc. (AMQ)	5,636
Institutional Index (XII)	5,426
Apple Computer Inc. (AAQ)	4,902
Digital Equipment Corporation (DEC)	4,898
American Express Compnay (BCP)	3,554
Wells Fargo & Company (WFC)	3,519
Intel Corporation (INQ)	2,934

Source: Amex Fact Book 1991

Number of Contracts Traded on the Amex

Year	Calls (thousands)	Puts (thousands)	Total (thousands)
1975	3,531	0	3,531
1976	9,036	0	9,036
1977	9,655	423	10,078
1978	13,540	841	14,381
1979	16,506	961	17,467
1980	24,955	4,093	29,048
1981	26,430	8,430	34,860
1982	27,680	11,111	38,791
1983	28,069	10,899	38,968
1984	28,731	11,373	40,104
1985	35,186	13,414	48,600
1986	48,875	16,568	65,443
1987	52,952	17,997	70,949
1988	34,225	10,776	45,001
1989	37,448	12,408	49,856
1990	26,958	13,930	40,888
1991	25,422	13,383	38,805

Source: Amex Fact Book, 1991

Chicago Board of Trade (CBOT)

141 West Jackson Blvd.
Chicago, IL 60604
(312) 435-3500

- Full members–1,402
- Associate members–751
- Commodity Options membership interests–643
- Index, Debt, Energy membership interests–635
- Gov't Instruments membership interests–231
- Total Members–3,662
- Seat Price in 1992–$392,500 high, $295,000 low.

In 1948, the CBOT was founded for the trading of forward grain contracts. In 1965, the CBOT developed futures contracts which were standardized according to quality, quantity, time, and location of delivery.

Until 1975, the exchange was devoted solely to agricultural products; then trading began on the world's first future contracts based on an interest rate instrument, Government National Mortgage Association (GNMA) certificates. Now 15 futures products and 13 options on futures products are traded at the CBOT. The CBOT has offices in Washington and London. For specific production literature call (800) THE CBOT.

U.S. Futures and Options Exchanges (cont'd)

Average Daily CBOT Volume

	Average Daily Volume (thousands)			Volume Growth Rate (%)			Ag. Share of Total (%)
Year	Ag	Non-Ag	Total	Ag	Non-Ag	Total	
1982	109.1	83.4	192.5	-14.0	24.4	-1.5	56.7
1983	148.5	106.3	254.8	36.1	27.5	32.4	58.3
1984	125.0	170.1	295.1	-15.8	60.0	15.8	42.4
1985	95.7	235.7	331.4	-23.4	38.6	12.3	28.9
1986	87.4	311.1	398.5	-8.7	32.0	20.2	21.9
1987	105.8	396.6	502.4	21.1	27.5	26.1	21.1
1988	170.4	394.9	565.4	61.1	-0.4	12.5	30.1
1989	140.8	408.2	549.0	-17.4	3.4	-2.9	25.6
1990	156.6	453.0	609.6	11.2	11.0	11.0	25.7
1991	146.2	404.9	551.1	-6.6	-10.6	-9.6	26.5
1991*	150.5	400.9	551.4	-6.6	-13.2	-11.5	27.3
1992*	151.0	450.1	601.1	0.3	12.3	9.0	25.1

Source: Chicago Board of Trade

* *January through September*
Ag=Agricultural

Chicago Board Options Exchange (CBOE)

LaSalle at Van Buren
Chicago, IL 60605
(312) 786-5600

- Founded: 1973
- Members/Seats–931 regular members; 450 exercisers from the CBOT
- 1991 Volume–approximately 122 million contracts
- Value of underlying shares for a typical CBOE trading day–$11.4 billion

In addition to options over 350 widely-traded equities and short- and long-term interest rates, CBOE lists options on the S&P 100 and 500 stock indexes, the CBOE BioTech Index and the FT-SE 100.

The CBOE is the world's largest options exchange. Originally created by the Chicago Board of Trade, it is managed and operated as a separate entity from the CBOT. The CBOE opened in 1973 with the trading of call options. In 1977, put options were introduced.

The CBOE accounts for approximately 92% of the U.S. index options market share. The Exchange holds the largest share of the total U.S. options market: 61.2% of all options traded in 1991.

Number of Contracts Traded on the CBOE

Year	Total Volume
1973	1,119,177
1974	5,682,907
1975	14,431,023
1976	21,498,027
1977	24,838,632
1978	34,277,350
1979	35,379,600
1980	52,916,921
1981	57,584,175
1982	75,735,739
1983	82,468,750
1984	123,273,736
1985	148,889,196
1986	180,357,774
1987	182,112,636
1988	111,760,234
1989	126,765,253
1990	129,500,018
1991	121,689,918

Source: Chicago Board Options Exchange

Chicago Mercantile Exchange (CME), International Monetary Fund, and Index and Option Market

30 South Wacker Dr.
Chicago, IL 60606
312/786-5600

The CME consists of 2,724 memebers including independent traders and brokers as well as representatives of major brokerage firms, banks, investment houses, and corporations.

The CME was established in 1919 for the trading of futures contracts on various agricultural commodities. Today, the Exchange trades four product groups: agricultural, currency, interest rate, and stock index. In 1991, the CME traded more than 108 million contracts, an all-time record for the exchange. As of June 30, 1992, CME's yearly volume was 25% ahead of 1991's pace: 66.7 million futures contracts and options traded.

U.S. Futures and Options Exchanges (cont'd)

Chicago Cotton and Rice Exchange (CRCE)

141 West Jackson Blvd.
Chicago, IL 60604
(312) 341-3078

The CRCE is an affiliate of the MidAm. It was originally the New Orleans Cotton Exchange, founded in 1871.

Citrus Associates of the New York Cotton Exchange

4 World Trade Center
New York, NY 10048
(212) 938-2702

The Exchange is an affiliate of the New York Cotton Exchange.

Coffee, Sugar and Cocoa Exchange (CSCE)

4 World Trade Center
New York, NY 10048
(212) 938-2800

The CSCE was founded in 1882 as the Coffee Exchange of the City of New York. The Exchange added the trading of sugar futures in 1914. A separate exchange for the trading of cocoa, the New York Cocoa Exchange, was founded in 1925. These two exchanges were merged in 1979.

- 1991 Volume–9,494,754 contracts
- Coffee–8.9%
- Coffee Options–4.4%
- Sugar–45.6%
- Sugar Options–6.2%
- Cocoa–13.2%
- Cocoa Options–1.7%

Commodity Exchange, Inc. (COMEX)

4 World Trade Center
New York, NY 10048
(212)938-2900

- Number of seats–772 full members; 238 others
- Full seat price prices in 1992–$68,000; low $42,000

Founded in 1933, the COMEX represented the union of four older exchanges: the National Metal Exchange, the Rubber Exchange of New York, the National Raw Silk Exchange, and the New York Hide Exchange. Today it is the world's most active metals market.

Financial Instrument Exchange (FINEX)

4 World Trade Center
New York, NY 10048
(212) 926-2634

The FINEX is a division of the New York Cotton Exchange.

In March, 1992, FINEX became the first-ever futures market to trade round-the-clock. U.S. Dollar and Ecu futures and options trade from 7:00 PM. EST to 10:00 PM. After a break of an hour and a half, Tokyo lunch time, trading resumes at 11:30 PM. and continues until the 3:00 PM. close.

Kansas City Board of Trade (KCBT)

4800 Main St.
Kansas City, MO 64112
(816) 753-7500
(816) 753-1101 (hotline)

Midamerica Commodity Exchange (MidAm)

141 West Jackson Blvd.
Chicago, IL 60604
(312) 341-3000

The MidAm is an affiliate of the Chicago Board of Trade.

Minneapolis Grain Exchange (MGE)

400 S. Fourth St.
Minneapolis, MN 55415
(612) 338-6212

New York Cotton Exchange (NYCE)

4 World Trade Center
New York, NY 10048
(212)938-2650

The oldest commodity exchange in New York, the NYCE was founded in 1870 by a group of cotton brokers and merchants. In 1966, the Exchange created an affiliate exchange, the Citrus Associates of the New York Cotton Exchange, expanding its product line to frozen orange juice futures and options. Through the formation of the Financial Instrument Exchange (FINEX) division, the NYCE began trading financial futures and options. The New York Futures Exchange became an affiliate of the NYCE in 1988 and moved its trading operations to the NYCE quadrant.

New York Futures Exchange (NYFE)

20 Broad St.
New York, NY 10005
(212) 623-4949
(800) 221-7722

Incorporated 1979 as a wholly owned subsidiary of the New York Stock Exchange and an affiliate of the New York Cotton Exchange

The NYFE is the eighth largest futures exchange in the United States.

Total NYFE volume for 1991 was 1,585,609.

New York Mercantile Exchange (NYMEX)

4 World Trade Center
New York, NY 10048
(212) 938-2222

The NYMEX began trading oil futures contracts in 1978. Since then several other key energy sources

U.S. Futures and Options Exchanges (cont'd)

have been added to the trading list: gasoline, 1981; crude oil, 1983; propane, 1987; residual fuel oil, 1989; natural gas futures contracts and options on crude oil, 1986; options on heating oil, 1987; options on gasoline, 1989. 1991 Total NYMEX Futures Options–40,786,714

At an average of 200,000 contracts a day, fourth quarter 1991 volume was the highest quarterly total in Exchange history.

New York Stock Exchange (NYSE)

11 Wall St.
New York, NY 10005
(212) 656-8533
(800) 692-6973 (out-of-state)

- Members/seats–1,417 members/1,366 seats
- 1991 Average Daily Volume of Index and Equity Options Trading–7,971 contracts
- Lists–98 NYSE Equity Options and the NYSE Composite Index Options

Ten Most Active NYSE Options Products, 1991

Product	Average Daily Volume
Maytag Corporation (MYG)	999
NYSE Composite Index (NYA)	603
Campbell Soup Company (CPB)	417
NYNEX Corporation (NYN)	401
Fruit of the Loom (FTL)	315
Consolidated Freightways, Inc. (CNF)	265
Chubb Corp.(CB)	229
Borden Chemicals and Plastics (BCP)	222
Triton Energy Corp. (DIL)	215
Potlatch Corporation (PCH)	211

Pacific Stock Exchange (PSE)

301 Pine St.
San Francisco, CA 94101
(415) 393-4000

- Average Daily Volume of Contracts 1991–54,753
- Option Volume 1991–13,852,604 contracts
- Number of Underlying Securities Listed (12/31/91)– 194
- PSE Market Share of Equities Options–13.14%

Ten Most Active PSE Options in 1991

Product	Contracts
Compaq Computer Corp.	1,788,968
Microsoft	1,159,933
Square D Company	994,782
Marion Merrell Dow, Inc.	654,683
Sun Microsystems	634,349
Conner Peripherals	582,088
Advanced Micro Devices, Inc.	459,630
McDonnell Douglas	383,389
Nike, Inc.	342,486
Hilton Hotels	317,077

Philadelphia Board of Trade (PBOT)

1900 Market St.
Philadelphia, PA 19103
(215) 496-5357

Twin Cities Board of Trade (TCBOT)

430 First Ave. North
Minneapolis, MN 55415
(612) 333-6742

U.S. and Foreign Future and Option Exchanges in Order of 1991 Year-End Volume

Exchange	Jan-Dec 1990	Jan-Dec 1991
Chicago Board of Trade	154,227,816	139,437,298
Chicago Mercantile Exchange	102,988,293	108,128,616
New York Mercantile Exchange	42,458,651	40,786,714
LIFFE, UK	34,169,529	38,583,877
MATIF, France	28,056,573	37,129,032
Osaka Securities Exchange	22,776,790	33,478,949
BM&F, Brazil	9,875,196	19,027,057
London Metal Exchange, UK	13,352,954	16,937,909
Tokyo Stock Exchange	21,623,268	16,601,899
TIFFE	14,450,989	15,152,964
Commodity Exchange, Inc.	18,283,621	15,123,655
Tokyo Commodity Exchange Industry	14,839,666	14,949,199
Sydney Futures Exchange	11,555,396	12,499,470
Tokyo Grain Exchange	7,144,758	9,817,622
Coffee Sugar & Cocoa Exchange	11,994,437	9,494,754

U.S. Futures and Options Exchanges (cont'd)

Exchange	Jan-Dec 1990	Jan-Dec 1991
Stockholm Options Exchange	5,190,986	9,061,437
International Petroleum Exchange, UK	6,946,173	8,440,493
SOFFEX, Switzerland	4,713,827	6,971,740
SIMEX, Singapore	5,720,610	6,068,044
DTB, Germany	111,028	5,979,551
New York Cotton Exchange	3,193,897	4,566,679
Osaka Grain Exchange	3,351,462	4,123,743
Futures & Options Exchange, UK	4,500,870	3,811,247
MONEP, France	2,470,394	3,804,396
MidAmerica Commodity Exchange	4,004,838	3,711,543
European Options Exchange, Netherlands	2,856,176	3,469,949
Tokyo Sugar Exchange	6,378,228	2,354,386
Kansas City Board of Trade	1,252,877	1,589,280
New York Futures Exchange	1,686,013	1,585,609
Osaka Sugar Exchange	2,840,713	1,429,020
Osaka Textile Exchange	1,726,279	1,413,779
Nagoya Textile Exchange	1,273,746	1,402,637
Kobe Rubber Exchange	1,383,394	1,374,337
Winnipeg Commodity Exchange	1,217,413	1,238,979
Guarantee Fund Danish Options & Futures	739,446	1,084,547
Nagoya Grain & Sugar Exchange	918,526	1,043,322
Meff Renta Fija, Spain	188,744	1,005,781
Toyahashi Dried Cocoon Exchange	1,328,122	836,629
Maebashi Dried Cocoon Exchange	1,159,978	771,574
New Zealand Futures Exchange	622,454	742,277
Kobe Grain Exchange	387,066	733,917
Montreal Exchange	680,790	678,286
Kanmon Commodity Exchange	573,750	645,486
Hokkaido Grain Exchange	476,801	639,576
Minneapolis Grain Exchange	482,608	633,470
Hong Kong Futures Exchange	507,534	569,557
Financial Futures Market Amsterdam	533,136	563,388
Toronto Futures Exchange	751,543	527,350
Kuala Lumpur Commodity Exchange	263,525	324,971
Yokohama Raw Silk Exchange	433,471	275,053
Kobe Raw Silk Exchange	387,611	207,012
Irish Futures & Options Exchange	47,433	40,635
Chicago Rice & Cotton Exchange	55,385	39,310
MERFOX, Argentina	NA	24,023

Source: Futures Industry Association

Almanac Fact

October and April are traditionally the two busiest months on U.S. exchanges.

Source: NASDAQ Fact Book

Foreign Options Exchanges

Futures and Options Exchanges by Year-End Annual Volume

Australia

Australian Stock Exchange, Ltd.
20 Bridge St.
Sydney, N.S.W. 2000, Australia

Sydney Futures Exchange, Ltd.
Grosvenor St.
Sydney, N.S.W. 2000, Australia

Canada

Montreal Exchange (ME)
800 Victoria Square
Montreal, Quebec, Canada H4Z 1A9
(514) 871-2424

Toronto Futures Exchange (TE)
2 First Canadian Place, Exchange Tower
Toronto, Ontario, Canada M5X 1J2
(416) 947-4487 or 4585

Toronto Stock Exchange
2 First Canadian Place, Exchange Tower
Toronto, Ontario, Canada M5X 1J2
(416) 947-4700

Vancouver Stock Exchange
609 Granville St.
Vancouver, British Columbia
Canada V7Y 1H1
(614) 689-3334

The Winnipeg Commodity Exchange
500 Commodity Exchange Tower
360 Main St.
Winnipeg, Manitoba
Canada R3C 3Z4
(204) 949-0495

France

France Matif Automatique
52 Ave des Champs Elysses
75008 Paris, France

Germany

Deutsche Terminboerse
Grueneburgweg 102, Postfach 17 02 03
D-6000 Frankfurt 1, Germany

Hong Kong

Hong Kong Futures Exchange
New World Tower
16-18 Queen's Road
Hong Kong

Japan

Osaka Securities Exchange
8-16 Kitahama, 1-chome, Chuo-ku
Osaka 541, Japan

Tokyo Commodity Exchange
10-8 Nihonbashi Horidomecho
1-chome, Chuo-ku
Tokyo 103, Japan

Tokyo International Financial Futures Exchange
Ntt Data Otemachi Bldg.
2-2-2 Otemachi, Chiyoda-ku
Tokyo 100, Japan

Tokyo Stock Exchange
2-1 Nihombashi-Kabuto-Cho
Chuo-Ku, Tokyo 103

Netherlands

European Options Exchange (EOE)
Rokin 65, Amsterdam
1012 KK, The Netherlands

Financiele Termijnmarkt Amsterdam N.V.
Nes 49, Amsterdam
1012 KD, The Netherlands

Singapore

Singapore International Monetary Exchange Ltd.
1 Raffles Place #07-00
OUB Centre, Singapore 0104

Switzerland

Swiss Options and Financial Futures Exchange Ag
Neumattstrasse 7
8953 Dietikon, Switzerland

United Kingdom

Baltic Futures Exchange
24-28 St. Mary Axe
London, England EC3A 8EP

International Petroleum Exchange of London
International House, 1 St. Katharine's Way
London, England E1 9UN

London International Financial Futures Exchange
The Royal Exchange
London, England EC3V 3PJ

London Futures and Options Exchange
1 Commodity Quay, St. Katharine Docks
London, England E1 9AX

London Metal Exchange
Plantation House, Fenchurch St.
London, England EC3M 3AP

London Traded Options Market
Old Broad St.
London, England EC2N 1H

Source: Futures Industry Association

Mutual Fund Rankings and Data

A MUTUAL FUND IS A POOL OF MONEY professionally invested by a money manager. Group Performance is measured by 1-year, 3-year, 5-year, and 10-year performance of the following fund categories:

General Equity Funds

CA–Capital Appreciation Fund
G–Growth Fund
SG–Small Company Growth Fund
GI–Growth and Income Fund
EI–Equity Income Fund

Specialty Equity-Oriented Funds

H–Health/Biotechnology Fund
NR–Natural Resources Fund
EN–Environmental Fund
TK–Science and Technology Fund
UT–Utility Fund
FS–Financial Services Fund
RE–Real Estate Fund
OI–Option Income Fund
AU–Gold Oriented Fund
GL–Global Fund
IF–International Fund
EU–European Region Fund
PC–Pacific Region Fund
JA–Japanese Fund
LT–Latin America Fund
CN–Canadian Fund

Other Funds

B–Balanced Fund
CV–Convertible Securities Fund
I–Income Fund
FI–Fixed Income Fund

Money Market Funds (Taxable)

UST–U.S. Treasury Money Market Funds
USS–U.S. Government Money Market Funds

Money Market Funds (Municipal)

TEM–Tax-Exempt Money Market Funds

General Domestic Taxable Fixed-Income Funds

GUT–General U.S. Treasury
GUS–General U.S. Government Funds
GNM–GNMA Funds
USM–U.S. Mortgage Funds
A–Corporate Debt Funds A Rated
BBB–Corporate Debt Funds BBB Rated
GB–General Bond Funds
HY–High Current Yield Funds

World Taxable Fixed Income Funds

GWI–General World Income Funds

General Municipal Debt Funds

GM–General Municipal Debt Funds

Single State Municipal Debt Funds

AZ, CO, FL, KY, MD, MI, MO, NY, OH, PA, TX, CAG(CA), CT, GA, LA, MA, MN, NJ, NC, OR, SC, and VA

Percent Distribution of Funds by Total Net Assets

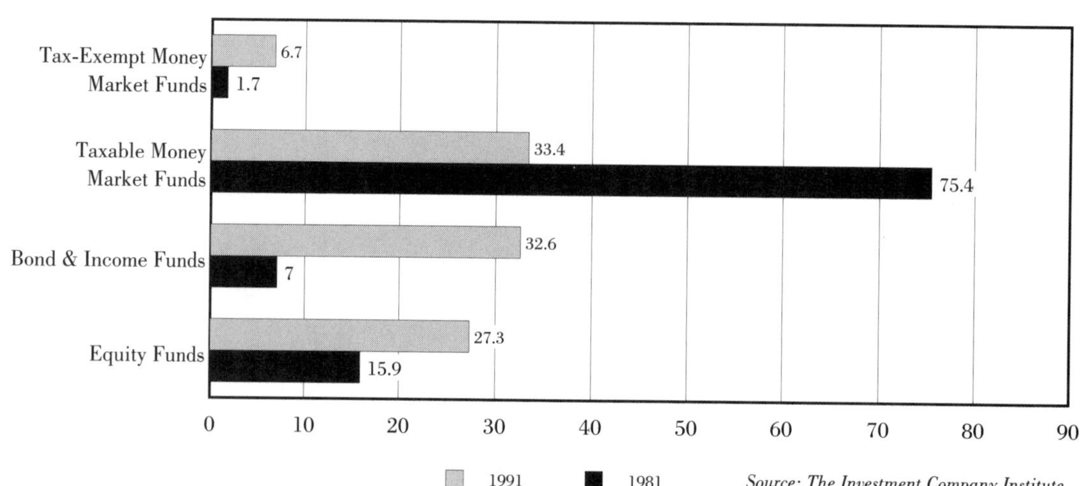

Source: The Investment Company Institute, Mutual Fund Fact Book

Mutual Fund Rankings and Data (cont'd)

Number of Mutual Funds by Type of Fund ($ billions)

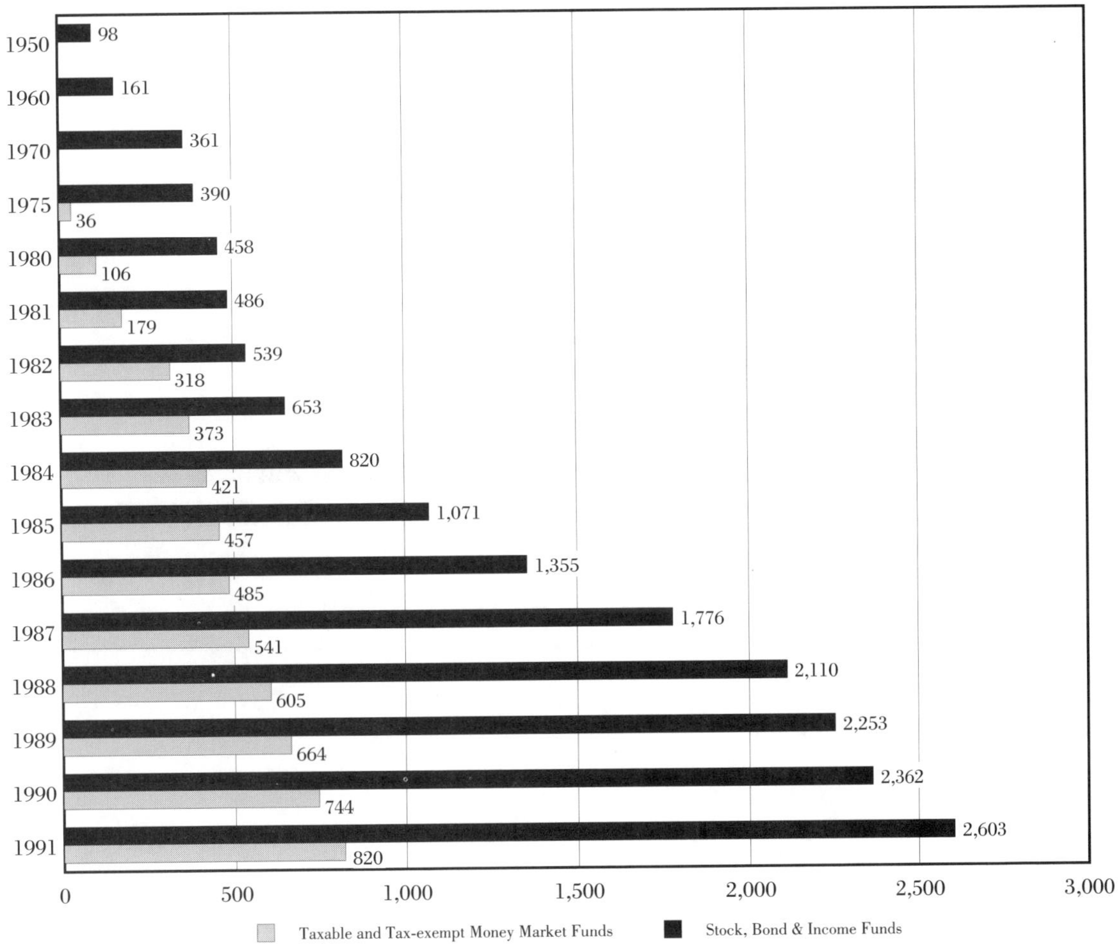

1950
98
1960
161
1970
361
1975
390
36
1980
458
106
1981
486
179
1982
539
318
1983
653
373
1984
820
421
1985
1,071
457
1986
1,355
485
1987
1,776
541
1988
2,110
605
1989
2,253
664
1990
2,362
744
1991
2,603
820
0
500
1,000
1,500
2,000
2,500
3,000
Taxable and Tax-exempt Money Market Funds
Stock, Bond & Income Funds

Fund Assets: Equity, Income and Bond Funds ($ billions)

1975
42.2
1976
47.6
1977
45
1978
45
1979
49
1980
58.4
1981
55.2
1982
76.8
1983
113.6
1984
137.1
1985
251.7
1986
424.2
1987
453.8
1988
472.3
1989
553.9
1990
568.5
1991
807.1
0
100
200
300
400
500
600
700
800
900

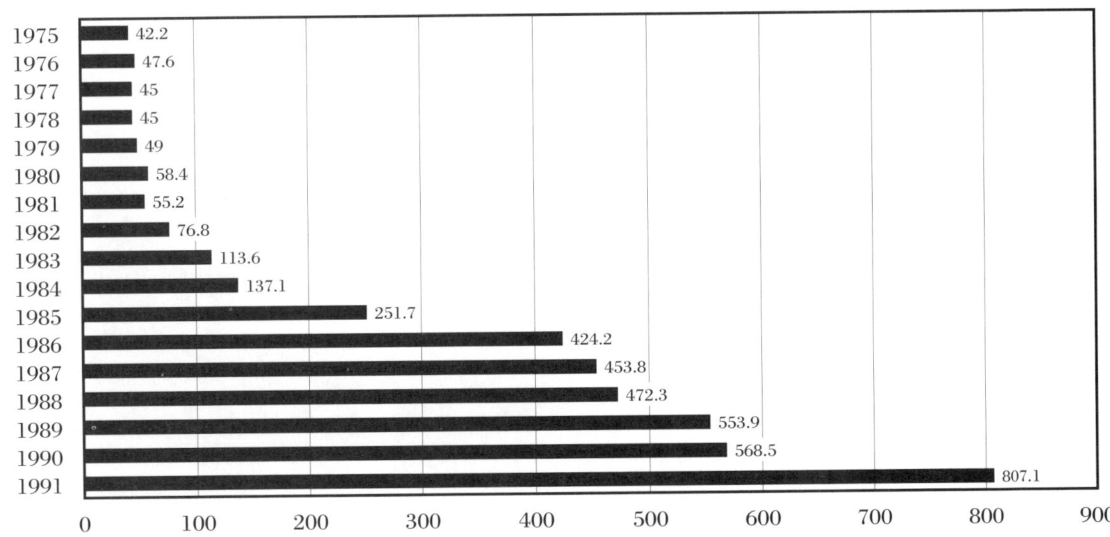

Source: The Investment Company Institute, Mutual Fund Fact Book

Mutual Fund Rankings and Data (cont'd)

Fund Assets: Taxable Money Market Funds ($ billions)

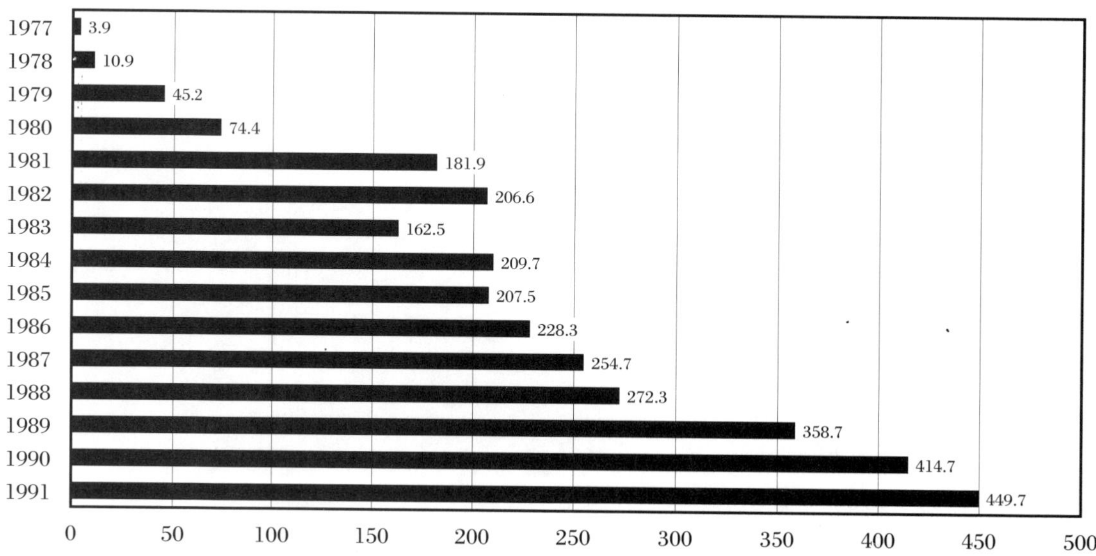

Fund Assets: Tax-exempt Money Market Funds ($ billions)

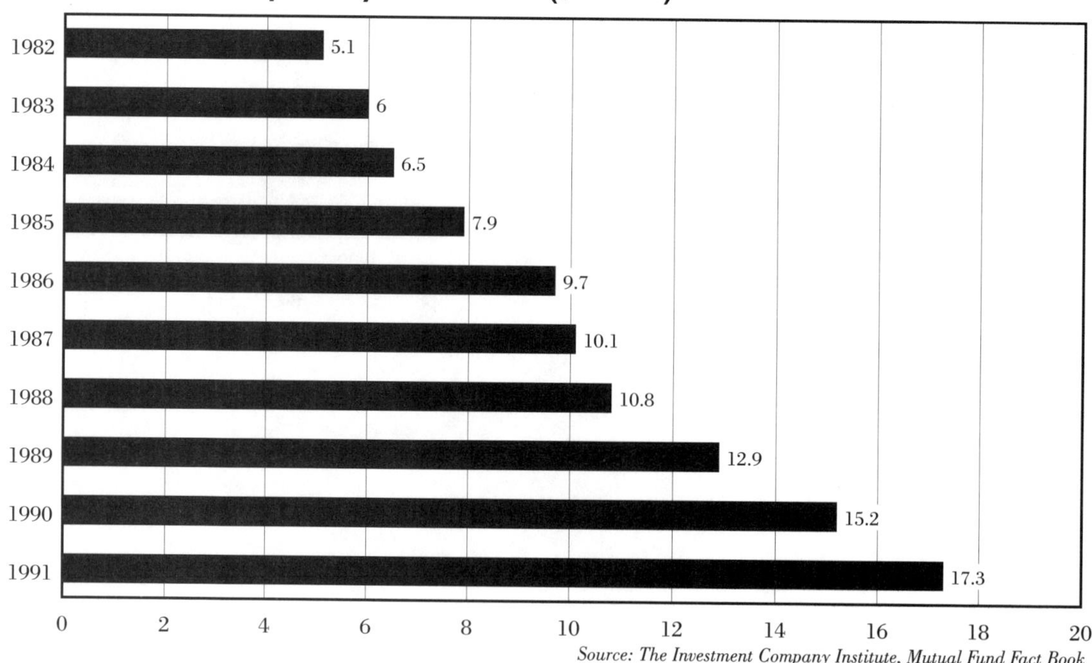

Source: The Investment Company Institute, Mutual Fund Fact Book

Eight Types of Mutual Funds

Aggressive Growth Funds

Aggressive Growth Funds strive to maximize capital gains (they aim to buy low and sell high). These funds may leverage their assets by borrowing funds, and may trade in stock options.

These funds often have low current yields. Because they don't invest for dividend income, and often have little cash in interest-bearing accounts, short-term yield is not optimized.

If you believe that the market is going up, these are the funds that will benefit the most. Conversely, aggressive growth funds are the ones hardest hit in bear markets. The volatility of these funds makes them inappropriate for risk-averse investors.

Growth Funds

Growth Funds are similar to aggressive growth funds, but do not usually trade stock options or borrow money with which to trade. Most growth funds surpass the S&P 500 during bull markets, but do a little worse than average during bear markets.

Just as in aggressive growth funds, growth funds are not aimed at the short-term market timer. The aggressive investor may find that they are an ideal complement for aggressive growth funds, as the differing investment strategies used by the two types of funds can produce maximum gains.

The volatility of these funds makes them inappropriate as the sole investment vehicle for risk-averse investors.

Growth-Income Funds

Growth-Income Funds are specialists in blue-chip stocks. These funds invest in utilities, Dow industrials and other seasoned stocks. They work to maximize dividend income while also generating capital gains.

These funds are appropriate as a substitute for conservative investment in the stock market.

Income Funds

Income funds focus on dividend income, while also enjoying the capital gains that usually accompany investment in common and preferred stocks. These funds are particularly favored by conservative investors.

International Funds

International Funds hold primarily foreign securities. There are two elements of risk in this investment: the normal economic risk of holding stocks, as well as the currency risk associated with repatriating money after taking the investment profits.

These funds are an important part of many portfolios, but any individual fund may prove too volatile for the average investor as the sole investment.

Asset Allocation Funds

Asset Allocation Funds don't invest in just stocks. Instead, they focus on stocks, bonds, gold, real estate, and money market funds. This portfolio approach greatly decreases the reliance on any one segment of the marketplace, easing any declines. The upside is limited by this strategy as well.

Precious Metal Funds

Precious Metal Funds invest in gold, silver, and platinum. Gold and (to a lesser degree) silver often move in the opposite direction from the stock market, and thus these funds can provide a hedge against investments in common stocks.

Bond Funds

Bond Funds invest in corporate and government bonds. A common misunderstanding among investors is that the return on a bond fund is similar to the returns of the bonds purchased. One might expect that a fund that owns primarily 8% yielding bonds would return 8% to investors. In fact, the yield from the fund is based primarily on the trading of bonds, which are extraordinarily sensitive to interest rates. Thus, one could find a bond fund that was earning double-digit returns as the prime rate climbed from 4% to 6%.

In addition to mutual funds, there are money market funds, which are essentially mutual funds that invest solely in government-insured short-term instruments. These funds nearly always reflect the current interest rates, and rarely engage in interest-rate speculation.

Recommended Resource

The Mutual Fund Encyclopedia
Gerald W. Perritt
Dearborn Financial Publishing, Inc.
520 N. Dearborn St.
Chicago, IL 60610

Equity Funds

20 Largest Equity Funds

Fund Name	Income Objective	1992 Assets ($ millions)
Fidelity Magellan Fund	Growth Fund	22,268.90
Investment Co of America	Growth & Income Fund	15,428.40
Washington Mutual Inv	Growth & Income Fund	10,100.40
Vanguard Windsor	Growth & Income Fund	8,832.60
Vanguard Index: 500 Port	Growth & Income Fund	6,547.30
Income Fund of America	Equity Income Fund	6,501.50
Fidelity Puritan	Equity Income Fund	5,912.30
Janus Fund	Captial Appreciation Fund	5,831.90
AIM Eq:Weingarten;Rtl	Growth Fund	5,608.80
Vanguard Wellington Fund	Balanced Fund	5,570.00
Vanguard Windsor II	Growth & Income Fund	5,416.70
Twentieth Cent:Ultra Inv	Capital Appreciation	5,299.20
Dean Witter Divid Gro	Growth & Income	5,035.80
Fidelity Equity-Inc	Equity Income Fund	4,977.30
Twentieth Cent:Growth	Capital Appreciation Fund	4,853.40
Fidelity Growth & Income	Growth & Income Fund	4,842.20
American Mutual	Growth & Income Fund	4,709.60
Twentieth Cent:Select	Growth Fund	4,691.80
Growth Fund of America	Growth Fund	4,332.90
Pioneer II	Growth & Income Fund	4,124.10

20 Best-Performing Equity Funds, 1992

Fund Name	1992 Return (%)	1992 Rank	5-Year Return (%)
Fidelity Sel Saving & Loan	57.83	1	185.87
NASDAQ Bank IX	52.02	index	36.42
Harris Assoc:Oakmark	48.90	2	
Fidelity Sel Regl Banks	48.53	3	211.06
J Hancock Fr Reg Bnk;B	47.37	4	192.41
Fidelity Sel Financial	42.82	5	133.55
Heartland:Value	42.48	6	138.87
Skyline:Special Eq	42.41	7	206.34
Fidelity Sel Automotive	41.57	8	126.65
Painewbr Reg Finl Gr;A	38.63	9	182.47
Painewbr Reg Finl Gr;B	37.82	10	
Parnassus Fund	36.81	11	140.89
Fidelity Sel Software	35.54	12	143.83
Sife Trust Fund	33.86	13	122.48
Retire Plan Amer:Gl Val	33.82	14	
NASDAQ Insurance IX	33.74	index	129.00
Crabbe Huson Growth	33.38	15	127.21
MSCI Hongkong IX GD	32.29	index	199.87
MSCI Hongkong IX ND	32.29	index	199.87
Regis:ICM Small Company	32.28	16	
GT Global America	31.74	17	150.34
Main Street Fds:Inc & Gr	31.08	18	
J Hancock Spec Equities	30.41	19	239.82
Thomson:Opportunity;A	29.57	20	
Selected Funds:Avg	38.85	20	164.41

Source: Lipper Analytical Services, Inc.

Equity Funds (cont'd)

20 Best-Performing Equity Funds: 5-Year

Fund Name	5-Year Return (%)	5-Year Rank	1992 Return (%)
Kaufmann Fund	335.96	1	11.32
Vista:Growth & Income	302.95	2	15.11
Fidelity Sel Bio Tech	285.89	3	-10.38
Financial Port:Health	285.18	4	-13.74
Fidelity Sel Retailing	250.41	5	22.07
J Hancock Spec Equities	239.82	6	30.41
Alger:Small Capital	234.07	7	4.00
Financial Port:Financial	228.47	8	26.78
Fidelity Sel Medical	228.33	9	-13.19
Fidelity Adv Eq:Gro;Inst	224.71	10	10.14
Fidelity Contrafund	223.29	11	15.89
Vista:Capital Growth	222.69	12	12.95
Twentieth Cent:Ultra Inv	220.43	13	1.27
Financial Port:Tech	216.48	14	18.81
Janus Twenty	211.81	15	1.97
Fidelity Sel Regl Banks	211.06	16	48.53
Pasadena Inv:Growth	206.61	17	2.25
Skyline:Special Eq	206.34	18	42.41
Delaware Trend	205.68	19	22.40
Twentieth Cent:Giftrust	202.28	20	18.00
Selected Funds:Avg	237.12	20	13.35

Source: Lipper Analytical Services, Inc.

Taxable Bond Funds

20 Largest Taxable Bond Funds

Fund Name	Investment Objective	1992 Assets ($ millions)
Cma Money Fund	Money Market Instrument Fund	26,104.5
AMEX Daily Dividend	Money Market Instrument Fund	16,363.8
Franklin Cust:US Govt	GNMA Fund	13,631.9
Vanguard MM Rsvs:Prime	Money Market Instrument Fund	12,447.7
Dean Witter US Govt	General U.S. Government Bond Fund	12,440.7
Fidelity Cash Reserves	Money Market Instrument Fund	9,799.2
Dean Witter Liquid Asset	Money Market Instrument Fund	8,604.3
Temp Inv Fd:Tempfund;Shs	Institutional Money Market Fund	7,786.6
Merrill Ready Assets	Money Market Instrument Fund	7,465.9
Vanguard Fxd:GNMA Port	GNMA Fund	6,958.3
Fidelity Inst:Treas II;A	Institutional U.S. Treasury Money Market Fund	6,855.6
Kemper US Govt Sec	GNMA Fund	6,775.8
Prudential Moneymart	Money Market Instrument Fund	6,743.8
Merrill Retire:Reserves	Money Market Instrument Fund	6,614.5
Dreyfus Govt Cash Mgt	Institutional U.S. Government Money Market Fund	6,241.3
Charles Schwab:Money Mkt	Money Market Instrument Fund	6,134.2
Dreyfus Worldwide Dlr MM	Money Market Instrument Fund	5,588.3
AARP GNMA	GNMA Fund	5,546.9
Dreyfus Liquid Assets	Money Market Instrument Fund	5,473.4
Trust US Treasury Oblig	Institutional U.S. Treasury Money Market Fund	5,433.9

Source: Lipper Analytical Services, Inc.

Taxable Funds (cont'd)

20 Best-Performing Taxable Bond Funds, 1992

Fund Name	1992 Return (%)	1992 Rank	5-Year Return (%)
Rochester Convertible	31.17	1	88.25
Fidelity Capital & Inc	28.05	2	74.18
Advantage:High Yield	27.57	3	-
National Bond	25.06	4	54.88
Dean Witter High Yield	24.23	5	18.44
Painewbr High Income;A	24.05	6	78.31
Venture Income (+) Plus	23.37	7	27.03
Painewbr High Income;B	23.14	8	NA
Fidelity Adv Hi Yield	23.05	9	116.40
Fidelity Convertible	22.02	10	140.58
Berwyn Income Fund	21.76	11	86.22
Mainstay:Hi Yld Corp	21.65	12	64.53
Fidelity Spartan Hiinc	21.45	13	-
P Hzn:Cap Inc	21.33	14	136.51
Colonial Hi Yld Sec;A	21.16	15	67.84
Putnam Conv Inc-Gro Tr	21.16	16	84.31
Sunamer Inc:Hi Yield	20.93	17	71.46
Merrill Corp:Hi Inc;A	20.65	18	89.15
Metlife SS Inc:High Inc	20.37	19	62.07
Lutheran Bro Hi Yld	20.12	20	65.42
AVERAGE	23.11		77.89

Source: Lipper Analytical Services, Inc.

Tax-Exempt Funds

20 Largest Tax-Exempt Funds

Fund Name	Investment Objective	1992 Assets ($ millions)
Franklin CA Tf Inc	California Municipal Debt Fund	13,176.9
Cma Tax-Exempt Fund	Tax-Exempt Money Market Fund	7,110.0
IDS High Yld Tax-Exempt	High Yield Municipal Debt Fund	6,116.4
Franklin Fed Tf Inc	General Municipal Debt Fund	5,959.5
Dreyfus Municipal Bond	General Municipal Debt Fund	4,283.4
Franklin NY Tf Inc	New York Municipal Debt Fund	3,950.5
AMEX Muni MM	Tax-Exempt Money Market Fund	3,529.8
Vanguard Muni:Intmdt-Tm	Intermediate Municipal Debt Fund	3,516.4
Kemper Municipal Bond	General Municipal Debt Fund	3,315.6
Vanguard Muni:Money Mkt	Tax-Exempt Money Market Fund	3,178.2
Colonial Tax-Ex;A	General Municipal Debt Fund	2,960.8
Putnam CA Tax Ex Inc	California Municipal Debt Fund	2,952.8
Fidelity Tx Ex Money Mkt	Tax-Exempt Money Market Fund	2,740.2
Franklin Tf:Hi Yld	High Yield Municipal Debt Fund	2,568.2
Nuveen Muni Bond	General Municipal Debt Fund	2,225.7
Fidelity Inst:Tx-Ex Cash	Institutional Tax-Exempt Money Market Fund	2,153.1
Merrill Muni:Ins;A	Insured Municipal Debt Fund	2,084.2
Fidelity High Yld Tax-Fr	High Yield Municipal Debt Fund	2,060.7
Vanguard Muni:Ins Lg-Tm	Insured Municipal Debt Fund	2,004.9
Dreyfus NY Tax Ex Bond	New York Municipal Debt Fund	1,992.1

Source: Lipper Analytical Services, Inc.

Tax-Exempt Funds (cont'd)

20 Best-Performing Tax-Exempt Funds, 1992

Fund Name	1992 Returns (%)	1992 Rank	5-Year Return (%)
Strong Ins Muni Bd	13.06	1	-
Vista:Tx Fr Income	12.83	2	67.72
Strong Municipal Bond	12.17	3	53.32
Morgan Grenfell Muni	11.96	4	-
Fundamental:NY Muni	11.86	5	56.30
Flagship Tx Ex:NY	11.35	6	-
Putnam Muni Income	11.31	7	-
Voyageur Inv:FL Ins	11.25	8	-
Rochester Fd Municipals	11.19	9	66.31
Fidelity Adv Hi Inc Muni	11.11	10	73.76
Franklin NY Tf Inc	11.09	11	62.73
Executive Inv:Ins Tax Ex	11.03	12	-
First Inv Multi Ins:AZ	10.97	13	-
Transam Tax-Free Bd;A	10.96	14	-
Quest Value:NY	10.89	15	-
Dreyfus Prem Muni:VA;A	10.87	16	-
Scudder Hi Yld Txfr	10.87	17	66.81
Scudder Mass Txfree	10.84	18	63.25
Putnam MA Tax Ex Inc II	10.74	19	-
Alliance Muni:NY;A	10.68	20	65.07
Merrill Multi Mun:Tx;A	10.68	20	-
AVERAGE	11.32		63.92

20 Best-Performing Tax-Exempt Funds: 5-Year

Fund Name	5-Year Return (%)	5-Year Rank	1992 Returns (%)
Fidelity Adv Hi Inc Muni	73.76	1	11.11
Dreyfus Gen Muni Bond	70.13	2	9.83
Vanguard Muni:High Yield	68.75	3	9.88
Dreyfus Prem Muni:Tx;A	68.73	4	9.72
Alliance Muni:Natl;A	68.56	5	10.43
Dreyfus Prem Muni Bd;A	68.56	6	10.43
Financial Tax-Fr Income	68.53	7	10.00
Vankamp PA Tax Free	68.13	8	8.78
United Municipal Bond	67.76	9	10.09
Vista:Tx Fr Income	67.72	10	9.53
UST Mstr Tx-Ex:Long	67.11	11	12.83
Dreyfus Prem Muni:FL;A	66.99	12	10.01
Dreyfus Prem Muni:PA;A	66.96	13	9.77
Scudder Hi Yld Txfr	66.81	14	10.87
Dreyfus Prem Muni:OH;A	66.65	15	9.35
Dreyfus Prem NY Muni;A	66.57	16	10.16
Sm Barney Muni:Natl;A	66.41	17	9.63
First Inv Multi Ins:OH	66.35	18	9.99
Rochester Fd Municipals	66.31	19	11.19
Vanguard Muni:Long-Tm	65.82	20	9.30
AVERAGE	67.83		10.08

Source: Lipper Analytical Services, Inc.

Performance of Equity Fund Groups

Overall Performance of Equity Fund Groups, 1992: 5-Year, 10-Year

Fund Category: By Investment Objective	Assets, Third Quarter 1992 ($ millions)	1992 Return (%)	5-Year Return (%)	10-Year Return (%)
Capital Appreciation Funds	34,247.6	8.28	102.85	233.10
Growth Funds	121,462.8	7.79	103.21	254.71
Small Company Growth Funds	21,965.0	12.54	125.46	220.90
Growth & Income Funds	128,051.0	8.61	92.75	270.29
Equity Income Funds	36,517.5	9.46	82.43	250.31
Health/biotechnology Funds	4,787.4	-8.28	206.98	414.35
Natural Resources Funds	1,897.9	1.94	43.92	159.87
Environmental Funds	229.7	-6.18	90.02	216.03
Science & Technology Funds	2,629.5	13.54	115.61	213.35
Specialty/miscellaneous Funds	1,471.7	11.52	102.45	96.62
Utility Funds	15,609.0	9.09	97.15	287.99
Financial Services Funds	1,194.3	35.18	166.99	387.48
Real Estate Funds	269.3	12.67	79.94	-
Option Income Funds	764.2	10.05	66.90	187.83
Gold Oriented Funds	2,427.3	-14.58	-29.43	-23.34
Global Funds	15,599.3	-0.30	46.16	298.65
Global Small Company Funds	2,348.1	1.49	64.44	181.74
International Funds	16,589.7	-5.09	34.74	274.95
European Region Funds	3,501.4	-8.02	26.26	-
Pacific Region Funds	2,163.4	0.40	36.35	419.70
Japanese Funds	711.8	-21.33	-0.39	276.46
Latin American Funds	243.2	0.39	-	-
Canadian Funds	46.9	-6.55	19.78	86.95
Flexible Portfolio Funds	9,448.6	7.58	68.68	165.99
Global Flexible Port Funds	2,315.7	2.86	39.49	89.27
Balanced Funds	27,019.4	7.11	81.76	254.09
Balanced Target Maturity Funds	885.0	5.31	79.51	-
Income Funds	7,533.5	8.77	74.70	223.30
Securities Indices	-	-1.21	45.44	238.75

Top Performing Funds: Financial Services

Fund Name	1992 Return (%)	5-Year Return (%)	10-Year Return (%)
Fidelity Sel Saving&Loan	57.83	185.87	-
Fidelity Sel Regl Banks	48.53	211.06	-
J Hancock Fr Reg Bnk;B	47.37	192.41	-
Fidelity Sel Financial	42.82	133.55	411.27
Painewbr Reg Finl Gr;A	38.68	182.47	-
Selected Funds:Avg	47.05	181.07	411.27
AVERAGE	35.18	169.90	387.48

Source: Lipper Analytical Services, Inc.

Performance of Equity Fund Groups (cont'd)

Top Performing Funds: Science & Technology

Fund Name	1992 Return (%)	5-Year Return (%)	10-Year Return (%)
Fidelity Sel Software	35.54	143.83	-
Fidelity Sel Electronic	27.44	93.13	-
Fidelity Sel Computer	21.96	91.52	-
Shearson Telecom:Gr;A	19.63	103.73	-
Financial Port:Tech	18.81	216.48	-
Selected Funds:Avg	24.68	129.74	-
All Science & Technology Funds: Avg	13.54	115.61	213.35

Top Performing Health/Biotechnology Funds

Fund Name	1992 Return (%)	5-Year Return (%)	10-Year Return (%)
Fidelity Sel Bio Tech	-10.38	285.89	-
Financial Port:Health	-13.74	285.18	-
Fidelity Sel Medical	-13.19	228.33	-
Fidelity Sel Health	-17.46	192.01	536.74
Vanguard Spl:Health	-1.57	187.18	-
Selected Funds:Avg	-11.27	235.72	536.74
AVERAGE	-8.28	206.98	414.35

Top Performing Funds: Financial Services

Fund Name	1992 Return (%)	5-Year Return (%)	10-Year Return (%)
Financial Port:Financial	26.78	228.47	-
Fidelity Sel Regl Banks	48.53	211.06	-
J Hancock Fr Reg Bnk;B	47.37	192.41	-
Fidelity Sel Saving&Loan	57.83	185.87	-
Painewbr Reg Finl Gr;A	38.68	182.47	-
Selected Funds:Avg	43.84	200.06	-
AVERAGE	0.35	169.90	3.874

Source: Lipper Analytical Services, Inc.

Total Institutional Assets in Mutual Funds ($ billions)

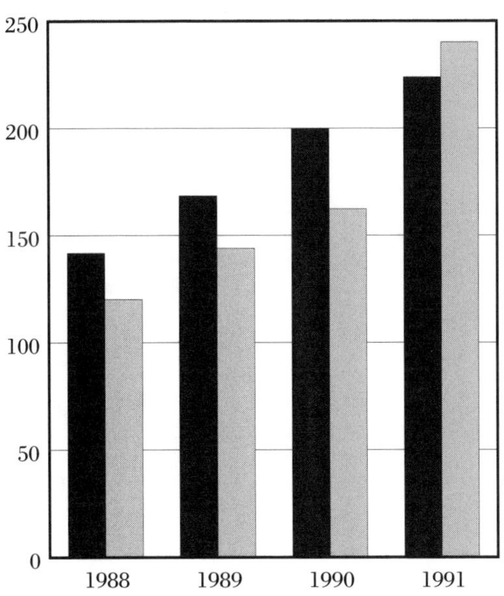

Choosing a Mutual Fund

10 Questions to Ask About a Mutual Fund

1. Does this fund match my investment objectives?

Spend some time to determine your investment goals, then find a fund or funds that match them.

2. What is the load (fee) for purchasing shares?

Some funds charge an upfront fee (a load) for buying into a fund, while others don't. This can dramatically affect your real return.

3. Is there a redemption fee or a management fee?

Some funds charge you to redeem your shares. You should also check to see if the fund is liquid—making it easy to redeem your shares.

4. How often, and in what form, are reports generated?

If you're concerned about keeping very close tabs on your investment, ask to see sample reports.

5. Can I write checks against the fund?

This convenient feature makes it easy to remove money from a fund. Some funds charge a per-check fee, and others don't permit this at all.

6. Can I switch among a family of funds? Is there a charge?

Major fund providers, like Fidelity, give you the flexibility of switching from one fund to another by phone. This is convenient for those interested in short-range management of their money, and is less important to those seeking a long-term home for their cash.

7. Is the fund registered with the SEC?

While overseas funds may occasionally post tremendous profits, in the long run the oversight provided by the SEC provides an important safety net.

8. Is the fund leveraged?

Funds that borrow money to invest can post spectacular gains during bull markets. On the other hand, this strategy can virtually wipe out an investment if the market reacts poorly. Be aware of the risk to your principal as well as your interest.

9. What are the fund's philosophy and current holdings?

Closely examine a fund's approach to the market. You may be concerned about investments in certain industries or countries, or you may find the management of the fund too conservative or aggressive for your comfort.

10. What is the fund's long-term track record?

While there is little correlation between immediate past performance and future performance, there is some. Look for a fund that has consistently ranked in the top third or quarter of its category. This consistency makes it more likely that the firm will continue the policies that attracted you to it in the first place.

The Top Reference Sources

Inc. Magazine
(800) 234-0999

This popular magazine walks a fine line between feature stories and how-to-manual. Filled with useful advice and real-life examples, *Inc.* regularly offers the reader excellent insights. Feature stories in one recent issue include "The Hottest Entrepreneurs in America," and "Guerilla Interviewing," plus articles on how to reduce workers' compensation costs, and knowing what your workers really think and taking action on their good ideas.

Non-Stock Investments

IN ADDITION TO INVESTING IN STOCKS and bonds, commodities, futures, options, and all types of funds, people over time have invested their money in the pursuit of comfort and culture–in real estate, diamonds, paintings, and ceramics. While these investments can bring great personal and aesthetic pleasure, they are known to be notoriously volatile. Experts advise that you only purchase what you love. Here's how real estate and collectibles compare to more traditional investments.

Compound Rates of Return on Various Investments

	20-Year Return	Ten-Year Return	Five-Year Return	One-Year Return
Stocks	11.50	18.40	11.10	9.90
Old Masters	11.10	13.30	17.20	-15.80
Diamonds	9.90	6.40	8.80	0.00
Stamps	9.60	-2.80	-1.10	3.40
Chinese Ceramics	9.60	8.50	13.80	0.60
Bonds	9.30	15.20	11.50	14.50
Gold	9.20	0.60	-5.30	-5.40
3-Month Treasury Bill	8.60	7.60	6.80	4.50
Oil	8.50	-5.10	0.70	0.80
Housing	7.10	4.40	3.60	2.20
Consumer Price Index	6.30	4.00	4.40	3.50
U.S. Farmland	5.90	-1.80	2.70	0.60
Silver	4.50	-3.90	-11.30	-1.60
Foreign Exchange	4.00	4.50	2.20	6.70

Source: Salomon Brothers

The Top Reference Sources

ARTnews International Directory of Art Collections
International Art Alliance
(813) 581-7328

While investing in art is never a sure thing, corporate art collections offer an opportunity for capital appreciation at the same time that they beautify the workplace.

This oversized volume chronicles the art collections of more than 1,000 companies, and is an excellent place to start research on this topic.

Institutional Funds

INVESTMENT ADVISORY FIRMS manage pension funds and foundation assets, and often run families of mutual funds. Most of these firms have a minimum account size of one to ten million dollars. This list ranks investment advisors by the size of their tax-exempt portfolio.

40 Biggest Investment Advisory Firms

Investment Advisor	Style	1 Yr. Total Return	3 Yr. Total Return	5 Yr. Total Return	Portfolio Value ($ mil.)	Avg. Beta	Stocks Held
Alliance Capital Management	combined	10.7	9.4	8.3	27,178	1.24	1,845
Fayez Sarofim	large growth	13.4	14.1	13.1	21,778	1.06	242
INVESCO MIM	large value	11.5	11.2	9.9	18,790	0.98	639
IDS Financial Services	combined	12.2	13.0	9.7	14,712	1.23	651
Delaware Management	large value	9.3	6.2	7.5	14,678	1.03	463
Capital Guardian Trust	combined value	8.8	8.7	9.6	13,695	1.17	390
Investors Research	large growth	7.1	10.9	10.5	13,606	1.34	382
Boston Co.	combined value	11.0	8.8	8.5	13,337	1.05	1,696
Shearson Lehman Brothers	large value	9.1	7.7	7.5	13,208	1.07	1,323
Oppenheimer LP	combined value	15.5	9.6	9.4	12,364	1.19	679
Merrill Lynch Asset Management	large value	9.3	7.4	7.3	11,102	1.09	682
RCM Capital Management	combined growth	10.3	11.4	9.5	10,854	1.22	631
Lazard Freres	combined value	8.3	6.8	7.6	10,214	1.13	497
Sanford C. Bernstein	combined value	14.2	3.6	4.7	10,106	1.28	383
Putnam Management	combined	9.5	9.6	8.0	9,885	1.17	842
Barrow Hanley Mewhinney & Strauss	large value	13.8	7.6	10.1	9,752	1.01	100
Jennison Associates Capital	large growth	12.5	11.9	8.9	9,530	1.40	154
Scudder Stevens & Clark	combined	9.7	10.5	9.4	8,844	1.15	703
Miller Anderson & Sherrerd	combined	12.7	11.7	10.1	8,306	1.18	425
Loomis Sayles	large growth	10.8	6.8	7.1	8,028	1.20	449
Newbolds Asset Management	large value	12.8	12.3	12.0	7,816	0.87	139
Independence Investment Assoc.	large combined	11.5	11.9	11.1	7,321	1.05	311
Chancellor Capital Management	combined	9.2	14.3	NA	7,312	1.23	770
Ark Asset Management	combined	7.2	7.6	NA	7,257	1.17	202
T. Rowe Price Associates	combined	8.7	8.3	6.3	7,239	1.14	1,025
TCW Management	combined	11.3	7.9	7.6	6,827	1.28	597
Provident Investment Counsel	small growth	20.5	23.4	17.1	6,479	1.34	169
Lincoln Capital Management	combined growth	13.7	16.8	13.0	6,465	1.17	89
State Street Research & Management	combined	9.2	7.4	7.9	6,453	1.22	406
Stein Roe & Farnham	combined growth	11.8	10.9	8.8	5,906	1.19	472
Grantham, Mayo, Van Otterloo	NA	12.3	9.2	9.1	5,687	0.94	679
Thomson Advisory Group LP	combined	9.2	13.4	NA	5,612	1.31	209
Templeton, Galbraith & Hansberger	combined value	8.8	5.3	6.2	5,284	1.20	407
Dodge & Cox	NA	9.6	8.0	7.0	5,253	1.07	141
First Manhattan	combined value	14.2	8.6	9.1	4,899	1.06	482
Rosenberg Institutional Equity Mgmt.	combined	7.0	5.7	8.1	4,800	1.04	694
Columbia Management	combined	9.6	9.3	7.7	4,628	1.19	421
Neuberger & Berman Inst. Asset Mgmt	combined value	13.8	8.9	NA	4,442	1.22	580
Hotchkis & Wiley	large value	13.4	7.8	9.0	4,427	1.10	216
Nicholas-Applegate Capital	combined growth	8.1	13.8	11.2	4,391	1.38	765

Source: CDA Investment Technologies

Institutional Funds (cont'd)

25 Best Investment Advisory Firms

Investment Advisor	Style	1 Yr. Return	3 Yr. Return	5 Yr. Return	Portfolio ($ mil.)	Avg. Beta	Stocks Held
Kopp Investment Advisors	small growth	NA	NA	NA	128	1.27	46
McKenzie Walker Investment Mgmt.	combined	8.7	NA	NA	258	1.08	61
JMC Capital Management	small growth	11.6	NA	NA	370	1.52	89
Gardner Lewis Asset Management	small growth	NA	NA	NA	152	1.29	66
Kennedy Capital Management	small combined	NA	NA	NA	140	0.71	160
Narvellier & Associates	small growth	9.8	NA	NA	437	1.30	169
Provident Investment Counsel	combined growth	20.5	23.4	17.1	6,479	1.34	169
W.H. Reaves	combined value	13.4	9.1	12.5	901	0.60	71
Chieftain Capital Management	NA	20.7	11.6	14.9	312	0.80	18
General American Investors	combined growth	11.8	20.3	15.6	1,065	1.31	68
Rothschild	combined	7.7	8.0	7.5	514	1.16	113
Glass Management	large growth	14.0	11.5	NA	157	0.98	120
Fleming Capital	small growth	16.7	11.7	NA	588	1.08	213
McKee Investment Management	other	18.7	NA	NA	125	0.51	48
Greenhaven Associates	combined value	27.5	16.2	NA	329	1.00	23
Hanson Investment Management	large value	15.3	13.3	13.4	1,335	1.17	49
Caldwell & Orkin	combined growth	7.7	14.4	13.7	183	1.27	31
Friess Associates	combined growth	11.4	NA	NA	1,699	1.38	162
Hartwell Management	combined growth	NA	NA	NA	148	1.53	60
George D. Bjurman & Associates	combined growth	14.3	15.0	10.7	263	1.23	137
Schroder Capital Mgmt/ Int'l.	large growth	19.8	11.9	8.4	301	1.26	316
F.D. Ballou-Loring, Wolcott & Coolidge	large growth	18.2	16.2	NA	236	1.08	137
Austin, Calvert & Flavin	large value	18.6	9.2	7.4	339	1.02	129
Palm Beach Capital Management	combined	12.3	8.0	9.0	219	0.79	114
Jurika & Voyles	combined	12.8	NA	NA	157	1.25	76

25 Worst Investment Advisory Firms

Investment Advisor	Style	1 Yr. Return	3 Yr. Return	5 Yr. Return	Portfolio ($ mil.)	Avg. Beta	Stocks Held
Sandler Capital Management	combined growth	2.9	-3.5	7.4	294	1.71	21
Donald Smith	combined value	15.8	-2.5	7.2	627	0.96	30
Gramercy Capital Management	combined	NA	NA	NA	200	1.56	15
Leominster	large value	7.6	NA	NA	279	1.27	47
Cheswick Investment	large growth	-0.2	16.8	14.2	357	1.25	44
Meyer Handelman	NA	5.1	14.7	10.3	767	0.99	193
Husic Capital Management	small growth	-1.5	-0.5	NA	1,531	1.40	123
MacKenzie Financial	NA	-6.2	-1.3	1.4	2,374	0.80	425
Sanford C. Bernstein	combined value	14.2	3.6	4.7	10,106	1.28	383
Clover Capital Management	combined value	16.8	NA	NA	246	1.18	48
Amerindo Investment Advisors	small growth	2.0	NA	NA	1,112	1.41	70
Lyon Stubb & Tompkins	NA	2.9	10.3	10.4	194	1.21	94
Capital International	combined	26.5	10.5	NA	201	1.44	76
Brandes Investment Management	large value	NA	NA	NA	231	0.92	55
Kahn Brothers	small value	NA	NA	NA	138	0.76	171
Bentley Capital Management	NA	NA	NA	NA	175	1.28	85
Steinhardt Partners	NA	13.8	3.6	5.6	498	0.62	65
Aberdeen America	large combined	NA	NA	NA	167	1.19	74
Piper Capital Management	large value	2.8	NA	NA	603	1.23	399
City Capital Counseling	large growth	NA	NA	NA	160	1.11	48
Blackhill Capital	combined growth	-5.1	NA	NA	133	1.13	59
Reams Asset Management	small value	11.0	-0.7	2.2	325	1.33	97
Gerald L. Ray & Associates	large growth	7.5	11.9	8.5	213	1.14	157
Hotchkis & Wiley	large value	13.4	7.8	9.0	4,427	1.10	216
Cypress Capital Management	large value	NA	NA	NA	132	1.00	59

Source: CDA Investment Technologies

Institutional Funds (cont'd)

25 Biggest Insurance Funds

Insurance Fund–Name of Account	Objective	1 Yr. Return	3 Yr. Return	5 Yr. Return	Assets ($ mil.)	Risk Beta	Risk Held
Equitable Life Assurance Society–SA-8	real estate	-3.3	-2.1	2.2	2,708	-0.17	-5.6
Prudential Insurance–prisa	real estate	-14.2	-3.3	1.6	2,572	-0.25	-15.8
Principal Financial Group–SA-A	common stock	13.9	9.7	6.7	2,414	1.04	2.3
Prudential Insurance–privest	fixed income	15.9	13.3	13.0	1,821	0.17	10.6
Equitable Life Assurance Society–SA-4	common stock	2.0	8.9	9.9	1,560	1.10	-8.7
Aetna Life Insurance–real estate SA	real estate	-7.5	-3.4	0.5	1,374	-0.28	-9.0
Massachusetts Mutual Life–SA investment A	common stock	12.9	10.8	9.3	1,216	0.74	3.6
Prudential Insurance–pridex	common stock	10.7	8.8	8.5	1,180	0.92	0.3
Travelers Insurance–large-cap index	common stock	11.1	9.8	9.1	1,069	0.99	0.1
Aetna Life Insurance–SA-76 public bond	fixed income	13.1	12.2	12.2	830	0.21	7.6
Prudential Insurance–priform	common stock	13.9	8.2	8.5	739	0.97	2.8
Cigna–SA-3	common stock	3.1	7.4	5.8	686	1.07	-7.5
Cigna–SA-10	fixed income	14.2	12.2	12.6	632	0.49	6.5
Aetna Life Insurance–SA-2	common stock	7.4	12.4	10.8	585	1.20	-4.6
Cigna – open-end equity SA-R	real estate	-10.5	-6.9	-3.1	557	-0.16	-12.6
John Hancock Mutual Life–diversified 1-K	common stock	11.7	12.6	12.3	522	0.95	1.0
Cigna–SA-4	common stock	1.8	5.9	5.0	504	1.09	-8.9
John Hancock Mutual Life–equity 1-L	common stock	11.8	11.8	11.1	445	0.84	1.8
Metropolitan Life Insurance–SA-2	common stock	12.9	8.8	7.6	442	1.08	1.2
Transamerica Life Ins & Annuity–VA SA T-2	fixed income	15.8	13.1	13.7	416	0.29	9.5
Travelers–domestic bond index	fixed income	13.2	11.9	NA	409	0.22	7.6
Mutual of New York–pooled account 6	common stock	9.0	6.1	7.0	390	0.75	0.0
Travelers Insurance–VA growth stock trust	common stock	4.1	6.0	6.0	338	1.01	-6.3
State Mutual of America–growth stock	common stock	14.0	12.1	10.6	306	1.16	1.6
Lincoln Nat'l Invest. Mgmt–grwth. eq. SA-11	common stock	5.3	8.2	6.8	287	0.92	-4.6

25 Best Insurance Funds

Insurance Fund–Name of Account	Objective	1 Yr. Return	3 Yr. Return	5 Yr. Return	Assets ($ mil.)	Risk Beta	Risk Held
Cigna–SA-10	fixed income	14.2	12.2	12.6	632	0.49	6.5
Linc. Nat'l Invest. Mgmt–lg. bond acc SA-25	fixed income	16.4	13.5	NA	15	0.59	7.8
Gen. Amer. Life Ins–long-term bond SA-18	fixed income	17.2	13.8	NA	5	0.41	9.9
John Hancock Mutual Life–fixed-income 1-D	fixed income	16.3	12.1	12.2	252	0.18	10.9
Linc. Nat'l Invest. Mgmt–emerg growth SA-24	common stock	3.8	3.5	9.3	35	0.59	-3.8
Lincoln Nat'l Invest. Mgmt–spec oppty SA-17	common stock	13.4	18.2	14.1	109	0.91	2.8
Equitable Life Assurance–SA-5	fixed income	12.8	11.0	12.3	278	0.50	5.1
Connecticut Mutual Life– CM select	common stock	18.3	8.1	7.8	86	0.82	7.9
First Variable Life–VA fixed-income D-2	fixed income	25.3	17.0	17.4	1	-0.01	21.0
New England Mutual Life–SA bond	fixed income	15.5	13.0	12.4	65	0.27	9.4
Transamerica Life Ins & Annuity–VA SA T-2	fixed income	15.8	13.1	13.7	416	0.29	9.5
Prudential Insurance–privest	fixed income	15.9	13.3	13.0	1,821	0.17	10.6
State Mutual of America–diversified bond	fixed income	15.5	13.0	13.0	93	0.22	9.8
Lincoln Nat'l Invest. Mgmt–corp. bond SA-12	fixed income	13.7	11.4	11.4	247	0.23	8.0
Ameritas Life Insur.–retirement equity acct.	common stock	15.9	14.4	10.1	12	0.81	5.8
Travelers Insur.–VA aggressive stock trust	common stock	10.4	6.2	1.7	20	0.79	0.9
Great American Reserve–variable annuity C	fixed income	15.1	12.3	12.0	9	0.21	9.5
Security Benefit Life–series B-4	common stock	8.0	10.4	10.3	43	0.75	-1.1
Travelers–domestic bond index	fixed income	13.2	11.9	NA	409	0.22	7.6
Minnesota Mutual Life–SA-C	common stock	10.1	11.1	8.8	64	0.93	-0.4
Metropolitan Life Insurance–market-plus 110	fixed income	13.2	NA	NA	222	0.22	7.6
Metropolitan Life Insurance–market-plus	fixed income	NA	NA	NA	110	NA	NA
Metropolitan Life Insurance–SA-41	fixed income	14.0	12.7	12.5	273	0.24	8.2
Bankers Nat'l Life–VA-ser. 2000 CS portfolio	common stock	11.0	5.8	6.9	8	0.90	0.7
Manufacturers Life Insurance–bond B	fixed income	12.2	10.5	10.7	40	0.25	6.5

Source: CDA Investment Technologies

Institutional Funds (cont'd)

25 Worst Insurance Funds

Insurance Fund–Name of Account	Objective	1 Yr. Return	3 Yr. Return	5 Yr. Return	Assets ($ mil.)	Risk Beta	Risk Held
Equitable Life Assurance–SA-3	common stock	-3.2	22.1	12.4	179	1.09	-13.3
Prudential Insurance–prisa	real estate	-14.2	-3.3	1.6	2,572	-0.25	-15.8
Lincoln Nat'l Investment Mgmt–intl equity 22	international	5.6	3.6	2.6	20	0.16	0.8
Connecticut Mutual Life–CM overseas	international	-1.5	1.9	1.3	37	0.48	-8.0
Confederation Life–international	international	6.1	7.8	8.0	15	0.50	-1.1
Travelers–international small-cap index	international	-12.9	-9.0	NA	132	0.48	-18.7
Equitable Life Assurance–SA-4	common stock	2.0	8.9	9.9	1,560	1.10	-8.7
New England Mutual Life–sep. capital growth	common stock	4.6	12.4	7.5	283	1.06	-6.1
Phoenix Investment Counsel–SA-R	real estate	-2.6	-2.8	1.6	255	-0.26	-4.4
Equitable Life Assurance Society–SA-8	real estate	-3.3	-2.1	2.2	2,708	-0.17	-5.6
Aetna Life Insurance–real estate SA	real estate	-7.5	-3.4	0.5	1,374	-0.28	-9.0
American United Life–SA-A	common stock	6.7	8.7	7.1	39	0.81	2.6
Confederation Life–common stock	common stock	12.5	7.3	8.4	53	0.83	2.6
Security Benefit Life–series A-4	common stock	9.3	5.7	6.5	68	1.07	-2.0
Mutual of New York–pooled account 6	common stock	9.0	6.1	7.0	390	0.75	-0.0
Great American Reserve–variable annuity D	real estate	3.0	5.3	6.0	4	0.00	-0.6
United of Omaha–variable fund A	common stock	14.0	10.6	9.3	30	0.89	3.5
Security Benefit Life–series C-4	fixed income	3.7	6.0	6.8	25	0.01	0.0
Security Benefit Life–equity fund	common stock	9.8	12.0	11.7	67	1.05	-1.5
Lincoln Nat'l Invest. Mgmt–short-term SA-14	fixed income	4.1	6.3	7.1	93	0.00	0.4
Met. Life Insurance–def contrib real estate	real estate	2.3	1.8	NA	105	-0.10	-0.7
Cigna–SA-A	common stock	1.8	5.9	5.0	504	1.09	-8.9
Conn. Mutual Life Insurance–CM equity SA-C	common stock	10.6	9.0	9.9	121	0.89	0.3
Equitable Life Assurance Society–SA-34	common stock	10.7	19.8	15.4	128	0.93	0.2
Northwest. Nat'l Life Insur.–VA sel cap growth	common stock	2.0	1.1	3.0	4	0.82	-7.0

25 Biggest Bank Funds

Bank Fund–Name of Account	Objective	1 Yr. Return	3 Yr. Return	5 Yr. Return	Assets ($ mil.)	Risk Beta	Risk Held
Morgan Guaranty Trust–fixed-income	fixed income	13.6	12.9	13.1	3,890	0.18	8.3
Morgan Guaranty Trust–real estate	real estate	-11.3	-5.1	0.7	1,592	-0.28	-12.8
Sun Bank Capital Mgmt.–suntrust corp equity	common stock	11.1	12.5	11.4	1,567	1.04	-0.2
Mellon Bank–EB stock	common stock	11.4	11.3	9.5	849	0.92	0.9
Nationsbank–EB stable capital	fixed income	6.1	7.8	8.1	842	0.00	2.3
Morgan Guaranty Trust–small-company equity	aggressive growth	11.6	9.5	6.5	768	0.74	2.3
Nationsbank–EB growth equity	common stock	7.4	10.2	10.1	738	1.18	-4.4
Norwest Bank Minnesota–stable return	fixed income	7.9	8.6	8.7	737	0.01	4.1
Harris Trust & Savings Bank–collective bond	fixed income	12.7	12.3	12.4	718	0.21	7.2
Landon Butler–multi-employee property trust	real estate	-2.8	2.2	4.2	660	-0.22	-4.9
Nationsbank–EB fixed income	fixed income	13.4	12.3	12.2	595	0.21	7.8
Fidelity Mgmt. Trust–small-company growth	aggressive growth	11.5	9.3	11.4	595	0.75	2.2
Mellon Bank–DF stock	common stock	13.1	13.3	11.2	593	0.95	2.3
Bankers Trust–SLH bond index	fixed income	13.4	11.8	12.1	576	0.21	7.9
Fidelity Management Trust–aggressive equity	aggressive growth	7.8	10.2	12.5	551	0.93	-2.3
Wells Fargo Bank–taxable total return	fixed income	14.0	12.6	12.0	518	0.25	8.1
First Union National Bank–common stock	common stock	13.3	9.6	8.9	497	1.07	1.6
First Union National Bank–income-plus bond	fixed income	11.4	11.3	NA	480	0.20	6.0
Bankers Trust–capital appreciation	aggressive growth	-1.9	11.3	7.6	479	1.11	-12.2
Security Trust-EB bond	fixed income	12.2	11.6	12.2	468	0.15	6.8
Wells Fargo Bank–taxable intermediate bond	fixed income	11.5	11.5	11.2	468	0.23	5.9
First Union National Bank–fixed income	fixed income	11.9	11.8	11.0	461	0.15	6.8
Bankers Trust–Russell 2000 equity	aggressive growth	9.6	5.7	NA	459	0.71	0.8
Nationsbank–EB real estate	real estate	-4.7	-5.4	0.4	449	-0.22	-6.7
Woodbridge Capital Mgmt–mfrs investment E	common stock	9.2	10.2	9.5	445	1.06	-2.0

Source: CDA Investment Technologies

Institutional Funds (cont'd)

25 Best Bank Funds

Bank Fund–Name of Account	Objective	1 Yr. Return	3 Yr. Return	5 Yr. Return	Assets ($ mil.)	Risk Beta	Risk Held
National Bank of Detroit–total return stock	common stock	21.3	12.1	12.5	87	0.75	11.2
Provident Nat'l Bank–personal special equity	aggressive growth	20.1	19.7	18.6	93	1.18	6.9
Comerica Bank–special sit CTF 5	aggressive growth	13.6	16.1	10.8	77	0.63	5.0
First National Bank of Clearwater–equity	common stock	17.6	14.4	11.6	24	1.12	5.0
Texas Commerce Invest. Mgmt–spec equity grp	aggressive growth	5.6	14.7	10.8	26	0.96	-4.6
Boatmen's Trust–variable maturity bond F	fixed income	18.5	14.3	14.6	195	0.40	11.2
Woodbridge Cap. Mgmt–fund I small-cap equity	aggressive growth	8.5	16.2	10.7	61	1.10	-2.9
First Commercial Bank–EB special	common stock	13.3	13.5	11.4	13	0.68	4.4
Chase of Connecticut–E-2	aggressive growth	10.2	11.9	7.8	10	0.93	-0.2
Barnett Banks Trust–EB small cap	aggressive growth	13.1	10.8	6.5	18	1.08	1.4
National Bank of Detroit–opportunity	common stock	16.9	10.4	10.5	135	0.79	6.9
Trust Co. Bank of Atlanta–sunbelt equity	common stock	13.1	16.7	14.8	30	1.03	1.7
Liberty Bank & Trust–common growth	aggressive growth	12.9	12.1	8.9	14	0.83	2.9
Security Pacific National Bank–common trust E	aggressive growth	10.1	12.8	10.8	41	1.23	-2.4
Signet Trust–capital growth	common stock	9.6	10.8	6.8	5	1.15	-2.3
Mellon Bank–DF special	aggressive growth	14.2	12.5	12.9	164	0.94	3.3
Union National Bank of WV–group trust 2	common stock	18.3	14.1	12.2	2	0.91	7.3
Tx. -Amer. Bank–team bank EB small-cap eq.	common stock	NA	NA	NA	8	NA	NA
Second National Bank of Ohio–EB growth	aggressive growth	11.9	15.0	12.7	3	1.02	0.7
One Valley Bank–special equity S	aggressive growth	-8.2	9.8	15.8	11	1.12	-18.0
One Valley Bank–common trust K	common stock	7.2	11.8	8.8	50	0.87	-2.5
First NH Investment Svc.–first common stock	common stock	6.5	8.6	9.4	24	1.12	-4.8
First Nat'l Bank of Chicago–PT taxable bond	fixed income	15.3	12.5	13.2	59	0.23	9.5
Union Bank–capital growth equity	aggressive growth	6.2	11.4	9.3	101	1.12	-5.1
Liberty Bank & Trust–pooled equity	common stock	12.5	11.9	9.2	9	0.82	2.7

25 Worst Bank Funds

Bank Fund–Name of Account	Objective	1 Yr. Return	3 Yr. Return	5 Yr. Return	Assets ($ mil.)	Risk Beta	Risk Held
Bank of Boston–BKB equity income	aggressive growth	1.1	-1.0	0.4	77	0.89	-8.2
United Bank of Denver–EBF equity S	aggressive growth	1.6	-0.1	4.2	39	0.80	-7.2
Fidelity Management Trust–select int'l	international	-2.4	NA	NA	32	0.63	-9.8
Boatmen's Trust–int'l equity W	international	-3.3	0.2	1.8	132	0.36	-8.9
First Nat'l Bank of Chicago–PT intl equity	international	-2.2	0.9	4.2	48	0.40	-8.1
Norwest Bank Minnesota–int'l equity	international	-3.2	-1.9	1.5	121	0.42	-9.3
Bankers Trust–gov't guarantee mortgage	fixed income	2.9	9.5	9.6	439	0.02	-0.9
Wilmington Trust–int'l equity collective	international	4.7	1.5	NA	8	0.28	-0.9
Bankcal–special growth equity	aggressive growth	-9.3	6.7	4.7	4	1.04	-18.5
Citizens Trust–equity CTF-A	common stock	8.0	10.1	8.9	23	1.05	-3.0
Laird Norton Trust–pacific northwest	common stock	3.4	NA	NA	7	0.67	-4.7
Star Bank–EB capital growth	aggressive growth	-7.6	0.7	2.0	13	0.70	-15.0
Star Bank–PT capital growth	aggressive growth	-7.6	2.7	NA	9	0.72	-15.1
FourthNat'l Bank of Tulsa–PT equity growth	common stock	8.5	12.1	10.3	7	0.80	-0.9
Morgan Guaranty Trust–real estate	real estate	-11.3	-5.1	0.7	1,592	-0.28	-12.8
Nationsbank–EB real estate	real estate	-4.7	-5.4	0.4	449	0.22	-6.7
Second National Bank–EB equity	common stock	11.0	8.0	9.3	5	0.81	1.4
Landon Butler–multi-employee property trust	real estate	-2.8	2.2	4.2	660	-0.22	-4.9
Putnam Trust–common trust B	common stock	5.5	10.4	8.9	20	1.05	-5.3
BancOklahoma Trust–A equity	common stock	-1.0	4.1	7.5	30	0.96	-10.6
Citibank Priv. Bank–common trust spec. eq.	aggressive growth	-5.0	8.3	9.4	48	1.45	-16.9
UBS Asset Mgmt.–large-cap growth equity	common stock	10.8	12.7	NA	66	1.17	-1.3
Union Bank–international equity	international	-5.6	-2.8	0.5	13	0.30	-10.7
Bankers Trust–capital appreciation	aggressive growth	-1.9	11.3	7.6	479	1.11	-12.2
Citizens Trust–equity retirement CTF-P	common stock	9.3	11.0	8.0	45	0.96	-1.3

Source: CDA Investment Technologies

Retirement

FEDERAL INCOME TAX LAWS PERMIT the establishment of a number of types of retirement plans, each of which may be funded with mutual fund shares.

Individual Retirement Accounts

All wage-earners under the age of 70S may set up an Individual Retirement Account (IRA). The individual may contribute as much as 100 percent of his or her compensation each year, up to $2,000. Earnings are tax-deferred until withdrawal. The amount contributed each year may be wholly or partially tax-deductible. Under the Tax Reform Act of 1986, all taxpayers not covered by employer-sponsored retirement plans can continue to take the full deduction for IRA contributions. Those who are covered, or who are married to someone who is covered, must have an adjusted gross income of no more than $25,000 (single) or $40,000 (married, filing jointly) to take the full deduction. The deduction is phased out for incomes between $25,000 and $35,000 (single) and $40,000 and $50,000 (married, filing jointly). An individual who qualifies for an IRA and has a spouse who either has no earnings or elects to be treated as having no earnings, may contribute up to 100 percent of his or her income or $2,250, whichever is less.

Simplified Employee Pensions (SEPs)

SEPs are employer-sponsored plans that may be viewed as an aggregation of separate IRAs. In an SEP, the employer contributes up to $30,000 or 15 percent of compensation, whichever is less, to an Individual Retirement Account maintained for the employee. SEPs established for employers with 25 or fewer employees may contain a "cash or deferred" arrangement allowing employees to make additional elective salary deferrals to the SEP. The cash or deferred arrangement for smaller employers is called a SARSEP, for salary reduction SEP.

Corporate and Self-Employed Retirement Plans

Tax-qualified pension and profit-sharing plans may be established by corporations or self-employed individuals. Changes in the tax laws have made retirement plans for employees of corporations and those for self-employed individuals essentially comparable. Contributions to a plan are tax-deductible and earnings accumulate on a tax-sheltered basis.

The maximum annual amount which may be contributed to a defined contribution plan on behalf of an individual is limited to the lesser of 13 percent of the individual's compensation or $30,000.

Section 403(b)of the Internal Revenue Code permits employees of certain charitable organizations and public school systems to establish tax-sheltered retirement programs. These plans may be invested in either annuity contracts or mutual fund shares.

Section 401(k) Plans

One particularly popular type of tax-qualified retirement plan which may be offered by either corporate or non-corporate entities is the 401(k) plan. A 401(k) plan is usually a profit-sharing plan that includes a "cash or deferred" arrangement. The cash or deferred arrangement permits employees to have a portion of their compensation contributed to a tax-sheltered plan on their behalf, or paid to them directly as additional taxable compensation. Thus, an employee may elect to reduce his or her taxable compensation with contributions to a 401(k) plan where those amounts will accumulate tax-free. Employers often "match" these amounts with employer contributions. The Tax Reform Act of 1986 established new, tighter anti-discrimination requirements for 401(k) plans and curtailed the amount of elective deferrals which may be made by all employees. Nevertheless, 401(k) plans remain excellent and popular retirement savings vehicles.

Source: Mutual Fund Fact Book

Recommended Resource

Mutual Fund Fact Book
Investment Company Institute
P.O. Box 66140
Washington DC 20035
(202) 955-3534

Retirement (cont'd)

Growth in Mutual Fund IRA Plans ($ billions)

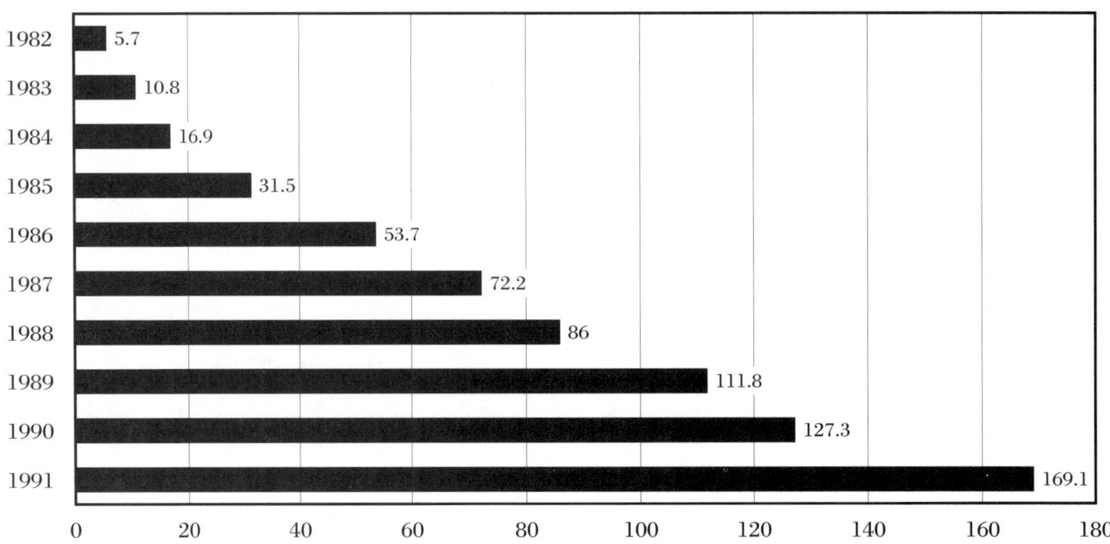

Growth in Mutual Fund Self-Employed Retirement Plans ($ billions)

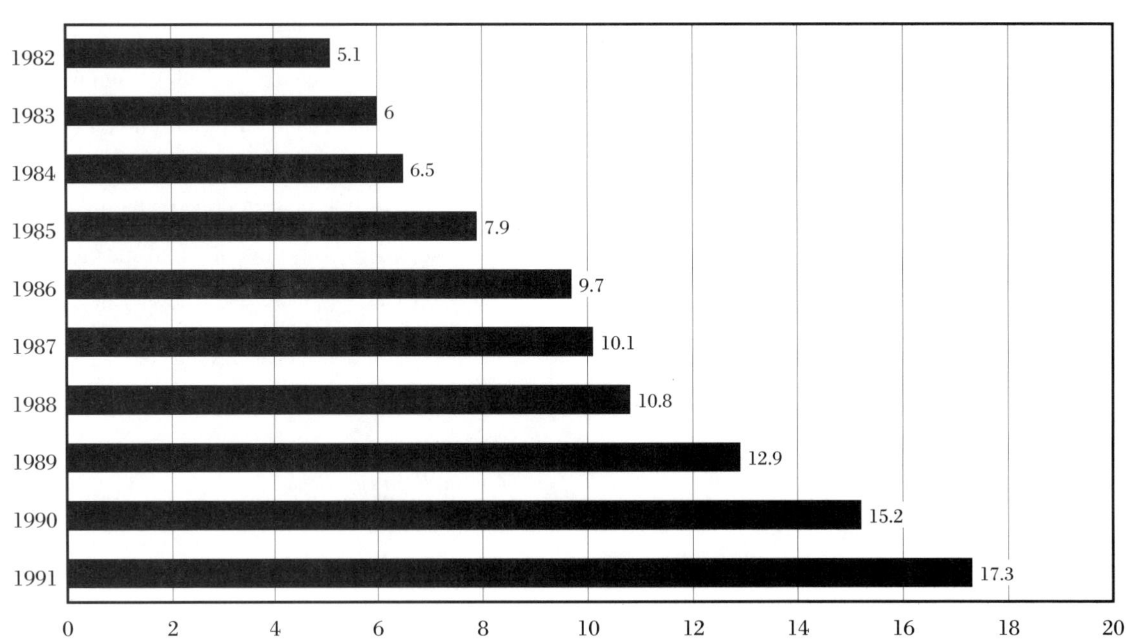

Source: The Investment Company Institute, Mutual Fund Fact Book

Actuaries

ACTUARIES USE MATHEMATICAL probability to project the financial effects that various events–birth, marriage, sickness, accident, fire, liability, retirement, death–have on insurance, benefit plans, and other financial security systems.

The American Academy of Actuaries is the best source of information on the actuarial profession. The Academy's *Fact Book* provides the most general information on the field, including assessments on the industry's past and future, and information on the academy programs and publications both for people inside and outside the field. The Academy's bi-monthly magazine, *Contingencies*, their monthly newsletter *The Actuarial Update*, and the *Enrolled Actuaries Report* (published 5 to 6 times yearly) explore current actuarial issues in-depth. Another publication, *The Issues Digest*, summarizes recent Washington legislative activities as they relate to the actuarial profession.

The *Directory of Actuarial Memberships*, published jointly by the two largest actuarial societies, the Academy and the Society of Actuaries (see below) lists all actuaries in North America, their professional affiliations, and qualifications.

Recommended Resources

The American Academy of Actuaries
1720 I St., NW, 7th Floor
Washington, DC 20006
(202) 223-8196

Represents actuaries in all practice specialties.

Society of Actuaries
Suite 800
475 N. Martingale Rd.
Schaumburg, IL 60173
(708) 706-3500

Represents actuaries working in the fields of life and health insurance, employee benefits, and pensions.

Casualty Actuarial Society
Suite 600
1100 N. Glebe Rd.
Arlington, VA 22201
(703) 276-3100

Represents actuaries specializing in property and liability insurance, workers' compensation, and liability coverage fields.

Conference of Actuaries in Public Practice
Suite 800
475 N. Martingale Rd.
Schaumburg, IL 60173
(708) 706-3535

An association for consulting actuaries in all fields of the practice.

American Society of Pension Actuaries
8th Floor
4350 N. Fairfax Dr.
Arlington, VA 22203
(703) 516-9300

Provides membership services to pension plan consultants and administrators.

Financing a Business

Venture Capital

Year	The Number of IPOs backed by Venture Capital Funds	Capital Committed to Venture Capital Funds ($ billions)
1981	68	0.867
1982	27	1.423
1983	121	3.408
1984	53	3.185
1985	47	2.327
1986	98	3.332
1987	81	4.184
1988	36	2.947
1989	39	2.399
1990	42	1.847
1991	121	1.271
1992	151	2.548

Source: Venture Capital Journal

Financing a Business (cont'd)

Looking for Investors On-Line

Finding interested and appropriate investors for your company can be the greatest of all start-up challenges. Now a number of computer-based services are making the process of meeting and matching much easier through the sharing of financial and investment information on-line. Subscribers to these services, both the company and the investor, pay a fee for listing their needs and criteria for investment.

Sources for Investors On-Line

Network	Area Served	Phone
Georgia Capital	Georgia	(404) 894-5344
Kentucky Investment Capital	National	(502) 564-4252
Mid-Atlantic Investment Network	Mostly Mid-Atlantic	(301) 405-2144
Northwest Capital	Oregon	(503) 282-6273
Pacific Venture Capital Network	California	(714) 856-8366
Private Investor	South Carolina	(803) 648-6851
Texas Capital Network	National	(512) 794-9398
Technology Capital Network	Mostly Northeast	(617) 253-7163
Venture Capital	Minnesota	(612) 223-8663
Washington Investment	Washington	(206) 464-6282

Source: Inc. Magazine

Investment Banks/Brokerage Houses

Top 10 Underwriters of Debt and Equity, 1992

Manager	Amount ($ billions)	Market Share (%)
Merrill Lynch	150.7	13.3
Goldman Sachs	119.6	10.6
Lehman Brothers	106.2	9.4
First Boston	98.7	8.7
Kidder Peabody	81.0	7.1
Salomon Brothers	80.3	7.1
Morgan Stanley	72.5	6.4
Bear Stearns	53.4	4.7
J.P. Morgan	29.2	2.6
Prudential Securities	28.6	2.5
TOTAL	820.3	72.4

Top 10 Underwriters of U.S. Debt and Equity, 1992

Manager	Amount ($ billions)	Market Share (%)	Number of Issues
Merrill Lynch	140.4	16.5	834
Goldman Sachs	104.5	12.3	534
Lehman Brothers	99.9	11.7	503
First Boston	81.3	9.5	381
Kidder Peabody	76.8	9.0	285
Salomon Brothers	74.7	8.8	268
Morgan Stanley	64.6	7.6	356
Bear Stearns	52.8	6.2	191
Prudential Securities	28.5	3.4	107
Donaldson Lufkin	20.2	2.4	117
TOTAL	43.6	87.4	3,576

Source: Securities Data Co.

Investment Banks/Brokerage Houses (cont'd)

Top 10 Underwriters of Non-U.S. Debt and Equity, 1992

Manager	Amount ($ billions)	Market Share (%)
Deutsche Bank	22.1	7.9
First Boston	17.4	6.2
Nomura Securities	17.3	6.1
Goldman Sachs	15.2	5.4
Banque Paribas	13.4	4.7
J.P. Morgan	12.5	4.4
Daiwa Securities	11.3	4.0
UBS Phillips & Drew	10.7	3.8
Merrill Lynch	10.3	3.7
Yamaicha Securities	9.2	3.3
TOTAL	139.4	49.4

Top Markets of U.S. Debt and Equity, 1992

Market	Amount ($ millions)	Top Ranked Manager
U.S. Domestic	851.2	Merrill Lynch
Straight Debt	309.2	Merrill Lynch
Convertible Debt	7.0	First Boston
Junk Bonds	38.0	Merrill Lynch
Investment Grade Debt	271.2	Merrill Lynch
Mortgage Debt	377.3	Kidder Peabody
Asset-Backed Debt	50.9	First Boston
Collateral Securities	428.2	Kidder Peabody
Preferred Stock	29.2	Merrill Lynch
Common Stock	72.4	Merrill Lynch
IPOs	39.4	Merrill Lynch
Closed-End Funds	15.7	Merrill Lynch
International Debt	268.3	Deutsche Banke
International Equity	13.6	Goldman Sachs
World-Wide Issues	1,133.1	Merrill Lynch
U.S. Issues	843.4	Merrill Lynch
Municipal New Issues	231.7	Goldman Sachs

Source: Securities Data Co.

The Top Reference Sources

Commodity Prices
Gale, $69.50
(800) 877-4253

Encompassing 14,000 listings for 10,000 products and 200 sources, this book gives you specific information to lead you to the periodicals, yearbooks, and other sources that list commodity prices. The entries are arranged by commodity, and there is an extensive index.

Alternative Financing

IN ADDITION TO BANKS, SBA loans, and traditional venture capital firms, there are a range of other, less traditional, financing alternatives available to entrepreneurs.

Here is a checklist of five alternatives, as assembled by Jay Levinson and Bruce Blechman, authors of *Guerrilla Financing*.

Receivable Financing

Extending credit to your customers is similar to lending them money. You are essentially loaning them cash while they have your product or service.

Short-term revolving financing is provided by factors or receivable lenders. These firms recognize your receivables as a valuable asset, and are usually willing to lend against it, regardless of your company's financial position.

Factors will purchase your receivables (at a discount) and collect the money from your customers directly. For example, if a company sells $1,000,000 in clothing to Macy's, a factor might pay $900,000 for the receivable. It is then up to the factor to collect the entire invoice directly from Macy's.

A receivables lender will loan money against the invoice and hold it as collateral. Once the invoice is paid, your company repays the lender.

This is a common form of lending. Check your local yellow pages under Factors, or the Corporate Finance Sourcebook for firms that offer this service.

Customer Financing

No one knows your business better than your customers. If your product or service is valuable and difficult to replace, many of your customers may be interested in financing your growth.

This is obviously a risky, time-consuming method of finding financing, but if the proper match is made, both parties can benefit.

Equipment Financing

When purchasing expensive capital equipment, a company often has the opportunity to finance the purchase, or enter into a lease. In both cases, money is freed up, and the company gains the ability to use the machinery without sacrificing its cash position.

Many banks and manufacturers are willing to finance the purchase of capital equipment. They will lend your company money against the value of the equipment purchased, holding the equipment as collateral. The downside of this approach is that the loan appears on your balance sheet, affecting your company's leverage and your ability to borrow against the value of the company.

Leasing is an increasingly common method of financing. In this situation, the company never takes title to the equipment. Instead, the leasing company purchases the equipment and leases it to the company for a monthly fee. There are two significant advantages to this arrangement: the company doesn't need to dispose of the equipment at the end of the lease, and the lease is off balance sheet, meaning that since there is no loan, a company's debt load is not affected.

Real Estate Financing

Many companies don't realize that their real estate is not fully leveraged. Banks prefer to make loans against land because they are more comfortable placing a value on it. Check the real estate section of the Sunday paper to find mortgage brokers in your area.

Venture Capital Clubs

These clubs seek to eliminate the middleman by bringing small investors together with entrepreneurs in search of capital. These small organizations make it easy for a company to speak directly to a motivated lender. The downside is that these are people lending their own money, so there is often an emotional side to the process.

Long Island Venture Group
Business Reseach Institute
Hofstra University
Hempstead, NY 11550
(516) 560-5705

New Enterprise Forum
912 N. Main St.
Ann Arbor, MI 48104
(313) 662-0550

New Jersey Venture Association
Weiner & Company
177 Madison Ave.
PO Box CN 1982
Morristown, NJ 07960
(201) 267-4200

New York Venture Group
605 Madison Ave., Suite 300
New York, NY 10022
(212) 832-7300

Southeastern Michigan Venture Group
PO Box 43181
Detroit, MI 48243
(313) 886-2331

Alternative Financing (cont'd)

Greater Cincinnati Venture Association
c/o Nobis Associates, Inc.
1802 Triangle Park Dr.
Cincinnati, OH 45246
(513) 772-7054

Baltimore-Washington Venture Group
1545 18th St., NW, #319
Washington, DC 20036
(301) 369-4900

Gold Coast Venture Capital Club
110 E. Atlantic Ave., #208E
Delray Beach, FL 33444
(305) 272-1040

Atlanta Venture Forum, Inc.
2859 Paces Ferry Rd., Suite 1400
Atlanta, GA 30339
(404) 584-1364

Central Kentucky Venture Capital Club
PO Box 508
Elizabethtown, KY 42701
(502) 769-1410

Tennessee Venture Group
27 Music Sq. East
Nashville, TN 37203
(615) 244-4622

Chicago Venture Capital Club
c/o Arthur Young & Company
One IBM Plaza
Chicago, IL 60611
(312) 645-3394

The Entrepreneur's Network
512 Nicollet Mall, Suite 500
Minneapolis, MN 55402
(612) 542-0682

Eastern South Dakota Venture Capital Forum
University of South Dakota
414 E. Clark St.
Vermillion, SD 57069
(605) 677 5272

Venture Club of Iowa City
First Capital Development
325 E. Washington
Iowa City, IA 52240
(319) 337-4195

Southwest Venture Forum
SMU-External Affairs
Edwin L. Cox School of Business
Dallas, TX 75275
(214) 692-3027

Greater New Orleans Venture Capital Club
c/o Center of Economic Development
Room BA 368
New Orleans, LA 70148
(504) 286-6663

Rockies Venture Club, Inc.
1600 Broadway, #2125
Denver, CO 80202
(303) 832-2737

MountainWest Venture Group
50 S. Main St.
PO Box 210
Salt Lake City, UT 84144
(801) 363-3455

Global Investment Interest Group
16810 E. Avenue of the Fountains, Suite 201
Fountain Hills, AZ 85268
(602) 837-7751

Orange Coast Venture Group
PO Box 7282
Newport Beach, CA 92658
(714) 754-1191

Northern California Venture Capital Association
1470 Wild Rose Way
Mountain View, CA 94043
(415) 965-4651

Puget Sound Venture Club
14606 NE 51st St., #C-1
Bellevue, WA 98007
(206) 882-0605

Puerto Rico Venture Capital Club
PO Box 2284
Hato Rey, PR 00919
1-809-787-9040

Contact Option

For a complete list of venture capital clubs, contact (by mail if possible):
Kevin Ontiveros
Association of Venture Clubs
265 E. 100 South, #300
Salt Lake City, UT 84110
(801) 583-4939

Recommended Resource

Guerrilla Financing
by Bruce Bleachman and Jay Conrad Levinson
Houghton Mifflin

Non-Performing Loans

Non-Performing Loans, % by State, FDIC-Insured Commercial Banks

State	%	State	%
Alabama	.94	Montana	1.00
Alaska	1.44	Nebraska	.79
Arizona	2.18	Nevada	2.34
Arkansas	1.06	New Hampshire	3.19
California	4.83	New Jersey	4.95
Colorado	1.34	New Mexico	2.46
Connecticut	4.90	New York	4.49
Delaware	1.55	North Carolina	1.42
DC	7.61	North Dakota	.96
Florida	2.55	Ohio	1.60
Georgia	1.52	Oklahoma	1.56
Hawaii	.96	Oregon	1.85
Idaho	.73	Pennsylvania	2.03
Illinois	1.77	Rhode Island	5.43
Indiana	1.50	South Carolina	1.90
Iowa	.73	South Dakota	1.91
Kansas	1.78	Tennessee	1.52
Kentucky	1.34	Texas	1.78
Louisiana	2.68	Utah	1.23
Maine	2.82	Vermont	4.62
Maryland	3.67	Virginia	2.89
Massachusetts	2.80	Washington	2.47
Michigan	1.27	West Virginia	1.12
Minnesota	1.25	Wisconsin	1.03
Mississippi	1.14	Wyoming	1.02
Missouri	1.91	NATIONAL AVERAGE	2.83

Source: Sheshunoff Information Services

Insurance Companies

A STUDY AT INDIANA UNIVERSITY examined the largest insurance companies in the country and identified those that were the most secure (least risky). Here are twenty of the most secure, ranked by size.

Prudential
Metropolitan
Aetna Life
Teachers Insurance & Annuity
New York Life
Connecticut General
John Hancock Mutual
Northwestern Mutual
Principal Mutual
Massachusetts Mutual
Lincoln National
IDS Life
Allstate Life
Nationwide
Variable Annuity Life
Hartford Life
State Farm Life
Aetna Life & Annuity
New York Life & Annuity
Continental Assurance

Source: Indiana University (Fact Book)

Accounting

Accounting Firms Ranked

Firm	City	Sales ($ millions)	Growth (%)
Arthur Andersen & Co.	New York	2,680	9
Ernst & Young	New York	2,280	2
Deloitte & Touche	Wilton, CT	1,955	0
KPMG Peat Marwick	New York	1,813	0
Coopers & Lybrand	New York	1,560	6
Price Waterhouse	New York	1,370	7
Grant Thornton	Chicago	222	8
Kenneth Leventhal & Co.	Los Angeles	188	3
McGladrey & Pullen	Davenport, IA	188	5
BDO Seidman	New York	181	0
Baird Kurtz & Dobson	Springfield, MO	60	5
Altschuler, Melvoin & Glasser	Chicago	54	11
Crowe, Chizek & Co.	South Bend, IN	52	12
Clifton Gunderson & Co.	Peoria, IL	51	3
Moss Adams	Seattle	50	14
Plante & Moran	Southfield, MI	49	2
Geo. S. Olive & Co.	Indianapolis	36	24
Goldstein Golub Kessler & Co.	New York	29	1
Richard A. Eisner & Co.	New York	29	12
Friedman, Eisenstein, Raemer & Schwartz	Chicago	27	1
Larson, Allen, Weishair & Co.	Minneapolis	25	4
Cherry Bekaert & Holland	Richmond, VA	23	-13
J.H. Cohn & Co.	Roseland, NJ	23	0
Wipfli Ullrich Bertelson	Wausau, WI	21	3
David Berdon & Co.	New York	20	0
Parente, Randolph, Orlando, Carey & Assoc.	Wilkes-Barre, PA	19	5
Campos & Stratis	Teaneck, NJ	19	7
Thomas Havey & Co.	Chicago	19	6
Urbach, Kahn & Werlin	Albany, NY	18	-2
Checkers Simon & Rosner	Chicago	18	0
Margolin Winer Evens	Garden City, NY	17	10
Reznick Fedder & Silverman	Bethesda, Md	17	17
M.R. Weiser & Co.	New York	17	1
Weber Lipshie	New York	15	1
Hausser & Taylor	Cleveland	15	5
Schenck & Associates	Appleton, WI	15	9
Virchow Krause & Co.	Madison, WI	14	16
Mitchell/Titus & Co.	New York	14	22
Kennedy & Coe	Salina, KS	13	1
Charles Bailly & Co.	Fargo, ND	13	-1
Blackman Kallick Bartelstein	Chicago	13	-7
Eide Heimeke & Co.	Fargo, ND	13	6
Rehmann Robson & Co.	Saginaw, MI	12	1
Kemper CPA Group	Robinson, IL	12	2
Mayer Hoffman McCann	Kansas City, MO	12	8
Follmer, Rudzewicz & Co.	Southfield, MI	12	4
Rubin, Brown, Gornstein	St. Louis	12	-2
Mahoney Cohen & Co.	New York	12	9
Joseph Decosimo & Co.	Chattanooga, TN	12	0
Dixon Odom & Co.	High Point, NC	11	7
Edward Isaacs & Co.	New York	11	-2
Tofias, Fleishman, Shapiro & Co.	Cambridge, MA	11	4
Anchin, Block & Anchin	New York	11	-4
LeMaster & Daniels	Spokane, WA	11	21
Mauldin & Jenkins	Albany, GA	11	-1
Rothstein, Kass & Co.	Roseland, NJ	11	9
Hemming Morse Inc.	San Francisco	10	6
Clark, Schaefer, Hackett & Co.	Middletown, OH	10	0
Goodman & Co.	Norfolk, VA	10	7
C.W. Amos & Co.	Baltimore	10	-9

Source: Accounting Today

Accounting (cont'd)

Accountants' Favorite Software

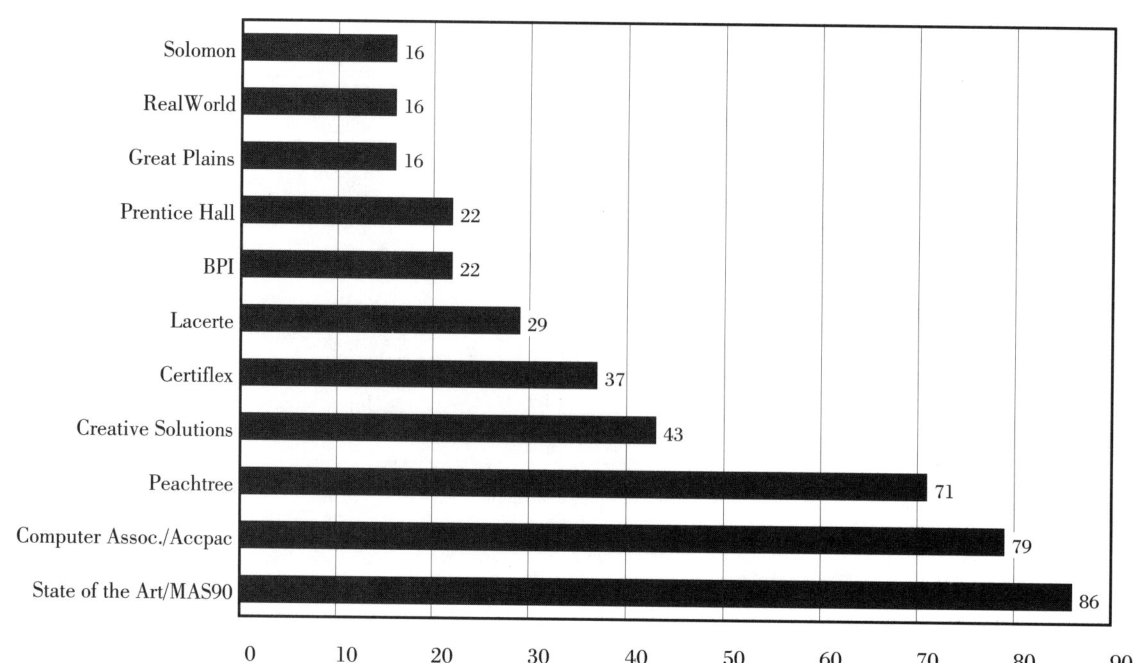

Tax Preparers' Favorite Software

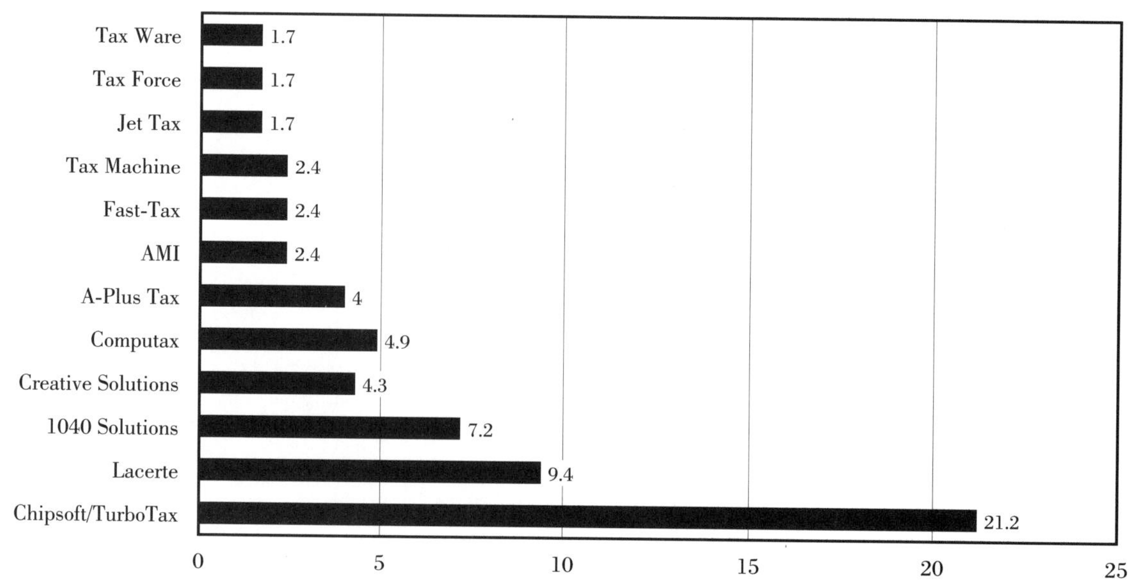

Source: Accounting Today

The Accounting Hall of Fame

Arthur Edward Andersen
Thomas Coleman Andrews
Robert Newton Anthony
Marshall Smith Armstrong
George David Bailey
Andrew Barr
Norton Moore Bedford
Sir Henry Alexander Beson
Carmen George Blough
Samuel John Broad
Percival Flack Brundage
John Lansing Carey
Sidney Davidson
Phillip Leroy Defliese
Sir Arthur Lowes Dickinson
Marquis George Eaton
Harry Anson Finney
Arthur Bevins Foye
Oscar Strand Gellein
Paul Franklin Grady
Henry Rand Hatfield
Charles Thomas Horngren
Yuji Ijiri
Roy Bernard Kester
Eric Louis Kohler
Ananias Charles Littleton
Perry Empey Mason
Robert Kuhn Mautz
George Oliver May
Hebert Elmer Miller
Hermann Clinton Miller
Robert Heister Montgomery
Maurice Moonitz
Lloyd Morey
William Andrew Paton
James Loring Peirce
Donald Putnam Perry
John William Queenan
Howard Irwin Ross
Thomas Henry Sanders
Hiram Thompson Scovill
Elijah Watt Sells
Leonard Paul Spacek
Charles Ezra Sprague
Elmer Boyd Staats
Maurice Hubert Stans
Victor Hermann Stempf
Joseph Edmund Sterrett
Robert Martin Trueblood
William Welling Werntz

Source: The Ohio State University College of Business

Tax Freedom Day

IN 1992, THE AVERAGE AMERICAN WORKER worked 126 days–from January 1 to May 15–to satisfy all federal, state, and local tax obligations for the year. Tax Freedom Day is that day on which the taxpayer stops working to earn the tax money he owes and starts working for himself–taking home his own paycheck for real. Over time, this day of freedom has fallen later and later in the year.

Tax Freedom Date

Year	Date
1960	April 16
1965	April 14
1970	April 26
1975	April 27
1980	May 1
1985	April 30
1990	May 3
1991	May 2
1992	May 5

The Top Reference Sources

Accounting Today
Lebhar-Friedman, $96
(212) 756-5155

This twice-a-month publication offers the inside scoop on the accounting field. Lively articles, news, and in-depth surveys offer the reader insight into the rules affecting accounting, and more important, the intricacies of running a successful accounting practice.

Choosing an Accountant

THE TERM ACCOUNTANT CAN MEAN many different things, depending on a company's size and needs. A huge company like IBM thinks of an accountant as not just one person but rather as a large professional team of consultants. The team may consist of specialists who audit financial statements, prepare tax returns, and give tax advice, or analyze and improve sophisticated computer and information systems.

A smaller company might need just one individual, probably a tax expert who periodically reviews the company's financial statements.

Finding an accountant whose specialties and interests match your needs is a critical step in setting up a long-term financial structure.

Here are fifteen questions you can ask when interviewing a prospective accountant:

1. Have you helped a client in a similar situation?

It saves time to work with an accountant who has already dealt with similar situations. Probe to discover exactly how he has dealt with problems similar to yours.

2. Will our firm be serviced by a partner or by junior accountants?

Many firms train new associates at the client's expense. Be sure that you get what you pay for.

3. What is the nature, scope, and timing of your work, and what will it cost me?

Often, an accountant's work plan can be more extensive and more expensive than you might expect. Get the accountant to be specific about what he or she will do, and get a detailed written engagement letter and cost estimate.

4. Can you give me two or three quick ideas on how you might be able to save our company money?

A good accountant should have sharp business acumen and be willing to be creative. A question like this can show whether the accountant can call on his or her many skills to truly help you to increase profits, improve productivity, trim costs, enhance return, and lower taxes.

5. Can you tell me a little about your practice, and your successes and failures?

Open-ended questions can elicit a wealth of information. Let the accountant talk. You will also learn a lot about the accountant's priorities, risk-tolerance levels, and various personality characteristics, all of which can be helpful in gauging compatibility.

6. How are your fees calculated? Will you be charging me for every phone discussion?

To avoid friction later, it is essential to discuss the accountant's fee structure, including the hourly rate of the accountant and staff, overhead expense reimbursement (how much should you pay for a fax?), and whether certain time is not billed.

7. What can I do to help you with your work and keep your fees to a minimum?

A great deal of your accountant's time can be saved by preparing information beforehand. Find out if your accountant is willing to work with you to offload this work to your firm.

8. How will you be communicating the results of your work to me?

The results of an audit usually take the form of an audit report, and tax return preparation yields tax returns. But this work also can lead to many suggestions by the accountant on how to cut taxes, increase income, restructure investments, build business, and improve information flow. Some accountants are more comfortable with interactive discussions and others prefer written action reports.

9. Do you perceive any conflicts of interest?

Accountants work for dozens of firms, and you should probe to see if any of your direct competition is represented by the firm. If so, inquire as to how this conflict is handled.

10. Are you a Certified Public Accountant, and what other licenses do you hold?

If the accountant is certified, you should inquire with the state CPA organization to discover if there have been any disciplinary actions entered. Some accountants also have credentials as financial planners, securities representatives, even lawyers.

11. How well have you integrated computers into your practice, and has it enabled you to do more for clients at less cost?

Integrating your computer files with those of your accountant's can save time and money, and increase accuracy.

12. Will you need to overhaul our current system?

Your internal bookkeeping and cost-accounting systems are expensive to alter. Find out upfront whether you can integrate with the firm's systems.

13. Are you conservative or aggressive in interpreting tax laws and regulations, and accounting and auditing standards?

Save yourself the hassle and be certain that your accountant approaches your books in the same way you would.

Source: Frank Sisco

Mortgage Tables

To compute a mortgage payment, divide the amount borrowed by $100,000, then multiply that number by the number in the table.

	Length of Mortgage (years)					
Rate	**5**	**10**	**15**	**20**	**25**	**30**
5.0%	1,887.12	1,060.66	790.79	659.96	584.59	536.82
5.5%	1,910.12	1,085.26	817.08	687.89	614.09	567.79
6.0%	1,933.28	1,110.21	843.86	716.43	644.30	599.55
6.5%	1,956.61	1,135.48	871.11	745.57	675.21	632.07
7.0%	1,980.12	1,161.08	898.83	775.30	706.78	665.30
7.5%	2,003.79	1,187.02	927.01	805.59	738.99	699.21
8.0%	2,027.64	1,213.28	955.65	836.44	771.82	733.76
8.5%	2,051.65	1,239.86	984.74	867.82	805.23	768.91
9.0%	2,075.84	1,266.76	1,014.27	899.73	839.20	804.62
9.5%	2,100.19	1,293.98	1,044.22	932.13	873.70	840.85
10.0%	2,124.70	1,321.51	1,074.61	965.02	908.70	877.57
10.5%	2,149.39	1,349.35	1,105.40	998.38	944.18	914.74
11.0%	2,174.24	1,377.50	1,136.60	1,032.19	980.11	952.32
11.5%	2,199.26	1,405.95	1,168.19	1,066.43	1,016.47	990.29
12.0%	2,224.44	1,434.71	1,200.17	1,101.09	1,053.22	1,028.61
12.5%	2,249.79	1,463.76	1,232.52	1,136.14	1,090.35	1,067.26
13.0%	2,275.31	1,493.11	1,265.24	1,171.58	1,127.84	1,106.20
13.5%	2,300.98	1,522.74	1,298.32	1,207.37	1,165.64	1,145.41
14.0%	2,326.83	1,552.66	1,331.74	1,243.52	1,203.76	1,184.87
14.5%	2,352.83	1,582.87	1,365.50	1,280.00	1,242.16	1,224.56
15.0%	2,378.99	1,613.35	1,399.59	1,316.79	1,280.83	1,264.44
15.5%	2,405.32	1,644.11	1,433.99	1,353.88	1,319.75	1,304.52
16.0%	2,431.81	1,675.13	1,468.70	1,391.26	1,358.89	1,344.76
16.5%	2,458.45	1,706.42	1,503.71	1,428.90	1,398.24	1,385.15
17.0%	2,485.26	1,737.98	1,539.00	1,466.80	1,437.80	1,425.68
17.5%	2,512.22	1,769.79	1,574.58	1,504.94	1,477.53	1,466.33
18.0%	2,539.34	1,801.85	1,610.42	1,543.31	1,517.43	1,507.09
18.5%	2,566.62	1,834.17	1,646.52	1,581.90	1,557.48	1,547.94
19.0%	2,594.06	1,866.72	1,682.88	1,620.68	1,597.68	1,588.89
19.5%	2,621.64	1,899.52	1,719.47	1,659.66	1,638.01	1,629.92
20.0%	2,649.39	1,932.56	1,756.30	1,698.82	1,678.45	1,671.02
20.5%	2,677.29	1,965.82	1,793.35	1,738.15	1,719.01	1,712.18
21.0%	2,705.34	1,999.32	1,830.61	1,777.64	1,759.66	1,753.40
21.5%	2,733.54	2,033.03	1,868.08	1,817.28	1,800.41	1,794.67
22.0%	2,761.89	2,066.97	1,905.76	1,857.06	1,841.24	1,835.98

Almanac Fact

Toll-free tax advice is available from the IRS year round. The number to call is (800) 829-1040.

Human Resources

Business School Placement Offices

Carnegie Mellon University
Career Opportunities Center
Graduate School of Industrial Administration
Schenley Park
Pittsburgh, PA 15213
(412) 268-2272

Columbia University
Columbia Business School
Office of Placement
Uris Hall
New York, NY 10027
(212) 280-5567

Cornell University
Johnson Graduate School of Management
Placement Office
315 Malott Hall
Ithaca, NY 14853
(607) 255-2327

Dartmouth University
Amos Tuck School of Business Administration
Placement Office
Hanover, NH 03755
(603) 646-3162

Duke University
The Fuqua School of Business
Placement Office
Durham, NC 27706
(919) 684-5874

Harvard University
Graduate School of Business Administration
Placement Office
Soldiers Field Road
Boston, MA 02163
(617) 495-6127

Indiana University at Bloomington
Graduate School of Business
Business Placement Office
10th St. and Fee Lane
Bloomington, IN 47405
(812) 335-8006

Massachusetts Institute of Technology
Sloan School of Management
Placement Office
50 Memorial Dr.
Cambridge, MA 02139
(617) 253-3730

New York University
Graduate School of Business Administration
Office for Student Counseling & Career Placement
100 Trinity Pl.
New York, NY 10006
(212) 285-6250

Northwestern University
Kellogg Graduate School of Management
Placement Office
2001 Sheridan Rd., Leverone Hall
Evanston, IL 60208
(312) 491-3308

Purdue University
Krannert Graduate School of Management
Placement Office
Lammert Center
West Lafayette, IN 47907
(317) 494-4365

Stanford University
Graduate School of Business
Career Management Center
Stanford, CA 94305
(415) 723-2766

University of California at Berkeley (Haas)
Graduate School of Business Administration
Placement Center
350 Barrows Hall
Berkeley, CA 94720
(415) 642-1405

University of California at Los Angeles
John E. Anderson Graduate School of Management
Placement and Career Planning Office
405 Hilgard Ave.
Los Angeles, CA 90024
(213) 825-8874

University of Chicago
Graduate School of Business
Placement Office
1101 E. 58th St.
Chicago, IL 60637
(312) 702-7269

University of Michigan
School of Business Administration
Placement Office
701 Tappan
Ann Arbor, MI 48109
(313) 763-5796

University of North Carolina-Chapel Hill
Graduate School of Business Administration
MBA Program Placement Service
CB # 3490 Carroll Hall
Chapel Hill, NC 27599
(919) 962-3236

University of Pennsylvania
The Wharton School, Graduate Division
Placement Office
102 Vance Hall
Philadelphia, PA 19104
(215) 898-6182

Business School Placement Offices (cont'd)

University of Pittsburgh
Joseph M. Katz Graduate School of Business
Placement Services
276 Mervis Hall
Pittsburgh, PA 15260
(412) 648-1700

University of Rochester
William E. Simon Graduate School of Business
Administration Placement Office
Dewey Hall
Rochester, NY 14627
(716) 275-3533

University of Southern California
Graduate School of Business Administration
Career Program
University Park
Los Angeles, CA 90089
(213) 743-7846

University of Texas at Austin
Graduate School of Business
Placement Office
Austin, TX 78712
(512) 471-5921

University of Virginia
Darden Graduate School of Business Administration
Placement Office
Box 6550
Charlottesville, VA 22906
(804) 924-3900

Vanderbilt University
Owen Graduate School of Management
Career Counseling and Placement Office
401 21st Ave.
Nashville, TN 37203
(605) 322-6469

Yale University
Yale School of Organization and Management
Career Development Office
Box 1A
New Haven, CT 06520
(203) 432-5932

MBA Schools Ranked

Top 20 U.S. Business Schools*

1992 Rank	School	1990 Rank	Corp. Poll	Graduate Poll	Avg. Pay Pre-MBA ($)	Avg. Pay Post-MBA ($)
1	Northwestern (Kellogg)	1	1	3	42,950	70,200
2	Chicago	4	4	10	40,460	68,600
3	Harvard	3	3	12	52,790	84,960
4	Pennsylvania (Wharton)	2	2	15	45,780	72,200
5	Michigan	7	6	9	36,370	58,110
6	Dartmouth (Amos Tuck)	6	12	1	49,700	74,260
7	Stanford	5	7	5	51,570	82,860
8	Indiana	15	8	6	33,410	49,070
9	Columbia	8	5	18	40,150	66,620
10	North Carolina	12	11	8	39,990	55,500
11	Virginia (Darden)	14	15	2	40,560	65,280
12	Duke (Fuqua)	13	14	7	39,060	59,870
13	MIT (Sloan)	11	10	14	42,630	73,000
14	Cornell (Johnson)	16	17	4	37,820	59,940
15	NYU (Stern)	17	13	16	40,130	56,730
16	UCLA (Anderson)	10	16	11	42,740	64,540
17	Carnegie Mellon	9	9	23	35,730	56,980
18	California (Haas)	19	19	13	41,050	65,500
19	Vanderbilt (Owen)	None	20	19	27,900	47,230
20	Washington (Olin)	None	18	24	31,900	48,200

**Note: Rankings are based on a Business Week survey of business school alumni and corporations.*

Source: Business Week

Universities Ranked

U.S. News & World Report SELECTS fourteen categories of schools in its annual guide to colleges and universities, using the standard guidelines established by the Carnegie Foundation for the Advancement of Teaching. The Best University category is selected from national universities with selective student bodies, greater resources, and broader reputations than schools in other categories. According to Carnegie guidelines, these schools offer a wide range of baccalaureate programs, place a high priority on research, and award large numbers of Ph.D.'s.

The Best Universities

Rank	University
1	Harvard University
2	Princeton University
3	Yale University
4	Stanford University
5	California Institute of Technology
*	Massachusetts Institute of Technology
7	Dartmouth College
*	Duke University
9	University of Chicago
10	Columbia University
11	Cornell University
12	Rice University
13	Northwestern University
14	University of Pennsylvania
15	Johns Hopkins University
16	University of California at Berkeley
17	Georgetown University
18	Brown University
19	Carnegie-Mellon University
20	Washington University
21	Emory University
22	University of Virginia
23	University of California at Los Angeles
24	University of Michigan
25	Vanderbilt University

Note: *=*tie.*

Source: U.S. News & World Report

Small Colleges Ranked

THE BEST SMALL COLLEGE CATEGORY is comprised of national liberal arts colleges which are highly selective and award more than half their degrees in the liberal arts. Within each category, schools are ranked by reputation, selectivity, faculty resources, financial resources, and student satisfaction.

The Best Small Colleges

Rank	College
1	Williams College
2	Amherst College
3	Swarthmore College
4	Wellesley College
5	Pomona College
6	Bowdoin College
7	Wesleyan College
8	Middlebury College
9	Haverford College
10	Smith College
*	Bryn Mawr College
12	Carleton College
13	Vassar College
14	Grinnell College
15	Colby College
16	Claremont McKenna College
17	Colgate University
18	Davidson College
19	Mount Holyoke College
20	Oberlin College
21	Hamilton College
22	Washington and Lee University
23	Bates College
24	Trinity College (CT)
25	Lafayette College

Note: *=*tie.*

Source: U.S. News & World Report

Law School Placement Offices

Boston College
Law School
Placement Office
885 Centre St.
Newton, MA 02159
(617) 552-4350

Columbia University
School of Law
Office of Law Placement
435 W. 116th St.
New York, NY 10027
(212) 280-2648

Cornell University
Cornell Law School
Placement Service
Myron Taylor Hall
Ithaca, NY 14853
(607) 255-5141

Duke University
School of Law
Placement Office
Towerview and Science Dr.
Durham, NC 27706
(919) 684-2834

Georgetown University
Law Center
Career Planning and Placement Center
600 New Jersey Ave., NW
Washington, DC 20001
(202) 662-9010

George Washington University
The National Law Center
Career Development Office
716 20th St., NW
Washington, DC 20052
(202) 676-6260

Harvard University
Harvard Law School
Placement Office
Cambridge, MA 02138
(617) 495-3109

New York University
School of Law
Office of Placement Services
40 Washington Square S.
New York, NY 10012
(212) 598-2517

Northwestern University
School of Law
Placement Office
357 E. Chicago Ave.
Chicago, IL 60611
(312) 908-8465

Stanford University
Stanford Law School
Office of Career Services
Crown Quadrangle
Stanford, CA 94305
(415) 723-4985

University of California at Berkeley
School of Law
Placement Office
220 Boalt Hall
Berkeley, CA 94720
(415) 642-2274

University of California at Hastings
College of Law
Placement Office
200 MacAllister St.
San Francisco, CA 94102
(415) 565-4623

University of California at Los Angeles
School of Law
Placement Office
405 Hilgard Ave.
Los Angeles, CA 90024
(213) 825-4041

University of Chicago
Law School
Placement Office
111 E. 60th St.
Chicago, IL 60637
(312) 702-9484

University of Iowa
College of Law
Placement Office
Boyd Law Building
Melrose and Byington Sts.
Iowa City, IA 52242
(319) 335-9142

University of Michigan
Law School
Placement Service
Hutchins Hall
625 S. State St.
Ann Arbor, MI 48109
(313) 764-0537

Law School Placement Offices (cont'd)

University of Minnesota
Law School
Placement Office
229 19th Ave. S.
Minneapolis, MN 55455
(612) 625-5005

University of Notre Dame
Notre Dame Law School
Placement Office
Notre Dame, IN 46556
(219) 239-6626

University of Pennsylvania
Law School
Placement Office
3400 Chestnut St.
Philadelphia, PA 19104
(215) 898-7400

University of Southern California
Law Center
Office of Career Planning and Placement
University Park
Los Angeles, CA 90089
(213) 743-7331

University of Texas at Austin
School of Law
Placement Office
727 E. 26th St.
Austin, TX 78705
(512) 471-5151

University of Virginia
School of Law
Placement Office
North Grounds
Charlottesville, VA 22901
(804) 924-7351

University of Washington
School of Law
Placement Office
1100 NE Campus Parkway
Seattle, WA 98105
(206) 543-4550

Vanderbilt University
School of Law
Placement Office
Nashville, TN 37240
(615) 322-6452

Yale University
Law School
Placement Office
Box 401-A Yale Station
New Haven, CT 06520
(203) 436-3015

Law Schools Ranked

AT LEAST 15 LAW SCHOOLS consider themselves among the top ten. Here is an alphabetical list of those most often mentioned in national rankings.

Columbia University
Cornell University
Duke University
Georgetown University
Harvard University
New York University
Northwestern University
Stanford University
University of California at Berkeley
University of Chicago
University of Michigan
University of Pennsylvania
University of Texas
University of Virginia
Yale University

Almanac Fact

The U.S. spends 2.6% of the total GDP on litigation. There are seven times as many lawyers per capita in the U.S. as in France.

Source: We're Number One

Business Co-Op Programs

COOPERATIVE EDUCATION BEGAN IN 1906 at the University of Cincinnati in Ohio. The purpose then, and now, was to strengthen classroom learning with periods of study-related employment in companies outside of the academic environment. Co-operative students take part in a college program that alternates periods of study with periods of work, either on a full-time or part-time basis.

The goal of businesses that participate in co-operative learning programs is to enhance the education of college and university students through integrated, structured programs which combine academic study with paid, productive work experience. Co-op education can provide a cost-effective means of meeting recruiting goals, and training potential career employees, as well as providing an opportunity to influence the education process.

Co-op education is practiced in over 1,000 colleges and universities in the U.S., as well as in various countries around the world. It is found mostly in two- and four-year college programs but is also in a limited number of five-year programs. Co-op is available in virtually every college curriculum and is offered at all levels, from the associate to the doctoral degree. Age is no factor for participation. Co-op is open to both traditional and non-traditional college students. In most programs, students receive academic credit for work experience and are charged comparable tuition rates. In other programs, no academic credit is awarded and no tuition is charged.

According to the Cooperative Education Research Center, over 275,000 co-op students are enrolled in a program each year with over 50,000 employers. Although student earnings vary with college major, years in school, and geographic location, co-op students earn a national average of $7,000 per year.

Where Co-Op Students Find Work

80% of co-op students receive an offer for full-time employment from one of their co-op employers. 63% of co-op students receive an offer from their final co-op employer. 48% of the co-op students accept those offers. 40% find employment in fields directly related to their co-op assignments. 15% enroll in graduate or professional programs.

Recommended Resources

Co-op Experience Magazine
Academic Periodicals, Ltd.
330 Cherokee St.
Marietta, GA 30060
(800) 955-5134

This quarterly magazine also publishes a directory of schools, employers and training programs.

Cooperative Education Association
11710 Beltsville Dr.
Suite 520
Beltsville, MD 20705
(301) 572-CEA9

Provides services for professionals who either hire or place co-operative education students.

Cooperative Education Undergraduate Directory
National Commission for Cooperative Education
360 Huntington Ave.
Boston, MA 02115

This directory lists co-operative education programs by school and by state and includes a list of co-operative education employers.

Continuing Education

FOR A COMPLETE LISTING OF CONTINUING education programs in a particular area, consult:

Recommended Resource

The College Blue Book: Occupational Education
Macmillan Publishing Company
866 Third Avenue
New York, NY 10022
(212) 702-2000

This extensive directory has a complete listing of educational programs arranged alphabetically by subject and by location. The book is available in the reference section of most public libraries.

Colleges by Specialty Programs

Top Undergraduate Business Administration Programs

Carnegie-Mellon University
Indiana University
Massachusetts Institute of Technology
New York University
University of California at Berkeley
University of Illinois
University of Michigan
University of Pennsylvania
University of Texas
University of Wisconsin

Source: The Ultimate College Shopper's Guide

Top Undergraduate Accounting Programs

Arizona State University
Brigham Young University
James Madison University
Kansas State University
Miami University
Michigan State University
Northern Illinois University
Ohio State University
Oklahoma State University
Stanford University
Texas A&M University
University of Alabama
University of Florida
University of Georgia
University of Illinois
University of Michigan
University of Missouri
University of Notre Dame
University of Pennsylvania
University of Southern California
University of Tennessee
University of Texas
University of Virginia
University of Washington
University of Wisconsin
Wake Forest University

Source: The Ultimate College Shopper's Guide

ESL Programs

TO FIND THE LOCATION of an English as a Second Language program, contact:

The National Literacy Hotline
(800) 228-8813

This hotline has a listing of available ESL programs in high schools, colleges, and universities around the country.

Recommended Resource

English Language and Orientation Programs in the United States
Institute of International Education
809 United Nations Plaza
New York, NY 10017
(212) 883-8200

The Top Reference Sources

The Idea-a-Day Guide to Super Selling and Customer Service
Dartnell
(800) 621-5463

This excellent reference includes a self-diagnostic test to identify special selling needs; sections devoted to specific sales skills, techniques, and strategies; more than 100 tips, ideas, and information sources, worksheets, and 250 practical money-making ideas for each working day of the year. The oversized format and easy-to-use design make it an excellent workbook.

Correspondence Courses

THE FOLLOWING IS A LIST of selected programs that provide accredited home study programs. Most of them offer financial assistance through the G.I. Bill or through employee assistance programs.

Accounting/Secretarial Computer
North American Correspondence Schools
Scranton, PA 18515
(717) 342-7701

Airline/Travel
American Travel Centre
11300 Lomas Blvd., NE
P.O. Box 23427
Albuquerque, NM 87192
(800) 727-7702

Airline/Travel
Educational Institute of the American Hotel & Motel Association
Stephen S. Nisbet Building
1407 S. Harrison Rd.
P.O. Box 1240
East Lansing, MI 48226
(517) 353-5500

Airline/Travel
Hospitality Training Center, Inc.
220 N. Main St.
Hudson, OH 44236
(216) 653-9151

Airline/Travel
International Aviation and Travel Academy
300 W. Arbrook Blvd.
Arlington, TX 76014
(817) 784-7000

Airline/Travel
Southeastern Academy, Inc.
233 Academy Dr.
P.O. Box 421768
Kissimmee, FL 34742
(407) 847-4444

Airline/Travel
TransWorld Travel Academy
11495 Natural Bridge Rd.
St. Louis, MO 63044
(314) 895-6754

Airline/Travel
Travel Lab
One Chatham Center
Pittsburgh, PA 15219
(412) 456-1800

Airline/Travel
WORLDSPAN Travel Academy
7310 Tiffany Springs Parkway
Kansas City, MO 64153
(816) 891-5357

Airline/Travel Career Training
American Educational Institute
3851 Main St.
Bridgeport, CT 06606
(800) 354-3507

Broadcasting/Computer
Columbia School of Broadcasting
2840 E. Flamingo Rd., Suite F
Las Vegas, NV 89121
(800) 426-0651

Business/Vocational
International Correspondence Schools
Scranton, PA 18515
(717) 342-7701

Electronics/Computers
McGraw-Hill Continuing Education Center
4401 Connecticut Ave., NW
Washington DC 20008
(202) 244-1600

Engineering/Electronics
International Correspondence Schools Center for Degree Studies
Scranton, PA 18515
(717) 342-7701

English Usage
English Language Institute
332 S. Michigan Ave., Suite 1518
Chicago, IL 60604
(800) 398-9834

High School Diploma
American School
850 E. 58 St.
Chicago, IL 60637
(312) 947-3300

High School Diploma
Citizen's High School
188 College Dr.
Orange Park, FL 32067
(904) 276-1700

Correspondence Courses (cont'd)

High School Diploma
Futures High School
1249 F St.
San Diego, CA 92101
(619) 235-4100

High School Diploma
ICS-Newport/Pacific High School
Scranton, PA 18515
(717) 342-7701

Paralegal
Paralegal Institute, Inc.
2922 N. 35th Ave., Suite 4
Drawer 11408
Phoenix, AZ 85061
(602) 272-1855

Paralegal
Southern Career Institute
164 W. Royal Palm Rd.
P.O. Drawer 2158
Boca Raton, FL 33427
(800) 669-2555

People's College of Independent Studies
233 Academy Dr.
P.O. Box 421768
Kissimmee, FL 34742
(407) 847-4444

Secretarial Training
Laural School
2538 N. 8th St.
P.O. Box 5338
Phoenix, AZ 85010
(602) 994-3460

Contact Option

National Home Study Council
1601 18 St., NW
Washington DC 20009
(202) 234-5100
Information source

Trainers and Seminars

ON-SITE TRAINING FOR PERSONNEL, whether in the form of books, audio cassettes, films, videotapes, software, or live seminars, is available through a wide range of human resources companies and consultants.

One of the most extensive sources for finding the right training program is published by the American Society for Training and Development. Their book offers a listing of companies and consultants that provide hardware, training facilities, and other training and equipment supplies. Also included is an alphabetized listing of companies and consultants and a listing of specialists who cater to industry-specific audiences. The directory also includes a subject index of companies and consultants who provide human resources development in areas as specific as: AIDS in the Workplace, Ergonomics, Quality Control, and Time Management Skills.

Recommended Resource

ASTD Buyer's Guide and Consultant Directory
1640 King St., Box 1443
Alexandria, VA 22313
(703) 683-8100

Contact Options

Personal Progress Library
7657 Winnetka Ave., #331
Winnetka, CA 91306
(818) 996-0352
Programs for rent

Training and Development Resource Catalogues:

Blanchard Training and Development, Inc.
125 State Pl.
Escondido, CA 92025
(800) 821-5332

CareerTrack
3085 Center Green Dr.
Boulder, CO 80301
(800) 423-3001

Nightingale-Conant
7300 N. Lehigh Ave.
Niles, IL 60714
(312) 588-6217

QCI International
P.O. Box 1503, Dept. 1029
1350 Vista Way
Red Bluff, CA 96080
(916) 527-6970

Sybervision Systems
P.O. Box 2278
Maple Plains, MN 55348
(800) 888-9980

The Zig Ziglar Company
3330 Earhart #20
Carrolton, TX 75006
(800) 527-0306

Executive Education

AUDIOCASSETTES, VIDEOCASSETTES, training programs, and seminars designed to expand the skills of the corporate executive are a multi-billion dollar industry in this country.

There are several companies that design and present executive training programs that run anywhere from one day to several weeks. Seminars are offered in a wide array of topics ranging from quality control to stress reduction and from business writing to budget planning.

Contact Options

Executive Training Firms:

CareerTrack
3085 Center Green Dr.
Boulder, CO 80301
(800) 423-3001

Fred Pryor Seminars
Pryor Resources Inc.
2000 Shawnee Mission Parkway
Shawnee Mission, KA 66205
(913) 722-3990

National Seminars Group
6901 W. 63 St.
Shawnee Mission, KA 66202
(913) 432-7755

An executive looking for a seminar on a particular subject can call:

First Seminar Service
600 Suffolk St.
Lowell, MA 01854
(800) 321-1990

For a fee, First Seminar will do a search and find all of the available seminars on a particular topic anywhere in the country over the course of the year.

Recommended Resources

The Corporate University Guide to Short Management Seminars
The Corporate University, Inc.
123 N. Main St.
Suite 108
Fairfield, Iowa 52556
(515) 472-7720

Seminar Directory
Gale Research, Inc.
835 Penobscot Bldg.
Detroit, MI 48226
(313) 961-2242

Both directories provide a thorough listing of seminars available by topic, training organization, date, and location.

Speakers Bureaus

COMPANIES OFTEN NEED SPEAKERS, either to motivate a sales force or to entertain at a company event. For the right price, it's possible to hire anyone, from Henry Kissinger to a foreign expert on quality control, to lecture an audience of company personnel. A number of agencies exist whose sole function is to book speakers for corporate events.

Contact Options

Lecture Agents:

Walters International Speakers Bureau
18825 Hicrest Rd.
P.O. Box 1120
Glendora, CA 91740
(818) 335-1855

Washington Speakers Bureau, Inc.
310 S. Henry St.
Alexandria, VA 22314
(703) 684-0555

The Harry Walker Agency
One Penn Plaza, Suite 2400
New York, NY 10119
(212) 563-0700

National Speakers Bureau
222 Wisconsin Ave.
Lake Forest, IL 60045
(708) 295-1122

Keppler Association
4350 N. Fairfax Dr.
Arlington, VA 22203
(703) 516-4000

Recommended Resource

Who's Who in Professional Speaking
National Speaker's Assoc. Membership Directory
1500 S. Priest Dr.
Tempe, AZ 85281
(602) 986-2552

This directory lists names, addresses, and phone numbers of members alphabetically, geographically, and by specialty.

Speech and Image Consultants

SEMINARS THAT ASSIST EXECUTIVES and managers in developing a solid professional image and effective presentation skills are available from a number of human resources consultants. These programs focus on effective communication styles for public speaking engagements.

Contact Options

Human Resource Consultants:

Achievement Concepts, Inc.
1963 Cynthia Lane
P.O. Box 430
Merrick, NY 11566
(516) 868-5100

Anderson Management Group, Inc.
413 Victoria Court, NW
Box 1745-A
Vienna, VA 22183
(703) 938-9672

Communication Resources
Harvard Square
P.O. Box 537
Cambridge, MA 02238
(617) 332-4334

Conrad Communications
6 Black Birch Lane
Scarsdale, NY 10583
(914) 725-2360

Dale Carnegie & Assoociates, Inc.
1475 Franklin Ave.
Garden City, NY 11530
(800) 231-5800

Kaufman Professional Image Consultants
200 Locust Street
Suite 3B
Philadelphia, PA 19106
(215) 592-1075

The Mentor Group
1202 Calibre Creek Parkway
Roswell, GA 30076
(404) 552-2569

Myers
P.O. Box 1526
Princeton, NJ 08542
(609) 737-6832

Tracy Presentation Skills
2414 Londonderry Rd., Suite 767
Alexandria, VA 22308
(703) 360-3222

Top Business Speakers

Cavett Award Winners

The Cavett Award is the top speaker's award given annually by the National Speakers Association:

1979 - Robert Cavett
1980 - Bill Gove
1981 - Dave Yoho
1982 - Ty Boyd
1983 - Joe Larson
1984 - Ira M. Hayes
1985 - Nido R. Oubein
1986 - Don Hutson
1987 - James "Doc" Blakely
1988 - Robert H. Henry
1989 - Jeanne Robertson
1990 - D. Michael Frank
1991 - Rosita Perez
1992 - D. John Hammond

Personal Selling Power Magazine's Top Ten Meeting Speakers for 1992 and Their Fees

1. Lou Holtz - $22,000
2. Pat Riley - $20,000
3. Terry Bradshaw - $15,000
4. Zig Ziglar - $15,000
5. Dr. Denis Waitley - $10,000
6. Tony Alessandra - $7,000
7. Danielle Kennedy - $6,500
8. Art Mortell - $6,500
9. Don Hutson - $6,000
10. Charlie Plumb - $5,000

Contact Option

National Speakers Association
1500 S. Priest Dr.
Tempe, AZ 85281
(602) 968-2552

Coping with Illiteracy

Reasons Most Often Cited by Manufacturers for Rejecting Job Applicants

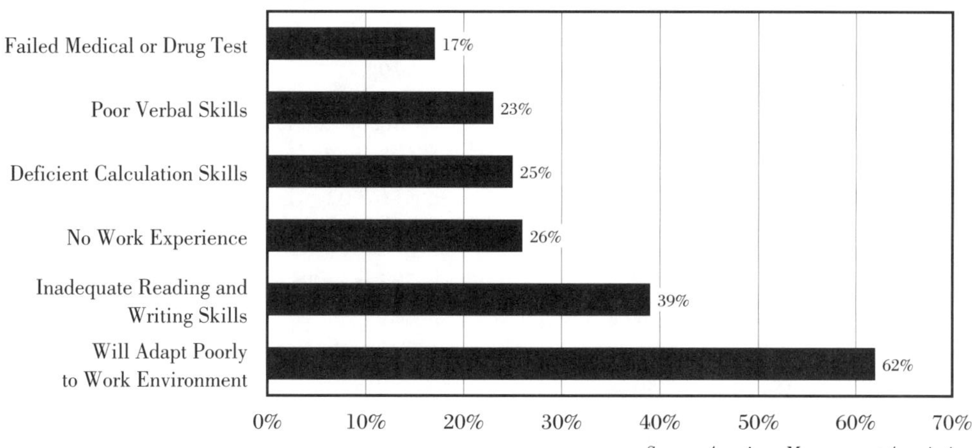

Source: American Management Association

Percentage of Companies that Provide Remedial Training

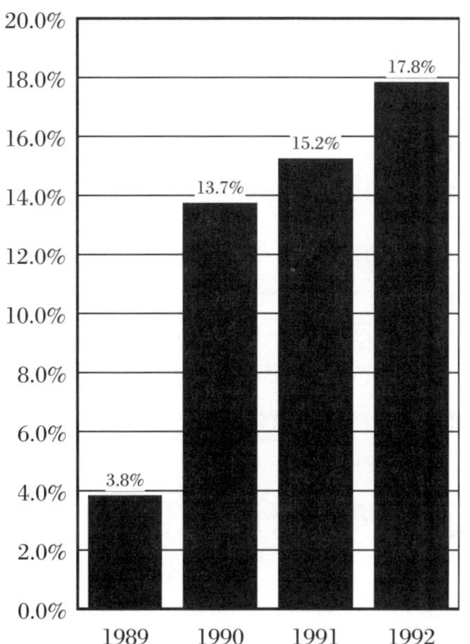

Source: American Management Association

Percentage of Companies that Conduct Literacy and Math Competency Testing

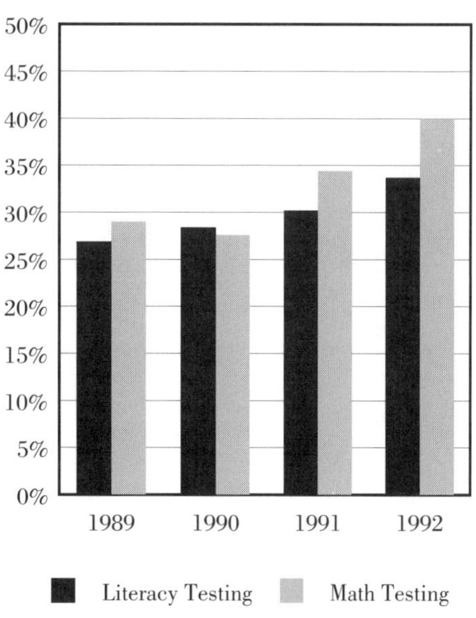

Source: American Management Association

Coping with Illiteracy (cont'd)

Percentage of Companies that Give Basic Skills Tests to Applicants and Current Workers

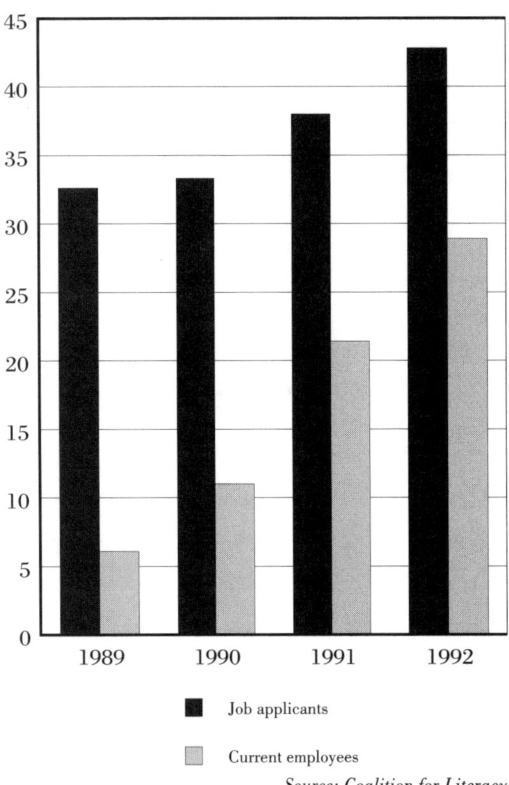

Source: Coalition for Literacy

A number of companies specialize in training programs to improve the reading and writing speed, and efficiency of company personnel. These companies will conduct on-site seminars or provide materials for corporations to conduct their own courses.

Contact Options

Companies Specializing in Literacy Training:

Aztec Software Associates/Computer Action Learning Inc.
24 Tulip St., Box 863
Summit, NJ 07902
(908) 273-7443

Bell Atlantic Education Services
104 Carnegie Center, CN5302
Princeton, NJ 08543
(609) 987-6062

Conover Company, Ltd.
P.O. Box 155
Omro, WI 54963
(800) 933-1943

Computer Action Learning, Inc.
58 Harvey Dr.
P.O. Box 770
Summit, NJ 07902
(908) 273-4829

Karen Dexter & Associates
77 Salem
Suite 200
Evanston, IL 60203
(708) 679-8878

National Education Centers, Inc.
1732 Reynolds
Irvine, CA 92714
(714) 261-7606

Reading Development Resources
7201 S. Broadway, Suite 11
Littleton, CO 80122
(303) 794-1764

Shipley Associates
390 N. Main St.
P.O. Box 460
Bountiful, UT 84011
(800) 343-0009

Writing Development Associates
254-39 Bates Rd.
Little Neck, NY 11363
(718) 279-3143

Recommended Resource

Coalition for Literacy
P.O. Box 81826
Lincoln, NE 68501
(800) 228-8813

Compensation and Benefits

A COMPANY NEEDING TO DESIGN a benefits package for its employees can contact a consulting firm that specializes in this field.

The following is a list of the ten largest U.S.-based consultants and their estimated 1991 revenues in millions of dollars:

Ten Largest U.S.-Based Consultants

Consulting Firm	Est. 1991 Revenue ($ millions)
Mercer	395.9
Towers, Perrin	316.8
Wyatt	316.0
Hewitt	256.7
Alexander	134.9
A. Foster Higgins	125.6
Buck	122.3
Coopers & Lybrand	96.9
Segal	70.6
KPMG Peat Marwick	60.0

Source: Business Insurance Magazine

Percentage of Companies That Offer Each Employee Benefit

A recent survey of 1,300 companies yielded the following information on the type of employee benefits offered by a sampling of U.S. businesses.

Plan Type	Insurance	%
Basic health care plans	Medical insurance	98
	HMO	77
	PPO	50
Special health care plans	Dental	94
	Prescriptions	76
	Vision	43
Retirement plans	401(k) plan	86
	Pension plan	78
	Profit sharing	31
Other benefits	Life insurance	97
	Disability	97
	Education assistance	94

Source: The New York Times

Compensation and Benefits Offered

Benefits Program	Total % With	Total % Without	% Do Not Have But Are Considering
BASIC HEALTH CARE PLANS			
Medical Insurance Coverage (excluding dental)	98.3	1.5	0.2
Health Maintenance Organization (HMO)	77.0	19.9	3.1
Preferred Provider Organization (PPO)	49.8	37.6	12.6
SPECIAL HEALTH CARE PLANS (not included under Basic Health Care)			
Dental Coverage	94.4	4.4	1.2
Vision Coverage	43.1	50.3	6.6
Alcohol/Drug Program	68.2	29.2	2.6
Physical Fitness Program	31.9	59.6	8.5
Prescription Drug Coverage	76.0	21.5	2.5
Hearing Examination Coverage	22.6	73.7	3.7
OTHER EMPLOYEE BENEFITS			
Formal Training/Professional Development Program	68.8	23.1	8.1
Flextime (employee chooses alternative work schedules)	44.3	47.0	8.7
Group Term Life Insurance	96.5	3.1	0.4
Educational Assistance	93.5	5.5	1.0
Pre-Retirement Counseling	44.6	42.3	13.1
Accidental Death & Dismemberment	94.6	5.2	0.2
Short-Term Disability Insurance	83.9	14.2	1.9
Long-Term Disability Insurance	97.2	2.0	0.8
Annual Computerized Benefits Statement	60.0	21.6	18.4
Group Personal Insurance (payroll deduction auto or homeowner's insurance)	10.0	84.8	5.2
Flexible Benefits (employee chooses from among various benefits plans)	40.6	39.6	19.8
Flexible Spending Account(s) (Section 125)	59.0	30.0	11.0

Compensation and Benefits (cont'd)

Benefit Program	Total % With	Total % Without	% Don't Have But Are Considering
RETIREMENT INCOME			
Pension Plan	77.7	21.6	0.7
Profit Sharing Plan	30.7	66.5	2.8
Thrift Plan	18.9	78.4	2.7
401(k) Salary Reduction Plan	85.7	11.8	2.5
ESOP (Employee Stock Ownership Plan)	24.3	71.6	4.1
EXECUTIVE STOCK PLANS			
Incentive Stock Options	36.2	60.1	3.7
Non-Qualified Stock Option Plan	37.1	59.8	3.1
Stock Appreciation Rights	16.6	79.0	4.4
Restricted Stock Award Plan	27.8	67.7	4.5
Performance Share Plan	13.0	81.3	5.7
EXECUTIVE INCENTIVE PLANS			
Performance Unit Plan	20.8	74.5	4.7
Annual Cash Incentive Plan	66.9	30.5	2.6
Medium-Term Cash Incentive Plan (2-3 yrs.)	5.7	89.6	4.7
Long-Term Cash Incentive Plan (3 yrs. or longer)	19.1	75.4	5.5
SPECIAL EXECUTIVE BENEFIT PROGRAMS			
Low/No Interest Loan Program	8.9	88.3	2.8
Executive Physical Examination	68.4	29.6	2.0
Executive Medical Reimbursement Plan	20.4	76.9	2.7
Executive Supplemental Disability Plan	19.1	77.0	3.9
Executive Supplemental Retirement Plan	38.3	58.0	3.7
Executive Supplemental Survivor Income Plan	16.7	80.5	2.8
Voluntary Deferred Compensation Plan	39.8	56.6	3.6
Executive Employment Contracts	33.4	65.1	1.5
Financial Counseling/Tax Planning	32.7	62.3	5.0
COMPENSATION PROGRAMS			
Formal Point-Factor Job Evaluation System	57.3	35.2	7.5
Formal Performance Appraisal	95.9	2.0	2.1
Special Project-Oriented Incentive for Engineers, Programmers, or Inventors	6.3	67.2	6.5
Other Group Incentives	29.3	60.2	10.5
Lump Sum Merit Increases	30.3	62.6	7.1
Gain Sharing	8.8	81.5	9.7
Specialized Compensation Software	20.8	64.0	15.2

Source: 1992 Human Resources Survey by William Mercer, Inc.

The Top Reference Sources

The Burwell Directory of Information Brokers
Burwell Enterprises, $65
(717) 537-9051

The only complete listing of reference librarians, researchers, and information brokers available.

This is an excellent first step in gathering market, competitive, or research and development data. These brokers, for a fee, will tap computerized databases and deliver information on virtually any topic.

Social Security

Covered Employment, Earnings, and Contribution Rates

Item	1970	1980	1983	1984	1985
Workers with insured status (millions)	105.7	137.4	145.0	147.0	148.7
Male (millions)	61.9	75.4	78.4	78.8	79.7
Female (millions)	43.8	62.0	66.6	68.2	69.0
Under 25 years old (millions)	17.7	25.5	24.4	23.1	22.3
25 to 34 years old (millions)	22.3	34.9	38.0	39.7	39.9
35 to 44 years old (millions)	19.0	22.4	25.9	27.2	28.5
45 to 54 years old (millions)	19.0	18.6	18.6	18.8	19.0
55 to 59 years old (millions)	7.8	9.2	9.2	9.1	9.1
60 to 64 years old (millions)	6.3	7.9	8.4	8.6	8.7
65 to 69 years old (millions)	5.1	6.7	7.1	7.1	7.3
70 years old and older (millions)	8.5	12.1	13.4	13.4	13.9
WORKERS REPORTED WITH					
Taxable earnings (millions)	93.0	112.0	112.0	116.0	120.0
Maximum earnings (millions)	24.0	10.0	7.0	7.0	7.0
Earnings in covered employment ($ billions)	532.0	1,326.0	1,608.0	1,772.0	1,912.0
Reported taxable ($ billions)	416.0	1,176.0	1,454.0	1,609.0	1,724.0
Percent of total (%)	78.2	88.7	90.4	90.8	90.2
AVERAGE PER WORKER					
Total earnings ($)	5,711.0	11,817.0	14,345.0	15,260.0	15,955.0
Taxable earnings ($)	4,464.0	10,500.0	12,982.0	13,871.0	14,367.0
Annual maximum taxable earnings ($)	7,800.0	25,900.0	35,700.0	37,800.0	39,600.0
Maximum tax ($)	374.0	1,588.0	2,392.0	2,533.0	2,792.0

Item	1986	1987	1988	1989	1990
Workers with insured status (millions)	150.6	152.7	155.4	158.0	160.4
Male (millions)	80.7	81.5	82.6	83.7	84.7
Female (millions)	69.9	71.2	72.8	74.3	75.7
Under 25 years old (millions)	21.9	21.3	21.3	21.1	20.9
25 to 34 years old (millions)	40.0	40.6	41.0	41.3	41.4
35 to 44 years old (millions)	29.8	31.2	32.3	33.5	34.8
45 to 54 years old (millions)	19.3	19.8	20.5	21.4	22.1
55 to 59 years old (millions)	9.0	8.9	8.8	8.7	8.7
60 to 64 years old (millions)	8.8	8.7	8.7	8.7	8.6
65 to 69 years old (millions)	7.5	7.6	7.7	7.9	8.0
70 years old and older (millions)	14.3	14.7	15.0	15.4	15.8
WORKERS REPORTED WITH					
Taxable earnings (millions)	123.0	125.0	130.0	133.0	134.0
Maximum earnings (millions)	7.0	8.0	8.0	8.0	8.0
Earnings in covered employment ($ billions)	2,035.0	2,198.0	2,411.0	2,593.0	2,722.0
Reported taxable ($ billions)	1,844.0	1,960.0	2,101.0	2,243.0	2,370.0
Percent of total (%)	90.6	89.2	87.1	86.5	87.1
AVERAGE PER WORKER					
Total earnings ($)	16,587.0	17,584.0	18,610.0	19,494.0	20,373.0
Taxable earnings ($)	14,992.0	15,680.0	16,215.0	16,863.0	17,739.0
Annual maximum taxable earnings ($)	42,000.0	43,800.0	45,000.0	48,000.0	51,300.0
Maximum tax ($)	3,003.0	3,132.0	3,380.0	3,605.0	3,924.0

Source: 1992 Statistical Abstract

Social Security (cont'd)

Social Security–Beneficiaries, Annual Payments, and Average Monthly Benefit

Year	Total Number of Beneficiaries (thousands)	Total Annual Payments ($ millions)	Average Monthly Benefit ($)
1970	26,229	31,863	118
1980	35,585	120,472	341
1985	37,058	186,195	479
1986	37,703	196,692	489
1987	38,190	204,156	513
1988	38,627	217,214	537
1989	39,151	230,850	567
1990, TOTAL	39,829	247,796	603

Social Security–Beneficiaries, Annual Payments, and Average Monthly Benefit

Division, State, Other Area	Total Number of Beneficiaries (thousands)	Total Annual Payments ($ millions)	Average Monthly Benefit ($)
UNITED STATES	38,889	244,020	606
New England	2,142	13,843	N/A
Maine	215	1,246	555
New Hampshire	162	1,032	605
Vermont	88	542	589
Massachusetts	970	6,224	605
Rhode Island	181	1,150	601
Connecticut	527	3,649	661
Middle Atlantic	6,299	42,173	N/A
New York	2,832	19,034	645
New Jersey	1,229	8,462	659
Pennsylvania	2,237	14,677	621
East North Central	6,798	44,724	N/A
Ohio	1,803	11,616	618
Indiana	913	5,929	628
Illinois	1,753	11,760	641
Michigan	1,490	10,010	643
Wisconsin	838	5,409	618
West North Central	3,024	18,656	N/A
Minnesota	669	4,101	587
Iowa	524	3,292	605
Missouri	914	5,582	589
North Dakota	113	653	567
South Dakota	128	739	557
Nebraska	268	1,664	595
Kansas	407	2,625	617
South Atlantic	7,148	43,252	N/A
Delaware	104	691	627
Maryland	609	3,875	601
District of Columbia	77	430	515
Virginia	834	4,928	567
West Virginia	370	2,247	595
North Carolina	1,075	6,250	561
South Carolina	541	3,117	561
Georgia	884	5,066	560
Florida	2,653	16,648	602

Social Security (cont'd)

Division, State, Other Area	Total Number of Beneficiaries (thousands)	Total Annual Payments ($ millions)	Average Monthly Benefit ($)
East South Central	2,630	14,812	NA
Kentucky	646	3,656	553
Tennessee	825	4,763	561
Alabama	709	4,019	555
Mississippi	451	2,374	520
West South Central	3,847	22,465	NA
Arkansas	470	2,581	539
Louisiana	652	3,689	560
Oklahoma	532	3,165	575
Texas	2,193	13,030	583
Mountain	1,948	11,906	NA
Montana	138	846	588
Idaho	157	953	586
Wyoming	62	388	604
Colorado	422	2,551	588
New Mexico	219	1,243	568
Arizona	591	3,701	610
Utah	192	1,175	611
Nevada	168	1,049	604
Pacific	5,054	32,193	NA
Washington	714	4,633	624
Oregon	492	3,170	614
California	3,665	23,293	615
Alaska	34	204	602
Hawaii	149	893	593
Puerto Rico	564	2,146	384
Guam	5	21	438
American Samoa	4	12	384
Virgin Islands	10	47	509
Abroad	358	1,550	434

Source: 1992 Statistical Abstract

The Top Reference Sources

Companies and Their Brands, 1993
Gale, $369
(800) 877-4253

This valuable resource alphabetically lists the manufacturers, distributors, marketers, and importers of 250,000 consumer products.

Complete addresses, phone numbers, and fax numbers are provided for the 47,000 companies listed.

Personnel Testing

Physical Examinations

Physical examinations can be used to screen out applicants when the results indicate that job performance would be adversely affected. For example, jobs that require a great deal of physical force may require job applicants to receive back X-rays while desk jobs may not.

Drug Testing

Drug testing for employees and job applicants has increased 250 percent since 1987. Perhaps as a result of increased testing and related educational programs, drug use among workers and job seekers has declined in the last five years.

Only a handful of states presently outlaw drug testing for private sector businesses. Many government workers, on the other hand, are required to submit to random or periodic drug testing as mandated by the Federal Workplace Drug Testing Regulations.

Just about all drug testing is done by urinalysis which, when performed under the guidelines established by the Federal Workplace Drug Testing Regulations, offers a 99.9 percent accuracy rate.

Contact Options

Drug Testing and Program Management Firms:

Drug Intervention Services of America
11200 Westheimer, Suite 630
Houston, Texas 77042
(713) 972-3472

National MRO
P.O. Box 261426
Lakewood, CO 80226
(303) 238-2000

Substance Abuse Management Inc.
Two Plaza East
330 E. Kilbourn Ave., Suite 1075
Milwaukee, WI 53202
(414) 273-7264

University Services
Arsenal Business Center
5301 Tacony St.
Building 4
Philadelphia, PA 19137
(215) 743-4200

Percentage of Drug Abuse Policies in the Workplace

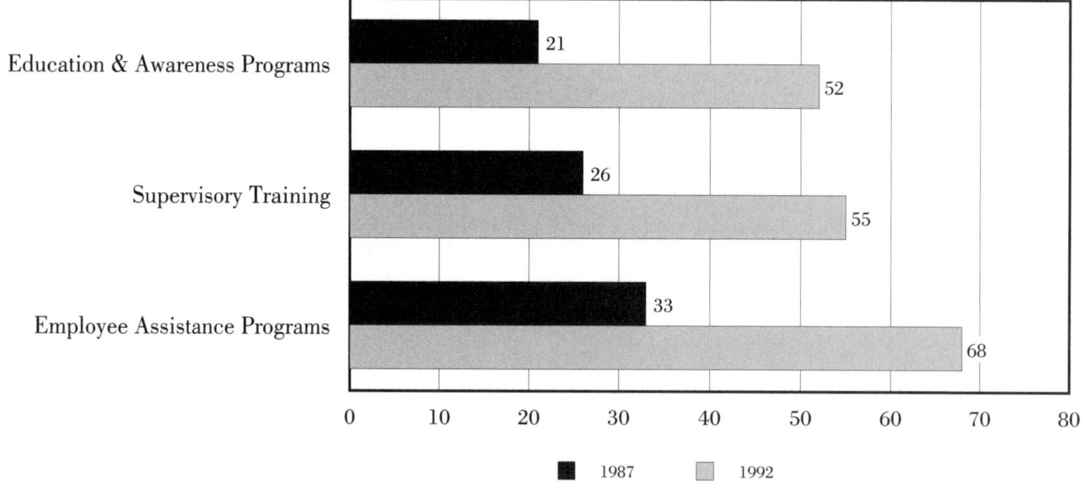

Source: American Management Association

Personnel Testing (cont'd)

Percentage of Workplace Drug Testing 1987-1992

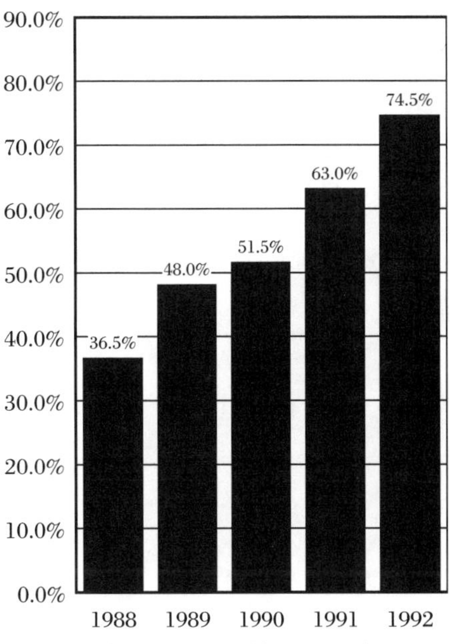

Source: American Management Association

Percentage of Executives Who Say Drug Testing Is Effective

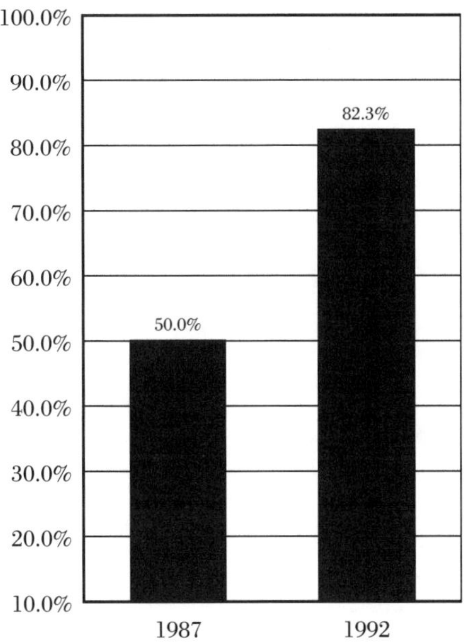

Source: American Management Association

Corporate Methods for Combating Drug Abuse

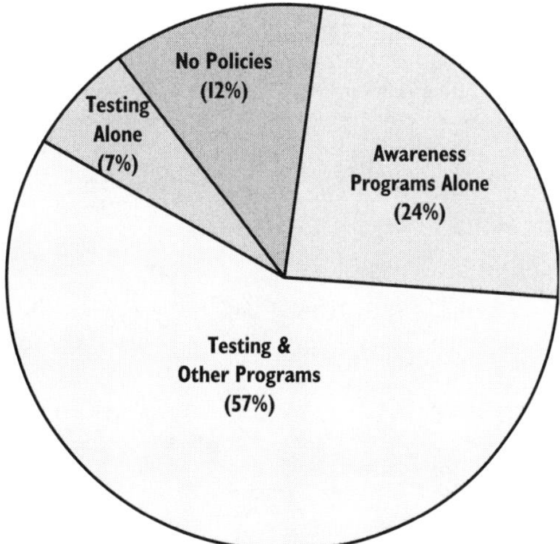

Source: American Management Association

Almanac Fact

In a recent study, 12% of employees admitted to recent drug use.

Source: Institute for a Drug Free Workplace

Personnel Testing (cont'd)

AIDS

It is against the law in all states to require employees to submit to a blood test for the presence of the HIV virus. According to the Gay Men's Health Crisis in Manhattan, however, many corporations circumvent this law by requiring prospective employees to submit to a comprehensive physical that includes a complete blood work-up by the company's physician of choice. These tests, however, are usually required upon completion of employment contract.

Polygraph Tests

With the passage of the Employee Polygraph Protection Act of 1988, employers are restricting their use of polygraph or lie detector tests. The law virtually outlaws the use of lie detectors in connection with employment, and covers all private employers in interstate commerce. Supporters of the law claim that the tests are accurate only two-thirds of the time and are far more likely to be inaccurate for honest employees. The new law restricts pre-employment screening and random use of the device.

The Employee Polygraph Protection Act allows polygraph tests to be used in connection with jobs in security, handling drugs, or in investigating a theft or other suspected crime. Before an employee can be required to take such a test as part of an investigation of an employment-related crime, however, the employee must be given a written notice stating that he or she is a suspect.

Parental and Medical Leave

MORE THAN 70 PERCENT of all American women between the ages of 20 and 54 now work outside the home. The Family and Medical Leave Act of 1993 becomes effective on August 5, 1993, and guarantees family leave for employees under certain circumstances. The FMLA requires private sector employers of 50 or more employees, and public agencies to provide up to 12 weeks of unpaid, job-protected leave to "eligible" employees for certain family and medical reasons. Employees are "eligible" if they have worked for a covered employer for at least one year, and for 1,250 hours over the previous 12 months, and if there are at least 50 employees within 75 miles. Similar provisions may apply to federal and congressional employees. For more information on the new federal regulations, contact the nearest office of the Wage and Hour Division, listed in most telephone directories under U.S. Government, Department of Labor, Employment Standards Administration.

The following state regulations augment and supercede the federal requirements for employers:

Alaska

Effective September 16, 1992, Alaska's family leave law provides state and other public employees with up to 18 weeks of leave every 24 months to care for the serious health condition of a child, spouse, parent, or for the worker's own serious health condition. Additionally, the law provides 18 weeks of leave per year to care for a newborn or newly adopted child. It covers the state and political subdivisions of the state with at least 21 employees. Workers must work at least 35 hours per week for six consecutive months or 17.5 hours per week for 12 consecutive months to be eligible.

California

Effective January 1, 1992, California's family leave law provides up to 16 weeks of leave over two years for birth or adoption, or for the serious health condition of a child, spouse, or parent. It applies to employers of 50 or more; employees must be employed for 12 months to be eligible.

Connecticut

Effective July 1, 1990, Connecticut provides 12 weeks of family and medical leave every two years; to be phased to 16 weeks by 1993. Covers employers of 250 or more; to be phased to cover employers of 75 or more by 1993.

Employees must be employed for 1,000 hours in the 12-month period preceding the first day of leave to be eligible. Effective January 7, 1988, Connecticut also provides state employees with a total of 24 weeks over two years for family or medical leave.

Effective 1973, Connecticut's pregnancy disability law provides job-guaranteed leave for the period that a worker is physically disabled due to pregnancy, childbirth, and related medical conditions. The law covers employers with three or more employees; certain family businesses are exempted.

Delaware

Effective July 20, 1984, Delaware provides state employees who have had one year of continuous employment with six weeks of family leave for adoption or birth of a child.

District of Columbia

Effective April 1, 1991, the District of Columbia's family and medical leave law provides up to 16 weeks of unpaid leave every two years to care for a newborn or newly adopted child or for a seriously ill family member. "Family member" is defined broadly to include a person related by blood, legal custody, or marriage, or a person with whom an employee shares a residence in the context of a committed relationship. Sixteen weeks of medical leave every two years is separately available for the employee's own serious health condition. Covers employers of 50 or more for the first three years after enactment;

Parental and Medical Leave (cont'd)

covers employers of 20 or more thereafter. Employees must have worked for the employer for at least 1,000 hours during the last 12 months to be eligible.

Florida

Effective October 1, 1991, Florida law grants up to six months of family leave per year to state employees for birth, adoption, or for the serious illness of a worker's spouse, child, or parent.

Georgia

Effective January 1, 1993, Georgia provides up to 12 weeks of family and medical leave per year for state employees. Employees must be employed for at least 12 months and 1,040 hours to be eligible.

Hawaii

Effective January 1, 1992, for state employees, and January 1, 1994, for private sector employers of 100 or more, Hawaii law provides employees four weeks of family leave for birth, adoption, or the serious health condition of a child, spouse, or parent.

Effective November 15, 1982, Hawaii also provides pregnancy disability leave to all employees for the period that a worker is physically disabled by pregnancy, childbirth, or related medical conditions.

Illinois

Effective September 26, 1983, Illinois provides certain permanent, full-time state employees with family leave of up to one year for "bona fide family responsibilities" (including birth or adoption, or care of a seriously ill family member).

Iowa

Effective July 1, 1987, Iowa provides up to eight weeks pregnancy disability leave. Employers with four or more employees are covered.

Kansas

Effective January 1, 1994, Kansas provides pregnancy disability leave for the period that a worker is physically disabled by pregnancy, childbirth, or related medical conditions. Employers with four or more employees are covered.

Kentucky

Effective July 15, 1982, Kentucky provides all employees with six weeks leave for adopting a child under age seven.

Louisiana

Effective September 1, 1987, Louisiana provides up to four months of leave to employees who are temporarily disabled because of pregnancy, childbirth, or related medical conditions. Only six weeks of disability leave is generally available for normal pregnancy or childbirth. Employers with 26 or more employees are covered.

Maine

Effective October 9, 1991, Maine provides ten weeks of family and medical leave over a two-year period. Employers with 25 or more employees are covered. Employees must work for the same employer for 12 consecutive months to be eligible.

Massachusetts

Effective October 17, 1972, female employees in Massachusetts are eligible for eight weeks of leave for birth or adoption of a child under age three. Employees are eligible after completing employer's initial probationary period or three consecutive months as a full-time employee. Covers employers of 6 or more employees.

Minnesota

Effective August 1, 1987, Minnesota employers with 21 or more employees must provide their employees with six weeks of leave for the birth or adoption of a child. Employees must work 12 months at 20 or more hours per week to be eligible.

Montana

Effective September 14, 1984, Montana provides pregnancy disability leave for workers when temporarily disabled by pregnancy, childbirth, or related medical condition. Covers employers with one or more employees.

New Hampshire

Effective November 15, 1984, New Hampshire provides pregnancy disability leave for workers when temporarily disabled by pregnancy, childbirth, or related medical conditions. Covers employers of six or more.

New Jersey

Effective April 25, 1990, New Jersey provides 12 weeks of leave over a 24-month period for birth, adoption, or the serious health condition of a child, parent, or spouse. Employers of 100 or more are covered during the first year after enactment; employers of 75 or more, the second and third years after enactment; employers of 50 or more will be covered thereafter. Employee must have been employed at least 1,000 hours in the 12 months before the leave to be eligible.

North Carolina

Effective February 1, 1988, North Carolina provides all state employees with pregnancy disability leave when temporarily disabled by pregnancy, childbirth, or related medical conditions.

North Dakota

Effective January 1, 1990, North Dakota provides full-time state employees (with one-year minimum employment at an average of 20 hours per week) four months of leave per year for birth, adoption, or serious health condition of spouse, child, or parent.

Parental and Medical Leave (cont'd)

Oklahoma

Effective August 20, 1989, Oklahoma provides state employees with 12 weeks of family leave per year for birth or adoption, or for the care of a critically ill child or dependent adult. Employees must work six months to be eligible.

Oregon

Effective January 1, 1992, Oregon's family leave law provides employees with 12 weeks of leave every two years for the illness of a child requiring "home care," or to care for a child, spouse, or parent suffering from "any mental or physical condition requiring constant care." Covers employers with 50 or more employees.

Effective January 1, 1988, Oregon's parental leave law provides 12 weeks of leave for the birth of a child or for adopting a child up to age 12. This law covers employers of 25 or more employees; employees are eligible after 90 days of employment. Employees hired on a seasonal or temporary basis are not covered.

Effective October 3, 1989, Oregon provides pregnancy disability leave for the period of physical disability if such leave can be reasonably accommodated.

Pennsylvania

Effective December 15, 1986, Pennsylvania provides certain permanent state employees with six months of parental leave for birth or adoption.

Puerto Rico

Effective June 11, 1942, Puerto Rico provides all female employees with eight weeks of leave for pregnancy disability (which may be divided in any amount before and after childbirth); leave must be extended an additional 12 weeks in the event of complications. The employee is entitled to receive half pay during the leave period.

Rhode Island

Effective July 12, 1990, Rhode Island provides up to 13 weeks of family medical leave over a two-year period. Covers private employers with 50 or more employees; city, town, or municipal agencies with 30 or more employees; and all state agencies. Employee must be employed for an average of 30 or more hours per week by same employer for 12 consecutive months to be eligible.

Tennessee

Effective January 1, 1988, Tennessee provides up to four months of leave for pregnancy disability and nursing. Covers employees who have worked full-time for 12 consecutive months at companies with 100 or more employees.

Vermont

Effective July 1, 1992, Vermont provides 12 weeks of family and medical leave per year. Employers of ten or more must provide leave to care for a newborn or newly adopted child; employers of 15 or more must also provide leave to care for the serious health condition of a child, spouse, or parent, or for the worker's own serious health condition. Employees must work for at least one year for an average of 30 hours per week to be eligible.

Virginia

Effective July 7, 1991, Virginia provides state employees with six weeks of parental leave per year for birth or adoption.

Washington

Effective September 1, 1989, Washington's parental leave law provides 12 weeks of leave over a two-year period for the birth, adoption, or serious illness of a child. Employees must be employed 52 weeks at 35 or more hours per week to be eligible. Covers employers of 100 or more employees.

Effective October 28, 1973, Washington also provides pregnancy disability leave for the period of physical disability. Covers employees of eight or more.

West Virginia

Effective July 7, 1989, West Virginia provides state and school employees with 12 weeks of leave per year for the birth or adoption, or serious health condition of a spouse, child, or parent. Employees must have 12 consecutive weeks of employment to be eligible.

Wisconsin

Effective April 26, 1988, Wisconsin provides six weeks of leave for birth or adoption of a child; two weeks of leave for serious health condition of a child, spouse, or parent; and two weeks of medical leave for a worker's own serious health condition (including pregnancy disability). No more than eight weeks may be taken in a 12 month-period for any combination of these reasons. Law covers employers with 50 or more employees; an employee must be employed for 52 consecutive weeks and have worked 1,000 hours to be eligible.

Parental and Medical Leave (cont'd)

Mothers Participating in Labor Force (%)

Year	With Children Under 18 Years	With Children 6-17 Years	With Children Under 6 Years
1955	27.0	38.4	18.2
1965	35.0	45.7	25.3
1975	47.4	54.8	38.9
1980	56.6	64.4	46.6
1985	62.1	69.9	53.5
1986	62.8	70.4	54.4
1987	64.7	72.0	56.7
1988	65.0	73.3	56.1
1989	NA	NA	NA
1990	66.7	74.7	58.2

Source: 1992 Information Please Almanac

Family Friendly Companies

The Families and Work Institute (FWI) rigorously researched work-family problems and evaluated a range of work-family solutions.

The Index measures the overall responsiveness to employees' family and personal needs in light of business objectives. It covers seven primary categories: flexible work arrangements, leaves, financial assistance, corporate giving/community service, dependent care services, management change, and work-family management.

The score for each work-family initiative is based on six criteria that the Families and Work Institute considers important:

- Impact: The program's capacity to reduce work-family conflicts.
- Coverage: The more widely available a program or services, the higher the score.
- Institutionalization: A policy that is formally written, thus sanctioning usage, will score higher.
- Commitment: A program that requires a great investment of resources in terms of money, people, time, or leadership will receive more points.
- Level of effort: The higher the complexity that the implementation of a program requires, the higher the score.
- Innovativeness: A program that is uniquely responsive scores higher.

The rankings are arranged in stages and are listed in descending order with the highest score (245) signifying the most family-friendly company in the study. Note: only companies that participated in the study are included. The top two stages of companies are listed here.

Rankings of companies within each stage of development are based on FWI Family-Friendly Index Scores.

Most Friendly (Scores of 179+)

Aetna Life & Casualty
Corning
IBM
Johnson & Johnson

Friendly (Scores of 100-178)

Allied-Signal
Allstate Insurance
American Express
AT&T
Bank of America N.T. & S.A.
Campbell Soup
Champion International
Chase Manhattan
Citicorp
Coors Brewing
Digital Equipment
Dow Chemical U.S.A.
E.I. Du Pont de Nemours
Eastman Kodak
Equitable Life Assurance Society of United States
Gannett
General Dynamics
Hewlett-Packard
Hoffmann-LaRoche
Honeywell
Household International
John Hancock Mutual Life Insurance
McDonnell Douglas
Merck & Co.
Metropolitan Life Insurance
Minnesota Mining & Manufacturing (3M)
Mobil
Norton
Polaroid
Procter & Gamble
Time, Inc.
Travelers Insurance
US West
Warner-Lambert
Wells Fargo Bank

Parental and Medical Leave (cont'd)

Percent of Full-Time Employees by Leave Policy–Medium and Large Firms

Employer Leave Policy	All Employees	Professional & Administrative Employees	Technical & Clerical	Production & Service
% of all Employees Eligible for Parental Leave	41	45	41	39
ELIGIBLE FOR MATERNITY LEAVE	41	44	41	39
Paid Days Only	2	2	1	2
Unpaid Days Only	35	37	36	34
Both Paid & Unpaid Days	1	2	1	1
Information not Available on Type of Days	2	3	2	2
Not Eligible for Maternity Leave	<.5	1	<.5	<.5
ELIGIBLE FOR PATERNITY LEAVE	20	23	20	19
Paid Days Only	1	2	1	1
Unpaid Days Only	18	20	17	17
Both Paid & Unpaid Days	<.5	<.5	<.5	<.5
Information not Available on Type of Days	1	1	1	1
Not Eligible for Parental Leave	59	55	59	61

Source: Bureau of Labor Statistics

Duration of Leave Benefits by % of Eligible Employees–Medium & Large Firms

Duration	All Eligible Employees	Professional & Administrative Employees	Technical & Clerical	Production & Service
UNPAID MATERNITY LEAVE				
TOTAL	100	100	100	100
Under 6 Weeks	2	1	1	2
6 Weeks	15	12	13	18
Over 6 but Under 8 Weeks	<.5	-	<.5	-
8 Weeks	4	5	2	5
Over 8 but Under 13 Weeks	9	7	9	11
13 Weeks	15	18	19	11
Over 13 but Under 26 Weeks	19	18	19	21
26 Weeks	20	19	22	19
Over 26 but Under 52 Weeks	5	6	6	3
52 Weeks	11	13	10	10
Over 52 Weeks	<.5	-	-	<.5
UNPAID PATERNITY LEAVE				
TOTAL	100	100	100	100
Under 6 Weeks	3	5	2	3
6 Weeks	21	17	21	24
8 Weeks	3	3	2	4
Over 8 but Under 13 Weeks	8	8	11	7
13 Weeks	15	18	15	14
Over 13 but Under 26 Weeks	14	14	10	15
26 Weeks	21	17	21	24
Over 26 but Under 52 Weeks	3	3	4	2
52 Weeks	11	16	12	7

Source: Bureau of Labor Statistics

Companies for Working Mothers

The Working Mother 100
Best Companies for Working Mothers

Aetna Life and Casualty
Allstate Insurance
American Express
Apple Computer
Arthur Andersen & Co., SC
American Telephone & Telegraph
Avon Products
Baptist Hospital of Miami
Barnett Bank
Bausch & Lomb
Baxter International
BE & K
Bell Atlantic
Bellcore
Ben & Jerry's Homemade
Boston's Beth Israel Hospital
Bright Horizons Children's Centers
The Bureau of National Affairs
Leo Burnett
Burroughs Wellcome
Cigna
Citibank
Colgate-Palmolive
Consolidated Edison Company of New York
Corning, Inc.
Dayton Hudson
Dominion Bankshares
R.R. Donnelley
Dow Chemical
Du Pont
Eastman Kodak
Fel-Pro
Gannett
Genentech
General Mills
Glaxo
Great Western Bank
G.T. Water Products
Hallmark Cards
John Hancock Mutual Life Insurance
Hanna Andersson
Home Box Office
Hewitt Associates
Hewlett-Packard
Hill, Holliday, Connors, Cosmopulous
Hoechst Celanese
Hoffmann-La Roche
International Business Machines
IDS Financial Services.
Johnson & Johnson
S.C. Johnson & Son
Lancaster Laboratories
Lincoln National
Little Company of Mary Hospital
Lotus Development
Lucasarts Entertainment
Magee-Women's Hospital
Marquette Electronics
Massachusetts Mutual Life Insurance
MBNA America
Catherine McAuley Health System
Merck
Minnesota Mining & Manufacturing (3M)
Morrison & Foerster
Motorola
NationsBank
Neuville Industries
Northern Trust Corp.
Northern States Power
Nynex
Pacificare Health Systems
Patagonia
Pacific Gas & Electric
Phoenix Home Life Mutual Insurance
Pitney Bowes
Procter & Gamble
Prudential Insurance
The Putnam Companies
Quad/Graphics
Rohm & Haas
The St. Paul Companies
The St. Petersburg Times
SAS Institute
The Seattle Times
Sequent Computer Systems
Sprint
Steelcase
Stride Rite
Syntex
Time Warner
The Travelers Companies
United States Hosiery
Unum Life Insurance
The Upjohn Company
USA Group
Warner-Lambert
Wegmans
Wells Fargo & Company
Work/Family Directions
Xerox

Source: Working Mother, October, 1992

Affirmative Action

EMPLOYERS ALL OVER THE COUNTRY sign contracts with the federal government guaranteeing nondiscrimination and equal opportunity in all their employment practices. In these contracts, employers also agree to take affirmative action to hire and promote workers who traditionally have been discriminated against in the job market.

Each year, the U.S. Government awards hundreds of thousands of these contracts for supplies, services, use of property, and construction work, totaling over $200 billion. Construction contractors, banks, utilities, insurance and real estate companies, manufacturers, producers, builders, and universities are among those who do federal contract and subcontract work.

Under two statutes and one executive order, minorities, women, members of religious and ethnic groups, handicapped persons, and Vietnam and disabled veterans of all wars are protected by the Equal Employment Opportunity Commission (EEOC) and affirmative action requirements. These state that special efforts must be made by employers in outreach, recruitment, training, and other areas to help members of protected groups compete for jobs and promotions on equal footing with other applicants and employees. Affirmative action is not preferential treatment. Nor does it mean that unqualified persons should be promoted over other people. What affirmative action does mean is that positive steps must be taken to provide equal employment opportunity.

Enforcement of these contracts is carried out by the Office of Federal Contract Compliance Programs (OFCCP), a division of the U.S. Department of Labor's Employment Standards Administration. OFCCP's compliance officers regularly review the employment practices of federal contractors, subcontractors, and federally assisted construction contractors to determine whether or not they are fulfilling their EEOC and affirmative action obligations.

Complaints of Discrimination

Individuals who are protected by the contract compliance programs may file complaints if they believe that they have been discriminated against by federal contractors, subcontractors, or federally assisted construction contractors or subcontractors. Complaints may also be filed by organizations or other individuals on behalf of the person or persons affected.

If a complaint filed under the Executive Order involves discrimination against only one person, OFCCP will refer it to the EEOC, an independent agency. Cases that involve groups of people or indicate patterns of discrimination are generally investigated by the OFCCP.

Complaints must be filed within 180 days from the date of the alleged discrimination, unless the time for filing is extended because of a good reason, which requires approval by the OFCCP director.

Persons filing complaints should include a description of the discrimination involved and any other related information which would assist in an investigation.

Complaints may be filed directly with the OFCCP in Washington, DC, or with any of the program's regional offices throughout the country.

Enforcing Contract Compliance

When a complaint is filed, or a compliance review turns up problems, the OFCCP attempts to enter into a conciliation agreement with the contractor.

A conciliation agreement may include back pay, seniority credit, promotions, or other forms of relief for the victims of discrimination. It may also involve new training programs, special recruitment efforts, or other affirmative action measures.

The conciliation agreement allows the contractor to continue doing government business, and guarantees that employees' rights are protected.

When conciliation efforts are unsuccessful, the OFCCP moves to enforcement. Federal rules and regulations set forth administrative and judicial procedures to be followed when enforcement actions are necessary.

Contractors or subcontractors cited for violating their EEO and affirmative action requirements may have a formal hearing before an administrative law judge. If conciliation is not reached before or after the hearing, sanctions may be imposed. For example, contractors or subcontractors could lose their government contracts or subcontracts; they could have payments withheld by the government; or they could be declared ineligible for any federal contract work.

In some cases the Department of Justice, on behalf of the Department of Labor, may file suit in federal court against a contractor for violation of the contract requirements.

For more information about contract compliance, filing complaints, or special assistance, contact any of the OFCCP's ten regional offices, or get in touch with a program area office listed in telephone directories under U.S. Department of Labor, Employment Standards Administration, Office of Federal Contract Compliance Programs.

Contact Option

The Office of Federal Contract
Compliance Programs
U.S. Department of Labor
200 Constitution Ave., NW
Washington DC 20201
(202) 219-9368

Unemployment Benefits

Unemployment Insurance by State and Other Areas: 1990

State	Beneficiaries' First Payments ($ thousands)	Benefits Paid ($ millions)	Average Weekly Unemployment Benefits ($)
TOTAL	8,628	18,057	162
AL	169	182	116
AK	40	91	163
AZ	83	147	135
AR	91	140	133
CA	1,210	2,232	131
CO	71	144	168
CT	155	443	201
DE	22	42	176
DC	24	89	213
FL	254	468	146
GA	251	318	143
HI	22	48	196
ID	39	59	145
IL	352	946	170
IN	139	147	107
IA	82	146	161
KS	67	152	171
KY	131	194	136
LA	85	127	102
ME	59	115	159
MD	119	267	170
MA	303	1,143	217
MI	466	1,166	204
MN	133	362	190
MS	77	103	111
MO	179	295	135
MT	24	38	137
NE	27	36	120
NV	46	91	162
NH	49	60	128
NJ	325	1,052	207
NM	27	54	126
NY	615	1,873	181
NC	299	323	152
ND	14	24	136
OH	338	665	155
OK	61	106	150
OR	126	256	162
PA	472	1,225	189
RI	62	171	194
SC	115	135	130
SD	7	9	120
TN	261	254	113
TX	346	784	162
UT	33	58	163
VT	26	53	149
VA	169	189	146
WA	188	426	169
WV	54	99	146
WI	196	362	171
WY	10	20	159

Source: 1992 Statistical Abstract

Benefits Checklist

Percent of Full-Time Employees Participating in Selected Employee Benefit Programs: Medium and Large Firms

Employee Benefit Program	All Employees	Professional & Administrative	Technical & Clerical	Production & Service
PAID				
Holidays	97	97	96	97
Vacations	97	98	99	95
Personal leave	22	28	30	14
Jury duty leave	90	95	92	87
Military leave	53	61	57	45
Sick leave	68	93	87	44
Maternity leave	3	4	2	3
Paternity leave	1	2	1	1
UNPAID				
Maternity leave	37	39	37	35
Paternity leave	18	20	17	17
SICKNESS AND ACCIDENT INSURANCE	43	29	29	58
Wholly employer financed	36	22	22	51
Partly employer financed	7	7	7	7
LONG-TERM DISABILITY INSURANCE	45	65	57	27
Wholly employer financed	35	50	43	23
Partly employer financed	9	15	14	4
MEDICAL CARE	92	93	91	93
EMPLOYEE COVERAGE				
Wholly employer financed	48	45	41	54
Partly employer financed	44	48	50	39
FAMILY COVERAGE				
Wholly employer financed	31	28	25	37
Partly employer financed	60	64	66	54
DENTAL CARE	66	69	66	65
EMPLOYEE COVERAGE				
Wholly employer financed	34	32	31	38
Partly employer financed	32	37	36	27
FAMILY COVERAGE				
Wholly employer financed	25	23	21	28
Partly employer financed	42	46	46	37
LIFE INSURANCE	94	95	94	93
Wholly employer financed	82	82	81	83
Partly employer financed	12	13	14	11
ALL RETIREMENT	81	85	81	80
DEFINED BENEFIT PENSION	63	64	63	63
Wholly employer financed	60	61	61	60
Partly employer financed	3	3	2	3
DEFINED CONTRIBUTION	48	59	52	40
RETIREMENT USE OF FUNDS	36	43	39	31
Wholly employer financed	14	15	14	12
Partly emplyer financed	22	28	24	18
CAPITAL ACCUMULATION USE OF FUNDS	14	18	14	11
Wholly employer financed	2	1	1	3
Partly employer financed	12	17	13	8

Benefits Checklist (cont'd)

Employee Benefit Program	All Employees	Professional & Administrative	Technical & Clerical	Production & Service
TYPES OF PLANS				
Savings and thrift	30	41	35	21
Deferred profit-sharing	15	13	13	16
Employee stock ownership	3	4	3	3
Money purchase pension	5	8	6	3
Stock purchase	2	3	2	1
Cash only profit-sharing	1	1	1	1
Flexible benefits plans	9	14	15	3
Reimbursement accounts	23	36	31	11
INCOME CONTINUATION PLANS				
Severance pay	39	54	46	27
Supplemental unemployment benefits	5	2	2	9
TRANSPORTATION BENEFITS				
Free or subsidized employee parking	90	85	86	94
Subsidized commuting	5	7	6	3
Job-related travel accident insurance	53	69	60	39
GIFTS AND CASH BONUSES				
Gifts	24	25	23	25
Non-production bonuses	27	26	28	28
FINANCIAL AND LEGAL SERVICES				
Financial counseling	9	12	11	6
Prepaid legal services	4	2	2	5
FAMILY BENEFITS				
Employer assistance for child care	5	6	6	3
Employer financial assistance for adoption	5	8	6	3
Elder care	3	4	3	2
Long-term care insurance	3	3	3	2
HEALTH PROMOTION PROGRAMS				
In-house infirmary	36	40	35	34
Wellness programs	23	30	25	19
Employee assistance programs	49	57	50	44
MISCELLANEOUS BENEFITS				
Employee discounts	54	53	58	52
Employer-subsidized recreation facilities	28	36	26	24
Subsidized meals	23	29	29	16
Relocation allowance	36	68	29	21
EDUCATION ASSISTANCE				
Job related	69	81	75	59
Not job related	19	21	17	19

Source: Bureau of Labor Statistics

Sampling of Benefit Plans and Programs Offered by Employers

Accidental death and dismemberment insurance
Adoption benefits
Birthdays (time off)
Business and professional memberships
Cash profit-sharing
Civic activities (time off)
Club memberships
Company medical assistance
Company-provided or subsidized automobiles
Company-provided housing
Company-provided subsidized travel
Credit unions
Day-care centers
Death leave
Deferred bonus
Deferred compensation plan
Deferred profit-sharing
Dental and eye-care insurance
Discount on company products
Discount of other products
Education costs
Educational activities (time off)
Employment contract

Benefits Checklist (cont'd)

Executive dining room
Financial counseling
Free or subsidized lunches
Group automobile insurance
Group homeowners insurance
Group legal insurance
Group life insurance
Health maintenance organization fees
Holidays
Home health care
Hospital-surgical-medical insurance
Interest-free loans
Layoff pay
Legal, estate planning, and other professional assistance
Loans of company equipment
Long-term disability benefits
Matching educational, charitable contributions
Nurseries
Nursing home care
Outside medical services
Paid attendance at business, professional, and other outside meetings
Parking facilities
Pension
Personal accident insurance
Personal counseling
Personal credit cards
Personal liability insurance
Physical examinations
Physical fitness programs
Political activities (time off)
Pre-retirement counseling
Price discount plan
Professional activities
Psychiatric services
Recreation facilities, sports activities
Resort facilities
Retirement gratuity
Sabbatical leave
Salary continuation
Savings plan
Scholarships for dependents
Severance pay
Sickness and accident insurance
Social Security
Social service sabbaticals
Split-dollar insurance
State disability plans
Stock appreciation rights
Stock bonus plans
Stock option plans (qualified, nonqualified, tandem)
Stock purchase plans
Survivors benefits
Tax assistance
Training program
Travel accident insurance
Vacations
Weekly indemnity insurance

Source: Buck Consultants

What Employees Want

FAMILIES & WORK INSTITUTE, a New York research and consulting concern, asked 925 employees of one large manufacturer whether they would be willing to trade off any of their existing benefits for each of some 37 new ones. The answers depended very much on whom they asked.

The following rankings of benefits – broken down by type of workers – shows the percentage of workers who were willing to make that trade-off.

Employees with Non-Working Spouse and Children Under Six Years Old

1. Assist in paying for sick or emergency care–69%
2. Child-care center at or near the work site–69%
3. Child-care center for sick children or last minute emergency care–64%
4. Extend summer hours year-round–60%
5. Working at home–55%
6. Gain sharing–54%
7. Combined sick, vacation and personal days–53%

* Pay part of costs of child care/elder care–53%

9. Someone to help negotiate problems between managers and employees–50%

* Fitness or recreational facility–50%

11. In-home nursing service for sick family members–48%
12. Increased possibility of reduced working hours–47%

Employees with Working Spouse and Children Under Six Years Old

1. Increased possibility of reduced working hours–74%
2. Working at home–71%
3. Pay part of costs of child care/elder care–69%
4. Child-care center at or near the work site–68%
5. Child-care center for sick children or last minute emergency care–67%
6. Extend summer hours year-round–66%

What Employees Want (cont'd)

7. Someone to help negotiate problems between managers and employees–64%
8. Combined sick, vacation & personal days–63%
9. More employee-relations staff–60%
10. Part-time work after taking parental leave–56%
11. Assist in paying for sick or emergency care–50%
12. Gain sharing–49%

Employees with Children More Than Six Years Old

1. Insurance for eye care–62%
2. Increased possibility of reduced working hours–59%
3. Working at home–59%
4. Dental insurance–58%
5. Extend summer hours year-round–56%
6. Combined sick, vacation and personal days–56%
7. Gain sharing–53%
8. Assist in paying for sick or emergency care–53%
9. Child-care center for sick children or last-minute emergency care–52%
10. Child-care center at or near the work site for everyday use–51%
11. Fitness or recreational facility–46%
12. Pay employees part of costs of child care/elder care–45%

Employees with No Children

1. Extend summer hours year-round–68%
2. Insurance for eye care–67%
3. Working at home–63%
4. Increased possibility of reduced working hours–62%
5. Dental insurance–59%
6. Combined sick, vacation and personal days–59%
7. Child-care center at or near the work site–51%
8. Assist in paying for sick or emergency care–50%
9. Fitness or recreational facility–48%

* Part-time work after taking parental leave–48%

11. Gain sharing–46%
12. Pay part of costs of child care/elder care–43%

*Note: *=tie. Source: Families and Work Institute*

Most Frequently Mentioned Ways to Make Jobs More Satisfying (by % of respondents)

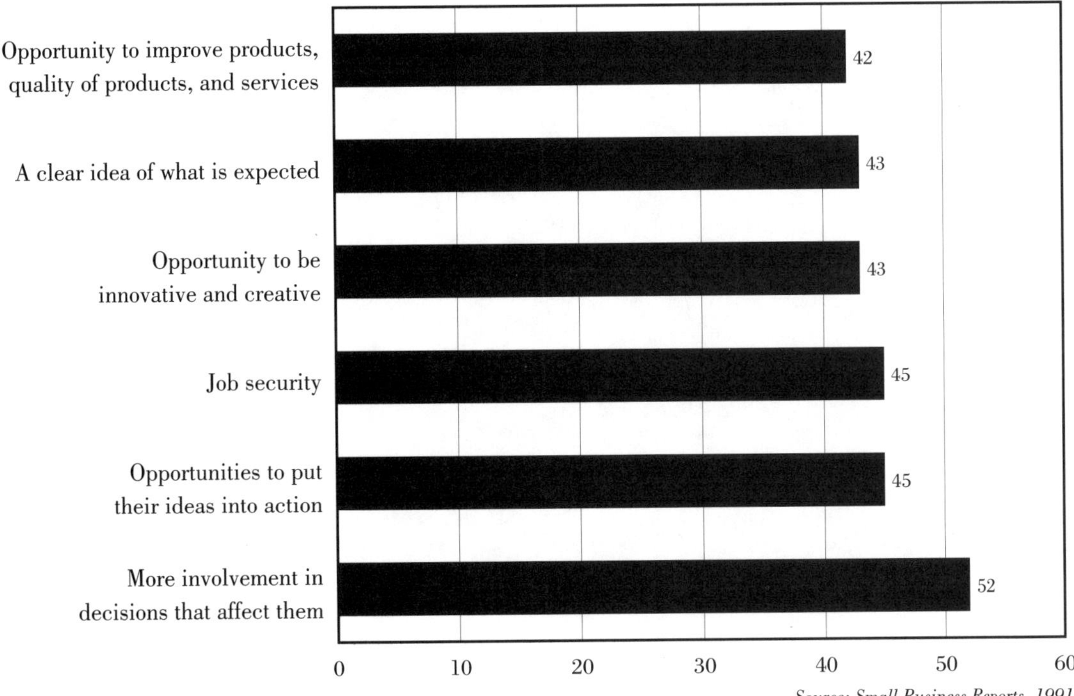

Source: Small Business Reports, 1991

Outplacement Firms & Headhunters

Largest Retained Search Firms in the United States

Rank	Firm	1991 U.S. Billings ($ millions)	% Change From 1990	Consultants	Billings/ Consultant ($)	Research Facilities	Offices
1	Korn/Ferry Int'l.	56.4	-13	143	394	17	18
2	Russell Reynolds Assoc.	48.5	-7	86	564	16	11
3	Heidrick & Struggles	44.5	0	80	556	53	12
4	SpencerStuart	37.2	1	64	581	31	10
5	Paul R. Ray & Co.	15.6	6	48	325	30	8
6	Lamalie Associates	14.6	6	36	403	8	7
7	Kearney Exec. Search	13.3	11	46	289	29	14
8	Ward Howell Int'l.	10.7	-23	33	324	13	7
9	Egon Zehnder Int'l.	9.6	4	22	436	12	4
10	Witt/Keiffer	9.0	6	28	321	5	5
11	J.D. Ross International	6.4	NA	16	400	3	2
12	Whitney Group	5.7	-5	11	518	3	1
13	Nordeman Grimm	5.6	2	14	400	NA	2
14	Handy HRM	5.0	11	12	417	5	1
15	Gilbert Tweed Associates	4.5	25	15	300	8	5
16	BoydenWorld	4.4	-49	34	129	9	10
17	Johnson Smith & Knisely	4.1	14	14	293	5	1
18	DHR International	4.0	-7	11	361	7	7
19	Norman Broadbent Int'l.	3.9	11	5	780	3	2
20	Stevenson Group	3.8	-20	11	345	5	3
21	Herbert Mines Associates	3.7	0	7	529	1	1
22	Goodrich & Sherwood	3.2	-9	8	400	4	5
23	Heath/Norton Associates	3.0	-9	8	375	5	2
23	Higdon & Joys	3.0	-20	5	600	1	1
23	Howe-Lewis International	3.0	NA	15	200	4	2
23	Kenny Kindler Hunt & Howe	3.0	-35	4	750	4	1
27	Tyler & Co.	2.6	8	14	187	4	1
28	Viscusi Group	2.6	0	26	100	NA	3
29	Diversified Search Cos.	2.5	-19	12	208	7	1
29	Daniel A. Silverstein Assoc.	2.5	0	6	417	2	1
31	Canny Bowen	2.4	-16	7	347	5	2
32	Foster Partners	2.2	-15	14	157	NA	4
32	Sampson Neill & Wilkins	2.2	-15	6	367	3	1
34	Battalia Winston Int'l.	2.1	NA	6	350	2	2
34	Coopers & Lybrand	2.1	11	10	210	2	3
34	Isaacson Miller	2.1	-6	14	148	0	2
37	Barton Raben	2.0	NA	6	333	3	1
37	Gould & McCoy	2.0	-20	4	500	6	1
37	Heidrick Partners	2.0	0	5	400	4	1
37	Ingram	2.0	0	4	500	3	1
37	Thorndike Deland	2.0	-13	7	286	2	1

Source: Executive Recruiter News

Outplacement Firms & Headhunters (cont'd)

Telephone Directory of the Largest Search Firms in the U.S. & the World

Firm	City	Telephone Number
Korn/Ferry International	New York	(212) 687-1834
Russell Reynolds Associates	New York	(212) 351-2000
Heidrick & Struggles	Chicago	(312) 372-8811
SpencerStuart	New York	(212) 407-0296
Paul R. Ray & Co.	Fort Worth	(817) 334-0500
Lamalie Associates	New York	(212) 953-7900
Kearney Executive Search	Chicago	(312) 648-0111
Ward Howell International	New York	(212) 697-3730
Egon Zehnder International	New York	(212) 838-9199
Witt, Keiffer, Ford, Hadelman, Lloyd	Oak Brook, IL	(708) 574-5070
J.D. Ross International	New York	(212) 644-9100
The Whitney Group	New York	(212) 421-4949
Nordeman Grimm	New York	(212) 935-1000
Handy HRM	New York	(212) 557-0400
Gilbert Tweed Associates	New York	(212) 697-4260
Boyden World	New York	(212) 685-3400
Johnson Smith & Knisely	New York	(212 686-9760
DHR International	Chicago	(312) 782-1581
Norman Broadbent International	New York	(212) 953-6990
Stevenson Group	West Hartford, CT	(203) 232-3393
Herbert Mines Associates	New York	(212) 355-0909
The Goodrich & Sherwood Co.	New York	(212) 697-4131
Heath/Norton Associates	New York	(212) 695-3600
Higdon & Joys	New York	(212) 752-9780
Howe-Lewis International	Palo Alto, CA	(415) 324-4430
Kenny, Kindler, Hunt & Howe	New York	(212) 355-5560
Tyler & Co.	Atlanta	(404) 396-3939
The Viscusi Group	New York	(212) 251-0100
The Diversified Search Companies	Philadelphia	(215) 732-6666
Daniel A. Silverstein Associates	Boca Raton, FL	(407) 391-0600
Canny, Bowen	New York	(212) 949-6611
Foster & Partners	New York	(212) 758-9700
Sampson, Neill & Wilkins	Upper Montclair, NJ	(201) 783-9600
Battalia Winston International	New York	(212) 683-9440
Coopers & Lybrand	Chicago	(312) 701-5601
Isaacson Miller	Boston	(617) 262-6500
Barton Raben	Houston	(713) 961-9111
Gould & McCoy	New York	(212) 688-8671
Heidrick Partners	Chicago	(312) 845-9700
Ingram, Inc.	New York	(212) 319-7177
Thorndike Deland	New York	(212) 661-6200
Amrop International	Sydney, Australia	61-22-52-3500
Transearch International	Versailles (Paris)	40-50-70-00
Carre, Orban & Partners	Brussels, Belgium	32-2-640-10-35
Berndtson International	Stockholm, Sweden	46-8-662-5515
Norman Broadbent/International Search Partnership	London, United Kingdom	44-71-629-9626
TASA	New York	(212) 486-1490
GKR Neumann	London, United Kingdon	44-71-930-5100
KPMG Peat Marwick c/o Foster & Partners	New York	(212) 758-6232
Accord Group Johnson Smith & Knisely	New York	(212) 686-9760

Source: Executive Recruiter News

Human Resource Software Systems

A NUMBER OF FIRMS MANUFACTURE low-cost, management software systems designed to assist corporations in employee selection, motivation, evaluation, and integration. Using a brief questionnaire, the software can create a comprehensive profile. The computer program is designed to analyze the individual's behavioral traits, stress and energy styles, and organizational skills.

Contact Options

Management Software Sources:

Consulting Psychologists Press, Inc.
3803 E. Bayshore Rd.
Palo Alto, CA 94303
(415) 969-8901

This company has an extensive catalogue of management software systems and training programs.

Professional Dynametric Programs, Inc.
400 W. Highway 24
Suite 201
Box 5289
Woodland Park, CO 80866
(708) 291-1616

This software manufacturer will also provide training in how to use and interpret the test results.

Job Interview Tips

Preparation:

- Learn about the organization.
- Have a specific job or jobs in mind.
- Review your qualifications for the job.
- Prepare answers to broad questions about yourself.
- Review your resume.
- Practice an interview with a friend or relative.
- Arrive before the scheduled time of your interview.

Personal Appearance:

- Be well groomed.
- Dress appropriately.
- Do not chew gum or smoke.

The Interview:

- Answer each question concisely.
- Respond promptly.
- Use good manners. Learn the name of your interviewer and shake hands as you meet.
- Use proper English and avoid slang.
- Be cooperative and enthusiastic.
- Ask questions about the position and the organization.
- Thank the interviewer, and follow up with a letter.

Test (if given):

- Listen closely to instructions.
- Read each question carefully.
- Write legibly and clearly.
- Budget your time wisely and don't dwell on one question.

Information to Bring to an Interview:

- Social Security number
- Driver's license number
- Resume. Although not all employers require applicants to bring a resume, you should be able to furnish the interviewer with information about your education, training, and previous employment.
- References. Usually an employer requires three references. Get permission from people before using their names, and make sure they will give you a good reference. Avoid using relatives. For each reference, provide the following information: name, address, telephone number, and job title.

Source: U.S. Department of Labor, Bureau of Labor Statistics

Job Interview Questions

MANY MANAGERS ENCOUNTER a mental block when facing an interview. A checklist of questions makes it easier to elicit revealing answers from a job candidate.

Martin Yate, an employment analyst and best-selling author, has collected twenty questions that are of use in most interview settings.

According to Yate, some of the most important skill sets we can have for employees in the coming years are:

- analytical skills
- speed and mental processing
- ability to work with others
- an understanding of the necessity of taking direction.

These twenty questions will help you explore these areas with a job candidate.

- How would you describe the ideal job for you?
- What kind of work interests you most?
- How many levels of management did you interact with?
- What was the job's biggest challenge?
- If you were hiring for this position, what would you be looking for?
- What have you done that shows initiative and willingness to work?
- Why are you interviewing with us?
- What special characteristics should I consider about you?
- How do you plan your day?
- How do you plan your week?
- How do you determine your priorities?
- What happens when two priorities compete for your time?
- What's the toughest communication problem you faced?
- When have your verbal communications been important enough to follow up in writing?
- Tell me about the time when someone has lost his/her temper at you in a business environment.
- Have you ever worked in a place where it seemed to be just one crisis after another? And, obviously, there is a follow-up with that.
- How did you handle it? How did you feel?
- What do you see as some of your most pressing developmental needs?
- Define cooperation.
- What quality should a successful manager possess?
- How have past managers gotten the best out of you?
- A two-part question. Describe the best manager you've ever had. Describe the toughest manager you've ever had.
- And last, for what have you been most frequently criticized?

The Top 100 Reference Sources

Hiring the Best
Bob Adams Publishers, $12.95
(800) 872-5627

This third edition of Martin Yate's indispensable book includes over 400 interview questions. The book also includes a chapter on what constitutes a discriminatory, or perhaps illegal, interviewing question, an in-depth review of what it will take to recruit the best in the '90s, information on drug testing, plus four ready-to-use outlines for use as a starting point in critical interview areas: management, sales, recent graduates, and clerical.

Employee Relocation Firms

MORE THAN HALF THE COMPANIES that relocate employees on a regular basis contract with a relocation firm that will help in the purchasing, managing, and disposing of the former homes of relocated employees. In general, the client company retains full ownership responsibilities for the homes during the time the employee agrees to accept the company's offer until the time of closing the sale. Home purchase firms charge a fee for their role in establishing a fair market value for the home, maintaining it after the employee has relocated, and managing the sale. The following relocation firms assisted in more than 7,000 client transfers in 1991.

Contact Options

Largest Relocation Firms:

Associates Relocation Management Company, Inc.
P.O. Box 650042
250 E. Carpenter Freeway
Dallas, TX 75265
(800) 241-6529

Coldwell Banker Relocation Services, Inc.
27271 Las Ramblas
Mission Viejo, CA 92691
(714) 367-2500

PHH Homequity
249 Danbury Rd.
Wilton, CT 06897
(203) 834-8500

Prudential Relocation Management
200 Summit Lake Dr.
Valhalla, NY 10595
(914) 741-6111

Relocation Resources, Inc.
(Eastern Operations Center)
120 Longwater Dr.
Norwell, MA 02061
(617) 871-4500

Relocation Resources, Inc.
(Western Operations Center)
1099 Eighteenth St.t
Denver, CO 80202
(303) 297-0500

Cost-of-Living Values in Selected Locations

Location	Total Annual Costs ($)	Index
Los Angeles, CA	75,975	126.6
New York, NY	74,028	123.4
Washington, DC	71,622	119.4
Chicago, IL	65,812	109.7
Atlanta. GA	63,494	105.8
Syracuse, NY	63,365	105.6
Rochester, NY	62,862	104.8
Buffalo, NY	62,638	104.4
Standard City, U.S.A.	60,000	100.0
Dallas, TX	58,768	97.9
Denver, CO	58,638	97.7
Kansas City, MO	56,344	93.9

Average Annual Home Rental Costs in Most Expensive Locations Nationwide

Location	Annual Rental Costs ($)	Index
Honolulu, HI	12,480	244.7
San Francisco, CA	9,320	182.7
Washington, DC	8,920	174.9
New York, NY	8,810	172.7
Boston, MA	8,870	172.2
Los Angeles, CA	7,910	155.1
Chicago, IL	7,370	144.5
Philadelphia, PA	6,900	135.3
Providence, RI	6,900	135.3
San Diego, CA	6,840	134.1
Standard City, U.S.A.	5,100	100.0

Source: Runzheimer International

Employee Relocation Firms (cont'd)

Average Annual Rental Costs in Least Expensive Locations Nationwide

Location	Annual Rental Costs ($)	Index
Corbin, KY	2,460	48.2
Newport, TN	2,760	54.1
Hennessey, OR	2,880	56.5
Scottsboro, AL	2,940	57.6
Casper, WY	3,000	58.8
Midland, TX	3,300	64.7
Roanoke Rapids, NC	3,360	65.9
Rangely, CO	3,480	68.2
Hobbs, NM	3,540	69.4
Lafayette, LA	3,600	70.6
Standard City, U.S.A.	5,100	100.0

Average Cost to Relocate Employees ($)

Year	Homeowners	Renters	New Hires
1986	34,984	9,218	NA
1987	36,253	10,503	12,847
1988	36,891	9,924	13,192
1989	40,939	10,666	13,937
1990	45,620	13,139	15,955
1991	44,804	13,358	17,903
1992	48,426	14,272	28,900

Source: Runzheimer International

Five Lowest Car Cost Locations

Location	Fixed Costs ($)	Operating Costs ($)	Total Annual Costs ($)
Sioux City, SD	3,343	1,283	4,626
Eau Claire, WI	3,476	1,208	4,684
Burlington, VT	3,445	1,268	4,713
Boise, ID	3,479	1,238	4,717
Billings, MT	3,519	1,245	4,764

Five Highest Car Cost Locations

Location	Fixed Costs ($)	Operating Costs ($)	Total Annual Costs ($)
Los Angeles, CA	6,074	1,455	7,529
Philadelphia, PA	5,118	1,418	6,536
Detroit, MI	5,081	1,343	6,424
Boston, MA	4,897	1,500	6,397
Hartford, CT	4,929	1,425	6,354

Source: Runzheimer International

Sources for Interns

SEVERAL COMPANIES PUBLISH DIRECTORIES with extensive listings of internships available in a wide range of industries. Prospective interns may contact corporations listed therein. A few of these companies also provide access to data bases with listings of interns and internships, and will do an executive search for a small fee. Subscribing to one of these services may provide an inexpensive alternative to hiring a search firm or placing classified ads.

Contact Options

The National Directory of Internships
National Society for Internships and Experiential Education
3509 Haworth Dr.
Suite 207
Raleigh, NC 27609
(919) 787-3263
Internship Placement

Peterson's
202 Carnegie Center
P.O. Box 2123
Princeton, NJ 08543
(609) 243-9111

Both a directory and a new database service called Connexion are available from Peterson's.

Labor Union Directory

Union	Phone
Actors' Equity Assn.	(212) 869-8530
Amalgamated Clothing and Textile Workers Union	(212) 242-0700
Amalgamated Transit Union	(202) 537-1645
American Assn. of University Professors	(202) 737-5900
American Federation of Government Employees	(202) 737-8700
American Federation of Grain Millers	(612) 545-0211
American Federation of Musicians of the United States and Canada	(212) 869-1330
American Federation of Teachers	(202) 879-4415
American Federation of Television and Radio Artists	(212) 532-0800
American Nurses' Assn.	(202) 554-4444
American Postal Workers Union	(202) 842-4200
American Federation of State, County and Municipal Employees	(202) 429-1100
Associated Actors and Artistes of America	(212) 869-0358
Association of Flight Attendants	(202) 328-5400
Bakery, Confectionery, and Tobacco Workers' International Union	(301) 933-8600
Brotherhood of Locomotive Engineers	(216) 241-2630
Brotherhood of Maintenance of Way Employees	(313) 868-0490
California School Employees Assn.	(408) 263-8000
Communications Workers of America	(202) 434-1100
Federation of Nurses and Health Professionals	(202) 879-4491
Fraternal Order of Police	(614) 221-0180
Glass, Molders, Pottery, Plastics and Allied Workers International Union	(215) 565-5051
Graphic Communications International Union	(202) 462-1400
Hotel Employees and Restaurant Employees International Union	(202) 393-4373
Int'l Alliance of Theatrical Stage Employees & Moving Picture Machine Operators of the U..S. & Canada	(212) 730-1770
International Assn. of Bridge, Structural andOrnamental Iron Workers	(202) 383-4800
International Assn. of Fire Fighters	(202) 737-8484
International Assn. of Machinists and Aerospace Workers	(202) 857-5200
International Brotherhood of Boilermakers, Iron Ship Builders, Blacksmiths, Forgers and Helpers	(913) 371-2640
International Brotherhood of Electrical Workers	(202) 833-7000
International Brotherhood of Painters and Allied Trades of the United States and Canada	(202) 637-0700
International Brotherhood of Teamsters, Chauffeurs, Warehousemen and Helpers of America	(202) 624-6800
International Chemical Workers Union	(216) 867-2444
International Federation of Professional and Technical Engineers	(301) 565-9016
International Ladies' Garment Workers' Union	(212) 265-7000
International Longshoremen's and Warehousemen's Union	(415) 775-0533
International Union of Bricklayers and Allied Craftsmen	(202) 783-3788
International Union of Electronic, Electrical, Salaried, Machine and Furniture Workers	(202) 296-1200
International Union of Operating Engineers	(202) 429-9100
International Union, Allied Industrial Workers of America	(414) 645-9500
International Union, Aluminum, Brick and Glass Workers	(314) 739-6142
International Union, United Automobile, Aerospace and Agricultural Implement Workers of America	(313) 926-5000
International Union, United Plant Guard Workers of America	(313) 772-7250
International Woodworkers of America	(503) 656-1475
Laborers' International Union of North America	(202) 737-8320
International Longshoremen's Assn.	(212) 425-1200
Maryland Classified Employees Assn.	(301) 298-8800
National Assn. of Letter Carriers	(202) 393-4695
National Education Assn.	(202) 833-4000
National Federation of Federal Employees	(202) 862-4400
National Marine Engineers' Beneficial Assn.	(202) 347-8585
National Rural Letter Carriers' Assn.	(703) 684-5545
National Treasury Employees Union	(202) 783-4444
Office and Professional Employees International Union	(212) 675-3210
Oil, Chemical and Atomic Workers International Union	(703) 876-9300

Labor Union Directory (cont'd)

Union	Phone
Operative Plasterers' and Cement Masons' International Assn. of the United States and Canada	(202) 393-6569
Retail, Wholesale and Department Store Union	(212) 684-5300
Screen Actors Guild	(213) 465-4600
Seafarers International Union of North America	(301) 899-0675
Service Employees International Union	(202) 898-3200
Sheet Metal Workers' International Assn.	(202) 783-5880
State Employees Assn. of North Carolina	(919) 833-6436
The Newspaper Guild	(301) 585-2990
Transport Workers Union of America	(212) 873-6000
Transportation Communications International Union	(202) 783-3660
United Assn. of Journeymen & Apprentices of the Plumbing & Pipe Fitting Industry of the U.S. & Canada	(202) 628-5823
United Brotherhood of Carpenters and Joiners of America	(202) 546-6206
United Electrical, Radio and Machine Workers of America	(703) 684-3123
United Farm Workers of America	(805) 822-5771
United Food and Commercial Workers International Union	(202) 223-3111
United Garment Workers of America	(615) 889-9221
United Mine Workers of America	(202) 842-7200
United Paperworkers International Union	(615) 834-8590
United Rubber, Cork, Linoleum and Plastic Workers of America	(216) 869-0320
United Steelworkers of America	(412) 562-2400
United Transportation Union	(216) 228-9400
United Union of Roofers, Waterproofers and Allied Workers	(202) 638-3228
Utility Workers Union of America	(202) 347-8105

Source: Washington Directory of Labor Unions

Labor Unions Ranked

Unions Ranked by Membership, 1991

Union	Membership
National Education Association	2,000,000
International Brotherhood of Teamsters, Chauffeurs, Warehousemen and Helpers of America	1,700,000
American Federation of State, County and Municipal Employees	1,250,000
International Union, United Food and Commercial Workers	1,235,000
Service Employees International Union	950,000
International Union, United Automobile, Aerospace and Agricultural Implement Workers of America	921,926
International Brotherhood of Electrical Workers	845,000
International Association of Machinists and Aerospace Workers	767,000
American Federation of Teachers	750,000
Communications Workers of America	650,000
United Steelworkers of America	650,000
United Brotherhood of Carpenters and Joiners of America	609,000
Laborers' International Union of North America	570,000
International Union of Operating Engineers	365,000
American Postal Workers Union	330,000
United Association of Journeymen and Apprentices of the Plumbing and Pipe Fitting Industry	325,000
National Association of Letter Carriers	315,000
International Union, Hotel Employees and Restaurant Employees	301,300
Amalgamated Clothing and Textile Workers Union	250,000
United Paper Workers International Union	250,000
American Federation of Government Employees	210,000
American Nurses Association	198,000
Graphic Communications International Union	185,585
International Association of Fire Fighters	180,000

Source: Washington Directory of Labor Unions

Collective Bargaining

Major Collective Bargaining Agreements–Wage Rate Changes

Changes	1970	1975	1980	1985	1990	1991
Average wage rate change (pro-rated over all workers)	8.8	8.7	9.9	3.3	3.5	3.6
SOURCE						
Current settlements	5.1	2.8	3.6	0.7	1.3	1.1
Prior settlements	3.1	3.7	3.5	1.8	1.5	1.9
COLA provisions	0.6	2.2	2.8	0.7	0.7	0.5
INDUSTRY						
Manufacturing	7.1	8.5	10.2	2.8	4.4	3.7
Nonmanufacturing	10.5	8.9	9.7	3.6	3.0	3.5
Construction	NA	8.1	9.9	3.0	3.4	3.4
Transportation and public utilities	NA	9.7	10.8	3.6	2.2	3.3
Wholesale and retail trade	NA	9.2	7.6	3.3	3.6	3.5
Services	NA	6.4	8.1	5.1	4.3	4.9
Nonmanufacturing, excluding construction	NA	9.3	9.6	3.7	2.9	3.6
Average wage rate increase for workers receiving an increase	9.4	9.0	10.1	4.2	4.2	4.0
SOURCE						
Current settlements	11.9	10.2	9.4	4.1	4.1	4.2
Prior settlements	5.8	5.2	5.6	3.7	3.3	3.7
COLA provisions	3.7	4.8	7.7	2.2	2.7	2.0
Total no. of workers receiving a wage rate increase (millions)	10.2	9.7	8.9	5.5	4.9	5.1
SOURCE (mil.)						
Current settlements	4.7	2.7	3.5	1.4	1.9	1.5
Prior settlements	5.7	7.3	5.6	3.4	2.7	3.0
COLA provisions	1.8	4.7	3.4	2.3	1.4	1.3
No. of workers not receiving a wage rate increase (millions)	0.6	0.4	0.2	1.5	1.0	0.5

Changes	1970	1975	1980	1983	1985	1990	1991
COMPENSATION RATES							
First year	13.1	11.4	10.4	3.4	2.6	4.6	4.1
Over life of contract	9.1	8.1	7.1	3.0	2.7	3.2	3.4
WAGE RATES							
All industries							
First year	11.9	10.2	9.5	2.6	2.3	4.0	3.6
Contracts with COLA	NA	12.2	8.0	1.9	1.6	3.4	3.4
Contracts without COLA	NA	9.1	11.7	3.3	2.7	4.4	3.7
Over life of contract	8.9	7.8	7.1	2.8	2.7	3.2	3.2
Contracts with COLA	NA	7.1	5.0	2.0	2.5	1.9	3.0
Contracts without COLA	NA	8.3	10.3	3.7	2.8	4.0	3.3
Manufacturing							
First year	8.1	9.8	7.4	0.4	0.8	3.7	3.9
Over life of contract	6.0	8.0	5.4	2.1	1.8	2.1	3.1
Nonmanufacturing							
First year	15.2	10.4	10.9	3.8	3.3	4.3	3.4
Over life of contract	11.5	7.8	8.3	3.2	3.3	4.0	3.3
Number of workers affected (millions)	4.7	2.9	3.8	3.1	2.2	2.0	1.8
Manufacturing (millions)	2.2	0.8	1.6	1.1	0.9	0.9	0.6
Nonmanufacturing (millions)	2.5	2.1	2.2	2.0	1.3	1.1	1.2

Source: 1992 Statistical Abstract

The Most Highly Paid Executives

According to a 1992 survey, the pay raises of CEOs lagged behind those of middle managers. The average increase in CEO annual pay, including salary and long-term compensation, was 3.9%, the lowest increase in ten years. Despite this change, the salaries of many CEOs continue at a notably high level.

1992 Salaries of 10 Selected CEOs

Company	CEO	Base Salary ($ thousands)
General Electric	John Welch, Jr.	1,600.0
Hewlett-Packard	John Young	1,558.8
ITT	Rand Araskog	1,462.5
Coca-Cola	Roberto Goizueta	1,401.1
Loews	Preston Tisch	1,303.3
IBP	Robert Peterson	1,200.0
Bristol-Meyers	Richard Gelb	1,173.8
RJR Nabisco	Louis Gerstner, Jr.	1,161.2
Citicorp	John Reed	1,150.0
American Int'l	Maurice Greenberg	1,147.1

15 Highest Compensated CEOs, 1992

Company	CEO	Total Pay ($ thous.)
Hosp. Corp. of America	Thomas F. First, Jr.	127,002
Primerica	Sanford I Weill	67,635
Toys 'R' Us	Charles Lazarus	64,231
U.S. Surgical	Leon C. Hirsch	62,171
Mirage Resorts	Stephen A. Wynn	38,005
H.J. Heinz	Anthony J.F. O'Reilly	36,918
Medco	Martin J. Wygod	30,207
General Dynamics	William A. Anders	29,015
Torchmark	Ronald K. Richey	26,568
UST Inc.	Louis F. Bantle	24,602
Colgate-Palmolive	Reuben Mark	22,818
AMD	Walter Sanders III	22,356
General Electric	John Welch, Jr.	17,970
Chrysler	Lee Iacocca	16,908
IFF	Eugene Grisanti	16,475

Source: Business Week

Working Woman magazine produces an annual survey of the salaries of top-paid corporate women at the end of the year. According to the magazine's findings, the following are the highest paid female executives in the country.

Name	Position	Company	Salary ($ millions)
Turi Josefson	Executive Vice President	U.S. Surgical	23.6
Rena Rowan	Executive Vice President of Design	Jones Apparel Group	6.0
Linda Wachner	Chairwoman & CEO	Warnaco	3.1
Jill Barad	President and Chief Operating Officer	Mattel USA	2.4
Nina McLemore	Senior Vice President	Liz Claiborne	1.5
Robin Burns	President & CEO	Estee Lauder	1.3
Sally Frame Kasaks	CEO	Anne Taylor	1.1
Linda Allard	Design Director	Ellen Tracy	1.0
Charlotte Beers	Chairwoman	Ogilvy & Mather Worldwide	1.0
Marion Sandler	Co-CEO	Golden West Financial	0.8

Source: Working Woman, 1992

30 Most Overpaid CEOs

THE CRYSTAL REPORT ANALYZES the salaries of top CEOs in over 300 companies based on several criteria. The editors collect data on the Total Cash Compensation (TCC) and the Total Direct Compensation (TDC) which includes base salary, plus miscellaneous compensations such as annual bonus and stock options. Comparing these figures to the company's size and performance, the Report calculates a figure called the Final Competitive TDC, or the TDC considered most appropriate. The relationship between the Final Competitive TDC and the Actual TDC of the CEOs in thirty major companies is the percent deviation and appears in the accompanying table.

Source: The Crystal Report 1992. Reprinted with permission.

Contact Option

Graef Crystal, Editor
The Crystal Report
564 Montecito Blvd.
Napa, CA 94559
(702) 832-3779

30 Most Relatively Overpaid CEOs according to The Crystal Report, 1992

Company	CEO	Actual TCC ($ thous.)	Actual TDC ($ thous.)	Final Competitive TDC ($ thousands)	Percent Deviation
Coca Cola	Robert C. Goizueta	3,140	63,550	5,970	964
Time Warner	Steven J. Ross & N.J. Nicholas	6,960	11,000	1,260	773
UAL Corporation	Stephen M. Wolf	580	17,200	2,230	671
General Dynamics	William A. Anders	1,500	13,530	1,770	664
Grace (W.R) & Company	J. Peter Grace	1,710	10,250	1,560	557
Occidental Petroleum	Ray R. Irani	4,240	8,800	1,420	520
Masco Corporation	Richard A. Manoogian	1,500	6,550	1,070	512
Merrill Lynch	William A. Schreyer	5,850	10,350	1,950	431
United States Surgical	Leon C. Hirsch	2,070	42,730	8,120	426
Int'l Flavors & Fragrances	Eugene P. Grisanti	790	9,240	1,790	416
National Medical Enterprises	Richard K. Eamer	1,540	6,570	1,350	387
Burlington Resources	Thomas H. O'Leary	1,290	6,510	1,430	355
McCaw Cellular Communications	Craig O. McCaw	160	7,560	1,790	322
ITT	Rand V. Araskog	2,880	7,390	1,850	299
Quaker Oats	William D. Smithburg	1,400	10,240	2,570	298
Burlington Northern	Gerald Grinstein	1,180	2,310	620	273
IBM	John F. Akers	1,180	4,930	1,330	271
RJR Nabisco Holdings	Louis V. Gerstner, Jr.	3,180	10,440	2,840	268
Tandy	John V. Roach	800	1,470	440	234
Imcera Group	George D. Kennedy	1,330	6,800	2,090	225
TRW	Joseph T. Gorman	1,100	3,880	1,200	223
Suntrust	James B. Williams	600	7,020	2,260	211
Monsanto	Richard J. Mahoney	1,530	7,470	2,430	207
Cooper Industries	Robert Cizik	1,120	5,820	2,000	191
Bear Stearns Companies	Alan C. Greenberg	5,300	5,300	1,840	188
Union Pacific	Andrew L. Lewis	2,030	6,100	2,120	188
Digital Equipment	Kenneth H. Olsen	1,000	2,230	780	186
Travelers Corporation	Edward H. Budd	920	2,220	780	185
Freeport-McMoran	James R. Moffett	1,170	4,650	1,640	184
Primerica Corporation	Sanford I. Weill	2,230	6,330	2,240	183

Source: The Crystal Report, 1992

Wage Data

Selected Occupations and Median Weekly Earnings

Occupation (Male and Female)	1991 Median Weekly Earnings ($)	% Change 1983-1991
Accountants and auditors	580	40.8
Administrators & officials, public administration	659	40.5
Advertising and related sales	488	36.3
Airplane pilots and navigators	932	–
Architects	623	25.1
Bank tellers	281	37.7
Bookkeepers, accounting and auditing clerks	345	37.5
Chemical engineers	874	38.7
Clergy	459	45.3
Computer programmers	662	40.0
Computer systems analysts and scientists	792	51.1
Economists	732	21.6
Editors and reporters	593	54.8
Electricians	538	27.5
Engineers	847	41.2
Financial managers	743	51.0
Firefighters and fire prevention occupations	608	53.1
Insurance sales	513	34.6
Lawyers	1,008	61.3
Librarians, archivists, curators	521	39.3
Managers, marketing, advertising, public relations	784	37.5
Managers, properties and real estate	483	43.8
Mechanical engineers	836	40.3
Personnel and labor relations managers	752	53.5
Personnel, training, and labor relations specialists	592	43.0
Pharmacists	845	65.0
Physicians	994	98.0
Police and detectives, public service	595	46.9
Public relations specialists	591	32.8
Purchasing managers	784	38.3
Real estate sales	517	34.6
Receptionists	296	40.3
Secretaries	359	42.5
Securities and financial services sales	698	34.5
Social scientists and urban planners	612	32.2
Supervisors, general office	507	43.6
Supervisors, police and detectives	682	35.6
Teachers, secondary school	592	52.2
Telephone line installers and repairers	629	31.3
Telephone operators	362	29.3
Truck drivers, heavy	429	31.6
Waiters and waitresses	218	34.6

Source: U.S. Department of Labor

Wage Data (cont'd)

Percent Job Distribution of Non-Farm Establishments and Employees

Year	Total Goods Prod.	Mining	Const.	Mfg.	Total Service Prod.	Trans. & Utilities	Wholesale Trade	Retail Trade	Finance	Svcs.	Gov't.
1960	37.7	1.3	5.4	31.0	62.3	7.4	5.8	15.2	4.8	13.6	15.4
1965	36.1	1.0	5.3	29.7	63.9	6.6	5.7	15.2	4.9	14.9	16.6
1970	33.3	0.9	5.1	27.3	66.7	6.4	5.7	15.6	5.1	16.3	17.7
1975	29.4	1.0	4.6	23.8	70.6	5.9	5.8	16.4	5.4	18.1	19.1
1980	28.4	1.1	4.8	22.4	71.6	5.7	5.9	16.6	5.7	19.8	18.0
1985	25.5	1.0	4.8	19.7	74.5	5.4	5.9	17.8	6.1	22.6	16.8
1986	24.7	0.8	4.8	19.1	75.3	5.3	5.8	18.0	6.3	23.2	16.8
1987	24.2	0.7	4.9	18.6	75.8	5.3	5.7	18.1	6.4	23.7	16.6
1988	23.9	0.7	4.8	18.3	76.1	5.2	5.7	18.1	6.3	24.3	16.5
1989	23.4	0.6	4.8	17.9	76.6	5.2	5.7	18.0	6.2	25.0	16.4
1990	22.7	0.6	4.7	17.4	77.3	5.3	5.6	17.9	6.1	25.7	16.7
1991	21.9	0.6	4.3	16.9	78.1	5.3	5.6	17.8	6.2	26.4	16.9

Weekly Earnings of Non-Farm Employees ($)

Year	Total	Total Goods Prod.	Mining	Const.	Mfg.	Total Svc. Prod.	Trans. & Utilities	Whsl. Trade	Retail Trade	Finance	Svcs.	Govt.
1960	81	NA	105	113	90	NA	NA	91	58	75	NA	NA
1965	95	NA	124	138	108	NA	125	106	67	89	74	NA
1970	120	NA	164	195	133	NA	156	137	82	113	97	NA
1975	164	NA	249	266	191	NA	233	182	109	148	135	NA
1980	235	NA	397	368	289	NA	351	267	147	210	191	NA
1985	299	NA	520	464	386	NA	450	351	175	289	256	NA
1986	305	NA	526	467	396	NA	459	358	176	304	266	NA
1987	313	NA	532	480	406	NA	472	365	179	316	276	NA
1988	322	NA	541	496	419	NA	476	380	184	325	289	NA
1989	334	NA	570	513	430	NA	490	395	189	341	306	NA
1990	346	NA	604	526	442	NA	504	411	195	357	320	NA
1991	355	NA	631	534	455	NA	511	425	200	373	333	NA

Source: Statistical Abstract

Almanac Fact

Since 1980, the Fortune 500 have collectively added no jobs to the U.S. economy.

Source: Fortune

Job Outlook Data

Change in Age Distribution (%) of the Labor Force, 1975 to Projected 2005

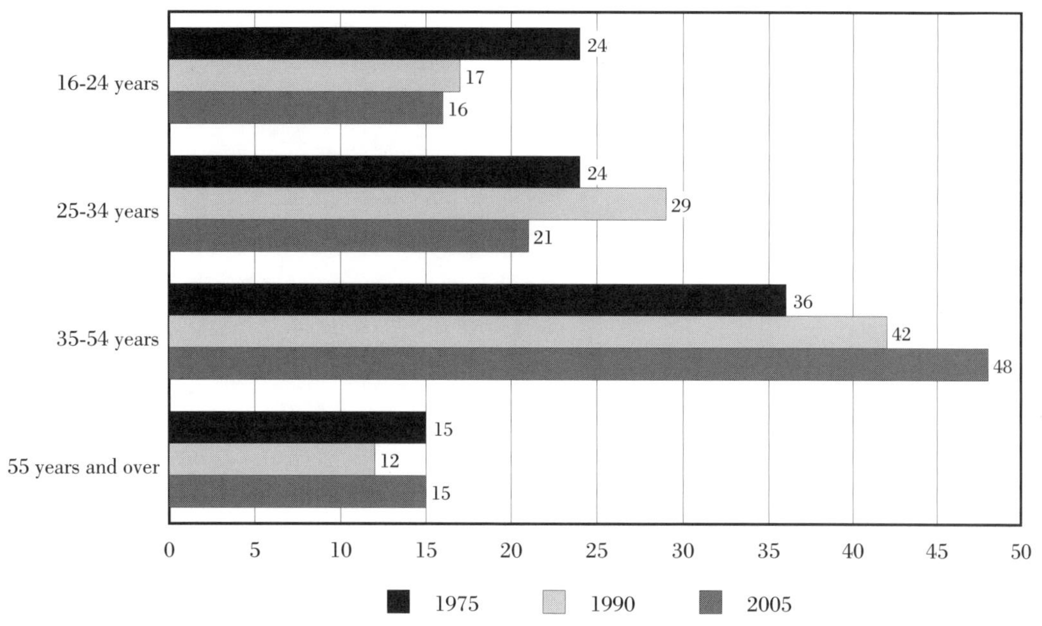

Source: U.S. Dept. of Labor, Bureau of Labor Statistics

Proportion of Workers 25 and 64 Years Old With a College Background, 1975 vs. 1990

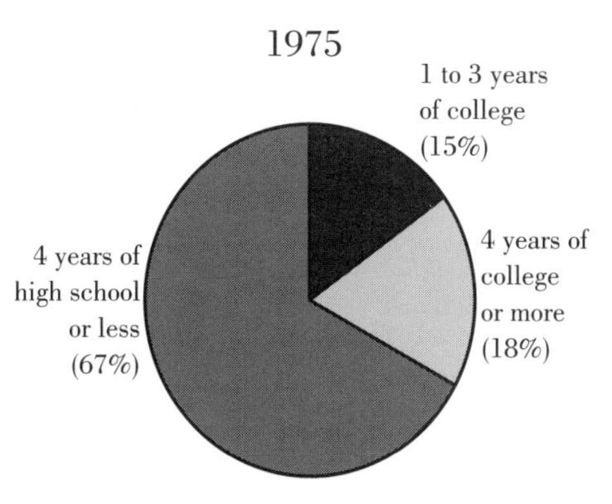

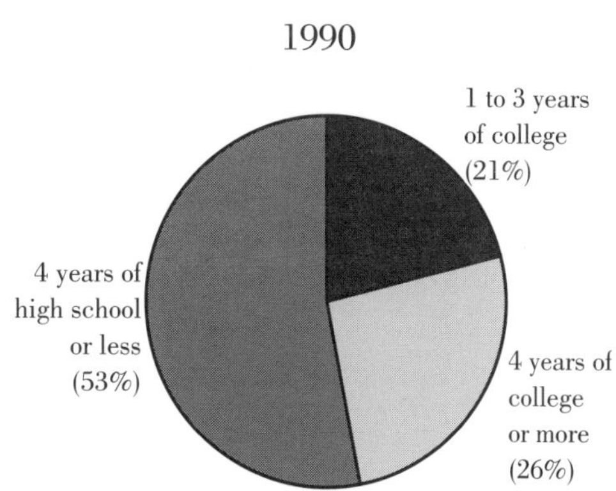

Source: U.S. Dept. of Labor, Bureau of Labor Statistics

Job Outlook Data (cont'd)

Projected Percent Change in Employment by Industry, 1990 to 2005

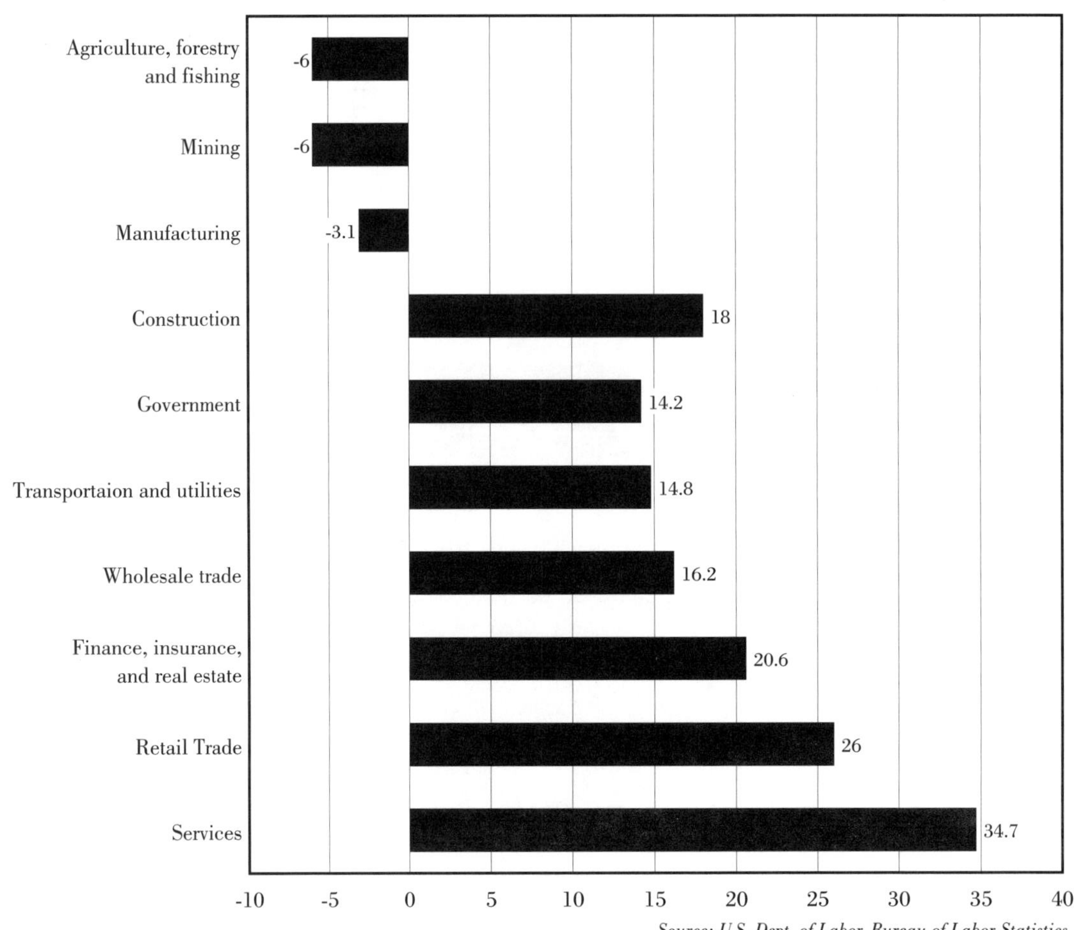

Source: U.S. Dept. of Labor, Bureau of Labor Statistics

Almanac Fact

The average American has held 8 jobs by his or her 40th birthday.

Source: Runzheimer International

Job Outlook Data (cont'd)

Projected Percent Change in Employment by Broad Occupational Group, 1990 to 2005

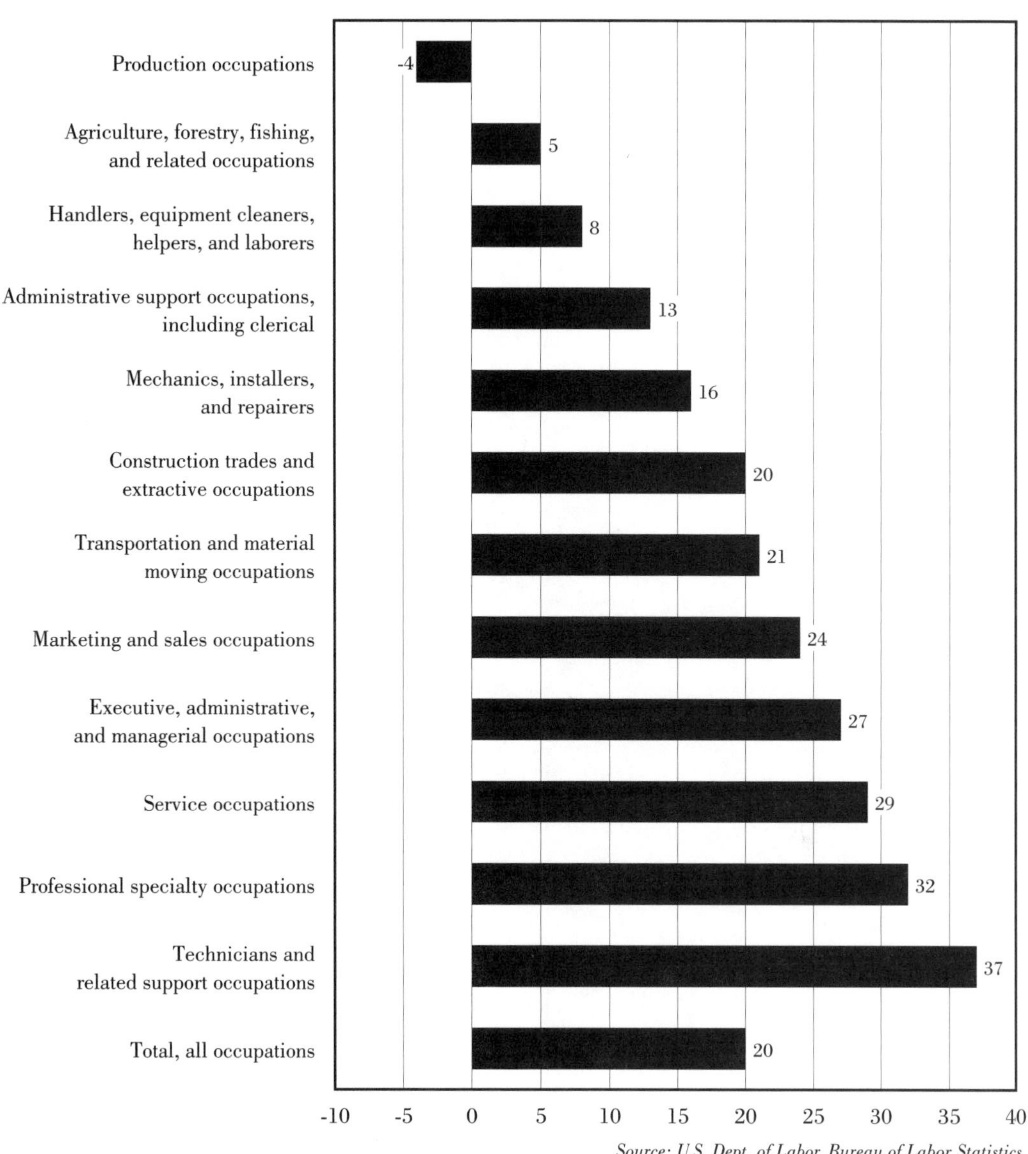

Source: U.S. Dept. of Labor, Bureau of Labor Statistics

Job Outlook Information

STATE AND LOCAL JOB MARKET and career information is available from state employment security agencies and State Occupational Information Coordinating Committees (SOICCs). State employment security agencies develop occupational employment projections and other job market information. SOICCs provide or help locate labor market and career information. The following list provides the title, address, and telephone number of state employment security agency directors of research and SOICC directors.

Alabama
Director, Labor Market Information
Alabama Department of Industrial Relations
649 Monroe St., Room 422
Montgomery, AL 36130
(205) 242-8855

Director, Alabama Occupational Information Coordinating Committee
Bell Bldg.
207 Montgomery St., Suite 400
Montgomery, AL 36130
(205) 242-2990

Alaska
Chief, Research and Analysis
Alaska Department of Labor
P.O. Box 25501
Juneau, AK 99802
(907) 465-4500

American Samoa
Program Director, American Samoa State Occupational Information Coordinating Committee
Office of Manpower Resources
American Samoa Govemment
Pago Pago, AS 96799
(684) 633-4485

Arizona
Research Administrator, Arizona Department of Economic Security
1789 W. Jefferson
P.O. Box 6123
Site Code 733A
Phoenix, AZ 85005
(602) 542-3871

Executive Director
Arizona State Occupational Information Coordinating Committee
Site Code 897J
1788 W. Jefferson St., First Floor North
Phoenix, AZ 85005
(602) 542-3680

Arkansas
State and Labor Market Information
Arkansas Employment Security Division
P.O. Box 2981
Little Rock, AR 72203
(501) 682-1543

Executive Director, Arkansas Occupational Information Coordinating Committee
Arkansas Employment Security Division
Employment and Training Services
P.O. Box 2981
Little Rock, AR 72203
(501) 682-3159

California
Acting Chief, Employment Data and Research Division
California Employment Development Department
P.O. Box 942880, MIC 57
Sacramento, CA 94280
(916) 427-4675

Executive Director, California Occupational Information Coordinating Committee
800 Capitol Mall, MIC-67
Sacramento, CA 95814
(916) 323-6544

Colorado
Director, Labor Market Information
Chancey Building, 8th Floor
1120 Lincoln St.
Denver, CO 80203
(303) 894-2589

Director, Colorado Occupational Information Coordinating Committee
State Board Community College
1391 Speer Blvd., Suite 600
Denver, CO 80204
(303) 866-4488

Connecticut
Director, Research and Information
Employment Security Division
Connecticut Labor Department
200 Folly Brook Blvd.
Wethersfield, CT 06109
(203) 566-2120

Executive Director, Connecticut Occupational Information Coordinating Committee
Connecticut Department of Education
25 Industrial Park Rd.
Middletown, CT 06457
(203) 638-4042

Job Outlook Information (cont'd)

Delaware
Chief, Office of Occupational and
Labor Market Information
Delaware Department of Labor
University Plaza, Building D
P.O. Box 9029
Newark, DE 19702
(302) 368-6962

Executive Director, Office of Occupational and
Labor Market Information
Delaware Department of Labor
University Office Plaza, P.O. Box 9029
Newark, DE 19714
(302) 368-6963

District of Columbia
Chief of Labor Market Information
District of Columbia Department of Employment
Services, 500 C St., NW., Room 201
Washington, DC 20001
(202) 639-1642

Director, District of Columbia Occupational
Information Coordinating Committee
Department of Employment Security Services
500 C St., NW, Room 215
Washington, DC 20001
(202) 639-1001

Florida
Chief, Bureau of Labor Market Information
Florida Department of Labor Employment Security,
2012 Capitol Circle, SE, Room 200
Hartman Building
Tallahassee, FL 32399
(904) 488-1048

Manager, Florida Department of Labor
and Employment Security
Bureau of Labor Market Information
2012 Capitol Circle, SE
Hartman Bldg., Suite 200
Tallahassee, FL 32399
(904) 488-7397

Georgia
Director, Labor Information System
Georgia Department of Labor
22 Courtland St., NE
Atlanta, GA 30303
(404) 656-3177

Executive Director, Georgia Occupational
Information Coordinating Committee
Department of Labor
148 International Blvd., Sussex Place
Atlanta, GA 30303
(404) 656-9639

Guam
Executive Director, Guam State Occupational
Information Coordinating Committee
Human Resource Development Agency
Jay Ease Bldg., Third Floor
P.O. Box 2817
Agana, GU 96910
(871) 646-9341

Hawaii
Chief, Research and Statistics Office
Hawaii Department of Labor and
Industrial Relations
830 Punchbowl St., Room 304
Honolulu, HI 96813
(808) 548-7639

Executive Director, Hawaii Occupational
Information Coordinating Committee
830 Punchbowl St., Room 315
Honolulu, HI 96813
(808) 548-3496

Idaho
Chief, Research and Analysis
Idaho Department of Employment
317 Main St.
Boise, ID 83735
(208) 334-6169

Director, Idaho Occupational Information
Coordinating Committee
Len B. Jordan Bldg., Room 301
650 W. State St.
Boise, ID 83720
(208) 334-3705

Illinois
Director, Economic Information and Analysis
Illinois Department of Employment Security
401 S. State St., 2 South
Chicago, IL 60605
(312) 793-2316

Executive Director, Illinois Occupational
Information Coordinating Committee
217 E. Monroe, Suite 203
Springfield, IL 62706
(217) 785-0789

Job Outlook Information (cont'd)

Indiana
Director, Labor Market Information
Indiana Department of Employment and
Training Services
10 N. Senate Ave.
Indianapolis, IN 46204
(317) 232-8456

Executive Director, Indiana Occupational
Information Coordinating Committee
309 W. Washington St., Room 309
Indianapolis, IN 46264
(317) 232-8528

Iowa
Supervisor, Audit and Analysis Department
Iowa Department of Employment Services
1000 E. Grand Ave.
Des Moines, IA 50319
(515) 281-8181

Executive Director, Iowa Occupational Information
Coordinating Committee
Iowa Department of Economic Development
200 E. Grand Ave.
Des Moines, IA 50309
(515) 242-4890

Kansas
Chief, Labor Market Information Services
Kansas Department of Human Resources
401 Topeka Ave.
Topeka, KS 66603
(913) 296-5058

Director, Kansas Occupational Information
Coordinating Committee
401 Topeka Ave.
Topeka, KS 66603
(913) 296-1865

Kentucky
Manager, Labor Market Research and Analysis
Kentucky Department for Employment Services
275 E. Main St.
Frankfort, KY 40621
(502) 564-7976

Information Liaison/Manager, Kentucky
Occupational Information Coordinating Committee
275 E. Main St., I East
Frankfort, KY 40621
(502) 564-4258

Louisiana
Director, Research and Statistics Division
Louisiana Department of Employment and Training
P.O. Box 94094
Baton Rouge, LA 70804
(504) 342-3141

Coordinator, Louisiana Occupational Information
Coordinating Committee
P.O. Box 94094
Baton Rouge, LA 70804
(504) 342-5149

Maine
Director, Division of Economic
Analysis and Research
Maine Department of Labor
Bureau of Employment Security
20 Union St.
Augusta, ME 04330
(207) 289-2271

Executive Director, Maine Occupational
Information Coordinating Committee
State House Station 71
Augusta, ME 04333
(207) 289-2331

Maryland
Director, Office of Labor Market Analysis
and Information
Maryland Department of Economic and
Employment Development
1100 N. Eutaw St., Room 601
Baltimore, MD 21201
(301) 333-5000

Coordinator, Maryland Occupational Information
Coordinating Committee
Department of Employment and Training
1100 N. Eutaw St., Room 600
Baltimore, MD 21201
(301) 333-5478

Massachusetts
Director of Research
Massachusetts Division of Employment Security
19 Stamford St., 2nd Floor
Boston, MA 02114
(617) 727-6868

Director, Massachusetts Occupational Information
Coordinating Committee
Massachusetts Division of Employment Security
Charles F. Hurley Bldg., 2nd Floor
Government Center
Boston, MA 02114
(617) 727-6718

Michigan
Director, Bureau of Research and Statistics
Michigan Employment Security Commission
7310 Woodward Ave.
Detroit, MI 48202
(313) 876-5445

Job Outlook Information (cont'd)

Executive Coordinator, Michigan Occupational Information Coordinating Committee
Victor Office Center, Third Floor
201 N. Washington Square, Box 30015
Lansing, MI 48909
(517) 373-0363

Minnesota
Director, Research and Statistical Services
Minnesota Department of Jobs and Training
390 N. Robert St., 5th Floor
St. Paul, MN 55101
(612) 296-6546

Director, Minnesota Occupational Information Coordinating Committee
Minnesota Department of Economic Security
690 American Center Bldg.
150 E. Kellogg Blvd.
St. Paul, MN 55101
(612) 296-2072

Mississippi
Chief, Labor Market Information Department
Mississippi Employment Security Commission
P.O. Box 1699
Jackson, MS 39215
(601) 961-7424

Acting Executive Director, Department of Economic and Community Development
Labor Assistance Division
Mississippi Occupational Information Coordinating Committee Office
301 W. Pearl St.
Jackson, MS 39203
(601) 949-2002

Missouri
Chief, Research and Analysis
Missouri Division of Employment Security
P.O. Box 59
Jefferson City, MO 65104
(314) 751-3591

Director, Missouri Occupational Information Coordinating Committee
421 E. Dunklin St.
Jefferson City, M0 65101
(314)751-3800

Montana
Chief, Research and Analysis
Montana Department of Labor and Industry
P.O. Box 1728
Helena, MT 59624
(406) 444-2430

Program Manager, Montana Occupational Information Coordinating Committee
P.O. Box 1728
1327 Lockey St., Second Floor
Helena, MT 59624
(406) 444-2741

Nebraska
Research Administrator, Labor Market Information
Nebraska Department of Labor
550 S. 16th St.
P.O. Box 94600
Lincoln, NE 68509
(402) 471-9964

Administrator, Nebraska Occupational Information Coordinating Committee
P.O. Box 94600, State House Station
Lincoln, NE 68509
(402) 471-4845

Nevada
Chief, Employment Security Research
Nevada Employment Security Department
500 E. Third St.
Carson City, NV 89713
(702) 687-4550

Executive Director, Nevada Occupational Information Coordinating Committee
1923 N. Carson St., Suite 211
Carson City, NV 89710
(702) 687-4577

New Hampshire
Director, Labor Market Information
New Hampshire Department of Employment Security
32 S. Main St.
Concord, NH 03301
(603) 228-4123

Director, New Hampshire State Occupational Information Coordinating Committee
64B Old Suncook Rd.
Concord, NH 03301
(603) 228-3349

New Jersey
Assistant Commissioner, Policy and Planning
New Jersey Department of Labor
John Fitch Plaza, Room 1010
Trenton, NJ 08625
(609) 292-2643

Job Outlook Information (cont'd)

Staff Director, New Jersey Occupational
Information Coordinating Committee
1008 Labor and Industry Bldg., CN 056
Trenton, NJ 08625
(609) 292-2682

New Mexico
Chief, Economic Research and Analysis Bureau
New Mexico Department of Labor
401 Broadway Blvd., NE
P.O. Box 1928
Albuquerque, NM 87103
(505) 841-8645

Director, New Mexico Occupational Information
Coordinating Committee
Tiwa Bldg., 401 Broadway NE
P.O. Box 1928
Albuquerque, NM 87103
(505) 841-8455

New York
Director, Division of Research and Statistics
New York State Department of Labor
State Campus, Bldg. 12, Room 400
Albany, NY 12240
(518) 457-6181

Executive Director, New York Occupational
Information Coordinating Committee
Department of Labor
Research and Statistics Division
State Campus
Bldg. 12, Room 400
Albany, NY 12240
(518) 457-6182

North Carolina
Director, Labor Market Information Division
North Carolina Employment Security Commission
P.O. Box 25903
Raleigh, NC 27611
(919) 733-2936

Executive Director, North Carolina Occupational
Information Coordinating Committee
1311 St. Mary's St., Suite 250
P.O. Box 27625
Raleigh, NC 27611
(919) 733-6700

North Dakota
Director, Research and Statistics
Job Service of North Dakota
P.O. Box 1537
Bismarck, ND 58502
(701) 224-2868

Coordinator, North Dakota Occupational
Information Coordinating Committee
1600 E. Interstate, Suite 14
P.O. Box 1537
Bismarck, ND 58502
(701) 224-2197

Ohio
Labor Market Information Division
Ohio Bureau of Employment Services
145 South Front St.
Columbus, OH 43215
(614) 644-2689

Director, Ohio Occupational Information
Coordinating Committee
Division of LMI, Ohio
Bureau of Employment Services
1160 Dublin Rd., Bldg. A
Columbus, OH 43215
(614) 644-2689

Oklahoma
Director, Research Division
Oklahoma Employment Security Commission
308 Will Rogers Memorial Office Bldg.
Oklahoma City, OK 73105
(405) 557-7116

Executive Director, Oklahoma Occupational
Information Coordinating Committee
Department of Voc/Tech Education
1500 W. 7th Ave.
Stillwater, OK 74074
(405) 743-5198

Oregon
Assistant Administrator for Research and Statistics
Oregon Employment Division
875 Union St. NE
Salem, OR 97311
(503) 378-3220

Executive Director
Oregon Occupational Information
Coordinating Committee
875 Union St. NE
Salem, OR 97311
(503) 378-8146

Pennsylvania
Director, Research and Statistics Division
Pennsylvania Department of Labor and Industry
1216 Labor and Industry Building
Harrisburg, PA 17121
(717) 787-3265

Job Outlook Information (cont'd)

Director, Pennsylvania Occupational Information Coordinating Committee
Pennsylvania Department of Labor and Industry
1224 Labor and Industry Bldg.
Harrisburg, PA 17120
(717) 787-8646

Puerto Rico
Director, Research and Statistics Division
Puerto Rico Department of Labor and Human Resources
505 Munoz Rivera Ave., 20th Floor
Hato Rey, PR 00918
(809) 754-5385

Executive Director, Puerto Rico Occupational Information Coordinating Committee
202 Del Cristo St.
P.O. Box 6212
San Juan, PR 00936
(809) 723-7110

Rhode Island
Administrator, Labor Market Information and Management Services
Rhode Island Department of Employment and Training
101 Friendship St.
Providence, RI 02903
(401) 277-3730

Director, Rhode Island Occupational Information Coordinating Committee
22 Hayes St., Room 133
Providence, RI 02908
(401) 272-0830

South Carolina
Director, Labor Market Information
South Carolina Employment Security Commission
P.O. Box 995
Columbia, SC 29202
(803) 737-2660

Director, South Carolina Occupational Information Coordinating Committee
1550 Gadsden St.
P.O. Box 995
Columbia, SC 29202
(803) 737-2733

South Dakota
Director, Labor Information Center
South Dakota Department of Labor
P.O. Box 4730
Aberdeen, SD 57402
(605) 622-2314

Tennessee
Director, Research and Statistics Division
Tennessee Department of Employment Security
500 James Robertson Pkwy.,11th Floor
Nashville, TN 37245
(615) 741-2284

Director, Tennessee Occupational Information Coordinating Committee
500 James Robertson Pkwy.
11th Floor Volunteer Plaza
Nashville, TN 37219
(615) 741-6451

Texas
Director, Economic Research and Analysis
Texas Employment Commission
15th and Congress Ave.
Room 208T
Austin, TX 78778
(512) 463-2616

Director, Texas Occupational Information Coordinating Committee
Texas Employment Commission Building
Room 526T
15th and Congress
Austin, TX 78778
(512) 463-2399

Utah
Director, Labor Market Information and Research
Utah Department of Employment Security
140 E. 300 South
P.O. Box 11249
Salt Lake City, UT 84147
(801) 536-7400

Vermont
Director, Policy and Information
Vermont Department of Employment and Training
5 Green Mountain Dr.
P.O. Box 488
Montpelier, VT 05602
(802) 229-0311

Director, Vermont Occupational Information Coordinating Committee
Green Mountain Dr.
P.O. Box 488
Montpelier, VT 05601
(802) 229-0311

Virginia
Director, Economic Information Service Division
Virginia Employment Commission
P.O. Box 1358
Richmond, VA 23211
(804) 786-7496

Job Outlook Information (cont'd)

Executive Director, Virginia Occupational
Information Coordinating Committee
Virginia Employment Commission
703 E. Main St.
P.O. Box 1358
Richmond, VA 23211
(804) 786-7496

Virgin Islands
Chief, Research and Analysis
Virgin Islands Department of Labor
P.O. Box 3159
St. Thomas, VI 00801
(809) 776-3700

Washington
Labor Market Information
Washington Employment Security Department
212 Maple Park
MailStop KGII
Olympia, WA 98504
(206) 753-5114

Director, Washington Occupational Information
Coordinating Committee
212 Maple Park
MailStop KGII
Olympia, WA 98504
(206) 438-4803

West Virginia
Assistant Director, Labor and Economic Research
West Virginia Bureau of Employment Programs
112 California Ave.
Charleston, WV 25305
(304) 348-2660

Executive Director, West Virginia Occupational
Information Coordinating Committee
One Dunbar Plaza, Suite E
Dunbar, WV 25064
(304) 293-5314

Wisconsin
Director, Labor Market Information Bureau
Wisconsin Department of Industry, Labor, and
Human Relations
201 E. Washington Ave., Room 221
P.O. Box 7944
Madison, WI 53707
(608) 266-5843

Administrative Director, Wisconsin Occupational
Information Coordinating Council
Division of Employment and Training Policy
201 E. Washington Ave.
P.O. Box 7972
Madison, WI 53707
(608) 266-8012

Wyoming
Manager, Research and Planning,
Division of Administration
Wyoming Department of Employment
P.O. Box 2760
Casper, WY 82602
(307) 235-3646

The Top Reference Sources

Infolink
(914) 736-1565

This group of researchers uses databases, computers, and libraries to track down obscure information on almost any topic.

For a rate of about $60 an hour, they will research any question you need answered, from competitive pricing and market share to the best ways to design a playground.

National Labor Relations Board

What Is the NLRB?

The National Labor Relations Board is an independent federal agency created in 1935 by Congress to administer the National Labor Relations Act, the basic law governing relations between labor unions and the employers whose operations affect interstate commerce.

The statute guarantees the right of employees to organize and to bargain collectively with their employers or to refrain from all such activity. Generally applying to all employers involved in interstate commerce – other than airlines, railroads, agriculture, and government – the Act implements the national labor policy of assuring free choice and encouraging collective bargaining as a means of maintaining industrial peace.

Through the years, Congress has amended the Act, and the Board and courts have developed a body of law drawn from the statute. This section is intended to give a brief explanation of the Act to employees, employers, unions, and the public.

What Does It Do?

In its statutory assignment, the NLRB has two principal functions: (1) to determine, through secret ballot elections, the free democratic choice by employees as to whether or not they wish to be represented by a union in dealing with their employers and if so, by which union; and (2) to prevent and remedy unlawful acts, called unfair labor practices, by either employers or unions.

The Act's election provisions provide the authority for conducting representation elections, which determine the views of the employees regarding representation by a labor union. Its unfair labor practice provisions place certain restrictions on actions of both employers and labor organizations in their relations with employees, as well as with each other.

The agency does not act on its own motion in either function. It processes only those charges of unfair labor practices and petitions for employee elections which are filed with the NLRB in one of its Regional, Subregional, or Resident Offices.

The staff in each office is available to assist the public with inquiries concerning the Act and to provide appropriate forms and other technical assistance to those who wish to file charges or petitions.

What Does the Act Provide?

The Act sets forth the basic rights of employees as follows:

- To self-organize;
- To form, join, or assist labor organizations;
- To bargain collectively about wages and working conditions through representatives of their own choosing;
- To engage in other protected "concerted activities," that is, to act together for purposes of collective bargaining, or other mutual aid or protection;
- To refrain from any of these activities. (However, a union and employer may, in a state where such agreements are permitted, enter into a lawful union security clause.)

The Act prohibits both employers and unions from violating these employee rights. As an example, an employer may not discriminate against employees with regard to hiring, discharge, or working conditions because of their union activities. A union may not engage in acts of violence against employees who refrain from union activity. These examples are for illustration only. For further information about employer and union unfair labor practices, refer to *The National Labor Relations Board and You: Unfair Labor Practices*, available from your nearest NLRB office. A related publication, *The National Labor Relations Board and You: Representation Cases*, describes the election process in more detail.

What Is the NLRB's Structure?

The agency has two major, separate components. The Board itself has five members and primarily acts as a quasi-judicial body in deciding cases on the basis of formal records in administrative proceedings. Board members are appointed by the president to five-year terms, with Senate consent, the term of one member expiring each year. The general counsel, appointed by the President to a four-year term with Senate consent, is independent from the Board and is responsible for the investigation and prosecution of unfair labor practice cases and for the general supervision of the NLRB field offices in the processing of unfair labor practice and representation cases.

Each Regional Office is headed by a Regional Director who is responsible for making the initial determination in unfair labor practice and representation cases arising within the geographical area served by the Region (including any Resident or Subregional Offices within the Region).

What Are the NLRB's Procedures?

Representation Cases:

In a typical representation election case, a union employer or individual files a petition with the field office requesting that an election be held among a particular group of employees (referred to as a "bargaining unit") to determine whether the group wishes to be represented, or wishes to continue to be represented, by a union. A petition filed by a union or an individual must be supported by showing that at least 30 percent of affected employees desires an election.

If the Region's investigation reveals that the petition should be processed, attempts are made to

National Labor Relations Board (cont'd)

secure agreement of the parties on the issues involved, including the appropriate unit and the time and place of the election. Over 80 percent of meritorious election petitions result in such agreements. If an agreement cannot be reached, the Region conducts a hearing. On the basis of the record of the hearing, the Regional Director issues a decision disposing of the issues. The Regional Director's decision may be appealed to the Board.

When an unfair labor practice charge is filed, the appropriate field office conducts an investigation to determine whether there is reasonable cause to believe the Act has been violated. If the Regional Director determines that the charge lacks merit, it will be dismissed, unless the charging party decides to withdraw the charge. A dismissal may be appealed to the General Counsel's office in Washington, DC.

If the Regional Director finds reasonable cause to believe a violation of the law has been committed, the Region seeks a voluntary settlement to remedy the alleged violations. If these settlement efforts fail, a formal complaint is issued, and the case goes to a hearing before an NLRB administrative law judge.

The judge issues a written decision which may be appealed to the Board for a final Agency determination. That final determination is subject to review in the Federal courts. More than 90 percent of the unfair labor practice cases filed with the NLRB are disposed of in an average of 45 days without the necessity of formal litigation before the Board. Only about four percent of the cases proceed to Board decision.

Since its establishment, the NLRB has processed more than 900,000 unfair labor practice charges and conducted in excess of 360,000 secret ballot elections. The Agency handles approximately 40,000 cases each year, including more than 7,000 representation petitions.

For Additional Information

For further information, or to receive copies of the publications referred to here, contact the nearest field office of the NLRB. The Agency has also published a pamphlet, "A Guide to Basic Law and Procedures Under the National Labor Relations Act" (available from the Superintendent of Documents, U.S. Government Printing Office, Washington, DC 20402).

National Labor Relations Board Field Offices

City	State	Telephone
Anchorage	AK	(907) 271-5015
Birmingham	AL	(205) 731-1492
Little Rock	AR	(501) 378-6311
Phoenix	AZ	(602) 261-3361
Los Angeles	CA	(213) 894-5200
Los Angeles	CA	(213) 209-7352
Oakland	CA	(415) 273-7200
San Diego	CA	(619) 293-6184
San Francisco	CA	(415) 995-5300
Denver	CO	(303) 844-3551
Hartford	CT	(203) 240-3522
Washington	DC	(202) 254-7612
Jacksonville	FL	(904) 791-3768
Miami	FL	(305) 536-5391
Tampa	FL	(813) 228-2641
Atlanta	GA	(404) 331-2896
Honolulu	HI	(808) 541-2814
Des Moines	IA	(515) 284-4391
Chicago	IL	(312) 353-7570
Peoria	IL	(309) 671-7080
Indianapolis	IN	(317) 269-7430
Mission	KS	(913) 236-2777
New Orleans	LA	(504) 589-6361
Boston	MA	(617) 565-6700
Baltimore	MD	(301) 962-2822
Detroit	MI	(313) 226-3200

City	State	Telephone
Grand Rapids	MI	(616) 456-2679
Minneapolis	MN	(612) 348-1757
St. Louis	MO	(314) 425-4167
Winston-Salem	NC	(919) 761-3201
Newark	NJ	(201) 645-2100
Albuquerque	NM	(505) 262-6395
Las Vegas	NV	(702) 388-6416
Albany	NY	(518) 472-2215
Brooklyn	NY	(718) 330-7713
Buffalo	NY	(716) 846-4931
New York	NY	(212) 264-0300
Cincinnati	OH	(513) 684-3686
Cleveland	OH	(216) 522-3715
Tulsa	OK	(918) 581-7951
Portland	OR	(503) 221-3085
Philadelphia	PA	(215) 597-7601
Pittsburgh	PA	(412) 644-2977
Hato Rey	PR	(809) 766-5347
Memphis	TN	(901) 521-2725
Nashville	TN	(615) 736-5922
El Paso	TX	(915) 534-6434
Fort Worth	TX	(817) 334-2921
Houston	TX	(713) 220-2365
San Antonio	TX	(515) 229-6140
Seattle	WA	(206) 442-4532
Milwaukee	WI	(414) 291-3861

Time Management Techniques

Ten Tips for Better Time Management:

1. Any time you handle any piece of paper, limit your contact with it to one time. If it requires a response, respond now – not later. If it must be filed, file it now. If it might be better off in the wastebasket, toss it now.
2. Learn how to say no. This is not an easy word to say, and you'll have to say it to some of the nicest people in the world. Be nice, direct, and compassionate, but say it immediately. Don't leave people hanging and waste their time.
3. Respect your instincts and your mood. If you're not in the mood to do something, do something else, saving the original task for a time when you are more likely to tackle it efficiently.
4. Make a public commitment. If you want to complete a task by a certain hour, go public with your pronouncement. "I'll have that report to you by three o'clock," leaves you with little choice.
5. Take breaks. If you work straight through without any break at all, chances are your work will suffer. If you take brief breaks, you'll better be able to keep an attentive pace and your work will be more accurate.
6. Learn to tolerate your faults in an effort to overcome perfectionism. You'll have a far better time of almost anything in life if you strive for excellence rather than perfection.
7. Get things done right now. It is estimated that a minimum of 80 percent of the business coming across the desk of an efficient executive gets handled immediately, through either personal action or delegation.
8. Force yourself to be neat. Neatness leads to organization, and organization leads to time efficiency.
9. Do things one at a time. This simple mind-set can keep you well organized, because the main reason some people can't seem to organize anything is that they fear having to organize everything.
10. When negotiating, realize that the shortest route to an agreement isn't necessarily the straightest. It takes 90 percent of the total discussion time to resolve 10 percent of the issues, and the final 10 percent of the time to resolve the other 90 percent. By recognizing this fact of negotiation, you can save a great deal of valuable time.

Source: Adapted from Jay Conrad Levinson's The 90-Minute Hour

Recommended Resources

How to Get Organized When You Don't Have the Time
By Stephanie Culp
Writer's Digest Books, 1986

The Effective Executive
By Peter Drucker
Harper & Row, 1967

Working Smart
By Michael Leboeuf
Warner Books, 1979

The Top Reference Sources

Business Rankings Annual
Gale, $160
(800) 877-4253

This mammoth book (900+ pages) lists more than 4,500 top ten lists–from largest public companies to highest paid CEOs.

Covering more than 1,500 different topics, this volume is an excellent place to look for a wide breadth of information.

First Aid

The Heimlich Maneuver for Choking

What to look for: victim cannot speak or breathe; turns blue; collapses.

To perform the Heimlich Maneuver when the victim is standing or sitting:

1. Stand behind the victim and wrap your arms around his or her waist.
2. Place the thumb side of your fist against the victim's abdomen, slightly above the navel and below the rib cage.
3. Grasp your fist with the other hand and press your fist into the victim's abdomen with a quick upward thrust. Repeat as often as necessary.
4. If the victim is sitting, stand behind the victim's chair and perform the maneuver in the same manner.
5. After the food is dislodged, have the victim see a doctor.

When the victim has collapsed and cannot be lifted:

1. Lay the victim on his or her back.
2. Face the victim and kneel astride his or her hips.
3. With one hand on top of the other, place the heel of your bottom hand on the abdomen slightly above the navel and below the rib cage.
4. Press into the victim's abdomen with a quick upward thrust. Repeat as often as necessary.
5. Should the victim vomit, quickly place on his or her side and wipe out the mouth to prevent aspiration (drawing of vomit into the throat).
6. After the food is dislodged, have the victim see a doctor.

NOTE: If you start to choke when alone, and help is not available, an attempt should be made to self-administer this maneuver.

Burns

First Degree:

Signs/Symptoms: reddened skin.

Treatment: Immerse quickly in cold water or apply ice until pain stops.

Second Degree:

Signs/Symptoms: reddened skin, blisters.

Treatment: (1) Cut away loose clothing; (2) Cover with several layers of cold, moist dressings or, if limb is involved, immerse in cold water for relief of pain; (3) Treat for shock.

Third Degree:

Signs/Symptoms: skin destroyed; tissues damaged; charring.

Treatment: (1) Cut away loose clothing (do not remove clothing adhered to skin); (2) Cover with several layers of sterile, cold, moist dressings for relief of pain and to stop burning action; (3) Treat for shock.

Poisons

Treatment:

(1) Dilute by drinking large quantities of water; (2) Induce vomiting except when poison is corrosive or a petroleum product; (3) Call a Poison Control center or a doctor.

Poison Control Center: (800) 336-6997

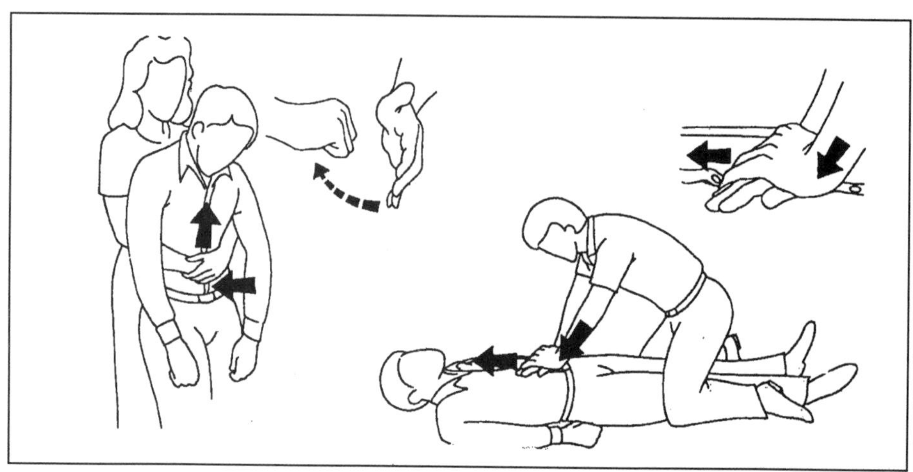

Source: New York City Department of Health

First Aid (cont'd)

Shock

Shock may accompany any serious injury: blood loss, breathing impairment, heart failure, burns. Shock can kill, so treat as soon as possible and continue until medical aid is available.

Signs/Symptoms: (1) Shallow breathing; (2) Rapid and weak pulse; (3) Nausea, collapse, vomiting; (4) Shivering; (5) Pale, moist skin; (6) Mental confusion; (7) Drooping eyelids, dilated pupils.

Treatment: (1) Establish and maintain an open airway; (2) Control bleeding; (3) Keep victim lying down. Exception: Head and chest injuries, heart attack, stroke, sun stroke. If no spine injury, victim may be more comfortable and breathe better in a semi-reclining position. If in doubt, keep the victim flat. Elevate the feet unless injury would be aggravated. Maintain normal body temperature. Place blankets under and over victim.

Heat Cramps

Heat cramps affect people who work or do strenuous exercises in a hot environment. To prevent it, drink large amounts of cool water and add a pinch of salt to each glass of water.

Signs/Symptoms: (1) Painful muscle cramps in legs and abdomen; (2) Faintness; (3) Profuse perspiration.

Treatment: 1) Move victim to a cool place; (2) Give him or her sips of salted drinking water (one teaspoon of salt to one quart of water); (3) Apply manual pressure to the cramped muscle.

Heat Exhaustion

Signs/Symptoms: (1) Pale and clammy skin; (2) Profuse perspiration; (3) Rapid and shallow breathing; (4) Weakness, dizziness, and headache.

Treatment: (1) Care for victim as if he or she were in shock; (2) Move victim to a cool area, do not allow chilling; (3) If body gets too cold, cover victim.

Heat Stroke

Signs/Symptoms: (1) Face is red and flushed; (2) Victim rapidly loses consciousness; (3) Skin is hot and dry with no perspiration.

Treatment: (1) Lay victim down with head and shoulders raised; (2) Apply cold applications to the body and head; (3) Use ice and fan if available; (4) Watch for signs of shock and treat accordingly; (5) Get medical aid as soon as possible.

Artificial Respiration

Artificial respiration is mouth-to-mouth breathing–in cases like drowning, electric shock, or smoke inhalation.

There is need for help when breathing movements stop or lips, tongue, and fingernails become blue. When in doubt, apply artificial respiration until you get medical help. No harm can result from its use, and delay may cost the patient his or her life. Start immediately. Seconds count. Clear mouth and throat of any obstructions with your fingers.

For Adults: Place patient on back with face up. Lift the chin and tilt the head back. If air passage is still closed, pull chin up by placing fingers behind the angles of the lower jaw and pushing forward. Take a deep breath, place your mouth over patient's mouth, making leak-proof seal. Pinch patient's nostrils closed. Blow into patient's mouth until you see his or her chest rise.

Repeat about 12 times a minute. (If the patient's stomach rises markedly, exert moderate hand pressure on the stomach just below the rib cage to keep it from inflating.)

For infants and small children: Place your mouth over patient's mouth and nose. Blow into mouth and nose until you see patient's chest rise normally.

Repeat 20 to 30 times per minute. (Don't exaggerate the tilted position of an infant's head.)

NOTE: For emergency treatment of heart attack, cardiopulmonary resuscitation (CPR) is recommended. Instruction in CPR can be obtained through local health organizations or schools.

First-Aid Kit Contents

THE FEDERAL GOVERNMENT has no prescribed standard for the contents of an office first-aid kit. But, Johnson & Johnson, the leading manufacturer of first aid kits, suggests that the following be included in a first aid kit for an office of 50 people:

- 100 Sheer bandages, 3/4" x 3"
- 10 Plastic bandages, extra large
- 20 Flexible fabric bandages, 1" x 3"
- 10 Flexible fabric knuckle bandages
- 10 Flexible fabric fingertip bandages
- 10 Non-stick pads, small
- 2 General-use sponges, sterile, 4" x 4"
- 2 Soft-gauze bandages, 2"
- 2 Oval eye pads
- 1 Triangular bandage
- 1 Hypo-allergenic first-aid tape, 1/2" x 180" (5 yds.) in dispenser
- 1 Elastic bandage, 2"
- 20 Antiseptic wipes
- 6 Burn cream, 1/8 oz. foil packs
- 1 First aid cream, 1/8 oz. tube
- 1 Instant cold pack, small (4 1/2" x 6")
- 1 Ophthalmic irrigating solution, 1/2 fl. oz.
- 12 Tylenol® Extra-Strength Caplets
- 1 Scissors
- 1 Tweezer
- 2 Disposable gloves
- 1 First-Aid guide

Dealing with Stress

ACCORDING TO *PERSONNEL* MAGAZINE, the cost of stress-related illnesses to American business is approximately 90 billion dollars a year. Being able to identify serious signs of stress and/or burnout in employees and co-workers, and alleviating the causes of stress where possible will increase productivity. In the long run, stress reduction can save millions of dollars in stress-related workers' compensation claims.

Stress is generally defined as any outside stimulus that disrupts the body's mental, physical, or chemical functioning.

Studies indicate that extreme forms of stress are characterized by restlessness, impatience, extreme competitiveness, and feelings of being under pressure. Furthermore, extreme stress can, over time, lead to deteriorating performance in the workplace as well as health problems such as: migraines, high blood pressure, arthritis, eczema, gastric and/or peptic ulcers, asthma, heart disease, and stroke.

The most common forms of workplace-related stress arise from one of the following conditions:

- Job changes that place new demands on a worker's time and personal or family relationships;
- Poor organizational climate and insufficient social support from friends or co-workers;
- Conflicts between workers' personal values and the values of the company;
- Frustrated career plans;
- Bad lighting, uncomfortable temperatures, noise, or other environmental factors.

An employee's ability to cope with stress is affected by the intensity and duration of one or more of the conditions listed above.

Stress by Industry

Industry	% Reporting "Managers Appear Stressed"	% Reporting "Managers Working Near Burnout"
Transportation/Communications/Utilities	50	28
Manufacturing	48	29
Wholesale/Retail/Trade	46	24
Finance/Insurance/Banking	44	25
Business Services	42	30
Health Services	36	27
Public Administration	33	28
Educational Services	24	16

Source: Training Magazine

Strategies Designed to Cope with Stress:

- Physical maintenance:
  Diet
  Sleep
  Exercise
- Internal assistance:
  Relaxation response
  Biofeedback
  Autogenic training
- Personal organization:
  Stress plan
  Delegation of responsibility
  Ability to choose or alternate environments
  Creative problem solving and decision making
  Goal setting
  Time management
  Conflict management
  Ability to restructure job
  Self-assessment measures
- Outside assistance:
  Psychoanalysis
  Stress counseling
  Development program
  Behavior change techniques
- Stress-directed strategies:
  Systematic desensitization
  Dynamic psychotherapy
- Situational and support group:
  Assertiveness training and role-playing
  Development of supportive relationships
- Negative strategies:
  Avoidance of substance abuse (alcohol, cigarettes, drugs)

Dealing with Stress (cont'd)

45 Elements of the Stress-Free Workplace

Northwestern National Life has created a simple questionnaire that allows workers to judge the level of stress they face at work. The basic principles behind this test are as follows.

1. Management is supportive of employees' efforts.
2. Management encourages work and personal support groups.
3. Management and employees talk openly.
4. Employees receive training when assigned new tasks.
5. Employees are recognized and rewarded for their contributions.
6. Work rules are published and are the same for everyone.
7. Employees have current and understandable job descriptions.
8. Management appreciates humor in the workplace.
9. Employees and management are trained in how to resolve conflicts.
10. Employees are free to talk with one another.
11. Workloads do not vary greatly for individuals or between individuals.
12. Employees have work spaces that are not crowded.
13. Employees have access to technology they need.
14. Opportunties for advancement are available.
15. Employees are given some control in how they do their work.
16. Employees generally are not physically isolated.
17. Mandatory overtime is seldom required.
18. Employees have some privacy.
19. Performance of work units is above average.
20. Personal conflicts on the job are not common.
21. Consequences of making a mistake on the job are not extremely severe.
22. Employees do not expect the organization will be sold or relocated.
23. There has been no major reorganization in the past 12 months.
24. Meal breaks are predictable.
25. Medical and mental health benefits are provided by the employer.
26. Employees are given information regularly on how to cope with stress.
27. Sick and vacation benefits are above that of similar organizations.
28. Employee benefits were not significantly cut in the past 12 months.
29. An employee assistance program (EAP) is offered.
30. Pay is above the going rate.
31. Employees can work flexible hours.
32. Employees have a place and time to relax during the workday.
33. Employer has a formal employee communications program.
34. Child care programs or referral services are available.
35. Referral programs or day care for elderly relatives are offered.
36. Special privileges are granted fairly based on an employee's level.
37. New machines or ways of working were introduced in the past year.
38. Employer offers exercise or other stress-reduction programs.
37. Work is neither sedentary nor physically exhausting.
40. Not all work is machine-paced or fast-paced.
41. Staffing or expense budgets are adequate.
42. Noise or vibration is low, or temperatures are not extreme or fluctuating.
43. Employees do not deal with a lot of red tape to get things done.
44. Downsizing or layoffs have not occurred in the past 12 months
45. Employees can put up personal items in their work area.

Contact Option

Northwestern National Life
20 Washington Ave., S.
Minneapolis, MN 55401
(612) 372-5432

Almanac Fact

Of all medical expenses, mental health ranks first in cost to employers.

Source: Medstat Systems

Computer-Related Illnesses

THE APPLICATIONS OF COMPUTER technology and the use of video display terminals are revolutionizing the workplace. Along with their growing use, however, have come reports about adverse health effects for VDT operators.

For every potential hazard, health specialists recommend interventions that can be used both by employers and computer operators alike. Here is a list of the most commonly recognized harmful effects of frequent computer use and some suggested means of alleviating potential problems.

Eyestrain

Visual problems, such as eyestrain and irritation are among the most frequently reported complaints by VDT operators. These visual problems can result from improper lighting, glare from the screen, poor positioning of the screen itself, or from copy that is difficult to read. These problems can usually be corrected by arranging workstations and lighting to avoid direct or reflected glare. VDT operators can also reduce eyestrain by taking vision breaks and by doing exercises that relax eye muscles.

Radiation

Some workers, including pregnant women, are concerned that their health could be affected by X-rays or electromagnetic fields emitted from VDTs. To date, however, there is no conclusive evidence that the low levels of radiation emitted from VDTs pose a health risk. The issue is still being researched and studied. In the meantime, some workplace designs have incorporated changes such as increasing the distance between the operator and the terminal, and between workstations to reduce potential exposures to electromagnetic fields.

Fatigue and Musculoskeletal Problems

Work performed at VDTs may require sitting still for considerable amounts of time and usually involves small frequent movements of the eyes, head, arms, and fingers. Retaining a fixed posture over long periods of time requires a significant static holding force, which causes fatigue. Proper workstation design is very important in eliminating these types of problems. An individual workstation should provide the operator with a comfortable sitting position sufficiently flexible to reach, use, and observe the display screen, keyboard, and document. Proper chair height and support to the lower region of the back are critical factors in reducing fatigue and related musculoskeletal complaints. Document holders also allow the operator to position and view material without straining the eyes or the muscles in the neck, shoulder, and back.

Repetitive Stress Syndrome

VDT operators are also subject to a potential risk of developing various nerve or cumulative trauma disorders. Carpal tunnel syndrome (CTS), a commonly recognized cumulative trauma disorder, is caused by repetitive wrist-hand movement and exertion. CTS is the compression and entrapment of the median nerve where it passes through the wrist into the hand. When irritated, the tendons and their sheaths, housed inside the narrow carpal tunnel in the wrist, swell and press against the median nerve. The pressure causes tingling, numbness, or severe pain in the wrist and hand. CTS usually can be reduced by maintaining correct posture and by limiting the activity that aggravates the tendon and the median nerve. For correct posture, VDT operators should sit in an upright position at the keyboard, with arms parallel to the floor and wrists and forearms supported where possible. Additional exercises may help eliminate the problem. In extreme cases, surgery may be required.

Seven Ways to Help VDT Users Reduce Job-Related Stress

- Maintain a well-designed work area. (See next page).
- Limit continuous hours. The longer the time spent at a VDT, the higher the rate of health problems reported. Users should spend no more than four hours at one time for demanding work.
- Allow frequent breaks. Give workers the opportunity to get up and move about and give their eyes a chance to rest. A 15-minute break every two hours is recommended.
- Train workers thoroughly.
- Maintain variety. Limit the time workers spend on VDTs by giving staffers varied duties.
- Provide interaction or privacy as needed.

Source: Office and Branch Managers Bulletin

Computer-Related Illnesses (cont'd)

VDT Workstation Checklist

- Does the workstation lend itself to proper posture considerations such as:
  thighs horizontal;
  lower legs vertical;
  feet flat on floor or footrest;
  wrists neutral or slightly extended?
- Does the chair in use:
  adjust easily;
  have a padded seat with a rounded front;
  have a backrest which is adjustable;
  provide lumbar support;
  have casters?
- Is the keyboard worksurface:
  height adjustable;
  tilt adjustable?
- Is the keyboard detachable?
- Does keying require minimal force?
- Does the thickness of the keyboard affect wrist posture?
- Is there an adjustable document holder?
- Are armrests provided where needed?
- Are glare and reflections avoided?
- Do the VDT's have brightness and contrast controls?
- Is there proper distance between eyes and work?
- Is their sufficient space for knees and feet?
- Is the workstation biased toward right- or left-handed activity?
- Are adequate rest breaks provided for task demand?
- Are employees measured or rewarded by the number of keystrokes they type per minute?
- Is the employee's ability to maintain typing speed assisted by:
  job rotation;
  proper work methods;
  when and how to adjust workstations;
  how to get questions answered quickly?

Source: OSHA: Ergonomic Program Management Recommendations for General Industry

Contact Options

Occupational Safety and Health Administration (OSHA)
U.S. Department of Labor
Technical Data Center, Room N2439
200 Constitution Ave., NW
Washington DC 20210
(202) 219-6091

U.S. Department of Health and Human Services
Public Health Service, Center for Disease Control
National Institute for Occupational Safety and Health (NIOSH)
Robert A. Taft Laboratories
4676 Columbia Parkway
Cincinnati, OH 45226
(513) 533-8236

Almanac Fact

The new adjustable keyboard from Apple Computer is purported to reduce user stress and prevent carpal tunnel syndrome.

Source: Apple Computer (800) 767-2775

Accessibility for the Handicapped

THE AMERICANS WITH DISABILITIES ACT covers a broad range of topics relating to the working conditions of the disabled. All qualified handicapped workers are covered. An employer is not required to hire or retain an individual who is not qualified to perform a job. The regulations define a qualified individual with a disability as a person with a disability who "satisfies the requisite skills, experience, education, and other job-related requirements of the employment position such individual holds or desires, and who, with or without a reasonable accommodation, can perform the essential functions of such a position."

It is important that employers are familiar with the issues covered by ADA and with those discussed in Title I and Title III in particular.

Title I

Employment deals specifically with employment. It prohibits discrimination against a qualified individual with a disability in regard to:

- Applications
- Testing
- Hiring
- Assignments
- Evaluation
- Disciplinary actions
- Training
- Promotion
- Medical examinations
- Layoff/recall
- Termination
- Compensation
- Leave
- Benefits.

Title III

Public Accommodations and Services Operated by Private Entities prohibits discrimination in public accommodations and services operated by private entities. The term public accommodations means any business that provides goods or services to the general public. In general, persons with disabilities must be accorded the full and equal enjoyment of the goods, services, facilities, privileges, advantages, and accommodations by any person who owns, leases, or operates a place of public accommodation. To accomplish this end, this title requires:

- Provision of auxiliary aids and services;
- Removal of architectural and communications barriers in existing vehicles;
- Removal of transportation barriers in existing vehicles;
- Modifications in policies, practices and procedures.

Many areas and items must be addressed in an accessibility audit of public accommodations. The following is a sample accessibility checklist:

- Accessible routes (paths or walks) at least 3 feet wide and with at least 80 inches of headroom;
- Ramps that are at least 3 feet wide and with a maximum slope equal to 1 to 12 inches and maximum rise equal to 30 inches;
- Stairs with treads at least 11 inches wide and having a tactile warning at the top of the stairs;
- Parking facilities with spaces at least 8 feet wide and having special reserved spaces for the handicapped;
- Passenger loading zone that is at least 4 feet wide and 20 feet long;
- Drinking fountain: spout 3 feet high or less;
- Public telephones that are controlled by push button;
- Seating and tables that are 27 to 34 inches wide and 19 inches deep;
- Corridors with carpet pile one-half inch or less;
- Door openings at least 32 inches wide.

For situations requiring extensive analysis, the best resource is the Job Accommodation Network. Employers with questions on how to accommodate applicants and employees with disabilities may contact the Job Accommodation Network (JAN). This program, located at West Virginia University, is a free service for employers. It may be reached at (800) 526-7234.

Recommended Resource

The Employer's Guide to Understanding and Complying with the Americans with Disabilities Act
Dartnell Publishing
4660 Ravenswood Ave.
Chicago, IL 60640
(800) 441-7878

Facts About AIDS

APPROXIMATELY ONE IN EVERY 250 Americans–most of whom are of working age–is living with HIV. What's more, nearly one in ten small employers already have employees who are living and working with HIV infection, including AIDS.

According to the American Red Cross, there is no danger in working with someone who is HIV-positive or who has AIDS. An individual cannot become infected through everyday work activities that do not involve contact with blood, semen, or vaginal fluids. Scientific studies from around the world have shown that HIV is not spread through ordinary employee, client, or public contact; nor through a handshake, a hug, or a social kiss.

For most workers, there is no need for special precautions. Scientific studies do not indicate any risk of HIV infection from contact with body fluids or waste – feces, nasal fluid, saliva, sweat, tears, urine or vomit – unless these contain visible blood. Workers (such as sanitation workers) who may handle fluids and waste that sometimes contain blood should wear rubber or vinyl gloves. Furthermore, hairstylists, cosmetologists, electrologists, or any workers who use instruments that can penetrate the skin or become contaminated with blood should sterilize those instruments or throw them away after one use.

At the present time, 68 percent of businesses have no HIV/AIDS policy. It is important, however, that employees and employers alike are educated about HIV/AIDS and how to help support co-workers infected with the virus. An effective HIV/AIDS policy should address such issues as:

- Insurance and health care costs
- Productivity
- Work disruption
- Employee benefits
- Customer concern
- Employee morale
- Legal considerations
- Confidentiality and privacy
- Discrimination concerns
- Disability requirements
- Job accommodation.

Reducing the Risk of Infection

- Avoid direct contact with blood. Use a barrier such as a clean cloth or wear disposable latex or vinyl gloves to protect yourself from any blood.
- Wash your hands with soap and water as soon as you can after giving first aid, whether or not you have worn gloves.
- If you perform rescue breathing, avoid contact with any blood.
- When cleaning someone's blood from surfaces, always wear rubber gloves and use a disinfectant solution. If a disinfectant is not available, you can make one by mixing 1/4 cup of liquid household chlorine bleach with one gallon of water. (This solution must be made fresh just prior to use and discarded each day.)

Source: The American Red Cross

Responding to AIDS: Ten Principles for the Workplace

The Citizens Commission on AIDS of New York City and New Jersey suggests the following policies be adopted:

- People with HIV infection or AIDS are entitled to the same rights and opportunities as people with other serious or life-threatening illnesses.
- Employment policies must, at a minimum, comply with federal, state, and local laws and regulations.
- Employment policies should be based on the scientific and epidemiological evidence that people with HIV infection or AIDS do not pose a risk of transmission of the virus to co-workers through ordinary workplace contact.
- The highest levels of management and union leadership should unequivocally endorse nondiscriminatory employment policies and education programs about HIV/AIDS.
- Employers and unions should communicate their support of these policies clearly, simply, and unambiguously.
- Employers should provide employees with sensitive, accurate, and up-to-date education about risk reduction in their personal lives.
- Employers have a duty to protect the confidentiality of employees' medical information.
- To prevent work disruption and rejection by co-workers of employees with HIV infection or AIDS, employers and unions should undertake education for all employees before incidents occur and as needed thereafter.
- Employers should not require HIV screening as part of pre-employment or general workplace physical examinations.
- In those special occupational settings where there may be a potential risk of exposure to HIV, employers should provide specific ongoing education and training, as well as necessary equipment, to reinforce appropriate infection-control procedures and ensure that they are implemented.

Alcohol and Substance Abuse

ALL ALCOHOL AND SUBSTANCE ABUSE programs in work settings are called Employee Assistance Programs or EAPs. According to the U.S. Department of Labor, the use of EAPs has grown dramatically over the last decade. Although there is no standardized EAP, most are based on the assumption that helping employees with alcohol and substance abuse problems will reduce employee turnover as well as reducing absenteeism, tardiness, accidents, and other problems that affect productivity. Many of these programs are also concerned with ensuring efficient health-care cost containment and providing a new benefit to enhance employee morale and company commitment. Most companies employ one of the following four types of EAP:

- Internal company programs staffed by a company employee who accepts referrals from supervisors as well as self-referrals, conducts initial assessments, and refers employees to community resources for professional counseling or treatment.
- External company programs in which companies contract with outside agencies to provide most services. These are more common in small- and medium-sized firms.
- Labor union programs which usually revolve around a peer referral process that enourages union members with alcohol-use problems to seek help.
- Professional association programs which are usually aimed at maintaining standards of professional conduct. Threats to withdraw licensure are frequently used to pressure members into seeking assistance.

In most EAPs, alcohol and substance abuse problems are defined by poor job performance. Supervisors should confront employees constructively, demanding improved job performance as a condition of continued employment. Studies reveal that constructive confrontation rather than more severe forms of discipline leads to improvement in employee work performance.

In the last few years, more and more small- and medium-sized companies have begun investing their own resources in EAPs without any outside regulatory pressure from the government. This suggests the growing recognition among employers of the value of these efforts. The average annual cost for an EAP ranges from $12 to $20 per employee. Statistics from the National Council on Alcoholism and Drug Dependence indicate that an employer saves anywhere from $5 to $16 for every dollar invested in an EAP.

Establishing an EAP, however, is only one part of the way that a company can deal with substance abuse in the workplace.

Five Steps to a Workplace Substance Abuse Program:

1. Write a clear and comprehensive policy.

- Let employees and applicants know that drug and alcohol use on the job, or any use that affects job performance, is not permitted.
- Explain that you are establishing the policy for workplace safety, worker health, product quality, productivity, public liability.
- Tell employees what will happen if they violate the policy.

2. Train your supervisors. Supervisors should be responsible for:

- Observing and documenting unsatisfactory work performance or behavior.
- Talking to employees about work problems and what needs to be done about them.
- Supervisors are *not* responsible for diagnosing or treating substance abuse problems.

3. Educate your employees. An employee education and awareness program:

- Explains your workplace substance abuse policy and the consequences of using drugs and alcohol on or off the job.
- Tells your employees how to get help with their drug and alcohol problems, including a description of services available to help employees by a representative of the EAP, if the company has one, or by a community resource.
- Informs employees on how drugs and alcohol actually affect the company's productivity, product quality, absenteeism, health care costs, or accident rates.
- Explains testing procedures – if drug testing is part of the program – with special attention to the consequences of testing positive, and procedures for ensuring accuracy and confidentiality.

4. Provide an employee assistance program.

5. Start a drug testing program.

Some companies must set up a drug testing program because of the kind of work they do. The Drug-Free Workplace Act of 1988 is a federal statute requiring certain federal contractors and grantees to maintain a drug-free workplace. Companies covered by the act must have a single contract with the Federal Government of $25,000 or more, or must receive

Alcohol and Substance Abuse (cont'd)

a grant from the Federal Government. Any company that sets up a drug testing program must make sure that the program explains the:

- Statutory or regulatory requirements;
- Disability discrimination provisions;
- Collective bargaining agreements;
- Any other requirements in effect.

Source: An Employer's Guide to Dealing with Substance Abuse, U.S. Dept. of Labor, October, 1990

Alternative or Complementary Strategies to EAPs

- Alcohol education in the workplace, directed both toward information about the effects of drinking and identification of problem drinking and alcoholism;
- Alcohol control policies associated with work, such as prohibited lunchtime drinking, limiting availability of alcohol in executive dining rooms, excluding alcohol at company-sponsored functions, and prohibiting reimbursement of employee expenses for the purchase of alcohol for themselves and their clients;
- Wellness programs, including health-risk appraisals, blood-pressure screening, and counseling of employees regarding health risks associated with different drinking lifestyles.

Source: Alcohol Health & Research World, Vol. 13, No. 4 package

Ten Facts About Alcohol and Substance Abuse in the Workplace

- 11.9 percent of the American workforce reports heavy drinking, defined as drinking five or more drinks per occasion on five or more days in the past 30 days.
- Up to 40 percent of industrial fatalities and 47 per cent of industrial injuries can be linked to alcohol consumption and alcoholism.
- 70 percent of all current adult illegal drug users are employed.
- 63 percent of firms responding to a 1991 survey were engaged in some sort of drug testing, a 200 percent increase since 1987.
- Absenteeism among alcoholics or problem drinkers is 3.8 to 8.3 times greater than normal and up to 16 times greater among all employees with alcohol and other drug-related problems. Drug-using employees use three times as many sick benefits as other workers. They are five times more likely to file a workers' compensation claim.
- Non-alcoholic members of alcoholic families use ten times as much sick leave as members of families in which alcoholism is not present.
- 43 percent of CEOs responding to one survey estimate that use of alcohol and other drugs cost them one percent to ten percent of their payroll.
- For every dollar they invest in an Employee Assistance Program, employers generally save anywhere from $5 to $16. The average annual cost for an EAP ranges from $12 to $20 per employee.
- While roughly 90 percent of the Fortune 500 companies have established EAPs, this percentage is much lower among smaller companies. Only nine percent of businesses with fewer than 50 employees have EAP programs. Fully 90 percent of U.S. businesses fall into this category.
- A recent survey reports that nearly nine out of ten employers limit benefits for alcoholism, other drug dependence, and mental disorders despite the fact that 52 percent of the survey participants could not say how much it cost them to provide treatment for these conditions.

Source: National Council on Alcoholism and Drug Dependence

Contact Options

Dr. Richard K. Fuller
Prevention Research Branch
Division of Clinical and Prevention Research
National Institute on Alcohol Abuse and Alcoholism
5600 Fishers Lane, Room 16C-03
Rockville, MD 20857
(301) 443-1206

Drug-Free Workplace Helpline
(800) 843-4971
Provides information and publications that will help companies research and develop drug-free workplace programs.

The National Association of State Alcohol and Drug Abuse Directors (NASADAD)
Drug-Free Workplace Project
444 N. Capitol St., NW
Suite 642
Washington DC 20001
(202) 783-6868

NIDA Hotline
(800) 662-HELP
Referrals for treatment programs locally and nationwide.

Workers' Compensation

IF A WORKER IS INJURED ON THE JOB, he or she cannot sue the employer for negligence. The exclusive remedy is workers' compensation. The worker gets no more if the employer is to blame and no less if he or she is at fault. Instead, the worker is entitled to medical care, certain wage replacement, or indemnity benefits and often vocational rehabilitation, regardless of fault.

This is a state program, and laws vary greatly from one state to another. All states except New Jersey, South Carolina, and Texas require that every employer provides workers' compensation coverage. Very large employers usually choose to be self-insured while others purchase insurance from insurance companies or, in some states, from funds sponsored by the state or trade associations. In most states the price of workers' compensation insurance is set by the state, but an increasing number of states are allowing varying forms of price competition.

Workers receive a portion of their wages (usually two thirds) while they are recovering from an injury. These are called temporary total benefits. Very often the employee returns to work and there is no further problem. If that does not happen, temporary total benefits continue until maximum medical improvement occurs, or until the worker is medically stable. At that point most states make an assessment of whether the worker has a permanent impairment, and award additional benefits based on its severity. About ten states, however, base continuing benefits on the amount of the worker's wage loss rather than his or her degree of impairment.

Originally this was intended to be a simple system in which there would be no need for lawyers or formal litigation. Recently, however, workers have come to rely more and more on attorneys and employers have found the system increasingly more costly. It has become very popular for politicians to attempt to "reform" state workers' compensation laws. In some cases these changes have been successful and in others they have not.

Research in Michigan has shown that there is much employers can do to control their workers' compensation experience regardless of the laws. A study conducted by the Upjohn Institute examined 5,000 employers in 29 different industries. It found that in each of the 29 industries some employers had ten times as many claims as others. What made the difference? Three things seemed to stand out: safety, disability management, and the corporate culture.

Ed Welch's Suggestions for Controlling Costs

- Safety is the first and most important approach. Nothing reduces costs more than preventing injuries from occurring.
- Create an atmosphere in which safety is important. Du Pont has 100,000 employees in the United States and it averages 30 lost claims per year. Safety has always been the most important aspect of its corporate culture.
- Return workers to the job as quickly as possible. Most workers want to go back during the first few weeks or months after an injury but if they are allowed to sit idle for several months their attitude changes. They begin to view themselves as disabled people who can never return to work.
- Most successful employers have very aggressive return-to-work programs which are designed to keep the worker in the habit of "getting up and brushing his teeth every morning."
- Larger employers often find it best to become self-insured and to take more control over their workers' compensation program.
- Smaller employers need to demand more service from their insurance companies. This might include help with safety and return-to-work programs and more active claims management.
- Employers should find out if price competition is allowed in their state and shop for the best deal. Note, however, that good service may be more important than a small difference in price.
- Employers and insurers should work together. If you have more than a few open claims you should expect your insurance company to meet with you a few times each year to discuss those claims and to plan what should be done about them.

Ed Welch teaches continuing education courses and publishes a newsletter on workers' compensation. For more information, he can be contacted at:

Ed Welch on Workers' Compensation
2875 Northwind Dr., Suite 210-A
East Lansing, MI 48823
(517) 332-5266

Almanac Fact

Health care expenditures have increased from $74.4 billion in 1970 to $838.5 billion in 1992, at an average annual rate of 11.5%.

Source: U.S. Industrial Outlook

Insurance

Work Fatalities and Injuries

Year	Employed Labor Force (millions)	Fatalities	Fatalities per 100,000 Workers	Injuries (millions)	Injuries per 100,000 Workers
1960	65.8	13,800	21.0	1,950	2,964
1970	78.7	13,800	17.5	2,200	2,795
1980	99.3	13,200	13.3	2,200	2,216
1981	100.4	12,500	12.5	2,100	2,092
1982	99.5	11,900	12.0	1,900	1,910
1983	100.8	11,700	11.6	1,900	1,885
1984	105.0	11,500	11.0	1,900	1,810
1985	107.2	11,500	10.7	2,000	1,866
1986	109.6	11,100	10.1	1,800	1,642
1987	112.4	11,300	10.1	1,800	1,601
1988	114.3	11,000	10.0	1,800	1,565
1989	116.7	10,700	9.0	1,700	1,449
1990	117.4	10,500	9.0	1,800	1,527

Source: Bureau of Labor Statistics; National Safety Council

Economic Losses from Work Accidents

Year	Loss ($ millions)	Loss in 1990 Dollars ($ millions)	Cost Per Worker 1990 Dollars ($)
1960	4,400	19,428	295.26
1970	8,000	26,948	342.42
1980	28,000	44,413	447.26
1981	30,200	43,423	432.50
1982	29,400	39,819	400.20
1983	31,200	40,942	406.17
1984	30,800	38,745	369.00
1985	35,000	42,514	396.59
1986	32,800	39,115	356.89
1987	39,800	45,791	407.39
1988	44,500	49,164	427.52
1989	48,500	51,121	435.81
1990	63,800	63,800	541.14

Sources: Bureau of Labor Statistics; National Safety Council Consumer Prices; Insurance Information Institute estimates

The Top Reference Sources

The Evaluation Guide to Corporate Wellness Programs
The Corporate University, $189
(515) 472-7720

This looseleaf binder features more than 400 pages of in-depth evaluations of hundreds of corporate wellness seminars given around the country. These seminars offer executives an opportunity to learn how to control health costs through preventive techniques.

This book is the preeminent resource on the topic.

Insurance Rating Agencies

THERE ARE FOUR NATIONAL RATING agencies whose job it is to monitor the status of the country's insurance companies. The ratings are no guarantee of an insurer's strength. Most experts agree, however, that if an insurance company receives either the highest or the second highest grade from two or more of the major rating companies and receives no grade below the fourth level from any of the raters, the insurance policy or annuity is relatively secure.

A company can call A.M. Best Co. and Standard & Poor's to order their reports or can find the Moody's and Duff & Phelps reports in some public libraries.

Recommended Resources

The Insurance Forum
P.O. Box 245
Ellettsville, IN 47429
(812) 876-6502

This monthly newsletter costs $50 and reports thoroughly on the insurance industry. Each year, *The Insurance Forum* publishes a special ratings issue, containing the listings of hundreds of life insurance companies and how they are rated by A.M. Best, Standard & Poor's, Moody's and Duff & Phelps. *The Insurance Forum* special issue can be purchased for $10.

A.M. Best Co.
Ambest Rd.
Old Wick, NJ 08858
(908) 439-2200

A custom-printed report of all insurance companies in a particular category will cost $325.

Duff & Phelps
55 E. Monroe St.
35th Floor
Chicago, IL 60603
(312) 629-3833

An annual subscription to the Duff & Phelps report of insurance company ratings costs $495 per year.

Moody's Investor Service
99 Church St.
New York, NY 10007
(212) 553-0377

Standard & Poor's
25 Broadway
New York, NY 10004
(212) 208-1527

S&P also publishes the *S&P Insurer Solvency Review*, which gives the annual ratings of several hundred insurance companies and costs $80.

The Top Reference Sources

Insuring Your Business
Insurance Information Institute Press, $22.50
(212) 669-9200

This is an essential reference for anyone who is planning to open and insure a business. There are, among others, chapters on property insurance, liability insurance, workers' compensation, insuring key employees, and employee benefits insurance. There are also sections on specific types of businesses, such as restaurants, manufacturers, construction firms, and trading companies.

Health Insurance Coverage

EVERY SMALL BUSINESS OWNER has unique needs when it comes to selecting a health insurance policy for employees. You probably will use health insurance more often during your lifetime than any other type of insurance. That is why it is so important for you to make an informed decision about the health insurance coverage you choose for yourself and your employees.

This section discusses the small group market, defines the basic choices and provides a checklist to help you compare policies presented by your agent. A glossary is included as an easy reference to health insurance terms and common benefits.

If you come across terms not defined, call the National Insurance Consumer Helpline at (800) 942-4242. The Helpline staff will try to explain them, and answer any other questions you may have about health insurance.

Small Group Health Insurance

"Small group" refers to the number of employees (sometimes 1 or 2, but most often between 3 and 25) covered under a company's group insurance plan.

In the small group market, health insurance prices are based mainly upon two factors. The first is the expected cost of medical services in a given geographic area; the second is the projected utilization of services. Usually, insurers estimate the probability of an insured person using medical services based upon factors such as age, sex, and medical history. These factors influence an insurer's charges to you and your employees. Often, those individuals who are considered a greater risk due to age or other factors will pay a higher premium for insurance. Of course, the type of benefit plan chosen also affects the premium.

Most small group health insurance companies use a process known as medical underwriting, which enables them to better predict claims. An underwriter analyzes a number of risk factors, including the medical history of each individual, to determine the group's insurability.

The insurer's goal is to offer coverage at a price that is fair to the insured group and to assure adequate income to pay future claims and other expenses.

Private Commercial Insurance Options

Today, there are many options for the small group employer. It is important to be aware of the pros and cons of each choice when selecting a plan. While premiums can vary among different carriers, recognize that there can be substantial differences in the covered benefits and in what your employees must pay out-of-pocket for medical services.

1. Fee-for-service plans

Fee-for-service is the traditional form of commercial health insurance. Fee-for-service plans enable you to choose your own physicians and hospitals. Most of these plans require deductible and co-insurance payments.

Simply put, coverage results from your insurer's paying "reasonable and customary" or usual charges (i.e., reasonable compared with other providers in the same geographic area) for physician and hospital services. Typically, fee-for-service coverage for employer-sponsored health insurance has been characterized by three major features:

- Employers and employees share the premiums in most cases;
- Employees have complete freedom to select any medical care provider;
- The insurance company pays the allowable claim.

Fee-for-service coverage has dominated employee benefits packages for many years. In the past, fee-for-service coverage often did not include cost containment provisions, and the major advantage of these plans was the freedom for the consumer to choose providers.

Today, however, many fee-for-service plans also offer a wide variety of cost containment features. These plans can hold down costs for both the insurance company and the business owner, as well as encourage consumers to be efficient users of medical services.

2. Managed care options

A managed care health insurance plan integrates both the financing and the delivery of appropriate health care services to covered individuals. Managed health care plans are becoming more common among small groups. Today, more than 70 percent of Americans who obtain health insurance through their employers are enrolled in some type of managed care plan. Most managed care plans have the following basic characteristics:

- Arrangements with selected doctors, hospitals, and other providers to furnish a comprehensive set of health care services to members;
- Explicit standards for the selection of health care providers;
- Formal programs for quality assurance and utilization review;
- Significant financial incentives when using the specific providers and procedures associated with the plan.

Health Insurance Coverage (cont'd)

Preferred Provider Organizations (PPO)

A PPO typically consists of groups of hospitals and providers that contract with employers, insurers, third-party administrators, or other sponsoring groups to provide health care services to covered persons and accept negotiated fees as payment for services rendered.

There are different sponsoring arrangements:

- Hospital-sponsored PPOs, which often include a network of institutions in order to cover a wider geographic area, as well as many of the physicians on their medical staffs;
- Physician-sponsored PPOs, which are developed by local medical societies, local professional associations or clinics, or groups of physicians;
- Third-party payer-sponsored PPOs, which include those initiated by commercial insurers and Blue Cross and Blue Shield plans;
- Entrepreneur-sponsored PPOs, which create a broker relationship, with the entrepreneur acting as an intermediary between the provider and the payer of service;
- Employer- or labor-sponsored PPOs, which contract directly with providers on behalf of their employees or members;
- Other provider-sponsored PPOs, which are developed by non-hospital and non-physician providers, such as dentists, optometrists, pharmacists, chiropractors, and podiatrists, through their professional associations, local groups or clinics.

Health Maintenance Organizations (HMO)

This was the original managed care arrangement, first emerging as prepaid group practices in the 1930s. The name "health maintenance organization" was coined in the early 1970s, and was given to 1973 federal legislation promoting its development. HMOs constitute an organized system for providing, or assuring delivery of, health care in a certain geographic area; they provide an agreed-on set of basic and supplemental health-maintenance and treatment services to a voluntarily enrolled group of people.

In exchange for a set amount of premium or dues, HMOs provide all the agreed-on health services to their enrollees; there are generally no deductibles and no, or minimal, co-payments. The HMO bears the risk if the cost of providing the care exceeds the premium received. There are now several types of HMOs:

- The staff model, where providers are directly employed by the HMO;
- The group model, where medical groups contract with the HMO (Kaiser plans are the best-known example of this type);
- The independent practice association (IPA), where the HMO contracts with physicians in independent practice, or with associations of independent physicians. IPA physicians frequently have arrangements with more than one HMO; and
- The network model, which contracts to cover two or more independent practices.

3. Fee-for-service with managed care features

These plans combine some of the features of managed care plans with traditional fee-for-service insurance arrangements. They hold down costs and discourage unnecessary use of services. Examples of managed care features that may appear in a fee-for-service plan include:

- Case management
- Centers of excellence
- Employee assistance plans
- Pre-admission certification
- Second surgical opinion
- Special benefit networks
- Utilization review.

Choosing Quality Coverage

Choosing health insurance can be confusing because the health care marketplace constantly changes. Finding a policy that provides quality coverage for you and your employees and stays within your budget can seem impossible. It doesn't have to be–you simply need to find an agent with whom you are comfortable, and a plan that is backed by a reputable insurance company.

1. Choosing an insurance agent or broker

Agents and brokers are licensed by the state to solicit and negotiate contracts of insurance and serve policyholders. Agents may represent one company or several companies. They earn commissions based on the policies they sell.

When choosing an agent you should:

- Consult relatives, friends, and business associates for referrals;
- Make sure the agent has been licensed by your state insurance department and is a full-time agent;
- Look for an agent with special professional qualifications or many years' experience. The best agents have specialized training in health insurance and other related subjects.

Health insurance agents do more than just sell policies; they are paid to provide service to their clients. Services you should expect from your agent include:

- Advising you on the right insurance policy to fit your special needs. The agent should ask enough questions to understand your entire insurance picture before advising you;

Health Insurance Coverage (cont'd)

- Explaining the cost and coverage of a policy you are considering;
- Keeping you informed about the new insurance plans that may be of interest to you;
- Reviewing your insurance every year to consider changes in your employees' financial or family status which may change your insurance requirements;
- Helping you handle claims, answering your questions, and helping you resolve any other insurance problems.

2. Choosing an insurance company

When you purchase insurance, you are buying the insurer's promise to make the payments as specified in the policy if you incur covered medical expenses.

In order to satisfy this promise, the company must be able and willing to pay the claim. The best way to investigate a company's ability to pay the claim is to check on its financial stability. (See Company Reliability/Rating below).

Checking the company's willingness to pay claims can be more difficult. The best source for this kind of information is your agent or a personal referral from someone who has had a policy with the company for some time and has filed several claims. Either can give you a sense of the "friendliness" of the company, its willingness to answer questions, and resolve complaints or problems.

Another good source of information is your state insurance department. The state insurance department regulates insurers and collects information about the number of complaints received about a particular company. Local consumer groups, newspaper columnists and Better Business Bureaus may have additional information specific to your area.

3. Company reliability/rating

The financial stability of your insurance company is an important indicator of its ability to pay your future claims. A number of financial publishing firms investigate and report their findings on the financial standing of specific insurance companies. Some of these firms are A.M. Best Company, Moody's Investor Service, Duff & Phelps and Standard & Poor's Corporation. These reports are expensive but often are available in the reference sections in business and public libraries.

If you have trouble finding published information about an insurance company, ask your agent for information or call or write the company home office and ask for a copy of its most recent annual report or report from a rating firm. The company's earnings or losses will be reported, along with information about its cash reserves and liabilities.

It is important to find out if the company and agent are licensed to do business in your state. Your state insurance department is the source for this information. It requires the companies it licenses to file yearly financial reports, maintain legally required reserve funds, undergo periodic inspection audits, and comply with state laws regarding fairness.

A Final Note

Remember that price alone is not the sole factor of good insurance protection. The service provided by the company and agent you select is important too. Therefore, in making your choice, personal knowledge of both the company's and agent's reputation for good service is a significant consideration.

Beware, also, that quite a few small employer health benefit plans are sold through a multiple-employer trust (MET) or a multiple employer welfare association (MEWA). Care should be exercised with such programs, as many are uninsured, i.e., don't have the backing of a financially sound life and health insurance company. Such plans present a high risk to employers as there may be no assurance that adequate funds will be set aside to pay future claims.

Source: Health Insurance Association of America

Glossary of Health Insurance Terms

Case Management
This is a process for directing the ongoing course of treatment to be sure that it occurs in the most appropriate setting and that the best form of service is selected. Case management often can produce alternatives to institutional care that result in better patient outcomes as well as lower costs.

Centers of Excellence
These are hospitals that specialize in treating particular illnesses, such as cancer, or performing particular treatments, such as organ transplants.

Co-insurance
Sometimes called "co-payment," it is the portion of covered health care expenses an insured must pay in addition to a deductible. Co-insurance is usually described as a percentage. For example, on a standard 80/20 co-insurance plan, the insurance company will pay 80 percent of covered expenses and the insured employee will pay 20 percent.

Concurrent Review
See Utilization Review.

Glossary of Health Insurance Terms (cont'd)

Deductible
A deductible is the amount of covered expenses that the insured must pay in each benefit period before the insurer pays for allowable claims. A higher deductible will usually result in a lower premium.

Employee Assistance Program (EAP)
An EAP is a generic term for the variety of counseling services made available to employees (and frequently their families) through an employer-sponsored program. These programs often refer employees to appropriate treatment.

Fee-for-Service
Fee-for-service is a method of charging, whereby a physician or other practitioner bills for each visit or service. Premium costs for fee-for-service agreements can increase if physicians or other providers increase their fees, increase the number of visits, or substitute more costly services for less expensive ones.

Health Maintenance Organization (HMO)
HMOs constitute an organized system for providing, or assuring delivery of, health care in a certain geographic area; they provide an agreed-on set of basic and supplemental health-maintenance and treatment services to a voluntarily enrolled group of people. In exchange for a set amount of premium or dues, HMOs provide all the agreed-on health services to their enrollees; there are generally no deductibles and no, or minimal, co-payments. The HMO bears the risk if the cost of providing the care exceeds the premium received.

Indemnity
An indemnity is a benefit paid by an insurance policy for an insured loss. Often it is used to refer to benefits paid directly to the insured.

Insurance Department
Each state has an insurance department that is responsible for implementing state insurance laws and regulations.

Limitations
Limitations describe conditions or circumstances under which the insurer will not pay or will limit payments. Detailed information about limitations and exclusions is found in the certificate of insurance. An employer gets a group policy, with all details of the contract. An employee gets a booklet on the insurance, which is a more concise presentation of the insurance contract.

Major Medical
Major medical insurance plans provide broad coverage and substantial protection from large, unpredictable medical care expenses. They cover a wide range of medical care charges with few internal limits and a high overall maximum benefit.

Maximum Out-of-Pocket
The maximum amount of money an insured will pay in a benefit period, in addition to regular premium payments, is called the maximum out-of-pocket. The out-of-pocket payment is usually the sum of the deductible and co-insurance payments. Non-covered expenses are the employee's responsibility in addition to out-of-pocket amounts.

National Association of Insurance Commissioners (NAIC)
This national organization of state insurance commissioners promotes national uniformity in the regulation of insurance. Each state has an appointed or elected commissioner.

Pre-Admission Certification
See Utilization Review.

Pre-Admission Testing
Tests taken prior to a hospital admission are called pre-admission tests.

Pre-Existing Condition
A medical condition that existed before obtaining insurance coverage for which a reasonably prudent person would seek medical treatment is called a pre-existing condition. Examples of pre-existing conditions include a sickness, injury, or complication of pregnancy for which an insured person received medical advice, consultation, prescription drugs, or treatment during a specified time period before the effective date of coverage.

Preferred Provider Organization (PPO)
A PPO consists of hospitals and providers that contract with employers, insurers, third-party administrators, or other sponsoring groups to provide health care services to covered persons and accept negotiated fee schedules as payment for services rendered.

Premium
A premium is a periodic payment made by a policyholder (employer, individual) for the cost of insurance.

Reasonable and/or Customary Charge
A charge for health care that is consistent with the going rate or charge in a certain geographical area for the same or similar services is called a reasonable and/or customary charge.

Retrospective Review
See Utilization Review.

Second Surgical Opinion
See Utilization Review.

Special Benefit Networks
Special networks of providers for a particular service, such as mental health, substance abuse, or prescription drugs are known as special benefit networks.

Glossary of Health Insurance Terms (cont'd)

State-Mandated Benefits
Each state requires insurance policies sold in that state to include benefits for a variety of medical conditions or providers. These mandated benefits can add to costs greatly. For example, an insurance policy may have to cover mental health or podiatry services.

Third-Party Administrator (TPA)
A TPA is a company or broker that handles the administration of an insurance plan. Depending on the terms of its agreement with an insurance plan, a TPA may collect premiums, pay claims, and handle routine underwriting and administrative functions. The TPA typically acts on guidelines that the insurance plan establishes.

Underwriting
The process by which an insurer determines whether and on what basis it will accept an application for insurance is called underwriting.

Utilization Review (UR)
UR is a process that assesses the delivery of medical services to determine if the care provided is appropriate, medically necessary, and of high quality. Utilization review may include review of appropriateness of admissions, services ordered and provided, length of stay and discharge practices, both on a concurrent and retrospective basis. For example:

- Pre-Admission Certification: Determines whether a hospital should admit a patient and whether services can be provided on an outpatient basis; its goal is eliminating unnecessary non-emergency procedures.
- Concurrent Review: Includes continued-stay review of hospital cases, discharge-planning efforts to include proper and efficient placement of the hospital patient on discharge and case management.
- Retrospective Review: Follow-up analysis that ensures medical care services were necessary and appropriate (to detect and reduce the incidence of fraud and unnecessary services).
- Second Surgical Opinion: A process that requires patients to obtain an opinion from a second doctor before certain elective surgeries. Insurers rely on second surgical opinion to eliminate unnecessary surgical procedures.

Explanation of Common Benefits

Ambulatory Care
Also known as outpatient care, ambulatory care is medical, surgical, or diagnostic services provided in a non-hospital setting, not requiring an overnight stay.

Dental Care
This coverage provides reimbursement of dental services and supplies, including preventive care. Benefits may be provided through a plan integrated with other medical insurance coverage, or a plan may be written separately from other coverage (non-integrated).

Diagnostic X-Ray and Laboratory Examinations
This coverage provides reimbursement for outpatient diagnostic and laboratory examinations.

Home Health Care
Home Health Care services are given at home to aged, disabled, sick, or convalescent individuals who do not need institutional care. The most common types of home care are visiting nurse services and speech, physical, occupational, and rehabilitation therapy. Home health agencies, hospitals, or other community organizations provide these services.

Hospice Care
Hospices care for the terminally ill and their families, in the home or a non-hospital setting, emphasizing alleviating pain rather than medical cure.

Hospital Care
Both in-patient medical care expenses and outpatient medical care expenses incurred in a hospital are reimbursed under this coverage.

In-Patient Benefits

- Charges for room and board
- Charges for necessary services and supplies sometimes referred to as "hospital extras," "miscellaneous charges," and "ancillary charges."

Out-Patient Benefits

- Surgical procedures
- Rehabilitation therapy
- Physical therapy.

Physician Visits
This coverage provides reimbursement for physician's fees for visits in cases of injury or sickness. The two types of plans commonly offered are one covering in-hospital visits only and the other that covers visits in-hospital and doctor visits out of the hospital setting.

Pregnancy Care
Federal maternity legislation, enacted in 1978, requires that employers with 15 or more employees who are engaged in interstate commerce provide the same benefits for pregnancy, childbirth, and related medical conditions as for any other sickness or injury. This includes all employers who are, or become, subject to Title VII of the Civil Rights Act of 1964.

Glossary of Health Insurance Terms (cont'd)

Prescription Drug Plan
Some prescription drug expense insurance plans are subject to the same deductible and co-payments as are other covered medical expenses. Other plans use a prescription drug card and cover these expenses with very little, if any, cost to the insured.

Rehabilitation Care
A program of care that provides physical and mental restoration of disabled insured individuals to maximum independence and productivity.

Skilled Nursing Facility
A licensed institution engaged in providing regular medical care and treatment to sick and injured persons is known as a skilled nursing facility. The institution maintains a daily medical record and requires that each patient be under the care of a licensed physician.

Supplemental Accident
Many plans contain supplemental accident insurance that provides first dollar coverage (no deductible or co-payments) when an injury is due to an accident. Another type of accident plan pays a fixed dollar amount–$5,000 or $10,000, for example–if a serious accidental injury occurs.

Vision Care
This coverage is designed to provide benefits for preventive and corrective eye care. Insurers usually offer vision care with basic coverage such as hospital, surgical, medical, or X-ray and laboratory benefits.

Checklist for Comparing Plans

THIS CHECKLIST CAN GUIDE your discussions with your broker or agent.

1. Evaluating your company's needs.

- Number of employees
- Number of dependents
- Sex of employees
- Age of employees
- Employees and dependents of childbearing age
- Employees/dependents with pre-existing medical conditions
- Employees with health problems making them high-risk
- Employees insured elsewhere.

2. Covered medical services.

- In-patient hospital services
- Out-patient surgery
- Psychiatric and mental health care
- Drug and alcohol abuse treatment
- Skilled nursing care
- Home health care visits
- Rehabilitation facility care
- Hospice care
- Dental care
- Maternity care
- Supplemental accident.
- Prescription drugs
- Vision care
- Preventive care and checkups
- Chiropractic care
- Physician visits
- Medical tests and X-rays
- Mammograms.

3. Are there medical service limits, exclusions , or pre-existing conditions that will affect employees?

4. What cost-containment and quality assurance procedures are included? (i.e., utilization review, pre-certification, second surgical opinions)

5. What is the total cost of the policy?

- Cost for the employer
- Cost for employees
- Single deductible
- Family deductible
- Co-insurance
- Single out-of-pocket maximum per year
- Family out-of-pocket maximum per year
- Share of premium.

6. Is the rate guaranteed? For how long?

7. What is the policy's lifetime maximum amount of coverage?

Checklist for Comparing Plans (cont'd)

8. What has the rate history been for comparable groups over the past five years and how is it calculated?

9. What will happen to premiums if one of the employees has a major claim?

10. How will service needs be handled?

11. Will the agent/broker or a customer service representative be available to meet with employees and dependents?

12. How long will it take to process a claim?

13. How often will the employer be billed?

14. Is the agent or broker qualified in the small group market? Does the agent or broker know about small group insurance?

- Good references
- Licensed in my state
- Professional qualifications
- Experience in the small group market
- Doing business for at least 3 years
- Member of recognized professional organization.

Holding Down Insurance Costs

A MAJOR CHALLENGE IN HEALTH CARE today is holding down the rising costs of employee medical care while at the same time maintaining high standards of quality. There are many factors in achieving that goal; so many, in fact, that it can seem as though your employees' health care is "everybody's business."

When one of your employees seeks medical care, treatment decisions involve many people. As an employer, you make decisions that affect the medical services your employees seek and the treatments their doctors prescribe. Your health insurance plan may limit coverage for services or require authorization from your insurance company before services are rendered.

Cost-containment measures can prevent overutilization of medical services and assure that your investment in health care is being used wisely. Negotiating a plan with your insurance agent or broker that incorporates proven cost-containment provisions into your company benefits plan will help to protect that investment.

Everyone involved plays an important role in keeping health care costs down. By familiarizing yourself with each role, you can better evaluate whether your health care plan is making the most of appropriate cost-saving strategies.

The Employee's Role in Choosing Appropriate Medical Care

The individual employee needs information in order to use the health care system wisely. Encourage employees to discuss diagnostic and treatment decisions with their doctor, so that they fully understand both the medical and financial implications of their health care. Employees must be knowledgeable about what their health insurance does and does not cover in order to be intelligent consumers of health care. Working with your insurance agent and benefits carrier, you can provide appropriate educational tools to increase your employees' understanding of the plan and their personal responsibility in using it.

The Doctor's Role in Managing Patient Care

While doctors use specialized medical knowledge and training to make informed diagnostic and treatment decisions, their practice of medicine is still part art and part science. With the patient's best interest in mind, doctors must often make medical judgments considering the advantages of additional tests when the benefits may not be clear cut. Insurance companies are encouraging doctors to rely on standards of care to assist them in deciding when tests are really needed.

The Hospital's Role in Providing Cost-Effective Quality Care

Hospitals are continually analyzing their efficiency to cut the costs of patient care while maintaining quality care. Some strategies include evaluating the costs of nursing and other professional care, reducing money spent on equipment, and upgrading quality-assurance departments to increase hospital efficiency. In addition, many hospitals are joining purchasing cooperatives, i.e., agencies that represent many hospitals to purchase supplies, pharmaceuticals, and equipment at a discount.

Hospitals are paid for Medicare cases (and in some states for Medicaid cases) based upon a projected rate for a particular case. For instance, if the regional norm for recovery from a specific surgery is three days of hospitalization, it is in the hospital's interest to perform the procedure and discharge the patient within three days. Otherwise, the hospital is not paid for the additional care provided unless there is justification.

Many insurance payers are adopting similar systems of reimbursement for patients with private

Holding Down Insurance Costs (cont'd)

insurance. This challenges the hospital to evaluate its performance and conduct procedures as efficiently as possible.

The Insurance Company's Mission to Hold Down Medical Costs

Insurance companies may review your employees' medical care to be certain that it was performed within approved medical guidelines. There are several cost-containment measures used by your health insurer. These may include reviewing the history of medical claims submitted by hospitals and doctors to assess whether they were medically necessary. Second opinion, or pre-authorization, may also be necessary to evaluate the validity of specific procedures.

According to the arrangements of your benefits plan, you also may be encouraged to use a selected group of medical practitioners who provide your company's medical care at agreed-upon fees. These measures can help you hold down the cost of health care.

At each step along the way, there are opportunities to control costs. It is in your best interest to learn about the process and become an active participant in getting the most out of your health care dollar.

Health care cost inflation affects both employers and employees. In the past 10 years, the U.S. health care delivery system has seen a dramatic increase in the cost of employer-paid health care plans, and in the contributions made by employees because of increases in co-payments and deductibles. Today, health care costs are seen as a great threat to the survival and profitability of small businesses.

Health Care Costs

Top 25 Diagnosis Related Groups (Ranked by Total In-Patient Payments per Year)

1990	1989	Diagnosis Related Group
1	1	Psychoses (DRG 430)
2	2	Vaginal Delivery w/o Complicating Diagnoses (DRG 373)
3	4	Uterine & Adnexa Procedures for Non-Malignancy w/o C.C.(DRG 359)
4	5	Coronary Bypass w/Cardiac Catheterization (DRG 106)
5	3	Alcohol/Drug Abuse or Dependence, Detox or Other Sympt. Treat w/o C. C. (DRG 435)
6	6	Cesarean Section w/o C.C. (DRG 371)
7	7	Back & Neck Procedures w/o C. C. (DRG 215)
8	12	Percutaneous Cardiovascular Procedures (DRG 1 12)
9	9	Coronary Bypass w/o Cardiac Catheterization (DRG 107)
10	11	Bilateral or Multiple Major Joint Procedures of Lower Extremity (DRG 471)
11	14	Tracheostomy w/Mouth, Larynx or Pharynx Disorder (DRG 482)
12	10	Depressive Neuroses (DRG 426)
13	15	Major Small & Large Bowel Procedures w/C.C. (DRG 148)
14	19	Extreme Immaturity or Respiratory Distress Syndrome, Neonate (DRG 386)
15	18	Craniotomy Age > 17 exc. for Trauma (DRG 1)
16	17	Circulatory Disorders exc. AMI, w/Cardiac Catheterization & Complex Diagnosis (DRG 124)
17	16	Total Cholecystectomy w/o Common Duct Exploration w/o C.C. (DRG 198)
18	23	Specific Cerebrovascular Disorders exc. TIA (DRG 14)
19	13	Circulatory Disorders exc. AMI w/Cardiac Catheterization w/o Complex Diagnosis (DRG 125)
20	33	Esophagitis, Gastroenteritis & Miscellaneous Digestive Disorders Age > 1 w/C.C. (DRG 182)
21	22	Major Chest Procedures (DRG 75)
22	31	Back & Neck Procedures w/C.C. (DRG 214)
23	28	Chest Pain (DRG 143)
24	32	Total Cholecystectomy w/o Common Duct Exploration w/C.C. (DRG 197)
25	26	Angina Pectoris (DRG 140)

C.C. = Complications or Co-morbidity

Source: The MEDSTAT Report, 1992

Health Care Costs (cont'd)

Health Care Payments ($) Per Capita, 1987 to 1992

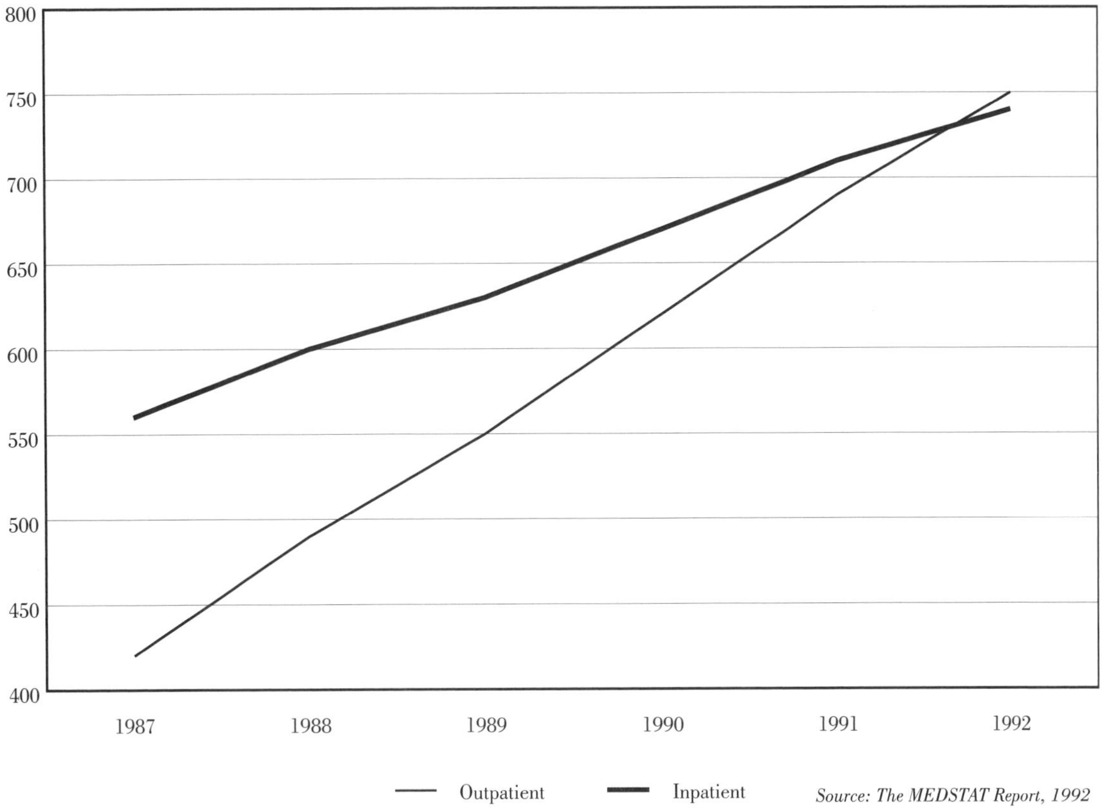

800
750
700
650
600
550
500
450
400
1987
1988
1989
1990
1991
1992
Outpatient
Inpatient

Source: The MEDSTAT Report, 1992

Employee, Employer Expenditures, 1987 to 1992

1400
1200
1000
800
600
400
200
0
1987
1988
1989
1990
1991
1992
Employers (Premiums and Equivalents)
Employees (Deductibles and Copays)

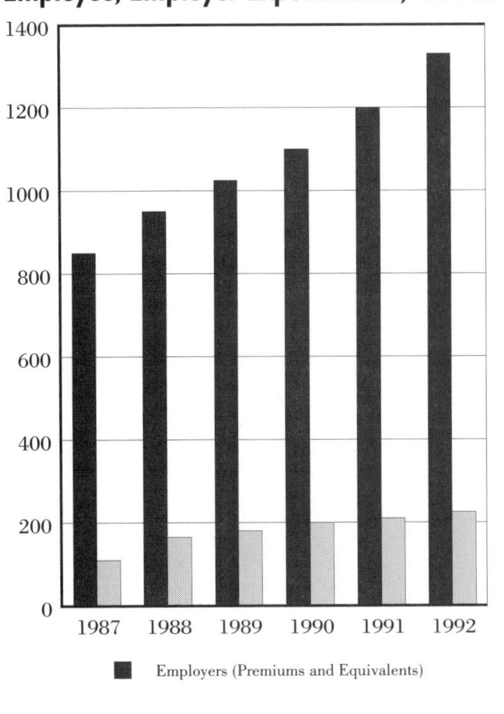

Source: The MEDSTAT Report, 1992

International

For more information on international communications, see International Dialing beginning on page 99.

Foreign Investors in the U.S.

THE MAJOR FOREIGN INVESTOR IN THE UNITED STATES is the United Kingdom, followed by Japan and the Netherlands. The United Kingdom and the Netherlands concentrate on manufacturing and petroleum while Japan is focused on trade, real estate, and financial services.

Foreign Direct Investment Position in the United States, Historical-Cost Basis

Location	1991 Total ($ millions)
WORLD	407,577
Petroleum	39,955
Manufacturing	162,853
Wholesale trade	52,962
Other	151,807
Canada	30,002
Petroleum	913
Manufacturing	9,662
Wholesale trade	1,962
Other	17,466
Europe	258,127
Petroleum	31,989
Manufacturing	126,809
Wholesale trade	21,527
Other	77,801
Netherlands	63,848
Petroleum	12,254
Manufacturing	24,137
Wholesale trade	5,276
Other	22,180
United Kingdom	106,064
Petroleum	14,238
Manufacturing	50,120
Wholesale trade	5,275
Other	36,431
Japan	86,658
Petroleum	113
Manufacturing	18,657
Wholesale trade	26,935
Other	40,953
Other areas	32,791
Petroleum	6,939
Manufacturing	7,726
Wholesale trade	2,539
Other	15,587

Source: Survey of Current Business, August 1992

Foreign Direct Investment in the United States, Historical-Cost Basis

The foreign direct investment position is calculated from the equity in, and net outstanding loans to, subsidiaries in the United States owned by foreign corporations. This is the foreign corporation's contribution to subsidiary assets.

Country	1987 ($ millions)	1988	1989	1990	1991
ALL COUNTRIES	263,394	314,754	368,924	396,702	407,577
CANADA	24,684	26,566	30,370	30,037	30,002
EUROPE	181,006	208,942	239,190	250,973	258,127
Austria	245	392	386	623	472
Belgium	3,371	3,471	3,799	3,866	3,653
Denmark	498	588	656	819	1,219
Finland	295	452	1,297	1,513	1,547
France	10,137	13,233	15,365	18,665	22,740
Germany	21,905	25,250	28,386	28,309	28,171
Ireland	544	725	1,416	1,208	1,292
Italy	1,310	752	1,436	1,869	2,859
Liechtenstein	190	181	177	181	98
Luxembourg	590	-131	407	2,118	974
Netherlands	46,636	48,128	56,734	63,938	63,848
Norway	352	220	576	773	556
Spain	442	511	601	790	1,161
Sweden	4,910	4,713	5,435	5,467	5,597
Switzerland	13,772	14,372	18,746	17,745	17,594
United Kingdom	75,519	95,698	103,458	102,790	106,064
Other	288	388	316	299	282

Foreign Investors in the U.S. (cont'd)

Country	1987 ($ millions)	1988	1989	1990	1991
LATIN AMERICA AND WESTERN HEMISPHERE	10,103	11,243	16,218	19,616	17,673
SOUTH AND CENTRAL AMERICA	3,935	4,331	5,819	6,020	6,466
Brazil	293	286	428	378	488
Mexico	180	218	350	550	608
Panama	2,627	2,878	3,392	4,099	4,367
Venezuela	411	540	1,163	489	544
Other	425	409	486	503	458
OTHERWESTERN HEMISPHERE	6,168	6,911	10,399	13,596	11,208
AFRICA	521	441	505	512	309
MIDDLE EAST	4,973	6,570	7,588	4,423	4,798
Israel	632	587	630	626	1,085
Kuwait	3,898	3,954	4,280	1,831	2,000
Lebanon	*	-7	-9	-18	-27
Saudi Arabia	257	1,826	2,455	1,803	1,588
United Arab Emirates	43	111	112	97	97
Other	142	100	119	85	55
ASIA AND PACIFIC	42,108	60,992	75,053	91,141	96,668
Australia	5,369	7,171	4,962	6,539	6,626
Hong Kong	941	895	1,124	1,199	1,272
Japan	34,421	51,126	67,268	81,775	86,658
Korea, Republic of	198	505	-307	-1,000	-542
Malaysia	7	42	29	56	85
New Zealand	263	154	166	138	131
Philippines	73	73	82	74	50
Singapore	391	510	934	1,147	914
Taiwan	199	329	476	824	1,115
Other	246	186	318	389	360

** = Suppressed to avoid disclosure of individual companies*

Source: Survey of Current Business, August 1992

The Top Reference Sources

Business America
U.S. Government Printing Office, $53 per year
(202) 783-3238

Published biweekly by the U.S. Department of Commerce, this informative magazine is focused on international trade issues. Features include articles on the U.S. trade balance, exporting to Japan, economic reforms in Africa, and the outlook for stronger commercial ties with North Africa and the Near East.

The many contact names and numbers for government support throughout each issue are extremely valuable.

Foreign Investors in the U.S. (cont'd)

Sales of U.S. Companies to Foreign Buyers: By Industry ($ millions)

Industry Classification of Seller	1987	1988	1989	1990	1991
Electrical Equipment	248.3	1,494.5	316.5	26.5	2,828.2
Drugs, Medical Supplies & Equipment	790.8	1,541.3	1,679.9	3,844.0	1,309.7
Insurance	127.5	5,549.1	611.2	4,688.1	1,251.5
Fabricated Metal Products	344.5	97.7	2,078.9	567.5	1,226.5
Banking & Finance	1,750.0	1,790.0	3,191.4	150.0	767.9
Electric, Gas, Water & Sanitary Services	30.5	15.6	0.0	0.0	643.2
Oil & Gas	8,198.4	2,228.6	1,400.0	1,522.0	558.8
Food Processing	125.0	7,291.7	3,925.1	1,052.6	440.0
Chemicals, Paints & Coatings	1,501.1	166.4	3,203.9	1,060.4	388.2
Brokerage, Investment & Mgmt. Consulting	986.0	276.5	122.0	11.0	357.7
Wholesale & Distribution	65.5	677.6	407.3	280.0	314.0
Communications	0.0	71.0	1,912.0	217.8	266.0
Health Services	82.5	0.0	1,241.1	293.0	257.0
Industrial & Farm Equipment & Machinery	690.0	1,648.7	450.6	254.1	225.7
Mining & Minerals	241.8	374.5	246.3	1,489.0	218.8
Leisure & Entertainment	3,115.5	1,202.7	4,023.4	8,029.5	204.9
Instruments & Photographic Equipment	627.9	903.2	38.0	100.0	180.0
Retail	5,202.7	7,341.2	208.2	701.6	125.0
Miscellaneous Services	1,529.1	884.1	2,084.8	622.1	122.6
Electronics	943.8	897.9	970.3	221.5	114.9
Beverages	2,763.6	1,249.8	296.0	21.0	103.0
Autos & Trucks	0.0	13.5	0.0	340.1	99.8
Transportation	46.4	34.1	89.8	234.8	96.7
Computer Software Supplies & Services	5.5	333.8	355.0	197.7	52.5
Toiletries & Cosmetics	0.0	734.0	2,254.2	107.0	43.0
Printing & Publishing	747.0	7,905.7	2,562.2	285.0	32.0
Plastics & Rubber	1,793.0	49.6	311.6	76.8	12.9
Construction Contractors & Engineering Svs.	0.0	1,659.1	55.6	7.6	10.7
Office Equipment & Computer Hardware	1,023.3	418.2	1,212.6	362.6	10.0
Aerospace, Aircraft & Defense	391.0	701.4	498.5	103.0	0.0
Agricultural Production	170.0	0.0	4.9	131.7	0.0
Apparel	205.0	5.7	604.0	125.0	0.0
Auto Products & Accessories	650.0	3,085.7	1,244.0	380.0	0.0
Broadcasting	2.0	180.0	0.0	0.0	0.0
Building Products & Materials	99.0	466.2	0.0	40.0	0.0
Conglomerate	1,984.3	32.0	0.0	0.0	0.0
Construction, Mining & Oil Equip. & Mach.	253.4	0.0	0.0	21.1	0.0
Energy Services	0.0	0.0	0.0	193.0	0.0
Furniture	0.0	17.0	0.0	0.0	0.0
Household Goods	515.0	625.0	207.0	1,250.0	0.0
Miscellaneous Manufacturing	1,625.8	0.0	0.0	5.5	0.0
Packaging & Containers	0.0	1,272.4	416.8	0.0	0.0
Paper	0.0	0.0	0.0	275.5	0.0
Primary Metal Processing	718.6	136.3	88.2	785.5	0.0
Real Estate	0.0	196.0	1,065.3	2.0	0.0
Stone, Clay & Glass	63.4	1,164.6	153.5	2,323.3	0.0
Textiles	266.3	465.0	195.2	0.0	0.0
Timber & Forest Products	0.0	0.0	0.0	0.0	0.0
Toys & Recreational Products	112.5	231.4	202.9	20.0	0.0
Valves, Pumps & Hydraulics	330.0	34.0	100.0	640.2	0.0
TOTAL	40,366.0	55,462.8	40,028.1	33,059.0	12,261.2

Source: Mergerstat Review

Foreign Investors in the U.S. (cont'd)

Industries Attracting Foreign Buyers: By Number of Transactions

Industry Classification of Seller	1987	1988	1989	1990	1991	Five-Year Cumulative
Chemicals, Paints & Coatings	12	12	15	17	14	70
Insurance	3	7	6	10	14	40
Miscellaneous Services	10	31	21	17	12	91
Banking & Finance	10	8	13	4	11	46
Brokerage, Investment & Mgmt. Consulting	6	9	9	10	10	44
Drugs, Medical Supplies & Equipment	8	14	12	18	9	61
Electronics	7	9	16	13	9	54
Electrical Equipment	4	12	5	6	9	36
Industrial & Farm Equipment & Machinery	12	24	6	8	7	57
Printing & Publishing	6	14	19	4	7	50
Leisure & Entertainment	6	6	11	11	7	41
Instruments & Photographic Equipment	9	13	4	6	7	39
Health Services	2	0	6	5	7	20
Food Processing	7	17	11	13	6	54
Wholesale Distribution	8	10	12	4	6	40
Communications	0	3	4	4	6	17
Office Equipment & Computer Hardware	6	5	8	8	5	32
Fabricated Metal Products	6	9	4	7	5	31
Mining & Minerals	1	2	4	6	5	18
Construction Contractors & Eng. Services	2	2	4	5	5	18
Computer Software Supplies & Services	5	12	5	13	4	39
Plastics & Rubber	7	4	8	6	3	28
Oil & Gas	5	5	10	4	3	27
Electric, Gas, Water & Sanitary Services	1	1	1	0	3	6
Beverages	6	5	6	2	2	21
Transportation	3	4	2	5	2	16
Autos & Trucks	0	1	0	3	2	6
Retail	15	9	9	8	1	42
Primary Metal Processing	7	5	7	7	1	27
Stone, Clay & Glass	6	9	3	6	1	25
Toiletries & Cosmetics	2	6	7	3	1	19
Textiles	3	8	3	2	1	17
Aerospace, Aircraft & Defense	3	4	3	4	1	15
Miscellaneous Manufacturing	6	0	0	2	1	9
Construction, Mining & Oil Equip. & Mach.	4	0	2	1	1	8
Automotive Products & Accessories	2	3	7	5	0	17
Household Goods	4	3	3	1	0	11
Real Estate	1	4	5	1	0	11
Apparel	2	3	3	1	0	9
Toys & Recreational Products	1	3	3	2	0	9
Building Products & Materials	3	3	1	1	0	8
Agricultural Production	1	0	2	5	0	8
Valves, Pumps & Hydraulics	3	2	1	1	0	7
Packaging & Containers	2	1	3	0	0	6
Paper	0	1	0	4	0	5
Conglomerate	2	1	0	0	0	3
Broadcasting	1	1	0	1	0	3
Furniture	0	2	0	0	0	2
Energy Services	0	0	0	2	0	2
Timber & Forest Products	0	0	1	0	0	1
TOTAL	220	307	285	266	188	1,266

Source: Mergerstat Review

Foreign Investors in the U.S. (cont'd)

Foreign Buyers of U.S. Companies: Number of Transactions, by Country

Country of Buyer	1987	1988	1989	1990	1991	Five Year Cumulative
United Kingdom	78	114	69	62	40	363
Canada	28	37	50	33	30	178
Japan	15	35	53	38	29	170
France	19	25	17	26	16	103
West Germany	15	29	18	19	11	92
Italy	6	7	6	4	10	33
Netherlands	9	9	14	15	9	56
Switzerland	9	15	8	16	8	56
Austria	17	10	12	4	4	47
Spain	1	3	1	0	4	9
Sweden	9	6	7	14	3	39
Hong Kong	3	3	4	3	3	16
Ireland	2	2	1	2	2	9
Norway	1	0	1	1	2	5
Denmark	0	3	0	1	2	6
New Zealand	0	1	0	0	2	3
Taiwan	0	0	1	4	2	7
Thailand	0	0	0	1	2	3
Bermuda	0	0	1	0	1	2
Argentina	0	2	0	0	1	3
Indonesia	0	1	0	2	1	4
Puerto Rico	0	0	1	0	1	2
Greece	0	0	0	0	1	1
Panama	0	0	0	0	1	1
Saudi Arabia	0	0	0	0	1	1
Luxembourg	0	0	0	0	1	1
Portugal	0	0	0	0	1	1
South Africa	6	1	6	4	0	17
Finland	0	0	5	2	0	7
Belgium	0	1	2	2	0	5
Israel	0	1	0	4	0	5
Brazil	1	1	1	1	0	4
Singapore	0	0	1	2	0	3
Venezuela	0	1	2	1	0	4
Kuwait	0	0	0	1	0	1
Mexico	0	0	2	0	0	2
South Korea	0	0	0	1	0	1
Philippines	0	0	0	0	0	0
Colombia	0	0	0	0	0	0
Libya	0	0	0	0	0	0
Barbados	0	0	0	1	0	1
U.S. Virgin Islands	0	0	1	0	0	1
Bahamas	0	0	0	0	0	0
Austria	0	0	1	0	0	1
Malaysia	0	0	0	0	0	0
Trinidad	0	0	0	0	0	0
Bahrain	0	0	0	0	0	0
Liechtenstein	0	0	0	1	0	1
Netherlands Antilles	0	0	0	1	0	1
TOTAL	220	307	285	266	188	1,266

Source: Mergerstat Review

Foreign Investors in the U.S. (cont'd)

Largest Foreign Acquisitions (since 1986) of U.S. Companies, in Order of Size

Company	Foreign Buyer	Year
Rorer Group	Rhone-Poulenc SA (France)	1990
Fireman's Fund Insurance	Allianz AG Holding (Germany)	1991
Triangle Publications	News Corp., Ltd. (Australia)	1988
Pillsbury Co.	Grand Metropolitan PLC (U.K.)	1989
Triangle Industries	Pechiney SA (France)	1989
SmithKline Beckman Corp.	Beecham Group PLC (U.K.)	1989
Federated Department Stores	Campeau Corp. (Canada)	1988
MCA	Matsushita Electric Industrial (Japan)	1991
Executive Life Insurance	Altus Finance (France)	1992

Source: Securities Data Company

Trade-Weighted Dollar Exchange Rate

THE TRADE-WEIGHTED DOLLAR represents the foreign currency price of the U.S. dollar or the export value of the U.S. dollar. When these index numbers increase, the value of the dollar increases, making it easier for Americans to afford imports, but making American exports more expensive to those in other countries.

Trade-Weighted Dollar Index (1973=100)

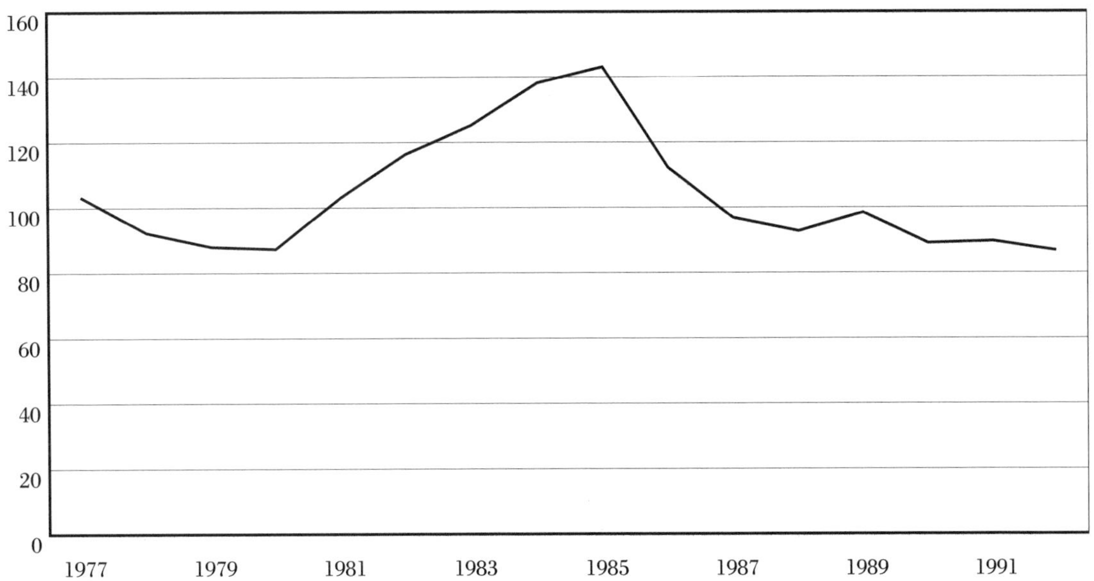

Source: Federal Reserve Board

Almanac Fact

The largest investor in U.S. land is Great Britain, not Japan.

Worldwide Gross Domestic Product

Gross Domestic Product Comparison for 25 Selected Countries Worldwide

Country	1991 GDP ($ billions)	1990 GDP ($ billions)	% Change GDP 1991-90	% Change GDP 1990-80	Per Capita at Current Prices	Trade Balance % of GDP	Net Nat'l. Saving % of GDP
Australia	295.5	295.3	-1.2	3.2	17,282	-1.1	4.6
Austria	161.9	157.4	2.8	2.2	20,391	1.1	13.8
Belgium	196.5	192.4	1.4	2.0	19,303	3.2	12.3
Canada	595.9	570.1	-0.9	2.9	21,418	0.3	5.9
Denmark	131.9	131.0	1.8	2.1	25,478	5.4	9.1
Finland	127.1	137.3	-6.3	3.2	27,527	-1.4	7.6
France	1,191.4	1,190.8	1.3	2.2	21,105	0.0	8.5
Germany	1,538.8	1,488.2	3.2	2.1	23,536	5.5	12.7
Greece	68.8	66.0	1.2	1.5	6,505	-11.2	4.7
Iceland	6.3	5.9	0.3	2.3	22,875	1.6	3.9
Ireland	43.0	42.5	1.5	3.5	12,131	8.1	13.3
Italy	1,133.4	1,090.8	1.1	2.2	18,921	0.0	7.4
Japan	3380.8	2,942.9	4.2	4.2	23,822	0.7	20.5
Luxembourg	8.9	8.7	2.0	3.4	22,895	-0.5	50.0
Netherlands	285.4	279.1	2.2	1.8	18,676	5.1	14.6
New Zealand	41.5	42.8	-1.5	1.9	12,656	-1.6	6.9
Norway	107.5	105.8	4.1	2.4	24,953	7.3	9.6
Portugal	68.9	59.7	2.7	2.7	6,085	-8.9	22.3
Spain	525.9	491.2	2.5	2.9	12,609	-3.4	11.1
Sweden	235.3	228.1	-1.2	1.9	26,652	0.4	5.9
Switzerland	230.1	224.8	-0.2	2.1	33,085	0.5	22.5
Turkey	111.9	108.4	2.3	5.3	1,896	-3.4	16.7
United Kingdom	1,008.8	975.1	-1.9	2.6	16,985	-2.4	4.4
United States	5,552.2	5,392.2	-0.7	2.9	21,449	-1.5	2.2

Source: "OECD in Figures" 1992 Edition, supplement to The OECD Observer, No. 176, June/July, 1992

The Top Reference Sources

Journal of Commerce
(212) 837-7000

This daily magazine provides information on the conditions and influences affecting national and international commerce.

It covers a variety of topics including manufacturing, world trade, processing, shipping, foreign exchange, energy, and commodities. It also reports on trade and investment studies within and outside the U.S.

Fortune's Top 50 Exporters

1991 Rank	Company	Major Exports	1991 Exports ($ millions)	As % of Sales	1991 Sales ($ millions)
1	Boeing	Commercial and military aircraft	17,856.0	60.9	29,314.0
2	General Motors	Motor vehicles, parts	11,284.7	9.1	123,780.1
3	General Electric	Jet engines, turbines, plastics, medical	8,614.0	14.3	60,236.0
4	IBM	Computers, related equipment	7,668.0	11.8	64,792.0
5	Ford Motor	Motor vehicles, parts	7,340.0	8.3	88,962.8
6	Chrysler	Motor vehicles, parts	6,168.0	21.0	29,370.0
7	McDonnell Douglas	Aerospace, electronic systems	6,160.0	32.9	18,718.0
8	E.I. du Pont De Nemours	Specialty chemicals	3,812.0	10.0	38,031.0
9	Caterpillar	Heavy machinery, engines, turbines	3,710.0	36.4	10,182.0
10	United Technologies	Jet engines, helicopters, cooling equip.	3,587.0	16.9	21,262.0
11	Hewlett-Packard	Measurement and computation systems	3,223.0	22.2	14,541.0
12	Philip Morris	Tobacco, beverages, food products	3,061.0	6.4	49,109.0
13	Eastman Kodak	Imaging, chemicals, health products	3,020.0	15.4	19,649.0
14	Motorola	Commun. equip., cellular phones	2,928.0	25.8	11,341.0
15	Archer-Daniels-Midland	Protein meals, vegetable oils, flour, grain	2,600.0	30.3	8,567.7
16	Digital Equipment	Computers, related equipment	2,200.0	15.7	14,024.2
17	Intel	Microcomputer components, modules	1,929.0	40.4	4,778.6
18	Allied-Signal	Aircraft and automotive parts	1,729.0	14.6	11,882.0
19	Sun Microsystems	Computers, related equipment	1,606.0	49.3	3,259.8
20	Unisys	Computers, related equipment	1,598.0	18.4	8,696.1
21	Raytheon	Electronics, environmental, aircraft	1,556.0	16.6	9,355.5
22	Weyerhaeuser	Pulp, paper, logs, lumber	1,550.0	17.8	8,701.6
23	Dow Chemical	Chemicals, plastics, consumer specialties	1,376.0	7.1	19,305.0
24	General Dynamics	Tanks, aircraft, missiles, gun systems	1,370.0	14.3	9,548.0
25	Merck	Health products, specialty chemicals	1,342.0	15.6	8,602.7
26	Minnesota Mining & Mfg.	Industrial, electronic, and health products	1,275.0	9.6	13,340.0
27	International Paper	Pulp, paperboard, wood products	1,200.0	9.4	12,703.0
28	Union Carbide	Chemicals, plastics	1,200.0	16.3	7,346.0
29	Textron	Aerospace and consumer products	1,171.0	14.9	7,840.1
30	Hoechst Celanese	Chemicals, plastics, fibers, pharmaceuticals	1,158.0	16.9	6,856.0
31	Westinghouse Electric	Electrical products, electronic systems	1,141.0	8.9	12,794.0
32	Monsanto	Herbicides, chemicals, pharmaceuticals	1,128.0	12.6	8,929.0
33	Xerox	Copiers, printers, document processing svcs.	1,040.0	5.8	17,830.0
34	Aluminum Co. of America	Aluminum products	967.0	9.7	9,981.2
35	Abbott Laboratories	Drugs, diagnostic equipment	957.0	13.8	6,921.7
36	Occidental Petroleum	Agricultural products, coal	951.0	9.2	10,304.8
37	Compaq Computer	Computers, related equipment	950.0	29.0	3,271.4
38	FMC	Armored military vehicles, chemicals	913.0	23.2	3,931.5
39	Miles	Chemicals, health and imaging products	877.0	14.2	6,197.4
40	Cooper Industries	Petroleum and industrial equip., electronics	835.0	13.5	6,162.0
41	Rockwell Int'l	Electronics, automotive parts	828.0	6.9	12,027.9
42	Honeywell	Building, industry, and aviation control sys.	808.0	13.0	6,220.9
43	Bristol-Myers Squibb	Drugs, medical devices, consumer products	807.0	7.1	11,298.0
44	Lockheed	Aerospace products, electronics, missile sys.	794.0	8.1	9,809.0
45	Exxon	Petroleum, chemicals	744.0	0.7	103,242.0
46	Deere	Farm and industrial equipment	713.0	10.1	7,055.2
47	Amoco	Chemicals	712.0	2.8	25,604.0
48	Tenneco	Farm, construction, and auto equipment	692.0	4.9	14,035.0
49	Ethyl	Specialty and petroleum chemicals	655.0	25.4	2,574.8
50	Reynolds Metals	Aluminum, aluminum and plastic products	603.0	10.4	5,784.5

Source: Fortune, June 1992

Fastest-Growing Companies

50 Fastest-Growing American Companies with International Focus

Company	Location	Phone	2-Year Growth (%)	1991 Sales ($ millions)	% International
Communications & Entertainment	New York, NY	(212) 486-3999	1,256.3	43.4	95
Wellfleet Communications	Bedford, MA	(617) 275-2400	1,096.7	35.9	26
Sunrise Technologies	Fremont, CA	(510) 623-9001	866.7	20.3	50
InterDigital Communications	King of Prussia, PA	(215) 278-7800	651.1	33.8	52
Cisco Systems	Menlo Park, CA	(415) 326-1941	561.4	183.2	36
Artisoft	Tucson, AZ	(602) 293-4000	511.9	41.0	28
LaserMaster Technology	Eden Prairie, MN	(612) 941-8687	493.6	55.8	30
Platinum Technology	Lombard, IL	(708) 620-5000	380.0	28.8	33
Trimble Navigation	Sunnyvale, CA	(408) 481-8000	373.4	151.0	39
Birtcher Medical Systems	Irvine, CA	(714) 753-9400	349.3	31.0	20
In Focus Systems	Tualatin, OR	(503) 692-4968	330.4	49.5	42
Summit Technology	Waltham, MA	(617) 890-1234	323.1	22.0	93
PictureTel	Danvers, MA	(508) 762-5000	319.4	78.0	40
IPL Systems	Waltham, MA	(617) 890-6620	311.6	60.5	47
Parametric Technology	Waltham, MA	(617) 894-7111	306.4	44.7	38
Allied Research	Baltimore, MD	(410) 625-1888	290.0	174.7	96
KnowledgeWare	Atlanta, GA	(404) 231-8575	276.7	124.3	29
nVIEW	Newport News, VA	(804) 873-1354	273.3	16.8	30
Kaneb Services	Richardson, TX	(214) 699-4000	260.0	135.0	46
Chiron	Emeryville, CA	(510) 655-8730	233.8	118.5	42
Wainoco Oil	Houston, TX	(713) 658-9900	226.8	130.4	30
Nabors Industries	Houston, TX	(713) 874-0035	222.3	240.1	70
SynOptics Comm.	Santa Clara, CA	(408) 988-2400	221.2	248.3	30
Amtech	Dallas, TX	(214) 733-6600	213.3	18.8	24
Komag	Milpitas, CA	(408) 946-2300	186.1	279.2	58
Chipcom	Southborough, MA	(508) 460-8900	180.7	48.0	43
Digi International	Eden Prairie, MN	(612) 943-9020	179.5	40.8	24
Restor Industries	Ocoee, FL	(407) 877-0908	178.6	19.5	42
Sybase	Emeryville, CA	(510) 596-3500	178.2	159.4	24
Cabletron Systems	Rochester, NH	(603) 332-9400	177.5	290.5	28
Integrated Waste Services	Buffalo, NY	(716) 852-2345	173.5	30.9	20
Rentrak	Portland, OR	(503) 284-7581	164.8	47.4	37
American Power Conversion	W. Kingston, RI	(401) 789-5735	164.4	93.6	25
Frame Technology	San Jose, CA	(408) 433-3311	161.3	41.8	24
Symantec	Cupertino, CA	(408) 253-9600	159.7	216.6	27
Geonex	St. Petersburg, FL	(813) 823-3300	150.2	67.8	31
ICN Pharmaceuticals	Costa Mesa, CA	(714) 545-0100	148.2	460.4	79
ViewLogic Systems	Marlborough, MA	(508) 480-0881	144.8	42.1	34
Geotek Industries	Ramsey, NJ	(201) 825-7080	137.4	36.8	25
Varco International	Orange, CA	(714) 978-1900	130.4	196.3	79
Progress Software	Bedford, MA	(617) 275-4500	129.5	58.3	56
Immucor	Norcross, GA	(404) 441-2051	123.8	27.3	50
Pyramid Technology	Mountain View, CA	(415) 965-7200	119.3	227.9	20
Landmark Graphics	Houston, TX	(713) 560-1000	117.1	89.9	70
BMC Software	Sugar Land, TX	(713) 240-8800	116.6	188.7	44
Xyplex	Boxborough, MA	(508) 264-9900	113.9	41.5	50
U.S. Robotics	Skokie, IL	(708) 982-5010	110.1	78.8	26
Marcam	Newton, MA	(617) 965-0220	108.5	56.5	32
Offshore Pipelines	Houston, TX	(713) 952-1000	106.4	214.5	33
Sequoia Systems	Marlborough, MA	(508) 480-0800	103.2	63.2	20

Note: Companies included generate more than 20% of sales internationally

Source: International Business Magazine, December 1992

U.S. Direct Investment Abroad

THE U.S. DIRECT INVESTMENT POSITION abroad was valued at $450.2 billion at the end of 1991, the most recent year for which data are available. The position is defined as the book value of U.S. direct investors' equity in, and net outstanding loans to, their foreign affiliates. A foreign affiliate is a foreign business enterprise in which a single U.S. investor owns at least 10% of the voting securities, or the equivalent. The positions in Canada and in the United Kingdom are the largest.

U.S. Direct Investment Position Abroad, Historical-Cost Basis at Year End ($ millions)

Location	All Industries	Petroleum	Manuf.	Wholesale Trade	Banking	Finance, Insurance, Real Estate	Services	Other Industries
All countries	450,196	59,160	175,413	43,218	18,756	117,094	13,368	23,187
Developed countries	335,433	41,229	139,082	35,421	8,895	83,952	11,227	15,628
Canada	68,510	10,847	32,360	4,388	1,047	12,208	2,206	5,455
Europe	224,554	22,829	89,090	24,875	6,947	67,423	8,159	5,231
European Communities (12)	188,710	17,810	85,664	16,243	5,200	51,486	7,258	5,048
France	20,495	-	11,952	3,769	-	2,170	747	513
Germany	32,942	3,621	20,086	2,008	1,466	4,289	430	1,042
Italy	13,825	569	8,730	2,173	137	1,325	403	488
Netherlands	24,711	1,822	7,715	1,560	112	11,028	1,754	720
United Kingdom	68,261	9,540	20,851	2,940	1,813	28,362	2,667	2,087
Other Europe	35,845	5,018	3,426	8,632	1,748	15,937	901	184
Japan	22,918	4,195	10,437	4,851	30	2,555	401	449
Australia, New Zealand, South Africa	19,451	3,359	7,195	1,307	870	1,766	460	4,493
Developing countries	111,608	15,526	36,331	7,797	9,862	33,142	2,141	6,809
Latin America/Western Hemisphere	77,342	4,339	25,687	3,381	6,838	29,888	1,741	5,467
South America	25,998	2,252	15,441	1,067	1,481	2,398	939	2,420
Central America	23,408	1,176	9,302	1,033	149	9,465	299	1,985
Mexico	11,570	-	8,493	681	-	392	188	1,641
Panama	10,980	900	369	402	88	9,047	35	140
Other Western Hemisphere	27,935	911	945	1,280	5,208	18,026	503	1,063
Other Africa	4,371	3,294	347	153	48	237	116	177
Saharan	1,882	1,415	74	63	145	-5	99	90
Sub-Saharan	2,489	1,879	273	90	-97	242	17	87
Middle East	4,715	1,928	1,192	201	121	920	-12	365
Other Asia and Pacific	25,180	5,965	9,104	4,062	2,855	2,097	297	800
Hong Kong	6,430	342	950	2,299	721	1,731	96	290
South Korea	2,392	-	960	346	987	86	-11	-
Taiwan	2,470	-4	1,642	374	264	131	16	47
International	3,155	2,405	-	-	-	-	-	750
Addendum-OPEC	11,028	5,383	2,392	353	179	1,059	3	1,659

Source: Survey of Current Business, June 1992

The Top Reference Sources

A Basic Guide to Exporting
U.S. Government Printing Office, $9.50
(202) 783-3238
Stock #003-009-00604-0

This excellent publication of the U.S. Department of Commerce is designed to help companies learn the costs and risks associated with exporting and develop a successful strategy. Reference appendixes include an export glossary, directory of federal export assistance, state and local sources of assistance, and U.S. and foreign contacts for major overseas markets. Topics discussed include preparing products for export, service exports, business travel, pricing, regulations, tax incentives, customs benefits, and financing.

U.S. Direct Investment Abroad (cont'd)

U.S. Direct Investment Position Abroad and Foreign Direct Investment Position in the U.S. on a Historical-Cost Basis ($ millions)

Year End	U.S. Direct Investment Position Abroad	Foreign Direct Investment Position in the U.S.
1982	207,752	124,677
1983	207,203	137,061
1984	211,480	164,583
1985	230,250	184,615
1986	259,800	220,414
1987	314,307	263,394
1988	335,893	314,754
1989	372,419	368,924
1990	424,086	396,702
1991	450,196	407,577

Source: Survey of Current Business, June 1992

Import/Export

GREAT POTENTIAL EXISTS for businesses in the United States to become more active in exporting. Only 15 percent of U.S. exporters account for 85 percent of the value of U.S.-manufactured exports. One-half of all exporters sell in only one foreign market. Fewer than 20 percent of exporters (less than 3 percent of U.S. companies) export to more than five markets.

Competing effectively abroad helps companies keep the edge they need at home. However, because there are real costs and risks associated with exporting, it is up to each company to weigh the necessary commitment against the potential benefit.

Ten Recommendations for Successful Exporting

- Obtain qualified export counseling and develop a master international marketing plan before starting an export business. The plan should clearly define goals, objectives, and problems that may be encountered.
- Secure a commitment from top management to overcome the initial difficulties and financial requirements of exporting. Take a long-range view of this process.
- Select overseas distributors carefully. International communication and transportation require international distributors to act more independently than their domestic counterparts.
- Establish a basis for profitable operations and orderly growth. Unsolicited trade leads should not be ignored, but the successful exporter will not rely solely on these inquiries.
- Continue to pursue export business even when the U.S. market is healthy.
- Treat international distributors on an equal basis with domestic counterpart, offering similar advertising, special discounts, sales incentive programs, special credit terms, warranty offers, etc.
- Do not assume that a marketing technique that works in Japan will be equally successful in France. Treat each market individually to ensure maximum success.
- Be willing to adapt products to meet regulations or cultural preferences of other countries.
- Print service, sale, and warranty messages in local languages.
- Provide readily available servicing for the product.

Source: A Basic Guide to Exporting

Almanac Fact

Japan was the largest overseas customer in 1992 for U.S. sporting goods, buying $280 million worth of U.S. exports, primarily golf and exercise equipment.

Source: U.S. Industrial Outlook

Methods of Payment Abroad

Letters of Credit

The most secure and most often-used method of payment in export/import transactions is the documentary letter of credit. A letter of credit is a document issued by a bank on the instruction of a buyer of goods (importer), authorizing the seller (exporter) to draw a specified sum of money under specified terms, usually the receipt by the bank of certain documents within a given time.

Before payment, the bank responsible for making payment on behalf of the buyer verifies that all documents are exactly as required by the letter of credit.

If a U.S. exporter is unfamiliar with the credit risk of the foreign bank, or if there is concern about the political or economic risk associated with the country in which the bank is located, it is advised that a letter of credit issued by a foreign bank be *confirmed* by a U.S. bank. This means that the U.S. bank adds its pledge to pay to that of the foreign bank. Letters of credit that are not confirmed are called *advised* letters of credit. The local Department of Commerce district office or an international banker will help exporters determine whether a confirmed or advised letter of credit is appropriate for a particular transaction.

Letters of credit may be irrevocable (cannot be changed unless both the buyer and seller agree) or revocable (either party can make changes). An *at sight* letter of credit means that payment is made immediately upon presentation of documents. *Time* or *date* letters of credit specify when payment is to be made in the future.

Changes made to a letter of credit are called amendments. The fees charged by the banks involved in amending the letter of credit may be paid either by the buyer or the seller, but the letter of credit should specify which party is responsible. Since changes are costly and time-consuming, every effort should be made to get the letter of credit right the first time.

An exporter is usually not paid until the advising or confirming bank receives the funds from the issuing bank. To expedite the receipt of funds, wire transfers may be used. Bank practices vary, however, and the exporter may be able to receive funds by discounting the letter of credit at the bank, which involves paying a fee to the bank for this service. Exporters should consult with their international bankers about bank policy on these issues.

Other Methods of Payment for International Transactions

Cash in Advance (CIA)
Usually used only for small purchases and when the goods are built to order.

Draft (or Bill of Exchange)
An unconditional order in writing from one person (the drawer) to another (the drawee), directing the drawee to pay a specified amount to a named drawer at a fixed or determinable future date. May be date, sight or time draft.

Credit cards
Used mainly in transactions where the dollar value of the items sold is low and shipment is to be made directly to the end-user.

Open Account
The exporter bills the customer, who is expected to pay under agreed terms at a future date. Some of the largest firms abroad make purchases only on an open account, which is a convenient method of payment if the buyer is well established and has demonstrated a long and favorable payment record.

Consignment Sales
Exporter delivers goods to an agent under agreement that the agent sell the merchandise for the account of the exporter. The agent sells the goods for commission and remits the net proceeds to the exporter.

Countertrade/barter
Sale of goods or services that are paid for in whole or in part by the transfer of goods or services from a foreign country.

Payment Problems

The best solution to a payment problem is to negotiate directly with the customer. If negotiations fail and the sum involved is large enough to warrant the effort, obtain the assistance of its bank, legal counsel, and other qualified experts. If both parties can agree to take their dispute to an arbitration agency, this step is faster and less costly than legal action. The International Chamber of Commerce handles the majority of international arbitrations and is usually acceptable to foreign companies because it is not affiliated with any single country.

Source: A Basic Guide to Exporting

Contact Options

The International Chamber of Commerce
(212) 354-4480

American Arbitration Association
(212) 484-4000

Trade Remedy Assistance Office
International Trade Commission
(202) 205-2200

U.S. Exports and Imports

Exports and Imports by Selected Commodity Groupings, 1991 and 1992 ($ millions)

Item	1992 Exports	1992 Imports	1991 Exports	1991 Imports
TOTAL	448,156.3	532,497.7	421,730.0	487,129.0
AGRICULTURAL COMMODITIES	42,078.2	23,432.6	38,510.0	22,140.4
Animal feeds	3,521.0	337.1	3,192.3	312.1
Cereal flour	925.2	725.9	812.7	640.7
Cocoa	31.1	774.1	22.7	823.4
Coffee	17.8	1,566.4	9.8	1,738.1
Corn	4,943.7	68.5	5,145.7	39.2
Cotton, raw and linters	2,010.3	11.4	2,514.3	16.3
Dairy products, eggs	709.2	506.6	454.5	452.4
Grains, unmilled	892.1	121.6	701.2	112.0
Live animals	608.4	1,434.4	687.6	1,172.4
Meat and preparations	4,205.4	2,722.8	3,629.6	2,908.3
Oils/fats, animal	521.4	31.1	446.8	28.5
Oils/fats, vegetable	826.7	958.0	596.2	735.1
Plants	135.1	102.5	99.2	104.8
Rice	725.0	91.7	753.5	80.1
Seeds	297.8	152.5	273.6	132.2
Soybeans	4,416.4	15.9	3,994.9	27.4
Sugar	5.6	667.7	12.1	713.2
Tobacco, unmanufactured	1,650.6	948.7	1,429.6	989.3
Vegetables and fruit	5,718.5	5,697.6	5,341.7	5,391.4
Wheat	4,496.4	189.6	3,350.2	66.0
Other agricultural	3,953.9	5,921.9	3,546.4	5,313.1
MANUFACTURED GOODS	347,512.1	434,256.3	325,978.0	392,432.6
ADP equip., office mach.	26,987.8	36,393.4	25,978.8	30,019.1
Airplanes	26,412.6	3,917.5	24,335.1	3,347.3
Airplane parts	9,328.8	3,396.8	10,283.6	4,046.0
Aluminum	2,665.7	2,538.4	3,127.8	2,408.8
Artwork/Antiques	1,075.7	2,086.8	1,239.4	1,978.7
Basketware, etc.	1,520.6	2,188.0	1,289.9	1,910.8
Chemicals–cosmetics	2,630.6	1,711.8	2,360.8	1,415.2
Chemicals–dyeing	1,867.4	1,626.3	1,649.2	1,416.4
Chemicals–fertilizers	2,372.0	952.2	2,977.3	917.6
Chemicals–inorganic	4,119.2	3,300.0	4,082.7	3,296.5
Chemicals–medicinal	5,356.9	3,812.1	4,608.5	3,046.9
Chemicals–organic	10,993.3	9,365.8	10,898.2	8,132.8
Chemicals–plastics	10,253.4	4,293.2	10,315.5	3,783.6
Chemicals	6,363.5	2,622.8	6,019.4	2,121.9
Clothing	4,093.3	31,241.6	3,214.8	26,202.2
Copper	1,176.9	1,635.3	1,328.0	1,572.8
Electrical machinery	32,038.6	39,728.5	30,050.1	35,067.0
Furniture and parts	2,549.2	5,504.6	2,119.6	4,936.1
Gem diamonds	367.5	4,147.7	209.3	4,002.0
General industrial mach.	18,436.2	15,521.9	17,152.8	14,396.1
Glass	1,193.7	849.6	1,144.6	769.5
Gold, non-monetary	4,059.5	1,899.5	3,279.2	1,922.1
Iron and steel mill prod.	3,595.4	8,320.7	4,210.8	8,301.1
Lighting, plumbing	977.6	1,520.9	876.5	1,246.0
Metal manufactures	5,491.0	6,730.4	5,188.8	6,372.2
Metalworking machinery	3,032.8	3,170.3	2,709.3	3,605.0
Motorcycles, bicycles	1,437.0	1,914.8	1,307.6	1,636.3
Nickel	195.8	797.2	218.5	1,061.0
Optical goods	766.1	1,644.6	713.4	1,483.5

U.S. Exports and Imports (cont'd)

Item	1992 Exports	1992 Imports	1991 Exports	1991 Imports
Paper and paperboard	6,337.7	7,998.5	5,965.4	8,020.6
Photographic equipment	2,948.3	3,849.4	2,926.1	3,640.9
Plastic articles	2,773.2	3,570.5	2,240.1	3,114.0
Platinum	294.4	1,426.3	310.9	1,658.9
Pottery	103.3	1,402.8	87.1	1,242.3
Power generating mach.	17,949.7	15,910.0	16,960.3	14,194.8
Printed materials	3,800.7	1,876.0	3,588.9	1,701.6
Records/magnetic media	4,839.8	3,110.7	4,266.9	2,788.1
Rubber articles	616.3	878.7	579.1	704.8
Rubber tires and tubes	1,407.9	2,512.2	1,274.0	2,308.8
Scientific instruments	14,369.6	7,604.0	13,499.0	6,732.6
Ships, boats	1,421.8	319.5	1,155.0	248.9
Silver and bullion	208.8	448.6	237.2	363.2
Spacecraft	269.6	91.8	257.3	-
Specialized ind. mach.	16,680.1	11,825.9	16,686.3	10,863.9
Telecommunications equip.	11,204.5	25,818.6	9,998.7	23,445.7
Textile yarn, fabric	5,756.2	7,840.3	5,481.9	6,981.1
Toys/games/sporting goods	2,435.9	10,747.1	2,087.0	8,820.9
Travel goods	194.0	2,510.1	159.3	2,346.1
Vehicles/new cars–Canada	5,927.6	13,890.1	6,194.9	13,517.7
Vehicles/new cars–Japan	693.6	20,538.1	495.8	20,422.5
Vehicles/new cars–Other	5,091.0	11,564.0	3,069.7	10,812.5
Vehicles/trucks	3,678.1	9,783.8	3,878.7	8,292.8
Vehicles/chassis/bodies	311.2	352.8	241.3	351.9
Vehicles/parts	16,551.5	15,840.6	14,370.9	14,066.5
Watches/clocks/parts	207.4	2,320.5	225.0	2,285.0
Wood manufactures	1,386.7	2,409.4	1,250.5	1,907.4
Zinc	37.7	854.6	39.5	651.5
Other manufactured goods	27,558.6	32,947.7	24,569.8	30,042.4
MINERAL FUEL	11,122.2	55,028.2	12,081.3	54,055.7
Coal	4,324.8	419.2	4,775.6	310.0
Crude oil	26.6	38,544.1	33.4	36,901.9
Petroleum preparations	3,990.4	11,281.7	4,399.4	12,312.0
Liquified propane/butane	257.6	706.4	253.0	858.6
Natural gas	351.1	2,807.5	308.2	2,482.5
Electricity	63.6	589.8	43.8	486.7
Other mineral fuels	2,108.0	679.6	2,267.9	704.0
SELECTED COMMODITIES				
Fish and preparations	3,377.2	5,656.8	3,062.7	5,637.6
Cork, wood, lumber	5,297.6	3,969.9	5,113.8	3,056.8
Pulp and waste paper	3,849.9	2,128.9	3,600.4	2,163.4
Metal ores; scrap	3,421.0	3,322.6	4,038.7	3,560.6
Crude fertilizers	1,384.9	914.4	1,385.4	982.3
Cigarettes	4,192.0	264.7	4,238.1	129.9
Alcoholic beverages, distilled	343.3	1,836.9	279.0	1,594.9
ALL OTHER	2,798.2	1,540.9	2,821.6	1,374.5
RE-EXPORTS	22,500.4	NA	20,621.0	NA
Agricultural commodities	892.0	NA	857.0	NA
Manufactured goods	21,051.6	NA	19,153.1	NA
Mineral fuels	77.8	NA	205.7	NA
Other, re-exports	479.1	NA	405.2	NA
Timing adjustment	279.3	145.5	NA	NA

NA=not applicable.

Source: U.S. Department of Commerce

U.S. Exports and Imports (cont'd)

U.S. Exports of Merchandise by State, 1992 ($ millions)

Item	Manufactured Commodities	Non-Manufactured Commodities	Total Cumulative to Date
U.S. TOTAL	403,015.1	45,140.7	448,156.3
Alabama	3,222.8	405.7	3,628.5
Alaska	1,073.6	2,120.9	3,194.5
Arizona	4,767.3	341.4	5,108.7
Arkansas	1,241.7	81.8	1,323.5
California	51,867.6	4,439.8	56,307.4
Colorado	2,499.0	95.1	2,594.1
Connecticut	4,740.8	287.3	5,028.1
Delaware	1,497.4	10.3	1,507.7
Florida	13,593.3	837.8	14,431.1
Georgia	6,942.0	710.2	7,652.2
Hawaii	150.1	56.1	206.2
Idaho	1,012.3	63.7	1,076.0
Illinois	14,711.8	615.7	15,327.5
Indiana	6,022.2	125.5	6,147.7
Iowa	2,350.0	125.7	2,475.7
Kansas	2,235.0	278.8	2,513.8
Kentucky	3,265.3	383.0	3,648.3
Louisiana	7,329.2	8,821.3	16,150.5
Maine	790.7	111.1	901.8
Maryland	3,596.0	282.8	3,878.8
Massachusetts	9,969.8	430.5	10,400.3
Michigan	19,969.7	444.4	20,414.1
Minnesota	5,689.2	447.6	6,136.8
Mississippi	1,845.3	117.9	1,963.2
Missouri	3,491.4	172.1	3,663.5
Montana	173.7	94.3	268.0
Nebraska	1,157.3	75.3	1,232.6
Nevada	490.7	16.1	506.8
New Hampshire	850.2	67.0	917.2
New Jersey	8,503.1	451.9	8,955.0
New Mexico	325.1	30.5	355.6
New York	20,886.3	1,741.8	22,628.1
North Carolina	8,965.5	1,408.0	10,373.5
North Dakota	269.8	66.1	335.9
Ohio	15,468.5	837.5	16,306.0
Oklahoma	1,931.2	55.6	1,986.8
Oregon	3,616.3	1,273.4	4,889.7
Pennsylvania	9,929.7	399.3	10,329.0
Rhode Island	735.1	124.0	859.1
South Carolina	4,051.4	170.5	4,221.9
South Dakota	220.7	11.5	232.2
Tennessee	4,825.2	330.4	5,155.6
Texas	40,267.7	3,285.1	43,552.8
Utah	2,327.4	378.5	2,705.9
Vermont	1,287.0	26.8	1,313.8
Virginia	7,344.6	2,439.6	9,784.2
Washington	25,324.4	2,716.9	28,041.3
West Virginia	903.1	842.5	1,745.6
Wisconsin	5,740.8	432.3	6,173.1
Wyoming	344.3	23.9	368.2
DC	243.9	100.2	344.1
Puerto Rico	3,822.7	49.6	3,872.3
U.S. Virgin Islands	121.2	0.2	121.4

NA=not applicable.

Source: U.S. Department of Commerce

U.S. Exports and Imports (cont'd)

U.S. Domestic Exports and General Imports by Area ($ millions)

Selected Major Commodities	Canada	Mexico	U.K.	Germany	France	Japan	China; Taiwan	South Korea
DOMESTIC EXPORTS, TOTAL	83,674	28,279	23,490	18,760	13,664	48,580	11,491	14,404
Meat and meat preparations	496	270	8	10	65	1,567	15	129
Fish, crustaceans, etc.	391	26	100	66	86	1,799	43	107
Cereals and cereal preparations	347	931	42	72	48	2,419	659	827
Vegetables and fruit	2,123	208	240	297	127	938	171	56
Feeding stuff for animals	328	131	76	31	94	370	55	15
Misc. edible products & preparations	246	55	14	8	7	66	40	24
Tobacco and tobacco manufactures	12	3	59	253	24	1,622	159	115
Hides, skins, and fur skins, raw	120	99	4	12	20	457	114	780
Oils seeds and oleaginous fruits	135	232	132	227	39	848	413	197
Cork and wood	686	166	111	116	38	2,690	112	316
Pulp and waste paper	298	323	160	289	198	777	203	405
Textile fibers & their wastes	151	118	55	208	13	629	140	508
Crude fertilizers & crude minerals	278	71	37	61	15	292	41	61
Metalliferous ores and metal scrap	934	231	175	153	58	1,036	202	646
Crude animal and vegetable materials	216	110	49	64	23	147	14	29
Coal, coke and briquettes	615	25	245	45	296	597	178	186
Petroleum, related materials	988	610	81	48	175	722	309	550
Organic chemicals	1,150	604	359	451	197	1,137	873	698
Inorganic chemicals	473	224	127	243	57	987	129	217
Dyeing, tanning/coloring materials	429	99	104	54	20	116	37	88
Medicinal/pharmaceutical products	462	106	221	328	271	765	50	53
Essential oils, polishing, preparations	412	131	128	73	64	249	53	51
Fertilizers	189	46	5	37	58	160	2	82
Plastics in primary forms	1,184	537	257	206	84	448	255	264
Plastics in nonprimary forms	745	325	136	144	70	196	46	62
Chemical materials and products.	1,127	253	209	273	308	569	94	204
Rubber manufactures.	991	204	78	73	26	235	17	32
Cork, wood manuf. other than furniture	279	109	137	117	10	109	40	54
Paper, paperboard and particles	1,336	633	244	154	64	513	94	127
Textile yarn, fabrics	1,248	516	300	189	94	272	65	106
Nonmetallic mineral manufacturing	1,164	231	184	114	69	548	71	89
Iron and steel	1,462	563	108	62	59	215	28	150
Nonferrous metals	1,435	370	226	135	123	1,574	358	168
Manufactures of metals	2,288	907	360	286	141	366	90	138
Power- generating machinery	4,262	863	1,263	699	2,067	912	471	354
Mach. specialized for industries	3,389	965	904	685	554	1,001	288	549
Metalworking machinery	563	214	207	205	75	217	96	194
Gen. industrial equipment, parts	4,928	1,415	898	688	540	855	498	704
Office machines	4,180	941	3,171	2,710	1,471	3,678	469	656
Telecom., sound recording, equip.	1,582	1,529	746	548	218	973	577	306
Elect. machinery, appliances.	7,669	3,749	1,763	1,402	1,009	2,390	1,440	1,395
Road vehicles (incl. air-cushion vehicles)	18,062	3,274	445	1,191	361	1,584	846	242
Transport equipment	1,883	522	4,091	2,132	1,435	3,689	430	962
Furniture, bedding, mattresses	747	325	80	44	24	80	13	10
Articles of apparel/clothing accessories	236	403	94	46	69	306	7	8
Prof. scientific, control instruments	2,036	770	1,001	1,018	705	1,613	276	471
Photo equip., watches, clocks	592	197	437	238	333	601	46	51
Miscellaneous manufactured articles	4,033	1,148	1,821	1,315	811	3,448	442	501
Trans., commodities not class. by kind	1,040	201	132	135	48	145	80	33
Gold, non-monetary	530	94	689	97	336	16	3	4
Ship. < $10,000 &< $1,500 exports	1,183	1,264	722	485	374	618	168	135

U.S. Exports and Imports (cont'd)

Selected Major Commodities	Canada	Mexico	U.K.	Germany	France	Japan	China; Taiwan	South Korea
IMPORTS, TOTAL	91,380	30,157	20,188	28,162	13,153	89,684	22,666	18,485
Meat and meat preparations	649	3	*	1	4	4	*	*
Fish crustaceans, etc., preps	1,174	278	24	3	9	147	168	124
Vegetables and fruit	278	1,441	15	76	17	38	71	26
Coffee, tea, cocoa, spices	149	374	30	80	10	4	13	1
Beverages	543	248	633	192	893	30	3	4
Cork and wood	2,785	111	1	3	1	*	11	*
Pulp and waste paper	2,546	2	*	2	*	*	1	*
Metalliferous ores and metal scrap	1,209	282	37	39	33	16	3	2
Petroleum, products, related materials	6,583	5,101	2,068	64	354	26	*	9
Gas, natural and manufactured	2,836	161	14	8	11	2	0	*
Organic chemicals	847	156	764	1,072	420	844	42	73
Inorganic chemicals	1,057	236	242	400	187	158	10	3
Medicinal/pharmaceutical products	100	15	456	337	114	213	4	3
Chemical materials and products	236	51	158	348	126	250	11	4
Rubber manufacturers	831	72	112	228	153	1,061	185	255
Cork/wood manuf. other than furniture	700	100	11	27	43	11	288	12
Paper, paperboard and particles	6,286	191	156	292	121	237	60	73
Textile yarn, fabrics, made-up articles	403	292	294	318	203	580	445	490
Nonmetallic mineral manufactures	701	437	602	412	327	739	384	123
Iron and steel	1,505	358	391	877	665	2,155	161	574
Nonferrous metals	3,923	521	390	432	172	467	28	8
Manufactures of metals	1,361	499	289	625	239	1,584	1,559	568
Power-generating machinery, equip.	2,742	1,074	1,830	1,605	1,897	3,284	95	82
Mach. specialized for industries	1,420	140	1,072	3,073	593	3,349	314	69
Metalworking machinery	246	8	222	672	62	1,519	162	36
Gen. industrial machinery, parts	1,717	737	925	2,142	379	3,856	846	416
Office machines/auto processing mach.	1,877	709	794	521	247	10,978	3,092	1,351
Telecomm., sound recordingequip.	969	2,773	209	140	107	9,348-	1,450	1,706
Electronic machinery, appliances	3,316	4,563	936	2,018	603	8,897	2,192	2,507
Road vehicles (incl. air-cushion vehicles)	26,121	3,646	1,374	6,722	699	27,356	870	1,292
Transport equipment	2,422	31	1,159	181	1,055	526	65	80
Furniture, bedding, mattresses, etc.	1,208	580	93	201	69	166	1,008	67
Travel goods, handbags	17	46	7	16	72	9	407	446
Articles of apparel and accessories	251	712	213	138	227	160	2,491	3,259
Footwear	53	164	43	28	48	5	1,525	2,565
Prof. scientific & control instruments	526	523	651	958	242	1,643	180	91
Photo equip., watches, clocks	181	135	224	368	270	2,781	348	135
Miscellaneous manufactured articles	1,277	779	1,482	1,007	833	4,622	2,987	1,562
Trans., commodities not class. by kind	3,579	1,007	1,265	887	574	827	98	104
Low-valued import transactions (est.)	878	292	212	343	115	528	152	40

**Less than $500,000. Statistics for Germany include the former East and West Germanies.*

Source: U.S. Bureau of the Census

The United States' Top Ten Export Markets for Manufactured Goods

Country	Exports 1991 ($ billions)	Share of U.S. Exports (%)
Canada	75.9	66.3
Japan	31.4	22.0
Mexico	28.4	9.1
United Kingdom	20.3	8.2
Germany (West)	19.4	5.9

Country	Exports 1991 ($ billions)	Share of U.S. Exports (%)
France	13.7	5.6
South Korea	11.1	4.0
Netherlands	10.3	3.2
Taiwan	10.0	3.0
Singapore	8.3	2.9

Source: U.S. Industrial Outlook

Global High-Tech Markets

THE NATION'S COMPETITIVENESS in the global marketplace depends on its ability to sell products abroad and to compete against imports in the home market. According to studies by the National Science Foundation, the international market for high-tech goods is growing faster than that for other manufactured goods. The following charts provide the most recent information on U.S. participation in international high-tech markets.

In the 1980s, the United States was the leading producer of high-tech products, although its lead was challenged, and continues to be challenged, by Japanese industry.

U.S. Global Market Share: High-Tech Industries (%)

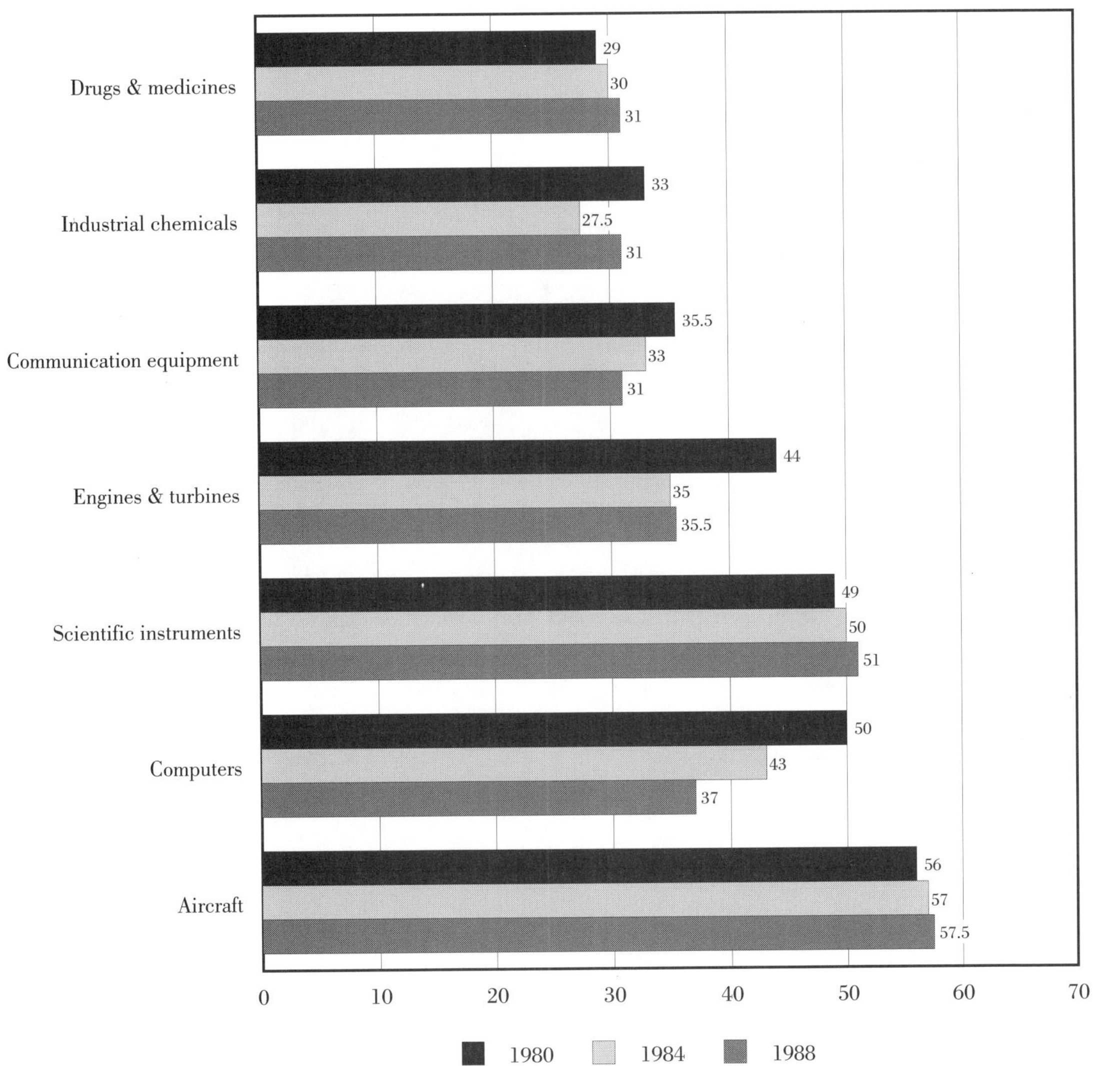

Source: National Science Board, Science & Engineering Indicators

Global High-Tech Markets (cont'd)

Country Share of Global High-Tech Markets (%)

	1980	1984	1988
Italy	4	3.25	3
France	6	5.25	4.75
United Kingdom	8.5	8.25	9
Germany	11.5	11	10
Japan	19	24	27
Europe (EC-12)	34	33	31
USA	41	37	36

0 5 10 15 20 25 30 35 40 45

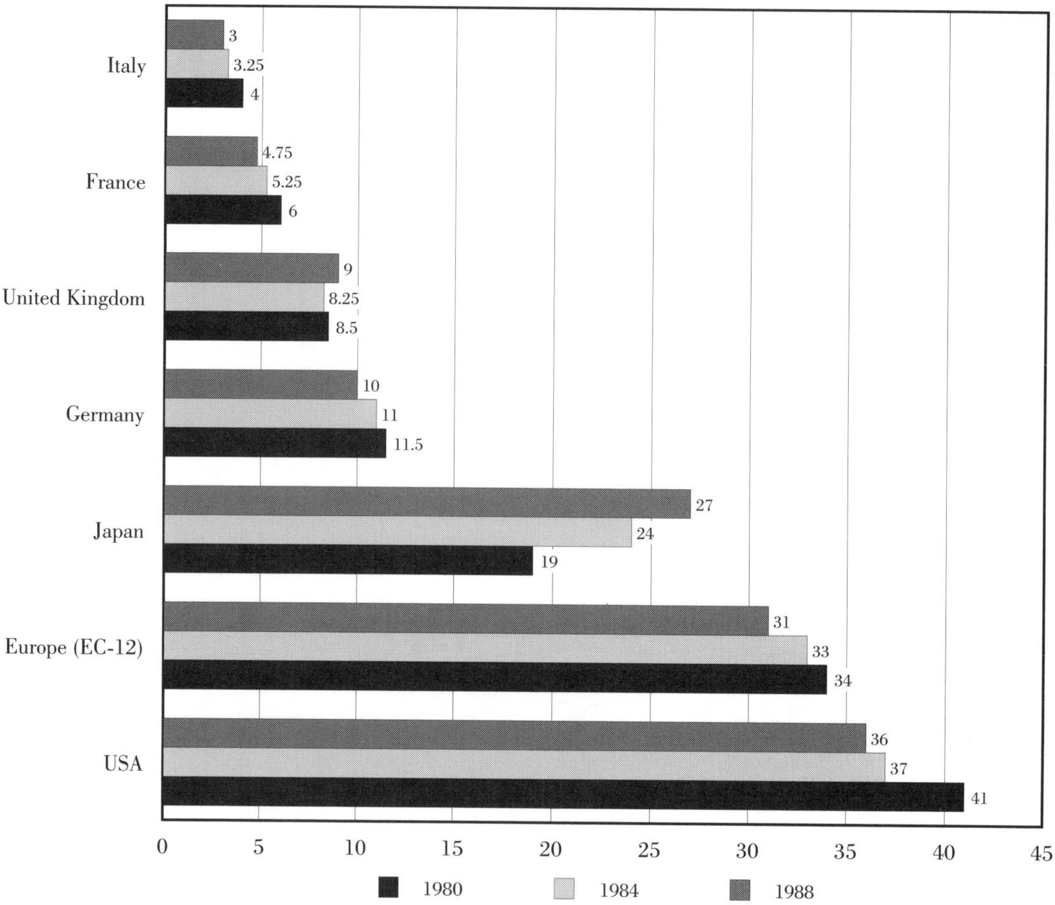

Import Penetration of High-Tech Markets (% of home market supplied by imports)

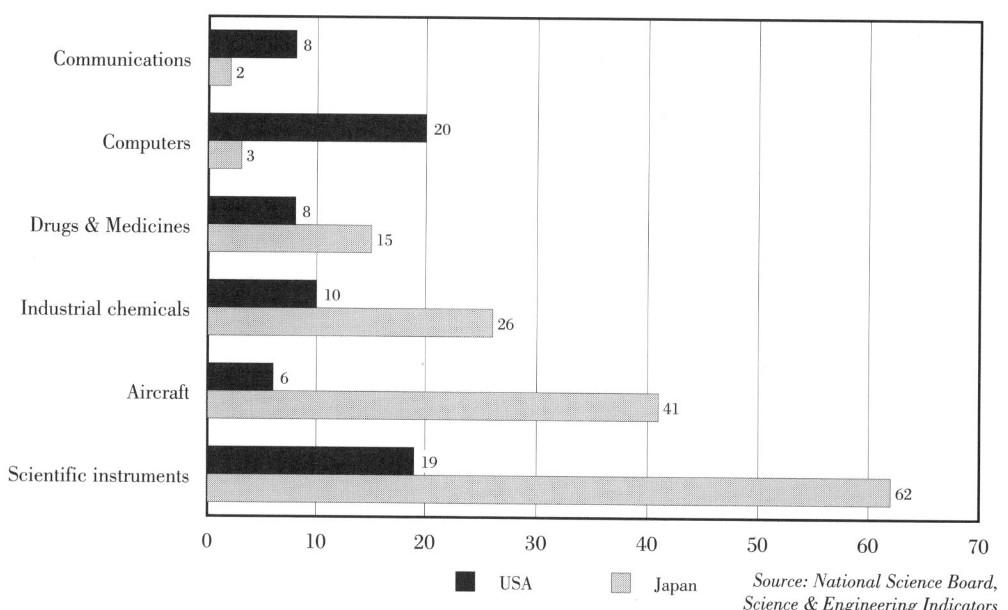

Source: National Science Board, Science & Engineering Indicators

Intellectual Property Exports

THE UNITED STATES IS A NET EXPORTER of technology sold as intellectual property. Royalties and fees received from foreigners have been, on average, almost four times that paid out to foreigners by U.S. firms for access to their technology. Japan is the largest consumer of U.S. technology sold in this manner. While sales of technological know-how contribute positively to the balance sheets of U.S. firms and the U.S. economy in the short term, there has been ongoing controversy regarding the long-term consequences. The most recent statistics are reflected in the following graph.

Royalties & License Fees Generated From the Exchange of Industrial Processes ($ millions)

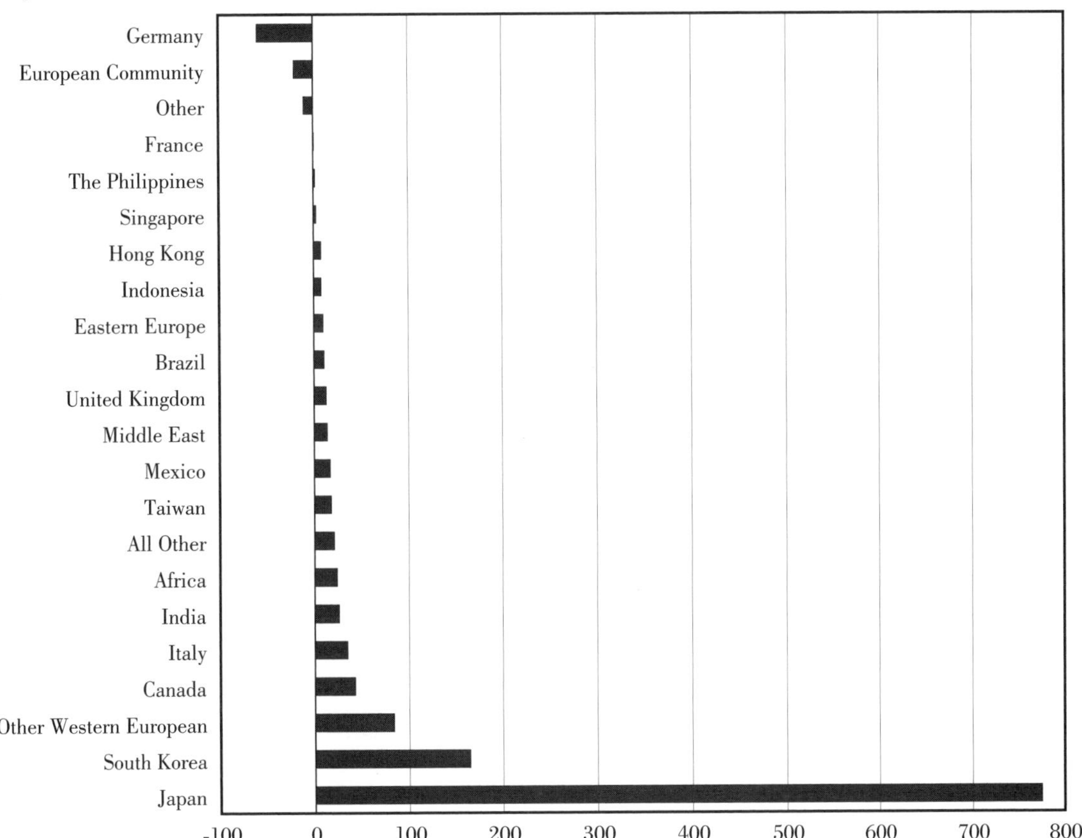

Source: National Science Board, Science & Engineering Indicators

Almanac Fact

In 1991, 6 of the 10 companies with the largest worldwide software revenues were from the United States, 3 were from Japan, and 1 was from Germany.

Source: Datamation

Intellectual Property Protection

WHILE THE UNITED STATES HAS a long-standing tradition of protecting the intellectual property of its citizens, such protection is not offered by all foreign countries. The patents, trademarks, and copyrights of U.S. citizens are, at times, ignored in other countries and piracy and product counterfeiting result in a considerable loss of revenue for American companies.

Despite the efforts of the General Agreement on Tariffs and Trade (GATT), the Paris Convention for the Protection of Industrial Property (trademarks and patents), and the Berne Convention for the Protection of Literary and Artistic Works (copyrights), there is no uniform protection available to an individual whose invention, mark, literary works, or computer software might be used in foreign countries.

Property protection in a foreign country frequently is dependent upon the owner meeting the registration requirements of the individual country. Individual applications for patent protection, for example, must be filed in each country in which the patent owner desires protection, unless the country conforms to an international agreement. Usually a foreign patent agent or attorney is needed to execute the filing of the application in another country. The Patent Trade Office (PTO) will provide a list of individuals who are qualified to practice before the U.S. PTO and knowledgeable about foreign registration requirements.

More recent treaties, such as the Patent Cooperation Treaty, allow applicants from member countries to file one standardized international application to use in member countries in which intellectual property protection is desired.

Despite these strides in international cooperation, a number of countries are frequently cited as locations where property rights protection is often inadequate:

- Copyrights are inadequately protected in Brazil, China, India, Korea, Indonesia, Malaysia, Singapore, and Saudi Arabia.
- Patents are unprotected or inadequately protected in Indonesia, Mexico, Thailand, Brazil, India, Korea, Philippines, Singapore, Saudi Arabia, Taiwan, the United Arab Emirates, and China.
- Trademarks are inadequately protected in Brazil, India, Indonesia, Philippines, and Thailand.
- Product piracy and counterfeiting is a recurring problem in Taiwan, particularly with audio-visual materials.

A good source of information about protecting a business against foreign infringement of property rights is the U.S. and Foreign Commercial Service (US&FCS), which maintains 47 district offices and 20 branches in 67 cities around the United States. These offices are staffed by trade specialists and maintain business libraries of the latest reports of the Department of Commerce. For assistance, call the nearest Department of Commerce district office (see list this chapter) or call (800) 872-8723. The United States Patent Trademark Office will also provide additional information.

Recommended Resources

Copyrights, Patents & Trademarks
Hoyt L. Barber
Liberty Press, McGraw-Hill
(800) 262-4729

Exportise: An International Trade Source Book for Smaller Company Executives
The Small Business Foundation of America
Washington, DC
(202) 223-1103

The Top Reference Sources

The Multinational Executive Travel Companion
Suburban Publishing, $60
(203) 324-6439

This is an indispensable resource for executives traveling overseas. Published annually, it includes 160 country profiles, with information on population, GNP, imports and exports, country affiliations, and trade groups.

The business traveler will also find listings of major companies' performances, weather conditions, time diffences, passport and visa requirements, postage, English-speaking physicians, embassies and consulates, tipping guidelines, travel and transportation tips, and more. Particularly useful are the listings of important addresses and phone numbers.

Export Intermediaries

EXPORT MANAGEMENT COMPANIES and Export Trading Companies are firms that market American products and services abroad on behalf of manufacturers, farm groups, and distributors. These export intermediaries may handle products in a single sector, such as automotive equipment or clothing, or they may handle a variety of items from a number of different sectors. Intermediaries may service markets worldwide, or they may specialize in certain countries or regions.

Export Management Companies (EMC) help U.S. manufacturers establish an overseas market for the company's products, usually on an exclusive basis. The management company maintains a close relationship with its clients as well as with overseas distributors. Its business is supply-driven.

Management companies may take title to the products they sell, making a profit on the markup, or they may charge a commission, depending on the type of products being sold, the overseas market, or the manufacturer-client's needs. Export management companies may also work on a retainer basis.

In contrast, Export Trading Companies (ETC) most often act as independent distributors, bringing buyers and sellers together for a transaction. Business for ETCs is demand-driven and transaction-oriented. Most export trading companies take title to the products involved, but others may work on commission.

There are more than 1,500 ETCs and EMCs in the United States. Potential exporters should develop a list of those ETCs and EMCs which specialize in exporting the types of products proposed to be sold overseas.

For assistance in locating and selecting the proper ETC/EMC, contact the Commerce Department's Office of Export Trading Company Affairs, International Trade Administration, Washington, DC 20230, (202) 482-5131. Or, call a local office of the Small Business Administration or local World Trade Center (see listings for each in this chapter).

Source: Business America

Recommended Resources

The Export Yellow Pages
Office of Export Trading Company Affairs
International Trade Administration
Washington, DC 20230

This directory of more than 12,000 firms involved in foreign trade is designed to facilitate contact between producers of goods and services and firms providing export trade services. The directory is available free of charge from Commerce Department district offices (see list in this chapter). Call the nearest Commerce Department district office to list your company in the next edition. For advertising information, call (800) 288-2582.

Directory of Leading U.S. Export Management Companies
Bergano Book Co.
P.O. Box 190
Fairfield, CT 06430
(203) 254-2054

This reference provides contacts, names, and addresses for 400 EMCs and 41 product categories. Geographic specialties and language capacities are also included. Lists export consultants. Cross-referenced by company name, state, and product category.

Export Trading Company Guidebook
U.S. Government Printing Office
Washington, DC 20402
(202) 783-3238
(# 003-009-00523, available for $8.50)

Export Profits
Upstart Publishing Company
Dover, NH 03820
(603) 749-5071

Trading Company Sourcebook
National Federation of Export Associations
4905 Del Ray Ave., Suite 302
Bethesda, MD 20814

Part yearbook of members of the Federation and part directory of EMCs and ETCs, this reference includes an index of companies by product specialization and specific examples of how these companies operate. The cost is $18.00, payable by check.

The Top Reference Sources

International Business
American International Publishing, $59.97 a year
(914) 381-7700

This impressive magazine is loaded with information for businesses participating in the global marketplace. Features include articles on the use of bar codes to keep track of overseas shipments, why the weak dollar isn't helping U.S. export sales, and how Japan's recession has drastically cut Asian venture capital into U.S. companies.

A special highlight is International Business' Top 100, a ranking of America's fastest-growing midsize international companies.

Brokers and Forwarders

EVERY SHIPMENT ENTERING THE UNITED STATES is subject to more than 500 pages of customs and tariff regulations. Customs Brokers are import professionals, licensed by the U.S. Department of the Treasury, who have a thorough knowledge of these regulations, and who help clients choose the best modes of transportation, types of carriers, and shipping routes. Brokers also assist with exchange rates, appraisal, and determining proper classifications and duties. The broker's job often transcends the Customs Bureau, and involves contact with other government agencies such the USDA (for meat import questions), EPA (for vehicle emissions standards), or the FDA (product safety).

Ocean Freight Forwarders are licensed by the Federal Maritime Commission. Air Cargo or Air Transport Agents are accredited by the International Air Transportation Association. These freight forwarding professionals advise clients of the best rates, routings, and modes of transporting goods to or from any area in the world. Freight forwarders are experts on such items as foreign documentation requirements, hazardous materials regulations, special packaging or handling requirements, licensing provisions, etc.

The following licensed customs brokers and freight forwarders have been selected on the basis of range of services and the number of branch offices. The services provided include four or more of the following: Customs Broker (CB), Ocean Freight Forwarder (OFF), International Air Freight Forwarder (AFF), International Air Transport Agent (IATA), Container Station (CS), Drawback Specialist (DS), Steamship Agent (SA), Motor Property Broker (MPB), Non-Vessel Operating Common Carrier (NVO), Warehouseman (WH).

Source: National Customs Brokers and Forwarders Association

Customs Brokers and Freight Forwarders in the United States

Air Express International
120 Tokeneke Rd.
Darien, CT 06820
AFF, CB, CS, IATA, OFF, WH
(203) 655-7900

Amerford International Corporation
One Cross Island Plaza
Rosedale, NY 11422
AFF, IATA, NVO, OFF
(718) 481-4200

Burlington Air Express
18200 Von Karman Ave.
Irvine, CA 92715
AFF, CB, DB, IATA, WH
(714) 752-1212

John V. Carr & Son
P.O. Box 33479
Detroit, MI 48232
AFF, CB, DB, IATA, MPB, NVO, OFF, WH
(313) 965-1540

Danzas Corporation
330 120th, NE
Bellevue, WA 98005
AFF, CB, IATA, MPB, NVO, OFF, WH
(206) 646-7171

A.N. Deringer
P.O. Box 1309
St. Albans, VT 05478
AFF, CB, CS, DB, IATA, MPB, NVO, OFF, WH
(802) 524-5975

Expeditors International of Washington
P.O. Box 69620
Seattle, WA 98168
AFF, CB, DB, IATA, MPB, NVO, OFF
(206) 246-3711

Fritz Companies
P.O. Box 7221
San Francisco, CA 94120
AFF, CB, DB, IATA, MPB, NVO, OFF, SA, WH
(415) 904-8200

The Harper Group
260 Townsend St.
San Francisco, CA 94107
AFF, CB, CS, DB, MPB, NVO, OFF, WH
(415) 978-0600

Intertrans Corporation
124 E. John Carpenter Freeway
Irving, TX 75062
AFF, CB, DB, IATA, MPB, NVO, OFF
(214) 830-8888

Norman G. Jensen
3050 Metro Dr., Suite 300
Minneapolis, MN 55425
AFF, CB, IATA, MPB, OFF
(612) 854-7363

The Myers Group
Myers Building
Rouses Point, NY 12979
AFF, CB, CS, DB, IATA, MPB, NVO, OFF, WH
(518) 297-2222

Brokers and Forwarders (cont'd)

Panalpina
Harborside Financial Center
34 Exchange Pl., Plaza Two,
Jersey City, NJ 07302
AFF, CB, CS, DB, IATA, MP, NVO, OFF
(201) 451-4000

Schenkers International Forwarders
Exchange Place Centre
10 Exchange Pl., Suite 1500
Jersey City, NJ 07302
AFF, CB, IATA, MPB, NVO, OFF
(201) 434-5500

Tower Group International
128 Dearborn St.
Buffalo, NY 14207
AFF, CB, CS, DB, IATA, MPB, NVO, OFF, WH
(716) 874-1300

Yusen Air & Sea Service USA
60 E. 42nd St.
New York, NY 10165
AFF, CB, IATA, OFF
(212) 983-1170

Customs Brokers and Freight Forwarders Outside the United States

Affiliated Customs Brokers, Ltd.
411 Des Recollets
Montreal, PQ, Canada H2Y 1W3
AFF, CB, DB, IATA, OFF, WH
(514) 288-1211

Constantine Shipping and
International Services, Ltd.
10 Grafton St.
London, England W1X 3LA
AFF, OFF, SA
(01) 493-9484

Footwork-Hamacher GmbH
Martinistr. 24
P.O. Box 10 51 05
Bremen 1, Germany 2800
AFF, CB, CS, IATA, NVO, OFF, WH
421-33-77-60

A. Hartrodt GmbH & Co.
P.O. Box 10 29 29
Hamburg 1, Germany D-200
AFF, CB, IATA, NVO, OFF
(040) 239 0383

Livingston Group Inc.
405 The West Mall, Suite 600
Toronto, ON, Canada M9C 5K7
AFF, CB, DB, IATA, MPB, NVO, OFF, WH
(416) 626-2828

Malenstein Rotterdam B.V.
Bergambachstraat 10
Rotterdam, Netherlands 3079 DA
AFF, CB, CS, DB, IATA, NVO, OFF, WH
010-492-8700

Naigai Nitto Co. Ltd.
38-8 Higaski-Shinagawa 1-Chome
Shinagawa-ku
Tokyo, Japan 140
AFF, CB, CS, IATA, MPB, NVO, OFF, SA, WH
(03) 450-7400

Starber International
410 St. Nicholas Street
Montreal, PQ, Canada H2Y 2P5
AFF, CB, DB, IATA, NVO, OFF, WH
(514) 285-1500

Swift Freight International
Carrera (Bin Hendi Building)
Zabeel Road-Karama
P.O. Box 50177
Dubai, United Arab Emirates
AFF, CB, CS, IATA, NVO, OFF, WH
(971)-369-595

Recommended Resource

The Who's Who of Customs Brokers and International Freight Forwarders
National Customs Brokers & Forwarders
Association of America
One World Trade Center, Suite 1153
New York, NY 10048
(212) 432-0050

Contact Options

U.S. Customs Service
1301 Constitution Ave., NW
Washington, DC 20229
(202) 566-8195

Federal Maritime Commission
800 N. Capitol St.
Washington, DC 20573
(202) 523-3782

International Air Transportation Association (IATA)
1001 Pennsylvania Ave., Suite 285N
Washington, DC 20004
(202) 624-2977

Government Resources for Exporters

Trade Information Center

Department of Commerce
Washington, DC 20230
(800) 872-8723

Established in the Department of Commerce, the Trade Information Center is the first point of contact for information on U.S. Government programs and activities that support exporting, including:

- Export Counseling
- Seminars and Conferences
- Overseas Buyers and Representatives
- Export Financing
- Technical Assistance.

National Trade Data Bank

U.S. Department of Commerce
(202) 482-1986

Established by the Omnibus Trade and Competitiveness Act of 1988, the NTDB collects in one place the federal government's offerings of information on international trade, export promotion, trade contracts, country profiles, and other international economic data.

Each monthly NTDB disc sells for $35.00, and a 12-month subscription is available for $360.

Country Desk Officers

The key Department of Commerce sources for information on trade potential for U.S. products in specific countries are the International Economic Policy Country Desk Officers. These specialists can identify the needs of an individual firm wishing to sell in a particular country in the full context of that country's economy, trade policies, political situation, and U.S. policies toward that country.

Trade Development Industry Officers

Specialists from over 100 different industries work with manufacturing and service industry associations and firms to identify trade opportunities and obstacles by product or service, industry sector, and market. Industry specialists develop export marketing plans and programs. Call (800) 872-8723.

Trade with Eastern Europe, the Commonwealth of Independent States and Selected Areas

The following offices have been established within the International Trade Administration to respond to the greatly expanded need for business information on new opportunities for trade and investment in selected parts of the world.

Business Information Service for the Newly Independent States
(202) 482-4655

This office handles Armenia, Azerbaijan, Belarus, Georgia, Kazakhstan, Kyrgyzstan, Moldova, Russia, Thaikistan, Turkmenistan, Ukraine, and Uzbekistan, all former Republics of the Soviet Union. These countries, excluding Georgia, make up the Commonwealth of Independent States.

Eastern Europe Business Information Center
(202) 482-2645

The Baltics (Latvia, Lithuania and Estonia) are now considered part of Eastern Europe.

Japan Export Information Center
(202) 482-2425

Latin America/Caribbean Business Dev. Center
(202) 482-0841

Single Internal Market 1992 Information Service
(202) 482-5276

U.S. and Foreign Commercial Service

The US&FCS, a division of the U.S. Department of Commerce, maintains a network of 67 offices in the United States and locations in 66 countries worldwide. Services for U.S. exporters are provided through the Commerce Department District and Branch offices and include:

- Free General Export Support Services include product and/or country information, private counseling by appointment, trade statistics.
- Custom Support Services may include surveys of potential sales representatives; interpreting and secretarial services; office space; market research; single-company promotional events; arranging appointments with local contacts.
- Product promotion (US&FCS will mail company brochures to potential clients and key industry associations).
- Customized Sales Survey (sales potential, competitors, normal sales channels, comparable product prices are all provided in a report on your particular product).
- Foreign Market Research (in-depth market data on selected products and industries, focusing on the best opportunities for U.S. goods).
- Agent/Distributor Service includes contacting potential agents and finally providing a list of six most interested and best-suited contacts for your product.
- Export Contact List Service (company profiles).

Government Resources for Exporters (cont'd)

Commerce Department District Offices

The first stop for companies interested in making use of government programs for export promotion is the nearest Commerce Department District Office, which is part of the U.S. and Foreign Commercial Service. Specialists in these offices help companies assess the export capacity of their products; target markets; locate and check out potential overseas partners; and counsel on the steps involved in exporting.

U.S. & Foreign Commercial Service Overseas Posts

These are the commercial attaches in American embassies and consulates around the world who encourage foreign businesses to buy American products and services.

Contact Options

U.S. and Foreign Commercial Service
Office of Domestic Operations
(202) 482-4767

U.S. and Foreign Commercial Service
Office of International Operations
(202) 482-6228

Country Desk Officers

Country	Desk Officer	Phone
Afghanistan	Tim Gilman	(202) 482-2954
Albania	Lynn Fabrizio/EEBIC	(202) 482-2645
Algeria	Jeffrey Johnson	(202) 482-4652
Angola	Claude Clement	(202) 482-5148
Anguilla	Michelle Brooks	(202) 482-2527
Antigua	Michelle Brooks	(202) 482-2527
Argentina	Randy Mye	(202) 482-1548
Aruba	Michelle Brooks	(202) 482-2527
ASEAN	George Paine	(202) 482-3875
Australia	Gary Bouck	(202) 482-3646
Austria	Philip Combs	(202) 482-2920
Bahamas	Rodrigo Soto	(202) 482-2527
Bahrain	Claude Clement	(202) 482-5545
Baltics Republic	Pam Green	(202) 482-4915
Bangladesh	Cheryl McQueen	(202) 482-2954
Barbados	Michelle Brooks	(202) 482-2527
Barbuda	Michelle Brooks	(202) 482-2527
Belgium	Simon Bensimon	(202) 482-5041
Belize	Michelle Brooks	(202) 482-2527
Bermuda	Michelle Brooks	(202) 482-2527
Bolivia	Laura Zeiger	(202) 482-2521
Botswana	Finn Holm-Olsen	(202) 482-5148
Brazil	Larry Farris	(202) 482-3871
Brunei	Raphael Cung	(202) 482-3875
Bulgaria	Lynn Fabrizio	(202) 482-2645
Burina Faso	Philip Michelini	(202) 482-4388
Burma (Myanmar)	George Paine	(202) 482-3875
Burundi	Debra Henke	(202) 482-4228
Cambodia	Hong-Phong B. Pho	(202) 482-3875
Cameroon	Debra Henke	(202) 482-4228
Canada	Jonathan Don	(202) 482-3101
Cape Verde	Philip Michelini	(202) 482-4388
Caymans	Michelle Brooks	(202) 482-2527
Central Africa Rep.	Debra Henke	(202) 482-4228
Chad	Debra Henke	(202) 482-4228

Government Resources for Exporters (cont'd)

Country	Desk Officer	Phone
Chile	Roger Turner	(202) 482-1495
Colombia	Laurie MacNamara	(202) 482-1659
Comoros	Chandra Watkins	(202) 482-4564
Congo	Debra Henke	(202) 482-4228
Costa Rica	Theodore Johnson	(202) 482-2527
Cuba	Rodrigo Soto	(202) 482-2527
Cyprus	Ann Corro	(202) 482-3945
Czechoslovakia	Mark Mowrey/EEBIC	(202) 482-2645
Denmark	Maryanne Lyons	(202) 482-3254
D'Jibouti	Chandra Watkins	(202) 482-4564
Dominica	Michelle Brooks	(202) 482-2527
Dominican Rep.	Rodrigo Soto	(202) 482-2527
East Caribbean	Michelle Brooks	(202) 482-2527
Ecuador	Laurie McNamara	(202) 482-1659
Egypt	Thomas Sams	(202) 482-4441
El Salvador	Theodore Johnson	(202) 482-2527
Ethiopia	Chandra Watkins	(202) 482-4564
European Community	Charles Ludolph	(202) 482-5276
Finland	Maryanne Lyons	(202) 482-3254
France	Elena Mikalis	(202) 482-8008
Gambia	Philip Michelini	(202) 482-4388
Germany	Brenda Fisherr	(202) 482-2434
Ghana	Debra Henke	(202) 482-4228
Greece	Ann Corro	(202) 482-3945
Grenada	Michelle Brooks	(202) 482-2527
Guatemala	Theodore Johnson	(202) 482-2527
Guinea	Philip Michelini	(202) 482-4388
Guinea-Bissau	Philip Michelini	(202) 482-4388
Guyana	Michelle Brooks	(202) 482-2527
Haiti	Rodrigo Soto	(202) 482-2527
Honduras	Theodore Johnson	(202) 482-2527
Hong Kong	Sheila Baker	(202) 482-3583
Hungary	Brian Toohey	(202) 482-2645
Iceland	Maryanne Lyons	(202) 482-3254
India	John Simmons	(202) 482-2954
Indonesia	Karen Goddin	(202) 482-3875
Iran	Paul Thanos	(202) 482-4652
Iraq	Thomas Sams	(202) 482-4441
Ireland	Boyce Fitzpatrick	(202) 482-2177
Israel	Kate Fitzgerald-Wilks	(202) 482-4652
Italy	Boyce Fitzpatrick	(202) 482-2177
Ivory Coast	Philip Michelini	(202) 482-4388
Jamaica	Rodrigo Soto	(202) 482-2527
Japan	Cantwell Walsh	(202) 482-2425
Jordan	Claude Clement	(202) 482-2515
Kenya	Chandra Watkins	(202) 482-4564
Korea	Jeffrey Donius	(202) 482-4957
Kuwait	Corey Wright	(202) 482-2515
Laos	Hong-Phong B. Pho	(202) 482-3875
Lebanon	Thomas Sams	(202) 482-2515

Government Resources for Exporters (cont'd)

Country	Desk Officer	Phone
Lesotho	Finn Holm-Olsen	(202) 482-5148
Liberia	Reginald Biddle	(202) 482-4388
Libya	Claude Clement	(202) 482-5545
Luxembourg	Simon Bensimon	(202) 482-5401
Macao	Laura McCall	(202) 482-2462
Madagascar	Chandra Watkins	(202) 482-4564
Malawi	Finn Holm-Olsen	(202) 482-5148
Malaysia	Raphael Cung	(202) 482-3875
Maldives	John Simmons	(202) 482-2954
Mali	Philip Michelini	(202) 482-4388
Malta	Robert McLaughlin	(202) 482-3748
Mauritania	Philip Michelini	(202) 482-4564
Mauritius	Chandra Watkins	(202) 482-4564
Mexico	Andrew Lowry	(202) 482-4464
Mongolia	JeNelle Matheson	(202) 482-2462
Montserrat	Michelle Brooks	(202) 482-2527
Namibia	Emily Solomon	(202) 482-5148
Nepal	Tim Gilman	(202) 482-2954
Netherlands	Simon Bensimon	(202) 482-5401
Netherlands Antilles	Michelle Brooks	(202) 482-2527
New Zealand	Gary Bouck	(202) 482-3647
Nicaragua	Theodore Johnson	(202) 482-2527
Niger	Philip Michelini	(202) 482-4388
Nigeria	Debra Henke	(202) 482-4228
Norway	James Devlin	(202) 482-4414
Oman	Kate Fitzgerald-Wilks	(202) 482-4652
Pacific Islands	Gary Bouck	(202) 482-3647
Pakistan	Cheryl McQueen	(202) 482-2954
Panama	Theodore Johnson	(202) 482-2527
Paraguay	Randy Mye	(202) 482-1548
People's Rep. of China	Robert Chu	(202) 482-3583
Peru	Laura Zeiger	(202) 482-2521
Philippines	George Paine	(202) 482-3875
Poland	Audrey Abraham Zuck	(202) 482-2645
Portugal	Mary Beth Double	(202) 482-4508
Puerto Rico	Rodrigo Soto	(202) 482-2527
Qatar	Kate Fitzgerald-Wilks	(202) 482-4652
Romania	Lynn Fabrizio/EEBIC	(202) 482-2645
Russia, CIS	Jack Brougher	(202) 482-4655
Rwanda	Debra Henke	(202) 482-4228
Sao Tome & Principe	Debra Henke	(202) 482-4228
Saudi Arabia	Jeffrey Johnson	(202) 482-4652
Senegal	Philip Michelini	(202) 482-4388
Seychelles	Chandra Watkins	(202) 482-4564
Sierra Leone	Philip Michelini	(202) 482-4388
Singapore	Raphael Cung	(202) 482-3875
Somalia	Chandra Watkins	(202) 482-4564
South Africa	Emily Solomon	(202) 482-5148
Spain	Mary Beth Double	(202) 482-4508
Sri Lanka	John Simmons	(202) 482-2954

Government Resources for Exporters (cont'd)

Country	Desk Officer	Phone
St. Barthelemy	Michelle Brooks	(202) 482-2527
St. Kitts-Nevis	Michelle Brooks	(202) 482-2527
St. Lucia	Michelle Brooks	(202) 482-2527
St. Martin	Michelle Brooks	(202) 482-2527
St. Vincent-Grenadines	Michelle Brooks	(202) 482-2527
Sudan	Chandra Watkins	(202) 482-4564
Suriname	Michelle Brooks	(202) 482-2527
Sweden	James Devlin	(202) 482-4414
Switzerland	Philip Combs	(202) 482-2920
Syria	Corby Wright	(202) 482-2515
Taiwan	Ian Davis	(202) 482-4957
Tanzania	Finn Holm-Olsen	(202) 482-5148
Thailand	Jean Kelly	(202) 482-3875
Togo	Debra Henke	(202) 482-4228
Trinidad & Tobago	Michelle Brooks	(202) 482-2527
Tunisia	Corey Wright	(202) 482-2515
Turkey	Heidi Lamb	(202) 482-5373
Turks & Caicos Islands	Rodrigo Soto	(202) 482-2527
Uganda	Chandra Watkins	(202) 482-4564
United Arab Emirates	Claude Clement	(202) 482-5545
United Kingdom	Robert McLaughlin	(202) 482-3748
Uruguay	Roger Turner	(202) 482-1495
Venezuela	Herbert Lindow	(202) 482-4303
Vietnam	Hong-Phong B. Pho	(202) 482-3875
Virgin Islands (U.K.)	Michelle Brooks	(202) 482-2527
Virgin Islands (U.S.)	Rodrigo Soto	(202) 482-2527
Yemen, Rep. of	Kate Fitzgerald-Wilks	(202) 482-4652
Yugoslavia	Jeremy Keller	(202) 482-2645
Zaire	Debra Henke	(202) 482-4228
Zambia	Finn Holm-Olsen	(202) 482-5148
Zimbabwe	Finn Holm-Olsen	(202) 482-5148

The Top Reference Sources

Exportise
The Small Business Foundation of America, $50
(202) 223-1103

This is a comprehensive source book on international trade for small business managers. It focuses primarily on exporting, but includes an expanded chapter on importing and foreign competition at home.

Topics covered include foreign markets, overseas marketing, channels of distribution, international finance, methods of payment, legal issues, regulations, taxation, and international communications. Also helpful are the country-by-country overviews that describe the potential for exports and list vital statistics.

Government Resources for Exporters (cont'd)

Commerce Department District Offices

State	Phone
Alabama	(205) 731-1331
Alaska	(907) 271-6237
Arizona	(602) 379-3285
Arkansas	(501) 324-5794
California	(310) 575-7105
	(714) 660-1688
	(619) 557-5395
	(415) 705-2300
Colorado	(303) 844-3246
Connecticut	(203) 240-3530
Delaware	(215) 962-4980
Florida	(305) 536-0268
	(813) 461-0011
	(407) 648-6235
	(904) 488-6469
Georgia	(404) 452-9101
	(912) 652-4204
Hawaii	(808) 541-1782
Idaho	(208) 334-3857
Illinois	(312) 353-4450
	(312) 353-4332
	(815) 987-4347
Indiana	(317) 226-6214
Iowa	(515) 284-4222
Kansas	(316) 269-6160
Kentucky	(502) 582 5066
Louisiana	(504) 589-6546
Maine	(207) 622-8249
Maryland	(410) 962 3560
	(301) 975-3904
Massachusetts	(617) 565-8563
Michigan	(313) 226-3650
	(616) 456-2411
Minnesota	(612) 348 1638
Mississippi	(601) 965-4388
Missouri	(314) 425 3302
	(816) 426-3141
Montana	(503) 326-3001
Nebraska	(402) 221-3664
Nevada	(702) 784-5203

State	Phone
New Hampshire	(603) 271-2591
New Jersey	(609) 989-2100
New Mexico	(505) 766-2070
New York	(716) 846-4191
	(716) 263-6480
	(212) 264-0634
North Carolina	(919) 333 5345
North Dakota	(402) 221-3664
Ohio	(513) 684-2944
	(216) 522-4750
Oklahoma	(405) 231-5302
	(918) 581-7650
Oregon	(503) 326-3001
Pennsylvania	(215) 951-7954
	(412) 644-2850
Puerto Rico	(809) 766-5555
Rhode Island	(401) 528-5104
South Carolina	(803) 765-5345
South Dakota	(402) 221-3664
Tennessee	(615) 736-5161
	(615) 549-9268
	(901) 544-4137
Texas	(214) 767-0542
	(512) 482-5939
	(713) 229-2578
Utah	(801) 524-5116
Vermont	(617) 565-8563
Virginia	(804) 771-2246
Washington	(206) 553-5615
West Virginia	(304) 347 5123
Wisconsin	(414) 297-3473
Wyoming	(303) 844-3246

Government Resources for Exporters (cont'd)

U.S. & Foreign Commercial Service Overseas Posts and Officers

Algeria
American Embassy Algiers
Andrew Tangalos
011-213-2-60-18-63
Fax: 011-213-2-60-18-63

Argentina
American Embassy
Buenos Aires
Ralph Fermoselle
011-54-1-773-1063
Fax: 011-54-1-775-6040

Australia
American Consulate General
Sydney
Michael Hand
011-61-2-261-9200
Fax: 011-61-2-261-8148

American Consulate
Brisbane
Keith Sloggett
011-61-7-831-1345
Fax: 011-61-7-832-6247

American Consulate General
Melbourne
Daniel Young
011-61-3-526-5900
Fax: 011-61-3-510-4660

American Consulate General
Perth
Marion Shingler
011-61-9-221-1177
Fax: 011-61-9-325-3569

Austria
American Embassy
Vienna
Benjamin Brown
011-43-222-31-55-11
Fax: 011-43-222-34-12-61

Barbados
American Embassy
Bridgetown
Richard Ades
Miami District Office
(809) 436-4950
Fax: (809) 426-2275

Belgium
American Embassy
Brussels
Jerry Mitchell
011-32-2-513-3830
Fax: 011-32-2-512-6653

Brussels
U.S. Mission to the European Communities
James Blow
011-32-2-513-3830
Fax: 011-32-2-513-1228

Brazil
American Embassy
Brasilia
Kevin Brennan
011-55-61-223-0120
Fax: 011-55-61-225-3981

American Consular Agency
Belem
Raymundo Teixiera
011-55-91-223-0800
Fax: 011-55-91-223-0413

American Consular Agency
Belo Horizonte
Jose Mauricio De Vasconcelos
011-55-31-335-3250
Fax: 011-55-31-335-3054

American Consulate General
Rio De Janeiro
Walter Hage
011-55-21-292-7117
Fax: 011-55-21-240-9738

American Consulate General
São Paulo
Arthur Alexander
011-55-11-853-2011
Fax: 011-55-11-853-2744

Cameroon
American Consulate
Douala
Jean Sumo
011-237-425-331
Fax: 011-237-427-790

Canada
American Embassy
Ottawa
Robert Marro
1-613-238-5335
Fax:1-613-233-8511

American Consulate General
Calgary
Randall Labounty
1-403-265-2116
Fax: 1-403-264-6630

American Consulate General
Halifax
Richard Vinson
1-902-429-2482
Fax: 1-902-423-6861

Government Resources for Exporters (cont'd)

American Consulate General
Montreal
Geoffrey Walser
1-514-398-9695
Fax: 1-514-398-0711

American Consulate General
Toronto
Dan Wilson
1-416-595-5413
Fax: 1-416-595-5419

American Consulate General
Vancouver
Stephen Wasylko
1-604-685-3382
Fax: 1-604-685-5285

Chile
American Embassy
Santiago
Ricardo Villalobos
011-56-2-671-0133
Fax: 011-56-2-697-2051

China
American Embassy
Beijing
Tim Stratford
011-86-1-532-3831
Fax: 011-86-1-532-3297

American Consulate General
Guangzhou
Dennis Barnes
011-86-20-677-842
Fax: 011-86-20-666-409

American Consulate General
Shanghai
Nora Sun
011-86-21-433-2492
Fax: 011-86-21-433-1576

American Consulate General
Shenyang
(Vacant)
011-86-24-220-057
Fax: 011-86-24-290-074

Colombia
American Embassy
Bogota
Arthur Trezise
011-57-1-232-6550
Fax: 011-57-1-285-7945

Costa Rica
American Embassy
San Jose
Judith Henderson
011-506-20-3939
Fax: 011-506-31-4783

Cote D'ivoire
American Embassy
Abidjan
Catherine Houghton
011-225-21-4616
Fax: 011-225-22-3259

Czech Republic
American Embassy
Prague
Dan Harris
011-42-2-532-470
Fax: 011-42-2-532-457 Or

Denmark
American Embassy
Copenhagen
Stephen Helgesen
011-45-31-42-31-44
Fax: 011-45-31-42-01-75

Dominican Republic
American Embassy
Santo Domingo
Richard Ades
Miami District Office
(809) 541-2171
Fax: (809)-688-4838

Ecuador
American Embassy
Quito
Jere Dabbs
011-593-2-561-404
Fax: 011-593-2-504-550

American Consulate General
Guayaquit
Francivon Buc
011-593-4-323-570
Fax: 011-593-4-324-558

Egypt
American Embassy
Cairo
Norman Glick
011-20-2-354-1583
Fax: 011-20-2-355-8368

American Consulate General
Alexandria
Hanna Abdelnour
011-20-3-482-1911
Fax: 011-20-3-482-9199

Finland
American Embassy
Helsinki
Maria Andrews
011-358-0-171-821
Fax: 011-358-0-635-332

Government Resources for Exporters (cont'd)

France
American Embassy
Paris
Peter Frederick
011-33-1-4296-1202
Fax: 011-33-1-4266-4827

U.S. Mission to the OECD
Paris
Robyn Layton
011-33-1-4524-7437
Fax: 011-33-1-4524-7410

American Consulate General
Bordeaux
Valeria DeRousseau
011-33-56-526-595
Fax: 011-33-56-51-60-42

American Consulate General
Lyon
Alain Beullard
011-33-72-40-59-20
Fax:011-33-72-41-71-81

American Consulate General
Marseille
Igor Lepine
011-33-91-54-92-00
Fax: 011-33-91-550-947

U.S. Commercial Office
Nice
Reine Joguet
011-33-93-88-89-55
Fax: 011-33-93-87-07-38

American Consulate General
Strasbourg
Jacqueline Munzlinger
011-33-88-35-31-04
Fax: 011-33-88-24-06-95

Germany
American Embassy
Bonn
John Bligh
011-49-228-339-2895
Fax: 011-49-228-334-649

American Embassy Office
Berlin
James Joy
011-49-30-251-2061
Fax: 011-49-30-238-6296

U.S. Commercial Office
Duesseldorf
Barbara Ernst
011-49-211-596-798
Fax: 011-49-211-594-897

American Consulate General
Frankfurt
Donald Businger
011-49-69-7535-2453
Fax: 011-49-69-748-204

Amercian Consulate General
Hamburg
Hans Amrhein
011-49-40-4117-1304
Fax: 011-49-40-410-6598

American Consulate General
Leipzig
B. Lehne
011-37-41-211-7866
Fax: 011-37-41-211-7865

American Consulate General
Munich
Edward Ruse
011-49-89-2888-748
Fax: 011-49-89-285-261

American Consulate General
Stuttgart
Camille Sailer
011-49-711-214-5238
Fax: 011-49-711-236-4350

Greece
American Embassy
Athens
John Priamou
011-30-1-723-9705
Fax: 011-30-1-721-8660

Guatemala
American Embassy
Guatemala
Henry Nichol
011-502-2-348-479
Fax: 011-502-2-317-373

Honduras
American Embassy
Tegucigalpa
Eric Weaver
011-504-32-3120
Fax: 011-504-38-2888

Hong Kong
American Consulate General
Hong Kong
Lee Boam
011-852-521-1467
Fax: 011-852-845-9800

Government Resources for Exporters (cont'd)

Hungary
American Embassy
Budapest
Gary Gallagher
011-36-1-122-8600
Fax: 011-36-1-142-2529

India
American Embassy
New Delhi
John Bensky
011-91-11-600-651
Fax: 011-91-11-687-2391

American Consulate General
Bombay
John Wood
011-91-22-262-4590
Fax: 011-91-22-262-3851

American Consulate General
Calcutta
Nargiz Chatterjee
011-91-33-22-3611
Fax: 011-91-33-225-994

American Consulate General
Madras
Rajendra Dheer
011-91-44-475-947
Fax: 011-91-44-825-0240

Indonesia
American Embassy
Jakarta
Theodore Villinski
011-62-21-360-360
Fax: 011-62-21-385-1632

American Consulate General
Medan
Zulhava Luthfi
011-62-61-322-200
Fax: N/A

American Consulate General
Surabaya
Midji Kwee
011-62-31-67100
Fax: N/A

Ireland
American Embassy
Dublin
Gene Harris
011-353-1-687-122
Fax: 011-353-1-687-840

Israel
American Embassy
Tel Aviv
Judith Henderson
011-972-3-517-4338
Fax: 011-972-3-658-033

Italy
American Embassy
Rome
Keith Bovetti
011-39-6-4674-2202
Fax: 011-39-6-4674-2113

American Consulate General
Florence
Allessandra Gola
011-39-55-211-676
Fax: 011-39-55-283-780

American Consulate General
Genoa
Erminia Lezzi
011-39-10-247-1412
Fax: 011-39-10-290-027

American Consulate General
Milan
Peter Alois
011-39-2-498-2241
Fax: 011-39-2-481-4161

American Consulate General
Naples
Christiano Sartario
011-39-81-761-1592
Fax: 011-39-81-761-1869

Jamaica
American Embassy
Kingston
Larry Eisenberg
Miami District Office
(809) 928-4850
Fax: 1-809-926-6743

Japan
American Embassy
Tokyo
George Mu
011-81-3-3224-5000
Fax: 011-81-3-3589-4235

American Consulate
Fukuoka
Yoshihiro Yamamoto
011-81-92-751-9331
Fax: 011-81-92-713-922

Representative Office
Nagoya
Todd Thurwachter
011-81-52-203-4011
Fax: 011-81-52-201-4612

American Consulate General
Osaka-Kobe
Patrick Santillo
011-81-6-315-5957
Fax: 011-81-6-361-5978

Government Resources for Exporters (cont'd)

American Consulate General
Sapporo
Kenji Itaya
011-81-11-641-1117
Fax: 011-81-11-641-0911

Kenya
American Embassy
Nairobi
Richard Benson
011-254-2-334-141
Fax: 011-254-2-216-648

Korea
American Embassy
Seoul
Robert Connan
011-82-2-732-2601
Fax: 011-82-2-739-1628

Kuwait
American Embassy
Kuwait
William Yarmy
011-965-242-4151, Or 244-8073
Fax: 011-965-244-7692

Malaysia
American Embassy
Kuala Lumpur
Paul Walters
011-60-3-248-9011
Fax: 011-60-3-242-1866

Mexico
American Embassy
Mexico City
Roger Wallace
011-52-5-211-0042
Fax: 011-52-5-207-8938

American Consulate General
Guadalajara
Americo Tadeu
011-52-36-25-0321
Fax: 011-52-536-26-3576

American Consulate General
Monterrey
Dawn Cooper-Bahar
011-52-83-452-120
Fax: 011-52-83-42-5172

Morocco
American Consulate General
Casablanca
Sam Starrett
011-212-26-45-50
Fax: 011-212-22-02-59

American Embassy
Rabat
Asma Benghhalem
011-212-7-622-65
Fax: 011-212-7-656-61

Netherlands
American Embassy
The Hague
Michael Hegedus
011-31-70-310-9417
Fax: 011-31-70-363-2985

American Consulate General
Amsterdam
Bert Engelhardt
011-31-20-664-5661
Fax: 011-31-20-675-2856

New Zealand
American Consulate General
Auckland
Babette Orr
011-64-9-303-2038
Fax: 011-64-9-366-0870

American Consulate General
Wellington
Janet Coulthart
011-64-4-722-068
Fax: 011-64-4-781-701

Nigeria
American Embassy
Lagos
Frederic Gaynor
011-234-1-616-477
Fax: 011-234-1-619-856

American Consulate General
Kaduna
Mathias Mgbeze
011-234-62-201-070

Norway
American Embassy
Oslo
Scott Bozek
011-47-2-44-85-50
Fax: 011-47-2-55-88-03

Pakistan
American Consulate General
Karachi
Daniel DeVito
011-92-21-568-5170
Fax: 011-92-21-568-1381

Government Resources for Exporters (cont'd)

American Consulate General
Lahore
Shalla Malik
011-92-42-365-530
Fax: 011-92-42-368-901

Panama
American Embassy
Panama
Peter Noble
011-507-27-1777
Fax: 011-507-27-1713

Peru
American Embassy
Lima
Richard Lenahan
011-51-14-33-0555
Fax: 011-51-14-33-4687

Philippines
American Embassy
Manila
Jonathan Bensky
011-63-2-818-6674
Fax: 011-63-2-818-2684

Poland
American Embassy
Warsaw
Joan Edwards
011-48-22-21-45-15
Fax: 011-48-22-21-63-27

Portugal
American Embassy
Lisbon
Miguel Pardo De Zela
011-351-1-726-6600
Fax: 011-351-1-726-8914

American Consulate
Oporto
Adolfo Coutinho
011-351-2-63094
Fax: 011-351-2-600-2737

Romania
American Embassy
Bucharest
Kay Kuhlman
011-40-0-10-40-40
Fax: 011-40-0-120-395

Saudi Arabia
American Embassy
Riyadh
Kevin Brennan
011-966-1-488-3800
Fax: 011-966-1-488-3237

American Consulate General
Dhahran
Thomas Moore
011-966-3-891-3200
Fax: 011-966-3-891-8332

American Consulate General
Jeddah
Renato Davia
011-966-2-667-0040
Fax: 011-966-2-665-8106

Singapore
American Embassy
George Ruffner
011-65-338-9722
Fax: 011-65-338-5010

Slovenia and *Croatia*
Zagreb
Economic and Commercial Officer
Timothy Arnts
011-38-41-444-800
011-38-41-440-235

Slovakia
American Embassy
Bratislava
Chris Sandrolini
011-42-7-330-861
Fax: 011-42-7-335-439

South Africa
American Consulate General
Johannesburg
George Kachmar
011-27-11-331-3937
Fax: 011-27-11-331-6178

American Consulate General
Cape Town
Sylvia Frowde
011-27-21-21-4280
Fax: 011-27-21-254-151

Spain
American Embassy
Madrid
Robert Kohn
011-34-1-577-4000
Fax: 011-34-1-575-8655

American Consulate General
Barcelona
Ralph Griffin
011-34-3-310-0442
Fax: 011-34-3-319-5621

Government Resources for Exporters (cont'd)

Sweden
American Embassy
Stockholm
Harrison Sherwood
011-46-8-783-5346
Fax: 011-46-8-660-9181

Switzerland
American Embassy
Bern
Kay Kuhlman
011-41-31-43-73-41
Fax: 011-41-31-43-73-36

U.S. Mission to GATT
Geneva
Andrew Grossman
011-41-22-749-5281
Fax: 011-41-22-749-4885

American Consulate General
Zurich
Paul Frei
011-41-1-552-070
Fax: 011-41-1-383-9814

Thailand
American Embassy
Bangkok
Herbert Cochran
011-66-2-251-4920
Fax: 011-66-2-255, 2915

Trinidad and *Tobago*
American Embassy
Port of Spain
Richard Ades
Miami District Office
1-809-622-6371
Fax: 1-809-622-9583

Turkey
American Embassy
Ankara
Dave Katz
011-90-4-467-0949
Fax: 011-90-4-467-1366

American Consulate General
Istanbul
Russell Smith
011-90-1-251-1651
Fax: 011-90-1-152-2417

American Consulate General
izmir
Berrin Erturk
011-90-51-849-426
Fax: 011-90-51-830-493

United Arab Emirates
American Consulate General
Dubai
Paul Scogna
011-971-4-378-584
Fax: 011-971-4-375-121

American Embassy
Abu Dhabi
Sam Dhir
011-971-2-345-545
Fax: 011-971-2-331-374

United Kingdom
American Embassy
London
Kenneth Moorefield
011-44-71-499-9000
Fax: 011-44-71-491-4022

Russia
American Embassy
Moscow
Dale Slaght
011-7-502-224-1106
Fax: 011-7-502-224-1105

American Consulate General
St. Petersburg
Karen Zens
011-7-812-274-8235
Fax: N/A

Venezuela
American Embassy
Caracas
Edgar Fulton
011-58-2-285-2222
Fax: 011-58-2-285-0336

Locating Foreign Embassies in the U.S.

Most foreign embassies are located in Washington, DC. Those that are not are located in New York. They are:
Bulgaria
Congo
Estonia
Guinea-Bissau
Seychelles
Western Samoa

If you need to contact an embassy directly, call (202) 555-1212 and obtain phone numbers of interest. Many countries maintain consulates and offices in other cities throughout the U.S. Before contacting an embassy, it is probably a good idea to check with a Commerce Department District Office for information on locating the appropriate foreign office.

Export Financing Assistance

Export-Import Bank of the United States

Eximbank is an independent U.S. government agency with the primary purpose of facilitating the export of U.S. goods and services. Eximbank meets this objective by providing loans, guarantees, and insurance coverage to U.S. exporters and foreign buyers, normally on market-related credit terms.

Eximbank's insurance and guarantee programs encourage private financial institutions to fund U.S. exports by reducing the commercial and political risks exporters face. The financing made available under Eximbank's guarantees and insurance is generally on market terms, and most of the commercial and political risks are borne by Eximbank.

Eximbank's loan program is structured to neutralize interest rate subsidies offered by foreign governments. By responding with its own subsidized loan assistance, Eximbank enables U.S. financing to be competitive with that offered by foreign exporters.

Contact Option

Export-Import Bank
Marketing and Program Division
811 Vermont Ave., NW
Washington, DC 20571
(800) 424-5201

The Overseas Private Investment Corporation

The Overseas Private Investment Corporation (OPIC) is a U.S. government agency that provides project financing, investment insurance, and a variety of investor services in more than 130 developing nations and emerging economies throughout the world. OPIC assists U.S. investors through three principal programs:

- Financing of investments through direct loans and loan guarantees;
- Insuring investment projects against a broad range of political risks;
- Providing investor services including advisory services, country and regional information, computer assisted project/investor matching, investment missions, and outreach.

Contact Option

Overseas Private Investment Corporation
1100 New York Ave., NW
Washington, DC 20537
(800) 424-6742
(202) 457-7010

Department of Agriculture

The Foreign Agriculture Service of the Department of Agriculture administers several programs to make U.S. exporters competitive in international markets and make U.S. products affordable to countries that have greater need than they have ability to pay. The Export Credit Guarantee program offers risk protection for U.S. exporters against non-payment by foreign banks.

Contact Option

Foreign Agricultural Service
Export Credits
14th St. and Independence Ave., SW
Washington, DC 20250
(202) 447-3224

State and Local Export Finance Programs

Several states and cities have export financing programs. To be eligible for assistance, an export sale must generally be made under a letter of credit or with credit insurance coverage. A certain percentage of state or local content may also be required. Some programs may require only that certain facilities, such as a state or local port, be used. Exporters should contact a Department of Commerce district office or state economic development agency for more information.

Private Export Funding Corporation

The Private Export Funding Corporation (PEFCO) is owned by more than five-dozen investors, primarily commercial banks. PEFCO supplements the financing activities of commercial banks and Eximbank, lending only to finance the export of goods and services of U.S. manufacture and origin. PEFCO loans normally mature in the medium-term (181 days to five years), and all are unconditionally guaranteed by Eximbank with regard to payment of interest and repayment of principal.

Contact Option

PEFCO
280 Park Ave.
New York, NY 10017
(212) 557-3100

Export Assistance from the SBA

U.S. Small Business Administration

The Small Business Administration is also involved in encouraging and supporting export activities of small businesses. Companies eligible for SBA programs include manufacturers with a maximum of 1,500 employees; wholesalers with maximum annual sales of $9.5 million; and service companies with maximum average annual sales for the past three years of $2 million.

Specific Programs

Management:

- Counseling by volunteers with international trade experience;
- Counseling through Small Business Development Center Programs;
- Referral to other public or private sector organizations offering more in-depth international trade programs and services;
- International trade and export marketing publications;
- Business management training.

Financial:

- Pre-export financing of supply purchases, inventories, materials, and working capital needed for manufacture of export goods and for financing shipping costs, and receivable collection on exports;
- Activities to develop foreign markets, professional marketing advisors and services, foreign business travel, participation in trade shows, and other promotions overseas.

Other:

- Joint programs with the Commerce Department's International Trade Administration, the National Oceanic and Atmospheric Administration, and the Department of Agriculture.

Contact Option

Small Business Administration
(800) 827-5722

Small Business Administration Regional Offices

60 Batterymarch Street
Boston, MA 02110
(617) 565-5590

26 Federal Plaza
New York, NY 10007
(212) 972-5270

231 St. Asaphs Rd.
Bala Cynwyd, PA 19004
(215) 962-3700

1375 Peachtree St., NE
Atlanta GA 30309
(404) 347-2441

219 S. Dearborn St.
Chicago, IL 60604
(312) 353-5000

1720 Regal Rd.
Dallas, TX 75235
(214) 767-7629

911 Walnut St.
Kansas City, MO 64106
(816) 426-3316

1405 Curtis St.
Denver, CO 60202
(303) 294-7186

450 Golden Gate Ave.
San Francisco, CA 94102
(415) 744-6820

710 Second Ave.
Seattle, WA 98104
(206) 220-6500

Small Business Development Centers

Funded jointly by the Small Business Administration and private agencies, SBDCs also provide assistance in the area of international trade, including:

- Joint ventures/license programs
- Assistance with overseas trade shows
- Packaging international trade finance loans, language training
- Translation services.

Alabama
Alabama International Trade Center
University of Alabama at Birmingham
400 North Martha Parham
Tuscaloosa, AL 35487
(205) 348-7621

Export Assistance from the SBA (cont'd)

California
Export Small Business Dev. Center
110 E. Ninth St., Suite A761
Los Angeles, CA 90079
(213) 892-1111 or (800) 371-1110

Export Small Business Development
Center Satellite
300 Esplanade Dr., Suite 1020
Oxnard, CA 93030
(805) 981-4633

Florida
Florida Atlantic University
P.O. Box 3091
Boca Raton, FL 33431
(407) 338-2273

Small Business Development Center
University of Central Florida
P.O. Box 2500 Building Ceba II
Orlando, FL 32816
(407) 823-5554

University of West Florida
College of Business, Bldg. 8
Pensacola, FL 33251
(904) 474-2908

Georgia
International Trade Development Center
University of Georgia
Chicopee Complex
1180 E. Broad St.
Athens, GA 30602
(404) 542-5760

Small Business Development Center
Kennesaw College
P.O. Box 444
Marietta, GA 30061
(404) 423-6450

Small Business Development Center
Clayton State College
P.O. Box 285
Morrow, GA 30260
(404) 961-3440

Illinois
Illinois World Trade Center Chicago
321 N. Clark St., Suite 550
Chicago, IL 60610
(312) 467-0550

International Trade Center
Bradley University, Lovelace Hall
Peoria, IL 61625
(309) 677-3075

Louisiana
Louisiana International Trade Center
University of New Orleans
368 Business Administration
New Orleans, LA 70148
(504) 286-6978

Maine
Small Business Development Center
University of Southern Maine
96 Falmouth St.
Portland, ME 04103
(207) 780-4420

Massachusetts
Small Business Development Center
University of Massachusetts
Amherst, MA 01003
(413) 545-5580

Michigan
Center for International Business Dev.
Michigan State University
6 Kellogg Center
East Lansing, MI 48824
(517) 353-4336

Mississippi
Small Business Development Center
International Trade Center
Millsaps College
Jackson, MS 39210
(601) 354-5201, ext. 407

New York
Small Business Development Center
State University College at Buffalo
1300 Elmwood Ave.
Buffalo, NY 14222
(716) 878-4030

Small Business Development Center
Rockland Community College
145 College Rd.
Suffern, NY 10901
(914) 356-0381

Ohio
Small Business Development Center
Lake County Economic Dev. Center
Lakeland Community College
Mentor, OH 44080
(216) 951-1290

Small Business Development Center
218 N. Huron St.
Toledo, OH 43604
(419) 243-8191

Export Assistance from the SBA (cont'd)

Oklahoma
Small Business Development Center
Rose State College
6420 Southeast 15th
Midwest City, OK 73110
(405) 733-7348

Oregon
Small Business Development Center
Portland Community College
One World Trade Center
121 SW Salmon St., Suite 210
Portland, OR 97204
(503) 274-7482

Pennsylvania
Small Business Development Center
Lehigh University
International Trade Center
301 Broadway
Bethlehem, PA 18015
(215) 758-3930

Small Business Development Center
Gannon University
Carlisle Building, 3rd Floor
Erie, PA 16541
(814) 871-7714

Small Business Development Center
Pennyslvania State University at Harrisburg
Crags Building
Route 230
Middletown, PA 17057
(717) 948-6069

Wharton School of Business
University of Pennsylvania
Vance Hall, 4th Floor
Philadelphia, PA 19104
(215) 898-4861

Small Business Development Center
Duquesne University
Rockwell Hall, Room 10 Concourse
600 Forbes Ave.
Pittsburgh, PA 15282
(412) 434-6233

Rhode Island
Small Business Development Center
Bryant College
450 Douglas Pike
Smithfield, RI 02917
(401) 232-6407

Tennessee
Small Business Development Center
International Trade Center
Memphis State University
Memphis, TN 38152
(901) 678-2500

Texas
North Texas Small Business
Development Center
International Trade Resource Center
2050 Stemmons Freeway, Suite 150
Dallas, TX 75258
(214) 653-1777

Small Business Development Center
University of Houston
601 Jefferson St., Suite 2330
Houston, TX 77002
(713) 752-8404

South Texas Border Small Business
Development Center
University of Texas at San Antonio
San Antonio, TX 78285
(512) 224-0791

Washington
International Trade Institute
North Seattle Community College
9600 College Way North
Seattle, WA 98103
(206) 527-3732

The Top Reference Sources

The Henry Holt International Desk Reference
Henry Holt, $39.95
(212) 886-9200

Organized by geographical region and by country, this reference provides up-to-date information on the global community.

Each country listing is divided into sections such as agriculture, banking, business development, consultants and advisors, imports and exports, laws, politics, sales agents, social agents, and tourism.

The entries are highly annotated, with descriptions of services, addresses, telephone numbers, and background information.

Organizations Focusing on Trade

THE FOLLOWING PRIVATE ORGANIZATIONS and associations are useful contacts for trade and export issues.

United States Council for International Business
1212 Avenue of the Americas
New York, NY 10036
(212) 354-4480

The Council is the official U.S. affiliate of the International Chamber of Commerce. In addition to addressing policy issues, the Council and the ICC provide a number of programs available for members:

- Court of Arbitration
- International Environmental Bureau
- Counterfeiting Intelligence Bureau
- Institute of International Business Law and Practice.

American Association for Exporters and Importers
11 W. 42nd St., 30th Floor,
New York, NY 10036
(212) 944-2230
Trade association

Committee for Small Business Exports
P.O. Box 6
Aspen, CO 81612
(303) 925-7567

Federation of International Trade Associations
1851 Alexander Bell Dr.
Reston, VA 22091
(703) 391-6108

International Trade Facilitation Council
350 Broadway, Suite 205
New York, NY 10013
(212) 925-1400

Helps importers and exporters to simplify the procedures and paperwork associated with world trade.

International Trade Council
3144 Circle Hill Rd.
Alexandria, VA 22305
(703) 548-1234

Conducts research and offers educational programs on topics such as market conditions abroad, transportation costs, and trade regulations.

National Foreign Trade Council
1625 K St., NW
Washington, DC 20006
(202) 887-0278

Trade association that deals exclusively with U.S. public policy affecting international trade and investment. Members are companies with substantial international operations or interests.

World Trade Centers

HEADQUARTERED IN NEW YORK, the World Trade Centers Association includes 241 affiliated organizations in 60 countries with a total membership of over 400,000 companies worldwide. World Trade Centers provide one-stop shopping in a region for international trade. The World Trade buildings usually house freight forwarders, customs brokers, international companies, and government agencies. Additional services include:

- Office space for the international trading community;
- Information and trade research services;
- Consumer/business services (hotels, restaurants, banks);
- Educational services (seminars, language training).

Contact Option

World Trade Centers Association
(212) 432-2626

World Trade Centers

Alaska
World Trade Center
University of Alaska Anchorage
WTC Building
4201 Tudor Centre Dr., Suite 320
Anchorage, AK 99508
(907) 561-1615
Fax: (907) 561-1541

Arizona
World Trade Center–Phoenix
34 W. Monroe, Suite 900
Phoenix, AZ 85003
(602) 495-6480
Fax: (602) 495-8913

California
World Trade Center–Irvine
1 Park Plaza, Suite 150
Irvine, CA 92714
(714) 724-9822
Fax: (714) 752-8723

World Trade Centers (cont'd)

Greater Los Angeles World Trade Center
One World Trade Center, Suite 295
Long Beach, CA 90831
(310) 495-7070
Fax: (310) 495-7071

Los Angeles World Trade Center
350 S. Figueroa St., Suite 172
Los Angeles, CA 90071
(310) 680-1888
Fax: (310) 680-1878

World Trade Center–San Francisco
110 Sutter St., Suite 408
San Francisco, CA 94104
(415) 392-2705
Fax: (415) 392-1710

Colorado
Colorado Springs World Trade Center
P.O. Box 6539
Colorado Springs, CO 80934
(719) 633-9041

World Trade Center–Denver
1625 Broadway, Suite 680
Denver, CO 80202
(303) 592-5760
Fax: (303) 892-3820

Connecticut
World Trade Center–Bridgeport
360 Fairfield Ave.
Bridgeport, CT 06604
(203) 336-5353
Fax: (203) 331-9959

Delaware
World Trade Center–Delaware
1207 King St., P.O. Box 709
Wilmington, DE 19899
(362) 656-7905
Fax: (302) 656-1620

Florida
World Trade Center of San Jose, Costa Rica
1515 S. Federal Hwy., Suite 211
Boca Raton, FL 33432
(407) 394-9033
Fax: (407) 394-9094

World Trade Center
1100 Lee Wagener Blvd., P.O. Box 13065
Ft. Lauderdale International Airport
Fort Lauderdale, FL 33315
(305) 359-3615
Fax: (305) 359-0277

World Trade Center Association
3 Independent Dr.
Jacksonville, FL 32202
(904) 366-6646
Fax: (904) 632-0617

World Trade Center–Miami
One World Trade Plaza, Suite 1800; 800 SW 8th St.
Miami, FL 33130
(305) 579-0064
Fax: (305) 536-7701

World Trade Center–Orlando
201 S. Orange Ave., Suite 901
Orlando, FL 32801
(407) 649-1899
Fax: (407) 649-1486

World Trade Center–Tampa Bay
800 Second Ave. S., Suite 340
St. Petersburg, FL 33701
(813) 822-2492
Fax: (813) 823-8129

Georgia
World Trade Center–Atlanta
240 Peachtree St., NE, Suite 2200
Atlanta, GA 30303
(404) 525-4144
Fax: (404) 220-3030

Hawaii
International Business Center–Hawaii
201 Merchant St., Suite 1510 Box 2359
Honolulu, HI 96804
(808) 587-2797
Fax: (808) 587-2790

World Trade Center–Honolulu
521 Ala Moana Blvd., Suite 110
Honolulu, HI 96813
(808) 599-3969
Fax: (808) 537-4488

Illinois
Illinois World Trade Center–Chicago
321 N. Clark St., Suite 550
Chicago, IL 60610
(312) 467-0550
Fax: (312) 467-0615

Indiana
World Trade Center–Indianapolis
3905 Vincennes Rd., Suite 504
Indianapolis, IN 46268
(317) 871-6807
Fax: (317) 876-3905

Iowa
Cedar Rapids World Trade Center
312 8th St., Suite 200
Des Moines, IA 50309
(515) 246-6000
Fax: (515) 246-6014

Iowa Dept. of Economic Development
Div. of Community & Rural Development
200 E. Grand Ave.

World Trade Centers (cont'd)

Des Moines, IA 50309
(515) 242-4728
Fax: (515) 242-4859

Iowa World Trade Center
3200 Ruan Center
666 Grand Ave.
Des Moines, IA 50309
(515) 245-2555
Fax: (515) 245-3878

Kansas
World Trade Center–Wichita
301 North Main, Suite 1860
Wichita, KS 67202
(316) 262-3232
Fax: (316) 262-3585

Kentucky
World Trade Center–Lexington
410 W. Vine St., Suite 290
Lexington, KY 40507
(606) 258-3139
Fax: (606) 233-0658

Louisiana
World Trade Center–New Orleans
2 Canal St., Suite 2900
New Orleans, LA 70130
(504) 529-1601
Fax: (504) 529-1691

Maryland
The World Trade Center–Baltimore
401 E. Pratt St., Suite 1355
Baltimore, MD
(301) 576-0022
Fax: (301) 576-0751

Massachusetts
World Trade Center–Boston
Executive Offices, Suite 50
Boston, MA 02210
(617) 439-5001
Fax: (617) 439-5033

Michigan
World Trade Center–Detroit/Windsor
1000 Buhl Bldg.
Detroit, MI 48226
(313) 965-6500
Fax: (313) 965-1525

Minnesota
Minnesota World Trade Center #400
30 East 7th St.
St. Paul, MN 55101
(612) 297-1580
Fax: (612) 297-4812

Missouri
Greater Kansas City World Trade Center
920 Main St., Suite 600
Kansas City, MO 64105
(816) 221-2424
Fax: (816) 221-7440

World Trade Center–St. Louis
St. Louis County Economic Council
121 S. Meramec, Suite 412
St. Louis, MO 63105
(314) 889-7663
Fax: (314) 889-7666

Nevada
Nevada World Trade Center
6330 S. Eastern Ave., Suite 7
Las Vegas, NV 89119
(702) 795-8487

New York
Buffalo World Trade Center
Triple Vision Group
5340 Goodrich Rd.
Buffalo, NY 14031
(716) 741-4101
Fax:(716) 833-1342

World Trade Center–New York
The Port Authority of New York and New Jersey
One World Trade Center, 35 E.
New York, NY 10048
(212) 435-2329
Fax: (212) 435-2810

World Trade Center–Schenectady-Capital District
One Broadway Center, Suite 750
Schenectady, NY 12305
(518) 377-4904
Fax: (518) 377-0085

North Carolina
World Trade Center–Charlotte
Box 220814
Charlotte, NC 28222
(704) 335-0000
Fax: (704) 332-3464

World Trade Center–Piedmont Triad
Piedmont Triad Airport Authority, P.O. Box 35005
Greensboro, NC 27425
(919) 665-5600
Fax: (919) 668-3749

The Research Triangle World Trade Center
P.O. Box 13487
Research Triangle Park, NC 27709
(919) 544-8969
Fax: (919) 544-8970

World Trade Center–Wilmington
Greater Wilmington Chamber of Commerce
P.O. Box 330
Wilmington, NC 28402
(919) 762-3525
Fax: (919) 762-9765

World Trade Centers (cont'd)

Ohio
World Trade Center–Columbus
International Trade Dev. Office
37 N. High St.
Columbus, OH 43215
(614) 225-6951
Fax: (614) 469-8250

Toledo World Trade Center
828 Prouty St.
Toledo, OH 43609
(419) 255-7226
Fax: (419) 255-7227

Oregon
World Trade Center–Portland
One World Trade Center, Suite 250
121 Southwest Salmon St.
Portland, OR 97204
(503) 464-8888
Fax: (503) 464-8880

Pennsylvania
Greater Philadelphia WTC and Financial Center
Carl Marks & Co.
135 East 57th St., 27th Floor
New York, NY 10022
(212) 909-8400
Fax: (212) 980-2631

World Trade Center–Pittsburgh
441 Smithfield St., 2nd Floor
Pittsburgh, PA 15222
(412) 355-4344
Fax: (412) 471-1032

Rhode Island
World Trade Center–Rhode Island
Bryant College
P.O. Box 61
Smithfield, RI 02917
(401) 232-6400
Fax: (401) 232-6319

South Carolina
South Carolina World Trade Center
Charleston Trident Chamber of Commerce
81 Mary St., P.O. Box 975
Charleston, SC 29402
(803) 577-2510 Ext. 3055
Fax: (803) 723-8353

The Greenville-Spartanburg World Trade Center
The Jenkins Companies
315 Old Boiling Springs Rd.
Greer, SC 29650
(803) 297-8600
Fax: (803) 297-8606

Tennessee
World Trade Center–Chattanooga
1001 Market St.
Chattanooga, TN 37402
(615) 752-4316
Fax: (615) 752-4322

Texas
The Alliance World Trade Center–Ft.Worth/Dallas
12377 Merit Dr., Suite 1700
Dallas, TX 75251
(214) 788-3050
Fax: (214) 788-3097

Houston World Trade Association
1100 Milan, 25th Floor
Houston, TX 77002
(713) 658-2401
Fax: (713) 658-2429

World Trade Center Rio Grande Valley at McAllen
One Park Place, Suite 670
McAllen, TX 78503
(512) 686-1982
Fax: (512) 618-1982

World Trade Center–San Antonio
118 Broadway, Suite 621
San Antonio, TX 78205
(512) 978-7601
Fax: (512) 978-7610

Virginia
World Trade Center–Washington, DC
One Prince St.
Alexandria, Va. 22314
(703) 684-6630
Fax: (703) 684-2918

Washington
Seattle World Trade Center
1201 Third Ave., Suite 1700
Seattle, WA 98101
(206) 224-7450
Fax: (206) 224-7464

World Trade Center–Tacoma
3600 Port of Tacoma Rd., Suite 309
Tacoma, WA 98424
(206) 383-9474
Fax: (206) 926-0384

Wisconsin
Wisconsin World Trade Center–Madison
8401 Greenway Blvd.
Middleton, WI 53562
(608) 831-0666
Fax: (608) 831-6982

Wisconsin
WTC at Milwaukee Pfister Hotel
424 E. Wisconsin Ave.
Milwaukee, WI 53202
(414) 274-3840
Fax: (414) 274-3846

State International Trade Contacts

State	Phone
Alabama	(205) 242-0400
Alaska	(907) 561-5585
Arizona	(602) 280-1371
Arkansas	(501) 682-7690
California	(916) 324-5511
Colorado	(303) 892-3856
Connecticut	(203) 258-4261
Delaware	(302) 739-4271
Florida	(904) 488-9050
Georgia	(404) 656-3571
Hawaii	(808) 548-7719
Idaho	(208) 334-2470
Illinois	(312) 814-7164
Indiana	(317) 232-3527
Iowa	(515) 242-4729
Kansas	(913) 296-4027
Kentucky	(502) 564-2170
Louisiana	(504) 342-4320
Maine	(207) 289-5700
Maryland	(410) 333-8180
Massachusetts	(617) 367-1830
Michigan	(517) 373-6390
Minnesota	(612) 297-4227
Mississippi	(601) 359-6672
Missouri	(314) 751-4999

State	Phone
Montana	(406) 444-3923
Nebraska	(402) 471-3111
Nevada	(702) 687-4325
New Hampshire	(603) 271-2591
New Jersey	(201) 648-3518
New Mexico	(505) 827-0272
New York	(212) 827-6210
North Carolina	(919) 733-7193
North Dakota	(701) 221-5300
Utah	(801) 538-8737
Vermont	(802) 828-3221
Virginia	(804) 371-8107
Washington	(206) 464-7143
West Virginia	(304) 558-2234
Wisconsin	(608) 266-9487
Virgin Islands	(809) 774-8784
Puerto Rico	(809) 725-7254

The Top Reference Sources

Nation's Business
Chamber of Commerce of the United States
(202) 463-5650

This monthly publication is written for members of the national business community concerned with regional and national business and fractional trends.

Sample features include tax planning ideas, key professional investment oportunities, corporate shifts and/or mergers, and association meetings coverage.

American Chambers of Commerce

THE AMERICAN CHAMBERS of Commerce abroad are voluntary associations of American business enterprises and individuals doing business in a given country, as well as firms of that country operating in the United States. American Chambers of Commerce Abroad will usually handle inquiries from any U.S. business. Detailed service, however, may be provided free of charge only for members of affiliated organizations. Some chambers have a set schedule of charges for services for non-members. Services available to U.S. companies may include:

- Briefings on market conditions;
- Export-import trade leads, business and government contacts;
- Periodic news bulletins and other publications on living and trading abroad;
- Information on customs duties, tariffs, and regulations;
- Clearinghouse of information on trade, investment, and commerce;
- Information on the host country business environment.

American Chambers of Commerce Abroad

Argentina
Av. Pte. Roque Saenz Pena 567, P6
1352 Buenos Aires
Phone: (541) 331-3436
Fax: (541) 30-7303

Australia
Level 2, 39-41 Lower Fort St.
Sydney, N.S.W. 2000
Phone: (612) 241-1907
Fax: 011 61 2 251-5220

Level 1, 123 Lonsdale St.
Melbourne, Victoria 3000
Phone: (613) 663-2644
Fax: (613) 663-2473

23rd Floor, 68 Queen St.
Brisbane, Queensland 4000
Phone: (617) 221-8542
Fax: (617) 221-6313

6th Floor, 231 Adelaide Terrace
Perth, W.A. 6000
Phone: (619) 325-9540
Fax: (619) 221-3725

Austria
Porzellangasse 35
A-1090 Vienna
Phone: (43) 222 31 57 51
Fax: (43) 222 31 57 52/15

Belgium
Avenue des Arts 50, Boite 5
B-1040, Brussels
Phone: (32) 2 513 67 70/9
Fax: (32) 2 513 79 28

Bolivia
Casilla 8268, La Paz
Phone: (5912) 34-2523
Fax: (5912) 34-2523

Brazil
C.P. 916, Praca Pio X-1 5, 5th Floor
20,040 Rio de Janeiro, RJ
Phone: (5521) 203 2477
Fax: (5521) 263-4477

Rua da Espanha 2, Salas 604-606
40,000 Salvador, Bahia
Phone: (5571) 242-0077; 242-5606
Fax: (5571) 243-9986

Rua Alexandre Dumas 2372
04717 Sao Paulo, SP.
Phone: (5511) 246-9199
Fax: (5511) 246-9080

Chile
Av. Americo Vespucio Sur 80, 9 Pisco
4131 Correo Central, Santiago
Phone: (562) 48 41 40

China (PRC)
International Club
Jian Guo Men Wai
Beijing
Phone: (861) 5322491/5322559, (861) 5233570
Fax: (861) 512-7345

Colombia
Apdo. Aereo 8008
Calle 35, No. 6-16
Bogota
Phone: (571) 285-7800
Fax: (571) 288-6434

American Chambers of Commerce (cont'd)

Apdo. Aereo 5943
Cali, Valle
Phone: (573) 610-162; 672-993
Fax: (573) 672-992

Edificio Banco de Colombia, Of. 500
Apdo. Aereo 20483
Cartagena
Phone: (573) 42842

Costa Rica
Avda. 2, Calles 30-32 3034
Apdo. 4946
San Jose 1000
Phone: (506) 33 21 33
Fax: (506) 23 23 49

Dominican Republic
Torre B.H.D., Av. Winston Churchill
PO Box 95-2
Santo Domingo
Phone: (809) 544-2222
Fax: (809) 544-0502

Ecuador
Edificio Multicentra, 4P
La Nina y 6 de Diciembre
Quito
Phone: (5932) 543-512
Fax: (5932) 504-571

F. Cordova 812
Piso 3, Oficina 1
Edificio Torres de la Merced
Guayaquil
Phone: (5934) 312-760; 312-865
Fax: (5934) 326-259

Egypt
Marriott Hotel, Suite 1537
PO Box 33
Zamalek, Cairo
Phone: (20) 2 340-8888
Fax: (20) 2 340-8888, Ext. 1543

El Salvador
65 Avenida Sur, No. 159
PO Box (05) 9
San Salvador
Phone: (503) 23-2419/9604
Fax: (503) 23-6081

Germany
Rossmarkt 12
Postfach 100 162
D-6000 Frankfurt/Main 1
Phone: (49) 69 28 34 01
Fax: (49) 69 28 56 32

Budapesterstrasse 31
D-1000 Berlin 30
Phone: (49) 30 261 55 86
Fax: (49) 30 262 26 00

France
21 Avenue George V
F-75008 Paris
Phone: (33) 1 47 23 70 28
(33) 1 47 23 80 26
Fax: (33) 1 47 20 18 62

Greece
16 Kanari Street, 3rd Floor
Athens 106 74
Phone: (30) 1 36 18 385 /36 36 407
Fax: (30) 1 36 10 170

Guam
102 Ada Plaza Center
PO Box 283
Agana, Guam 96910
Phone: (671) 472-6311/8001

Guatemala
Apdo, Postal 832, 7 Avda
14-44, Zona 9, Nivel 2, Oficina 19
Guatemala City
Phone: (5022) 312-235
Fax: (5022) 312-763

Haiti
Complexe 384, Delmas (59)
Port-au-Prince, Haiti
Phone: (5091) 60-3164

Honduras
Hotel Honduras Maya, Ap. Pos. 1838
Tegucigalpa
Phone: (504) 32-31-91, Ext. 1056
Fax: (504) 3294-43

Edificio Samara
2 Piso, Of. 5
Blvd. Morazan 16 Ae. SO
Box 1209
San Pedro Sula, Honduras
Phone: (504) 52-2401/2790

Hong Kong
1030 Swire Road,
Phone: (852) 5-260165
Fax: 011-852-810-1289

Indonesia
The Landmark Centre
22nd Floor, Suite 2204
JI. Jendral Sudirman, Jakarta
Phone: (622) 1-578-0656
Fax: (622) 1-578-2437 Att: L. Sinclair

American Chambers of Commerce (cont'd)

Ireland
20 College Green
Dublin 2
Phone: (353) 1-79-37-33/1-79-34-02
Fax: (353) 1 60-17-82

Israel
35 Shaul Hamelech Blvd.
PO Box 33174
64927 Tel Aviv
Phone: (972) 3 25 23 41/2
Fax: (972) 3 25 12 72

Italy
Via Cantu 1
20123 Milano
Phone: (39) 2 86 90 661
Fax: (39) 2 80 57 737

Ivory Coast
BP 1083
Abidjan 06
Phone: (255) 326 766/785

Jamaica
The Wyndham Hotel
77 Knutsford Blvd.
Kingston 5
Phone: (809) 926-5430
Fax: (809) 929-8597

Japan
Fukide Bldg., No. 2
4-1-21 Toranomon
Minato-ku, Tokyo 105
Phone: (03) 433-5381
Fax: (03) 436-1446

PO Box 235
Okinawa City 904
Phone: (819) 889-8935-2684

Korea
Room 307, Chosun Hotel
Seoul
Phone: (822) 753-6471/6516
Fax: (822) 755-6577

Malaysia
15.01 15th Fl., Amoda
Jalan Imbi
55100 Kuala Lumpur
Phone: (603) 248-4207/2540
Fax: (603) 243-7682

Mexico
Lucerna 78-4
Mexico 6, D.F.
Phone: (905) 705-0995
Fax: (905) 535-3166

Avda. 16 de Septiembre 730-1209
Guadalajara, Jalisco
Phone: (5236) 146-300/148-068
Fax: (5236) 425-396

Picachos 760
Despachos 4 y 6
Colonia Obispado
Monterrey, Nuevo Leon
Phone: (52828) 48-7141/4749
Fax: (5283) 4855-74

Netherlands
Carnegieplein 5
2517 KJ The Hague
Phone: (31) 70 65 98 08/9
Fax: (31) 70 646992

New Zealand
PO Box 3408
Wellington
Phone: (04) 767081 (Director)
(04) 727549 (Main)

Nicaragua
Apdo. 202
Managua
Phone: (5052) 62-486

Pakistan
NIC Building, 6th Floor
Abbasi Shaheed Road off Sharea Faisal
Karachi
Phone: (92) 21-52 1635/5476
Fax: (92) 21-52 6649/3070

Panama
Apdo. 168, Estafeta Balboa
Panama
Phone: (507) 69-3881
Fax: (507) 23-3508

Paraguay
Edif. Finansud, Av. Mariseal Lopez y Saravi
Asuncion
Phone: (5921) 609-730

Peru
Av. Ricardo Palma 836 Miraflores
Lima 18
Phone: (5114) 47-9349
Fax: (5114) 47-9352

Philippines
PO Box 1578
MCC, Manila
Phone: (632) 818-7911
Fax: (632) 816-6359

American Chambers of Commerce (cont'd)

Portugal
Rua de D. Estefania, 155, 5 Esq.
Lisbon 1000
Phone: (351) 1 57 25 61/82 08

Saudi Arabia
c /o ARAMCO
PO Box 1329
Dhahran, 31311
Phone: (966) 3 875 2933
Fax: (966) 3-876-1018

Hyatt Regency
PO Box 8483
Jeddah 21482
Phone: (966) 2-651-9800, Ext. 1759
Fax: (966) 2-651-6260

PO Box 3050
Riyadh 11471, 07045
Phone: (966) 1-465-3390
Fax: (966) 1-465-6738

Singapore
Scotts Road, 16-07 Shaw Center, 0922
Phone: (65) 235-0077
Fax: (65) 732-5917

South Africa
PO Box 62280
Johannesburg
Phone: (27) 11-788-0265

Spain
Avda. Diagonal 477
08036 Barcelona
Phone: (34) 3 321 81 95/6
Fax: (34) 3 321 81 97

Hotel EuroBuilding
Padre Damian 23
Madrid 16
Phone: (34) 1 458-6520

Switzerland
Talacker 41
8001 Zurich
Phone: (41) 1 211 24 54
Fax: (41) 1 211 95 72

Taiwan
Room 1012-Chia Hsin Bldg. Annex
96 Chung Shan N. Rd., Section 2
PO Box 17-277
Taipei
Phone: (886) 2 551-2515
Fax: (886) 2 542-3376

Thailand
PO Box 11-1095
140 Wireless Road, 7th Floor
Kian Gwan Bridge, Bangkok
Phone: (662) 251-9266
Fax: (662) 255-2454

Turkey
Rumeli Cad. No. 63, D7, 4th Floor
Nisantasi 80200
Istanbul
Phone: (1) 130 30 81/36 47
Fax: (1) 130 47 34

United Arab Emirates
International Trade Center, Ste. 1609
PO Box 9281, Dubai
Phone: (971) 4 377 735
Fax: (971) 4 375 317

United Kingdom
75 Brook Street
London WlY 2EB
Phone: (44) 493 03 81
Fax: (44) 1 493 23 94

Uruguay
Calle Bartolome Mitre 1337
Cassilla de Correo 809
Montevideo
Phone: (5982) 959 059/048
Fax: (5982) 921 735

Venezuela
Torre Credival, Piso 10
2 Avenida de Campo Alegre, Apdo. 5181
Caracas 1010-A
Phone: (582) 32-49-76
Fax: (582) 32-07-64

Trade Assistance

Trade Adjustment Assistance

Trade adjustment assistance, part of the Commerce Department's Economic Development Administration, helps firms that have been harmed by imported products to adjust to international competition. Companies eligible for trade adjustment assistance may receive technical consulting to upgrade operations such as product engineering, marketing, information systems, export promotion, and energy management. The federal government may assume up to 75 percent of the cost of these services.

Contact Option

Trade Adjustment Assistance Division
U.S. Department of Commerce
14th and Constitution Avenue
Room 7023
Washington, DC 20230
(202) 482-3373

Trade Remedy Assistance

The Trade Remedy Assistance Office, part of the U.S. International Trade Commission, will provide continuing technical assistance and legal support to certified small businesses pursuing remedies under the international trade laws.

For example, selling merchandise in another country at a price below the price at which the same merchandise is sold in the home market, or selling such merchandise below the costs incurred in production and shipment, is known as *dumping*. If a U.S. firm is adversely affected by a competitor's practices, a complaint may be filed with the Trade Remedy Assistance Office. In addition to information and assistance on anti-dumping laws, this office also provides remedies on countervailing duty laws (where subsidized foreign goods are sold in the U.S.); intellectual property laws (where articles imported into the U.S. infringe valid patents, trademarks, or copyrights); and investigations of situations where U.S. exports are subject to unfair restrictions in overseas markets.

Contact Option

Trade Remedy Assistance Office
U.S. International Trade Commission
500 E Street, SW
Washington, DC 20436
(800) 343-9822

Port Import Export Reporting Service

Companies interested in finding out about their own market share, a competitor's exports and practices, who's dumping in which ports and cities, or where to find a new source of supply, can request such information from Port Import Export Reporting Service. For a fee, PIERS generates computer reports from original ships' manifests customized to meet an individual company's requirements.

PIERS reports provide product data, name and location of U.S. consignee/exporter, overseas shipper, country of origin or destination, quantities, weights, and other items.

Contact Option

Denise Simms
PIERS
Two World Trade Center, 27th Floor
New York, NY 10048
(212) 837-7068

The Top Reference Sources

National Directory of Corporate Giving
The Foundation Center
(212) 620-4230

This directory profiles 1,791 companies making contributions to nonprofit organizations. It is intended for use by grantseekers in locating potential support, grantmakers in learning more about other grantseekers, scholars researching the field, journalists reporting on contributions activities of the corporate world, and everyone generally interested in philanthropy.

It lists company, address, contacts, financial data, types of philanthropic support, geographic limitations, and application information.

The President's "E" Award

ESTABLISHED BY AN EXECUTIVE ORDER of the President in 1961, the "E" Certificate of Service is awarded to persons, firms, and organizations that may or may not export directly, but assist or facilitate export efforts through financing, transportation, market promotion, or other export-related services. In addition to manufacturers, other firms such as banks, utilities, chambers of commerce, trade associations, and individuals that promote and assist exporting may receive this award.

Applications must be submitted through the nearest Commerce Department district office. Award ceremonies may be held in conjunction with trade events, such as conventions, trade shows, conferences, and seminars. "E" Star Awards are presented to "E" Award winners to recognize continued superior performance in increasing or promoting exports.

Recent "E" Award Recipients

H. Shenson International, San Francisco, CA
International Game Technology, Reno, NV
Lil' Orbits, Minneapolis, MN
Miami Free Zone, Miami, FL
Redcom Laboratories, Victor, NY
Tape Division, Shuford Mills, Hickory, NC
W.H. Miner Division, Miner Enterprises, Geneva, IL

Recent "E" Star Award Recipients

Bird Electronic, Solon, OH
Crystal International, New Orleans, LA
International Division, Tecumseh Products, Tecumseh, MI
Nalge Co., Division of Sybron, Rochester, NY
Reliable Industrial, Metairie, LA
Taylor Co., Rockton, IL

Contact Option

"E" Awards Program
Office of Domestic Operations
International Trade Administration
Room 3810
U.S. Department of Commerce
Washington, DC 20230
(202) 482-1289

International Business Locations

Top Ten U.S. Cities for International Business

World Trade Magazine publishes an annual ranking of the best cities for international business. Here is the 1992 list:

Atlanta, Georgia
Dozens of trade consulates are located in Atlanta: 25 trade and tourism offices, ten foreign chambers, and 25 international banks. One thousand international facilities have located in Atlanta since 1988.

Baltimore, Maryland
State and local governments have focused on training businesses in international practices and assisting their entry into overseas markets. Maryland exports topped $4.03 billion in 1991.

Columbus, Ohio
The United Nations recently selected Columbus as the site for an "info port"–a computer laboratory that will test cutting-edge technologies.

Des Moines, Iowa
Pioneer Hi-Bred International tops the city's export list, with 35 percent of its $1.3 billion business going to foreign markets. Des Moines exports a wide variety of agricultural products.

Indianapolis, Indiana
Mayor Stephen Goldsmith recently called for the creation of an international marketing commission, and an annual survey of local export activities. New maintenance and cargo facilities for United Airlines and Federal Express will be in Indianapolis.

Long Beach, California
Considered a transportation gateway, the city has developed a support network to make the most of its superior location.

Miami, Florida
Called the "shopping center of the Americas," Miami boasts a bicultural and bilingual workforce, along with international seaports and airports.

Pittsburgh, Pennsylvania
Pittsburgh has a new international airport, healthy manufacturing base, and outstanding support from the university and philanthropic communities.

Rochester, New York
Rochester claims world-class schools and a high level of local cultural awareness. Export revenues exceeded $12 billion in 1991.

Tulsa, Oklahoma
Tulsa boasts a strong communication and transportation infrastructure.

Source: World Trade Magazine

Export Regulations

EXPORT CONTROLS ARE ADMINISTERED by the Bureau of Export Administration (BXA) in the U.S. Department of Commerce, and are described in detail in the official *Export Administration Regulations (EAR)*. Whenever there is any doubt about how to comply with export regulations and licensing procedures, Department of Commerce officials or qualified professional consultants should be contacted for assistance.

The *EAR* is available by subscription from the Superintendent of Documents, U.S. Government Printing Office, Washington, DC 20401, (202) 275-2091.

The Department of Commerce controls exports for the following reasons:

- To restrict exports that would be detrimental to the national security of the United States;
- To advance the foreign policy of the United States, or to fulfill its declared international obligations;
- To protect the domestic economy from the excessive drain of materials that are in short supply and to reduce the serious inflationary impact of foreign demand.

Exports not controlled by the Department of Commerce are controlled by the following agencies:

- Department of State, Office of Defense Trade Controls (arms, ammunition and implements of war, and related technical data);
- Department of Justice, Drug Enforcement Administration (exports of certain narcotics and dangerous drugs);
- U.S. Maritime Administration (certain watercraft);
- Department of Agriculture (any tobacco seed and/or live tobacco plants);
- Department of the Interior (endangered fish and wildlife, migratory birds, and bald and golden eagles);
- Patent and Trademark Office (unclassified technical data contained in patent applications);
- Department of the Treasury, Office of Foreign Assets Control (certain business dealings involving U.S. persons and embargoed countries, and all exports to Libya).

In addition, exporters of food products should contact the Food and Drug Administration (FDA) Compliance Division, (301) 295-8073, to ensure that all foreign regulations, documents, and certification requirements are met.

Export Licenses

An export license is the government document that permits the export of designated goods to certain destinations. All Commerce Department export licenses fall into two broad categories. *General licenses* do not require prior Commerce Department approval before shipment. *Validated licenses* are given to a particular exporter for a specified commodity to specified destinations for a specific end-use.

The majority of all exports leave the country under a general license authorization. A general license is a broad grant of authority by the government to all exporters for certain categories of products. Individual exporters do not need to apply for general licenses, since such authorization is already granted through *EAR*; they only need to know the authorization is available.

There are currently more than twenty different categories of general licenses. To qualify for a general license, an exporter must meet all of the described provisions and not violate any of the prohibitions listed in Part 771.2 of *EAR*. Violations of the *Export Administration Regulations* carry both civil and criminal penalties.

The procedure for applying for a validated license is to submit a completed application to: U.S. Department of Commerce, Office of Export Licensing, P.O. Box 273, Washington, DC 20044. Application forms may be ordered by sending a self-addressed mailing label to "Forms Request" at this same U.S. Department of Commerce address.

For assistance in determining the proper license, exporters may contact the Exporter Counseling Division of the Department of Commerce, Room 1099D, U.S. Department of Commerce, Washington, DC 20230, (202) 482-4811. The exporter may also check with the local Department of Commerce district office.

Contact Options

Bureau of Export Administration (BXA)
(202) 482-4811

BXA Eastern Regional Office
(603) 598-4300

BXA Western Regional Office
(714) 660-0144

Export Licensing Voice Information System (ELVIS)
(202) 482-4811

An automated attendant offers a range of licensing information and emergency handling procedures. Callers may order forms and publications or

Export Regulations (cont'd)

subscribe to the Office of Export Licensing (OEL) *Insider Newsletter*, which provides regulatory updates. Callers also will be given the option to speak to a consultant.

Recommended Resource

A Basic Guide to Exporting
U.S. Department of Commerce
Government Printing Office (#003-009-00604-0)
(202) 783-3238

This comprehensive publication of the International Trade Administration helps businesses develop export strategies, find economic market research, ship overseas, complete export documentation, respond to overseas inquiries, and take advantage of available government export assistance programs. The 1992 edition costs $9.50.

Import Regulations

Import regulations imposed by foreign governments vary from country to country. Exporters should be aware of the regulations that apply to their own operations and transactions. Many governments require such items as consular invoices, certificates of inspection, health certification, and various other documents.

Targeted Trade Barriers

TRADE BARRIERS CAN BE BROADLY DEFINED as government laws, regulations, policies, or practices that either protect domestic products from foreign competition or artificially stimulate exports of particular domestic products. While restrictive business practices sometimes have a similar effect, they are not usually regarded as trade barriers.

The most common foreign trade barriers are government-imposed measures and policies that restrict, prevent, or impede the international exchange of goods and services. These include:

- Import policies such as tariffs, quantitative restrictions, import licensing, and customs barriers;
- Standards, testing, labeling, and certification in an unnecessarily restrictive application of standards;
- Export subsidies which offer export financing on preferential terms and displace U.S. exports in third country markets;
- Lack of intellectual property protection;
- Service barriers which regulate international data flow and foreign data processing;
- Investment barriers;
- Other barriers.

The Office of the U.S. Trade Representative issues an annual report on 45 countries describing the trade barriers that exist in each country and estimating the impact on U.S. exports. Some of the countries included in the report are: Argentina, Brazil, Canada, China, Federal Republic of China, Guatemala, India, Indonesia, Israel, Japan, Mexico, Nigeria, Singapore, Taiwan, Turkey, and Venezuela.

Foreign Trade Barriers may be obtained through:

Office of the U.S. Trade Representative
Executive Office of the President
Washington, DC 20506
(202) 395-3230

Foreign Trade Barriers may also be directly ordered through the Government Printing Office (GPO), (202) 783-3238, or one of the local offices

Other useful information may be obtained through the Trade Information Center, a one-stop information source on a multitude of federal export assistance programs. This service connects the caller with international trade specialists on a toll-free line.

Trade Information Center
Department of Commerce
14th St., NW, and Constitution Ave.
Washington, DC 20230
(800) 872-8723

Almanac Fact

The cost for rebuilding the eastern sector of Germany is now estimated at $80 billion to $100 billion annually for as long as ten years. Unofficial unemployment is more than 25 percent of the workforce.

Source: U.S. Industrial Outlook

Import/Export Directories

American Export Register
Thomas Publishing Co.
Five Penn Plaza
New York, NY 10001
Fax: (212) 629-1140

This annual two-volume, 3,000-page directory features product listings in more than 4,200 categories. The reference also includes:

- Alphabetical listing of nearly 43,000 U.S. companies;
- Product listings in ten languages;
- Directory of import/export services (banks, cargo carriers, customs brokers, embassies, railroads).

Directory of United States Importers
Directory of United States Exporters
Journal of Commerce Business Directories
445 Marshall St.
Phillipsburg, NJ 08865
(800) 222-0356

World trade directories featuring numerical product listings and company profile listings.

Bergano's Register of International Importers
P.O. Box 190
Fairfield, CT 06430
(203) 254-2054

A comprehensive resource of 2,000 leading distributors, dealers, agents, and representatives in over 75 important international markets.

Making International Contacts

Matchmaker Trade Delegations

Organized and led by Commerce Department personnel, Matchmaker trade delegations enable new-to-export and new-to-market firms to meet prescreened prospects who are interested in their products or services in overseas markets. Matchmaker delegations usually target major markets in two countries and limit trips to a week or less. U.S. firms can interview a maximum number of prospective business partners with a minimum of time away from the office. Thorough briefings on market requirements and business practices and interpreters' services are provided. Delegation members pay their own expenses. For further information call, Export Promotion Services, International Trade Administration, (202) 482-3119.

Trade Fairs and Exhibitions

About 80 international worldwide events are selected annually for recruitment by the Commerce Department or by the private sector under the Commerce's certification program. Exhibitors receive pre- and post-event logistical and transportation support, design and management of the USA pavilion, and extensive overseas market promotional campaigns to attract appropriate business audiences. For further information on trade fairs and exhibitions, call the Trade Information Center, (800) 872-8723.

The ITA also publishes The Export Promotion Calendar, a quarterly publication listing trade shows, trade fairs, seminars, and other events by industry, with dates and contact numbers.

The Top Reference Sources

1993 Guide to Worldwide Postal-Code & Address Formats
Marian Nelson, $99.50, U.S. and Canada
(212) 362-9855

The second edition of this postal guide is an extremely useful reference for anyone involved in using the mails to do business with a foreign country, from executives, to data managers to mailroom personnel.

The book includes practical tips for standardizing foreign addresses, including: city and county names, postal-code formats, abbreviations, sample addresses, information sources, and more.

International Price Indexes

THE U.S. EXPORT AND IMPORT PRICE INDEXES are general purpose indexes that measure changes in price levels within the foreign trade sector. The all-export index provides a measure of price change for domestically produced U.S. products shipped to other countries. The all-import index measures price change of goods purchased from other countries by U.S. residents.

Selected Import Price Indexes

Commodity	1982	1983	1984	1985	1986	1987	1988	1989	1990	1991	1992
ALL COMMODITIES	NA	102.8	103.9	99.2	98.7	110.0	116.8	119.8	118.9	122.4	124.3
Coffee, tea, cocoa	84.6	89.0	105.6	96.8	117.2	87.0	93.3	85.3	66.3	62.1	51.5
Fuels, related products	123.6	108.4	108.7	99.7	51.5	74.1	63.4	73.3	63.7	72.5	75.5
Textiles	99.5	97.8	99.4	98.9	105.4	111.8	120.6	122.1	125.8	131.3	135.1
Telecommunications	113.0	110.1	107.4	100.2	106.4	110.3	113.8	115.7	111.4	108.7	108.0
Footwear, c.i.f.	100.7	97.5	102.0	98.1	108.0	119.8	129.6	127.9	137.6	140.3	142.6

Selected Export Price Indexes

Commodity	1982	1983	1984	1985	1986	1987	1988	1989	1990	1991	1992
ALL COMMODITIES	NA	NA	104.1	100.4	99.1	102.2	109.5	113.2	113.3	114.7	115.3
Rice	104.9	118.4	107.2	101.6	67.9	59.1	105.7	95.7	93.1	102.7	97.7
Fuels, related products	NA	NA	101.5	101.8	76.8	82.8	82.1	86.0	88.7	87.5	84.2
Hydrocarbons,	117.6	111.7	113.9	101.4	86.4	142.8	169.0	157.6	128.0	104.6	106.8
Telecommunications	96.7	98.9	99.8	99.6	98.9	101.4	104.6	107.5	111.2	118.2	120.4

The average for the year 1985 is set to equal 100.

Source: Bureau of Labor Statistics

The Top Reference Sources

UNESCO Statistical Yearbook
UNIPUB, distributors, $95.00
(301) 459-7666
Order # 47448

Member states of the United Nations Education, Scientific and Cultural Organization report periodically on their laws, regulations, and statistics relating to educational, scientific, and cultural life. Statistics in this valuable yearbook include school enrollment ratios, educational expenditures, R&D expenditures, number of books, periodicals and newspapers published, number of films imported, number of films produced, radio and television broadcasting revenues and expenditures, among others.

Translation Services

WHEN A COMPANY NEEDS TO have a one-page letter from Romania translated into English or its annual report translated into 17 different languages, these and many other services can be provided by translation companies. The companies listed here all provide the following:

- Translation in all languages;
- All subjects (legal, technical, advertising, etc.);
- Interpreters (consecutive and simultaneous);
- Desktop publishing, typesetting, graphic arts;
- Film, video and slide adaptations (narrative and voice-over).

Contact Options

Translation Companies:

Berlitz Translation Services
New York Center, 17th Floor
257 Park Ave. S.
New York, NY 10010
(212) 777-7878

With 29 translation centers located in 18 countries, Berlitz is the best known translation company.

Inlingua
551 Fifth Ave.
New York, NY 10176
(212) 682-8585

Offers services in 250 offices worldwide.

The Language Lab
211 E. 43rd St.
New York, NY 10017
(212) 697-2891
(800) 682-3126

Also offers instruction services to corporations.

Rennert Bilingual Translation Group
2 W. 45th St.
New York, NY 10036
(212) 819-1776

Language Instruction Services:

Berlitz International
293 Wall Street
Princeton, NJ 08540
(609) 924-8500
(800) 257-9449

Berlitz International operates language centers in over 205 cities throughout the world, with training in all spoken languages.

Lingua Service Worldwide
2 West 45th Street, #500
New York, NY 10036
(800) 394-5327
(212) 768-2728

A list of language immersion and study programs (domestic and abroad) may also be obtained from the Modern Language Association of America, 10 Astor Place, New York, NY 10003, (212) 475-9500.

Or, call the Continuing Education offices of local colleges and universities for information on language programs that may be offered.

Over-the-Phone Interpretation

AT&T Language Line offers 24-hour-a-day access to interpretations of over 140 languages, over the phone, within minutes. To reach an AT&T Language Line Services interpreter from the United States or Canada, call (800) 628-8486. Interpreter time costs $3.50 a minute, billable to major credit cards. The Language Line Service also provides software localization, translation and multinational document management services, and multilingual telephone marketing.

Sprint's Language Connection offers 11 languages: Japanese, Korean, Taiwanese, Cantonese, Mandarin, German, French, Italian, Portuguese, Spanish, and English. Call (800) 776-3333; the cost is $3.50 a minute.

MCI does not offer a general interpretation service, but provides translators for customer-service calls in Spanish, Japanese, Vietnamese, Korean, German, French, Italian, Cantonese, Tagalog, Portuguese and Mandarin.

Bilingual Business Cards

In some countries, Japan especially, exchanging business cards at any first meeting is considered a basic part of good business etiquette. As a matter of courtesy, it is best to carry business cards printed both in English and in the language of the country being visited.

There are many companies in the United States that translate and print English-Japanese business cards, among them:

Japan Printing Services, New York
(212) 406-2905

Japan Printing Company, Los Angeles
(213) 538-4879

Kojimoto Printing Service, San Francisco
(415) 668-2448

Inlingua, Houston
(713) 528-1515

Oriental Printing, Chicago
(708) 439-4822

International Price Comparisons

Price Comparisons of Selected Items, by City (in U.S. Dollars)

ITEM	Amsterdam	Beijing	Berlin	Brussels	Dublin	Geneva	Hong Kong	London
Chocolate candy bar (150 g.)	1.07	4.37	1.08	1.30	0.95	1.48	1.85	1.22
Carbonated soft drink (6 pack)	2.65	3.27	3.68	3.06	2.90	3.48	2.38	2.41
Bottled mineral water (1 liter)	0.48	1.66	0.94	0.48	0.67	0.49	0.72	0.50
Wine (750 ml.)	6.09	43.76	8.05	6.98	7.25	8.63	14.97	8.48
Dry cleaning (man's suit–1 piece)	9.99	5.16	11.66	11.13	8.24	14.45	7.55	9.27
Woman's haircut–wash/dry	43.55	33.25	45.93	46.02	26.13	52.56	67.73	45.92
Toothpaste (100 ml.)	2.57	7.15	2.11	1.86	1.57	1.83	1.04	1.94
Deodorant (155 ml.)	2.12	14.30	1.85	3.63	1.71	3.07	4.18	1.82
Aspirin (20 units)	12.84	9.20	13.90	6.31	3.70	15.09	6.76	2.97
Blank video tape (1 unit)	6.05	6.71	8.29	4.82	6.47	8.39	4.94	5.75
Camera film (36 exposures)	26.92	10.62	20.81	23.22	14.49	25.73	10.47	14.95
Paperback book (1 unit)	12.18	10.41	15.75	6.76	8.11	12.06	12.62	8.60
Movie ticket (1 unit)	6.97	NA	6.82	6.39	5.71	9.20	5.16	10.40
Taxi ride (2 km.)	4.79	2.10	6.78	4.95	4.47	6.57	1.29	4.31
Business lunch (for two)	77.18	37.17	70.68	51.68	40.99	29.57	52.63	51.66
Hotel (daily rate)	183.31	131.49	231.26	352.35	183.00	193.82	248.84	236.78

ITEM	Madrid	Moscow	Paris	Rome	São Paulo	Tokyo	Toronto	Vienna
Chocolate candy bar (150 g.)	1.25	3.00	1.44	1.26	1.14	3.75	2.17	1.57
Carbonated soft drink (6 pack)	4.91	5.33	2.54	2.49	3.12	6.77	3.80	3.33
Bottled mineral water (1 liter)	0.33	1.01	0.33	0.29	0.28	1.39	0.74	0.73
Wine (750 ml.)	9.41	16.09	4.51	8.72	20.87	12.10	7.24	10.01
Dry cleaning (man's suit–1 piece)	12.86	34.79	20.97	9.19	12.97	24.34	8.41	11.61
Woman's haircut–wash/dry	38.36	21.00	53.99	37.69	44.07	75.01	33.73	50.70
Toothpaste (100 ml.)	2.42	6.28	2.35	2.17	1.65	6.70	1.60	2.70
Deodorant (155 ml.)	2.73	9.97	2.42	3.43	3.76	11.64	2.27	3.57
Aspirin (20 units)	8.21	16.71	9.39	13.35	12.86	19.56	3.34	10.92
Blank video tape (1 unit)	4.81	19.62	7.92	5.50	6.22	9.14	5.83	11.00
Camera film (36 exposures)	23.88	22.44	26.49	15.22	18.44	10.51	21.01	21.15
Paperback book (1 unit)	10.35	15.69	10.63	92.41	12.87	11.25	6.69	10.53
Movie ticket (1 unit)	5.06	NA	7.70	6.23	3.23	19.41	6.42	7.10
Taxi ride (2 km.)	2.53	NA	3.47	6.04	0.81	5.06	4.58	3.78
Business lunch (for two)	37.29	54.98	68.32	58.37	25.40	58.34	36.94	75.68
Hotel (daily rate)	224.34	326.81	266.92	194.87	194.30	354.28	154.18	232.63

Prices recorded between October, 1992 and February, 1993

Source: Organization Resources Counselors

Almanac Fact

In France, 26 percent of adults over 18 speak English. In the Netherlands, 68 percent of adults also speak English.

Source: International Business

Cultural Differences

BUSINESS ETIQUETTE AND METHODS, religious customs, dietary practices, humor, and acceptable dress vary widely from country to country.

Even as global communications make the world more homogeneous, local customs continue to provide a challenge to traveling business people.

A classic book on the topic, *Do's and Taboos Around the World*, has already sold over 100,000 copies.

Filled with humorous anecdotes about misunderstandings and odd (to us) customs and foods, this book is a useful safety measure for frequent travelers.

In addition to customs, countries have radically different time schedules. Holidays vary worldwide, as do normal hours of business. The Multinational Executive Travel Companion lists holidays and business hours for hundreds of countries, and can help the businessperson avoid snafus.

Recommended Resources

Do's and Taboos Around the World
by Roger Axtell
John Wiley and Sons

The Multinational Executive Travel Companion
Suburban Publishing
(203) 324-6439

Expensive Cities

THE FOLLOWING TABLE RANKS the most expensive cities in the world based on the cost of 151 products. The index for New York City equals 100.

Rank	City	Index
1	Tokyo, Japan	183
2	Osaka, Japan	171
3	Libreville, Gabon	139
4	Brazzaville, Congo	138
5	Oslo, Norway	137
6	Dakar, Senegal	132
7	Taipei, Taiwan	130
8	Douala, Cameroon	128
9	Copenhagen, Denmark	128
10	Abidjan, Ivory Coast	127
11	Buenos Aires, Argentina	127
12	Zurich, Switzerland	126
13	Geneva, Switzerland	125
14	Moscow, Russia	122
15	Vienna, Austria	121

Source: Corporate Resources Group

The Top Reference Sources

Export Profits
Upstart Publishing Company, $19.95
(603) 749-5071

This very thorough reference, written by international trade consultant Jack S. Wolf, is essential reading for managers of small- and mid-size businesses who want to begin exporting.

With an extensive glossary, lists of resources, and sample documents, this book shows how to decide whether a business should export, find the right foreign markets for its products, choose distributors or agents, minimize currency risks, and cut through red tape.

Other topics discussed include pricing, shipping, finding a banker, property rights protection, and test marketing.

Carnets

THE ATA CARNET IS A STANDARDIZED international customs document used to obtain duty-free temporary admission of certain goods into the countries that are signatories to the ATA Convention. Under the ATA Convention, commmercial and professional travelers may take commercial samples, tools of the trade, advertising material and cinematographic, audiovisual, medical, scientific, or other professional equipment into member countries temporarily without paying customs duties and taxes, or posting a bond at the border of each country to be visited.

Countries participating in the ATA Carnet System include: Australia, Austria, Belgium, Bulgaria, Canada, Cyprus, Denmark, Finland, France, Germany, Gibraltar, Greece, Hong Kong, Hungary, Iceland, India (commercial samples only), Iran, Ireland, Israel, Italy, Ivory Coast, Japan, Luxembourg, Mauritius, Netherlands, New Zealand, Norway, Poland, Portugal, Romania, Senegal, Singapore, Sri Lanka (certain professional equipment not accepted), South Africa, South Korea, Spain, Sweden, Switzerland, Turkey, United Kingdom, and United States.

Since other countries are continuously added to the ATA Carnet system, travelers should contact the U.S. Council for International Business if the country to be visited is not included in this list. Applications for carnets should also be made through the U.S. Council. The fee depends on the value of the goods to be covered. A bond, letter of credit, or bank guaranty of over 40 percent of the value of the goods is also required to cover duties and taxes that would be due if goods imported into a foreign country by carnet were not re-exported and the duties were not paid by the carnet holder. The carnets generally are valid for 12 months.

Contact Option

U.S. Council for International Business
1212 Avenue of the Americas
New York, NY 10036
(212) 354-4480

Source: A Basic Guide to Exporting

PAL, SECAM, NTSC Conversion

PAL, SECAM, and NTSC refer to the different kinds of video systems around the world. For a videotape to play in a foreign country's system, it must be converted to the correct format. Check the local Yellow Pages under Video Conversion, PAL-SECAM-NTSC, to find a local company that will convert U.S. tapes for viewing abroad and foreign tapes for viewing in the United States. Costs for this service vary according to the quality or definition required and the type of equipment used to make the conversions. Midrange equipment conversions run from $40 to $70 for the first hour.

Formats Used

PAL
Western Europe–excluding France–also, Australia, South Africa, parts of Asia, including India, China

PAL-M
Brazil

PAL-N
Argentina

NTSC
North America

SECAM
France, Eastern Bloc and parts of the Middle East

Almanac Fact

Two countries targeted by the U.S. for extensive videotape piracy are Thailand and Taiwan.

Electric Current Conversions

Country	Cycles	Volts
Afghanistan	50/60	220/380
Algeria	50	127/220
	50	220/380
Andorra	50	110/130
	50	220/380
Angola	50	220/380
Antigua	60	110/220
Argentina	50	220/380
Australia	50	220/250
Austria	50	220/380
Bahamas	60	120/208
	60	120/240
Bahrain	50	230
Bangladesh	50	220/240
Barbados	50	110
Belgium (Brussels)	50	220/380
Belize	60	110/220
Benin	60	220
Bermuda	50	110/220
Bolivia	60	110/220
Botswana	50	230
Brazil (Belem)	60	127/220
(Brazilia)	60	220/240
	60	220/380
(Recife)	60	127/220
(Rio de Janeiro)	60	127/220
(São Paulo)	60	115/230
Brunei	50	240
Bulgaria	50	220/380
Burkina Faso	50	220
Burma	50	230/250
Burundi	50	220
Cambodia	50	220
Cameroon	50	110/220
Canada	60	120/240 & 110
Central Afr. Rep.	50	220/380
Chad	50	220/380
Chile	50	220/380
China	50	220/380
	60	110/220
Colombia	60	110/120
Bogota	60	150/240
Congo	50	220
Costa Rica	60	120/240 & 110
Cuba	60	110/220
Curacao	50	127/220
Cyprus	50	220/240
	50	240/415
Czech Republic	50	220/380
Denmark	50	220/380

Country	Cycles	Volts
Dominica	50	220/240
Dominican Rep.	60	110/220
Ecuador	60	120/208
	60	120/240
	60	110/220
	60	121/210
Egypt	50	110/220/380
El Salvador	60	110
Ethiopia	50	220/380
Finland	50	220/380
France	50	220/380
	50	110/115
	50	127/220
Gabon	50	220
Gambia	50	230/400, 200
Germany	50	220/380
Ghana	50	220/400
Great Britain	50	240 & 240/415
Greece	50	220, 220/380/127
Greenland	50	220/380
Grenada	50	220/240
Guatemala	60	120/240, 110
Guinea	50	220/380
Guyana	60	110
Haiti	60	110/220
Hawaii	60	120
Honduras	60	110/220
Hong Kong	50	220, 200/346
Hungary	50	220/380
Iceland	50	220/380/ 240
India	50	230/400/ 220
Indonesia	50	127/220
Iran	50	220/380
Iraq	50	220/380
Ireland	50	220/380
Israel	50	230/400/ 220
Italy	50	220/380
	50	127/220
Ivory Coast	50	220/380
Jamaica	50	110/220
Japan	50/60	100/200
Jordan	50	220/380
Kenya	50	240/415
Kiribati	50	240
Korea	60	110/220
Kuwait	50	240/415
Laos	50	220/380
Lebanon	50	110/190
	50	220/380
Lesotho	50	220

Electric Current Conversions (cont'd)

Country	Cycles	Volts
Liberia	60	110,120/240
		120/208
Libya	50	125/220
Liechtenstein	50	110/220
Luxembourg	50	120/208
	50	220/380
Madagascar	50	110/220
Malawi	50	230/400
Malaysia	50	230/240/415
Mali	50	220/380
Malta	50	240/415
Mauritania	50	220
Mauritius	50	230
Mexico	60	varies
Federal District	60	127/220
Monaco	50	220/380
	50	110/115
Morocco	50	115/200
	60	110/125
Mozambique	50	220/380
Namibia	50	220/240
Nauru	50	240
Nepal	50	220
Netherlands	50	220/380
New Zealand	50	230/400
Nicaragua	60	120/240/110
Niger	50	220/380
Nigeria	50	210/250
	50	230/415
Norway	50	220/230
Oman	50	220/240
Pakistan	50	220/230/400
Panama	60	110/120
Papua New Guinea	50	240/415
Paraguay	50	220
Peru	60	220
Philippines	60	110/220
	50	110/120
Poland	50	220/380
Portugal	50	220/380
	50	110/190
Puerto Rico	60	120/240
Qatar	50	220/240
Romania	50	220/380
Russia	50	127/220, 220
Rwanda	50	280/380
St. Christopher & Nevis	60	230
St. Lucia	50	220
St. Vincent	60	220/240
Saudi Arabia	60	110/120

Country	Cycles	Volts
Mecca	50	220
Senegal	50	110/220
Sierra Leone	50	220/400
Singapore	50	230/400
Soloman Island	50	230/415
Somalia	50	200
South Africa	50	250
Spain	50	110/130
	50	220/380
Sri Lanka	50	230/400
Sudan	50	240/415
	60	127/220
Suriname	60	127/220
Swaziland	50	220
Sweden	50	220/380
Switzerland	50	110/220
	50	220/380
Syria	50	110/190
	50	220/380
Tahiti	60	220 & 110
Taiwan	60	110
Tanzania	50	230/400
Thailand	50	220/380
Togo	50	127/220
	50	220/380
Tonga	50	240
Trinidad & Tobago	60	115/220
	60	230/400
Tunisia	50	110/190
	50	220/380
Turkey	50	110/220
	50	220/380
Uganda	50	240/415
United Arab Emirates	50	220/240
Uruguay	50	220
U.S.	60	110
Venezuela	60	120/240
Caracas	50	120/208
Vietnam	50	120/127/220
	50	220/380
Virgin Islands	60	120/240
Yugoslavia	50	220/380
Zaire	50	220/380
Zambia	50	220/380
Zimbabwe	50	230

Note: Pay particular attention to cycles when using any electronic or computer equipment.

Currencies of the World

FOR UPDATED CURRENCY EQUIVALENTS call Thomas Cook, Inc. at (212) 736-9790

Country	Currency	Subcurrency	Value in Dollars as of 4/1993
Afghanistan	afghani	100 puls	0.00086
Algeria	dinar	100 centimes	0.0451
Argentina	austral	100 centavos	1.0013
Australia	dollar	100 cents	0.676
Austria	schilling	100 groschen	0.09
Bahamas	dollar	100 cents	1
Bahrain	dinar	1000 fils	2.6525
Barbados	dollar	100 cents	0.4971
Belgium	franc	100 centimes	0.0298
Belize	dollar	100 cents	0.435
Benin	franc	100 centimes	0.0036
Bolivia	boliviano	100 centavos	0.2427
Botswana	pula	100 thebe	0.4411
Brazil	cruzeiro	100 centavos	0.00006
Brunei	dollar	100 cents	0.6067
Bulgaria	lev	100 stotinki	0.039
Cameroon	franc	100 centimes	0.0036
Canada	dollar	100 cents	0.7911
Cayman Islands	dollar	100 cents	1.176
Central African Republic	franc	100 centimes	0.0036
Chad	franc	100 centimes	0.0036
Chile	peso	100 centesimos	0.003
China	yuan	10 jiao	0.171
Colombia	peso	100 centavos	0.002
Congo	franc	100 centimes	0.0036
Costa Rica	colon	100 centimos	0.0072
Cuba	peso	100 centavos	2.1
Czechoslovakia	koruna	100 halers	0.035
Denmark	krone	100 ore	0.159
Djibouti	franc	100 centimes	0.0056
Dominican Republic	peso	100 centavos	0.0769
Ecuador	sucre	100 centavos	0.0006
Egypt	pound	100 piasters	0.3007
El Salvador	colon	100 centavos	0.1135
Ethiopia	birr	100 cents	0.2
Fiji	dollar	100 cents	0.629
Finland	markka	100 penni	0.1780
France	franc	100 centimes	0.1814
Gabon	franc	100 centimes	0.0036
Gambia	dalasi	100 butut	0.1144
Germany	deutsche mark	100 pfennigs	0.6133
Ghana	cedi	100 pesewa	0.0018
Greece	drachma	100 lepta	0.004
Guatemala	quetzel	100 centavos	0.1879
Guinea	franc	100 centimes	0.0002

Currencies of the World (cont'd)

Country	Currency	Subcurrency	Value in Dollars as of 4/1993
Guyana	dollar	100 cents	0.0079
Haiti	gourde	100 centimes	0.0833
Honduras	lempira	100 centavos	0.1703
Hong Kong	dollar	100 cents	0.129
Hungary	forint	100 fillér	0.0120
Iceland	krona	100 aurer	0.0158
India	rupee	100 paise	0.0343
Indonesia	rupiah	100 sen	0.0005
Iraq	dinar	1000 fils	3.2165
Ireland	pound	100 pence	1.4945
Israel	shekel	100 agorot	0.3618
Italy	lira	100 centesimi	0.0006
Ivory Coast	franc	100 centimes	0.0036
Jamaica	dollar	100 cents	0.0453
Japan	yen	100 sen	0.0080
Jordan	dinar	1000 fils	1.4577
Kenya	shilling	100 cents	0.0278
Kuwait	dinar	1000 fils	3.3068
Lebanon	pound	100 piasters	0.0006
Luxembourg	franc	100 centimes	0.0298
Malawi	kwacha	100 tambala	0.2293
Malaysia	ringgit	100 sen	0.3810
Maldives	rufilyaa	100 larees	1.46
Malta	lira	100 cents	2.7177
Mauritania	ouguiya	5 khoums	0.0094
Mauritius	rupee	100 cents	0.0598
Mexico	peso	100 centavos	0.3224
Morocco	dirham	100 centimes	0.1162
Nepal	rupee	100 paisas	0.0214
Netherlands	guilder	100 cents	0.5351
New Zealand	dollar	100 cents	0.5155
Nicaragua	cordoba	100 centavos	0.1667
Niger	franc	100 centimes	0.0036
Nigeria	naira	100 kobos	0.0488
Norway	krone	100 Ore	0.1443
Oman	riyal-omani	1000 baiza	2.5974
Pakistan	rupee	100 paisas	0.0384
Papua New Guinea	kina	100 toea	1.006
Paraguay	guarani	100 centimos	0.0006
Peru	inti		0.5882
Philippines	peso	100 centavos	0.0395
Poland	zloty	100 groszy	0.00006
Portugal	escudo	100 centavos	0.0068
Qatar	riyal	100 dirhams	0.2747
Romania	leu	100 bani	0.002
Saudi Arabia	riyal	20 qurush	0.2666
Senegal	franc	100 centimes	0.0036
Seychelles	rupee	100 cents	0.1901
Sierra Leone	leone	100 cents	0.0019
Singapore	dollar	100 cents	0.6067

Currencies of the World (cont'd)

Country	Currency	Subcurrency	Value in Dollars as of 4/1993
Solomon Islands	dollar	100 cents	0.335
Somalia	shilling	100 cents	0.0004
South Africa	rand	100 cents	0.3257
South Korea	won	100 chon	0.0012
Spain	peseta	100 centimos	0.0086
Sri Lanka	rupee	100 cents	0.0217
Sudan	pound	100 piasters	0.01
Suriname	guilder	100 cents	0.5602
Sweden	krona	100 ore	0.1353
Switzerland	franc	100 centimes	0.6615
Syria	pound	100 piasters	0.0476
Taiwan	dollar	100 cents	0.0392
Tanzania	shilling	100 cents	0.0028
Thailand	baht	100 satang	0.0393
Togo	franc	100 centimes	0.0036
Trinidad and Tobago	dollar	100 cents	0.2352
Tunisia	dinar	1000 millimes	1.0727
Turkey	lira	100 kurus	0.0001
Uganda	shilling	100 cents	0.0008
United Arab Emirates	dirham	1000 fils	0.2724
United Kingdom	pound	100 pence	1.4625
United States	dollar	100 cents	1.0000
Uruguay	peso	100 centesimos	0.0003
Venezuela	bolivar	100 centimos	0.0123
Western Samoa	tala	100 sene	0.3958
Yugoslavia	dinar	100 para	0.0013
Zambia	kwacha	100 ngwee	0.0025
Zimbabwe	dollar	100 cents	0.1655

World Weather

Location	December-March (high/low)	June-August (high/low)
Amsterdam	40/32	69/53
Athens	58/44	90/72
Bali	90/74	94/76
Bangkok	89/70	90/75
Bogotá	67/48	64/50
Buenos Aires	87/62	57/40
Cairo	67/48	94/69
Caracas	77/57	78/63
Dublin	47/36	67/51
Guam	90/72	86/69
Hong Kong	68/57	87/59
Israel	57/41	90/65
Istanbul	48/38	80/64
Kathmandu	65/36	84/70
Lima	75/53	77/61
Lisbon	55/44	84/63
London	44/35	70/52

Location	December-March (high/low)	June-August (high/low)
Manila	87/70	90/75
Montevideo	84/72	77/70
Munich	36/23	73/53
Nairobi	77/54	69/51
New Delhi	71/43	96/80
Panama City	88/71	86/70
Paris	44/36	76/58
Quito	77/57	78/65
Rio de Janeiro	82/71	76/70
Rome	55/42	85/66
Santiago	86/70	78/69
Seoul	30/20	81/69
Singapore	88/74	87/73
Taiwan	70/61	90/72
Tokyo	47/32	81/69

World Weather (cont'd)

Location	December-March (high/low)	June-August (high/low)
Acapulco	87/70	89/75
Albuquerque	72/40	91/62
Austin	63/42	93/72
Bermuda	68/58	84/73
Boston	40/22	80/58
Cancún	87/70	89/75
Chicago	34/18	82/64
Dallas	58/37	92/72
Denver	43/17	85/57
Dominican Repb.	85/69	88/72
Honolulu	76/68	84/72
Jackson Hole, WY	36/11	80/52
Lake Tahoe	50/16	89/40
Las Vegas	65/34	103/71
Los Angeles	66/47	76/58
Mexico City	72/43	75/53
Miami	76/59	88/75

Location	December-March (high/low)	June-August (high/low)
Montreal	24/10	72/54
Nassau	77/67	88/76
New Orleans	65/48	90/76
New York City	41/27	80/65
Palm Beach	79/43	95/73
Philadelphia	42/29	83/64
Port au Prince	86/68	70/73
St. Thomas	85/72	89/76
San Juan	82/72	87/76
Tucson	65/39	97/71
Vancouver	44/36	67/53
Washington, DC	45/29	85/64
Yellowstone National Park	32/6	75/46

Source: National Weather Service

The Top Reference Sources

The Economist Atlas
Henry Holt, $47.50
(212) 886-9200

This revised edition of a bestselling reference provides a comprehensive, fully-illustrated portrait of the world today. Included are up-to-date political and economic analyses, plus 70 pages of full-color political and geographical maps for every country in the world. There are also 37 pages of thematic maps which allow comparisons between countries on subjects ranging from defense spending to foreign debt to environmental pollution.

Manufacturing

Industrial Buying Guides

RESEARCH SHOWS THAT 97% of all industrial purchases are initiated by the buyer, not the seller. And most purchases, either of a new product or plant facility, a new component or material, are made with the help of a buying guide. The best known, most comprehensive and widely used industrial buying system is the *Thomas Register of Manufacturers*. More than $400 million in purchases of products or services are transacted each day through this system. The *Thomas Register* combines a product and services section, company directories, and a catalogue file section, in one multi-volume reference set. The location of a company's distributors, engineering or service offices, plants, and sales offices may be found in the company profiles section of this reference. Companies may advertise and/or distribute their catalogues in the *Thomas Register*.

Recommended Resources

Thomas Register of American Manufacturers
One Penn Plaza
New York, NY 10001
(212) 290-7225

Sweet's Catalogue
1221 Avenue of the Americas
New York, NY 10020
(212) 512-4753
Distributes manufacturers' catalogues for construction-related products.

MacRae's Blue Book
817 Broadway
New York, NY 10003
(212) 673-4700
National industrial directory listing manufacturers only.

U.S. Industrial Directory
P.O. Box 3824
Stamford, CT 06905
(203) 328-2500
Annual reference listing products and services for industrial manufacturing.

Standard & Poor's Register of Corporations, Directors and Executives
25 Broadway
New York, NY 10004
(212) 208-1649
Descriptive listing of corporations, but not a buying guide.

Manufacturers' Sales Agencies

MANUFACTURERS' AGENTS ARE INDEPENDENT contractors who work on commission for more than one company. Most manufacturers who have turned to agents in recent years have done so after first working with a salaried sales force of their own. Companies switch for a variety of reasons, but often because they want to trim sales costs and fixed overhead. Start-up companies with little knowledge of what to expect from different territories, and with no sales benchmarks, also use agents rather than establish their own sales force. Ideally, the manufacturer's agent will represent other manufacturers' products which are compatible, but not competitive, with the company's own products. Experienced agents will be able to provide information on what to expect in various territories, when and how to advertise, and what a competitor's efforts are likely to be. Sales agencies are paid commissions only when they make a sale.

The source of first resort for manufacturers in search of a sales agent or independent contractor is the *Directory of Manufacturers' Sales Agencies*, the membership directory of the Manufacturers' Agents National Association. This reference of 9,000 member agents and agencies is organized in three sections: Alphabetically by agency name, by state, and by product classification. Profiles of the agencies include the kinds of products sold, sales territories, names of key officials, warehousing facilities, size of sales staff, and location of branch offices.

Contact Option

Manufacturers' Agents National Association
23016 Mill Creek Rd.
Laguna Hills, CA 92654
(714) 859-4040
MANA also publishes the monthly *Agency Sales Magazine*, along with numerous special reports on making the agency decision, finding the right agent, negotiating the agreement, and so on.

Overseas Manufacturing

TO ASSIST U.S. MANUFACTURERS in the areas of trade and import/export, the International Trade Administration assigns country desk officers to every country in the world. These specialists collect information on a specific country's regulations, tariffs, business practices, political and economic climate, and may provide selected industry sector analyses for that country as well. Complete listings for industry specialists and country desk officers appear in the International chapter.

Contact Options

Hong Kong, Ireland, Canada, and Mexico are leading exporters of manufactured goods to the United States. For information on manufacturing, contact:

Hong Kong Government Industrial Promotion Office
680 Fifth Ave., 22nd Floor
New York, NY 10019
(212) 265-7273

Industrial Promotion Unit/ Hong Kong Economic & Trade Office
222 Kearny St., Suite 402
San Francisco, CA 94108
(415) 956-4560

Irish Development Office
140 E. 45th St.
New York, NY 10017
(212) 972-1658

Investment Canada
P.O. Box 2800, Postal Station D
Ottawa, Ontario
Canada K1P6A5
(613) 995-0465

Trade Commission of Mexico
150 E. 58th St.
New York, NY 10155
(212) 826-2916

New Techniques and Consultants

The Manufacturing Technology Centers Program

The United States' long-dominant position in the world's marketplace is declining due to increasingly sophisticated foreign competition and swiftly changing technologies. There are more than 350,000 manufacturing firms in the U.S. with fewer than 500 employees. These firms employ 12 million workers and account for over 50 percent of the total of this country's value added to goods and services. While many small manufacturing firms have been able to maintain their competitive edge in smaller domestic markets and in special technology areas, they simply have not kept pace with the rapidly changing, computer-driven global marketplace of the past decade. To address this problem, the Omnibus Trade and Competitiveness Act established the Manufacturing Technology Centers (MTC) Program as a new initiative at the National Institute of Standards and Technology (NIST). The program, authorized by Congress in 1988, was created to improve U.S. industrial productivity and competitiveness in the growing international marketplace.

Each MTC's approach is unique, dictated by its location and the type of manufacturing in its client base. In general, the MTCs provide a wide range of services including:

- Individual project engineering
- Training courses
- Demonstrations
- Assistance in selecting and using software and equipment
- Factory survey visits
- Technical training
- Introduction of modern manufacturing equipment.

Seven MTCs have been established to date:

Great Lakes MTC (GLMTC)
Prospect Park Bldg.
4600 Prospect Ave.
Cleveland, OH 44103
(216) 432-5300

Northeast MTC (NEMTC)
RPI CII, Room 9009
Troy, NY 12180
(518) 276-6314

Southeast MTC (SMTC)
P.O. Box 1149
Columbia, SC 29202
(803) 252-6976

Midwest MTC (MMTC)
P.O. Box 1485
2901 Hubbard Rd.
Ann Arbor, MI 48106
(313) 769-4377

New Techniques and Consultants (cont'd)

Mid-America MTC (MAMTC)
10561 Barkley, Suite 602
Overland Park, KS 66212
(913) 649-4333

Upper Midwest MTC (UMMTC)
111 Third Ave. S., Suite 400
Minneapolis, MN 55401
(612) 338-7722

California MTC (CMTC)
13430 Hawthorne Blvd.
Hawthorne, CA 90250
(310) 355-3060

Contact Option

Michael Baum
National Institute of Standards and Technology
Gaithersburg, Maryland 20899
(301) 975-2763

The Federal Laboratory Consortium

THE FEDERAL LABORATORY Consortium is a little-known government agency comprised of over 700 member research laboratories and centers from sixteen federal departments. If a company has a specific technology need or question, one of the more than 100,000 scientists or engineers who works in the federal laboratories will have the solution. The FLC provides a link between the individual laboratory members and the potential users of government- developed technologies. The Federal Laboratories contain technologies, facilities, and expertise in all areas of science and engineering and offer opportunities such as:

- Consulting
- Cooperative research projects
- Employee exchange
- Exclusive or non-exclusive licensing
- Visits to laboratories
- Printed documentation
- Sponsored research
- Use of unique laboratory facilities
- Workshops, seminars, briefings.

The FLC Locator is a clearinghouse within the FLC network that assists companies in locating the appropriate laboratory or individual scientist or technician to handle a company's specific request. Once the contact is made, the specific technology transfer arrangements are made between the laboratory and the business.

To take advantage of the Federal Laboratory Consortium network and access the Federal Laboratories, contact one of the FLC Regional Coordinators. The Regional Coordinator working with the FLC Locator will find the appropriate laboratory to meet specific requests.

Federal Laboratory Consortium Locator
Dr. Andrew Cowan
DelaBarre & Associates, Inc.
P.O. Box 545
Sequim, WA 98382
(206) 683-1005

Federal Laboratory Consortium Regional Contacts

Far West
Diana Jackson
DOD-Naval Command Control
Ocean Surveillance Center
(619) 553-2101

Midwest
Dr. Paul Betten
DOE-Argonne National Laboratory
(708) 252-5361

Northeast
Al Lupinetti
DOT-Federal Aviation Administration
Technical Center
(609) 484-6689

Mid-Atlantic
Dr. Richard Rein
DOD-Naval Research Laboratory
(202) 767-3744

Mid-Continent
Douglas Blair
DOD-Air Force Armstrong Laboratory
(210) 536-3817

Southeast
H. Brown Wright
Tennessee Valley Authority
(615) 632-6435

Washington, DC
Dr. Beverly Berger
1850 M St., NW Suite 800
Washington, DC 20036
(202) 331-4220

Industry Studies

OPTIONS FOR INDUSTRY RESEARCH, from market analyses to forecasts, to planning and strategy, include producing studies internally, or commissioning an outside firm to do customized research. Given the prohibitive cost of customized research, companies are turning more and more to commercially available off-the-shelf studies produced by market research firms.

The most comprehensive guide to published market research reports, studies, and surveys is the *Findex* directory. This reference contains descriptions of consumer and industrial studies and surveys, syndicated and multi-client studies, audits and subscription research services, as well as published reports on general management and business topics. Individual reports may cover an entire industry, a specific segment of an industry, or an individual product or series of related products.

Recommended Resource

Findex
Cambridge Information Group
Attn: Marketing Department
7200 Wisconsin Ave.
Bethesda, MD 20814
(800) 843-7751

Contact Options

Selected Market Research Firms:

Business Trend Analysts
2171 Jericho Turnpike
Commack, NY 11725
(516) 462-5454

Leading Edge Reports
12417 Cedar Rd., Suite 29
Cleveland Heights, OH 44106
(216) 791-5500

The Freedonia Group, Inc.
20600 Chagrin Blvd., 10th Floor
Cleveland, OH 44122
(216) 921-6800

Frost & Sullivan, Inc.
106 Fulton St.
New York, NY 10038
(212) 233-1080

Euromonitor Plc
87-88 Turnmill St.
London EC1M 5QU
England
44-071-251-8024

Find/SVP
625 Avenue of the Americas
New York, NY 10011
(212) 463-6294

The Top Reference Sources

Directory of Manufacturers' Sales Agencies
Manufacturers' Agents National Association
(714) 859-4040

This book offers the most efficient way to hire outside sales representatives. The directory includes informative articles on finding the best agents for your products, communication between agents, manufacturers, and customers, and agent marketing, among others. Membership listings are cross-referenced and organized geographically and by product classification.

Listings include agency name, address, telephone number, branch offices, warehousing facilities, number of field salespeople, territory covered, and complete descriptions of the types of products sold.

Environmental Issues

Hazardous Waste

In 1976 the United States Congress passed a law called the Resource Conservation and Recovery Act (RCRA). Under RCRA, the United States Environmental Protection Agency has developed specific requirements for handling hazardous waste. These requirements control hazardous waste from the moment it is generated until its ultimate disposal. Since 1980, the EPA has been improving the hazardous waste program to further protect public health and the environment. As a result, the requirements were expanded to include small businesses that handle specified quantities of hazardous waste, and the number of wastes classified as hazardous has been increased.

Defining Hazardous Waste

A waste is a solid or liquid material that is no longer used. EPA defines waste as hazardous if it has certain properties that could pose dangers to human health and the environment after it is discarded. EPA considers a waste to be hazardous if it possesses certain characteristics (ignitability, corrosivity, reactivity, or toxicity) or if it is on a list of specific wastes determined by the EPA to be hazardous. RCRA regulations, found in the Code of Federal Regulations (CFR) Title 40, Part 261, present the listed hazardous wastes, describe hazardous waste characteristics, and specify test methods for determining whether waste is hazardous.

Complete lists of wastes identified by the EPA as hazardous can also be obtained from the EPA's RCRA/Superfund Hotline at (800) 424-9346 or from the Regional EPA offices and state hazardous waste management agencies listed in this chapter.

In general, a business is likely to produce hazardous waste if it:

- Uses petroleum products;
- Uses dyes, paints, printing inks, thinners, solvents, or cleaning fluids;
- Uses pesticides or other related chemicals;
- Uses materials that dissolve metals, wood, paper, or clothing (acids and caustics);
- Uses flammable materials;
- Uses materials that burn or itch upon contact with skin;
- Uses materials that bubble or fume upon contact with water;
- Receives delivery of products accompanied by a shipping paper or label indicating that the product is hazardous.

Waste Production Threshold

The EPA considers small-quantity generators to be producers of more than 220 and less than 2,200 pounds (more than 100 and less than 1,000 kilograms) of hazardous waste in a calendar month. Small-quantity generators are subject to hazardous waste requirements, and businesses should be aware that state agencies may have additional, or more restrictive requirements. Producers of 1,000 kilograms or more of hazardous waste in any calendar month, or more than one kilogram of certain acutely hazardous wastes (waste that is fatal to humans in small doses) are subject to the more extensive regulations that apply to large-quantity generators.

A business which produces hazardous waste and is regulated under the Federal Hazardous Waste Requirements, must:

- Obtain an EPA identification number for each site at which hazardous waste is generated. To obtain an EPA identification number, contact the EPA regional office or your state hazardous waste management agency and ask for Form 8700-12.
- Properly handle waste on the company premises. A permit may be required if waste is stored, treated, or disposed of on site. Contact the regional EPA office, state agency or RCRA/ Superfund Hotline for information on permits, storing and shipping of hazardous wastes.

Source: U.S. Environmental Protection Agency

Emergency Planning and Community Right-to-Know Act

Established as part of the Superfund Amendments passed by Congress in 1986, the purpose of the Emergency Planning and Community Right-to-Know-Act (EPCRA) is to inform the public and community emergency-response services, such as fire departments, about the existence of certain toxic substances in area businesses. If toxic substances are being released into the air, land, or water while they are being manufactured, processed or used in other ways, the EPCRA requires businesses to file a "Form R" with the EPA. (A list of more than 300 toxic substances is available from the EPA.)

Manufacturers should be aware that failure to submit a Form R is a felony, and even an unintentional violation of this law is a civil offense. The EPA estimates that compliance costs for businesses total $147 million dollars and acknowledges that small businesses are typically most burdened by these regulations.

For more information about environmental reporting laws, contact the EPCRA Hotline at (800) 535-0202 or your regional EPA office.

EPA Regional Offices

EPA Region I
Connecticut, Maine, Massachusetts, New Hampshire, Rhode Island, Vermont
Frank Ciavattieri, Chief
ME/VT Waste Management Branch
HPL-CAN2
JFK Federal Building
Boston, MA 02203
(617) 573-5770

EPA Region 2
New Jersey, New York, Puerto Rico, Virgin Islands
Stanley Siegel, Chief
Hazardous Waste Programs Branch
26 Federal Plaza Room 2343
New York, NY 10278
(212) 264-3384

EPA Region 3
Delaware, District of Columbia, Maryland, Pennsylvania, Virginia, West Virginia
Robert Allen, Chief
RCRA Programs Branch (3HW30)
841 Chestnut St.
Philadelphia, PA 19107
(215) 597-0980

EPA Region 4
Alabama, Florida, Georgia, Kentucky, Mississippi, North Carolina, South Carolina, Tennessee
James H. Scarbrough, Chief
RCRA and Federal Facilities Branch
345 Courtland St., NE
Atlanta, GA 30365
(404) 347-3016

EPA Region 5
Illinois, Indiana, Michigan, Minnesota, Ohio, Wisconsin
Judith A. Kertcher, Chief
RCRA Program
Management Branch
230 S. Dearborn St.
Chicago, IL 60604
(312) 353-8510

EPA Region 6
Arkansas, Louisiana, New Mexico, Oklahoma, Texas
Guanita Reiter, Chief
RCRA Programs Branch (6H-H)
1445 Ross Ave.
Dallas, TX 75270
(214) 655-6655

EPA Region 7
Iowa, Kansas, Missouri, Nebraska
Mike Sanderson, Chief
RCRA Branch
726 Minnesota Ave.
Kansas City, KS 66101
(913) 551-7050

EPA Region 8
Colorado, Montana, North Dakota, South Dakota, Utah, Wyoming
Terry Anderson, Chief
Implementation Branch
Denver Place (8HWM-R1)
999 18th St., Suite 500
Denver, CO 80202
(303) 293-1662

EPA Region 9
Arizona, California, Hawaii, Nevada, Guam, Marianas
Eve Levin
State Programs Branch
1235 Mission St.
San Francisco, CA 94103
(415) 744-1468

EPA Region 10
Alaska, Idaho, Oregon, Washington
Michael Gearheard, Chief
Waste Management Branch (HW-112)
1200 Sixth Ave.
Seattle, WA 98101
(206) 442-2782

Waste Management

Largest Waste Management Companies
Attwoods PLC (Attwoods Inc.)
2601 S. Bay Shore Dr., Penthouse 2
Coconut Grove, FL 33133
(305) 856-4455

Browning-Ferris Industries
P.O. Box 3151
Houston, TX 77253
(713) 870-8100

Waste Management (cont'd)

Chambers Development Co.
1700 Frankstown Rd.
Pittsburgh, PA 15235
(412) 242-6237

Laidlaw, Inc.
3221 N. Service Rd.
P.O. Box 5028
Burlington, Ontario L7R 3Y8
(416) 336-5151

Waste Management, Inc.
3003 Butterfield Rd.
Oak Brook, IL 60521
(708) 218-1500

Western Waste Industries
19803 S. Main St.
Carson, CA 90744
(310) 327-2522

Source: Waste Age

State and Territorial Hazardous Waste Management Agencies

Alabama
Land Division
Alabama Department of Environmental Managment
(205) 271-7730

Alaska
Alaska Department of Environmental Conservation
Division of Environmental Quality
(907) 465-2666

American Samoa
Environmental Quality Commission
Government of American Samoa
Overseas Operator: 663-2304

Arizona
Office of Waste and Water Quality Management
Arizona Department of Environmental Quality
(602) 257-2211

Arkansas
Hazardous Waste Division
Arkansas Department of Pollution Control and Ecology
(501) 562-7444, ext. 504

California
Toxic Substances Control Division
Department of Health Services
(916) 324-1826

Colorado
Waste Management Division
Colorado Department of Health
(303) 331-4830

Commonwealth of Northern Mariana Islands
Division of Environmental Quality
Department of Public Health & Environmental Services
Commonwealth of the Northern Mariana Islands
Office of the Governor
Overseas Operator: 6984

Connecticut
Hazardous Materials Management Unit
Department of Environmental Protection
(203) 566-4924

Delaware
Hazardous Waste Management Section
Division of Air and Waste Management
(302) 736-3672

District of Columbia
Pesticides and Hazardous Materials Division
Department of Consumer and Regulatory Affairs
(202) 783-3194

Florida
Division of Waste Management (UST)
Department of Environmental Regulations
(904) 488-0190

Georgia
Land Protection Branch
Industrial and Hazardous Waste
(404) 656-2833

Guam
Hazardous Waste Management Program
Guam Environmental Protection Agency
Overseas Operator: (671) 646-8863

Hawaii
Department of Health
Hazardous Waste Program
(808) 543-8226

Idaho
Hazardous Materials Bureau
Department of Health and Welfare
Idaho State House
(208) 334-5879

Illinois
Division of Land Pollution Control
Illinois Environmental Protection Agency
(217) 782-6760

Indiana
Indiana Department of Environmental Management
(317) 232-3210

Iowa
Air Quality and Solid Waste Protection
Department of Water, Air, and Waste Management
(515) 281-8693

Waste Management (cont'd)

Kansas
Bureau of Waste Management
Department of Health and Environment
(913) 862-9360, ext. 290

Kentucky
Division of Waste Management
Department of Environmental Protection
Cabinet for Natural Resources and
Environmental Protection
(502) 564-6716, ext. 214

Louisiana
Hazardous Waste Division
Office of Solid and Hazardous Waste
Louisiana Department of Environmental Quality
(504) 342-9079

Maine
Bureau of Oil and Hazardous Materials Control
Department of Environmental Protection
(207) 289-2651

Maryland
Hazardous and Solid Waste Management Administration
Maryland Department of the Environment
(301) 225-5647

Massachusetts
Division of Solid and Hazardous Waste
Massachusetts Department of Environmental Protection
(617) 292-5589

Michigan
Waste Management Division
Environmental Protection Bureau
Department of Natural Resources
(517) 373-2730

Minnesota
Solid and Hazardous Waste Division
Minnesota Pollution Control Agency
(612) 296-7282

Mississippi
Division of Solid and Hazardous Waste Management
Bureau of Pollution Control
Department of Natural Resources
(601) 961-5062

Missouri
Waste Management Program
Department of Natural Resources
Jefferson Building
(314) 751-3176

Montana
Solid and Hazardous Waste Bureau
Department of Health and Environmental Sciences
(406) 444-2821

Nebraska
Hazardous Waste Management Section
Department of Environmental Control
State House Station
(402) 471-2186

Nevada
Waste Management Program
Division of Environmental Protection
Department of Conservation and Natural Resources
Capitol Complex
(702) 687-4670

New Hampshire
Division of Public Health Services
Office of Waste Management
Department of Health and Welfare
Health and Welfare Building
(603) 271-4662

New Jersey
Division of Waste Management
Department of Environmental Protection
(609) 292-1250

New Mexico
Hazardous Waste Section
Groundwater and Hazardous Waste Bureau
New Mexico Health and Environment Department
(505) 827-2924

New York
Division of Solid and Hazardous Waste
Department of Environmental Conservation
(518) 457-6603

North Carolina
Solid and Hazardous Waste Management Branch
Division of Health Services
(919) 733-2178

North Dakota
Division of Hazardous Waste Management
Department of Health
(701) 224-2366

Ohio
Division of Solid and Hazardous Waste Management
Ohio Environmental Protection Agency
(614) 466-7220

Waste Management (cont'd)

Oklahoma
Waste Management Service
Oklahoma State Department of Health
(405) 271-5338

Oregon
Hazardous and Solid Waste Division
Department of Environmental Quality
(503) 229-5356

Pennsylvania
Bureau of Waste Management
Pennsylvania Department of Environmental Resources
(717) 787-9870

Puerto Rico
Environmental Quality Board
(809) 725-0439

Rhode Island
Solid Waste Management Program
Department of Environmental Management
(401) 277-2797

South Carolina
Bureau of Solid and Hazardous Waste Management
Department of Health and Environmental Control
(803) 758-5681

South Dakota
Office of Air Quality and Solid Waste
Department of Water and Natural Resources
(605) 773-3153

Tennessee
Division of Solid Waste Management
Tennessee Department of Public Health
(615) 741-3424

Texas
Hazardous and Solid Waste Division
Texas Water Commission
(512) 463-7760

Utah
Bureau of Solid and Hazardous Waste Management
Department of Health
(801) 533-4145

Vermont
Waste Management Division
Agency of Environmental Conservation
(802) 244-8702

Virgin Islands
Department of Conservation and Cultural Affairs
(809) 774-6420

Virginia
Division of Technical Services
Virginia Department of Waste Management
(804) 225-2667

Washington
Solid and Hazardous Waste Management Division
Department of Ecology
(206) 459-6316

West Virginia
Waste Management Division
Department of West Virginia Natural Resources
(304) 348-5935

Wisconsin
Bureau of Solid Waste Management
Department of Natural Resources
(608) 266-1327

Wyoming
Solid Waste Management Program
State of Wyoming
Department of Environmental Quality
(307) 777-7752

The Top Reference Sources

The Information Please Environmental Almanac
Houghton Mifflin, $9.95
(617) 725-5000

Compiled by the World Resources Institute, this informative book includes state, national, and global statistics on the environment, along with waste and clean-up information.

Articles of interest include green shopping, saving energy, toxins in food and water, recycling legislation, and facts on 145 countries.

Special highlights include the U.S. Green City rankings and comparisons.

Corporate Environmental Awards

National Corporate Environmental Awards

Sponsor	Award/Recipient of 1992 Award	Telephone
American Marketing Association	Edison Award for Environmental Achievement Naturally Colored Cottons Webster Industries Sanyo	(212) 255-3800
Composting Council	Hi Kellogg Award Hannaford Brothers	(703) 739-2401
Council on Economic Priorities	Corporate Conscience Awards Digital Equipment Aveda	(212) 420-1133
Direct Marketing Association	Robert Rodale Environmental Achievement Award Fingerhut Seventh Generation	(212) 768-7277
Du Pont Co.	Du Pont Awards Kraft General Foods Hoechst Celanese Plastipak Packaging	(302) 774-0821
Ecological Society of America	Corporate Award Pacific Gas & Electric	((202) 833-8773
Environmental Exchange	Recognition, not an award per se The Robbins Company	(202) 387-2182
Environmental Institute	Good Earthkeeping Seal American Airlines	(904) 375-2221
United Nations Environment Programme	Environmental Communications Award (First award to be presented in late 1993.)	(801) 466-3600
Flexible Packaging Association	Green Globe Award Duralam	(202) 842-3880
Glass Packaging Institute	Clear Choice Awards General Foods	(202) 452-9450
Keep America Beautiful	National Awards Recycle Roofs to Repair Roads	(203) 323-8987
Nat'l Arbor Day Foundation	National Awards Competition International Grocers Association Coca-Cola Corp. Louisiana Pacific Corp.	(402) 474-5655
Nat'l Environmental Develop. Assoc. (NEDA)	International Environmental Achievement Award Merck & Co.	(202) 638-1230
Nat'l Recycling Coalition	Fred Schmitt Award for Outstanding Leadership Bank of America	(202) 625-6406
Nat'l Wildlife Federation	National Conservation Achievement Awards Stephan Schmidheiny	(202) 797-6800
Renew America	National Environmental Achievement Awards AT&T	(202) 232-2252
United Earth	Earth Prize United Nations Development Program United Nations Environmental Program	(215) 517-7776
Wildlife Habitat Enhancement Council	Corporate Wildlife Habitat Certification Program Deere & Co.	(301) 588-8994
World Environment Center	Gold Medal Award Xerox	(212) 683-4700

Source: Green MarketAlert

Environmental Hotlines

MANY CLEARINGHOUSES, HOTLINES, and electronic bulletin boards have been developed by the Environmental Protection Agency (EPA) to respond to legislative initiatives requiring the Agency to provide outreach, communications and technology transfer to businesses, individuals, and other organizations. Clearinghouses facilitate the exchange of critical information and are also useful as a central access point for hard-to-locate technical reports and documents. The following information clearinghouses and hotlines may be of particular interest to manufacturers:

Air and Radiation

Control Technology Center (CTC)
U.S. Environmental Protection Agency
Emission Standards Division
Office of Air Quality Planning and Standards, MD-13
Research Triangle Park, NC 27711
(919) 541-0800

Air emissions and air pollution control technology for all air pollutants including air toxics emitted by stationary sources, and information on the Federal Small Business Assistance Program.

Emission Factor Clearinghouse
U.S. Environmental Protection Agency
Emission Factor Clearinghouse, MD-14
Research Triangle Park, NC 27711
(919) 541-5477

Air pollutant emission factors, for criteria and toxic polllutants from stationary and area sources, as well as mobile sources.

Green Lights Program
The Bruce Company
1850 K St., NW, Suite 290
Washington, DC 20006
(202) 775-6650

Provides information on energy-efficient lighting and how companies can join and become a partner or ally with the Green Lights Program. Five hundred companies have joined, and seven states have agreed to convert all state and government buildings to energy-efficient lighting in the next five years.

Indoor Air Quality Information Center
P.O. Box 37133
Washington, DC 20013
(301) 585-9020
(800) 438-4318

Provides access to a full range of information about indoor air quality problems.

National Air Toxics Information Clearinghouse
U.S. Environmental Protection Agency
Office of Air Quality Planning and Standards, MD-13
Research Triangle Park, NC 27711
(919) 541-0850

Collects, classifies, and disseminates air toxics (noncriteria pollutant) information submitted by state and local air agencies, and makes the audience aware of published air toxics information from the EPA, other federal agencies, and similar relevant sources. State and local information includes general agency facts, regulatory program descriptions, acceptable ambient limits, permitted facilities, source testing data, emissions inventories, and monitoring.

National Radon Hotline
U.S. Environmental Protection Agency
Radon Division, ANR 464
401 M St., SW
Washington, DC 20460
(800) 767-7236

Information on radon health effects and testing for radon. Information callers receive a brochure.

Office of Air Quality Planning and Standards Technology Transfer Network Bulletin Board System
Research Triangle Park, NC 27711
(919) 541-5742
(919) 541-5384 (voice)

Provides information and technology exchange in areas of air pollution control ranging from emission test methods to regulatory air quality models.

International

INFOTERRA
U.S. Environmental Protection Agency
USA National Focal Point, PM-211A
401 M St., SW, M 2904
Washington, DC 20460
(202) 260-5917

International environmental referral and research service made up of 140 countries coordinated by the United Nations Environment Programme in Nairobi, Kenya. The mission of the network is to link national and international institutions and experts in a cooperative venture to improve the quality of environmental decision-making worldwide.

Pesticides and Toxic Substances

Toxic Substances Control Act Assistance Information Service
U.S. Environmental Protection Agency
Environmental Assistance Division, TS-799
401 M Street, SW
Washington, DC 20460
(202) 554-1404
(202) 554-5603 (fax) for document requests only

Provides information on TSCA regulations to industry, labor and trade organizations, environmental groups, and the public. Technical as well as general information is available.

Environmental Hotlines (cont'd)

National Pesticide Information Retrieval System
CERIS (NPIRS)
1231 Cumberland Ave., Suite A
West Lafayette, IN 47906
(317) 494-6614
A membership organization for pesticide manufacturers and users, libraries, law firms, and state/federal agencies.

Hazardous and Solid Waste

Emergency Planning and Community Right-to Know Information Hotline
Booz, Allen & Hamilton, Inc.
1725 Jefferson Davis Highway
Arlington, VA 22202
(703) 920-9877
(800) 535-0202
Provides regulatory, policy, and technical assistance to federal agencies, local, and state governments, the public, and the regulated community in response to questions related to the Emergency Planning and Community Right-to-Know Act (Title III of SARA).

Solid Waste Information Clearinghouse and Hotline
P.O. Box 7219
8750 Georgia Ave., Suite 140
Silver Spring, MD 20910
(800) 67-SWICH
Developed and partially funded by the Solid Waste Association of North America and EPA, SWICH is comprised of a library system and an electronic bulletin board, providing information on all aspects of solid waste management, including source reduction, recycling, composting, planning, education and training, legislation and regulation, waste combustion, collection, transfer, disposal, landfill gas, and special wastes.

Resource Conservation and Recovery Act/Superfund/Underground Storage Tank Hotline (RCRA/SF/OUST)
1725 Jefferson Davis Highway
Arlington, VA 22202
(703) 920-9810
(800) 424-9346
Provides assistance to the public and regulated community in understanding the EPA's regulations pursuant to RCRA, UST, CERCLA, and Pollution Prevention/Waste Minimization.

Hazardous Waste Ombudsman Program
U.S. Environmental Protection Agency
401 M St., SW, Room SE 315
Washington, DC 20460
(800) 262-7937
The hazardous waste management program established under the RCRA is the most complex regulatory program developed by the EPA. It assists the public and regulated community in resolving problems concerning any program or requirement under the Hazardous Waste Program. The Ombudsman Program, located at Headquarters and in each Regional office (see listing in this chapter), handles complaints from citizens and the regulated community, obtains facts, sorts information, and substantiates policy.

National Response Center
U.S. Coast Guard Headquarters
2100 Second St., SW, Room 2611
Washington, DC 20593
(202) 267-2675
(800) 424-8802
Receives reports of oil, hazardous chemical, biological, and radiological releases. The NRC then passes those reports to a predesignated federal On-Scene Coordinator who coordinates cleanup efforts with other responsible federal agencies.

Methods Information Communications Exchange (MICE)
Falls Church, VA 22043
(703) 821-4789
Analytical test-methods for the characterization of hazardous waste in support of the Resource Conservation and Recovery Act (RCRA).

Pollution Prevention

Stratospheric Ozone Information Hotline
The Bruce Co.
501 3rd St., NW
Washington, DC 20001
(800) 296-1996
Consultation on ozone protection regulations and requirements under Title VI of the Clean Air Act Amendments (CAAA) of 1990. Title VI covers the following key aspects of the production, use, and safe disposal of ozone-depleting chemicals: (1) production and phase-out controls; (2) servicing of motor vehicle air conditioners; (3) recycling and emission reduction; (4) technician and equipment certification; (5) approval of alternatives; (6) ban of nonessential uses; (7) product labeling; and (8) federal procurement.

OZONACTION
c/o SAIC
7600-A Leesburg Pike
Falls Church, VA 22043
(703) 821-4800
Ozone depleting substance alternatives, pollution prevention, and source reduction, recycling, and substitution.

Environmental Hotlines (cont'd)

Pollution Prevention Information Clearinghouse
Science Applications International Corporation
7600A Leesburg Pike
Falls Church, VA 22043
(703) 821-4800

PPIC is designed to provide technical, policy, programmatic, legislative, and financial information dedicated to reducing industrial pollutants through technology transfer, education, and public awareness. It is a national and international communication network that targets multi-media source reduction and recycling opportunities.

Water

National Small Flows Clearinghouse
West Virginia University
P.O. Box 6064
Morgantown, WV 26506
(800) 624-8301

Distributes publications and videotapes, performs literature searches, operates a toll-free hotline, produces free newsletters, and operates a computer bulletin board.

Small Business

Small Business Ombudsman Clearinghouse/Hotline
U.S. Environmental Protection Agency
Small Business Ombudsman, A-149-C
401 M St., SW
Washington, DC 20460
(703) 305-5938
Fax: (703) 305-6462

Special attention is directed to apprising the trade associations representing small business interests of current regulatory developments.

Recommended Resources

Access EPA
U.S. Environmental Protection Agency
Public Information Center
(202) 260-2049
EPA Document Number: EPA/IMSD-91-100

A directory of U.S. Environmental Protection Agency and other public sector environmental information resources. First published in 1991, this annual directory provides information on documents, dockets, clearinghouses and hotlines, records, databases, models, EPA libraries, and state libraries.

Environmental Organizations

SELECTED INDUSTRY AND ASSOCIATION contacts for further information on Recycling, Waste Management, and Environmental Issues, include:

Aluminum Association, Inc.
Suite 300
900 19th St., NW
Washington, DC 20006
(202) 862-5100

Aluminum Recycling Association
1000 16th St., NW
Washington, DC 20036
(202) 785-0951

American Paper Institute
260 Madison Ave.
New York, NY 10016
(212) 340-0650

American Petroleum Institute
1220 L St., NW
Washington, DC 20005
(202) 682-8200

American Public Works Association
1301 Pennsylvania Ave., NW, Suite 401
Washington, DC 20004
(202) 393-2792

Association of Petroleum Re-Refiners
1915 I St., NW, Suite 600
Washington, DC 20006
(202) 639-4490

Association of State and Territorial
Solid Waste Management Officials
444 N. Capitol St.
Washington, DC 20001
(202) 624-5828

Can Manufacturers Institute
625 Massachusetts Ave., NW
Washington, DC 20036
(202) 232-4677

Council on Plastic and Packaging in
the Environment
Suite 300
1275 K St., NW
Washington, DC 20005
(202) 789-1310

Environmental Action Foundation
1525 New Hampshire Ave., NW
Washington, DC 20036
(202) 745-4871

Environmental Defense Fund
1616 P St., NW
Washington, DC 20036
(202) 387-3500

Environmental Organizations (cont'd)

Food Service and Packaging Institute
1025 Connecticut Ave., NW, Suite 513
Washington, DC 20036
(202) 347-3756

Glass Packaging Institute
1801 K St., NW, Suite 1105-L
Washington, DC 20005
(202) 887-4850

Governmental Refuse Collection and Disposal Association
P.O. Box 7219
Silver Spring, MD 20910
(301) 585-2898

Institute of Clean Air Companies
1707 L St., NW Suite 570
Washington, DC 20036
(202) 457-0911

Institute of Scrap Recycling Industries, Inc.
1325 G. St., NW, Suite 1000
Washington, DC 20005
(202) 466-4050

National Association of Counties
440 First St., NW
Washington, DC 20001
(202) 393-6226

National Association of Towns and Townships
1522 K St., NW, Suite 730
Washington, DC 20005
(202) 737-5200

National Association for Recovery
5024 Parkway Plaza Blvd.
Charlotte, NC 28217
(704) 357-3250

National Association of Solvent Recyclers
1333 New Hampshire Ave., NW
Washington, DC 20036
(202) 463-6956

National Governors Association
444 N. Capitol St.
Washington, DC 20001
(202) 624-5300

National League of Cities
1301 Pennsylvania Ave., NW
Washington, DC 20004
(202) 626-3000

National Oil Recyclers Assn.
2600 Virginia Ave., NW, Suite 1000
Washington, DC 20037
(202) 333-8800

National Recycling Coalition
1101 30th St., NW, Suite 305
Washington, DC 20007
(202) 625-6406

National Soft Drink Assn.
Solid Waste Management Dept.
1101 16th St., NW
Washington, DC 20036
(202) 463-6740

National Solid Wastes Management Association
1730 Rhode Island Ave., NW, Suite 1000
Washington, DC 20036
(202) 659-4613

National Tire Dealers and Retreaders Association
1250 I Street, NW, Suite 400
Washington, DC 20005
(202) 789-2300

Partnership for Plastics Progress
1275 K Street, NW, Suite 500
Washington, DC 20005
(202) 371-5319

Plastics Recycling Institute
Rutgers, The State University of New Jersey
Center for Plastics Recycling Research
Bldg. 3529, Busch Campus
Piscataway, NJ 08855
(201) 932-4402

Polystyrene Packaging Council
1025 Connecticut Ave,. NW, Suite 513
Washington, DC 20036
(202) 822-6424

Rubber Manufacturers Assn., Inc.
1400 K. St., NW, Suite 900
Washington, DC 20005
(202) 682-4800

Steel Can Recycling Institute
Foster Plaza 10
680 Andersen Dr.
Pittsburgh, PA 15220
(412) 922-2772

Textile Fibers and By-Products Association
P.O. Box 11065
Charlotte, NC 28220
(704) 527-5593

The Society of the Plastics Industry, Inc.
1275 K St., NW, Suite 400
Washington, DC 20005
(202) 371-5200

Environmental Organizations (cont'd)

The Vinyl Institute
Wayne Interchange Plaza II
155 Route 45 West
Wayne, NJ 07470
(201) 890-9299

U.S. Conference of Mayors
1620 I St., NW
Washington, DC 20006
(202) 293-7330

U.S. Department of Energy Biofuels & Municipal Waste Technology Division
1000 Independence Ave., NW
Washington, DC 20585
(202) 586-6750

Source: List prepared in part by the Institute of Scrap Recycling Industries, Inc.

Labeling Regulations

ON FEBRUARY 11, 1993, CONGRESS issued the final ruling on Section 611 of the Clean Air Act, which requires labeling of products made with or containing class I and class II ozone-depleting substances (such as chloroflourocarbons or CFCs). It also requires that containers containing class I or class II substances be labeled.

A product containing an adhesive for example, must be labeled as "containing." When that product is applied by a subsequent manufacturer in affixing a cushion to a seat, the seat must be labeled as a "product manufactured with" because the CFCs have been released. The subsequent sale of the seat to an automobile manufacturer, however, would not result in the labeling of a car based on that product.

All products made prior to May 15, 1993, are exempt from the labeling requirements if the manufacturer is able to show within 24 hours that its products were made before that date. Likewise, an importer, when so requested by the EPA, must be able to show that the products imported were manufactured before the deadline.

For additional information, including a complete list of class I and class II ozone-depleting chemicals, contact the Stratospheric Ozone Information Hotline at (800) 296-1996. To receive copies of the final rule and any follow-up notices regarding the labeling rule, see the Federal Register in a local university or government library.

Source: Environmental Protection Agency

Almanac Fact

More than 80 percent of Americans say they are willing to pay "a little more" for an environmentally friendly product.

Source: Cambridge Reports/Research International

Waste Exchanges

THE IDEA BEHIND WASTE EXCHANGE is that one company's waste or unwanted material may be another company's resource. By promoting the reuse and recycling of industrial materials through waste exchanges, it is estimated that industry currently saves $27 million in raw material and disposal costs and the energy equivalent of more than 100,000 barrels of oil annually. With over 7 billion tons of industrial solid waste generated yearly, and only 6 million tons of waste currently on the exchange, there is an enormous potential for savings as more companies make use of waste exchanges.

Established in 1992, the National Materials Exchange Network is a partnership of industrial waste exchanges, supported in part by Congress and assisted by the Environmental Protection Agency, that increases recycling opportunities within industry. Materials listed on the Exchange include waste by-product, off-spec, overstock, obsolete, and damaged materials; used and virgin, solid and hazardous. Access to the National Materials Exchange Network is free with participation in your local exchange and available 24 hours a day.

Contact Option

National Materials Exchange Network
For computer modem access: (800) 858-6625
Canada only: (509) 325-1724
Direct assistance: (509) 325-0507

Waste Exchanges in North America

Alberta Waste Materials Exchange
Alberta Research Council
P.O. Box 8330
Postal Station F
Edmonton, Alberta
Canada T6H 5X2
(403) 450-5408

AR Industrial Development Commission
#1 Capitol Mall
Little Rock, AR 72201
(501) 682-1370

Arizona Waste Exchange
4725 E. Sunrise Dr., Suite 215
Tucson, AZ 85718
(602) 299-7716

B.A.R.T.E.R.
2512 Delaware St., SE
Minneapolis, MN 55414
(612) 627-6811

British Columbia Waste Exchange
2150 Maple St.
Vancouver, B.C. V6J 3T3
(604) 731-7222

California Waste Exchange
P.O. Box 806
Sacramento, CA 95812
(916) 322-4742

CALMAX
909 12th St., Suite 205
Sacramento, CA 95814
(916) 255-2369

Canadian Chemical Exchange
P.O. Box 1135
Ste-Adele, Quebec
Canada JOR 1LO
(514) 229-6511

Canadian Waste Materials Exchange
ORTECH International
2395 Speakman Drive
Mississauga, Ontario
Canada L5K 1B3
(416) 822-4111, ext. 265

Department of Environmental Protection
18 Riley Rd.
Frankfort, KY 40601
(502) 564-6761

Enstar Corporation
P.O. Box 189
Latham, NY 12110
(518) 785-0470

Hawaii Waste Exchange
Maui Recycling Group
Paia, HI 96779
(808) 667-7744

Indiana Waste Exchange
Purdue University
School of Civil Engineering
Civil Engineering Building
West Lafayette, IN 47907
(317) 494-5036

Industrial Materials Exchange
172 20th Ave.
Seattle, WA 98122
(206) 296-4633

Industrial Materials Exchange Service
P.O. Box 19276
Springfield, IL 62794
(217) 782-0450

Industrial Waste Information Exchange
New Jersey Chamber of Commerce
5 Commerce St.
Newark, NJ 07102
(201) 623-7070

Waste Exchanges (cont'd)

Iowa Waste Reduction Center
75 BRC, University of Northern Iowa
Cedar Falls, IA 50614
(319) 273-2079

Louisiana/Gulf Coast Waste Exchange
1419 CEBA
Baton Rouge, LA 70803
(504) 388-4594

Manitoba Waste Exchange
c/o Biomass Energy Institute, Inc.
1329 Niakwa Road
Winnipeg, Manitoba
Canada R2J 3T4
(204) 257-3891

MISSTAP
P.O. Drawer CN
Mississippi State, MS 39762
(601) 325-8454

Missouri Environmental Improvement Authority
325 Jefferson St.
Jefferson City, MO 65101
(314) 751-4919

Montana Industrial Waste Exchange
Montana Chamber of Commerce
P.O. Box 1730
Helena, MT 59624
(406) 442-2405

New Hampshire Waste Exchange
c/o NHRRA
P.O. Box 721
Concord, NH 03301
(603) 224-6996

Northeast Industrial Waste Exchange, Inc.
90 Presidential Plaza, Suite 122
Syracuse, NY 13202
(315) 422-6572

Ontario Waste Exchange
ORTECH International
2395 Speakman Dr.
Mississauga, Ontario
Canada L5K 1B3
(416) 822-4111, ext. 512

Pacific Materials Exchange
South 3707 Godfrey Blvd.
Spokane, WA 99204
(509) 623-4244

Peel Regional Waste Exchange
10 Peel Center Dr.
Brampton, Ontario
Canada L6T 4B9
(416) 791-9400

Portland Chemical Consortium
P.O. Box 751
Portland, OR 97207
(503) 725-3811

RENEW
Texas Water Commission
P.O. Box 13087
Austin, TX 78711
(512) 463-7773

Resource Exchange & News
400 Ann St., NW
Suite 201-A
Grand Rapids, MI 49504
(616) 363-3262

San Francisco Waste Exchange
2524 Benvenue #35
Berkeley, CA 94704
(415) 548-6659

SEMREX
171 W. 3rd St.
Winona, MN 55987
(507) 457-6460

Southeast Waste Exchange
Urban Institute
UNCC Station
Charlotte, NC 28223
(704) 547-2307

Southern Waste Information Exchange
P.O. Box 960
Tallahassee, FL 32302
(800) 441-7949
(904) 644-5516

Tennessee Waste Exchange
226 Capital Blvd., Suite 800
Nashville, TN 37202
(615) 256-5141

Wastelink, Division of Tencon, Inc.
140 Wooster Pike
Milford, OH 45150
(513) 248-0012

Almanac Fact

Of the total amount of hazardous waste sent to landfills, electrical, gas and sanitary services supply 61 percent.

Source: The Environmental Almanac

Recycling

MOST AUTHORITIES AGREE THAT RECYCLING can realistically reduce the amount of municipal solid waste by approximately 25 percent. Recycling allows discarded materials to be diverted from the waste stream and begins with separation and collection of recyclable material at the source.

Easily Recycled Materials

- Aluminum: Today we recycle more than 65,000 aluminum beverage cans every minute.
- Iron and Steel: In 1989, the U.S. scrap processing industry prepared 60 million tons for recycling, double the amount of paper, nonferrous metals (aluminum, copper, lead, zinc, etc.), glass, and plastics combined.
- Plastics: Currently, three principal types of plastics are being recycled:
  - PETE (polyethylene terephthalate) soft drink containers, especially the two-litre bottle, are the most common plastic containers manufactured–and discarded–today.
  - HDPE (high-density polyethylene) containers are used as milk and water jugs, base cups or bottoms of PET soft drink bottles, oil bottles, and detergent and other household cleaner bottles.
  - Polystyrene Foam is used primarily to make fast food carryout containers.
- Glass: The use of crushed glass, or cullet, in manufacturing offers economic advantages over virgin materials (sand, soda ash, limestone). Cullet melts at a lower temperature than the raw materials, so manufacturers can reduce energy usage as well as particulate emissions into the atmosphere. Today, 25 percent of any given glass container is made from recycled glass.
- Paper: Paper and paperboard constitute the largest proportion of municipal solid waste. More than 30 percent of all the paper and paperboard used in the United States today is being collected and used as either a component to make recycled paper and paperboard or as an export to foreign nations.

Source: Institute of Scrap Recycling Industries

Products and Materials in the Waste Stream

Product	Tons Generated (millions)	% of Waste Stream	Tons Recycled (millions)	% of Product Recycled
Yard Waste	31.6	17.6	0.5	1.6
Corrugated Boxes	23.1	12.9	10.5	45.4
Newspaper	13.3	7.4	4.4	33.3
Food Waste	13.2	7.4	0.0	0.0
Consumer Electronics	10.6	5.9	0.1	0.7
Furniture	7.5	4.2	0.0	0.0
Office Paper	7.3	4.1	1.6	22.5
Glass Beer & Soft Drink Bottles	5.4	3.0	1.1	20.0
Books & Magazines	5.3	3.0	0.7	13.2
Paper Toys & Games	5.2	3.0	0.0	0.0
Folding Cartons	4.4	2.4	0.3	7.7
Junk Mail	4.1	2.3	0.6	14.6
Clothing & Shoes	4.0	2.2	0.0	0.6
Glass Jars	3.9	2.2	0.3	8.1
Large Appliances	3.0	1.7	0.2	7.0
Paper Tissue & Towels	3.0	1.7	0.0	0.0
Paper Bags	2.9	1.6	0.2	7.0
Disposable Diapers	2.7	1.5	0.0	0.0
Rocks & Dirt	2.7	1.5	0.0	0.0
Steel Food Cans	2.5	1.4	0.4	15.0
Rubber Tires	2.2	1.2	0.1	4.8
Wood Crates & Pallets	2.1	1.2	0.0	0.0
Glass Wine & Liquor Bottles	2.0	1.1	0.1	5.0
Misc. Plastic Products	1.7	1.0	0.0	0.0

Recycling (cont'd)

Product	Tons Generated (millions)	% of Waste Stream	Tons Recycled (millions)	% of Product Recycled
Lead-acid Batteries	1.6	0.9	1.5	90.0
Aluminum Beer & Soft Drink Cans	1.4	0.8	0.8	55.0
Plastic Wraps	1.1	0.6	0.0	0.0
Plastic Bags	0.8	0.4	0.0	0.0
Paper Plates & Cups	0.7	0.4	0.0	0.0
Paper Milk Cartons	0.5	0.3	0.0	0.0
Plastic Soft Drink Bottles	0.4	0.2	0.1	21.0
Plastic Milk Bottles	0.4	0.2	0.0	0.0
Other	9.0	4.6	0.0	0.0
TOTAL	179.6	100.0	23.5	13.1

Source: U.S. Environmental Protection Agency

The Top 25 Counties for Cancer-Causing Chemicals

Rank	County	State	Industry Releases (million lbs.)
1	Jefferson	LA	13.50
2	Harris	TX	10.88
3	Monroe	NY	10.45
4	Los Angeles	CA	10.21
5	Jefferson	TX	7.27
6	Kalamazoo	MI	6.80
7	Posey	IN	6.73
8	Brazoria	TX	5.87
9	Nueces	TX	5.33
10	Albany	NY	4.88
11	Marion	IN	4.64
12	Berkshire	MA	4.63
13	Broome	NY	4.55
14	Allen	OH	4.49
15	Ouachita	LA	4.27
16	Cuyahoga	OH	4.15
17	Erie	PA	4.14
18	Orange	CA	3.99
19	Bradley	TN	3.75
20	Allegheny	PA	3.68
21	Salt Lake	UT	3.58
22	Cook	IL	3.54
23	Lake	IN	3.54
24	Washington	OH	3.51
25	Wayne	MI	3.37

Source: U.S. Environmental Protection Agency

The Top Reference Sources

U.S. Industrial Outlook
U.S. Government Printing Office, $37.00
(202) 783-3238
Stock #003-009-00618-0

This annual business report is a major publication of the International Trade Administration, U.S. Department of Commerce. The reference includes industry-by-industry overviews with economic analyses and projections for manufacturing, services, and high-technology industries.

Features include industry forecasts, five-year industry projections, 450 tables and charts, profiles of international competitiveness, international trade forecasts, and new environmental reviews.

Recycled Content Mandates

TWELVE STATES NOW REQUIRE manufacturers to use recycled materials. Connecticut and California were the first states to enact these laws with mandates that responded to the glut of old newspapers in 1989. The following is a list of these twelve states and the amount of recycled materials that will be required in manufacturing:

- Arizona
  Newsprint: 50% by 2000.
- California
  Newsprint: 50% by 2000.
  Plastic Containers: options similar to Oregon; see below.
  Glass Containers: 65% by 2005.
  Trash Bags: 10% by 1993; 30% by 1995.
- Connecticut
  Newsprint: 50% by 2000.
  Phone Books: 40% by 2001.
- Illinois
  Newsprint: 45% by 1997.
- Maryland
  Newsprint: 40% by 1998.
  Phone Books: 12% by 1994; 15% by 1995; 20% by 1996; 25% by 1997; 30% by 1998; 40% after 1999.
- Missouri
  Newsprint: 50% by 2000.
- North Carolina
  Newsprint: 12% by 1992; 40% by 1997.
- Oregon
  Newsprint: 7.5% by 1995.
  Glass Containers: 35% by 1995; 50% by 2000 (food/beverages).
  Plastic Containers, options: made of 25% post-consumer material; recycled at 25% rate; reusable or refillable, or reduced 10% in content by 1995 (certain exemptions).
  Phone Books: 25% by 1995.
- Rhode Island
  Newsprint: 11% by 1993; 22% by 1996; 31% by 1998; 40% by 2000.
- Texas
  Newsprint: 10% by 1993; 30% by 2000.
- West Virginia
  Newsprint: highest "practicable" content; advisory committee created.
- Wisconsin
  Newsprint: 45% by 2001.
  Plastic Containers: 10% by 1995.

Source: National Solid Wastes Management

Recycled Symbols

1. Polyethylene terephthalate (PETE)

2. High-Density Polyethylene (HDPE)

3. Polyvinyl Chloride (PVC)

4. Low-Density Polyethylene (LDPE)

5. Polypropylene (PP)

6. Polystyrene (PS)

7. Other

Tax Incentives for Recycling

Arizona
30 percent tax credit on income/corporate taxes for purchase of equipment that makes products with at least 10 percent recycled content.

California
Banks and corporations may take a 40 percent tax credit for the cost of equipment used to manufacture recycled products. Development bonds for manufacturing products with recycled materials.

Colorado
Individual and corporate income tax credits for investments in plastics recycling technology. Up to 20 percent tax credit for purchase of certain equipment to make products using post-consumer recycled material.

Florida
Sales tax exemption on recycling machinery purchased after July 1, 1988. Tax incentives to encourage affordable transportation of recycled goods from collection points to sites for processing and disposal.

Illinois
Tax credits for real property used in collecting, separating, and processing recyclable materials. Sales tax exemptions for manufacturing equipment.

Indiana
Property tax exemptions for buildings, equipment, and land involved in converting waste into new products.

Iowa
Sales tax exemptions.

Kentucky
Property tax exemptions to encourage recycling industries.

Maine
Business tax credits equal to 30 percent of cost of recycling equipment and machinery. Subsidies to municipalities for scrap metal transportation costs. Taxpayers are also allowed a credit equal to $5.00 per ton of wood waste from lumber production that is incinerated for fuel or to generate energy. The total credit may not exceed 50 percent of the tax liability.

Maryland
From their state income taxes, individuals and corporations can deduct 100 percent of expenses incurred to convert a furnace to burn used oil or to buy and install equipment to recycle used Freon.

Montana
25 percent tax credit on purchase of equipment to process recyclable materials; up to 5 percent off income taxes for purchase of business-related products made with recycled material.

New Jersey
Businesses may take a 50 percent investment credit for recycling vehicles and machinery. They are also eligible for a 6 percent sales tax exemption on purchases of recycling equipment.

New Mexico
Tax credits on equipment to recycle or use recycled materials in a manufacturing process.

North Carolina
Industrial and corporate income tax credits and exemptions for equipment and facilities.

Oklahoma
15 percent income tax credit on purchase of equipment and facilities to use recyclable materials in a product.

Oregon
Individuals and corporations receive income tax credits for capital investment in recycling equipment and facilities. Special tax credits are available for equipment, property, or machinery necessary to collect, transport, or process reclaimed plastic.

Texas
Sludge recycling corporations are eligible for franchise tax exemptions.

Virginia
Individuals and corporations may take a tax credit worth 10 percent of the purchase price of any machinery and equipment for processing recyclable materials. The credit also applies to manufacturing plants that use recycled products.

Washington
Motor vehicles are exempt from rate regulation when transporting recovered materials from collection to reprocessing facilities and manufacturers. Tires and certain other hard-to-dispose materials are exempt from portions of sales and use taxes.

Wisconsin
Sales tax exemptions for waste reduction and recycling equipment and facilities; business property tax exemptions for some equipment.

Source: National Solid Waste Management Association

Recommended Resources

PaperMatcher: A Directory of Paper Recycling Resources
American Paper Institute, Inc.
1250 Connecticut Ave., NW, Suite 360
Washington, DC 20036
(800) 878-8878

American Recycling Market Directory
P.O. Box 577 O
Ogdensburg, NY 13669
(800) 267-0707

The Clean Air Act

ENACTED TO CORRECT SERIOUS AIR pollution problems in the United States, the Clean Air Act Amendments of 1990 contain some of the most important elements of environmental legislation in recent years.

The Environmental Protection Agency estimates the new Clean Air Act will remove 56 billion pounds of pollution from the air each year. In human terms, these measures will significantly reduce lung disease, cancer, and other serious health problems caused by air pollution.

Air quality improvements mandated by the Clean Air Act Amendments include:

- Greatly reduced emissions of toxic air pollution and acid rain-causing pollutants
- Attainment of air quality standards nationwide by the year 2010
- Cleaner cars, fuels, factories, and power plants
- Less damage to lakes, streams, parks, and forests
- Reduced emissions of greenhouse gases
- Less damage to the stratospheric ozone layer.

The regulatory requirements of the CAAA will exact profound changes in many U.S. industries. For example, the amendments significantly affect the electric utility industry and, consequently, the coal industry. Sulfur emissions controls in the CAAA are divided into two phases. Phase I controls set out specific 1995 sulfur dioxide emissions limits for power plants built before 1978 (about 110 power plants). Phase II controls, set for the year 2000, generally limit sulfur dioxide emissions to the same level as for post-1978 power plants: 1.2 pounds of sulfur dioxide per million Btu. To achieve these emissions levels, plants will retrofit scrubbers, switch to low-sulfur coal, blend low-sulfur with high-sulfur coal, co-fire with natural gas, re-power with advanced technology boilers, or perhaps even close the plant. Plants may also trade emission allowance credits issued to them by the EPA.

The potential global climate change caused by so-called "greenhouse gases" is yet another environmental issue important to the coal industry. Carbon dioxide, which absorbs solar radiation and traps the sun's heat, has been steadily increasing in the earth's atmosphere. All fossil fuels emit carbon dioxide, but coal emits 80% more per unit of energy consumed than natural gas, and about 20 percent more carbon dioxide than fuel oil. Consequently, coal-fired power stations are prime candidates for controls on carbon dioxide emissions. While no actions affecting the coal industry are likely in the near future, the issue of global warming has far from disappeared.

Passage of the CAAA also had a significant impact on the U.S. petroleum refining industry. The first oxygenated gasoline season began in November of 1992, and mandates that motor gasoline sold during at least four winter months in 39 areas of the country classified as moderate or serious carbon monoxide non-attainment areas must have a minimum oxygen content of 2.7 percent by weight (2 percent in California). Beginning January 1995, the nine worst ozone non-attainment areas with populations in excess of 250,000 must begin using motor gasoline that meets mandated emissions and composition requirements. As a result of these and other mandates, U.S. refiners have had to closely examine their operations relative to the CAAA, committing considerable resources to plant additions and reconfigurations, product reformulations, and research and development to advance processing technologies.

The search for alternatives to CFC (chlorofluorocarbon) and HCFC (hydrofluorocarbon) refrigerants, as required by Title VI of the Clean Air Act, is one of the greatest challenges the air conditioning and refrigeration industry has ever faced. On July 1, 1992, Section 608 of the act prohibited intentional venting of CFCs and HCFCs during service, repair, or disposal of any air conditioning or refrigeration equipment. There will be controls on the sale of refrigerants and the disposition of recovered refrigerants, as well as mandatory certification of recovery/recycling equipment, technicians, and the purity of refrigerant recovered, reclaimed, and resold. Section 612 (list of safe alternatives to CFCs and HCFCs and Section 611 (labeling of products containing or manufactured with controlled substances) regulations are also under development.

Paper and pulp mills are affected as the CAAA provides extensive changes to new and existing source requirements for ozone, carbon monoxide, and particulate matter. Paper companies will be required to demonstrate that they are in compliance with all existing air standards, or that the benefits of a mill outweigh the environmental and social costs of anti-pollution regulations.

Clean Air Act Amendments have created new markets in the United States for the general components industry, particularly valves and pipe fittings. Environmental and health concerns that are emerging abroad are also creating incipient markets for U.S. valve and pipe fitting companies, which are global leaders in the pollution control and pollution abatement industry.

Industry Preparations

Large and small companies need to become aware of the many new clean air requirements and deadlines for compliance. Industry needs to know about the flexible options, pollution prevention incentives, programs that encourage technological innovation, and market-based programs that clean the air at a much lower cost. These programs include:

- *Early Reductions Program* offers companies incentives to take early voluntary action to reduce emissions and, in so doing, receive a six-year deferral on new clean air requirements.

The Clean Air Act (cont'd)

- *Allowance Trading System* enables utilities to buy and sell emission credits among themselves, provided that total emissions reductions are achieved.
- *Fuel Averaging Program* enables oil companies to meet tight new reformulated fuel standards by averaging the oxygen content in different grades of gasoline.

Recommended Resource

The Clean Air Act Amendments
National Association of Manufacturers
Publications Coordinator
1331 Pennsylvania Ave., NW
Suite 1500, North Tower
Washington, DC 20004
(800) 637-3005

Contact Options

Government Agencies:

Global Change Division
U.S. Environmental Protection Agency
Office of Atmospheric and Indoor Air Programs
Office of Air and Radiation (6202J)
(800) 296-1996

Clean Air Act Advisory Committee
U.S. Environmental Protection Agency
Office of Air & Radiation
(202) 260-7400

State Air Quality Agencies:

Department of Environmental Management
Air Division
(205) 271-7861

Department of Environmental Conservation
Air Quality Management Section
(907) 465-5100

Department of Environmental Quality
Office of Air Quality
(602) 257-2308

Department of Pollution Control and Ecology
Air Division
(501) 562-7444

Air Resources Board
(916) 445-4383

Department of Health
Air Pollution Control Division
(303) 331-8500

Department of Environmental Protection
Bureau of Air Management
(203) 566-2506

Department of Natural Resources and Environmental Control
Division of Air and Waste Management
Air Resources Section
(302) 739-4791

Department of Consumer and Regulatory Affairs
Environmental Control Division
Air Quality Control and Monitoring Branch
(202) 404-1120

Department of Environmental Regulation
Air Resources Management
(904) 488-1344

Department of Natural Resources
Environmental Protection Dividion
Air Protection Branch
(404) 656-6900

State Department of Health, Laboratories Division
Air Surveillance and Analysis Branch
(808) 586-4019

Division of Environmental Quality
Air Quality Bureau
(208) 334-5898

Environmental Protection Agency
Division of Air Pollution Control
(217) 782-7326

Department of Environmental Management
Office of Air Management
(317) 232-8384

Department of Natural Resources
Air Quality Section
(515) 281-8852

Department of Health and Environment
Bureau of Air and Waste Management
(913) 296-1593

Department for Environmental Protection
Division for Air Quality
(502) 564-3382

Department of Environmental Quality
Office of Air Quality and Radiation Protection
Air Quality Division
(504) 765-0110

Department of Environmental Protection
Bureau of Air Quality Control
(207) 289-2437

Department of the Environment
Air Management Administration
(301) 631-3255

Department of Environmental Protection
Division of Air Quality Control
(617) 292-5630

The Clean Air Act (cont'd)

Department of Natural Resources
Air Quality Division
(517) 373-7023

Pollution Control Agency
Air Quality Division
(612) 296-7331

Department of Environmental Quality
Office of Pollution Control, Air Division
(601) 961-5171

Department of Natural Resources
Division of Environmental Quality
Air Pollution Control Program
(314) 751-4817

Department of Health and Environmental Sciences
Air Quality Bureau
(406) 444-3454

Department of Environmental Control
Air Quality Control
(402) 471-2189

Division of Environmental Protection
Bureau of Air Quality
(702) 687-5065

Air Resources Division
(603) 271-1370

Department of Environmental Protection
Division of Environmental Quality Air Program
(609) 292-6710

New Mexico Environment Department
Environmental Protection Division
Air Quality Division
(505) 827-0070

New York State Department of Environmental
Conservation Division of Air Resources
(518) 457-7230

Department of Environment, Health, and
Natural Resources
Air Quality Section
(919) 733-3340

North Dakota State Department of Health
Division of Environmental Engineering
(701) 221-5188

Ohio Environmental Protection Agency
Division of Air Pollution Control
(614) 644-2270

Oklahoma State Department of Health
Air Quality Service
(405) 271-5220

Oregon Department of Environmental Quality
Air Quality Control Division
(503) 229-5287

Pennsylvania Department of Environmental Resources
Bureau of Air Quality Control
(717) 787-9702

Department of Environmental Management
Division of Air and Hazardous Materials
(401) 277-2808

South Carolina Department of Health and
Environmental Control
Bureau of Air Quality Control
(803) 734-4750

Department of Environment and Natural Resources
Point Source Control Program
(605) 773-3351

Tennessee Department of Environment and
Conservation Division of Air Pollution Control
(615) 741-3931

Texas Air Control Board
(512) 908-1000

Department of Environmental Quality
Division of Air Quality
(801) 536-4000

Agency of Natural Resources
Air Pollution Control Division
(802) 244-8731

Department of Air Pollution Control
(804) 786-2378

Washington State Department of Ecology
Air Program
(206) 459-6632

Air Pollution Control Commission
(304) 348-2275

Wisconsin Department of Natural Resources
Bureau of Air Management (AM/10)
(608) 266-7718

Wyoming Air Quality Division
(307) 777-7391

Department of Planning and Natural Resources
Division of Environmental Protection
(809) 773-0565

Puerto Rico Environmental Quality Board
Air and Water Division
(809) 767-8071

Environmental Quality Commission
Governor's Office
011 (684) 633-4116

Guam Environmental Protection Agency
011 (671) 646-8863

Productivity

PRODUCTIVITY EXPRESSES the relationship between the quantity of goods and services produced –output– and the quantity of labor, capital, land, energy, and other resources that produced it–input.

Productivity is a key element in analyzing an economy. It demonstrates both the efficiency of industry and the wealth-generating capability of the economy.

The best known measure of productivity relates output to the input of labor time: output per hour, or its reciprocal unit labor requirements. This kind of measure is used widely because labor productivity is relevant to the most economic analyses, and because labor is the most easily measured input. Relating output to labor input provides a tool not only for analyzing productivity but also for examining labor costs, real income, and employment trends.

Trends in Productivity Growth

Productivity growth varies among individual industries. Large increases reflect many factors, including new technologies, advanced production methods, and increased output with economies of scale.

U.S. productivity growth has trailed that of other major industrial countries.

The absolute level of U.S. productivity, unlike its growth trend, is still ahead of that of other major industrial countries. Although the United States has the lowest rate of change in real domestic product per employed person among major industrialized countries, it still has the highest level of gross domestic product per employed person. The gap continues to shrink, however.

Change in Output per Employee Hour (%), Selected Industries

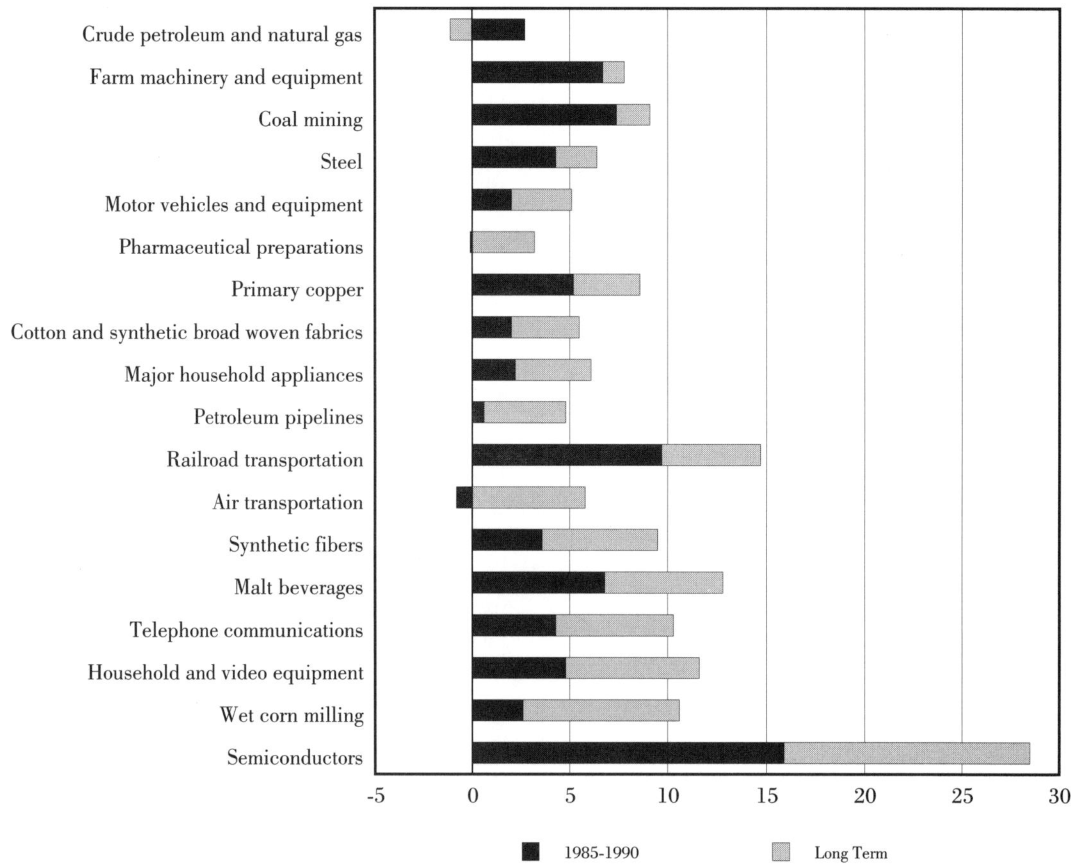

Note: The black bar indicates the average annual percent change from 1985 to 1990. The gray bar shows the changes over a longer period of time, in most cases, over the last forty years.

Source: Bureau of Labor Statistics

Productivity (cont'd)

Relative Levels in Real Gross Domestic Product per Employed Person, Selected Countries

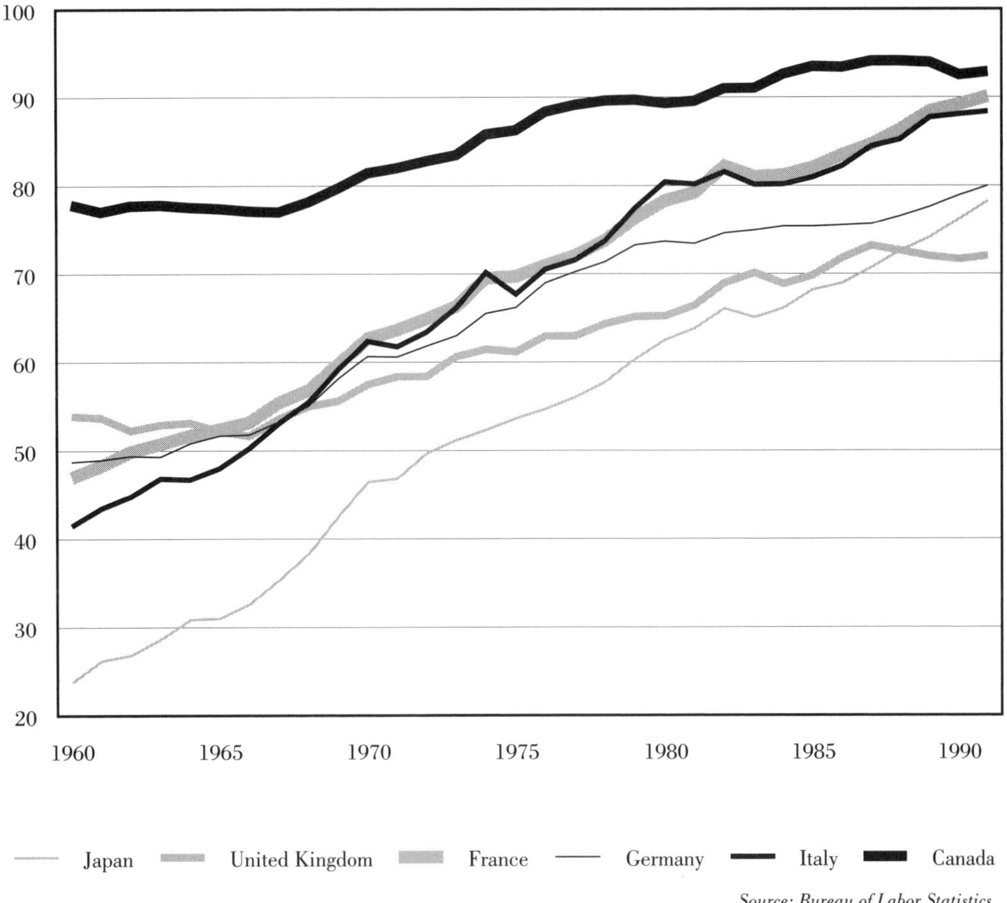

Source: Bureau of Labor Statistics
Note: U.S=100.

The Top Reference Sources

Who Knows What
Henry Holt, $45
(212) 886-9200

Written by Daniel Starer, this 1,239-page reference contains names of thousands of experts and organizations for business information on any subject, from abrasives to yarn.

Organized alphabetically, sections provide resource information for individual industries, states, or selected topics. A subject index is provided, along with an index of associations, periodicals, and companies.

Productivity (cont'd)

Trends in Real Gross Domestic Product per Employed Person, Selected Countries

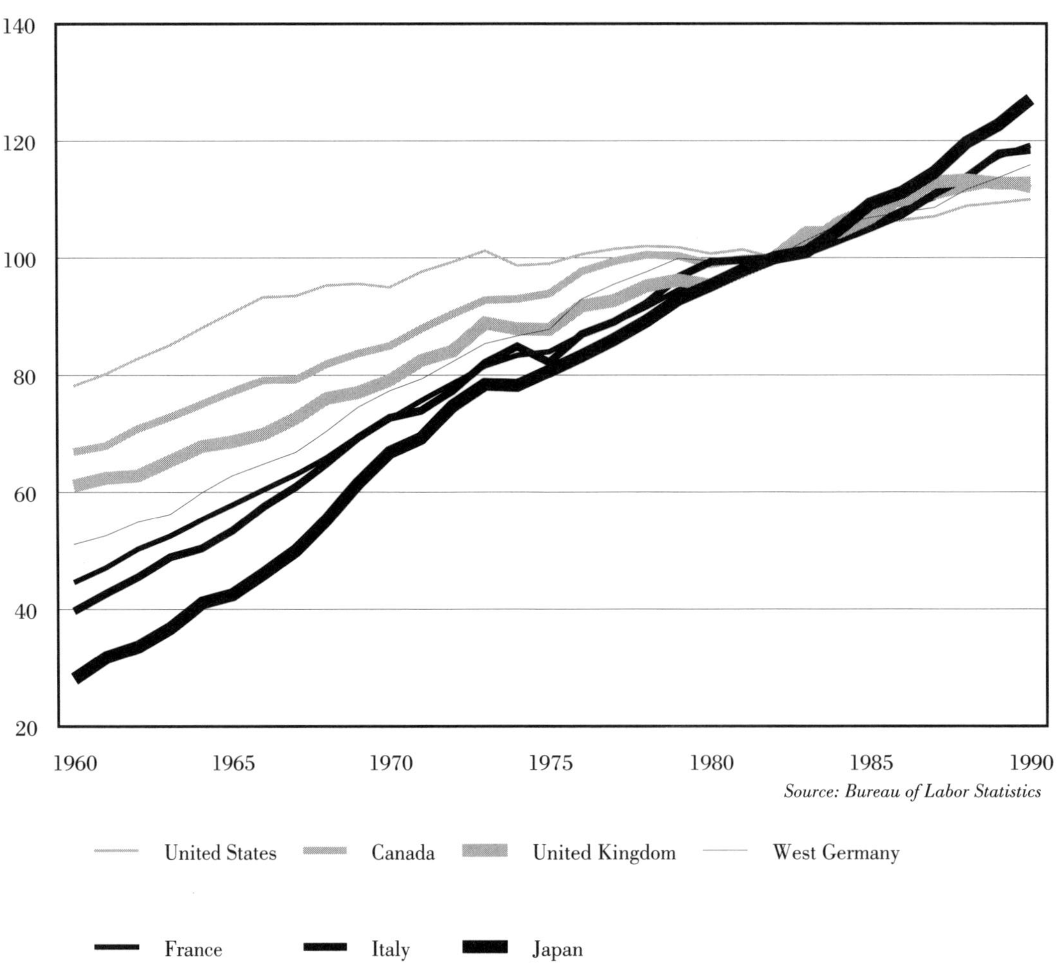

Source: Bureau of Labor Statistics

The Top Reference Sources

Lesko's Info Power
Information USA,
(301) 369-1519

Mathew Lesko's superb compilation of over 30,000 free and low-cost sources of information is an indispensable reference for use at home or at work.

Chapters provide information sources on consumer power, vacation and business travel, government financial help to individuals, investments and financial services, taxes, health and medicine, arts and humanities, housing and real estate, careers and workplace, law, science and technology, environment, patents, business and industry, and many more.

Research & Development

Corporate and Government Spending on Research and Development ($ millions)

Government financing provided $31 billion for all industry R&D performance in 1990 (the most recent year for which data are available).

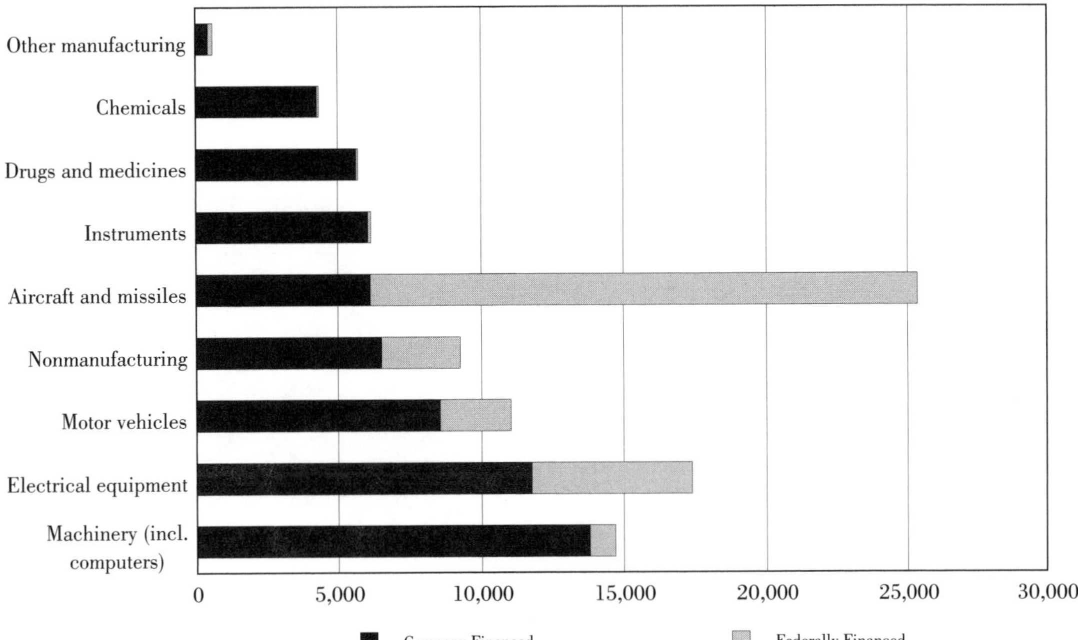

Percent of U.S. GDP Spent on Research and Development

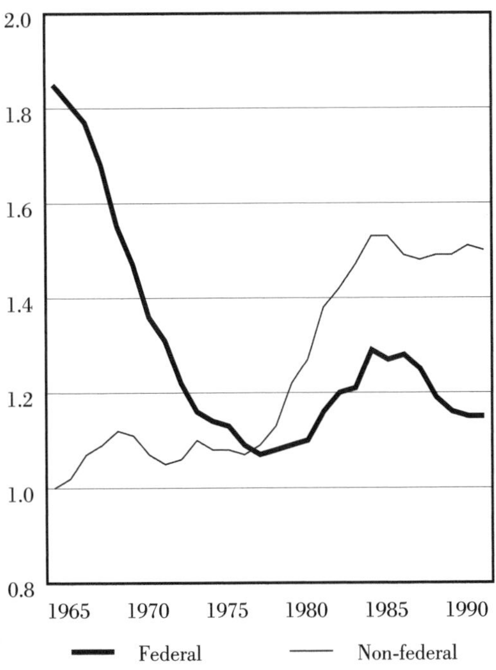

Source: National Patterns of R&D Resources, National Science Foundation

Industry Growth Rates

MODEST GROWTH IS PROJECTED IN 1993 for basic materials industries, including rubber, chemicals, plastic products, and wood products. High-tech sectors, such as computers and semiconductors, have favorable outlooks, especially when the growth rates of individual industries are compared. Motor vehicles and parts industries are recovering, with much of the strength coming from rising sales of light trucks. The aerospace industry will continue to decline in shipments as a result of defense spending reductions and a leveling off in backlogs for large commercial aircraft; however, production levels for large commercial aircraft will still be at relatively high levels. Consumer durables should continue to improve.

Percent Change in Yearly Growth Rates for Selected Industries

Sector	1987-88	1988-89	1989-90	1990-91 (estimate)	1991-92 (estimate)	1992-93 (forecast)
Construction	1.2	-1.3	-2.9	-9.8	4.1	0.7
Food and beverages	2.5	-1.9	1.0	1.4	2.6	1.6
Wood products	-0.9	-1.1	-3.0	-6.0	2.6	1.8
Paper and allied products	3.0	1.7	0.2	1.1	3.8	4.0
Chemicals	3.8	1.1	3.6	1.8	1.9	3.2
Rubber and plastic products	2.7	2.7	2.4	1.7	1.3	3.1
Construction materials	-0.7	-0.1	0.8	-8.5	1.2	1.1
Steel mill products	13.8	-2.6	-1.5	-7.4	4.1	2.4
Production machinery	10.5	4.7	-1.0	-2.3	-1.6	2.1
Metal working equipment	5.6	7.4	-1.7	-10.9	-0.5	3.5
Electrical equipment	6.7	-0.5	-2.5	-3.2	-0.3	1.4
Electronic components	11.6	4.3	3.4	1.9	6.2	7.9
Computers	12.4	-4.8	-1.3	-2.0	4.0	8.2
Telecommunications and navigation equipment	3.0	-4.7	5.5	-3.2	-1.4	-0.4
Motor vehicles and parts	6.4	-0.8	-7.2	-8.4	8.2	6.5
Aerospace	2.7	2.6	6.4	-0.5	-5.5	-5.3
Instruments, controls and medical equipment	5.1	-1.2	1.5	1.7	1.9	2.6
Durable consumer goods	2.7	0.3	-1.1	-4.2	3.2	4.3
Printing and publishing	0.5	-1.2	0.6	-2.2	0.7	1.9

Source: U.S. Industrial Outlook

10 Fastest-Growing Manufacturing Industries (% change in yearly growth)

Industry	% Change 1992-93
Semiconductors	12.0
Surgical and medical instruments	8.5
Surgical appliances and supplies	8.5
Computers and peripherals	8.2
Electromedical equipment	7.8
Motor vehicles and car bodies	6.8
Household laundry equipment	6.7
Household refrigerators and freezers	6.5
Automotive parts and accessories	6.1
X-ray apparatus and tubes	5.6

Source: U.S. Industrial Outlook

10 Slowest-Growing Manufacturing Industries (% change in yearly growth)

Industry	% Change 1992-93
Personal leather goods	-3.4
Women's handbags and purses	-3.6
Leather and sheep-lined clothing	-3.8
Aircraft engines and engine parts	-3.8
Aircraft parts and equipment	-4.8
Space propulsion units and parts	-5.0
Paper industries machinery	-5.2
Guided missiles and space vehicles	-5.7
Space vehicle equipment	-6.0
Aircraft	-6.0

Source: U.S. Industrial Outlook

Industry Growth Rates (cont'd)

Forecast Growth Rates for Manufacturing Industries (Ranked by Compound Growth Rate)

Rank	Industry	Growth Rate (%) 1992-93	Compound Annual Growth (%) 1988-93
1	X-ray apparatus and tubes	5.6	16.0
2	Electromedical equipment	7.8	11.9
3	Surgical and medical instruments	8.5	10.0
4	Semiconductors	12.0	9.5
5	Motorcycles, bicycles, and parts	3.4	7.5
6	Surgical appliances and supplies	8.5	6.9
7	Poultry slaughtering and processing	3.5	6.7
8	Oil and gas field machinery	2.0	6.5
9	Plastic plumbing fixtures	1.9	6.3
10	Analytical instruments	4.7	6.0
11	Household vacuum cleaners	5.4	5.8
12	Soap and other detergents	2.5	5.8
13	Greeting cards	5.0	5.8
14	Phosphatic fertilizers	5.0	5.7
15	Household appliances	5.2	5.6
16	Sporting and athletic goods	4.4	4.7
17	Biological products, except diagnostic	3.0	4.4
18	Radio and TV communications equipment	2.0	4.2
19	Pulp mills	4.0	4.0
20	Household audio and video equipment	1.7	4.0
21	Packaging machinery	5.0	3.8
22	Industrial inorganic chemicals, except pigments	3.0	3.8
23	Agricultural chemicals	2.0	3.6
24	Frozen foods	1.8	3.3
25	Sanitary paper products	3.5	3.2
26	Book printing	2.7	3.0
27	Wood pallets and skids	2.5	2.9
28	Paper industries machinery	-5.2	2.9
29	Mattresses and bedsprings	4.5	2.8
30	Medicinals and botanicals	3.0	2.8
31	Corrugated and solid fiber boxes	4.0	2.7
32	Pharmaceutical preparations	5.2	2.7
33	Malt beverages	1.5	2.7
34	Ice cream and frozen desserts	3.5	2.7
35	Adhesives and sealants	3.0	2.6
36	Gypsum products	3.9	2.5
37	Misc. plastic products, except bottles and plumbing	2.9	2.4
38	Cheese, natural and processed	1.6	2.3
39	Measuring and controlling devices	2.3	2.3
40	Platemaking services	3.5	2.3
41	Ship building and repairing	-3.2	2.2
42	Candy and other confectionary products	2.9	2.2
43	Bookbinding and related work	2.0	2.1
44	Nitrogenous fertilizers	-1.5	2.1
45	Mining machinery	3.1	2.0
46	Book publishing	3.4	1.9
47	Instruments to measure electricity	5.0	1.8
48	Canned foods	1.7	1.8
49	House slippers	2.0	1.8
50	Paper and paperboard mills	4.5	1.8

Source: U.S. Industrial Outlook

Government Industry Specialists

THESE U.S. GOVERNMENT SPECIALISTS will provide advice on industry analysis, trade promotion, and trade policy development

Industry	Contact	Telephone
Aerospace	Sally Bath, Clayton Mowry, Ronald Green	(202) 482-4222
Apparel	Joanne Tucker	(202) 482-4058
Automotive parts	Mary Anne Slater	(202) 482-1418
Bicycles, motorcycles, boat building, sporting goods	John Vanderwolf	(202) 482-0348
CAD/CAM/CAE	Vera Smolenski	(202) 482-0396
Chemicals	Mike Kelly	(202) 482-0128
Computer networking	Vivian Spathopoulos	(202) 482-0572
Computers/workstations	Timothy Miles	(202) 482-2990
Construction	Patrick MacAuley	(202) 482-0132
Construction materials	Charles Pitcher	(202) 482-0132
Consumer electronics	Howard Fleming	(202) 482-5163
Dairy, bakery, candy & other products; bottled & canned drinks	William Janis	(202) 482-2250
Drugs & biotechnology	William Hurt	(202) 482-0128
General industrial components	Richard Reise	(202) 482-0312
Household appliances	John Harris	(202) 482-1178
Household furniture	Kevin Ellis	(202) 482-1176
Industrial & analytical instruments	Marguerite Nealon	(202) 482-3411
Jewelry & musical instruments	John Harris	(202) 482-1178
Lawn & garden	John Vanderwolf	(202) 482-0348
Leather and leather products	James Byron	(202) 482-4034
Meat, poultry, fruits, vegetables & spec. alcoholic beverages	Donald Hodgen	(202) 482-3346
Medical equipment/instruments	Joseph Burke	(202) 482-5014
Medical, dental instruments & supplies	Patricia Eyring	(202) 482-2846
Metal industries	David Cammarota	(202) 482-5157
Metalworking equipment	John Mearman	(202) 482-5157
Microelectronics	Margaret Donnelly	(202) 482-5014
Midrange portables	Heidi Hoffman	(202) 482-2053
Motor vehicles	Randy Miller	(202) 482-0311
Paper products	Gary Stanley	(202) 482-0132
Personal computers	R. Clay Woods	(202) 482-3013
Photographic equipment & supplies	John McPhee	(202) 482-0571
Plastics & rubber	Ray Pratt	(202) 482-0128
Printing & publishing	Rose-Marie Bratland	(202) 482-0380
Production machinery	Edward Abrahams	(202) 482-0312
Semiconductor mfg. equipment	Jack Uldrich	(202) 482-0429
Semiconductors	Dorthea Blouin	(202) 482-1333
Semiconductors and related devices	Judee Mussehhl-Aziz	(202) 482-0429
Software	Mary Smolenski	(202) 482-2053
Supercomputers	Jonathan Streeter	(202) 482-0572
Superconductors	Roger Chiarodo	(202) 482-0402
Telecommunications and navigation equipment	John Henry	(202) 482-3411
Telecommunications services	Dan Edwards	(202) 482-4466
Textiles	Matthew Hein	(202) 482-4058
Textiles (man-made fibers)	Maria D'Andrea	(202) 482-4058
Wood products	Barbara Wise	(202) 482-0375

Emerging Technologies

THE DEPARTMENT OF COMMERCE defines an emerging technology as one in which research has progressed far enough to indicate a high probability of technical success for new products and applications that might have substantial markets within approximately ten years.

Some emerging technologies–usually self-contained products such as new medicines, or processes, such as X-ray lithography–have important, but focused, impacts. Others substantially affect the economy by advancing the technical infrastructure or by improving the quality and efficiency of the manufacturing process. Examples are components of a computer-integrated manufacturing system, such as robots or machining centers or the factory control system itself.

Emerging technologies are also important because they will drive the next generation of research and development and spin-off applications. When an industry uses a new technology to design or improve a product, and successfully carries it to the marketplace, that new or improved product becomes the starting point for development of the next generation of products or services.

The Commerce Department has identified the following as emerging technologies:

Emerging Materials

Advanced Materials
Superconductors

Emerging Electronics and Information Systems

Advanced Semiconductor Devices
Digital Imaging Technology
High-Density Data Storage
High-Performance Computing
Optoelectronics

Emerging Manufacturing Systems

Artificial Intelligence
Flexible Computer-Integrated Manufacturing
Sensor Technology

Emerging Life-Sciences Applications

Biotechnology
Medical Devices and Diagnostics

The Advanced Technology Program

MANAGED BY THE TECHNOLOGY Administration's National Institute of Standards and Technology, the Advanced Technology Program is an industry-driven, cooperative partnership between government and the private sector to advance the nation's competitive position. The purpose of the program, now in its third year, is to assist U.S. companies in creating and applying "generic technology" and research results to help commercialize new technology more quickly and improve manufacturing processes.

The ATP Awards are based on merit as determined through a full and open competition. In December, 1992, twenty-one new awards were announced, two-thirds of which were for small businesses. The projects cover a broad spectrum of technology areas, including machine tools, biotechnology, electronics, optics, materials engineering, lighting technology, and refrigeration.

Any business or industrial joint venture may apply for these grants.

Contact Option

Advanced Technology Program
Administration Building, Room A430
Rt. 270 & Quince Orchard Rd.
Gaithersburg, MD 20899
(301) 975-2636

1992 ATP Awards

Company	ATP Award ($ thousands)
Calmac Manufacturing, Englewood, NJ	729
Illinois Superconductor, Evanston, IL	1,980
FSI International, Chaska, MN	2,000
Ingersoll Milling Machine, Rockford, IL	1,874
Giddings & Lewis, Dayton, OH	994
General Motors, Warren, MI	5,784
Genosensor Consortium, Fullerton, CA	9,234
Mathematical Tech, Providence, RI	997
Accuwave, Santa Monica, CA	1,987
Geltech, Alachua, FL	1,323
IBM, San Jose, CA	1,831
Eagle-Picher Research, Miami, OH	1,759
Diamond Semiconductor, Wenham, MA	1,327
AlliedSignal, Morristown, NJ	2,000
Optex, Rockville, MD	1,433
3M, St. Paul, MN	3,483
Galileo Electro-Optics, Sturbridge, MA	1,915
General Electric, Schenectady, NY	1,720
Tissue Engineering, Boston, MA	1,999
Cynosure, Bedford, MA	1,965
GenPharm, Int'l, Mountain View, CA	1,987

Producer Price Index

PRODUCER PRICE INDEXES MEASURE average changes in prices received by domestic producers of commodities in all stages of processing. Most of the information used in calculating the indexes is obtained through the systematic sampling of nearly every industry in the manufacturing and mining sectors of the economy. Because producer price indexes are designed to measure only the change in prices received for the output of domestic industries, imports are not included. The stage-of-processing indexes organize products by class of buyer and degree of fabrication.

Within the stage-of-processing system, finished goods are commodities that will not undergo further processing and are ready for sale to the final individual or business consumer. Finished goods include unprocessed foods such as eggs and fresh vegetables, as well as processed foods such as bakery products and meats. Other finished consumer goods include durable goods such as automobiles, household furniture, and appliances, and nondurable goods such as apparel and home heating oil. Producer durable goods include heavy motor trucks, tractors, and machine tools.

Intermediate materials consist partly of commodities that have been processed but require further processing, such as flour, cotton yarn, steel mill products, and lumber. Nondurables in this category include diesel fuel, paper boxes, and fertilizers. Crude materials are products entering the market for the first time that have not been manufactured and that are not sold directly to consumers, such as grains and livestock. Raw cotton, crude petroleum, coal, hides and skins, iron and steel scrap are examples of nonfood crude materials. The following chart shows that industrial prices have risen only incrementally in the last couple of years, due mainly to foreign competition and the recession.

Producer Price Indexes by Major Commodity Groups

Commodity	1970	1975	1980	1985	1989	1990
All commodities	38.1	58.4	89.8	103.2	112.2	116.3
Farm products	45.8	77.0	102.9	95.1	110.7	112.2
Processed foods and feeds	44.6	72.6	95.9	103.5	117.8	121.9
Textile products and apparel	52.4	67.4	89.7	102.9	112.3	114.9
Hides, skins, and leather products	42.0	56.5	94.7	108.9	136.3	141.7
Fuels and related products and power	15.3	35.4	82.8	91.4	72.9	82.2
Chemicals and allied products	35.0	62.0	89.0	103.7	123.1	123.6
Rubber and plastic products	44.9	62.2	90.1	101.9	112.6	113.6
Lumber and wood products	39.9	62.1	101.5	106.6	126.7	129.7
Pulp, paper and allied products	37.5	59.0	86.3	113.3	137.8	141.3
Metals and metal products	38.7	61.5	95.0	104.4	124.1	123.0
Machinery and equipment	40.0	57.9	86.0	107.2	117.4	120.7
Furniture and household durables	51.9	67.5	90.7	107.1	116.9	119.1
Nonmetallic mineral products	35.3	54.4	88.4	108.6	112.6	114.7
Transportation equipment	41.9	56.7	82.9	107.9	117.7	121.5
Miscellaneous products	39.8	53.4	93.6	109.4	NA	NA

The average for the year 1982 is set to equal 100

Source: Department of Commerce, Bureau of Economic Analysis

The Top Reference Sources

American Demographics
Dow Jones
(800) 828-1133

Published monthly, this extremely informative magazine is must-reading for businesses, especially their sales, marketing, and advertising departments.

Based primarily on Census data, sample features include articles on aging, Black suburbs, consumer confidence, influential Americans, market-driven companies, the real Hispanic market, the 1950s, and how market research can increase marketing efficiency.

The editors do a great job of making a dry topic extremely interesting.

Producer Price Index (cont'd)

Producer Price Indexes, Selected Commodities

Commodity	1960	1970	1980	1985	1988	1989	1990	1991
FINISHED GOODS	33.4	39.3	88.0	104.7	108.0	113.6	119.2	121.7
Finished consumer goods	33.6	39.1	88.6	103.8	106.2	112.1	118.2	121.5
Finished consumer foods	35.5	43.8	92.4	104.6	112.6	118.7	124.4	124.1
Fresh fruits	42.8	42.3	100.3	108.1	113.5	113.2	118.1	129.4
Fresh and dried vegetables	39.0	47.5	88.9	99.5	105.5	116.7	118.1	103.8
Eggs	68.5	71.0	95.7	95.7	88.6	119.6	117.6	110.7
Bakery products	32.3	40.0	90.0	113.9	126.4	135.4	141.0	146.6
Milled rice	51.5	52.4	131.5	105.0	118.1	104.9	102.5	110.0
Beef and veal	38.8	46.7	106.2	90.3	101.4	108.9	116.0	112.1
Pork	34.5	44.6	78.4	89.1	95.0	97.7	119.8	113.0
Processed young chickens	66.0	61.2	106.8	106.5	113.1	120.3	111.0	105.1
Processed turkeys	67.2	69.1	109.2	121.3	100.4	110.6	107.6	107.2
Fish	19.3	29.7	87.8	114.6	148.7	142.9	147.2	151.3
Dairy products	34.6	44.7	92.7	100.2	102.2	110.6	117.2	114.6
Processed fruits and vegetables	33.8	40.3	83.3	108.0	113.8	119.9	124.7	119.5
Soft drinks	25.6	37.8	81.8	107.7	114.3	117.7	122.3	125.6
Roasted coffee	28.7	37.7	110.4	107.2	113.5	115.9	113.0	107.9
Shortening and cooking oils	37.8	47.7	99.5	124.0	118.8	116.6	123.2	116.4
Finished consumer goods except foods	33.5	37.4	87.1	103.3	103.1	108.9	115.3	118.7
Alcoholic beverages	49.6	53.3	88.9	107.7	111.8	115.2	117.2	123.7
Women's apparel	56.9	62.8	86.9	105.4	111.3	113.5	116.1	117.8
Mens'and boys' apparel	41.1	51.2	91.3	105.0	113.0	116.8	120.2	122.7
Girls', children's, and infants' apparel	47.6	58.8	87.1	103.1	107.5	110.5	115.3	117.6
Textile housefurnishings	40.3	43.4	86.8	100.6	104.4	106.6	109.5	111.8
Footwear	35.8	46.2	95.2	104.8	115.1	120.8	125.6	128.6
Natural gas	-	7.9	63.3	102.9	77.4	82.0	80.4	79.0
Gasoline	14.5	14.4	93.3	83.3	57.3	65.1	78.7	69.9
Fuel oil No. 2	-	-	82.8	81.6	49.5	58.0	73.3	65.2
Pharmaceutical preps, ethical (Prescription)	-	52.0	80.6	132.0	169.0	184.4	200.8	217.0
Pharmaceutical preps, propri.; Over-counter	-	42.3	81.3	121.6	144.4	152.1	156.8	165.7
Soaps and synthetic detergents	37.5	41.5	85.8	107.9	114.7	119.4	117.7	117.1
Cosmetics and other toilet preparations	40.9	47.8	83.8	109.0	116.3	119.3	121.6	124.5
Tires, tubes, tread, etc.	38.0	42.7	92.8	93.0	94.0	97.2	96.8	98.3
Sanitary papers and health products	26.5	32.5	91.9	106.6	115.0	126.0	135.3	136.4
Household furniture	39.2	48.6	89.1	108.5	117.6	121.8	125.1	128.1
Floor coverings	59.3	54.9	90.0	105.6	114.7	117.6	119.0	120.2
Household appliances	54.0	52.9	87.5	106.7	106.0	108.7	110.8	111.3
Home electronic equipment	133.8	106.0	103.8	90.8	87.2	86.9	82.7	83.2
Household glassware	20.6	33.1	84.7	121.8	128.1	134.7	132.5	136.0
Household flatware	20.7	32.7	148.0	98.6	113.0	125.7	122.1	119.4
Lawn and garden equipment	39.2	46.8	87.5	110.3	114.6	119.8	123.0	124.9
Passenger cars	48.5	50.0	88.9	106.9	113.0	115.5	118.3	124.1
Toys, games, children's vehicles	43.3	48.5	89.2	103.8	110.8	115.6	118.1	120.3
Sporting and athletic goods	45.5	52.7	90.6	99.7	105.9	109.8	112.6	115.2
Tobacco products	27.9	35.2	76.0	132.5	171.9	194.8	221.4	249.3
Mobile homes	-	-	-	101.7	109.3	114.0	117.5	120.4
CAPITAL EQUIPMENT	32.8	40.1	85.8	107.5	114.3	118.8	122.9	126.7
Agricultural machinery and equipment	27.7	36.4	83.3	108.7	112.7	117.7	121.7	125.2
Construction machinery and equipment	25.0	33.7	84.2	105.4	111.8	117.2	121.6	125.2
Metal cutting machine tools	-	30.8	85.1	107.3	117.4	123.4	129.8	134.6

Producer Price Index (cont'd)

Commodity	1960	1970	1980	1985	1988	1989	1990	1991
Metal forming machine tools	-	28.6	85.7	107.0	113.2	118.1	128.7	133.5
Tools, dies, jigs, fixtures, ind. molds	-	-	-	106.3	110.9	113.8	117.2	122.6
Pumps, compressors, equipment	23.9	33.0	82.8	102.6	108.9	115.0	119.2	124.6
Industrial material handling equipment	30.9	39.8	88.4	102.7	107.5	111.7	115.0	117.4
Textile machinery	35.8	45.4	87.2	107.6	119.4	123.9	128.8	135.0
Paper industries machinery	-	-	-	109.8	119.4	128.5	134.8	140.1
Printing trades machinery	26.9	42.5	89.7	109.0	120.1	123.0	124.9	126.7
Transformers and power regulators	49.5	44.7	82.4	105.0	108.8	117.3	120.9	123.8
Oil field and gas field machinery	20.7	27.0	76.3	96.8	97.0	99.1	102.4	108.6
Mining machinery and equipment	24.5	30.9	85.2	105.4	110.2	116.3	121.0	125.2
Office and store machines and equipment	63.0	68.3	93.1	101.6	107.0	109.5	109.5	109.7
Commercial furniture	33.4	41.6	85.7	111.9	124.2	129.0	133.4	136.2
Light motor trucks	-	42.0	83.3	112.2	125.0	129.5	130.0	135.5
Heavy motor trucks	-	36.3	82.3	108.8	112.4	117.2	120.3	123.5
Truck trailers	-	-	-	106.2	106.6	110.4	110.8	112.2
Railroad equipment	-	33.2	90.4	104.9	107.5	114.0	118.6	122.2
Photographic and photocopy equipment	71.4	72.0	94.9	89.5	91.8	94.1	97.2	99.4
INTERMED. MATERIALS, SUPPLIES	30.8	35.4	90.3	102.7	107.1	112.0	114.5	114.4
Intermediate foods and feeds	-	45.6	105.5	97.3	109.5	113.8	113.3	111.1
Flour	47.9	55.3	102.3	99.8	105.7	114.6	103.6	97.6
Crude vegetable oils	57.6	75.8	127.1	137.6	116.6	103.1	115.8	103.2
Prepared animal feeds	37.2	49.1	107.3	90.1	116.0	116.6	107.4	106.8
INTERMEDIATE MATERIALS LESS FOODS AND FEEDS	30.7	34.8	89.4	103.0	106.9	111.9	114.5	114.6
Leather	30.1	34.6	99.8	113.4	167.5	170.4	177.5	168.4
Liquified petroleum gas	-	-	102.3	86.3	51.6	52.7	77.4	75.3
Electric power	24.9	26.1	79.1	111.6	111.2	114.8	117.6	124.3
Jet fuels	-	-	87.5	81.0	52.1	58.1	76.0	66.4
No. 2 Diesel fuel	-	-	85.8	81.2	49.7	58.9	74.1	65.5
Residual fuel	9.3	10.6	81.3	83.2	41.1	47.6	57.7	46.9
Industrial chemicals	29.3	28.6	91.9	96.0	106.8	114.8	113.2	111.8
Prepared paint	35.0	42.8	89.5	105.3	112.2	119.5	124.8	129.9
Paint materials	36.7	33.3	89.9	109.5	115.7	129.1	136.3	135.8
Medicinal and botanical chemicals	53.9	44.4	91.0	91.8	93.5	100.3	102.2	109.1
Fats and oils, inedible	37.5	49.7	111.6	110.6	110.9	95.5	88.1	86.8
Mixed fertilizers	35.2	35.2	90.0	96.1	104.8	105.9	103.3	105.1
Nitrogenates	48.4	32.7	90.0	96.3	93.3	94.9	92.3	98.5
Phosphates	28.4	27.5	93.0	91.6	103.3	105.6	96.5	98.2
Other agricultural chemicals	-	23.2	80.1	98.7	107.4	115.1	119.9	125.4
Plastic resins and materials	38.2	32.0	98.5	107.5	132.4	133.4	124.1	120.1
Synthetic rubber	34.8	34.0	85.3	96.8	108.9	108.5	111.9	106.0
Plastic construction products	-	65.5	103.9	108.6	121.1	120.1	117.2	115.4
Softwood lumber	28.8	35.2	107.3	107.4	120.0	127.1	123.8	125.7
Hardwood lumber	34.6	43.7	96.0	117.1	131.0	128.2	131.0	128.5
Millwork	33.3	41.5	93.2	111.7	121.9	127.3	130.4	135.4
Plywood	47.2	46.7	106.2	99.6	103.4	115.9	114.2	114.3
Woodpulp	27.0	28.9	100.3	91.4	136.7	127.4	151.3	119.8
Paper	32.4	38.8	89.7	106.0	123.2	129.6	128.8	127.0
Paperboard	41.0	39.7	92.0	107.7	133.2	140.1	135.7	130.2
Paper boxes and containers	40.3	43.3	89.4	108.8	123.5	129.8	129.9	128.6
Building paper and board	46.1	42.2	86.1	107.4	113.3	115.6	112.2	111.8
Commercial printing	-	-	-	111.6	119.5	124.9	128.0	130.0

Producer Price Index (cont'd)

Commodity	1960	1970	1980	1985	1988	1989	1990	1991
Foundry and forge shop products	26.6	32.4	89.7	105.2	109.6	114.6	117.2	119.0
Steel mill products	27.6	32.7	86.6	104.7	110.7	114.5	112.1	109.6
Primary nonferrous metals	29.5	44.9	132.7	93.6	144.3	149.2	133.4	114.1
Aluminum mill shapes	37.1	36.7	89.3	107.8	130.9	135.4	127.9	123.2
Copper and brass mill shapes	39.7	63.4	112.6	106.9	162.7	182.0	174.6	161.0
Nonferrous wire and cable	39.8	62.6	107.5	100.9	129.6	146.1	142.6	139.3
Metal containers	27.3	34.3	90.9	109.0	110.2	111.5	114.0	115.6
Hardware	32.2	39.8	85.8	109.1	113.7	120.4	125.9	130.2
Plumbing fixtures and brass fittings	33.5	39.9	88.5	111.9	128.7	137.7	144.3	149.7
Heating equipment	44.6	46.6	87.0	109.5	119.2	125.1	131.6	134.1
Fabricated structural metal products	31.4	36.7	88.8	103.2	114.3	120.3	121.8	122.4
Mechanical power transmission equipment	27.3	36.9	84.5	108.2	116.0	121.1	125.3	129.1
Ball and roller bearings	34.2	33.1	80.0	105.9	114.0	124.1	130.6	136.7
Wiring devices	-	35.9	81.9	111.7	123.8	129.7	132.2	133.9
Motors, generators, motor generator sets	34.3	37.7	86.0	113.3	121.8	129.0	132.9	135.0
Switchgear, switchboard, etc., equipment	34.7	40.5	88.4	106.7	113.2	119.0	124.4	128.5
Electronic components and accessories	-	57.4	88.8	112.4	117.5	119.4	118.4	118.8
Internal combustion engines	28.4	34.5	81.7	104.9	111.4	114.7	120.2	126.0
Machine shop products	-	31.1	81.0	112.8	116.8	121.3	124.3	126.0
Flat glass	-	52.2	88.7	101.7	109.7	109.7	107.5	106.0
Concrete products	32.6	37.7	92.0	107.5	110.0	111.2	113.5	116.6
Asphalt felts and coatings	24.4	25.8	99.6	102.6	94.7	95.8	97.1	98.3
Gypsum products	38.7	38.9	100.1	132.3	112.9	110.0	105.2	99.5
Glass containers	27.6	33.9	82.3	106.8	112.3	115.2	120.4	125.4
Motor vehicle parts	-	32.9	72.9	102.5	107.2	109.7	111.2	112.3
Photographic supplies	34.7	41.0	97.2	107.4	113.1	123.0	127.6	126.1
CRUDE MATERIALS FOR PROCESSING	30.4	35.2	95.3	95.8	96.0	103.1	108.9	101.2
Crude foodstuffs and feedstuffs	38.4	45.2	104.6	94.8	106.1	111.2	113.1	105.5
Wheat	51.2	39.7	108.3	87.6	93.7	109.5	87.6	79.5
Corn	46.0	54.5	119.2	105.9	97.1	102.4	100.9	97.0
Cattle	40.0	46.9	104.9	91.2	109.5	113.8	122.5	115.8
Hogs	32.8	45.5	74.5	80.7	81.8	80.5	94.1	82.7
Live chickens (broilers and fryers)	63.1	48.5	103.4	110.5	125.4	131.7	119.5	111.9
Live turkeys	67.5	59.9	112.2	144.6	108.4	119.1	116.9	109.5
Fluid milk	30.0	40.8	96.0	93.7	89.4	98.8	100.8	89.3
Soybeans	35.0	45.3	117.0	94.2	124.8	114.3	100.8	95.1
Cane sugar, raw	31.0	39.9	148.3	104.6	111.9	115.5	119.2	113.7
CRUDE NONFOOD MATERIALS	-	23.8	84.6	96.9	85.5	93.4	101.5	94.6
Raw cotton	65.8	43.6	135.7	97.7	95.5	105.6	118.2	116.2
Leaf tobacco	33.1	40.3	82.1	101.2	87.2	93.8	95.8	100.4
Cattle hides	33.5	30.4	104.6	126.1	205.8	213.1	217.8	173.5
Coal	17.9	28.1	87.4	102.2	95.4	95.5	97.5	97.2
Natural gas	-	7.9	63.3	102.9	77.4	82.0	80.4	79.0
Crude petroleum	13.4	14.5	75.9	84.5	46.2	56.3	71.0	61.9
Logs, timber, etc.	-	-	-	96.0	117.7	131.9	142.8	144.0
Wastepaper	95.4	103.2	172.2	122.9	183.6	157.1	138.9	121.3
Iron ore	38.7	35.9	87.8	97.5	82.8	82.8	83.3	83.6
Iron and steel scrap	47.3	59.6	140.9	112.6	177.1	173.7	166.0	147.3
Nonferrous metal ores (Dec. 1983=100)	-	-	-	93.2	108.1	109.6	98.3	82.9
Copper base scrap	48.8	100.9	138.9	95.4	157.9	179.8	181.3	170.0
Aluminum base scrap	35.0	34.4	183.9	123.4	219.5	204.4	172.6	142.7
Construction sand, gravel, and crushed stone	33.5	40.9	85.3	110.7	120.6	122.8	125.4	128.6

* *The average for the year 1982 is set to equal 100*

Source: Department of Commerce, Bureau of Economic Analysis

Purchasing Benchmarks

PURCHASING PERFORMANCE and effectiveness has become one of the most closely watched economic indicators. The following chart is a comparison of total purchasing (dollars spent with vendors) as a percent of corporate sales in selected industries. For complete data on purchasing benchmarks, contact the Center for Advanced Purchasing Studies, an affiliate of the National Association of Purchasing Management, at (602) 752-2277.

Total Purchasing Dollars as a Percent of Sales, Selected Industries

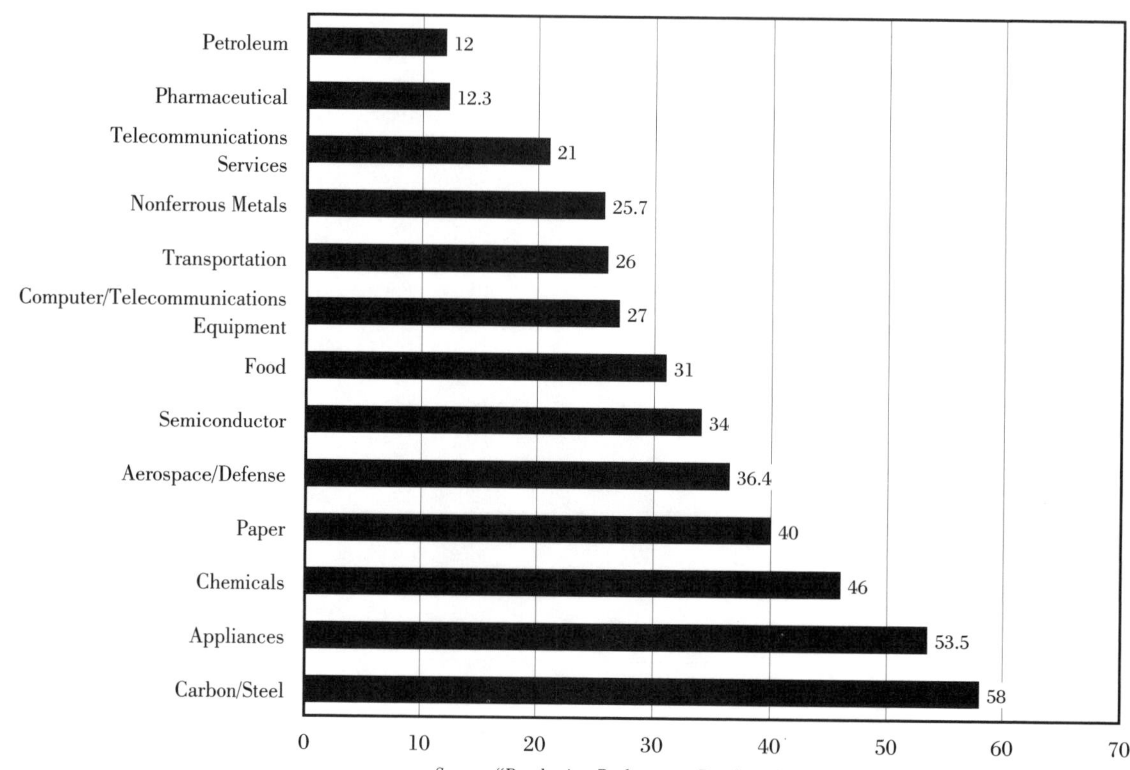

Source: "Purchasing Performance Benchmarks," Center for Advanced Purchasing Studies

Warehousing

A NATIONAL STUDY BY TOMPKINS Associates, Inc., reveals a number of interesting trends and conditions:

- Warehousing is still a very labor-intensive industry with great room for productivity improvements.
- The average warehouse is approximately 50,000 square feet with an average clear height of 22 feet.
- The age of the average warehouse is 19 years. New construction is prohibitively expensive.
- Few warehouses have ventured beyond basic material handling and storage methods.
- The pressure to computerize the warehouse is great, but the level of understanding of need, benefit, and specific requirements is low. A total of 85% of warehouses responding in the Tompkins Associates survey maintain inventory data on computer and 68 percent have a computerized stock location system. And 33 percent of warehouses surveyed use bar codes.

Source: Tompkins Associates, Inc.

The Public Warehouse Alternative

As warehousing costs continue to rise, public warehouses are more and more seen as a viable alternative. Jim McBride, President of Affiliated Warehouse Companies, estimates that public warehousing accounts for 16 percent of current warehousing needs. Criteria to be evaluated in selecting a public warehouse include:

- Financial stability
- Management depth
- Sanitation
- Facilities
- Rates
- Interest in the account
- Reputation
- Delivery capabilities
- Consolidations
- Ownership
- Similar accounts
- Building ownership
- Labor
- Security
- Data processing capabilities
- Contents insurance rate
- Legal liability insurance
- Taxes
- Location.

Source: Affiliated Warehouse Companies

Average Warehouse Rates in Major Cities

Market	Price/sq. ft.($)	Rent/sq. ft.($)
Atlanta	26.18	3.19
Baltimore	31.27	3.60
Boston	39.07	5.26
Chicago	41.37	5.30
Cincinnati	25.87	3.53
Cleveland	24.13	3.84
Columbus	22.28	2.84
Dallas	27.26	3.85
Denver	25.63	3.02
Detroit	28.89	4.78
Indianapolis	29.96	3.95
Los Angeles	48.62	5.39
Miami	30.24	3.85
Milwaukee	28.05	4.28
Minneapolis	35.90	5.19
New York	37.38	5.05
Norfolk	30.15	4.28
No. New Jersey	36.12	5.54
Philadelphia	35.42	4.98
Phoenix	28.89	3.63
Pittsburgh	31.74	4.99
Portland	28.17	3.92
Sacramento	29.91	3.65
St. Louis	26.60	3.99
San Antonio	17.14	2.76
San Diego	41.43	4.98
San Francisco	48.36	5.69
Seattle	38.06	5.13
Tampa	24.31	3.59
Washington, DC	39.20	5.09

Source: The National Real Estate Index Market Monitor

Prices and rents above represent Class A (i.e. space built or substantially renovated in the preceding ten years) warehouse/distribution space at the metropolitan level. Reported rents are effective gross (i.e. after concessions, if any). New York rates are for Nassau-Suffolk counties.

Contact Option

National Real Estate Index
1900 Powell St.
Emeryville, CA 94608
(800) 992-7257

Recommended Trade Journals

THE FOLLOWING IS AN INCOMPLETE LIST of trade magazines in various fields. For a more complete listing, consult *Who Knows What* by Daniel Starer, published by Henry Holt.

Adhesives Age
Communication Channels, Inc.
6151 Powers Ferry Rd., NW
Atlanta, GA 30339
(404) 955-2500

Advanced Material and Processes
ASM International
Metals Park, OH 44073
(216) 338-5151

American Printer
Maclean Hunter Publishing Co.
29 N. Wacker Dr.
Chicago, IL 60606
(312) 726-2802

Appliance Manufacturer
29100 Aurora Road
Suite 200
Solon, OH 44139
(216) 349-3060

Automation
Penton Publishing
Diamond Bldg.
11 Superior Ave.
Cleveland, OH 44114
(216) 696-7000

Automotive Industries
Chilton Co.
Chilton Way
Radnor, PA 19089
(215) 964-4041

Automotive News
Crain Communications
1400 Woodbridge
Detroit, MI 48207
(313) 446-6000

Aviation Week and Space Technology
McGraw-Hill, Inc.
1221 Avenue of the Americas
New York, NY 10020
(800) 257-9402

Bakery Production and Marketing
Delta Communications, Inc.
455 N. Cityfront Plaza Dr.
Chicago, IL 60611
(312) 222-2000

Beverage Industry
Stagnito Publishing Co.
1935 Shermer Rd.
Suite 100
Northbrook, IL 60062
(708) 205-5660

Chemical Engineering News
American Chemical Society
1155 16th St., NW
Washington, DC 20036
(202) 872-4600

Chilton's Food Engineering
Chilton Co.
Chilton Way
Radnor, PA 19089
(215) 964-4041

Compressed Air
253 East Washington Ave.
Washington, NJ 07882
(201) 689-4496

Datamation
Cahners Publishing
257 Washington St.
Newton, MA 02158
(617) 964-3030

Designfax
6521 Davis Industrial Parkway
Solon, OH 44139
(216) 248-1125

Distribution
Chilton Co.
Chilton Way
Radnor, PA 19089
(215) 964-4379

Electronic Design
VNU Business Publications
10 Mulholland Dr.
Hasbrouck Heights, NJ 67604
(201) 393-6060

EDN (Electronic Design Engineering)
Cahners Publishing
257 Washington St.
Newton, MA 02158
(617) 964-3030

Electronic Products
645 Stewart Ave.
Garden City, NY 11530
(516) 227-1300

Recommended Trade Journals (cont'd)

Food Processing
Putnam Publishing Co.
301 Erie St.
Chicago, IL 60611
(312) 644-2020

Forest Industries
Miller Freeman Publications
500 Howard St.
San Francisco, CA 94105
(415) 397-1881

Industrial Engineering
Institute of Industrial Engineers
25 Technology Park
Norcross, GA 30092
(404) 449-0461

Industrial Maintenance and Plant Operation
Chilton Co.
Chilton Way
Radnor, PA 19089
(215) 964-4041

Industrial Product Bulletin
P.O. Box 1952
Dover, NJ 07801
(201) 361-9060

Instrumentation and Automation News
Chilton Co.
Chilton Way
Radnor, PA 19089
(215) 964-4419

Industry Week
Penton Publishing
1100 Superior Ave.
Cleveland, OH 44114
(216) 696-7000

Iron Age
Hitchcock Publishing Co.
191 S. Gary Ave.
Carol Stream, IL 60188
(708) 665-1000

Journal of Manufacturing Systems
Society of Manufacturing Engineers
P.O. Box 930
Dearborn, MI 48121
(313) 271-1500

Machine Design
Penton Publishing
Diamond Bldg.
1100 Superior Ave.
Cleveland, OH 44114
(216) 696-7000

Manufacturing Week
CMP Publications
600 Community Dr.
Manhasset, NY 11030
(516) 365-4600

Materials Handling Engineering
Penton Publishing
Diamond Bldg.
1100 Superior Ave.
Cleveland, OH 44114
(216) 696-7000

Mechanical Engineering
American Society of Mechanical Engineers
345 E. 47th St.
New York, NY 10017
(212) 705-7782

Medical Device and Diagnostic Industry
Canon Communications
2416 Wilshire Blvd.
Santa Monica, CA 90403
(213) 829-0135

Metal Fabricating News
W.A. Whitney
P.O. Box 1178
Rockford, IL 61105
(815) 965-4031

Mining Engineering
8307 Shaffer Pkwy.
Littleton, CO 80127
(303) 973-9550

Modern Materials Handling
Cahners Publishing
275 Washington St.
Newton, MA 02158
(617) 964-3030

Modern Paint and Coatings
6255 Barfield Rd.
Atlanta, GA 30328
(404) 256-9800

Modern Plastics
McGraw-Hill, Inc.
1221 Avenue of the Americas
New York, NY 10020
(212) 512-6241

New Equipment Digest
Penton Publishing
Diamond Bldg.
1100 Superior Ave.
Cleveland, OH 44114
(216) 696-7000

Recommended Trade Journals (cont'd)

Packaging
Cahners Plaza
1350 E. Touhy Ave.
P.O. Box 5080
Des Plaines, IL 60017
(708) 635-8800

Packaging Digest
Delta Communications
455 N. Cityfront Plaza Dr.
Chicago, IL 60611
(312) 222-2000

Paper Maker
Maclean Hunter Publishing, Co.
57 Executive Park S.
Atlanta, GA 30329
(404) 325-9153

Plant Engineering
Cahners Publishing
275 Washington St
Newton, MA 02158
(617)·964-3030

Prepared Foods
Delta Communications, Inc.
455 N. Cityfront Plaza Dr.
Chicago, IL 60611
(312) 222-2000

Pulp and Paper
Miller Freeman Publications
500 Howard St.
San Francisco, CA 94105
(415) 397-1881

Purchasing Magazine
Cahners Publishing
275 Washington St.
Newton, MA 02158
(216) 696-7000

Quality Progress
ASQC
310 W. Wisconsin Ave.
Milwaukee, WI 53203
(414) 272-8575

Textile World
Maclean Hunter Publishing
4170 Ashford-Dunwoody Road, Suite 420
Atlanta, GA 30319
(404) 847-2770

The Top Reference Sources

Industrial Design in the United States
Van Nostrand Reinhold
(212) 254-9499

Published first in 1992, this annual directory is a comprehensive reference to the field of industrial design.

The information presented allows readers to make discriminating choices among the consulting firms, design departments, schools, institutions, organizations, and resources listed.

Detailed information is carried in the profiles; product category and name entries are cross referenced with the profiles.

Major Standards Developers

Aerospace Industries Association
1250 I St., NW, Suite 1100
Washington, DC 20005
(202) 371-8400

American Association of Cereal Chemists
3340 Pilot Knob Rd.
St. Paul, MN 55121
(612) 454-7250

Amercian Association of State Highway and Transportation Officials
444 North Capitol St., NW, Suite 225
Washington, DC 20001
(202) 624-5800

American Conference of Governmental Industrial Hygienists
6500 Glenway Ave., Bldg. D-7
Cincinnati, OH 45211
(513) 661-7881

American National Standards Institute
11 W. 42nd St.
New York, NY 10036
(212) 642-4900

American Oil Chemists Society
1608 Broadmoor Dr.
Champaign, IL 61821
(217) 359-2344

American Petroleum Institute
1220 L St., NW
Washington, DC 20005
(202) 682-8000

American Railway Engineering Association
50 F St., NW, Suite 7702
Washington, DC 20001
(202) 639-2190

American Society of Mechanical Engineers
345 E. 47th St.
New York, NY 10017
(212) 705-7722

ASTM
1916 Race St.
Philadelphia, PA 19103
(215) 299-5585

Association of Official Analytical Chemists
2200 Wilson Blvd., Suite 400
Arlington, VA 22201
(703) 522-3032

Cosmetic, Toiletry and Fragrance Association
1101 17th St., Suite 300
Washington, DC 20005
(202) 333-1770

Electronic Industries Association
2001 Pennsylvania Ave., NW, 11th Floor
Washington, DC 20006
(202) 457-4900

Institute of Electrical and Electronics Engineers
445 Hoes Lane
P.O. Box 1331
Piscataway, NJ 08855
(908) 562-3800

National Fire Protection Association
One Batterymarch Park
P.O. Box 9101
Quincy, MA 02269
(617) 770-3000

SAE International
400 Commonwealth Dr.
Warrendale, PA 15096
(412) 776-4841

Technical Association of the Pulp and Paper Industry
15 Technology Parkway
P.O. Box 105113
Norcross, GA 30092
(404) 446-1400

Underwriters Laboratories
333 Pfingsten Rd.
Northbrook, IL 60062
(708) 272-8800

U.S. Pharmacopeial Convention
12601 Twinbrook Parkway
Rockville, MD 20852
(301) 881-0666

Contact Option

The National Center for Standards and Certification Information
National Institute of Standards and Technology
TRF Bldg., Room 163
Gaithersburg, MD 20899
(301) 975-4040

The National Center for Standards and Certification Information (NCSCI) provides information on national and international voluntary standards, government regulations, and rules of certification for non-agricultural products. The Center serves as a referral service and focal point in the United States for information about standards and standards-related information.

Major Industrial Design Awards

Industrial Design Excellence Awards

Presented each year by the Industrial Designers Society of America and sponsored by *Business Week* magazine, the IDEA is the nation's most coveted annual accolade for industrial design–from computers to packaging, toys to cars. A list of the most recent winners is included in this chapter.

Contact:
IDEA/IDSA
Department 0811
Alexandria, VA 22334
(703) 759-0100

I.D. Annual Design Review

I.D. (International Design) Magazine presents this most comprehensive design award in categories such as consumer products, graphics, environments, furniture, equipment, packaging, surfaces, concepts, and student work.

Contact:
I.D. Magazine
Design Review Editor
250 W. 57th St., Suite 215
New York, NY 10107
(212) 956-0535

Neste Forma Finlandia Plastics Design

Prizes include a First Prize of FIM 300,000 (about U.S. $70,000) in this popular international plastics design competition, sponsored by Neste, one of Scandinavia's largest companies. Entries are considered in two categories: "Tomorrow's Challengers," for new, previously unpublished plastics product ideas; and "The World's Best Plastic Products," recognizing products that have been on the market for less than three years. The "working language" of the competition is English.

Contact:
Neste Forma Finlandia 3
P.O. Box 20
02151 Espoo, Finland
358-0-450-5044
Fax: 358-0-450-4985

International Design Competition, Osaka

This biennial competition sponsored by the Japan Design Foundation aims to question "the role of design in clarifying visions of the future of humankind in the 21st century" by inviting designers to enter imaginative works from a broad range of design fields. Each competition focuses on a singular theme, such as "wind," "air," or "terra." Prizes include a Grand Prize/Prime Minister's Prize of U.S. $35,000. Official languages for the award are Japanese and English.

Contact Option

International Design Competition, Osaka
Japan Design Foundation
3-1-800 UMEDA 1 Chome
Kita-ku, Osaka 530
Japan
81-6-346-2611
Fax: 81-6-346-2615

1992 IDEA Gold Award Winners

PowerBook–Apple Computer, Cupertino, CA

CleanWorks–Scott/Sani-Fresh International, San Antonio, TX

"D" Series Angle Wrenches–Ingersol-Rand Power Tool Division, Liberty Corner, NJ

Electrical Vehicle Charging System–General Motors, Torrance, CA

Rear Projection TV–Thomson Consumer Electronics, Indianapolis, IN

Good Grips Kitchen Utensils–Oxo International, New York, NY

EZ Router–Sears Roebuck, Chicago, IL

Airflex–Spalding Sports Worldwide, Chicopee, MA

BeeperKid–A&H International, Honolulu, HI

Handkerchief TV–Brion Vega, Milano, Italy

Seville STS–Cadillac Motor Div., General Motors, Detroit, MI

Aquatred–Goodyear Tire and Rubber, Akron, OH

Ultralite–General Motors, Detroit, MI

Demon Dispenser–ICI Americas, Wilmington, DE

Clinitron Elexis Air Fluidized Therapy–Support Systems International, Charleston, SC

Protex Work Envelope System–Proformix, Whitehouse Station, NJ

Relay Furniture–Herman Miller, Zeeland, MI

Precedence Bath–Kohler, Kohler, WI

Orchestra Lamp–The Knoll Group, New York, NY

From White to Green–Apple Computer, Cupertino, CA

Fit–Medtronic, Minneapolis, MN

Lee Trade Show Exhibit Booths–Lee Company, Merriam, KS

Airbass–Art Center College of Design, Pasadena, CA

New Move Wheelchair–Art Center College of Design, Pasadena, CA

Major Industrial Design Awards (cont'd)

1992 I.D. Annual Design Review Winners (Best of Category)

Consumer Products
Nikonos RS Underwater SLR Camera, Nikon

Environment
Airline Facility Design, Continental Airlines

Packaging
Armani Exchange Packaging, Giorgio Armani

Furniture
Shaker Screen, Cappellini
Whimsical Traditions Fabric Collection, Knoll

Concepts/Students
Air Bass, Art Center College
Apple Concepts, Apple Computer

Equipment
NCR1325 NotePad, NCR Corp.

Graphics
(No best of category winner in 1992)

Recommended Resources

Deadlines
17 W. Hawley Rd.
Hawley, MA 01339
(413) 339-4018

This monthly newsletter publishes announcements and deadline information for all national and international design competitions and award programs open to U.S. architects and designers.

Design Access
National Building Museum
401 F St., NW
Washington, DC 20001
(202) 272-5427
(202) 272-5432

Newly established by the National Endowment for the Arts and the National Building Museum, the Design Access database maintains information on all aspects of design, including industrial and product design, architecture, urban design and planning, graphic design, historic preservation, and landscape architecture.

Directory to Industrial Design in the United States
Van Nostrand Reinhold
115 Fifth Ave.
New York, NY 10003
(212) 254-3232

A comprehensive guide to consulting firms, design departments, schools, institutions, organizations, and resources in industrial design.

The Top Reference Sources

Hoover's Handbook of American Business
The Reference Press, $24.95
(800) 486-8666

The most recent edition of this relatively new reference book profiles 500 business enterprises based in the United States. The book should be of interest to anyone who invests in, buys from, sells to, competes with, interviews with, or works for a large company in the U.S.

The profiles include brief histories, names of officers and human resources contacts, headquarters address and telephone numbers, sales figures, income, markets, stock prices, products, affiliates and subsidiaries, key competitors, and rankings.

Patent Licensors

LICENSING IS THE PROCESS of transferring intellectual property (copyrights, patents, trademarks, trade secrets, business information, etc.) from one business, individual, or organization to another. The Licensing Executive Society, Inc., is a professional society of over 3,200 members (scientists, engineers, lawyers, marketers, and licensing consutants), most of whom are actively engaged on behalf of their employers or clients in the transfer of intellectual property. These licensing professionals may provide a number of business services, including:

- Identifying potential markets and licenses;
- Evaluating and packaging licensable intellectual property;
- Funding research and development of intellectual property;
- Protecting the intellectual property to be licensed
- Monitoring the flow of intellectual property and the payment of royalties;
- Determining what intellectual property rights should be licensed;
- Negotiating reasonable terms between the licensor (seller) and licensee (buyer) and drafting an appropriate license agreement which authorizes the use of intellectual property rights.

Source: Licensing Executive Society

Contact Options

The following consultants have been selected based on their size, technical interests, and the range of services provided. Each is a member of the Licensing Executive Society:

James D. Donovan
Executive Vice President
Intercon Research Associates
6865 Lincoln Ave.
Lincolnwood, IL 60646
(708) 982-1101
Pharmaceutical, chemical, and medical

C. Richard Goodlet, Vice President
UC Industries, Inc.
137 East Ave., P.O. Box 395
Tallmadge, OH 44278
(216) 633-1105
Plastics, building materials, specialized machinery

Tarif Karobi, Vice President
Stelco Technical Services Limited (Steltech)
1375 Kerns Road
Burlington, Ontario
Canada L7P 3H8
(416) 528-2511
Steel industry, manufacturing processes, environmental equipment

George W. K. King
King Associates
1050 Eagle Rd.
Newtown, PA 18940
(215) 968-4483
Mechanical, electronics, plastics

Steven R. Maimon, President
The Hunter Group
8200 Treebrooke Lane
Alexandria, VA 22308
(703) 765-2678
Medical and environmental, computers and telecommunications, manufacturing and mining

James E. Malackowski
IPC Group, Inc.
205 W. Wacker Dr., Suite 1400
Chicago, IL 60606
(312) 641-0051
Automotive, electronics

William R. Mattson, Jr., President
The Mattson Jack Group
9 The Pines Court, Suite A
St. Louis, MO 63141
(314) 469-7600
Pharmaceuticals, over-the-counter products

Gordon S. Riess, President
Intercontinental Enterprises Limited
256 S. Robertson, Suite 3194
Beverly Hills, CA 90211
(213) 276-6525
Medical and laboratory equipment, over-the-counter drugs

Edward G. Tutle, President
Tutle International–Technology Marketing
2601 Seabreeze Court
Orlando, FL 32805
(407) 423-8016
Manufacturing, communications

Richard Wechsler, President & C.E.O.
BIEC International, Inc.
3400 Bath Pike, Park Plaza
Bethlehem, PA 18017
(215) 694-7597
Steelmaking

Manufacturing Apprenticeships

WHILE A NUMBER OF GOVERNMENT programs are now in place to make the school-to-work transition a more productive process for American workers and industry, a few U.S. companies may be said to be at the forefront of an industry-driven apprenticeship movement. Among them, are:

Robert Bosch Corporation
38000 Hills Tech Dr.
Farmington Hills, MI 48331
(313) 553-9000

Corning, Inc.
MP-PS-02-7
Corning, NY 14831
(607) 974-9000

Milford Fabricating
19200 Glendale Ave.
Detroit, MI 48223
(313) 272-8400

Remmele Engineering
1211 Pierce Butler Route
St. Paul, MN 55104
(612) 642-5689

Siemens Corporation
1301 Avenue of the Americas
New York, NY 10019
(212) 258-4046

Jobs for the Future is a non-profit group which promotes workforce quality and helps to sponsor youth apprenticeship sites, along with state, school district, and industry support. The following programs are current and may be of particular interest to manufacturers:

Pennsylvania Youth Apprenticeship Program
P.O. Box 5046
York, PA 17405
(717) 843-2898
Metalworking

Pickens County Youth Apprenticeship Initiative
1348 Griffin Mill Rd.
Easley, SC 29640
(803) 855-8150
Electronics

Project A.L.I.V.E.: Pasadena Partnership Academies
Pasadena Unified School District
351 Hudson Ave.
Pasadena, CA 91109
(818) 795-6981
Auto-technology, electronics, CAD-drafting, laser-tech, printing

Roosevelt Renaissance 2000
Roosevelt High School
6941 N. Central St.
Portland, OR 97203
(503) 280-5138
Manufacturing technology, business information systems, health

Broome County Youth Apprenticeship Demonstration Project
Martha Van Rensselaer Hall
Cornell University
Ithica, NY 14853
Health, manufacturing, and engineering technology

Craftsmanship 2000
616 S. Boston
Tulsa, OK 74119
(918) 585-1201
Metalworking

Contact Options

Jobs for the Future
1815 Massachusetts Avenue
Cambridge, MA 02140
(617) 661-3411

U.S. Department of Labor
Training Policy Unit
Office of Work-Based Learning
200 Constitution Ave., NW, Room N-4649
Washington, DC 20210
(202) 523-0281

ISO 9000 Quality Standards

IN 1987, THE INCREASED FOCUS on global quality issues led the International Organization for Standardization, or ISO, headquartered in Geneva, Switzerland, to establish a series of international quality standards. Called the ISO 9000 Series of Standards, the series is not specific to any one industry, but when used with proper industry-specific standards, helps build a strong foundation for a quality system. The idea behind ISO is to promote standardization which will facilitate the international exchange of goods and services.

Currently, ISO 9000 certification is voluntary and not required or mandated in any country. However, the European community has recently required that quality systems of many suppliers of products related to health, safety, and the environment be formally registered, by a third party, according to the ISO 9000 Series standard. This action has made adoption of the ISO standards a virtual prerequisite for doing business in Europe. Countries in Asia, Africa, and South America are more and more considering adoption of these standards as a means to increased trade among themselves and the United States. Over 20,000 companies have been registered worldwide, and at least 52 nations are implementing the standards. In its January, 1993, issue, the newsletter *Quality Systems Update* reports that a total of 621 companies, from 45 states, are registered in the United States.

In the United States, the ISO 9000 Series of Standards was adopted verbatim as the ANSI/ASQC Q90 series of standards. The series is comprised of five individual, but related, international standards on quality management and quality assurance, known as ISO 9000, 9001, 9002, 9003, and 9004. For a company's quality system to become registered in one or more of these standards involves having an accredited, independent third party conduct an audit of the company's operations against the requirements of the ISO 9000 standards. Upon successful completion of this audit, the company will receive a registration certificate that identifies its quality system as being in compliance with ISO 9000 standards.

Accredited Registrars in the United States and Canada

ABS Quality Evaluations, Inc.
263 N. Belt East
Houston, TX 77060
(713) 873-9400

American European Services, Inc. (A.E.S.)
1054 31st St., NW, Suite 120
Washington, DC 20007
(202) 337-3214

American Gas Association Laboratories (A.G.A.) Quality
8501 E. Pleasant Valley Rd.
Cleveland, OH 44131
(216) 524-4990

AT&T Quality Registrar
1259 S. Cedarcrest Blvd.
Allentown, PA 18103
(215) 770-3285

American Association for Laboratory Accreditation
656 Quince Orchard Rd. #304
Gaithersburg, MD 20878
(301) 670-1377

Bureau Veritas Quality International
509 N. Main St.
Jamestown, NY 14701
(716) 484-9002
(800) 937-9311

DNV Industrial Services, Inc.
16340 Park 10 Pl., Suite 100
Houston, TX 77084
(713) 579-9003

Intertek
9900 Main St., Suite 500
Fairfax, VA 22031
(703) 476-9000

Lloyd's Register Quality Assurance Ltd.
33-41 Newark St.
Hoboken, NJ 07030
(201) 963-1111

MET Electrical Testing Company
916 W. Patapsco Ave.
Baltimore, MD 21230
(301) 354-2200

National Sanitation Foundation
3475 Plymouth Rd.
Ann Arbor, MI 48106
(313) 769-8010

Perry Johnson Registrars, Inc.
3000 Town Center, Suite 2960
Southfield, MI 48075
(313) 356-4410

ISO 9000 Quality Standards (cont'd)

Quality Systems Registrars, Inc.
1555 Naperville/Wheaton Rd.
Naperville, IL 60563
(708) 778-0120

SGS Yarsley Quality Assured Firms
1415 Park Ave.
Hoboken, NJ 07030
(201) 792-2400

Southwest Research Institute
6220 Culebra Rd.
San Antonio, TX 78228
(512) 522-3145

TUV Rheinland of North America, Inc.
12 Commerce Rd.
Newtown, CT 06470
(203) 426-0888

TUV America–Hartford Steam Boiler
5 Cherry Hill Dr.
Danvers, MA 01923
(800) 243-5882
(508) 777-7999

Underwriters Laboratories, Inc.
1285 Walt Whitman Rd.
Melville, NY 11747
(516) 271-6200, ext. 284

Vincotte USA, Inc.
10497 Town & Country Way, Suite 900
Houston, TX 77024
(713) 465-2850

Canadian Registrars

Canadian General Standards Board
Qualification and Certification Listing Branch
Ottawa, Canada K1A 1G6
(819) 956-0439

Quality Management Institute
1420 Mississauga Executive Center
2 Robert Speck Parkway
Mississauga, Ontario L4Z 1S1
(416) 272-3920

Source: Quality Systems Update

Contact Options

American Society for Quality Control
P.O. Box 3005
Milwaukee, WI 53201
(800) 952-6587

The American Society for Quality Control (ASQC) is an accredited standards-writing body. The ANSI/ASQC Q90 series is available from the customer service department of ASQC.

American National Standards Institute
1430 Broadway
New York, NY 10018
(212) 354-3300

The American National Standards Institute (ANSI), an influential member of the ISO, is a non-government voluntary organization which provides a process for accrediting standards-writing bodies. The ISO 9000 Series is available from ANSI (The ANSI/ASQC Q90 Series is identical to the ISO 900 Series.)

National Institute of Standards and Technology
U.S. Department of Commerce
Administration Bldg., Room A629
Gaithersburg, MD 20899
(301) 975-2000

International Standards Organization
Rue de Varembe 1
CH-1211 Geneva 20, Switzerland
(41) 22-33-88-63

CEEM Information Services
P.O. Box 200
Fairfax Station, VA 22039
(800) 745-5565

Publishes *Quality Systems Update* newsletter, ISO 9000 handbook, and a directory of registered companies.

Consultants:

Booz, Allen & Hamilton, Inc.
4330 E. West Highway
Bethesda, MD 20814
(301) 907-4070

Du Pont Quality Management & Technology Center
Louviers 33W44
P.O. Box 6090
Newark, DE 19714
(800) 441-8040

Perry Johnson, Inc.
3000 Town Center, Suite 2960
Southfield, MI 48075
(313) 356-4410

Malcolm Baldrige Quality Award

THE MALCOLM BALDRIGE NATIONAL Quality Award is widely acknowledged as having raised overall quality awareness and practice in U.S. manufacturing. According to David A. Garvin, Robert and Jane Cizik Professor of Business Administration at the Harvard Business School, the Award "has become the most important catalyst for transforming American business."

Established in 1987 by the Malcolm Baldrige National Quality Improvement Act, the award is administered by the Secretary of Commerce and the National Institute of Standards and Technology, with cooperation and financial support from the private sector. The Malcolm Baldrige National Quality Award is the highest level of national recognition for quality that a U.S. company can receive.

Officially, the Baldrige award has three goals: to promote an understanding of quality excellence, to recognize the quality achievements of U.S. businesses, and to publicize successful quality strategies. Awards are presented to qualifying companies in manufacturing, service, and small business categories. A maximum of two awards per category may be given each year. Recipients of the award are allowed to publicize and advertise receipt of the Award, in return for agreement to share their successful quality strategies with other U.S. organizations.

Applicants for the Award are judged on these seven criteria:

- Leadership
- Information and Analysis
- Strategic Quality Planning
- Human Resource Development and Management
- Management of Process Quality
- Quality and Operational Results
- Customer Focus and Satisfaction.

The information submitted in each of these criteria must demonstrate that the applicant's approaches could be replicated or adapted by other companies.

The award has achieved such high status that many large manufacturers encourage their supplier base to participate. And, since all applicants, win or lose, receive feedback from the Award's Board of Examiners, many of these companies find the application process itself a worthwhile exercise. For others, the time and expense is not justified. Indeed, a report prepared by the Grant Thornton Survey of Manufacturers in 1992 reveals that midsized U.S. manufacturers may have become disenchanted with the Malcolm Baldrige Award. Sixty percent of companies responding in the Grant Thornton study agree that the Award needs to address more substance (the quality, integrity, or innovativeness of a company's products) than form (the quality of a company's control procedures).

Number of Completed Applications/ Registrants Each Year

1988–66
1989–40
1990–97
1991–106
1992–90
1993–76

Previous Award Winners

1992

Manufacturing
AT&T Network Systems Group, Morristown, NJ.
Texas Insturments, Inc., Dallas, TX

Service
AT&T Universal Card Services, Jacksonville, FL
The Ritz-Carlton Hotel Company, Atlanta, GA

Small Business
Granite Rock Company, Watsonville, CA

1991

Manufacturing
Solectron Corp., San Jose, CA
Zytec Corp., Eden Prairie, MN

Small Business
Marlow Industries, Dallas, TX

1990

Manufacturing
Cadillac Motor Car Company, Detroit, MI
IBM Rochester, Rochester, MN

Service
Federal Express Corp., Memphis, TN

Small Business
Wallace Co., Houston, TX

1989

Manufacturing
Milliken & Company, Spartanburg, IL
Xerox Business Products and Systems, Stamford, CT

1988

Manufacturing
Motorola, Inc., Schaumburg, IL
Westinghouse Commercial, Pittsburgh, PA

Small Business
Globe Metallurgical, Inc., Cleveland, OH

Malcolm Baldrige Quality Award (cont'd)

Malcolm Baldrige Award Application Fees

A nonrefundable Eligibility Determination Fee of $50.00 is required of all applicants. Additional fees for 1993 applicants covering all expenses associated with distribution of applications, review of applications, and development of feedback reports are $4,000 for Manufacturing and Service company categories and $1,200 for the Small Business category. Site visit review fees are established when the visits are scheduled.

Individual copies of the Award Criteria and application forms and instructions may be obtained free of charge from:

Malcolm Baldrige National Quality Award
National Institute of Standards and Technology
Route 270 and Quince Orchard Rd.
Administration Building, Room A537
Gaithersburg, MD 20899
(301) 975-2036

Multiple copies of the Award Criteria may be ordered in packets of 10 (Item Number T997) for $24.95 per packet from:

American Society for Quality Control
Customer Service Department
P.O. Box 3066
Milwaukee, WI 53201
(800) 248-1946

Consultants for Malcolm Baldrige National Quality Award

The application for the Baldrige award is sufficiently complicated that many companies rely on outside consultants for help in completing it. Here is a partial list, recommended by the Association of Management Consulting Firms:

Robert E. Nolan Co.
90 Hopmeadow St.
Simsbury, CT 06070
(203) 658-1941

K.W. Tunnell Co.
900 E. Eighth Ave., Suite 106
King of Prussia, PA 19406
(215) 337-0820

Rath & Strong
92 Hayden Ave.
Lexington, MA 02173
(617) 861-1700

Coopers & Lybrand
1251 Avenue of the Americas
New York, NY 10020
(212) 536-2000

Contact Options

Association of Management Consulting Firms
521 Fifth Ave.
New York, NY 10175
(212) 697-9693

Consultants News
Kennedy Publications
Templeton Rd.
Fitzwilliam, NH 03447
(603) 585-6544

Quality Benchmarking

BENCHMARKING, THE PROCESS OF LEARNING from the best practices of others, is increasing rapidly in the U.S. due to growing foreign competition, limited resources, and even the requirements of the Malcolm Baldrige National Award criteria. To assist firms, non-profit organizations, and government agencies in the process of benchmarking, the American Productivity & Quality Center established an International Benchmarking Clearinghouse in 1992 as a source of information about "best practices" for a large number of organizational processes. The Clearinghouse provides standards of conduct, conducts in-depth secondary research, and collects and disseminates best practices through databases, case studies, publications, seminars, conferences, videos, and other media. The Clearinghouse also provides training and consulting.

Contact Options

International Benchmarking Clearinghouse
American Productivity & Quality Center
123 North Post Oak Lane
Houston, TX 77024
(713) 681-4020

International Quality and Productivity Center
P.O. Box 43115
Upper Montclair, NJ 07043
(800) 882-8684

The IQPC has sponsored numerous workshops and seminars on benchmarking practices.

Marketing

Ad Agencies Ranked

The 30 Hottest Agencies in the U.S., 1992

Rank	Agency/Headquarters	ADWEEK Performance Index	1992 Billings ($ thousands)	Increase in Billings 1991-92 ($ thousands)	% Increase in Billings 1991-92
1	Lotas Minard Patton McIver, New York	1,215	77,800	42,000	117.3
2	Kirshenbaum & Bond, New York	655	105,000	40,000	61.5
3	Deutsch/Dworin, New York	545	135,000	45,000	50.0
4	Wieden & Kennedy, Portland, OR	501	240,000	72,000	42.9
5	Goodby Berlin & Silverstein, San Francisco	468	166,445	49,145	41.9
6	GSD&M, Austin	397	201,083	51,583	34.5
7	Long Haymes & Carr, Winston-Salem	392	119,300	31,600	36.0
8	Ammirati & Puris, New York	375	325,000	75,000	30.0
9	The Martin Agency, Richmond	339	148,043	34,546	30.4
10	MVBMS/Euro RSCG, New York	329	500,635	94,994	23.4
11	Cliff Freeman & Partners, New York	324	105,000	24,200	30.0
12	Valentine-Radford, Kansas City	307	119,060	26,110	28.1
13	J. Walter Thompson, New York	300	1,944,000	191,000	10.9
14	McCann-Erickson, New York	288	1,567,800	167,800	12.0
15	Ayer, New York	235	855,300	100,887	13.4
16	Bayer Bess Vanderwalker, Chicago	234	151,338	26,026	20.8
17	Temerlin McClain, Dallas	212	405,000	55,000	15.7
18	Tucker Wayne/Luckie & Co., Atlanta	203	196,000	29,000	17.4
19	Margeotes Fertitta & Weiss, New York	203	122,000	19,000	18.4
20	Bernstein-Rein, Kansas City	199	159,112	23,717	17.5
21	Rubin Postaer & Associates, Los Angeles	197	210,800	30,100	16.7
22	Lauglin/Constable, Milwaukee	189	80,500	12,100	17.7
23	Rotando Lerch & Lafeliece, Stamford, CT	184	100,300	14,500	16.9
24	Angotti, Thomas, Hedge, New York	182	105,000	15,000	16.7
25	Foote, Cone & Belding, Chicago	180	2,288,469	122,716	5.7
26	Waring & LaRosa, New York	173	80,400	11,200	16.2
27	BBDO, New York	171	1,634,768	103,452	6.8
28	Bloom FCA, New York	163	215,000	25,900	13.7
29	Bozell, New York	162	850,000	71,000	9.1
30	Scali, McCabe, Sloves, New York	159	182,500	21,949	13.7

Source: AdWeek

The Top Reference Sources

Guerrilla Marketing for the 90's
Houghton Mifflin, $9.95
(800) 352-5455

One in a series of marketing books by bestselling author Jay Conrad Levinson, this book provides 100 affordable marketing weapons for maximizing profits from your small business.

Levinson has created an approach to marketing that relies on low cost, high impact techniques for identifying, reaching, and keeping customers.

Ad Agencies Ranked (cont'd)

The Top 25 Agencies Worldwide, 1992

Rank	Agency	Headquarters	1992 Billings ($ thousands)	1991 Billings ($ thousands)	% Change
1	McCann-Erickson	New York	6,357,400	5,570,405	14.1
2	FCB-Publicis	Chicago	6,200,000	5,790,000	7.1
3	J. Walter Thompson	New York	5,690,000	4,957,000	14.8
4	Saatchi & Saatchi Advertising	New York	5,189,400	5,189,400	0.0
5	BBDO Worldwide	New York	5,100,827	4,400,000	15.9
6	Ogilvy & Mather Worldwide	New York	5,015,740	4,831,338	3.8
7	Young & Rubicam	New York	4,981,134	4,981,134	0.0
8	Backer Spielvogel Bates Worldwide	New York	4,730,658	4,492,000	5.3
9	DDB Needham Worldwide	New York	4,565,403	4,289,696	6.4
10	Lintas: Worldwide	New York	4,422,981	4,456,996	-0.8
11	Grey Advertising	New York	4,319,500	3,965,700	8.9
12	Leo Burnett	Chicago	4,304,343	3,890,586	10.6
13	D'Arcy Masius Benton & Bowles	New York	4,031,989	3,859,888	4.5
14	Ayer	New York	1,548,000	1,361,000	13.7
15	The Lowe Group	New York	1,498,247	1,409,602	6.3
16	Bozell	New York	1,230,000	1,154,000	6.6
17	CME KHBB	Minneapolis	1,141,342	1,107,980	3.0
18	TBWA	New York	1,111,800	1,001,900	11.0
19	Dentsu, Young & Rubicam Partnerships	New York	927,110	870,173	6.5
20	Wells Rich Greene BDDP	New York	919,900	923,700	-0.4
21	Ketchum	Pittsburgh	718,200	705,145	1.9
22	Chiat/Day	Venice, CA	620,000	568,000	9.2
23	Medicus Intercom	New York	502,113	461,203	8.9
24	MVBMS/Euro RSCG	New York	500,635	405,641	23.4
25	Earle Palmer Brown	Bethesda, MD	408,840	417,600	-2.1

The 15 Largest Agency Holding Companies, 1992

Rank	Agency	Headquarters	1992 Billings ($ thousands)	1991 Billings ($ thousands)	% Change
1	WPP Group PLC	London	18,095,000	17,915,800	1.0
2	The Interpublic Group of Companies	New York	13,802,538	12,564,262	9.9
3	Saatchi & Saatchi	London	11,755,000	11,755,000	0.0
4	Omnicom	New York	12,277,293	11,000,000	11.6
5	Dentsu	Tokyo	10,495,609	10,680,078	-1.7
6	Young & Rubicam	New York	7,878,540	7,840,125	0.5
7	Euro RSCG	Paris	6,647,137	6,900,000	-3.7
8	FCB-Publicis	Chicago	6,554,000	6,139,000	6.8
9	Hakuhodo	Tokyo	5,089,638	4,887,424	4.1
10	Grey Advertising	New York	4,795,500	4,464,600	7.4
11	D'Arcy Masius Benton & Bowles	New York	4,700,689	4,509,299	4.2
12	Leo Burnett	Chicago	4,304,343	3,890,586	10.6
13	BDDP	Paris	2,397,000	2,218,400	8.1
14	Bozell Jacobs Kenyon & Eckhardt	New York	1,720,000	1,559,000	10.3
15	Ayer	New York	1,548,000	1,361,000	13.7

Source: AdWeek

Ad Agencies Ranked (cont'd)

The Top 10 Health-Care Agencies of 1992

Rank	Agency	Headquarters	1992 Domestic Billings (thousands)	1991 Domestic Billings (thousands)	% Change
1	Nelson Communications	New York	259,283	242,347	6.9
2	Medicus Intercon	New York	253,840	229,818	10.5
3	Ferguson Communications Group	Parsippany, NJ	220,077	173,090	27.1
4	William Douglas McAdams	New York	196,200	158,832	23.5
5	Kallir Philips Ross	New York	193,858	186,200	4.1
6	Klemtner Advertising	New York	193,475	170,100	13.7
7	Sudler & Hennessey	New York	192,106	183,807	4.5
8	Lavey/Wolff/Swift	New York	146,747	144,322	1.7
9	Vicom/FCB	San Francisco	133,467	115,753	15.3
10	Gross Townshend Frank Hoffman	New York	117,500	104,600	12.3

The Top Ten Direct Response Agencies, 1992

Rank	Agency	Headquarters	1992 Domestic Billings ($ thousands)	1991 Domestic Billings ($ thousands)	% Change
1	Ogilvy & Mather Direct	New York	390,000	344,100	13.3
2	Rapp Collins Marcoa	New York	333,231	292,600	13.9
3	Bronner Slosberg	Boston	301,024	223,399	34.7
4	Wunderman Cato Johnson Worldwide	New York	241,401	241,401	0.0
5	FCB Direct	Chicago	219,800	216,075	1.7
6	Kobs & Draft	Chicago	172,400	155,900	10.6
7	DIMAC Direct	Bridgeton, MO	163,500	138,800	17.8
8	Barry Blau	Fairfield, CT	151,419	127,048	19.2
9	Grey Direct	New York	135,000	125,000	8.0
10	The Direct Marketing Group	New York	130,100	131,900	-1.4

Source: AdWeek

The Top Reference Sources

SRDS Direct Mail List Rates and Data
Standard Rate and Data Service
(708) 256-6067

Virtually every mailing list available for rent to marketers is catalogued in this cumbersome volume.

This is a complete resource for direct mail users that includes a subject/market classification index, title/list index, suppliers, and services directory. Also included are mailing list brokers, compilers and managers, business lists, business co-ops and package insert programs, consumer lists, farm lists, consumer co-ops and package insert programs, and alternate delivery systems.

Major Ad Award Winners

Starch Awards

SINCE 1988, STARCH INRA HOOPER, a market research firm, has presented the Starch Award. The award is given to the print ads that achieved the highest recognition scores among consumers during the previous year. Winners are culled from more than 50,000 face-to-face interviews with consumers annually.

1988 Starch Winners

Agency	Category	Client/Product
AC&R Advertising	Cosmetic and Beauty Aids	Estée Lauder
Ogilvy & Mather	Financial	American Express
Greengage Associates	Apparel, Footwear	Lycra
FCB/Leber Katz Partners	Tobacco Products	Salem Cigarettes
Ogilvy & Mather	Beer, Wine and Liquor	Seagram's Seven
Leo Burnett, USA	Airlines	United Airlines
Stern/Monroe	Travel, Hotels and Resorts	Embassy Suites Hotels

1989 Starch Winners

Agency	Category	Client/Product
AC&R Advertising	Women's Toiletries	Estée Lauder
FCB/Leber Katz Partners	Beer, Wine and Liquor	Bolla
Ogilvy & Mather	Confectionery, Snacks	Hershey's Kisses
D'Arcy Masius Benton & Bowles	Household Accessories	Charmin
CRK Advertising	Men's Toiletries	Calvin Klein Obsession
Deutsch	Household Materials	Oneida
Foote, Cone & Belding	Automotive	Mazda
Ogilvy & Mather	Financial	American Express
Rick Bennett Agency	Computers	Oracle
Ammirati & Puris	Insurance and Real Estate	Aetna
Sales Aid International	Food	Swanson
Eric Michelson	Apparel, Footwear	Evan-Picone
BBDO	Freight	Federal Express
Backer Spielvogel Bates	Electronic Entertainment	Magnavox

1990 Starch Winners

Agency	Category	Client/Product
Hakuhoda Advertising America	Electronic Entertainment	Hitachi
Deutsch	Household Materials	Oneida
Geer, DuBois	Automotive	Jaguar
Levine, Huntley, Vick & Beaver	Financial	Dreyfus
Tracy-Locke	Travel	Embassy Suites Hotels
Ogilvy & Mather	Beer, Wine and Liquor	Seagram's Seven
DCA Advertising	Office Equipment	Canon
Ad Group	Sportswear	Gitano
Saatchi & Saatchi	Computers	Hewlett Packard
BBDO	Floor Coverings	Armstrong
D'Arcy Masius Benton & Bowles	Food	Kraft Foods Cool Whip
Lawner Reingold Britton & Partners	Sporting goods, toys	Pinnacle Golf Balls
Revlon Professional Products (in-house)	Hair Products	Revlon
Bozell	Lingerie	Vanity Fair
PR+	Sportswear	Zena

Major Ad Award Winners (cont'd)

1991 Starch Winners

Agency	Category	Client/Product
Lintas	Hair Products	Johnson's Baby Shampoo
TBWA Advertising	Beer, Wine & Liquor	Absolut
Hakuhodo Advertising	Electronic Entertainment	Hitachi
D'Arcy Masius Benton & Bowles	Food	Cool Whip
BBDO	Floor Coverings	Armstrong
Eisaman, Johns & Laws Advertising	Women's Toiletries	Giorgio Beverly Hills
Young & Rubicam	Automotive	Mercury
Bozell	Lingerie	Vanity Fair
Avrett, Free & Ginsberg	Tobacco Products	Kent Cigarettes
Ogilvy & Mather	Financial	American Express
FCB/Leber Katz Partners	Bakery Goods	Chips Ahoy
Waring & LaRosa	Sporting Goods, Toys	Fisher-Price
DDB Needham	Computers	NEC
Young & Rubicam	Insurance & Real Estate	MetLife
Carlson & Partners	Sportswear	Ralph Lauren

Source: Starch Inra Hooper

For the past 12 years, the Magazine Publishers of America have chosen 25 nominees for the Kelly Award. The award is given to the print ad which best demonstrates the ability to capture and hold the reader's attention.

1991 Kelly Nominees

Agency	Client	Headquarters
Fallon McElligott	Timex Watches	Minneapolis
TBWA Advertising	Arbogast Lures	St. Louis
Fallon McElligott	Continental Bank	Minneapolis
Fallon McElligott	Jim Beam Brands Pusser's Rum	Minneapolis
Fallon McElligott	Porsche 911 Turbo	Minneapolis
Fallon McElligott	Porsche 968 Introduction	Minneapolis
Fallon McElligott	Lee Jeans	Minneapolis
Wieden & Kennedy	Nike Women's Fitness Insert	Portland
Carmichael Lynch	Harley Davidson	Minneapolis
Wieden & Kennedy	Nike Echelon Apparel	Portland
Wieden & Kennedy	Nike Women's Fitness Campaign	Portland
Goldsmith/Jeffrey	Everlast Sportswear	New York
Goodby, Berlin & Silverstein	Royal Viking Line	San Francisco

Source: AdWeek

Kelly Winners

Year	Agency	Client	Product/Campaign
1981	Ogilvy & Mather	Par Parfums	Paco Rabanne Cologne
1982	Ogilvy & Mather	International Paper	International Paper
1983	Doyle Dane Bernbach Group	Foodways National	Weight Watchers Frozen Foods
1984	Chiat/Day	Nike	Nike Apparel
1985	Ogilvy & Mather	American Express	Retail
1986	McKinney & Silver	North Carolina Travel & Tourism	Travel
1987	Ogilvy & Mather	American Express	"Green" Card
1988	TBWA Advertising	Carillon Importers	Absolut Vodka
1989	Wieden & Kennedy	Nike	Emotional Running
1990	TBWA Advertising	Carillon Importers	Absolut Vodka
1991	Wieden & Kennedy	Nike	Women's Fitness Campaign

Source: Magazine Publishers of America

Major Ad Award Winners (cont'd)

The EFFIE Awards

THE EFFIE AWARD IS PRESENTED ANNUALLY by the New York City Chapter of the American Marketing Association to advertisers and advertising agencies in recognition of those campaigns judged to be the most effective. Print, television, and radio campaigns are judged in over 30 categories.

Year	Agency	Client	Category	Product
1980	Ally & Gargano	Federal Express	Business Products and Services	Federal Express
	Advertising to Women	Gillette	Women's Toiletries	Silkience Conditioner
1981	BBDO	G.E. Corp.	Household Durables	G.E. Products
	Doyle, Dane Bernbach	Volkswagen	Automotive	Volkswagen Autos
1982	Doyle, Dane Bernbach	Polaroid Corp.	Recreational Products	Sun Camera
1983	Della Femina, Travisano & Partners	A.A.A.	Automotive Related	AAA, Auto Club
1984	SCC & B	Coca-Cola	Beverages: Non-Alcoholic	Diet Coke
	Ally & Gargano	Federal Express	Business Products and Services	Federal Express
1985	Chiat/Day	Apple Computer	Bus. Computers: Software	Apple Computer
1986	Chiat/Day	Pizza Hut	Restaurants	Pizza Hut
1987	Chiat/Day	NYNEX	Telecommunications Services	Yellow Pages
1988	Jordan, McGrath, Case & Taylor	Quaker Oats	Breakfast Food	Quaker Oatmeal
1989	Chiat/Day	NYNEX	Media: Non-Newspaper	Yellow Pages
1990	TBWA Advertising	Carillon Importers	Distilled Spirits: Non-Wine	Absolut Vodka
1991	Northwoods Advertising	Senator Wellstone	Political	Senator Wellstone
1992	Hill, Holiday, Conners, Cosmopolous	Reebok	Fashion Apparel	Blacktop Sneakers

Source: American Marketing Association, NY Chapter

AAAA A+ Creative Awards

THE A+ CREATIVE AWARDS, established by the American Association of Advertising Agencies, are awarded to advertising agencies rather than to a particular ad campaign. Each agency in the competition was asked to submit ten ads in any combination of media that ran for the first time the previous year.

Year	Agency	Location
1991	Carmichael Lynch	Minneapolis
1992	Cliff Freeman and Partners	New York

Source: AAAA

Almanac Fact

In 1990, the company that ran advertising's Clio Awards for television, radio, and print campaigns went bankrupt. The award program has been sold twice, and is currently in a state of transition.

Major Ad Award Winners (cont'd)

The One Show Awards–Best In Show

THE ONE SHOW AWARDS, gold, silver, and bronze, have been given each year since 1973 by The One Club for Art & Copy. The award is given to print, television, and radio ad campaigns in a variety of categories on the basis of effectiveness.

Best In Show

Year	Agency	Client
1990	Wieden & Kennedy, Portland, OR	Nike
1991	GGK, London	Electricity Association
1992	Saatchi & Saatchi, London	British Airways

1992 One Show Winners

Category	Agency	Client
Newspaper Over 600 Lines: Single	Fallon McElligott	Jim Beam Brands
Newspaper Over 600 Lines: Campaign	Leagas Delaney	Ordinance Survey
Newspaper 600 Lines or Less: Single	Fallon McElligott	Jim Beam Brands
Newspaper 600 Lines or Less: Campaign	Leonard Monahan Lubars & Kelly	The Narragansett
Magazine B/W 1 Page or Spread: Single	Goldsmith/Jeffrey	Everlast
Magazine Color 1 Page or Spread: Single	Goldsmith/Jeffrey	Everlast
Magazine Color 1 Page or Spread: Campaign	Fallon McElligott	Porsche Cars
Outdoor: Single	Mad Dogs & Englishmen	Tiny Mythic Theatre Company
Outdoor: Campaign	Chiat/Day/Mojo	NYNEX
Trade B/W 1 Page or Spread: Single	Goldsmith/Jeffrey	Everlast
Trade Color 1 Page or Spread: Single	Gordon/Gier	Crain's Chicago Business
Trade Any Size B/W or Color: Campaign	Fallon McElligott	The Lee Company
Collateral Brochures Other Than By Mail	Bartleby	Waldorf Astoria
Collateral Direct Mail: Single	Fallon McElligott	Art Directors/Copywriters Club of MN
Collateral Direct Mail: Campaign	The Richards Group	Tabu Lingerie
Collateral P.O.P.	Goldberg Moser O'Neill	The Red and White Fleet
Public Service Newspaper: Single	Della Femina McNamee	City Meals on Wheels
Public Service Newspaper: Campaign	Earle Palmer Brown	Goodwill
Public Service Outdoor	GSD&M	ACLU, San Francisco
Consumer Radio: Single	Bomb Factory	Wolfgang Puck Food
Consumer Radio: Campaign	Chiat/Day/Mojo	NYNEX
Consumer TV: Over 30-Single	BMP DDB Needham Worldwide	Barclaycard
Consumer TV: Over 30-Single	Wieden & Kennedy	Nike
Consumer TV: Over 30-Campaign	BMP DDB Needham	Barclaycard
Consumer TV :30 to 25-Single	Chiat/Day/Mojo	Reebok
Consumer TV :30 to 25-Campaign	Wieden & Kennedy	Nike
Consumer TV :30 to 25-Campaign	Goodby, Berlin & Silverstein	Chevy's Mexican Restaurant
Consumer TV :20 & Under-Single	DDB Needham	NY State Lottery
Consumer TV :20 & Under-Single	Della Femina McNamee	Beck's
Consumer TV :20 & Under-Single	Fallon McElligott	Nature's Course
Consumer TV: 20 & Under-Campaign	Chiat/Day/Mojo	Eveready Batteries
Consumer TV: Under $50,000 Budget	Fitzgerald & Co.	Opti-World
Public Service TV: Single	Fallon McElligott	Violence Against Women Coalition
Cinema/Video	Saatchi & Saatchi	British Airways
Out-Of-Home	Goldsmith/Jeffrey	Lumex
Consumer TV Foreign Language	Nordskar & Thokildsen Leo Burnett	Sparebankkort
College Competition	Portfolio Center	Portfolio Center Graduates

Source: One Club for Art & Copy

Choosing an Ad Agency

ANY COMPANY THAT SPENDS more than $500,000 to $1 million on advertising should seriously consider employing an agency to facilitate its advertising needs.

AdWeek and *Advertising Age* are the two magazines that thoroughly cover the advertising industry. These sources, combined with the tips listed below, may help narrow the range of what you should be looking for and clarify how to evaluate what you've seen.

Finding the agency that is best suited to your company's needs can be a tricky business. Many agencies do a better job of selling themselves than the companies they represent, and the burden falls on the client to find a selection process that works.

10 Questions to Ask Yourself Before Hiring an Ad Agency:

- Are we more interested in creative or in short-term market share results?
- Does our agency need a media-buying capability or will we handle that separately?
- Do we want to pay our agency a flat fee or a percentage of our budget?
- Are we looking for a particular campaign or for a company?
- How important is it to have regular access to the head of the agency we choose?
- Which medium do we need our agency to handle?
- Do we need our agency to handle existing projects only or new product launches as well?
- Does it matter if our agency is conveniently located?
- Do we want a company with a particular philosophy or one that is willing to work with the philosophy of its clients?
- Whom do we want to be in charge?

Evaluate Each Agency by Asking the Following:

- Does it understand our company's objectives?
- Does it address our company's objectives?
- Does it have the necessary credentials and experience?
- Does it have a knowledge of our business?
- Does it have an interest in our business?
- Does it have a knowledge of our competitive situation?
- Does it present sound marketing strategies?
- Does it present clear, creative solutions?
- Does it have good internal resources?
- Does it have a strong account management team?
- Can we work together?

Adapted from Small Business Reports, August 1991

Contact Options

The American Association of Advertising Agencies
666 Third Ave.
New York, NY 10017
(212) 682-2500
Fax: (212) 682-8391
Industry Association

Selection Agencies:

Advertising Agency Register
155 E. 55th St., Suite 6A
New York, NY 10022
Leslie Winthrop
(212) 644-0790

Advertising Agency Search Service
30 E. Huron, Suite 1609
Chicago, IL 60611
Mary Jane Rumminger
(312) 649-1148

Bismark Corp.
30 Bismark Way
Dennis, MA 02638
William Weilbacher
(508) 385-6889

The Canaan Parish Group
Ogden Rd.
New Canaan, CT 06840
Allen A. McCusker
(203) 972-2859

Dorward & Associates
2000 Powell St.
Suite 1530
Emeryville, CA 94608
Don Dorward
(510) 452-0587

EBJ Management Consultants
7229 S. Janmar Circle
Dallas, TX 75230
Eugene Jacobson
(214) 361-1427

Choosing an Ad Agency (cont'd)

Neal Gilliatt
1 Rockefeller Plaza, Suite 1510
New York, NY 10020
(212) 262-0660

Goodnight Consulting Group
5050 Quorum Dr., Suite 700
Dallas, TX 75240
James P. Goodnight
(214) 404-8697

W.E. Hooper & Associates
Box 107
Gibson Island, MD 21056
William E. Hooper
(301) 427-1196

Jones-Lundin Associates
625 N. Michigan Ave., Suite 500
Chicago, IL 60611
Bob Lundin (Chicago)
(312) 751-3470

Jack McBride
7019 Serr Ct.
Modesto, CA 95356
(209) 577-1464

Horace Malfa
15 Country Rd.
Mamaroneck, NY 10543
(914) 698-4927

Robert Marker
P.O. Box 4033
Tequesta, FL 33469
(212) 989-6868
(305) 747-3237

Morgan, Anderson & Co.
136 W. 24th St.
New York, NY 10011
Lee Anne Morgan; Arthur Anderson
(212) 206-1578

New England Consulting Group
55 Green Farms Rd.
Westport, CT 06880
Gary Stibel
(203) 226-9200

Pile & Company
45 Newbury St.
Boston, MA 02116
"Skip" Pile
(617) 267-5000

Richard Roth Associates
73 Cross Ridge Rd.
Chappaqua, NY 10514
Richard Roth
(914) 238-9206

Waldman, Moore & Associates
885 Third Ave., Suite 2900
New York, NY 10017
Eric Waldman
(212) 288-0824

Wanamaker Associates
3360 Peachtree Rd.
Atlanta, GA 30305
Ken Bowes
(404) 233-3029

Herb Zeltner
R.D. #1
North Salem, NY 10560
(914) 669-8530

Talent Agencies

MOST OF THE BIG TALENT NAMES are concentrated in three or four top talent agencies.

Creative Artists Agency (CAA)
(615) 383-8787

The William Morris Agency
(212) 586-5100

International Creative Management (ICM)
(212) 556-5600

United Talent Agency
(310) 273-6700

In addition, these agencies also have clout and are recommended:

The Gersh Agency
(310) 274-6611

Shapiro–Lichtman
(310) 859-8877

The Writers and Artists Agency
(310) 824-6300

Recommended Resource

Pacific Coast Studio Directory
Published by Jack Reitz
6313 Yucca St.
Hollywood, CA 90028
(213) 467-2920

This is a quarterly reference on the film and television industries.

Magazines

AdWeek's Ten Hottest Small Magazines

Rank	Magazine	AdWeek Performance Index	Revenue Up ($ Millions)	Ad Pages Up (%)
1	Details	2,878	4.5	80.9
2	The Walking Magazine	666	.9	20.4
3	Backpacker	553	1.2	21.3
4	Health	466	2.8	33.8
5	Cooking Light	422	2.2	16.1
6	Spin	420	1.2	3.8
7	Soap Opera Digest	291	2.1	7.5
8	American Health	259	3.1	33.2
9	Spy	210	0.3	21.3
10	Sassy	205	1.0	11.8

Source: AdWeek, April 1993

Top Magazine Spending By Company

Rank	Company	Magazines	Media Total	% in Magazines
1	General Motors	221.5	850.2	25
2	Philip Morris	203.9	1,001.7	20
3	Procter & Gamble	149.6	1,042.6	14
4	Ford	143.5	538.4	27
5	Chrysler	136.1	502.4	27
6	Nestlé	103.8	331.2	31
7	Toyota	97.1	400.8	24
8	Unilever	81.3	386.6	21
9	Nissan	69.0	265.3	26
10	Johnson & Johnson	64.2	313.4	20
11	American Brands	60.8	85.8	71
12	Sony	58.6	291.0	20
13	Mazda	57.0	148.2	38
14	Grand Metropolitan	55.9	265.6	21
15	Honda	54.8	234.1	23
16	Time Warner	54.3	299.2	18
17	Dow Chemical	43.2	128.0	34
18	Bradford Exchange	42.0	84.3	50
19	Ralston Purina	40.8	128.7	32
20	IBM	40.4	72.5	56
21	RJR Nabisco	39.0	216.5	18
22	Nike	38.7	108.2	36
23	American Protection Industries	38.4	100.0	38
24	AT&T	37.9	353.7	11
25	American Express	35.6	166.9	21

Source: AdWeek

Almanac Fact

42% of American households own an answering machine; 53% have cable TV service; 87% own a car; and 32% own Nintendo. 71% have more than one television, and 79% have a VCR.

Source: Fortune Guide to Investing in the 1990s

Top Magazines

Top 50 Magazines in Paid Circulation

Rank	Magazine	Average Paid Circulation 1992	% Change vs. 1991
1	Modern Maturity	22,879,886	1.9
2	Reader's Digest	16,258,476	-0.1
3	TV Guide	14,498,341	-3.7
4	National Geographic	9,708,254	-1.0
5	Better Homes	8,002,585	0.0
6	The Cable Guide	5,889,947	15.3
7	Family Circle	5,283,660	4.3
8	Good Housekeeping	5,139,355	-1.0
9	Ladies' Home Journal	5,041,143	-0.5
10	Woman's Day	4,810,445	4.1
11	McCall's	4,707,772	-7.2
12	Time	4,203,991	3.2
13	People Weekly	3,506,816	3.7
14	Sports Illustrated	3,432,044	4.1
15	Playboy	3,402,630	-4.1
16	National Enquirer	3,401,263	-9.5
17	Redbook	3,395,029	-12.1
18	Newsweek	3,240,131	0.5
19	Prevention	3,234,901	1.0
20	AAA World	3,107,468	11.0
21	American Legion	2,953,941	0.6
22	Star	2,931,305	-5.5
23	Cosmopolitan	2,705,224	-1.3
24	Auto Club News	2,540,275	2.7
25	Southern Living	2,374,530	0.6
26	U.S. News	2,307,569	3.1
27	Smithsonian	2,211,552	3.3
28	Money	2,146,410	11.0
29	Glamour	2,083,849	0.1
30	VFW Magazine	2,062,914	0.0
31	NEA Today	2,059,728	1.2
32	Field & Stream	2,007,234	0.2
33	Seventeen	1,915,426	3.4
34	Country Living	1,839,363	0.0
35	Popular Science	1,812,019	-1.4
36	Ebony	1,791,536	-2.3
37	Life	1,777,087	-2.1
38	Parents Magazine	1,749,322	-0.2
39	Popular Mechanics	1,642,081	0.2
40	Outdoor Life	1,502,542	0.0
41	American Rifleman	1,485,190	14.6
42	Sunset	1,452,086	-2.6
43	Golf Digest	1,421,883	0.0
44	Self	1,408,975	17.3
45	Soap Opera Digest	1,396,346	-3.5
46	Elks Magazine	1,383,318	-4.1
47	YM	1,340,415	31.6
48	American Hunter	1,329,124	12.8
49	New Woman	1,313,181	-2.7
50	Boy's Life	1,284,193	2.5

Top 50 Magazines in Ad Revenue

Title	1992 revenues ($ millions)	% Change vs. 1991
People Weekly	368.2	6.7
Time	342.8	5.0
Sports Illustrated	314.1	-2.8
TV Guide	276.2	-1.1
Newsweek	258.4	10.4
Business Week	211.1	-4.1
U.S. News & World Report	195.8	14.1
Good Housekeeping	193.8	17.1
Better Homes & Gardens	188.5	17.8
Forbes	173.4	11.0
Family Circle	158.4	21.9
Cosmopolitan	135.7	6.4
Fortune	133.8	-12.7
Woman's Day	130.9	30.5
Reader's Digest	120.4	24.5
Ladies' Home Journal	117.2	4.3
Vogue	106.7	3.7
Glamour	101.1	10.5
Money	94.9	8.0
McCall's	93.6	10.5
Golf Digest	79.8	12.0
Southern Living	78.7	24.2
Redbook	77.7	7.8
Rolling Stone	74.2	2.3
Parents Magazine	71.5	14.9
Vanity Fair	63.2	21.4
Bride's	58.8	3.5
Car and Driver	57.1	7.6
New Yorker	55.9	3.6
Elle	55.3	-6.1
Inc.	54.6	15.9
Travel & Leisure	53.8	-8.3
Country Living	51.5	13.6
Sunset	49.6	13.4
Mademoiselle	49.2	9.8
Gentleman's Quarterly	48.2	8.0
Modern Bride	46.8	12.9
Modern Maturity	46.2	-2.8
Life	46.1	4.0
Golf	45.4	15.0
Playboy	43.3	-11.3
National Geographic	43.1	4.8
Self	41.6	10.3
Road & Track	40.0	15.8
New York Magazine	39.5	-2.5
Ebony	39.0	5.0
Smithsonian	38.8	3.7
Entertainment Weekly	35.2	34.4
Esquire	35.1	10.0
Seventeen	35.0	3.8

Source: AdWeek

Video Retention Rankings

Most Popular Television Commercials

1991	1990	Brands	Ad Agencies
1	1	Pepsi/Diet Pepsi	BBDO
2	3	Energizer	Chiat/Day/Mojo
3	17	DuPont Stainmaster	BBDO
4	2	Nike	Wieden & Kennedy
5	5	McDonald's	Leo Burnett
6	4	Coca-Cola	McCann-Erickson
7	6	Little Caesar's	Cliff Freeman & Partners
8	9	Budweiser	DMB & B
9	-	Taco Bell	Foote, Cone & Belding
10	25	Pizza Hut	BBDO
11	-	Coors Light	Foote, Cone & Belding
12	8	California Raisins	Foote, Cone & Belding
13	7	Miller Lite	Leo Burnett
14	-	Toyota	Saatchi & Saatchi
15	-	Huggies	Ogilvy & Mather
16	-	Taster's Choice	McCann-Erickson
17	16	Diet Coke	Lintas
18	-	Johnson & Johnson Baby Shampoo	Lintas
19	15	Burger King	DMB & B/Saatchi & Saatchi
20	-	AT&T	Ayer/Ogilvy & Mather/Young & Rubicam/McCann-Erickson
21	12	Bud Light	DDB Needham
22	20	Duracell	Ogilvy & Mather
23	-	Honda	Rubin Postaer & Associates
24	-	Wendy's	Backer Spielvogel Bates
25	19	Jell-O	Young & Rubicam

Source: Video Storyboard Tests

Top Advertising Industries

Rank	Category	1992 Spending ($ millions)	% Change	1991 Rank
1	Automotive	1,035.9	10	1
2	Toiletries & Cosmetics	719.1	12	2
3	Direct Response Companies	628.0	9	3
4	Business & Consumer Services	507.3	12	4
5	Apparel, Footwear & Accessories	483.2	15	6
6	Foods & Food Products	461.9	6	5
7	Computers, Office Equipment & Stationery	350.7	21	8
8	Travel, Hotels & Resorts	338.1	-2	7
9	Drugs & Remedies	278.6	66	13
10	Cigarettes, Tobacco & Accessories	224.0	-15	9
11	Publishing & Media	202.8	3	12
12	Retail	187.3	-7	11
13	Liquor	185.0	-18	10
14	Sporting Goods, Toys & Games	172.2	12	14
15	Household Equipment & Supplies	160.5	40	15

Source: AdWeek

Music Permissions

A COMPANY THAT NEEDS TO USE POPULAR MUSIC or lyrics, either for commercial advertising or for an in-house corporate video, will have to get permission to do so.

Obtaining music permissions can be done simply and cheaply by purchasing music that comes with an automatic license for use, but the choice of music available will be significantly limited. On the other hand, obtaining permission to use protected music, which includes just about any song currently available in local music stores, can be costly and lead to extensive litigation since the copyright law protecting the use of current, popular music is very strict.

When choosing protected music, it is best to get a lawyer or an expert to help determine the appropriate legal procedures and to keep the following information in mind.

To use music that is protected by copyright in any way, it is necessary to obtain permission from the copyright owners in writing. These include the music publisher who represents the composer of the music and of the lyrics and the record company that owns the recording and represents the performer who made the recording.

A fee is generally charged by the copyright owners for permission, and the amount varies depending upon how it is used. Using a piece of protected music for a television or radio commercial is the most expensive. For a commercial in one state or city, the fees may be in the low thousands. For a national television commercial for one year, fees can range from $40,000 to $200,000 each to the music publisher and the record company.

Once a piece of music has been chosen, a company may either use an already recorded piece of music by a known artist or obtain the rights to use the music and rerecord it with other artists.

In the case of a performance by a known artist, for example, it may be necessary to pay various fees such as union new-use fees, which can enhance costs. On the other hand, hiring unknowns to perform a hit song will still require obtaining permission from the music publisher, who then pays the original talent. Union fees may be incurred, depending upon the arrangements made with the talent.

If using protected music seems too expensive or too complicated, the alternative may be to use a stock music library or similar music service. These services provide hundreds of CD's containing appropriate background music recorded by professional musicians.

The cost of purchasing these CD's is nominal, averaging $20 per CD. Additional licensing fees are also nominal, depending upon use. A company may pay a blanket fee of several hundred dollars to cover the music used throughout a video, or what's called a "needle drop" fee for each use of a piece of music within a video. These fees generally range from $15 to $75 per needle drop.

Listed below are the telephone numbers and addresses of key rights organizations and several stock music libraries.

Contact Options

Barbara Zimmerman
B Z Rights and Permissions
125 W. 72nd St.
New York, NY 10025
(212) 580-0615
Rights Consultant

Broadcast Music, Inc. (BMI)
320 W. 57th St.
New York, NY 10019
(212) 586-2000
Trade Association

The American Society of Composers, Authors and Publishers (ASCAP)
1 Lincoln Plaza
New York, NY 10023
(212) 682 7227
Trade Association

Music Libraries:

Associated Production Music
6255 Sunset Blvd.
Hollywood, CA 90028
(800) 543-4274

Firstcom
13747 Montfort Drive
Suite 220
Dallas, TX 75240
(800) 858-8880

De Wolfe Music Library
25 W. 45th St.
New York, NY 10036
(800) 221-6713

TRF Production Music Libraries
747 Chestnut Ridge Rd.
Suite 301
Chestnut Ridge, NY 10977
(800) 899-6874

Green Marketing

A RECENT STUDY PUBLISHED in the newsletter, *Green MarketAlert*, forecast that for four key consumer product markets (household products, health and beauty aids, food, and beverages), sales of "green" products would be more than 16 percent of total sales in those markets (almost $100 billion in green product sales).

Guidelines for the use of environmental marketing claims such as "recyclable," "biodegradable," "compostable," etc., have been established by the Federal Trade Commission, but the guides themselves are not enforceable regulations, nor do they have the force and effect of law. These guides specifically address the application of Section 5 of the Federal Trade Commission Act–which makes deceptive acts and practices in or affecting commerce unlawful–to environmental advertising and marketing practices. Guides for the Use of Environmental Marketing Claims provide the basis for voluntary compliance with such laws by members of industry, and are available from the EPA and the FTC.

Contact Option

Carol C. Weisner
Environmental Protection Specialist
Municipal & Industrial Solid Waste Division
United States Environmental Protection Agency
401 M St., SW (OS-301)
Washington, DC 20460
(202) 260-4489

Recommended Resource

Green MarketAlert
345 Wood Creek Rd.
Bethlehem, CT 06751
(203) 266-7209

This monthly newsletter provides expert information about the impact of green consumerism on businesses.

Environmental Marketing Task Force

In addition to the federal government sources named previously, a task force of Attorneys General from California, Florida, Massachusetts, Minnesota, Missouri, New York, Tennessee, Texas, Utah, Washington, and Wisconsin has issued recommendations for responsible environmental advertising in *The Green Report II*. The recommendations may be summarized in general as follows:

- Claims should be specific
- Claims should reflect current solid waste management options
- Claims should be substantive
- Claims should be supported.

A copy of *The Green Report II* may be obtained from any one of the task force member offices listed below:

California
Honorable Dan Lungren
California Attorney General
1515 K St., Suite 638
Sacramento, CA 91244
(619) 237-7754

Florida
Honorable Robert A. Butterworth
Florida Attorney General
Department of Legal Affairs
State Capitol
Tallahassee, FL 32399
(305) 985-4780

Massachusetts
Honorable Scott Harshbarger
Massachusetts Attorney General
One Ashburton Pl., 20th Floor
Boston, MA 02108
(617) 727-2200

Minnesota
Honorable Hubert H. Humphrey, III
Minnesota Attorney General
102 State Capitol
St. Paul, MN 55155
(612) 296-2306

Missouri
Honorable William L. Webster
Missouri Attorney General
Supreme Court Building
101 Highstreet, P.O. Box 899
Jefferson City, MO 65102
(417) 837-6567

New York
Honorable Robert Abrams
New York Attorney General
120 Broadway, 25th Floor
New York, NY 10271
(212) 241-2294

Tennessee
Honorable Charles W. Burson
Tennessee Attorney General
450 James Robertson Parkway
Nashville, TN 37243
(615) 741-3549

Green Marketing (cont'd)

Texas
Honorable Dan Morales
Texas Attorney General
Capitol Station
P.O. Box 12548
Austin, TX 78711
(214) 742-9698

Utah
Honorable Paul Van Dam
Utah Attorney General
236 State Capitol
Salt Lake City, UT 84114
(801) 538-1331

Washington
Honorable Kenneth O. Eikenberry
Washington Attorney General
Highways/Licenses Building
PB71
Olympia, WA 98504
(206) 593-5057

Wisconsin
Honorable James E. Doyle
Wisconsin Attorney General
114 East, State Capitol
P.O. Box 7857
Madison, WI 53707
(608) 267-3187

Top Grossing Licenses

Distribution of Licensed Product Sales by Category

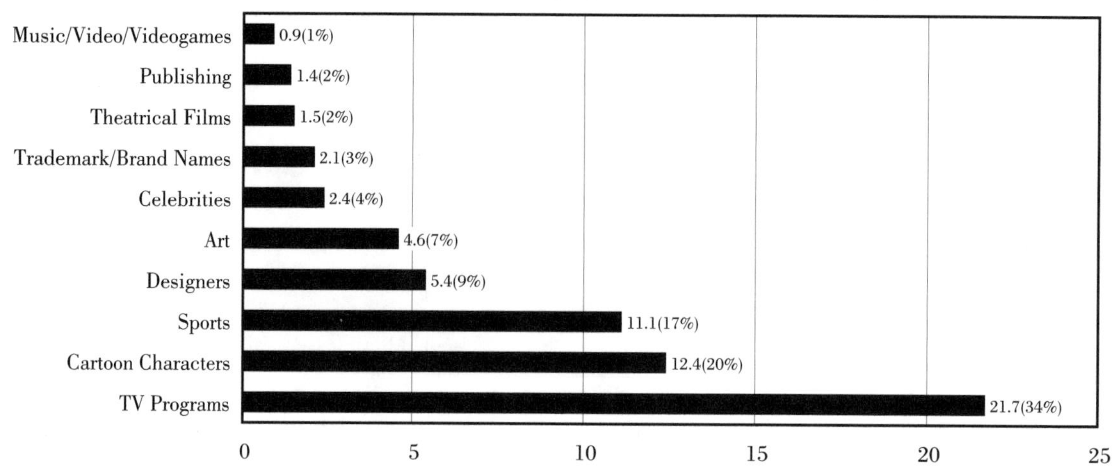

Source: The Licensing Letter

The Top Reference Sources

The U.S. Licensing Industry Buyers Guide
Licensing Industry Merchandising Association
(212) 244-1944

This is a complete resource for the more than $64 billion a year licensing industry. Licensing agents and the properties they represent are cross referenced for anyone interested in locating an agent or a property. Manufacturers are identified alphabetically, indicating their manufacturing capabilities and, in many cases, the licenses they represent.

The Consultants section lists law and accounting firms with licensing expertise. Important trade publications and trademark search firms are also listed.

The Top Brands

Apparel/Manufacturers

Brand	Company	Sales ($ millions)	Ad Spending ($ millions)	Spending as % of Sales
Levi's: Dockers	Levi Strauss	4,902.0	94.0	1.92
Hanes: L'Eggs	Sara Lee	4,104.0	61.9	1.51
Liz Claiborne	Liz Claiborne	2,007.0	47.7	2.38
Fruit of the Loom: BVD	Farley Industries	1,628.0	52.4	3.22
Lee: Wrangler	VF	1,400.0	67.0	4.79

Apparel/Retailers

Brand	Company	Sales ($ millions)	Ad Spending ($ millions)	Spending as % of Sales
Marshall's et. al.	Melville	9,886	25.0	0.25
The Limited, Express	The Limited	6,149	10.0	0.16
T.J. Maxx, Hit or Miss	The TJX	2,757	15.5	0.56
The Gap, Banana Republic	The Gap	2,518	15.1	0.06
Petrie's, Marianne	Petrie Stores	1,354	N/A	N/A

Athletic Footwear

Brand	Company	Sales ($ millions)	Ad Spending ($ millions)	Spending as % of Sales
Nike	Nike	3,386	120.0	3.54
Reebok	Reebok	2,672	78.0	2.92
L.A. Gear	L.A. Gear	984	24.2	2.46
Keds	Stride Rite	690	10.8	1.57
Converse	Converse	400	22.0	5.50

Automotive/Family Sedans

Brand	Company	Sales (units)	Ad Spending ($ millions)
Honda Accord	American Honda Motor	399,297	50.0
Ford Taurus	Ford Motor	299,659	42.0
Toyota Camry	Toyota Motor Sales USA	263,818	76.0
Chevy Lumina	General Motors	217,555	39.0
Olds Cutlass Ciera	General Motors	135,670	31.0

Automotive/General

Brand	Company	Sales (units)	Ad Spending ($ millions)
Ford	Ford Motor	2,312,611	348.6
Chevrolet	General Motors	2,229,915	264.7
Toyota	Toyota Motor Sales USA	939,274	303.9
Dodge	Chrysler	773,364	174.3
Honda	American Honda Motor	659,659	126.4

The Top Brands (cont'd)

Automotive/Imported Luxury Cars

Brand	Company	Sales (units)	Ad Spending ($ millions)
Acura Legend	American Honda Motor	65,689	56.0
Lexus LS400	Toyota Motor Sales USA	36,955	48.0
Volvo 740 Series	Volvo Cars of North America	29,198	1.2
BMW 3 Series	BMW of North America	26,618	11.0
Mercedes 300 Series	Mercedes Benz of North America	18,916	6.9

Automotive/Minivans and Sport Utilities

Brand	Company	Sales (units)	Ad Spending ($ millions)
Ford Explorer	Ford Motor	250,059	18.0
Dodge Caravan	Chrysler	207,919	12.0
Plymouth Voyager	Chrysler	173,373	19.0
Ford Aerostar	Ford Motor	147,373	4.0
Chevy Blazer	General Motors	123,346	1.3

Automotive/Subcompacts

Brand	Company	Sales (units)	Ad Spending ($ millions)
Ford Escort	Ford Motor	247,864	59.0
Honda Civic	American Honda Motor	232,690	36.0
Toyota Corolla	Toyota Motor Sales USA	199,083	28.0
Nissan Sentra	Nissan North America	146,618	32.0
Chevy Geo Prizm	General Motors	98,433	17.0

Automotive/U.S. Luxury Cars

Brand	Company	Sales (units)	Ad Spending ($ millions)
Cadillac DeVille	General Motors	146,636	3.1
Lincoln Town Car	Ford Motor	116,900	12.2
Buick Park Avenue	General Motors	83,831	30.6
Lincoln Continental	Ford Motor	52,540	12.2
Cadillac Seville	General Motors	26,688	14.6

Beverages/Beer

Brand	Company	Barrels Sold (millions)	Ad Spending ($ millions)
Budweiser	Anheuser-Busch	45.2	105.0
Miller Lite	Miller Brewing	19.1	94.0
Bud Light	Anheuser-Busch	12.4	58.0
Coors Light	Coors Brewing	12.2	66.0
Busch	Anheuser-Busch	9.8	7.0

The Top Brands (cont'd)

Beverages/Bottled Water

Brand	Company	Sales ($ millions)	Ad Spending ($ millions)	Spending as % of Sales
Arrowhead	Perrier Group	221.0	4.0	1.80
Sparkletts	McKesson Water Products	136.8	2.9	2.10
Poland Spring	Perrier Group	131.0	1.5	1.15
Evian	Evian Waters of France	92.0	5.9	6.40
Hinckley & Schmitt	Hinckley & Schmitt	88.6	0.2	0.23

Beverages/Soft Drinks

Brand	Company	Cases Sold (millions)	Ad Spending ($ millions)
Coca-Cola	Coca-Cola	2,521.8	150.0
Pepsi-Cola	Pepsico	1,950.5	139.0
Dr. Pepper	Dr. Pepper/Seven-Up	404.4	47.0
Mountain Dew	Pepsico	327.5	15.0
Sprite	Coca-Cola	300.9	33.0

Beverages/Spirits

Brand	Company	Sales ($ millions)	Ad Spending ($ millions)	Spending as % of Sales
Bacardi	Bacardi Imports	429.5	8.6	2.00
Smirnoff	Heublein	330.2	8.7	2.63
Jack Daniel's Black	Brown-Forman	265.6	9.2	3.46
Absolut	Carillon Importers	252.7	16.7	6.60
Seagram's Gin	Joseph E. Seagram & Sons	209.6	5.4	1.81

Beverages/Wine

Brand	Company	9-Liter Cases Sold (millions)	Ad Spending ($ millions)
Carlo Rossi	E & J Gallo Winery	16,000	NA
Gallo	E & J Gallo Winery	11,800	25.0
Almaden	Heublein	8,000	NA
Reserve Cellars	E & J Gallo Winery	7,000	NA
Inglenook	Heublein	6,510	0.1

Computer/Mainframe and Personal

Brand	Company	Sales ($ billions)	Ad Spending ($ millions)	Spending as % of Sales
IBM	IBM	64.8	110.0	0.17
Hewlett-Packard	Hewlett-Packard	14.7	55.0	0.37
Digital	Digital Equipment	13.9	28.8	0.21
Apple/Macintosh	Apple Computer	6.3	50.0	0.79
NCR	NCR	6.3	8.0	0.13

The Top Brands (cont'd)

Computer/Software

Brand	Company	Sales ($ millions)	Ad Spending ($ millions)	Spending as % of Sales
Windows/Word	Microsoft	2,275.0	38.2	1.78
Lotus 1-2-3	Lotus Development	828.0	15.0	1.81
WordPerfect	WordPerfect	532.0	4.6	0.86
dBase	Borland Int'l	502.0	7.1	1.41
PageMaker	Aldus	167.5	2.0	1.19

Cosmetics/Color Makeup

Brand	Company	Manuf. Sales ($ millions)	Ad Spending ($ millions)	Spending as % of Sales
Cover Girl	Procter & Gamble	406.6	61.4	15.10
Revlon	Revlon	326.8	17.8	5.45
Maybelline	Maybelline	313.5	19.2	6.12
L'Oreal	Cosmair	165.3	33.5	20.27
Max Factor	Procter & Gamble	153.9	7.4	4.81

Cosmetics/Mass Market Fragrances

Brand	Company	Manuf. Sales ($ millions)	Ad Spending ($ millions)	Spending as % of Sales
Gloria Vanderbilt	Cosmair	40	1.3	3.25
Primo	Parfums DeCoeur	26	2.1	8.08
Lady Stetson	Coty	25	6.7	26.80
Charlie	Revlon	25	1.6	6.40
Jovan Musk	Quintessence	20	2.6	13.00

Cosmetics/Prestige Fragrances

Brand	Company	Manuf. Sales ($ millions)	Ad Spending ($ millions)	Spending as % of Sales
Red by Giorgio	Giorgio Beverly Hills	68	2.7	3.97
Giorgio Beverly Hills	Giorgio Beverly Hills	47	2.3	4.89
Obsession	Calvin Klein Cosmetics	40	3.5	8.75
Opium	Yves Saint Laurent	35	2.0	5.71
Chanel No. 5	Chanel	35	1.3	3.71

Fast Food

Brand	Company	Sales ($ billions)	Ad Spending ($ millions)	Spending as % of Sales
McDonald's	McDonald's	12.5	386	3.09
Burger King	Burger King	6.2	200	3.23
KFC	Kentucky Fried Chicken	6.2	120	1.94
Pizza Hut	Pizza Hut	5.3	118	2.23
Hardee's/Roy Rogers	Hardee's Food Systems	3.8	49	1.29

The Top Brands (cont'd)

Foods

Brand	Company	Sales ($ millions)	Ad Spending ($ millions)	Spending as % of Sales
Oscar Mayer	Kraft General Foods	2,500	31.0	1.24
Weight Watchers	H.J. Heinz	1,800	30.0	1.67
Campbell Soup	Campbell Soup	1,500	31.0	2.07
Kraft Cheese	Kraft General Foods	1,450	53.0	3.66
Dole Produce	Dole Food	1,400	13.0	0.93

Hygiene/Deodorants & Anti-Perspirants

Brand	Company	Sales ($ millions)	Ad Spending ($ millions)	Spending as % of Sales
Secret	Procter & Gamble	130	20.7	15.92
Mennen Speed Stick	Mennen	100	22.8	22.80
Sure	Procter & Gamble	99	21.4	21.62
Ban	Bristol-Myers Squibb	91	12.6	13.85
Right Guard	Gillette	84	14.6	17.38

Over the Counter/Top Five Antacids

Brand	Company	Wholesale Sales ($ millions)	Ad Spending ($ millions)	Spending as % of Sales
Tums	SmithKline Beecham	110	15	13.64
Maalox	Rhone-Poulenc Rorer	100	17	17.00
Mylanta	Johnson & Johnson	95	24	25.26
Rolaids	Warner-Lambert	95	19	20.00
Pepto-Bismol	Procter & Gamble	90	13	14.44

Over the Counter/Top Five Cough/Cold Preparations

Brand	Company	Wholesale Sales ($ millions)	Ad Spending ($ millions)	Spending as % of Sales
Vicks	Richardson-Vicks	260	32	12.31
Robitussin	A.H. Robins	125	36	28.80
Hall's	Parke-Davis	125	13	10.40
Sudafed	Burroughs-Wellcome	80	23	28.75
Alka-Seltzer Plus	Miles	75	31	41.33

Over the Counter/Top Five Non-Prescription Brands

Brand	Company	Wholesale Sales ($ millions)	Ad Spending ($ millions)	Spending as % of Sales
Tylenol	McNeil Consumer Prod.	725	148	20.41
Advil	Whitehall Labs	305	61	20.00
Vicks	Richardson-Vicks	260	32	12.31
Alka-Seltzer	Miles	160	46	28.75
Bayer	Sterling Winthrop	135	15	11.11

The Top Brands (cont'd)

Soap

Brand	Company	Sales ($ millions)	Ad Spending ($ millions)	Spending as % of Sales
Dove	Lever Brothers	165.0	18.7	11.33
Dial	Dial	120.3	10.6	8.81
Ivory	Procter & Gamble	85.6	14.1	16.47
Zest	Procter & Gamble	76.4	12.3	16.10
Lever 2000	Lever Brothers	72.7	21.2	29.16

Soaps/Laundry Detergents

Brand	Company	Sales ($ millions)	Ad Spending ($ millions)	Spending as % of Sales
Tide	Procter & Gamble	997	62.0	6.22
Wisk	Lever Brothers	304	27.0	8.88
Surf	Lever Brothers	225	14.4	6.40
Cheer	Procter & Gamble	182	35.0	19.23
All	Lever Brothers	151	8.1	5.36

Soaps/Multi-Purpose

Brand	Company	Sales ($ millions)	Ad Spending ($ millions)	Spending as % of Sales
Lysol	Lehn & Fink Products Group	79	28.3	35.82
Pine-Sol	Clorox	71	10.9	15.35
Spic & Span	Procter & Gamble	56	4.4	7.86
Mr. Clean	Procter & Gamble	42	10.0	23.81
Formula 409	Clorox	42	6.0	14.29

Telecommunications

Brand	Company	Sales ($ billions)	Ad Spending ($ millions)	Spending as % of Sales
AT&T	AT&T	63.0	340.7	0.54
GTE	GTE	19.6	25.4	0.13
BellSouth	BellSouth	14.4	13.7	0.10
Nynex	Nynex	13.2	19.2	0.15
Bell Atlantic	Bell Atlantic	12.2	44.6	0.37

Television Networks

Brand	Company	Sales ($ billions)	Ad Spending ($ millions)	Spending as % of Sales
ABC	Capital Cities–ABC	2.7	29.9	1.11
NBC	General Electric	2.6	39.6	1.52
CBS	CBS	2.4	31.5	1.31
Turner Broadcasting	Turner Broadcasting	2.5	19.3	0.77
Fox Broadcasting	Fox Broadcasting	0.7	28.4	4.06

The Top Brands (cont'd)

Tobacco

Brand	Company	Sales ($ billions)	Ad Spending ($ millions)	Spending as % of Sales
Marlboro	Philip Morris	11.60	99.8	0.86
Winston	R.J. Reynolds Tobacco	3.37	42.5	1.26
Salem	R.J. Reynolds Tobacco	2.43	7.8	0.32
Newport	Lorillard	2.11	41.9	1.99
Doral	R.J. Reynolds Tobacco	2.07	1.2	0.06

Toys

Brand	Company	Sales ($ millions)	Ad Spending ($ millions)	Spending as % of Sales
Nintendo	Nintendo of America	3,500	45.0	1.29
Sega	Sega of America	741	30.0	4.05
Fisher-Price	Fisher-Price	640	25.4	3.97
Barbie	Mattel	550	63.0	11.45
Ninja Turtles	Playmates Toys	360	9.8	2.72

Travel/Airlines

Brand	Company	Revenue ($ billions)	Ad Spending ($ millions)	Spending as % of Revenue
American Airlines	AMR	12.09	109.0	0.90
United Air Lines	UAL	11.66	70.9	0.61
Delta Air Lines	Delta Air Lines	10.06	130.0	1.29
Northwest Airlines	NWA	7.53	32.2	0.43
USAir	USAir Group	6.04	40.8	0.68

Travel/Hotels

Brand	Company	Sales ($ billions)	Ad Spending ($ millions)	Spending as % of Sales
Best Western	Best Western	4.3	12.5	0.29
Marriott Hotels	Marriott	4.3	25.4	0.59
Hyatt Hotels	Hyatt Hotels	3.2	40.0	1.25
Days Inns	Hospitality Franchise Systems	1.1	5.4	0.49
Hilton Hotels	Hilton Hotels	1.1	20.0	1.82

Travel/Rental Cars

Brand	Company	System-Wide Sales ($ billions)	Ad Spending ($ millions)	Spending as % of Sales
Hertz	Hertz	4.0	44.1	1.10
Avis	Avis	3.3	31.1	0.94
Budget	Budget Rent A Car	2.1	20.0	0.95
National	National Car Rental System	0.9	6.0	0.67
Enterprise	Enterprise Rent-A-Car	0.8	10.5	1.31

Source: Superbrands 92

Top Consumer Brands

FINANCIAL WORLD EVALUATED MAJOR consumer brands and computed the value of the brand based on its value if it were to be sold.

Cash Value of Major Consumer Brands

Brand	Company	Value ($ billions)	Revenue ($ billions)	Ratio Value to Revenue
Marlboro cigarettes	Philip Morris	31.20	15.40	2.03
Coca-Cola soft drinks	Coca-Cola	24.40	8.40	2.91
Budweiser beer	Anheuser-Busch	10.20	6.20	1.64
Pepsi-Cola soft drinks	PepsiCo	9.60	5.50	1.74
Nescafé instant coffee	Nestlé	8.50	4.30	1.97
Kellogg cereals	Kellogg	8.40	4.70	1.79
Winston cigarettes	RJR Nabisco	6.10	3.60	1.69
Pampers disposable diapers	Procter & Gamble	6.10	4.00	1.52
Camel cigarettes	RJR Nabisco	4.40	2.30	1.92
Campbell soups	Campbell Soup	3.90	2.40	1.62
Nestlé sweets	Nestlé	3.70	6.00	0.63
Hennessy cognac	LVMH	3.00	0.90	3.24
Heineken beer	Heineken	2.70	3.50	0.76
Johnnie Walker Red scotch	Guinness	2.60	1.50	1.77
Louis Vuitton baggage	LVMH	2.60	0.90	2.94
Hershey sweets	Hershey	2.30	2.60	0.90
Guinness beer	Guinness	2.30	1.80	1.28
Barbie dolls accessories	Mattel	2.20	0.80	2.64
Kraft cheese	Philip Morris	2.20	2.80	0.79
Smirnoff vodka	Grand Metropolitan	2.20	1.00	2.10
Del Monte fruits, vegetables	Del Monte	1.60	2.30	0.71
Wrigley's chewing gum	Wm. Wrigley, Jr.	1.50	1.00	1.45
Schweppes mixers	Cadbury-Schweppes	1.40	1.30	1.11
Tampax tampons	Tambrands	1.40	0.60	2.19
Heinz ketchup	H.J. Heinz	1.30	0.80	1.63
Quaker cereals	Quaker Oats	1.20	1.10	1.16
Colgate toothpaste	Colgate-Palmolive	1.20	1.10	1.10
Gordon's gin	Guinness	1.10	0.60	1.89
Hermes clothing	Hermes	1.00	0.50	2.00
Kleenex tissue	Kimberly-Clark	0.80	0.70	1.16
Carlsberg beer	Carlsberg	0.70	0.80	0.90
Häagen-Dazs ice cream	Grand Metropolitan	0.60	0.50	1.25
Fisher-Price toys	Fisher-Price	0.60	0.60	0.91
Nivea cream	Nivea	0.60	0.90	0.68
Sara Lee baked goods	Sara Lee	0.50	0.80	0.67
Oil of Olay skin cream	Procter & Gamble	0.50	0.60	0.89
Planters nuts	RJR Nabisco	0.50	0.70	0.74
Green Giant vegetables	Grand Metropolitan	0.40	1.00	0.44
Jell-O desserts	Philip Morris	0.40	0.30	1.35
Band-Aid bandages	Johnson & Johnson	0.20	0.20	1.15
Ivory soap	Procter & Gamble	0.20	0.40	0.65
Birds Eye vegetables	Philip Morris	0.20	0.30	0.54

Source: Financial World, September 14, 1992

Network and Cable TV Data

Advertising Volume in the United States ($ millions)

Year	Total Ad Volume	TV Ad Volume	% in TV
1980	53,550	11,469	21.4
1981	60,430	12,846	21.3
1982	66,580	14,636	22.0
1983	75,850	16,759	22.1
1984	87,820	19,848	22.6
1985	94,750	21,022	22.2
1986	102,140	22,881	22.4
1987	109,650	23,904	21.8
1988	118,050	26,686	21.8
1989	123,930	26,891	21.7
1990	128,640	28,405	22.1

Television Advertising Volume ($ millions)

Year	Network	Spot	Local	Total
1980	5,130	3,269	2,967	11,469
1981	5,540	3,746	3,368	12,846
1982	6,144	4,364	3,765	14,636
1983	6,955	4,827	4,345	16,759
1984	8,318	5,488	5,084	19,848
1985	8,060	6,004	5,714	21,022
1986	8,342	6,570	6,514	22,881
1987	8,500	6,846	6,833	23,904
1988	9,172	7,147	7,270	25,686
1989	9,110	7,354	7,612	26,891
1990	9,383	7,788	7,856	28,405

Sources: TVB 1990-91& McCann-Erickson

Cost per :30 Commercial 1992 ($ thousands)

Early Morning (M-F 6:30-9 AM)	25.5
Daytime (M-F 10 AM-4:30 PM)	25.0
Early News (M-F 6:30-7:30 PM)	95.5
Prime Time (M-S 8-11 PM)	217.5
Late Eve. (M-F 11:30 PM-1 AM)	43.2
Weekend Children's Shows	34.6

Cost per TV Home Rating Point ($) 1992

Early Morning (M-F 6:30-9 AM)	6,375
Daytime (M-F 10 AM-4:30 PM)	4,808
Early News (M-F 6:30-7:30 PM)	8,377
Prime Time (M-S 8-11 PM)	16,603
Late Eve. (M-F 11:30 PM-1 AM)	10,285
Weekend Children's Shows	9,611

Time Spent Viewing per TV Home per Day

Year	Average Viewing Time
1980	6 hours, 36 minutes
1981	6 hours, 45 minutes
1983	7 hours, 2 minutes
1985	7 hours, 10 minutes
1989	7 hours, 1 minutes
1990	6 hours, 53 minutes
1991	6 hours, 56 minutes

Sources: TVB & Nielsen Media Research 1991-92, annual avg.

Network and Cable TV Data (cont'd)

Network Commercial Activity by Commercial Length (% of Total)

Year	:10	:15	:20	:30	:45	:60	:90+	Total
1980	0.7	-	-	94.6	2.7	1.9	0.1	100
1981	0.9	0.1	-	94.2	3.2	1.5	0.1	100
1982	0.9	0.1	-	93.7	3.7	1.5	0.1	100
1983	0.9	0.2	-	93.8	2.9	1.8	0.4	100
1984	1.0	5.2	-	89.2	2.0	2.1	0.5	100
1985	1.3	10.1	0.8	83.5	1.7	2.2	0.4	100
1986	0.5	20.9	1.2	73.6	1.4	1.8	0.6	100
1987	0.2	30.9	1.0	65.1	0.9	1.5	0.4	100
1989	0.3	37.9	1.2	57.4	1.0	1.8	0.4	100
1990	0.1	35.4	1.4	60.1	1.0	1.7	0.3	100

Sources: TVB 1990-91 & Arbitron, annual average

Commercial Television Stations

Year	Total	VHF	UHF
1980	734	516	218
1981	756	519	237
1982	777	517	260
1983	813	519	294
1984	841	523	318
1985	883	520	363
1986	919	522	397
1987	968	524	444
1988	1,028	539	489
1989	1,061	545	516
1990	1,092	547	545
1991	1,099	547	552
1992	1,118	551	567

Sources: TVB & Television Digest

Top Ten ADI's for Television by Market: 2nd Quarter 1992

Markets	TV Households (thousands)	% U.S.
New York	6,750	7.4
Los Angeles	4,883	5.4
Chicago	3,000	3.3
Philadelphia	2,637	2.9
San Francisco-Oakland-San Jose	2,208	2.4
Boston	2,126	2.3
Washington, DC	1,781	2.0
Dallas-Ft. Worth	1,763	1.9
Detroit	1,719	1.9
Atlanta	1,457	1.6

Source: SQAD Report Projections as of March 1992

Almanac Fact

The United States ranks first among countries for hours spent watching television per week, with 29:05 hours. Japan ranks second with 28:28 hours, and the U.K. is third with 25:35 hours.

Source: A.C. Nielsen Co.

Network and Cable TV Data (cont'd)

Growth of Cable TV Penetration by County Size (%)

Total U.S.	% of TV Homes With Cable	County Size "A"	County Size "B"	County Size "C"	County Size "D"
1969	5.0	1	3	14	9
1974	11.0	4	10	26	15
1979	18.0	8	19	35	22
1981	27.0	15	22	38	24
1982	33.0	23	39	48	35
1983	37.0	27	44	51	38
1985	45.0	36	52	55	42
1986	48.0	41	55	57	43
1987	50.0	44	58	57	47
1988	54.0	46	59	59	46
1989	57.1	51	62	61	47
1990	59.0	56	65	64	49
1991	60.6	59	64	66	53

Source: Nielsen

TV Network Telephone Directory

Network	Telephone Number
Arbitron	(212) 887-1390
Capital Cities–ABC	(212) 456-7777
CBS Network	(212) 975-6121
Fox TV	(212) 452-5555
Group W Broadcasting	(212) 307-3000
NBC Network	(212) 664-4444
A.C. Nielsen	(212) 708-7500
Telemundo	(212) 492-5500
Turner Broadcasting Sales	(212) 852-6600
Arts & Entertainment (A&E) Sales	(212) 210-9120
Black Entertainment TV (BET) Sales	(212) 582-8644
Country Music Television (CMT) Sales	(212) 916-1000
CNBC Sales	(212) 664-7920
Cable News Network (CNN) Sales	(212) 852-6600
Comedy Central Sales	(212) 408-8528
The Discovery Channel (DSC) Sales	(212) 751-2120
ESPN Sales	(212) 916-9200
Entertainment Television (E!) Sales	(212) 852-5100
The Family Channel (FAM) Sales	(212) 997-1710
Headline News Sales	(212) 852-6600
LIFETIME Sales	(212) 832-8832
Music Television (MTV) Sales	(212) 258-8210
Monitor Channel Sales	(212) 819-4150
NICKELODEON Sales	(212) 258-8158
NICK AT NIGHT Sales	(212) 258-8158
Prevue Sales	(800) 447-7388
Prime Network Sales	(212) 935-5931
SportsChannel America (SCA) Sales	(212) 664-7920
TBS Sales	(212) 692-6900
The Learning Channel (TLC) Sales	(212) 867-0600
The Nashville Network (TNN) Sales	(212) 916-1000
Turner Network Television (TNT) Sales	(212) 692-6900
The Weather Channel (TWC) Sales	(212) 308-3055
USA Sales	(212) 408-9100
Video Hits 1 (VH-1) Sales	(212) 258-8154

Network and Cable TV Data (cont'd)

Programming Most Valued by Advertisers

	% Rating Programming Very or Extremely Important		
Programming	**Client Marketing Execs.**	**Agency Media Planners**	**Agency Media Buyers**
Major Sporting Events/Series	57.0	67.0	68.3
Major League Professional Sports	47.2	62.8	60.1
Business, Consumer, Informational	38.6	42.5	44.8
Theatrical First-Run Films	42.5	36.2	48.0
Regional Sporting Events/Series	35.2	39.3	37.4
Cultural, Performing Arts, Documentary	24.5	34.1	44.7
Sports News	32.4	42.6	34.1
Comedy, Music, Entertainment	22.2	34.0	48.8
Off-Network High Profile Series	25.2	30.8	34.1
Original Made-For-Cable Specials	17.2	24.4	38.3
Original Made-For-Cable Series	17.3	22.3	30.9
New Productions of Off-Network Series	17.1	22.3	30.9
Classic Off-Network Series	9.4	21.2	17.0

Source: Myers Communication

Major Radio Networks

Radio Audience by Location of Listening (% All Radio Reach)

	Men 18+	Women 18+	Teens 12-17
At Home	75.0	80.1	95.6
In Car	82.8	75.1	77.9
Other	45.4	38.7	51.9

Source: RADAR, Fall 1991

Radio Usage (Average Daily Time Spent Listening)

By Age	Men (hr:min)	Women (hr:min)
18+	3:04	2:52
18-24	3:15	2:59
25-34	3:24	2:56
35-49	3:08	2:52
50+	2:37	2:47

Source: calculated from RADAR

Profile of Daily Listeners of Radio Stations by Format

Format	% Male	% Female	Median Age	Median income ($ thousands)	% 1+ Yrs. College
Adult Contemporary	50	50	39.1	31,300	41
All News	57	43	44.7	37,700	45
Album Oriented Rock	63	37	30.8	33,600	45
Black/R&B	37	63	36.0	21,000	29
Classic Rock	56	44	31.8	35,500	51
CHR/Rock	46	54	32.0	30,800	38
Classical	64	36	40.0	38,800	54
Country	55	45	41.5	28,400	32
Beautiful	43	57	48.2	30,100	37
Golden Oldies	49	51	38.3	32,900	39
MOR/Nostalgia	55	45	53.0	27,900	37
News/Talk	57	43	46.1	34,300	47
Religious	40	60	38.8	26,300	33
Urban Contemporary	45	55	31.9	22,500	29
U.S. Adult Pop	48	52	39.2	31,100	39

Source: Simmons, 1991 Study of Media & Markets

Magazine Ad Departments

Magazine	NY Telephone
American Health	(212) 366-8900
American Way	(212) 455-6200
Architectural Digest	(212) 687-6330
Automobile	(212) 407-9737
Barron's	(212) 808-7200
Better Homes & Gardens	(212) 557-6600
Black Enterprise	(212) 242-8000
Bon Appetit	(212) 297-5500
Boy's Life	(212) 532-0985
Business Week	(212) 512-2700
Cable Guide	(212) 683-6116
Chicago Tribune	(212) 682-3033
Colonial Homes	(212) 830-2900
Condé Nast Publications	(212) 880-8800
Cosmopolitan	(212) 649-3570
Country America	(212) 551-7128
Country Home	(212) 551-7117
Country Living	(212) 649-3192
Ebony	(212) 397-4500
Elle	(212) 767-6044
Endless Vacation	(212) 481-6090
Entertainment Weekly	(212) 522-5206
Esquire	(212) 459-7600
Family Circle	(212) 463-1000
Field & Stream	(212) 779-5450
Financial World	(212) 594-5030
Food & Wine	(212) 382-5618
Forbes	(212) 620-2200
Fortune	(212) 522-5203
GQ	(212) 880-6657
Glamour	(212) 880-7999
Golf Digest	(212) 789-3000
Golf Magazine	(212) 779-5000
Good Housekeeping	(212) 649-2556
Gourmet	(212) 371-1330
Harper's Bazaar	(212) 903-5370
Home	(212) 767-5519
Home Mechanix	(212) 779-5250
HG	(212) 880-8800
House Beautiful	(212) 903-5100
Inc.	(212) 326-2600
Insight	(212) 599-1730
Jet	(212) 397-4500
Kiplinger's Personal Finance	(212) 398-6320
Ladies' Home Journal	(212) 351-3500
Life Magazine	(212) 522-1212
Los Angeles Times Magazine	(212) 692-7170
Mademoiselle	(212) 880-8363
McCall's	(212) 463-1000
Metropolitan Home	(212) 551-7086
Modern Maturity	(212) 599-1880
Money	(212) 522-4829

Magazine	NY Telephone
Motor Trend	(212) 935-9150
National Enquirer	(212) 682-4022
National Geographic	(212) 974-1700
National Geographic Traveler	(212) 974-1700
Nation's Business	(212) 370-1440
Natural History	(212) 599-5555
New Choices	(212) 366-8800
New York Magazine	(212) 880-0700
New York Times Magazine	(212) 556-5854
The New Yorker	(212) 840-3800
Newsweek	(212) 350-4000
Omni	(212) 496-6100
Outdoor Life	(212) 779-5000
Parade	(212) 573-7000
Parenting	(212) 840-4200
Parents	(212) 878-8700
Penthouse	(212) 496-6100
People	(212) 522-1212
Philip Morris Magazine	(212) 880-5000
Playboy	(212) 688-3030
Popular Mechanics	(212) 649-3133
Popular Photography	(212) 767-6086
Popular Science	(212) 779-5000
Practical Homeowner	(212) 887-1856
Prevention	(212) 697-2040
Reader's Digest	(212) 953-0030
Redbook	(212) 649-3357
Rolling Stone	(212) 484-1616
Scientific American	(212) 754-0472
Scouting	(212) 532-0985
Self	(212) 880-8814
Seventeen	(212) 759-8100
Smithsonian	(212) 490-2510
Soap Opera Digest	(212) 645-2100
Southern Living	(212) 986-9010
Spin	(212) 633-8200
Sporting News	(212) 532-4330
Sports Afield	(212) 649-4302
Sports Illustrated	(212) 522-1155
Spy	(212) 633-6550
Sunset	(212) 986-3810
Tennis	(212) 789-3000
Time	(212) 522-1212
Town & Country	(212) 903-5000
Travel & Leisure	(212) 382-5600
Travel Holiday	(212) 366-8700
TVSM	(212) 683-6116
TV Guide	(212) 484-9900
U.S. News & World Report	(212) 326-5300
USA Today	(212) 715-5350
USA Weekend	(212) 715-2100
US	(212) 836-9200
Vanity Fair	(212) 880-7231

Magazine Ad Departments (cont'd)

Magazine	NY Telephone
Vogue	(212) 880-8405
Wall Street Journal	(212) 808-6700
Woman's Day	(212) 767-6000
Working Mother	(212) 551-9500
Working Woman	(212) 551-9500

Source: Marketer's Guide to Media

Newspapers

Advertising Cost Data: Top Daily Newspapers by ADI Circulation

Newspaper	ADI Circulation (thousands)	Daily Inch Rate ($)	Full Page Rate ($)
USA Today (Fri.)	2,162	N/A	65,810
The Wall Street Journal	1,919	N/A	110,627
USA Today (Mon.-Thurs.)	1,740	N/A	57,505
The New York Daily News	1,135	377.93	31,746
The Los Angeles Times	1,007	447.00	49,923
The Detroit Newspaper Agency	964	415.00	47,763
The Washington Post	735	311.10	41,065
Philadelphia Newspapers	718	302.00	35,728
The New York Times	714	382.00	47,124
New York Newsday	710	225.36	17,037
The Chicago Tribune	656	299.00	37,674

Source: Marketer's Guide to Media

College Newspaper Advertising

THE AVERAGE COLLEGE NEWSPAPER issue is read by 62% of the students in its market. If a company wants to reach that market by placing ads in college newspapers, it may be easier and more cost-efficient to contact one of the few existing college newspaper advertising syndicates.

These organizations will ship your company's copy to thousands of college newspapers and then collect tearsheets and monitor advertising performance. They can also match your company's specific needs to particular college newspapers, based on categories such as college enrollment, circulation, cost to attend or college degrees offered.

It is not necessary to pay these syndicates for placing ads. They are commissioned by college newspapers to represent them to advertisers.

Contact Options

American Passage Media Corporation
1114 Avenue of the Americas
New York, NY 10036
(212) 382-1692
Newspaper Syndicate

Cass Communications
1800 Sherman Pl.
Evanston, IL 60201
(708) 475-8807
Newspaper Syndicate

Almanac Fact

The leading direct mail catalogue, ranked by number of buyers, is Spiegel, with 3,800,000 buyers in 12 months. L'eggs, Fingerhut, Lillian Vernon, and Avon Fashions round out the top five list.

Source: Direct Marketing Association's Statistical Fact Book

Outdoor Advertising

ACCORDING TO THE OUTDOOR ADVERTISING Association of America, billboards and posters are the most cost-effective way of reaching the consumer.

The billboard, the most commonly used form of outdoor advertising, comes in two standard forms, the 30-sheet poster and the bulletin.

The 30-Sheet Poster

These are lithographed or silk-screened by a printer and shipped to an outdoor advertising company. They are then prepasted and applied in sections to the poster panel's face on location. Standard 30-sheet posters measure approximately 12 feet high by 24 feet wide.

The Bulletin

This can be hand-painted in an outdoor company's studio and erected in sections on location, painted directly at the location, or produced by computer. Most measure 14 feet high by 48 feet wide. The majority of painted bulletins in the United States are rotary panels, which can be dismantled and moved to a different location every 30-60 days. Permanent bulletins are placed at extremely high traffic locations and remain at a fixed location for the duration of an advertiser's contract.

Other Types of Outdoor Advertising

- 8-sheet posters or junior panels
- Transit exteriors
- Painted walls
- Telephone kiosks
- Truck displays
- Taxi tops
- Transit/rail platforms
- Airport/bus terminal displays
- Transit clock platforms
- Bus shelter displays
- Shopping mall displays
- In-store clock and aisle displays.

In recent years, advertisers from various product categories have increased their use of outdoor advertising because of its relative cost-efficiency. Billboards are permitted in all states except Maine, Vermont, Hawaii, and Alaska. In fact, in 1991, the industry fared better than any other form of advertising. The chart below reveals the top ten spending categories for the outdoor advertising industry.

The actual billboard design is generally developed by a company's ad agency which then contacts one of the many outdoor companies operating throughout the country.

The cost of an outdoor ad will largely depend upon location. Unlike print advertising, which charges a space rate, billboard advertising sells by "showings." There are three types of showings, a 100, a 50, and a 25. A 50 showing, for example, is seen approximately 14 times a month by approximately 90 percent of the area's population. The billboard company will help distinguish the location that attracts the particular demographic population a company is trying to reach. The charts below may provide a general sense of what costs to expect.

To visualize how a billboard will appear from 300 feet away, cut out the rectangular frame below or cut a frame that is 3Sinches wide by 1 inch, frame your artwork and hold it at arm's length.

A billboard seen from 300 feet

Outdoor Advertising (cont'd)

Billboard Reach (Frequency)–Women

Age	#100 Showing	#50 Showing	#25 Showing
18-24	90.6 (27.88)	89.1 (14.52)	85.8 (7.68)
18-34	91.8 (27.84)	90.3 (14.42)	87.2 (7.69)
18-49	91.9 (28.07)	90.5 (14.53)	87.6 (7.76)
25-34	92.5 (27.82)	90.9 (14.36)	88.0 (7.70)
35-44	93.1 (28.43)	92.3 (14.69)	89.5 (7.83)
45-54	89.4 (28.00)	87.2 (14.58)	85.3 (7.78)
55-64	89.7 (27.76)	89.0 (14.29)	84.5 (7.80)
65 +	87.6 (27.34)	87.4 (14.07)	84.4 (7.63)

Source: Simmons Market Research Bureau

Billboard Reach (Frequency)–Men

Age	#100 Showing	#50 Showing	#25 Showing
18-24	93.4 (27.84)	92.6 (14.15)	87.2 (7.73)
18-34	93.6 (28.03)	92.9 (14.28)	88.3 (7.81)
18-49	93.2 (27.97)	92.4 (14.30)	88.4 (7.78)
25-34	93.7 (28.13)	93.1 (14.36)	88.9 (7.86)
35-44	92.7 (27.81)	91.9 (14.25)	88.9 (7.68)
45-54	92.0 (28.35)	91.2 (14.53)	88.8 (7.78)
55-64	92.7 (28.44)	92.7 (14.46)	90.0 (7.91)
65 +	88.3 (26.28)	87.9 (13.50)	85.6 (7.23)

Source: Simmons Market Research Bureau

Billboard Cost per Thousand (CPM): 30-Sheet Positioning–National Average

Age	Adults ($)	Men ($)	Women ($)
18 +	1.43	3.01	3.38
18-34	3.51	6.50	7.58
35-49	6.10	11.79	12.81
50 +	4.92	9.92	10.81
18-49	2.23	4.26	4.69
25-49	2.85	5.36	6.11
25-54	2.67	5.01	5.76

Source: Simmons Market Research Bureau

For a free booklet containing illustrations of the annual Obie Award-winning billboards, contact:

Outdoor Advertising Association of America,
Marketing Division
12 E. 49th St., Floor 22
New York, NY 10017
(212) 688-3667

Contact Options

Several of the Largest Outdoor Companies:

Ackerley Communications
3601 6th Ave. S.
Seattle, WA 98134
(206) 624-2888

Gannett Outdoor Group
666 Third Ave., 4th Floor
New York, NY 10017
(212) 297-6400

Naegele Outdoor Advertising
1700 W. 78th St.
Richfield, MN 55423
(612) 869-1900

Penn Advertising
P.O. Box 6157
York, PA 17406
(717) 252-1528

Patrick Media Group
338 N. Washington Ave.
Scranton, PA
(717) 347-7100

3M National Advertising
6850 S. Harlem Ave.
Bedford Park, IL 60501
(708) 496-6500

Whiteco Metrocom
1000 E. 80th Pl.
Merrillville, IN 46410
(219) 769-6601

Banners

MOST BANNERS ARE MADE of a vinyl- or acrylic-coated fabric. They average 3 feet by 5 feet in size but can be made 4 feet by 60 feet or even larger. The following is a partial listing of companies that provide stock banners carrying generic messages such as Grand Opening or Clearance Sale. These companies will also custom-make banners to any specifications.

Contact Options

Banner Producers:

American Banner
9810-A E. 58 St.
Tulsa, OK 74146
(918) 254-6151

Best Buy Banner
6750-C Central Ave.
Riverside, CA 92504
(800) 624-1691

Davey Enterprises
75 B Mill St.
P.O. Box 574
Newton, NJ 07860
(201) 579-5889

Eastern Banner Supply
2582 Spring Lake Rd.
Mooresville, IN 46158
(317) 831-6055

Royal Wholesale Banner
4801 E. 39th Ave.
Denver, CO 80207
(303) 320-0308

McCullough Manufacturing
27 Miller St.
Strasburg, PA 17579
(800) 423-8204

Blimps

CORPORATIONS LOOKING FOR an innovative way to advertise may now contact several companies that sell and/or lease small, less expensive airships to advertisers who can't afford the likes of Goodyear Aerospace's 192-foot-long blimps.

The advantages of advertising on one of the new breed of airships that patrols the country's stadiums, golf courses, and racetracks are two-fold. First, they are seen by the large crowds that attend sporting events. Second, because the airship companies request network coverage in exchange for providing aerial camera platforms, they are seen by the even larger audiences that watch the televised events. What's more, a recent poll conducted by Opinion Research revealed that consumer preference for a product rises by 19 percent after a blimp appearance.

Contact Options

Airship Advertising Brokers:

Airship International
7380 Sand Lake Rd., Suite 200
Orlando, FL 32819
(407) 351-0011

Skyrider Airships
2840 Wilderness Pl.
Boulder, CO 80301
(303) 449-2190

Miller Airship Corp
1400 E. Blvd., Box 2167
Kokomo, IN 46904
(317) 453-2463

Memphis Airships
P.O. Box 13037
Memphis, TN 38113
(901) 775-0386

Almanac Fact

The top month for direct mail marketing in the business and finance category is December. The top month for self-improvement is May. Parents and children mailings do best in September.

Source: Direct Marketing Association's Statistical Fact Book

Media Buying Services

ONE WAY FOR A COMPANY TO SAVE MONEY on advertising costs is to use a media buying service.

Many companies use an outside advertising agency and pay them a fee to design their ad campaign and place it in the media. That fee generally includes a fee of 15 percent of the cost of the ads that the ad agency charges to get the campaign placed in the various media outlets that carry the campaign. Since an accredited agency receives a 15-percent discount from the media, however, that 15-percent fee is generally profit for the advertising agency.

To reduce that 15-percent fee to a 5-percent fee, a company can hire an independent marketing consultant and art director and use a media buying service. A free-lance marketing consultant is paid a flat fee to help a company develop a marketing plan. The art director, also for a flat fee, will design the logo, ads, brochures, and everything else that needs designing. The media buying service will then place all of the ads in the media for a charge of from 3 to 5 percent of the cost of the ads, amounting to a 10-percent savings for the client.

Contact Options

Ogilvy & Mather
309 W. 49th St.
New York, NY 10019
(212) 237-4000

DDB Needham
437 Madison Ave.
New York, NY 10022
(212) 415-2000

Graphic Artists and Designers

FINDING THE RIGHT PHOTOGRAPHER, graphic designer, illustrator, or printer to design a brochure or package, or any other marketing tool is relatively simple.

Most art and office supply stores carry a substantial selection of graphic design portfolios. These books provide the names, addresses, and phone numbers of a varied assortment of working professionals. The catalogues are broken down by specialty and offer samples of each artist's work.

Recommended Resource

PrintBooks
PRINT
3200 Tower Oaks Blvd.
Rockville, MD 20852
(800) 222-2654

Contact Options

Designers and Design-Related Organizations:

National Firms
American Center for Design
233 E. Ontario St., Suite 500
Chicago, IL 60611
(312) 787-2018 (In-State)
(800) 257-8657

American Institute of Graphic Arts
1059 Third Ave.
New York, NY 10021
(212) 752-0813

Association of Professional Design Firms
685 High St., Suite 5
Worthington, OH 43085
(614) 888-3301

Graphic Artists Guild
11 W. 20th St.
New York, NY 10011
(212) 463-7730

Society of Environmental Graphic Designers
47 Third St.
Cambridge, MA 02141
(617) 577-8225

Society of Illustrators
128 E. 63rd St.
New York, NY 10021
(212) 838-2560

Society of Publication Designers
Lincoln Building
60 E. 42nd St.
New York, NY 10165
(212) 983-8585

University and College Designers Association
615S Roosevelt Rd., Suite 2
Walkerton, IN 46574
(219) 586-2988

Graphic Artists and Designers (cont'd)

Regional Firms
Art Center Dayton
P.O. Box 3503
Dayton, OH 45401
(513) 294-0053

Art Directors Club
250 Park Ave. S.
New York, NY 10003
(212) 674-0500

Art Directors Club of Cincinnati
c/o South-Western Publishing
5101 Madison Rd.
Cincinnati, OH 45227
(513) 241-4591

Art Directors Club of Los Angeles
7086 Hollywood Blvd., Suite 410
Los Angeles, CA 90028
(213) 465-8707

Art Directors Club of Metropolitan Washington
1420 K St., NW, 5th Floor
Washington, DC 20005
(202) 842-5063

Artists in Print
665 Third St.
San Francisco, CA 94107
(415) 242-8244

Creative Forum Nashville
P.O. Box 23512
Nashville, TN 37202
(615) 244-4220

Creative Club of Atlanta
P.O. Box 421367
Atlanta, GA 30342
(404) 394-3256

Dayton Advertising Club
P.O. Box 513
Dayton, OH 45409
(513) 436-9672

Graphic Arts Service
1612 Grand
Kansas City, MO 64108
(816) 421-3879

Western Art Directors Club
P.O. Box 996
Palo Alto, CA 94302
(415) 321-4196

Packaging

FOR A COMPANY NEEDING TO LOCATE professionals to design packaging, there are a number of alternatives. The Package Design Council publishes an annual membership directory that lists the names, addresses, and phone numbers of packaging professionals, broken down by design and industry specialty. The reference costs $100 and is published in January.

Also available is *Packaging Magazine's* annual *Supplier Source Guide*, which provides an alphabetical listing of suppliers, associations, contract packagers, consultants, and design firms.

Recommended Resources

Package Design Council Membership Directory
P.O. Box 1332
Pleasant Valley, NY 12569
(914) 635-9153

Packaging
Cahners Plaza
1350 E. Touhy Ave.
P.O. Box 5080
Des Plaines, IL 60017
(708) 635-8800

The Top Reference Sources

Who's Who in Professional Speaking
National Speakers Association, $25 (free to meeting planners)
(602) 968-2552

This membership directory of the National Speakers Association contains the most recent information on more than 3,100 professional speakers. Listings include individual speakers, what topics they address, and how to get in touch with them. The directory is organized alphabetically and includes a geographic index.

Most speakers are happy to provide references and a tape to prospective clients.

Packaging Award Winners

1991 PDC Gold Award Winners: International Division

Category	Product	Client	Designer
Home Maintenance	ASDA Colours	ASDA Stores/Leeds	Lewis Moberly/London
Beauty Aids	Les Huiles Essentielles	Yves Rocher/Paris	Lewis Moberly/London
Wine	ASDA Valencia	ASDA Stores/Leeds	Lewis Moberly/London
Coffee/Tea	DESCA	Kraft General Foods/Spain	Board/Behaeghel & Partners/Brussels
Liquor	Glen Elgin	United Distillers/London	Lewis Moberly/London
Specialty Packaging	Hills High Mountain Coffee	Hill Brothers/Osaka	Jun Saeki/Al/Osaka
Cosmetics	Albion Excia	Albion Cosmetics/Tokyo	In-House Albion Cosmetics/Tokyo

1991 PDC Gold Award Winners: International Division

Category	Product	Client	Designer
Home Maintenance	ASDA Colours	ASDA Stores/Leeds	Lewis Moberly/London
Beauty Aids	Les Huiles Essentielles	Yves Rocher/Paris	Lewis Moberly/London
Wine	ASDA Valencia	ASDA Stores/Leeds	Lewis Moberly/London
Coffee/Tea	DESCA	Kraft General Foods/Spain	Board/Behaeghel & Partners/Brussels
Liquor	Glen Elgin	United Distillers/London	Lewis Moberly/London
Specialty Packaging	Hills High Mountain Coffee	Hill Brothers/Osaka	Jun Saeki/Al/Osaka
Cosmetics	Albion Excia	Albion Cosmetics/Tokyo	In-House Albion Cosmetics/Tokyo

Source: Package Design Council International

Top Purchasers of Packaging

Rank	Company	Expenditures ($ millions)
1	Philip Morris	2,631.50
2	Anheuser-Busch	2,510.00
3	PepsiCo	1,646.50
4	Procter & Gamble	1,608.00
5	Coca-Cola	1,320.00
6	ConAgra	1,315.00
7	Coca-Cola Enterprises	1,133.50
8	RJR Nabisco	1,032.00
9	Seagrams	762.00
10	Unilever US	674.75
11	Sara Lee	610.75
12	Nestlé USA	578.00
13	Adolph Coors	536.61
14	Brown-Forman	450.25
15	Eastman Kodak	437.00
16	Campbell Soup	405.00
17	Borden	404.50
18	American Home Products	402.27
19	Stroh Brewing	399.75
20	General Mills	391.04
21	Clorox	359.00
22	Cadbury-Schweppes	355.00
23	Archer-Daniels-Midland	343.00
24	Grand Metropolitan	326.00
25	Rhone-Poulenc Rorer	317.48
26	G. Heileman Brewing	305.75
27	Whitman	302.50
28	Del Monte USA	297.50
29	Revlon Group	294.25
30	H.J. Heinz	275.00
31	John Labatt	266.85
32	Ocean Spray Cranberries	253.38
33	Kellogg	252.00
34	Quaker Oats	251.75
35	S.C. Johnson & Son	249.00
36	Johnson & Johnson	247.00
37	Sherwin-Williams	237.00
38	Dean Foods	204.75
39	Warner-Lambert	193.25
40	Bristol-Myers Squibb	191.00
41	American Cyanamid	190.93
42	Tyson Foods	186.08
43	Du Pont de Nemours	186.00
44	Geo. A. Hormel & Co.	185.12
45	Hershey Foods	184.68
46	Allied-Signal	178.75
47	Dow Chemical USA	172.00
48	CPC International	171.00
49	Colgate-Palmolive	170.00
50	Dr. Pepper/Seven-Up	169.13

Source: Packaging Magazine

Celebrity Booking Services

IT MAY SEEM IMPOSSIBLE for a company to get Meryl Streep to appear at its annual convention or have Bill Cosby endorse its newest product at the local mall, but, in reality, many well-known celebrities are available for corporate appearances at a relatively reasonable cost.

A number of agencies are available whose job it is to book celebrities either to make a speech, perform, or simply appear at corporate conventions, publicity events, or charity benefits. These booking services cater to companies that believe that contact with major television, movie, music, and sports personalities will enhance their company's image. They rely on the fact that many celebrities are interested in getting exposure and income in ways that their agents may not be handling.

These companies will contact a personality, present him or her with a company's proposal and negotiate a deal, usually within a day or two.

Contact Options

Celebrity Booking Services:

Celebrity Service International
1780 Broadway, Suite 300
New York, NY 10019
(212) 245-1460

Washington Speakers Bureau
310 S. Henry St.
Alexandria, VA 22314
(703) 684-0555

Ingels
7080 Hollywood Blvd., 11th Floor
Hollywood, CA 90028
(310) 464-0047

Recommended Resources

Earl Blackwell's Celebrity Register
Published by Gale Research
(800) 776-6265

Celebrity Service International Contact Book
Published by Celebrity Service International
(212) 245-1460

Cavalcade of Acts and Attractions
Published by Amusement Business
(615) 321-4250

Clipping Services

VERY OFTEN A COMPANY WANTS TO MONITOR its own or a competitor's press coverage or needs to do subject research for a public relations campaign or a company presentation. The best solution may be the services of one of several clipping services available across the country.

For a fee that averages $200 per month, these companies will read the country's major daily and weekly newspapers, magazines, and trade publications and monitor the wire services, radio, and network and cable television news broadcasts. They will clip all articles or transcribe or tape every broadcast that mentions any subject requested by their client company.

Clips may be received on a daily or weekly basis. Companies may find them useful when they need to know the exact words written or spoken by politicians, executives, or public figures either for background research or for a company briefing, press release, daily news update, or public relations campaign.

Most of these clipping services offer a range of services, including day-of-publication delivery, historical research, news clip analysis of public relations performance, advertising analysis of competitors, and foreign press monitoring.

Contact Options

Press Clipping Services:

Allen's Press Clipping Bureau
215 W. 6th St., Room 1100
Los Angeles, CA 90014
(213) 628-4214

Bacon's Information
332 S. Michigan Ave.
Chicago, IL 60604
(312) 922-2400

Burrelle's Information Services
75 E. Northfield Rd.
Livingston, NJ 07039
(201) 992-6600

Luce Press Clippings
420 Lexington Ave.
New York, NY 10170
(212) 889-6711

Hiring a Copywriter

ANY TIME A COMPANY NEEDS TO DISSEMINATE information to the public, it's a good idea to hire a copywriter to ensure clean, effective, professional copy.

Herschell Gordon Lewis, author of *Direct Mail Copy That Sells*, suggests the following procedure for choosing a copywriter:

- Advertise for a copywriter listing enough specifics about the job to keep novices away.
- Ask for samples; then ask questions about the samples to validate authorship. If the candidate is boastful or seems more concerned with ego defense than with any admission of participation by others . . . beware.
- Conduct a convivial personal interview in which you lead the candidate to believe he or she actually has the job and the conversation is just a formality. Pay close attention to the degree of literacy. Look for two Achilles' heels (a) phony sincerity, and (b) contempt for whatever you're selling. Disqualify any candidate on either basis.
- Have the candidate take a timed writing test assignment. Pepper the instructions with weak words from the list below. If the writer regurgitates more than a couple of those words or uses platitudes and clichés, this person is not an original thinker.
- Give the top three candidates an actual, for-pay assignment. You'll find your writer.

A number of sources are available to help you find the writer that best suits your company's needs. The classified sections in AdWeek and Advertising Age, for example, are probably the best places to find the names of copywriters or place an advertisement.

Finally, it's always a good idea to check with a headhunter who specializes in advertising.

Recommended Resources

Dial-A-Writer
1501 Broadway, Suite 302
New York, NY 10036
(212) 398-1934
Fax: (212) 768-7414

Dial-A-Writer connects writers from ASJA's membership of 800 well-published, independent, free-lance writers with anyone needing a skilled professional.

The One Club for Art and Copy
3 W. 18th St.
New York, NY 10011
(212) 255-7070
Fax: (212) 633-6950

The One Club boasts a membership of some 700 advertising art directors and copywriters and is another good referral source for professional writers.

Contact Options

Headhunters:

Baedar Chiu
9538 BrightonWay, Suite 306
Beverly Hills, CA 90210
(310) 274-0051

Greenberg & Associates
1133 Broadway, Room 1204
New York, NY 10010
(212) 463-0020

Howsam & Weingarten
51 E. 25th St., Suite 501
New York, NY 10010
(212) 779-2299

Sandy Wade Company
101 E. Ontario
Chicago, IL 60611
(312) 280-9036

The Watts Group
812 Washington Ave.
Santa Monica, CA 90403
(310) 576-7925

Bob Westerfield & Associates
5150 S. Florida Ave.
Lakeland, FL 33813
(813) 644-1216

Weak Words

administration	facilitate	product
affinity	features	purchase
amendment	fond	quality
approximately	formulate	replacement
attractive	humorous	requested
configuration	indeed	respond
constructed	merchant	rethink
contradictory	moderate	service
"Dear Friend"	needs (as a noun)	standards
define	pamphlet	utilize
dispatch	peruse	value
earn	prearranged	work

Printers

CATALOGUES, BROCHURES, LABELS, and a host of other business printing needs can be arranged without ever leaving the office. A number of companies now provide fast, high-quality, full-color professional printing services nationwide based on specifics that the client can provide by mail, fax, or telephone.

Contact Options

Printing Companies:

Multiprint
5555 W. Howard St.
Skokie, IL 60077
(800) 858-9999

Service Webb Offset Corporation
2500 S. Dearborn St.
Chicago, IL 60616
(800) 621-1567

Econocolor
7405 Industrial Rd.
Florence, KY 41042
(800) 877-7405, ext. 245

Recommended Resource

Printing Trades Bluebook
A.F. Lewis & Co.
79 Madison Ave.
New York, NY 10016
(212) 679-077

Product Placement Firms

AFTER E.T. FOUND HIS HUMAN FRIEND, Elliot, through a trail of Reese's Pieces, sales of the candy leaped 66 percent in three months.

When Tom Cruise sported Ray-Ban sunglasses in *Top Gun*, sales of the company's aviator-style glasses jumped 40 percent in seven months.

The use of these brand name products and many others on film and television is negotiated by companies called product placement firms. For a fee that can run as high as $50,000, these firms will provide their corporate clients with promotional consultation and placement of their products in television series, feature films, and even game shows. These deals enable corporations to market their products by using the entertainment industry, and allow filmmakers to cut production costs by getting free products and services in exchange for their placement.

Product placement firms are hired by corporate clients to review upcoming scripts and determine: what products will be needed, whether they should be handled visually or simply mentioned in dialogue; evaluate whether the film is aimed at the correct target audience for the product, and negotiate a mutually beneficial deal for both the corporate client and the cost-conscious studios.

Contact Options

Entertainment Resources and Marketing Assoc.
P.O. Box 11001
Burbank, CA 91510
(818) 954-6944
Trade Association

Product Placement Firms:

AIM Promotions
Kaufman Astoria Studios
34-12 36th St.
Astoria, NY 11106
(718) 786-0137

BEI Entertainment
11466 San Vicente
Los Angeles, CA 90025
(310) 820-0607

Creative Entertainment Services
1015 N. Hollywood Way, Suite 101
Burbank, CA 91505
(818) 842-9119

Motion Picture Placement
9250 Wilshire Blvd.
Beverly Hills, CA 90212
(310) 858-1115

Rogers & Cowan
3701 W. Oak St.
Burbank, CA 91505
(818) 954-6944

UPP Entertainment Marketing
10865 Burbank Blvd.
North Hollywood, CA 91601
(818) 508-8877

Working with the Press

WORKING WITH THE PRESS IS a sales process. And like any other sales process, it is important for a company to establish clear goals and create ongoing relationships with the press with which they are dealing. Here are several guidelines that should help:

1. Set your objectives.
The key to successful interviews is to know what you want to accomplish before entering into a conversation with the press. Never enter into an interview process without knowing your objectives. If you get a spontaneous phone call from a reporter, the best way to handle it is to call the person back after you've had a chance to think about the key company objectives.

2. Know your key message.
Find every opportunity during a conversation with a reporter to underline the company's key objectives.

3. Manage the conversation.
Try to drive an interview rather than let it be driven for you. Answer questions by bringing them back to the points you want to emphasize. The goal is to communicate information rather than load the listener with data he or she may not understand.

4. Be responsive to your audience.
Different types of press have different needs. Try to understand their needs, either by getting advice from your public relations firm beforehand, or by taking the first few minutes of your interview to chat with the interviewer to understand his or her concerns. Then, present your material as effectively as possible to meet those needs.

5. Respect deadlines.
Press people are often under deadline pressure. Since the purpose of taking the time to do an interview is to develop a rapport, try to get an understanding of what deadline pressures the interviewer is under and be responsive to those pressures.

6. Remember the First Amendment.
Every interview may not result in a story and every story that gets written may not be exactly the story the company wants to see published. Members of the press are entitled to freedom of the press. Remember that if you want something to be "off the record," you need to get agreement from the person you are speaking with before you are guaranteed anonymity.

Contact Option

Abigail Johnson
Roeder-Johnson
29 Barcelona Circle, Suite 100
Redwood City, CA 94065
(415) 802-1850

Publicity Services

SEVERAL SERVICES EXIST that, for a fee, will take a company's press release or other publicity material and deliver it to media outlets for presentation.

Contact Options

Publicity Services:

Radio-TV Interview Report
135 E. Plumstead Ave.
Landsdowne, PA 19050
(215) 259-1070

This bimonthly magazine lists project pitches and profiles and is mailed to over 5,000 radio-TV talk show and TV news programming executives nationwide.

Publicity Express
1563 Solano Ave., No. 223
Berkeley, CA 94707
(800) 541-2897

This monthly magazine lists projects and pitches and is mailed to over 5,000 electronic media outlets.

PR Newswire (PRN)
150 E. 38 St.
New York, NY 10155
(800) 832-5522 or (212) 832-9400

This is a daily service that provides news releases and camera-ready photo transmissions to the world's largest media telecommunications network through satellite, fax, mail, and database.

Audio TV Features
149 Madison Ave., No. 804
New York, NY 10016
(212) 889-1342

This is a daily radio feed servicing 2,000 news and talk radio stations and all Associated Press and United Press International audio feed wire service subscribers.

Publicity Services (cont'd)

North American Precis Syndicate
4209 Vantage Ave.
Studio City, CA 91604
(818) 761-8400

This is a monthly distributor of multimedia script and slide packages to over 3,000 radio and television news and talk shows.

Derus Media
500 N. Dearborn, No. 516
Chicago, IL 60601
(312) 644-4360

This is a monthly distributor of multimedia script and slide packages to radio and television outlets. They are the only service to offer a full-service division for the Hispanic market.

News USA
2300 Clarendon Blvd.
Arlington, VA 22201
(800) 868-6872

This company distributes media releases and editorial feature camera-ready art in a monthly package by mail, discs, and computer hook-ups to 10,000 newspapers.

Metro Publicity Services
33 W. 34th St.
New York, NY 10001
(212) 947-5100

This service mails to 7,000 newspapers monthly. They offer monthly theme sections 22 times a year featuring subject matter for targeted audiences.

Recommended Resources

Three newsletters list the new columns, shows, magazines, and what they are looking for. They also report on free-lance project needs and provide names and addresses.

Bulldog Reporter
2115 Fourth St.
Berkeley, CA 94710
(800) 327-9893

Contacts
35-20 Broadway
Astoria, NY 11106
(718) 721-0508

Partyline
35 Sutton Pl.
New York, NY 10022
(212) 755-348

Contact Options

Media Outlet Directories:

Bacon's Media Information Systems
332 S. Michigan Ave.
Chicago, IL 60604
(800) 621-0561 or (312) 922-2400

BPI: BPI Media Services
1515 Broadway
New York, NY 10036
(800) 284-4915 or (212) 536-5263

Burrelle's Media Information Systems
75 E. Northfield Rd.
Livingston, NJ 07039
(800) 631-1160

Power Media Selects
Broadcast Interview Source
2233 Wisconsin Ave., NW, No. 406
Washington, DC 20007
(202) 333-4904

Selecting a Public Relations Firm

THOUGH THEY ARE OFTEN CONFUSED, public relations and advertising are not the same thing. A public relations firm is responsible for determining the way an organization is perceived by the public.

The first thing to consider when choosing a public relations firm is whether you want that firm to handle your company's entire public relations program or just its publicity. A firm that handles publicity sees to it that a company's products or services receive media coverage in the form of articles or radio and television broadcasts. When a firm handles public relations as a whole, its job is to help craft a company's image. Most PR firms do both. Here are some of the other ways they can help an organization:

- Provide an outside viewpoint or perspective;
- Increase an organization's overall visibility;
- Support a product or an overall marketing effort;
- Counsel in a crisis;
- Communicate with employees;
- Inform investors;
- Strengthen community relations;
- Act as a liaison with government agencies;
- Measure and evaluate existing public relations programs;

Selecting a Public Relations Firm (cont'd)

- Research public attitudes and behavior;
- Stage media events.

Once you have determined the specific communication needs of your organization, choosing the right public relations firm involves a certain amount of investigation. Begin by looking through the magazines in which you would like to have coverage, call the companies that are written about and find out which firm those companies employ.

When you have narrowed down your options, interview several firms. Don't assume that a large company is necessarily better equipped to handle your organization's needs. While advertising often requires a large staff of people to create and develop a campaign, public relations can usually be handled by a smaller team that is responsible for writing press releases and getting them out to an appropriate contact list.

Before deciding on a firm, consider the following questions:

- Does the firm have expertise in your company's field and understand your particular needs?
- Do you want greater awareness for your product nationally or in a targeted market?
- Do you want to pay your firm a flat fee, a retainer fee, a minimum monthly fee, or a project fee?
- What is your company's objective?
- How important is it to have regular access to the agency head and who is the backup?
- Which of the media do you need your agency to handle?
- How long will it take to learn about your account?
- What reporting/measurement methods are used?
- Must you have easy access to your firm's offices?
- Do you want a company with a particular philosophy or one that is willing to work with the philosophy of its clients?
- Whom do you want to be in charge?

If, after meeting with key people, you are still undecided, ask each to send a written proposal outlining how it would provide the public relations services your organization needs. When you have decided upon a firm, get references from other clients, and work out a reasonable budget so there are no surprises down the line.

Recommended Resource

O'Dwyer's Directory of Public Relations
J.R. O'Dwyer Co.
271 Madison Ave.
New York, NY 10016
(212) 679-2471

Lists most existing public relations firms, noting their rank, specialties, number of employees, and clients.

Leading Public Relations Firms

Top Fifteen PR Firms by Net Fees

Agency	1991 Net Fees ($)	1992 Net Fees ($)	% Change 1991 to 1992
Burson-Marsteller	199,818,000	203,638,000	1.93
Shandwick	72,970,000	166,100,000	-3.93
Hill and Knowlton	173,500,000	149,100,000	-14.00
Omnicom PR Network	63,948,548	65,569,433	2.50
Edelman Public Relations Worldwide	52,791,480	59,814,538	13.30
Fleishman-Hillard	52,228,000	58,651,000	12.30
Ketchum Public Relations	41,800,000	45,600,000	9.10
The Rowland Company	48,000,000	44,000,000	-8.30
Ogilvy Adams & Rinehart	56,917,000	36,124,000	-36.50
Manning, Selvage & Lee	30,346,000	31,424,000	3.60
GCI Group	29,584,296	28,095,400	-1.00
Ruder Finn	28,234,066	27,076,769	-4.10
Robinson, Lake, Lerer & Montgomery	20,733,000	21,200,000	3.00
Cohn & Wolfe	15,521,000	14,200,000	-0.85
Financial Relations Board	8,815,745	10,263,134	+16.4

Source: J.R. O'Dwyer Company

Leading Public Relations Firms (cont'd)

Leading PR Firms by Specialty

Agriculture

Firm	1991 Fee Income ($)
Gibbs and Soell	3,575,000
Bader Rutter and Assoc.	2,418,106
Fleishman-Hillard	2,300,000
Shandwick	2,008,000
Morgan and Myers	1,755,567

Beauty/Fashion

Firm	1991 Fee Income ($)
Hill and Knowlton	8,500,000
The Rowland Co.	4,495,000
Burson-Marsteller	3,000,000
Porter/Novelli (Omnicom)	1,947,664
DeVries PR	1,725,278

Entertainment/Cultural

Firm	1991 Fee Income ($)
Shandwick	7,750,000
The Rowland Co.	5,127,000
Ruder Finn	2,500,000
Burson-Marsteller	2,000,000
Manning, Selvage and Lee	1,980,000

Environmental

Firm	1991 Fee Income ($)
Burson-Marsteller	17,000,000
Hill and Knowlton	15,000,000
Ketchum Public Relations	11,900,000
Fleishman-Hillard	8,400,000
Shandwick	5,573,000

Financial PR/ Investor Relations

Firm	1991 Fee Income ($)
Hill and Knowlton	38,400,000
Burson-Marsteller	26,000,000
Ogilvy Adams and Rinehart	18,300,000
Fleishman-Hillard	9,700,000
Edelman PR Worldwide	8,918,156

Foods & Beverages

Firm	1991 Fee Income ($)
Burson-Marsteller	36,000,000
Hill and Knowlton	25,500,000
Fleishman-Hillard	11,400,000
Shandwick	10,363,000
Ketchum Public Relations	10,100,000

Health Care

Firm	1991 Fee Income ($)
Burson-Marsteller	41,000,000
Hill and Knowlton	19,000,000
Ruder Finn	9,000,000
Porter/Novelli (Omnicom)	8,796,339
Edelman PR Worldwide	8,022,172

High-Tech

Firm	1991 Fee Income ($)
Hill and Knowlton	24,500,000
Shandwick	19,464,000
Burson-Marsteller	14,000,000
Manning, SelvageandLee	6,210,000
Fleishman-Hillard	5,700,000

Sports

Firm	1991 Fee Income ($)
Burson-Marsteller	4,000,000
Hill and Knowlton	2,500,000
Cohn and Wolfe	2,450,000
Edelman PR Worldwide	2,400,000
Manning, Selvage and Lee	2,175,000

Travel

Firm	1991 Fee Income ($)
Hill and Knowlton	14,000,000
Burson-Marsteller	7,000,000
Shandwick	4,396,000
Fleishman-Hillard	3,000,000
Lou Hammond and Assoc.	2,261,812

Source: J.R. O'Dwyer Company

The Top Reference Sources

Zig Ziglar's Secrets of Closing the Sale
Berkeley, $8.95
(212) 951-8800

This best-selling book is must reading for anyone who is serious about wanting to improve as a salesperson. Ziglar's inspiring work includes over 100 successful closings for every kind of persuasion; over 700 questions that will open your eyes to new possibilities you may have overlooked; how to paint word pictures and use your imagination to get results; plus tips from America's 100 most successful salespeople.

This is one of the most important books on the topic–every salesperson should own a copy.

VNR and Industrial Video

A VIDEO NEWS RELEASE IS BASICALLY a press release in video form–typically a 90-second video piece that is paid for by corporate sponsors and then distributed, via satellite or mail, to stations around the country to be included in local newscasts. They are, in effect, paid advertisements in a news format. When they are well made, it is almost impossible to distinguish them from a regular national news segment.

Presidential candidates use them for air time on local news channels. Fortune 500 companies create them to inform the public about their latest product research. And, in the last decade, a growing number of small companies have begun to use them as an effective public relations tool.

There are two basic categories of VNR: timely and "evergreen."

A timely VNR takes advantage of a newsworthy event to get across a company's ideas or products to the public. For example, the 3M Company provided a high-tech coating for American luges in the 1988 Winter Olympics and produced a VNR featuring action race shots and experts applying the coating. The advantage of a timely VNR is that there's a good chance it will be picked up by stations that may be looking for news fillers. The disadvantage to a timely VNR is that it may become obsolete very quickly.

The "evergreen" VNR, on the other hand, is produced to have a longer shelf life, typically dealing with human interest stories that can be used by stations on a slow news day. Recent studies conducted by Nielsen Media Research, however, reveal that "evergreens" were preferred by 25 percent of all news producers, while just under 50 percent preferred timely pieces.

Most commonly, VNR's try to tie a company's new products and/or services to one of the following topics:

- Health tips
- Consumer affairs
- Community services
- Government issues
- New regulations
- Public service messages.

Creating an effective VNR can cost $20,000 or more including production, distribution, and follow-up costs.

The emphasis should be on the video's newsworthiness. Also effective are issue-oriented videos. The Insurance Institute for Highway Safety, for instance, recently transmitted a hard-hitting VNR on seatbelt safety by focusing on a car manufacturer whose seatbelts were not well designed.

A recent Medialink-Nielsen survey suggests the following rules to keep in mind when producing a video news release:

- Create a package containing a news-story type release and a few minutes of background tape or B-Roll.
- Time your VNR to be approximately 90 seconds.
- Place audio signals on separate channels so that news producers may insert their own voice-overs on one sound channel with the natural sound of your VNR tape on the other.
- When distributing a VNR, always clearly identify it as a public relations service in the materials provided.

Nick Peters, Medialink vice-president, suggests the following "litmus test" when choosing a production firm to create your VNR:

- Ask your own or another public relations firm that has had experience with VNR's to recommend a production company.
- Ask the production company whether it has done any VNR's before and for whom. Ask what results it has had and how those results have been documented.
- Make sure the company has past experience in television news.
- Ask to see a demo reel.

For further information, contact Medialink, a major satellite distributor of VNR's and other video public relations services. Medialink has a variety of free reference books about VNR as well as a listing of production companies nationwide.

Contact Options

Medialink locations:

708 Third Ave.
New York, NY 10017
(212) 682-8300

1401 New York Ave., Suite 520
Washington, DC 20005
(202) 628-3800

6430 Sunset Blvd.
Los Angeles, CA 90028
(213) 465-0111

The Time and Life Building
541 N. Fairbanks Ct.
Chicago, IL 60611
(312) 222-9850

VNR and Industrial Video (cont'd)

For a price that most experts say averages $2,000 per minute, it is possible to create an in-house company video that uses the same sophisticated techniques common to most television broadcasts.

Contact Options

Production Companies Specializing in VNR and Industrial Video:

Perri Pharris Productions
4590 MacArthur Blvd., Suite 540
Newport Beach, CA 92660
(714) 263-3737

Washington Independent Productions
400 N. Capitol St., NW, Suite 183
Washington, DC 20001
(202) 638-3400

Doug Manning Productions
8 S. Michigan Ave., Suite 1308
Chicago, IL 60603
(312) 782-2700

VNR-1
5639 Wembley Downs
Arlington, TX 76017
(817) 784-9920

The Story Painters
P.O. Box 195
Piermont, NY 10968
(914) 359-8820

The "A" Team
425 E. 79th St.
New York, NY 10021
(212) 737-8492

Reality Film & Video
1401 S. Brentwood Blvd.
St. Louis, MO 63144
(314) 725-3838

Manetta Development
723 Gist Ave.
Silver Springs, MD 20910
(301) 588-4111

Infomercials

INFOMERCIALS ARE PROGRAM-LENGTH TV commercials that are devoted solely to one product. These programs are designed to heighten public awareness, develop brand-name identification, and create a consumer market for a product by providing potential customers with all the information they will need about the product.

Contact Options

The Five Largest Infomercial Companies Ranked by Gross Sales:

American Telecast
16 Industrial Blvd.
Paoli, PA 19301
(215) 251-9933

National Media
4360 Main St.
Philadelphia, PA 19127
(215) 482-9800

Regal Group
355 Lexington Ave., 18th Floor
New York, NY 10017
(212) 682-6000

USA Direct (a division of Fingerhut)
4400 Baker Rd.
Minnetonka, MN 55343
(612) 932-3100

Gunthy-Renker
42-080 State St., #A
Palm Desert, CA 92260
(619) 773-9022

Source: Infomercial Marketing Report

Recommended Resource

Infomercial Marketing Report
11956 Gorham Ave., Suite 14
Los Angeles, CA 90049
(310) 826-6301

Almanac Fact

55% of Americans watch infomercials, while 62% of households earning over $30,000 watch infomercials.

Source: Hudson Street Partners

Infomercials (cont'd)

The PLAY (Program Length Advertisement of the Year) Awards are given by *Infomercial Marketing Report*.

1992 PLAY Awards

Award	Title (Show)	Recipient
Most Effective Show	Personal Power #3	Gunthy/Renker/ Lieberman Productions
Most Effective Show (tie)	NordicFlex Gold	NordicTrack/Tyee Productions
Most Innovative Product	Jet Stream Oven	American Harvest/National Media Corp.
Best Performance–Host	Juice Tiger	Mike Levey/National Media Corp.
Most Innovative Show	Amazing Discoveries	Positive Response Tele./National Media Corp.
Best Celebrity Performance	Where There's A Will There's An A	Michael Landon
Best Director	Juice Tiger	Steven Moore
Best Writer	NordicFlex Gold	Richard McKinney
Best Producer	Amazing Discoveries	Mike Levey

Direct Response Fulfillment Houses

APPROXIMATELY 80 PERCENT OF THE CALLS generated by commercials and infomercials occur within the first five minutes after the commercial has aired. These "call spikes" make setting up an in-house center for receiving telephone orders impractical and expensive.

"800" service bureaus that specialize in handling spot TV and half-hour infomercial-generated calls present the advertiser with an effective and relatively inexpensive resource for handling a high volume of calls.

In selecting an inbound call center or fulfillment house, the advertiser must determine if the number of lines and staff available at the times when specific ads are scheduled to run are sufficient to handle the expected number of calls. Advertisers should expect to pay the following costs:

- A one time set-up fee that will include normal program set-up and any unique programming or training that may be necessary.
- Call-processing fees based upon a negotiated per-call charge or actual usage, per minute of on-phone conversation.
- A monthly minimum fee credited against call charges.
- Special transaction fees such as output, payment processing, etc.

Contact Options

Operator centers with more than 400 work stations:

MATRIXX Marketing
1400 West 4400 S.
Ogden, UT 84405
(800) 629-6423

WATS Marketing of America
2121 N. 117th Ave.
Omaha, NE 68164
(402) 498-4000

West Telemarketing
9910 Maple St.
Omaha, NE 68134
(402) 571-7700

Operator centers with 100-400 work stations:

Advanced Telemarketing Corp.
8001 Bent Branch Dr.
Irving, TX 75063
(801) 629-6423

American Transtech
8000 Baymeadows Way
Jacksonville, FL 32256
(904) 636-1000

Neodata
100 Crescent Ct.
Suite 650
Dallas, TX 75201
(214) 871-5588

Precision Response Corp.
4300 NW 135th St.
Miami, FL 33054
(305) 681-1188

The Product Line
2370 S. Trenton Way
Denver, CO 80231
(303) 671-8000

Sitel
5601 N. 103rd St.
Omaha, NE 68134
(402) 498-6810

Teletech
15355 Morrison St.
Sherman Oaks, CA 91403
(818) 501-5595

Greeting Card Suppliers

Contact Options

Major Christmas Card Suppliers:

Birchcraft Studios
10 Railroad St.
Abington, MA 02351
(617) 878-5151

Brett-Forer Greetings
161 Avenue of the Americas
New York, NY 10013
(212) 620-2770

Century Engraving and Embossing
1500 W. Monroe
Chicago, IL 60607
(312) 666-8686

Handshake Greeting Cards
P.O. Box 9027
Columbus, GA 31908
(800) 634-2134

Masterpiece Studios
5400 W. 35 St.
Chicago, IL 60650
(708) 656-4000

Gift Baskets, Gift Brokers, Flowers

Contact Options

Gift Basket Brokers:

Dial-A-Gift
(800) 453-0428

800 Spirits
(800) 238-4373

JB Goodhouse
(800) 332-4332

The Peterson Nut Company
(800) 367-6887

Popcorn World
(800) 443-8226

Calyx & Corolla
(800) 800-7788

Phillips's Flower Shops
(800) 356-7257

Premium Sources

MANY COMPANIES PROVIDE CATALOGUES with a wide range of personalized premium or specialty advertising items, ranging from key rings and mugs to calendars, pens, pads, and other office items.

Total industry sales in 1991 were $5.1 billion, up 25 percent since 1987.

Contact Options

The Specialty Advertising Association
3125 Skyway Circle N.
Irving, TX 75038
(212) 580-0404
Trade Association

The association will provide free advice on developing a cost-efficient promotional plan and will provide a list of specialty advertising distributors by location. To find a local specialty advertising distributor, check the Yellow Pages under Advertising Specialties.

Promotion and Marketing Association of America
322 8th Ave., Suite 1201
New York, NY 10001
(212) 206-1100
Trade Association

Licensed Product Category Sales by Large Distributors

Product	% Sales
Wearables	19.7
Writing Instruments	13.4
Glassware/Ceramics	10.8
Office Accessories	9.2
Calendars	8.7
Recognition Awards	8.5
Sporting Goods/ Leisure Products	7.2
Buttons, Badges, Ribbons/ Stickers, Magnets	6.4
Automotive Accessories	4.4

Source: The Specialty Advertising Association

Mailing Lists

DIRECT MAIL MARKETERS RELY on mailing lists to target the particular geographical and demographical market they are trying to reach. It is possible to rent or purchase mailing lists that include the names, addresses, and telephone numbers of people in categories as specific as museum curators, tax shelter investors, or people who have recently moved.

Mailing lists are divided into two major categories:

- Compiled lists, which are derived from directories, associations, government data, Yellow Pages registration, and public records.
- Response lists, which are comprised of individuals who have taken a direct action such as making a purchase, subscribing to a publication, or joining an organization. In general, these lists are more accurate since they are compiled from less general sources.

Anyone can obtain either kind of list directly from a mailing list company, or they can hire a list broker. Mailing list companies all provide free catalogues of their available lists and generally charge between $50 and $100 per 1,000 names for one-time use of a list. Overall, it is a better idea to use a broker than rent a list directly. It is not necessary to pay a broker since the broker receives a commission directly from the list owner, and will investigate, select, and order the list that is most suitable for each individual client.

Recommended Resources

Standard Rate & Data Service
3004 Glenview Rd.
Wilmette, IL 60091
(708) 256-6067
This company publishes *Direct Mail List Rates and Data*, a directory of available mailing lists.

Directory of Mailing List Companies
Todd Publications
18 N. Greenbush Rd.
West Nyack, NY 10994
(914) 358-6213

This book sells for $25 and includes an alphabetical listing of the names, addresses, and telephone numbers of hundreds of mailing list brokers.

Contact Options

List Brokers:

Abelow Response
181 S. Franklin Ave.
Valley Stream, NY 11581
(516) 791-7900

AZ Marketing Services
31 River Rd.
Cos Cob, CT 06807
(203) 629-8088

Direct Media
200 Pemberwick Rd.
Greenwich, CT 06830
(203) 532-1000

The Kaplan Agency
1200 High Ridge Rd.
Stamford, CT 06905
(203) 968-8800

Kleid Company
530 Fifth Ave., 17th Floor
New York, NY 10036
(212) 819-3400

Leon Henry
455 Central Ave.
Scarsdale, NY 10583
(914) 723-3176

Mal Dunn & Associates
Hardscrabble Rd.
Croton Falls, NY 10519
(914) 277-5558

Media Horizons
94 East Ave.
Norwalk, CT 06851
(203) 857-0770

Millard Group
10 Vose Farm Rd.
Peterborough, NH 03458
(603) 924-9262

Names and Addresses
4096 Commercial Ave.
Northbrook, IL 60062
(708) 272-7933

Qualified Lists Corp.
135 Bedford Rd.
Armonk, NY 10504
(914) 273-6606

Package Inserts and Co-ops

WITH THE RISE OF POSTAL RATES over the last decade, the direct mail industry has found increasing success in the use of alternative media such as package inserts, co-ops, and ride-alongs. These allow marketers to share the cost of direct mail advertising by sending their material out together in one package.

Package inserts are advertisements in the form of postcards, flyers, folders, or envelopes (either from the company selling the product or from outsiders) placed in packages delivered to mail order or retail buyers. The most popular format is a 5S-by-8S-inch one- or two-panel four-color advertisement.

The number of inserts enclosed, will vary from four to eight. They are generally carried by an envelope or box that delivers an order sent by an established purveyor of mail-order merchandise, by a utility or credit card bill, or by a monthly bank statement. They can also be placed in an envelope containing photo-finishing, a package containing laundry or dry cleaning, a cereal box, a disposable diaper carton, or anything else bought retail. The average cost to direct marketers of package inserts is between $45 and $55 per thousand.

When non-competing advertisements are mailed together to reduce costs and reach the same prospective customers, it's called a co-op mailing. These are generally carried in the same way or inserted in newspapers instead of being mailed.

When the mailing is run by a company with the primary purpose of mailing a catalogue or making an announcement, it's a ride-along. The average cost of such mailings is now edging above the $30 million mark.

The most obvious advantage to using these alternative media is the low initial cost relative to the benefits, particularly after a successful format has been created.

Leon Henry's Ten Rules for the Most Effective Alternative Media Ad Placement

1. Choose the right distribution program.

Look for demographics that are geared to your product or service, and try to insure that the merchandise that your package insert accompanies will heighten the response to your offer.

2. Test at least ten programs at a time.

Out of every ten programs tested, however, you will have an average of three losers. Experiment with new inserts to get an accurate measure of success.

3. Go with the maximum size.

Different programs have different physical limitations. Go with the maximum size allowed by each program to prevent your insert from being lost in the shuffle.

4. Test with copy that you know works.

Do not write new copy, create new graphics, or introduce a new offer when you first test your insert. Test what you already know works in direct mail or space advertising. If your program fails, you'll know it was the program and not your copy or offer that was at fault.

5. Be patient when evaluating a program.

Inserts that accompany retail merchandise may take six months before they are fully distributed. Calculate a final cost-per-order you can be comfortable with, and as long as you come in under that number, you can consider your insert program a success.

6. Try to transform marginal performers into new profit makers.

By reducing printing costs, changing layout, or changing stock, color, or copy, you might be able to manipulate the cost of participation in a program. Creative renegotiation can turn a marginal program into a real success.

7. Always key every insert package.

Using a five- or six-digit code, mark every insert you send out with a key that will allow you to identify what package it was part of. It's better to pay the extra money to stop the press and change keys than it is to be unsure of your results.

8. Include an appropriate number of inserts.

Unless you have at least 10,000 inserts in each program you test, your returns may not be statistically reliable. On the other hand, if the number of inserts you put in one program is too high, it will force you to wait too long a time until all of your inserts have been distributed and you can evaluate the results. One way around this is to break up a large number of inserts into several keys and evaluate them as you go along.

9. Choose a dependable broker.

Many inserts miss the program they were intended for because of foul-ups in production or shipping. Your broker must make sure your materials are printed accurately, shipped to where they're supposed to go, received by the appropriate people, and inserted in the right program.

10. Always re-test favorable returns.

If you don't, a competitor may jump in and pre-empt you from profiting from your success. On the other hand, you should maintain sizeable reserves of pre-keyed inserts so that you may take advantage of a new program or a competitor's failure to re-test promptly.

Contact Option

Leon Henry
455 Central Ave.
Scarsdale, NY 10583
(914) 723-3176

Color Marketing

EFFECTIVE USE OF COLOR is the mission of The Color Marketing Group, an international non-profit association of 1,300 design and color professionals. The group forecasts color directions one to three years ahead in all industries, including consumer, contract, transportation, fashion, graphics, office, and health care. The Color Marketing Group provides a forum for the exchange of non-competitive information on all phases of color marketing, including color trends and combinations; styling and design; merchandising and sales; education and research.

Each year the Color Marketing Group selects emerging color preferences such as Ensign Blue, Plantation Shutter and Canyon Rose, for industry groups like exterior home, kitchen and bath, and retail.

Contact Option

The Color Marketing Group
4001 N. Ninth St., Suite 102
Arlington, VA 22203
(703) 528-7666

1992 National Sales Hall of Fame

THE NATIONAL SALES HALL OF FAME IS selected by The Sales and Marketing Executives of Greater New York, a not-for-profit membership association of sales professionals.

Thomas J. Watson, Sr. (posthumous award)
IBM, Founder and Chairman

Ewing M. Kauffman
Marion Merrell Dow, Chairman Emeritus

James E. Preston
Avon Products, Chairman and CEO

Reginald F. Lewis
TLC Beatrice International Holdings, Chairman and CEO

James W. Kinnear
Texaco, President and CEO

Cathleen Black
American Newspaper, President & CEO

Joseph E. Anonini
Kmart, Chairman, President & CEO

Classic Marketing Books

BOOKS ABOUT MARKETING ACCOUNT for a large percentage of the greatest business books ever written. Here is an idiosyncratic list of some of the most useful books on the topic.

Direct Mail Copy That Sells
by Herschell Gordon Lewis
Prentice Hall

How to Write a Good Advertisement
by Victor O. Schwab
Wilshire Book Company

The Copy Workshop
by Bruce Bendinger
The Copy Workshop

Positioning
by Trout & Reis
McGraw, Hill

Tested Advertising Methods
by John Caples
Reward Books

Typical Sales Rep Territories

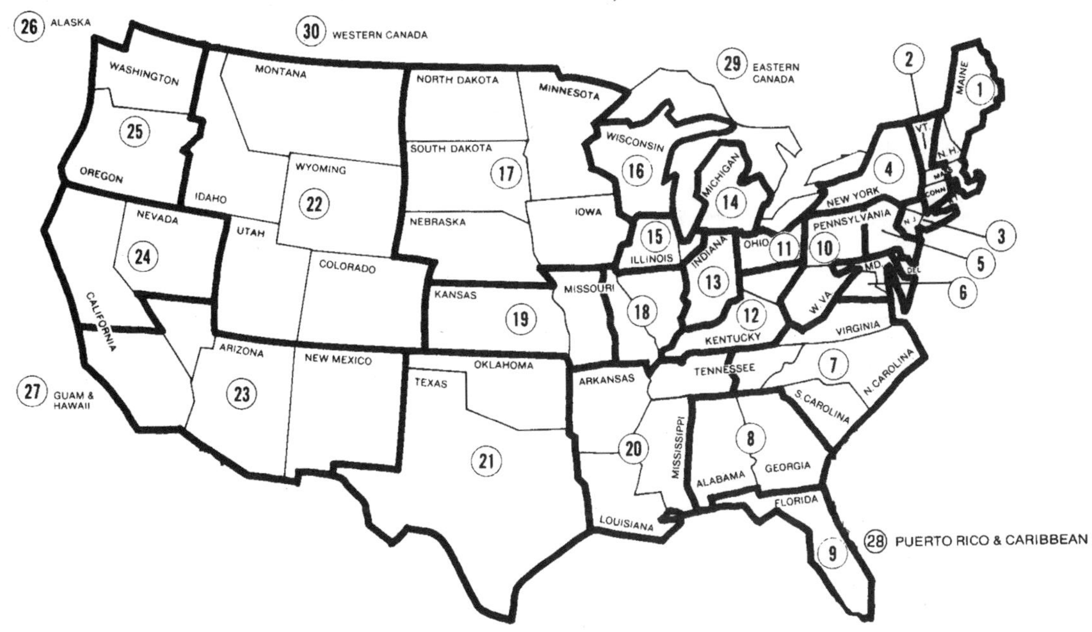

No.	Regions
1	Eastern Massachusetts, Rhode Island, New Hampshire, Maine
2	Connecticut, western Massachusetts, Vermont
3	New York City, Long Island, Westchester County, New Jersey north of Trenton
4	New York Upstate
5	New Jersey, Trenton and south, Pennsylvannia east of Harrisburg
6	Maryland, Delaware, District of Columbia, Northern Virginia
7	Southern Virginia, North Carolina, South Carolina, eastern Tennessee
8	Georgia and Alabama
9	Florida
10	Western Pennsylvania to Harrisburg, West Virgina
11	Ohio north of Route 40
12	Ohio south of Route 40, Kentucky
13	Indiana except Northwestern counties
14	Michigan and Toledo, Ohio

No.	Regions
15	Illinios, north of Route 36 and Lake, Porter and LaPorte counties of Indiana
16	Wisconsin and northwestern Michigan (area northwest of Lake Michigan)
17	Minnesota, may include North and South Dakota and all or part of Iowa and Nebraska
18	Eastern Missouri, southern Illinois
19	Western Missouri, Kansas
20	Louisiana, Mississippi, Arkansas, western Tennessee
21	Texas and Oklahoma
22	Colorado, Utah, may include Montana, Idaho, Wyoming
23	California, Bakersfield and south, Arizona, Southern Nevada, and New Mexico
24	California north of Bakersfield, part of Nevada
25	Washington and Oregon
26	Alaska
27	Hawaii and Guam
28	Puerto Rico and the Caribbean
29	Eastern Canada
30	Western Canada

Source: Manufacturers' Agents National Association ©1993

Trade Shows and Conventions

Convention Dates and Cities

Convention	Year	City	Dates
Agriculture and Food Show SADAQ (514) 289-9669	1993	Montreal	10/30 to 11/7
American Booksellers Assn. Convention and Trade Exh. American Booksellers Association (914) 631-7800	1994	Los Angeles	5/28 to 5/31
	1995	Chicago	6/3 to 6/6
American Chemical Society National Expo American Chemical Society (202) 872-4485	biannual		
American Financial Services Association Expo American Financial Services Association (202) 296-5544	1993	Boston	5/25 to 5/29
	1994	Vancouver	5/18 to 5/21
	1995	New Orleans	5/17 to 5/20
American Hospital Association American Hospital Association (312) 280-6711	1993	Philadelphia	8/9 to 8/11
American International Toy Fair Toy Manufacturers of America (212) 555-1322	1993	New York	1/7 to 1/10
	1994	New York	1/7 to 1/10
	1995	New York	1/7 to 1/10
	1996	New York	1/7 to 1/10
Amusement and Music Operators Association Smith, Bucklin and Associates (312) 644-6610	1993	Anaheim	10/21 to 10/23
	1994	San Antonio	9/22 to 9/24
Annual Showbiz Expo Live Time (213) 668-1811	biannual		
Architectural Woodwork Institute Convention and Trade Show Architectural Woodwork Institute (703) 222-1100	1993	Atlanta	10/7 to 10/9
	1994	St. Louis	10/27 to 10/29
ASCD Annual Conference and Exhibit Show Assn. for Supervision and Curriculum Development (703) 549-9110	1994	Chicago	3/19 to 3/22
	1995	San Francisco	3/25 to 3/28
	1996	New Orleans	3/9 to 3/12
	1997	Baltimore	3/22 to 3/25
Associated General Contractors of America Associated General Contractors of America (202) 393-2040	1994	Orlando	3/17 to 3/22
Association of Broadcasters Convention National Association of Broadcasters (202) 429-5300	1993	Las Vegas	4/18 to 4/22
	1994	Las Vegas	3/21 to 3/24
	1995	Las Vegas	4/10 to 4/13
	1996	Las Vegas	4/15 to 4/18
ASTA's World Travel Congress American Society of Travel Agents (703) 739-2782	1993	St. Louis	9/19 to 9/24
	1994	Lisbon, Portugal	11/6 to 11/12
	1995	Philadelphia	11/5 to 11/10
Bobbin Show/American Apparel Mfgrs. Assn. Convention Bobbin International (800) 845-8820	1993	Atlanta	10/5 to 10/8
	1994	Atlanta	9/27 to 9/30

Trade Shows and Conventions (cont'd)

Show / Sponsor	Year	Location	Dates
Building Owners and Managers Assn. Convention Building Owners & Managers Association (202) 408-2662	1993	Baltimore	6/27 to 6/29
	1994	San Diego	6/19 to 6/21
	1995	Denver	6/25 to 6/26
	1996	Boston	6/23 to 6/25
Consumer Electronics Show Electronic Industries Assn. (202) 457- 4900	1993	Las Vegas	1/7 to 1/10
	1993	Chicago	1/7 to 1/10
	1994	Las Vegas	1/7 to 1/10
	1994	Chicago	1/7 to 1/10
	1995	Las Vegas	1/7 to 1/10
	1995	Chicago	1/7 to 1/10
Converting Machinery and Materials Conf. & Expo Bruno Blenheim (201) 346-1400	1993	Chicago	8/30 to 9/2
Electric Power and Farm Equipment Show Midwest Equipment Dealers Assn. (608) 276-7000	1994	Madison	3/16 to 3/18
	1995	Madison	315 to 3/17
COMDEX The Interface Group (617) 449-6600	1993	Atlanta	5/24 to 5/27
	1993	Las Vegas	11/15 to 11/19
	1994	TBA	4/11 to 4/14
	1994	Las Vegas	11/14 to 11/18
Frankfurt Book Fair Ausstellungs-und Messe-GmbH (069) 2102-219	1993	Frankfurt	10/6 to 10/11
	1994	Frankfurt	10/5 to 10/10
	1995	Frankfurt	10/11 to 10/16
	1996	Frankfurt	10/2 to 10/7
Insurance Accounting and Systems Assn. Conf. and Business Show Insurance Accounting & Systems Association (919) 489-0991	1993	Seattle	6/6 to 6/9
	1994	Atlanta	6/5 to 6/8
	1995	St. Louis	6/4 to 6/7
	1996	Las Vegas	6/2 to 6/5
International Broadcast PT Multi Media Promo (021) 420-4300	1993	Indonesia	9/8 to 9/12
International Commercial Vehicles Show FEBIAC ASBL (02) 7710085	1995	Brussels	1/18 to 1/29
	1997	Brussels	1/15 to 1/26
International Craft Expo Offinger Management (614) 452-4541	1993	Rosemont	7/23 to 7/26
	1994	Rosemont	7/22 to 7/25
	1995	Rosemont	7/21 to 7/24
	1996	Rosemont	7/26 to 7/29
International Fancy Food and Confections Show National Association of Specialty Food Trade (212) 921-1690	1993	San Francisco	2/28 to 3/2
	1993	New York	6/20 to 6/23
International Fashion and Boutique Show Larkin-Pluznick-Larkin (617) 964-5100	1993	New York	6/5 to 6/8
	1994	New York	6/4 to 6/7
	1995	New York	6/3 to 6/7
International Fashion Boutique Show The Larkin Group, Samuel J. Starr (617) 964-5100		5 per year	
International Food and Drink Exhibition Interbuild Exhibition (071) 486-1951	1993	London	4/25 to 4/28

Trade Shows and Conventions (cont'd)

Show / Contact	Year	Location	Dates
International Housewares Show National Housewares Manufacturers (708) 292-4200	1994	Chicago	1/16 to 1/19
	1995	Chicago	1/15 to 1/18
International Jewelry Show–New York Bruno Blenheim (201) 346-1400		biannual	
International Kids Fashion Show The Larkin Group, Stanley Kaye (212) 594-8556		4 per year	
Internat'l Woodworking, Machinery and Furniture Supply Fair Cahners Expo Group (708)299-9311	1994	Atlanta	8/26 to 8/29
	1996	Atlanta	8/23 to 8/26
Medical Group Management Assn. Conference Medical Group Management Association (303) 799-1111	1993	Seattle	10/3 to 10/6
	1994	Boston	10/2 to 10/5
	1995	New Orleans	10/8 to 10/11
	1996	Minneapolis	10/13 to 10/16
	1997	Washington, DC	10/5 to 10/8
Nat'l Cable Television Assn. Annual Convention Dobson & Associates (202) 463-7905	1993	San Francisco	5/6 to 5/9
	1994	New Orleans	5/23 to 5/25
Nat'l Healthcare and American Hospital Assn. Convention American Healthcare Association & American Hospital Association (202) 842-4444; (312) 280-6000	1993	Orlando	8/9 to 8/11
	1994	Dallas	8/8 to 8/10
	1995	San Francisco	8/21 to 8/23
	1996	Philadelphia	8/5 to 8/7
National Association of Realtors Annual Conference National Association of Realtors (312) 329-8886	1993	Miami	11/11 to 11/16
	1994	Anaheim	11/3 to 11/8
	1995	Atlanta	11/9 to 11/14
	1996	San Francisco	11/14 to 11/19
National Business Aircraft Assn. Meeting and Conv. National Business Aircraft Assoc. (202) 783-9000	1993	Atlanta	9/21 to 9/23
	1994	New Orleans	10/4 to 10/6
	1995	Las Vegas	9/27 to 9/29
	1996	Miami	9/30 to 10/3
National Education Association Convention & Exhibit Services (813) 530-0405	1993	San Francisco	6/30 to 7/2
	1994	New Orleans	7/1 to 7/3
	1995	Minneapolis	6/30 to 7/2
Nat'l Environmental Health Assn. Educational Conf. National Environmental Health Assn. (303) 756-9090	1993	Orlando	6/26 to 6/30
	1994	Fort Worth	6/17 to 6/25
National Food Distributors Assn. Convention Smith Buklin & Assoc. (312) 644-6610	1993	San Diego	7/31 to 8/2
	1994	Ft. Lauderdale	1/21 to 1/24
National Hardware Show Association of Expositions and Services (203) 325-5099	1993	Chicago	8/15 to 8/18
	1994	Chicago	8/14 to 8/17
	1995	Chicago	8/13 to 8/16
	1996	Chicago	8/11 to 8/14
National Home Center Show Marvin Park & Assoc. (708) 823-2151	1993	Chicago	3/21 to 3/23
	1994	Dallas	2/13 to 2/15
	1995	Dallas	3/12 to 3/14
	1996	Atlanta	3/17 to 3/19

Trade Shows and Conventions (cont'd)

Show / Organizer	Year	Location	Dates
National Home Health Care Expositions SEMCO Productions (404) 998-9800	1993	Atlanta	11/18 to 11/20
	1994	Atlanta	11/10 to 11/12
	1995	Atlanta	11/16 to 11/16
	1996	Atlanta	11/14 to 11/16
National Merchandise Show Thalheim Exposition (516) 627-4000	1993	New York	9/11 to 9/14
	1994	New York	9/10 to 9/13
	1995	New York	9/9 to 9/12
Nat'l Office Products Association Convention and Exhibit National Office Products Association (703)549-9040	1993	Las Vegas	9/8 to 9/11
	1994	Chicago	10/19 to 10/22
National Restaurant, Hotel/Motel Show National Restaurant Association (312) 853-2525	1993	Chicago	5/22 to 5/26
	1994	Chicago	5/21 to 5/25
National Stationery Show George Little Management (212) 686-6070	1993	New York	5/15 to 5/18
NATPE National Association of TV Programming Executives (310) 453-4440	1993	San Francisco	1/25 to 1/28
	1994	Miami Beach	1/24 to 1/28
	1995	TBA	1/17 to 1/20
	1996	TBA	1/16 to 1/19
New Music Seminar New Music Seminar (212) 473-4343	1993	New York	7/20 to 7/24
New York Gift Fair George Little Management (212) 686-6070	1993	New York	2/20 to 2/25
	1993	New York	8/14 to 8/19
	1994	New York	1/22 to 1/27
North American Farm and Power Show Farm Equipment Assn. of Minnesota & South Dakota (507) 451-1136	1993	Minneapolis	12/1 to 12/2
	1994	Minneapolis	11/30 to 12/1
	1995	Minneapolis	11/30 to 12/1
	1996	Minneapolis	12/4 to 12/5
PACK Expo Packaging Machinery Manufacturing Institute (202)347-3838	1994	Chicago	11/13 to 11/17
	1996	Chicago	11/17 to 11/21
Premium and Incentive Show Miller Freeman (212) 869-1300	1993	New York	5/4 to 5/6
SUPERCOMM E.J. Krause & Associates (301) 986-7800	1993	Atlanta	4/19 to 4/22
	1994	New Orleans	5/2 to 5/5
	1995	Anaheim	3/20 to 3/23
	1996	Atlanta	3/25 to 3/28
	1997	Anaheim	2/3 to 2/6
PC Expo in New York Bruno Blenheim (201) 346-1400	1993	New York	6/22 to 6/24
The Builders Show National Association of Home Builders (202) 822-0200	1994	Las Vegas	1/21 to 1/24
	1995	Houston	1/20 to 1/23
	1996	Houston	1/19 to 1/22
	1997	Houston	1/17 to 1/20
The Imprinted Sportswear Show The Imprinted Sportswear Show (800) 527-0207		4 per year	

Trade Shows and Conventions (cont'd)

Show / Sponsor	Year	Location	Dates
The Licensing Show			
International Licensing Industry Merchandising Assn.	1993	New York	6/15 to 6/17
(212) 244-1944	1994	New York	6/14 to 6/16
	1995	New York	6/20 to 6/22
The Super Show			
Sporting Goods Manufacturers Assn.	1993	Atlanta	2/5 to 2/8
(305) 893-8771	1994	Atlanta	1/29 to 2/1
	1995	Atlanta	2/9 to 2/12
	1996	Atlanta	2/8 to 2/11
Variety Merchandise Show			
Thalheim Exposition	1993	New York	2/13 to 2/16
(516) 627-4000	1994	New York	2/19 to 2/22
	1995	New York	2/18 to 2/21

Source: 1992-93 Trade Show & Convention Guide

Recommended Resource

1992-93 Trade Show & Convention Guide
Published by Amusement Business
(615) 321-4250

The Top Reference Sources

1992 Mail Order Business Directory
B. Klein Publications, $75
(305) 752-1708

This directory is an essential tool for reaching the 9,500 most active mail order firms. This book also includes a very good summary of the mail order market. Companies are listed by product categories, and all entries include company name, address, and telephone number.

Foreign mail order companies are also included.

Top Franchises

ESSENTIALLY FRANCHISING IS A METHOD of distributing products or services as a result of an agreement between two parties. The franchisor is the parent company whose owner desires to expand his or her operations without maintaining additional stores. The franchisee, in return for an initial fee or a continuing royalty payment based on sales, assumes the right to operate the franchise, maintaining the products, services and quality of the original operation.

The franchisor benefits from the ability to more rapidly expand his or her operations, while the franchisee enters the retail world, bolstered by the established procedures, training, advice, and guidance of the parent company. The franchisor generally offers limited or expanded plan packages to the franchisee which may include support services such as: site selection, guidelines for decor and design, management training and consulting, employee training, advertising and merchandising support, and financial assistance.

The types of franchised businesses range from auto and truck dealerships to soft drink bottlers, with a wide variety of establishments in between. While statistics can direct the entrepreneur to businesses displaying growth and financial opportunity, the IFA emphasizes that it is critical to consider financial growth and analyze the track record of any prospective franchisor. A pattern of rapid growth may indicate a lack of sound support systems, whereas a long, steady growth pattern suggests a solid foundation in business franchising

According to IFA reports, the number of franchises grew from 521,125 in 1990 to 542,496 in 1991. Other experts report that the largest (number of outlets) franchise chains are as follows:

Rank	Largest Franchise Chains	Number of Outlets
1	McDonald's Corporation	12,254
2	H&R Block	8,955
3	KFC Corporation	8,187
4	Century 21 Real Estate	7,000
5	Radio Shack	7,000
6	SUBWAY Sandwiches & Salads	5,820
7	Burger King Corporation	5,559
8	International Dairy Queen, Inc.	5,313
9	Ace Hardware	5,111
10	Duskin Company	4,877
11	The Service Master Company	4,000
12	Snap-On-Tools	4,000
13	The Prudential Real Estate	3,768
14	Budget Rent-a-Car	3,557
15	Hardee's Food Systems	3,527

When contemplating a new business, the entrepreneur's first concern is how much money it will require and how to obtain that money. Sources for start-up capital include:

- Bank loans;
- Life Insurance Policies that may allow borrowing on the cash value of the policy while charging a lower interest rate than banks;
- Equipment suppliers who will allow a new business to pay for equipment on an installment plan or offer similar short-term credit;
- Small Business Administration (see below for a description of this service);
- Private Investors who are willing to commit money to a business in return for a percentage of the business's profits during a predetermined time period or during the life of the business. Limited partnerships are one form of private investing in which the partners are investors only and do not contribute to the management of the business;
- SBICs–Small Business Investment Companies that are licensed by the Small Business Administration to provide venture capital to small businesses. Venture capitalists are frequently prepared to wait for a considerable length of time for profits to begin and will charge a rate of 15 percent and higher on their investment. These investors, however, will require a higher percentage of ownership in the new company, as much as 51 percent. In addition to financing, they often provide marketing and product ideas and management consultation.

The Federal Trade Commission offers a free packet of information for individuals interested in franchises. It contains information regarding the pros and cons of franchising, a detailed explanation of the information required by the franchisor in fulfillment of the disclosure rule.

Almanac Fact

Retail sales from franchise establishments account for more than one-third of all U.S. retail sales.

Source: International Franchise Association

Top Franchises (cont'd)

According to a *Success Magazine* survey, the following are the most desirable franchises based on service, earnings, and stability.

Success Magazine's Top Ten Franchises

Franchisor	Headquarters	Product/Service	No. of Locations
Computertots/ECW	Great Falls, VA	Child development, education classes	67
The Krystal Co.	Chattanooga, TN	Fast-food restaurants	261
Beaux Visages	Albany, NY	Skin-care centers	19
Candy Express	Silver Spring, MD	Candy stores	30
GNC General Nutrition	Pittsburgh, PA	Vitamins, health products stores	1,240
Family Haircut/Rancar	Glastonbury, CT	Hair salons	26
Magic Wok	Toledo, OH	Fast-food restaurants	20
Heel Quick!	Marietta, GA	Shoe repair	382
American Leak Detection	Palm Springs, CA	Detection of gas, water leaks	128
Checkcare Systems	Columbus, GA	Check guarantors for retailers	48

Source: Success Magazine

ENTREPRENEUR MAGAZINE'S 14th Annual Franchise 500 issue (January, 1993) is devoted exclusively to the top franchises in the United States. These companies were ranked using a formula which included the following objective criteria: length of time in business, number of years franchising, number of franchised units and company-owned operating units, start-up costs, growth rate, percentage of terminations, and financial stability of the company.

Recommended Resources

Entrepreneur Magazine
Entrepreneur Group
2329 Morse Ave.
Irvine, CA 92714
(714) 261-2325
Annual issue on franchises, January, 1993

Franchise Opportunities Guide 1993 Edition
International Franchise Association
1350 New York Ave., NW, Suite 900
Washington, DC 20005
(202) 628-8000

Rank	Company
1	Subway
2	Dunkin' Donuts
3	Little Caesars Pizza
4	McDonald's
5	Mail Boxes Etc.
6	Burger King Corp.
7	Chem-Dry
8	Jani-King
9	Dairy Queen
10	Coverall North America Inc.
11	Baskin-Robbins USA Co.
12	Choice Hotels Int'l.
13	H & R Block
14	Midas Int'l. Corp.
15	Coldwell Banker Residential Affiliates Inc.

Rank	Company
16	ServiceMaster
17	Re/Max Int'l. Inc.
18	Arby's Inc.
19	Blockbuster Video
20	Merle Norman Cosmetics
21	Jazzercise Inc.
22	Hardee's
23	Domino's Pizza Inc.
24	Holiday Inn Worldwide
25	Budget Rent A Car
26	Sonic Drive In Restaurants
27	Electronic Realty Associates
28	Century 21 Real Estate Corp.
29	MicroAge Computer Centers Inc.
30	CleanNet
31	Miracle Ear
32	Decorating Den
33	The Medicine Shoppe
34	Fantastic Sam's
35	Goodyear Tire Centers
36	Super 8 Motels Inc.
37	Days Inns of America Inc.
38	Servppro
39	GNC Franchising Inc.
40	Minuteman Press Int'l. Inc.
41	Meineke Discount Mufflers
42	Supercuts
43	Ben Franklin Stores Inc.
44	Kwik-Kopy Corp.
45	Merry Maids
46	Uniglobe Travel
47	Culligan Water conditioning
48	Novus Windshield Repair
49	One Hour Martinizing Dry Cleaning
50	Sir Speedy Printing Inc.

Source: Entrepreneur Magazine, January, 1993

Top Franchises (cont'd)

According to IFA reports, the number of franchises grew from 521,125 in 1990 to 542,496 in 1991. Other experts report that the largest (number of outlets) franchise chains are as follows:

Rank	Largest Franchise Chains	Number of Outlets
1	McDonald's Corporation	12,254
2	H&R Block	8,955
3	KFC Corporation	8,187
4	Century 21 Real Estate	7,000
5	Radio Shack	7,000
6	SUBWAY Sandwiches & Salads	5,820
7	Burger King Corporation	5,559
8	International Dairy Queen, Inc.	5,313
9	Ace Hardware	5,111
10	Duskin Company	4,877
11	The Service Master Company	4,000
12	Snap-On-Tools	4,000
13	The Prudential Real Estate	3,768
14	Budget Rent-a-Car	3,557
15	Hardee's Food Systems	3,527

Domestic Franchising by Number of Establishments (thousands): 1980 to 1990

Franchised Businesses	1980	1985	1987	1988	1989	1990
TOTAL FRANCHISING	442.4	455.2	479.1	480.8	498.8	533.0
Auto and truck dealers	29.4	27.5	27.6	27.8	27.6	27.6
Restaurants (all types)	60.0	73.9	83.3	90.3	94.3	102.1
Gasoline service stations	158.5	124.6	115.9	113.2	112.0	111.7
Retailing (non-food)	35.2	45.1	47.9	46.2	49.2	54.1
Auto, truck rental services	7.3	11.2	10.0	9.5	9.9	10.6
Automotive products & services	40.2	36.5	39.3	34.7	35.8	38.6
Business aids & services						
Employment services	4.4	4.8	6.1	6.5	6.6	7.4
Tax preparation services	9.2	8.1	8.5	8.3	8.2	8.5
Accounting, credit, collection	2.4	2.1	2.0	1.7	1.7	1.9
Real estate	17.3	13.9	15.2	15.3	16.0	17.0
Printing & copying	2.8	4.5	5.6	5.9	6.5	7.4
Other business aids	4.8	16.4	19.4	17.9	20.8	25.1
Construction, home improvement, maint.	14.3	17.5	21.7	22.0	24.7	28.3
Convenience stores	15.6	15.1	16.3	17.2	17.3	17.5
Educational products & services	3.2	8.2	9.6	11.6	11.9	13.3
Equipment rental services	2.2	2.5	2.8	3.0	3.0	3.4
Food retailing	15.5	18.7	20.5	21.6	23.0	25.4
Hotels & motels	6.4	7.5	9.3	9.3	10.1	11.1
Laundry, dry cleaning services	3.4	2.3	2.2	2.3	2.5	2.6
Recreation, entertainment, travel	4.6	7.8	8.2	8.8	9.5	10.3
Soft drink bottlers	1.9	1.4	1.1	0.9	0.8	0.8
Miscellaneous	3.6	5.5	6.8	6.9	7.3	8.4

Source: 1992 Statistical Abstract

The Top Reference Sources

1992 Washington Representatives
Columbia Books, $60
(202) 898-0662

This essential reference book is a compilation of names of representatives of the major national associations, labor unions and U.S. companies, registered foreign agents, lobbyists, lawyers, law firms and special interest groups, together with their clients and areas of legislative and regulatory concerns.

The book provides quick and easy answers to questions such as: who represents General Motors on Capitol Hill and what American law firms represent Japanese business interests in Washington.

Top Franchises (cont'd)

Domestic Franchising by Sales ($ billions): 1980 to 1990

Franchised Businesses	1980	1985	1987	1988	1989	1990
TOTAL FRANCHISING SALES	336.2	543.0	599.4	648.1	678.8	716.4
Auto and truck dealers	143.9	282.6	319.7	345.1	353.6	362.3
Restaurants (all types)	27.9	47.7	56.8	64.3	69.1	76.5
Gasoline service stations	94.5	100.8	89.2	101.9	108.5	115.1
Retailing (non-food)	10.5	20.6	25.4	23.3	26.0	28.6
Auto, truck rental services	3.1	5.7	6.5	6.6	7.0	7.6
Automotive products & services	7.1	10.7	12.3	11.4	12.2	13.6
Business aids & services	6.7	12.0	14.7	15.7	17.1	19.5
Employment services	1.6	2.7	3.7	4.7	5.0	5.8
Tax preparation services	0.3	0.4	0.5	0.6	0.7	0.7
Accounting, credit, collection	0.1	0.2	0.2	0.2	0.2	0.2
Real estate	3.6	4.6	5.6	5.9	6.2	6.8
Printing & copying	0.4	0.9	1.2	1.5	1.6	1.9
Other business aids	0.8	3.1	3.5	3.0	3.4	4.1
Construction, home improvement, maint.	1.5	4.1	5.2	5.3	6.0	6.8
Convenience stores	7.8	10.8	12.3	13.9	14.1	14.4
Educational products & services	0.3	0.8	1.0	1.7	1.9	2.3
Equipment rental services	0.4	0.7	0.7	0.7	0.7	0.8
Food retailing	7.4	10.1	11.1	10.2	10.9	11.9
Hotels & motels	9.5	14.8	17.7	19.7	21.3	23.9
Laundry, dry cleaning services	0.3	0.3	0.3	0.3	0.3	0.3
Recreation, entertainment, travel	0.5	2.3	4.0	3.5	4.1	4.7
Soft drink bottlers	14.4	18.3	20.9	22.7	24.2	25.8
Miscellaneous	0.4	0.9	1.5	1.7	1.9	2.2

Source: 1992 Statistical Abstract

Franchise Disclosure

FRANCHISES ARE BECOMING INCREASINGLY popular with the aspiring small business owner. To protect the interests of the inexperienced entrepreneur, the Federal Trade Commission (FTC) requires every franchisor to provide an extensive disclosure document to prospective franchisees prior to making any purchases. This statement must contain information about the following:

- Required fees;
- Basic investment;
- Bankruptcy;
- Litigation history of the company;
- Expected term of the franchise;
- Audited financial statement of the franchisor including bankruptcy history;
- Earnings claims;
- List of directors, trustees or partners, and principal officers of the franchisor; history of the franchisor, its directors and key executives;
- Description of the franchise requirements, its directors and key executives and their business experience, and ongoing continuing expenses required of the franchisee to be paid to the franchisor;
- A list of individuals who are part of the franchisor or its affiliates and with whom the franchisee is required to do business, including real estate, services, equipment required to be purchased, and the names of those with whom these agreements must be made;
- Celebrity involvement in the franchise and a list of royalties and/or commissions paid to such third party individuals by the franchisee, and statistical information about the rate of termination;
- Obligations of franchisee to purchase or lease from approved suppliers;
- Obligations of the franchisor to the franchisee, namely, types of assistance and charges associated with these services.

Franchise Disclosure (cont'd)

- Conditions of renewal, extension, termination of franchise.
- The number, names, addresses, and phone numbers of franchisees.
- A copy of all agreements to be signed before the purchase of the franchise.

On the federal level, the FTC allows the franchisors to distribute this information through a Uniform Franchise Offering Circular (UFOC). Fourteen individual states (California, Hawaii, Illinois, Indiana, Maryland, Michigan, Minnesota, New York, North Dakota, Rhode Island, South Dakota, Virginia, Washington, and Wisconsin) have disclosure laws similar to those required by the FTC. Write to the franchise division of the department of commerce of any of the state offices to request copies of the disclosure agreements of a specific company. While the forms vary from state to state, the essence of the reporting is the same. New York will send its report anywhere in the country:

New York State
Bureau of Investor and Protection Securities
120 Broadway
New York, NY 10271
(212) 416-8200

The next page provides a sample form for request of disclosure documents regarding any franchisor. Simply fill in the name of the franchise, complete the form and send the request to the above address.

The franchisee must, in turn, sign a franchise agreement. There should be clear, concise statements regarding the following items:

- Franchise fee;
- Advertising fees;
- Royalty fees;
- Hidden costs such as equipment and supplies;
- Quotas;
- Franchise term;
- Assignment or permission to transfer franchise agreement to another individual;
- Termination rights of franchisor and franchisee;
- Competition.

The International Franchise Association (IFA) is the industry's regulatory agency. Members must maintain a satisfactory financial condition and are expected to comply with franchise law. The association continually updates its membership regarding changes in franchise law as well as methods of improving cooperative advertising, public relations, marketing, and field operations.

The IFA recommends that any individual considering a franchise, should carefully discuss the disclosure materials, and the history and reputation of both the company and its officers, with both an accountant and an attorney. The organization also strongly suggests that the franchisee discuss the franchise with a number of other franchisees of the target organization.

Contact Option

International Franchise Association
1350 New York Ave. NW, Suite 900
Washington, DC 20005
(202) 628-8000

Recommended Resources

The Legal Guide for Starting and Running a Small Business
by Fred S. Steingold
Nolo Press
(800) 992-6656 or (510) 549-1976

Nation's Business
Chamber of Commerce of the United States
1615 H St., NW
Washington, DC 20062
(202) 463-5650

This publication includes four annual inserts specifically devoted to franchise trends, financing, seminars and expos, conversion, growth forecasts, and other related topics.

Franchise Opportunities Guide Winter 1993 Edition
International Franchise Association
350 New York Ave., NW, Suite 900
Washington, DC 20005
(202) 628-8000

Useful guide to the what, where, and how of franchise opportunities.

Almanac Fact

A new franchise outlet opens somewhere in the United States every 17 minutes.

Source: International Franchise Association

Franchise Disclosure (cont'd)

Many states require franchises doing business within the state to file complete background information, including financial facts about their companies. An individual seeking to invest in a particular franchise should request disclosure of such information from the state office of the Bureau of Investor Protection. If no such office exists, the individual may contact a state which has such an office. The following is a sample freedom of information request form for New York state.

FREEDOM OF INFORMATION REQUEST

I HEREBY APPLY TO INSPECT THE FOLLOWING RECORD:

____

____

____

NAME ______________ REPRESENTING ______________

MAILING ADDRESS ______________ TELEPHONE NUMBER ______________

SIGNATURE ______________ DATE ______________

FOR AGENCY USE ONLY

APPROVED ____

DENIED (for reason(s) checked below)

- ____ Confidential disclosure
- ____ Unwarranted invasion of personal privacy
- ____ Record of which this agency is legal custodian cannot be found
- ____ Record is not maintained by this agency
- ____ Exempted by statute other than the Freedom of Informaiton Act
- ____ Request has been referred to department which has custody or control of original record
- ____ Part of investigatory files
- ____ Other (specify) ______________

SIGNATURE ______________ TITLE ______________ DATE ______________

NOTE: YOU HAVE THE RIGHT TO APPEAL A DENIAL OF THIS APPLICATION TO HEAD OF THIS AGENCY

NAME ______________ BUSINESS ADDRESS ______________

WHO MUST FULLY EXPLAIN HIS REASONS FOR WHICH DENIAL IN WRITING WITHIN SEVEN WORKING DAYS OF RECEIPT OF AN APPEAL.

I HEREBY APPEAL:

SIGNATURE ______________ DATE ______________

Franchise Law

AS THE ACCOMPANYING TABLE ILLUSTRATES, franchising is becoming an increasingly popular form of business in the United States. The International Franchise Association (IFA), the industry regulator, recently noted that over 30% of total retail sales in the U.S. were made by retail franchise businesses.

Domestic and International Franchising Summary: 1980 to 1991

Item	1983	1984	1985	1986	1987	1988	1989	1990	1991
DOMESTIC									
No. of franchises est. (thousands)	442	444	455	462	479	481	493	521	543
Company-owned (thousands)	86	87	86	88	89	94	95	97	101
Franchisee-owned (thousands)	355	357	369	374	390	387	398	424	442
Sales of prod. & svcs. ($ billions)	423	492	543	569	599	648	678	714	758
Company-owned ($ billions)	59	64	68	85	90	98	107	117	127
Franchisee-owned ($ billions)	364	428	475	484	509	550	570	597	631
Avg. sales per est. ($ thousands)	958	1,108	1,193	1,231	1,251	1,348	1,376	1,369	1,396
Employment (thousands)	5,165	5,671	6,283	6,501	NA	NA	NA	NA	NA
INTERNATIONAL									
U.S.-operated foreign outlets	305	328	342	354	NA	374	NA	NA	NA
Foreign outlets (thousands)	26	27	30	32	NA	35	NA	NA	NA

Source: Statistical Abstract

The Top Reference Sources

Franchise Opportunities Guide
International Franchise Association, $15.00
(202) 628-8000

This reference provides a comprehensive listing of more than 2,000 franchises and contains answers to the most frequently asked questions about franchising. Special features include sources for legal advice and franchise consultants, and information on how to finance your franchise.

Office Management

Fleet Cars

TO OBTAIN SUBSTANTIAL DISCOUNTS and benefits on car purchases, companies buying a fleet of cars can contact the Fleet Manager of the manufacturer of the type of cars they are interested in purchasing. The fleet manager will provide information on elegibility for fleet purchasing, as well a list of the local dealerships that handle fleet sales. Chrysler Corporation, for instance, offers rebates from $200 to $1,250 per car on fleet purchases.

Contact Options

Fleet Car Dealers:

Chrysler/Dodge/Plymouth Fleet Representative Line
(800) 255-2616

Ford/Lincoln/Mercury Fleet Company
Information Center
(800) 343-5338

General Motors
(313) 556-2373

Toyota Customer Assistance Center
(800) 331-4331

Volkswagen Customer Service Center
(800) 822-8987

Auto Theft and Damage

Frequency of Car Theft

Model	1988	1989	1990
SMALL			
2-Door	123	124	125
4-Door	168	175	115
Station Wagons, Passenger Vans	68	49	52
Sports and Specialty Models	179	193	160
MIDSIZE			
2-Door	73	69	83
4-Door	62	68	76
Station Wagons, Passenger Vans	37	45	45
Sports and Specialty Models	150	141	173
LARGE			
2-Door	95	51	61
4-Door	93	92	106
Station Wagons, Passenger Vans	42	46	54
Sports and Specialty Models	163	226	212

Theft Losses, Passenger Cars, Relative Claim Frequency by model year (All Car Average=100)

Small = wheelbase less than 100 inches, Midsize = wheelbase 100 to 109 inches

Large = wheelbase more than 109 inches

Source: Insurance Information Institute Fact Book

Auto Theft and Damage (cont'd)

Average Loss Payment Index per Claim*

Model	1988	1989	1990
SMALL			
2-Door	58	65	73
4-Door	47	47	57
Station Wagons, Passenger Vans	50	79	51
Sports and Specialty Models	183	197	195
MIDSIZE			
2-Door	139	130	99
4-Door	90	86	98
Station Wagons, Passenger Vans	63	74	42
Sports and Specialty Models	172	146	181
LARGE			
2-Door	172	240	317
4-Door	131	162	96
Station Wagons, Passenger Vans	90	139	117
Sports and Specialty Models	145	118	80

Average Loss Payment Index per Year*

Model	1988	1989	1990
SMALL			
2-Door	71	81	92
4-Door	78	83	65
Station Wagons, Passenger Vans	34	39	26
Sports and Specialty Models	326	380	312
MIDSIZE			
2-Door	101	90	82
4-Door	56	59	75
Station Wagons, Passenger Vans	24	33	19
Sports and Specialty Models	258	206	312
LARGE			
2-Door	163	121	193
4-Door	122	150	102
Station Wagons, Passenger Vans	38	64	64
Sports and Specialty Models	237	267	169

Source: Insurance Information Institute Fact Book

Small = wheelbase less than 100 inches

Medium = wheelbase 100 to 109 inches

Large = wheelbase more than 109 inches

**The average index for all cars is set to equal 100*

Almanac Fact

There are 60,000,000 potholes in the United States.

Source: Road Information Program

Electronic Surveillance

A FEW STORES SPECIALIZE in state-of-the-art electronic surveillance and security equipment. For prices that can run into the thousands, it is possible to purchase everything from hidden camera and alarm systems to anti-bugging and wiretapping equipment, to telephone and fax scramblers, weapons detectors, and surveillance vehicles. Briefcases equipped with covert microphones and miniature cameras and other specialized executive accessories are also sold.

Contact Options

Electronic Surveillance Sources:

The Spy Store
164 Christopher St.
New York, NY 10014
(212) 366-6466

Communication Control Systems of New York, Ltd.
675 Third Ave.
New York, NY 10001
(212) 268-4779

Eavesdropping Detection Equipment
266 Pepper Tree Dr.
Buffalo, NY 14228
(716) 691-3476

Sheffield Electronics
P.O. Box 377785
Chicago, IL 60637
(312) 643-4928

Security and Bodyguards

Contact Options

National Companies Providing Corporate Security:

Advance Security Inc.
2964 Peachtree Rd.
Atlanta, GA 30305
(800) 241-0267

Burn's International Security Services
2 Campus Dr.
Parsippany, NJ 07054
(201) 397-2000

Guardsmark
50 Pine St.
Suite 1001
New York, NY 10005-2828
(212) 269-8818

Guardsmark Inc.
22 S. Second St.
Memphis, TN 38103
(901) 522-6000

Pinkerton Security and Investigation Services
6727 Odessa Ave.
Van Nuys, CA 91406
(818) 782-5400

Recommended Resources

The American Society for Industrial Security
155 N. Fort Meyer Dr. Suite 1200
Arlington, VA 22209
(703) 522-5800

The Security Industry Buyer's Guide
The American Society for Industrial Security and Phillips Publishing
(800) 777-5006
(301) 424-3338

This book costs $129 and lists all products and services available in the security industry alphabetically and by product and location.

National Council of Investigation and Security Services
P.O. Box 449
Severna Park, MD 21146
(800) 445-8408

This organization will provide the names, addresses, and telephone numbers of companies providing security services in locations across the country.

Check the Yellow Pages under Guard and Patrol Services as well.

Alarm Systems

Largest Security Installation Companies Based on 1991 Revenues

Firm	Location	1991 Revenue ($ millions)	No. of Accounts
ADT Security Systems Inc.	Parsippany, NJ	577.0	488,000
Honeywell Inc.	Minneapolis, MN	203.0	140,000
The National Guardian Corp.	Greenwich, CT	177.2	155,000
Wells Fargo Alarm Systems	King of Prussia, PA	168.0	110,000
Emergency Networks Inc.	Dallas, TX	88.5	N/A
The Alert Center	Engelwood, CO	75.0	273,000
Thorn Automated Systems Inc.	Westlake, OH	75.0	10,000
Westec Security Inc	Irvine, CA	65.0	55,000
Rollins Protective Services Inc.	Atlanta, GA	60.0	102,500
Holmes Protection Group Inc.	New York, NY	80.0	32,000
Brink's Home Security Inc.	Carrollton, TX	56.0	180,000
API Security Inc.	Culver City, CA	52.4	22,800
Security Link Corp.	Dallas, TX	49.0	203,000
Bay Alarm Company	Walnut Creek, CA	30.0	34,000

Source: Security Distributing & Marketing Magazine, May, 1992

Market Share of Monitored Alarm Security Systems

Firms ranked here either sell, install, service, and/or monitor residential and commercial alarm systems that produce contracted recurring revenue. To qualify, they must own the asset value of their customer contracts and provide the monitoring from their own facilities.

Firm Name	1991 Gross Revenue ($ millions)
ADT	577
AFA Protective	26
API Alarms	48
Alert Center	80
Bay Alarm	29
Brink's	56
Comsec/Narragansett	16
Consolidated Southern	18
Denver Burglar Alarm	16
Guardian-Detroit	20
Holmes Protection	60
Honeywell	203

Firm Name	1991 Gross Revenue ($ millions)
Intercap Monitoring	23
National Guardian	177
Network/PSI	48
PC Security/Westec	15
Protection One	14
Rollins	60
SecurityLink	60
Smith-Dallas	14
Sonitrol Management	18
Wells Fargo	168
Westec/Secom	63
Westinghouse	11

Reprinted from Security Dealer Magazine, April, 1992
Support Services Group, San Clemente, CA

Corporate Charge Cards

EXPERTS ESTIMATE THAT COMPANIES spent a total of $120 billion on travel and entertainment (T&E) in 1992. What's more, T&E is the third largest controllable expense, after salaries and data processing, for most companies.

In an effort to serve this growing business as well as other corporate needs, major credit card companies currently provide their corporate clients with a wide range of services–from expense management, to disability insurance, to protection plans, to travel benefits and discounts, to billing options.

Below is a list of numbers to contact to obtain corporate credit cards. In general, the more cards a company orders for its employees, the lower the card's annual fee.

Contact Options

American Express Corporate Card
(800) 528-2122

Citibank Diner's Club Corporate Card
(800) 525-5289

Visa and MasterCard may be obtained through individual banks.

Office Machinery Buyers Guide

BUYERS LABORATORY INC., an independent provider of critical evaluations of office products and procedures, gives its "Line of the Year" and "Pick of the Year" awards to the manufacturers of copiers, printers, and facsimile machines that excelled in the company's extensive in-house testing.

Buyers Laboratory 1992 Awards

Device	Category	Company	Model
All	Line of the Year	Lanier Worldwide, Inc.	All
Copier	Very-low-volume	Minolta	EP2121
Copier	High-volume	Pitney Bowes	9056, 9070
Copier	Mid-volume console	Ricoh	FT6750
Copier	Mid-volume simplex	Toshiba	3210
Copier	Mid-volume duplex	Toshiba	3220
Copier	Outstanding value	Toshiba	4010
Copier	Very-high-volume	Xerox	5100
Copier	Low-volume	Xerox	5320, 5322
Copier	Overall outstanding	Xerox	5775
Printer	High-volume, dot-matrix	IBM	4226, model 302
Printer	Laser/LED-Array value	Okidata	OL830
Printer	Outstanding dot-matrix values	Star Micronics	NX-2430 Multi-font, NX2420Rainbow
Facsimile	Low-to-mid volume, plain paper value	Hewlett-Packard	HP FAX-310
Facsimile	High-volume thermal	Konica	FAX 955
Facsimile	Mid-volume therman	Xerox	7019
Facsimile	Plain paper	Ricoh	Fax3200L

Source: Buyers Laboratory Inc.

The Top Reference Sources

Buyers Laboratory Test Reports for Office Equipment
Buyers Laboratory
$635 for one-year subscription
(201) 488-0404

Buyers Laboratory provides testing information to business consumers in much the same way as Consumer Reports provides information to the general public. Each test report is based on actual testing conducted by Buyers Laboratory test technicians. The Office Products subscription service provides reports on copiers, copier supplies, facsimile equipment, swivel chairs, file cabinets, typewriters, paper shredders, desks, printers, and postage meter machines, among others. A good source for critical, unbiased evaluations of business equipment.

Voice Mail

VOICE MAIL HAS PROGRESSED from pre-recorded answering machine messages to sophisticated systems which use applications of computer-telephone integration. Current and future technological developments in this facet of telecommunications include interactive voice response, and enhanced information services in combination with traditional office communications media such as facsimile and electronic messaging.

Contact Options

Companies Providing Office Telephone Systems:

AT&T Communication Services
7948 Baymeadows Way
Jacksonville, FL 32256
(908) 221-5670

Digital Equipment
(800) DEC- INFO, ext. 705

IBM
(201) 930-3348

InterVoice
(214) 497-8862

MacroTel International
(407) 997-5500

TelePulse
(800) 835-7857

Televox
(219) 432- 3375

Toshiba America Information Systems
(714) 753-0733

Voice Professionals
(800) 868-3684

Voice Technologies Group
(716) 689-6700

Voicetek
(508) 250-9393

Recommended Resources

Association of Telemessaging Services International
320 King St.
Suite 500
Alexandria, VA 22314
(703) 684-0016

Voice Processing Magazine
P.O. Box 42382
Houston, TX 77242
(713) 974-6637
Fax: (713) 974-6272

A one-year free qualified subscription is available to this publication which reports on the latest developments in computer-telephone integration and voice automation.

MCI's Tips on Preventing Toll Fraud

MCI COMMUNICATIONS HAS A LIST of recommendations for limiting your risk of toll fraud. These will sound familiar to those managing file servers and other network services, but make sure the PBX administrator knows them, too.

- Learn all the capabilities of your PBX, particularly any you may not be aware of now. The vendor who sells or services your equipment is the most logical source for this information.
- Delete all authorization codes that were programmed into your PBX for testing or initial servicing.
- Audit and change all active codes in your PBX frequently and de-activate those not authorized.
- Treat authorization codes as you would credit card numbers. Each code should be assigned individually, and employees should be kept confidential
- Assign the longest possible authorization numbers your PBX can handle. And select codes at random: Do not use telephone extension numbers, social security numbers, employee identification numbers, and the like.
- Be alert during PBX-related conversations to the possibility that the person on the other end may be an impersonator; it may be a thief trying to learn about your phone system in order to defraud you.
- Tailor access to your PBX to conform strictly with the needs of your company. Block access to international and long-distance domestic numbers that your company does not call.
- Use an unpublished number for the Remote Access Unit/Direct Inward System Access and program the PBX to wait at least five rings before responding to the call.
- Review carefully all billing information to identify unauthorized calling patterns.
- Avoid a steady tone as the prompt for inputting an authorization code. Instead, use a voice recording or no prompt, which will minimize your vulnerability to unauthorized activity.

Business & Office Supplies by Mail

BELOW IS A BRIEF LISTING OF SELECTED mail-order business dealers. For a more complete listing, consult the Directory of Mail Order Catalogues or the Mail Order Business Directory.

Recommended Resources

Mail Order Product Guide
Todd Publications
18 N. Greenbush Rd.
West Nyack, NY 10094
(914) 358-6213

Mail Order Business Directory
B. Klein Publications
Coral Springs, FL 33075
(305) 752-1708

Contact Options

Office equipment:

Allied Business Machines
9281 Earl St.
La Mesa, CA 92041
(619) 461-6361

FAX Depot
3125 Madlock Bridge Rd.
Norcross, GA 30071
(800) 543-8161

International Typewriters
122 E. 42nd St.
New York, NY 10017
(212) 867-3560

Longacre Office Machines Co.
20 E. 40th St.
New York, NY 10016
(212) 684-2471

Pitney Bowes, Inc.
World Headquarters
Stamford, CT 06926
(203) 356-5000

Office Supplies:

Adirondack Direct
31-01 Vernon Blvd.
Long Island City, NY 11106
(718) 932-4003

All Types Office Supply Co.
1528 W. Belmont Ave.
Chicago, IL 60605
(312) 525-4586

Charrette Corp.
31 Olympia Ave.
Woburn, MA 01888
(617) 935-6000

Commercial Office Products
1000 E. Higgins Rd.
Elk Grove Village, IL 60007
(312) 364-7544

Staples
P.O. Box 160
Newton, MA 02195
(800) 333-3330

Wholesale Supply Co.
P.O. Box 23437
Nashville, TN 37202
(800) 962-9162

Stationery:

Atlas Pencil Co.
3040 N. 29 Ave.
Hollywood, FL 33022
(305) 920-4444

Day Timers
One Willow Lane
East Texas, PA 18046
(215) 398-1151

Forms Inc.
P.O. Box 1109
La Jolla, CA 92038
(619) 233-9742

Standard Stationery
10 Furniture Row
Milford, CT 06460
(203) 874-1608

The Stationery House
1000 Florida Ave.
Hagerstown, MD 21740
(301) 739-4487

Office Furniture by Mail

Contact Options

Mail Order Furniture Companies:

A.T.D. American
135 Greenwood Ave.
Wyncote, PA 19095
(803) 523-2300

Business & Institutional Furniture Co.
611 N. Broadway
Milwaukee, WI 53202
(414) 272-6080

Carl Manufacturing Co.
110 W. Washington St.
Lisbon, OH 44432
(216) 424-5363

Foster Manufacturing Co.
414 N. 13 St.
Philadelphia, PA 19108
(215) 625-0500

National Business Furniture
1819 Peachtree Rd., NE
Atlanta, GA 30309
(800) 241-0676

National Business Furniture
222 E. Michigan St.
Milwaukee, WI 53202
(800) 558-1010

Office Furniture Center
411 Waverly Oaks Rd.
Rte. 60
Waltham, MA 02154
(800) 343-4222

Standard Equipment
3175 Fulton St.
Brooklyn, NY 11208
(800) 221-4782

Color Printing

A NUMBER OF COMPANIES will provide four-color brochures, catalogues, sales sheets, posters, and other computer-generated color graphics by mail-order quickly and inexpensively.

Contact Options

Companies specializing in color printing

Color Impressions
1313 W. Randolph St.
Chicago, IL 60607
(800) 626-1333

Multiprint Co., Inc.
5555 W. Howard St.
Skokie, IL 60077
(800) 858-9999

Scangraphics
5300 Newport Dr.
Rolling Meadows, IL 60008
(708) 392-3980

Catalogue Sources

A WIDE RANGE OF BUSINESS-RELATED articles–from office furniture to stationery to heavy machinery–can be efficiently purchased by mail. These publications profile a wide variety of catalogues.

Recommended Resources

The Directory of Mail Order Catalogues
Grey House Publishing, Inc.
Pocket Knife Square
Lakeville, CT 06039
(203) 435-0868

Mail Order Business Directory
B. Klein Publications, Inc.
P.O. Box 8503
Coral Springs, FL 33065
(305) 752-1708

Airlines Ranked by Size

Domestic Airlines Ranked by Revenue

Company	Location	Sales Rank	1991 Revenue ($ thousands)	Load Factor (%)	# of Major Airports Served
American	D/FW Airport, TX	1	12,098,000	61.7	188
United	Chicago, IL	2	11,663,000	66.3	148
Delta	Atlanta, GA	3	10,019,600	60.4	188
Northwest	St. Paul, MN	4	7,534,000	65.8	133
USAir	Arlington, VA	5	6,068,968	59.0	126
Continental	Houston, TX	6	5,400,000	62.6	143
TWA	Mount Kisco, NY	7	3,660,000	66.3	110
Southwest	Dallas, TX	8	2,627,210	61.1	34
Pan Am	New York, NY	9	2,122,143	62.6	48
America West	Phoenix, AZ	10	1,416,925	63.2	47
Alaska Airlines	Seattle, WA	11	921,519	56.3	38
Comair	Cincinnati, OH	12	403,420	43.5	55
Hawaiian Airlines	Honolulu, HI	13	365,945	63.1	18
Tower Air Inc.	Jamaica, NY	14	245,900	78.8	10
Westair	Fresno, CA	16	239,068	46.8	36
Atlantic Southeast	College Park, GA	17	221,916	49.3	51
Aloha Airlines	Honolulu, HA	18	214,022	63.0	6
Air Wisconsin	Appleton, WI	19	204,143	46.0	33
Horizon Air	Seattle, WA	20	183,142	51.5	34
Trump Shuttle	New York, NY	21	163,322	45.0	4
Midwest Express	Milwaukee, WI	22	125,300	54.7	18
Metro Airlines	D/FW Airport, TX	23	117,725	64.0	26
Skywest	St. George, UT	24	109,441	41.0	42
Mesa Air	Farmington, NM	25	73,625	43.9	55

Source: Business Travel News

The Top Reference Sources

FAA Statistical Handbook of Aviation
The National Technical Information Service
(800) 336-4700

This annual report presents statistical information pertaining to the Federal Aviation Administration, The National Airspace System, airports, airport activity, U.S. Civil Air Carrier Fleet, U.S. Civil Air Carrier Operating Data, aircraft accidents, and aeronautical production. Also included are imports/exports, general aviation aircraft, and a glossary of terms.

Domestic Airline Hubs

Company	Major Hub(s)
American	Dallas/Fort Worth, Chicago, Nashville, Miami, Raleigh/Durham, San Jose, San Juan
United	San Francisco, Chicago, Denver, Washington
Delta	Atlanta, Cincinnati, Dallas/Fort Worth, Orlando, Salt Lake City
Northwest	Minneapolis, Detroit, Memphis
USAir	Charlotte, Pittsburgh, Philadelphia, Baltimore, Indianapolis
Continental	Houston, Newark, Denver, Cleveland
TWA	New York, St. Louis
Southwest	Dallas, Houston, Phoenix
Pan Am	New York
America West	Columbus, Las Vegas, Phoenix
Alaska Airlines	Anchorage, Portland, Seattle
Comair	Cincinnati, Orlando
Hawaiian Airlines	Honolulu
Tower Air Inc.	Miami, New York
Westair	San Francisco
Atlantic Southeast	Atlanta
Aloha Airlines	Honolulu
Air Wisconsin	Chicago
Horizon Air	Portland, Seattle
Trump Shuttle	New York
Midwest Express	Milwaukee
Metro Airlines	Dallas/Fort Worth
Skywest	Salt Lake City, Los Angeles
Mesa Air	Denver
CC Air	Charlotte
Big Sky Airlines	Billings, Bismarck
Mesaba	Minneapolis

Source: Business Travel News

Special Meals on Airlines

Airline	Meals	Notice Required
American	Infants, bland and soft, diabetic, gluten-free, Hindu, Muslim, low calorie, lactose free, low carbohydrate, low sodium, ovo-lacto vegetarian.	12 hours for kosher meal, 6 hours for others
Continental	Diabetic, fruit plate, Hindu, low sodium, seafood, ovo-lacto vegetarian.	6 hours
Delta	Asian vegetarian, baby, bland, diabetic, fruit plate, gluten free, Hindu, low calorie, low sodium, ovo-lacto vegetarian, Muslim, cold seafood, hot seafood, toddler	8 hours for kosher meal, 6 hours for others
Northwest	Baby, bland, diabetic, fruit, gluten free, Hindu, low calorie, low sodium, ovo-lacto vegetarian, seafood	24 hours for kosher meal, 12 hours for others
TWA	Low calorie, low sodium, low carbohydrate-low sugar, cold seafood	24 hours
United	Dietary (diabetic-hypoglycemic), McDonald's children platter, infant, low calorie-low carbohydrate, ovo-lacto vegetarian, Lighter Choice (chef's salad, fruit plate or cold seafood)	6 hours
USAir	Bland, diabetic, fruit plate, high protein, Hindu, low calorie, low sodium, Muslim, seafood	By 8 PM day before flight

Source: The New York Times

Largest Airlines Worldwide

Rank by Revenue	Company	Country
1	American	U.S.
2	Air France Groupe	France
3	United	U.S.
4	Japan	Japan
5	Lufthansa	Germany
6	Delta	U.S.
7	British Airways	Britain
8	Northwest	U.S.
9	All Nippon Airways	Japan
10	USAir Group	U.S.
11	Continental Air Holdings	U.S.
12	Scandinavian Air System	*
13	Alitalia	Italy
14	Swire Pacific	Hong Kong
15	Swissair	Switzerland
16	KLM Royal Dutch	Netherlands
17	Iberia	Spain
18	TWA	U.S.
19	Air Canada	Canada
20	Singapore	Singapore
21	Qantas	Australia
22	Korean Air	South Korea
23	PWA Corp.	Canada
24	Thai Airways	Thailand
25	Japan Air System	Japan

Rank by Revenue	Company	Country
26	Saudia	Saudi Arabia
27	Varig	Brazil
28	Garuda	Indonesia
29	China	Taiwan
30	Sabena	Belgium
31	LTU	Germany
32	Ansett Transport	Australia
33	America West	U.S.
34	Aer Lingus	Ireland
35	Southwest	U.S.
36	Malaysian	Malaysia
37	Finnair	Finland
38	Air New Zealand	New Zealand
39	Austrian	Austria
40	Alaska Air Group	U.S.
41	TAP Air Portugal	Portugal
42	Australian	Australia
43	Mexicana	Mexico
44	South African Airways	South Africa
45	El Al	Israel
46	Aerolineas	Argentina
47	Aeromexico	Mexico
48	Olympic Airways	Greece
49	Air India	India
50	Pakistan International	Pakistan

**Jointly owned by governments of Sweden, Denmark and Norway*

Source: Fortune, Nov. 2, 1992

Frequent Flier Programs

Inside Flier's Ratings of Frequent Flier Programs

		Ease of Earning Awards		Service	Blackouts		Seat Availability		Hotel Partners	# Travel Awards
Rank	Program	Dom.	Int'l	All	Dom.	Int'l	Dom.	Int'l	All	All
1	Northwest	B+	A	A-	B	A	A	C	B	873,000
2	American	B+	C	A	D	D	A	C	C	975,000
3	Continental	B+	B	A-	D	C	B	C	B	200,000
4	United	B+	C	A-	D	B	A	C	B	1,200,000
5	Alaska	B	B	B-	B+	C	A-	C	A	87,000
6	America West	B	A	A-	D	C	A	C	C	125,000
7	TWA	B+	C	B	D	C	B	C	C	311,300
8	USAir	B	D+	B	B	A	A	C	A	1,000,000
9	Delta	B-	C-	A-	A	D	A	C	A	912,000
10	Southwest	C	F	A-	C	N/A	A	N/A	F	168,000

Ratings: A = Best; F = Worst

Source: Inside Flier, 1990

Frequent Flier Programs (cont'd)

Airline, Hotel, Car Rental Partners

Airline	Car Rentals	Hotels	Airlines
American	Avis Hertz	Intercontinental Hilton Marriott Sheraton Wyndham Hotel Chains	American American Eagle Cathay Pacific Qantas Singapore TWA Malev South African
Continental	National Thrifty	Aston Canadian Pacific Marriott Radisson	United Southwest America West Delta American Northwest Aloha Alaskan Canadian
Northwest	Budget Hertz National	Holiday Inn Hyatt Marriott Radisson, Westin	USAir (international) KLM (international)
TWA	Dollar Thrifty	The Adam's Mark Hotels Doubletree Hotels & Club Hotels Forte Hotels Marriott Hotels, Resorts, Suites	–
United	Alamo Dollar Hertz National	Hilton Hyatt Intercontinental Sheraton Westin	Air Canada Air France Alitalia Aloha Ansett British Midland Iberia KLM Lufthansa MGM Grand Sabena SAS Swissair United Express
USAir	Hertz National Alamo Tilden (Canada)	Hyatt Hilton Marriott Omni Radisson Stouffer Westin Hotel Resorts	Air France Lufthansa British Airways Northwest Swissair Air New Zealand Sabena KLM Alitalia All Nippon

Almanac Fact

The best North American business hotels are The Plaza and the Waldorf-Astoria in New York, and the Westin St. Francis in San Francisco.

Source: Business Traveler International

Airline & Train Directory

Airline	Code	800 Number
AerLingus	EI	(800) 223-6537
Aeromexico	AM	(800) 237-6639
Air Canada	AC	(800) 422-6232
Air France	AF	(800) 237-2747
Alaska Airlines	AS	(800) 426-0333
Alitalia	AZ	(800) 223-5730
American Airlines	AA	(800) 433-7300
Amtrak	-	(800) 872-7245
British Airways	BA	(800) 247-9297
British Caledonian	BR	(800) 231-0270
Continental Airlines	CO	(800) 525-0280
Delta Airlines	DL	(800) 221-1212
Iberia Airlines	IB	(800) 221-9741
Japan Airlines	JL	(800) 525-3663
Lufthansa	LH	(800) 645-3880
Northwest Airlines, Domestic	NW	(800) 225-2525
Northwest Airlines, International	NW	(800) 447-4747
Qantas	QF	(800) 227-4500
Republic Airlines	RC	(800) 441-1414
Scandinavian Air	SA	(800) 221-2350
Swissair	SR	(800) 221-4750
TWA, Domestic	TW	(800) 221-2000
TWA, International	TW	(800) 892-4141
United Airlines	UA	(800) 241-6522
USAir	AL	(800) 428-4322
World Airways	WO	(800) 772-2600

Airline Accidents

Accidents: Scheduled Airlines

Year	Accidents	Accidents per 100,000 Flight Hours
1981	25	0.366
1982	16	0.224
1983	22	0.318
1984	13	0.168
1985	17	0.206
1986	21	0.211
1987	32	0.308
1988	28	0.257
1989	25	0.236
1990	24	0.222

Source: National Transportation Safety Board

Paging at Major U.S. Airports

THE FOLLOWING IS A LIST of paging numbers at most U.S. airports, by airport and airline. When no number is listed, call the airline in question and ask them to page the passenger for you.

Paging Phone Numbers at Major U.S. Airports

Airport	Airline	Telephone
Atlanta International	Northwest	(404) 530-3960
	TWA	(404) 530-2620
	Delta	(404) 714-7250
	USAir	(404) 530-3300
	Continental	(404) 530-3530
Baltimore/Washington Intl., Baltimore	All	(410) 859-7111
Logan Airport, Boston	All	(617) 568-8408
	American	(800) 433-7300
	Delta	(617) 561-2550
	United	(800) 241-6522
	Continental	(617) 561-2132
	USAir	(617) 561-6721
	Northwest	(617) 561-5310
O'Hare, Chicago	All	(312) 686-2868
	United	(312) 601-3100
	American	(312) 686-4477
	Northwest	(312) 686-5575
	Continental	(312) 601-5305
	Delta	(312) 686-8635
	TWA	(312) 686-5080
	America West	(312) 686-5670
	USAir	(312) 686-7171
Midway, Chicago	All	(312) 767-0500
	Northwest	(312) 471-4692
Greater Cincinnati International	Northwest	(606) 283-3144
	TWA	(606) 283-3526
	Delta	(606) 283-3427
	United	(606) 283-3691
	USAir	(606) 283-3645
	Continental	(606) 283-3202
Cleveland International, Cleveland	All	(216) 265-6030
Columbus, OH	Northwest	(614) 239-4381
	TWA	(614) 239-4082
	Delta	(614) 239-4476
	USAir	(614) 238-7500
	Cleveland	(614) 239-4082
Dallas	All	(214) 574-6673
	Delta	(214) 574-2247
	United	(214) 574-6673
	USAir	(214) 574-6673
	American	(214) 425-2477
	Continental	(214) 574-6673
Stapleton International, Denver	Northwest	(303) 270-1000
	TWA	(303) 270-1300/1310
	Delta	(303) 270-1300

Paging at Major U.S. Airports (cont'd)

Airport	Airline	Telephone
Stapleton International, Denver (cont'd)	United	(800) 247-2336
	USAir	(303) 270-1300
	American	(303) 270-1310
	Continental	(303) 270-1300
Detroit	Northwest	(313) 942-4268
	TWA	(313) 942-3406
	Delta	(313) 942-2640
	USAir	(313) 942-2460
	Continental	(313) 955-1797
Houston Intercontinental	All	(713) 230-3000
	Northwest	(713) 845-3500
Indianapolis International	Northwest	(317) 248-7243
	TWA	(317) 487-PAGE
	Delta	(317) 248-7243
	United	(317) 248-7243
	USAir	(317) 487-7243
	American	(317) 487-7243
	Continental	(317) 487-7243
Los Angeles	Northwest	(310) 646-7711/3517
	TWA	(310) 646-2424
	Delta	(310) 646-5802
	United	(310) 646-3116
	USAir	(310) 646-2020
	American	(310) 646-3533
	Continental	(310) 568-3131
Miami International	All	(305) 876-7000, ext. 35
Milwaukee	Northwest	(414) 747-4740/ 4604
	TWA	(414) 747-4670
	United	(414) 747-4920
	USAir	(414) 747-4713
	Continental	(414) 747-4572
Minneapolis	Delta	(612) 725-4931
	Northwest	(612) 726-3007/7981
	TWA	(612) 726-5642
	USAir	(612) 726-5373
	Continental	(612) 726-5818
John F. Kennedy, New York	Northwest	(718) 244-5604
	TWA	(718) 244-2000
	Delta	(718) 632-4180
	USAir	(718) 656-2100
LaGuardia, New York	Northwest	(718) 476-7191
	TWA	(718) 803-6810
	Delta	(718) 565-3940
	United	(718) 476-4966
	USAir	(718) 533-2634
	Continental	(718) 334-7132
Norfolk	TWA	(804) 857-3210
	Delta	(804) 857-3245
	United	(804) 857-3330
	USAir	(804) 857-3318
	Continental	(804) 857-3584

Paging at Major U.S. Airports (cont'd)

Airport	Airline	Telephone
Philadelphia	All	(215) 492-3222
Phoenix	All	(602) 273-3455
Pittsburgh	Northwest	(412) 472-5450
	TWA	(412) 472-5380
	Delta	(412) 472-3209
	United	(412) 472-5126
	USAir	(412) 472-2527
	American	(412) 472-5321
	Continental	(412) 262-4405
Portland, OR	All	(503) 335-1040
Sacramento	Northwest	(916) 929-5411
	Delta	(916) 922-7730
	United	(916) 929-5411
	USAir	(916) 929-5411
	American	(916) 929-5411
	Continental	(916) 929-5411
Lambert/St. Louis International	All	(314) 426-8000
	Northwest	(314) 427-5357
	TWA	(314) 429-9400
	Delta	(314) 426-9201
	USAir	(314) 423-3757
	Continental	(314) 423-6376
San Antonio International	All	(512) 821-3411
Lindbergh Field Intl., San Diego	All	(619) 231-2294
	Northwest	(619) 231-7314
San Francisco	No Paging Services Available	–
Seattle	TWA	(206) 433-5722
	Delta	(206) 433-4324
	United	(206) 433-4343
	USAir	(206) 433-7850
	Continental	(206) 433-5545
Tampa	All	(813) 870-8770
Washington, D.C., Dulles	Northwest	(703) 661-3356
	TWA	(703) 834-1969
	Delta	(703) 661-5577
	American	(703) 661-5299
	Continental	(703) 661-8636
Washington, D.C., National	Northwest	(703) 769-6100
	TWA	(703) 684-6441
	Delta	(703) 271-6150
	USAir	(703) 892-7164
	Continental	(703) 769-6745

Almanac Fact

The world's best individual hotels are The Regent, The Peninsula, and The Mandarin Oriental, all in Hong Kong.

Source: Business Traveler International

Transportation from Airport to City

Taxi Fares from Airport to City: Domestic

City	Airport	Code	Mileage	Approx. Taxi Fare ($)
Atlanta	Atlanta Intl.	ATL	8 mi SW	15.00
Baltimore	Baltimore/Washington	BWI	10 mi S	16.00
Boston	Logan Intl.	BOS	3 mi NE	10.00
Chicago	O'Hare Intl.	ORD	18 mi NW	24.00
Chicago	Midway	MDW	10 mi SW	17.00
Cincinnati	Greater Cincinnati Intl.	CVG	13 mi SW	20.00
Cleveland	Cleveland/Hopkins Intl.	CLE	10 mi SW	15.00
Columbus, OH	Port Columbus Intl.	CMH	7 mi NE	15.00
Dallas	Dallas/Ft. Worth Intl.	DFW	21 mi NW	27.00
Denver	Stapleton Intl.	DEN	7 mi NE	10.00
Detroit	Detroit Metropolitan	DTW	19 mi SW	28.00
Houston	Houston Intercontinental	HOU	22 mi N	29.00
Indianapolis	Indianapolis Intl.	IND	8 mi SW	14.00
Los Angeles	Los Angeles Intl.	LAX	15 mi SW	27.00
Miami	Miami Intl.	MIA	6 mi NW	14.00
Milwaukee	General Mitchell Intl.	MKE	7 mi S	14.00
Minneapolis	Minneapolis/St. Paul	MSP	13 mi SE	20.00
New York	JFK Intl.	JFK	15 mi SE	24.00
New York	La Guardia	LAG	8 mi NE	14.00
Norfolk	Norfolk Intl.	ORF	6 mi NE	15.00
Philadelphia	Philadelphia Intl.	PHL	8 mi SW	22.00
Phoenix	Phoenix Sky Harbor Intl.	PHX	4 mi SE	7.00
Pittsburgh	Greater Pittsburgh Intl.	PIT	17 mi W	25.00
Portland, OR	Portland Intl.	POX	9 mi NE	19.00
Sacramento	Metropolitan	SMF	11 mi NW	25.00
St. Louis	Lambert/St. Louis Intl.	STL	13 mi NW	18.00
San Antonio	San Antonio Intl.	SAT	8 mi N	12.00
San Diego	San Diego Intl.	SAN	3 mi NW	7.00
San Fransisco	San Fransisco Intl.	SFO	14 mi S	29.00
Seattle	Seattle/Tacoma Intl.	SEA	13 mi S	22.00
Tampa	Port Columbus Intl.	TPA	7 mi NE	15.00
Washington, DC	Dulles Intl.	IAD	26 mi W	38.00
Washington, DC	National	DCA	4 mi S	9.00

Taxi Fares from Airport to City: International

City	Airport	Mileage	Approx. Taxi Fare ($)
Amsterdam, Netherlands	Schiphol	9 mi SW	25-28
Beijing, China	Beijing Capital	18 mi NE	8
Berlin, Germany	Tegel	4 mi NW	10-11
Brussels, Belgium	Brussels National Airport	7.5 mi NE	29
Paris, France	Charles De Gaulle	15 mi NE	7-31
Paris, France	Orly	8 mi S	22-60
Rome, Italy	Leonardo Da Vinci	18 mi SW	40
Dublin, Ireland	Dublin	18 mi N	12
Geneva, Switzerland	Cointrin	2.5 mi NW	17-25
Hong Kong	Hong Kong Intl.	3 mi NE	5
London, England	Heathrow	15 mi W	50
Madrid, Spain	Barajas	7.5 mi NE	15-17
São Paulo, Brazil	Sao Paulo Intl.	18 mi NE	22
Tokyo, Japan	Norita Airport	42 mi. W	150
Toronto, Ontario	Lester B. Pearson Intl.	20 mi NW	30
Vienna, Austria	Schwecat	10 mi SE	27

Basic Airline Fare Codes

Fare Code	Description
B	Excursion Fare
BE	Excursion Fare
C	Business Class
C	Children
CD	Seniors
CH	Children
F	First Class
G	Group
H	Excursion Fare
H	High Season
HE	Excursion Fare
I	No-Reservations Variants
IT	Inclusive Tour Fares
J	Business Class
K	Modified Full Fare
L	Excursion Fare
L	Low Season
LE	Excursion Fare

Fair Code	Description
M	Modified Full Fare
O	Shoulder Season
P	First Class
Q	Modified Full Fare
Q	Excursion Fare
QE	Excursion Fare
R	First Class on Supersonic Concorde
S	Coach Class
V	Modified Full Fare
V	Excursion Fare
VE	Excursion Fare
W	Weekend
X	Midweek
Y	Coach Class
+ Numeral	Temporary Fare Cut
+N	Off-Peak Night Flights
+R	Roundtrip Special Discount
+RN	Roundtrip Special Discount

Air Charter Companies

A FULL-SERVICE AIR CHARTER BROKER is like a travel agent for a company's private flying needs. A charter broker maintains broad contacts among the air charter operators and matches a company's air travel needs with a suitable aircraft supplier. Because a broker plans a variety of trips every day, he is better able to pick the most appropriate equipment and supplier for a flight. Brokers will also help a company deal with issues such as which insurance policies to choose and what kind of payment procedures to make.

Aircraft are usually chartered by the hour, with rates varying according to many factors. Hourly rates are figured against the time the aircraft is actually in the air. A strong tailwind, for example, will lower the cost. Air traffic delays, holding patterns and en route deviations will increase it.

Because of the high expense of chartered flight, one bad debt might erase a substantial portion of a charter operator's annual profit. Therefore, a 15-20 per-cent deposit is usually required of a new customer. Sometimes, operators may ask for complete payment in advance.

Recommended Resource

The Air Charter Guide
Boston Aviation Services Inc.
55B Reservoir St.
Cambridge, MA 02138
(617) 547-5811

This directory is published semi-annually and offers a complete listing of air charter companies and air charter brokers, aircraft description, pricing policies, and selected airport information.

Contact Options

U.S. Charter Brokers That Specialize in Executive Aircraft:

Afrer International
P.O. Box 791648
San Antonio, TX 78279
(512) 520-9729

Air Charter Association
950 E. Paces Ferry Rd., Suite 3180
Atlanta, GA 30326
(800) 432-1222

Atlantic Aviation Corp.-Charter Services
233 Industrial Ave.
Teterboro, NJ 07608
(201) 288-7660

Corporate America Aviation, Inc.
P.O. Box 7304, Suite 406
N. Hollywood, CA 91603
(818) 953-7206

Air Charter Companies (cont'd)

Direct Airway, Inc.
CN5244
Princeton, NJ 08540
(609) 799-3030

Exclusive Air, Inc.
Nine Fuller Dr.
Hudson, NH 03051
(603) 881-8400

Flight Services Group, Inc.
111 Beach Rd.
Fairfield, CT 06430
(800) 666-6767

Intercharter
640 Main Ave., Suite 201
Durango, CO 81301
(303) 259-2454

Jetair International
P.O. Box 607
East Farmingdale, NY 11753
(516) 752-8985

Martin Aviation, Inc.
19301 Campus Dr.
Santa Ana, CA 92707
(800) 627-8467

National Charter Network, Inc.
6987 Perimeter Rd. S., Suite 215
Seattle, WA 98108
(206) 767-6423

Richmor Aviation
Box 423
Hudson, NY 12534
(518) 828-9461

Universal Weather and Aviation, Inc.
8787 Tallyho
Houston, TX 77061
(800) 231-5600

U.S. Jet Charter
General Aviation Terminal
Washington International Airport
Washington, DC 20001
(703) 892-6200

U.S. Charter Brokers Specializing in Airline Charters:
Afer International
P.O. Box 791648
San Antonio, TX 78279
(512) 520-9729

Air Denver
Terminal Building
Stapleton International Airport
Denver, CO 80207
(303) 333-3332

Airfax-Airline Marketing Associates
5450 Peachtree Parkway, Suite 109
Norcross, GA 30092
(404) 662-0885

Chapman Freeborn Airmarketing USA, Inc.
5432 W. 104th St.
Los Angeles, CA 90045
(213) 641-7343

Charter Clearing House
3800 Walnut St.
Harrisburg, PA 17109
(717) 657-9912

Charter Services, Inc.
3700 Rio Grande Blvd., NW
Albuquerque, NM 87107
(505) 761-9000

Chartersearch Network, Inc.
7751 Carondelet Ave., Suite 306
St. Louis, MO 63105
(314) 726-2644

Curtis Air Services, Inc.
2202 Timberloch Pl., Suite 112
The Woodlands, TX 77380
(713) 350-3184

Flight Services Group, Inc.
111 Beach Rd.
Fairfield, CT 06430
(800) 666-6767

Flight Time Corporation
200 Boylston St.
Chesnut Hill, MA 02167
(617) 965-7060

Morris Air Service
260 E. Morris Ave.
Salt Lake City, UT 84115
(801) 483-6322

One By Air, Inc.
2424 North Federal Highway, Suite 151
Boca Raton, FL 33431
(407) 483-2165

Three Way Corporation
1120 Karlstad Dr.
Sunnyvale, CA 94089
(408) 745-7500

European Charter Brokers Specializing in Executive Aircraft:
Air London International, PLC
Mack House, Aviation Court
Gatwick Rd.
Crawley, Sussex, UKRH10 2GG
44-29-354-9555

Air Charter Companies (cont'd)

Business Aire Centre, Ltd.
Brettenham House
Lancaster Place, London, UK WC2E 7EN
44-071-836-7971

Exec Air International, Ltd.
Melbourne House
27/29 Collingham Rd.
London, UK SW5 0NU
44-071-370-6191

Fields Aircraft Charter Services
Huntavia House, 420 Barth Rd.
W. Drayton, Middlesex UB7 007
44-081-897-6446

MAM Aviation Ltd.
P.O. Box 800
Heathrow Airport
Hounslow, Mdlsx, UK TW6 3EZ
44-081-897-2466

Reed Aviation Ltd.
Eaton House, Proctor Way
Luton Intl. Airport, Luton Bedfrdshr, UK LU2 9PE
44-482-402-404

Turin Lentotilauskeskus
Brahenkatu 9A9
Turku, Fl SF-20110
358-21-504000

Service People
POB 630 506 GAT
Hamburg Airport
2000 Hamburg, GE 63
49-40-593-333

World Aviation Group Ltd.
2 Horsted Square
Bellbrook Business Park
Uckfield, East Sussex, TN22 1QW England
0825-765055

KLM General Aviation
Building 106, Box 7700
117ZL, Amsterdam, The Netherlands, NL
31-20-649-2455

European Charter Brokers Specializing in Airline Charters:

Air London International, PLC
Mack House, Aviation Court
Gatwick Rd.
Crawley, Sussex, UK RH10 2GG
44-29-354-9555

Aircraft Chartering Services, Ltd.
Cunliffe House, Cunliffe Rd.
Stoneleigh, Surrey, UK KT19 0RL
44-081-394-2795

Chapman Freeborn Airmarketing Ltd.-UK
7 Buckingham Gate
London, UK SW1E 6JP
44-071-828-0865

Hunt & Palmer, Ltd.
26 Little Portland St.
London, UK W1 N5AF
44-071-580-8991

Instone Aviation
Bridge House, 4 Borough High St.
London, UK SE1 9QQ
44-071-407-4411

International Skycharter
435 High Holbourne HSE
52/54 High Holbourne
London, UK WC1 V 6RL
44-071-242-9501

Kent Aviation Services, Ltd.
156 Westcomb Rd.
Blackheath, London, UK SE3 7DH
44-081-858-0976

Chapman Freeborn France Sarl
2 Rue De La Pomme Bleue
BP 95705
Roissy CDG Cedex, FR
33-1-48-62-95-36

Chapman Freeborn Airmarketing GMBH
Im Taubengrund 27
Kelsterbach, GE 6092
49-61-075-036

Nordavia Flug GMBH
Innhocentiastr. 32
2000 Hamburg, GE 63
49-40-440-040

Chapman Freeborn Airmarketing Ltd.
Dublin Airport
Dublin, IR
35-31-423-144

Chapman Freeborn Airmarketing Ltd.
Station Bldg., Rotterdam Airport
Rotterdam, NL
31-10-437-7845

Recommended Resource

The Air Charter Guide
Boston Aviation Services Inc.
55B Reservoir St.
Cambridge, MA 02138
(617) 547-5811

This directory is published semi-annually and offers a complete listing of air charter companies and air charter brokers, aircraft description, pricing policies, and selected airport information.

Busiest Airports

Airports Ranked by Number of Passengers

Rank	Airport	Passengers
1	Chicago O'Hare International	27,827,241
2	Dallas/Ft. Worth	24,092,801
3	Los Angeles International	22,519,698
4	Atlanta	18,886,533
5	San Francisco	15,186,626
6	Denver	13,270,540
7	New York: Kennedy	12,577,222
8	Miami	12,500,636
9	Phoenix	11,111,436
10	Newark	11,057,046
11	Honolulu	10,914,002
12	Detroit Metropolitan	10,354,655
13	Boston: Logan	10,339,844
14	New York: La Guardia	9,789,076
15	Minneapolis/St. Paul	9,770,403
16	Las Vegas: McCarren Intl.	9,653,154
17	Lambert-St. Louis Intl.	9,621,236
18	Orlando International	8,839,819
19	Houston Intercontinental	8,452,340
20	Charlotte/Douglas Intl.	8,425,447

Source: Federal Aviation Administration

Best Times to Fly

Leaving: Best Hour to Go

Airport	Best Hour	On-Time Percentage	Worst Hour	On-Time Percentage
Atlanta	7-8 AM	96.0	4-5 PM	80.1
Charlotte	6-7 AM	100.0	5-6 PM	79.9
Chicago	11 PM-6 AM	97.9	7-8 PM	78.2
Denver	11 PM-6 AM	100.0	9-10 PM	81.3
Dallas	7-8 AM	96.0	10-11 PM	87.5
Los Angeles	7-8 AM	95.8	10-11 AM	81.5
Miami	6-7 AM	98.3	9-10 PM	83.3
New York: Kennedy	9-10 AM; 12-1 PM	95.0	8-9 PM	62.5
New York: La Guardia	6-7 AM	95.9	10-11 PM	79.6
New York: Newark	6-7 AM	97.5	7-8 PM	62.1
San Francisco	7-8 AM	97.9	8-9 PM	88.2
St. Louis	10-11 PM	98.0	7-8 PM	86.2

Arriving: Best Hour to Land

Airport	Best Hour	On-Time Percentage	Worst Hour	On-Time Percentage
Atlanta	1-2 PM	94.8	4-5 PM	71.4
Charlotte	12-1 AM	94.2	10-11 PM	74.1
Chicago	7-8 AM	88.8	10-11 PM	76.4
Denver	4-5 PM	92.9	9-10 PM	82.1
Dallas	6-7 AM	96.6	2-3 PM	83.8
Los Angeles	7-8 AM	93.2	9-10 PM	73.2
Miami	7-8 AM	98.2	8-9 PM	77.9
New York: Kennedy	8-9 AM	93.1	6-7 AM	64.7
New York: La Guardia	8-9 AM	89.8	8-9 PM	73.7
New York: Newark	11 AM-12 PM	89.2	5-6 PM	53.1
San Francisco	7-8 AM	94.7	11 AM-12 PM	82.7
St. Louis	7-8 AM	96.8	8-9 PM	82.7

Source: Department of Transportation Report for April 1992

State Travel Information Centers

ALL 50 STATES OFFER TOURISM SERVICES which will send maps, brochures, and travel information upon request. Note that requests for materials should be made at least four weeks in advance of travel.

State	Telephone
Alabama	(800) 832-5510
Alaska	(907) 465-2010
Arizona	(602) 255-3618
Arkansas	(501) 682-1219
California	(916) 322-1396
Colorado	(303) 866-2205
Connecticut	(800) 243-1685
Delaware	(800) 441-8846
District of Columbia	(202) 789-7000
Florida	(904) 488-5606
Georgia	(404) 656-3590
Hawaii	(808) 923-1811
Idaho	(800) 635-7820
Illinois	(800) 637-8560
Indiana	(317) 232-8870
Iowa	(515) 281-3100
Kansas	(913) 296-2009
Kentucky	(502) 564-4930
Louisiana	(800) 234-8626
Maine	(207) 289-2423
Maryland	(800) 381-1750, ext. 250
Massachusetts	(617) 727-3201
Michigan	(517) 373-0670
Minnesota	(612) 296-5029
Mississippi	(800) 647-2290
Missouri	(314) 751-4133

State	Telephone
Montana	(406) 449-2654
Nebraska	(402) 471-3111
Nevada	(702) 885-4322
New Hampshire	(603) 271-2665
New Jersey	(609) 292-2470
New Mexico	(800) 545-2040
New York	(212) 827-6100
North Carolina	(919) 733-4171
North Dakota	(800) 437-2077
Ohio	(614) 466-8844
Oklahoma	(405) 521-2406
Oregon	(800) 547-7842
Pennsylvania	(717) 787-5453
Rhode Island	(800) 556-2484
South Carolina	(803) 734-0127
South Dakota	(800) 843-1930
Tennessee	(615) 741-2158
Texas	(512) 320-9692
Utah	(801) 533-5681
Vermont	(802) 828-3236
Virginia	(804) 786-2051
Washington	(206) 753-5600
West Virginia	(800) 624-9110
Wisconsin	(608) 266-2147
Wyoming	(800) 443-2784

Car Rental Companies

The Top Car Rental Companies

U.S. Rank	Foreign Rank	Company	Telephone
1	1	Hertz	(800) 654-3131
2	2	Avis	(800) 331-1212
3	–	Enterprise	(800) 325-8007
4	4	Budget	(800) 227-3678
5	3	National	(800) 328- 4567
6	10	Agency	(800) 321-1972
7	6	Dollar	(800) 622-6231
8	–	U-Save	(800) 438-2300
9	7	Thrifty	(800) 367-2277
10	11	Rent A Wreck	(800) 822-1662
11	8	Carey	(800) 585-9333
12	–	Snappy	(800) 762-7791
13	–	Practical	(800) 233-1663
14	12	Alamo	(800) 327-9633
15	9	Payless	(800) 462-3757

Source: Business Travel News

Car Rental Companies (cont'd)

Popular Rental Car Companies: Revenue and % Market Share

Rank	Airport	1990 Revenue ($)	Hertz	Avis	National	Budget	Dollar	Alamo	Other
1	Los Angeles	217,045,894	35.0	24.7	16.9	17.8	5.6	0.0	-
2	Orlando	142,308,364	22.8	23.4	17.0	24.5	9.0	0.0	3.4
3	San Francisco	141,164,716	36.7	28.0	15.4	15.9	4.0	0.0	-
4	Miami	118,017,735	24.5	26.7	11.6	18.0	14.1	0.0	5.1
5	Boston	113,102,093	27.7	26.2	15.7	12.0	3.8	11.0	3.5
6	Atlanta	106,301,500	26.4	21.5	16.1	15.3	2.8	11.8	6.0
7	Denver	106,068,007	25.6	19.5	12.1	14.7	7.9	10.8	9.3
8	Chicago (O'Hare)	100,628,101	31.8	27.5	17.7	19.0	3.4	0.0	0.6
9	Phoenix	94,574,067	28.6	24.0	13.7	25.0	6.6	1.6	0.4
10	Newark	88,780,599	33.7	29.9	18.9	14.6	3.0	0.0	-
11	Dallas (D/FW)	82,164,117	34.8	30.8	16.1	18.3	0.0	0.0	-
12	Tampa	78,468,284	26.8	24.2	13.7	25.1	10.2	0.0	-
13	Philadelphia	74,901,789	28.4	24.5	19.1	11.9	4.9	11.3	-
14	Detroit	73,947,088	27.9	26.6	18.6	23.3	3.6	0.0	-
15	Seattle	70,825,537	28.1	27.3	14.6	22.4	6.8	0.0	0.7
16	Ft. Lauderdale	65,786,894	25.4	23.2	12.7	23.4	8.2	0.0	7.1
17	San Diego	64,897,083	35.8	25.4	17.1	14.8	6.8	0.0	-
18	W. Palm Beach	57,891,197	26.4	20.3	11.1	14.2	7.2	20.7	-
19	Maui	57,414,305	14.6	8.6	6.6	30.8	20.2	0.0	19.2
20	Wash., DC (Nat'l)	56,815,189	32.0	31.0	19.1	12.9	5.0	0.0	-
21	Minneapolis	52,530,630	30.1	25.3	19.0	19.3	0.0	0.0	6.2
22	San Jose	52,249,150	37.0	31.0	13.3	14.0	4.6	0.0	-
23	NY (La Guardia)	51,205,669	38.7	30.0	14.1	12.5	4.6	0.0	-
24	Houston IC	50,061,990	29.0	27.6	19.0	13.8	4.4	0.0	6.2
25	Wash., DC (Dulles)	45,412,889	35.8	29.6	16.2	14.2	4.2	0.0	-
26	St. Louis	44,765,404	32.4	26.6	16.2	19.5	5.3	0.0	-
27	Ft. Meyers	44,425,257	22.3	17.1	9.9	31.8	8.3	0.0	10.6
28	New York (JFK)	44,119,953	36.6	30.3	13.2	14.2	5.7	0.0	-
29	Baltimore	43,997,592	26.7	26.5	15.9	15.6	4.2	6.5	4.6
30	Honolulu	43,879,665	18.2	17.0	11.1	36.6	17.0	0.0	-
31	Las Vegas	39,057,138	33.6	26.2	16.0	0.0	11.9	0.0	12.3
32	Houston HOB	38,842,166	24.4	28.2	15.1	20.3	5.1	0.0	7.0
33	Orange County	36,919,228	33.8	25.7	15.3	17.5	6.5	0.0	1.3
34	Pittsburgh	36,222,624	31.3	27.3	18.4	17.8	3.2	0.0	2.0
35	New Orleans	36,041,083	29.0	27.3	19.7	22.4	1.5	0.0	-
36	Kansas City	35,942,779	28.3	25.7	16.6	16.3	5.1	8.0	-
37	Is. of Hawaii	35,201,373	13.3	7.6	6.7	29.4	16.2	0.0	-
38	Hartford	34,532,507	34.1	24.3	15.4	15.3	4.1	6.7	-
39	Portland, OR	33,643,271	27.6	24.0	14.6	22.4	11.4	0.0	-
40	Nashville	33,146,268	24.1	25.9	15.6	19.8	4.1	10.5	-
41	Cleveland	32,660,217	32.5	27.7	20.2	15.5	4.1	0.0	-
42	Albuquerque	32,633,960	31.2	18.6	14.6	24.1	5.1	0.0	6.4
43	Raleigh, NC	32,493,297	30.9	24.0	14.8	15.7	3.0	6.7	4.9
44	Salt Lake City	32,171,538	34.1	24.0	18.0	18.7	5.2	0.0	-
45	Oakland, CA	30,778,221	31.0	24.9	14.4	22.6	7.0	0.0	-
46	Kauai	30,698,893	22.4	15.2	5.5	32.7	0.0	0.0	-
47	Ontario	30,454,446	32.4	23.6	15.7	20.0	8.4	0.0	-
48	San Antonio	28,998,816	21.9	20.4	14.8	20.5	4.6	6.9	10.8
49	Indianapolis	28,932,782	27.2	23.2	25.9	19.1	4.6	0.0	-
50	Charlotte	27,216,920	34.4	25.2	19.0	15.9	2.8	0.0	2.7

Source: Auto Rental News

Travel Agencies

Agencies Ranked by U.S. Sales

Agency	Sales ($ thousands)
American Express	4,500,000
Carlson	2,300,000
Thomas Cook	1,138,000
Rosenbluth	1,000,000
USTravel	935,000
Maritz	660,000
IVI Travel	600,000
Wagons-Lits Travel USA	303,316
Omega World Travel	303,000
World Travel Advisors	220,000
VTS	219,738
Travel and Transport	207,000
Total Travel Management	155,000
McDonnell Douglas Travel	149,480
Travel One	145,000
Corporate Travel Consultants	141,000
Associated Travel Services	139,500
Northwestern Travel Service	139,000
Travel Incorporated	127,000
Arrington	122,700
McCord	118,000
Supertravel	113,000
Murdock Travel	109,600
Worldtek	109,000
Garber	106,942

Source: Business Travel News

Agencies Ranked by Number of Offices

Agency	Telephone No.	Offices
American Express	(212) 640-4446	650
Carlson	(612) 449-1000	400
Thomas Cook	(617) 868-9800	373
Rosenbluth	(215) 981-1700	NA
USTravel	(301) 251-9450	284
Omega World Travel	(703) 998-7171	160
Travel and Transport	(402) 592-4100	148
Wagon-Lits Travel USA	(513) 435-7397	142
IVI Travel	(708) 480-8400	81
Maritz	(314) 827-4436	71
Garber	(800) 359-4272	71
Supertravel	(800) 798-7189	61
Associated Travel Services	(800) 969-2552	56
World Travel Advisors	(404) 320-4195	54
Direct Travel	(800) 345-0355	53
Morris Travel	(800) 444-7111	48
Total Travel Management	(800) 535-8617	42
World Wide Travel	(800) 643-3788	40
Hoy & Eckdall Tours	(800) 421-3787	39
AAA Auto Club South	(813) 289-5000	38
Northwestern Travel Service	(800) 726-0569	37
Travel Incorporated	(404) 455-6575	34
AAA Travel Agency	(800) 732-1246	33
Travel One	(800) 243-1600	32
VTS	(800) 233-1632	32

Source: Business Travel News

Per Diems by City

THE PER DIEM TOTALS SHOWN BELOW are based on an analysis of 200 U.S. locations and 100 international locations, and represent average costs for the typical business traveler. Costs include breakfast, lunch, and dinner in business-class restaurants, and single-rate lodging in first-class hotels and motels.

10 Most Expensive U.S. Locations Ranked by Per Diem Costs

Location	Total Cost Per Diem ($)
New York, NY	297
Washington DC	248
Honolulu, HI	238
Chicago, IL	215
Boston, MA	197
San Francisco, CA	194
Atlantic City, NJ	191
Los Angeles, CA	190
Anchorage, AK	167
Philadelphia, PA	161

Note: Honolulu rates are seasonal: 12/15 - 4/15

10 Most Expensive International Locations Ranked by Per Diem Costs

Location	Total Cost Per Diem ($)
Paris	404
Tokyo	392
Milan	376
Stockholm	262
Madrid	359
London	356
Rome	350
Copenhagen	317
Oslo	317
Hong Kong	305

Source: Runzheimer Meal-Lodging Cost Index, 1992

Per Diems by City (cont'd)

The IRS has a maximum deduction for travel expenses. Any expenses over these amounts are the responsiblity of the corporation, and cannot be deducted from income taxes.

IRS-Approved Allowances for Travel on or After March 1, 1992

City	Lodging ($)	Meal & Incidentals ($)	Combined ($)
Atlanta	79	34	113
Baltimore	78	34	112
Boston	97	34	131
Buffalo	68	26	94
Chicago	101	34	135
Cincinnati	60	26	86
Cleveland	76	34	110
Columbus	68	26	94
Dallas	74	34	108
Denver	74	34	108
Detroit	80	34	114
Hartford	68	34	102
Houston	73	34	107
Indianapolis	69	26	95
Jacksonville	49	26	75
Los Angeles	100	34	134
Memphis	56	26	82
Miami	63	34	97
Milwaukee	63	26	89
Minneapolis	62	26	88
Nashville	52	26	78
New Orleans	65	34	99
New York City	140	34	174
Norfolk	68	26	94
Orlando	63	26	89
Philadelphia	89	34	123
Phoenix	72	26	98
Pittsburgh	73	26	99
Portland	65	26	91
Sacramento	66	34	100
St. Louis	69	26	95
Salt Lake City	70	26	96
San Antonio	61	26	87
San Diego	77	34	111
San Francisco	92	34	126
Seattle	79	34	113
Tampa	56	26	82
Washington	110	34	144

Source: Payroll Managers Letter

Recommended Resources

Travel and Entertainment Expenses: A Guide to Tax Rules
Grant Thornton
800 One Prudential Plaza
Chicago, IL 60601
(312) 856-0001

This pamphlet is an excellent guide to applying the tax laws to business travel and entertainment. It outlines what expenses are deductible and defines the methods for claiming deductions.

Travel, Entertainment and Gift Expenses
Department of the Treasury
Internal Revenue Service
Publication: 463

To receive this free pamphlet about how to prepare travel, entertainment, and gift expenses for your tax returns, contact the IRS Forms Distribution Center for your state.

U.S. Passport Agencies

Boston
John F. Kennedy Building
Government Center
Room E123
Boston, MA 02203
(617) 565-3940

Chicago
Kluczynski Federal Office Building
230 S. Dearborn
Suite 380
Chicago, IL 60604
(312) 353-5426

Honolulu
New Federal Building
300 Ala Moana Blvd.
Room C-06
Honolulu, HI 96850
(808) 546-2130

Houston
One Allen Center
500 Dallas St.
Houston, TX 77002
(713) 229-3607

Los Angeles
Federal Building
11000 Wilshire Blvd.
Room 13100
West Los Angeles, CA 90024
(213) 209-7070

Miami
Federal Office Building
51 SW 1st Ave.
16th Floor
Miami, FL 33130
(305) 536-5395

New Orleans
Postal Service Building
701 Loyola Ave.
Room T-12005
New Orleans, LA 70113
(504) 589-6728

New York City
630 Fifth Ave.
Room 270
New York, NY 10111
(212) 541-7700

Philadelphia
Federal Office Building
600 Arch St.
Room 4426
Philadelphia, PA 19106
(215) 597-7480

San Francisco
525 Market St.
Suite 200
San Francisco, CA 94105
(415) 974-7972

Seattle
Federal Office Building
915 Second Ave.
Room 992
Seattle, WA 98174
(206) 442-7941

Stamford
One Landmark Square
Broad and Atlantic Sts.
Stamford, CT 06901
(203) 325-3538

Washington
1425 K St., NW
Washington, DC 20524
(202) 523-1355

Almanac Fact

The best European business hotels are The Ritz in Paris, and the Dorchester and Inter-Continental in London.

Source: Business Traveler International

The Best Restaurants

The Top 5 Restaurants in Selected U.S. Metro Areas Ranked by Zagat Survey America

City	Restaurant	Cuisine Type	Address	Telephone
Atlanta	The Dining Room	American Contemporary	3434 Peachtree Rd.	(404) 237-2700
	La Grotta	Northern Italian	2637 Peachtree Rd.	(404) 231-1368
	Pano's and Paul's	American Traditional	1232 W. Paces Ferry Rd.	(404) 261-3662
	103 West	Continental	103 W. Paces Ferry Rd.	(404) 233-5993
	The Hedgerose Heights Inn	Continental	490 E. Paces Ferry Rd.	(404) 233-7673
Baltimore	The Prime Rib	American Traditional	1101 N. Calvert St.	(410) 539-1804
	Milton Inn	Continental	14833 York Rd.	(410) 771-4366
	Hamptons	American Contemporary	550 Light St.	(410) 234-0550
	The Conservatory	French Classic	612 Cathedral St.	(410) 727-7101
	Tio Pepe	Spanish	10 E. Franklin St.	(410) 539-4675
Boston	Olives	No. Italian/Mediterranean	10 City Sq., Charlestown	(617) 242-1999
	L'Espalier	French Nouvelle	30 Gloucester St.	(617) 262-3023
	Hamersley's Bistro	Eclectic/French Bistro	578 Tremont St.	(617) 267-6068
	Jasper's	Seafood	240 Commercial St.	(617) 523-1126
	Seasons	Eclectic	9 Blackstone St. N.	(617) 523-3600
Chicago	Le Francais	French Classic	269 S. Milwaukee Ave.	(708) 541-7470
	Carlos'	French Classic	429 Temple Ave.	(708) 432-0770
	Ambria	French Nouvelle	2300 N. Lincoln Park W.	(312) 472-5959
	Jimmy's Place	French/Japanese	3420 N. Elston Ave.	(312) 539-2999
	Tallgrass	French Nouvelle	1006 S. State St.	(815) 838-5566
Dallas	Riviera	French	7709 Inwood Rd.	(214) 826-7804
	The French Room	French Classic	1321 Commerce St.	(214) 742-8200
	Routh Street Cafe	Southwestern	3005 Routh St.	(214) 871-7161
	Gaspar's	American Contemporary	150 S. Denton Tap Rd.	(214) 393-5152
	The Mansion on Turtle Creek	Southwestern	2821 Turtle Creek Blvd.	(214) 559-2100
Houston	Deville	Southwestern	1300 Lamar	(713) 650-1300
	Tony's	Continental	1801 Post Oak Blvd.	(713) 622-6778
	La Reserve	French Classic	4 Riverway	(713) 871-8177
	Chez Nous	French Bistro	217 S. Ave. G	(713) 446-6717
	Empress of China	Chinese/French	5419A FM 1960 W.	(713) 583-8021
Kansas City	Tatsu's	French	4603 W. 90th St.	(913) 383-9801
	Cafe Allegro	Eclectic	1815 W. 39th St.	(816) 561-3663
	Pepper Corn Duck Club	American Traditional/Eclectic	2345 McGee St.	(816) 421-1234
	La Mediterranee	French	4742 Pennsylvania Ave.	(816) 561-2916
	Venue	Eclectic	4532 Main St.	(816) 561-3311
Los Angeles	Patina	Californian/French	5955 Melrose Ave.	(213) 467-1108
	Matsuhisa	Pacific New Wave	129 N. La Cienega Blvd.	(310) 659-9639
	Shiro	Pacific New Wave	1505 Mission St.	(818) 799-4774
	Chinois on Main	Pacific New Wave	2709 Main St.	(310) 392-9025
	Diaghilev	French Classic/Russian	1001 N. San Vicente Blvd.	(310) 854-1111
Miami	Mark's Place	American Contemporary	2286 NE 123rd St.	(305) 893-6888
	Chef Allen's	American Contemporary	19088 NE 29th Ave.	(305) 935-2900
	Grand Cafe	Continental	2669 S. Bayshore Dr.	(305) 858-9600
	The Fish Market	Seafood	1601 Biscayne Blvd.	(305) 374-4399
	Casa Larios	Cuban	7929 NW 2nd St.	(305) 266-5494
Milwaukee	Sally's Steak House	Steakhouse	1028 E. Juneau St.	(414) 272-5363
	Grenadier's	Continental	747 N. Broadway	(414) 276-0747
	The English Room	American Traditional/French	424 E. Wisconsin Ave.	(414) 273-8222
	Karl Ratzsch's	German	320 E. Mason St.	(414) 276-2720
	The Immigrant Room	American Traditional	Highland Dr.	(414) 457-8888

The Best Restaurants (cont'd)

City	Restaurant	Type of Cuisine	Address	Telephone
New Orleans	Grill Room	American Traditional	300 Gravier St.	(504) 523-6000
	Commander's Palace	Haute Creole	1403 Washington Ave.	(504) 899-8221
	Bistro at Maison de Ville	Haute New Orleans	733 Toulouse St.	(504) 528-9206
	La Provence	French Classic	Hwy. 190, Lacombe	(504) 626-7662
	Brigtsen's	Cajun	723 Dante St.	(504) 861-7610
New York	Bouley	French	165 Duane St.	(212) 608-3852
	Aureole	Amer. Contemp./French	34 E. 61st St.	(212) 319-1660
	Le Cirque	French	58 E. 65th St.	(212) 794-9292
	Lutece	French	249 E. 50th St.	(212) 752-2225
	Le Bernardin	French/Seafood	155 W. 51st St.	(212) 489-1515
Philadelphia	The Fountain	International	Logan Square	(215) 963-1500
	Ciboulette	French Nouvelle	200 S. Broad St.	(215) 790-1210
	Dmitri's	Mediterranean	795 S. 3rd St.	(215) 625-0556
	Swann Lounge & Cafe	American Traditional	1 Logan Sq.	(215) 963-1500
	Tacconelli's Pizza	Pizza	2604 E. Sommerset St.	(215) 425-4983
Phoenix	Vincent Guerithault	American Trad./SW	3930 E. Camelback Rd.	(602) 224-0225
	Franco's Trattoria	Northern Italian	6919 N. Hayden Rd.	(602) 948-6655
	Yamakasa	Japanese	9301 E. Shea Blvd.	(602) 860-5605
	Marquesa	Spanish	7575 E. Princess Dr.	(602) 271-9000
	Christopher's /The Bistro	French Nouvelle/Amer.	2398 E. Camelback Rd.	(602) 957-3214
Portland	Cafe des Amis	French Classic	1987 NW Kearney St.	(503) 295-6487
	Genoa	Northern Italian	2832 SE Belmont St.	(503) 238-1464
	Indigene	Indian	3725 SE Division St.	(503) 238-1470
	Winterborne	Seafood	3520 NE 42nd Ave.	(503) 249-8486
	L'Auberge	French Classic	2601 NW Vaughn St.	(503) 223-3302
St. Louis	Tony's	Continental/N/S Italian	410 Market St.	(314) 231-7007
	Fio's La Fourchette	French Classic	1153 St. Louis Galleria	(314) 863-6866
	Cafe de France	French Classic	410 Olive St.	(314) 231-2204
	Andria's	Steakhouse	6805 Old Collinsville Rd.	(618) 632-4866
	Giovanni's	Northern Italian	5201 Shaw Ave.	(314) 772-5958
San Diego	Wine Sellar & Rasserie	Californian/French	9555 Waples	(619) 450-9557
	Mille Fleurs	Californian/French	6009 Paseo Delicias	(619) 756-3085
	El Bizcocho	French Classic	17550 Bernardo Oaks Dr.	(619) 277-2146
	Marius	French Nouvelle	2000 Second St.	(619) 435-3000
	Belgian Lion	Belgian/French	2265 Bacon St.	(619) 223-2700
San Francisco	Masa's	French Nouvelle	648 Bush St.	(415) 989-7154
	Fleur de Lys	French Classic/Nouvelle	777 Sutter St.	(415) 673-7779
	La Folie	French	2316 Polk St.	(415) 776-5577
	Chez Panisse	Californian	1517 Shattuck Ave.	(510) 548-5525
	Cafe at Chez Panisse	Californian	1517 Shattuck Ave.	(510) 548-5049
Seattle	Fullers	Continental/Northwest	1400 Sixth Ave.	(206) 447-5544
	Gerard's Relais	French Classic	17121 Bothell Way, NE	(206) 485-7600
	Saleh al Lago	Northern Italian	6804 E. Green Lake Way, N	(206) 524-4044
	Labuznik	Middle European	1924 First Ave.	(206) 441-8899
	Cafe Juanita	Nuova Cucina Italian	9702 NE 120th Pl.	(206) 823-1505
Tampa Bay	Euphemia Haye	Eclectic	5540 Gulf-of-Mexico Dr.	(813) 383-3633
	Armani's	Northern Italian	6200 Courtney Campbell Way	(813) 874-1234
	Bern's Steak House	Steakhouse	1208 S. Howard Ave.	(813) 251-2421
	Cafe L'Europe	Continental	431 St. Armands Circle	(813) 388-4415
	Mise en Place	American Contemporary	1815 Platt W.	(813) 254-5373
Washington, DC	Inn at Little Washington	American Contemporary	Middle & Main Sts.	(703) 675-3800
	Le Lion d'Or	French Classic	1150 Connecticut Ave., NW	(202) 296-7972
	Jean-Louis	French Classic	2650 Virginia Ave., NW	(202) 298-4488
	L'Auberge Chez Francois	French Classic	332 Springvale Rd.	(703) 759-3800
	Yannick's	French Nouvelle	5000 Seminary Rd.	(703) 845-1010

Guide to Audio-Visual Rentals

WHEN TRAVELING TO ANOTHER CITY TO GIVE a presentation, a firm can save money by using a local company to provide multimedia equipment like televisions, slide projectors, or computers. This city-by-city listing highlights selected firms around the country.

Atlanta
Atlanta Sound & Lighting
(404) 455-7695

Projexions Video Supply Company
(404) 872-6247

Seriously Sound Incorporated
(404) 872-0346

Total Audio Visual Services Inc.
(404) 875-7555

Baltimore
American Audio-Video
(410) 539-8400

Audio Visual, Inc.
(410) 643-4220

Crew Works Inc.
(410) 235-2037

Total Audio-Visual Systems, Inc.
(410) 625-4700

Boston
Immediate Connections, Inc.
(617) 783-1599

Media 1 Inc.
(617) 254-0770

Projection Video Services
(617) 254-6693

Audio Services Incorporated
(617) 424-1062

Chicago
Artistic Communication Center
(312) 280-0808

LeGrand Services
(800) 252-6222

Video Replay
(312) 822-0221

Williams Gerard Productions
(312) 467-5560

Cincinnati
Cavalier Audio Visual Services, Inc.
(513) 784-0055

Chesapeake Audio/Visual Communications, Inc.
(301) 796-0040

CSI/Clarity Systems
(513) 784-1200

Visual Aids Electronics
(513) 684-0800

Cleveland
CPS Meetings
(216) 771-7711

Colortone
(216) 581-5055

Eighth Day Sound
(216) 961-2900

Media Control
(216) 241-2777

Columbus, OH
Audio Visual Technologies
(800) 338-1228

Brite Lights, Inc.
(614) 272-1404

Mills James Productions
(614) 777-9933

United States Audio Visuals
(614) 461-8444

Dallas
Bauer Southam Audio Visual
(214) 630-6700

SAV Communications
(214) 423-5874

Brad Young Multi-Image Inc.
(214) 528-4888

Arapaho Audio Visual
(214) 458-1468

Audio Visual America
(214) 637-0581

Denver
Audio Visual Rentals, Inc.
(303) 733-9910

Guide to Audio-Visual Rentals (cont'd)

Ceavco Audio Visual Company, Inc.
(303) 238-0443

Colorado Audio Visual (Aspen)
(303) 925-8508

Spectrum Audio-Visual
(303) 477-4456

Detroit
Allied Vision Convention Services
(313) 568-1012

Audio Visual Wholesalers
(612) 559-9666

Blumberg Communications, Inc.
(612) 521-8225

GAVCO Audio-Visual
(313) 567-2159

Showtech Presentation Systems, Inc.
(313) 547-8880

Houston
A/V Texas, Inc.
(713) 526-3687

Aves Audio Visual Systems, Inc.
(713) 783-3440

Image in Action, Inc.
(713) 932-9779

Photo & Sound Co.
(713) 956-9566

Indianapolis
Dodd Technologies
(317) 842-4905

Markey's Audio Visual
(317) 783-1155

United States Audio-Visuals
(317) 632-2527

Visual Aids Electronics
(317) 638-8111

Los Angeles
Bauer/Southam Audio Video Inc.
(310) 949-0351

Jacobs Audio Visual Systems Inc.
(213) 882-8577

Studio Instrument Rental
(213) 466-1314

Thomas Gregor Audio
(818) 760-0470

Video Equipment Rentals of Southern California
(818) 956-0212

Miami
Blumberg Communications
(305) 594-3939

Metro Audio Visual
(305) 623-1300

Miami Audio Visual
(305) 757-5000

Southern Audio/Video & Business Rental
(305) 266-5561

Total Audiovisual
(407) 859-3399

Milwaukee
Audio Visual of Milwaukee, Inc.
(414) 258-1077

Midwest Visual Equipment Co., Inc.
(414) 784-5880

Studio Gear
(414) 223-4884

United States Audio-Visuals
(414) 276-8688

Minneapolis
Audio-Visual and Video Resources
(612) 456-9033

Twin City Audio-Visual Services, Inc.
(612) 869-4501

WIX/MIX Systems Inc.
(612) 789-548

New York
Ace Audio Visual Company
(212) 685-3344

Bauer/Southern Audio Video, Inc.
(212) 714-9648

Executive Audio-Visual Services Inc.
(212) 575-2500

Guide to Audio-Visual Rentals (cont'd)

Norfolk
Craft-Work Sound
(804) 436-2577

Atlantic Audio Visual
(804) 422-5252

Philadelphia
Audio Visual Center
(215) 563-6872

Bauer/Southam Audio Video, Inc.
(215) 625-0885

Visual Sound Company
(215) 544-8700

Phoenix
A.V. Concepts, Inc.
(602) 894-6642

EDS Video Services
(800) 845-1972

Southwest Audio Visual Inc.
(602) 258-4911

Pittsburgh
Corporate Video Creations Inc.
(412) 281-2662

Pro-Com Systems
(412) 621-1950

Visual Aids Center of Pittsburgh
(412) 566-1800

Willowglen Productions
(412) 381-3333

Portland, OR
Advision Video Marketing
(800) 678-7712

Audio-Visual Rentals & Services
(503) 222-1664

AVCOM Corp.
(503) 232-8382

Rose City Sound
(503) 238-6330

Sacramento
Munday & Collins, Inc.
(916) 451-6511

The Pacific Crest Picture Company
(916) 652-4466

Photo & Sound
(916) 649-6999

St. Louis
Audio-Visual Alternatives
(314) 773-9155

Audio-Visual Management Consultants
(314) 421-2862

San Francisco
AVTS, Inc.
(415) 255-7766

Audio Visual Headquarters
(415) 296-7485, ext. 1111

Concept Organization Inc.
(415) 495-6521

Projection Video Services
(415) 826-2244

Seattle
Audio Productions
(206) 523-9035

Barr Audio Visual
(206) 763-7181

Pro-Image
(206) 284-5000

Tampa
Advanced Visual Communications (AVCOM)
(813) 875-0888

Audio Visual Support Service, Inc.
(813) 872-7914

Cypress Productions
(813) 289-6115

Vaughn Broadcast Rentals
(813) 887-3141

Washington, D.C.
Chesapeake Audio/Video Communications Inc.
(301) 596-3900

The Crew Works Inc.
(410) 235-2037

Future View, Inc.
(202) 882-7450

Visitor and Convention Bureaus

BELOW IS A LISTING OF THE NAMES, ADDRESSES, and phone numbers of the Visitors and Convention Bureau in 30 major cities. Any company in need of a trade show facilitator should contact the Visitors and Convention Bureau in the city hosting the event. The telephone numbers of a variety of facilitators are available through the convention services department of each bureau. The best way to contact these bureaus is often by fax.

Recommended Resources

Trade Show and Convention Guide
P.O. Box 24970
Nashville, TN 31202
(615) 321-4250

This book sells for $75 and includes a complete listing of convention facilities in every U.S. city as well as an annual calendar of major trade shows and events. It also lists the names, addresses, and telephone numbers of most major trade organizations.

Visitor and Convention Bureaus

Atlanta
233 Peachtree St., NE
Suite 2000
Atlanta, GA 30303
(404) 521-6600
Fax: (404) 584-6331

Baltimore
1 East Pratt St., Plaza Level
Baltimore, MD 21202
(410) 659-7300
(800) 343-3468
Fax: (301) 727-2308

Boston
Prudential Tower, 4th Floor, Suite 400
P.O. Box 490
Boston, MA 02199
(617) 536-4100
Fax: (617) 424-7664

Chicago
McCormick Place On-The-Lake
Chicago, IL 60616
(312) 567-8500
Fax: (312) 567-8533

Cincinnati
300 W. Sixth St.
Cincinnati, OH 45202
(513) 621-2142
Fax: (513) 621-2156

Cleveland
3100 Terminal Tower
Tower City Center
Cleveland, OH 44113
(216) 621-4110
(800) 321-1001
Fax: (216) 621-5967

Columbus
One Columbus Building
10 W. Broad St., Suite 1300
Columbus, OH 43215
(614) 221-6623
(800) 234-2657
Fax: (614) 221-5618

Dallas
1201 Elm St., Suite 2000
Dallas, TX 75270
(214) 746-6677
Fax: (214) 746-6688

Denver
225 W. Colfax Ave.
Denver, CO 80202
(303) 892-1112
Fax: (303) 892-1636

Detroit
100 Renaissance Center, Suite 1950
Detroit, MI 48243
(313) 259-4333
Fax: (313) 259-7583

Houston
3300 Main St.
Houston, TX 77002
(713) 523-5050
(800) 231-7799
Fax: (713) 524-5376

Indianapolis
One Hoosier Dome, Suite 100
Indianapolis, IN 46225
(317) 639-4282
(800) 323-4639
Fax: (317) 639-5273

Los Angeles
515 S. Figueroa, 11th Floor
Los Angeles, CA 90071
(213) 624-7300
Fax: (213) 624-9746

Miami
701 Brickell Ave., Suite 2700
Miami, FL 3313
(305) 539-3000
(800) 933-8448
Fax: (305) 539-3113

Visitor and Convention Bureaus (cont'd)

Milwaukee
510 West Kilbourn Ave.
Milwaukee, WI 53203
(414) 273-3950
(800) 231-0903
Fax: (414) 273-5596

Minneapolis
1219 Marquette Ave.
Minneapolis, MN 55403
(612) 348-4313
(800) 445-7412
Fax: (612) 348-8359

New Orleans
1520 Sugar Bowl Dr.
New Orleans, LA 70112
(504) 566-5011
Fax: (504) 566-5046

New York
Two Columbus Circle
New York, NY 10019
(212) 484-1265
Fax: (212) 484-1280

Norfolk
236 E. Plume St.
Norfolk, VA 23510
(804) 441-5266
(800) 368-3097
Fax: (804) 622-3663

Philadelphia
1234 Market St., Suite 1800
Philadelphia, PA 19107
(215) 545-1234
Fax: (215) 972-3900

Phoenix
400 E. Van Buren St., Suite 600
Phoenix, AZ 85004
(602) 254-6500
(800) 535-8898
Fax: (602) 254-4415

Pittsburgh
Four Gateway Center, Suite 514
Pittsburgh, PA 15222
(412) 281-7711
(800) 821-1888
Fax: (412) 644-5512

Portland
Three World Trade Center
26 South West Salmon
Portland, OR 97204
(503) 275-9750
(800) 962-3700
Fax: (503) 275-9774

Sacramento
1421 K St.
Sacramento, CA 95814
(916) 264-7777
Fax: (916) 264-7788

St. Louis
10 S. Broadway, Suite 1000
St. Louis, MO 63102
(314) 421-1023
(800) 325-7962
Fax: (314) 421-0039

San Antonio
121 Alamo Plaza (78205)
P.O. Box 2277
San Antonio, TX 78298
(512) 270-8700
(800) 447-3372
Fax: (512) 270-8782

San Diego
1200 Third Ave., Suite 824
San Diego, CA 92101
(619) 232-3101
Fax: (619) 696-9371

San Francisco
201 Third St., Suite 900
San Francisco, CA 94103
(415) 974-6900
Fax: (415) 227-2602

Seattle
520 Pike St., Suite 1300
Seattle, WA 98101
(206) 461-5800
Fax: (206) 461-5855

Tampa
111 Madison St., Suite 1010
P.O. Box 519
Tampa, FL 33602
(813) 223-1111
(800) 826-8358
Fax: (813) 229-6616

Washington, DC
1212 New York Ave., NW
Sixth Floor
Washington, DC 20005
(202) 789-7000
Fax: (202) 789-7037

Convention Centers

Major Convention Centers in 25 Cities

City	Covention Center	Telephone	Total Exhibit Space (sq. ft.)	No. of Meeting Rooms
New York, NY	Jacob K. Javits Convention Center	(212) 216-2000	900,000	102
Los Angeles, CA	Los Angeles Convention Center	(213) 741-1151	685,000	64
Chicago, IL	McCormick Place	(312) 791-6464	2,500,000	50
Houston, TX	George R. Brown Convention Center	(713) 853-8000	470,500	43
Philadelphia, PA	Pennsylvania Convention Center	(215) 636-3300	517,000	52
Detroit, MI	Cobo Conference/Exhibition Center	(313) 224-1030	800,000	84
San Diego, CA	San Diego Convention Center	(619) 525-5200	354,000	32
Dallas, TX	Dallas Convention Center	(619) 939-2700	753,000	85
San Antonio, TX	Henry B. Gonzalez Convention Center	(210) 299-8500	240,000	46
Phoenix, AZ	Phoenix Civic Plaza	(602) 262-6225	300,000	43
Baltimore, MD	Baltimore Convention Center	(410) 659-7000	194,000	34
San Francisco, CA	Moscone Convention Center	(415) 974-4000	510,235	42
Indianapolis, IN	Indiana Convention Center & Hoosier Dome	(317) 262-3410	400,000	60
San Jose, CA	San Jose Convention Center	(408) 277-5277	143,000	30
Memphis, TN	Memphis Cook Convention Center	(901) 576-1200	200,000	19
Washington, DC	Washington Convention Center	(202) 789-1600	381,000	40
Jacksonville, FL	Prime F. Osborne III Convention Center	(904) 630-4000	100,000	22
Milwaukee, WI	Milwaukee Exposition & Convention Center	(414) 271-4000	256,000	42
Boston, MA	Hynes Convention Center	(617) 954-2000	218,000	45
Columbus, OH	Greater Columbus Convention Center	(614) 645-5000	306,000	54
New Orleans, LA	Ernest N. Morial Convention Center	(504) 582-3000	756,000	96
Cleveland, OH	International Exposition (I-X) Center	(216) 676-6000	1,600,000	18
Denver, CO	Colorado Convention Center	(303) 640-8007	300,000	46
El Paso, TX	El Paso Convention & Performing Arts Ctr.	(915) 534-0600	68,400	14
Seattle, WA	Washington State Convention and Trade Ctr.	(206) 447-5000	176,000	59

Source: Meetings & Conventions, 1/93

Personal Computing

PC Computing 1992 Awards

EVERY YEAR *PC COMPUTING* selects noteworthy IBM PC-compatible software in a variety of categories.

Category	Winner
Hardware Innovation	OverDrive
Software Innovation	Wizards
Desktop System	Gateway 2000 4DX2-66V
Input Device	HP ScanJet IIp & OmniPage
Storage	Pinnacle Micro PMO-650
Display Adapter	ATI Graphics Ultra Pro
Printer	HP LaserJet 4
Monochrome Portable	Compaq LTE Lite/25E
Entry-Level System	Compaq ProLinea 4/33 120
Modem	Intel SatisFAXtion Modem/400
Monitor	Nanao FlexScan T660i
Color Portable	IBM ThinkPad 700C
Multimedia	Microsoft Bookshelf, Multimedia
Network	Windows for Work

Category	Winner
Spreadsheet	Excel 4.0
Painting/Drawing	CorelDraw 3.0
Presentation Graphics	Freelance for Windows
Word Processor	Ami Pro 3.0
Financial/Accounting	Fidelity On-Line Xpress
Entertainment/Education	Power Japanese 1.1
System Utility	FontMonger 1.06
Communications	Procomm Plus for Windows
Business Utility	Zagat-Axxis City Guide
Operating System Enviroments	Windows 3.1 and OS/2 2.0
Desktop Publishing	QuarkXPress 3.1, Windows
Database	Microsoft Access
Application Dev.	Borland C++ for Windows

PC World 1992 Top 200

EVERY YEAR *PC WORLD* magazine selects 200 noteworthy IBM PC compatible products in a variety of categories.

Category	Product	Company
Desktop Computer	4D33	Gateway 2000
Portable Computer	Compaq Portable 486c	Compaq Computer
Notebook Computer	T4400SXC	Toshiba America
Laser Printer	HP LaserJet III	Hewlett-Packard
Dot Matrix Printer	Panasonic KX-P1124i	Panasonic
Ink Jet Printer	HP DeskJet 500	Hewlett-Packard
Monitor	MultiSync 4FG	NEC Technologies
Modem	14.4EX Modem	Intel
Fax Board	SatisFAXtion Modem/200	Intel
Memory Expansion Board	AboveBoard 2 Plus	Intel
Graphics Board	Graphics Ultra	ATI Technologies
Hard Drive	Seagate ST3144A	Seagate Technology
Removable/Portable Hard Drive	Bernoulli Transportable 90 Pro	Iomega
Tape Backup Drive	Jumbo 250	Colorado Memory Systems
Scanner	ScanMan 256	Logitech
Pointing Device	Microsoft Mouse	Microsoft
Most Promising Newcomer	FotoMan	Logitech
Word Processing	WordPerfect (DOS)	WordPerfect
Spreadsheet	Microsoft Excel	Microsoft
Operating System/Environment	Microsoft Windows 3	Microsoft
Utility	Norton Utilities	Symantec
Database	Paradox	Borland
Communications	ProComm Plus	DataStorm Technologies
Backup Software	Central Point Backup	Central Point Software

PC World 1992 Top 200 (cont'd)

Category	Product	Company
Desktop Publishing	PageMaker	Aldus
Draw Software	CorelDraw	Corel Systems
Personal Finance	Quicken (DOS)	Intuit
Presentation Graphics	Harvard Graphics (DOS)	Software Publishing
Programming Language	Borland C++	Borland
LAN Operating System	Lantastic	Artisoft
Tax Planning/Preparation	TurboTax (DOS)	ChipSoft
Forms Software	FormTool Gold	BLOC Publishing
Computer-Aided Design	AutoCAD	Autodesk
Paint Software	PC Paintbrush	ZSoft
Personal Information Manager	PackRat	Polaris Software
Project Manager	Microsoft Project for Windows	Microsoft
Management Tool	Microsoft Project for Windows	Microsoft
Accounting	DacEasy Accounting	DacEasy
Most Promising Newcomer	OS/2 2.0	IBM

MacUser Eddy Awards

EVERY YEAR *MACUSER* MAGAZINE awards the Eddy Awards, gold statuettes that honor the most innovative Macintosh software of the year. Here are the winners for 1992.

Product	Company
Word 5.1	Microsoft
FileMaker Pro 2.0	Claris
In Control 1.1	Attain
PowerPoint 3.0	Microsoft
M.Y.O.B. 3.0	Teleware
Now Utilities 4.0.1	Now Software
Public Utilities 1.0	Fifth Generation Systems
CPU 1.0	Connectix
QuarkXPress 3.1	Quark
Fontographer 3.5	Altsys
Sketcher 1.0	Fractal Design
Cachet 1.0.1	Electronics for Imaging
deBabelizer 1.2.15	Equilibrium Technologies
Infini-D 2.0	Specular International
ElectricImage Animation 1.5	ElectricImage
Premiere 2.0	Adobe Systems
Audiomedia II	Digidesign

Product	Company
VideoFusion 1.0	VideoFusion
PowerPad	Sophisticated Circuits
Arcus	Agfa Division, Miles
Luminator LCD Projector	nView
LaserJet 4M	Hewlett-Packard
PowerPort Gold	Global Village
LanRover/L	Shiva
cc:Mail for Macintosh 2.0	Lotus Development
StuffIt Deluxe 3.0	Aladdin Systems
Frontier 2.0	UserLand Software
StatView 4.0	Abacus Concepts
Expanded Books	The Voyager Company
Tree 1.0	Onyx Computing
Millie's Math House	Edmark
Interactive Physics II 1.01	Knowledge Revolution
Prince of Persia 1.0	Brøderbund Software
Star Trek: The Screen Saver 1.0	Berkeley Systems

Almanac Fact

Since its introduction in 1982, DOS has sold more than 100,000,000 copies worldwide.

Source: Microsoft

The Windows 100

THE TOP WINDOWS products, as chosen by *Windows* magazine in 1993.

Category	Product	Company
Accounting/Financial Management	Heizer Tax Series	Heizer Software
Accounting/Financial Management	MYOB 2.0	Teleware
Accounting/Financial Management	Quicken 2.0	Intuit
Accounting/Financial Management	Turbo Tax	ChipSoft
Alternative Desktops	hDC Power Launcher 2.0	hDC Computer
Alternative Desktops	NewWave 4.1	Hewlett-Packard
Alternative Desktops	Norton Desktop 2.0	Symantec
Alternative Desktops	WinTools	Tool Technology Publishing
App. Dev./Languages	Borland C++ & Application Frameworks 3.1	Borland International
App. Dev./Languages	Codewright 2.0	Premia
App. Dev./Languages	KnowledgePro	Knowledge Garden
App. Dev./Languages	Visual Basic/Standard & Pro 2.0	Microsoft
App. Dev./Languages	VBAssist 1.0	Sheridan Software Systems
CD-ROM Hardware	NEC Intersect CDR-74	NEC
Communications	MicroPhone Pro	Software Ventures
Communications	Terminal Plus 3.1	FutureSoft
Content Publishing	Cinemania 1.0	Microsoft
Content Publishing	Word + Bookshelf	Microsoft
Content Publishing	Oxford English Dictionary 2nd Edition on CD-ROM	Oxford University Press
Databases	Approach 2.0	Approach Software
Databases	FileMaker Pro 2.0	Claris
Databases	MapInfo 2.0	MapInfo
Databases	Quik Reports	Crystal Computer Services
Databases	Superbase 2.0	Software Publishing
Desktop Publishing	FrameMaker	Frame Technology
Desktop Faxing	Intel SatisFAXtion Modem/400	Intel
Desktop Faxing	WinFax PRO 3.0	Delrina Technology
Font Tools	Fontographer 3.5	Altsys
Font Tools	Typecase 1.0	SWFTE International
Games	Golf 1.0	Microsoft
Illustration	Illustrator 4.0	Adobe Systems
Illustration	ClickArt Series	T-Maker
Illustration	CorelDRAW! 3.0	Corel Systems
Illustration	Gallery Effects 1.0	Aldus
Illustration	HiJack 1.0	Inset Systems
Illustration	IntelliDraw 1.0	Aldus
Illustration	JAG (Jaggies Are Gone)	Ray Dream
Illustration	OFOTO	Light Source
Illustration	Painter 1.2	Fractal Design
Illustration	PhotoStyler 1.1	Aldus
Illustration	ImagePals	U-Lead Systems,
Illustration	Logitech ScanMan Color	Logitech
Pointing Devices	Altra Felix	Altra
Pointing Devices	Mouse Systems PC Trackball II	Mouse Systems
Management	ManagePro	Avantos Performance Systems
Management	Project 3.0	Microsoft
Mass Storage	Quantum Hardcard EZ	Quantum
Networking & E-Mail	BeyondMail Release 1.0/MHS	Beyond
Networking & E-Mail	LANtastic 4.1	Artisoft
Networking & E-Mail	Microsoft Mail	Microsoft

The Windows 100 (cont'd)

Category	Product	Company
Networking & E-Mail	Saber Menu System	Saber Software
Networking & E-Mail	Windows for Workgroups	Microsoft
PIMs	Commence	Jensen-Jones
PIMs	InfoSelect	Micro Logic
PIMs	Lotus Organizer	Lotus Development
Presentation	Add Impact!	Gold Disk
Presentation	DeltaGraph Professional 2.0	DeltaPoint
Presentation	SmartPics	Lotus Development
Presentation	Stanford Graphics 2.0	3-D Visions
Presentation	PowerPoint 3.0	Microsoft
Printing	Hewlett-Packard LaserJet 4	Hewlett-Packard
Printing	LaserMaster WinJet 800	LaserMaster
Printing	PaperKit	Paper Direct
Printing	Tektronix Phaser II PXe	Tektronix
Scientific	LabVIEW 1.0	National Instruments
Sound	Turtle Beach MultiSound	Turtle Beach Systems
Sound	Windows Sound System 1.0	Microsoft
Spreadsheets	Excel 4.0	Microsoft
Spreadsheets	Quattro Pro	Borland International
Systems	AST Premium Exec 386 SX/25	AST Research
Systems	Compaq Deskpro/i	Compaq
Systems	Gateway 2000 4SX/25	Gateway 2000
Systems	NEC UltraLite SL/25C	NEC Technologies
Systems	Toshiba T4400C	Toshiba America Information Systems
Systems	Texas Instruments TravelMate 4000 WinSX	Texas Instruments
Systems	Zeos Color Notebook	Zeos International
Utilities	Doc-To-Help 1.1	WexTech Systems
Utilities	Icon Hear-it	Moon Valley Software
Utilities	METZ Task Manager 2.0	METZ Software
Utilities	Outside In 2.0	Systems Compatibility
Utilities	Perform Pro Plus	Delrina Technology
Utilities	Plug-In Program Manager Utilities	Plannet Crafters
Utilities	Stacker 3.0 for DOS and Windows	Stac Electronics
Utilities	Super PC-Kwik	PC Kwik
Utilities	WinZip	Niko Mak
Utilities	386Max	Qualitas
Utilities	XTree	XTree
UPS	Powercard Internal Power System	Powercard
Video & Graphics	ATI Graphics Ultra Pro	ATI Technologies
Video & Graphics	Nanao Flexscan F550i	Nanao USA
Video & Graphics	NEC MultiSync 6FG	NEC Technologies
Video & Graphics	Number Nine 9GXiTC	Number Nine Computer
Video & Graphics	Orchid Fahrenheit VA	Orchid Technologies
Video & Graphics	Radius MultiView 24	Radius
Word Processing	Ami Pro 3.0	Lotus Development
Word Processing	MasterWord 1.0	Alki Software
Word Processing	RightWriter 6	Que Software
Word Processing	WOPR	PineCliffe International
Word Processing	WordPerfect 5.2	WordPerfect
Word Processing	Writer's Toolkit	Systems Compatibility

Source: Windows Magazine

Industry Data

PC RESEARCH COLLECTS DATA on the bestselling software products. The lists below are from December, 1992. For each list, low-priced utilities, like screen savers, which dominate the lists, were not included.

Top-Selling Personal Productivity Software

Product	Company
Quicken for Windows	Intuit
Quicken 6.0	Intuit
Print Shop Deluxe	Brøderbund
Print Shop Deluxe for Windows	Brøderbund
TurboTax	Chipsoft

Top-Selling Windows Productivity Software

Product	Company
Access	Microsoft
Windows 3.1	Microsoft
WordPerfect Upgrade	WordPerfect
Norton Desktop	Symantec
Corel Draw 3.0	Corel

Top-Selling Mac Productivity Software

Product	Company
Office	Microsoft
Works 3.0	Microsoft
Word 5.0	Microsoft
Excel Upgrade	Microsoft
Works 3.0 Upgrade	Microsoft

Top-Selling DOS Productivity Software

Product	Company
DOS 5.0 Upgrade	Microsoft
DOS 5.0	Microsoft
Stacker	Stac
QEMM	Quarterdeck
WordPerfect 5.1	WordPerfect

Source: PC Research (703) 435-1025

The Top Reference Sources

Before & After
(916) 784-3880

A four-color newsletter devoted to teaching amateur computer users to look like professionals in print.

In-depth, step-by-step instructions on how to choose type, draw shadows, buttons, or logos, even use photos in articles. This is consistently the best written, best designed publication we receive. A must.

Personal Computer Sales

Top U.S. Personal Computer Vendors by Unit Shipments, 1990 and 1991

Rank	Vendor	1990 Shipments	% Share	1991 Shipments	% Share	1990-91 % Change
1	IBM	1,517,500	16.5	1,360,000	14.3	-10.4
2	Apple	1,019,120	11.1	1,340,045	14.1	31.5
3	Packard Bell	371,500	4.0	455,000	4.8	22.5
4	Compaq	425,300	4.6	390,000	4.1	-8.3
5	Tandy/Grid	468,500	5.1	349,250	3.7	-25.5
6	AST Research	172,200	1.9	261,490	2.8	51.9
7	Gateway 2000	94,950	1.0	246,774	2.6	159.9
8	VTech Computers	206,850	2.3	220,000	2.3	6.4
9	Groupe Bull/ZDS	216,100	2.4	202,761	2.1	-6.2
10	Toshiba America	209,600	2.3	181,500	1.9	-13.4

Top U.S. Personal Computer Vendors by Value of Shipments, 1990 and 1991

Rank	Vendor	1990 Sales ($ thousands)	% Share	1991 Sales ($ thousands)	% Share	1990-91 % Change
1	IBM	4,591,700	20.4	4,089,450	18.7	-10.9
2	Apple	2,647,066	11.7	2,659,677	12.1	0.5
3	Compaq	1,547,850	6.9	1,231,700	5.6	-20.4
4	Packard Bell	660,650	2.9	820,560	3.7	24.2
5	Tandy/Grid	1,066,498	4.7	804,615	3.7	-24.6
6	AST Research	578,506	2.6	796,677	3.6	37.7
7	NCR/AT&T	721,375	3.2	657,315	3.0	-8.9
8	Gateway 2000	239,248	1.1	618,034	2.8	158.3
9	Groupe Bull/ZDS	703,400	3.1	576,962	2.6	-18.0
10	Toshiba America	532,380	2.4	494,800	2.3	-7.1

Source: IDG

Total U.S. Personal Computer Shipments

Year	PC Shipments
1982	3,039,772
1983	5,450,167
1984	6,654,318
1985	5,710,395
1986	6,751,642
1987	8,117,395
1988	8,622,176
1989	8,860,205
1990	9,186,916
1991	9,485,122
1992*	11,000,000

*Estimated

Top-Selling DOS Productivity Software

Product	Company
DOS 5.0 Upgrade	Microsoft
DOS 5.0	Microsoft
Stacker	Stac
QEMM	Quarterdeck
WordPerfect 5.1	WordPerfect

Source: PC Research (703) 435-1025

Top-Selling Windows Productivity Software

Product	Company
Access	Microsoft
Windows 3.1	Microsoft
WordPerfect Upgrade	WordPerfect
Norton Desktop	Symantec
Corel Draw 3.0	Corel

Top-Selling Mac Productivity Software

Product	Company
Office	Microsoft
Works 3.0	Microsoft
Word 5.0	Microsoft
Excel Upgrade	Microsoft
Works 3.0 Upgrade	Microsoft

Source: IDG

Ordering by Mail

THE BEST PRICES, delivery, and support on computer hardware and software are often found from mail order dealers. Use a credit card to avoid late or non-existent delivery.

Contact Options

Ordering Software and Peripherals by Mail:

Mac's Place
(800) 367-4222

Micro Connection
(800) 422-2531

PC Connection
(800) 243-8088

River Computer (Mac)
(800) 998-0090

Tiger Software
(800) 888-4437

Ordering a Computer by Mail:

Acer
(800) 733-2227

AST
(800) 876-4277

Compudyne
(800) 932-2667

Dell
(800) 289-1210

Gateway
(800) 523-2000

PC Brand
(800) 722-7263

Zeos
(800) 423-5891

DOS Commands

DOS IS THE OPERATING SYSTEM used by more than 100 million computers around the world. Here are 28 common DOS commands, together with a brief description of their functions.

BACKUP	Archives data
BREAK	Turns cntrl–c on and off
CD	Change directory
CHKDSK	Checks a disk
CLS	Clear screen
COMP	Compares two files
COPY	Copy a file
DATE	Sets the date
DEL	Delete
DIR	Directory
DISKCOPY	Copy all files on a disk
FIND	Searches for text in a file
FORMAT	Wipes a disk and prepares for use
MD	Makes a directory
MEM	Describes memory status
MODE	Sets defaults
MORE	Pauses the printout of a text file
PATH	Accesses other subdirectories
PROMPT	Changes the C: prompt
REN	Rename
RESTORE	Opposite of backup
SYS	Makes a disk bootable
TIME	Sets the time
TYPE	Prints a text file to the screen
VER	Lets you know what version of DOS is running
VERIFY	Double-checks all disk writes
VOL	Tells you a disk's volume
XCOPY	Better than Copy

The Top Reference Sources

The Macintosh Bible
Peachpit Press, $19
(800) 283-9444

The Macintosh Bible is a mammoth collection of tips, techniques, tricks, and advice. There should be a copy next to every Macintosh in the office.

Other books in the series include easy-to-use books on FileMaker, Excel, MacDraw, and a book called *What Do I Do Now?* that is ideal for novice users.

Networking

NETWORKING PERSONAL COMPUTERS seems easy. For many businesses, however, it often takes more time and money to establish a network than it does to purchase the computers in the first place.

There are several competing networking standards, including Appletalk, Ethernet, and Netware from Novell. For more information on each format, and to determine which is best for your organization, contact the Novell Netware hotline at (800) 638-9273. They publish a 100-page guide to networking that is free on request.

Also available is an electronic faxback system that will automatically send information on a wide variety of topics to any fax machine. To access the system, dial (800) 638-9273 and press 6, then 100.

Recommended Resource

Novell
122 East 1700 South
Provo, UT 84606
(800) 638-9273

Computer Products Phone Directory

Company	Telephone
3-D Visions	(800) 729-4723
Abacus Concepts	(510) 540-1949
Acer	(800) 733-2227
Adobe	(800) 833–6687
AEC	(800) 346-9413
Agfa Division, Miles	(508) 658-5600
Aladdin Systems	(408) 761-6200
Aldus	(800) 888-6293
Alki Software	(800) 669-9673
ALR	(800) 444-4257
Altra	(800) 726-6153
Altsys	(214) 680-2060
American Power Conversion	(800) 800-4172
Apple	(800) 767-2775
Approach Software	(800) 277-7622
APS	(800) 235-2750
Ares	(415) 578-9090
Artisoft	(800) 846-9726
AST	(800) 876-4277
ATI Technologies	(416) 756-0718
Attain	(617) 776-1110
Autodesk	(800) 964-6432
Avantos Performance Systems	(800) 282-8268
Berkeley Systems	(510) 540-5535
Beyond	(617) 621-0095
Borland International	(800) 331-0877
Brøderbund Software	(415) 382-4400
Caere	(800) 535-7226
Central Point Software	(800) 445-4208
ChipSoft	(619) 453-8722

Company	Telephone
Claris	(408) 727-8227
Colorado Memory Systems	(800) 845-7905
Compaq	(800) 345-1518
Compudyne	(800) 932-2667
CompuServe	(800) 848-8199
Computer Associates	(800) 225-5224
Connectix	(415) 571-5100
Corel Systems	(800) 836-3729
Crystal Computer Services	(604) 681-3435
Curtis	(800) 548-4900
DacEasy	(800) 322-3279
DataStorm	(314) 443-3282
Dayna	(801) 531-0600
Daystar Digital	(800) 962-2077
DCA	(800) 348-3221
Dell	(800) 289-1210
DeLorme	(207) 865-1234
Delrina Technology	(800) 268-6082
DeltaPoint	(800) 367-4334
DeScribe	(800) 448-1586
Digidesign	(415) 688-0600
Digital	(508) 486-5198
Dow Jones	(800) 522-3567
DuPont	(302) 774-1000
Edmark	(206) 556-8400
Electric Image	(818) 577-1627
Electronics for Imaging	(415) 286-8600
Epson	(800) 289-3776
Equilibrium Technologies	(415) 332-4343
E–Machines	(503) 646–6699
Farallon	(800) 949-7761

Computer Products Phone Directory (cont'd)

Company	Telephone
Fifth Generation Systems	(504) 291-7221
Focus	(800) 538-8866
Fractal Design	(408) 688-5300
Frame Technology	(408) 366-2717
FutureSoft	(713) 496-9400
Gateway 2000	(800) 232-2000
Global Village	(415) 329-0700
Gold Disk	(800) 465-3375
Graphsoft	(410) 461-9488
Haven Tree	(800) 267-0668
Hayes	(800) 374-8388
hDC Computer	(800) 321-4606
Heizer Software	(800) 888-7667
Helix	(708) 205–1669
Hewlett Packard	(800) 752-0900
Hyundai	(800) 933-3445
IBM	(800) 426-2468
Inset Systems	(800) 374-6738
Intel	(800) 538-3373
Intuit	(800) 624-8742
Jensen-Jones	(800) 289-1548
Kaetron	(713) 890–3434
Kingston	(714) 435-2600
Knowledge Garden	(516) 246-5400
Knowledge Revolution	(415) 554-8153
LaserMaster	(800) 365-4646
Leading Edge	(800) 874-3340
Lexmark	(800) 358-5835
Light Source	(800) 231-7226
Logitech	(800) 231-7717
Lotus	(800) 448-2500
Lotus Development	(800) 343-5414
MapInfo	(800) 327-8627
Matrox	(800) 361-4903
Maynard	(800) 821-8782
MCI	(800) 444-6245
Media Vision	(800) 348–7116
METZ Software	(800) 447-1712
Micro Logic	(800) 342-5930
Micrografx	(800) 998-6131
Microsoft	(800) 426-9400
Moon Valley Software	(602) 375-9502
Mouse Systems	(510) 656-1117
M•USA	(800) 933-6872
Nanao USA	(310) 325-5202
National Instruments	(800) 433-3488
NEC	(800) 388-8888
Newgen	(800) 756-0556
Niko Mak	(800) 242-4775
Novell	(800) 526-5463
Now Software	(503) 274-2800

Company	Telephone
Number Nine Computer	(800) 438-6463
nView	(804) 873-1354
Okidata	(800) 654-8326
Onyx Computing	(617) 876-3876
Orchid Technologies	(510) 683-0300
Oxford University Press	(212) 679-7300
Panasonic	(800) 742-8086
Paper Direct	(800) 272-7377
PC Brand	(800) 722-7263
PC Kwik	(503) 644-5644
PC Paintbrush	(800) 444-4780
Peachpit Press	(510) 548-4393
Peachtree	(404) 564-5800
PineCliffe International	(800) 659-4696
Pinnacle Micro	(800) 553-7070
Pixar	(510) 236-4000
Plannet Crafters	(404) 740-9821
Powercard	(800) 637-2797
PowerUp!	(800) 851-2917
Premia	(800) 547- 9902
QMS	(205) 633-4300
Qualitas	(301) 907-6700
Quantum	(800) 624-5545
Quark	(303) 894-8888
Que Software	(800) 428-5331
Radius	(800) 452-5524
RasterOps	(800) 729–2656
Ray Dream	(800) 846-0111
Saber Software	(800) 338-8754
Sceptre	(800) 788-2878
Seagate	(408) 438-8111
Sharp	(800) 321-8877
Sheridan Software	(516) 753-0985
Shiva	(617) 252-6300
Shiva	(617) 252-6300
Softsync	(305) 444–0080
Software Publishing	(408) 986-8000
Software Ventures	(510) 644-3232
Sophisticated Circuits	(206) 485-7979
Specular International	(413) 549-7600
Stac Electronics	(800) 522-7822
Storm	(415) 691-1111
SuperMac	(800) 334-3005
SWFTE International	(800) 237-9383
Symantec	(800) 441-7234
Symantec	(800) 441-7234
Systems Compatibility	(312) 329-0700
T-Maker	(415) 962-0195
Tektronix	(800) 835-6100
Teleware	(201) 586-2200
Texas Instruments	(800) 527-3500

Computer Products Phone Directory (cont'd)

Company	Telephone
The Voyager Company	(310) 451-1383
Timeworks	(708) 559-1300
Tool Technology Publishing	(415) 459-3700
Toshiba	(800) 334-3445
Turtle Beach Systems	(717) 843-6916
U-Lead Systems,	(800) 858-5323
Userland	(415) 369-6600
VideoFusion Partnership	(419) 891-9767
ViewSonic	(800) 888-8583
Warner New Media	(818) 955–9999
WordPerfect	(800) 451-5151
Xtree	(800) 395-8733
Zeos	(800) 423-5891
Zyxel	(800) 255-4101

Shareware

SHAREWARE IS AN ALTERNATIVE METHOD of software distribution. Instead of packaging the product and offering it for sale through dealers or mail order vendors, the author of the software posts a copy on various electronic bulletin boards (e.g. CompuServe) and allows users to try it for free. If the software does what it claims, and you find it useful, you're expected to send the requested fee directly to the author.

The only downsides of shareware are the lack of uniformity in technical support and the sometimes unpolished nature of the software.

The Top 10 PC Shareware Programs

- Desktop Paint 256 (Paint Program)
- Sky Globe (Star Map)
- ViruScan (Virus Dectector)
- Graphics Workshop (File Converter and Editor)
- Graphics Workshop for Windows (File Converter and Editor)
- News of the Past (Historical Timeline)
- Secrets of Credit Repair (How to Improve a Credit Rating)
- Quikmenu (DOS Shell)
- Family History (Genealogy)
- Print Partner (Banner Printer)

Source: Association of Shareware Professionals

The Top Mac Shareware Programs

- AKA (Aliases)
- Beatsville (Font)
- DateKey (Date utility)
- Disinfectant (Viruses)
- dropple menu (System 7 shortcut)
- FlashWrite II (Word processor)
- Image (Image processor)
- Inigo Gets Out (HyperCard game)
- KidPix (Painting program)
- Mariner (Spreadsheet)
- MaxAppleZoom (Monitor enhancement)
- NetTrek (Game)
- Oscar the Grouch (Animated singing puppet)
- PopChar (Key finder)
- Programmer's Key (Interrupt switch)
- Solarian II (Game)
- SoundMaster (Sound)
- StuffIt Lite (Compression)
- Thomas (Font)
- To Do! (Scheduler)
- ZTerm (Communications)

Source: The Mac Shareware 500, Ventana Press

Recommended Resources

CWI
(800) 777-5636

Public Brand Software
(800) 426-3475

Shareware Express
(800) 346-2842

Ziffnet on CompuServe
(800) 848-8199

America Online
(800) 827-6364

Upgrading an Existing PC or Mac

AS PERSONAL COMPUTERS become more advanced, the chances that a company's PCs are "obsolete" increase. With the price of used computers plummeting, it usually makes more sense to upgrade than to replace an existing machine. Here are the ten most effective ways to get more out of a computer.

1. Buy more memory.

No computer has enough. Buy memory (SIMMs) from a reputable company like Techworks or the Chip Merchant. On some machines, the memory is easy to install. On others, see a dealer. Remember: always buy as much as you can afford–the bigger memory chips are usually worth it.

2. Get a bigger screen.

Studies have shown that, depending on the task, a user's productivity can increase as much as 100% with a larger work area. 19 inches is ideal for most spreadsheet, graphics, and word processing users.

3. Install a bigger hard drive.

More complicated software (especially Windows or complex graphic modeling tools) use lots of disk space. The price of hard disk storage has declined significantly. Look for a brand of drive with at least two years of history in the market, and a warranty of at least two years.

4. Install a better/faster printer.

Buy a PostScript printer (for more fonts and better graphics), or a printer with greater resolution (measured in dpi or dots per inch). Owners of sophisticated printers should consider adding a color printer.

5. Get an accelerator board.

These boards work with (or replace) an existing computer chip to dramatically speed up the computer. Some accelerators can increase speed by as many as ten times (that means that an activity that took 60 seconds–like opening a large spreadsheet–now takes 6). Daystar is the leader in the Mac market, while ATI is a leader in the PC market.

6. Buy a backup device.

No one likes to backup, but every competent user must. Tape drives or removable bulk storage make it more painless. Investigate digital audio tapes, cartridge, Bernoulli, or Syquest devices (available from many vendors) that make backup automatic and foolproof.

7. Take a training course.

Often the bottleneck isn't the computer, it's the user. Investigate courses that can help a user become even more expert at the software already used.

8. Buy and use a macro program.

Macro programs remember keystrokes and make it easy to automate repetitive tasks. Type a return address with one keystroke, or reserve a function key to automatically open a file, print it out, update it, and save a backup. A popular tool for the Mac is Quickkeys, and there are several specialized ones available for the PC.

9. Get a very fast fax modem.

With prices falling every day, fax modems are an easy choice. Send a fax without printing the document and walking across the office to feed it into a busy machine. The built-in modem allows a user to access bulletin boards and gain free access to huge amounts of data. In addition, electronic mail will dramatically increase a user's ability to communicate with others.

10. Buy an Uninterruptible Power Supply.

A little box that resembles a surge supressor, sometimes called a UPS, can automatically protect a computer from blackouts or power surges.

The Top Reference Sources

MacWEEK
Ziff Davis, Controlled
(415) 243-3500

InfoWorld
IDG, Controlled
(800) 227-8365

MacWEEK is the ultimate resource for the computer manager responsible for Macintoshes. Every week, the magazine offers fresh graphics, helpful advice, and the inside news on new technology.

MacWEEK is a controlled circulation magazine, so you must qualify to get a subscription.

InfoWorld focuses on the issues facing managers who deal with computers. The reviews are among the best in the industry, and the news is usually more current and specific than you'll find anywhere else.

Computer Resources

Insurance
Safeware
2929 N. High St. Box 02211
Columbus OH 43202
(800) 848-3469

The Computer Insurance Agency
6150 Old Millersport Rd., NE
Pleasantville, OH 43148
(800) 722-0385

Typefaces
FontHaus
15 Perry Ave., A7
Norwalk, CT 06850
(800) 942-9110

Monotype
(800) 666-6897

Handwriting Faces
Lazy Dog Foundry
316 Bates Ave.
St. Paul, MN 55106
(800) 876-9807

Off Site Data Storage
Iron Mountain
(617) 357-6966

Hard Disk Crash Recovery
Drivesavers
30-D Pamaron Way
Novato CA 94949
(415) 883-4232

Data Recovery Technology
(408) 943-9401

Computer Peripheral Repair
7570 S. U.S. Highway 1, Suite 10
Hypoluxo, FL 33462
(800) 765-9292

Software Piracy
Software Publishers of America
(800) 388-7478

Technical Support
TeleGuru
Seneca Corporation
(703) 448-6100

CD ROM
CD–ROM Professional
Magazine for CD ROM Publishers
Pemberton Press
462 Danbury Rd.
Wilton, CT 06897
(203) 761-1466

Data Entry (keyboarding)
Quadrant USA
P.O. Box 7788
Nashua, NH 03060
(603) 888-5969

Sencor Systems
Box 6818
New York, NY 10151
(212) 980-5146

Specialized Software Directories
Redgate Communications
660 Bechland Blvd.
Vero Beach, FL 32963
(407) 231-6904

Smileys

WHEN SENDING ELECTRONIC MAIL, users often want to express more emotion than the keyboard allows. These "smileys" can be more easily understood if you tilt your head to the left.

Smiley	Meaning
:-)	Your basic smiley
:)	Midget smiley
,-)	Winking happy smiley
(-:	Left-handed smiley
(:-)	Smiley big-face
(:-(	Very unhappy smiley
,-}	Wry and winking smiley

Smiley	Meaning
'-)	Winking smiley
:-#	My lips are sealed
:-*	Kiss
:-/	Skeptical smiley
:->	Sarcastic smiley
:-@	Screaming smiley
:-V	Shouting smiley
:-X	A big wet kiss!
:-\	Undecided smiley
:-]	Smiley blockhead
;-(	Crying smiley
>;->	A very lewd remark was just made

Source: The Smiley Dictionary

Electronic Mail

USING ELECTRONIC MAIL (E-MAIL), a business can instantly send a message or computer file to an employee or customer anywhere in the world. Unlike faxes, e-mail permits the recipient to edit the message and work with the data sent.

Just like faxes, e-mail requires that both parties have the right equipment. There are several different e-mail services, but fortunately a common standard is developing which permits them to speak to each other.

All electronic bulletin boards and information services provide their users with access to e-mail within the system. It is a straightforward and simple task to send mail to anyone on the same system. For this reason, many companies are asking their employees and customers to join one system or another.

Inter-bulletin board communication is handled through the Internet. Once an Internet address is known, most information systems (and some bulletin boards) permit users to send mail through the internet. For example, to reach the editors of the Business Almanac, send mail from any service with Internet access to the Internet address: SETHWOOD@AOL.COM.

Contact Options

Popular Electronic Mail Services:

MCI Mail
(800) 444-6245

CompuServe
(800) 848-8199

ATT Mail
(800) 367-7225

America Online
(800) 827-6364

(See also, the Internet, below)

The Internet

MORE THAN 20 YEARS AGO, DARPA, a division of the Pentagon, created a network of computers being used by its researchers. These computers were located at universities and research facilities around the world.

The purpose of the network was to permit researchers at one facility to contact others, and to exchange information as well.

Once the protocol for this network was established, the number of users and number of uses skyrocketed. With more than five million people currently "on" the Internet, it has become the de facto standard for electronic mail.

In addition to a huge base of mail users, the Internet provides access to hundreds of millions of pieces of data. A quick search could find a state of the art paper on the uses of silicon in biomedical engineering, or an article spoofing the latest state of the union address.

Access to the Internet

There are two levels of access. Using the Internet standard for sending electronic mail is simple and cheap. America Online, CompuServe, and MCI Mail all provide easy access.

If a user needs to access the many articles, conversation threads, and research services of the Internet, more complex and expensive software is needed.

The Hayes Command Set

VIRTUALLY ALL MODEMS for personal computers use Hayes-compatible modems. These modems can be controlled using an arcane code–speaker volume, auto answer, speed, and other features can be easily set once you know the proper code.

Code	Modem Operation
ATA	Answer phone immediately
ATDT	Tone dial the phone
ATH0	Hang up

Code	Modem Operation
ATL1	Make speaker soft
ATL3	Make speaker loud
ATM0	Turn monitor speaker (dial tone) off
ATDP	Pulse dial the phone
ATS0=1	Auto answer on one ring
ATS8=4	Set the pause for a comma in the phone number to 4 seconds
ATZ	Reset the modem

Online Services

CompuServe

CompuServe is one of the oldest and largest online services. As the de facto standard, it offers a wide range of software and advice, allows users to send and receive electronic mail, and provides a wide range of non-computer related information.

CompuServe offers a nationwide network of local phone numbers, which can be easily accessed by anyone with a computer and a modem. To obtain a local access number, call (800) 848-8199, 24 hours a day.

Once connected to CompuServe, the user can get detailed information on more than 1,000 topics, from wood carving to Amiga computers.

Divided into forums, the CompuServe service has segmented its users into nearly 1,000 special interest areas. This specialization allows the user to post a message directly to the people most interested in the topic. It's not unusual to post a question about a piece of software and receive more than a dozen answers within an hour.

In addition to forums and access to free files, CompuServe offers access to the Eaasy Saabre travel reservations system, as well as dozens of other commercial services and databases. CompuServe will also monitor the wire services on request, clipping any stories that contain the keywords that the user has identified.

The easiest way to use CompuServe is to home in on the areas that are of interest. Here is a complete listing of CompuServe forums, together with the jump word for accessing them.

ACIUS Forum	ACIUS
AI Expert Forum	AIEXPERT
APPC Info Exchange Forum	APPCFORUM
ASP/Shareware Forum	ASPFORUM
Adobe Forum	ADOBE
Aldus Customer Service Forum	ALDSVC
Aldus Forum	ALDUSFORUM
Aldus Special Programs Forum	ALDUSSP
Amiga Arts Forum	AMIGAARTS
Amiga Tech Forum	AMIGATECH
Amiga User's Forum	AMIGAUSER
Amiga Vendor Forum	AMIGAVENDOR
Apple II Programmers Forum	APPROG
Apple II Users Forum	APPUSER
Apple II Vendor Forum	APIIVEN
Aquaria/Fish Forum	FISHNET
Artisoft Forum	ARTISOFT
Ask3Com Forum	ASKFORUM
Astronomy Forum	ASTROFORUM
Atari 8-Bit Forum	ATARI8
Atari Portfolio Forum	APORTFOLIO
Atari ST Arts Forum	ATARIARTS
Atari ST Productivity Forum	ATARIPRO
Atari Vendor Forum	ATARIVEN
Autodesk AutoCAD Forum	ACAD
Autodesk Retail Forum	ARETAIL
Autodesk Software Forum	ASOFT
Automobile Forum	CARS
Aviation Forum	AVSIG
BASIS International Forum	BASIS
Bacchus Wine Forum	WINEFORUM
Banyan Forum	BANFORUM
Blyth Forum	BLYTH
Borland Applications Forum	BORAPP
Borland C++/DOS Forum	BCPPDOS
Borland C++/Windows Forum	BCPPWIN
Borland Dbase Products Forum	BORDB
Borland Developer Tool Forum	BDEVTOOLS
Borland GmbH Forum	BORGMBH
Borland Paradox/Windows Forum	PDOXWIN
Borland PASCAL Forum	BPASCAL
Borland Quattro Pro Forum	QUATTROPRO
Borland dBASE Forum	DBASE
Broadcast Professionals Forum	BPFORUM
CADD/CAM/CAE Vendor Forum	CADDVEN
CASE DCI Forum	CASEFORUM
CB Forum	CBFORUM
CDROM Forum	CDROM
CIM Support Forum (FREE)	CIMSUPPORT
CIM for Windows Support Forum	WCIMSUPPORT
CP/M Users Group Forum	CPMFORUM
Cabletron Systems Forum	CTRONFORUM
Campaign 92 Forum	VOTEFORUM
Cancer Forum	CANCER
Cannon Support Forum	CAN-10
Canopus Research Forum	CANOPUS
Central Point DOS Forum	CPSDOS
Central Point Win/Mac Forum	CPSWIN
Chess Forum	CHESSFORUM
Clarion Forum	CLARION
Claris Forum	CLARIS
Client Server Computing Forum	MSNETWORKS
Cobb Applications Forum	COBBAPP
Cobb Group Programming Forum	COBBPROG
Coin/Stamp/Collectibles Forum	COLLECT
Color Compuer Forum	COCO
Comics/Animation Forum	COMICS
Commodore Applications Forum	CBMAPP
Commodore Art/Games Forum	CBMART
Commodore Service Forum	CBMSERVICE
Compaq Computer Forum	CPQFORUM
CompuAdd Forum	COMPUADD
CompuServe Help Forum	HELPFORUM
CompuServe Pacific Forum	PACFORUM
Computer Art Forum	COMART
Computer Assoc App Dev Forum	CAIDEV
Computer Assoc Clipper Forum	CLIPPER
Computer Assoc Clipper Germany	CLIPGER
Computer Assoc Prof Solutions	CAIPRO
Computer Assoc VAX/UNIX Forum	CAIMINI
Computer Club Forum	CLUB
Computer Consultant's Forum	CONSULT
Computer Language Forum	CLMFORUM
Computer Shopper Forum	COMPSHOPPER
Computer Training Forum	DPTRAIN
Consumer Electronics Forum	CEFORUM
Cooks Online Forum	COOKS
Corel Support Forum	COREL
Corporate Computing Forum	CORPORATE
Court Reporters Forum	CRFORUM
Crafts Forum	CRAFTS
Crosstalk Forum	XTALK
DATASTORM Forum	DATASTORM
DBMS Magazine Forum	DBMSFORUM
DEC PC Forum	DECPC

Online Services (cont'd)

DEC PC Integration Forum	DECPCI
DELL Forum	DELL
Data Access Forum	DACCESS
Data Based Advisor Forum	DBADVISOR
DataEase International Forum	DATAEASE
Dear FocWizards Forums	FOCWIZARD
Desktop Publish. Vendor Forum	DTPVENDOR
Desktop Publishing Forum	DTPFORUM
Deutsches Computer Forum	GERNET
Developers Contest Forum	DEVCONTEST
Diabetes Forum	DIABETES
Digitalk Forum	DIGITALK
Disabilities Forum	DISABILITIES
Dr. Dobbs Journal Forum	DDJFORUM
Dr. Neuhaus Forum	NHDFORUM
EETnet Engineering Forum	ENGINEERING
EETnet Profession Forum	PROFESSIONS
EICON Technology Forum	EICON
Education Forum	EDFORUM
Educational Research Forum	EDRESEARCH
Electronic Frontier Forum	EFFSIG
Engineering Automation Forum	LEAP
Epson Forum	EPSON
Executives Online Forum	EXECUTIVES
Federation Intl Distributions	FEDERATION
Fifth Generation Forum	FIFTHGEN
Fine Art Forum	FINEART
Fishnet - ADC Forum	AQUADATA
Flight Simulator Forum	FSFORUM
Florida Forum	FLORIDA
FocServices Forum	FOCSERVICES
Focus User's Group	FUSE
Foreign Lang. Education Forum	FLEFO
Forth Forum/Creative Solution	FORTH
Fox Software Forum	FOXFORUM
Game Publishers A Forum	GAMAPUB
Game Publishers B Forum	GAMBPUB
Gamers Forum	GAMERS
Gardening Forum	GARDENING
Genealogy Forum	ROOTS
Global Crisis Forum	CRISIS
Graphics Corner Forum	CORNER
Graphics Developers Forum	GRAPHDEV
Graphics Gallery Forum	GALLERY
Graphics Plus Forum	GRAPHPLUS
Graphics Support Forum	GRAPHSUPPORT
Graphics Vendor Forum	GRAPHVEN
Graphics Vendor B Forum	GRAPHBVEN
HP Handheld Forum	HPHAND
HP Peripherials Forum	HPPER
HP Systems Forum	HPSYS
HamNet Ham Radio Forum	HAMNET
Hayes Forum	HAYFORUM
Health & Fitness Forum	GOODHEALTH
Human Sexuality Adult Forum	HSX200
Human Sexuality Open Forum	HSX100
Human Society of U.S. Forum	HSUS
IBM Applications Forum	IBMAPP
IBM Bulletin Board Forum	IBMBBS
IBM Communications Forum	IBMCOM
IBM Desktop Software Forum	IBMDESK
IBM European Users Forum	IBMEUROPE
IBM Hardware Forum	IBMHW
IBM Lan Mgmt Utilities/2 Forum+	LMU2FORUM
IBM New Users Forum	IBMNEW
IBM OS/2 Developer's Forum #1	OS2DF1
IBM OS/2 Developer's Forum #2	OS2DF2
IBM OS/2 Support Forum	OS2SUPPORT
IBM OS/2 User's Forum	OS2USER
IBM Programming Forum	IBMPRO
IBM Systems/Utilities Forum	IBMSYS
IBM/Special Needs Forum	IBMSPECIAL
IBM ThinkPad Forum	THINKPAD
Int'l Entrepreneurs Network	USEN
Intel Access/iRUG Forum	INTELACCESS
Intel Forum	INTELFORUM
Investors Forum	INVFORUM
Issues Forum	ISSUESFORUM
Japan Forum	EET331
Javelin/EXPRESS Forum	IRIFORUM
Journalism Forum	JFORUM
LDC Word Processing Forum	LOTUSWP
LDOS/TRSDOS6 Users Forum	LDOS
LOGO Forum	LOGOFORUM
Lan Magazine Forum	LANMAG
Lan Technology Forum	LANTECH
Legal Forum	LAWSIG
Literary Forum	LITFORUM
Logitech Forum	LOGITECH
Lotus Spreadsheets Forum	LOTUSA
Lotus Words & Pixels Forum	LOTUSB
MECA Software Forum	MECA
MIDI Vendor Forum	MIDIAVENDOR
MIDI Vendor B Forum	MIDIBVENDOR
MIDI/Music Forum	MIDIFORUM
Mac A Vendor Forum	MACAVEN
Mac Applications Forum	MACAP
Mac B Vendor Forum	MACBVEN
Mac C Vendor Forum	MACCVEN
Mac D Vendor Forum	MACDVEN
Mac CIM Support Forum (FREE)	MCIMSUPPORT
Mac Communications Forum	MACCOMM
Mac Community Clubhouse Forum	MACCLUB
Mac Developers Forum	MACDEV
Mac Fun/Entertainment Forum	MACFUN
Mac Hardware Forum	MACHW
Mac Hypertext Forum	MACHYPER
Mac New Users/Help Forum	MACNEW
Mac System Software Forum	MACSYS
MacUser Forum	MACUSER
MacWEEK Forum	MACWEEK
Macromedia Forum	MACROMEDIA
Markt & Technik Deutschland	MUTFORUM
Masonry Forum	MASONRY
McAfee Virus Help Forum	VIRUSFORUM
MedSIG Forum	MEDSIG
Mensa Forum	MENSA
Microsoft Applications Forum	MSAPP
Microsoft Access Forum	MSACCESS
Microsoft BASIC Forum	MSBASIC
Microsoft Benelux Forum	MSBF
Microsoft Central Europe Forum	MSCE
Microsoft Central Europe System+	MSCESYSTEM
Microsoft DOS Forum	MSDOS
Microsoft Developer Library	MSDNLIB
Microsoft Developer Relations	MSDR
Microsoft Excel Forum	MSEXCEL
Microsoft Languages Forum	MSLANG
Microsoft SQL Server Forum	MSSQL
Microsoft WIN32 Forum	MSWIN32
Microsoft Windows Advanced	WINADV
Microsoft Windows NewUsers	WINNEW
Microsoft Windows SDK Forum	WINSDK
Microsoft Word Forum	MSWORD
Military Forum	MILITARY

Online Services (cont'd)

Model Aviation Forum	MODELNET
Modem Games Forum	MODEMGAMES
Modem Vendor Forum	MODEMVENDOR
Motor Sports Forum	RACING
Multi-Player Games Forum	MPGAMES
MultiMedia Conference Forum	MULTICON
MultiMedia Forum	MULTIMEDIA
MultiMedia Vendor Forum	MULTIVEN
Music/Arts Forum	MUSICARTS
NAIC Investor Education Forum	NAIC
Navigator Support Forum	NAVSUPPORT
NeXT Forum	NEXTFORUM
New Age Forum	NEWAGE
Novell A Forum	NOVA
Novell B Forum	NOVB
Novell C Forum	NOVC
Novell Desktop Systems Group	DRFORUM
Novell Library Forum	NOVLIB
Novell NetWare 2.X Forum	NETW2X
Novell NetWare 3.X Forum	NETW3X
Novell Vendor Forum	NOVVEN
OS-9 Forum	OS9
Oracle Support Forum	ORACLE
Outdoors Forum	OUTDOORFORUM
PC Contact Forum	PCCONTACT
PC MagNet: After Hours Forum	AFTERHOURS
PC MagNet: Editorial Forum	EDITORIAL
PC MagNet: Programming Forum	PROGRAMMING
PC MagNet: Utilities Forum	UTILFORUM
PC Magazine UK Forum	PCMAGUK
PC Plus/PC Answers Forum	PCPFORUM
PC Sources Forum	SOURCES
PC Vendor A Forum	PCVENA
PC Vendor B Forum	PCVENB
PC Vendor C Forum	PCVENC
PC Vendor D Forum	PCVEND
PC Vendor E Forum	PCVENE
PC Vendor F Forum	PCVENF
PC Vendor G Forum	PCVENG
PC Week: Buyers' Forum	PCWEEK
PDP-11 Forum	PDP11
PR & Marketing Forum	PRSIG
Packard Bell Forum	PACKARDBELL
Palmtop Forum	PALMTOP
Pen Technology Forum	PENFORUM
Pets/Animal Forum	PETS
Photography Forum	PHOTOFORUM
Play-By-Mail Games Forum	PBMGAMES
Portable Programming Forum	CODEPORT
Practical Peripherals Forum	PPIFORUM
Practice Forum	PRACTICE
Prisma Deutschland Forum	PRISMA
Public Brand Software App Forum	PBSAPPSZNT
Public Brand Software Arcade	PBSARCADE
Quarterdeck Support Forum	QUARTERDECK
Quick Pictures Forum	QPICS
Religion Forum	RELIGION
Revelation Tech Forum	REVELATION
RockNet Forum	ROCKNET
Role-Playing Games Forum	RPGAMES
Safetynet Forum	SAFETY
Sailing Forum	SAILING
Santa Cruz Operation Forum	SCOFORUM
Science/Math Education Forum	SCIENCE
Science Fiction & Fantasy Forum	SCI-FI
Scuba Forum	DIVING
ShowBiz Forum	SHOWBIZ
Siemens Automatisierungs Forum	AUTFORUM
Software Publisher Assn Forum	SPAFORUM
Software Publishing Forum	SPCFORUM
Solutions Australia Forum	SOLUTIONS
Space/Astronomy Forum	SPACEFORUM
Spinnaker Software Forum	SPINNAKER
Sports Forum	FANS
Stac Electronics Forum	STACKER
Standard Microsystem Forum	SMC
Students' Forum	STUFO
Symantec Applications Forum	SYMFORUM
Symantec/Norton Utility Forum	NORUTL
TAPCIS Forum	TAPCIS
TBS Network Earth Forum	EARTH
Tandy Model 100 Forum	M100SIG
Tandy Professional Forum	TRS80PRO
Telecommunication Issues Forum	TELECOM
Texas Instruments Forum	TIFORUM
Thomas-Conrad Support Forum	TCCFORUM
Toshiba Forum	TOSHIBA
Toshiba GmbH Forum	TOSHGER
TrainNet Forum	TRAINNET
Travel Forum	TRAVSIG
UK Computer Shopper Forum	UKSHOPPER
UK Computing Forum	UKCOMPUTING
UK Forum	UKFORUM
UK Share Forum	UKSHARE
Ultimedia Tools Series A Forum	ULTIATOOLS
Ultimedia Tools Series B Forum	ULTIBTOOLS
Unix Forum	UNIXFORUM
UserLand Forum	USERLAND
VAX Forum	VAXFORUM
Venture Software Inc Forum	VENTURA
Wang Support Forum	WANGFORUM
Windows 3rd Party A Forum	WINAPA
Windows 3rd Party B Forum	WINAPB
Windows 3rd Party C Forum	WINAPC
Windows 3rd Party D Forum	WINAPD
Windows Extensions Forum	WINEXT
WinNT Pre-Release Forum	WINNT
Wolfram Research Forum	WOLFRAM
WordPerfect Customer Support	WPCS
WordPerfect Users Forum	WPUSERS
WordStar Forum	WORDSTAR
Working-From-Home Forum	WORK
Worldwide Car Network Forum	WWCAR
ZMac Download & Support Forum	DOWNLOAD
ZiffNet Support Forum	SUPPORT
Zenith Data Systems Forum	ZENITH

Contact Option

CompuServe
Box 20212
Columbus, OH 43220
(800) 848-8199

Online Services (cont'd)

Dialog

Dialog is an online service that provides access to hundreds of research databases and publications. Corporations use Dialog as a fast, easy way to search through the full text of thousands of publications.

By navigating through its occasionally difficult interface, a researcher can access all of these sources in seconds.

Research-oriented services like Dialog and Nexis are quite expensive. Investigate subscription pricing as an alternative.

Here is a partial listing of publications carried by Dialog. The actual list (more than thirty pages long) can be requested by contacting Dialog directly.

ABA Banking Journal
Accent on Living
Adhesives Age
Advanced Manufacturing Technology
Agra Europe
Air Toxics Report
American Education
American Forests
American Heritage
Antitrust Bulletin
AP News
Arab News
Archives of Dermatology
Atlantic Trade Report
Avionics Report
Backpacker
Belfast Telegraph
Black Enterprise
BNA Federal Contracts Daily
Bottomline
Business & The Environment
Business Atlanta
Business History
Business Mexico
CD-ROM Professional
Cendata
Commuter Regional Airline News
CSN
Ebony
Electronic Office
Engineering Lasers
Environment Today
Food in Canada
Hippocrates
Il Mondo
Infosystems
Italia Oggi
Japanese Advanced Technology Magnetic Material
Journal of New York Taxation
Journal of Occupational and Organizational Psychology
Journal of State Government
Kyodo
Long-Distance Letter
Metropolitan Home
Meyler's Side Effects of Drugs
Modem User Digest
Motor Age
National Forum: Phi Kappa Phi Journal
National Review
Navy News & Undersea Technology
NEA Today
New Zealand Herald
Newsline
North Sea Letter
Ocean Industry
Online
PC Magazine
PR Week
Psychology Today
Pulp & Paper
Report on IBM
Road & Track
Scholastic Update
Skiing Trade News
Skin Diver
Sludge
Space Station News
Sports Illustrated
Sunset
Syria Times
Television Digest
Textline World Trade
The Charlotte Observer
The Economist
The Power Letter
Times of Oman
Toshiba Weekly
UN Cronicle
Video Store
Week in Germany
World Health
World Tobacco

Contact Option

Dialog
3460 Hillview Ave.
Palo Alto, CA 94394
(800) 334-2564

Almanac Fact

There are literally hundreds of computer magazines. As the roster of titles changes almost daily, the best strategy is to start at your local newsstand. Consistent favorites are MacUser, PCWorld, Boardwatch, InfoWorld *and* Computer Shopper.

Online Services (cont'd)

Nexis

Nexis is a nearly complete compendium of news. It features the full text of hundreds of magazines, ranging from *Time* to *Forbes* to obscure technical journals. It also contains every word that has passed through more than twenty newswires, including AP and the Xinhua News Agency.

Using Nexis, a business user can find every mention of a competitor or a topic over a given period of time. Far more efficient than a clipping service, Nexis allows users to perform complicated boolean searches. For example, one could search for every instance of the word "wool" within three words of the phrase "cardigan sweaters." Within seconds, Nexis will find all relevant references. NOTE: of all the services listed here, Nexis is far and away the most expensive, with monthly fees beginning at $500.

Here is a partial listing of the many hundreds of publications covered by Nexis. For a complete listing, contact Nexis at the number given.

Advertising Age
Aerospace Daily
Africa News
Airports
American Salesman
Annals of Neurology
Argus Researchoration
Automotive Engineering
AutoWeek
Back Stage
Banking Policy Report
BASELINE In Production Credits
Bill Tracking (all states)
Billboard
BNA Pension Reporter
Business International (Country Profiles)
Business Week
BYTE
California Journal
Central News Agency
Chemical Week
Civil Aeronautics Board Decisions
CNN Transcripts
Coal
Coloradooration/Limited Partnership Information
Cosmetics International
Datamatian
Dean Witter Reynolds,
Defense News
Drug Topics
EC Energy Monthly
Evans Economics, Electronic News Service
Federal News Service-Daybook
Foundry Management & Technology
Garbage
Gas World
Grocery Marketing
Hanifen, Imhoff
Harvard Business Review
Hewlett-Packard Journal
Illinois Legal Times
Industrial Bioprocessing
INSIGHTS
Insurance Review
Integrated Waste Management
Jack O'Dwyer's Newsletter
Jiji Press Ticker Service
Journal of Accountancy
Laserdisk Professional
Maclean's
Member Profile Report
Mining Magazine
Minneapolis Star Tribune
Modern Office Technology
Money
Nation's Restaurant News
Newsweek
Nikko Securities
Nuclear News
Oilweek
Olympic Factbook
Orange County Business Journal
PAC Summary Reports
People
Pharmaceutical Business News
Physician Directory
Power in Europe
Roll Call
SEC News Digest
Small Computers in Libraries
Southwest Newswire
Standard Industrial Classification Manual
Stereo Review
Tea and Coffee Trade Journal
TECH-LINE
The Abortion Report
The Atlantic
The Billings Gazette
The Bond Buyer
The Boston Globe
The Computer Lawyer
The FDIC Watch
The Japan Economic Journal
The MacNeil/Lehrer NewsHour
The National Law Journal
The Reuter Canadian Financial Report
The Rose Sheet
The Thrift Accountant
The Toronto Star
The Washington Post
Training Electronics & C41
U.S. Distribution Journal
U.S. Supreme Court Case List
United Press International (UPI)
UNIX Review
VISTA National Priority List
Washingtonian Magazine
Woman
Woman's Wear Daily
World Policy Guide
World Tax Report

Contact Option

Nexis
Mead Data Central
9393 Springboro Pike
Dayton OH 45401
(800) 346-9759

Online Services (cont'd)

Other Online Services

IBM, SEARS, APPLE, H&R BLOCK, MCI and Dow Jones are all major investors in the information services industry. They are financing huge bulletin boards that allow computer users to exchange information, software and advice, and to send and receive electronic mail.

In addition to CompuServe, Dialog and Nexis, there are a wide variety of other services available.

Prodigy currently posts the largest membership of all electronic information services. Designed primarily for consumer use, Prodigy offers an excellent way to get basic information on a variety of sources. In addition, Prodigy's news and Wall Street services provide an extremely low-cost way to stay in touch with the world on a daily basis.

Prodigy
445 Hamilton Ave.
White Plains, NY 10601
(914) 993-8000
(800) 776-3449

Dow Jones News Retrieval is similar to Dialog and Nexis, in that it offers easy access to hundreds of publications. But Dow Jones focuses primarily on business, offering everything from *Barron's* to *Plastics World* online.

Dow Jones & Co.
P.O. Box 300
Princeton, NJ 08543
(609) 452-1511

America Online (AOL) is a hybrid. It combines the friendly interface of Macintosh or Windows with a speedy and powerful information service. AOL provides extremely low-cost access to Internet messaging, as well as a large range of forums and information sources. AOL is highly recommended for first-time users of information services.

America Online
Quantum
8619 Westwood Center Dr.
Vienna, VA 22182
(800) 827-6364

Contact Options

GEnie
General Electric
401 N Washington St.
Rockville MD 20849
(800) 638-9636

NewsNet
945 Haverford Rd.
Bryn Mawr, PA 19010
(800) 345-1301

Online Access Magazine
920 N. Franklin St. #203
Chicago IL 60610
(312) 573-1700

Bulletin Boards

USING A COMPUTER AND A MODEM, you can reach more than 70,000 bulletin boards around the world. These boards allow you to exchange software and data, find help on an awesome variety of topics, or just visit electronically with other computer users.

While there are a handful of large commercial bulletin boards, most are run by small businesses and individuals.

The typical bulletin board offers a large collection of shareware programs, frequently updated. Many also specialize, ranging from 'adult' material to information on tropical fish. In addition, many give access to the Internet, allowing low-cost or free electronic mail around the world.

Finding a local bulletin board is surprisingly easy. The following list (updated in 1993) catalogues bulletin boards which keep a list of other bulletin boards. Once you access one, you can easily find others in that field or locality.

Recommended Resource

Boardwatch Magazine
5970 S. Vivian St.
Littleton, CO 80127
(800) 933-6038

Almanac Fact

When buying a computer book, start from the back. Good computer books never have skimpy indexes. Look up a technique you're familiar with and see if the explanation makes sense. Finally, don't be influenced by price. Sometimes the cheapest books are the best.

Bulletin Board Access

BOARDWATCH MAGAZINE COMPILES A LIST OF bulletin boards that keep track of *other* bulletin boards.

Board	Access Number
96 List - 9600+bps BBS	(213) 484-0260
AC 516 Free Shareware BBS	(516) 385-7882
Airline Pilot/JUMPSEAT BBSs	(708) 980-1613
Alaska AC 907	(907) 562-1854
Apple II BBS with Internet con	(619) 670-5379
Area Code 517 - Mid-Michigan	(517) 695-9952
Arkansas Area 501	(501) 444-8420
ASP BBS Member List	(317) 856-2087
Astronomy/Space BBS	(209) 432-2487
Atlanta Area 404	(404) 924-8472
Atlanta Area 404	(404) 627-2662
Austin Area BBS List AC 512	(512) 258-9553
Autocad Related BBS	(206) 643-5477
Baltimore Area 301	(301) 633-7870
BBS With Handicapped Focus	(203) 337-1607
Black Run/Oriented BBS	(707) 552-3314
Business/Professional BBS	(517) 797-3740
California AC 31 0	(310) 804-3324
Central California AC 209	(209) 675-8436
Central California Area 805	(805) 652-1478
Chicago	(708) 801-0823
Chicago	(708) 403-2826
Cleveland Area 216	(216) 382-2558
Commodore 64/128/Amiga BBS	(818) 287-4570
CompuCom Modem BBS List	(803) 297-4395
Connecticut AC 203	(203) 743-4044
Dallas/Ft Worth Area 214/817	(817) 784-1178
Darwin National USBBS List	(916) 929-7511
Desktop Publishing BBS	(301) 924-0398
Detroit Area 313	(313) 754-1131
Ecology/Conservation BBS	(803) 552-4389
Geneology Related BBS	(703) 528-2612
Graphical User Interface BBS	(212) 876-5885
Ham/Amateur Radio BBS	(301) 590-9629
Handicapped Issues BBS	(301) 593-7357
Houston Area 713	(713) 530-8875
Kansas City Area 816/913	(816) 436-4516

Board	Access Number
Kitsap County Washington	(206) 780-2011
List of Gay/Lesbian BBS	(514) 597-2409
Macintosh BBS	(803) 548-0900
Medical Issues BBS	(302) 731-1998
Milwaukee Area 414	(414) 442-0170
Minnesota Twin Cities AC 612	(612) 489-7983
NAPLPS Graphics BBS	(404) 498-4254
National 800 Number BBS List	(800) 874-2937
National BBS List	(412) 349-6862
New Jersey AC 609	(609) 561-3377
New Jersey Area 201/609/908	(609) 953-0769
New Orleans BBS List	(504) 885-5928
Ontario Area 705	(705) 835-6192
Open Access UNIX Site List	(215) 348-9727
Orlando Florida AC 407	(407) 423-5226
OS/2 BBS Systems	(703) 385-4325
OS/2 Related BBS	(918) 481-5715
Pennsylvania AC 215	(215) 443-5830
Portland Oregon BBS	(503) 297-9145
Raleigh NC Area Code 919	(919) 779-6674
Republic of South Africa	(041) 34-1122
Rhode Island Area 401	(401) 732-5292
Rochester NY AC 716	(716) 256-2659
San Diego. CA AC 619	(619) 573-1675
San Francisco Area 408/415/51 0	(510) 339-1045
Seattle AC 206/West Washington	(206) 367-3837
Selected BBS	(513) 236-1229
South Florida Area 305/407	(305) 474-6512
Southern California	(213) 422-7942
St. Louis AC 314	(314) 579-0700
Tacoma Washington AC 206	(206) 566-1155
Technical Support BBS List	(812) 479-1310
The List National BBS List	(516) 938-6722
Tulsa Oklahoman Area BBS List	(918) 747-2542
U.S.S.R. BBS List	7-3832-356722
Washington DC BBS List	(703) 425-2505
Wildcat! BBS	(805) 395-0650
Wisconsin 608	(608) 837-1923

The Top Reference Sources

Microcomputer Market Place
Random House Electronics Publishing, $30
(212) 751-2600

This new publication is a comprehensive guide to PC software and hardware vendors, service providers, and information sources. Thousands of listings are included such as software and hardware companies, new equipment sources (mail order and retail), secondary market sources, associations and organizations, information and media resources, computer safety and product information sources, and more.

Used Computers

Contact Options

Used Computer Brokers:

Boston Computer Exchange
(800) 262-6399

Computer Brokerage Services
330 W. 42nd St.
New York, NY 10036
(212) 947-7848

Solute
145 Palisade
Dobbs Ferry, NY 10522
(914) 674-6000

Rentex
337 Summer St.
Boston, MA 02210
(800) 545-2313

Technical Support

Five Tips on Technical Support

1. Go to the bookstore and buy a third-party book. It is easier, simpler and faster than using the manual.

2. Use CompuServe. Post your message and look for an answer tomorrow.

3. Send a fax to tech support. Faxes are often given to the best advisor, and you're guaranteed not to spend time and money on the phone.

4. Turn off all TSRs, inits, and special software before calling. The tech support people usually won't help you until you prove that the problem is theirs.

5. If you have a modem, send your problem directly to the company's bulletin board. A complete list of bulletin board numbers begins below.

Bulletin Boards

Company	BBS Phone
3Com	(408) 980-8204
3rd Planet Software	(213) 841-2260
Abacus Concepts	(616) 698-8106
Abaton Technology	(415) 438-4650
Accolade	(408) 296-8800
Acer America	(800) 833-8241
Adaptec	(408) 945-7727
Addstor	(415) 324-4077
Advanced Digital	(714) 894-0893
Advanced Logical Research	(714) 458-6834
All Computer	(416) 960-8679
Alloy Computer Products	(508) 460-8140
Allied Telesis	(415) 964-2994
Alpha Software	(617) 229-2915
Altima	(510) 356-2456
Altsys	(214) 680-8592
Amdekoration	(408) 922-4400
American Megatrends (AMI)	(404) 246-8780
Apogee Software	(508) 365-2359
Applied Engineering	(214) 241-6677
Artisoft	(602) 293-0065
Artist Graphics	(612) 631-7669
Ask Sam Systems	(904) 584-8287
Asymetrix	(206) 451-1173
AST Research	(714) 727-4723

Company	BBS Phone
ATI Technologies	(416) 756-4591
AT&T Computer Systems	(201) 769-6397
Automated Design Systems	(404) 394-7448
Award	(408) 371-3139
Beagle Bros	(619) 558-6151
Blackmond Software	(505) 589-0319
Boca Research	(407) 241-1601
Borland	(408) 439-9096
Bourbaki	(208) 342-5823
Brightbill Roberts	(315) 472-1058
Brightwork Development	(914) 667-4759
Brown Bag Software	(408) 371-7654
Buerg Software	(707) 778-8944
Buttonware	(206) 454-7875
Calcomp	(714) 821-2359
Campbell Services	(313) 559-6434
Cannon Printer Division	(516) 488-6528
Cardinal Technologies	(717) 293-3074
Cardz	(604) 734-5400
CBIS	(404) 446-8405
cc:Mail	(415) 691-0401
Central Point	(503) 690-6650
Certus	(216) 546-1508
Cheyenne Software	(516) 484-3445
Chipsoft	(619) 453-5232

Tech Support Bulletin Boards (cont'd)

Company	BBS Phone
Chwatal Development	(318) 487-0800
Citizens America	(310) 453-7564
Citrix Systems	(305) 346-9004
Clarion Software	(305) 785-9172
Clark Development	(801) 261-8976
Clear Software	(617) 965-5406
CNET	(408) 954-1787
Coconut Computing	(619) 456-0815
Codenoll	(914) 965-1972
Colorado Memory Systems	(303) 679-0650
Columbia Data Products	(407) 862-4724
Communications Research	(504) 926-5625
Complete PC	(408) 434-9703
Computers International	(213) 823-3609
Computer Peripherals	(805) 499-9646
Computer Support	(214) 404-8652
Computone	(404) 664-1210
Comtrol	(612) 631-9310
Conner International	(408) 456-4415
Continental Software	(619) 386-5218
Core International	(407) 241-2929
Corel System	(613) 728-4752
Cornerstone	(408) 435-8943
Corvus System	(408) 972-9154
Creative Labs	(408) 428-6660
Cross Communications	(303) 444-9003
Cumulus	(216) 464-3019
DAC Software	(214) 931-6617
Dariana Technology Group	(714) 994-7410
Darwin Systems	(301) 251-9206
Data Access	(305) 238-0640
Datadesk/Prometheus	(503) 691-5199
DataEase	(203) 374-6302
Dataproducts	(818) 887-8167
Datastorm	(314) 875-0503
Data Technology	(408) 942-4197
David Systems	(408) 720-0406
Dayna Communications	(801) 535-4205
DCA	(404) 740-8428
Dell Computer	(512) 338-8528
Delphi	(800) 365-4636
Diamond Computer	(408) 730-1100
Digiboard	(612) 943-0812
Digital Communications	(513) 433-5080
Digital Research	(408) 649-3443
Digital Vision	(617) 329-8387
Disk Technician	(619) 272-9240
Disston Ridge Software	(813) 327-0822
Distibuted Processing Tech.	(407) 831-6432
D-Link Systems	(714) 455-1779

Company	BBS Phone
DNA Networks	(215) 296-9558
Dove Computer	(919) 343-5616
DTK	(818) 333-6548
Dudley Software	(615) 966-3574
Dynamic Microprocessor	(516) 462-6638
EagleSoft	(812) 479-1310
Elite Business App's	(410) 987-2335
Emac/Everex	(510) 226-9694
Emerald Systems	(619) 673-4617
Enable Software	(518) 877-6316
Epson America	(408) 946-8777
Equinox Systems	(305) 378-1696
eSoft	(303) 699-8222
ETS Incorporated	(801) 265-0919
Exis	(416) 439-8293
EZX Publishing	(713) 280-8180
Family Scrapbook	(904) 249-9515
Fifth Generation Systems	(504) 295-3344
Folio	(801) 375-9907
Foresight Resources	(816) 891-8465
Frederick Engineering	(301) 290-6944
Fresh Technology	(602) 497-4235
Fujitsu America	(408) 944-9899
Future Domain	(714) 253-0432
FutureSoft Engineering	(713) 588-6870
Galacticomm	(305) 583-7808
GAP Development Company	(714) 493-3819
Gateway BBS	(605) 232-2109
Gateway Communications	(714) 863-7097
Gazelle Systems	(801) 375-2548
GEcho	(316) 263-5313
Genoa Systems	(408) 943-1231
Gensoft Development	(206) 562-9407
Gibson Research	(714) 362-8848
GigaTrend	(619) 566-0361
Global Village Comm	(415) 390-8397
Goldstar Technologies	(408) 432-0236
Great American Software	(603) 889-7292
Gupta Technologies	(415) 321-0549
GVC Technologies	(201) 579-2380
Hayes Microcomputer	(800) 874-2937
HDC Computer	(206) 869-2418
Headland Technology	(415) 656-0503
Hercules Computer	(510) 540-0621
IBM	(404) 835-6600
Intelligent Graphics	(408) 441-0386
IMC Networks	(714) 724-0930
IMSI Software	(415) 454-2893
Infinity Computer Services	(215) 965-8028
Infochip Systems	(408) 727-2496

Tech Support Bulletin Boards (cont'd)

Company	BBS Phone
Informix	(913) 492-2089
InfoShare	(703) 803-8000
Innovative Data Concepts	(215) 357-4183
Insetoration	(203) 740-0063
Insignia Solutions	(415) 694-7694
Intel	(503) 645-6275
Intracorp	(305) 378-8793
Iomega	(801) 778-4400
Irwin Magnetics	(313) 930-9380
Jetfax	(415) 324-1259
Jetform	(613) 563-2894
JDR Microdevices	(408) 559-0253
Kent Marsh	(713) 522-8921
Kodiak Technology	(408) 452-0677
Kurta	(602) 243-9440
LAN Master	(817) 771-0233
LAN Systems	(801) 373-6980
LAN Works	(416) 238-0253
Laser Go	(619) 450-9370
Lattice	(708) 916-1200
Leading Edge	(508) 836-3971
Lexmark	(800) 453-9223
Liant Software	(206) 236-6485
Logical Connection	(504) 295-3344
Logitech	(510) 795-0408
Lotus	(617) 693-7000
Lotus	(404) 395-7707
Mace, Paul Software	(503) 482-7435
Madge Networks	(408) 441-1340
Magee Enterprises	(404) 446-6650
Magitronic Technology	(516) 454-8262
Magnavox	(310) 532-6436
Main Lan	(407) 331-7433
Mannesman Tally	(206) 251-5513
Manx Software Systems	(201) 542-2793
Marstek	(404) 424-3146
Matrix Technology	(617) 569-3787
Maxi Host Support	(209) 836-2402
Maxtor/Miniscribe	(303) 678-2222
Maynard Electronics	(407) 263-3502
McAfee Assoc	(408) 988-4044
Media Vision	(510) 770-0968
Micro Display Systems	(612) 438-3513
Microcom	(617) 762-5134
Microdyne	(703) 739-0432
Micron Technology	(208) 368-4530
Micronics	(510) 651-6837
Micropolis	(818) 709-3310
Microrim	(206) 649-9836
MicroProse	(301) 785-1841

Company	BBS Phone
Microsoft	(206) 637-9009
Microsystems Software	(508) 875-8009
Microtech	(203) 469-6430
Microtest	(602) 996-4009
Mitsubishi	(714) 636-6216
Mouse Systems (MSC)	(510) 683-0617
Multi-Tech Systems	(612) 785-9875
Mustang Software	(805) 395-0650
National Semiconductor	(408) 245-0671
NEC Technologies	(508) 635-6328
NetWorth	(214) 869-2959
New Media Graphics	(508) 663-7612
Night Owl BBS	(716) 881-5688
NISCA	(214) 446-0646
Norton-Lambert	(805) 683-2249
Novell	(801) 429-3030
Novell Desktop Systems	(408) 649-3443
Number Nine	(617) 497-6463
OCR Systems	(215) 938-7245
Okidata	(800) 283-5474
Omen Technology	(503) 621-3746
Ontrack Computer Systems	(612) 937-0860
Open Network	(718) 638-2239
Orchid Technology	(510) 683-0327
Origin	(512) 328-8402
Pacific Data Products	(619) 452-6329
Packard Bell	(818) 773-7207
Palindrome	(708) 505-3336
Panasonic	(201) 863-7847
Paperbackoration	(415) 644-0782
Paradise Systems	(714) 753-1234
Patton & Patton Software	(408) 778-9697
Pentax Technologies	(303) 460-1637
Phoenix Technologies	(405) 321-2400
Pinnacle Publishing	(206) 251-6217
Pinpoint Publishing	(707) 523-0468
PKWare	(414) 354-8670
PLI	(510) 651-5948
Plus Development	(408) 434-1664
Practical Peripherals	(805) 496-4445
Priam Systems	(408) 434-1646
Princeton Graphic Systems	(404) 664-1210
Prometheus Products	(503) 691-5199
Proteon	(508) 366-7827
Public Brand Software	(317) 856-2087
Pure Data	(214) 242-3225
Qmail	(901) 382-5583
QMS	(205) 633-3632
Quadram	(404) 564-5678
Qualitas	(301) 907-8030

Tech Support Bulletin Boards (cont'd)

Company	BBS Phone
Quantum	(408) 894-3214
Quarterdeck Office Systems	(310) 341-3227
QuickBBS	(407) 896-0494
Race	(305) 271-2146
Rams' Island Software	(303) 841-6269
RelayNet National	(301) 229-5623
Remote Control Int	(619) 431-4030
Revelation Technologies	(206) 641-8110
Rix Softworks	(714) 476-0728
Rybs Electronics	(303) 443-7437
Saber Software	(214) 361-1883
Salt Air BBS	(801) 261-8976
Samsung Info Systems	(201) 691-6238
SEAboard	(201) 473-1991
Seagate	(408) 438-8771
Searchlight Software	(516) 689-2566
SemWare	(404) 641-8968
Sharp	(404) 962-1788
Shiva	(617) 621-0190
Sitka	(415) 769-8774
Sierra Online	(209) 683-4463
Sigma Design	(510) 770-0111
Silicon Valley Computers	(415) 967-8081
Sitka	(510) 769-8774
SMS Technology	(510) 964-5700
Sofnet	(404) 984-9926
Softklone	(904) 878-9884
Softlogic Solutions	(603) 644-5556
Softronics	(719) 593-9295
Software Products Intl	(619) 450-2179
Software Security	(203) 329-7263
Software Venture	(510) 849-1912
Solutions Systems	(617) 237-8530
SparkWare	(901) 382-5583
Spectra Publishing	(408) 730-8326
SprintNet	(800) 546-1000
Stac Electronics	(619) 431-5956
STB Systems	(214) 437-9615
Storage Dimensions	(408) 944-1220
Sunrise Software	(404) 256-9525
Sunriver	(512) 835-8082
Supermac Software	(408) 773-4500
Supra	(503) 967-2444
Sydex	(503) 683-1385
Symantec	(408) 973-9598
Sysgen	(408) 946-5032
Systems Compatibility	(312) 670-4239
Syquest	(415) 656-0470
Swan Technologies	(814) 237-6145
TEAMate	(213) 318-5302
Tecmar	(216) 349-0853
Telebit	(408) 745-3803
Telix Support	(416) 439-8293
Template Garden Software	(914) 337-2008
Texas Instruments	(512) 250-6112

Company	BBS Phone
TheSoft Programming	(415) 581-3019
Thomas Conrad	(512) 836-8012
Thumper Technologies	(918) 627-0059
Tiara Computer Systems	(415) 966-8533
Timeline Software	(415) 892-0408
Timeslips	(508) 768-7581
Tops Microsystems	(510) 769-8774
TopSoft Software	(502) 425-9941
Toshiba Printer Products	(714) 581-7600
Trantor Systems	(415) 656-5159
Traveling Software	(206) 485-1736
Trident Microsystems	(415) 691-1016
Trius	(508) 794-0762
True Vision	(317) 577-8783
TSR Systems	(516) 331-6682
Turbo Tax	(619) 453-5232
Turtle Beach	(717) 845-4835
Unicorn Software	(317) 784-2147
US Robotics	(708) 982-5274
US Sage	(417) 331-7433
Ven Tel	(408) 922-0988
Ventura Software	(619) 673-7691
Vermont Microsystems	(802) 655-7461
Video Seven	(510) 656-0503
Visual Business Systems	(404) 953-1613
Volkswriter	(408) 648-3015
Vortex Systems	(412) 322-3216
Wacom	(415) 960-0236
Walker, Richer, & Quinn	(206) 324-2357
Wallsoft Systems	(212) 962-1923
Walt Disney Software	(818) 567-4027
Wangtek	(805) 582-3370
Weitek	(408) 522-7517
Western Digital	(714) 753-1068
White Water Systems	(708) 328-9442
Windows Tech. Support	(206) 637-9009
Word Perfect	(801) 225-4414
Wordtech	(415) 254-1141
Wyse	(408) 922-4400
Xebec	(702) 883-9264
Xircom	(818) 878-7618
Xyquest	(508) 667-5669
XTree	(805) 546-9150
Zenographics	(714) 851-3860
Zoom Telephonics	(617) 451-5284
Zsoft	(404) 427-1045
ZyXEL	(714) 693-0762
3Com	(408) 980-8204

Source: Gary Barr, Digicom BBS (812) 479-1310

Program Templates

WordPerfect Commands

Key	Function
F1	Cancel
Alt F1	Thesaurus
Shift F1	Setup
Ctrl F1	Shell
F2	Search Forward
Alt F2	Replace
Shift F2	Search Backward
Ctrl F2	Spell
F3	Help
Alt F3	Reveal Codes
Shift F3	Switch
Ctrl F3	Screen
F4	Indent Right
Alt F4	Block
Shift F4	Indent Both Sides
Ctrl F4	Move
F5	List Files
Alt F5	Mark Text
Shift F5	Date/Outline
Ctrl F5	Text In/Out
F6	Bold
Alt F6	Flush Right
Shift F6	Center
Ctrl F6	Tab Align
F7	Exit
Alt F7	Columns/Table
Shift F7	Print
Ctrl F7	Footnote
F8	Underline
Alt F8	Style
Shift F8	Format
Ctrl F8	Font
F9	Merge R
Alt F9	Graphics
Shift F9	Merge Codes
Ctrl F9	Merge/Sort
F10	Save
Alt F10	Macro
Shift F10	Retrieve
Ctrl F10	Macro Define

XyWrite Commands

Key	Function
F1	Begin/End Text Define
Alt F1	Begin/End Column Define
Shift F1	—
Ctrl F1	—
F2	Make or Load Save/Gets
Alt F2	Display All Save/Gets
Shift F2	Append to a Save/Get
Ctrl F2	Displays Save/Get on one key
F3	Release Define
Alt F3	Undelete
Shift F3	—
Ctrl F3	Open a Footnote or Header
F4	Define Line
Alt F4	Define Word
Shift F4	Define Paragraph
Ctrl F4	Define Sentence
F5	Clear Command Line
Alt F5	Delete Line
Shift F5	—
Ctrl F5	—
F6	Clear Command Line
Alt F6	Delete Define
Shift F6	—
Ctrl F6	—
F7	Copy Defined Block
Alt F7	—
Shift F7	—
Ctrl F7	—
F8	Move Defined Block
Alt F8	—
Shift F8	—
Ctrl F8	—
F9	Execute Command
Alt F9	Help
Shift F9	Show Page and Line Numbers
Ctrl F9	Normal or Expanded Display

Almanac Fact

A wide range of decorative papers, labels, and brochures, ideal for desktop publishing, is available from Paper Direct. (800) 272-7377.

Reference/Index

Glossary

Absolute net lease—Lease in which the tenant agrees to pay the landlord or owner a basic rent, and also agrees to pay separately for all maintenance, operating, and other building expenses.

Abuse of process—The misuse of legal procedures for the benefit of an individual or business. For instance, suing someone simply in the hopes of frightening them into meeting your demands, when the case has absolutely no merit.

Accounts payable—The amount of money owed to suppliers and vendors that is generally due within the next 30 days.

Accounts receivable—The amount of money due a business from its customers which is anticipated during the next 30 days.

Affidavit—A written statement certified by a notary public as to its authenticity.

Aggregate rent—Total dollar value of a lease.

Air rights—Space or air over a piece of property that legally belongs to or is attached to the property, and can be transferred, sold, or rented. Frequently sold to permit a larger than zoned building on another property.

Amortize—Dividing a loan payment into a series of equal smaller payments to be made on a regular basis, thereby extending the payback over a longer period of time. A residential mortgage is generally amortized over a 30-year period, requiring monthly mortgage payments.

Annualized—Converting a monthly or daily figure to an annual basis.

Anticipatory breach—Notifying an individual or business that is part of a contract that another individual cannot meet the terms of the contract, thereby rendering it invalid.

Apparent authority—The situation in which a principal (individual or company) states or indicates that another individual or business may act on his or her behalf. The principal is then liable for the actions of the other individual, who is acting on his/her authority.

Arbitrage—Buying something in one market and selling it another, profiting on the small differences between the two market prices.

Asset—Everything owned by a corporation that has value, including physical items, real estate, trademarks, and goodwill.

Assignment—Ability to transfer benefits and obligations of a contract or lease to another party.

Assumpsit—Reference to a contractual agreement made verbally or in writing with an individual or business that is not certified.

Assumption of risk—The situation that arises when an individual agrees to perform certain duties knowing that it could be potentially dangerous. Frequently this claim is made in legal suits by the defendant, often an employer, arguing that the plaintiff, often an employee, assumed the risk by agreeing to perform certain duties, such as on-the-job activities, despite the knowledge that it would be risky.

Attornment—Lease provision whereby the tenant agrees in advance to accept and pay rent or other required payments to a new landlord or legal owner.

Attorney-in-fact, subordination clause—Lease provision that permits the landlord to submit, on the tenant's behalf, without further approval, a certificate of subordination to a lender, trustee, or financing institution.

Bailor—An individual who delivers property to another individual who either owns the property or who holds it until it is claimed by the owner. Leaving your coat in a check room makes you a bailor.

Bait and switch pricing—An illegal sales tactic used by unscrupulous companies. Customers are lured into a store with advertising promises of low prices for an item. However, when the customer arrives at the store, the item is reported unavailable and an alternate, often higher-priced or lower-quality product is recommended in its place.

Balance of trade—The difference between the amount of goods a country exports and imports. When the value of exports exceeds imports, the balance is favorable. In the reverse, the balance is negative.

Balance sheet—An overview of a company's assets, liabilities, and owner's equity at a specific point in time.

Balloon payment—The term for the last payment on a loan if it is substantially larger than the previous series of payments. Generally a balloon payment is negotiated when a large sum of money is anticipated before the payoff date, making such a payment possible.

Barter—An agreement between two firms where products or services of equal value are exchanged, with no cash changing hands.

Basis—The original cost of an investment that must be reported to the IRS when it is sold, in order to calculate capital gains.

Glossary (cont'd)

Basis point—The smallest measure used in quoting bond yields, .01%. When changes in bond yields are reported, it is in basis points.

Bear market—A prolonged period of declining stock prices.

Bearer bond—A type of bond that can be redeemed by whoever has possession. No proof of ownership is required. The opposite of a registered security.

Beta—A measure of a stock's volatility or changes in price, as compared with changes in other stocks. Stocks with a high beta are more likely to change dramatically.

Big Blue—Slang for International Business Machines Corp. (IBM).

Big Board—Slang for the New York Stock Exchange (NYSE).

Big Eight—Originally, the eight largest accounting firms in the U.S. Through mergers, they are now the Big Six: Arthur Andersen, Ernst & Young, Deloitte & Touche, KPMG Peat Marwick, Price Waterhouse, Coopers & Lybrand.

Binding letter of intent—Letter of intent that a court of law would uphold as the actual leasing of space, regardless of whether a lease document exists.

Black-Scholes model—A formula created by Fisher Black and Myron Scholes for evaluating stock option values.

Block trade—Buying or selling 10,000 or more shares of stock or $200,000 or more in bonds.

Blue sky laws—State laws governing the issuance and trading of securities established in order to prevent fraudulent transactions.

Board of directors—A group of advisors elected by stockholders to oversee the management of a public company. The Chief Executive Officer receives direction from the board.

Bond rating—A ranking system used to assess the financial solvency of bond issuers. The better the rating, the less the likelihood that the bond issuer will default.

Book value—The value of an asset or an entire business calculated by subtracting cumulative depreciation from the original purchase price.

Brainstorm—A group idea-generation technique. Ideas and problem-solving suggestions are offered by group members until no more are forthcoming. Then the group evaluates and considers each idea, looking for ways to combine and enhance ideas with those offered by other group members.

Brand—The name, symbol, packaging, and promotional theme surrounding a product that creates an identity of its own, separate from the parent company's name and identity.

Brand extension—The addition of a new product within a family of similar products using the same brand name. Ivory shampoo is a classic example.

Breach—The failure to perform certain duties as outlined in a contract, so that the contract is not fulfilled.

Break-even—The point at which revenues for a product exactly equal the cost to produce it. This calculation is frequently used to assess whether it is worth producing a product.

Break-even pricing—A pricing technique that provides for all costs to be covered but no profit realized.

Bridge loan—A short-term loan provided while longer-term financing is being finalized. Allows for business to proceed uninterrupted.

Bucket shop—A brokerage firm that accepts customer buy and sell orders but does not immediately execute them, as the SEC requires. Instead, the firm waits until the price has increased or decreased to the point of allowing the firm to buy or sell the stock and pocket the difference. In extreme cases the firm just takes the money, with no intention of executing the order. Such practices are illegal.

Building standard workletter—Detailed specifications of the construction items that the developer will provide and use in building out a tenant's office space. Available before a lease is executed, it should be included in the lease.

Bull market—A prolonged period of rising stock prices. Opposite of bear market.

Bylaws—The rules for running a company which are drafted when the business is incorporated. Items covered include the election of a board of directors, their responsibilities, and other committees to be established to assist in managing the company.

Call—The option to purchase shares of a stock at a specified price within a certain time frame. If a stock's price rises above the option price during the option period, there is an immediate financial advantage to making the purchase.

Capital assets—Capital consists of property, inventory, cash on hand, accounts receivable, and other items of value owned by a company.

Glossary (cont'd)

Capital expenditure—Money spent to purchase or repair a capital asset, such as plant and machinery.

Capital gains/losses—The difference between an asset's purchase price and selling price. If the difference is positive, it is considered a capital gain and is taxable. If the difference is negative, it is a capital loss and can result in a tax reduction.

Capital stock—Stock sold by a corporation, rather than resold by an investor.

Capitalization—The amount of money used to start a company.

Carryforward—A tax benefit allowing a company to apply losses realized in a previous year to future years' revenue in order to reduce taxes.

Cartel—A group of businesses or countries that agree to work together to affect the pricing and availability of certain products that they produce. OPEC is a classic example.

Cash cow—Business that has had strong sales, generating revenue consistently. In most cases, cash cows are based on products with a strong brand name and repeat buying habits.

Cash discount—A discount offered to buyers who pay their bills within a specified time period. A prompt payment incentive.

Cash flow—The actual cash in and out of a corporation, rather than the more artificial accounting measures often used. Companies can secure paper profits but go bankrupt because of negative cash flow.

Channel of distribution—The means of getting a product into a customer's hands. This might include retail stores, direct salespeople, wholesalers, and distributors.

Chapter 11—A bankruptcy status that provides time for reorganizing a company in order to make it profitable and to be able to pay off its debts.

Chapter 7—A bankruptcy status that allows for liquidation of all of a company's assets in order to pay off creditors.

Churn—Unnecessary and excessive trading on a customer's brokerage account, thereby generating fee income for a broker without adding value to the investments. While this practice is illegal it is also difficult to prove.

Class action—A suit filed by one or more individuals on behalf of a larger group of people who have been treated similarly by a situation. Once the suit has been filed and the court has approved its class action status, all people who may benefit from a ruling (the parties to the suit) must be notified.

Clifford Trust—A trust established for more than 10 years that allows the transfer of assets from one individual or organization to another and then back again when the trust expires. Before new regulations established in 1986, these trusts were a popular means of transferring income-producing assets to children, who would be taxed at a lower tax rate, and then reclaiming them when the child reached the age of 18.

Cognitive dissonance—A psychological state that occurs when an individual questions an action they have taken, such as a purchase he or she has made, and seeks reassurance that they have indeed made the right decision.

Cold call—A marketing technique that involves a salesperson placing a telephone call to a potential client without having had any previous contact.

Collateral—An item of value that is used to guarantee a loan. If the borrower fails to repay the loan, the lender keeps the asset pledged as collateral.

Commodity—Bulk goods, such as crops, food, and metals, that are traded on the commodities exchange. Such items are generally used as raw materials in other products.

Common areas—Portions of a building used by more than one tenant, such as hallways, elevators, and restrooms.

Common carrier—A business that specializes in providing transport of goods and services.

Common market—The group of European nations working cooperatively to establish a unified monetary and trading policy. Also called the European Economic Community (EEC).

Common stock—A class of stock that enables the owner to participate in management of the public corporation that has issued the stock, but which receives proceeds last in the case of bankruptcy.

Comparative advantage—The theory that if two countries specialize in manufacturing different products and each can sell its product at a relative price advantage, then trade between the countries results in more products at lower prices.

Compound interest—Interest that is earned on the original amount invested plus any additional interest earned.

Consideration—An item of value given from one individual or business to another in return for

Glossary (cont'd)

a promise or agreement to do something or sell something. In a contract, there must be consideration for both sides.

Constant dollar—A measurement tool used to gauge fluctuations in consumer purchasing power. The dollar in the base year is valued at $1, with its value being expressed over future years relative to the first year.

Consumer price index—The U.S. Department of Labor's measure of change in the U.S. cost of living. A survey is conducted monthly to gauge the cost of various consumer goods, such as food, housing, transportation, and tracked over time to monitor overall living expenses.

Contempt of court—An act that interferes with the ability of the court to conduct normal business, or which insults the court's authority.

Contest—A game of skill used to get consumers interested in a company's product. A prize is offered to the winner, who is selected based on criteria described in the contest guidelines.

Contingent agreement—Agreement between two parties in which lease, sale, purchase, or payment depends on a special condition usually involving a third party.

Contract—An agreement signed by two individuals or businesses outlining goods or services to be exchanged, and on what terms.

Convertible security—A security, such as a bond or preferred stock, that a stockholder can convert to common stock at any time.

Copyright—The legal right of artists, authors, and creative individuals to determine who can use works that they have created.

Corporate culture—The values, beliefs, and ways of doing business that affect the way employees act, think, and feel about their employer.

Corporation—A form of doing business that establishes a separate legal entity for transacting business, providing for limited liability on the part of the owners, easy transfer of ownership through the use of shares of stock, and continued existence following the death of the owner(s). Such businesses differ from proprietorships and partnerships, two other legal forms, in that owners typically have personal liability that may cease to exist at the death of one of the owners.

Cost per thousand (CPM)—The cost quoted in advertising to reach one thousand people using a promotional method. Allows comparison of various promotional methods by standardizing the way costs are reported.

Cost-plus contract—A type of contract negotiated that provides for full payment of all expenses incurred in fulfilling a contract, such as in manufacturing a product, plus an additional percentage of the total costs as the profit margin. Cost-plus contracts are common in government work, where there are situations in which there is no way to accurately gauge upfront what a product will actually cost to produce, such as in the development of new weapons technology.

Custodian—An individual or institution that has the responsibility for overseeing the financial management of a group of assets.

Debenture—An unsecured bond that has a maturity of 15 years or more.

Default judgment—A court's decision to grant a plaintiff's motion or request without a trial simply because the defendant failed to appear in court to provide any debate on the subject.

Deferred compensation—Salary and earnings to be received at some point in the future, rather than when they are earned. Deferring payment often has tax advantages.

Deflation—A widespread decline in prices. The opposite of inflation.

Demographics—Characteristics of individuals, such as age, education level, and marital status, that are used to better target marketing efforts to appropriate groups of consumers.

Depreciation—An asset's decline in value due to usage or obsolescence.

Devaluation—Lowering a country's currency relative to the price of gold or to another country's currency.

Dilution—The decline in value of earnings per share and stock price when new shares are issued by a company.

Direct marketing—A marketing method that involves mailing brochures and promotional materials to a group of consumers believed to have a need for or interest in a company's product.

Discount—Due to inflation and varying interest rates, $1 received today is worth more than $1 received next week, next month, or next year. The discount is the amount deducted from the face value of a future payment.

Discount rate—The rate used to calculate the time value of money; the value of future cash if it were to be received today.

Disposable income—Income available to consumers after expenses for food, clothing, shelter,

Glossary (cont'd)

and other debts have been covered. Also known as discretionary income.

Divestiture—The act of selling off an asset or business, typically because it is underperforming financially or no longer fits within a company's strategic plan.

Dividend—The distribution of a company's earnings to its shareholders.

Dividend yield—The amount of a company's annual dividend for one share of stock divided by the current price of one share.

Dog—A business with minimal sales in a low-growth market. Generally, companies attempt to rid themselves of dogs, which can be a drain on cash flow.

Domicile—An individual's permanent address or where they consistently return for periods of time, but do not necessarily reside.

Dow Jones Industrial Average—An index of 30 actively traded stocks of selected companies that is used to gauge overall price changes in the stock market.

Drawee—The individual or institution who has been instructed to pay another individual out of funds on deposit. Generally, when a check is written by an individual, the bank on which the check is drawn is the drawee.

Drawer—The individual or institution that has written the check or who has requested that payment be made by the drawee.

Dumping—Selling large numbers of shares of a stock, despite the fact that such a large-scale sale may cause the share price to drop or the market to decline in response. Also used to define the act of selling goods at below cost to force competitors out of the market.

Dutch auction—A sale in which the price of an item is lowered until it reaches a price at which someone is willing to buy it.

Early adopters—The small group of consumers most likely to purchase new products immediately after they are available on the market. The majority of consumers will wait for the reaction of the early adopters before making the decision of whether to purchase the product. Early adopters are most evident in the electronics market.

Earnings per share—A company's annual earnings divided by the total number of shares outstanding.

Easement—An agreement providing one individual or business with the right to use land owned by someone else. In the case of real estate transactions, long-term easements can affect the value of a property if they interfere with the potential usage of the land. An agreement between a landowner and the telephone company to permit telephone poles to be installed, is one example of an easement.

Economies of scale—The improvements in a company's operational efficiency as a result of savings from purchasing inventory in volume, the division of labor, and the learning curve.

80-20 rule—Business experience that indicates that 80% of a company's revenue will come from just 20% of its total customer base.

Elasticity of demand—A measure of the responsiveness of buyers to changes in a product's price. Demand is elastic if it increases due to price reductions or decreases due to price increases. Luxury items are generally more elastic, because consumers can wait for price changes before purchasing. Cigarette demand, on the other hand, is virtually inelastic.

Encumbrance—Any agreement involving the use of land that does not prohibit its sale, but which may reduce its value. An easement is one type of encumbrance. Other common encumbrances include liens and mortgages.

Equity—The value of common and preferred stock owned by stockholders.

Equity financing—Raising money by issuing stock, thereby offering part ownership in the company in return for an investment.

ERISA—The Employee Retirement Income Security Act, enacted in 1973 to set standards for how company pensions and retirement accounts will be managed.

Escalator(s)—A clause in an agreement that increases prices or rents over time.

Escrow money—Assets held by a third party until the conditions of a contract are satisfied, at which time they are paid out.

ESOP—An Employee Stock Ownership Plan, a program to encourage employee investment in company stock.

Estoppel—A legal situation barring one individual or business from denying the existence of contracts or agreements when it is clear that a contract existed. Such situations can arise after one individual realizes that the terms of a signed contract will be detrimental to their business and claims that the contract is invalid. An estoppel comes into play when the court recognizes that the contract existed and prevents the individual from trying to deny its existence as part of a legal suit.

Glossary (cont'd)

Exchange rate—The price at which one country's currency can be converted to another currency.

Experience curve—The efficiency gains realized in production as more products are manufactured.

Fannie Mae—Federal National Mortgage Association. A publicly owned organization that purchases mortgages from banks and resells them on the open market to investors.

FASB—Financial Accounting Standards Board. A governing body established in 1973 to define and monitor the usage of generally accepted accounting principles.

FDIC— Federal Deposit Insurance Corporation, the federal agency that guarantees deposits made by consumers in member banks.

Federal funds rate—The interest rate charged by Federal Reserve district banks for short-term, overnight loans to banks who cannot meet reserve cash requirements.

Federal Reserve Board—The governing body of the Federal Reserve System. Seven presidential appointees who establish and oversee the U.S. money supply through its banking system.

Federal Reserve System—An organization established by the Federal Reserve Act of 1913 to regulate the U.S. banking system. Twelve regional Federal Reserve Banks and 24 branches oversee all of its member banks nationwide.

Fee—Used in real estate to mean property that is owned by an individual without any restrictions on its use.

FIFO—First In, First Out, a method of accounting for inventory that assumes that the first item to be produced was the first item sold. The opposite of LIFO.

Fixed cost—Production costs that do not vary, even when sales volumes change. Expenses such as rent, interest, and executive compensation are considered fixed costs.

Float—The time lag between when a check is deposited and when it clears.

Floor area ratio (F.A.R.)—Ratio between floor area and height.

Focus group—A non-scientific market research technique involving a group of 8 to 12 individuals who are brought together to provide feedback on such issues as new products, advertising campaigns, and a company's reputation.

Forward contract—An agreement to conduct business on a future date.

Franchise—The sale of the license and rights to establish and manage a business under a recognized name using set business practices. McDonald's restaurants are one of the most famous franchises, which sell the rights to operate a restaurant within a specific geographic area provided all operating standards are maintained.

Franchisee—The individual or company that purchases the rights to operate a business from the owner, the franchisor.

Franchisor—The owner of the rights to a business concept who sells them to the franchisee.

Fraudulent conveyance—The transfer of funds or property from one individual or business to another in order to avoid having to turn over such assets to creditors. A form of hiding assets.

Free on board (FOB)—Shipping arrangements that indicate exactly when the buyer assumes responsibility for the transport of a product. The location specified on an invoice as FOB Anywhere, is the point to which the seller will assume responsibility for transport. Beyond that point, it is the buyer's responsibility.

Frequency—The calculation of how many times an advertisement has been seen by a specific population. An ad with a frequency of four, reaches each consumer four times. The higher the frequency, the better the chances that an ad will be noticed.

Full faith and credit—The legal requirement that judgments issued in one state be upheld and recognized by all other states.

Futures contract— An agreement made between traders on the floor of the commodity exchange regarding the purchase of commodities on a specific date in the future for an agreed-upon price.

GATT—General Agreement on Tariffs and Trade. A multinational trade agreement regarding trade issues and policies.

Generic—A non-branded product sold at prices generally below name-brand products.

Gold standard—A national monetary standard using gold as the basis.

Golden handcuffs—An employment contract between employer and employee that provides lucrative compensation and benefits during an employee's tenure with the firm. However, if the employee leaves, they will be

Glossary (cont'd)

liable for repayment of the compensation and benefits received during their employment.

Golden parachute—Lucrative severance packages negotiated for top executives in the event of a takeover.

Goodwill—The intangible assets of a business that impact its overall value. Such assets might include company reputation, loyal customer base, brand recognition, and employee morale.

Greenmail—Repurchase of company stock from a potential acquirer in return for assurances that the acquirer will not pursue the takeover of the company. Generally the purchase price of the stock is inflated by the acquirer.

Gross profit—The amount remaining after the cost to produce a product (cost of goods sold) is subtracted from the net sales.

Gross rating point—A measure of the size of an audience watching a television program during a certain time period, reported in percentages of the total audience size.

Guaranty—An agreement to be responsible for the obligations of another individual or business.

Hedge—An investment tactic in which securities are purchased on both sides of a risk, so that any loss in one security is countered by gains in the other securities.

Holder in due course—An individual or business that accepts a check or form of payment in exchange for merchandise or property without noticing that the check is invalid. The individual accepting the check is the holder in due course and has the right to pursue full payment from the person who wrote the check.

Holding company—A company whose sole purpose is to hold stock in other companies, rather than creating a product or service itself.

Holdover rent—High rent that penalizes a tenant for staying beyond the term of a lease.

Horizontal market—A wide range of customers–the market for sneakers, for example. As opposed to a vertical market, which might include those buying equipment for brain surgery.

In camera—The act of reviewing legal documents and motions in a judge's chambers, rather than in a public courtroom. In the case of sensitive information that could be publicly embarrassing or damaging to people involved in a suit, the information is often reviewed privately by a judge to decide whether the information should become public through a court action.

Income statement—A summary of a company's revenue and expenses for a specified period of time, usually one year. Together with the balance sheet, these two documents make up a company's financial statements. Also known as a profit and loss statement.

Inelastic demand—A demand for products that remains relatively constant despite any changes in price. Basic needs for food and utilities, for instance, cannot be put off until prices drop.

Inflation—Widespread rise in prices that cause, an overall increase in the cost of living.

Initial Public Offering—The first offering of a stock for sale to the public.

Injunction—A court order barring a defendant from doing something that would harm the plaintiff. If the defendant ignores the order, they may face fines, penalties, or formal charges.

Innovators—Consumers who are some of the first to try a new product.

Insider trading—Illegal trading of securities based on confidential information from internal company sources. Since such information would not be generally available to the public, the trader has an unfair advantage.

Intangible asset—Non-physical company assets such as patents, technical know-how, and trademarks.

Interest—Fees paid by a borrower to a lender for the use of their money.

Internal rate of return (IRR)—The discount rate at which an investment has a net present value of $0.

Inventory turnover—The rate at which a firm's inventory is totally depleted over a period of time, usually a year. A company's average inventory divided by its annual sales will give you its inventory turnover.

Joint venture—An agreement between two or more groups to work together on a specific project.

Judgment debtor—An individual who owes an individual or business money following a legal judgment. The individual to whom the money is owed is the judgment creditor.

Junk bond—A bond with a rating of BB or worse that is considered to be more volatile than higher rated bonds. In return for the higher risk of default, the bonds promise higher yields.

Just-in-time purchasing—A purchasing method that schedules delivery of raw materials just at the point in the production when they are needed.

Glossary (cont'd)

Such arrangements reduce the cost of holding the inventory in-house and increase pressure on suppliers to create top quality materials.

Keogh plan—A pension program specifically for the self-employed.

Laches—The extended delay in processing a legal matter that results in the defendant being placed at a disadvantage in proving his/her innocence because evidence no longer exists, witnesses are no longer living, and other difficulties due to the delay.

Laissez faire—The belief that government intervention in business should be minimal.

Latent defect—A problem or defect that cannot be discovered through normal examination and that is not noticed by the seller when turning the product or service over to the buyer. Such defects often become noticeable after a product or service has been delivered. Assets such as real estate, automobiles, and machinery most frequently have latent defects because it is so difficult to check every possible source of future problems before it is sold to the new owner.

Leading economic indicator—Twelve ratios tracked by the U.S. Department of Commerce as indications of economic activity.

Lease—A long-term rental agreement.

Lease term—Length of time a lease is in full force.

Lease year—Any period of 12 consecutive months, starting from the first day of a month.

Lessee—Tenant who pays rent in return for the right to use office space.

Lessor—Landlord who receives payment for renting out office space.

Letter of credit—A document provided by a bank on behalf of a customer guaranteeing that a debt will be paid up to a certain amount. Such letters are often necessary in international dealings.

Letter of intent—Good faith agreement signed by tenant and landlord prior to lease, setting forth major terms and conditions.

Letter of representation—Agreement between tenant and broker giving broker exclusive rights to locate and negotiate for office space.

Leveraged buyout—A purchase method that uses the existing assets of a company to finance its purchase by an outside investor.

Lien—A lender's claim to assets, usually as a guarantee against a loan.

LIFO—Last In, First Out. An accounting method for valuing inventory that assumes that the last or most recently produced item is the next item to be sold.

Limited partnership—A form of a partnership composed of a general manager responsible for the day-to-day management of the business, and several limited partners who invest money but who have limited involvement in the management of the firm, and, hence, limited liability for its financial obligations.

Line of credit—An agreement between a lender and borrower allowing the borrower to draw on a pool of money up to an established limit.

Liquid—Easily converted into cash.

Liquidated damages—The amount of money one individual or business agrees to pay another in the event that they breach a contract signed by both parties. Liquidated damages are calculated as part of the contract, so that both parties know at the outset what it will cost them if they are responsible for a breach of contract.

Load—The sales charge paid by an investor for the privilege of buying shares in a mutual fund.

Loss leader—Products sold at a loss as a means of drawing customers into a store. For example, Toys R Us toy store sells childrens' diapers at an extreme discount in order to draw parents into the store on a regular basis, hoping that once they are in the store, they will buy something else.

M1—The amount of U.S. currency in circulation at any given point in time, plus consumer bank deposits.

M2—M1 plus overnight European transactions, savings, and money market mutual fund transactions.

M3—A broad measure of the money supply, including M1, M2, and time deposits over $100,000 in value.

Manufacturer's agent—An independent salesperson representing a manufacturing firm or firms on a non-exclusive basis. Such arrangements reduce the need for manufacturers to keep large sales forces on staff.

Margin—Money borrowed from a brokerage house in order to purchase more securities.

Marginal cost—The cost of producing one more unit of a product or service beyond the planned quantity.

Marginal revenue—The change in total revenues for a firm from the sale of one more product.

Glossary (cont'd)

Market rent—Current rental rates for similar kind of office space.

Market share—The percentage of total industry sales that one company is responsible for. For instance, XYZ Co. has $10 million in sales in the widget industry, which has a total of $100 million in sales from all companies in the industry. So, XYZ has a 10% market share.

Marketing mix—The tools used to market a product or service, including the price, channels of distribution, promotional methods, and the product features.

Markup—The difference between the cost to produce a product and its selling price.

Material—Information relevant to a particular matter that may affect the outcome of a legal suit.

Mean—The average of a set of numbers. Calculated by adding several numbers together, counting how many numbers are being added, and then dividing by that number.

Median—The middle point in a series of numbers where half the numbers are higher and half are lower. For example, 3 is the median between 1 and 5.

Mitigation of damages—The legal requirement that an individual who has been negatively affected by the actions of another and who has been repaid for that action must make every effort not to make the situation worse for themselves and then hold the other still responsible.

Mode—The number appearing most frequently in a series of numbers. For instance in the series, 1,2,5,2,7,2,8, 2 is the mode, appearing more frequently than any of the other numbers.

Monetarism—The economic perspective that the federal money supply has great impact on the growth of the economy and should be handled carefully.

Monetary policy—Decisions made by the Federal Reserve Board regarding the amount of money in circulation at a given point. By supplying more credit to the banking system or withdrawing credit, the Federal Reserve Board can affect the growth of the economy.

Money market—The market for safe, short-term investments.

Monopoly—A market with one firm in control of the manufacture and supply of a product. Until the advent of Federal Express, the Postal Service was a monopoly.

Monopsony—A market with just one buyer for a product or service and many sellers.

Mortgage—A loan to purchase real estate, with the property used as collateral to guarantee the loan. Residential mortgages are generally for a term of 30 years.

Mortgage REIT—A real estate investment trust that invests in real estate mortgages. Instead of investing in one or two properties, investors can buy shares in an REIT, which owns many different types of properties.

Multinational—A company with branch offices in many countries.

Mutual fund—A diversified portfolio of investments purchased in shares through brokers.

Naked option—The situation in which an investor has purchased a put or call, but does not own any shares. If the share price rises, there is the potential for great gains, without having to invest large sums of money to actually purchase shares. However, if the price drops and the investor has to replace the shares "borrowed" for the transaction, the cash outlay can be huge.

Nationalization—Action by the government to acquire ownership in a company or industry.

Negotiable—Investments that can be easily transferred to another.

Negotiable instrument—A document promising to pay an amount of money to another individual or business that can be transferred to someone else and still be valid. A check is the most common form of a negotiable instrument.

Net present value—Today's discounted value of a string of cash inflows in the future.

Net sales—Gross sales minus such costs as cash discounts, shipping charges, and inventory returns.

Net worth—An individual's or business's total value of its assets minus all obligations.

No par—Stocks issued without a specific face value.

Non-callable—Securities that issuers cannot redeem before the date of maturity.

Non-conforming use—Changes in zoning requirements that occur after a structure has been built and is in use and that now make the structure noncompliant. A non-conforming use permits continued use of the structure as it has been, but requires that any future changes to it must be approved by the zoning board.

Offering circular—Brief marketing materials describing a new stock issue.

Glossary (cont'd)

Oligopoly—A market in which there are several firms, none of which is dominant enough to control the entire market through its actions.

Operating income—Income generated from day-to-day operations of a firm.

Opinion—A written evaluation of the accuracy of a firm's financial statements provided by the firm's certified public accounting firm.

Opportunity cost—The cost of giving up one opportunity in order to invest in another. For instance, the opportunity cost of eating a hot fudge sundae is the brownie you could have had instead.

Option—The purchased right to buy or sell securities at a set price for a specified period of time. Key executives often receive options to purchase company stock at an advantageous price as part of their compensation package.

Original equipment manufacturer (OEM)—A manufacturer that supplies its product to other firms who sell it as part of their product line, often under a different brand name.

Over the counter (OTC)—The market for securities that are not bought and sold over the major exchanges. Penny stocks are one example of securities that are only available over the counter.

Overdraft—A situation in which the amount of money deposited in an account does not adequately cover the obligations on the account.

Overreaching—The advantage that one business acquires when it cheats or defrauds another business. Any agreements or contracts that arise from overreaching are invalid.

Owners equity—The total value of a company's shares of stock minus obligations.

Paper—Short-term obligations issued for terms of 2 to 270 days. Such investments are targeted to investors with large amounts of cash available on a short-term basis.

Par value—The value of a security printed on the certificate.

Parking—Investing funds temporarily in short-term, safe havens while longer-term investment options are considered.

Partial breach—A minor breach of contract that does not affect an agreement to a major extent. As a result, the contract is maintained. An example of a partial breach would be if a business is a day late in delivering some materials necessary for a contract. If a one day delay has no material affect on the ability of the other business to hold up its part of the bargain, then it is only a partial breach.

Partnership—A firm owned by two or more people who are jointly liable for the assets and obligations of the firm.

Patent—The legal claim to a new process or device that provides protection from other companies or individuals stealing the patent for 17 years. Patents must be registered in order to be protected.

Penny stock—A stock with an initial offering price of less than one dollar, available through over-the-counter markets and considered a high risk investments.

Pension fund—An investment fund established by a corporation or organization to manage the retirement benefits and investments for its employees.

PERT—Program Evaluation and Review Technique, a scheduling method that graphically shows when certain project tasks must be completed before other activities can begin.

Piercing the corporate veil—The process of suing individuals involved in the management of a corporation. Since corporations generally shield individuals from liability, such action can only be taken if it can be proven that there is a good reason to disregard the corporate entity.

Point-of-purchase promotion—A piece of marketing literature that is placed in a store where a customer is likely to be making a purchase decision about a product.

Poison pill—A resolution passed by a company's board of directors that makes it difficult or impossible to stage an unfriendly takeover.

Ponzi scheme—A pyramid marketing program in which the proceeds from new customers are used to pay off existing customers. The last wave of customers is left with nothing.

Portfolio—Several securities owned by one individual or institution. A variety of securities reduces investment risk, so a diversified portfolio is the goal.

Position—The amount of money an individual has invested in a particular security; their stake.

Positioning—How a company wants to be perceived by its public, which is supported by investments in advertising, direct marketing, and public relations.

Power of acceptance—An individual's right and ability to accept or reject the terms of a contract.

Glossary (cont'd)

Power of attorney—Appointing an individual to make important decisions for another individual.

Preferred stock—A class of stock that receives its dividends before common stock. Common stock dividends cannot be paid until and unless preferred stockholders have been paid.

Premium—The additional amount a stock is worth relative to other stocks. When one stock is selling at a higher price than another it is said to be selling at a premium of X%.

Pre-paid expense—Paying for an expense in advance, usually for tax or accounting reasons.

Price-earnings ratio (P/E ratio)—Current share price divided by a stock's earnings per share. Stocks in similar industries often have similar P/E ratios. Any differences reflect investor anticipation of the company's prospects.

Prime rate—The interest rate banks offer to their best commercial customers.

Principal—The base amount of money borrowed as part of a loan on which interest will be charged.

Private placement—Offering securities directly to private investors, rather than through a public offering.

Privileged communication—Discussions that take place between an attorney and his/her client that may not be forced to be divulged in court proceedings.

Product life cycle—The stages through which a product progresses from its introduction, acceptance, growth, and maturity in the marketplace.

Product portfolio—All the products a company has to sell.

Profit margin—The selling price of an item less all variable costs.

Profit-sharing plan—A plan that provides for the division of a portion of the company's profits, generally depositing the funds in a tax-deferred account, to be held until the employee retires or leaves the company.

Program trading—Computerized buying and selling of stocks, bonds, and commodities.

Promotion—Marketing tactics that communicate product and company information to the public through such vehicles as newsletters, advertisements, sweepstakes, and brochures.

Proprietorship—A type of business that is controlled and managed by one person.

Prospecting—The marketing practice of seeking out and classifying potential clients in terms of their likelihood to buy.

Prospectus—A summary of the registration statement for a security that has been filed with the SEC.

Protectionism—Government policy of establishing barriers to entry for foreign products, making domestic products more desirable. Such barriers protect domestic firms and products by making foreign products more expensive.

Proxy—Written authorization to act on behalf of someone else in a specific capacity, such as with stock voting rights.

Public relations—Activities on behalf of a company or organization that increase the company's exposure in the community through media coverage, sponsorships, and community involvement. Publicity is one goal of public relations activities, which seeks to increase the public's awareness of, and familiarity with, an organization and its products.

Put—An option to sell a specific stock for a specified price within a set time frame.

Pyramid—An illegal investment practice that involves soliciting investors by promising high returns, but then using newly invested funds to pay earlier investors, rather than actually investing the funds in securities.

Quantum meruit—The right to sue for payment resulting from an implied or existing contract. When an individual or business provides goods or services through an implied contract but are not paid, they can sue the other party in quantum meruit in order to be paid.

Question mark—A classification of a product line that is in a high growth market, but which isn't yet performing as well as anticipated. Such businesses either can yield great returns by acquiring a large share of the growing market, or they can lose money by falling behind new competitors that have recognized the potential growth opportunities.

Quick ratio—A measure of liquidity calculated by subtracting inventory values from current assets and dividing that figure by current liabilities.

Raider—An investor who aims to take control of a company by purchasing a majority stake in the firm.

Real estate—Land and property, including any building and structures on a parcel of land.

Real estate investment trust (REIT)—-A real estate investment trust that invests in a variety of

Glossary (cont'd)

real estate properties. Instead of investing in one or two properties, investors can buy shares in a REIT, which owns many different types of properties, and reduce their risk.

Real income—Income adjusted for inflation, which is considered to be a truer measure of purchasing power.

Receiver—A court-appointed individual who is responsible for managing the day-to-day affairs of a company involved in bankruptcy proceedings. The receiver does not own the company and is not liable for the company's obligations, but simply keeps the company running until a determination is made on the bankruptcy claim.

Recession—Several months of decline in business activity.

Recoupment—A discount or reduction negotiated by a buyer or defendant in a legal matter.

Red herring—A preliminary prospectus issued before SEC approval for a security sale. Identified by the red band across the first page.

Registration statement—A document prepared prior to the public offering of securities, detailing the financial situation of the company, its history and background, and the qualifications of the business managers.

Regression analysis—A statistical tool used to look at past events and determine cause and effect.

Regressive tax—A type of tax that takes a larger proportion of income from those with lower incomes. Opposite is progressive tax, which taxes higher income brackets at a higher rate.

Re-insurance—The practice of spreading the risk of insuring someone across several insurance companies, in return for a portion of the premium payment. Lloyd's of London is a re-insurance marketplace.

Release—A document that certifies that an individual or business has given up a claim to something.

Rent abatement—Reducing rent by omitting payments for a number of months to induce tenants to lease office space.

Replacement cost—The cost of replacing an asset with the same asset if the original were to break or malfunction.

Reserve requirement—The percentage of funds the Federal Reserve Board requires that member banks maintain on deposit at all times.

Retained earnings—Earnings that are left after dividends are paid out.

Retention—The number of units retained by an investment banker during the process of underwriting a securities sale, minus the units set aside for institutional sales.

Return on equity (ROE)—The return investors receive on their investment in a security expressed as a percentage.

Royalty—Payment made to the owner of an asset in return for its use in generating income. Such payments are made to patent holders who grant permission to use the patent, as well as to authors, who are paid royalties based on book sales.

Sale and leaseback—The sale of an asset which is immediately leased from the new owner. Such a transaction helps to increase short-term cash flow for the seller, and can provide tax advantages.

Sallie Mae—Student Loan Marketing Association. A government-funded agency that guarantees student loans, purchasing them from financial institutions, and selling them on the secondary market.

Scrip—A document issued by a corporation to represent a fractional share of stock. Scrip may be collected and presented for full shares.

Sector—Stocks from one particular industry. Stocks from firms in the automotive industry are in the automotive sector, for instance. Brokerage firms may specialize in tracking particular sectors.

Securities and Exchange Commission (SEC)—The government agency responsible for monitoring the issuance and sale of securities.

Security interest—The right to collateral in return for granting some form of financing. A creditor has a security interest in assets that have been pledged as collateral on a loan.

Segment—A grouping of customers within a market with similarities in their purchasing needs or preferences.

Self-liquidating premium—A premium paid in part or in full by the buyer. Includes gimmicks offered on the side of cereal boxes.

Senior debt—Debt that must be paid before subordinated debt such as common stock can be paid. This is a consideration in bankruptcy situations.

Service of process—The action of delivering or communicating information on a legal proceeding to the plaintiff or defendant in a suit.

Settlement—Completing a transaction by paying all obligations.

Glossary (cont'd)

Seven sisters—The seven major international oil companies: British Petroleum, Chevron, Exxon, Gulf, Mobil, Shell, and Texaco.

Shakeout—The shutdown or closing of several firms in an industry, leaving only a few dominant players.

Share—One unit of stock in a corporation.

Shark repellent—Provisions established by a corporation to discourage unwanted takeover attempts, by making it more expensive and difficult to purchase the company.

Short hedge—Hedges taken to lessen or eliminate the financial loss occurring from falling share prices.

Short position—A stock purchase procedure that involves "borrowing" shares of stock through a broker, selling them, and repurchasing them when the price has dropped. The buyer never actually takes possession of the shares and can make a profit if the shares can be repurchased for less than what they were "borrowed" for. However, if the stock price rises, the buyer must pay to buy back the shares, thereby losing money.

Shrinkage—Losses experienced from worker and customer shoplifting.

Simple interest—Interest earned only on the initial capital investment. Unlike compound interest, which continues to accrue on both the capital and the earned interest, simple interest only applies to the capital.

Simulation—The process of creating an investment model in order to adjust certain variables to see their effect on investments. This type of learning can help brokers make decisions regarding where to place their clients' money.

Sixteenth—Reference to one sixteenth of a point change in the price of stocks, bonds, and options.

Small-capitalization stock—Shares of stock issued by small firms with little equity or stock outstanding.

Smokestack industry—Basic manufacturing industries that have experienced minimal growth during the past decades.

Sovereign risk—Risk that lenders assume when making loans to foreign governments due to the fact that a change in the national power structure could cause the country to default on its commitments.

Specialist—A member of the securities exchange responsible for executing securities trades on a particular stock.

Spinoff—Separating a corporate division from the parent company and establishing it as its own independent operating unit.

Split—Increasing the number of shares outstanding without increasing the shareowner's equity, causing a drop in the share price proportional to the number of new shares.

Sponsor—A trader, generally an institution or brokerage firm, whose large scale purchases influence the purchases of other traders. The demand for a stock can be significantly affected by the actions of a sponsor.

Spread—The difference between yields of various maturities. For instance, the spread between a 3-month CD of 3% and a 5-year CD of 6% is 3 percentage points.

Stagflation—The economic condition of slowed economic growth and rising unemployment coupled with rising prices.

Standard deviation—A statistical measure used to assess variability.

Standard Metropolitan Statistical Area (SMSA)—A geographical area consisting of at least 50,000 residents. Used in marketing to determine potential sales and advertising costs for an area.

Star—A business or product line with growth potential–a market leader in a fast-growing market. Stars often become a cash cow or a question mark, depending on their performance.

Stock—Units of ownership in a publicly-held company.

Stock dividend—A dividend paid in shares of stock instead of cash.

Stock option—The opportunity to purchase shares of stock at a specified price and time period.

Stop order—An order given to a broker to buy or sell a security when it reaches a certain price.

Straight-life annuity—A series of payments that continue only while the recipient is alive.

Straight-line depreciation—A method of depreciating an asset by reducing its value in equal amounts each year.

Strategic business unit (SBU)—An organizational unit within a company that is typically focused on selling to one market segment or specializing in one type of product.

Strategic plan—A long-term road map for a company, spelling out its financial and operational objectives for the next 3-5 years.

Glossary (cont'd)

Strip—The practice of dividing a bond into a series of lesser-valued zero-coupon bonds.

Strong dollar—When the foreign exchange rate results in the U.S. dollar being able to purchase foreign goods more cheaply.

Subordinated debenture—Debt which is paid out after preferred stock and bonds.

Supply-side economics—Economic policy that supports reduction in taxes as a means of improving the long-term growth of the economy.

Sweepstakes—A type of contest that encourages participants to purchase a product in order to be considered for free prizes. A lottery, which is illegal, requires a payment for a game of chance. A sweepstakes offers an alternative means of entry, eliminating the cost to play.

Syndicate—A group of individuals who have formed a joint venture to undertake a project they would have been unable to complete individually.

Synergy—A theory that states that merging businesses or groups into a large organization will be more productive and successful than the businesses were individually; the whole is greater than the sum of its parts.

Takeover—The action of assuming control of a business, usually by a raider.

Tangible asset—Physical assets, such as land, buildings, and machinery, that can be sold separately from the business entity.

Target market—A group of consumers or businesses believed to have a need for a company's products that the company attempts to communicate with through advertising.

Tariff—A tax levied on imported products as a means to making them less desirable than domestic products by making them more expensive.

Tax haven—A geographic location that charges little or no taxes on businesses in the area.

Technical correction—An unexplained drop in stock prices after several days of increases.

10-K—An annual report filed with the SEC on behalf of any company that has stock issued, providing information on revenues and income.

Tenancy—Possession or occupancy of real estate by title, under a lease, or on payment of rent, with or without a written lease.

Tenant—Individual or entity paying rent to use or occupy property owned by another.

Tender offer—An offer made by one company seeking to buy another company by purchasing its shares of stock at a price above the current market price.

Term-to-maturity—The amount of time that will elapse before an obligation becomes due.

Time value of money—A dollar received today is worth more than a dollar received at some point in the future, considering the fact that rising prices will mean that a dollar will buy even less in the future.

Tombstone—A form of advertisement announcing the issuance of a security by a particular firm or group of firms.

Tout—To promote a firm or security to a group of clients, by praising them. Sometimes done at racetracks as well.

Trade deficit—The difference between the amount of exports and imports a country has. When there are more imports than exports, a trade deficit exists for the country receiving the imports.

Trade secrets—Secret ideas, processes, or ways of doing business that give a firm an advantage but which are not patented. Businesses try to protect such information from being given to the competition.

Trade surplus—When a country's exports exceed its imports.

Trademark—A registered symbol, theme, mark, or identification related to a person or company. Only that company can use or grant the use of a trademarked item.

Transfer pricing—The cost to sell a company's product to another division or department internally. Since there is no need for markup and external distribution costs with an internal sale, the transfer price is typically less than the retail price.

Trend—A series of occurrences that indicate a pattern.

Triple witching hour—The hour before the market closes on a day when both stock options and futures both expire.

Trust—A relationship established that gives one individual, the trustee, responsibility for the management and care of assets on behalf of another individual, the beneficiary.

Undercapitalized—A situation in which a business does not have the necessary funds to transact normal business.

Undervalued—When a share is trading at a price lower than its market value.

Glossary (cont'd)

Underwrite—The process of purchasing securities from the issuer in order to sell them back to the public.

Unfriendly takeover—The acquisition of a business under protest from the current managers and/ or owners.

Unrealized loss—A loss that has occurred on paper, through a drop in price, but which has not yet been realized because the security has not yet been sold.

Value-added tax—A tax levied at each stage in the production cycle, when another feature is added to the functioning of the product.

Variable cost—Production costs involving raw materials, labor, and utilities that vary according to the production quantity.

Venture capital—Capital provided by a pool of investors for use by firms just starting or expanding, in return for an equity position in the venture.

Voting rights—The right that accompanies ownership of common stock, providing the opportunity to vote on issues of importance to the company.

Warrant—A type of security that gives the owner the right to purchase a certain number of shares of stock at a price slightly higher than the market price at issuance. The warrant is usually good for several years, however, providing time for the stock price to appreciate.

Wasting asset—An asset that declines in value.

Workout—The process of renegotiating a loan package.

Yield curve—A graph showing the various bond maturities and corresponding yields. When the shorter-term bond rates are higher than the longer-term rates, the yield curve is said to be negative. And when the shorter-term bond rates are lower than the longer-term rates, the curve is positive.

Weights and Measures

Linear Measure

12 inches (in) = 1 foot (ft)
3 feet = 1 yard (yd)
5 1/2 yards = 1 rod (rd), pole, or perch (16 1/2 ft)
40 rods = 1 furlong (fur) = 220 yds = 660 ft
8 furlongs = 1 statute mile (mi) = 1,760 yds = 5,280 ft
3 land miles = 1 league
5,280 feet = 1 statute or land mile
6,076.11549 feet = 1 international nautical mile

Area Measure

144 square inches = 1 sq ft
9 square feet = 1 sq yd = 1,296 sq in.
30 1/4 square yards = 1 sq rd = 272 1/4 sq ft
160 square rods = 1 acre = 4,840 sq yds = 43,560 sq ft
640 acres = 1 sq mi
1 mile square = 1 section (of land)
6 miles square = 1 township = 36 sections = 36 sq mi

Cubic Measure

1,728 cubic inches = 1 cu ft
27 cubic feet = 1 cu yd

Liquid Measure

2 pints = 1 quart (qt) (= 57.75 cu in.)
4 quarts = 1 gallon (gal) (= 231 cu in.) = 8 pts

Apothecaries' Fluid Measure

60 minims (min.) = 1 fluid dram (fl dr)
8 fluid drams = 1 fluid ounce (fl oz)
16 fluid ounces = 1 pt
2 pints = 1 qt
4 quarts = 1 gal

Dry Measure

2 pints = 1 qt (= 67.20 cu in.)
8 quarts = 1 peck (pk) (= 537.60 cu in.) = 16 pts
4 pecks = 1 bushel (bu) (= 2,150.42 cu in.) = 32 qts

Avoirdupois Weight

27 11/32 grains = 1 dram (dr)
16 drams = 1 oz = 437 1/2 grains
16 ounces = 1 lb = 256 drams = 7,000 grains
100 pounds = 1 hundredweight (cwt)1
20 hundredweights = 1 ton(tn) = 2,000 lbs 1

Units of Circular Measure

Minute (') = 60 seconds
Degree (°) = 60 minutes
Right angle = 90 degrees
Straight angle = 180 degrees
Circle = 360 degrees

Troy Weight

24 grains = 1 pennyweight (dwt)
20 pennyweights = 1 ounce troy (oz t)12 ounces troy = 1 pound (lb t)

Metric and U.S. Equivalents

1 angstrom (light wave measurement) = 0.1 millimicron
1 angstrom = 0.0000001 millimeter
1 angstrom = 0.0000004 inch
1 cable's length = 120 fathoms
1 cable's length = 720 feet
1 cable's length = 219.45 meters
1 centimeter = 0.39 inch
1 chain (Gunter's or surveyor's) = 66 feet
1 chain (Gunter's or surveyor's) = 20.11 meters
1 decimeter = 3.93 inches
1 dekameter = 32.80 feet
1 fathom = 6 feet
1 fathom = 1.82 meters
1 foot = 0.30 meter
1 furlong = 10 chains (surveyor's)
1 furlong = 660 feet
1 furlong = 220 yards
1 furlong = 1/8 statute mile
1 furlong = 201.16 meters
1 inch = 2.54 centimeters
1 kilometer = 0.62 mile
1 league (land) = 3 statute miles
1 league (land) = 4.82 kilometers
1 link (Gunter's or surveyor's) = 7.92inches
1 link (Gunter's or surveyor's) = 0.201168 meter
1 meter = 39.37 inches
1 meter = 1.09 yards
1 micron = 0.00 millimeter
1 micron = 0.00003937 inch
1 mil = 0.00 inch
1 mil = 0.02 millimeter
1 mile (statute or land) = 5,280 feet
1 mile (statute or land) = 1.60 kilometers
1 mile (nautical international) = 1.85 kilometers
1 mile (nautical international) = 1.15 statute miles
1 mile (nautical international) = 0.99 U.S. nautical miles
1 millimeter = 0.03937 inch
1 millimicron = 0.00 micron
1 millimicron = 0.00000003937 inch
1 nanometer = 0.00 micrometer
1 nanometer = 0.00000003937 inch
1 point (typography) = 0.013837 inch
1 point (typography) = 1/72 inch
1 point (typography) = 0.35 millimeter
1 yard = 0.91 meter

Areas or Surfaces

1 acre = 43,560 square feet
1 acre = 4,840 square yards
1 acre = 0.40 hectare
1 hectare = 2.47 acres

Weights and Measures (cont'd)

1 square centimeter = 0.15 square inch
1 square decimeter = 15.5 square inches
1 square foot = 929.03 square centimeters
1 square inch = 6.45 square centimeters
1 square kilometer = 0.38 square mile
1 square kilometer = 247.10 acres
1 square meter = 1.19 square yards
1 square meter = 10.76 square feet
1 square mile = 258.99 hectares
1 square millimeter = 0.00 square inch
1 square rod, square pole or square perch = 25.29 square meters
1 square yard = 0.83 square meters

Capacities or Volumes

1 cord (firewood) = 128 cubic feet
1 cubic centimeter = 0.06 cubic inch
1 cubic decimeter = 61.02 cubic inches
1 cubic foot = 7.48 gallons
1 cubic foot = 28.31 cubic decimeters
1 cubic inch = 0.55 fluid ounce
1 cubic inch = 4.43 fluid drams
1 cubic inch = 16.38 cubic centimeters
1 cubic meter = 1.30 cubic yards
1 cubic yard = 0.76 cubic meter
1 cup, measuring = 8 fluid ounces
1 cubic inch = 1/2 liquid pint
1 dram, fluid or liquid (U.S.) = 1/8 fluid ounce
1 dram, fluid or liquid (U.S.) = 0.22 cubic inch
1 dram, fluid or liquid (U.S.) = 3.69 milliliiters
1 dram, fluid or liquid (U.S.) = 1.04 British fluid drams
1 dekaliter = 2.64 gallons
1 dekaliter = 1.13 pecks
1 gallon (U.S.) = 231 cubic inches
1 gallon (U.S.) = 3.78 liters
1 gallon (U.S.) = 0.83 British gallon
1 gallon (U.S.) = 128 U.S. fluid ounces
1 gallon (British Imperial) = 277.42 cubic inches
1 gallon (British Imperial) = 1.20 U.S. gallons
1 gallon (British Imperial) = 4.54 liters
1 gallon (British Imperial) = 160 British fluid ounces
1 liter = 1.05 liquid quarts
1 liter = 0.90 dry quart
1 milliliter = 0.27 fluid dram
1 ounce, fluid or liquid (U.S.) = 1.80 cubic inch
1 ounce, fluid or liquid (U.S.) = 29.57 milliliters
1 ounce, fluid or liquid (U.S.) = 1.04 British fluid ounces
1 peck = 8.81 liters
1 pint, dry = 0.55 liter
1 pint, liquid = 0.47 liter
1 quart, dry (U.S.) = 1.10 liters
1 quart, liquid (U.S.) = 0.94 liter
1 quart (British) = 1.03 U.S. dry quarts
1 quart (British) = 1.20 U.S. liquid quarts
1 tablespoon, measuring = 3 teaspoons
1 tablespoon, measuring = 4 fluid drams
1 tablespoon, measuring = 1/2 fluid ounce
1 teaspoon, measuring = 1/3 tablespoon
1 teaspoon, measuring = 1 1/3 fluid drams
1 assay ton = 29.16 grams
1 carat = 200 milligrams
1 carat = 3.08 grains
1 dram, apothecaries' = 60 grains
1 dram, apothecaries' = 3.88 grams
1 gram = 15.43 grains
1 kilogram = 2.20 pounds
1 microgram (µg) = 0.000001 gram
1 milligram = 0.01 grain
1 ounce, avoirdupois = 437.5 grains
1 ounce, avoirdupois = 0.91 troy or apothecaries' ounce
1 ounce, avoirdupois = 28.35 grams
1 pennyweight = 1.55 grams
1 point = 0.01 carat
1 point = 2 milligrams
1 ton = 2,240 pounds
1 ton, gross = 1.12 net tons
1 ton, gross = 1.01 metric tons
1 ton, metric = 2,204.62 pounds
1 ton, metric = 0.98 gross ton

Miscellaneous Units of Measure

Acre–An area of 43,560 square feet. Originally, the area a yoke of oxen could plow in one day.

Agate–Originally a measurement of type size (5 1/2 points). Now equal to 1/12 inch. Used in printing for measuring column length.

Ampere–Unit of electrical current.

Astronomical Unit (A.U.)–93,000,000 miles, the average distance of the earth from the sun. Used for astronomy.

Bale–A large bundle of goods (hay, cotton).

Board Foot (fbm)–144 cubic inches (12 in. x 12 in. x 1 in.). Used for lumber.

Bolt–40 yards. Used for measuring cloth.

Btu–British thermal unit. Amount of heat needed to increase the temperature of one pound of water by one degree Fahrenheit (252 calories).

Carat (c)–200 milligrams or 3.08 grains troy (precious stones). See also Karat.

Chain (ch)–A chain 66 feet or one-tenth of a furlong in length, divided into 100 parts called links. One mile is equal to 80 chains. Cubit – 18 inches or 45.72 cm.

Decibel–Unit of relative loudness. One decibel is the smallest amount of change detectable by the human ear.

Freight, Ton (also called Measurement Ton) – 40 cubic feet of merchandise (cargo freight).

Great Gross–12 gross or 1,728 pieces.

Weights and Measures (cont'd)

Gross–12 dozen or 144 pieces.

Hand–4 inches or 10.16 cm. Derived from the width of the hand. Used for measuring the height of horses at withers.

Hertz–Modern unit for measurement of electromagnetic wave frequencies (equivalent to "cycles per second").

Horsepower–The power needed to lift 33,000 pounds a distance of one foot in one minute. Used mostly for measuring power of engines.

Karat (kt)–A measure of the purity of gold, indicating how many parts out of 24 are pure. For example – 18 karat gold is 3/4 pure. See also, carat.

Knot–The rate of speed of one nautical mile per hour.

League–Usually estimated at 3 miles in English-speaking countries.

Light-Year–5,880,000,000,000 miles, the distance light travels in a vacuum in a year at the rate of 186,281.7 miles (299.79 kilometers) per second. (If an astronomical unit were represented by one inch, a light-year would be represented by about one mile.) Used for measurements in interstellar space.

Magnum–Two-quart bottle. Used for measuring wine.

Ohm–Unit of electrical resistance. A circuit in which a potential difference of one volt produces a current of one ampere has a resistance of one ohm.

Parsec–Approximately 3.26 light-years or 19.2 million miles. Used for measuring interstellar distances.

Pi (π)–3.14159+. The ratio of the circumference of a circle to its diameter. The value is usually rounded to 3.1416

Pica–1/6 inch or 12 points. Used in printing for measuring column width, etc.

Point–0.013837 (approximately 1/72) inch or 1/12 pica.

Quire–25 sheets of paper.

Ream– 500 sheets of paper.

Roentgen–International unit of radiation exposure produced by X-rays.

Score–20 units.

Sound, speed of–1,088 ft per second at 32°F at sea level.

Span–9 inches or 22.86 cm.

Square–100 square feet. Used in building.

Therm–100,000 Btu's.

Tun–252 gallons, but often larger. Used for measuring wine and other liquids.

Watt–Unit of power. The power used by a current of one ampere across a potential difference of one volt equals one watt.

Public Library Reference Contacts

THE LIBRARIES LISTED BELOW are delighted to answer almost any question by phone. Librarians are usually able to find the answer to a question in just a few minutes—longer searches may require a personal visit. The Brooklyn Business Library is an excellent source for business information, and the Honolulu library is great for after hours research.

City	Phone
Atlanta	(404) 730-1700
Baltimore	(410) 396-5430
Boston	(617) 536-5400
Brooklyn Business Library	(718) 780-7800
Buffalo	(716) 858-8900
Chicago	(312) 747-4090
Cincinnati	(513) 369-6900
Cleveland	(216) 623-2800
Columbus	(614) 645-2800
Dallas	(214) 670-1400
Denver	(303) 640-8800
Detroit	(313) 833-1000
Hartford	(203) 293-6000
Honolulu	(808) 586-3704
Houston	(713) 247-2700
Indianapolis	(317) 269-1700
Jacksonville	(904) 630-1994
Los Angeles	(310) 940-8462
Memphis	(901) 725-8855
Miami	(305) 375-2665
Milwaukee	(414) 278-3020
Minneapolis	(612) 372-6500

City	Phone
Nashville	(615) 862-5800
New Orleans	(504) 596-2550
New York City	(212) 340-0849
Norfolk	(804) 441-2887
Orlando	(407) 425-4694
Philadelphia	(215) 686-5300
Phoenix	(602) 262-6451
Pittsburgh	(412) 622-3100
Portland, OR	(503) 248-5402
St. Louis	(314) 241-2288
Salt Lake City	(801) 943-4636
San Antonio	(512) 299-7790
San Deigo	(916) 440-5926
San Francisco	(415) 557-4400
Seattle	(206) 386-4100
Tampa	(813) 223-8868
Washington, DC	(202) 727-1101

Industry Newsletters

Advertising

Ad Business Report
Executive Communications
411 Lafayette St., #3
New York, NY 10003
(212) 254-1823

Ad Change
National Register Publishing
3004 Glenview Rd.
Wilmette, IL 60091
(708) 441-2182

AD/PR Agency Report
P.O. Box 715
Kentfield, CA 94904
(415) 461-2588
Fax: (415) 461-6526

AdVantage Point
AdVantage Point Press
80 Belvedere St., #A
San Rafael, CA 94901
(415) 485-6969
Fax: (415) 485-0143

Briefings
National Business Services
1120 Wheeler Way
Langhorne, PA 19047
(215) 752-4200

Broadcast Investor Charts
Paul Kagan Associates
126 Clock Tower Pl.
Carmel, CA 93923
(408) 624-1536
Fax: (408) 625-3225

Broadcast Stats
Paul Kagan Associates
126 Clock Tower Pl.
Carmel, CA 93923
(408) 624-1536
Fax: (408) 625-3225

Bulldog Reporter
InterCom
2115 Fourth St.
Berkeley, CA 94710
(510) 549-4300
Fax: (510) 549-4331

Channels
PR Publishing
P.O. Box 600
Exeter, NH 03833
(603) 778-0514
Fax: (603) 778-1741

Directory MarketPlace
Todd Publications
18 N Greenbush Rd.
West Nyack, NY 10994
(914) 358-6213

Idea Source Guide
Bramlee
P.O. Box 366
Devon, PA 19333

The Image Digest
Promotional Image Contract Associates
P.O. Box 1463
Ann Arbor, MI 48106
(313) 971-0780

Levin's Public Relations Report
Levin Public Relations & Marketing
30 Glenn St.
White Plains, NY 10603
(914) 993-0900
Fax: (914) 993-9589

Media Industry Newsletter
Phillips Publishing
145 E. 49th St., #7B
New York, NY 10017
(212) 751-2670
Fax: (212) 752-7301

Media Matters
Media Dynamics
18 E. 41st St., #1806
New York, NY 10017
(212) 683-7895
Fax: (212) 683-7684

Media News Keys
Television Index
40-29 27th St.
Long Island City, NY 11101
(718) 937-3990

Industry Newsletters (cont'd)

The Multinational PR Report
Pigafetta Press
P.O. Box 39244
Washington, DC 20016
(202) 244-2580
Fax: (202) 244-2581

The Nido Qubein Letter
Creative Services
P.O. Box 6008
High Point , NC 27262
(919) 889-3010

On Achieving Excellence
InterCom Group
2115 Fourth St.
Berkeley, CA 94710
(510) 549-4300
Fax: (510) 549-4331

Park Ave. South
Park Ave South Publications
165 W. 46th St.
New York, NY 10036
(212) 302-5363

Partyline, The PR Media Newsletter
Partyline Publishing
35 Sutton Pl.
New York, NY 10022
(212) 755-3487

Peak Performance Selling
Bureau of Business Practice
24 Rope Ferry Rd.
Waterford, CT 06386
(203) 442-4365

PR Marcom Jobs West
Rachel PR Services
513 Wilshire Blvd., #238
Santa Monica, CA 90401
(310) 326-2661
Fax: (310) 326-2825

PR Reporter
PR Publishing
P.O. Box 600
Exeter , NH 03833
(603) 778-0514
Fax: (603) 778-1741

The Pricing Advisor
3277 Roswell Rd., #620
Atlanta, GA 30305
(404) 252-5708
Fax: (404) 252-0637

Promotional Links
C.J. Kell Associates
824 Lynnhaven Pkwy., #114-254
Virginia Beach, VA 23452
011 39 81 869 3072
Fax: 011 39 82 526 2112

Public Relations News
Phillips Business Information
7811 Montrose Rd.
Potomac, MD 20854
800 777-5006

Publisher's Multinational Direct
Direct International
150 E. 74th St.
New York, NY 10021
(212) 861-4188
Fax: (212) 986-3757

Radio Business Report
P.O. Box 782
Springfield, VA 22150
(703) 866-9300
Fax: (703) 866-9306

The Radio Promotion Bulletin
Sullivan Company
P.O. Box 37236
Houston, TX 77237
(713) 684-6914

Tactics
Communications Management
13523 Barrett Parkway Dr., #221
Ballwin, MO 63021
(314) 569-3443
Fax: (314) 569-3443

Telecom Advertising Report
Communications Trends
2 East Ave.
Larchmont, NY 10538
(914) 833-0600
Fax: (914) 833-0558

Television & Radio Newsletter
Restivo Communications
107 S. West St., #199
Alexandria, VA 22314
(203) 355-7762

Tested Copy
Starch INRA Hooper
566 E Boston Post Rd.
Mamaroneck, NY 10543
(914) 698-0800
Fax: (914) 698-0485

Industry Newsletters (cont'd)

Video Marketing News
Phillips Publishing
7811 Montrose Rd.
Potomac, MD 20854
(301) 340-2100
Fax: (301) 309-3847

Yellow Pages & Directory Report
Communications Trends
2 East Ave.
Larchmont, NY 10538
(914) 833-0600
Fax: (914) 833-0558

Air Travel

Airline Newsletter
Roadcap Aviation Publications
1030 S. Green Bay
Lake Forest, IL 60045
(708) 234-4730

Airport Highlights
Airport Operators Council International
1220 19th St., NW, #200
Washington, DC 20036
(202) 293-8500
Fax: (202) 331-1362

Fun Seekers
PO Box 1222
Benicia, CA 94510
(415) 798-3866
Fax: (415) 825-6492

Aviation Daily
McGraw-Hill
1200 G St.
Washington, DC 20005
(202) 383-2369
Fax: (202) 383-2438

The Business Flyer
Holcon
P.O. Box 276
Newton Centre, MA 02159
(203) 782-2155
(800) 359-3774

Automobiles

Automotive Parts International
International Trade Services
P.O. Box 5950
Bethesda, MD 20824
(202) 857-8454
Fax: (202) 229-3995

Automotive Week
Automotive Week Publishing
P.O. Box 3495
Wayne, NJ 07474
(201) 694-7792/ 694 6076
Fax: (201) 694-2817

Car Rental/Leasing Insider
United Communications Group
11300 Rockville Pike, #1100
Rockville, MD 20852
(301) 816-8950
Fax: (301) 816-8945

Banking

Bank Bailout Litigation News
Buraff Publications
1350 Connecticut Ave., NW, #1000
Washington, DC 20036
(202) 862-0990

Bank Mergers & Acquisitions
SNL Securities L P
P.O. Box 2124
Charlottesville, VA 22902
(804) 977-1600
Fax: (804) 977-4466

Bank Securities Monthly
SNL Securities L P
P.O. Box 2124
Charlottesville, VA 22902
(804) 977-1600
Fax: (804) 977-4466

Business Law

Antitrust FOIA Log
Washington Regulatory Reporting Assocs
P.O. Box 356
Basye, VA 22810
(703) 856-2216

Bankruptcy Alert
Clark Boardman Callaghan
Aqueduct Building
Rochester, NY 14694
(716) 546-1490

Bankruptcy Law Letter
Warren, Gorham & Lamont
210 South St.
Boston, MA 02111
(800) 950-1205
Fax: (617) 423-2026

Industry Newsletters (cont'd)

BNA's Bankruptcy Law Reporter
Bureau of National Affairs
1231 25th St., NW
Washington, DC 20037
(202) 452-4200
Fax: (202) 822-8092

BNA's Corporate Counsel Weekly
Bureau of National Affairs
1231 25th St., NW
Washington, DC 20037
(202) 452-4200
Fax: (202) 822-8092

BNA's Patent, Trademark & Copyright Journal
Bureau of National Affairs
1231 25th St., NW
Washington, DC 20037
(202) 452-4200
Fax: (202) 822-8092

Cable TV and New Media Law & Finance
Leader Publications
111 8th Ave., #900
New York , NY 10011
(212) 463-5704
Fax: (212) 463-5523

Commodities Law Letter
Commodities Law Press Associates
40 Broad St., #2000
New York, NY 10004
(212) 612-9545
Fax: (212) 425-0266

Commodities Litigation Reporter
Andrews Publications
Box 1000
Westtown, PA 19395
(215) 399-6600
Fax: (215) 399-6610

Corporate Control Alert
American Lawyer Media L P
600 3rd Ave., 3rd Floor
New York, NY 10016
(212) 973-2800
Fax: (212) 973-2829

Europe 1992 Law & Strategy
Leader Publications
111 8th Ave., #900
New York, NY 10011
(212) 463-5709
Fax: (212) 463-5523

FTC:Watch-FTC Freedom Of Information Log
Washington Regulatory Reporting Assocs.
P.O. Box 356
Bayse, VA 22810
(703) 856-2216
(703) 856-8331

Indoor Pollution Law Report
Leader Publications
111 8th Ave., #900
New York, NY 10011
(212) 463-5704
Fax: (212) 463-5523

Industrial Negligence
Quinlan Publishing
131 Beverly St.
Boston, MA 02114
(617) 542-0048

Liability Reporter
Americans for Effective Law Enforcement
5519 N. Cumberland Ave., #1008
Chicago, IL 60656
(312) 763-2800

Licensing Law and Business Report
Clark Boardman Company
375 Hudson St.
New York, NY 10014
(212) 929-7500

Manager's Legal Bulletin
Alexander Hamilton Institute
97 W. Spring Valley Ave.
Maywood, NJ 07607
(201) 587-7050
Fax: (201) 587-7063

National Bankruptcy Litigation Reporter
Andrews Publications
Box 1000
Westtown, PA 19395
(215) 399-6600
Fax: (215) 399-6610

Product Safety Letter
Washington Business Information
1117 N. 19th St., #200
Arlington, VA 22209
(703) 247-3423
Fax: (703) 247-3421

Product Safety News
Institute for Product Safety
P.O. Box 1931
Durham, NC 27702 1931
(919) 489-2357

Industry Newsletters (cont'd)

Securities Regulation & Law Report
Bureau of National Affairs
1231 25th St., NW
Washington, DC 20037
(202) 452-4200
Fax: (202) 822-8092

Work In America
Buraff Publications
1350 Connecticut Ave., NW, #1000
Washington, DC 20036
(202) 862-0990
Fax: (202) 862-0999

Worker's Compensation Law Bulletin
Quinlan Publishing Company
131 Beverly St.
Boston, MA 02114
(617) 542-0048

You & The Law
National Institute of Business Management
P.O. Box 25287
Alexandria, VA 22313
(800) 543-2055
Fax: (703) 549-9705

Cellular Phones

Cellular Technology
Paul Kagan Associates
126 Clock Tower Pl.
Carmel, CA 93923
(408) 624-1536
Fax: (408) 625-3225

Collectibles

Car Collecting & Investing
Insightful Investor
175 Great Neck Rd., #307
Great Neck, NY 11021
(516) 446-7788
Fax: (516) 466-7808

Coin Quote
International Financial Publishers
1423 W. Fullerton
Chicago, IL 60614
(312) 528-8800

Connoisseur's Guide to California Wines
P.O. Box V
Alameda, CA 94501
(415) 865-3150

Jukebox Collector Newsletter
2545 SE 60th Ct.
Des Moines, IA 50317
(515) 265-8324

Kovels on Antiques and Collectibles
P.O. Box 420347
Palm Coast, FL 32142
(800) 829-9158
Fax: (216) 752-3115

The Photograph Collector
Photographic Arts Center
163 Amsterdam Ave., #201
New York, NY 10023
(212) 838-8640
Fax: (212) 873-7065

The Print Collector's Newsletter
119 E. 79th St.
New York, NY 10021
(212) 988-5959

The Rosen Numismatic Advisory
Numismatic Counseling
P.O. Box 38
Plainview, NY 11803
(516) 433-5800

The Wine Investor/Buyer's Guide
Wine Investor
3284 Barham Blvd., #201
Los Angeles, CA 90068
(213) 876-7590
Fax: (213) 876-4090

The Wine Investor-Executive Edition
3284 Barham Blvd., #201
Los Angeles, CA 90068
(213) 876-7590
Fax: (213) 876-4090

Colleges

Administrator: The Management Newsletter for Higher Education
Magna Publications
2718 Dryden Dr.
Madison, WI 53704
(608) 246-3580
Fax: (608) 249-0355

MBA Newsletter
Kwartler Communications
14 Cross St.
Port Washington, NY 11050
(516) 944-5957
Fax: (516) 944-5987

Industry Newsletters (cont'd)

Communications

Communications Daily
Warren Publishing
2115 Ward Ct., NW
Washington, DC 20037
(202) 872-9200
Fax: (202) 293-3435

Communications Industries Report
Int'l Communications Industries Association
3150 Spring St.
Fairfax, VA 22031
(703) 273-7200
Fax: (703) 728-8082

Communications Product Reports
Management Information
PO Box 5062
401 E. Route 70
Cherry Hill, NJ 08034
(609) 428-1020
Fax: (609) 428-1683

Current News on File
Facts On File
460 Park Avenue South
New York, NY 10016
(212) 683-2244
Fax: (212) 683-3633

Disaster Trends Update
QW Communications
P.O. Box 6591
Concord, NH 03303
(603) 648-2629

N-A Newsletter for Newsletters
Poll Communication Group
126 N. Third St., #200
Minneapolis, MN 55401
(612) 338-7664
Fax: (612) 338-5423

Trends in Communications Policy
Economics and Technology
Washington Mall
Boston, MA 02108
(617) 227-0900
Fax: (617) 227-5535

Computers

BYTEweek
BYTE Publications/McGraw-Hill
70 Main St.
Peterborough, NH 03458
(603) 924-9281
Fax: (603) 924-2550

Computer & Communications Buyer
Technology News of America
110 Greene St.
New York, NY 10012
(212) 334-9750

Computer Industry Report
International Data
P.O. Box 955, 5 Speen St.
Framingham , MA 01701
(508) 872-8200

Computer Price Guide
Computer Merchants
200 Brady Ave.
Hawthorne, NY 10532
(914) 769-2686

Computer Services & Software Report
De Boever, Tucker Technologies
50 Washington St.
S. Norwalk, CT 06854
(203) 857-0080
Fax: (203) 857 0082

Electronic Services Update
Link Resources
79 5th Ave.
New York, NY 10003
(212) 627-1500
Fax: (212) 620-3099

Information Industry Alert
Industry News Service
P.O. Box 457
Wilton, CT 06897
(203) 762-3206
Fax: (203) 834-0616

Information Industry Bulletin
Digital Information Group
51 Bank St.
Stamford, CT 06901
(203) 348-2751
Fax: (203) 977-8310

ISDN News
Phillips Business Information
7811 Montrose Rd.
Potomac, MD 20854
(301) 340-2100
Fax: (301) 424-4297

National Report on Computers & Health
United Communications Group
11300 Rockville Pike, #1000
Rockville, MD 20852
(301) 816-8950
Fax: (301) 816-8945

Industry Newsletters (cont'd)

Packaged Software Reports
Management Information
PO Box 5062
401 E. Route 70
Cherry Hill, NJ 08034
(609) 428-1020
Fax: (609) 428-1683

Software Digest
National Software Testing Laboratories
Plymouth Corporate Center, Box 1000
Plymouth Meeting, PA 19462
(215) 941-9600
Fax: (215) 941-9952

Software Industry Bulletin
Digital Information Group
51 Bank St.
Stamford, CT 06901
(203) 348-2751
Fax: (203) 977-8310

Software-Industry Report
Millin Publishing Group
3918 Prosperity Ave., #310
Fairfax, VA 22031
(703) 573-8400
Fax: (703) 573-8594

Word Processing: Quality Clinic
Bureau of Business Practice
24 Rope Ferry Rd.
Waterford, CT 06386
(203) 442-4365

Construction

Construction Market Data
4126 Pleasantdale Rd.
Atlanta, GA 30340
(404) 447-6633

Construction Policies–From The State Capitals
Wakeman/Walworth
300 N. Washington St., #204
Alexandria, VA 22314
(703) 549-8606
Fax: (703) 549-1372

Consulting

Consultant News
Kennedy Publications
Templeton Rd.
Fitzwilliam, NH 03447
(603) 585-6544
Fax: (603) 585-9221

Consulting Opportunities Journal
Consultants National Resource Center
P.O. Box 430
Clear Spring, MD 21722
(301) 791-9332

Management Consultant International
Lafferty Publications
2970 Clairmont Rd., NE, #800
Atlanta, GA 30329
(404) 636-6610
Fax: (404) 636-6422

Professional Consultant & Information Marketing Report
123 NW 2nd Ave., #403
Portland, OR 97209
(503) 224-8834
Fax: (503) 224-2104

Consumer Trends

Buying Strategy Forecast
Cahners Publishing
275 Washington St.
Newton, MA 02158
(617) 964-3030

Consumer Trends
Interantional Credit Association
243 N. Lindbergh Blvd.
St Louis, MO 63141
(314) 991-3030

Shopper Report
Consumer Network
3624 Science Center
Philadelphia, PA 19104
(215) 386-5890

Credit

Credit Risk Management Report
Phillips Business Information
7811 Montrose Rd.
Potomac, MD 20854
(301) 340-2100
Fax: (301) 309-3847

Dangerous Substances

Job Safety and Health
Bureau of National Affairs
1231 25th St., NW
Washington, DC 20037
(202) 452-4200
Fax: (202) 822-8092

Industry Newsletters (cont'd)

Economic Indicators

Blue Chip Economic Indicators
Capitol Publications
1101 King St., #444
Alexandria, VA 22314
(703) 683-4100

Charting the Economy
P.O. Box 829
New Haven, CT 06504
(203) 666-8664

Economic Education Bulletin
American Institute for Economic Research
Division St.
Great Barrington, MA 01230
(413) 528-1216
Fax: (413) 528-0103

Inside the Economy
Statistical Indicator Associates
P.O. Box 187
North Egremont, MA 01252
(413) 528-3280

Electronic Mail

Electronic Messaging News
Phillips Business Information
7811 Montrose Rd.
Potomac, MD 20854
(301) 340-2100
Fax: (301) 424-4297

EMMS–Electronic Mail & Micro Systems
International Resource Development
P.O. Box 1716
New Canaan, CT 06840
(203) 966-2525

Facsimile and Voice Services
Probe Research
3 Wing Dr., #240
Cedar Knolls, NJ 07927
(201) 285-1500
Fax: (201) 285-1519

Fax Reporter
Buyers Laboratory
20 Railroad Ave.
Hackensack , NJ 07601
(201) 488-0404
Fax: (201) 488-0461

Faxpaper
Hartford Courant
285 Broad St.
Hartford, CT 06115
(203) 241-6200

ISDN Newsletter
Information Gatekeepers
214 Harvard Ave.
Boston, MA 02134
(617) 232-3111
(800) 323-1088
Fax: (617) 734-8562

Electronics

EDI Executive
EDI Executive Publishing
1639 Desford Court
Marietta, GA 30064
(404) 499-8296
Fax: (404) 578-4980

Henderson Electronic Market Forecast
Henderson Ventures
101 1st St., #444
Los Altos, CA 94022
(415) 961-2900
Fax: (415) 961-3090

Industrial Communications
Phillips Business Inormation
7811 Montrose Rd.
Potomac, MD 20854
(301) 340-2100
Fax: (301) 424-4297

Environment

Business & The Environment
Cutter Information
37 Broadway
Arlington, MA 02174
(617) 648-8700
Fax: (617) 648-8707

Environment Report
Trends Publishing
1079 National Press Building
Washington, DC 20045
(202) 393-0031

Industry Newsletters (cont'd)

Environment Reporter
Bureau of National Affairs
1231 25th St., NW
Washington, DC 20037
(202) 452-4200
Fax: (202) 822-8092

Environmental Manager
Executive Enterprises
22 W. 21st St., 10th Floor
New York, NY 10010
(212) 645-7880
Fax: (212) 645-1160

Environmental Manager's Compliance Advisor
Business & Legal Reports
39 Academy St.
Madison, CT 06443
(203) 245-7448
Fax: (203) 245-2559

Finance

Accounting & Tax Highlights
Warren Gorham & Lamont
210 South St.
Boston , MA 02111
(800) 950-1216

The Advisory Letter for Concerned Investors
Franklin Research and Development
1711 Atlantic Ave., 5th Floor
Boston, MA 02111
(617) 423-6655

All-Weather Fund Investor
Growth Fund Research
P.O. Box 6600
Rapid City, SD 57709
(605) 341-1971

Best Investor
Man Computer Systems
84-13 168th St.
Jamaica, NY 11432
(718) 739-4242

Blue Chip Financial Forecasts
Capitol Publications
1101 King St., #444
Alexandria , VA 22314
(703) 683-4100
Fax: (703) 739-6517

Bondweek
Institutional Investor
488 Madison Ave., 15th Floor
New York, NY 10022
(212) 303-3233
Fax: (212) 421-7038

Buy Low–Sell High
Securities Investment Management
1224 Vallecita Dr.
Santa Fe, NM 87501
(505) 989-9224

Commodity Price Charts
Futures Magazine
PO Box 6
219 Parkade
Cedar Falls, IA 50613
(319) 277-6341

CPA Digest
CPA Services
16800 W. Greenfield Ave.
Brookfield, WI 53005
(414) 797-9999
Fax: (414) 782-7997

The CPA Letter
American Institute of CPAs
1211 Ave. of the Americas
New York, NY 10036
(212) 575-5417
Fax: (212) 575-6848

Financial Market Trends
Organization for Economic
Cooperation and Development
2001 L St., NW, #700
Washington, DC 20036
(202) 785-6323

Futures Market Service
Knight-Ridder Financial Publishing
75 Wall St., 22nd Floor
New York, NY 10005
(212) 504-7742
Fax: (212) 809-5442

GOOD MONEY Newsletter
Good Money Publications
P.O. Box 363
Worcester, VT 05682
(800) 535-3551
Fax: (802) 223-8949

IBC/Donoghue's Quarterly Report on Money Fund Performance
P.O. Box 91004
290 Eliot St.
Ashland, MA 01721
(508) 881-2800
(800) 343-5413
Fax: (508) 881-0982

Industry Newsletters (cont'd)

Investment Guide
American Investment Services
Division St.
Great Barrington, MA 02130
(413) 528-1216
Fax: (413) 528-0103

IRS Practice Alert
Warren Gorham & Lamont
210 South St.
Boston, MA 02111
(800) 922-0066
Fax: (617) 423-2026

The Jacobs Report on Retirement and Tax Planning Strategies
Research Press
4500 W. 72nd Terrace
Shawnee Village, KS 66208
(913) 362-9667
Fax: (913) 383-3505

Letters of Credit Report
Executive Enterprises
22 W. 21st St., 10th Floor
New York, NY 10010
(212) 645-7880
Fax: (212) 645-1160

Long Term Investing
Concept Publishing
P.O. Box 203
York, NY 14592
(716) 243-3148

Making Ends Meet
Pascit Publications
P.O. Box 1125
Traverse City, MI 49685
(616) 929-7227

Marketing Timing Report
P.O. Box 225
Tucson, AZ 85702
(602) 795-9552

Marple's Business Newsletter
Newsletter Publishing
117 W. Mercer St., #200
Seattle, WA 98119
(206) 281-9609
Fax: (206) 285-8035

Mutual Fund Investing
Phillips Publishing
7811 Montrose Rd.
Potomac, MD 20854
(301) 340-2100
Fax: (301) 424-7034

Newsletter Digest
2201 Big Cove Rd.
Huntsville, AL 35801
(205) 534-1535
Fax: (205) 533-4871

O.T.C. Growth Stock Watch
O T C Research
P.O. Box 305
Brookline, MA 02146
(617) 327-8420
Fax: (617) 327-8486

Penny Stocks Newsletter
12149 6th St.
Yucaipa, CA 92390
(714) 797-2155

Personal Moneyplan
Felton Enterprises
501 Palmetto Dr., #100
Pasadena, CA 91105
(818) 795-5115

Plain Talk Investor
Plain Talk Investor
1500 Skokie Blvd., #203
Northbrook, IL 60062
(708) 564-1955

Platinum Perspective
Henry Gammage & Co
P.O. Box 81487
Atlanta, GA 30366
(404) 261-7744
Fax: (404) 261-7744

Real Estate Tax Ideas
Warren Gorham & Lamont
210 South St.
Boston, MA 02111
(617) 423-2026
(800) 950-1205

Real Estate Tax Letter
John Clark Financial Development
505 E. 1st St., #H
Tustin, CA 92680
(714) 832-6246

Industry Newsletters (cont'd)

The Review of Securities & Commodities Regulation
Standard & Poor's
25 Broadway
New York, NY 10004
(212) 208-8650
Fax: (212) 412-0299

SEC Today
Washington Service Bureau
655 15th St., NW
Washington, DC 20005
(202) 508-0600
Fax: (202) 508-0694

Securities Week
McGraw-Hill
1221 Avenue of the Americas
New York, NY 10020
(212) 997-3144

The Small Business Tax Review
A/N Group
17 Scott Dr.
Melville, NY 11747
(516) 549-4090

The Tax Adviser
1211 Avenue of the Americas
New York, NY 10036
(212) 575-6317

Tax Avoidance Digest
Agora
824 E. Baltimore St.
Baltimore, MD 21202
(404) 234-0515

Tax Haven Reporter
Thomas P. Azzara
P.O. Box CB 11552
Nassau, Bahamas
(809) 327-7359
Cellular: (809) 359-1132

Tax Management Compensation Planning Journal
Tax Management Estates, Gifts and Trusts Journal
Tax Management Financial Planning
Tax Management Financial Planning Journal
Tax Management Foreign Income Portfolios
Tax Management International Journal
Tax Management Real Estate Journal
Tax Management Washington Tax Review
Tax Management
1231 23rd St., NW
Washington, DC 20037
(202) 833-7240
Fax: (202) 833-7297

Tax Planning Review
Commerce Clearing House
4025 W. Peterson Ave.
Chicago, IL 60646
(312) 583-8500

Taxation of Mergers & Acquisitions
Faulkner & Gray
106 Fulton St.
New York, NY 10038
(212) 766-7800

Technical Trends
P.O. Box 792
Wilton, CT 06897
(203) 762-0229
(800) 736-0229

General Business

Association's Report
Galloway Publications
2940 NW Circle Blvd.
Corvallis, OR 97330
(503) 754-7464

The Bruce Report
Bruce Consulting Group
2865 Broderick
San Francisco, CA 94123
(415) 346-7230
Fax: (415) 346-7442

Business & Acquisition Newsletter
Newsletters International
2600 S Gessner Rd.
Houston, TX 77063
(713) 783-0100

Business Ideas
Dan Newman Co.
1051 Bloomfield Ave.
Clifton, NJ 07012
(201) 778-6677

Business Line
1151 NE Todd George Rd.
Lee's Summit, MO 64141
(816) 525-4484

Business Newsletter
Business Newsletter
537 E. Vine St.
Owatonna, MN 55060
(507) 455-3220

Industry Newsletters (cont'd)

Business Now
Dartnell's Marketing Publications
286 Congress St.
Boston, MA 02110
(617) 451-7751
(800) 468-3068
Fax: (617) 451-8149

Business Planning Advisory
WPI Communications
55 Morris Ave.
Springfield, NJ 07081
(201) 467-8700
(800) 323-4995
(210) 467-0368

The Business Publisher
JK Publishing
P.O. Box 71020
Milwaukee, WI 53211
(414) 332-1625
Fax: (414) 962-0084

Businessgram
BusinessGram
P.O. Box 273390
Tampa, FL 33688
(813) 968-2979

Economic Development–From the State Capitals
Wakeman/Walworth
300 N. Washington St., #204
Alexandria, VA 22314
(703) 549-8606
Fax: (703) 549-1372

Economic Growth Report
CD Publications
8204 Fenton St., 2nd Floor
Silver Spring, MD 20910
(301) 588-6380
Fax: (301) 588-6385

The Entrepreneurial Economy
Corporation for Enterprise Development
777 N. Capital St., NE, #801
Washington, DC 20002
(202) 408-9788
Fax: (202) 408-9793

Forecaster
Forecaster Pub
19623 Ventura Blvd.
Tarzana, CA 91356
(818) 345-4421

General Trends–From the State Capitals
Wakeman/Walworth
300 N. Washington St., #204
Alexandria, VA 22314
(703) 549-8606
Fax: (703) 549-1372

Global Report
Center for War/Peace Studies
218 E. 18th St.
New York, NY 10003
(212) 475-1077

Industry Forecast
Jerome Levy Economic Institute of Bard College
P.O. Box 26
223 N. Greeley Ave
Chappaqua, NY 10514
(914) 238-3665
Fax: (914) 238-4599

The Main Report Business & Executive Letter
Main Report Publications
P.O. Box 1046
47 Birmingham Dr.
Christchurch, New Zealand 8000
03 338 6068
Fax: 03 338 6071

The TJFR Business News Reporter
TJFR Publishing
545 N. Maple Ave., 2nd Floor
Ridgewood, NJ 07450
(201) 444-6061
Fax: (201) 444-5919

Working Smart
National Institute of Business Management
P.O. Box 25287
Alexandria, VA 22313
(800) 543-2049
Fax: (703) 549-9705

The Yellow Sheet
Communications Management
13523 Barrett Parkway Dr., #221
Ballwin, MO 63021
(314) 569-3443
Fax: (314) 569-3443

Gold

American Gold News
P.O. Box 849
Beaver, UT 84713
(801) 438-5020

Gold Newsletter
Lakeview Publishing
PO Box 2430
2400 Jefferson Highway
Chelan, WA 98816
(509) 687-9750
Fax: (509) 687-9321

Industry Newsletters (cont'd)

Gold Standard News
Gold Standard
1805 Grand Ave.
Kansas City, MO 64108
(816) 842-4653

Powell Gold Industry Guide, The
Reserve Research
P.O. Box 4135, Station A
Portland, ME 04101
(207) 774-4971

Precious Metals Data Base
Moneypower
P.O. Box 22644
Minneapolis, MN 55422
(612) 537-8096

Graphics

Board Report For Graphic Artists
P.O. Box 1561
Harrisburg, PA 17105
(717) 774-5413

Plus Business
Metro Creative Graphics
33 W. 34th St.
New York, NY 10001
(212) 947-5100
Fax: (212) 976-4602

Health

Benefits Today
Bureau of National Affairs
1231 25th St., NW
Washington, DC 20037
(202) 452-4200
Fax: (202) 822-8092

Employee Assistance Program Management Letter
American Business Publishing
3100 Highway 138, P.O. Box 1442
Wall Township, NJ 07719
(908) 681-1133
Fax: (908) 681-0490

Employee Health & Fitness
American Health Consultants
PO Box 940056
Atlanta, GA 30374
(404) 262-7436
Fax: (404) 262-7837

The Executive Report on Managed Care
American Business Publishing
3100 Highway 138
PO Box 1442
Wall Township, NJ 07719
(908) 681-1133
Fax: (908) 681-0490

OSHA Compliance Advisor (OCA)
Business & Legal Reports
39 Academy St.
Madison, CT 06443
(203) 245-7448
Fax: (203) 245-2559

OSHA Compliance Advisor (with Encyclopedia) (OCB)
Business & Legal Reports
39 Academy St.
Madison, CT 06443
(203) 245-7448
Fax: (203) 245-2559

Safety Compliance Letter
Bureau of Business Practice
24 Rope Ferry Rd.
Waterford, CT 06386
(203) 442-4365

Human Resources

Creative Training Techniques
Lakewood Publications
50 S. Ninth St.
Minneapolis, MN 55402
(612) 333-0471
Fax: (612) 333-6526

Discipline and Grievances
Bureau of Business Practice
24 Rope Ferry Rd.
Waterford, CT 06386
(203) 442-4365

EEOC Compliance Manual
Bureau of National Affairs
1231 25th St., NW
Washington, DC 20037
(202) 452-4200
Fax: (202) 822-8092

Employee Assistance Program Management Letter
American Business Publishing
3100 Highway 138, PO Box 1442
Wall Township, NJ 07719
(908) 681-1133
Fax: (908) 681-0490

Employee Benefit Notes
Employee Benefit Research Institute
2121 K St., NW, #600
Washington, DC 20037
(202) 659-0670

Industry Newsletters (cont'd)

Employee Benefits Cases
Bureau of National Affairs
1231 25th St., NW
Washington, DC 20037
(202) 452-4200
Fax: (202) 882-8092

Employee Relations and Human Resources Bulletin
Bureau of Business Practice
24 Rope Ferry Rd.
Waterford, CT 06386
(800) 243-0876

Employee Relations Report
HR Communication Services
P.O. Box 671
Richmond, VA 23206
(804) 751-5003

Employee Security Connection
National Security Institute
161 Worcester Rd.
Framingham, MA 01701
(508) 872-8001
Fax: (508) 872-6153

Employers' Health Benefits Management Letter
American Business Publishing
3100 Highway 138, PO Box 1442
Wall Township, NJ 07719
(908) 681-1133
Fax: (908) 681-0490

Equal Employment Compliance Update
Callaghan & Co
155 Pfingsten Rd.
Deerfield, IL 60015
(708) 948-7000
(800) 323-1336

Fair Employment Practices
Bureau of National Affairs
1231 25th St., NW
Washington, DC 20037
(202) 452-4200
Fax: (202) 822-8092

Government Employee Relations Report
Bureau of National Affairs
1231 25th St., NW
Washington, DC 20047
(202) 452-4200
Fax: (202) 822-8092

Hiring & Firing
Carswell
2075 Kennedy Rd.
Scarborough, Ontario Canada MIT 3V4
(416) 609-3800
Fax: (416) 298-5094

Individual Employment Rights
Bureau of National Affairs
1231 25th St., NW
Washington, DC 20037
(202) 452-4200
Fax: (202) 822-8092

Job Finder
Western Governmental Research
10900 Los Alamitos Blvd., #201
Los Alamitos, CA 90720
(310) 795-6694
Fax: (310) 795-6697

The Office Professional
Professional Training Associates
210 Commerce Blvd.
Round Rock, TX 78664
(512) 255-6006
Fax: (512) 255-7532

The Personnel Alert
Alexander Hamilton Institute
197 W. Spring Valley Ave.
Maywood, NJ 07607
(201) 587-7050
Fax: (201) 587-7063

Personnel Management
Bureau of National Affairs
1231 25th St., NW
Washington, DC 20037
(202) 452-4200
Fax: (202) 822-8092

Personnel Update
Dartnell
4660 N. Ravenswood Ave.
Chicago, IL 60640
(312) 561-4000
Fax: (312) 561-3801

PPF Survey (Personnel Policies Forum)
Bureau of National Affairs
1231 25th St., NW
Washington, DC 20037
(202) 452-4200
Fax: (202) 822-8092

Program Trends for Business & Industry
Learning Resources Network
1554 Hayes Dr.
Manhattan, KS 66502
(913) 539-5376

Industry Newsletters (cont'd)

Recruitment and Retention
Magna Publications
2718 Dryden Drive
Madison, WI 53704
(608) 246-3580
Fax: (608) 249-0355

Training & Development Alert
Advanced Personnel Systems
P.O. Box 1438
Roseville, CA 95678
(916) 781-2900, ext. 2901

Wages and Hours
Bureau of National Affairs
1231 25th St., NW
Washington, DC 20037
(202) 452-4200
Fax: (202) 822-8092

What To Do About Personnel Problems In (your state)
Business & Legal Reports
39 Academy St.
Madison, CT 06443
(203) 245-7448
Fax: (203) 245-2559

What's Ahead in Human Resources
Remy Publishing
350 W. Hubbard
Chicago, IL 60610
(312) 464-0300
Fax: (312) 464-0166

Work in America
Buraff Publications
1350 Connecticut Ave., NW, #1000
Washington, DC 20036
(202) 862-0990
Fax: (202) 862-0999

International

American Export Marketer
Welt Publishing
1413 K St., NW, #800
Washington, DC 20005
(202) 377-0555
Fax: (202) 408-9369

Brown University World Business Advisory, The
Manisses Communications Group
PO Box 3357
Providence , RI 02906
(401) 831-6020
Fax: (401) 861-6370

Business Asia
Economists Intelligence Unit
215 Park Ave. S.
New York, NY 10003
(212) 460-0600

Business International
Economists Intelligence Unit
215 Park Avenue S.
New York, NY 10003
(212) 460-0600

Business International Money Report
Economists Intelligence Unit
215 Park Avenue S.
New York, NY 10003
(212) 460-0600

East-West Technology Digest
Welt Publishing
1413 K St., NW, #800
Washington, DC 20005
(202) 371-0555
Fax: (202) 408-9369

Europa 1992
Wolfe Publishing
P.O. Box 7599 South Station
Nashua, NH 03060
(603) 888-0338
Fax: (603) 888-5816

Government Business Reports Worldwide
P.O. Box 5997
Washington, DC 20016
(202) 244-7050
Fax: (202) 244-5412

The Harriman Institute Forum
Harriman Institute, Columbia University
420 W. 118th St.
New York, NY 10027
(212) 854-6218

Inside US Trade
Inside Washington Publishers
P.O. Box 7167 Ben Franklin Station
Washington, DC 20044
(703) 892-8500
Fax: (203) 685-2606

International Business Opportunities Bulletin
U.J. Import-Export Publications
PO Box 428
Bellflower, CA 90707
(213) 925-2918
Fax: (213) 804-1234

Industry Newsletters (cont'd)

International Fund Monitor
Research International
P.O. Box 5754
Washington, DC 20016
(202) 363-3097

International Information Report
Washington Researchers Publishing
2612 P St., NW
Washington, DC 20007
(202) 333-3533

International Intertrade Index
P.O. Box 636 Federal Square
Newark, NJ 07101
(201) 686-2382

International Law & Trade Perspective
P.O. Box 27495
Washington, DC 20038
(202) 429-2098

International Market Alert
International Reports
114 E. 32nd St., #602
New York, NY 10016
(212) 685-6900
Fax: (212) 685-8566

International Money & Politics
MM
420 S. Orlando Ave.
Winter Park, FL 32789
(407) 629-9229
Fax: (407) 647-3567

International Trade and Investment Letter
International Business Affairs
4905 Del Ray Ave., #302
Bethesda , MD 20814
(301) 907-8647
Fax: (301) 907-8650

International Trade Reporter Current Reports
Bureau of National Affairs
1231 25th St., NW
Washington, DC 20037
(202) 452-4200
Fax: (202) 822-8092

Japan Financial Market Report
Japan Market Research
609 Columbus Ave.
New York, NY 10024
(212) 496-6760

Joint Venture News
Transmart Company
3581 Kachemak Circle
Anchorage, AK 99515
(907) 349-5481
Fax: (907) 522-1489

Major Trends
250 W. Coventry Ct.
Milwaukee, WI 53217
(414) 352-8460

Market Europe
W-Two Publications
202 The Commons, #401
Ithaca, NY 14850
(607) 277-0934
Fax: (607) 277-0935

Markets Abroad
Strawberry Media
2460 Lexington Dr.
Owosso, MI 48867
(517) 725-9072

Mideast Report
P.O. Box 2460, Grand Central Station
New York, NY 10163
(212) 714-3530
Fax: (212) 714-3510

Near East Report
Near East Research
440 First St., NW, #607
Washington, DC 20001
(202) 639-5254
Fax: (202) 347-4916

Nielsen's International Investment Letter
Nielsen & Nielsen
P.O. Box 7532
Olympia, WA 98507

Random Lengths Export Market Report
Random Lengths Publications
P.O. Box 867
Eugene, OR 97440
(503) 686-9925
Fax: (800) 874-7979

Washington Tariff & Trade Letter
Gilston Communications Group
P.O. Box 467
Washington, DC 20044
(301) 570-4544
Fax: (301) 570-4545

Industry Newsletters (cont'd)

World Market Perspective
World Market Perspective Publishing
3443 Parkway Center Court
Orlando, FL 32763
(407) 290-9600
Fax: (407) 290-9622

World Trade & Business Digest
Kassanga International
213 E. 88th St.
New York, NY 10028
(212) 427-7176

The World Trade Newsletter
Aronds Publishing
12928 Valleywood Dr.
Wheaton, MD 20906
(301) 942-2517

Worldwide Investment Notes
P.O. Box 16041
St. Louis, MO 63105
(314) 726-2731

Literacy

Report on Literacy Programs
Business Publishers
951 Pershing Dr.
Silver Spring, MD 20910
(301) 587-6300
Fax: (301) 587-1081

Management

Academy of Management News
Baugh Center for Entrepreneurship
Baylor University, BU Box 8011
Waco, TX 76798
(817) 755-2265
Fax: (817) 755-2421

Administration & Management
National Technical Information Service
U.S. Department of Commerce
5285 Port Royal Rd.
Springfield, VA 22161
(703) 487-4630

Advanced Management Report, English & Intl
Advanced Management Publishers
1357 Washington St.
Newton, MA 02165
(617) 964-5080

Applied Management Newsletter
National Association for Management
1617 Murray
Wichita, KS 67212
(316) 721-4684

BNA's Employee Relations Weekly
Bureau of National Affairs
1231 25th St., NW
Washington, DC 20037
(202) 452-4200
Fax: (202) 822-8092

Collective Bargaining Negotiations and Contracts
Bureau of National Affairs
1231 25th St., NW
Washington, DC 20037
(202) 452-4200
Fax: (202) 822-8092

Employer Advocate
Independent Small Business Employers
520 S. Pierce, #224
Mason City, IA 50401
(515) 424-3187
Fax: (515) 424-1673

The Entrepreneurial Manager's Newsletter
Center for Entrepreneurial Management
180 Varick St., Penthouse
New York, NY 10014
(212) 633-0060
Fax: (212) 633-0063

From Nine To Five
Dartnell
4660 N. Ravenswood Ave.
Chicago , IL 60640
(312) 561-4000
Fax: (312) 561-3801

Labor Notes
Labor Education & Research Project
7435 Michigan Ave.
Detroit, MI 48210
(313) 842-6262

Labor Relations
Bureau of National Affairs
1231 25th St., NW
Washington, DC 20037
(202) 452-4200
Fax: (202) 822-8092

Labor Relations Reporter
Bureau of National Affairs
1231 25th St., NW
Washington, DC 20037
(202) 452-4200
Fax: (202) 822-8092

Labor Relations–From The State Capitals
Wakeman/Walworth
300 N. Washington St., #204
Alexandria, VA 22314
(703) 549-8606
Fax: (703) 549-1372

Industry Newsletters (cont'd)

Management Confidential
Stonehart Publications
57-61 Mortimer St.
London, England W1N 7TD

Management Letter
Bureau of Business Practice
24 Rope Ferry Rd.
Waterford, CT 06386
(203) 442-4365
Fax: (203) 434-3341

Management Matters
Infoteam
P.O. Box 15640
Plantation, FL 33318
(305) 473-9560
Fax: (305) 473-0544

Management Report
Executive Enterprises
22 W. 21st St., 10th Floor
New York, NY 10010
(212) 645-7880
Fax: (212) 645-1160

OSHA Compliance Advisor
Business & Legal Reports
39 Academy St.
Madison, CT 06443
(203) 245-7448
Fax: (203) 245-2559

Strategic Planning Management
Commerce Communications
5247 Washburn Ave., S.
Minneapolis, MN 55410
(612) 924-0957

The Supervisor's Source
P.O. Box 682
Wynantskill, NY 12198
(518) 283-1370

Union Labor Report
Bureau of National Affairs
1231 25th St., NW
Washington, DC 20037
(202) 452-4200
Fax: (202) 822-8092

Update: The Executive's Purchasing Advisor
Buyers Laboratory
20 Railroad Ave.
Hackensack, NJ 07601
(201) 488-0404

Manufacturing

American Industry
Publications for Industry
21 Russell Woods Rd.
Great Neck, NY 11021
(516) 487-0990
Fax: (516) 487-0809

Industrial Purchasing Agent
Publications for Industry
21 Russell Woods Rd.
Great Neck, NY 11021
(516) 487-0990
Fax: (516) 487-0809

Inside R&D
Technical Insights
P.O. Box 1304
Fort Lee, NJ 07024
(201) 568-4744
Fax: (201) 568-8247

Quality Assurance Bulliten
Bureau of Business Practice
24 Rope Ferry Road
Waterford CT 06386
(203) 442-4635

Marketing

American Marketplace
Business Publishers
951 Pershing Dr.
Silver Spring, MD 20910
(301) 587-6300
Fax: (301) 587-1081

Business Mailers Review
1813 Shepherd St., NW
Washington, DC 20011
(202) 723-3397

Dartnell Sales and Marketing Executive Report
Dartnell
4660 N. Ravenswood Ave.
Chicago, IL 60640
(312) 561-4000
Fax: (312) 561-3801

Frohlinger's Marketing Report
Marketing Strategist Communications
2060 Holland Ave.
Merrick, NY 11566
(800) 962-7538
(516) 867-7253

Industry Newsletters (cont'd)

The Information Report
Washington Researchers Publishing
2612 P St., NW
Washington, DC 20007
(202) 333-3533

Inside Mass Marketing
IMM Marketing Group
200 Boylston St., #126
Chestnut Hill, MA 02167
(617) 969-4700

Jack O'Dwyer's Newsletter
J.R. O'Dwyer
271 Madison Ave.
New York, NY 10016
(212) 679-2471
Fax: (212) 683-2750

John Naisbitt's Trend Letter
The Global Network
1101 30th St., NW, #130
Washington, DC 20007
(202) 337-5960
Fax: (202) 333-5198

Marketing Breakthroughs
World Business Publications
4th Floor, Britannia House
960 High Rd.
London, N12 9RY England
081-446-5141
Fax: 081-446-3659

Marketing Insights
WPI Communications
55 Morris Ave.
Springfield, NJ 07081
(800) 323-4995
Fax: (201) 467-0368

The Marketing Pulse
Unlimited Positive Communications
P.O. Box 1173
Woodstock, NY 12498
(914) 255-2222, ext. 3130
Fax: (914) 255-2231

Marketing & Sales Journal
First Information Technology Group
P.O. Box 372
4 Flint St.
Marblehead, MA 01945

Marketing to Women
About Women
33 Broad St.
Boston, MA 02109
(617) 723-4337
Fax: (617) 723-7107

Marketing Update
Predicasts
11001 Cedar Ave.
Cleveland, OH 44106
(216) 795-3000
Fax: (216) 229-9944

Professional Telephone Selling
Bureau of Business Practice
24 Rope Ferry Rd.
Waterford, CT 06386
(203) 442-4365
(800) 243-0876

Public Pulse
Roper Organization
205 E. 42nd St.
New York, NY 10017
(212) 599-0700
Fax: (212) 687-2102

Sales & Marketing Digest
Marsili Publishing
P.O. Box 4315
Rockford, IL 61110
(815) 547-4311

School Marketing Newsletter
School Market Research Institute
P.O. Box 10
1721 Saybrook Rd.
Haddam, CT 06438
(203) 345-4018
Fax: (203) 345-3985

Siedlecki On Marketing
Richard Siedlecki Business and
Marketing Consulting
2996 Grandview, #305
Atlanta, GA 30305
(805) 658-7000

The SpeciaList's MarketPulse
SpeciaLists
120 E. 16th St.
New York, NY 10003
(212) 677-6760

TA Report
Communications Trends
2 East Ave.
Larchmont, NY 10538
(914) 833-0600
Fax: (914) 833-0558

Telemarketing Update
Prosperity & Profits Unlimited Distribution Services
Box 570213
Houston, TX 77257
(713) 867-3438

Industry Newsletters (cont'd)

Telephone Selling Report
Business By Phone
5301 S. 144th St.
Omaha, NE 68137
(402) 895-9399
Fax: (402) 896-3353

Tradeshow Week
Tradeshow Week
12233 W. Olympic Blvd., #236
Los Angeles, CA 90064
(213) 826-5696

Miscellaneous

Andrew Harper's Hideaway Report
Harper Associates
P.O. Box 50
Sun Valley, ID 83353
(208) 622-3183

Antitrust & Trade Regulation Report
Bureau of National Affairs
1231 25th St., NW
Washington, DC 20037
(202) 452-4200
Fax: (202) 822-8092

Backpacking Newsletter
PO Box 3818
Downey, CA 90242

Bottom Line Personal Incorporating Privileged Information
Boardroom Reports
330 W. 42nd St.
New York, NY 10036
(212) 239-9000

Business Information Alert
Alert Publications
399 Fullerton Parkway
Chicago, IL 60614
(312) 525-7594

The Business Initiative Newsletter
Ecomedia
315 E. 65th St.
New York, NY 10021
(212) 794-8902

Buyouts Newsletter
Venture Economics
40 W. 57th St., #802
New York, NY 10019
(212) 765--5311
Fax: (212) 765-6123

Drugs In The Workplace
Business Research Publications
817 Broadway, 3rd Floor
New York, NY 10003
(212) 673-4700
Fax: (212) 475-1790

Executives' Digest
Dartnell's Marketing Publications
286 Congress St.
Boston, MA 02110
(617) 451-7551
(800) 468-3038
Fax: (617) 451-8149

Hazardous Materials Transportation
Washington Business Information
1117 N. 19th St., #200
Arlington, VA 22209
(703) 247-3424
Fax: (703) 247-3421

Innovator's Digest
Infoteam
P.O. Box 15640
Plantation, FL 33318
(305) 473-9560
Fax: (305) 473-0544

Kosher Business
Kosher Business
PO Box 66136
Albany, NY 12206
(518) 438-9328
Fax: (518) 438-1284

Leisure Business, US Report on Travel, Tourism & Recreation Industries
Leisure Information Service
P.O. Box 1992
700 Orange St.
Wilmington, DE 19899
(302) 656-2209

Licensing Journal, The
GB Enterprises
P.O. Box 1169
Stamford, CT 06904
(203) 358-0848
Fax: (203) 348-2720

Metals Week
McGraw-Hill
1221 Ave. of the Americas
New York, NY 10020
(212) 512-2823
Fax: (212) 512-2504

Industry Newsletters (cont'd)

National Right To Work Newsletter
8001 Braddock Rd.
Springfield, VA 22160
(703) 321-9820
Fax: (703) 321-7342

The Newsletter On Newsletters
Newsletter Clearinghouse
P.O. Box 311
44 W. Market St.
Rhinebeck, NY 12572
(914) 876-2081
Fax: (914) 876-2561

Nutshell– A Digest of Employee Benefit Publications
Country Press
P.O. Box 5880
Snowmass Village, CO 81615
(303) 923-3210

Options Unlimited: The Newsletter of Alternatives to Traditional Employment
Davcol Group
1660 Oak Tree Rd., #155
Edison, NJ 08820
(201) 668-8164

The PresentFutures Report
PresentFutures Group
101 Park Washington Ct.
Falls Church, VA 22046
(703) 538-6181
Fax: (703) 538-6713

The Quality Executive
B&B Press
Box 801, Radio City Station
New York, NY 10102
(212) 582-3791

Safety Management
Bureau of Business Practice
24 Rope Ferry Rd.
Waterford, CT 06386
(203) 442-4365

Taxation & Revenue Policies–From the State Capitals
Wakeman/Walworth
300 N. Washington St., #204
Alexandria, VA 22314
(703) 549-8606
Fax: (703) 549-1372

Tourist Business Promotion–From the State Capitals
Wakeman/Walworth
300 N. Washington St., #204
Alexandria, VA 22314
(703) 549-8606
Fax: (703) 549-1372

Travel Expense Management
American Business Publishing
P.O. Box 1442
3100 Highway 138
Wall Township, NJ 07719
(908) 681-1133
Fax: (908) 681-0490

Washington Executive Travel Report
1728 21st St., NW
Washington, DC 20009
(202) 328-0810
Fax: (202) 328-1101

The Worker's Compensation Review
Carswell
2075 Kennedy Blvd.,
Scarborough, Ont. Canada M1T 3V4
(416) 609-3800
Fax: (416) 298-5094

Working At Home
P.O. Box 200504
Cartersville, GA 30120
(706) 386-1257

Networking

Linc: Linking Issue Networks for Cooperation
Issue Action Publications
219 South St., SE
Leesburg, VA 22075
(703) 777-8450

Public Speaking

The Executive Speechwriter Newsletter
Words Ink
Emerson Falls
St. Johnsbury, VT 05819
(802) 748-4472
Fax: (802) 748-1939

Speechwriter's Newsletter
Ragan Communications
212 W. Superior St., #200
Chicago,, IL 60610
(312) 335-0037
Fax: (312) 335-9583

Industry Newsletters (cont'd)

Publishing

Publishing Trends & Trendsetters
Oxbridge Communications
150 Fifth Ave.
New York, NY 10011
(212) 741-0231
Fax: (212) 633-2938

Real Estate

Digest of State Land Sales Regulations
Land Development Institute
1300 N St., NW
Washington, DC 20005
(202) 232-2144

Foreclosure Hotlist
Foreclosure Research of America
P.O. Box 10236
Rockville, MD 20849
(301) 590-1177
Fax: (301) 921-6380

Housing Market Report
CD Publications
8204 Fenton St., 2nd Floor
Silver Spring, MD 20910
(301) 588-6380
Fax: (301) 588-6385

Insider
Maclean Hunter Media
Four Stamford Forum
Stamford, CT 06901
(203) 325-3500
Fax: (203) 325-8423

Landlord–Tenant Relations Report
CD Publications
8204 Fenton St., 2nd Floor
Silver Spring, MD 20910
(301) 588-6380
Fax: (301) 588-6385

Leasing Professional
P.O. Box 5675
Scottsdale, AZ 85261
(602) 860-0659
Fax: (602) 451-7957

Managing Housing Letter
CD Publications
8204 Fenton St., 2nd Floor
Silver Spring, MD 20910
(301) 588-6380
Fax: (301) 588-6385

Minfax
Span
33300 Five Mile Rd., #202
Livonia, MI 48154
(313) 422-6100
Fax: (313) 397-2020

People & Profits
Lee Resources
P.O. Box 16711
Greenville, SC 29606
(800) 277-7888
Fax: (803) 234-6961

Professional Apartment Management
Brownstone Publishers
304 Park Avenue South
New York, NY 10010
(212) 473-8200
Fax: (212) 995-9205

Real Estate Digest
InterCom Group
2115 Fourth St.
Berkeley, CA 94710
(510) 549-4300
Fax: (510) 549-4331

Real Estate Insider
Walker Communications
1541 Morris Ave.
Bronx, NY 10457
(212) 583-8060

Real Estate Investment, Trends & Opportunities
Jarvis Investment
PO Box 1031
Kent WA 98035
(206) 852-3910

Real Estate Law Report
Warren Gorham & Lamont
210 South St.
Boston, MA 02111
(800) 950-1205
Fax: (617) 423-2026

The Real Estate Tax Digest
Matthew Bender & Co
2101 Webster St.
Oakland, CA 94612
(415) 446-7100

Realty Stock Review
MJH Research Associates
PO Box 7
92 Kennedy Rd.
Tranquility, NJ 07879
(908) 850-1155

Industry Newsletters (cont'd)

Reference

Baseline
American Library Association
50 Huron St.
Chicago, IL 60611
(217) 782-5823

Business Information From Your Public Library
Administrator's Digest
P.O. Box 993
South San Francisco, CA 94080
(415) 573-5474

Business Library Newsletter
427-3 Amherst St., #305
Nashua, NH 03063
(603) 672-0705

Census and You
Bureau of the Census
Data User Services Division
Washington Plaza, Room 317
Washington, DC 20233
(301) 763-1584

Current Events on File
Facts on File
460 Park Ave. S.
New York, NY 10016
(212) 683-2244
Fax: (212) 683-3633

Home-Run-Business Newsletters
IronGate Graphics
7627 Iron Gate Lane
Frederick, MD 21702
(301) 473-4393
Fax: (301) 473-4397

The Morgan Report on Directory Publishing
Morgan-Rand Publications
2200 Sansom St.
Philadelphia, PA 19103
(215) 557-8200
Fax: (215) 557-8414

Research Recommendations
National Institute of Business Management
P.O. Box 25287
Alexandria, VA 22313
(800) 543-2051
Fax: (703) 549-9705

Sales

Executive Compensation Report
DP Publications
P.O. Box 7188
Fairfax Station, VA 22039
(703) 425-1322
Fax: (703) 425-7911

Professional Selling
Bureau of Business Practice
24 Rope Ferry Rd.
Waterford, CT 06386
(203) 442-4365

REP World
Albee-Campbell
806 Penn Ave., Box 2087
Sinking Spring, PA 19608
(215) 678-3361

Research Alert
EPM Communications
488 E. 18th St.
Brooklyn, NY 11226
(718) 469-9330
Fax: (718) 469-7124

Sales Leads
Sales Leads Publishing
705 Park Ave.
Lake Park, FL 33403
(407) 845-0133
Fax: (407) 848-2799

Sales Manager's Bulletin
Bureau of Business Practice
24 Rope Ferry Rd.
Waterford, CT 06386
(203) 442-4365

Salesman's Insider
Marv Q. Modell Associates
P.O. Box 4111
Stanford, CA 94309
(408) 270-4526

Salesmanship
Dartnell
4660 N. Ravenswood Ave.
Chicago, IL 60640
(312) 561-4000
Fax: (312) 561-3801

Industry Newsletters (cont'd)

Selling to Seniors
CD Publications
8204 Fenton St., 2nd Floor
Silver Spring, MD 20910
(301) 588-6380
Fax: (301) 588-6385

Small Business

SBANE Enterprise
Smaller Business Association of New England
69 Hickory Dr.
Waltham, MA 02254
(617) 890-9070
Fax: (617) 890-4567

Small Business Advocate
Summit Business Associates
P.O. Box 30398
Mesa, AZ 85275
(602) 832-0021

Small Business Tax Saver
Small Business Tax Saver
725 Market St.
Wilmington, DE 19801
(302) 654-0110

Small Businessman's Clinic
444-113 Whispering Pines Dr.
Scotts Valley, CA 95066
(408) 438-1411

The Small Small Business
Lynco Publications
1552 Old York Rd.
Abington, PA 19001
(215) 657-0776

Venture Capital

Venture Capital Journal
Venture Economics
40 W. 57th St., #802
New York, NY 10019
(212) 765-5311
Fax: (212) 765-6123

Source: Almanac research and Hudson's Subscription Newsletter Directory

The Top Reference Sources

Hudson's Subscription Newsletter Directory
Hudson's, $118
(914) 876-2081

This extraordinary reference lists thousands of newsletters on a wide variety of topics. From advertising to women's issues, the Directory offers data on significant newsletters in nearly every field. In addition to names and addresses, subscription rates and frequency are also included. Cross references and geographical listings are helpful as well.

The Newsletter Directory is a surprisingly useful reference, certain to pay back its cost many times over. A sister publication, *The Newsletter on Newsletters*, is also recommended.

Media Contacts

1001 Home Ideas
Phone: (212) 340-9200
Fax: (212) 725-3962
Three Park Avenue
New York, NY 10016

ABC Radio Networks
Phone: (212) 456-5131
Fax: (212) 887-5150
125 West End Avenue
New York, NY 10023

ABC Television Network
Phone: (212) 456-7777
Fax: (212) 887-3222
77 W. 66th Street
New York, NY 10023

Adventure Road
Phone: (312) 856-2583
Fax: (312) 856-2379
Amoco Enterprises, Inc.
200 East Randolph Drive
Chicago, IL 60601

American Legion
Phone: (317) 635-8411
Fax: (317) 638-1801
700 N. Penna Street
P.O. Box 1055
Indianapolis, IN 46206

Arizona Republic
Phone: (602) 271-8000
Fax: (602) 271-8500
P.O.Box 1950
Phoenix, AZ 85004

Associated Press Broadcast News
Phone: (202) 955-7200
Fax: (202) 955-7347
1825 K Street, NW
Washington, DC 20006

Atlanta Constitution
Phone: (404) 526-5342
Fax: (404) 526-5819
72 Marietta Street, NW
Atlanta, GA 30303

Atlanta Journal
Phone: (404) 526-5320
Fax: (404) 526-5746
72 Marietta Street, NW (POB 4689)
Atlanta, GA 30303

Baltimore Sun
Phone: (410) 332-6003
Fax: (410) 752-6049
501 N. Calvert Street
Baltimore, MD 21278

Better Homes & Gardens
Phone:(515) 284-3000
Fax:(515) 284-2700
Meredith Corporation
1716 Locust Street
Des Moines, IA 50336

Boston Globe
Phone: (617) 929-2000
Fax: (617) 929-3183
P.O.Box 2378
Boston, MA 02107

Boston Herald
Phone: (617) 426-3000
Fax: (617) 423-0887
One Herald Square
Boston, MA 02106-2096

Boys Life
Phone: (214) 580-2355
Fax: (214) 580-2079
Boy Scouts of America
1325 Walnut Hill Lane
P.O. Box 152079
Irving, TX 75015-2079

Cable News & Business Channel
Phone: (201) 585-6420
Fax: (201) 585-6278
2200 Fletcher Avenue
Fletcher, NJ 07024

CBS Radio Networks
Phone: (212) 975-2127
Fax: (212) 975-4674
51 West 52nd Street
New York, NY 10019

CBS Television Network
Phone: (212) 975-4321
Fax: (212) 975-1893
51 W. 52nd Street
New York, NY 10019

Chicago Sun-Times
Phone: (312) 321-3000
Fax: (312) 321-3084
401 N. Wabash Avenue
Chicago, IL 60611

Chicago Tribune
Phone: (312) 222-3232
Fax: (312) 222-4299
435 N. Michigan Avenue
Chicago, IL 60611

Christian Science Monitor
Phone: (617) 450-2000
Fax: (617) 450-2595
One Norway Street
Boston, MA 02115

Media Contacts (cont'd)

Cincinnati Enquirer
Phone: (513) 721-2700
Fax: (513) 369-1079
617 Vine Street
Cincinnati, OH 45202

Cincinnati Post
Phone: (513) 352-2000
Fax: (513) 621-3962
125 E. Court Steet
Cincinnati, OH 45202

Cleveland Plain Dealer
Phone: (216) 344-4500
Fax: (216) 344-4210
1801 Superior Avenue, NE
Cleveland, OH 44114

CNN Television Network
Phone: (404) 827-1500
Fax: (404) 827-1593
One CNN Center
100 International Blvd
Atlanta, GA 30348

Cosmopolitan
Phone: (212) 649-2000
Fax: (212) 956-3268
224 W. 57th Street
New York, NY 10019

Country Living
Phone: (212) 649-2000
Fax: (212) 956-3857
224 W. 57th Street
New York, NY 10019

Dallas Morning News
Phone: (214) 977-8222
Fax: (214) 977-8776
508 Young Street
P.O. Box 655237
Dallas, TX 75265

Dallas Times-Herald
Phone: (214) 720-6111
Fax: (214) 720-6465
1101 Pacific Avenue (POB 225445)
Dallas, TX 75202

Denver Post
Phone: (303) 820-1010
Fax: (303) 820-1406
1560 Broadway
Denver, CO 80202

Denver/Rocky Mountain News
Phone: (303) 892-5000
Fax: (303) 892-5081
400 W. Colfax Avenue
Denver, CO 80204

Des Moines Register
Phone: (515) 284-8000
Fax: (515) 284-8103
P.O. Box 957
Des Moines, IA 50304

Detroit Free Press
Phone: (313) 222-6400
Fax: (313) 678-6400
321 W. Lafayette
Detroit, MI 48231

Detroit News
Phone:(313) 222-6400
Fax: (313) 222-2599
615 W. Lafayette Blvd
Detroit, MI 48231

Ebony
Phone: (312) 322-9200
Johnson Publishing Company, Inc.
820 S. Michigan Avenue
Chicago, IL 60605

ESPN, Inc.
Phone: (203) 585-2000
Fax: (203) 585-2550
ESPN Plaza
Bristol, CT 06010

Family Circle
Phone:(212) 463-1000
Fax:(212) 463-1808
110 Fifth Avenue
New York, NY 10011

Field & Stream
Phone: (212) 779-5000
Fax: (212) 779-5468
2 Park Avenue
New York, NY 10016

FOX Broadcasting Company
Phone: (213) 856-1236
Fax: (213) 856-1981
5746 Sunset Blvd
Los Angeles, CA 90028

Glamour
Phone: (212) 880-8800
Fax: (212) 880-6922
350 Madison Avenue
New York, NY 10017

Globe
Phone: (407) 997-7733
Fax:(407) 997-7733
5401 NW Broken Sound Blvd.
Boca Raton, Fl 33487

Good Housekeeping
Phone: (212) 649-2531
Fax: (212) 977-9824
959 Eighth Avenue
New York, NY 10019

Media Contacts (cont'd)

Guideposts
Phone: (212) 754-2200
Fax: (212) 832-4870
747 Third Avenue
New York, NY 10017

Home & Away
Phone: (402) 390-1000
Fax: (402) 390-0539
AAA Home & Away, Inc.
P.O. Box 3535
Omaha, NE 68103

Houston Chronicle
Phone: (713) 220-7171
Fax: (713) 220-7868
801 Texas Avenue
Houston, TX 77002

Houston Post
Phone: (713) 840-5600
Fax: (713) 840-6722
4747 S.W. Freeway
Houson, TX 77027

Journal of Commerce
Phone: (212) 425-1616
Fax: (212) 208-0206
Journal of Commerce, Inc.
110 Wall Street
New York, NY 10005

Kansas City Star
Phone: (816) 234-4300
Fax: (816) 234-4346
1729 Grand Avenue
Kansas City, MO 64108

Ladies' Home Journal
Phone: (212) 953-7070
Fax: (212) 351-3650
100 Park Avenue
New York, NY 10017

Life Magazine
Phone: (212) 522-1212
Fax:(212) 522-0304
Time, Inc.
Time and Life Building
Rockefeller Center
New York, NY 10020

Lifetime Television
Phone: (718) 706-7650
Fax: (718) 706-3525
Lifetime Astoria Studios
36-12 35th Avenue
Astoria, NY 11106

Long Island/Newsday
Phone: (516) 843-2800
Fax: (516) 843-5459
235 Pinelawn Road
Long Island, NY 11747

Los Angeles Daily News
Phone: (818) 713-3000
Fax: 818) 713-0058
21221 Oxnard Street
Woodland Hills, CA 91365-4200

Los Angeles Times
Phone: (213) 237-3000
Fax: (213) 237-4712
Times Mirror Square
Los Angeles, CA 90053

McCall's
Phone: (212) 551-9500
Fax: (212) 551-9590
230 Park Avenue
New York, NY 10169

Miami Herald
Phone:(305)350-2111
Fax:(305)376-2677
One Herald Plaza
Miami, FL 33132-1693

Minneapolis Star Tribune
Phone: (612) 673-4000
Fax: (612) 673-4359
425 Portland Avenue
Minneapolis, MN 55488

Modern Maturity
Phone: (310) 496-2277
Fax: (310) 496-4124
3200 E. Carson Street
Lakewood, CA 90712

Money
Phone: (212) 522-1212
Fax:(212)522-0332
Time, Inc.
Time and Life Building
Rockefeller Center
New York, NY 10020

Motorland
Phone:(415) 565-2620
Fax: (415) 552-5825
150 Van Ness Avenue
San Francisco, CA 94102

Mutual Broadcast System
Phone: (703) 685-2090
Fax: (703) 685-2197
1755 S. Jefferson Davis Hwy
Arlington, VA 22202

National Association of Radio Talk Show Hosts
Phone: (617) 956-3320
Fax : (617) 956-2703
134 St. Botolph Street
Boston, MA 02115

Media Contacts (cont'd)

National Enquirer
Phone: (407) 586-1111
Fax: (407) 540-1009
N.E. Inc.
600 South East Coast Avenue
Lantana, FL 33462

National Geographic
Phone:(202) 857-7000
Fax:(202) 828-5658
17th and M Streets, NW
Washington, DC 20036

National Public Radio
Phone: (202) 822-2113
Fax: (202) 842-3625
2025 M Street, NW
Washington, DC 20005

NBC Television Network
Phone: (212) 644-4444
Fax: (212) 582-7656
30 Rockefeller Plaza
New York, NY 10020

New York Daily News
Phone: (212) 210-2100
Fax: (212) 662-2597
220 E. 42nd Street
New York, NY 10017

New York Post
Phone:(212) 815-8499
Fax: (212) 815-8616
210 South Street
New York, NY 10002

New York Times
Phone: (212) 556-1234
Fax:
229 W. 43rd Street
New York, NY 10036

Newark Star-Ledger
Phone: (201) 877-4141
Fax: (201) 643-7248
Star Ledger Plaza
Newark, NJ 07101

Newsweek
Phone: (212) 350-4000
Fax: (212) 421-4993
444 Madison Avenue
New York, NY 10022

Omaha World-Herald
Phone: (402) 444-1000
Fax: (402) 345-0183
World-Herald Square
Omaha, NE 68102

Oregonian
Phone: (503) 221-8327
Fax: (503) 294-4199
1320 SW Broadway
Portland, OR 97201

Orlando Sentinel
Phone: (407) 420-5000
Fax: (407) 420-5661
633 N. Orange Avenue
Orlando, FL 32801

Outdoor Life
Phone: (212) 779-5000
Fax: (212) 686-6877
2 Park Avenue
New York, NY 10016

Parents Magazine
Phone: (212) 878-8700
Fax: (212) 867-4583
685 Third Avenue
New York, NY 10017

PBS Television Network
Phone: (703) 739-5000
Fax: (703) 739-0775
1320 Braddock Place
Alexandria, VA 22314

Penthouse
Phone: (212) 496-6100
Fax: (212) 580-3693
1965 Broadway
New York, NY 10023-5965

People Weekly
Phone: (212) 586-1212
Fax: (212) 522-0331
Time, Inc.
Time and Life Building
Rockefeller Center
New York, NY 10020

Philadelphia Daily News
Phone: (215) 854-2000
Fax: (215) 854-5910
400 N. Broad Street (POB 8527)
Philadelphia, PA 19130

Philadelphia Inquirer
Phone: (215) 854-2000
Fax: (215) 854-4794
400 N. Broad Street
Philadelphia, PA 19101

Phoenix Gazette
Phone: (602) 271-8000
Fax: (602) 271-8911
P.O. Box 1950
Phoenix, AZ 85004

Media Contacts (cont'd)

Pittsburgh Press
Phone: (412) 263-1100
Fax: (412) 263-0147
34 Blvd of the Allies, Box 566
Pittsburgh, PA 15230

Playboy
Phone: (312) 751-8000
Fax: (312) 751 2818
680 N. Lake Shore Drive
Chicago, IL 60611

Popular Mechanics
Phone: (212) 649-2000
Fax: (212) 586-5562
Hearst Corporation
224 W. 57th Street
New York, NY 10019

Popular Science
Phone: (212) 779-5000
Fax: (212) 779-5468
Two Park Avenue
New York, NY 10016

Post-Gazette
Phone: (412) 263-1100
Fax: (412) 391-8452
50 Blvd of the Allies (POB 957)
Pittsburgh, PA 15230

Prevention
Phone: (215) 967-5171
Fax: (215) 967-3044
Rodale Press
33 East Minor Street
Emmaus, PA 18098
Reader's Digest
Phone: (914) 769-7000
Fax: (914) 238-8585
Pleasantville, NY 10570

Redbook
Phone: (212) 649-2000
Fax: (212) 581-8114
224 W. 57th Street, 6th floor
New York, NY 10019

San Diego Tribune
Phone: (619) 299-3131
Fax: (619) 299-7520
P.O. Box 191
San Diego, CA 92112

San Diego Union
Phone: (619) 299-3131
Fax: (619) 293-2333
P.O. Box 191
San Diego, CA 92112

San Francisco Chronicle
Phone: (415) 777-1111
Fax: (415) 777-7131
901 Mission Street
San Francisco, CA 94103

San Francisco Examiner
Phone: (415) 777-5700
Fax: (415) 777-8058
925 Mission Street
San Francisco, CA 94103

Seattle Post-Intelligencer
Phone: (206) 448-8000
Fax: (206) 448-8165
101 Elliott Avenue, West
Seattle, WA 98119

Seattle Times
Phone: (206) 464-2944
Fax: (206) 464-2261
Fairview Avenue
North & John Street (POB 70)
Seattle, WA 98111

Seventeen
Phone: (212) 759-8100
Fax:
850 Third Avenue
New York, NY 10022
Smithsonian
Phone: (202) 786-2900
Fax: (202) 786-2564

Smithsonian Institution
Arts and Industries Building
900 Jefferson Drive
Washington, DC 20560

Southern Living
Phone: (205) 877-6000
Fax: (205) 877-6422
P.O. Box 523
Birmingham, AL 35201

Sports Illustrated
Phone: (212) 522-1212
Fax: (212) 522-0318
Time and Life Building
Rockefeller Center
New York, NY 10020

St. Louis Post-Dispatch
Phone: (314) 622-7000
Fax: (314) 342-3186
900 N. Tucker Blvd
St. Louis, MO 63101

Media Contacts (cont'd)

St. Paul Pioneer Press Dispatch
Phone: (612) 222-5011
Fax: (612) 229-5265
345 Cedar Street
St. Paul, MN 55101-1057

Star
Phone: (914) 332-5000
Fax: (914) 332-5044
660 White Plains Road
Tarrytown, NY 10591

Sunset
Phone: (415) 321-3600
Fax: (415) 321-0551
80 Willow Road
Menlo Park, CA 94025

Time
Phone: (212) 586-1212
Fax: (212) 522-0451
Time and Life Building
Rockefeller Center
New York, NY 10020

Times-Picayune
Phone: (504) 826-3300
Fax: (504) 826-3007
3800 Howard Avenue
New Orleans, LA 70140

TV Guide
Phone: (215) 293-8500
Fax:(215) 293-4849
4 Radnor Corporate Center
Radnor, PA 19088

UPI Broadcast Services
Phone: (202) 898-8015
Fax: (202) 842-3625
1400 Eye Street, NW
Washington, DC 20005

US News & World Report
Phone: (202) 955-2000
Fax: (202) 955-2713
2400 N Street, NW
Washington, DC 20037

Us
Phone:(212) 484-1616
Fax: (212) 767-8204
1 Dag Hammarskjold Plaza, 10th Floor
New York, NY 10017

USA Network
Phone: (212) 408-9100
Fax: (212) 408-3606
1230 Avenue of the Americas
New York, NY 10020

USA Today
Phone: (703) 276-3400
Fax: (703) 558-3955
1000 Wilson Blvd (POB 500)
Arlington, VA 22229

Veterans of Foreign Wars
Phone: (816) 756-3390
Fax:(816) 968-1169
VFW of the US
34th and Broadway
Kansas City, MO 64111

Wall Street Journal
Phone: (212) 416-2000
Fax: (212) 416-3299
200 Liberty Street
New York, NY 10281

Washington Post
Phone: (202) 334-6000
Fax: (202) 334-5661
1150 15th St., NW
Washington, DC 20071

Washington Times
Phone: (202) 636-3275
Fax: (202) 832-2167
3600 New York Ave, NE
Washington, DC 20002

Woman's Day
Phone: (212) 767-6000
Fax: (212) 767-5611
1633 Broadway
New York, NY 10019

Workbasket
Phone: (816) 531-5730
Fax: (816) 531-3873
K.C. Publishing, Inc.
4251 Pennsylvania Avenue
Kansas City, MO 64111

Corporate Contact Directory

THE 1,000 MOST VALUABLE public companies in America, as ranked by *Business Week*.

Rank	Company	Corporate Headquarters	Phone Number
29	Abbott Laboratories	One Abbott Park Rd., Abbott Park, IL 60064	(708) 937-6100
969	ADC Telecommunications	4900 W. 78th St., Minneapolis, MN 55435	(612) 938-8080
915	ADEPTEC	691 S. Milpitas Blvd., Milpitas, CA 95035	(408) 945-8600
709	Adobe Systems	1585 Charleston Rd., Mountain View, CA 94043	(415) 961-4400
418	Advanced Micro Devices	1160 Kern Ave., Sunnyvale, CA 94086	(408) 732-2400
811	Advanta	300 Welsh Rd., Horsham, PA 19044	(215) 657-4000
588	AES	1001 North 19th St., Arlington, VA 22209	(703) 522-1315
161	Aetna Life & Casualty	151 Farmington Ave., Hartford, CT 06156	(203) 273-0123
778	Affiliated Publications	135 Morrisey Blvd., Boston, MA 02107	(617) 929-3300
304	AFLAC	1932 Wynnton Rd., Columbus, GA 31999	(706) 323-3431
368	Ahmanson (H.F.)	4900 Rivergrave Rd., Irwindale, CA 91706	(818) 960-6311
171	Air Products & Chems.	7201 Hamilton Blvd., Allentown, PA 18195	(215) 481-4911
873	Alberto-Culver	2525 Armitage Ave., Melrose Park, IL 60160	(708) 450-3000
109	Albertson's	250 Parkcenter Blvd., Boise, ID 83720	(208) 385-6200
431	Alco Standard	825 Duportail Rd., Wayne, PA 19087	(215) 296-8000
138	Alcoa	1501 Alcoa Bldg, Pittsburgh, PA 15219	(412) 553-4545
686	Alexander & Alexander	1211 Ave. of the Americas, New York, NY 10036	(212) 840-8500
660	Alexander & Baldwin	822 Bishop St., Honolulu, HI 96813	(808) 525-6611
745	Alleghany	55 East 52nd St., New York, NY 10055	(212) 752-1356
621	Alleghany Ludlum	1000 Six PPG Place, Pittsburgh, PA 15222	(412) 394-2800
312	Alleghany Power	12 East 49th St., New York, NY 10017	(212) 752-2121
516	Allergan	2525 Dupont Dr., Irvine, CA 92713	(714) 752-4500
81	Allied Signal	101 Columbia Rd., Morristown, NJ 07962	(201) 455-2000
622	Allmerica Property	440 Lincoln St., Worchester MA 01605	(508) 855-1000
200	Alltel	One Allied Dr., Little Rock, AR 72202	(501) 661-8000
392	Alza	950 Page Mill Rd., Palo Alto, CA 94304	(415) 494-5000
476	Amax	200 Park Ave., New York, NY 10166	(212) 856-4200
959	Amax Gold	350 Indiana St., Golden, CO 80401	(303) 273-0600
477	Ambac	One State St. Plaza, New York, NY 10004	(212) 668-0340
758	Amdahl	1250 East Arques Ave., Sunnyvale, CA 94088	(408) 746-6000
178	Amerada Hess	1185 Ave. of the Americas, New York, NY 10036	(212) 997-8500
113	American Brands	1700 East Putnam Ave., Old Greenwich, CT 06870	(203) 698-5000
195	American Cyanamid	One Cyanamid Plaza, Wayne, NJ 07470	(201) 831-2000
122	American Electric	One Riverside Plaza, Columbus, OH 43215	(614) 223-1000
61	American Express	American Express Tower, World Finl Ctr, New York, NY 10285	(212) 640-2000
125	American General	2929 Allen Pkwy., Houston TX 77019	(713) 522-1111
448	American Greetings	10500 American Rd., Cleveland, OH 44144	(216) 252-7300
33	American Home Prods.	685 Third Ave., New York, NY 10017	(212) 878-5000
19	American Intl. Group	70 Pine St., New York, NY 10270	(212) 770-7000
788	American Medical	8201 Preston Rd., Dallas, TX 75225	(214) 360-6300
491	American National	One Moody Plaza, Galveston, TX 77550	(409) 763-4661
639	American Power	132 Fairgrounds Rd., West Kingston, RI 02892	(401) 789-5735
958	American President	1111 Broadway, Oakland, CA 94607	(510) 272-8000
323	American Stores	709 East South Temple, Salt Lake City, UT 84102	(801) 539-0112
803	American Water Works	1025 Laurel Oak Rd., Voorhees, NJ 08043	(609) 346-8200
31	Ameritech	30 South Wacker Dr., Chicago IL 60606	(312) 750-5000
931	Ametek	Station Square, Paoli, PA 19301	(215) 647-2121
194	Amgen	1840 DeHavilland Dr. Thousand Oaks, CA 91320	(805) 499-5725
17	Amoco	200 East Randolph Dr., Chicago, IL 60601	(312) 856-6111
133	AMP	470 Friendship Rd., Harrisburg, PA 17111	(717) 564-0101

Corporate Contact Directory (cont'd)

Rank	Company	Corporate Headquarters	Phone Number
201	AMR	4333 Amon Carter Blvd., Fort Worth, TX 76155	(817) 963-1234
579	Amsouth Bancorp.	1900 Fifth Ave., North Birmingham, AL 35203	(205) 326-5120
446	Anadarko Petroleum	17001 Northchase Dr., Houston, TX 77060	(713) 875-1101
785	Analog Devices	Three Technology Way, Norwood, MA 02062	(617) 329-4700
50	Anheuser-Busch	One Busch Place, St. Louis, MO 63118	(314) 577-2000
266	Aon	123 North Wacker Dr., Chicago, IL 60606	(312) 701-3000
651	Apache	2000 Post Oak Blvd., Houston, TX 77056	(303) 837-5000
124	Apple Computer	20525 Mariani Ave., Cupertino, CA 95014	(408) 996-1010
458	Applied Materials	3050 Bowers Ave., Santa Clara, CA 95054	(408) 727-5555
91	Archer Daniels Midland	4666 Faries Pkwy., Decatur, IL 62526	(217) 424-5200
226	Arco Chemical	3801 West Chester Pike, Newtown Square, PA 19073	(215) 359-2000
826	Argonaut Group	1800 Ave. of the Stars, Los Angeles, CA 90067	(310) 553-0561
710	Arkla	525 Milam St., Shreveport, LA 71101	(318) 429-2700
860	Armco	300 Interpace Pkwy., Parsippany, NJ 07054	(201) 316-5200
601	Armstrong World	313 West Liberty St., Lancaster, PA 17603	(717) 397-0611
708	Arrow Electronics	25 Hub Dr., Melville, NY 11747	(516) 391-1300
870	Arvin Industries	One Noblitt Plaza, Columbus, IN 47201	(812) 379-3000
693	Asarco	180 Maiden Lane, New York, NY 10038	(212) 510-2000
470	Ashland Oil	1000 Ashland Dr., Russell, KY 41169	(606) 329-3333
985	Ask Group	2440 W. El Camino Real, Mountain View, CA 94039	(415) 969-4442
884	Associated Communs.	200 Gateway Towers, Pittsburgh, PA 15222	(412) 281-1907
2	AT&T	32 Ave. of the Americas, New York, NY 10013	(212) 387-5400
700	Atlanta Gas Light	303 Peachtree St. NE, Atlanta, GA 30308	(404) 584-4000
571	Atlantic Energy	6801 Black Horse Pike, Pleasantville, NJ 08232	(609) 645-4100
38	Atlantic Richfield	515 South Flower St., Los Angeles, CA 90071	(213) 486-3511
718	Atlantic Southeast Air	100 Harts Field Ctr. Pkwy., Suite 800, Atlanta, GA 30354	(404) 766-1400
670	Autodesk	2320 Marinship Way, Sausalito, CA 94965	(415) 332-2344
100	Automatic Data	One ADP Blvd., Roseland, NJ 07068	(201) 994-5000
331	Autozone	3030 Poplar Ave., Memphis, TN 38111	(901) 325-4600
497	Avery Dennison	150 North Orange Grove Blvd., Pasadena, CA 91103	(818) 304-2000
626	Avnet	80 Cutter Mill Rd., Great Neck, NY 11021	(516) 466-7000
198	Avon Products	Nine West 57th St., New York, NY 10019	(212) 546-6015
284	Baker Hughes	3900 Essex Lane, Houston, TX 77027	(713) 439-8600
744	Ball	345 South High St., Muncie, IN 47305	(317) 747-6100
248	Baltimore G&E	39 West Lexington, Baltimore, MD 21203	(410) 234-5000
63	Banc One	100 East Broad St., Columbus, OH 43271	(614) 248-5800
541	Bancorp Hawaii	130 Merchant St., Honolulu, HI 96813	(808) 537-8111
499	Bandag	Bandag Center, Muscatine, IA 52761	(319) 262-1400
388	Bank of Boston	100 Federal St., Boston, MA 02110	(617) 434-2200
190	Bank of New York	48 Wall St., New York, NY 10286	(212) 495-1784
41	Bankamerica	555 California St., San Francisco, CA 94104	(415) 622-3456
147	Bankers Trust	280 Park Ave., New York, NY 10017	(212) 250-2500
730	Banponce	209 Munoz Riviera Ave., San Juan, PR 00918	(809) 765-9800
966	Banta	225 Main St., Menasha WI 54952	(414) 722-7777
554	Bard (C.R.)	730 Central Ave., Murray Hill, NJ 07974	(908) 277-8000
203	Barnett Banks	50 North Laura St., Jacksonville, FL 32202	(904) 791-7720
965	Bassett Furniture	245 Main St., Bassett, VA 24055	(703) 629-6000
279	Bausch & Lomb	One Lincoln First Sq., Rochester, NY 14604	(716) 338-6000
93	Baxter International	One Baxter Pkwy., Deerfield, IL 60015	(708) 948-2000
765	BayBanks	175 Federal St., Boston, MA 02110	(617) 482-1040

Corporate Contact Directory (cont'd)

Rank	Company	Corporate Headquarters	Phone Number
727	BB&T Financial	223 West Nash St., Wilson, NC 27893	(919) 399-4111
437	Bear Stearns	245 Park Ave., New York, NY 10167	(212) 272-2000
899	Beckman Instruments	2500 Harbor Blvd., Fullerton, CA 92634	(714) 871-4848
337	Becton, Dickinson	One Becton Dr., Franklin Lakes, NJ 07417	(201) 847-6800
995	Bed Bath & Beyond	715 Morris Ave., Springfield NJ 07081	(201) 379-1520
24	Bell Atlantic	1717 Arch St., Philadelphia, PA 19103	(215) 963-6000
15	Bellsouth	1155 Peachtree St. NE, Atlanta, GA 30367	(404) 249-2000
838	Belo (A.H.)	400 South Record St., Dallas, TX 75202	(214) 977-8730
568	Bemis	222 South Ninth St., Minneapolis, MN 55402	(612) 376-3000
457	Beneficial	400 Bellevue Pkwy., Wilmington, DE 19809	(302) 798-0800
901	Bergen Brunswig	4000 Metropolitan Dr., Orange, CA 92668	(714) 385-4000
789	Berkley (W.R.)	165 Mason St., Greenwich, CT 06830	(203) 629-2880
287	Berkshire Hathaway	1440 Kiewit Plaza, Omaha, NE 68131	(402) 346-1400
494	Bethlehem Steel	1170 8th Ave., Bethlehem, PA 18016	(215) 694-2424
469	Betz Laboratories	4636 Somerton Rd., Trevose, PA 19053	(215) 355-3300
798	Beverly Enterprises	1200 South Waldron Rd., Fort Smith, AR 72903	(501) 452-6712
459	BHC Communications	600 Madison Ave., New York, NY 10022	(212) 421-0200
736	Bic	500 Bic Dr., Milford, CT 06460	(203) 783-2000
712	Biogen	14 Cambridge Center, Cambridge, MA 02142	(617) 252-9200
517	Biomet	Airport Industrial Park, Warsaw, IN 46580	(219) 267-6639
514	Black & Decker	701 East Joppa Rd., Towson, MD 21204	(410) 716-3900
220	Block (H&R)	4410 Main St., Kansas City, MO 64111	(816) 753-6900
738	Block Drug	257 Cornelison Ave., Jersey City, NJ 07302	(201) 434-3000
258	Blockbuster Ent.	One Blockbuster Plaza, Fort Lauderdale, FL 33301	(305) 832-3000
533	BMC Software	One Sugar Creek Center, Sugar Land, TX 77478	(713) 240-8800
329	Boatmen's Bancshares	800 Market St., St. Louis, MO 63101	(314) 466-6600
849	Bob Evans Farms	3776 South High St., Columbus, OH 43207	(614) 491-2225
64	Boeing	7755 East Marginal Way South, Seattle, WA 98108	(206) 655-2121
751	Boise Cascade	1111 West Jefferson St., Boise, ID 83702	(208) 384-6161
251	Borden	277 Park Ave., New York, NY 10172	(212) 573-4000
968	Borland International	1800 Green Hills Rd., Scotts Valley, CA 95067	(408) 438-8400
560	Boston Edison	800 Boylston St., Boston, MA 02199	(617) 424-2000
447	Boston Scientific	480 Pleasant St., Watertown, ME 02172	(617) 923-1720
809	Bowater	One Parklands Dr., Darien, CT 06820	(203) 656-7200
914	BP Prudhoe Bay	101 Barclay St., New York, NY 10015	(212) 815-5513
747	Briggs & Stratton	12301 West Wirth St., Wauwatosa, WI 53222	(414) 259-5333
544	Brinker International	6820 LBJ Freeway, Dallas, TX 75240	(214) 980-9917
13	Bristol-Myers Squibb	345 Park Ave., New York, NY 10154	(212) 546-4000
654	Brooklyn Union Gas	One MetroTech Center, Brooklyn, NY 11201	(718) 403-2000
398	Brown Forman	850 Dixie Hwy, Louisville, KY 40210	(502) 585-1100
184	Browning-Ferris	757 North Eldridge, Houston, TX 77079	(713) 870-8100
739	Bruno's	800 Lakeshore Pkwy., Birmingham, AL 35211	(205) 940-9400
522	Brunswick	One Brunswick Plaza, Skokie, IL 60077	(708) 470-4700
924	Burlington Coat	1830 Rt. 130 N., Burlington, NJ 08016	(609) 387-7800
698	Burlington Industries	3330 W. Friendly Ave., Greensboro, NC 27410	(919) 379-2000
205	Burlington Northern	777 Main St., Fort Worth, TX 76102	(817) 878-2000
155	Burlington Resources	999 Third Ave., Seattle, WA 98104	(206) 467-3838
933	BWIP Holding	200 Oceangate Blvd., Long Beach, CA 90802	(310) 435-3700
366	Cabletron Systems	35 Industrial Way, Rochester, NH 03867	(603) 332-9400
721	Cablevision Systems	One Media Crossways, Woodbury, NY 11797	(516) 364-8450

Corporate Contact Directory (cont'd)

Rank	Company	Corporate Headquarters	Phone Number
881	Cabot	75 State St., Boston, MA 02109	(617) 345-0100
806	Cadence Design Systems	555 River Oaks Pkwy., San Jose, CA 95134	(408) 943-1234
694	Caesars World	1801 Century Park East, Los Angeles, CA 90067	(310) 552-2711
865	Calgon Carbon	400 Calgon Carbon Dr., Robinson Twp, PA 15205	(412) 787-6700
876	California Energy	10831 Old Mill Rd., Omaha, NE 68154	(402) 330-8900
69	Campbell Soup	Campbell Place, Camden, NJ 08103	(609) 342-4800
94	Capital Cities/ABC	77 West 66th St., New York, NY 10023	(212) 456-7777
255	Capital Holding	400 W. Market St., Louisville, KY 40202	(502) 560-2000
950	Capstead Mortgage	2001 Bryan Tower, Dallas, TX 75201	(214) 746-8000
162	Carnival Cruise Lines	3655 NW 87th Ave., Miami, FL 33178	(305) 599-2600
166	Carolina Power & Light	Fayetteville St. Mall, Raleigh, NC 27601	(919) 546-6111
607	Carter-Wallace	1345 Ave. of the Americas, New York, NY 10105	(212) 339-5000
140	Caterpillar	100 NE Adams St., Peoria, IL 61629	(309) 675-1000
706	CBI Industries	800 Jorie Blvd., Oak Brook, IL 60521	(708) 572-7000
333	CBS	51 West 52nd St., New York, NY 10019	(212) 975-4321
862	CCP Insurance	11825 N. Pennsylvania St., Carmel, IN 46032	(317) 573-6900
268	Centel	8725 Higgins Rd., Chicago, IL 60631	(312) 399-2500
328	Centerior Energy	6200 Oak Tree Blvd., Independence, OH 44131	(216) 447-3100
733	Centex	3333 Lee Pkwy., Dallas, TX 75219	(214) 559-6500
135	Central & South West	1616 Woodall Rodgers Fwy, Dallas, TX 7520.	(214) 754-1000
776	Central Bancshares	701 South 20th St., Birmingham, AL 35233	(205) 933-3000
606	Central Fidelity Banks	1021 East Cary St., Richmond, VA 23219	(804) 782-4000
998	Central LA Electric	2030 Donahue Ferry Rd., Pineville, LA 71360	(318) 484-7400
853	Central Maine Power	Edison Dr., Augusta, ME 04330	(207) 623-3521
957	Central Newspapers	135 North Pennsylvania St., Indianapolis, IN 46204	(317) 231-9201
859	Century Commun.	50 Locust Ave., New Canaan, CT 06840	(203) 972-2000
518	Century Telephone	100 Century Park, Monroe, LA 71203	(318) 388-9500
946	Ceridian	8100 34th Ave. S., Bloomington, MN 55424	(612) 853-8100
325	Champion International	One Champion Plaza, Stamford, CT 06921	(203) 358-7000
475	Charming Shoppes	450 Winks Lane, Bensalem, PA 19020	(215) 245-9100
169	Chase Manhattan	One Chase Manhattan Plaza, New York, NY 10081	(212) 552-2222
1000	Checkers Drive-in	600 Cleveland St., Clearwater, FL 34617	(813) 441-3500
74	Chemical Banking	270 Park Ave., New York, NY 10017	(212) 270-7000
235	Chemical Waste	3001 Butterfield Rd., Oak Brook, IL 60521	(708) 218-1500
20	Chevron	225 Bush St., San Francisco, CA 94104	(415) 894-7700
766	Chicago & North Western	One North Western Ctr., Chicago, IL 60606	(312) 559-7000
845	Chiquita Brands Intl.	250 East Fifth St., Cincinnati, OH 45202	(513) 784-8000
502	Chiron	4560 Horton St., Emeryville, CA 94608	(415) 655-8730
756	Chris-Craft Industries	600 Madison Ave., New York, NY 10022	(212) 421-0200
54	Chrysler	12000 Chrysler Dr., Highland Park, MI 48288	(313) 956-5741
95	Chubb	15 Mountain View Rd., Warren, NJ 07059	(908) 580-2000
972	Church & Dwight	469 North Harrison St., Princeton, NJ 08543	(609) 683-5900
207	Cigna	1650 Market St., Philadelphia, PA 19192	(215) 761-1000
627	Cincinnati Bell	201 East Fourth St., Cincinnati, OH 45202	(513) 397-9900
292	Cincinnati Financial	6200 South Gilmore Rd., Fairfield, OH 45014	(513) 870-2000
381	Cincinnati G&E	139 East Fourth St., Cincinnati, OH 45202	(513) 381-2000
992	Cincinnati Milacron	4701 Marburg Ave., Cincinnati, OH 45209	(513) 841-8100
546	Cintas	6800 Cintas Blvd., Mason, OH 45040	(513) 459-1200
659	Cipsco	607 East Adams St., Springfield, IL 62739	(217) 523-3600
367	Circuit City Stores	9950 Mayland Dr., Richmond, VA 23233	(804) 527-4000

Corporate Contact Directory (cont'd)

Rank	Company	Corporate Headquarters	Phone Number
361	Circus Circus	2880 Las Vegas Blvd. South, Las Vegas, NV 89109	(702) 734-0410
987	Cirrus Logic	3100 W. Warren Ave., Freemont, CA 94538	(510) 623-8300
153	Cisco Systems	1525 O'Brien Dr., Menlo Park, CA 94026	(415) 326-1941
79	Citicorp	399 Park Ave., New York, NY 10043	(212) 559-1000
321	Citizens Utilities	High Ridge Park, Stamford, CT 06905	(203) 329-8800
685	Clayton Homes	4726 Airport Hwy., Knoxville, TN 37901	(615) 970-7200
348	Clorox	1221 Broadway, Oakland, CA 94612	(510) 271-7000
643	CML Group	524 Main St., Acton, MA 01720	(508) 264-4155
479	CMS Energy	330 Town Center Dr., Dearborn, MI 48126	(313) 436-9200
154	CNA Financial	CNA Plaza, Chicago, IL 60685	(312) 822-5000
345	Coastal	Nine Greenway Plaza, Houston, TX 77046	(713) 877-1400
6	Coca-Cola	One Coca-Cola Plaza NW, Atlanta, GA 30313	(404) 676-2121
450	Coca-Cola Enterprises	One Coca-Cola Plaza NW, Atlanta, GA 30313	(404) 676-2100
871	Coleman	250 North St. Francis, Wichita, KS 67202	(316) 261-2100
72	Colgate-Palmolive	300 Park Ave., New York, NY 10022	(212) 310-2000
934	Colonial	1200 Colonial Life Blvd., Columbia, SC 29210	(803) 798-7000
953	Colorado National	950 17th St., Denver, CO 80202	(303) 629-1968
602	Coltec Industries	430 Park Ave., New York, NY 10022	(212) 940-0400
625	Columbia Gas System	20 Montchanin Rd., Wilmington, DE 19807	(302) 429-5000
275	Comcast	1234 Market St., Philadelphia, PA 19107	(215) 665-1700
885	Comdisco	6111 North River Rd., Rosemont, IL 60018	(708) 698-3000
240	Comerica	Renaissance Ctr., Detroit, MI 48243	(313) 222-4000
707	Commerce Bancshares	1000 Walnut St., Kansas City, MO 64106	(816) 234-2000
904	Commerce Clearing House	2700 Lake Cook Rd., Riverwoods, IL 60015	(708) 940-4600
143	Commonwealth Edison	125 South Clark St., Chicago, IL 60603	(312) 294-4321
684	Communications Satellite	950 L'Enfant Plaza SW, Washington, DC 20024	(202) 863-6000
267	Compaq Computer	20555 State Hwy. 249, Houston, TX 77070	(713) 370-0670
216	Computer Associates	One Computer Associates Plaza, Islandia, NY 11788	(516) 342-5224
604	Computer Sciences	2100 East Grand Ave., El Segundo, CA 90245	(310) 615-0311
691	Compuware	31440 Northwestern Hwy., Farmington Hills, MI 48334	(313) 737-7300
118	ConAgra	One ConAgra Dr., Omaha, NE 68102	(402) 595-4000
781	Conner Peripherals	3081 Zanker Rd., San Jose, CA 95134	(408) 456-4500
938	Cons. Freightways	3240 Hillview Ave., Palo Alto, CA 94304	(415) 494-2900
208	Cons. Natural Gas	625 Liberty Ave., Pittsburgh, PA 15222	(412) 227-1000
473	Conseco	11825 North Pennsylvania St., Carmel, IN 46032	(317) 573-6100
92	Consolidated Edison	Four Irving Place, New York, NY 10003	(212) 460-4600
461	Consolidated Papers	231 First Ave. North, Wisconsin Rapids, WI 54494	(715) 422-3111
192	Consolidated Rail	2001 Market St., Philadelphia, PA 19101	(215) 209-4000
792	Consolidated Stores	300 Phillipi Rd., Columbus, OH 43228	(614) 278-6800
489	Contel Cellular	245 Perimeter Center Pkwy., Atlanta, GA 30346	(404) 804-3400
577	Continental Bank	231 South LaSalle St., Chicago, IL 60697	(312) 828-2345
531	Continental Corp.	180 Maiden Lane, New York, NY 10038	(212) 440-3000
141	Cooper Industries	1001 Fannin St., Suite 4000, Houston, TX 77002	(713) 739-5400
305	Cooper Tire & Rubber	701 Lima Ave., Findlay, OH 45840	(419) 423-1321
955	Coors (Adolph)	12th & Ford St., Golden, CO 80401	(303) 279-6565
277	Corestates Financial	Broad & Chestnut Sts., Philadelphia, PA 19107	(215) 973-3100
119	Corning	Houghton Park, Corning, NY 14831	(607) 974-9000
364	Costco Wholesale	10809 120th Ave. NE, Kirkland, WA 98033	(206) 828-8100
451	Countrywide Credit	155 North Lake Ave., Pasadena, CA 91109	(818) 304-8400
104	CPC International	700 Sylvan Ave., Englewood Cliffs, NJ 07632	(201) 894-4000

Corporate Contact Directory (cont'd)

Rank	Company	Corporate Headquarters	Phone Number
487	Cracker Barrel	Hartmann Dr., Lebanon, TN 37087	(615) 444-5533
797	Crane	100 First Stamford Pl., Stamford, CT 06092	(203) 363-7300
791	Crawford	5620 Glenridge Dr. NE, Atlanta, GA 30342	(404) 256-0830
856	Cray Research	655-A Lone Oak Dr., Eagan, MN 55121	(612) 452-6650
488	Crestar Financial	919 East Main St., Richmond, VA 23219	(804) 782-5000
655	Crompton & Knowles	One Station Place, Stamford, CT 06902	(203) 353-5400
276	Crown Cork & Seal	9300 Ashton Rd., Philadelphia, PA 19136	(215) 698-5100
101	CSX	901 East Cary St., Richmond, VA 23219	(804) 782-1400
420	CUC International	707 Summer St., Stamford, CT 06901	(203) 324-9261
506	Cummins Engine	500 Jackson St., Columbus, IN 47201	(812) 377-5000
485	Cyprus Minerals	9100 East Mineral Circle, Englewood, CO 80112	(303) 643-5000
414	Dana	4500 Dorr St., Toledo, OH 43615	(419) 535-4500
842	Danaher	1250 24th St. NW, Washington, DC 20037	(202) 828-0850
850	Dauphin Deposit	213 Market St., Harrisburg, PA 17101	(717) 255-2121
150	Dayton Hudson	777 Nicollet Mall, Minneapolis, MN 55402	(612) 375-2200
644	Dean Foods	3600 North River Rd., Franklin Park, IL 60131	(708) 678-1680
652	Dean Witter, Discover	Two World Trade Center, New York, NY 10048	(212) 392-2222
219	Deere	John Deere Rd., Moline, IL 61265	(309) 765-8000
658	Dell Computer	9505 Arboretum Blvd., Austin, TX 78759	(512) 338-4400
582	Delmarva Power	800 King St., Wilmington, DE 19899	(302) 429-3011
360	Delta Air Lines	3450 Delta Blvd., Atlanta, GA 30320	(404) 715-2600
256	Deluxe	1080 West County Road F, St. Paul, MN 55126	(612) 483-7111
701	Destec Energy	2500 City West Blvd., Houston, TX 77042	(713) 735-4000
158	Detroit Edison	2000 Second Ave., Detroit, MI 48226	(313) 237-8000
943	Dexter	One Elm St., Windsor Locks, CT 06096	(203) 627-9051
428	Dial	1850 North Central Ave., Phoenix, AZ 85077	(602) 207-4000
973	Diamond Shamrock	9830 Colonnade Blvd., San Antonio, TX 78230	(512) 641-6800
783	Diebold	818 Mulberry Rd. SE, Canton OH 44707	(216) 489-4000
134	Digital Equipment	146 Main St., Maynard, MA 01754	(508) 493-5111
170	Dillard Dept. Stores	900 West Capital Ave., Little Rock, AR 72203	(501) 376-5200
21	Disney (Walt)	500 South Buena Vista St., Burbank, CA 91521	(818) 560-1000
424	Dole Food	31355 Oak Crest Dr., Westlake Village, CA 91361	(818) 879-6600
801	Dollar General	104 Woodmont Blvd., Nashville, TN 37205	(615) 783-2000
110	Dominion Resources	901 East Byrd St., Richmond, VA 23219	(804) 775-5700
187	Donnelley (R.R.)	77 W. Wacker Dr., Chicago, IL 60601	(312) 326-8000
343	Dover	280 Park Ave., New York, NY 10017	(212) 922-1640
47	Dow Chemical	2030 Willard H. Dow Center, Midland, MI 48674	(517) 636-1000
295	Dow Jones	200 Liberty St., New York, NY 10281	(212) 416-2000
407	DPL	1065 Woodman Dr., Dayton, OH 45432	(513) 224-6000
444	DQE	301 Grant St., Pittsburgh, PA 15279	(412) 393-6000
689	Dr. Pepper-Seven-Up	8144 Walnut Hill Ln., Dallas, TX 75231	(214) 360-7000
354	Dresser Industries	1600 Pacific Ave., Dallas, TX 75201	(214) 740-6000
521	Dreyfus	200 Park Ave., New York, NY 10166	(212) 922-6000
618	DSC Communications	100 Coit Rd., Plano, TX 75075	(214) 519-3000
96	Duke Power	422 South Church St., Charlotte, NC 28242	(704) 594-0887
73	Dun & Bradstreet	299 Park Ave., New York, NY 10171	(212) 593-6800
11	Du Pont	1007 Market St., Wilmington, DE 19898	(302) 774-1000
223	Duracell Intl.	Berkshire Industrial Park, Bethel, CT 06801	(203) 796-4000
922	Duty Free Intl.	63 Copps Hill Rd., Ridgefield, CT 06877	(203) 431-6057
587	E-Systems	6250 LBJ Freeway, Dallas, TX 75240	(214) 661-1000

Corporate Contact Directory (cont'd)

Rank	Company	Corporate Headquarters	Phone Number
947	Eastern Enterprises	Nine Riverside Rd., Weston, MA 02193	(617) 647-2300
42	Eastman Kodak	343 State St., Rochester, NY 14650	(716) 724-4000
315	Eaton	1111 Superior Ave. NE, Cleveland, OH 44114	(216) 523-5000
535	Echlin	100 Double Beach Rd., Branford, CT 06405	(203) 481-5751
634	Ecolab	370 Wabasha, St. Paul, MN 55102	(612) 293-2233
735	Edison Brothers Stores	501 North Broadway, St. Louis, MO 63102	(314) 331-6000
630	Edwards (A.G.)	One North Jefferson, St. Louis, MO 63103	(314) 289-3000
564	EG&G	45 William St., Wellesley, MA 02181	(617) 237-5100
597	El Paso Natural Gas	304 Texas St., El Paso, TX 79901	(915) 541-2600
623	Electronic Arts	1450 Fashion Blvd., San Mateo, CA 94404	(415) 571-7171
725	EMC	171 South St., Hopkinton, MA 01748	(508) 435-1000
58	Emerson Electric	8000 West Florissant Ave., St. Louis, MO 63136	(314) 553-2000
339	Engelhard	101 Wood Ave., Iselin, NJ 08830	(908) 205-6000
937	Enquirer/Star Group	600 Southeast Coast Ave., Lantana, FL 33462	(407) 586-1111
112	Enron	1400 Smith St., Houston, TX 77002	(713) 853-6161
303	Enron Oil & Gas	1400 Smith St., Houston, TX 77002	(713) 853-6161
641	Enserch	300 South St. Paul St., Dallas, TX 75201	(214) 651-8700
130	Entergy	225 Baronne St., New Orleans, LA 70112	(504) 529-5262
515	Equifax	1600 Peachtree St. NW, Atlanta, GA 30309	(404) 885-8000
336	Equitable	787 Seventh Ave., New York, NY 10019	(212) 554-1234
833	Equitable of Iowa	604 Locust St., Des Moines, IA 50309	(515) 245-6911
632	Equitable Resources	420 Blvd. of the Allies, Pittsburgh, PA 15219	(412) 261-3000
281	Ethyl	330 South Fourth St., Richmond, VA 23219	(804) 788-5000
1	Exxon	225 East Carpenter Fwy., Irving, TX 75062	(214) 444-1000
645	Family Dollar Stores	10401 Old Monroe Rd., Matthews, NC 28105	(704) 847-6961
28	Fannie Mae	3900 Wisconsin Ave., Washington, DC 20016	(202) 752-7000
299	Federal Express	2005 Corporate Ave., Memphis, TN 38194	(901) 369-3600
90	Federal Home Loan	8200 Jones Branch Dr., McLean, VA 22102	(703) 903-2000
673	Federal Paper Board	75 Chestnut Ridge Rd., Montvale, NJ 07645	(201) 391-1776
911	Federal Realty	4800 Hampden Ln., Bethesda, MD 20814	(301) 652-3360
813	Federal Signal	1415 West 22nd St., Oak Brook, IL 60521	(708) 954-2000
359	Federated Department Stores	Seven W. Seventh St, Cincinnati, OH 45202	(513) 579-7000
762	Ferro	1000 Lakeside Ave., Cleveland, OH 44114	(216) 641-8580
945	FHP International	9900 Talbert Ave., Fountain Valley, CA 92708	(714) 963-7233
289	Fifth Third Bancorp	38 Fountain Square Plaza, Cincinnati, OH 45263	(513) 579-5300
695	Fina	8350 North Central Expwy., Dallas, TX 75206	(214) 750-2400
754	Fingerhut	4400 Baker Rd., Minnetonka, MN 55343	(612) 932-3100
555	First Alabama	44 First Alabama Plaza, Montgomery, AL 36101	(205) 832-8011
877	First American	315 Deaderick, Nashville, TN 37237	(615) 748-2000
316	First Bank System	601 Second Ave., Minneapolis, MN 55402	(612) 973-1111
963	First Bankcorp. of Ohio	106 South Main St., Akron, OH 44308	(216) 384-8000
896	First Brands	83 Wooster Heights Rd., Danbury, CT 06813	(203) 731-2300
269	First Chicago	One First National Plaza, Chicago, IL 60670	(312) 732-4000
882	First Commerce	210 Baronne St., New Orleans, LA 70112	(504) 561-1371
239	First Data	200 Vesey St., New York, NY 10285	(212) 640-5090
713	First Empire State	One M&T Plaza, Buffalo, NY 14240	(716) 639-6000
246	First Fidelity	1009 Lenox Dr., Lawrenceville, NJ 08648	(609) 895-6800
365	First Financial Mgmt.	Three Corporate Square, Atlanta, GA 30329	(404) 321-0120
742	First Hawaiian	165 South King St., Honolulu, HI 96813	(808) 525-7000
221	First Interstate	633 West Fifth St., Los Angeles, CA 90071	(213) 614-3001

Corporate Contact Directory (cont'd)

Rank	Company	Corporate Headquarters	Phone Number
369	First of America Bank	211 S. Rose St., Kalamazoo, MI 49007	(616) 376-9000
676	First Security	79 South Main St., Salt Lake City, UT 84111	(801) 246-6000
635	First Tennessee Natl.	165 Madison Ave., Memphis, TN 38103	(901) 523-4444
115	First Union	One First Union Center, Charlotte, NC 28288	(704) 374-6565
763	First USA	2001 Bryan Tower, Dallas, TX 75201	(214) 746-8400
583	First Virginia Banks	6400 Arlington Blvd., Falls Church, VA 22042	(703) 241-4000
403	Firstar	777 East Wisconsin Ave., Milwaukee, WI 53202	(414) 765-4321
907	Fiserv	255 Friserv Dr., Brookfield, WI 53045	(414) 879-5000
820	Fisher-Price	636 Girard Ave., East Aurora, NY 14052	(716) 687-3000
552	Fleet Call	201 Rt. 17 N., Rutherford, NJ 07070	(201) 438-1400
188	Fleet Financial Group	50 Kennedy Plaza, Providence, RI 02903	(401) 278-6000
624	Fleet Mortgage Group	1333 Main St., Columbia, SC 29201	(803) 929-7900
737	Fleetwood Enterprises	3125 Myers St., Riverside, CA 92513	(714) 351-3500
605	Fleming	6301 Waterford Blvd., Oklahoma City, OK 73118	(405) 840-7200
550	Flightsafety Intl.	Marine Air Terminal, La Guardia Airport, Flushing, NY 11371	(718) 565-4100
297	Florida Progress	One Progress Plaza, St. Petersburg, FL 33701	(813) 824-6400
894	Flowers Industries	200 U.S. Hwy. 19 South, Thomasville, GA 31799	(912) 226-9110
252	Fluor	3333 Michelson Dr., Irvine, CA 92720	(714) 975-5000
471	FMC	200 East Randolph Dr., Chicago, IL 60601	(312) 861-6000
264	Food Lion	2110 Executive Dr., Salisbury, NC 28144	(704) 633-8250
23	Ford Motor	The American Rd., Dearborn, MI 48121	(313) 322-3000
528	Forest Laboratories	150 East 58th St., New York, NY 10155	(212) 421-7850
678	Foster Wheeler	Perryville Corporate Park, Clinton, NJ 08809	(908) 730-4000
822	Foundation Health	3400 Data Dr., Rancho Cordova, CA 95670	(916) 631-5000
917	Fourth Financial	100 North Broadway, Wichita, KS 67202	(316) 261-4444
111	FPL Group	700 Universe Blvd., Juno Beach, FL 33408	(407) 694-4600
320	Franklin Resources	777 Mariners Island Blvd., San Mateo, CA 94404	(415) 312-2000
335	Freeport-McMoran	1615 Poydras St., New Orleans, LA 70112	(504) 582-4000
217	Freeport-McMoran C&G	One East First St., Reno, NV 89501	(504) 582-1640
265	Fruit of the Loom	233 South Wacker Dr., Chicago, IL 60606	(312) 876-7000
912	Fund American	Main St., Norwich, VT 05055	(802) 649-3633
399	Galen Health Care	201 W. Main St., Louisville Ky 40202	(502) 572-2000
107	Gannett	1100 Wilson Blvd., Arlington, VA 22234	(703) 284-6000
183	Gap (The)	One Harrison, San Francisco, CA 94105	(415) 952-4400
886	Gatx	120 South Riverside Plaza, Chicago, IL 60606	(312) 621-6200
467	Gaylord Entertainment	2802 Opryland Dr., Nashville, TN 37214	(615) 871-6776
202	Geico	5260 Western Ave., Chevy Chase, MD 20815	(301) 986-3000
227	Genentech	460 Pt. San Bruno Blvd., South San Francisco, CA 94080	(415) 225-1000
272	General Dynamics	3190 Fairview Park Dr., Falls Church, VA 22042	(703) 876-3000
4	General Electric	3135 Easton Turnpike, Fairfield, CT 06431	(203) 373-2211
419	General Instrument	181 W. Madison St., Chicago, IL 60602	(312) 541-5000
65	General Mills	One General Mills Blvd., Minneapolis, MN 55426	(612) 540-2311
14	General Motors	3044 West Grand Blvd., Detroit, MI 48202	(313) 556-5000
288	General Public Utils.	100 Interpace Pkwy., Parsippany, NJ 07054	(201) 263-6500
76	General Re	695 East Main, Stamford, CT 06904	(203) 328-5000
586	General Signal	One High Ridge Park, Stamford, CT 06904	(203) 357-8800
910	Genetics Institute	87 Cambridge Park Dr., Cambridge, MA 02140	(617) 876-1170
990	Gensia Pharmaceuticals	11025 Roselle St., San Diego, CA 92121	(619) 546-8300
224	Genuine Parts	2999 Circle 75 Pkwy., Atlanta, GA 30339	(404) 953-1700
888	Genzyme	One Kendall Square, Cambridge, MA 02139	(617) 252-7500

Corporate Contact Directory (cont'd)

Rank	Company	Corporate Headquarters	Phone Number
824	Georgia Gulf	400 Perimeter Center Terrace, Atlanta, GA 30346	(404) 395-4500
146	Georgia-Pacific	133 Peachtree St. NE, Atlanta, GA 30303	(404) 521-4000
374	Gerber Products	445 State St., Fremont, MI 49413	(616) 928-2000
994	GFC Financial	1850 N. Central Ave., Pheonix, AZ 85004	(602) 207-4900
572	Giant Food	6300 Sheriff Rd., Landover, MD 20785	(301) 341-4100
829	Giddings & Lewis	142 Doty St., Fond du Lac, WI 54935	(414) 921-9400
56	Gillette	Prudential Tower Bldg, Boston, MA 02199	(617) 421-7000
821	Glatfelter (P.H.)	228 South Main St., Spring Grove, PA 17362	(717) 225-4711
302	Golden West Financial	1901 Harrison St., Oakland, CA 94612	(510) 446-6000
631	Goodrich (B.F.)	3925 Embassy Pkwy., Akron, OH 44333	(216) 374-2000
167	Goodyear Tire & Rubber	1144 East Market St., Akron, OH 44316	(216) 796-2121
271	Grace (W.R.)	One Town Center Rd., Boca Raton, FL 33486	(407) 362-2000
313	Grainger (W.W.)	5500 West Howard St., Skokie, IL 60077	(708) 982-9000
759	Great A&P Tea	Two Paragon Dr., Montvale, NJ 07645	(201) 573-9700
157	Great Lakes Chemical	Highway 52 NW, West Lafayette, IN 47906	(317) 497-6100
373	Great Western	9200 Oakdale Ave., Chatsworth, CA 91311	(818) 775-3411
692	Green Tree Financial	345 St. Peter St., St. Paul, MN 55102	(612) 293-3400
675	Grumman	1111 Stewart Ave., Bethpage, NY 11714	(516) 575-0574
9	GTE	One Stamford Forum, Stamford, CT 06904	(203) 965-2000
547	Gtech Holdings	55 Technology Way, West Greenwich, RI 02817	(401) 392-1000
425	Gulf States Utilities	350 Pine St., Beaumont, TX 77701	(409) 838-6631
932	Haemonetics	400 Wood Rd., Braintree, MA 02184	(617) 848-7100
247	Halliburton	500 North Akard St., Dallas, TX 75201	(214) 978-2600
895	Hanna (M.A.)	1301 East Ninth St., Cleveland, OH 44114	(216) 589-4000
772	Hannaford Brothers	145 Pleasant Hill Rd., Scarborough, ME 04074	(207) 883-2911
341	Harcourt General	27 Boylston St., Chestnut Hill MA 02167	(617) 232-8200
770	Harland (John H.)	2939 Miller Rd., Decatur, GA 30035	(404) 981-9460
575	Harley-Davidson	3700 West Juneau Ave., Milwaukee, WI 53208	(414) 342-4680
540	Harris	1025 West NASA Blvd., Melbourne, FL 32919	(407) 727-9100
671	Harsco	350 Popular Church Rd., Camp Hill, PA 17011	(717) 763-7064
609	Hartford Steam Boiler	One State St., Hartford, CT 06102	(203) 722-1866
334	Hasbro	1027 Newport Ave., Pawtucket, RI 02862	(401) 431-8697
741	Hawaiian Electric	900 Richards St., Honolulu, HI 96813	(808) 543-5662
311	HCA	One Park Plaza, Nashville, TN 37203	(615) 327-9551
836	Health Care Property	10990 Wilshire Blvd., Los Angeles, CA 90024	(310) 473-1990
916	Healthcare Compare	3200 Highland Ave., Downers Grove, IL 60515	(708) 241-7900
664	Healthtrust	4525 Harding Rd., Nashville, TN 37201	(615) 383-4444
731	Heilig-Meyers	2235 Staples Mill Rd., Richmond, VA 23230	(804) 359-9171
68	Heinz (H.J.)	600 Grant St., Pittsburgh, PA 15219	(412) 456-5700
921	Helmerich & Payne	1579 East 21st St., Tulsa, OK 74114	(918) 742-5531
294	Hercules	1313 North Market St., Wilmington, DE 19894	(302) 594-5000
176	Hershey Foods	100 Crystal A Dr., Hershey, PA 17033	(717) 534-4200
32	Hewlett-Packard	3000 Hanover St., Palo Alto, CA 94304	(415) 857-1501
283	Hillenbrand Industries	16 State Rd., 46 East, Batesville, IN 47006	(812) 934-7000
389	Hilton Hotels	9336 Civic Center Dr., Beverly Hills, CA 90209	(310) 278-4321
30	Home Depot	2727 Paces Ferry Rd., Atlanta, GA 30339	(404) 433-8211
869	Home Shopping Network	2501 118th Ave. North, St. Petersburg, FL 33716	(813) 572-8585
466	Homestake Mining	650 California St., San Francisco, CA 94108	(415) 981-8150
749	Hon Industries	414 East Third St., Muscatine, IA 52761	(319) 264-7400
204	Honeywell	2701 Fourth Ave., Minneapolis, MN 55408	(612) 951-1000

Corporate Contact Directory (cont'd)

Rank	Company	Corporate Headquarters	Phone Number
779	Horace Mann Educators	One Horace Mann Plaza, Springfield, IL 62715	(217) 798-2500
445	Hormel (Geo. A.)	501 NE 16th Ave., Austin, MN 55912	(507) 437-5611
961	Houghton-Mifflin	One Beacon St., Boston, MA 02108	(617) 725-5000
327	Household Intl.	2700 Sanders Rd., Prospect Heights, IL 60070	(708) 564-5000
136	Houston Industries	4400 Post Oak Pkwy., Houston, TX 77027	(713) 629-3000
481	Hubbell	584 Derby-Milford Rd., Orange, CT 06477	(203) 799-4100
724	Humana	500 West Main St., Louisville, KY 40202	(502) 580-1000
794	Hunt (J.B.)	615 J.B. Hunt Dr., Lowell, AR 72745	(501) 820-0000
443	Huntington Bancshares	Huntington Center, Columbus, OH 43287	(614) 463-8300
12	IBM	Old Orchard Rd., Armonk, NY 10504	(914) 765-1900
760	IBP	Hwy. 35, Dakota City, NE 68731	(402) 494-2061
681	Idaho Power	1221 West Idaho St., Boise, ID 83702	(208) 383-2200
775	IES Industries	200 First St. SE, Cedar Rapids, IA 52401	(319) 398-4411
666	Illinois Central	455 North Cityfront Plaza Dr., Chicago, IL 60611	(312) 755-7500
454	Illinois Power	500 South 27th St., Decatur, IL 62525	(217) 424-6600
218	Illinois Tool Works	3600 West Lake Ave., Glenview, IL 60625	(708) 724-7500
796	IMC Fertilizer Group	2100 Sanders Rd., Northbrook, IL 60062	(708) 272-9200
400	Imcera Group	2315 Sanders Rd., Northbrook, IL 60062	(708) 564-8600
954	Immunex	51 University St., Seattle, WA 98101	(206) 587-0430
872	Information Resources	150 North Clinton St., Chicago, IL 60661	(312) 726-1221
674	Informix	4100 Bohannon Dr., Menlo Park, CA 94025	(415) 926-6300
260	Ingersoll-Rand	200 Chestnut Ridge, Woodcliff Lake, NJ 07675	(201) 573-0123
846	Inland Steel Industries	30 West Monroe St., Chicago, IL 60603	(312) 346-0300
510	Integra Financial	Four PPG Place, Pittsburgh, PA 15222	(412) 644-8111
22	Intel	2200 Mission College Blvd., Santa Clara, CA 95052	(408) 765-8080
892	Interco	101 South Hanley Rd., St. Louis, MO 63105	(314) 863-1100
981	Intergraph	289 Dunlop Blvd., Huntsville, AL 35824	(205) 730-2000
99	International Paper	Two Manhattanville Rd., Purchase, NY 10577	(914) 397-1500
391	Interpublic Group	1271 Ave. of the Americas, New York, NY 10020	(212) 399-8000
211	Intl. Flavors	521 West 57th St., New York, NY 10019	(212) 765-5500
274	Intl. Game Technology	520 South Rock Blvd., Reno, NV 89502	(702) 688-0100
908	Intl. Specialty Products	1361 Alps Rd., Wayne, NJ 07470	(201) 628-3000
929	Iowa-Illinois G&E	206 East Second St., Davenport, IA 52801	(319) 326-7111
524	Ipalco Enterprises	25 Monument Circle, Indianapolis, IN 46204	(317) 261-8261
940	Itel	Two North Riverside Plaza, Chicago, IL 60606	(312) 466-4090
83	ITT	1330 Ave. of the Americas, New York, NY 10019	(212) 258-1000
463	Ivax	8800 NW 36th St., Miami, FL 33178	(305) 590-2200
903	Jacobs Engineering	251 South Lake Ave., Pasadena, CA 91101	(818) 449-2171
498	James River	120 Tredegar St., Richmond, VA 23219	(804) 644-5411
347	Jefferson-Pilot	100 North Greene St., Greensboro, NC 27401	(919) 691-3000
548	John Nuveen	333 West Wacker Dr., Chicago, IL 60606	(312) 917-7700
18	Johnson & Johnson	One Johnson & Johnson Plaza, New Brunswick, NJ 08933	(908) 524-0400
442	Johnson Controls	5757 North Green Bay Ave., Milwaukee, WI 53209	(414) 228-1200
935	Jones Apparel Group	250 Rittenhouse Circle, Bristol, PA 19007	(215) 785-4000
585	Jostens	5501 Norman Center Dr., Minneapolis, MN 55437	(612) 830-3300
980	Justin Industries	2821 West Seventh St., Fort Worth, TX 76107	(817) 336-5125
513	Kansas City Power	1201 Walnut Ave., Kansas City, MO 64106	(816) 556-2200
598	Kansas City Southern	114 West 11th St., Kansas City, MO 64105	(816) 556-0303
988	Kaufman & Broad Home	10877 Wilshire Blvd., Los Angeles, CA 90024	(310) 443-8000
46	Kellogg	One Kellogg Square, Battle Creek, MI 49016	(616) 961-2000

Corporate Contact Directory (cont'd)

Rank	Company	Corporate Headquarters	Phone Number
573	Kelly Services	999 West Big Beaver Rd., Troy, MI 48084	(313) 362-4444
509	Kemper	One Kemper Dr., Long Grove, IL 60049	(708) 540-2000
393	Kerr-McGee	Kerr-McGee Center, Oklahoma City, OK 73125	(405) 270-1313
212	Keycorp	30 South Pearl St., Albany, NY 12207	(518) 486-8000
729	Keystone International	9600 West Gulf Bank Rd., Houston, TX 77040	(713) 466-1176
920	Kimball International	1600 Royal St., Jasper, IN 47549	(812) 482-1600
89	Kimberly-Clark	545 East Carpenter Fwy., Irving, TX 75062	(214) 830-1200
574	King World	12400 Wilshire Blvd., West Los Angeles, CA 90025	(310) 826-1108
75	Kmart	3100 West Big Beaver Rd., Troy, MI 48084	(313) 643-1000
290	Knight-Ridder	One Herald Plaza, Miami, FL 33132	(305) 376-3800
566	Kohl's	N54-W13600 Woodale Dr., Menomonee Falls, WI 53051	(414) 783-5800
504	Kroger	1014 Vine St., Cincinnati, OH 45202	(513) 762-4000
648	Ku Energy	One Quality St., Lexington, KY 40507	(606) 255-2100
705	Lafarge	11130 Sunrise Valley Dr., Reston, VA 22091	(703) 264-3600
817	Lancaster Colony	37 West Broad St., Columbus, OH 43215	(614) 224-7141
868	Lance	8600 South Blvd., Charlotte, NC 28273	(704) 554-1421
978	Lawter International	990 Skokie Blvd., Northbrook, IL 60062	(708) 498-4700
819	LDDs Communications	4780 I-55 North, Jackson, MS 39211	(601) 364-7000
874	Lee Enterprises	215 North Main St., Davenport, IA 52801	(319) 383-2100
501	Legent	8615 Westwood Center Dr., Vienna, VA 22182	(703) 734-9494
538	Leggett & Platt	One Leggett Rd., Carthage, MO 64836	(417) 358-8131
927	Lennar	700 Northwest 107th Ave., Miami, FL 33172	(305) 559-4000
690	Leucadia National	315 Park Ave. South, New York, NY 10010	(212) 460-1900
593	LG&E Energy	220 West Main St., Louisville, KY 40202	(502) 627-2000
439	Liberty Media	2232 Dell Range Blvd., Cheyenne, WY 82009	(307) 637-8253
918	Liberty National	416 West Jefferson St., Louisville, KY 40232	(502) 566-2000
986	Life Re	969 High Ridge Rd., Stamford, CT 06905	(203) 321-3000
48	Lilly (Eli)	Lilly Corp Center, Indianapolis, IN 46285	(317) 276-2000
82	Limited (The)	Two Limited Pkwy., Columbus, OH 43216	(614) 479-7000
214	Lin Broadcasting	5295 Carillon Point, Kirkland, WA 98033	(206) 828-1902
262	Lincoln National	1300 South Clinton St., Fort Wayne, IN 46802	(219) 455-2000
812	Linear Technology	1630 McCarthy Blvd., Milpitas, CA 95035	(408) 432-1900
412	Litton Industries	360 North Crescent Dr., Beverly Hills, CA 90210	(310) 859-5000
307	Liz Claiborne	1441 Broadway, New York, NY 10018	(212) 354-4900
259	Lockheed	4500 Park Granada Blvd., Calabasas, CA 91399	(818) 876-2000
493	Loctite	Ten Columbus Blvd., Hartford, CT 06106	(203) 520-5000
114	Loews	667 Madison Ave., New York, NY 10021	(212) 545-2000
951	Lone Star Steakhouse	224 East Douglas, Wichita, KS 67202	(316) 264-8899
293	Long Island Lighting	175 East Old Country Rd., Hicksville, NY 11801	(516) 933-4590
851	Longs Drug Stores	141 North Civic Dr., Walnut Creek, CA 94596	(510) 937-1170
717	Longview Fibre	End of Fibre Way, Longview, WA 98632	(206) 425-1550
404	Loral	600 Third Ave., New York, NY 10016	(212) 697-1105
661	Lotus Development	55 Cambridge Pkwy., Cambridge, MA 02142	(617) 577-8500
640	Louisiana Land	909 Poydras St., New Orleans, LA 70112	(504) 566-6500
228	Louisiana-Pacific	111 SW Fifth Ave., Portland, OR 97204	(503) 221-0800
386	Lowe's	Hwy 268 East, North Wilkesboro, NC 28659	(919) 651-4000
991	LSI Logic	1551 McCarthy Blvd., Milpitas, CA 95035	(408) 433-8000
416	Lubrizol	29400 Lakeland Blvd., Wickliffe, OH 44092	(216) 943-1200
971	Luby's Cafeterias	2211 NE Loop 410, San Antonio, TX 78217	(512) 654-9000
913	Lukens	50 South First Ave., Coatesville, PA 19320	(215) 383-2000

Corporate Contact Directory (cont'd)

Rank	Company	Corporate Headquarters	Phone Number
411	Lyondell Petrochemical	1221 McKinney St., Houston, TX 77010	(713) 652-7200
787	Magma Power	4365 Executive Dr., San Diego, CA 92121	(619) 622-7800
976	Magnetek	11150 Santa Monica Blvd., Los Angeles, CA 90025	(310) 473-6681
613	Manor Care	10750 Columbus Pike, Silver Spring, MD 20901	(301) 681-9400
619	Manpower	5301 North Ironwood Rd., Milwaukee, WI 53217	(414) 961-1000
503	Mapco	1800 South Baltimore Ave., Tulsa, OK 74119	(918) 581-1800
132	Marion Merrell Dow	9300 Ward Pkwy., Kansas City, MO 64114	(816) 966-4000
861	Mark IV Industries	501 Audubon Pkwy., Amherst, NY 14228	(716) 689-4972
930	Marquette Electronics	8200 West Tower Ave., Milwaukee, WI 53223	(414) 355-5000
350	Marriott	One Marriott Dr., Washington, DC 20058	(310) 380-9000
116	Marsh & McLennan	1166 Ave. of the Americas, New York, NY 10036	(212) 345-5000
542	Marshall & Ilsley	770 North Water St., Milwaukee, WI 53202	(414) 765-7801
273	Martin Marietta	6801 Rockledge Dr., Bethesda, MD 20817	(301) 897-6000
697	Marvel Entertainment	387 Park Ave. South, New York, NY 10016	(212) 696-0808
174	Masco	21001 Van Born Rd., Taylor, MI 48180	(313) 274-7400
839	Masco Industries	21001 Van Born Rd., Taylor, MI 48180	(313) 274-7400
406	Mattel	333 Continental Blvd., El Segundo, CA 90245	(310) 524-2000
628	Maxus Energy	717 North Harwood St., Dallas, TX 75201	(214) 953-2000
84	May Department Stores	611 Olive St., St. Louis, MO 63101	(314) 342-6300
526	Maytag	One Dependable Square, Newton, IA 50208	(515) 792-8000
332	MBIA	113 King St., Armonk, NY 10504	(914) 273-4545
346	MBNA	400 Christiana Rd., Newark, DE 19713	(800) 441-7048
117	McCaw Cellular	5400 Carillon Point, Kirkland, WA 98033	(206) 827-4500
942	McClatchy Newspapers	2100 Q St., Sacramento, CA 95816	(916) 321-1846
415	McCormick	18 Loveton Circle, Sparks, MD 21152	(410) 771-7301
557	McDermott Intl.	1010 Common St., New Orleans, LA 70112	(504) 587-5400
37	McDonald's	One McDonald's Plaza, Oak Brook, IL 60521	(708) 575-3000
402	McDonnell Douglas	J.S. McDonnell Blvd. & Airport Rd., St. Louis, MO 63134	(314) 232-0232
318	McGraw-Hill	1221 Ave. of the Americas, New York, NY 10020	(212) 512-2000
60	MCI Communications	1801 Pennsylvania Ave. NW, Washington, DC 20006	(202) 872-1600
452	McKesson	One Post St., San Francisco, CA 94104	(415) 983-8300
804	MCN	500 Griswold St., Detroit, MI 48226	(313) 256-5500
355	Mead	Courthouse Plaza NE, Dayton, OH 45463	(513) 222-6323
173	Medco	100 Summit Ave., Montvale, NJ 07645	(201) 358-5400
905	Medical Care America	13455 Noel Rd., Dallas, TX 75240	(214) 851-2600
773	Meditrust	128 Technology Center, Waltham, MA 02154	(617) 736-1500
197	Medtronic	7000 Central Ave. NE, Minneapolis, MN 55432	(612) 574-4000
263	Mellon Bank	500 Grant St., Pittsburgh, PA 15258	(412) 234-5000
168	Melville	One Theall Rd., Rye, NY 10580	(914) 925-4000
687	Mercantile Bancorp.	721 Locust St., St. Louis, MO 63166	(314) 425-2525
699	Mercantile Bankshares	Two Hopkins Plaza, Baltimore, MD 21201	(410) 237-5900
558	Mercantile Stores	9450 Seward Rd., Fairfield, OH 45014	(513) 881-8000
7	Merck	One Merck Dr., Whitehouse, NJ 08889	(908) 594-4000
483	Mercury Finance	40 S. Skokie Blvd., Northbrook, IL 60062	(708) 564-3720
500	Meridian Bancorp	35 North Sixth St., Reading, PA 19601	(215) 655-2000
106	Merrill Lynch	250 Vesey St., North Tower, New York, NY 10281	(212) 449-1000
857	Merry-Go-Round	3300 Fashion Way, Joppa, MD 21085	(410) 538-1000
841	Meyer (Fred)	3800 SE 22nd Ave., Portland, OR 97202	(503) 232-8844
474	Mgic Investment	270 East Kilbourn Ave., Milwaukee, WI 53202	(414) 347-6480
723	MGM Grand	3155 W. Harmon Ave., Las Vegas, NV 89103	(702) 891-3333

Corporate Contact Directory (cont'd)

Rank	Company	Corporate Headquarters	Phone Number
746	Michigan National	27777 Inkster Rd., Farmington Hills, MI 48333	(313) 473-3000
704	Micron Technology	2805 East Columbia Rd., Boise, ID 83706	(208) 368-4000
26	Microsoft	One Microsoft Way, Redmond, WA 98052	(206) 882-8080
750	Midlantic	499 Thornall Rd., Edison, NJ 08837	(908) 321-8000
715	Midwest Resources	666 Grand Ave., Des Moines, IA 50306	(515) 242-4300
837	Millipore	80 Ashby Rd., Bedford, MA 01730	(617) 275-9200
25	Minnesota Mining & Mfg.	3M Center, St. Paul, MN 55144	(612) 733-1110
680	Minnesota Power	30 West Superior St., Duluth, MN 55802	(218) 722-2641
696	Mirage Resorts	3400 Las Vegas Blvd. South, Las Vegas, NV 89109	(702) 791-7111
752	Mitchell Energy	2001 Timberloch Place, The Woodlands, TX 77380	(713) 377-5500
581	MNC Financial	225 N. Calvert St., Baltimore, MD 21202	(410) 605-5000
16	Mobil	3225 Gallows Rd., Fairfax, VA 22037	(703) 846-3000
941	Modine Manufacturing	1500 De Koven Ave., Racine, WI 53403	(414) 636-1200
434	Molex	2222 Wellington Court, Lisle, IL 60532	(708) 969-4550
127	Monsanto	800 North Lindbergh Blvd., St. Louis, MO 63167	(314) 694-1000
543	Montana Power	40 East Broadway, Butte, MT 59701	(406) 723-5421
59	Morgan (J.P.)	60 Wall St., New York, NY 10260	(212) 483-2323
206	Morgan Stanley Group	1251 Ave. of the Americas, New York, NY 10020	(212) 703-4000
956	Morrison Knudsen	720 Park Blvd., Boise, ID 83729	(208) 386-5000
919	Morrison Restaurants	4721 Morrison Dr., Mobile, AL 36609	(205) 344-3000
285	Morton International	100 North Riverside Plaza, Chicago, IL 60606	(312) 807-2400
45	Motorola	1303 East Algonquin Rd., Schaumburg, IL 60196	(708) 576-5000
590	Multimedia	305 South Main St., Greenville, SC 29602	(803) 298-4373
462	Murphy Oil	200 Peach St., El Dorado, AR 71730	(501) 862-6411
378	Mylan Laboratories	130 Seventh St., Pittsburgh, PA 15222	(412) 232-0100
356	Nalco Chemical	One Nalco Center, Naperville, IL 60563	(708) 305-1000
210	National City	1900 East Ninth St., Cleveland, OH 44114	(216) 575-2000
677	National Fuel Gas	Ten Lafayette Square, Buffalo, NY 14203	(716) 857-7000
561	National Health Labs	7590 Fay Ave., La Jolla, CA 92037	(619) 454-3314
490	National Medical Ents.	2700 Colorado Ave., Santa Monica, CA 90404	(310) 315-8000
974	National Re	777 Long Ridge Rd., Stamford, CT 06902	(203) 329-7700
612	National Semiconductor	2900 Semiconductor Dr., Santa Clara, CA 95052	(408) 721-5000
570	National Service Inds.	1420 Peachtree St. NE, Atlanta, GA 30309	(404) 853-1000
53	Nationsbank	100 N. Tryon St., Charlotte, NC 28202	(704) 386-5000
979	Nationwide Health	4675 MacArthur Ct., Newport Beach, CA 92660	(714) 251-1211
887	Navistar International	455 North Cityfront Plaza Dr., Chicago, IL 60611	(312) 836-2000
152	NBD Bancorp	611 Woodward Ave., Detroit, MI 48226	(313) 225-1000
948	Neiman Marcus Group	27 Boylston St., Chestnut Hill, MA 02167	(617) 232-0760
764	Nevada Power	6226 West Sahara Ave., Las Vegas, NV 89102	(702) 367-5000
342	New England Electric	25 Research Dr., Westboro, MA 01582	(508) 366-9011
615	New Plan Realty Trust	1120 Ave. of the Americas, New York, NY 10036	(212) 869-3000
370	New York State E&G	4500 Vestal Pkwy. East, Binghamton, NY 13902	(607) 729-2551
387	New York Times	229 West 43rd St., New York, NY 10036	(212) 556-1234
310	Newell	29 East Stephenson St., Freeport, IL 61032	(815) 235-4171
257	Newmont Gold	1700 Lincoln St., Denver, CO 80203	(303) 863-7414
340	Newmont Mining	1700 Lincoln St., Denver, CO 80203	(303) 863-7414
301	Niagara Mohawk Power	300 Erie Blvd. West, Syracuse, NY 13202	(315) 474-1511
511	Nicor	1844 West Ferry Rd., Naperville, IL 60563	(708) 305-9500
159	Nike	One Bowerman Dr., Beaverton, OR 97005	(503) 671-6453
435	Nipsco Industries	5265 Hohman Ave., Hammond, IN 46320	(219) 853-5200

Corporate Contact Directory (cont'd)

Rank	Company	Corporate Headquarters	Phone Number
728	Noble Affiliates	110 West Broadway, Ardmore, OK 73401	(405) 223-4110
807	Nordson	28601 Clemens Rd., Westlake, OH 44145	(216) 892-1580
330	Nordstrom	1501 Fifth Ave., Seattle, WA 98101	(206) 628-2111
85	Norfolk Southern	Three Commercial Place, Norfolk, VA 23510	(804) 629-2600
245	Northeast Utilities	107 Selden St., Berlin, CT 06037	(203) 665-5000
314	Northern States Power	414 Nicollet Mall, Minneapolis, MN 55401	(612) 330-5500
358	Northern Trust	50 South LaSalle St., Chicago, IL 60675	(312) 630-6000
486	Northrop	1840 Century Park East, Los Angeles, CA 90067	(310) 553-6262
120	Norwest	Sixth & Marquette, Minneapolis, MN 55479	(612) 667-1234
790	Novacare	1016 W. Ninth Ave., King of Prussia, PA 19406	(215) 992-7200
86	Novell	122 East 1700 South, Provo, UT 84606	(801) 429-7000
241	Nucor	2100 Rexford Rd., Charlotte, NC 28211	(704) 366-7000
880	NWNL	20 Washington Ave. South, Minneapolis, MN 55401	(612) 372-5432
35	NYNEX	335 Madison Ave., New York, NY 10017	(212) 370-7400
137	Occidental Petroleum	10889 Wilshire Blvd., Los Angeles, CA 90024	(310) 208-8800
449	Office Depot	2200 Old Germantown Rd., Delray Beach, FL 33445	(407) 278-4800
703	Ogden	Two Pennsylvania Plaza, New York, NY 10121	(212) 868-6000
867	Ogden Projects	40 Lane Rd., Fairfield, NJ 07007	(201) 882-9000
616	Ohio Casualty	136 North Third St., Hamilton, OH 45025	(513) 867-3000
244	Ohio Edison	76 South Main St., Akron, OH 44308	(216) 384-5100
537	Oklahoma G&E	101 N. Robinson Ave., Oklahoma City, OK 73102	(405) 272-3000
536	Old Kent Financial	One Vandenberg Center, Grand Rapids, MI 49503	(616) 771-5000
567	Old Republic Intl.	307 North Michigan Ave., Chicago, IL 60601	(312) 346-8100
786	Olin	120 Long Ridge Rd., Stamford, CT 06904	(203) 356-2000
799	Olsten	One Merrick Ave., Westbury, NY 11590	(516) 832-8200
603	Omnicom Group	437 Madison Ave., New York, NY 10022	(212) 415-3600
177	Oracle Systems	500 Oracle Pkwy., Redwood Shores, CA 94065	(415) 506-7000
952	Orange & Rockland Utilities	One Blue Hill Plaza, Pearl River, NY 10965	(914) 352-6000
408	Oryx Energy	13155 Noel Rd., Dallas, TX 75240	(214) 715-4000
923	Outback Steakhouse	550 North Reo St., Tampa, FL 33609	(813) 282-1225
996	Overseas Shipholding	1114 Ave. of the Americas, New York, NY 10036	(212) 869-1222
438	Owens-Corning	Fiberglas Tower, Toledo, OH 43659	(419) 248-8000
549	Owens-Illinois	One SeaGate, Toledo, OH 43666	(419) 247-5000
417	Paccar	777 106th Ave. NE, Bellevue, WA 98004	(206) 455-7400
465	Pacific Enterprises	633 West Fifth St., Los Angeles, CA 90071	(213) 895-5000
49	Pacific Gas & Electric	77 Beale St., San Francisco, CA 94177	(415) 973-7000
748	Pacific Telecom	805 Broadway, Vancouver, WA 98660	(206) 696-0983
36	Pacific Telesis Group	130 Kearny St., San Francisco, CA 94108	(415) 394-3000
753	Pacificare Health	5995 Plaza Dr., Cypress, CA 90630	(714) 952-1121
182	Pacificorp	700 NE Multnomah St., Portland, OR 97232	(503) 731-2000
688	Paging Network	4965 Preston Park Blvd., Plano, TX 75093	(214) 985-4100
682	Painewebber Group	1285 Ave. of the Americas, New York, NY 10019	(212) 713-2000
413	Pall	2200 Northern Blvd., East Hills, NY 11548	(516) 484-5400
376	Panhandle Eastern	5400 Westheimer Court, Houston, TX 77056	(713) 627-5400
496	Parametric Technology	128 Technology Dr., Waltham, MA 02154	(617) 894-7111
145	Paramount Communs.	15 Columbus Circle, New York, NY 10023	(212) 373-8000
505	Parker Hannifin	17325 Euclid Ave., Cleveland, OH 44112	(216) 531-3000
835	Paychex	911 Panorama Trail South, Rochester, NY 14625	(716) 385-6666
578	Penn Central	One East Fourth St., Cincinnati, OH 45202	(513) 579-6600
78	Penney (J.C.)	6501 Legacy Dr., Plano, TX 75024	(214) 591-1000

Corporate Contact Directory (cont'd)

Rank	Company	Corporate Headquarters	Phone Number
196	Pennsylvania Power	Two North Ninth St., Allentown, PA 18101	(215) 774-5151
375	Pennzoil	700 Milam St., Houston, TX 77002	(713) 546-4000
656	Peoples Energy	122 South Michigan Ave., Chicago, IL 60603	(312) 431-4000
508	Pep Boys	3111 West Alleghany Ave., Philadelphia, PA 19132	(215) 229-9000
10	PepsiCo	700 Anderson Hill Rd., Purchase, NY 10577	(914) 253-2000
599	Perkin-Elmer	761 Main Ave., Norwalk, CT 06859	(203) 762-1000
480	Perrigo	515 Eastern Ave., Allegan, MI 49010	(616) 673-8451
453	Pet	400 South Fourth St., St. Louis, MO 63102	(314) 622-7700
617	Petrie Stores	70 Enterprise Ave., Secaucus, NJ 07094	(201) 866-3600
34	Pfizer	235 East 42nd St., New York, NY 10017	(212) 573-2323
254	Phelps Dodge	2600 North Central Ave., Phoenix, AZ 85004	(602) 234-8100
900	PHH	11333 McCormick Rd., Hunt Valley, MD 21031	(301) 771-3600
128	Philadelphia Electric	2301 Market St., Philadelphia, PA 19101	(215) 841-4000
5	Philip Morris	120 Park Ave., New York, NY 10017	(212) 880-5000
102	Phillips Petroleum	Fourth & Keeler Sts., Bartlesville, OK 74004	(918) 661-6600
844	Phillips-Van Heusen	1290 Ave. of the Americas, New York, NY 10104	(212) 541-5200
818	PHM	33 Bloomfield Hills Pkwy., Bloomfield Hills, MI 48304	(313) 647-2750
997	Piedmont Natural Gas	1915 Rexford Rd., Charlotte, NC 28233	(704) 364-3120
441	Pinnacle West Capital	400 East Van Buren St., Phoenix, AZ 85004	(602) 379-2500
357	Pioneer Hi-Bred Intl.	400 Locust St., Des Moines, IA 50309	(515) 270-3200
121	Pitney Bowes	One Elm Croft Rd., Stamford, CT 06926	(203) 356-5000
993	Pittston	100 First Stamford Place, Stamford, CT 06912	(203) 978-5200
989	Pittway	200 South Wacker Dr., Chicago, IL 60606	(312) 831-1070
105	Pnc Bank	Fifth Ave. and Wood St., Pittsburgh, PA 15265	(412) 762-2000
562	Polaroid	549 Technology Square, Cambridge, MA 02139	(617) 577-2000
432	Policy Management	I-77 & U.S. 21 North, Blythewood, SC 29016	(803) 735-4000
743	Portland General	121 SW Salmon St., Portland, OR 97204	(503) 464-8000
534	Potlatch	One Maritime Plaza, San Francisco, CA 94111	(415) 576-8800
306	Potomac Electric Power	1900 Pennsylvania Ave. NW, Washington, DC 20068	(202) 872-2000
108	PPG Industries	One PPG Place, Pittsburgh, PA 15272	(412) 434-3131
395	Praxair	39 Old Ridgebury Rd., Danbury, CT 06810	(203) 794-3000
525	Premark International	1717 Deerfield Rd., Deerfield, IL 60015	(708) 405-6000
362	Premier Industrial	4500 Euclid Ave., Cleveland, OH 44103	(216) 391-8300
482	Price	4649 Morena Blvd., San Diego, CA 92117	(619) 581-4600
897	Price (T. Rowe)	100 East Pratt St., Baltimore, MD 21202	(410) 547-2000
213	Primerica	65 East 55th St., New York, NY 10022	(212) 891-8900
8	Procter & Gamble	One Procter & Gamble Plaza, Cincinnati, OH 45202	(513) 983-1100
396	Progressive	6000 Parkland Blvd., Mayfield Heights, OH 44124	(216) 464-8000
422	Promus	1023 Cherry Rd., Memphis, TN 38117	(901) 762-8600
580	Provident Life	One Fountain Square, Chattanooga, TN 37402	(615) 755-1011
460	PS of Colorado	1225 Seventeenth St., Denver, CO 80202	(303) 571-7511
610	PSI Resources	1000 East Main St., Plainfield, IN 46168	(317) 839-9611
97	Public Service Ent.	80 Park Plaza, Newark, NJ 07101	(201) 430-7000
472	Puget Sound Power	411 108th Ave. NE, Bellevue, WA 98004	(206) 454-6363
832	Pyxis	9380 Carroll Park Dr., San Deigo, CA 92121	(619) 792-0966
175	Quaker Oats	321 North Clark St., Chicago, IL 60610	(312) 222-7111
825	Qualcomm	10675 Sorrento Valley Rd., San Deigo, CA 92121	(619) 587-1211
999	Quality Food Centers	10116 NE Eighth St., Bellevue, WA 98004	(206) 455-3761
928	Quantum	500 McCarthy Blvd., Milpitas, CA 95035	(408) 894-4000
637	Questar	180 East First South, Salt Lake City, UT 84111	(801) 534-5000

Corporate Contact Directory (cont'd)

Rank	Company	Corporate Headquarters	Phone Number
371	QVC Network	1365 Enterprise Dr., West Chester, PA 19380	(215) 430-1000
164	Ralston Purina	Checkerboard Square, St. Louis, MO 63164	(314) 982-1000
455	Raychem	300 Constitution Dr., Menlo Park, CA 94025	(415) 361-3333
103	Raytheon	141 Spring St., Lexington, MA 02173	(617) 862-6600
802	Read-Rite	345 Los Coches St., Milpitas, CA 95035	(408) 262-6700
151	Reader's Digest	Reader's Digest Rd., Pleasantville, NY 10570	(914) 238-1000
300	Reebok International	100 Technology Center Dr., Stoughton, MA 02072	(617) 341-5000
810	Reliance Electric	6065 Parkland Blvd., Cleveland, OH 44124	(216) 266-5800
351	Republic New York	452 Fifth Ave., New York, NY 10018	(212) 525-5000
852	Reynolds & Reynolds	115 South Ludlow St., Dayton, OH 45402	(513) 443-2000
298	Reynolds Metals	6601 West Broad St., Richmond, VA 23230	(804) 281-2000
129	Rhone-Poulenc Rorer	500 Arcola Rd., Collegeville, PA 19426	(215) 454-8000
456	Rite Aid	30 Hunter Lane, Camp Hill, PA 17011	(717) 761-2633
774	Riverwood International	3350 Cumberland Circle, Atlanta, GA 30339	(404) 644-3000
80	RJR Nabisco Holdings	1301 Ave. of the Americas, New York, NY 10019	(212) 258-5600
353	Roadway Services	1077 Gorge Blvd., Akron, OH 44309	(216) 384-1717
732	Rochester G&E	89 East Ave., Rochester, NY 14649	(716) 546-2700
584	Rochester Telephone	180 South Clinton Ave., Rochester, NY 14646	(716) 777-1000
131	Rockwell International	2201 Seal Beach Blvd., Seal Beach, CA 90740	(310) 797-3311
232	Rohm & Haas	Independence Mall West, Philadelphia, PA 19105	(215) 592-3000
761	Rollins	2170 Piedmont Rd. NE, Atlanta, GA 30324	(404) 888-2000
816	Rouse	10275 Little Patuxent Pkwy., Columbia, MD 21044	(410) 992-6000
944	Rowan	5450 Transco Tower Bldg., Houston, TX 77056	(713) 621-7800
782	RPM	2628 Pearl Rd., Medina, OH 44256	(216) 273-5090
165	Rubbermaid	1147 Akron Rd., Wooster, OH 44691	(216) 264-6464
563	Russell	One Lee St., Alexander City, AL 35010	(205) 329-4000
394	Ryder System	3600 NW 82nd Ave., Miami, FL 33166	(305) 593-3726
229	Safeco	4333 Brooklyn Ave. NE, Seattle, WA 98185	(206) 545-5000
591	Safety-Kleen	777 Big Timber Rd., Elgin, IL 60123	(708) 697-8460
636	Safeway	201 Fourth St., Oakland, CA 94660	(510) 891-3000
186	Salomon	Seven World Trade Center, New York, NY 10048	(212) 747-7000
309	San Diego G&E	101 Ash St., San Diego, CA 92101	(619) 696-2000
726	Santa Fe Energy	1616 South Voss, Houston, TX 77057	(713) 783-2401
363	Santa Fe Pacific	1700 East Golf Rd., Schaumburg, IL 60173	(708) 995-6000
51	Sara Lee	Three First National Plaza, Chicago, IL 60602	(312) 726-2600
429	Scana	1426 Main St., Columbia, SC 29201	(803) 748-3000
70	Scecorp	2244 Walnut Grove Ave., Rosemead, CA 91770	(818) 302-1212
893	Scherer (R.P.)	2075 West Big Beaver Rd., Troy, MI 48084	(313) 649-0900
66	Schering-Plough	One Giralda Farms, Madison, NJ 07940	(201) 822-7000
52	Schlumberger	277 Park Ave., New York, NY 10172	(212) 350-9400
777	Schulman (A.)	3550 West Market St., Akron, OH 44333	(216) 666-3751
600	Schwab (Charles)	101 Montgomery St., San Francisco, CA 94104	(415) 627-7000
793	Scientific-Atlanta	One Technology Pkwy. South, Norcross, GA 30092	(404) 903-5000
889	Scimed Life Systems	6655 Wedgwood Rd., Maple Grove, MN 55311	(612) 420-0700
317	Scott Paper	Scott Plaza, Philadelphia, PA 19113	(215) 522-5000
427	Scripps (E.W.)	312 Walnut St., Cincinnati, OH 45202	(513) 977-3825
669	Seagate Technology	920 Disc Dr., Scotts Valley, CA 95066	(408) 438-6550
875	Seagull Energy	1001 Fannin St., Houston, TX 77002	(713) 951-4700
39	Sears, Roebuck	Sears Tower, Chicago, IL 60684	(312) 875-2500
565	Sensormatic	500 NW 12th Ave., Deerfield Beach, FL 33442	(305) 427-9700

Corporate Contact Directory (cont'd)

Rank	Company	Corporate Headquarters	Phone Number
512	Service Corp. Intl.	1929 Allen Pkwy., Houston, TX 77019	(713) 522-5141
662	Service Merchandise	7100 Service Merchandise Dr., Brentwood, TN 37027	(615) 660-6000
349	Shaw Industries	616 East Walnut Ave., Dalton, GA 30720	(706) 278-3812
423	Shawmut National	777 Main St., Hartford, CT 06115	(203) 728-2000
322	Sherwin-Williams	101 Prospect Ave., Cleveland, OH 44115	(216) 566-2000
768	Shoney's	1727 Elm Hill Pike, Nashville, TN 37210	(615) 391-5201
344	Sigma-Aldrich	3050 Spruce St., St. Louis, MO 63103	(314) 771-5765
520	Signet Banking	Seven North Eighth St., Richmond, VA 23219	(804) 747-2000
440	Silicon Graphics	2011 North Shoreline Blvd., Mountain View, CA 94043	(415) 960-1980
683	Smith's Food & Drug	1550 South Redwood Rd., Salt Lake City, UT 84104	(801) 974-1400
795	Smucker (J.M.)	Strawberry Lane, Orrville, OH 44667	(216) 682-3000
539	Snap-On Tools	2801 80th St., Kenosha, WI 53141	(414) 656-5200
377	So. New England Tel.	227 Church St., New Haven, CT 06506	(203) 771-5200
230	Society	127 Public Square, Cleveland, OH 44114	(216) 689-3000
926	Solectron	847 Gibraltar Dr., Milpitas, CA 95035	(408) 957-8500
384	Sonat	1900 Fifth Ave., North, Birmingham, AL 35203	(205) 325-3800
405	Sonoco Products	North Second St., Hartsville, SC 29550	(803) 383-7000
902	Sotheby's Holdings	1334 York Ave., New York, NY 10021	(212) 606-7000
57	Southern	64 Perimeter Center East, Atlanta, GA 30346	(404) 393-0650
559	Southland	2711 North Haskell Ave., Dallas, TX 75204	(214) 828-7011
523	Southtrust	420 North 20th St., Birmingham, AL 35203	(205) 254-5000
291	Southwest Airlines	2702 Love Field Dr., Dallas, TX 75235	(214) 904-4000
27	Southwestern Bell	One Bell Center, St. Louis, MO 63101	(314) 235-9800
553	Southwestern PS	600 South Tyler St., Amarillo, TX 79101	(806) 378-2121
679	Spiegel	3500 Lacey Rd., Downers Grove, IL 60515	(708) 986-8800
831	Springs Industries	205 North White St., Fort Mill, SC 29715	(803) 547-1500
123	Sprint	2330 Shawnee Mission, Westwood, KS 66205	(913) 624-3000
909	SPS Transaction	2500 Lake Cook Rd., Riverwoods, IL 60015	(708) 405-0900
589	St. Joe Paper	1650 Prudential Dr., Jacksonville, FL 32207	(904) 396-6600
484	St. Jude Medical	One Lillehei Plaza, St. Paul, MN 55117	(612) 483-2000
280	St. Paul	385 Washington St., St. Paul, MN 55102	(612) 221-7911
843	Standard Federal Bank	2600 West Big Beaver Rd., Troy, MI 48084	(313) 643-9600
983	Standard Register	600 Albany St., Dayton, OH 45408	(513) 443-1000
925	Stanhome	333 Western Ave., Westfield, MA 01085	(413) 562-3631
436	Stanley Works	1000 Stanley Dr., New Britain, CT 06053	(203) 225-5111
815	Staples	100 Pennsylvania Ave., Framingham, MA 01701	(508) 370-8500
672	Star Banc	425 Walnut St., Cincinnati, OH 45202	(513) 632-4000
261	State Street Boston	225 Franklin St., Boston, MA 02110	(617) 786-3000
668	Stewart & Stevenson	2707 North Loop West, Houston, TX 77008	(713) 868-7700
657	Stone Container	150 North Michigan Ave., Chicago, IL 60601	(312) 346-6600
702	Stop & Shop	1358 Hancock Dr., Quincy, MA 02169	(617) 380-8000
716	Storage Technology	2270 South 88th St., Louisville CO 80028	(303) 673-5151
847	Stratus Computer	55 Fairbanks Blvd., Marlboro, MA 01752	(508) 460-2000
711	Stride Rite	Five Cambridge Center, Cambridge, MA 02142	(617) 491-8800
594	Stryker	2725 Fairfield Rd.,Portage, MI 49002	(616) 385-2600
193	Student Loan Mktg.	1050 Jefferson St. NW, Washington, DC 20007	(202) 333-8000
308	Sun	1801 Market St., Philadelphia, PA 19103	(215) 977-3000
253	Sun Microsystems	2550 Garcia Ave., Mountain View, CA 94043	(415) 960-1300
595	Sunamerica	11601 Wilshire Blvd., Los Angeles, CA 90025	(310) 312-5000
527	Sunbeam-Oster	One Citizens Plaza, Providence, RI 02903	(401) 831-0050

Corporate Contact Directory (cont'd)

Rank	Company	Corporate Headquarters	Phone Number
551	Sundstrand	4949 Harrison Ave., Rockford, IL 61108	(815) 226-6000
148	Suntrust Banks	25 Park Place NE, Atlanta, GA 30303	(404) 588-7711
379	Super Valu Stores	11840 Valley View, Eden Prairie, MN 55344	(612) 828-4000
855	Superior Industries	7800 Woodley Ave., Van Nuys, CA 91406	(818) 781-4973
834	Surgical Care	102 Woodmont Blvd., Nashville, TN 37205	(615) 385-3541
569	Sybase	6475 Christie Ave., Emeryville, CA 94608	(510) 596-3500
464	Synoptics Communications	4401 Great American Pkwy., Santa Clara, CA 95054	(408) 988-2400
646	Synovus Financial	901 Front Ave., Columbus, GA 31901	(706) 649-2311
209	Syntex	3401 Hillview Ave., Palo Alto, CA 94304	(415) 855-5050
181	Sysco	1390 Enclave Pkwy., Houston, TX 77077	(713) 584-1390
890	T2 Medical	1121 Alderman Dr., Alpharetta, GA 30202	(404) 442-2160
372	Tambrands	777 Westchester Ave., White Plains, NY 10604	(914) 696-6000
529	Tandem Computers	19333 Vallco Pkwy., Cupertino, CA 95014	(408) 725-6000
478	Tandy	1800 One Tandy Center, Fort Worth, TX 76102	(817) 390-3011
962	TCA Cable TV	3015 SSE Loop 323, Tyler, TX 75701	(903) 595-3701
468	Teco Energy	702 North Franklin St., Tampa, FL 33602	(813) 228-4111
883	Tecumseh Products	100 East Patterson St., Tecumseh, MI 49286	(517) 423-8411
858	Tektronix	26600 SW Pkwy., Wilsonville, OR 97070	(503) 685-3180
71	Tele-Communications	5619 DTC Pkwy., Englewood, CO 80111	(303) 267-5500
653	Teledyne	1901 Ave. of the Stars, Los Angeles, CA 90067	(310) 277-3311
507	Telephone & Data	30 North LaSalle St., Chicago, IL 60602	(312) 630-1900
338	Temple-Inland	303 South Temple Dr., Diboll, TX 75941	(409) 829-5511
142	Tenneco	1010 Milam St., Houston, TX 77002	(713) 757-2131
44	Texaco	2000 Westchester Ave., White Plains, NY 10650	(914) 253-4000
180	Texas Instruments	13500 North Central Expwy., Dallas, TX 75201	(214) 995-3333
77	Texas Utilities	2001 Bryan St., Dallas, TX 75243	(214) 812-4600
242	Textron	40 Westminster St., Providence, RI 02903	(401) 421-2800
545	Thermo Electron	81 Wyman St., Waltham, MA 02254	(617) 622-1000
638	Thermo Instrument	504 Airport Rd., Santa Fe, NM 87504	(505) 438-3171
596	Thomas & Betts	1001 Frontier Rd., Bridgewater, NJ 08807	(908) 685-1600
769	3Com	5400 Bayfront Plaza, Santa Clara, CA 95052	(408) 764-5000
650	Tidewater	1440 Canal St., New Orleans, LA 70112	(504) 568-1010
55	Time Warner	75 Rockefeller Plaza, New York, NY 10019	(212) 484-8000
215	Times Mirror	220 West First St., Los Angeles, CA 90012	(213) 237-3700
757	Timken	1835 Dueber Ave. SW, Canton, OH 44706	(216) 438-3000
380	TJX	770 Cochituate Rd., Framingham, MA 01701	(508) 390-3000
805	Tootsie Roll Industries	7401 South Cicero Ave., Chicago, IL 60629	(312) 838-3400
199	Torchmarx	2001 Third Ave South, Birmingham, AL 35233	(205) 325-4200
878	Tosco	72 Cummings Point Rd., Stamford, CT 06902	(203) 977-1000
67	Toys'R Us	461 From Rd., Paramus, NJ 07652	(201) 262-7800
238	Transamerica	600 Montgomery St., San Francisco, CA 94111	(415) 983-4000
614	Transatlantic Holdings	80 Pine St., New York, NY 10005	(212) 770-2000
234	Travelers	One Tower Square, Hartford, CT 06183	(203) 277-0111
270	Tribune	435 North Michigan Ave., Chicago, IL 60611	(312) 222-9100
719	Trinity Industries	2525 Stemmons Freeway, Dallas TX 75207	(214) 631-4420
863	Trinova	3000 Strayer, Maumee, OH 43537	(419) 867-2200
620	Triton Energy	6688 North Central Expwy., Dallas, TX 75206	(214) 691-5200
243	TRW	1900 Richmond Rd., Cleveland, OH 44124	(216) 291-7000
249	Turner Broadcasting	100 International Blvd., Atlanta, GA 30303	(404) 827-1700
492	Twentieth Century Inds.	6301 Owensmouth, Woodland Hills, CA 91367	(818) 704-3400

Corporate Contact Directory (cont'd)

Rank	Company	Corporate Headquarters	Phone Number
409	Tyco Laboratories	One Tyco Park, Exeter, NH 03833	(603) 778-9700
236	Tyson Foods	2210 Oaklawn Dr., Springdale, AR 72762	(501) 756-4000
352	U.S. Bancorp	111 SW Fifth Ave., Portland, OR 97204	(503) 275-6111
611	U.S. Cellular	8410 West Bryn Mawr, Chicago, IL 60631	(312) 399-8900
191	U.S. Healthcare	980 Jolly Rd., Blue Bell, PA 19422	(215) 628-4800
278	U.S. Surgical	150 Glover Ave., Norwalk, CT 06856	(203) 845-1000
324	UAL	1200 East Algonquin Rd., Elk Grove Village, IL 60007	(708) 952-4000
936	UGI	460 North Gulph Rd., King of Prussia, PA 19406	(215) 337-1000
530	UJB Financial	301 Carnegie Center, Princeton, NJ 08543	(609) 987-3200
823	Ultramar	120 White Plains Rd., Tarrytown, NY 10591	(914) 332-2000
426	Unifi	7201 West Friendly Rd., Greensboro, NC 27410	(919) 294-4410
608	Union Bank	350 California St., San Francisco, CA 94104	(415) 705-5000
296	Union Camp	1600 Valley Rd., Wayne, NJ 07470	(201) 628-2000
390	Union Carbide	39 Old Ridgebury Rd., Danbury, CT 06817	(203) 794-2000
222	Union Electric	1901 Chouteau Ave., St. Louis, MO 63103	(314) 621-3222
62	Union Pacific	Eighth & Eaton Aves., Bethlehem, PA 18018	(215) 861-3200
433	Union Texas Petroleum	1330 Post Oak Blvd., Houston, TX 77056	(713) 623-6544
401	Unisys	Township Line & Union Meeting Rds., Blue Bell, PA 19424	(215) 986-4011
984	United Asset Mgmt.	One International Place, Boston, MA 02110	(617) 330-8900
282	United Healthcare	9900 Bren Road East, Minnetonka, MN 55343	(612) 936-1300
967	United Illuminating	157 Church St., New Haven, CT 06506	(203) 499-2000
633	United Investors	2001 Third Ave. South, Birmingham, AL 35233	(205) 325-4200
149	United Technologies	One Financial Plaza, Hartford, CT 06101	(203) 728-7000
397	Unitrin	One East Wacker Dr., Chicago, IL 60601	(312) 661-4600
720	Universal	1501 North Hamilton St., Richmond, VA 23230	(804) 359-9311
767	Universal Foods	433 East Michigan St., Milwaukee, WI 53202	(414) 271-6755
126	Unocal	1201 West Fifth St., Los Angeles, CA 90017	(213) 977-7600
237	Unum	2211 Congress St., Portland, ME 04122	(207) 770-2211
179	Upjohn	7000 Portage Rd., Kalamazoo, MI 49001	(616) 323-4000
43	Us West	7800 East Orchard Rd., Englewood, CO 80111	(303) 793-6500
840	USAir Group	2345 Crystal Dr., Arlington, VA 22227	(703) 418-7000
647	USF&G	100 Light St., Baltimore, MD 21202	(410) 547-3000
771	USLife	125 Maiden Lane, New York, NY 10038	(212) 709-6000
144	UST	100 West Putnam Ave., Greenwich, CT 06830	(203) 661-1100
160	USX-Marathon Group	600 Grant St., Pittsburgh, PA 15219	(412) 433-1121
382	USX-U.S. Steel Group	600 Grant St., Pittsburgh, PA 15219	(412) 433-1121
649	Utilicorp United	911 Main St., Kansas City, MO 64105	(816) 421-6600
854	Valassis Communications	36111 Schoolcraft Rd., Livonia, MI 48150	(313) 591-3000
734	Valero Energy	530 McCullough Ave., San Antonio, TX 78215	(512) 246-2000
898	Valhi	5430 LBJ Freeway, Dallas, TX 75240	(214) 233-1700
556	Valley National	241 North Central Ave., Phoenix, AZ 85004	(602) 221-2900
891	Valspar	1101 Third St. South, Minneapolis, MN 55415	(612) 332-7371
964	Value City Dept. Stores	3241 Westerville Rd., Columbus, OH 43224	(614) 471-4722
828	Value Health	22 Waterville Rd., Avon, CT 06001	(203) 678-3400
977	Vanguard Cellular	2002 Pisgah Church Rd., Greensboro, NC 27455	(919) 282-3690
800	Varian Associates	3050 Hansen Way, Palo Alto, CA 94304	(415) 493-4000
830	Varity	672 Delaware Ave., Buffalo, NY 14209	(716) 888-8000
982	Verifone	Three Lagoon Dr., Redwood City, CA 94065	(415) 591-6500
286	VF	1047 North Park Rd., Wyomissing, PA 19610	(215) 378-1151
172	Viacom	1515 Broadway, New York, NY 10036	(212) 258-6000

Corporate Contact Directory (cont'd)

Rank	Company	Corporate Headquarters	Phone Number
663	Vons	618 Michillinda Ave., Arcadia, CA 91007	(818) 821-7000
430	Vulcan Materials	One Metroplex Dr., Birmingham, AL 35209	(205) 877-3000
139	Wachovia	301 North Main St., Winston-Salem, NC 27150	(919) 770-5000
3	Wal-Mart Stores	702 SW Eighth St., Bentonville, AR 72716	(501) 273-4000
185	Walgreen	200 Wilmot Rd., Deerfield, IL 60015	(708) 940-2500
949	Wallace Computer	4600 West Roosevelt Rd., Hillside, IL 60162	(708) 449-8600
975	Warnaco Group	90 Park Ave., New York, NY 10016	(212) 661-1300
88	Warner-Lambert	201 Tabor Rd., Morris Plains, NJ 07950	(201) 540-2000
755	Washington Federal S&L	425 Pike St., Seattle, WA 98101	(206) 624-7930
780	Washington Gas Light	1100 H St., NW, Washington, DC 20080	(703) 750-4440
740	Washington Mutual	1201 Third Ave., Seattle, WA 98101	(206) 461-2000
326	Washington Post	1150 15th St., NW, Washington, DC 20071	(202) 334-6000
939	Washington Reit	4936 Fairmont Ave., Bethesda, MD 20814	(301) 652-4300
722	Washington Water	East 1411 Mission Ave., Spokane, WA 99202	(509) 489-0500
40	Waste Management	3003 Butterfield Rd., Oak Brook, IL 60521	(708) 572-8800
960	Watts Industries	815 Chestnut St., North Andover, MA 01845	(508) 688-1811
906	Wausau Paper Mills	Second St., Brokaw, WI 54417	(715) 675-3361
848	Weingarten Realty	2600 Citadel Plaza Dr., Houston, TX 77008	(713) 866-6000
665	Weis Markets	1000 South Second St., Sunbury, PA 17801	(717) 286-4571
629	Wellfleet Communs.	Eight Federal St., Billerica, MA 01821	(508) 670-8888
879	Wellman	1040 Broad St., Shrewsbury, NJ 07702	(908) 542-7300
156	Wells Fargo	420 Montgomery St., San Francisco, CA 94163	(415) 477-1000
576	Wendy's International	4288 West Dublin-Granville, Dublin, OH 43017	(614) 764-3100
970	Wesco Financial	315 East Colorado Blvd., Pasadena, CA 91101	(818) 449-2345
784	West One Bancorp	101 South Capitol Blvd., Boise, ID 83733	(208) 383-7000
532	West Point-Pepperell	400 West 10th St., West Point, GA 31833	(706) 645-4000
827	Western Gas Resources	12200 North Pecos St., Denver, CO 80234	(303) 452-5603
421	Western Resources	818 Kansas Ave., Topeka, KS 66601	(913) 575-6300
189	Westinghouse Electric	11 Stanwix St., Pittsburgh, PA 15222	(412) 244-2000
383	Westvaco	299 Park Ave., New York, NY 10171	(212) 688-5000
87	Weyerhaeuser	Tacoma, WA 98477	(206) 924-2345
233	Wheelabrator	3003 Butterfield Rd., Oak Brook, IL 60521	(708) 572-8800
250	Whirlpool	2000 M-63, Benton Harbor, MI 49022	(616) 926-5000
495	Whitman	3501 Algonquin Rd., Rolling Meadows, IL 60008	(708) 818-5000
385	Willamette Industries	1300 SW Fifth Ave., Portland, OR 97201	(503) 227-5581
410	Williams	One Williams Center, Tulsa, OK 74172	(918) 588-2000
667	Wilmington Trust	1100 North Market St., Wilmington, DE 19890	(302) 651-1000
163	Winn-Dixie Stores	5050 Edgewood Court, Jacksonville, FL 32254	(904) 783-5000
319	Wisconsin Energy	231 West Michigan St., Milwaukee, WI 53201	(414) 221-2345
808	Wisconsin PS	700 North Adams St., Green Bay, WI 54301	(414) 433-1598
642	Witco	520 Madison Ave., New York, NY 10022	(212) 605-3800
231	Woolworth	233 Broadway, New York, NY 10279	(212) 553-2000
519	Worthington Industries	1205 Dearborn Dr., Columbus, OH 43085	(614) 438-3210
714	WPL Holdings	222 West Washington Ave., Madison, WI 53703	(608) 252-3311
225	Wrigley (W.M.), Jr.	410 North Michigan Ave., Chicago, IL 60611	(312) 644-2121
98	Xerox	800 Long Ridge Rd., Stamford, CT 06904	(203) 968-3000
814	Xilinx	2100 Logic Dr., San Jose, CA 95124	(408) 559-7778
866	Xtra	60 State St., Boston, MA 02019	(617) 367-5000
864	Yellow Freight System	10990 Roe Ave., Overland Park, KS 66211	(913) 345-3000
592	York International	631 South Richland Ave., York, PA 17403	(717) 771-7890

Index

NOTE: This is a listing of every company mentioned in a table or as a recommended resource throughout the Almanac. The indexes that follow include a listing of every topic heading and every publication recommended.

A

B

C

E

F

G

H

I

J

K

L

M

N

O

P•Q

R

S

T

U

X•Y•Z

The Top Reference Sources

NOTE: Throughout the *Almanac*, the editors have included profiles of noteworthy reference sources. This is an index of those profiles.

Topics Covered

NOTE: There are 455 separate topic entries in the *Almanac*. A subject by subject list appears in the table of contents. This is an index of those profiles.

Maps

Business Law & Government

Communications

Corporate Administration

Finance

Human Resources

International

Manufacturing

Marketing

Office Management

Personal Computers

Reference/Index

Maps

Pages 1 to 36

Includes:
Atlanta
Boston
Chicago
Cleveland
Columbus
Africa
Asia
Australia
Mileage Table

Business Law & Government

Pages 37 to 96

Includes:
Contracts
Intellectual Property
Working with the SBA
Federal Information Centers
Law Firm Fees
Regulatory Agencies
Free Government Publications
Minority Contract Provisions
OSHA
Government Spending
U.S. Lawyers with Foreign Offices

Communications

Pages 97 to 120

Includes:
Postal Abbreviations
Shipping
UPS
FEDEX
USPS
Manhattan Address Locator
World Time Chart
International Dialing
Video Conferencing
Time Zones
Area Codes

International

Pages 401 to 468

Includes:
Export Intermediaries
Trade Assistance
Government Assistance for Exporters
Making International Contacts
Expensive Cities
Carnets
Electric Current Conversions
Multinationals
Import/Export
Translation
Currencies
World Weather

Manufacturing

Pages 469 to 520

Includes:
Industrial Buying Guides
Sales Agents
The Federal Laboratory Consortium
Market Research
EPA Regional Offices
Recycling
New Techniques
Environmental Issues
Productivity
Warehousing
Design Awards
Quality
Trade Journals

The Almanac *is divided into twelve chapters, each focusing on a different area of business. The first page of each chapter lists the topics covered. In addition, there are three indexed listings at the end of the book: Companies and Publications, Top Resources and Topics Covered.*